D1072273

Helicopter Crash Litigation

Second Edition

Gary C. Robb

® Lawyers & Judges
Publishing Company, Inc.
Tucson, Arizona

 **Lawyers & Judges
Publishing Company, Inc.**

P.O. Box 30040 • Tucson, AZ 85751-0040
(800) 209-7109 • FAX (800) 330-8795
e-mail: sales@lawyersandjudges.com
www.lawyersandjudges.com

Library of Congress Cataloging-in-Publication Data

Robb, Gary C.
  Helicopter crash litigation / Gary C. Robb. -- Second edition.
      pages cm
  Includes bibliographical references and index.
  ISBN 978-1-936360-49-9 (hardcover : alk. paper) -- ISBN 1-936360-49-7 (hardcover : alk. paper)
  1. Liability for helicopter accidents--United States. I. Title.
  KF1290.A9R63 2015
  346.7303'22--dc23
                        2015024683

ISBN 13: 978-1-936360-49-9
ISBN 10: 1-936360-49-7
Printed in the United States of America
10 9 8 7 6 5 4 3 2 1

To My Anita,

*With much love and in recognition of your
support and encouragement without which this book
never would have been written.*

About the Author

Gary C. Robb is a partner at Robb & Robb LLC in Kansas City, Missouri, which was founded in 1984. He received his J.D. cum laude from the University of Michigan Law School in 1981. He is past-Chair of the Aviation Law Section of the American Association for Justice (AAJ), formerly known as the Association of Trial Lawyers of America (ATLA). He is also a past Co-Chair of the Aviation Litigation Committee of the ABA Section of Litigation.

Mr. Robb was recognized by *Forbes Magazine* in its March 16, 2009 issue as "by far the most successful helicopter crash trial attorney in the United States." Over the past 34 years, Mr. Robb has handled numerous helicopter crash lawsuits all over the country. His $350 million jury verdict in 1995 on behalf of a pilot killed in a helicopter crash and his $70 million jury verdict for a young woman killed in that same crash are the two highest jury verdicts in helicopter crash cases in U.S. history.

Mr. Robb's $38 million settlement in 2005 on behalf of a young woman severely burned in a helicopter crash in the Grand Canyon is the highest settlement of any helicopter crash case in the U.S. In 2008, he obtained an $18.4 million settlement in a triple-fatality helicopter crash in Nebraska. Recent helicopter crash jury verdicts include a $7.2 million jury verdict in 2009 for a cameraman killed in a helicopter crash in Iowa and a $16 million jury verdict in 2014 for the wrongful deaths of four passengers killed in a sight-seeing tour near the Hoover Dam in Nevada.

In addition to his work in helicopter crash litigation, Mr. Robb has extensive experience with airplane crash litigation obtaining record settlements of $27.5 million on behalf of skydivers killed in a small plane crash, a $26 million settlement for the wrongful deaths of a prominent North Carolina real estate executive and his wife in a plane crash and a $15 million settlement for the family of an Illinois man killed in a plane crash. In 2011, he obtained a $48 million jury verdict for the families of five skydivers who were killed when the DeHavilland DH-6 airplane lost an engine during take-off and crashed in Sullivan, Missouri.

He is past President of the Missouri Association of Trial Attorneys and recently received the Association's highest award presented to the Missouri trial attorney "who most exemplifies the qualities of professionalism, ethics, character, and courtroom success." Mr. Robb is a Board-Certified Civil Trial Lawyer by the National Board of Trial Advocacy and is listed in the peer-reviewed publication *The Best Lawyers in America*.

Foreword

This is an essential volume in the library of every trial lawyer litigating a helicopter crash case.

Gary Robb is one of the most accomplished trial lawyers in the United States and the leading plaintiff's lawyer concentrating in helicopter crash litigation. Based on decades of successful experience, his book combines mastery of the technical aspects and aerodynamic characteristics of helicopters—and their salient differences from other aircraft—with the keen insight and broad legal knowledge of a master trial lawyer. This book is both comprehensive and practical:

- It supplies guidelines, outlines and subject matters for questioning witnesses; outlines for depositions; checklists for factual investigations; and time-tested methods to avoid spoliation problems.
- It analyzes critical federal regulations and statutes.
- It elucidates critical jurisdictional issues and focuses on how best to obtain the preferred forum for the plaintiff.
- It supplies sample pleadings.
- It puts the reader in a position to have knowledgeable conversations with essential experts.
- It thoroughly explores effective demonstrative evidence and a wide array of recurring evidentiary issues, including critical damages issues.

Only an author with a $350 million jury verdict under his belt can provide trial advice with the authority and insight that this volume provides. "A trial is more than a matter of presenting a series of individual fact questions in arid fashion to a jury. The jury properly weighs fact questions in the context of a coherent picture of the way the world works. A verdict is not merely the sum of individual findings, but the assembly of those findings into that picture of the truth." *In re Diet Drugs Prods. Liab. Litig.*, 369 F.3d 293, 314 (3d Cir. 2004). This book gives you a coherent picture of the way the world works from the plaintiff's perspective—and how to project it to the jury. While the focus is helicopter accident litigation, the insights apply to all products liability cases and, often, all trials.

This book teaches effective investigation, pleading, science, expert and demonstrative evidence, and trial tactics. Helicopter litigation is as complex, and therefore as challenging, as litigation comes. This book arms you to determine the facts; prove the facts; negotiate state and federal law; communicate with experts and jurors; and obtain and sustain a verdict.

Trial preparation, like trial itself, is hard. "The final period before a large trial, like the trial itself, involves late nights, multiplying tasks and resulting confusions that are hard to imagine for one who has not experienced them." *Young v. City of Providence*, 404 F.3d 33, 41 (1st Cir. 2005). This unique and invaluable book puts you in a position to get a helicopter crash case to trial, in a forum of your choice, and to try it successfully.

Gregory P. Joseph
New York, New York
Former Chair, American Bar Association Section of Litigation
President, American College of Trial Lawyers, 2010-11

Preface to Second Edition

Since the publication of the First Edition of this book in 2010, the use of helicopters in the U.S. continues to expand at a rapid pace—and so has the accident rate. Every single day in this country, thousands of helicopters are in operation with missions ranging from air ambulance services to news and traffic reporting, from police surveillance to sightseeing tours and from border patrol to passenger transport. But the unacceptably high risk of helicopter flight continues with virtually no end in sight.

Even the National Transportation Safety Board (NTSB) earlier this year acknowledged the continued seriousness of the helicopter accident rate:

> The NTSB is concerned that, absent a concerted effort to enhance helicopter safety in public operations, accidents involving public helicopters will continue.[1]

That there were 30 fatal helicopter crashes in the U.S. in 2013 alone should be a clear signal that something is drastically wrong and that far-reaching regulatory reforms are necessary.[2] Although the FAA just recently adopted stricter safety rules applicable to all commercial helicopter operators, especially air ambulance providers, these proposals stop far short of meaningful and effective reform. It falls then to the victims of such unnecessary carnage to continue to hold those entities accountable for the deaths and massive injuries that occur in helicopter crashes with such alarming frequency.

In the five years since this book was first published:

- Significant statutory changes have occurred in many states that directly impact helicopter crash litigation.
- The FAA has taken an important first step in promulgating enhanced safety procedures applicable to all commercial helicopter operations, including air ambulances.
- The first helicopter crash occurred due, in large part, to the pilot's in-flight texting.
- Most significantly, the helicopter accident rate continues at an unacceptably high level.

The Second Edition of *Helicopter Crash Litigation* seeks to accomplish two things:

1. Update the legal, statutory and regulatory framework applicable to helicopter crash litigation; and
2. Expand and upgrade the practical approaches within the overall process of helicopter crash litigation, most notably the sections on pre-impact terror and jury selection.

Whether any of these things are accomplished, only the reader will know. But as with the First Edition, the greatest outcome would be to render the need for helicopter crash litigation infrequent if not altogether unnecessary. As before, any and all errors and misstatements in this Second Edition are solely those of the author who accepts full responsibility therefore.

Gary C. Robb
Kansas City, Missouri
Summer 2015

Preface to First Edition

The idea for this book on helicopter crash litigation was conceived while on an airplane in July 2002. Around that time, I created the basic outline for the book. I also assembled and organized all of my prior aviation-related articles and speeches for inclusion in various chapters.

A succession of trials and the other time demands of the practice of law put the project on an indefinite hold. Finally, as I approached 55 years of age, I realized that it was literally now or never and in March 2010, I set about the task in earnest. Once I signed on with my publisher, Lawyers & Judges Publishing Company, and deadlines were established, I was off and running and could not turn back. Although I took no formal sabbatical, there were many weeks where I arrived at the office and considered myself "unavailable" and those weeks were devoted entirely to work on the book.

One of the chief reasons why I wanted to write this book is that there is not another work devoted exclusively to the representation of plaintiffs in helicopter crash cases. Having grown up as a lawyer in the products liability world and then general aviation, I recognized that helicopter cases were unique and required different approaches in order to be successful. Many of these techniques were utilized in the *Turbomeca* jury trials in 1995 which resulted in jury verdicts of $70 million and $350 million. Portions of those trial transcripts are excerpted and commented upon in Chapter 10 which addresses the trial of helicopter crash cases.

My hope in writing this book is to provide a reliable reference source for lawyers undertaking the representation of plaintiffs in helicopter crash litigation. Although not my original intent, the book expanded to include a great number of practical discovery suggestions and trial technique discussion not unique to helicopter cases or even general aviation. The sections on jury selection and closing argument, in particular, may be useful to any plaintiff's jury trial lawyer. If by following any of these suggested techniques outlined within the book a lawyer is more able to effectively represent her client in a helicopter crash case or any other personal injury or wrongful death matter, then all of the time and effort will have been worthwhile.

My other principal goal was to set out specific safety recommendations for the helicopter industry garnered from many years of litigating in this area. Having seen firsthand on countless occasions the utter devastation in terms of needless lives lost and unimaginable injuries caused by helicopter crashes, it is time this industry woke up and began to seriously and effectively address the unacceptably high accident rate. Where accident after accident continues to be caused by the same deficiency it is inexcusable not to address and correct that deficiency.

Although a slow and cumbersome mechanism for change, I have seen the beneficial impact of litigation within the helicopter industry. As the result of lawsuits, helicopter operators have revised unsafe practices, helicopter component manufacturers have re-designed their products and helicopter manufacturers have changed the design of various systems. But a helicopter crash with resultant fatalities or injuries should not be required before every safety improvement. The greatest outcome of all would be to render the need for helicopter crash litigation infrequent. Hopefully, that day will come sooner rather than later.

Gary C. Robb
Kansas City, Missouri
Summer 2010

Acknowledgments

The author gratefully acknowledges the support, assistance and contributions of all those who helped to make this book a reality. Each of those named contributed in an important way to the completion of this project.

I am extremely indebted to my legal secretary of over 21 years, Debby Israel, who volunteered for this project perhaps not knowing the full extent of the late nights and weekends ultimately necessary. Her professionalism and dedication to the highest quality work product never varied notwithstanding the unending barrage of drafts for each chapter.

I express my deep gratitude to Colin Sommer for his extraordinary technical and engineering expertise throughout this project. Colin's work effort was most helpful for Chapters 1 and 2 which address the structure and operational characteristics of helicopters. I thank him for correcting my errors and confess that any that remain are purely my own. Colin helped me to express highly technical concepts in simple terms while preserving the technical accuracy of the description.

Jack Lipscomb was extremely generous of his time in reviewing early drafts of the book and commenting on various technical and accident reconstruction matters. It was comforting to draw upon someone with 50 years of experience investigating helicopter accidents.

To my professional peer reviewers I am greatly indebted for your time and effort in reviewing drafts of various chapters. These include Steve Rosen, Rick Alimonti, Alisa Brodkowitz, Don Sommer, Richard McSwain and David Hoeppner. Their comments and error-spotting were greatly appreciated and the work is better for their review.

Much of the original legal research was performed by our legal research assistant extraordinaire, Kathy Kedigh, whose work was exemplary. Kathy never complained despite the numerous occasions where specific research needed to be accomplished "yesterday."

Thanks also to Jacie Anello who assisted with much of the technical and statistical research as well as the laborious task of updating and verifying all contact addresses, phone numbers and web addresses.

I gratefully acknowledge the contribution of Anji Jesseramsing who has been steadfast in her support of this book.

Heartfelt appreciation to Greg Joseph for writing the foreword for this book. I am humbled and utterly non-deserving of his kind words about me and the book.

I wish to thank my daughter, Marilyn Robb, for applying her vast analytical abilities to Chapter 10, *Trial*, and rendering it a far more organized and useful chapter. It was a fatherly thrill to be able to work with her on a professional basis.

I also acknowledge two people who have been profoundly influential and helpful to me in my legal career, David Atkinson and Bill Sanders, Sr.

These acknowledgements would be incomplete without recognition of my wife and law partner, Anita Robb, who has suffered through a review of more drafts than any human being should endure. While her comments were unerringly correct, I am even more grateful for her kindly tolerating my four-month singular devotion to this work.

I wish to thank my editor and publisher, Eric Salo and Steve Weintraub of Lawyers & Judges Publishing Company, Inc. for their immediate and enthusiastic support of this project. It is truly a wonderful feeling having the unconditional support and encouragement of a publisher for a project of this magnitude.

I wish to acknowledge and express my heartfelt gratitude to my late mother, Gabriela Robb, who taught me the values of scholarship, persistence and achievement.

I extend my final gratitude to the families over the almost three decades now who have entrusted me with the handling of the most important legal matters of their lives. It continues to be the highest professional honor to appear in court for such worthy and deserving clients.

Naturally, all errors and misstatements are solely those of the author who accepts full responsibility therefore.

Gary C. Robb
Kansas City, Missouri
Summer 2010

Contents

Part III:
Safety Recommendations
for the Helicopter Industry

Introduction

I.1 Background and Scope of this Book

Helicopters are unique flying machines. They are very different in numerous respects from fixed-wing airplanes. Ask an aeronautical engineer to describe a helicopter and the response is likely to be that "a helicopter is just a bucket of bolts flying in formation." Ask exactly what makes a helicopter fly and the answer may be that "the main rotor blades simply beat the air into submission."

While almost every juror will have flown in an airplane, very few jurors, if any, will have flown in a helicopter. For these two reasons—the peculiarity of helicopter flight and the widespread unfamiliarity with these aircraft—plaintiff's counsel must utilize specific techniques throughout the litigation in order to successfully handle a helicopter crash case.

Helicopter crash litigation is difficult. The occupants and pilot rarely survive so there usually are no witnesses as to what occurred in-flight. The fuselage, cabin, main and tail rotor blades and primary control systems are broken apart into numerous pieces (see Figures I.1 and I.2).

Figure I.2 Helicopter crash of June 21, 2002 at Norfolk, Nebraska (courtesy of author).

The helicopter typically is destroyed beyond recognition (see Figures I.3 and I.4).

Figure I.3 Helicopter crash of August 10, 2001 at Grand Canyon, Arizona (courtesy of author).

Figure I.1 Helicopter crash of May 27, 1993 at Cameron, Missouri (courtesy of author).

Figure I.4 *Helicopter crash of June 30, 2006 at Walford, Iowa (courtesy of author).*

The cases are time-consuming, factually and legally complex, expensive and lengthy. But if handled properly, such cases can provide answers so as to bring closure to the client and perhaps a remedy to prevent similar tragedies.

I.2 Uniqueness of Helicopter Flight

The unique flight capabilities of a helicopter permit it to engage in missions which are virtually impossible for any fixed-wing aircraft. Primary among these is the helicopter's ability to hover as well as its capacity to land on any flat terrain without a runway, fly ultra-slowly, or even into reverse, and vertically climb or descend quickly.

Helicopters are very difficult to fly. They are inherently unstable aircraft with a significant delay in the response time from the pilot control inputs. Helicopter pilots must learn to anticipate wind effect and gust load conditions and compensate for them in advance. The unique flight missions of helicopters tend to stretch both the aircraft performance as well as the pilot's operational capability. These challenging and potentially hazardous flight regimes include urban law enforcement, border patrol, air ambulance, news-gathering, logging, fire-fighting, and sightseeing operations.

The typical helicopter flight mission places an already difficult-to-fly aircraft into an even more difficult and hazardous environment. The causes of helicopter crashes are markedly different from the causes of airplane crashes because of the former's unique and even peculiar design, flight, and handling features combined with their commonly high-risk mission profiles. The lower flight altitude of helicopters as compared with fixed-wing aircraft brings them in closer proximity to on-ground hazards such as radio control towers, utility wires, mountains or tall buildings.

Given the unique flight and performance characteristics, failure modes, and crash scenarios of helicopters, counsel must employ a different approach than for handling other complex cases or even other plane crash cases. Add to this the multiple legal complexities encompassing all manner of jurisdictional challenges, conflicts of laws, applicability of various federal regulations and the challenges of handling helicopter crash litigation are apparent. To the extent that products liability claims arise out of the helicopter crash, those entail an additional layer of legal complexity.

I.3 Helicopter Crash Statistics

Helicopter crashes within the U.S. are occurring with alarming frequency. One-half of the entire worldwide civil helicopter fleet operates in the U.S. and 36 percent of all accidents occur here.[3] As the usage of helicopters continues to increase, so too will there be a commensurate increase in helicopter accidents and a growing need for lawyers capable of handling helicopter crash litigation. From 2001 to 2005, the accident rate for civil helicopter use per 100,000 flight hours was 40 percent higher than that for general aviation fixed-wing aircraft.[4] This statistic has remained relatively constant. Between 2005-10, there were 599 helicopter crashes with 156 fatalities.[5] The NTSB Helicopter Accident Study documented 2211 helicopter accidents between 1990 and 2000.[6] The helicopter industry itself acknowledges that the current helicopter accident rate is "excessive and unsustainable" and that "business-as-usual" is no longer good enough.[7]

Yet the reality is that needless injuries and deaths as a result of helicopter crashes continue to occur unabated and with startling regularity. Helicopter crash litigation is becoming more and more extensive. Over the last 25 years there have been over 300 reported case decisions addressing various aspects of helicopter accident litigation.

As a result of the powerful impact forces involved in a helicopter crash, the likelihood of those occupants' sustaining severe and disabling injuries and fatalities is substantial. The potential damages claims include not only the typical economic losses common in general tort cases but also elements unique to aircraft crashes such as pre-impact terror and apprehension of impending death. Given these high stakes, counsel undertaking helicopter crash litigation may benefit from the experience of one who has traveled down these roads before.

I.4 Societal Benefits and Advantages of Helicopter Operations

This book is not "anti-helicopter." These aircraft have distinctive flight capabilities not remotely possible for fixed-wing aircraft, rendering them useful for important missions such as air ambulance rescues, police and law enforcement, and news-gathering operations. The many advantages of helicopters for military usage are well-documented. Helicopters undeniably serve an important societal function by taking on many types of missions for which any airplane or other form of transportation is ill-suited if not totally incapable. The shear versatility of these aircraft accounts for most of their operational utility.

The general public has long held a fascination for helicopters. From a cinematic point of view, helicopters are just plain photogenic, and their signature sound effect is universally recognized and sounds ominous in Dolby stereo. In virtually every motion picture action film there is the requisite helicopter pursuit, surveillance, transport of main characters, rocket-launching, fight in or fall out of, or crash. Every one of such movies also will use a helicopter in the production phase. The list of popular movies featuring extensive action footage of helicopters is long and includes such stalwarts as *Black Hawk Down*, *Terminator 2*, *Blue Thunder*, *Airwolf*, and perhaps most famous *Apocalypse Now*, which boasts of the most spectacular helicopter dynamics in the history of movies. One of the highest grossing films of all time, James Cameron's *Avatar*, makes extensive use of helicopter-like flying machines.

I.5 Scope and Intent of this Book

First and foremost, this book is intended to provide practical and useful advice to counsel in the lawful and ethical representation of plaintiffs in helicopter crash litigation. The ultimate objective and intent of this book is to guide a lawyer through this multi-disciplinary maze with one goal in mind: to maximize the prospects of success for persons injured in helicopter crashes and for the families of those who have had loved ones killed in those crashes. From start to finish, helicopter crash litigation represents as complex and challenging a type of civil litigation as there is to be found.

This book is written specifically for the trial lawyer called upon to represent victims of a helicopter crash. The book is intended as a practical and usable guidebook in the litigation of helicopter crash cases from the initial client contact to and through trial, if necessary. The book travels through the different knowledge and skill sets critical in the successful handling of these cases ranging from the basic elements of helicopter structure and flight, through the preliminary factual investigation, discovery and trial. While complex, time-consuming and expensive, helicopter crash litigation can be immensely satisfying both in terms of the particular justice afforded to the client and for the larger societal goal of improving the safety and operation of these unique aircraft for all.

Part One addresses the essentials of helicopter structure, operation, performance and flight characteristics or aerodynamics. It is virtually impossible for counsel to handle any helicopter crash lawsuit without a fundamental working knowledge of these basic principles. Such a working knowledge is essential in order to communicate effectively with one's own liability experts, to depose the defendants' corporate representatives of the subject aircraft manufacturer or any manufactured component, as well as the pilot should he survive, and all maintenance personnel.

Even more specific understanding of the particular liability claim or malfunction at issue is required to conduct proper discovery of the defendants' liability expert witnesses. A thorough understanding of the structure and flight characteristics of a helicopter is necessary at trial from the opening statement through examination of various witnesses and, ultimately, closing argument so that the jury will understand and appreciate the evidence.

This discussion of basic helicopter operation and flight principles is not intended solely as a "Helicopter 101" course for attorneys. The section incorporates specific terms, phrases and examples which have been found to resonate with lay jurors as effective learning aids and to promote sufficient conceptual understanding of helicopter flight and operations to render verdicts in these cases. A jury must first understand the principles involved and with that understanding comes an empowerment to enforce the proper standard of design and good practices set out in any jury charge. This approach awakens the jury to the realization that the trial is not just about fairly compensating victims of crashes, but it also sets the appropriate standards of safety for the helicopter industry demanded by society.

Part Two represents the heart of the book. Specific issues commonly encountered in helicopter crash litigation are highlighted and a practical means of addressing each issue is provided. It starts with the all important pre-filing factual investigation, the actual court filing of the case, and then discovery, common defenses, damages and trial. Real helicopter crash and case examples are utilized throughout so as to give context to the suggestions and techniques discussed.

Part Three identifies a series of recommended safety improvements within the helicopter industry which the author believes would prevent an extremely high percentage of these tragedies. So many helicopter accidents could be avoided by adoption of a few common sense regulations. For example, separating pilot duties from either tour guide or news reporter activity would eliminate all accidents where such dual roles caused an inattention to and diversion from the piloting responsibilities.

Some other general safety improvements would involve more frequent inspection and replacement of safety critical components in the helicopter given the higher vibrational forces sustained. Implementation of Health and Usage Monitoring Systems (HUMS) for routine helicopter maintenance would identify component failure before it could result in an in-flight malfunction. Mandatory equipment such as night vision goggles (NVGs) undeniably would prevent numerous helicopter accidents each year. Mission-specific recommendations include minimum separation requirements from objects of interest such as waterfalls or glaciers in the helicopter touring industry. Weather-sensitive risk analysis should be mandatory in any air ambulance mission for the enhanced safety of the helicopter crew as well as the passengers.

Helicopter crash litigation is complicated, time-consuming, labor intensive, and expensive. Hopefully, this book will remove some of the mystery and simplify some of the challenges in handling such litigation effectively so that justice may be served to those deserving parties. By bringing legal actions on behalf of those injured and killed in helicopter crashes and bringing them effectively and with just results, the safety of these unique and useful machines can be vastly improved and accidents can be prevented. And that is the best result of all.

Endnotes

1. NTSB 2015 Most Wanted Transportation Safety Improvements: Enhanced Public Helicopter Safety.

2. *The Wall Street Journal*, July 12, 2014, "Helicopter Safety is in the Spotlight."

3. Analysis by the Joint Helicopter Safety Analysis Team (JASAT), a subcommittee of the International Helicopter Safety Team (IAIT), reported at Rotorhub.com.

4. NTSB Aviation Accident Statistics, 2001-2005. The average 5-year accident rate for helicopters is 9.324 per 100,000 flight hours versus 6.654 for non-commercial carrier or general aviation (GA) fixed-wing aircraft.

5. NTSB Aviation Accident Statistics, May 2005 to May 2010.

6. NTSB Helicopter Accident Study, 1990-2000 (Report issued April 2002).

7. International Helicopter Safety Symposium at Montreal, Quebec (September 2005), at p. 2.

Part I:
The Basics of Helicopter Structure, Operation and Performance

While there are a number of excellent reference tools for understanding helicopter structure and flight, all are directed to a particular audience whether helicopter pilots,[1] design engineers,[2] aerodynamicists,[3] or the helicopter enthusiast generally.[4] The technical material in this book is specifically written and intended for attorneys representing victims of helicopter accidents.

Simply understanding the different parts of a helicopter or how it flies is insufficient. The difficult challenge and ultimate measure of success is to impart these complex technical concepts to the ordinary citizens who make up jury panels. Counsel must empower jurors with a sufficient understanding of the technical issues involved in order to return a just verdict. It is for this reason that various technical explanations are presented using ordinary everyday language. Whenever possible, diagrams or photographs are used to illustrate mechanical principles. Examples of technical concepts from one's life experience also are useful and employed in this section. Counsel will be much more comfortable, confident and competent in the handling of any helicopter crash case with a firm grasp of these fundamental technical issues.

---

1. Rotocraft Flying Handbook, FAA Flight Standards Service (2000); Shawn Coyle, *The Art and Science of Flying Helicopters* (1996).

2. Simon Newman, *The Foundations of Helicopter Flight* (1994).

3. J. Gorden Leeshman, *Principles of Helicopter Aerodynamics* (2000); J. Seddon and Simon Newman, *Basic Helicopter Aerodynamics* (2001); W.J. Wagtendonk, *Principles of Helicopter Flight* (1996).

4. H.F. Gregory, *The Helicopter: A Pictorial History* (1976); Robert Jackson, *Helicopters: Modern Civil and Military Rotorcraft* (2006).

Chapter 1

Introduction to Helicopter Flight, Operation and Control

Introduction

A brief history of the helicopter is useful for perspective. The word helicopter is derived from two Greek terms which together mean "rotating wing." The earliest known renderings of what we now call a helicopter were created by the famous Italian artist and inventor Leonardo da Vinci in the fifteenth century. His drawing of a "helical air screw" appeared to be powered by a wound-up spring (see Figure 1.1). Though da Vinci's records indicate that he may have constructed small models of this device, there is no known record that a full-scale machine was ever manufactured. The significance of da Vinci's rendering is that it is the first known design of a human-made craft designed to achieve vertical lift.

Figure 1.1 da Vinci's "helical air screw" circa 1480.

3

A number of inventors and later engineers worked on various permutations of the helicopter design including Thomas Edison, but it was the Russian engineer and inventor Igor Sikorsky who is given credit with production of the world's first operational helicopter in 1909. It was not until 1935 that Sikorsky advanced sufficiently in his design to develop the first mass-produced helicopter with an initial production order of 100 aircraft. Today helicopter usage is commonplace. In the United States there are over 13,000 civilian helicopters in active use.[1] The U.S. military deploys close to 6000 helicopters.[2]

1.1 Helicopter Structure and Flight Systems

While the many beneficial uses and advantages of helicopters are well-chronicled, their current design capability is inferior to airplanes in a number of respects. Their relative lack of airspeed and limited cargo and passenger-carrying capacity are obvious limitations. Helicopters also lack the typical occupant comfort of an airplane given their excessive vibration and sound. Helicopter flight, especially the "turn and bank" maneuver, exerts unusual forces on the occupant that can be unnerving to the uninitiated.

Lacking a fixed airfoil or wing structure as in an airplane, the engine must provide power for the lift generated by the main rotor blades. As explained in this section, a helicopter does have the ability to glide, but not in the conventional sense of fixed-wing aircraft. The ability of a helicopter to take off and land vertically in tight spaces is perhaps its greatest advantage. It enables the helicopter to be unequalled as a means of rescue operations, and countless people owe their lives to the fact that they were able to be reached, rescued and afforded the necessary and immediate medical treatment to survive.

A. Basic Structure

"This is a model of the helicopter involved in the accident." With that, counsel have likely exhausted the sum total of knowledge about a helicopter by the average person. Prior to launching on any highly technical discussion of the nature of the defect, aerodynamic irregularity or pilot error, counsel must walk through the basic anatomy of the helicopter and define some simple but basic terms.

The most common configuration of a helicopter consists of a single main rotor blade and a single tail rotor (see Figure 1.2).

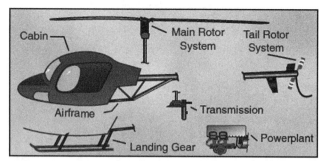

Figure 1.2 *Diagram of major components of helicopter (FAA Rotorcraft Flying Handbook, Figure 1-1).*

Figure 1.3 *Eurocopter AS350 helicopter.*

As per Figure 1.2, the structural components of the helicopter are the cabin, airframe, landing gear, power plant or engine, transmission, main rotor system and blades and tail rotor system and blades. There are helicopter designs utilizing two sets of main rotor blades and some have even employed three, but most multi-rotor configurations will consist of only two main rotor blade systems which alleviates the necessity for a tail rotor.

The most commonly used helicopters in the U.S. are the Eurocopter AS350 (Figure 1.3), the Bell Jet Ranger 206B, and the Robinson R44.

The structural configuration of a typical helicopter is not complicated and includes the cabin where the passengers, crew or cargo are positioned during flight and the airframe which is the basic structure to which everything else is attached much like a car frame. The other helicopter components are likely to be unfamiliar although most people would understand the need for an engine and transmission while not necessarily understanding their particular location or usage in a helicopter. The power produced by the engine is transmitted by the transmission to the main and tail rotors. The main rotor blade is the "spinning wing" which keeps the helicopter in the air. The additional purpose of the main rotor blade other than supplying lift is to provide directional control for the helicopter which is multi-directional. It is that function that permits the helicopter to fly forward or backward or sideways.

The tail rotor is usually a smaller propeller-like set of blades at the rear of the helicopter and affixed to the side of the tail boom. It rotates vertically as opposed to the main rotor which rotates horizontally. The function of the tail rotor is to counteract the rotational forces exerted by the main rotor which is why it is often referred to as the anti-torque rotor.

Understanding the operation and function of the anti-torque rotor or tail rotor is vital as it plays a critical role in helicopter flight and operation. As power is delivered to the main rotor system, the rotor blades on most U.S.-built helicopters turn in a counter-clockwise direction when looking down on the helicopter from above. Most European-made helicopter main rotor blades spin in a clockwise direction when viewed from above. A torque or rotational force equal to and opposite to the power delivered to the main rotor blades is constantly attempting to spin the fuselage of the helicopter in the opposite direction to that of the main rotor blades. To put this into an everyday context for illustrative purposes, one may imagine the commercial floor buffers that are used to clean wood and tile flooring. The buffer engine transmits power to the cleaning disc causing it to rotate. As long as the technician holds on to the handle, the disc rotates and cleans the floor. If the technician were to remove her grasp on the handle, the torque being delivered to the cleaning pad would cause the entire buffer to spin in a direction opposite to that of the cleaning pad. This same principle applies to the fuselage of the helicopter when the main rotor spins. The tail rotor delivers thrust or force opposite to the direction of spin of the main rotor blades and prevents the fuselage from spinning around the main rotor, as per Figure 1.4, which illustrates European or clockwise rotation of the main rotor blade.

All aircraft must have landing gear and helicopters are no exception. Instead of wheels most helicopters use stationary skids which resemble snow skis. The reason is that wheels, tires and their attached gears weigh more and require more routine maintenance than a simple skid configuration. Many larger helicopters do have wheels instead of skids and helicopters that often operate over water may be equipped with deployable floats.

B. The Rotor System

In order to understand the function of the rotor system, certain terms and concepts must be defined and understood.

1. Torque

In helicopters with a single main rotor blade, torque is the directional movement of the helicopter in the spin direction opposite that of the direction of the main rotor blade rotation. Torque is simply a force that twists an object around a rotational axis.

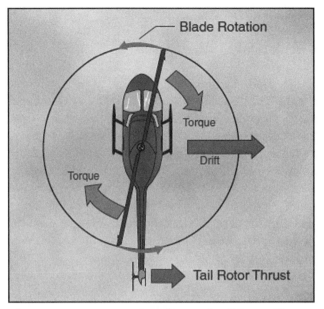

Figure 1.4 *Main Rotor Rotation and Tail Rotor Thrust (FAA Rotorcraft Flying Handbook, Figure 3-2).*

2. Blade Flap

The up or down movement made by the rotor blade while it rotates is referred to as blade flap.

3. Blade Pitch

Blade pitch is the angle of the blade in relation to the direction of rotation. One can imagine this as the amount of rotation in the blade at its attachment point on the main rotor hub. Understanding blade pitch is critical to understanding helicopter flight dynamics. Each helicopter blade can be thought of as a very long, skinny airplane wing. In fact, that is precisely what they are. They are shaped in the same way and function identically in accordance with the aerodynamic principles developed by a man named Bernoulli. As air flows over each main rotor blade, lower pressure on the top of the blade and higher pressure on the bottom of the blade create lift. This lift allows both the airplane wing and helicopter blade to fly and keeps the aircraft in the air. The pitch of the blade is the angle that it makes relative to its attachment point at the hub. As an example of this blade pitch, most everyone has stuck their arm out of the window of a moving vehicle with their fingers together and their palm held flat. This is pitch as for a helicopter rotor blade. When the palm is facing the pavement, the resistance against the air load is the lowest and the least amount of force is trying to move one's hand up, down or to the rear. This is considered low or flat pitch. As one rotates the thumb toward the sky, the amount of force acting on the palm increases and attempts to drive the hand upward. This is equivalent to increasing the pitch of the airfoil which in this case is the hand. The greater the pitch, the more force driving the hand upward and, although much simplified, the more lift causing one's hand to fly.

4. Blade Lead or Lag

Blade lead or lag is the fore and aft blade movement while it is in the plane of rotation. Main rotor blade systems have two or more blades depending on the size and design of the helicopter, but more than four is generally rare. The design of the method of attachment of the main rotor blades to the main rotor hub also depends on the size and function of the helicopter. Smaller helicopters generally have a more rigid system with less allowance for blade flap, lead and lag, while more complex or articulated systems used on generally larger and more advanced helicopters allow for movement of the blade up and down (flap) and forward and backward (lead and lag). This is especially important when there is an odd number of blades as the forces are not coupled between blades on opposite sides.

C. Helicopter Systems

The primary helicopter systems are the engine, transmission, main and tail rotor systems, fuel system, engine and fuel control systems, electrical and hydraulic systems. Almost all helicopters use either a reciprocating engine or a turbine engine. Smaller helicopters tend to use a reciprocating engine also known as a piston engine.

1. Piston Engines

A reciprocating engine is the same type of engine one finds under the hood of a car. In helicopters, they usually have either four or six cylinders and are generally cooled by airflow as opposed to liquid such as in one's car. Newer models are almost always fuel-injected but carbureted engines are still in use today. The pistons move longitudinally up and down, respectively, inside the cylinders transmitting linear power into rotational power by rotating the crankshaft.

Each piston undergoes four strokes or cycles for every two rotations of the crankshaft. The first stroke pulls air and fuel into the cylinder's combustion chamber. The second stroke compresses the air and fuel mixture inside the combustion chamber. At that point, the spark plugs, usually two in number, deliver their spark and the mixture of fuel and air ignites. This explosion causes the third or power stroke which drives the piston out of the cylinder causing the crankshaft to rotate. The fourth and final stroke pushes the combustion products (exhaust) out of the cylinder preparing it for the next intake of fresh air and fuel. Figure 1.5 shows the process.

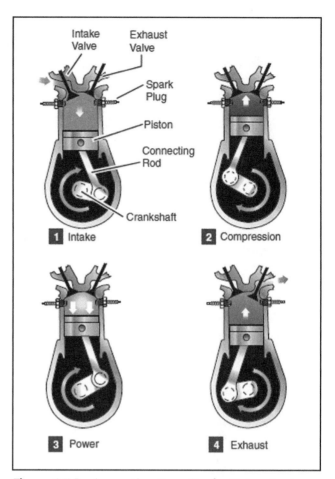

Figure 1.5 *Reciprocating Four-Stroke Piston Engine (FAA Rotorcraft Handbook, Figure 5-1).*

The crankshaft transmits rotational shaft horsepower to the transmission which then drives the main and tail rotor blades.

2. Turbine Engines

Turbine engines are quite dissimilar from reciprocating or piston engines. Turbine engines are round and generally operate under the four processes known as suck, squeeze, burn and blow. The engines operate by rotating a series of compressors or fans used to squeeze the air along with a combustion chamber to ignite the fuel and air followed by a series of turbines that convert the thermodynamic power into rotational shaft horsepower. The compressor sucks the air in through the intake while increasing pressure or squeezing it. That compressed air is then sprayed with fuel and delivered to the combustion chamber or burner can where it is ignited. As the fuel air mixture burns it expands very rapidly and blows past the turbine wheels. The turbines spin transferring shaft horsepower to run the engine as well as provide the transmission with power. See Figure 1.6.

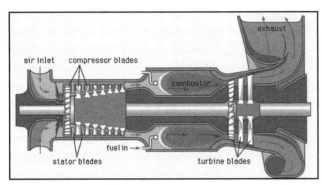

Figure 1.6 Gas Turbine Engine Operation (Reprinted with permission from Encyclopedia Britannica, ©1999 by Encyclopedia Britannica, Inc.).

3. Transmission

The helicopter transmission system is the transfer mechanism of power from the engine to the main rotor, tail rotor, and other systems. It consists of the main rotor transmission and drive shaft, tail rotor drive system and the over running clutch or freewheeling unit. The over running clutch or Sprague clutch also referred to as the freewheeling unit allows a one-way power transmission from the engine through the transmission to the rotor systems. It works exactly like the freewheeling unit on a common bicycle. When one pedals, power is delivered to the rear wheel. But if one stops pedaling, the rear wheel can still turn without driving the pedals. The engine drives the rotor systems but if the power on the engine is reduced or, in a worst case scenario, the engine fails, then the rotor systems can still spin freely without being dragged down by, or having to drive, the engine.

Helicopter transmissions must be lubricated in order to work properly, and require temperature control so as not to become overheated. Most of these transmissions require their own oil supply and that supply is monitored by a light in the cockpit instrument panel. The transmission drives the main rotor drive shaft and the tail rotor drive shaft which run up to the main rotor and back to the tail rotor, respectively.

The tail rotor drive system is powered by the main transmission and is comprised of the tail rotor drive shaft, a 90 degree gearbox located near the rear of the tail boom section and the tail rotor blades. The purpose of the tail rotor transmission is to re-route power 90 degrees from the tail rotor drive shaft to the tail rotor and in some cases allows for gearing to adjust tail rotor output RPM. Learning the relationship between the main and tail rotor systems is frequently critical to understanding the reasons for the helicopter crash.

4. Main Rotor System

The main rotor system contains a vertical mast or drive shaft which is the shaft extending from the transmission on one end to the attachment point for the rotor blades at the other, called the main rotor hub. The manner in which these rotor blades are attached to the hub and the way the blades move in relation to the main rotor hub are the basis for the three classifications of operation: (a) rigid, (b) semi-rigid or (c) fully articulated.

(a) In a rigid rotor system, the blades are rigidly attached to the main rotor hub such that they lack the ability to lead and lag as well as the ability to flap. Blade pitch can still be adjusted using the main controls, but dynamic blade forces must be absorbed in bending into the hub instead of through hinges.

(b) A semi-rigid rotor system usually consists of two main rotor blades that are rigidly attached to the main rotor hub, but are allowed to flap up and down on their hinge point similar to a child's see-saw. The blades are connected rigidly such that when one goes down, the other goes up, but lack the ability to lead and lag. Pitch is still controlled through pitch control links connected to cockpit controls.

(c) A fully articulated rotor system incorporates hinges that allow movement in all three directions. A vertical hinge at the hub allows for blade lead and lag usually accompanied by a cushion or damper. A horizontal hinge allows for blade flap up and down, and blade pitch is accomplished in the same way that rigid and semi-rigid blades are controlled. Each blade moves completely independent of each other meaning that each can lead, lag, flap and feather (change pitch) independent of the motion of the other blades in the hub.

5. Swashplate Assembly

The swashplate assembly is comprised of two separate components: a non-rotating and a rotating swashplate. The function of the swashplate assembly is to coordinate the stationary inputs coming from the collective and cyclic controls to the rotating main rotor blades. Any fracture, bend or break within the swashplate structure will have an immediate effect on the pilot's ability to control the helicopter. Details on how the swashplates work are covered later in this section.

6. Tail Rotor Drive System

The tail rotor is driven by means of a shaft from the main transmission and a small gearbox located next to the tail rotor in the back of the tail boom (see Figure 1.7).

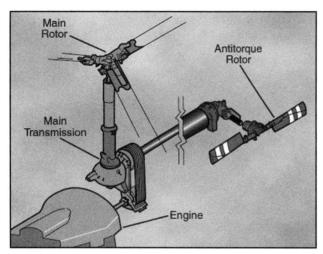

Figure 1.7 *Transmission-Driven Tail Rotor System (FAA Rotorcraft Flying Handbook, 2000).*

The shaft from the main transmission connects with flexible couplings to allow for shifting in-flight along the length of the tail boom.

The tail rotor gear box provides an angled drive for the tail rotor. Failure of any aspect of the tail rotor system is extremely serious, especially at low speed or low altitude, because of the difficulty of controlling the spin of the helicopter.

7. Fuel System

All helicopters require fuel storage and delivery in order for the engines to run. Unlike airplanes, helicopters do not have wings within which to store fuel. Thus, helicopter fuel must be stored in tanks located within and adjacent to the fuselage. This requirement places fuel and hot running parts such as the engine in close proximity to the passengers. Those areas should always be explored whenever there is an in-flight or post crash fire. The fuel system normally consists of one or more fuel tanks connected to lines that deliver fuel to the engine. Most systems incorporate an electric fuel pump and strainer located in the lines between the tank and the engine. Although piston and turbine engines use somewhat different delivery systems, they both use an engine-driven pump to draw gas out of the tank and then regulate the fuel pressure and flow for delivery into the engine.

Quantity indication, fuel flow and fuel pressure are normally indicated to the pilot via gauges on the instrument panel. A fuel shutoff valve and mixture control in a reciprocating engine give the pilot the ability to both control fuel delivery as well as shut it off completely in the event of an emergency. Most piston engines use a fuel injection system to properly mix air and fuel for consumption by the engine. The pilot can control the fuel mixture with a knob in the cockpit.

Turbine engines use a bit more complicated and automated fuel control system to properly monitor the various stages of the engine and to deliver the appropriate amount of fuel for air consumption. Older systems on turbine engines were mechanical and hydraulic or pneumatic while newer systems use a Full Authority Digital Engine Control (FADEC) system to electronically monitor and control fuel delivery. FADEC systems reduce pilot workload and increase engine efficiency; however, they too can be prone to failure and should be explored in any suspect engine failure involving that system.

8. Electrical System

Almost all aircraft require electricity to power their various monitoring and navigation systems and helicopters are no exception. Most of the equipment in a helicopter operates on Direct Current (DC) power. This system is similar to that in one's automobile. Just like a car, either an alternator (as in most piston engines) or a generator (as in most turbine engines) is connected to the gearbox for the engine. Engine operation spins the alternator or generator and DC current is generated which then supplies the rest of the helicopter systems with power. The DC power is delivered to electrical buses which act as central hubs for the electrical distribution.

This electrical delivery system can be equated to the main circuit breaker panel in one's home. Electricity comes in from outside and for a helicopter this is analogous to the generator system or battery that is routed to the various appliances requiring power in one's home. As one can view on any electrical panel at home, helicopters also are equipped with circuit breakers that will disengage when they become overloaded. This is indicative of too much current drawn by a particular system and often warns the pilot of a problem or failure of that system. That overload condition is similar to the overdrawn outlet in one's home where one too many lamps or other appliances are plugged in and drawing power.

Most helicopters use multiple buses to isolate faults in the electrical system divided into essential and non-essential uses. These buses are connected to the battery and the generator system, and—in the event that the generator system fails—the essential electrical systems can run off battery power for a short period. Certain helicopters, pending their equipment, may also need Alternating Current (AC) power. In these cases an inverter feeds in DC power and inverts it over to AC power to be used as necessary. Air ambulance helicopters often have numerous types of medical equipment requiring AC instead of DC power.

9. Hydraulic System

Hydraulic systems use fluid power to perform work. Technically a pneumatic system is a hydraulic system that uses air or another gas as the working fluid. In larger helicopters and even in some of the smaller ones, the loads acting on the flight controls are too high for a pilot of normal strength to manage. For this reason, larger helicopters use hydraulic actuators or servos to hydraulically assist the pilot in moving the flight controls. The systems normally consist of a hydraulic reservoir or tank, a pump, a filter, the hydraulic servos and the lines that connect them all together. Please see Figure 1.8 for reference.

The best comparison to help jurors understand and appreciate the operation of a helicopter hydraulic system is the familiar power steering system in a car. When the system is working properly, the power steering helps the driver turn the steering wheel to re-position the direction of the two front wheels. If the power steering has ever gone out, most people are very familiar with just how difficult it can be to steer a car without it. Helicopters are the same way. Without hydraulic assist, the main rotor and tail rotor can be very difficult if not impossible to control due to the heavy loads exerted on them by the surrounding force of air. Most helicopters have some sort of back up or emergency hydraulic system which allows the pilot enough time to land the helicopter before the controls become too heavy to operate. Hydraulic system failures in any helicopter can immediately render the aircraft completely uncontrollable.

1.2 Flight Controls and Operation

There are four basic flight controls used for flying a helicopter. These are the cyclic, the collective, the throttle and the anti-torque or tail rotor pedals. Figure 1.9 depicts the location of these flight controls in the helicopter.

Both the cyclic and the collective control the pitch of the main rotor blades. The foot pedals are used by the pilot to control the pitch of the tail rotor blades. As the name implies the throttle is used to control the power applied by the engine and is normally located at the tip of the collective control. A turn in a helicopter is much different from a turn in a fixed-wing airplane. Helicopters turn in two different ways, known as roll and yaw. The cyclic is used to control banking of the helicopter also known as roll, while the tail rotor pedals are used to control the direction the nose of the helicopter is heading, known as yaw. This will be covered in more detail in the section explaining how helicopters fly.

A. Collective Pitch Control

The collective pitch control, referred to simply as the collective, is a forward-facing lever to the left of the pilot's seat. The collective functions to change the pitch angle of all main rotor blades "collectively" meaning all at the same time and without regard to their position in the air. When the collective

pitch control lever is raised, this increases the pitch angle to the same extent on all main rotor blades simultaneously. Conversely, where the collective lever is lowered there would be a simultaneous and identical decrease in blade pitch angle.

The collective pitch control is connected to the main rotor blades through a system of mechanical linkages. The lever is adjusted up and down using the pilot's left hand. It is shaped and moves a bit like the emergency brake in many automobiles only located on the left side of the pilot instead of the right. Changing the pitch angle on a main rotor blade alters the angle of attack or angle that the blade makes with the relative airflow on each blade. Pulling up on the collective increases the pitch of each of the main rotor blades "collectively," thereby increasing both the lift and the drag acting on each blade. The more force or drag acting against each blade causes them to rotate more slowly or decrease in rotational speed or RPM. Conversely, decreasing the pitch angle lessens the angle of attack and lessens drag which logically increases the RPM of the main rotor blades. The increase or decrease of the rotor blade pitch requires adjustment of the power to maintain the proper rotor RPM.

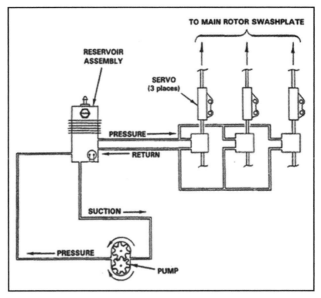

Figure 1.8 *Typical Helicopter Hydraulic System (Robinson R-44 Maintenance Manual, Figure 8-1B).*

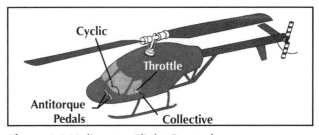

Figure 1.9 *Helicopter Flight Controls.*

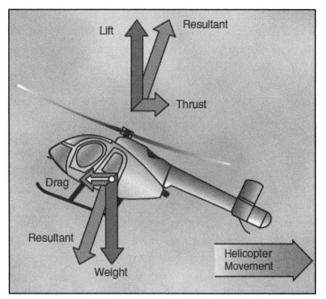

Figure 1.10 Rearward Flight (FAA Rotorcraft Flying Handbook, Figure 3-18).

B. Cyclic Pitch Control

The cyclic pitch control gets its name because it causes the pitch of the main rotor blades to move cyclically. This means that the pitch angle of the main rotor blades is changed in the cycle of rotation and this is accomplished by tilting the main rotor disc using the cyclic pitch control. The cyclic on most model helicopters is located between the pilot's legs and is also referred to as the cyclic stick or for obvious reasons simply a joystick. The cyclic is controlled by the pilot's right hand and moves left, right, forward and aft, and any combination thereof relative to the pilot's seat.

The cyclic allows the pilot to control the pitch of the main rotor blades in order to position the entire main rotor disc in the direction the pilot would like the helicopter to travel. To understand cyclic control, one may imagine all of the main rotor blades acting as one large disc, instead of multiple blades operating independently. Pushing the cyclic forward tilts the main rotor disc forward and the rotor produces a thrust in that forward direction causing the helicopter to move forward. Moving the cyclic to the left or to the right causes the rotor disc to tilt to that side and produces thrust in that direction moving the helicopter in that direction. In the same way, moving the cyclic backward creates thrust causing the helicopter to fly rearward as illustrated in Figure 1.10.

C. Swashplates

Located just above the transmission are two circular plates called swashplates. The bottom swashplate does not rotate and is firmly attached to the control linkages for the collective and cyclic controls. The top swashplate rotates with the main

rotor shaft and has control linkages attached to each rotor blade. The collective and cyclic pitch controls change the tilt of the lower swashplate. The two plates are stacked on top of each other and are connected by a bearing such that when the bottom one changes tilt, so does the top. This allows for the transfer of control system input from the non-rotating flight controls to the rotating main rotor pitch change mechanisms.

D. Tail Rotor Pedals

The tail rotor or anti-torque pedals are positioned on the floor and are controlled by the pilot's feet. This is similar to the position of rudder pedals in most airplanes and have a similar function which is to allow for change of direction of the aircraft also known as yaw. Because the main function of the tail rotor is to counteract or balance the torquing effect of the main rotor blades, there must be some equilibrium between those two forces. The primary function of the anti-torque pedals are to maintain directional or heading control of the helicopter in all phases of flight whether in hover, turn, slow flight or cruise flight. The amount of tail rotor input is a function of the phase of flight. Considerable input is required in hover flight while minimum input is required in cruise flight. The pedals are not the primary control to maintain the heading or direction of the helicopter in forward flight, but aid in trimming the aircraft and keeping the flight coordinated. Just like the main rotor blades, the tail rotor blades change pitch, producing more or less thrust as needed to counteract main rotor torque and change direction at very low speeds and in a hover. Pushing down on the right tail rotor pedal causes the helicopter's nose to rotate to the right, while pushing down with the left foot causes the reverse to occur.

Some helicopters lack conventional tail rotors but have alternate systems that provide the anti-torque. The NOTR or NO Tail Rotor system uses air blown out the side and back of the tail boom to provide the anti-toque. Some of the newer Eurocopters use what is called a Fenestron, which resembles a big fan with stator or guide vanes all protected by a large housing for anti-torque. These two systems are not the norm in the industry but it is useful for attorneys to be aware of their existence and the possibilities of their failure.

E. Throttle Control

The throttle control determines the amount of power delivered by the engine. Most throttle controls are located on the end of the collective lever in the form of a twist grip, somewhat similar to the throttle on a motorcycle. The main purpose of the throttle is to provide sufficient engine power so as to maintain the rotational speed or RPM of the main rotor blades such that the helicopter can maintain powered flight. Increases in collective pitch cause more drag on the main rotor blades which in turn attempt to slow them down. This force can be counteracted by either automatic or manual adjustments of the throttle, delivering more power to the main rotor blades and thus maintaining main rotor RPM.

1.3 Helicopter Aerodynamics: What Makes It Fly?

The simplest explanation for helicopter flight is that the helicopter will gain lift as a result of the rapid rotation of the main rotor blades which lift the airframe and all attachments, including the main fuselage and cabin. The design and speed of the blades' rotation causes airflow which produces the lift allowing the helicopter to engage in vertical flight. Using the flight controls, the pilot can manipulate the rotating blades to direct the helicopter to fly forward, backward, sideways or hover in the air during stationary flight. Those blades are controlled by altering their pitch angle which is done using the cyclic and collective pitch controls. The cyclic pitch allows the pilot to control the directional movement of the helicopter. In combination with the tail rotor pedals, the pilot is able to execute a turn to the left or right and control the direction in which the helicopter is headed.

In a hover, the lift is created and controlled solely by the main rotor blades as they spin around the fuselage. Once the helicopter starts forward flight, a number of different factors come into play that allow the helicopter to fly much more efficiently.

A. Aerodynamic Forces

There are four main forces taught to every aspiring helicopter pilot and which any helicopter crash litigator must understand that affect a helicopter at all times during flight. These forces are lift, weight, thrust and drag. Counsel handling these cases must realize that these are forces, not speeds or positions.

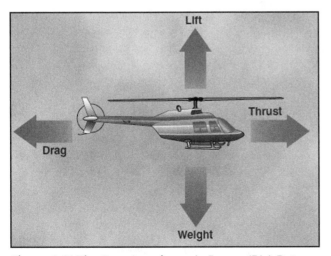

Figure 1.11 *The Four Aerodynamic Forces (FAA Rotorcraft Flying Handbook FAA-H-8083-21, Figure 2-1, 2000).*

This means that they must always have both a magnitude and a direction. The difference in each of these values causes a helicopter to speed up, slow down, ascend and descend. Figure 1.11 shows their relation during normal forward flight.

As lift is generated by the main rotor system, its vertical component counteracts the weight of the helicopter. When lift is greater than weight, the helicopter accelerates upward. Conversely, when the vertical component of lift is less than the weight, the helicopter accelerates downward. And when the two are equal, the acceleration becomes null or zero. This is not to intimate that zero acceleration is equivalent to level flight. A constant ascent rate, such as 500 feet per minute, is accomplished without any acceleration. The converse holds true during a constant descent rate. One might liken it to driving a car. When the light turns green, the driver applies the accelerator and the car starts to speed up. The car gains speed so long as the accelerator is pressed to the floor. Once the car attains a speed of 65 mph on the highway, the driver may reduce the accelerator application to maintain that constant speed. The car is not speeding up and acceleration is technically zero, but the speed is constant at the posted limit (or it well should be). The same is true when the driver applies the brake. The vehicle will decelerate until the brake is released or the vehicle comes to a stop. If the car reaches a 55 mph zone and the driver lays off the accelerator slightly and applies a bit of brake, the car will decelerate to 55 mph, where it can then resume a constant speed with zero acceleration. These same principles explain the acceleration and deceleration of a helicopter in flight.

Thrust and drag function in the same way. As the rotor disc on the helicopter tilts forward, a portion of the lift generated by the main rotor disc acts horizontally and becomes thrust. The air forces acting on the helicopter as it moves forward tend to drag it down and try to resist its forward movement. When thrust is greater than drag, the helicopter accelerates. When the horizontal component of lift or thrust is less than drag, the helicopter decelerates. When the two forces are equal, the helicopter maintains a constant speed, but just like a constant ascent or descent, this does not necessarily mean that the helicopter is stationary in the air.

B. Aerodynamic Lift

In the early 1700's, a Dutch-Swiss mathematician by the name of Daniel Bernoulli developed the concept in fluid mechanics that an increase in speed of a fluid results in a decrease in fluid pressure. More simply, the faster a fluid moves, the less pressure it exerts on its surroundings. The discovery is the basis of modern flight aerodynamics and is appropriately called Bernoulli's Principle.

To simplify and understand the great Bernoulli's idea,

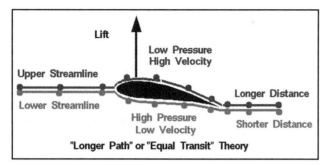

Figure 1.12 *Aerodynamic Lift.*

counsel has to put it into terms that a juror can understand. See Figure 1.12, showing the common airfoil.

This is the same shape of airfoil that is commonly used for the profile of an airplane wing and the same shape that is used for the profile of the blades on a helicopter. One should visualize two air particles traveling along happily together in space just like the two dots moving from left to right along the lines going above and below the rotor blade as shown in Figure 1.12. They both hit the front of the blade at the same time and approximately at the same location. The upper particle hits just slightly above the middle of the blade and the lower particle hits just slightly below it. The result is that the upper particles travels along the upper surface of the blade and the lower particle travels along the lower surface.

Bernoulli's principle states (and we trust him on this) that both particles will meet at the other side at exactly the same time. But as one can see, the upper particle has a lot further to travel than the lower one. For this reason, that particle must travel faster to reach the same spot at the same time at the trailing edge of the blade to join up with his buddy. This increase in speed causes a reduction in pressure on the upper surface of the blade. Now there is more pressure or force acting on the lower surface of the blade than on the upper surface. And what is the result? Aerodynamic lift. And this ladies and gentlemen of the jury, is what makes helicopters fly.

C. Angle of Attack and Stall

Blade pitch and the effect it has on the forces affecting the travel of a rotor blade was addressed earlier. A closely related aspect of aerodynamics is referred to as the airfoil angle of attack or, more simply, the angle that the blade attacks the surrounding relative wind. See Figure 1.13.

Depending on the direction the wind is blowing, the direction of travel and whether the helicopter is ascending or descending, the relative wind direction may or may not line up with the path of the rotor blade. As the helicopter ascends, the wind acting on a single advancing rotor blade will come from above relative to the blade's direction of travel. Conversely, during a descent, the relative wind will come

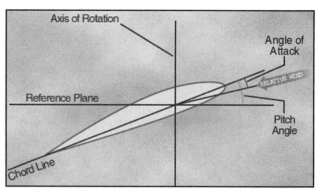

Figure 1.13 *Angle of Attack (FAA Rotorcraft Flying Handbook FAA-H-8083-21, Figure 2-6, 2000).*

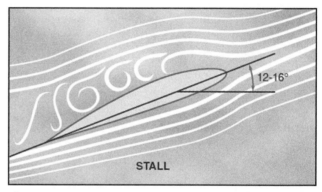

Figure 1.14 *Aerodynamic Stall (FAA Rotorcraft Flying Handbook FAA-H-8083-21, Figure 2-6, 2000).*

from below for an advancing blade. The angle between this relative wind and the centerline or chord line of the airfoil is called the angle of attack.

As blade pitch angle increases, so does the angle of attack. Correspondingly, decreased blade pitch angle results in a decreased angle of attack. And just as discussed with the illustration of a hand extending out the car window, the greater the angle of attack, the greater the production of lift. But, as also discussed with the hand out the window illustration, the more one's palm faces into the wind, the more force there is to drive it backwards. So, as lift increases with angle of attack, so does the aerodynamic drag. This relationship continues until the point at which the air can no longer flow smoothly over the airfoil and begins to separate from its surface. This occurs at what is referred to as the critical angle of attack also known as an aerodynamic stall. See Figure 1.14.

A most common misconception for jurors in any helicopter accident trial is the difference between an engine stall and an aerodynamic stall. Both arise often in aviation litigation, perhaps more with fixed-wing aircraft than with helicopters, but they are unrelated occurrences. An engine stall, normally referring to a piston engine, is the loss of power production usually due to engine failure. An aerodynamic stall has nothing to do with the engine. It is the point at which the critical angle of attack of the airfoil is reached and the air flow separates destroying the production of lift. An aerodynamic stall involves two factors: angle of attack of the airfoil and air flow. Without air flow there is no angle of attack.

The most common example of an aerodynamic stall occurs at an air show when a fixed-wing aircraft ascends steeply to the point where it is no longer able to fly and appears to just fall out of the air. When that happens the airfoils or wings have reached their critical angle of attack and the production of lift is no longer greater than the weight. The aircraft noses over and appears to fall out of the sky until the angle of attack is reduced below critical and sufficient airspeed is regained to allow the airplane to continue flight. The helicopter blade works exactly the same way. The main rotor blades follow the same principles but they rotate in a circle as opposed to being bolted onto the fuselage, as in a fixed-wing aircraft. Failure of the airfoils to produce lift on a helicopter has the same effect as on a fixed-wing aircraft. With less lift than weight, the helicopter descends and, given enough duration, the helicopter will be unable to maintain powered flight.

D. Translational Lift

When the helicopter begins to fly in a forward direction two aerodynamic principles apply. The first of these two factors affecting helicopter aerodynamics in forward flight is known as translational lift. The other is flight stability. Translational lift develops as the helicopter reaches 16-24 knots forward airspeed.[3] Although more complicated as to what this means aerodynamically, it should be understood that as the helicopter increases forward airspeed, the airflow over both rotors becomes less turbulent and more horizontal. The result is an increase in lift as smooth air helps each rotor fly more efficiently. This increase in performance can be vital in situations where additional performance is needed to fly out of

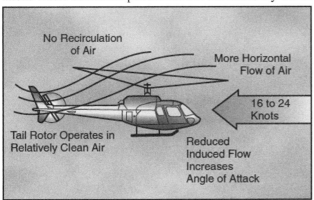

Figure 1.15 *Translational Lift (FAA Rotorcraft Flying Handbook, Figure 3-12).*

otherwise dangerous situations. See Figure 1.15 showing the effect of translational lift.

Extra caution is necessary for flight below translational lift airspeed. During that portion of the flight regime, higher power is required to produce the same amount of lift. Loss of rotor rpm or engine power at speeds below translational lift has a much greater propensity to become catastrophic than after achieving those speeds. This also is the reason why almost all helicopter pilots will attempt to take off in a forward direction into the wind as opposed to ascending straight up.

E. Flight Stability

Flight stability is the second aerodynamic principle that occurs when the helicopter achieves forward flight. This is where airflow over the vertical and horizontal tail surfaces stabilizes flight and significantly reduces or eliminates the need for tail rotor anti-torque force. One may envision the vertical tail like the rudder on a boat. When the boat is anchored and the current is calm, the rudder does very little to control the direction of the boat. The same is true for the vertical and horizontal tail surfaces on a hovering helicopter. But when the boat starts to move or the currents become stronger, the rudder causes the boat to align itself in the direction of the moving water. This is also true for the airflow over the tail of the helicopter. The wind over the vertical tail resists the yawing tendency caused by the main rotor torque and the wind over the horizontal tail helps stabilize the helicopter's pitch. This is not to say that the pilot no longer has pitch control by way of the cyclic but it does significantly reduce the effect of as well as the corresponding need for the tail rotor pedals to control the heading or yaw of the helicopter.

Extra caution is necessary for flight below translational lift airspeed. During that portion of the flight regime, higher power is required to produce the same amount of lift. Loss of rotor rpm or engine power at speeds below translational lift has a much greater propensity to become catastrophic than after achieving those speeds. This also is the reason why almost all helicopter pilots will attempt to take off in a forward direction into the wind as opposed to ascending straight up.

F. Height Velocity Diagram or Dead Man's Curve

The previous discussion on helicopter aerodynamics is the foundation for understanding the most important diagram in every Rotorcraft Flight Manual or Pilot Operating Handbook. The height velocity diagram or more commonly the Dead Man's Curve is essential information for piloting any helicopter. This diagram shows the altitude above ground

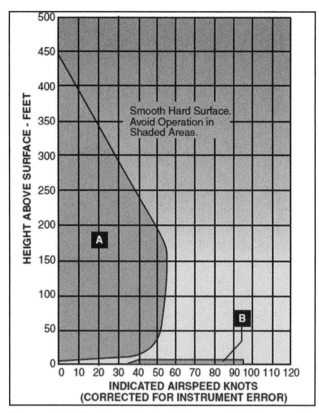

Figure 1.16 *Height Velocity Diagram (FAA Rotorcraft Flying Handbook, Figure 11-2).*

level on the left axis and airspeed on the lower axis. See Figure 1.16.

The diagram is designed to show pilots how to safely take off, climb, cruise, descend, approach and land while minimizing the dangers of being inside the Dead Man's Curve. The shaded areas A and B of the diagram are the regions of the flight envelope, or combinations of airspeed and altitude at which an engine failure could be disastrous. The reason for this very real danger is that in the shaded regions of the diagram, the helicopter does not have a sufficient combination of airspeed and altitude to perform a successful glide to a landing without power, more commonly known as an autorotation, the details of which will be covered in the next section.

Helicopters are designed such that if an engine failure occurs, the helicopter can glide to ground with little or no damage to the aircraft and its occupants assuming it is outside the Dead Man's Curve. The pilot's capability to conduct a proper autorotation is a combination of two factors, as shown on the diagram: airspeed and altitude. At lower airspeeds, in the example below of 0-35 knots, as long as the helicopter stays close to the ground, a loss of power or a control system still will allow the pilot to set the helicopter down without catastrophic damage occurring. At higher al-

titudes, such as 450 feet above ground level (AGL), airspeed becomes less of an issue, as there is sufficient altitude to enter and conduct an autorotation successfully.

Area B on the diagram is dangerous because at such a low altitude, the pilot may not have sufficient time to recognize that the engine has failed and manipulate the controls to enter and conduct an autorotation prior to ground impact. According to the example diagram, if the pilot maintains a low altitude at lower airspeeds and then increases altitude around 40-50 knots calibrated airspeed, that should minimize the risk of living up to the frightful nickname so appropriately given to the height/velocity diagram.

1.4 Piloting a Helicopter

The flight controls of a helicopter are extensions of the pilot's hands and both feet while one's eyes monitor fuel consumption, engine and rotor RPM, altitude, airspeed, attitude, vertical speed, heading, bank angle, and notably, navigation. If a person cannot walk and chew gum at the same time, she should not aspire to be a helicopter pilot. For consistency and simplicity, the following discussion will refer to piloting a typical U.S.-built helicopter with main rotor blades turning counter-clockwise when viewed from above and the helicopter equipped with an anti-torque rotor.

A. The Hover

The most difficult maneuver for any pilot to master and the one in which she will be trained first is the hover. In a hover, the throttle, cyclic, collective and tail rotor pedals are all used simultaneously to maintain the desired heading and position and keep within ground effect which is usually within one rotor diameter of the surface. The maneuver is used just after lift-off and before touchdown and is the most susceptible to adverse winds causing the various undesirable conditions discussed within the emergency conditions section ahead.

The reason ground effect is important is because within approximately one rotor diameter, the airflow developed by the main rotor creates a cushion like effect due to the air contacting the ground. The close proximity of the ground makes it easier for the helicopter to hover and requires less power to do so. Hovering within ground effect, commonly referred to as In Ground Effect Hover or "IGE", increases the factor of safety and reduces risk of damage or injury in the event of a failure. Hovering Out of Ground Effect or "OGE" by definition occurs with very little or no forward airspeed, often placing the helicopter within the Dead Man's Curve and greatly increasing the dangers associated with a system failure. With all of this in mind, one must also consider that one of the chief advantages of flying in a helicopter is to be able to take off and land in close quarters by using vertical flight. The primary reason for using a helicopter for transport is also the most dangerous portion of the flight envelope in which the helicopter can fly. The first step to departing mother earth is for the pilot to create enough rotor RPM. The pilot will apply the throttle slowly as the engine delivers more power to the blade systems. While maintaining proper RPM, the pilot then slowly and smoothly pulls up on the collective. The helicopter will lift its weight off the skids and the nose will tend to turn to the right. As this occurs, the pilot will simultaneously press down with her left foot on the tail rotor pedals in order to counteract the torque from the engine. During this process, one must understand that as the pilot applies more collective, the blades will generate more drag. This in turn requires more power from the engine and thus more twist on the throttle. More throttle means more engine torque which requires more left pedal. And the cycle continues throughout any flight.

Once the helicopter lifts off the ground, the pilot will attempt to face the helicopter into the wind as much as possible. This varies depending on the desired direction either in a hover taxi or for a departure and the severity of the wind. Relatively light wind may not require much pilot attention. Facing into the wind can be accomplished using the tail rotor pedals to change heading. A pilot will try to turn the helicopter so that it results in the smallest change in aircraft heading. This will minimize the dreaded prospect of positioning the tail into the wind with the risk of causing the helicopter to weathervane. This can occur when the wind blows the tail around forcing the helicopter to face directly into the opposite direction. This phenomenon can result in uncommanded and uncontrolled yaw which, if not dealt with properly, could result is loss of control about the yaw axis. See Figure 1.17.

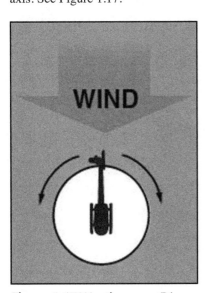

Figure 1.17 *Weathervane Diagram.*

Helicopter pilots must concentrate on a single point of reference for altitude, pitch and heading while making small, smooth, coordinated corrections. Flight instructors teach their students not to actually apply any force to the cyclic when trying to maintain the helicopter in a hover, but to "think" of the direction the pilot wants to move the aircraft and it will follow its master. Over-controlling is one of the most common mistakes of new or inexperienced pilots. Pilots should try to keep corrections light and not tense up too much on the controls. A pilot will move the cyclic ever so gently forward, aft, left and right to re-position the helicopter in each of those respective directions. She needs to apply left or right pedal to change heading. Altitude is controlled with the collective and corresponding throttle control. Many helicopters have a very useful device known as a correlator or automatic engine governor control which automatically increases the throttle slightly with the application of the collective reducing the pilot's workload during the hover and departure.

B. Take Off to Forward Flight

The second most common maneuver when learning to fly a helicopter is the take off to forward flight. Departure from the hover involves slowly and smoothly easing the cyclic forward and as the helicopter starts to move forward, adding collective as necessary to prevent sinking and throttle to maintain RPM. Increasing power requires slightly more left pedal while increasing speed until encountering translational lift. The added lift will cause the nose to rise and thus cyclic adjustment is needed to maintain a steady climb. Pilots must constantly watch their heading and stay away from the gray areas on the height-velocity diagram until ample forward airspeed and altitude are achieved. Collective adjustment and throttle control will govern the ascent rate while maintaining rotor RPM. Low rotor RPM can be fatal in a helicopter and should be avoided at all costs. As speed increases, a pilot will have less need for left pedal application, and once near cruise speed pedal application should approach close to neutral.

Once the helicopter has achieved the desired altitude, a pilot slightly reduces collective and uses it to control altitude while controlling airspeed with forward and aft cyclic. More forward cyclic will result in faster airspeed, but will require more throttle to maintain altitude. As one would expect, more throttle will require more forward cyclic in order to keep the altitude level. The path of the blade tip is a good tool for the pilot to use to measure how much forward cyclic is being applied. Changes in throttle without any change in cyclic will require changes in collective in order to prevent ascending or descending. Figure 1.18 shows the various controls and their primary purpose along with the different force and speed vectors involved in flight.

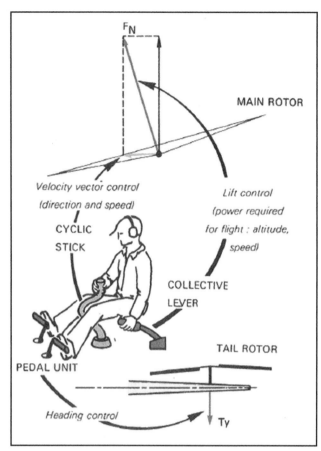

Figure 1.18 *Flight Control Functions. (Eurocopter AS350 Instruction Manual, Section 9.1, Rotor Controls, Issue 1990).*

C. Turns

Helicopters in straight and level forward flight turn similarly to their fixed-wing brethren in both appearance and control. The cyclic is used to change the lift vector to the left or to the right causing the helicopter to bank and enter into the turn. Pedal application is needed to keep the helicopter in longitudinal trim, but is not necessary to combat adverse yaw as is needed in a typical airplane. Once in the bank, the pilot returns the cyclic to neutral and continues the turn until headed toward the desired destination. Since part of the lift is being used to facilitate the turn, a bit more collective and throttle may be necessary to maintain altitude, and forward cyclic may be needed to maintain airspeed. A pilot will apply opposite cyclic to the direction of the turn prior to rolling out on the desired heading. Then the flight regime is to resume straight and level flight while keeping an eye out for other aircraft in the sky.

D. FAA Requirements

Federal regulations for aviation are strictly defined by the Code of Federal Regulations (CFR). These regulations are divided into different Titles separated by industry. Title 14 of the CFR deals with Aeronautics and Space and is commonly referred to as the Federal Air Regulations or FARs for short. These are readily available online and can be purchased in hardcopy as well.[4]

Part 61 of Title 14 of the CFR deals with the certification requirements of pilots and flight instructors. To become a certificated helicopter pilot a person must have completed at least 40 hours of flight time which includes at least 20 hours of flight training from an authorized instructor and 10 hours of solo flight training. The flight training must include a certain number of cross-country and night operation flights as well as a minimum number of take offs and landings while using the traffic pattern for each. The applicant must be 16 years old for solo flight and 17 years old to receive a private pilot license. One must receive an endorsement from an authorized instructor to take both the written and practical exams.

In addition to obtaining a pilot certificate with rotorcraft rating, the pilot must maintain proper experience currency as applicable, maintain a valid medical certificate, biennial flight review (BFR) and have a valid government-issued photo ID. The private license is just the initial certification as one may proceed to obtain an instrument rating, commercial rating, certified flight instructor and airline transport pilot license.

1.5 Emergency Conditions—Flight Irregularities and Systems Malfunction

Helicopters can experience numerous types of emergencies that are unknown to the fixed-wing world due to the number of moving components all working in unison to allow vertical and horizontal flight. It is important for the lawyer to be familiar with these conditions and have a way to reference their use when they inevitably come up during the trial.

A. Autorotation

Autorotation is an emergency maneuver performed by a helicopter pilot most frequently as a result of engine failure. Although a bit different than the standard action by a fixed-wing aircraft, for all practical purposes, an autorotation is a helicopter's ability to glide to a landing without engine power. All helicopters are designed to include this capability, although the dangers of engine failure are significantly reduced in larger turbine-powered helicopters with more than one engine. An engine failure is not the only time that an autorotation is necessary. The loss of anti-torque, usually from a failure of the tail rotor system, in essence poses the same dangers and requires the same action as an engine failure. Without any method of anti-torque, the pilot cannot and should not use the engine at lower airspeeds to provide the helicopter with lift. During a tail rotor failure, the pilot will have to perform an autorotation because at low airspeeds, the helicopter will yaw uncontrollably opposite the direction of rotation of the main rotor blades.

One way to educate juries about the aerodynamics of an autorotation is to revert back to mother nature, who was using this phenomenon long before da Vinci sketched out his heli-screw. Almost everyone has witnessed a virtual autorotation when they have seen the seed from a maple tree fall to the earth. See Figure 1.19.

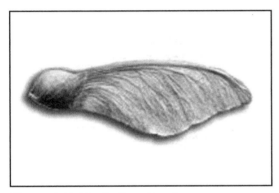

Figure 1.19 *Maple Tree Seed.*

As the seed falls, the air flowing past its single blade causes the seed to rotate and generates lift. This lift slows down the descent rate of the seed and also gives it rotational energy or inertia. The seed continues to spin and descend and eventually comes to rest in a relatively gentle landing, just like what happens in a helicopter autorotation. During normal operation, the main rotor blades of the helicopter cause air to be pulled down from above the rotor disc and then pushed out the bottom similar to a window fan. In an autorotation, the descent of the helicopter drives air up through the main rotor disc causing it to rotate.

This same phenomenon occurs when the wind blows through an idle window fan causing the blades to turn. The rotation of the main rotor blades generates lift and allows the helicopter to fly or glide down toward the ground even though no power is being delivered by the engine. Each helicopter has a published forward airspeed that should be maintained during an autorotation for maximum efficiency.

In conducting any autorotation, the engine is first disengaged from the main rotor blades through the function of the freewheeling unit. By initiating a prompt descent, the upward stream of air through the rotor will cause the blades to continue rotating even without engine power. In most helicopters, a freewheeling unit will automatically disengage the engine from the main rotor blades allowing them to rotate freely.

The pilot performs the autorotation by lowering the collective pitch and controls the rate of descent by variation of airspeed. The main rotor RPM is controlled with the collective and airspeed is controlled though pitch by way of the cyclic. Ultimately, the primary objective for any autorotation utilized in an emergency situation is to store enough energy in the rotating main rotor blades while easing the descent to accomplish a relatively soft landing. Pilots practice autorotation on a regular basis and it is part of their recurrent training.

During autorotation, the helicopter is trading potential energy or altitude for kinetic energy or rotor RPM and rotational potential energy known as inertia. As the airflow drives the main rotor blades, they develop and store rotational inertia which is used to complete autorotation. The descent rate and forward airspeed for most helicopters during autorotation is far above the acceptable limits for the helicopter to touch down. For these reasons, both the forward airspeed and descent rate must be reduced just prior to landing. This is accomplished using what pilots refer to as the flare. During the flare, the pilot applies rearward cyclic to slow the aircraft down, arrest the rate of descent and position the aircraft in a landing attitude. The pilot then uses the energy stored in the main rotor system in conjunction with the collective to control the descent and cushion the landing. The different stages of a normal, straight in autorotation can be seen in Figure 1.20.

In Figure 1.20, item 1 denotes the location of the engine or tail rotor failure. Item 2 shows the helicopter descending during a normal autorotation. Item 3 shows the pitch up of the nose from aft cyclic to arrest the forward airspeed and descent rate, usually at between 40-100 feet AGL. Item 4 shows the helicopter just prior to touchdown where the forward airspeed and descent rates have been reduced to the

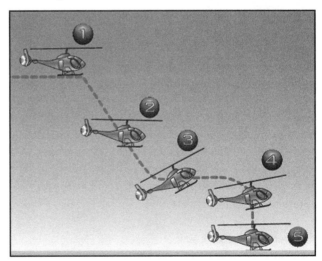

Figure 1.20 *Straight in Autorotation (FAA Rotorcraft Flying Handbook, Figure 11-1).*

lowest values possible. Item 5 shows the helicopter touching down in a landing attitude after a short vertical descent following the flare.

During the final touch down stage of the autorotation, the pilot will pull up on the collective to use up any remaining inertia in the main rotor blades allowing the helicopter to touch down gently, hopefully without damage to person or property. The success of an autorotation is directly dependent on the location of the helicopter in space, the wind and weather conditions, the availability of a suitable location to land the helicopter in close proximity to where the failure occurred and, of course, the skill and experience of the pilot

B. Hydraulic System Failure

Many helicopters have hydraulically assisted controls due to the excessive air loads imposed upon the control systems by the rotors. In the event of a hydraulic system failure, the pilot will usually feel an increase in control force and may hear evidence of the failing system. The Rotorcraft Flight Manual should be consulted for the exact procedures that are to be followed for each specific helicopter. Typically, the pilot conducts the checks detailed in the Rotorcraft Flight Manual such as cycling the hydraulic system circuit breakers or reset switch, followed by shutting off the hydraulic system if pressure to the system is not restored. Depending on the helicopter and the force of the control loads if hydraulic pressure is lost, a secondary hydraulic system or the use of accumulators may provide system back up. Accumulators store hydraulic energy which can then be used for a short period to help control the aircraft while attempting to find a suitable landing location.

An accumulator functions similar to a ball or balloon that is filled with air. The air or gas inside the accumulator is under pressure as long as pressure is being supplied by the hydraulic pump. If the hydraulic system fails, the gas pressure stored in the accumulators is used to deliver a limited amount of assist to the controls in hopes of giving the pilot enough time to put the helicopter down before the controls become unmanageable. Control force is usually directly proportional to airspeed and pilots are advised to reduce airspeed and high control input maneuvers such as in a hover. Pilots are instructed to perform a run-on landing with forward velocity while keeping the airspeeds low and control inputs at a minimum.

C. Dynamic Rollover

Dynamic rollover occurs when a helicopter is lifting off and something causes the fuselage to pivot laterally around some portion of the landing gear. Causes include the failure to remove a tie down, the sticking of the gear in mud, ice, asphalt or some aspect of the terrain such as a rock or rut. Improper takeoff or landing techniques as well as slope operations also can lead to the onset of dynamic rollover. Once the roll has started, the direction of the main rotor thrust is no longer perpendicular to the ground and the helicopter attempts to force itself over to one side. As can be expected, once one of the main rotors makes contact with the ground, there is a high probability of catastrophe.

D. Settling With Power

Settling with power or vortex ring state occurs when the helicopter is descending with up to maximum power being delivered to the rotor systems. The normal fresh airflow that travels through the main rotor blades becomes disrupted as the helicopter descends into what is essentially its own main rotor downwash. To occur, the helicopter must be in a descent and have relatively low forward airspeed. Instead of a constant supply of fresh air to the main rotor blades from above, the blades get caught in their own downwash. This unsteady turbulent airflow destroys the rotors' efficiency and can result in uncontrolled descent rates up to 6000 feet per minute. This situation occurs infrequently and pilots are trained to avoid it. But for any accident where there is an unexplainable, uncontrolled rapid descent with little forward airspeed, that helicopter may have settled with power.

E. Retreating Blade Stall

The main rotor disc may be visualized as having two halves separated by the centerline of the fuselage. On a counter-clockwise rotating blade system as seen from above, the right half of the main rotor disc is moving forward or advancing as the helicopter flies forward while the left half of the disc is moving backward or retreating. The faster the helicopter flies, the faster the air flows over the right hand side of the rotor disc due to their own rotation and conversely, the airflow slows down on the left hand side of the rotor disc. If the helicopter flies fast enough, usually denoted as the helicopter's Vne or velocity never to exceed, it is possible that the airflow over the left hand side of the rotor blade may become slow enough to allow the blades to enter an aerodynamic stall. Blade pitch and flap play a role in this condition, but at a high enough airspeed the retreating blades will begin to stall. The result will be that the helicopter's nose pitches up and the helicopter rolls to the left, or to the direction of the retreating blade in this example. Without sufficient altitude for recovery, the results can be disastrous.

F. Loss of Tail Rotor Effectiveness

At low airspeeds and especially during a hover, the tail rotor thrust is necessary as anti-torque to the effects of the main rotor. Certain conditions can cause the tail rotor thrust to become ineffective thus removing the necessary anti-torque force during the previously stated flight conditions. Wind is the primary culprit during a loss of tail rotor effectiveness (LTE) event and is one of the reasons pilots must be aware of and always try to take off and land into the direction from which the wind is coming. To oversimplify things, the wind can affect the tail rotor's ability to produce thrust in multiple ways. If the yaw rate is not properly contained by the pilot, the wind can cause the tail rotor to be incapable of preventing rotation of the fuselage opposite to the direction of the main rotor. This can also occur at higher altitudes where the air is thinner and where insufficient power is applied for the given flight conditions.

G. Failure of Tail Rotor System

An engine failure is not the only emergency situation faced by a pilot calling for autorotation. The failure of the tail rotor system requires a different action to safely land the helicopter. A common witness observation where a helicopter suffers a tail rotor system failure is that "the helicopter was spinning." At low forward speed the pilot would have little directional control without tail rotor capability. During autorotation the pilot will have good fuselage directional control until the RPM drops on the flare. With a tail rotor failure the pilot will only have fuselage directional control as a function of the air flow over the tail of the helicopter and the manipulation of the cyclic. The pilot will raise and lower the collective to change the torque level and accomplish a run-on landing if possible.

Endnotes

1. U.S. Civil Helicopter Statistics, compiled by Helicopter Association International.

2. The Military Balance 2009, at p. 50 (International Institute for Strategic Studies), January 2009.

3. FAA Rotorcraft Flying Handbook, p. 3-5.

4. http://ecfr.gpoaccess.gov.

Chapter 2

Helicopter Crash Dynamics—Common Crash Sequence and Impact Scenarios

Introduction

In investigating or handling a helicopter accident case, the crash dynamics are essential to understanding the causal role of various factors. An investigator's statement that the helicopter "impacted terrain" is no explanation but an obvious observation. Every aspect of the crash sequence must be analyzed and fully explainable by plaintiff's theory of the case.

2.1 Impact Categories

Crash impact refers to the extent of damage sustained by the helicopter as a result of the ground or terrain contact. Common impact scenarios for helicopter crashes are categorized by force of impact as follows.

A. Hard Landing

A hard landing may range from a slightly more forceful typical ground contact which merely jostles the occupants and kicks up dust to a slightly higher force impact with the ground which may damage the helicopter skids and little else. In the typical hard landing scenario, the helicopter pilot maintains full operational control of the aircraft and sustains no injury as neither do the passengers. See Figure 2.1.

Figure 2.1 *Photograph of Helicopter Hard Landing (courtesy of author).*

B. Survivable Crash

This is a helicopter accident which does result in considerable damage to the helicopter and is typically associated with moderate to significant injury sustained by the pilot and passengers. Such a crash may be due to a partial or complete loss of control of the aircraft or, alternatively, an autorotation initiated without sufficient airspeed or altitude. The severity of such injuries may include head trauma, internal injuries and other broken bones along with spinal injury due to the force of impact. Failure to perform a proper autorotation, either due to adverse conditions or pilot action, is a common cause of hard landings and survivable crashes. See Figure 2.2.

Figure 2.2 *Survivable Crash Impact of Helicopter (courtesy of author).*

Figure 2.3 *High Impact Crash of Helicopter (courtesy of author).*

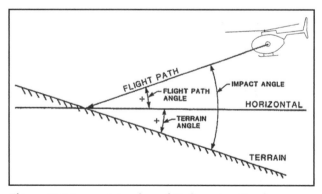

Figure 2.4 *Impact Angles of Helicopter Crash.*

C. High Impact Crash

Where the pilot loses visibility and executes a controlled flight into terrain (CFIT) or the helicopter suffers a catastrophic malfunction in-flight, the force of the impact will typically be so great that survival is not possible. That presupposes no crashworthiness or survivability issue which may have contributed to the fatal injury. The helicopter sustains severe damage and recognition of major components or systems becomes more difficult. See Figure 2.3.

2.2 Impact Dynamics

Counsel must have a basic understanding of helicopter impact dynamics to be able to explain to the jury how the crash occurred. The two principle concepts of impact dynamics for helicopters are direction of impact and rotational inertia.

A. Direction of Impact

Regardless of the speed or severity of the impact, one of the first steps to understanding a helicopter accident is determining the type and direction of impact. Did the helicopter fall straight down out of the sky? Did it fly straight ahead into a power line or a building? Did it skim down the side of the Grand Canyon before crashing into the terrain at the bottom of the slope? The type and direction of impact tell the lawyer and investigators what the helicopter was doing just prior to things going desperately wrong. The most expansive set of documents available on helicopter crash dynamics was assembled by the U.S. Army from testing that was completed from 1960 to 1987 in conjunction with the FAA, the U.S. Navy, NASA and the U.S. Air Force.[1] Figure 2.4 is a diagram from the Army's Aircraft Crash Survival Design Guide showing the impact angle, flight path angle and terrain angle.

1. Vertical Impact

The landing gear and lower belly of the helicopter are usually crushed depending on the attitude of the helicopter at impact. Injuries to the occupants usually involve broken or crushed vertebrae and internal organ damage. The tail boom often breaks at its weakest point and droops down toward the terrain and the main rotors can show downward fractures from impact due to their own weight. Many times the main rotor blades may contact the tail or nose of the helicopter cutting off pieces as it goes. The tail rotor also may impact the ground while still turning causing extensive leading edge damage and fracture and almost always breaking off the tail stinger. In a vertical impact, blunt force trauma to the occupants is less common due to impact with the instrument panel or surrounding structure. However, head and neck injuries can be common as the roof invades the occupant space.

2. Horizontal Impact

Often associated with an impact into a structure or sloping or rising terrain, horizontal impacts exhibit heavy damage to the nose of the helicopter. The forward cockpit is often destroyed and the occupants usually suffer blunt force trauma to the head and extremities as confirmed in the autopsy reports. The impact is a combination of the structure hitting the occupants and the occupants hitting the structure. Main rotor blades stop abruptly, often failing to complete even one full revolution which can sometimes leave varying degrees of damage. Depending on rotor torque and RPM, the abrupt stoppage can even leave a blade or two relatively unscathed. The main rotor and tail rotor transmissions as well as the engine are the heaviest things in the aircraft and thus contain the most energy. High impact crashes can tear the gear boxes or transmissions entirely from the aircraft structure and can even tear the engines from their mounts. Everything in the aircraft flies forward. It is similar to a vehicular head-on collision with a fixed object. These same forces will be duplicated, but instead of a car the wreckage is that of a helicopter.

3. Angled Impact

The varying degree with which the helicopter impacts the terrain governs the apportioning of the level of vertical and horizontal impact. Most crashes are neither completely vertical nor horizontal, but a combination of the two. If the helicopter suffers an engine failure, the norm is for the pilot to enter into an autorotation. In keeping with the diagram referenced earlier, just prior to touch down or impact, the pilot will attempt to flare. Depending on the aircraft's ability to autorotate and the pilot's capability to find a suitable landing zone referred to as LZ in pilot lingo, the pilot will approach the terrain at a relatively steep angle.

As addressed in the section on autorotation, just prior to touchdown the pilot will attempt to flare. The flare maneuver usually pitches the nose up slightly and lowers the tail. If for some reason things do not go exactly as planned and the pilot flares a bit too early, the helicopter may be too high above the ground when the final parcels of inertia are used up and the helicopter may fall the remaining distance to the earth in a flat or even slightly nose low attitude. If the flare occurs too late in the sequence, the most common type of impact is for the tail of the helicopter to strike the ground first. This normally results in breaking off the tail rotor guard or stinger, so called due to its resemblance to the thin tubular-shaped barb attached to certain insects. See Figure 2.5.

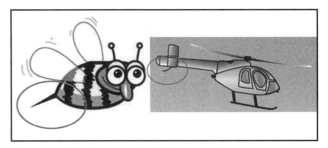

Figure 2.5 *Helicopter Tail Stinger (side by side photo of a helicopter and a bee or wasp with the stingers pointing out the back end).*

The tail rotor and tail rotor gear box often take on the first and most severe amounts of damage and the tail usually fractures upward followed by a nose high impact of the fuselage. The steeper the angle of impact, the shorter the debris path tends to be. An illustrative scenario would be that of a trash bag falling out of the back of a truck. If the truck is standing at a stop light, the bag ends up in a pile on the road contained within a relatively small circumferential area. However, if the truck is cruising the interstate at 70 mph when the bag falls out, the trash bag and all of its contents can cover multiple lanes for as far as the eye can see. The same goes for a helicopter in terms of the breadth of the disbursement pattern of the wreckage.

B. Rotational Inertia

A good indication of whether the helicopter was or was not under power when it impacted the terrain is the condition of the main rotor and tail rotor blades and the damage to the surrounding area. If the helicopter loses its engine, there is no method of power being delivered to the main rotor blades and thus very little need for anti-torque. During a powered crash, the leading edges of the main rotor and tail rotor blades will exhibit extensive damage and often become completely detached from their respective hubs. Some or all of the main rotor blades may be broken in multiple places and blades may be found along the wreckage path. Often, the blade with the most significant damage is the one that impacted the terrain first. This causes the most damage and also takes the most energy out of the main rotor system. The next blade to strike the terrain can exhibit slightly less damage than the first one and so on down the line. Depending on how fast the crash sequence occurs and how much power is being applied at the time of impact, all of the main rotor blades may be heavily damaged denoting high power impact at low speed. Sequential damage denotes powered impact at high speed, and only slight damage signifies little or no power at impact.

Helicopters do strange and unpredictable things upon impact with trees and surrounding terrain. Many an attorney and aircrash investigator have been fooled because they have attempted to reconstruct a helicopter accident as though it involved a fixed-wing airplane. Helicopters do not take off, fly or land in similar ways to airplanes and neither do they crash in similar fashion. When a helicopter crashes into trees and terrain, certain things will occur. All of the forward and vertical energy of the helicopter is exhausted, as well as that power remaining in the main and tail rotor systems. Torque to the main rotor causes the fuselage to turn opposite the direction of the main rotor blades and thus the need for a tail rotor.

When the main rotor blades hit solid objects, such as a tree or the ground, the phenomena is similar but greatly exaggerated. As the main rotor hits an object such as a tree, a tremendous amount of force is exerted on the tree by the blade. An equal and opposite force is simultaneously exerted on the blade by the tree. The reactive force is then transmitted back through the main rotor blade, drive shaft or mast and transmission into the fuselage causing it to rotate in the direction opposite of the main rotor blades. These forces can often fracture blades, pitch change links, portions of the hub, main and tail rotor drive shafts and tear the transmission out of the helicopter.

All this action may occur while the fuselage is spun around opposite the direction of rotation of the main rotor blades and can often be witnessed by impact marks to the left side of the helicopter, again for a U.S.-made helicopter. A useful comparison is to the typical home lawn mower with a rotating cutting blade. If one is pushing it along and the engine and cutting blade are running and the mower hits a small rock or stump, one may hear a loud noise. One might even see a portion of rock or stump exit out the thrower duct. If the mower is turned off and the blade inspected, one may see a small nick in one or both of the cutting blades underneath. The same scenario can be envisaged but with striking a very large and sturdy rock or stump. A substantial noise will result and one can feel the mower try to jump as the mower moves opposite to the direction of travel of the cutting blade. The engine might stop immediately and upon inspection one may find one or more blades broken off and each with extensive leading edge gouging and scratches. The more power to the mower and the more power to the main rotor blades, the worse the damage. See Figures 2.6 and 2.7.

The tail rotor system acts in much the same way. The major difference here is that the tail rotor spins much faster than the main rotor blade system, approximately six times faster,[2] but has significantly less mass. This high speed, low mass set-up often results in heavy damage to the tail rotor blades and

Figures 2.6 Low Rotor Inertia Crash (courtesy of author).

Figure 2.7 High Rotor Inertia Crash (courtesy of author).

the tail rotor drive shaft. The blades may end up as little stubs on the tail rotor hub and the tail rotor drive shaft may fail in torsion. It is important to understand the difference between a torsional failure and a bending-type failure when looking at helicopter crash wreckage. If the tail rotor is not spinning or spinning with very little energy, the damage to the drive shaft when the boom breaks, and it almost always will, exhibits signatures of a bending failure. Little rotational scoring or damage to the drive shaft and the surrounding structure will be apparent. On the other hand, if the drive shaft is spinning at rated speed anywhere from 2000-3000 RPM when the boom and tail rotor drive shaft break, the break will exhibit more twisting at the point of fracture and there will be significant circumferential or rotational scoring or scratching at the point of fracture and on the surrounding structure. See Figure 2.8.

If the tail rotor drive shaft is spinning with a lot of energy and is suddenly stopped, the drive shaft can torque itself off because power is still being delivered from the engine, but the tail rotor blades or drive shaft are no longer able to turn. There is an important exercise that would be educational for every helicopter crash attorney to try. For this experiment, one may use either two large carrots or two standard pieces of blackboard chalk. If one takes the piece of chalk or carrot

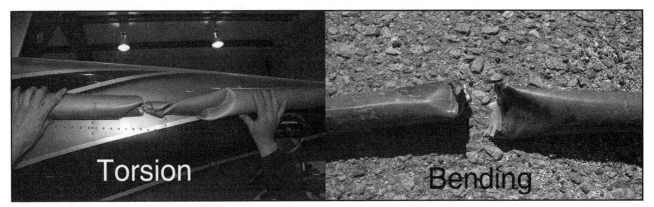

Figure 2.8 *Torsional vs. Bending Tail Rotor Drive Shaft Failure.*

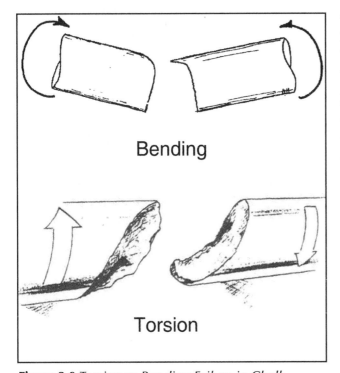

Figure 2.9 *Torsion vs Bending Failure in Chalk.*

with one end in each hand and bends it until it breaks, this is a bending failure. Notable are the signatures of fracture surface and plane of the fracture for a bending-type failure. The surface is relatively flat and perpendicular to the longitudinal axis. Using the second carrot or piece of chalk one can hold an end in either hand. Grip each end and twist them opposite to each other until it breaks as though one were wringing water out of a washcloth. This is a torsional fracture. Notable here are the curvature of the fracture plane and its concentricity about the centerline axis. This is a simple method for demonstrating to the jury the difference between torsional and bending failures. See Figure 2.9.

A common method of aircraft accident investigation applicable to helicopter crashes is to examine the filaments of the various cockpit indicators to determine if those par-ticular bulbs were lit at the time of impact. Typical tungsten filament light bulbs have a small coil of metal that connects to the two contacts inside the bulb. When DC power is delivered to this tightly coiled filament, it heats up and begins to glow. This introduction of heat is what causes the filament to give off light thus lighting the bulb. If the bulb is lit at the time of impact, it is common for the white hot filament to stretch due to G loading associated with the rapid deceleration. Instead of a nice, neat, tightly coiled filament, microscopic analysis can reveal a filament looking more like stringy pieces of linguini. This condition can alert attorneys and investigators that a particular Caution or Warning light was lit and act as a virtual flight data recorder indicating a failed condition at the time of the crash. New LED style lights unfortunately do not have these types of filaments and as such, are not of such investigative value after the accident. See figures 2.10 and 2.11.

2.3 Common Mechanical System Failures

Helicopters crash for many reasons. These reasons can be categorized into three general areas which are referred to by aircrash reconstruction experts as the man, the environment and the machine. These are more commonly described as pilot error, weather or terrain and mechanical failure. The earlier section already covered a few of the common errors that pilots can make and discussed some of the affects weather and terrain can have. The most common types of mechanical system failure are addressed below.

A. Engine Failure

Failure of an engine in a single engine helicopter is probably every helicopter pilot's greatest fear. It is evidenced by what pilots refer to as needle split and is so appropriately named because that is in fact what the pilot sees in the cockpit. During normal operation the needle for engine RPM and the needle for main rotor RPM are married and generally match up to each other or point to the same general location. Dur-

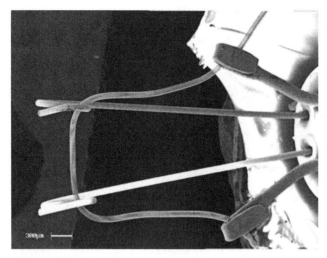

Figure 2.10 *Filament without stretch indicating bulb off at moment of crash (courtesy of author)*

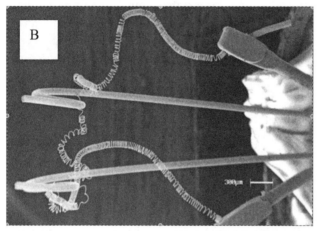

Figure 2.11 *Filament showing hot stretch indicating bulb on at moment of crash (courtesy of author)*

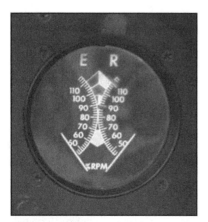

Figure 2.12 *Typical Helicopter RPM Gauge.*

ing normal operation this portion of the tachometer is painted with a small green stripe and referred to as the green arc. The tachometer can show percentage of RPM, such as in Figure 2.12, or indicate actual engine and main rotor RPM. In the example, the area from about 97-104 percent is considered the range of normal operation. As long as both needles are married and in the green arc, all operations are go.[3]

If the needle for the engine RPM starts to fall off from its mate, either the pilot has rolled off the throttle or the helicopter is in the process of experiencing an engine failure. The pilot's response to an engine failure is to lower the collective and enter an autorotation while attempting to face the helicopter into the wind and find a suitable place to set it down on the ground. While these procedures are ongoing, the pilot is instructed to follow the specific procedures in the flight manual which include any restart attempts and shutting off the fuel and ignition in the event a restart is not possible.

Turbine engines are by nature much more reliable than piston engines. Turbine engines do fail, but one of the advantages of a turbine engine over a piston engine is its reliability.

1. Turbine Engine Failure

Turbine engines fail for many different and complex reasons, but there are two basic failure modes: catastrophic and non-catastrophic. The former refers to the engine tearing itself to pieces by way of destruction of the compressor section, the turbine section or some portion of the gear box. In a non-catastrophic engine failure, the engine simply stops and is quiet.

Figure 2.13 *Turbine Blade Failure.*

The most common catastrophic form of engine failure is the loss of some portion of the turbine section. This occurs from the fracture of a turbine blade off of one of the turbine wheels or a failure of a bearing or drive component in the rear of the engine. This type of failure usually results in a large fire ball shooting out the tail pipe as the engine chews itself up and spits the contents of what used to be the turbine section out the rear section or the exhaust. The turbine wheels often look corn-cobbed because after one of the blades fails, it usually takes out the remainder of them. See Figure 2.13.

These blades shoot out the tail pipe and often leave a trail of tiny impact marks or dimples on the inside of the exhaust pipe. They rarely are found at the location of the crash site and even when they are located, they are in such bad condition from being destroyed during the failure that they may not have much value in post-accident metallurgical examination. If the turbine section appears like that photo above and there are no blades to be found this will most likely have been turbine blade failure.

The same failure mode may occur in the compressor section. Although less common, the compressor wheels or blades can and do fail and the result is similar to that found with a turbine section failure. All material downstream of the compressor wheel suffers the similar failure and becomes a type of garbage disposal destroying most everything in its path. The pieces can sometimes continue downstream and take out the turbine section as well. If there are multiple stages of the compressor or turbine section which have failed, one can look to the first section in the airflow where damage has occurred and most likely find the incipient point.

The other type of catastrophic engine failure that commonly occurs in a turbine engine is a failure of the gearbox. This may be due to the failure of a bearing, failure of a gear, loss of lubrication or various other types of mechanical anomalies. This is usually evidenced by the components of the gear box grinding themselves into shavings of metal and often stripping off gear teeth or chewing up bearings in the process. Metallurgical examination accompanied by a clear understanding of how the individual gearing systems work as well as what maintenance has been completed previously is the key to tracing the origin of such failures.

Turbine engines are not that dissimilar to human beings. They need air to breathe and fuel to eat. If they are substantially deprived of either, just like people, they will not function well. Fuel is delivered to the engine by the fuel control system. This is a complex system measuring various pressures and temperatures throughout the engine in order to deliver the right amount of fuel for the amount and pressure of the air that is being ingested by the engine. Too much fuel can cause the fire to burn too hot in the combustor and turbine section while too little fuel can cause the fire to go out, referred to in helicopter lingo as a flame out. While too much fuel may result in destruction of the turbine section as described above, too little fuel may cause the engine to just go silent. Turbine engine fuel control systems are quite complex and require very detailed examination, testing and expertise to track down the nature of their failure. So if the helicopter experienced an in-flight engine stoppage or power loss and the internal components of the engine do not show any obvious damage, a close inspection of the fuel delivery and control system is mandatory.

2. Piston Engine Failure

Piston engines are considered much less reliable than their round turbine rivals. They have shorter life spans and have many and varied ways to fail. Just as in turbine engines, failures in piston engines come in two types: catastrophic and non-catastrophic. If there is a large hole in the side of the crankcase or one of the cylinders is missing its top end, this is a clear indication of a catastrophic engine failure. There are times where catastrophic failures may not be so obvious. In the event of an engine failure for either a piston or turbine type, a teardown of the engine should be undertaken. If after taking the engine apart, one does not observe any metal shavings or large chunks of connecting rod lying in the bottom of the crankcase, one may have a non-catastrophic failure.

Catastrophic failures of a piston engine may occur for many reasons. The first sign of a catastrophic problem is an inability to turn the crankshaft. The crank will protrude from the front of the engine and will be attached to the drive train by means of couplings and flanges. Although impact damage can displace a cylinder or bend the crank flange, absent catastrophic engine damage within, the crank should move freely without effort. Most catastrophic failures occur for two main reasons: either some mechanical component inside the engine came apart, broke, wore out or came loose or some component failed to receive the required lubrication resulting in its destruction. Connecting rods can break, pistons sustain damage, valves fail, bearings fail, or cylinder heads crack. But where the engine looks as though it suffered a gunshot wound and started bleeding oil and metal, a good piston engine expert should be consulted who can conduct a full-scale disassembly and analysis of that engine.

Non-catastrophic failures can be more difficult to diagnose. The cylinders, pistons, intake and exhaust all reveal how the engine was running before it went quiet. Large deposits of black carbon and coke-like material covering these areas often indicate too much fuel for the intake air. Scarce deposits on these surfaces where everything looks light-gray in color with hardly any build up usually indicates that the engine was not receiving enough fuel. Each of the individual components should be tested. Valve sticking is a common problem in piston engine helicopters and the valves should always be examined. The magnetos, fuel pump, spark plugs, carburetor, fuel control or injection servo all should be examined closely and, if possible, tested by a facility familiar with piston engines and operation.

The two major helicopter manufacturers that use piston engines in the U.S. are Robinson and Schweizer. Each of their aircraft has a large fan that attaches to the crankshaft which acts as both a flywheel and helps to cool the engine. If the engine is running, that fan is spinning and carrying a fair amount of inertia with it. When helicopters crash and there is significant damage, the surrounding structure and fan shroud will almost always come into contact with that fan. If the fan has significant rotational scoring and damage around the perimeter, then the engine was probably running when the crash occurred. If the fan looks clean and there is a large flat spot on one or more sides without any indications of rotation at impact, this is a strong indication of an in-flight piston engine failure.

B. Transmission Failure

The transmission and its various interconnecting components transmit power from the engine to the main and tail rotor blades. Any failure or disconnect between the blades and the engine will cause the helicopter to suffer the inevitable effects of gravity and descend without power. Transmission failures come in many types and sizes but usually involve an internal failure or a failure of the interconnections between the engine and transmission. These may include the Sprague or overrunning clutch or the internal shafts or gears enclosed within the case of the transmission itself. Please refer back to Figure 2.3 for placement.

Depending on the helicopter and type of engine, the transmission is often the largest, heaviest and most robust component in the helicopter. It contains shafts, bearings and gears and requires its own lubrication system to keep everything running properly. Depending on the extent of the damage to the helicopter, one may be able to turn the main rotor blades, which then rotate the main rotor drive shaft which is directly attached to the transmission. If everything is working properly, the entire system should rotate freely causing the input shaft from the engine to rotate depending on the location of the Sprague clutch. As this is a helicopter transmission, not a wind-up toy, the rotation should be smooth, but heavy. There should not be any grinding or seizing of the components. Unfortunately, when helicopters crash hard, they often cause damage to the transmission preventing ro-

tation. If there is suspicion that any seized components could have pre-dated the impact, disassembly is advised. Bearings inside the transmission may have failed, spline shafts may become stripped or gears can lose teeth or fracture altogether. The easiest and quickest way to determine whether the transmission was grinding up before the impact is to check what is called the chip plug or chip detector. This is a very simple device which is as it sounds: a plug that screws into the bottom of the transmission. The end of the plug has a magnet attached which will attract and collect ferrous or metallic materials such as small shavings or shards that were present inside due to some kind of failure. The plug can be unscrewed and examined to see if it is clean or is accompanied by bits of broken metal. If the end of the plug resembles the hairstyle of Albert Einstein, then odds are high that the transmission failed internally. See Figure 2.14.

Figure 2.14 *Metallic Chip Plug Detector and Albert Einstein.*

The chip plug also can be equipped with wires that extend into the cockpit attached to a lightbulb. When the metal shavings from a failing gear collect on the plug, it bridges the circuit, lighting the light. This informs the pilot that the transmission is malfunctioning internally and that the helicopter should be landed immediately. These same plugs are usually found in the gearbox for the engine on turbine engines and also on the gearbox for the tail rotor. Piston engines do not normally have them. As a general rule, if there is a gearbox in a helicopter, it has a chip plug.

Although technically not part of the transmission, the Sprague or overrunning clutch is often located close by and should be examined for any suspected failure of power transmission to the blades. It should freewheel or rotate with very little resistance, but only in one direction. It should lock up completely in the other direction as it attempts to rotate the transmission.

Piston engine helicopters require some mechanism to transmit power from the engine's crankshaft to the transmission. The most common form and that most commonly used are belts. These belts are similar to those found on a car's alternator or fan. When the rotor blades are engaged, the belts tighten and the blades start to spin. Belt failures can be catastrophic if they occur in flight. They fail similar to those on a car, but instead of the car battery going dead, the helicopter loses engine power. There are usually 4 belts on Robinson helicopters and 8 on the Schweizer models. If all belts are not accounted for with the wreckage, a search of the scene should be conducted.

C. Main Rotor System Failure

The main rotor blades, hub and drive shaft are all essential components for helicopter operation. Failure of any of the three will usually result in an in-flight loss of control with dire consequences. Main rotor blades can fracture in flight, delaminate, or sling a tip weight, with pieces of the hub breaking or wearing out. When that occurs, they typically leave a trail of debris leading to the impact point. Main rotor systems are extremely intolerant of any sort of imbalance. If one blade loses a piece, it usually means the others will follow suit. Many helicopters have a system for retention of the main rotor which includes "TT" straps or tension/torsion straps that are the device for overcoming the forces trying to separate the main rotor blades from the rotor head. These straps have been known to fail. Hinges, dampers and links in the hub can fail, causing blade failure. It is not uncommon for the flailing components to chop off pieces of the tail.

D. Tail Rotor System Failure

Per Figure 2.3 and discussed previously, the tail rotor system normally consists of the transmission, the tail rotor drive shaft, the 90 degree gearbox, tail rotor hub and tail rotor blades. Tail rotor drive shafts can fail due to misalignment, and can fail at the joints also called flex or Thomas couplings. When this occurs, there is usually evidence of a torsional failure followed by an indication that the side of the drive shaft attached to the engine kept spinning, while the other side stopped. If the drive shaft and surrounding pieces of the tailboom look like a dinner fork left in the garbage disposal, it was probably turning at impact. If it is relatively pristine other than the bending fractures from the tail boom breaking on impact, it probably was not rotating in the last moments of flight. Tail rotor blades and hubs can fail as well and are equally as intolerant to imbalance as the main rotor blades. There should be a chip plug in the tail rotor gearbox. If it does not spin freely by hand, one should inspect it.

E. Control System Failure

Prior sections addressed the various primary controls for a helicopter and how they function to keep the helicopter in flight, pointed in the right direction and at the proper altitude. A control system failure may occur for any of these functions. If the control system for the tail rotor fails due to failure of the linkage going from the pedals to the tail rotor hub or due to a hydraulic servo failure used to assist, the method of anti-torque is lost and without much forward airspeed, the helicopter can enter an uncontrollable spin. Both the cyclic and collective control main rotor blade pitch. The failure of either of these systems either due to a possible jam, fracture of the linkage or hydraulic system or servo failure results in loss of control of the main rotor blade pitch. Depending on the nature of the failure, the blades can go to either a.) flat pitch, resulting in little lift or b.) a more steep pitch, which can result in blade stall. Neither is desirable. Loss of cyclic control on one side can result in the helicopter rolling or pitching violently in one direction without any capability for the pilot to recover. Loss of main rotor control accidents may result in unusual attitudes at impact as an autorotation is rarely an option.

F. In-Flight Fire

Fires during flight typically result from an ignition of some portion of the fuel system, from some failure in the electrical system or due to ignition of a flammable fluid. Flammable material includes oil, hydraulic fluid, oxygen typically stored for EMS operations and kerosene used for heaters. Most in-flight fires occur due to a leak and ignition of fuel or an electrical short and ignition of some component of the electrical system. Each Rotorcraft Flying Handbook has procedures to advise the pilot on how to properly deal with each of these situations. In-flight fires need three things to occur: fuel, oxygen, and an ignition source. Without all three, an in-flight fire cannot occur.

1. Electrical Fire

Most electronic components and wiring are located in the cockpit and behind the instrument panel. The cockpit and instrument panel area has the highest density of equipment and greatest propensity for an electrical fire. The indication to the pilot is usually smoke or flame visible in the cockpit. The pilot's immediate action must be to shut down whichever component is believed to be responsible for the fault. The circuit breaker for the suspect component should be pulled and sources of oxygen should be limited. Electrical fires usually start from shorting of electrical current. This means that electrical current is not following the path designed and a small arc of current travels from its desig-

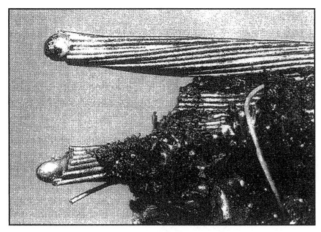

***Figure 2.15** Electrical arching.*

nated wire to some other metallic component in the aircraft. This arc can start an electrical fire and will often leave a black mark and even melt the conducting wire or sometimes ball up the end of the wire where the arc occurred. Refer to Figure 2.15.

Entire electric components can fail internally and catch fire as well. If an electrical fire is suspected, an electrical expert with experience in electrical engineering, electrical fires, aviation and avionics must be consulted. There are miles of wire in almost all helicopters and finding that spot where the fire started may require intensive digging.

2. Fuel Fire

Each component of the fuel system has its own unique manner by which fuel can leak out and lead to an in-flight fire. Fittings on lines can become loose, pumps can fail, fuel injection components can fail, gaskets can fail, safety wire holding components in place are missed by a mechanic, lines become chaffed and spring leaks. After the fuel is released, it must come into contact with some source of ignition. Aviation fuels must be atomized in some fashion to ignite and pure liquid avgas and jet fuel burn relatively poorly. Fuel vapor can be much more of a concern than fuel in liquid form due to its explosive characteristics. Ignition sources include electrical components, exhaust components and static discharge. Aircraft are struck by lightning from time to time, although less common in helicopters due to the nature of their operation. Strikes rarely result in an in-flight fire.

Once a fuel fire starts, the pilot should try to cut off the supply of fuel to the area in question. There are fuel cut-off valves and fire "T" handles that can be pulled during flight and inspected after the accident to determine their condition. Some helicopters have "fire" annunciators that light up on the panel and extinguishers in the engine compartment that can be manually or automatically deployed.

In-flight and post-crash fires burn quite differently. Fires that occur in flight often flow in the direction of the air passing over the area. They can leave distinctly different tracks on the components of the aircraft while they burn in the air as opposed to on the ground. Attention should be paid to the direction of the burn patterns and signatures of flame damage. A helicopter burning in flight while flying forward will show significantly different burn patterns than one burning while lying on the ground inverted.

G. Restraint System Failures and Crashworthiness

Many helicopter accident lawsuits have involved the failure of components in the cockpit designed to protect pilots from sustaining serious injuries in otherwise survivable accidents. Restraints vary from the typical lap belt and shoulder harness found in all modern automobiles to full five-point harnesses used in NASCAR vehicles. Seat belt retractors have a long history of problems with unspooling and have been the cause of many pilot and passenger injuries to the upper body, neck and head from impact with the surrounding structure. Seats are designed to allow some vertical crush, but often in civilian helicopters, crashworthiness design is not necessarily the highest priority. Seats can be made of rate foam that significantly reduces the G-loading on the occupant during a crash, and seat structures can be designed to absorb energy during impact. Significant testing has been done on both animate and inanimate objects to determine the effects of vertical and horizontal G-loading on humans to help reduce and prevent bodily injury.[4]

Endnotes

1. Zimmerman & Merritt, *Aircraft Crash Survival Design Guide—U.S. Army* (1989).

2. J. Gordon Leishman, *Principles of Helicopter Aerodynamics* (2000).

3. Robinson R-22 Dual Tachometer.

4. Zimmerman & Merritt, *Aircraft Crash Survival Design Guide—U.S. Army* (1989).

Part II:
The Basics of Helicopter Crash Litigation

Handling helicopter crash cases requires a familiarity with the rules and procedures for handling ordinary products liability lawsuits as well as the specific statutory and regulatory framework applicable to general aviation lawsuits. General aviation refers to those aircraft such as helicopters and small airplanes holding fewer than twenty passengers which were not engaged at the time of the flight in scheduled passenger-carrying operations. The vast majority of all litigated helicopter crash cases are referred to and handled as general aviation lawsuits. Helicopter crash cases are subject to different laws, legal procedures, federal regulations, and other considerations than commercial airliner crash cases, especially those involving international flights. The Warsaw Convention and other international treaties do not apply.[1] Other differences between commercial aircraft crashes and helicopter accidents include the imposition of commercial airliner common carrier liability, damages restrictions, use of multi-district litigation, plaintiffs' and defendants' steering committees, and the potential application of international treaties. However, precisely the same law applicable to other types of negligence or products liability cases is applicable to helicopter crash litigation.

Federal investigation of the accident is different. A commercial carrier crash is characterized by the NTSB as a major accident with multiple investigators, groups and group chairs. In contrast, every general aviation helicopter crash accident is investigated by a single NTSB employee referred to as the Investigator-in-Charge or IIC for short.

Prior to undertaking representation in any helicopter crash matter, plaintiff's counsel must be prepared to expend the necessary lawyer time in mastering those laws and regulations applicable to the facts of the case at hand. Substantial investigative efforts are required at the outset to determine if the case is viable. Helicopter crash litigation is expensive. Counsel must be prepared to outlay substantial sums of money, usually over several years, prior to disposition whether by trial or settlement. It is the chief objective of this book to render that representation in all respects more efficient and just.

---

1. Warsaw Convention for Unification of Certain Rules Relating to International Transportation by Air, Oct. 12, 1929, 49 Stat. 3000, T.S. No. 876 (1934).

Chapter 3

Pre-Filing Matters

Introduction

Upon being retained, plaintiff counsel's first order of business is to obtain as much information as possible about the helicopter crash. That inquiry will focus on the subject helicopter, the terrain and crash site, the helicopter's maintenance history, the accident and incident history of the helicopter and pertinent components as well as background data on the helicopter's owner and operator, the pilot, and the maintenance facility. All such factors bear on the following question: What was the cause of the helicopter crash and is there an identifiable and viable defendant subject to suit? Insofar as is possible, the answers to this question should be obtained before a lawsuit is undertaken. The purpose of this chapter is to assist counsel in meeting this significant early challenge.

3.1 Preliminary Factual Investigation

Unfortunately, defendants in helicopter crash litigation enjoy a number of inherent advantages over plaintiffs who bring the lawsuit. They receive almost immediate notification of the helicopter crash from the National Transportation Safety Board (NTSB) which invites them to participate in all aspects of the crash investigation. These defendants will have prompt access to both the crash site and the wreckage itself. They will retain defense counsel to undertake immediate steps to represent and protect their interests. Where the target defendants are also the product manufacturers they tend to have a sizeable financial advantage over injured plaintiffs as well. Nevertheless, plaintiffs are not totally powerless from an investigative standpoint. Counsel can acquire a wealth of information to assist in the threshold representation decision and, if counsel agrees to accept the case, that information will assist in identifying potential defendants and legal theories.

A. Initial Client Contact and Retention—The Statutory Time Constraints

From a timing standpoint, plaintiff's counsel is unconditionally at the mercy of when he is first contacted and retained by the potential client. Often, counsel are contacted only because the family is unable to obtain any information about the circumstances which caused the helicopter to crash. They seek counsel to discover what happened and why.

Those unfortunate enough to be involved with a serious helicopter crash have far more critical and urgent needs and concerns, including in many cases their very survival. Family members of those killed in a helicopter crash have significant shock and grief issues which overlay the unhappy planning of funerals and visitations. Those impacted have fears of long-term financial hardship which often are triggered immediately. Rarely do family members have the presence of mind to retain counsel to initiate an investigation in the midst of such a tragic calamity.

Upon first contact by a potential client, counsel must be knowledgeable of all relevant and applicable legal time restraints and deadlines bearing on the claim. These include statutes of limitations as short as one year in several states such as Kentucky, Louisiana and Tennessee. The majority of states have a two-year statute of limitations. A couple, such as Maine and North Dakota, have a six-year statute of limitations for injury claims but only two years for wrongful death claims.

Statutes of repose are particularly perilous and are traps for the unwary. Such statutes place an arbitrary and finite period of time on the filing of a products liability lawsuit based on the years in service of the product. These statutes will come into play in any helicopter crash involving a claim against the manufacturer of the helicopter airframe, the engine, or any component part installed therein that is alleged to have failed and contributed to the crash.

Most statutes of repose run from the date of manufacture or initial delivery of the helicopter or component part to the date of the injury-producing event which is the helicopter crash. There are a select few statutes of repose, however, which run from the date of manufacture or initial delivery to the actual filing of the lawsuit such as in North Carolina. Prompt investigation and filing are mandatory in those states. These statutes range from very short periods of repose such as five years from the date of sale in Kentucky to ten years in Indiana and many other states.

An updated chart of the current statute of limitations periods and statute of repose time periods for all fifty states is set out below, but counsel must always check that state's specific statute for any potential exceptions or limitations

such as extensions for minors' claims or for fraud. See Table 3.1.

In addition to various state statutes of repose, there is the federal statute of repose set forth in the General Aviation and Revitalization Act of 1994 (GARA).[1] GARA provides that no civil action for damages arising out of an accident involving a general aviation aircraft may be brought against the manufacturer of any aircraft or aircraft component if the date of the crash is more than 18 years after the date the aircraft or component was first delivered to a person engaged in selling these aircraft.[2]

This statute of repose has allowed helicopter and helicopter component part manufacturers to obtain dismissal of many otherwise meritorious actions. The federal statute of repose is inherently unjust given that these manufacturers have knowledge and every expectation that owners and operators use their helicopters and certain component parts for far longer than 18 years. Nonetheless, one of counsel's first duties is to ascertain the date of manufacture of the helicopter, the engine, and the critical component parts. A fuller exposition of the GARA statute of repose is contained in Section 6.1(B) with emphasis on the applicability of various exceptions.

One of the most difficult things a lawyer must do in the practice of law is to advise a potential client that she has no legal remedy because of the application of a statute of limitations or restrictive statute of repose. Far worse, however, are those instances where a lawyer contacted and retained by a helicopter crash victim simply sits on the file either by ignorance or neglect hoping for a favorable report from the NTSB while the short statute of repose runs out.

Some of the applicable, albeit non-legal, time considerations arise from the lapse of time between the helicopter accident and counsel's retention. In addition to a prompt on-site inspection, counsel will have to take steps to locate the wreckage and identify its owner or custodian. Counsel immediately must send an evidence preservation letter by certified mail to the owner or custodian demanding that the wreckage not be scrapped or otherwise altered or destroyed in any way and with the further demand that all wreckage should be preserved and maintained including protective covering if it is outside in the elements. Counsel should offer to pay any reasonable expenses associated with preservation of the wreckage. Following acceptance of the representation, counsel must promptly secure the services of aircrash reconstruction experts with specific helicopter accident experience.

In conducting a preliminary factual investigation counsel may encounter a number of roadblocks including the inability to gain access to the helicopter wreckage or even

Table 3.1
State By State Statutes Of Limitations (SOL) and Statutes Of Repose

State	SOL Personal Injury	SOL Product Liability	SOL Wrongful Death	Statute of Repose
Alabama	2 Years	1 Year	2 Years	10 year repose statute declared unconstitutional
Alaska	2 Years	2 Years	2 Years	None
Arizona	2 Years	2 Years	2 Years	12 years after product first sold
Arkansas	3 Years	3 Years	3 Years	None
California	2 Years	2 Years	2 Years	None
Colorado	2 Years	2 Years	2 Years	10 year rebuttable presumption that product was not defective or negligently manufactured
Connecticut	2 Years	3 Years	2 Years	10 years from date of product sale
Delaware	2 Years	2 Years	2 Years	None
Florida	4 Years	4 Years	2 Years	12 years from delivery of product to original purchaser if product has useful life of 10 years or less. 20 years from delivery of aircraft, vessels, railroad equipment, etc.
Georgia	2 Years	2 Years	2 Years	10 years from first sale of product
Hawaii	2 Years	2 Years	2 Years	None
Idaho	2 Years	2 Years	2 Years	10 years or after the expiration of the product's useful safe life
Illinois	2 Years	2 Years	2 Years	Either 10 years from date of sale or delivery to initial user or 12 years from date of first sale.
Indiana	2 Years	2 Years	2 Years	10 years after delivery of product to initial user, unless cause of action accrues at least 8 years but less than 10 years after initial delivery—then 2 years after the cause of action accrues.
Iowa	2 Years	2 Years	2 Years	15 years unless product is specifically warranted for longer period by manufacturer
Kansas	2 Years	2 Years	2 Years	10 years or after expiration of useful sale life of product. If manufacturer warrants life of product more than 10 years, then statute extended to the length of the warranty.
Kentucky	1 Year	1 Year	1 Year from appointment of Personal Representative. If no PR, 2 years from date of death.	Rebuttable presumption of repose; 5 years from date of sale or 8 years from date of manufacture.
Louisiana	1 Year	1 Year	1 Year	None
Maine	6 Years	6 Years	2 Years	None
Maryland	3 Years	3 Years	3 Years	None
Massachusetts	3 Years	3 Years	3 Years	None

continued on next page…

Table 3.1 (continued)
State By State Statutes Of Limitations (SOL) and Statutes Of Repose

State	SOL Personal Injury	SOL Product Liability	SOL Wrongful Death	Statute of Repose
Michigan	3 Years	3 Years	3 Years	None
Minnesota	2 Years	4 Years	3 Years	Expiration of product's ordinary useful life
Mississippi	3 Years	3 Years	3 Years	None
Missouri	5 Years	5 Years	3 Years	None
Montana	3 Years	3 Years	3 Years	None
Nebraska	4 Years	4 Years	2 Years	10 years from date sold or leased if manufactured in Nebraska. If outside of Nebraska, then state's statute of repose applies but not less than 10 years. If state where product is manufactured has no statute of repose, then only 4-year SOL applies.
Nevada	2 Years	2 Years	2 Years	None
New Hampshire	3 Years	3 Years	3 Years	Previous statute of repose declared unconstitutional
New Jersey	2 Years	2 Years	2 Years	None
New Mexico	3 Years	3 Years	3 Years	None
New York	3 Years	3 Years	2 Years	None
North Carolina	3 Years	3 Years	2 Years	12 years from initial purchase
North Dakota	6 Years	2 Years	2 Years	Expiration of the useful safe life of an aircraft or aircraft component against the manufacturer
Ohio	2 Years	2 Years	2 Years	10 years from date product delivered
Oklahoma	2 Years	2 Years	2 Years	None
Oregon	2 Years	3 Years for death; 2 Years for personal injury	3 Years	10 years from first purchase for use or consumption
Pennsylvania	2 Years	2 Years	2 Years	None
Rhode Island	3 Years	3 Years	3 Years	Previous repose statute declared unconstitutional.
South Carolina	3 Years	3 Years	3 Years	None
South Dakota	3 Years	3 Years	3 Years	10 years after delivery for aviation product liability claims; Expiration of aviation product's useful safe life
Tennessee	1 Year	1 Year	1 Year	10 years from purchase or within 1 year of expiration of useful life, whichever is shorter.
Texas	2 Years	2 Years	2 Years	15 years from date of sale, unless product has a written warranty longer than 15 years
Utah	4 Years	2 Years	2 Years	None
Vermont	3 Years	3 Years	2 Years	None
Virginia	2 Years	2 Years	2 Years	None
Washington	3 Years	3 Years	3 Years	Expiration of useful, safe life of product. 12 years is the rebuttable presumption of safe life.

continued on next page...

Table 3.1 (continued)
State By State Statutes Of Limitations (SOL) and Statutes Of Repose

State	SOL Personal Injury	SOL Product Liability	SOL Wrongful Death	Statute of Repose
West Virginia	2 Years	2 Years	2 Years	None
Wisconsin	3 Years	3 Years	3 Years	None
Wyoming	4 Years	4 Years	2 Years	None

the crash site if on restricted or private property, inability to obtain data from any governmental investigative agency or even the absence of any survivor accounts or on-scene witnesses. In such instances, the imperative of an applicable time constraint will compel counsel to file the lawsuit with only bare bones knowledge as to any potential contributing factors and, hence, the potential target defendants. It is in that time crunch scenario that a trusted team of experienced helicopter crash accident investigators will be required to identify all potential defendants to assist in preparing the lawsuit in an effort to preserve the claim.

B. Initial Interaction with the National Transportation Safety Board

It is the responsibility of the National Transportation Safety Board (NTSB) to investigate all civil aircraft crashes within the United States.[3] The Board also has the legal duty to determine the actual or probable cause of aircraft accidents and to report the facts, conditions and circumstances relating to any such crashes. In general aviation crash cases involving small airplanes and helicopters, the NTSB typically assigns a single investigator to lead the investigation and assemble the investigative team. In virtually every helicopter crash case, the NTSB will have conducted an initial on-site investigation and taken control of the helicopter wreckage weeks or even months before plaintiff's counsel is retained.

It is good practice as well as common courtesy for counsel to contact the investigator-in-charge (IIC) upon undertaking the representation either in writing or by telephone to apprise him of the representation. In this early contact with the NTSB, counsel should offer any assistance in making records available to the extent they are under counsel's control such as maintenance or pilot logs. A professional and respectful inquiry into the progress of the investigation is appropriate as well. On occasion, the IIC will have placed a courtesy call to a family member to inform her of the general process and perhaps of some early factual findings.

Families are astounded to learn that they or their representatives can have no role whatsoever in the initial on-site

helicopter crash investigation or even follow-up component part examinations such as engine teardowns which take place at a manufacturer's facility under NTSB supervision. The most disadvantageous aspect of the NTSB investigation is that until the NTSB formally releases the helicopter wreckage and any pertinent component parts, no other parties are allowed to examine it.

The inability to have access to the wreckage puts plaintiff's counsel at a tremendous disadvantage given the prospect of as little as two years within which to file the lawsuit in the majority of states. Frequently, the first time plaintiff's counsel and his experts physically examine and inspect the helicopter wreckage will be well after the lawsuit has been filed.

Compounding this disadvantage of initial inaccessibility to such key evidence is that the parties potentially responsible for the crash are invited to be party participants in the NTSB investigation. The regulations restrict the parties to any NTSB field investigation as follows:

> Parties [to the field investigation] shall be limited to those persons, government agencies, companies, and associations whose employees, functions, activities or products were involved in the accident or incident and who can provide suitable, qualified technical personnel actively to assist in the [field] investigation.[4]

The upshot of this provision is quite literally to permit the potential defendants to participate and actively provide input into the investigation, testing, factual findings and Probable Cause Report. Invariably, the "party participants" are the helicopter and engine manufacturer and any helicopter component part manufacturer or supplier that might be implicated in the crash investigation.

The impact of this provision is to keep out lawyers and their expert consultants who represent the victims of helicopter crashes. The natural and unavoidable consequence of this process is that these participants almost always wear two hats. They are anointed as NTSB party participants to make independent and objective inquiry into a helicopter crash but shortly thereafter are leading and coordinating the defense efforts for their respective companies.

This result is not entirely the fault of the NTSB. NTSB personnel work very hard and the agency is habitually understaffed. NTSB personnel are simply forced to rely heavily on helicopter manufacturers or manufacturers of critical components to participate on the investigative team and provide information about the function of their products.

Far too often the NTSB's conclusion that there was "no in-flight product or system malfunction" is based solely on the manufacturer of that product's own post-crash examination and testing of its product. While these challenges to establishing liability are significant, they are not insurmountable. All of these relationships can and should be dealt with firmly and directly throughout discovery and at trial. Occasionally, counsel may have a representative or the client present at an NTSB-supervised subsequent helicopter or component testing if the client was an owner or operator of the helicopter. The basis for participation is that such a representative may have information bearing on the operation and maintenance practices of the helicopter which could prove of assistance in the investigation.

Destructive testing of a helicopter component or system by the NTSB and the "party participants" frequently occurs prior to the plaintiff's retaining counsel. If retained early enough, counsel quickly should determine whether NTSB has any plans for destructive testing of any system or helicopter component part. An IIC may permit a representative of the plaintiff, not counsel, to be present and observe the procedure. Such instances are at the discretion of the investigator. Another avenue is to ask the NTSB investigator whether the experts may conduct a "hands off" visual inspection of the wreckage and parts. The NTSB has been sympathetic to plaintiff's statute-of-limitations concerns and often grants such access because the helicopter manufacturer and insurance industry representatives are already parties to the NTSB investigation team and have had full access to the wreckage.

An engine teardown is performed under the NTSB's authority at the helicopter engine manufacturer's facility whenever NTSB investigators suspect an in-flight loss of engine power. On rare occasions, the NTSB has permitted plaintiff experts, but not plaintiff's counsel, to witness the engine teardown. Plaintiffs have a better chance of having a representative attend if they, their family, or their employer owns the aircraft. The teardown is an invaluable early opportunity for an expert to examine the engine for indications of internal failure. If plaintiff's request to be present at an engine teardown is refused by the NTSB investigator, plaintiff should request that the procedure be carefully photodocumented as a measure of preserving evidence.

With the high workload of NTSB investigators and the number of general aviation accidents in the U.S., it is taking longer to obtain reports from the NTSB. The NTSB will prepare a preliminary accident report setting out only basic facts such as the pilot's certification, training and experience, information concerning the manufacture and history of the subject aircraft, weather information, and an abbreviated wreckage description and crash sequence record. Following conclusion of the investigation, the NTSB will issue its final Factual Report as well as its Probable Cause Report. These reports are presented to and approved by the full Board. Once approved, both documents are promptly placed on the NTSB website and mailed to those who have previously made a written request for the reports.

The significance of the Factual Report is that it will be fully admissible at trial. Any factual information obtained during the accident investigation is admissible for use by the litigants at trial.[5] Not so with the Probable Cause Report which sets out the NTSB's findings as to the probable causal factors of the helicopter crash. That Probable Cause Report is not admissible at trial pursuant to federal statute.[6]

By establishing an early and courteous line of communication with the NTSB, plaintiff's counsel may be privy to the timing of the wreckage or component part release and the progress of the various reports. In no case should counsel ever wait on and be totally reliant upon any of the NTSB reports. Counsel owes a duty to the plaintiff to accomplish a concurrent, thorough and independent investigation insofar as is possible under the circumstances. Counsel should timely file the lawsuit and obtain access to the helicopter wreckage at the earliest practicable opportunity for more in-depth examination, study and testing by the experts.

In some instances, the only reasonably reliable information available to counsel is the initial Incident Report prepared by the NTSB. This is to be distinguished from the Preliminary Factual Report and the subsequent Factual Report which delve into the crash in far greater detail. Having only the NTSB incident report still provides counsel with a number of leads which may by itself suggest the potential target defendants. The identification of the helicopter includes the year of manufacture, identity of the manufacturer and model number. In one case, the initial Incident Report identified a 1974 Bell Jet Ranger 206B. Early concerns centered on the applicability of the 18-year GARA statute of repose. Only later did counsel discover that the crash-producing malfunction originated from a separation of one of the main rotor blades in flight and that this rotor blade was recently replaced.

By checking with the FAA Main Aircraft Registry in Oklahoma City, Oklahoma, the aircraft registration or tail number can identify the owner of record of the helicopter.

This provides a solid lead to obtaining further information on the history, type of usage, and maintenance with respect to the helicopter.

C. Inspection and Documentation of the Helicopter Crash Site

An immediate inspection and examination of the crash site is necessary to assist in the process of identifying viable target defendants so that the initial lawsuit pleadings can be prepared and timely filed in the appropriate court. The timing of when counsel is first retained is the most critical factor relative to examination of the helicopter crash site. When counsel is first retained a year or even two years post-crash the likelihood of the crash site yielding any meaningful information is minimal. In those instances, counsel are forced to rely entirely on the photodocumentation of the site by NTSB investigators, local government authorities or media outlets.

Arrangements should be made to inspect the helicopter crash site as soon as possible. The objective is to acquire as much information from the scene for purposes of determining the sequence and force of the helicopter crash. Experienced helicopter accident investigators will look to pinpoint the initial impact of the aircraft with the terrain or surrounding objects. The surrounding search should include careful examination of trees, poles, rooftops and the like for any indication of flight path contact. Even where a changing of the seasons and the passage of time has eviscerated any remnants of the crash it is still essential for counsel and the accident reconstruction expert to personally inspect the crash site. So doing will give the lawyer a perspective of the crash scene including the direction of travel of the helicopter, the gradation and level of the terrain including positioning of trees and any other nearby buildings or other landmarks. Most experienced accident investigators will insist on going to the scene for an inspection. In one recent helicopter crash case it was necessary to have the height and configuration of utility wires measured and calculated by a survey team as part of the overall case analysis.

Another potential advantage of visiting the accident scene is that plaintiff's accident reconstruction expert may note markings or actually discover parts which the NTSB team inadvertently missed. For example, in a recent helicopter crash in a cornfield in Iowa, a key component of the helicopter was not discovered until months later after the corn had been harvested.

On several occasions, plaintiff's accident reconstruction consultants have noted physical evidence which had gone undetected by the NTSB accident team investigators who were on the scene immediately after the crash. Weather conditions or the nature of the terrain also may have hindered the immediate post-crash gathering of data. The NTSB on-site investigation is done without benefit of a full-scale wreckage or component examination. Once the liability team has focused in on a particular failure mode or malfunction, that may help direct the on-site inspection. Another factor that contributes to missing clues at the accident scene is the immediate priority of tending to the crash victims, including on-scene resuscitative efforts and the sensitive removal of any deceased.

In a recent helicopter crash involving a suspected tail rotor malfunction, gouge marks on the tarmac some distance from the initial crash site were not initially noted by the NTSB investigative team which included several representatives of the defendant manufacturers. A closer examination of the vicinity of the crash revealed this initial touchdown or impact point from which the helicopter actually bounced into its final wreckage configuration. That discovery was significant in explaining the overall helicopter crash sequence and, ultimately, the effect of the tail rotor malfunction on causing the loss of control of the helicopter.

Although the wreckage is likely to have been trucked to a storage facility by the owner or the NTSB, careful evaluation of the site will reveal clues as to the nature and cause of the crash. The initial contact point may reveal the aircraft's altitude, position, and angle of approach. "Scars" or ground markings made by impact should be measured for width, length, and depth. Dark discoloration on the ground may indicate fuel spillage or blood.

Careful measurements and photographs of clues are important because other liability experts may not be able to physically access the site. They must then rely on the photographs. Even where the NTSB has conducted an immediate and thorough site inspection, it is important for the plaintiff's accident reconstruction team to duplicate that effort as soon as possible for two reasons. First, the data generated by the NTSB early investigative team may not be available to plaintiff's counsel until months or even years later following the release of the Factual Report or even the final Probable Cause Report. Secondly, in order to fully develop the factual theory of liability, counsel's other liability experts will more often than not need to rely on the findings of the accident reconstruction expert.

In those rare instances where counsel are engaged early enough that the helicopter wreckage has not even been moved (which is rare indeed), the accident reconstruction may include a wreckage survey carefully detailing the precise location of the key structural components of the helicopter, engine, and the main and tail rotors.

All of this physical information is intended to provide the reconstruction expert with the most likely helicopter flight path to and including impact, the angle of impact with the ground or other object, and the approach and contact speeds. All of this information taken together can help establish whether the helicopter was spinning on impact, whether the pilot was attempting an autorotation, or whether a "run-on landing" was being attempted. The significance of each of these crash scenarios is apparent as each implicates a different potential malfunction and failure mode prior to crash of the helicopter.

The many ways of documenting on-scene information in this day and age include not only handwritten diagrams and maps but also digital photography and videotape. In some instances it has become important to obtain aerial photographs of the crash site where there is a disputed issue as to flight path or a structural framework issue involving separation or the destruction of the aircraft in flight. Aerial photography can be important to document one of those hard to explain helicopter crashes where there is no definable flight path. Aerial photographs may provide critical proof that the aircraft was out of control, spinning, and in an unusual or even fatal flight configuration. There can never be enough on-scene photographs especially early on because the specific locations that have the most relevance are frequently not known until later.

Counsel should arrange for the accident reconstruction expert who will be testifying at trial to be present for this early on-scene inspection and documentation. Where disputed issues arise as to the helicopter path or initial point of impact, the expert's presence on-scene and an earlier time may be especially persuasive to the jury.

Although most accident reconstruction experts in the aviation field are quasi-professional photographers it does warrant a few reminders so as to obtain the maximum benefit of these photographs. All on-scene photographs should be in color and if adequate lighting is an issue then appropriate steps need to be taken to insure that the objects and landscape are plainly visible. Smudges of paint on trees or sides of buildings may reveal the final movements of the helicopter before ground impact.

Most accident investigators are skilled at preparing diagrams which show the surface of the terrain, notable landmarks, and so-called proof points from which it may be surmised that there was contact with the helicopter in the moments before the crash. Although painstaking, sufficient time should be expended on site to document all of the important ground and other contact points.

One of the surest ways to lose a helicopter crash case at trial is to present a reconstruction of the helicopter crash sequence which is incompatible with the precise failure mode or malfunction claimed. The crash-producing failure or malfunction must explain and be consistent with the final flight path and crash sequence of the helicopter.

A notable helicopter crash site investigation was undertaken by the author in connection with the Grand Canyon helicopter crash of September 20, 2001 which killed six people and left a survivor with massive injuries. The crash involved a Eurocopter AS350-B2 that was returning to Las Vegas after an aerial sightseeing tour over the Grand Canyon. The crash occurred on the side of a butte. The crash site was on an outcropping which was the flattest spot in the vicinity. The NTSB investigator conducted an almost immediate site investigation and inspection and concluded that the helicopter had made a hard landing without contact by any object or terrain before impact. On October 14, 2002, thirteen months after the crash, plaintiff's accident investigation team traveled to the crash site by helicopter to conduct an in-depth inspection and photodocumentation.

Plaintiff's accident reconstructionists observed rotor blade strikes on the rising terrain adjacent to the site. These strikes indicated that the helicopter had been in a normal landing attitude just prior to ground impact which showed that the helicopter had landed on its skids. Plaintiff's consultants observed that from the location of the rotor blade strikes that the rotor system could not have been under engine power when the strikes occurred. From this observation they concluded that the pilot was executing an autorotative landing over the flattest terrain observable from the air. Subsequent investigation of the wreckage confirmed that there was a mechanical disconnect between the engine and the main rotor system. Moreover, the plaintiff's expert team was able to establish that the crash would have been a survivable occurrence if the helicopter fuel tank had been properly placed and protected.

Unfortunately, some helicopter crashes occur in locations which cannot easily be reached or for which no on-site inspection is physically possible. Some of these have occurred in mountainous regions where to conduct an inspection would be perilous and, hence, unadvisable. Other inaccessible locations include helicopter crashes over water such as in the Gulf of Mexico while on ferrying trips to and from off-shore petroleum platforms. Reconstructing a helicopter crash which occurs over water is challenging because of the difficulty of locating the wreckage. If the wreckage is findable, appropriate means must be undertaken to travel to that location and retrieve as much of the structural components as is possible. In many instances, the NTSB, the helicopter operator or a local governmental agency will assist in the cost of salvaging the wreckage. When they do not do so, counsel must consider the prospects of bearing that entire cost because of the critical need to examine the wreckage.

The precise location of the wreckage many times can be determined by means of fragments or parts floating on the surface. Visual fuel remnants may remain on the water's surface in the location where a helicopter has crashed. While it is far preferable to retrieve the entire helicopter wreckage for a careful and deliberate inspection, that is not always possible. Where the wreckage was not accessible or the cost of retrieval and salvage was deemed prohibitive, it is possible to retain experienced scuba divers to conduct underwater photography and to retrieve any parts suspected of contributing to the crash.

Investigation of a recent helicopter crash off the coast of Louisiana illustrates the importance of retrieving the wrecked helicopter. On February 12, 2007, a single-engine Eurocopter EC120B crashed while attempting to land on an offshore oil production platform. Both the commercial pilot and passenger were killed. There were substantial scrape marks and paint transfers on both the boom and the catwalk near the helipad of the platform. Pieces of the main rotor blade were scattered all about the platform. Fortunately, the NTSB was able to recover the wreckage from the water one week post-crash. All initial indications pointed to pilot negligence in the process of landing the helicopter and striking a nearby tower. The examination of the engine as pulled up from the floor of the Gulf waters revealed that the internal blades had separated prior to impact resulting in a total engine stoppage and power loss. The engine manufacturer's claim of pilot error dissolved and the case was settled for fair value.

D. Acquisition of Investigative Materials from Local Government Agencies and Media Outlets

Counsel should obtain any investigative reports prepared by local governmental agencies. The reports of local police, fire department personnel, and highway patrol are often exceptionally thorough. These local agencies may have personnel on-scene who have photodocumented the wreckage literally moments after the crash and the entire perimeter of the crash site as well. Some states, such as Illinois, have a dedicated aircrash accident investigator and reports prepared by that investigator are routinely thorough and well-documented.

For every aircraft accident, the local police and fire departments will issue reports on the time and location of the crash, weather conditions, rescue efforts, and passenger injuries. While their quality varies, these reports often include photographs that may provide clues and detail wreckage patterns or disbursements. The reports also may include eyewitness interviews that describe the flight path, unusual engine noises, the presence of smoke or fire, and the helicopter's descent and impact.

As part of the initial inspection process of the crash site, counsel should contact various media outlets which may

have taken scores of photographs in addition to the one that appeared on the front page of the local newspaper with the story of the helicopter crash. Local television stations often will send a camera team to the site of a helicopter crash and that footage can be of great value primarily because of its immediacy. Media will interview on-scene witnesses who may otherwise be difficult to locate. A thorough "download" of all information obtainable from local news media often will yield surprisingly useful results.

E. Interviews of All Eye and Ear Witnesses to the Helicopter Crash

In many helicopter crash cases, the ground witnesses report that "the helicopter's engine was sputtering or popping" or "the helicopter was spinning out of control." Such eyewitness accounts may help shed light on how and what caused the helicopter to crash. These on-scene fact witnesses should be interviewed and statementized promptly after counsel's retention. This aspect of the factual investigation can and should be accomplished prior to filing suit.

The effective procedures for obtaining accurate and detailed witness statements are as applicable to helicopter crashes as any other injury accident. A private investigator with significant experience in interviewing witnesses to aircrashes is a necessary tool in counsel's arsenal. The usual questions asked of a witness in motor vehicle accidents simply will not do. The sheer drama, shock and horror of observing a helicopter crash will unnerve most people and affect their recollection. Add to that the relative unfamiliarity most witnesses have with the flight characteristics of a helicopter, and the need for an experienced and skilled investigator becomes apparent.

Many witnesses will be uncertain and confused as to precisely what they saw. In one helicopter crash the witness was driving along the highway when he first saw the helicopter hovering. He then lost view of the helicopter and then saw it climb to about 100 to 200 feet above ground level (AGL). The witness then said, "It suddenly began to spin. I believe counter-clockwise, but upon reflection, I am really not certain. I believe it had its nose angled down and a moment later it started to descend rapidly, still spinning, and was apparently out of control. After several revolutions the helicopter dove to the ground, coming to rest on its right side."

Contrast that eyewitness observation with that of another witness who viewed the helicopter from about a quarter of a mile difference in direction. "I saw the helicopter hovering and then it proceeded back to the airport. It pitched sideways and the pilot hit the power and got the helicopter back up into the air. It then began to spin clockwise and the spinning slowed down and then the helicopter gained altitude and then it dove forward and down into the ground."

Yet another witness first saw the helicopter with its nose down at about a 30 degree angle. "The tail swung around about three times from northwest to the southwest and then it veered to the left." An experienced private investigator can extract meaning from these various descriptions and translate that into what probably and actually occurred. The methods and demeanor of the private investigator are similar to the techniques used in any other context. Although some investigators employ the technique of handwriting the statement and permitting the witness to sign it, it is far more effective, accurate and reliable to obtain a tape-recorded statement where the investigator at the outset asks for and receives the appropriate permission.

The interviews should be done in person rather than over the telephone and, preferably, they should be at the location of the crash as that often triggers specific memories which may later become fuzzy or lost. The goal of these on-scene witness statements is to document and record the witnesses' specific knowledge and observations including the precise movement of the helicopter, the precise location of the witness, and accurate description of any and all sounds. Such detailed observations can later be used to substantiate the more precise accident reconstruction scenario developed by the experts and form the basis for a computer-generated animation of the final flight and crash sequence. The investigator should inquire about post-crash activity including a careful description of sounds such as hydraulic fluid leakage, air release or "hissing," or mini-explosions. Careful questioning as to whether any of the occupants of the helicopter vocalized any sounds may be critical to a later claim of post-impact conscious pain and suffering.

In a recent case involving the crash of an air ambulance helicopter which killed the pilot as well as the flight nurse and paramedic, a critical issue was whether one of the occupants, a male flight nurse, survived the impact and lived for approximately 20-25 minutes. An on-scene eyewitness was located who had come to render aid to any crash survivors. When this witness was standing 10 to 12 feet from the wreckage she distinctly recalls hearing a male voice crying out "help me, help me." That testimony was critical evidence in support of plaintiff's damages claim of post-crash conscious pain and suffering.

Counsel should confer with the investigator prior to obtaining any witness statements. It is prudent to advise the investigator about any preliminary hypotheses concerning the crash scenario and what facts might be relevant thereto about which the investigator should make specific inquiry. In addition to the typical rules for conducting such recorded

interviews, there are some additional specific guidelines which have proven immensely useful in questioning witnesses to helicopter crashes:

1. The investigator should take along a small, scale model of a helicopter. Use of this model allows the witness to describe the movement of the helicopter in the air. This can yield much more precise information about the final movements of the helicopter prior to crash. This is especially so because most witnesses have no aviation experience or specialized aerodynamic training which they can call upon to describe the movement of a helicopter through the air. In several instances, it has proven helpful for the investigator to videotape the witness's description of the helicopter's precise maneuvering in the moments just prior to ground impact.

2. Despite the temptation, the investigator must permit the witness to describe what he saw in his own words. This is not the time for leading questions.

3. Scour the local media, police reports, fire department or highway patrol reports for the names of any eyewitnesses. In addition, a door-to-door or canvas search through the surrounding neighborhood or local businesses almost always will yield additional witnesses who had not previously been contacted by either a governmental agency or the local media.

4. As to those witnesses for whom a governmental agency or even the media have obtained any statement, the investigator should review those statements and be prepared to ask specific follow-up questions as necessary. For example, governmental investigative agencies are rarely interested in damages-type questions and will rarely ask about cries for help and a description or physical movement of any of the survivors.

5. The investigator should request that the witness draw a sketch or diagram of the flight path of the helicopter on a map of the area.

An outline of questions and subject matters for a helicopter crash witness is as follows:

1. Witness's name and residence address.
2. Acknowledge that statement is being recorded with witness's permission.
3. Acknowledge that investigator has identified herself and for whom she is working.
4. Personally observe a helicopter crash or flight of helicopter immediately prior to crash on (date and time)?
5. Where were you?
6. Familiar with area?

7. What was it that first caused you to be aware of the heli-copter? At what point did you notice something unusual or of concern?

8. Precisely where was the helicopter at moment in time you first observed it? Describe as best you can the flight path, altitude, whether it was climbing or descending, and its estimated speed. (Using the model of the heli-copter here is particularly helpful.)

9. Say in your own words what you observed to and through impact (if the witness observed impact).

10. Over what period of time were you observing this heli-copter in-flight?

11. Over what period of time did you observe the helicopter after the crash or post-impact?

12. Were the main rotor blades spinning or rotating at all times prior to the crash or ground impact? (Refer to model of helicopter.)

13. Was the tail rotor rotating or spinning at all times prior to the crash or ground impact? (Refer to model of he-licopter.)

14. Carefully describe the position of the helicopter in air just prior to impact (using model).

15. Describe movement of the helicopter upon ground impact in terms of roll, slide, turn, skid or none (using model).

16. Did you observe the helicopter strike or touch anything before crash or ground impact such as trees, wires, poles, side of building or any other object?

17. What were weather conditions like, especially wind speed and precipitation?

18. Are you aware of any other neighbors, business owners or friends who were in the area and also witnessed any aspect of this helicopter crash?

19. What did you do immediately after the crash (call 911, went to crash site, or other).

20. Did you see or hear anything after the helicopter hit the ground?

21. Did you see any of the survivors being extricated from the helicopter?

22. Did you witness any movement or sounds coming from any of the survivors?

23. Were you watching the helicopter in-flight the entire time from when you first looked at it until it crashed?

24. Were you able to hear the engine of the helicopter and, if you were, did you notice anything strange concerning how the engine sounded?

25. Have you been interviewed by anyone else concerning the helicopter crash and, if so, who?

26. Have you heard anything about the crash or why it hap-pened from any source?

27. Did you know the pilot or any of the other people on board the helicopter or any of their families?

28. Are the answers you have given to my questions true and accurate to the best of your knowledge and belief and will you confirm that I had your permission to re-cord this statement?

29. Can you think of anything else about this helicopter flight or the crash which you think might be important but which we have not talked about?

When the recorded statement is completed, the inves-tigator should obtain as much contact information from the witness as is possible so that counsel can locate the witness many years down the road for possible deposition or trial testimony. It has proven helpful to obtain contact informa-tion for other family members who would always know the whereabouts of this witness.

Eyewitness accounts, either singularly or in concert, are very useful in formulating preliminary crash scenarios as to what caused the helicopter to fly in the manner recounted. These eyewitness accounts need to be reconciled with the results of the on-site investigation as well as any available radar data, air traffic control communication, and other physical evidence.

Two recent case examples demonstrate the importance of these witness interviews. A helicopter crash in Arizona was a mystery. No ground eye or ear witnesses could be located. The NTSB investigator interviewed the only sur-vivor, a young woman. She described that the helicopter "just dropped" and the "the quiet was deafening." Utilizing this information, plaintiff's experts were able to pinpoint a potential flaw in the main rotor drive system by reason of a simple truth: while inside a helicopter in-flight, the pre-dominant noise is not that of the engine, it is the whirling of the main rotor blades.

The crash of a LifeNet helicopter in Nebraska also would be a mystery but for the carefully recorded observations of ground eye and ear witnesses to the crash. The experienced pilot reported to air traffic control a "binding in the right ped-al" and moments later the helicopter crashed on the airport tarmac. Numerous eyewitnesses reported that the helicopter prior to impact was spinning "in a clockwise fashion." That observation clearly implicated a classic tail rotor malfunc-tion and the subsequent NTSB report and plaintiff's experts confirmed a manufacturing defect in the tail rotor system.

F. Acquisition and Review of Engine and Maintenance Logbooks

Federal regulations require that the owner or operator of a helicopter maintain appropriate maintenance records.[7] Dur-ing this preliminary factual investigation, counsel should make every effort to obtain full, complete and readable copies of the entire aircraft and engine maintenance logbooks. The helicopter and helicopter engine certification are separately regulated. The Federal Aviation Regulations impose much stricter useful life limitations on helicopter components, such as rotor blades and other components which are subjected to very high levels of vibration, rotational or torsional stress, than on comparable components used in fixed-wing aircraft.

As with so many other aspects of the initial factual investigation of a helicopter crash, immediate acquisition of these records can be daunting. In those instances where the client or client's family is the owner or operator of the crash helicopter then obtaining those entire records seems simple enough. Unfortunately, that is not always the case. On a handful of occasions, following NTSB request for all of the maintenance records, they were handed over—and no copies of the original records were maintained. So it is never easy.

Obtaining physical possession of a copy of these records may require a bit of digging. If counsel or one of the retained experts has a good relationship with the maintenance shop (recall that we are still pre-filing), a request to have the records copied and picked up may be sufficient. The hull coverage insurance carrier may have copies of the records up to a certain point in time and be willing to make them available. And on occasion a professional and cordial request for copies of these records from the NTSB investigator may yield their production.

In those instances where the maintenance records are not obtainable prior to filing the lawsuit, other options to acquire maintenance information are to interview any of the mechanics who routinely put a wrench on the helicopter or any other pilots who regularly flew that helicopter. Such personnel can be interviewed as to any recent maintenance or operational anomalies or simply whether the logbooks seemed to be routinely updated and routine inspections performed.

The key things to look for in these maintenance records at this initial investigative stage are the following:

1. Any history of prior mishaps, hard landings, incidents or accidents over the life of the helicopter;
2. Pilot reports of chronic problems as to any flight control or performance issue, especially those close in time to the crash;
3. Recent repairs or parts replacement relating in any way to the engine, rotors or flight controls;
4. Whether mandatory 100-hour, annual inspections or other scheduled maintenance procedures were routinely and timely performed;

5. Whether service bulletins, airworthiness directives or any other recommended or required service or component replacement was timely complied with;
6. Whether the mechanics who performed the work on the helicopter were appropriately trained and FAA-certified; and
7. Whether there was any new or different maintenance procedure used on the helicopter engine, flight controls or other systems within the weeks preceding the crash.

As part of this review of the engine and maintenance logbooks, counsel should acquire the applicable maintenance manuals for the helicopter and all of its systems as well as the engine. Most experts have sufficient contacts within the helicopter industry that they either have these materials on hand or can access them readily. The primary point of inquiry with respect to the records is to note any maintenance discrepancy which would affect the airworthiness of the helicopter in the time period preceding and up to the time of the crash.

Every helicopter is accompanied not only by a maintenance manual but also an aircraft owner's manual and a pilot operating handbook (POH). The aircraft owner's manual contains basic data as to the helicopter specifications and performance capabilities, flight limitations and system descriptions. The POH contains detailed information as to both standard and emergency operational procedures for the helicopter as well as more detailed information concerning weight and balance computations. The manuals applicable at the time work was performed should be accessed and reviewed and any updated editions should be studied to see if more specific warnings or directions are included in the updated editions.

Once the lawsuit is filed, all maintenance records must be formally requested in discovery. The importance of a complete set of maintenance records cannot be sufficiently stressed. The defendants' use of any previously unseen records to examine plaintiff's expert at deposition or trial can be disastrous or, at the least, cause the expert to seem ill-prepared. For this reason it is advisable to identify and mark a "master set" of all engine and maintenance logbooks at the outset of discovery for use throughout the case.

G. Assessing Weather and Environmental Conditions

Many helicopter accident investigators have been trained to examine "the man" (pilot), "the machine" (helicopter) and "the environment" (weather). This last factor encompasses all of the weather and other outside or environmental factors prevailing at the time of the flight leading up to the crash. No reconstruction analysis of a helicopter crash can be complete without an accurate assessment of those conditions. These include temperature, wind speed and direction as well as the existence of lightning, cloud cover, fog, sudden or unexpected wind turbulence whether originating due to weather conditions or other aircraft, or unexpected smoke from a forest or ground fire. Fortunately, this information is readily and easily obtainable.

In every case, counsel must learn of the weather conditions prevailing at flight time and at the time of the crash. Counsel must determine the actual weather conditions and the weather information that was given to air traffic control or conveyed to the pilot immediately preceding take-off. One may look to the telephone weather briefings and the tape recordings of radio contact between the pilot or crew before and during the flight. Counsel can obtain the data from the local weather bureau, the local aircraft control tower, and the closest FAA regional office.

Counsel should start with those aviation weather conditions which were prevailing at a weather observation facility closest to the location of the crash. Ordering an official weather record can be accomplished by direct request of the closest Air Traffic Control facility or to the National Climatic Data Center (NCDC) at:

Commerce/NOAA/NNDC
c/o National Interest Security Company (NISC)
Attn: Fiscal Dept.
310 State Route 956, Building 300
Rocket Center, West Virginia 26726-9229
Phone (828) 271-4800, Facsimile (828) 271-4876).
Weather and climate data may now be obtained on line at ncdc.orders.noaa.gov.

If the Center is provided with basic information about the flight, it is capable of providing accurate weather information several weeks or months after the crash. NCDC can provide historical weather data close to the vicinity of the final flight path and crash location. It also can provide satellite images, radar observations, and surface weather observations. New weather resources are becoming available and counsel should search for other weather databases which may provide some specific information potentially applicable to the investigation. Other sources of prevailing weather conditions are the on-ground eyewitnesses in the vicinity of the crash and other pilots flying a similar flight path at the time of the crash.

Weather can be a factor in a helicopter crash in two ways: (1) certain unexpected or severe weather conditions such as low cloud cover, fog, smog, heavy piercing rain, hail, blinding snowfall, severe wind turbulence, hurricanes, tornadoes or thunderstorms can interfere with the pilot's visibility, ability to control the helicopter, or could potentially contribute to pilot disorientation, or (2) ice, lightning, wake turbulence from other larger aircraft or impact with migratory birds can physically interfere with the operation of the helicopter or damage a flight critical component.

A specific weather or environmental condition may play some contributory role in the helicopter crash by damaging the helicopter so severely that the pilot is unable to maintain controlled flight. This can be due to a direct lightning strike which disables electrical power or helicopter impact with a flock of geese which destroys one of the rotors. Another way these conditions play some role in a crash is by placing heightened demands on the pilot's skill, ability and judgment. These weather and environmental factors encompass both natural and man-made hazards.

When all available weather information is compiled, it must be reviewed to assess whether there are any potential weather-related phenomena which could have affected the operation or control of the helicopter or the visibility, physical condition or judgment of the pilot. If any of the above-delineated weather conditions is present or suspected during the crash flight, this will have a substantial impact on the causal analysis of the helicopter crash.

The focus then shifts to the pilot and what specific weather information he was provided with or observed prior to and during the mission. The meteorological information presented to the pilot prior to the mission should be obtained to assess its accuracy or whether conditions simply changed unexpectedly. That pre-flight weather briefing may trigger an inquiry as to whether the pilot should have undertaken the flight mission in the first place. This investigation will require closer scrutiny of the avionics and other instrumentation, the importance of which is enhanced during any adverse weather condition. Finally, inclement weather will entail careful examination of the flight control systems and the main and tail rotors to assess the effects of wind shear, icing, lightning, or some other environmental impact on the integrity and function of those components.

In those cases where weather is a predominant consideration, counsel must retain a well-qualified weather expert or meteorologist with specific experience in aviation. The pilot expert retained in such a scenario must be well familiar with the prevailing weather conditions or environmental circumstances at the time so as to address the impact of those weather or other conditions from the standpoint of whether the pilot exercised the proper standard of care.

Although strictly speaking, nighttime or prevailing darkness is not a weather condition, early evening cloud cover can bring the onset of darkness without warning to a pilot. "Nighttime condition" is often listed as a "contributing cause" or "contributing factor" to a helicopter crash. This refers either to the pre-planning or lack of foresight by the helicopter pilot in undertaking a mission in nighttime hours or flying at night over unfamiliar terrain with unmarked or unlit obstacles such as poles, utility wires, radio towers or even buildings.

The so-called lake effect is a visual phenomenon based on the reflection of light on water. It may momentarily blind or stun a pilot or cause loss of visualization of the horizon, as can a sudden appearance of the sun. The presence and impact of other aircraft or flocks of birds is an environmental condition which must be considered as well. If birds can bring down an Airbus 320 as occurred on January 15, 2009 and force Captain Chesley "Sully" Sullenberger to land in the Hudson River, a helicopter in that scenario would stand little chance.

The prospect of a bird strike causing or triggering a helicopter crash is not merely hypothetical. Even at the relatively lower speeds of helicopters, large birds may damage one of the rotors or other control functions. A bird strike which destroyed the windshield is suspected as a cause of the January 2009 crash of a Sikorsky S-76C helicopter in the Gulf of Mexico killing eight people.[8] The use of lightweight acrylic windshields is being examined in view of this crash. As the manufacturer of the helicopter, Sikorsky considered issuing a letter to helicopter pilots and operators warning of the potential danger of certain types of acrylic windshields which may be too light and flimsy to withstand bird strikes.[9]

At least one reported case involves a bird strike of a helicopter. While ferrying passengers to an offshore platform, a bird struck a helicopter, damaging its engine and causing the pilot to make a forced landing on an offshore platform. Because the cause of the accident was a bird striking the helicopter over open water, the appellate court affirmed the trial court's ruling that maritime law applied.[10]

The wake of a large commercial airliner is capable of severe wake turbulence impacting smaller aircraft such as a light helicopter, and that possibility should be investigated and ruled out. This is especially so if the crash occurred in the vicinity if an airport and at a time when other aircraft were landing or taking off. Severe air turbulence may cause a helicopter to roll sharply in one direction and this may cause loss of control of the aircraft. This factor may implicate air traffic control in failing to advise the pilot of the presence of a larger aircraft in that vicinity. Alternatively, the larger aircraft may have been flying outside of its directed flight path to the surprise of both the helicopter pilot and ATC.

The pilot's alertness and judgment may be affected by flying over forest fires due to the smoke contamination and resultant carbon dioxide which can lead to impairment of judgment and even total loss of consciousness. Helicopter pilots involved in fire-fighting operations have succumbed to such conditions due to visibility and heat factors in possible combination with enhanced intake of carbon dioxide in the lungs commonly referred to as hypoxia.

A severe rainstorm by itself may be contributory to the extent that the main or tail rotors become waterlogged creating a weight imbalance. The main and tail rotor blades are sealed units in large part to block moisture or other debris. Only if there is some un-airworthy condition in the blades would there be any potential for water to enter into the blades themselves. Ice buildup is as serious and potentially fatal a problem on a main rotor blade as it is on the wing of an airplane. In any icy condition, the pilot's inspection of the helicopter prior to takeoff is mandatory.

Wind shear is particularly dangerous for helicopters. Wind shear is a sudden or unexpected change of wind that creates an alteration of the helicopter flight path and which requires immediate and correct pilot response for safe recovery. Wind shear is especially detrimental to helicopters when the aircraft is on approach to land because a main rotor may strike the ground or other nearby object or the helicopter may strike the ground in an unintended landing configuration, causing a crash.

Lightning strikes still pose a threat of damage even though modern helicopters are equipped with various types of lightning protection including lightning diverters and surge protectors. Nevertheless, these systems are not infallible and lightning may disrupt the navigation equipment or a direct strike could cause damage to a rotor or flight control. The other danger of lightning is that it could cause momentary blindness of a helicopter pilot resulting in loss of control of the helicopter.

H. Pilot's Training, Certification and Ratings

Since in every case the pilot's actions will be scrutinized, counsel should acquire all the pilot's certificates, ratings, and log books. The types and grades of certificates are detailed in Part 61 of the Federal Aviation Regulations (FARs), and counsel should consult these early on. Two matters that arise frequently are whether a pilot holds a current and valid medical certificate and whether he is properly certificated for the particular helicopter model being flown.

Each pilot maintains his own logbooks which record the flight time as pilot-in-command. Since the pilot logbooks typically accompany the pilot, they are often damaged or destroyed in the crash of the helicopter especially where there was a post-impact fire. In some instances where these logbooks have incurred significant smoke or even water damage, there are a number of techniques which can be used to preserve or even enhance their readability including freeze-dry technology.

If available, these logbooks should be studied to determine the total flight time as pilot-in-command that the pilot had with the subject crash helicopter, his flight time with other same type or model helicopters and total helicopter flight time across the board. Experience has shown that the recent flight hours of a helicopter pilot are more revealing of problems than the total number of hours the pilot has accumulated.

In every helicopter crash lawsuit, the pilot's qualifications, health, and actions will be scrutinized. This is true whether the pilot or his employer is a defendant or plaintiff. Medical examiners routinely will test for alcohol or other performance-debilitating substances. The complete autopsy protocol normally includes a test for carbon monoxide poisoning as well. The presence of any drug in the pilot's system colors the entire case because it diverts attention from any other problem, such as a mechanical malfunction.

I. Collectibility and Insurance Coverage Issues

One of the most difficult decisions faced by plaintiff's counsel is whether to proceed against a potentially liable defendant without knowledge of that defendant's ability to pay a verdict or the extent of its available insurance coverage. As there are no current minimum insurance coverages required by helicopter operators, pilots or maintenance facilities, this matter has too often been a "shot in the dark." Plaintiff's counsel may not be able to discover the existence or amount of any given defendant's applicable insurance coverage until after suit is filed.

In a recent case arising out of a crash in Hawaii, the early fact investigation led to the conclusion that the pilot executed a controlled flight into terrain (CFIT) with no discernible in-flight malfunction of any component or system, a clear case of pilot error. Counsel sent a certified letter to the target defendant, a small locally-based tour operator, requesting that it be passed along to its insurance carrier. The insurance carrier telephoned counsel and relayed that there was $100,000.00 of coverage per each seat for a total of $200,000.00 which sum, following written confirmation, was promptly tendered. This process averted the time and expense of filing the lawsuit although the outcome provided scant redress to the children whose parents were killed in the crash.

The expense of such cases and the likely significant judgment entered upon a favorable verdict forces counsel to realistically assess the prospects of collectibility from the array of potentially liable defendants. Where that list includes a major aircraft manufacturer or parts components supplier and the joint and several laws are not officious, the prospect of full recovery by judgment or settlement is at least potential. Unfortunately, in the many cases where the pilot's experimental or home-built helicopter crashes and kills the passenger the prospects of meaningful recovery are dim. Similarly, in those instances where the pilot and passengers are co-employees such as in the air ambulance helicopter scenario, negligence by the pilot resulting in a crash will deprive the passengers of recovery by operation of the exclusive remedy provision of state workers' compensation statutes.

Most general liability policies of insurance have express aircraft or aviation exclusions. Unless aviation insurance is specifically provided for and applicable there is virtually no prospect of recovering other avenues of insurance such as through a general homeowner's or automobile policy. One recourse for this potential recoverability issue is to place the financial burden of a crash on the owner, operator or leasee of the aircraft. Such liability is based on state statutes such as one in Iowa rendering it unlawful to operate any aircraft within the state "in a careless or reckless manner so as to endanger the life or property of another."[11] The operation of aircraft is then defined as including those who "cause or authorize the operation of aircraft, whether with or without the right of legal control (in the capacity of owner, lessee, or otherwise).[12] At minimum in those states with a comparable statute it provides another lawful and ethical avenue of collectibility in the event of a helicopter crash attributable solely or primarily to the fault of the pilot.[13]

J. Practice Checklist: Helicopter Crash Initial Factual Investigation Checklist

The following checklist is a summary of the basic factual investigation which should be performed at the earliest stages of the case:

1. Send an investigator to the scene immediately to document and record the physical evidence of the accident and to interview all on-scene eye and ear witnesses.
2. Send evidence preservation letter to all parties with possession or control of helicopter wreckage, any component parts, the maintenance records, pilot logbooks and other pertinent documentation.
3. Have the wreckage examined by helicopter accident reconstruction specialist who will have the entire helicopter wreckage documented and photographed.
4. Order Aircraft Records package from the Federal Aviation Administration in Oklahoma City to determine the

history of ownership, modification, and damage of the aircraft involved.

5. Obtain all of the helicopter's maintenance records.

6. Review all applicable Service Letters and Service Bulletins on the particular make and model of helicopter.

7. Determine all applicable Airworthiness Directives and compliance with those directives.

8. Place courtesy call to NTSB Investigator-in-Charge (IIC).

9. Obtain all investigative reports from local governmental agencies.

10. Obtain current Pilot's Operating Handbook (POH) and FAA approved Flight Manual (where applicable) for the make and model helicopter.

11. Obtain information and specifications of undamaged helicopter of the same make and model.

12. Obtain manufacturer's Shop Manual (maintenance manual) and Parts Manual.

13. Order FAA Engineering Manufacturing Branch files on the make and model helicopter and certified copies.

14. Obtain certified copies and certified transcripts of tape recorded conversations between ATC and the helicopter pilot including copy of audiocassette tape.

15. Obtain certified copies of pertinent weather information.

16. Obtain certified copies of the pilot's airman records.

17. Obtain certified copies of the pilot's medical records.

18. Obtain from the FAA computer a certified computer printout of Malfunction or Defect Reports concerning the suspected failed part.

19. Order "Blue Ribbon" copy of the NTSB report.

20. Obtain all media accounts of helicopter crash including photographs and videotape.

3.2 Early Selection, Retention and Utilization of Liability Experts[14]

Helicopter crash litigation compels the hiring and retention of well qualified and experienced helicopter crash experts. This section addresses the basic factors to consider in selecting and retaining experts. While there are some variations among the states as to the procedural foundations for presenting expert testimony, counsel should look to the specific jurisdiction to determine the specific standards applicable thereto. Any helicopter crash expert possessing the background and qualifications discussed herein should meet the expert criteria for any court, including the most rigorous *Daubert* standard.[15] Counsel has the responsibility to insure that the well-qualified expert base her opinion on suitable testing, documentation and testimony so that the opinions are properly presented at trial to a jury.

Helicopter crash litigation requires hiring a broad range of expert witnesses and consultants. Counsel may need to enlist the help of a helicopter piloting expert, an airframe and power plant mechanic, an engine design expert and a metallurgist, all in the same case. Counsel must assemble an all-star team of experts from a variety of disciplines. The disciplines include aeronautical and mechanical engineering, metallurgy, helicopter pilot training and operation, federal aviation regulations, helicopter maintenance and operational procedures, and helicopter accident reconstruction. The use of experts and consultants in helicopter litigation is never optional. From the initial work-up of the case, counsel must collaborate with the expert team and in the first instance must rely on them for initial suspect causes of the crash and identification of the potential target defendants.

A. Criticality of Early Retention

Counsel cannot wait idly for the NTSB to do all the work. By the time the agency completes its investigation the statute of limitations may have run and the claim could be forever gone. Alternatively, the NTSB investigator may rely too heavily on the helicopter manufacturer's input or testing and adopt that favorable conclusion in the final Factual Report. There are countless cases where the well-intentioned NTSB investigator concludes that it was the negligence of the helicopter pilot which contributed to the crash but a judge or jury hearing all of the evidence determines otherwise. The early selection and continuous involvement of the experts yields an important collateral benefit in terms of the credibility of those experts' testimony at trial. The early involvement of experts from the start of the case also permits location and retention of any highly specialized or unusual fields of expertise. That specialty expert can be recommended by one of the existing experts if necessary.

The vast majority of lawyers who handle helicopter crash and other aviation accidents work with a regular team or core group of experts who can be quickly assembled in order to "roundtable" the case. For counsel not yet equipped with many years of experience in handling helicopter litigation, a prudent plan is to use a helicopter consulting expert simply to teach the lawyer about the disciplines involved and their interaction. Even for the experienced lawyer, use of such consultants through the discovery process is routine. Such expertise will help in preparing both the initial and follow-up written discovery.[16]

Early expert consultation can help assess the most probable causes and rule out alternative causes. This process is essential for identifying potential defendants. As the investigation progresses, experts should be hired as needed to help develop the case. Counsel must immediately hire any experts who may be retained by the defense because many well-known and highly qualified aviation experts testify for both plaintiffs and defendants.

Early inspection of the aircraft, engine, and other critical components can yield several tangible benefits, including the identity of potential defendants. The sooner potential defendants are identified, the sooner the lawsuit can be filed. Early inspection may also pinpoint areas where specialized expertise is needed. And it can bring into focus areas to explore in interrogatories and document requests.

Plaintiff's liability experts rarely will have the benefit of early access to the helicopter wreckage or components, because the items will be in the NTSB's custody. If the helicopter or engine wreckage is not available for inspection, counsel may not be certain which fields of expertise will be required. Counsel may have to make an educated guess about the types of experts that will be needed and retain them. A review of the accident photos and reports from the media, responding police and fire departments, witnesses, and survivors or family members can provide clues as to whether the crash occurred due to some malfunction or was the result of the pilot's negligence.

Retaining experts early gives them ample time to fully digest all the numerous materials routinely available in aviation cases and to perform other investigative tasks before they finalize their opinions and give deposition testimony. It is unrealistic to provide an expert with all the case materials and expect him to provide final opinions or deposition testimony in a few short weeks.

Counsel should hire a helicopter crash reconstructionist as early as possible to carefully examine, diagram, and photograph the accident scene. A seasoned crash investigator can learn a great deal at the scene. Such an expert can assess the angle of descent based on tree damage or damage to brush on the ground. The scars of ground impact can reveal other details, such as the aircraft's speed at impact and rate of descent, as well as whether the aircraft was spinning or flat and whether its wings were level. Burn or scorch marks may indicate a post-impact fire, and their location may point to a particular engine or the fuel tank as the source.

B. Selecting the Necessary and Appropriate Fields of Expertise

Usually the first question to be determined is whether the helicopter crash was due to some failure of some mechanical component or structure in-flight such as the engine or one of the rotors or whether there was pilot error. As soon as counsel have obtained some preliminary information about the helicopter crash, it will be possible to determine the fields of expertise necessary in order to reach the ultimate determination as to what caused the helicopter to crash and what parties are responsible.

The specific fields of expertise necessary may involve highly particular aspects of the helicopter itself, particular characteristics of the pilot including sufficiency of training, toxicology or pilot experience in-type and unique damages expertise such as pre-impact terror and forensic medicine to establish post-crash survival as well as biomechanical and medical expertise in crashworthiness cases. Given the gravity of most helicopter crashes, in the vast majority of cases there are no survivors to describe what may have occurred in the moments leading up to the crash. Information recounted by any survivor can be essential to the probable cause determination as illustrated by the Grand Canyon helicopter crash recounted earlier.[17]

Experts with specific expertise in helicopter crash investigation are necessary because these crashes often result in total destruction and devastation of the aircraft, and the investigation is quite literally putting pieces together akin to a jigsaw puzzle. Any aviation lawyer who has worked with outstanding helicopter crash reconstruction experts knows the magic of which they are capable. After an hour or two of visually examining the helicopter wreckage, the best reconstruction experts often can arrive at a theory as to precisely how the crash occurred and what caused it. Succeeding steps in the investigation will prove them to be uncannily accurate.

Carefully coordinating the various liability and causation experts will help advance the plaintiff's factual theory of the case and fend off the anticipated defense counterattacks. Before focusing on the precise areas of expertise needed, counsel should make every attempt to narrow the potential cause or causes of the helicopter accident to one of the following areas:[18]

1. Pilot error—insufficient training or experience, a medical condition, alcohol or drug use, insufficient rest, or operational error.
2. Mechanical malfunction—power plant failure such as a fuel problem, oil leak, metal fatigue, or part breakage, failure or control problem with main rotor blades or flight instrumentation malfunction such as the primary attitude indicator or other avionics, throttle control, rudder pedals, or helicopter control failure such as a tail rotor malfunction.
3. Weather or environmental factors—ice, fog, snow, heavy rain, air traffic control, fuel quality, lift-off weight, or severe air or wake turbulence.

Here are the most common areas of expertise required in helicopter crash litigation:

- helicopter certification and airworthiness of helicopter, engine, or component parts
- helicopter electrical and wiring systems or helicopter fuel and propulsion
- avionics (radio or global positioning system instrumentation), aeronautics (use of gyroscopes and other self-contained apparatus), and flight instrumentation (radar, altimeter, and digital gyroscope)
- manufacturing processes, material strength, and structural fatigue and integrity
- vibrational or torquing issues or welding and metal properties
- weather and meteorological issues

The other potential types of expertise needed include an aircraft engineer, aeronautical engineer, aerodynamicist, aircrash accident investigator, air traffic control expert, biomedical expert for crashworthiness issues, helicopter engine expert, federal air regulations expert, contamination and fuels expert, human factors expert, maintenance expert, forensic pathologist, piloting expert, photogrammetrist (photography and film expert), sound analysis expert, computer or electronic data retrieval expert, fire investigation expert, metallurgical expert, and forensic toxicologist.

An expert's conclusion that there was no in-flight or post-impact fire and that the helicopter's angle and speed of descent suggest a survivable impact may indicate that the aircraft's crashworthiness should be questioned. Counsel then should retain an expert on aircraft restraint systems to study the sufficiency of the seat belts and shoulder harnesses, seat-bracket attachments, seat and seat back design, and other crashworthiness factors.

Sometimes specific experience with a particular helicopter component is called for. For example in one recent helicopter case the experience of an A&P mechanic dealing with one very specific repair and replacement issue became critical. What was most needed was a mechanic out in the field who kept abreast of revisions to the maintenance manual, observed the condition of the part in normal usage and had responsibility for a similar model helicopter. Just such a mechanic was found maintaining the precise helicopter model in Buenos Aires, Argentina. Although that mechanic had never before testified or been involved in any litigation, his earnest and thorough knowledge of the maintenance of the part in question and subsequent opinions were pivotal in the case.

C. Considerations for Hiring Helicopter Crash Experts

Ready access to a trusted team of experts with whom counsel is already familiar and comfortable means that there is no lag time while the expert team is being assembled. That lag time refers to the due diligence process to be used by any lawyer in selecting an expert. The rule of thumb in these cases is identical to that applicable to any high stakes litigation. Counsel must investigate the background, qualifications, and experience of her own experts as diligently or more so than those experts retained by the defendants. Counsel must review the expert's published writings to ensure there are no statements that would be directly contrary to opinions or positions reached in the case at hand. And it is true that the single most effective way of locating other qualified experts is through the existing experts' recommendation.

Once these preliminary matters have been satisfied, then the final retention decision must be based on those typical factors involved in retaining an expert:

- Is the background and qualifications of the expert likely to be impressive to the judge and jury?
- Is this expert likely to be able to explain complex jargon to a jury so they may understand it?
- Will this expert be steadfast and resolute on cross-examination or will he wilt like a two-week old rose?

This process of expert selection and retention must have counsel's full attention because the case literally stands or falls by counsel's choice of experts. An expert who is unable to deliver the goods due to being disqualified for failure to have sufficient credentials or failing to complete all of the preparatory work necessary to render opinions, can be fatal to the case. Counsel can never interview and select only the best plaintiff, or best on-scene eyewitnesses. These are locked in and they be need to be dealt with as is. The employment of experts is counsel's singular opportunity to select a trial witness, and the jury will be the ultimate judge of plaintiffs counsel's decision making.

When selecting experts for any helicopter crash case, counsel must assess their education and background. For example, a metallurgist should have a doctorate degree in that subject or a comparable field, such as materials strength. Counsel should consider the expert's ability to communicate effectively with a jury, experience in the aviation industry, and familiarity with the particular aircraft, engine, or component at issue. From plaintiff counsel's standpoint, an expert is even more valuable if she has analyzed the same failed product in another case or handled a similar aircraft crash before. This not only enhances the expert's credibility, but also saves time and money because it is not necessary to bring the expert up to speed. Former NTSB and FAA officials can be excellent expert witnesses. They are familiar with the personnel, protocol, and jargon, and their government service gives them added credibility. Most of these former governmental employees have experience in expressing aviation concepts in understandable ways.

D. Use of Team Approach for Liability Experts

Habitual defendants in helicopter crash litigation such as the helicopter manufacturer, engine manufacturer or manufacturer of key component and system parts have little difficulty locating and hiring well-qualified experts. Such entities may call employee engineers within the company who have spent literally most of their professional lives designing and upgrading the product at issue. These companies also have access to insiders within the various governmental agencies, such as NTSB or FAA, whom they can call upon for available data to assist in defending the lawsuit.

But plaintiffs can counteract these defense advantages by careful organization and planning. By asking the pointed and sometimes difficult questions and conducting frequent conference calls among the expert team, counsel may create a seamless web of expert testimony which will be highly persuasive to any jury. It is ultimately counsel's sole responsibility to make certain that each member of the expert team is prepared for his deposition and trial testimony and will deliver the strongest and most persuasive opinions in each field of expertise as are possible.

The further advantage to assembling a well-qualified team of experts with different fields of expertise is the ability to critique and challenge each other's opinions. The early stages of a helicopter crash investigation present any number of possible causal options. Plaintiff's experts may not agree on the cause or crash sequence early on. Acquisition of additional information and documents along with specific component or flight testing will narrow the range of causes. Counsel's encouragement of a healthy dose of discussion and disagreement among the experts is very useful. Once a consensus among the team is attained counsel can be confident that each expert's opinion can withstand whatever defendant's attack will be forthcoming. And that those opinions will ultimately be persuasive to the jury.

E. Expert Assistance Throughout Investigation and Discovery

Plaintiff's experts should not be limited to preparing opinions to be presented at deposition or trial. The expert team should be part of the ongoing discovery process. The lawyer should index all documents received from the defense and forward them to the expert team. The team can then pinpoint critical documents or point to documents that are needed or missing. The experts also can highlight documents that will

help in deposing the defendant's engineers and executives. The expert team can assist in obtaining exemplar components for testing or as demonstrative exhibits for use at trial. An expert may have worked on a similar incident and be able to direct counsel to publicly available technical or industry literature related thereto.

Where the subject matter is particularly complicated such as the intricacies of helicopter aerodynamics or some aspect of metal fatigue, counsel should have a consultant present at the deposition of the defendant's corporate representative and even at depositions of the defendant's experts. There is the school of thought that says experts should not be brought in to assist at depositions as the defense will be able to discover their identity. That makes little sense given that such experts will have been present at the examination of the helicopter wreckage and it is plaintiff's counsel who should insist on a sign-in procedure.

Working with aviation experts is a unique challenge. Complex disciplines and extensive materials must be understood, digested, reviewed, analyzed, and, finally, explained to a jury. But when handling any helicopter crash case, counsel must be prepared to deal with numerous subject matters and to coordinate these areas of expertise into one seamless presentation at trial.

3.3 Acquisition, Preservation and Storage of the Helicopter Wreckage

Once the helicopter wreckage, the engine or any component parts are formally released by the NTSB, counsel must take affirmative steps to insure that the wreckage and various components are well preserved and not subject to the elements. Ownership and possession of the helicopter wreckage allows for storage in a more geographically convenient location and at a facility suitable for year-round inspections. Just one experience of freezing in an unheated barn for a day-long helicopter wreckage inspection will convince counsel to purchase the wreckage on the next occasion. Maintaining custody and ownership permits plaintiff's counsel to safeguard the chain of custody as well as maintain secure access to the wreckage to avert any defense claim of spoliation.

Careful preservation of the entire helicopter wreckage is crucial to plaintiff's case. Defendants are often very content to permit that wreckage to remain uncovered in a field and subject to the corroding effects of weather so that by the time plaintiff's experts examine it, key components are lost or altered by rust and exposure. On occasion, there is a dispute as to whether certain damage to the wreckage could have been caused by its initial handling and transport from the crash site. Depositions of those involved with the transport of the wreckage may be necessary to rebut any claim that certain damage occurred during the handling or transport process.

Where counsel cannot obtain prompt possession of the wreckage following its release by NTSB, steps must be taken to insure its secure and proper storage. If the wreckage is not properly maintained by plaintiff upon taking ownership or possession rights, the defense may claim that the wreckage has been so severely mishandled or destroyed as to constitute spoliation. Sanctions for spoliation of evidence include dismissal of the entire action, so it is best to err on the side of over-preservation.

The actual means of storage is a function of the condition of the wreckage itself. A high-impact crash on hard surface may demolish the helicopter into thousands of small pieces with the largest recognizable single piece being the engine or transmission. In such instances, the recovery team hired by the NTSB will put all of the parts in wooden crates. This makes for a difficult layout at such times as when the pieces are subject to inspection. Where the crash is substantial but not so severe as to cause a total break-up of the entire fuselage, the wreckage and any loose components can be shipped on a flatbed truck that is preferably tarped.

There are a number of aircraft recovery and salvage companies around the country that do an excellent job recovering and salvaging helicopters. Any recovery and salvage personnel must be experienced enough to know that no further harm should come to the wreckage during the recovery and storage process because all of that wreckage becomes material evidence in a filed or soon to be filed court case. The helicopter wreckage should be stored in a professional facility which does not permit public access and is secure. The facility should be enclosed, dry and ventilated. Storage in an outside environment can cause severe damage to the wreckage and any of the parts, and substantially interfere with any later inspection and examination as would be necessary and appropriate.

The NTSB will return the helicopter wreckage to the certificated owner. If a claim for the hull already has been made and paid, then the insurance carrier will have ownership and possessory rights to that wreckage. Fortunately, most hull carriers understand the importance of carefully preserving the helicopter wreckage but may seek cost sharing or reimbursement of all of the costs from counsel for their continuing agreement to do so. It is typical that the costs of long-term secure storage of the helicopter wreckage be borne on a pro rata basis from the parties to the litigation, and that is usually done by agreement.

Counsel must take immediate steps to preserve the helicopter wreckage and other evidence to ensure that not a single piece of the wreckage is sold, scrapped or disposed of. Evidence preservation letters should be sent out to all entities who may be in possession or control of the wreckage, any component parts, maintenance records, pilot logbooks or other pertinent documentation. A typical evidence preservation letter is as follows:

EVIDENCE PRESERVATION LETTER

November 10, 2009
CERTIFIED MAIL
RETURN RECEIPT REQUESTED

RE: HELICOPTER CRASH OF JUNE 17, 2009 AT KAILUA-KONA
WRONGFUL DEATHS OF MR. AND MRS. HARRIMAN

Dear [Owner, Operator or Hull Coverage Carrier]:

Please be advised that we have been retained by the family of Mr. and Mrs. Harriman who were killed when the helicopter piloted by your employee crashed on June 17, 2009.

Please make no direct contact with our clients. We respectfully demand that no portion of the helicopter wreckage be disposed of or altered in any way pending Orders from the applicable Court. This helicopter is material evidence in any potential claim or lawsuit brought by the family as a result of these deaths. We also request that you preserve all pertinent records and logbooks concerning the subject aircraft including pilot records and all records concerning the subject flight.

Further, please take any and all steps necessary and sufficient to preserve the wreckage in its current condition including inside storage. We will assist with the reasonable costs associated with proper preservation and storage of the wreckage.

Thank you for your attention and cooperation to this matter.

Sincerely yours,

_____

COUNSEL

At the earliest possible time it is advisable to obtain a court order as to the manner, method and divisible costs associated with long-term storage of the helicopter. The agreement and subsequent court order also should address the manner of access to the wreckage and whether parties will be seeking an early eyes-only or visual inspection and examination and the circumstances and protocol surrounding such an inspection.

3.4 Inspection and Examination of the Helicopter Wreckage

On occasion counsel along with the liability experts will have the opportunity to conduct a visual examination of the helicopter wreckage prior to filing suit. This occurs in several ways. The client may have been the owner or operator. Or the insurance carrier that paid out the hull coverage wants to be as cooperative as possible in the hopes of eventually seeing some reimbursement. Sometimes it would just happen that all parties learn through the grapevine as to which counsel represent the respective plaintiffs and defendants, and in the spirit of cooperation an early inspection with multiple experts is conducted.

In these situations where an examination of the wreckage goes forward prior to filing suit, counsel must take several precautions to avoid any claim of spoliation or alteration of any aspect of the wreckage. First, any such inspection absolutely should be limited to an eyes only or visual process without taking any measures which would alter or affect any system or component. Destructive testing at this juncture is improper.

A video operator should record the entire process (sound off) to establish a record of precisely what was done and to protect counsel and the assembled expert team from any later claims of spoliation or alteration of the evidence. In addition a proper photographic record should be made of either the laid out wreckage or other remnants for later observation and study. It is advisable to alert all potential defendants of the scheduled inspection so that they may have the opportunity to be present and observe the proceedings.

Experienced aviation lawyers do not attend helicopter wreckage inspections dressed as if they were attending an important court hearing. The rule of thumb is to wear only such clothing one would not mind getting oil- or fuel-smudged or even snagged or torn. Helicopter wreckage contains numerous sharp and pointed edges so counsel must exercise care. Work gloves are a must.

Counsel should obtain agreement on a protocol for this inspection. A suggested protocol for an early visual-only inspection and examination of the helicopter wreckage is as follows:

AGREED ORDER AS TO NON-DESTRUCTIVE EXAMINATION AND INSPECTION OF HELICOPTER WRECKAGE

The Court, having been fully advised of the issues and all parties given proper and timely notice and the opportunity to be heard, hereby finds as follows:

A. Plaintiff's claims arise out of the crash of a helicopter on September 7, 2009;

B. Plaintiff's deceased was a passenger aboard that helicopter;

C. The helicopter and engine have been released by the NTSB to Defendant, which is the owner of the aircraft;

D. The helicopter and engines are material evidence in the lawsuit and should be preserved and stored in their current condition;

E. Plaintiff's liability experts propose a "visual only" inspection and examination for purposes of photodocumentation and other visual analysis of the helicopter wreckage and engine components; and

F. All parties before the Court have reviewed this Order and all agree to the form and content of same.

WHEREFORE, the Court hereby orders as follows:

1. Defendant shall preserve and store the helicopter wreckage in its current condition and shall not transport, destroy, alter, or otherwise change that condition in any way without further Order of the Court;

2. Plaintiff's experts will be permitted to conduct an inspection and examination of the subject helicopter wreckage and engines at a time to be mutually agreed upon Plaintiff's and Defendants' counsel with the understanding that if counsel are not able to agree on a date, the Court shall set a date;

3. All other parties shall be permitted to attend the inspection and may have any representatives, experts or consultants present as they may desire; however, the Court will require that all persons present at this or any future inspection enter their names and affiliation on a sign-in sheet, copies of which will be circulated to all parties;

4.   Plaintiff's experts (as well as experts of any other parties in attendance) shall be permitted to photodocument, videotape and otherwise visually inspect and examine the helicopter wreckage, but shall perform no testing of any nature which would involve destruction or alteration of any of the helicopter or its component parts. For these purposes, it shall not be considered to be an alteration in order to move or dislodge a portion of the engine wreckage for purposes of identifying other components or to clean debris or dirt from an identification plate for purposes of obtaining information on the identification of any particular component part;

5.   All costs of the examination and inspection shall be borne by Plaintiff; and

6.   No examination or inspection of the helicopter or engines which would be destructive in any way shall occur absent further Order of this Court.

IT IS SO ORDERED THIS _____ DAY OF _____, 2010.

_____

CIRCUIT COURT JUDGE

SO AGREED AS TO FORM AND CONTENT:

All Counsel of Record

A meeting with the experts prior to the inspection is needed to coordinate matters to be examined and documented. At some early juncture in the proceeding, counsel should pull all experts aside and discuss preliminary opinions. Allowing the experts to discuss their early findings generates new leads and foci of inquiry.

Where the wreckage is being stored with a professional storage facility, counsel should make arrangements for those attendants to handle and unpack the wreckage. In most instances, the same personnel should reconfigure the helicopter by laying out those structures and parts in their pre-crash position. In some cases the helicopter has been so totally destroyed that it consists of nothing but small pieces and the engine, either by the force of the impact or a post-impact fire. In those cases the examination consists of sifting through the rubble for clues and attempting to identify broken parts of critical system components.

In any such initial inspection, once the wreckage is laid out and reconstructed as well as it can be given its condition, the first step is to carefully document the wreckage and, particularly, to photograph all indications of impact damage. Counsel should never request or permit a "pre-arrival" lay-out and configuration of the wreckage. This process must be observed by the experts as the attendants may place crash structure in the incorrect location. Smaller parts should be arranged on a table for closer examination and ease of photodocumentation.

The reason to document unpacking is that the process of packing and unpacking helicopter parts may by itself create stray markings and the transport of any wreckage may sometimes result in additional damage. This packing and transportation of the wreckage often introduces unexplained markings which may give the defense a field day. A later comparison of the first inspection photos with those at the crash scene may reveal that some damage or markings are indeed package or transport related.

One of the primary objectives at this early wreckage examination is to pinpoint and document all impact-related damage. The engine or engines often are crated separately. Special care should be taken to observe fluid levels. In any case where loss of power is suspected further internal examination of the engine will be necessary.

Documenting fluid levels whether it be in the fuel tank or other components is standard protocol for an initial helicopter wreckage inspection. Much more than fixed-wing aircraft, helicopters utilize hydraulic systems which contain various fluid mixtures and levels. Assessment and fluid mixtures may reveal the source of any malfunction. This was a critical finding in a recent helicopter crash where the tail rotor was alleged to have malfunctioned.

For example, the main and tail rotor systems on large helicopters are controlled through use of hydraulic servo systems. Each servo system contains a nitrogen-charged accumulator which allows for smooth operation of the servo. The nitrogen pre-charge in the servo is critical because the lack thereof may result in a loss of tail rotor control of the helicopter.

These accumulators literally "accumulate" air pressure with nitrogen stored under pressure inside a rubber bladder. One way to think of it is as a temporary hydraulic pump. The servo serves the function of providing the actual hydraulic power. This is a piston-like unit that moves the main rotor controls up and down under hydraulic power. If the fluid in the accumulator is hydraulic, this means that there was a lack of pressure and this will affect tail rotor function.

Even the most experienced helicopter crash attorney would never attend an initial examination of the wreckage without at least one experienced aircrash investigator and, most probably, with several in tow. There is no substitute for the hard won experience gained from looking at literally hundreds of helicopter crashes. It is frequently astounding what such investigators will uncover and how the mystery to the crash is unveiled by a masterful assembly of disparate clues.

Where the helicopter frame is relatively intact including the main and tail rotor blades, experienced investigators usually are able to determine the attitude or positioning of the helicopter at the moment of ground impact. This is an important clue directing further attention to the malfunction of a particular system or even the engine.

The failure of a main rotor blade invariably results in one or more of the remaining blades striking the helicopter fuselage structure. The loss of any part of the rotor blade will cause an imbalance in the rotor system which will generate tremendous gyroscopic forces. These will either tear the transmission from its housing location in the helicopter or sever the main rotor drive shaft. The location and magnitude of the rotor blade strikes on the fuselage indicate the in-flight conditions experienced by the pilot and passengers prior to ground impact. Failure of the tail rotor system results in rapid rotation or spinning of the helicopter fuselage with severe limitations on the pilot's ability to control any flight movement.

A failed main rotor blade invariably will contact the tail boom. Where and at what force provides clues to what happened during flight. If the blade first strikes a left horizontal stabilizer, that signifies a different scenario. The strike size can be determined by the extent of paint transfer which corresponds to markings on the leading edge of the rotor blade. The manner by which impact occurred also may hint at certain control problems experienced by the pilot and point to either the main rotor system or the tail rotor system.

A main rotor blade can fail in-flight usually by either spontaneous separation due to some bonding defect or latent fatigue crack or impact breakup caused by contact with a utility pole or a building. Loss of the main rotor blade at altitude is fatal for the occupants because the helicopter will fall like a rock as the sole source of its vertical lift is gone. If the main rotor blades were intact during engine power failure, defendant manufacturers often will claim that the pilot should have been able to safely land the helicopter by autorotation, the emergency landing procedure which uses the inertial rotational force of the main rotor blades.

The experienced helicopter crash investigator will note any markings on the frame of the helicopter which were inconsistent with ground impact and, therefore, must have occurred by some component breakage or separation in-flight. Circular gouge marks in the area of the initial ground impact normally suggest a tail rotor malfunction caused by the spinning of the helicopter at impact. The focus would then shift to an examination of the tail rotor and the drive train system and connection to the rotor.

The various clues to be assembled from analyzing the impact points from the helicopter frame and main and tail rotor blades may lead to the root cause of the crash:

- A flat or straight down impact squarely on the helicopter skids with little or no slide may be an indication of a failed autorotation maneuver due to some inability to control the main rotor blades or pilot inexperience.
- Forward skid marks coupled with on-scene documentation of sliding after ground impact is an indication that the pilot attempted a run-on landing which is a prescribed emergency procedure in the event of a loss of tail rotor function.
- Circular markings upon impact show that the helicopter was spinning which also harkens of a tail rotor malfunction.
- Minimal airframe damage especially in the cockpit vicinity may point to a crashworthiness issue given the relatively low g-forces at impact if serious injury or deaths resulted.

The cockpit configuration if discernible can be studied to reveal clues about what the pilot did in the moments prior to the crash. In one case involving a failed tail rotor system, the right pedal had been "stood on" as is evident from its bending at impact. This factual finding provided further corroboration that the pilot was struggling to maintain control of the aircraft with a malfunctioning tail rotor. Where an investigator finds a bent or even broken rudder pedal suggesting that the pilot's foot was placed there at the moment of impact, it is not uncommon that the autopsy report shows that the pilot sustained a broken ankle.

Examination of the cockpit control and switch positions may yield important information as to what the pilot was doing in the moments leading up to the crash. Certain types of controls or switches are not normally susceptible to impact movement especially those that are spring loaded or plastic guard-covered. These clues can help determine whether the pilot was in the process of attempting an autorotation or experiencing some specific system malfunction. NTSB investigators are well-trained in the importance of post-crash documentation of switch and control positions and routinely document these findings thoroughly. Many helicopters utilize cables and rods as part of the flight control system. If accessible, the integrity of all such flight control systems should be examined and documented.

At this early inspection juncture, any components in need of further and more detailed laboratory analysis can be separately boxed and sealed. That procedure will facilitate later transport of those components either pursuant to agreement of all of the parties or order of the court. The need for additional laboratory analysis and destructive testing also can be ascertained.[19]

The rotor blades provide a number of failure clues. Given the criticality of the main rotor blades, it would not be a stretch to conclude that the cause of the crash was the separation of a main rotor blade found 600 feet from the crash site. To the contrary, where the rotor blades are either found to be intact at the crash site or determined to have suffered impact damage only, then failure of the blades themselves may conditionally be ruled out as a cause of the crash.

Careful examination of the leading edge of the rotor blades for any damage may reveal a component separation in-flight. A normal post-impact finding of an upward bend in a rotor blade is a clue that it was rotating at impact. However, an upward bend of a blade can occur for a number of reasons. The reconstruction consultant must examine that blade in the context of many factors such as the known altitude of any in-flight malfunction or other problem, the amount of engine power being produced at impact, if any, and the various angles of impact. Some matters can only be learned through extensive experience. For example, a Robinson R-22 helicopter will have upward bending blades if the engine RPM falls too low and the helicopter crashes in an uncontrolled descent.

By conditionally ruling out certain causes, the investigator and counsel can focus more narrowly on those components and systems which continue to be explanatory of the crash and consistent with the observed impact damage. The process of helicopter accident reconstruction is akin to putting together a jigsaw puzzle after the cardboard pieces have been through a washing machine, a fire, and an oil bath. Seasoned helicopter crash reconstruction experts can picture in their mind's eye the precise sequence of events leading from normal flight to the devastation they see laying on the ground in front of them. The in-flight crash dynamic is important in developing proof of the panic experienced by the occupants, known as pre-impact terror.

Regrettably, some component parts or systems are irretrievably damaged and destroyed during the NTSB investigation. The cases are legion where the NTSB permits a part manufacturer to utterly destroy in the guise of testing a suspect part. In such instances, counsel must resort to other investigative techniques including acquisition and testing of exemplar components, later review of any NTSB photos or test results as a result of such destructive testing or a comparison of photo documentation from the crash scene. Such post-crash alteration and destruction of suspect parts is one of the more challenging and distressing aspects of helicopter crash litigation on behalf of injured parties.

3.5 Factual Investigation of Military Helicopter Crashes

If some lawyers are convinced that the factual investigation of a civilian helicopter crash poses challenges, they will find that the efforts to investigate a military helicopter crash are almost stifling. In countries other than the U.S., the military investigative procedures applicable to helicopter crashes are too varied to address. While many will conduct their own accident investigation or seek U.S. assistance, the military in other countries performs a minimal investigation or none at all. Assuming U.S. jurisdiction over a U.S. manufacturer, counsel and the entire accident reconstruction team will need access to the wreckage as well as the crash site. Foreign military forces are not typically inclined to cooperate with U.S. civilian lawyers and most will ignore any U.S. court orders.

Each branch of the U.S. military normally conducts its own independent investigation and although each takes a fairly similar approach there are differences in terms of the treatment of witnesses, the release of certain information and even the penalties for improper release and what the various reports are called. This section primarily addresses investigation of U.S. military helicopter accidents.

If counsel discover that the crash is combat-related as where the helicopter takes a direct hit from an enemy surface-to-air missile, the investigation should cease. No cause of action exists for military personnel who suffer injuries due to enemy combat. Only where the helicopter crash is due to some non-combat related mechanical deficiency should the case ever be pursued.

If both civil aircraft and U.S. military helicopters are involved in an aircrash, then the NTSB will investigate the incident in conjunction with representatives from the particular military branch involved. By federal statute the particular military branch operating the aircraft are given authority to conduct an investigation.[20] When only a military helicopter is involved in the crash and no civilian aircraft, the NTSB normally will not become involved.

Where the crash involves only military aircraft, the particular military branch in question will conduct two separate crash investigations which result in two separate reports. One investigation is intended to focus solely on facts of the crash while the other contains various opinions and conclusions as to the causes of the crash and makes recommendations for safety. In this respect, the reports are similar to the two different reports generated by the NTSB. The first investigation results in a report known as a Safety Mishap Investigation Report (SMIP). The opinion and cause aspect of the investigation will be assembled in an Aircraft Accident Investigation Report (AAIR). Counsel also should determine whether a Judge Advocate General (JAG) investigative report was conducted as that may not always be in agreement with the official military accident report.

The only initial investigative tool available to counsel in these cases is a request for information through the Freedom of Information Act (FOIA) directly to the particular military branch. In investigating such crashes, a FOIA request should be directed to the specific military branch involved and should request both the Safety Mishap Investigation Report (SMIP) as well as the Aircraft Accident Investigation Report (AAIR), making sure to specifically request all exhibits to each report. These reports may be obtained by FOIA requests in writing to:

U.S. Army: U.S. Army Combat Readiness/Safety Center
Attn: CSSC-SS (FOIA)
4905 5th Avenue
Fort Rucker, Alabama 36362
Phone: (334) 255-2373
Facsimile: (334) 255-2652
E-mail: usarmy.rucker.hdqa-secarmy.mbx.safe-foia@mail.mil

U.S. Navy: Commander Naval Safety Center
375 A Street
Norfolk, Virginia 23511
(757) 444-4520, ext. 7047

U.S. Air Force: The FOIA request should be directed to the particular base or activity that has the records you desire. A listing of the FOIA offices by base can be found at www.foia.af.mil/offices/bases. If one is unsure of which base or activity holds the records, the request should be directed to:

HAF/IMII
1000 Air Force Pentagon
Washington, D.C. 20330
Facsimile: (703) 696-7273
E-mail: haf.foia@pentagon.af.mil

A document request can be fashioned similarly as for a civil request for production of documents although it must be within the framework of a FOIA request.[21]

Many of the same investigative processes used by NTSB are used in military crash investigations. These include the inordinately tight relationship between the military and its aircraft manufacturers and supplies which often results in a revolving door of employment. This relationship and interplay as between the government and its aircraft suppliers is even stronger than that relationship normally existing between an NTSB investigator and the helicopter manufacturer. It is not unusual for some of the larger aircraft manufacturers to have employees actually stationed at various military branches. Just as does the NTSB, the military aircrash investigators rely on the helicopter or engine manufacturer as well as any suspect component part maker for design and background information with respect to their product.

As would be expected, there is a general reticence within the military to disclose information to non-military civilians and, especially, their private counsel. Add to that their general aversion to and distaste of lawyers and lawsuits, and the barriers to conducting an investigation are rendered higher and firmer. Nevertheless, the military is required to seasonably respond to proper FOIA requests, and counsel should aggressively follow-up as appropriate. Where early indications all point to some in-flight mechanical malfunction, the military tends to be a bit more cooperative with requests for information and additional documents from private counsel.

One of the other principle differences between an NTSB and military branch investigation is the treatment of witnesses and availability of their statements. For military purposes, witnesses who normally are active duty military are promised confidentiality. They are informed that they will be immune from any disciplinary action concerning all information they may divulge to the military branch investigator. Accordingly, counsel investigating such crashes may have difficulty obtaining the full unredacted witness statement if it can be obtained at all. Given these promises of confidentiality, private counsel investigating such a crash will have difficulty in so much as learning the identity of such witness.

Permeating these investigations is an inherent military suspicion and distrust of civilian investigation of any aspect of their affairs. Unfortunately, this is often the case even in those situations where the deaths are of loyal and true active duty men and women in the service of their country. Distrust abounds even though the crash unquestionably is due to some in-flight mechanical malfunction unrelated to any military-specific mission or modification or negligence of military personnel whether in piloting or maintaining the helicopter. And if the crash occurred during a training mission, any request for a flight mission profile or the intended usage of the helicopter will be brusquely rebuffed as seeking confidential combat tactics and non-discoverable for national security reasons.

Many of these same roadblocks arise when counsel seek to acquire any maintenance records of the subject helicopter. Military personnel receive and are charged with following the same or very similar routine maintenance procedures and overhauls as are applicable on the civil side. This is a tightrope during the investigative process because should the maintenance records disclose that a failure to follow a manufacturer's recommended practice or procedure contributed to the circumstances of the crash, counsel may just have investigated herself out of a case. Although as a general rule it is better to acquire all available information it may be preferable on this issue to permit the target product manufacturer to take the position that its maintenance instructions were not being followed.

3.6 Acquisition of Records from the Federal Aviation Administration

The Federal Aviation Administration (FAA) maintains a host of accessible public records which should be acquired as part of the initial factual investigation. As with all other aspects of the investigation, potential clues to the causes of the helicopter crash may be revealed by one or more of these records.

A. Air Traffic Control Data

If the pilot was in communication with Air Traffic Control (ATC) at or prior to the time of the crash, an ATC accident package will usually have been assembled. This package provides the written transcript of the communications as between the pilot and ATC, written statements by any ATC personnel who were active at the time of the crash, and a flight plan if one was filed.

The ATC accident package can be obtained by making a written request to the FAA Regional Headquarters within whichever region the helicopter accident happened. Counsel or one of the investigators can determine the online address by referring to www.faa.gov/about/office_org and selecting the appropriate regional office. Although normally included in the request, counsel should delineate that the request include all pertinent radar and weather information for the time period of the crash.

In addition to the transcripts of the communication between the pilot and ATC, counsel should request the actual audiotape cassettes of all recorded transmissions. Those voice tapes should be cross-checked against the transcript provided as there is often an important omission, transcription error or awkward punctuation which can alter the meaning of the exchange.

The voice tape of the pilot many times will reveal much more than the spoken word. The tape will reflect the relative calm or panic of the pilot in dealing with the conditions at hand. On several occasions it has been useful to employ a sound technician expert to analyze these tapes to listen for unusual or problematic engine noises or rotor flap irregularities.

B. Aircraft Ownership Records

Armed only with the registration or tail number of the helicopter, counsel may determine the legal ownership, certificates of airworthiness and some limited alteration history of the particular aircraft. The helicopter's registration number may be obtained from a variety of sources including the NTSB Incident Report, photographs of the crash helicopter on scene, or media reports. The request for this information should be directed to FAA Aircraft Registration Branch, AFS-750, P.O. Box 25504, Oklahoma City, Oklahoma 73125, although it is far easier and faster to submit the request online at www.faa.gov/licenses_certificates/aircraft_certification/aircraft_registry. Basic aircraft and ownership data such as helicopter make and model and certificate issue data are instantly accessible online at http://registry.faa.gov/aircraftinquiry.

Counsel must request both the aircraft registration and maintenance records as these are kept in separate files within the FAA Oklahoma City facility. Learning the identity of the legal owner of the helicopter as well as some basic maintenance background is useful to ultimate determination of the appropriate defendants in the case and may provide leads to additional information such as prior owners or previous service problems.

C. Pilot's Flight and Medical File

The investigation of the pilot's experience and background begins with obtaining the information on file at the same FAA Aircraft Registration Branch in Oklahoma City by directing the inquiry to FAA Aviation Data Systems Branch, AFS-620, Attn: Privacy Act, P.O. Box 25082, Oklahoma City, Oklahoma. Some information will be readily accessible such as any FAA disciplinary actions taken against the pilot and the date of issue and class of her medical certification. The pilot's medical classification, certification and ratings are available online at http://amsrvs.registry.faa.gov/airmeninquiry.

Acquisition of other pilot records usually requires either the pilot's authorization or a court-issued subpoena duces tecum. These additional records include the pilot's specific medical records, pilot qualifications and experience, copies of pilot logbooks and other general information. Once acquired, this file should be thoroughly reviewed for any clues which would suggest a lack of qualification or any medical issue concerning the subject pilot.

D. Service Difficulty Reports and Accident/Incident Reports

Service Difficulty Reports (SDRs) are forms filled out by maintenance personnel, pilots or helicopter owners describing any particular problem with the helicopter, engine, system or component. These SDRs are organized and maintained in a database by the FAA. Similarly, Accident/Incident Reports are summary statements of any helicopter accident or incident setting out the reason or suspected reason by the individual filing the report. Both the SDR and Accident/Incident FAA databases may be accessed by online inquiry to the FAA Service Difficulty Reporting Site at www.faa.gov/data_research/aviation_data_statistics/data_downloads as well as by some private non-governmental websites. The FAA site allows for public search and review of all submitted reports.

It should be evident during the course of the investigation that any frequently noted SDR or Accident/Incident Report directed to a particular helicopter type, engine or component parts may be the tell-tale sign of a serious design flaw. Taking the time to obtain and review this data may pay dividends by uncovering similar helicopter crash information and laying the foundation for its admissibility at trial.[22]

E. Service Letters, Service Bulletins and Airworthiness Directives

When a helicopter or engine manufacturer or component part maker discovers a potential malfunction with the product or dangerous defect affecting the airworthiness of the aircraft, it may issue a Service Letter, Service Bulletin or Airworthiness Directive (AD). A Service Letter or Service Bulletin is a voluntary communication and may provide only that the part replacement or revised maintenance procedure is recommended and "optional." A Service Letter is the least formal communication from any helicopter airframe or component part manufacturer and typically provides routine non-safety critical information. Service Bulletins usually address safety-related matters or concerns.

In contrast, an Airworthiness Directive is a mandatory rule issued by the FAA which requires a helicopter owner or operator to follow the mandate from the manufacturer within a certain period of time or even before the aircraft can be placed back in operation. The manufacturer's involvement in the issuance of the AD and even its efforts to avoid it are ripe areas for discovery. ADs can be requested directly from the FAA Regulatory and Guidance Library (RGL) website at http://rgl.faa.gov. In requesting any of this information, counsel must provide the helicopter make and model or a description and part number of a particular helicopter component part.

Normally, Service Bulletins must be acquired directly from the particular manufacturer, although access to a maintenance facility with oversight over the same or similar helicopter model should find any applicable Service Bulletins as well. In an uncanny number of cases, the basis for issuance of the Airworthiness Directive goes to the precise system or component which is the subject of the investigation. That is never good luck. It is good investigating.

F. Federal Aviation Regulations

Federal Aviation Regulations (FARs) are the bare minimum rules set out by the FAA governing U.S. aviation activity. These are instantly accessible by either LexisNexis or Westlaw or in the Commerce Clearing House (CCH) Aviation Law Reporter. All current as well as historical versions of the FARs are available on the FAA's main website www.faa.gov/regulations_policies/faa_regulations. The FARs comprise a comprehensive regulatory scheme applicable to all aspects of helicopter piloting, operation, maintenance and control. The FARs also spell out the specific records that owners and operators are required to maintain. This is useful when propounding initial written discovery. It pays dividends to have an expert on the FARs on the investigative team who can scour these regulations to determine if there are any applicable regulations. The importance of that is evident because violation of an FAR is violation of the ordinary standard of care and in most jurisdictions is proof of negligence if not negligence per se. Fortunately, the opposite is not true because compliance with an FAR will not exculpate a defendant.

3.7 Mining Technical and Professional Journals

There is a wealth of information on helicopter performance, engine operation, and system analysis in the public domain. Many professional organizations and societies publish newsletters containing technical and engineering reports on particular helicopters or parts used in helicopters. These include the American Helicopter Society (AHS), Helicopter Association International (HAI), the Society of Automotive Engineers (SAE), the American Society of Mechanical Engineers (ASME), and the American Institute of Aeronautics and Astronautics (AIAA). Many of these papers are well documented and researched with reference to actual helicopter crashes and incidents which may be similar to the crash under investigation. Moreover, some of the research and engineering may pinpoint recurring problems within the industry about which the manufacturer should have actual knowledge. A compilation of all relevant published technical data is a time-consuming but necessary task as part of this early investigation.

3.8 Accepting or Declining the Representation

Aviation litigation and particularly helicopter crash litigation is more expensive and time-consuming to handle than any other type of personal injury or wrongful death matter. As the helicopter so often is destroyed, extensive crash reconstruction, technical and engineering expertise and analysis are required. The reasons are multiple but it starts with the need to use a multitude of expert witnesses on liability alone and the need for frequent inspection and examination of the subject helicopter and component parts. More times than not repeated and expensive testing of a particular component is essential and that also may necessitate testing of an exemplar component similar if not identical to the helicopter component at issue. Jurisdictional and discovery disputes are the norm requiring careful and detailed briefing and inordinate chunks of attorney time.

A. Standard for Accepting Representation

Experienced aviation lawyers do not commit to representing victims of a helicopter crash without the opportunity to conduct a sufficient investigation to assess the merits of the case. This section is intended to provide some practical advice based on experience so that lawyers can steer clear of potential representation-related problems. These involve a host of other considerations not unique to helicopter crash litigation but which are well known to any plaintiff's personal injury and wrongful death lawyer.

For all these reasons the threshold for accepting representation in a helicopter crash case must be significantly higher than for other types of cases. After counsel has completed the preliminary factual investigation and absent some other extenuating circumstance, unless the case appears to be reasonably recoverable, the representation should be declined. The reasonably recoverable standard contemplates a successful outcome based on strong liability evidence and measurable and significant damages. This is in the client's best interest because if such a lawsuit is not reasonably recoverable it creates false hopes in a potential client and will lead only to bitter disappointment and dejection when the case is ultimately dismissed or lost.

B. Helicopter Crash Cases Which Should Be Declined

Experienced aviation lawyers know that far more of these cases are declined than accepted for representation. Sadly, all aviation lawyers including this author have had the experience of declining representation to the most innocent and deserving family members having lost a loved one in a helicopter crash. Many times these instances occur where the pilot is the sole passenger and exceeds the boundaries of either the pilot's or the helicopter's capabilities resulting in a loss of control and subsequent crash. Plaintiff's attorneys must decline representation in certain categories of helicopter accident cases as follows.

1. Minimal Injury Or Close Call Cases

A serious malfunction occurred in-flight and the helicopter pilot skillfully lands the helicopter but the impact damages the helicopter and jostles the occupants. In such a situation, representation of a client with whiplash or sore back symptoms will not justify the time and expense of moving forward with helicopter crash litigation.

Similarly, helicopter passengers and even pilots who have experienced close calls such as engine failure with resultant autorotation and safe landing do not warrant going forward with a lawsuit. That is why the initial factual investigation must always encompass some analysis of the extent of the damages suffered.

2. Crashes of Experimental Or Home-Built Helicopters

Where the pilot of an experimental or home-built helicopter is injured or killed and the cause of the helicopter crash is his improper assembly, the representation should be declined.

3. Claims for Pilot Or Pilot's Family In Face of Pilot's Clear Negligence

In instances where there is no indication of an in-flight mechanical malfunction or other explanation for the helicopter crash, representation of the pilot or the pilot's family will not be successful. The same negligence principles apply as are applicable to the driver of a motor vehicle who causes an accident and gets injured. The one issue where scrutiny is called for is crashworthiness and its role in enhancing the injury or contributing to the death. Though the pilot may have been negligent for the crash, if the impact was otherwise survivable but the fuel tank bursts into flame the case may have merit.

4. Lawyer-Switching Clients

When contacted by a client with a seemingly meritorious lawsuit, counsel learns that she has dismissed four previously retained aviation counsel. Unless counsel wishes to be the fifth dismissed aviation firm, representation should be declined.

5. No Plaintiff Scenarios

As in other wrongful death litigation, there must be an appropriate plaintiff to bring the action. Where the deceased is single, widowed or divorced with no living parents and no children, who then presents a worthy and deserving plaintiff?

In one instance, the author was contacted by a family member and the case appeared recoverable on its face but warranting of further investigation. The deceased was divorced with no children. The only surviving family member was a brother who had not seen him in eleven years. Counsel should decline the representation unless curious as to what a jury would award a brother for being estranged from the victim for over a decade.

Included in this category are co-habitants, one of whom is injured or killed while flying in a helicopter. Infrequently, the law of the state where they resided may provide for a common law marriage if the couple were together long enough. Although they may have lived and functioned as a married couple, the law makes no provision for compensation for the death of a good friend.

6. Target Defendant Judgment Proof Or Insolvent

After investigation or after filing suit and conducting discovery, it is learned that the target defendant is bankrupt, has no insurance and is otherwise insolvent. There is no point in continuing with the litigation. There are no pyrrhic or moral victories in helicopter crash litigation and pursuing such lawsuits in the face of known uncollectibility is not only foolhardy but fatuous.

7. The Unsure Plaintiff

Whether on philosophical, moral, religious or even political grounds, some people "don't believe in lawsuits." Or they will not permit others to stand in judgment of them and will refuse to attend a jury trial. It is good practice to find out about any such reservations prior to the start of a five-week helicopter crash trial.

Sentiments such as "Dad (the deceased) never did like lawyers and hated the idea of suing people" are dead giveaways. The potential exists for such a client to abandon the case without warning, leaving counsel saddled with large out-of-pocket expenses, no opportunity to earn a fee for the time expended or, worse, possible sanctions. Experienced lawyers can sense hesitation on this issue and will not proceed absent some reassurance that the client is willing to assist throughout the case, attend the trial, if necessary, and otherwise participate meaningfully.

8. The Previously Filed and Mishandled Case

Several years ago a frantic call came in to the author from a Tennessee lawyer who had been retained to handle a serious helicopter crash case. He asked for a prompt meeting at the Peabody Hotel in Memphis. Upon arrival, the story was told of missed deadlines, missed hearings, client displeasure and other misfortune. As it turns out, a hearing was scheduled for the following day on the defendant's motion to dismiss for failure of plaintiffs to comply with various discovery scheduling deadlines including the identification of experts. No one in history had ever left the Peabody Hotel so rapidly as the author did on that occasion.

This story illustrates the extent to which these cases can be mishandled and botched and they are too numerous to mention. Experience teaches that counsel should be wary of becoming involved in any case for which suit has been filed or substantial discovery conducted on account of the following probable pitfalls:

a. Case Filed but Fails to Include Critical Defendants— This is the most common. Counsel are called long after the statute of limitations has run asking to "bail out" current counsel. Unless one has the desire to become a co-defendant in a legal malpractice case the letter confirming non-representation should be sent promptly.

b. Case Filed Against U.S. Subsidiary of Foreign Corporation Only—This is another common travesty leading to the inability to obtain any meaningful discovery against the U.S. subsidiary that is only a distributor and, of course, has no design drawings, engineering reports, accident history or other basic information about the helicopter, the helicopter engine or component part.

c. Minimal Initial Factual Investigation—This type of mishandling is irreversible where no on-scene investigation or documentation is available. Eyewitnesses have long disappeared and maintenance records are incomplete or altogether missing.

d. Failure to Preserve Helicopter Wreckage—First counsel on the case are offered an opportunity to purchase the wreckage and decline. There being no lawsuit, contemplated lawsuit or other notice within some reasonable period of time to preserve the wreckage, the hull carrier scraps it. Helicopter crash litigation is difficult enough with the availability of the helicopter wreckage.

e. Case Filed in Improper Jurisdiction—These calls usually come in the form of, "We are on the verge of being dismissed, what can be done?" Given the passage of time and the passing of the statute of limitations in the appropriate jurisdiction the response is likely to be "nothing."

C. Avoiding Conflicts of Interest In Multiple Representation

As in other litigation where multiple parties are involved helicopter litigation is rife with potential conflicts of interest. These can be either direct conflicts as between competing interests or insurance coverage conflicts. In any helicopter accident scenario where there are multiple occupants, conflict waivers must be explained and executed even where the interests of the plaintiffs are perfectly coincident such as where both are surviving occupants and unrelated to the pilot or operator by employment or familial relation.

There are circumstances where it is appropriate to represent an occupant and the pilot such as where the helicopter crash is due to a mechanical malfunction or when the passenger is legally unable to sue the pilot such as in a co-employee situation as would be existing on an air ambulance flight. The advantages to multiple representation include the division of litigation expenses and enhanced leverage for settlement purposes. Another advantage is the retention of only one set of liability experts and avoiding the prospect of inconsistent or even contradictory opinions among experts for plaintiffs in the same helicopter crash.

Unavoidable conflicts include those where there is either a direct action by one plaintiff against another or where the plaintiffs out of necessity must make inconsistent claims. Counsel cannot undertake that dual representation.

D. Filing Suit Promptly After Representation Accepted

Following case acceptance and written retention, counsel should proceed with the factual investigation necessary for filing of the lawsuit. Nothing taints the attorney-client relationship worse than a client continually calling to inquire about why the lawsuit is not filed.

In many instances, the filing of a lawsuit is simply the first action in a "hurry up and wait" process while the NTSB prepares its Factual Report and otherwise releases the wreckage. There is rarely any procedural or tactical advantage to be gained from delaying the filing of the lawsuit. Of course, once the case is filed clients should receive regular status reports as to the progress of the litigation.

Endnotes

1. 49 U.S.C § 40101 (1997).

2. 49 U.S.C § 40101 secs. 2-3 (1997).

3. 49 U.S.C. § 1131 (2006).

4. 49 C.F.R. § 831.11 (1998).

5. 49 C.F.R. § 835.3 (1999).

6. 49 U.S.C. § 1154(b) (2000).

7. 9 14 C.R.F. § 91.417 (2010).

8. Andy Pasztor, "Bird Strike Is New Suspect in Helicopter Crash," *The Wall Street Journal*, February 17, 2009.

9. *Id.*

10. *Buras v. Petroleum Helicopters, Inc.*, 705 So.2d 766 (La. App. 1997), cert. denied, 526 U.S. 826 (1998).

11. Iowa Code, Section 328.41 (2010).

12. Iowa Code, Section 328.19 (1976).

13. See Chapter 4, section 4.6 (F) addressing special statutory liability.

14. Portions of this section are based on G. Robb, "How to Select and Use Aviation Experts," *Trial Magazine* (November 2002).

15. See Chapter 7, Section 7.8 on surviving *Daubert* challenges.

16. See Chapter 5, Section 5.2 on initial and follow-up use of written discovery.

17. See Chapter 3, Section A.3.

18. See Chapter 4, Section 4.1 for a more expanded list of common helicopter crash factors.

19. Destructive testing of any subject helicopter component parts is dealt with in Chapter 8.

20. 49 U.S.C. 1132 (1994); see in addition 32 § Part 518 (2006) (U.S. Army), § 701 (1999) (U.S. Navy), § 806 (1999) (U.S. Air Force).

21. See Chapter 5, Section 5.5 (C) on discovery and handling of military helicopter crashes.

22. See Chapter 7, Section 7.9 on evidence of substantially similar incidents and crashes.

Chapter 4

Filing the Helicopter Crash Lawsuit

Introduction

Once the case is judged to be reasonably recoverable and representation of the client is accepted, the remaining factual investigation and legal analysis should be focused solely on preparing the case for filing against the proper and lawful defendants in the proper and lawful court. This section is intended to give the practitioner a ready reference to all of the potential considerations presaging successful filing of the lawsuit.

4.1 Determining the Cause of the Crash

The chief objective in preparing to file the lawsuit must be to assess the most likely cause or causes of the helicopter crash and the resultant injuries or deaths.[1] Only by identifying the potential causes can counsel properly identify and file suit against the potential defendants responsible for the helicopter crash. The most common causes of helicopter crashes are as follows.

A. Loss of Main Rotor Control

The main rotor blade (MRB) is the only source of lift for maintaining powered flight. It allows the helicopter to fly. Any damage to the MRB itself or inability to control either its rotation or pitch will result in a loss of control and subsequent crash. Loss of main rotor control is most commonly due to either a swashplate or linkage control malfunction or a hydraulic system failure. If the swashplate cracks or becomes separated from any of its pitch change rods, the pilot will be unable to provide the required input to the main rotors. Such a malfunction also prevents any autorotation maneuver which is the emergency procedure designed to take advantage of the inertia of the main rotors in accomplishing a survivable landing. The author has handled several cases where the MRB has either disintegrated or broken apart in flight rendering the pilot and crew suspended and helpless as the helicopter plummets to earth.

B. Loss of Tail Rotor Function

Numerous helicopter crashes are due to the pilot's inability to control the tail rotor. A loss of tail rotor function means that the pilot is unable to control the tail or anti-torque rotor which is designed to prevent the helicopter from spinning in the opposite direction of the main rotor blade. At low altitudes, that loss of control is dangerous because the pilot is unable to maneuver the aircraft into a run-on landing. The tail rotor malfunction may come about because of a loss of hydraulic pressure, a kink or fracture in the control cable, or a leak in the hydraulic servo or accumulator.

Loss of tail rotor effectiveness or LTE is a related phenomenon. It is not necessarily caused by equipment malfunction and may occur in a heavy or fully loaded helicopter traveling at low airspeed which encounters certain weather or wind conditions. The effects of the wind may counteract the force of the tail rotor and result in that rotor's failing to provide enough thrust to counteract the opposite rotation of the main rotor.

C. Main Rotor Strike to Fixed Obstacle

While the hovering capability of a helicopter is a unique advantage, it is also a unique hazard. Whether a police chopper is hovering next to a building in observation of suspected criminal activity or a scenic helicopter hovers next to a glacier in Alaska or a waterfall in Hawaii, the danger of an inadvertent main rotor strike to a fixed object is ever present. The slightest imbalance between the collective and cyclic controls by the pilot or an unexpected gust of wind or downwash from the main rotor can cause a lateral movement of the helicopter with no warning and no time to recover.

D. Helicopter Component Part or System Failure

It is said that everything in a helicopter vibrates excessively including the passengers. That excessive vibration is not without safety consequences. The excess vibratory stresses inherent in the design and structure of a helicopter lead to increased metal fatigue and cracking of safety critical components. The added fatigue and stresses on critical components led the FAA to designate shorter retirement lives for certain helicopter component parts. Excessive vibration often has led to catastrophic component failure with no prior warning involving, for example, a cracked gear tooth, a cracked rotor blade, a crack within the internal combustion engine, or failed bearings.[2]

E. Helicopter Engine Failure or Power Loss

Just as for fixed-wing aircraft, engine failure is a potentially cataclysmic malfunction. If the engine failure occurs over an area where the pilot may utilize the autorotation maneuver, then it need not result in a fatal crash. All too often, however, the operating mission of the helicopter and the location and altitude of the engine failure renders autorotation all but impossible. This can occur if the helicopter is traveling over water, above a dense forest or even in the middle of a large city with a highly dense downtown building structure.

The causes of helicopter engine failure run the gamut from poorly designed nozzle guide vanes (NGV) to faulty fuel control or fuel pumps, and component metal fatigue or cracking. In-flight engine failure often is reported by the pilot and preserved on the ATC voice tape.

F. Wire Strike Incidents

The various usages of helicopters often mean that they tend to fly at much lower altitudes than fixed-wing aircraft. Low altitude flights include local traffic and news reporting operations, air ambulance services, film production, and law enforcement. It is for this reason that helicopters are much more frequently involved in wire strikes or contact with utility power lines which may be all but invisible to the helicopter pilot. In the U.S. alone between 1990 and 1995, there were almost 200 helicopter wire strike accidents resulting in 43 deaths.[3]

Helicopters performing at low altitude environments often are equipped with wire strike protection equipment. These devices are large scissor-like blades affixed above and below the fuselage designed to guide the wire to a set of cutting jaws. Their effectiveness is questionable. Such devices are potentially effective only as against frontal strikes on horizontally strung wires where the helicopter is flying straight and level. The systems fail to cover critical contact points of a helicopter such as the main rotor blades, the rotor mast or the skids. The most critical factor in preventing crashes due to wire strike is for the helicopter pilot to avoid contact with power lines in the first instance.

Utility lines in a moderate to heavy air traffic vicinity should be marked by the utility company. The use of bright red or orange-colored spheres placed on utility lines will alert helicopter pilots as to the location of the line and serve to prevent such wire strike incidents. Indeed, utility companies are often named in such wire strike cases for failing to adequately mark their power lines where the visibility is suspect. For example, if the utility is aware of aircraft flying in the vicinity of its power lines, it should mark those lines.

G. Pilot Error

Even with strong evidence pointing to a pre-impact mechanical malfunction, the pilot's qualifications, medical condition, and piloting actions will be meticulously scrutinized in every helicopter crash lawsuit. This is so regardless of if that pilot or his employer is a defendant or plaintiff. Common errors committed by helicopter pilots in addition to those referenced earlier such as main rotor strike or wire strike include improper pre-flight inspection, loss of situational awareness, loss of visibility, unintended ground impact, exceeding gross weight limits, and flying in hazardous weather conditions.

Medical examiners will perform toxicological testing upon the body of a deceased pilot for alcohol or any other performance-reducing drugs. Such tests must be acquired early on so that counsel may assess the legal ramifications of positive test results. Positive and significant drugs or alcohol in the pilot's system impacts the entire case because that drug or alcohol usage distracts the jury's attention from any other mechanical problem such as rotor or engine failure or linkage malfunction.

H. Pilot Incapacitation

The pilot's physical or mental incapacity to perform the functions of pilot-in-command is frequently the NTSB's probable cause of a helicopter accident. For this reason an autopsy of the pilot is routinely performed. The incapacity may take the form of excessive alcohol use, illicit drug impairment or a truly catastrophic medical mishap such as a heart attack, stroke or brain aneurysm. Cardiovascular disease, specifically acute myocardial infarction, has been determined to be the primary cause of pilot in-flight incapacitation.[4]

Carbon monoxide poisoning has led to pilot incapacitation normally caused by a faulty helicopter engine exhaust system. Hypoxia is not normally experienced by helicopter pilots given the relatively low altitudes of their flight missions. Nevertheless in some mountainous regions lack of oxygen to the brain may be a concern, especially where the helicopter is not equipped with oxygen masks.

I. Pilot Distraction

Regrettably, this has emerged as a new cause of helicopter crashes since the first edition of this book was published in 2010. The proliferation of personal electronic devices (PEDs) in our society has permeated the helicopter flight deck. The author knows this all too well as he handled the first known helicopter crash case where one of the causes cited by the NTSB was "the pilot's distracted attention due to personal texting during safety-critical ground and flight operations…"[5]

As a result of this helicopter crash, the NTSB reiterated an earlier safety recommendation prohibiting flight crew members from using portable electronic devices while the aircraft is being operated.[6] It is clear that texting by a helicopter pilot is equally or more fatal than by motor vehicle drivers. Counsel handling these cases must investigate PED distraction by the pilot as a potential cause or contributing cause of the helicopter crash.

J. Improper Maintenance

Serious mistakes by a mechanic either when working upon or approving installation or other return to service items have resulted in many helicopter accidents. This includes situations where the incorrect type or size of part is installed in the helicopter or installed incorrectly. The qualifications and experience of all mechanics performing work on the helicopter are subject to scrutiny. Improper maintenance also encompasses failure to perform required inspections at the recommended or scheduled intervals or neglecting to perform major overhauls or annual inspections. Reasons include poor training, work overload, improper oversight, or misplaced budgetary priorities.

Some of these maintenance errors can be appallingly simple. Failure of the assigned mechanic to re-attach a cable within the main rotor control system or to firmly affix a bolt in the swashplate may result in catastrophic loss of main rotor control. Absent total annihilation of the helicopter wreckage at impact, such errors easily will be detected by any experienced helicopter crash investigator.

K. Mid-Air Collision

Unfortunately, helicopters are not immune from colliding with other aircraft in-flight with catastrophic results. Two such recent incidents illustrate the perils albeit in two different respects.

In a mid-air collision in Phoenix in July 2007, news-gathering helicopters were covering a police chase on the ground over downtown Phoenix. Five such news-gathering helicopters were on the scene. Reviews of voice transcripts at the time indicated that all of the pilots were in communication with one other.[7]

Those voice tapes also show that the pilots were busily reporting to their respective news outlets while at the same time acting as pilot-in-command and seeking to avoid the other four helicopters along the chase route. Two of the news helicopters came into contact and crashed killing both pilots and two on-board photographers. This incident points out the hazard of helicopter pilots taking on too many responsibilities given the workload required for safe operation.[8]

In August 2009 a sightseeing helicopter collided with a small private plane and crashed into the Hudson River. Eyewitnesses reported that the plane appeared to strike into the side of the helicopter.[9] Notwithstanding the numerous private aircraft and helicopter sightseeing tours flying along the scenic Hudson River route, that corridor is not regulated at low altitude flight. General aviation aircraft, which basically includes all helicopters and small planes, are permitted to fly over the Hudson River beneath a 1,100-foot ceiling maintaining separation from airliners flying at a 5,000-foot minimum altitude. Upon inquiry about any federal regulation of the Hudson River flight corridor, the Mayor of New York City, Michael Bloomberg, explained that he did not favor any federal regulation because of the city's interest in tourism.[10] Some federal regulatory order restricting low altitude flight is essential for this crowded airspace.

L. Avionics or Instrument Failure

Where instrument flight rules (IFR) were prevailing and the accident may seem otherwise unexplainable, a failure of any of the flight instruments is a potential cause. As with engine failure, the loss of any flight instrument may be reported by a pilot to ATC. All flight instrumentation and their power sources should be examined thoroughly. In any suspect flight instrument failure the radar path should also be obtained and studied to assess any irregularities or deviations from the assigned flight path or known destination potentially explainable by loss of flight instruments in poor weather.

M. In-Flight Fire or Explosion

The combination of high heat, hot metal, and fuel creates the deadly potential for in-flight fire or explosion in a helicopter. Specialized fire investigators must be retained if this factor is suspected. These experts routinely look for indicia of in-flight fire such as smoke and thermal or heat damage in the cockpit and cabin. The investigation also will center on the ignition source as well as the condition and integrity of the fuel tank. In such scenarios it is often determined that the fire extinguisher has been pulled from its storage compartment by the pilot or one of the passengers and was found in a position post-impact where it could not possibly have been otherwise.

All electrical circuitry must be examined for any indication of melted wires or damaged installation. Finally, any in-flight helicopter fire whether in the cabin or on the exterior airframe itself will have a particular shape far different from the type of shape generated by a ground fire or explosion. The collateral complications of an in-flight helicopter fire are the identification of victims and, on occasion, even identifying who was the pilot-in-command at the controls.

N. Mid-Air Break-Up or Structural Failure

Although a helicopter does not have wings, it can suffer structure separation in-flight with horrific consequences. A helicopter can lose a tail boom, horizontal stabilizer, or even the entire main rotor mast. One of the hallmarks of any mid-air structural failure is that there will be helicopter components scattered along the flight path some distance away from the final resting place of the wreckage.

O. Fuel Starvation, Exhaustion or Contamination

Fuel starvation or fuel exhaustion is not a malady limited to fixed-wing aircraft. Technically, fuel starvation signifies that fuel is not reaching the engine whereas fuel exhaustion is literally running out of the usable fuel supply. The most common reasons for fuel exhaustion are insufficient fuel for the intended mission whether due to the pilot's error in trip planning or a line attendant or mechanic's failure to fill the fuel tank to the level expected. Or the explanation may be as simple as the fuel gauge needle was stuck. Fuel starvation occurs where there has been some restriction or stoppage of fuel flow to the helicopter engine. There may be some mechanical malfunction with the engine fuel control unit (FCU) or fuel pump. There have been instances where some foreign object was found in a fuel line thereby obstructing fuel flow to the engine.

Simply running out of fuel is often attributable to a faulty fuel gauge. However, at least one court has held that a helicopter pilot could not rely on his fuel gauge because of the potential for an inaccurate reading and imposed upon the helicopter pilot the duty to verify the accuracy of the fuel gauge and to be aware of the remaining flight time.[11]

Fuel system contamination can occur in several ways but the two most common are improperly mixing the fuel with water or not draining water from the fuel line as specified. Another contaminant scenario may be as a result of some other fluid which is inadvertently mixed into the fuel either at the source or at the fueling point. The NTSB regularly preserves and tests fuel reserves in any case of suspect engine power loss.

P. Sabotage and Combat Operations

Foul play fortunately has been a rare cause of helicopter accidents. However, where governmental officials or other dignitaries are involved it is routine procedure for the FBI to become involved in a helicopter crash investigation. The FBI or an investigator from the Alcohol, Tobacco and Firearms (ATF) Division will check for exterior damage to rule out a direct strike at the helicopter as well as to detect for the presence of any explosives.

All branches of the U.S. military, including the National Guard, employ thousands of helicopters for use in combat operations to transport troops, conduct surveillance or engage in active combat. Regrettably, many helicopters lose control and crash as a result of enemy fire and surface-to-air missiles.

Q. Weather or Environmental Factors

Any type of inclement or severe weather may play a role in causing the helicopter accident whether that is in the form of an icestorm or snowstorm, heavy rain or other meteorological condition. The possibility of outside factors affecting the helicopter such as a flock of birds or severe air turbulence from a commercial jetliner also must be assessed and ruled out.

R. Air Traffic Control Error

Air traffic control (ATC) operators make similar mistakes involving helicopters as for fixed-wing aircraft. The most frequent ATC error occurs when the controller commands a fixed-wing aircraft along a particular flight path that results in a direct collision into a helicopter. Other air traffic controllers have failed to properly respond to a helicopter pilot's emergency declaration either by not allowing the helicopter to land immediately and not providing appropriate vectors where a loss of instrumentation was suspected. ATC negligence also may explain severe wake turbulence helicopter crashes. If the ATC puts a helicopter in harm's way such as in close proximity to a large commercial airliner, the potential for a crash is evident.

4.2 Assessing Survivability and Crashworthiness Issues

Plaintiff's counsel must assess the level of occupant safety protection in a helicopter accident for any contributing cause to the injuries or death. This is an aspect of the crash which the NTSB largely ignores. This is, in part, explained by the mission of the NTSB which is to determine the probable cause of the crash itself. As the ability to survive a crash cannot possibly be its probable cause, NTSB often ignores crashworthiness issues in its investigation and analysis. On occasions, the NTSB has addressed crashworthiness issues relative to a particular safety hazard or specific model of aircraft or equipment.

The FAA has issued a number of regulatory criteria for crashworthiness and survivability including standards for post-impact explosion, fuel tank integrity and occupant restraint systems. FAA has issued stringent requirements for restraint systems in helicopters which include seat strength and the requirement of basic safety equipment such as life vests, flashlights, and first aid kits. All helicopters must have means of escape post-impact which are usable and functional.

The concept of helicopter accident survivability encompasses both the design of the helicopter and available equipment so as to maximize the prospects that the passengers will suffer non-fatal or even minimal injury as a result of the helicopter crash. While this is an important goal, many helicopter crashes would not be survivable under any circumstances because of the severe impact forces or nature of the crash dynamic.

In any helicopter crash sequence, there are four such criteria for survivability.

A. Occupant Protection

Counsel must assess whether any aspect of the interior passenger compartment contributed to cause any of the occupant injuries, such as an unwarranted protrusion, an unpadded interior cabin wall, inadequately cushioned seat, or even a broken seat bracket. For example, in air ambulance helicopters the interior is substantially modified with the installation of medical equipment and patient beds which can be a source of injury to the occupants on impact. Counsel also must examine whether any design deficiency or poor construction of a helicopter helmet contributed to a pilot's or other occupant's head trauma.

B. Restraint Systems

Evaluation of the entire restraint system includes examination of the seat belts and shoulder harnesses for proper function as well as utilization. The same crashworthiness principles apply to improper or inadequate safety restraint systems in helicopters as in any motor vehicle, but specialized experts with experience in the aviation arena are critical. The seat itself should be firmly attached to the fuselage. In helicopter crashes that are otherwise survivable, an occupant in an inadequately affixed seat may become a projectile causing injury to that seat occupant and potentially others within the helicopter cabin.

C. Structural Integrity

The helicopter crash load as experienced by each occupant must be analyzed as to whether the impact was within human tolerance levels. The structural integrity of the helicopter should permit crash survival on hard landing or moderate impact forces. There is a critical trade-off between the structural integrity of a helicopter and the permissible payload or weight certified for a particular helicopter.

D. Post-Impact Fire or Explosion

Helicopter crashes often will result in a fire which may engulf the cabin. As many helicopters utilize a fuel tank location directly beneath the helicopter passenger compartment, counsel must assess whether the fuel tank met minimal crashworthiness specifications. The fuel tank and fuel pump design also must be examined for contributing to cause any helicopter post-crash fire or explosion. The ability of the fuel tank to withstand puncture or tear forces on impact can dramatically improve the prospects of avoiding any post-crash fire.

As recently as the mid-1960's, a post-crash fire was the primary cause of death in U.S. Army helicopter crashes. The Army subsequently developed a more crashworthy fuel system which was installed in all Army helicopters. That improvement as well as the development of helicopter drop testing substantially enhanced crash survival in helicopters due to greater avoidance of post-crash fire and subsequent thermal injuries.[12]

4.3 Non-Occupant Injuries and Deaths

Many helicopter accidents occur without the occupant physically present in the aircraft. These incidents can occur while passengers are entering or exiting the aircraft, during routine maintenance activity, or simply where curious bystanders stand too close to a helicopter during take-off or landing.

A. Boarding or Deboarding Incidents

Boarding and deboarding incidents are not crashes but occur too frequently to ignore. The simple expedient of boarding and deboarding a helicopter becomes a highly risky affair when the main and tail rotor blades are still turning. Engine shut-down does not mean the blades have stopped rotating, because the blades will continue to spin due to inertia. There is a significant accident history associated with tail rotor injuries as well. Absent an emergency or military application, the engine must be shut down and all rotors at rest when passengers are entering or exiting the helicopter. A passenger's unfamiliarity with the location of these rotating blades and their lack of visibility has proven fatal on many occasions.

B. Persons On Ground

Helicopter crashes have been just as devastating to people and property on the ground. An out-of-control main rotor blade is lethal. The underbelly location of the fuel tank with or without an explosion can cause extensive fire damage. The danger to rescuers and other on-scene personnel from fire and explosion is ever present. Counsel need to be aware that the 18-year statute of repose set out in the General Aviation and Revitalization Act (GARA) does not apply where the plaintiff injured party is not aboard the aircraft.

In a case handled by the author, a 20-year old college student was walking along a sidewalk in downtown Cranbrook, Vancouver, British Columbia when a Bell 206B Jet Ranger helicopter lost engine power and descended rapidly. He was struck by the main rotor blade and suffered fatal injuries.

Another example of on-ground injury from a helicopter occurs where onlookers are merely in the vicinity of an operational helicopter. Failure to maintain a safe distance from a helicopter while it is preparing to take-off or while in the process of landing has caused many serious accidents. One such incident occurred in November 1962 in Little Rock, Arkansas. A 3-year old girl was struck in the face and severely injured by the helicopter rotor blades. The pilot had turned off the engine but the rotors continued to move by inertia. Sadly, the girl's mother was taking her to visit Santa Claus, who was arriving in that helicopter.[13]

Seven states presently impose absolute liability on an owner or lessee of aircraft for any injuries or damages sustained by persons or property on the ground. These states are Delaware, Hawaii, Minnesota, New Jersey, South Carolina, Tennessee, and Vermont.[14] At least two states, Maryland and Wisconsin, provide for a presumption of liability on the part of an aircraft owner or operator causing injury to persons or property on the ground.[15]

C. Maintenance-Related Accidents

Mechanics and other helicopter repair personnel have been injured while performing routine maintenance on helicopters. The primary danger comes from engine run-ups and testing of the main rotor and tail rotor blades. Clear lines of communication with the pilot must be established and any personnel in the vicinity should be alerted to any operational testing or engine starts of the helicopter.

Injuries to helicopter mechanics have resulted in lawsuits against the helicopter manufacturer. In one such case a helicopter mechanic was seriously injured while working on the transmission oil pressure relief valve near the swashplate which is connected to the helicopter's main rotor mast.[16] He filed suit under the Alabama Extended Manufacturer's Liability Doctrine alleging that the helicopter was defective because the maintenance manual did not adequately warn of the dangers and risks associated with working around the rotating swashplate while the engine was on. That court granted defendant's motion for summary judgment as the applicable maintenance manual was produced by the U.S. Army with no involvement by the defendant manufacturer. The court also found that the danger of working near that rotating swashplate was "open and obvious" to any reasonable person.

4.4 Identification of Potential Target Defendants

Once the initial factual investigation has revealed the primary suspect causes of the helicopter accident, the next step in the filing preparation process is to identify precisely those defendants whose conduct in any manner caused or contributed to cause the crash. Included in this analysis are the factual allegations to be made against each defendant, and the applicable legal theories as permitted by the chosen jurisdiction. That list of potential defendants and possible factual bases for liability include the following.

A. Pilot of Helicopter

In most cases, one side or the other will seek to blame the pilot in whole or in part for the helicopter accident. The pilot of the helicopter presents an easy target for two reasons. The pilot is often killed in the crash and unable to defend her actions at trial. No one has the benefit of hearing from the pilot's perspective precisely what occurred in the moments leading up to the crash. The second reason is that any crash is presumed to be due to the pilot-in-command's failure to maintain operational control of the aircraft. Absent an obvious malfunction, the NTSB routinely will cite pilot error as the probable cause of the helicopter accident.

Under the Federal Aviation Regulations, the pilot is the final authority on the safety of any flight and is therefore responsible for an unsafe flight.[17] If any weather, engine, mechanical or other known or readily observable condition which caused the crash existed prior to the flight, then the pilot should not have flown the non-airworthy helicopter.

There are a myriad of potential pilot errors in any given accident both prior to and during flight. In the pre-flight category, the most frequent charge is flying in bad weather. Embarking on a flight in the face of adverse weather conditions or failing to obtain any weather data at all are typical pre-flight failures contributing to an accident. Pre-flight claims of negligence also include improper planning of the flight, lack of a filed flight plan, improper weight and balance calculations ("improperly overloaded the helicopter") or even inadequate fuel calculations.

Another common pre-flight pilot error is the pilot's failure to conduct the proper pre-flight inspection and checklist required for the helicopter. Failure of the pilot to conduct the proper pre-flight may result in overlooking such simple matters as a loose or missing fuel cap, unresponsive or catching tail rotor pedal or obvious impact damage to the leading edge of a main or tail rotor blade.

In-flight operational errors include the ubiquitous "failure to keep the helicopter under proper control," failure to know the terrain, flying at too low of an altitude, or inadvertently stalling the engine. Pilot condition factors include fatigue, impairment by drugs or alcohol, or some medically induced incapacitation such as a heart attack or stroke. Where the pilot was confronted with an in-flight malfunction of any component or system, his actions should be evaluated based on the standard of care applicable in comparable emergency situations, often referred to as the sudden emergency doctrine.

When analyzing the actions of the pilot, the same checklist applies to any co-pilot who may have shared operational control. In the case of a flight training accident, although the student pilot may have been at the controls, the pilot-in-command at all times would have been the certified flight instructor.

Where another pilot is in the cockpit of a dual-controlled helicopter and both suffer fatal injuries in the crash, the question of which was the pilot-in-command often arises. FAR 91.3 is helpful by providing that "the pilot in command of the aircraft shall be directly responsible for its operation and shall have final authority as to operation of the aircraft." This issue is often framed as which pilot was "manipulating the controls" of the helicopter at the time of the accident. The pilot-in-command of the helicopter could be either its owner or the pilot sitting in the right seat which is customarily the seat of the pilot having operational control of the helicopter. In such instances circumstantial evidence becomes critical. Factors such as the relative experience of the two pilots, who filed a flight plan (if any) who was undertaking radio communication, and who happened to be in the right seat, all weigh on that determination. Most flight plans provide for the pilot's name and basic identifying information. Forensic evidence also may play a role in identifying the pilot-in-command. In the pilot training scenario, the instructor can be counted on to "take over the aircraft" if time allows for the execution of any emergency procedures.

B. Operator of Helicopter

Whether the operator is literally a one-person shop with a single helicopter used for crop-dusting operations or the large multi-state air ambulance operation with 70 or more helicopters in fleet, that operator must be considered as a target defendant. Any operator carrying passengers for hire as part of its customary flight mission must develop and comply with an FAA-Approved Aircraft Inspection Program (AAIP). Failure to have a written AAIP is a basis for negligence liability as violative of the Federal Aviation Regulations.

Other rules and regulations subjecting an operator to liability include policies permitting its pilots to fly the helicopter too low as for example in congested urban areas or too closely to fixed objects such as the rim of the Grand Canyon. Most large operators employ their own in-house mechanics for routine maintenance, inspection, and repair of the aircraft. That maintenance of the subject helicopter may be an additional factual basis for liability.

C. Maintenance Personnel

Where the cause of the helicopter accident involved the failure of some component or system the actions of all mechanics with responsibility for that helicopter are under a hot glare. The most common factual allegation is that those responsible for maintenance "failed to properly maintain the helicopter in an airworthy condition."

Most helicopter maintenance programs have required maintenance due at periodic intervals such as 100 hours. Pursuant to Part 91 of the Federal Aviation Regulations, any helicopter used for passenger-carrying operations requires both an annual inspection as well as compliance with the manufacturer's recommended and regularly scheduled maintenance procedures. Charter operations are governed under FAR Part 135 which requires even more extensive maintenance and compliance with an FAA-Approved Aircraft Inspection Program (AAIP).

All helicopter components have or should have a time between overhaul (TBO) specification which must be logged and recorded in the maintenance records. Whether it involves a swashplate support assembly or a mast bearing, helicopter flight is brutal on certain components given their constant exposure to excessive vibration, heat and wear. Pilot squawk notes may reveal maintenance concerns which

were not timely or properly addressed by the responsible mechanics.

D. Manufacturer of Helicopter

Any suspect in-flight malfunction requires consideration of the helicopter manufacturer as a defendant in the lawsuit. The manufacturer determines the design and type of systems used in a helicopter, selects and installs the various component parts and is presumed to know more about the design, function and operation of its helicopter than anyone else. Any factual basis for airframe structure, system or component design defect compels inclusion of the helicopter manufacturer as a defendant.

The Federal Aviation Regulations attach certain responsibilities to the owner of the Type Certificate (TC) of an aircraft. Any modifications to that aircraft in the form of structure or system design requires an application and approval of a Supplemental Type Certificate (STC).

Any potential issue going to the useful safe life of any component or system requires naming the helicopter manufacturer in the lawsuit. The supplementation of and revisions to all maintenance and operational material and especially the Pilot Operating Handbook (POH) is the direct responsibility of the manufacturer. This may take the form of service letters, service bulletins, circular advisories, and updated and current technical information.

E. Distributor of Helicopter

Every foreign helicopter manufacturer has a U.S. subsidiary whose primary mission is to sell and provide technical support for its parent company's helicopters. For the most part those distributors rely entirely on the foreign manufacturer for engineering and technical data and conduct no testing or certification themselves.

Nevertheless, such distributors must be considered as target defendants as they would have access to information the parent company may not. This includes service difficulty reports, sales information and records, warranty claims and even direct customer complaints. Inclusion of the U.S. distributor as a defendant avoids the whip-saw technique favored by such defendants who desire to avoid discovery where each points to the other as the source of information or as the responsible party.

F. Helicopter Engine Manufacturer

The manufacturer of the engine warrants its own separate treatment as a target defendant. A close and cozy relationship exists between all of the helicopter manufacturers and their carefully chosen engine maker. Counsel never should expect the airframe manufacturer to bring a third party action against the engine maker and must file any action against the engine manufacturer directly. Any suspect engine failure or power loss requires inclusion of the engine manufacturer because certain essential discovery can be obtained only from that party.

The existence of other similar helicopter engine problems or in-flight failures is discoverable and may occur in models other than the specific subject helicopter model at issue. On some occasions the extent of the engine problems known to the engine manufacturer was not fully communicated to the helicopter manufacturer.

G. Helicopter Component Part Manufacturer

Where a particular component or as-installed system can be identified as having been designed, manufactured and delivered by an outside manufacturer and that component or system is suspect then that manufacturer should receive a summons to the suit as well. The component part manufacturer will have design and technical information not in the possession of or accessible by the helicopter manufacturer. The component part maker may seriously overextend the recommended life limit of its part for competitive purposes. Maintenance is less expensive if an operator need only replace a component part at 200 hours rather than every 50 hours. Examination of the part maker's internal documentation, field feedback and engineering data will determine if it has improperly misled the helicopter manufacturer or helicopter operator or both.

H. Air Traffic Control

Most helicopter missions are not flown pursuant to a pre-assigned flight path and would not be under the auspices of air traffic control (ATC). Nevertheless, there still are a number of situations where ATC actions or failures may have contributed to a helicopter crash. If the pilot goes on channel and declares an emergency, it is ATC's responsibility to immediately take charge of that aircraft, clear other aircraft out of the vicinity, and take all necessary steps to effectuate a safe landing. In some situations, either the controller failed to timely recognize that an actual emergency had been declared or took inappropriate and inadequate steps to facilitate that aircraft's safe return to ground.

A common controller error is where an airplane is directed along a flight path far too close to the vicinity of a helicopter. In other instances, air traffic controllers have failed to recognize the often deadly consequences of releasing a large commercial airliner for take-off with a helicopter in the vicinity. The wake turbulence created by the larger aircraft may lead to a loss of control and potential crash of the helicopter. Controllers have failed to advise helicopter

pilots of dangerous weather conditions such as fog cover or thunderstorms. Similarly, Flight Service Stations (FSS) have given rise to federal government liability for erroneous weather briefings.

In considering any claim against ATC, counsel must consider that the lawsuit will be handled pursuant to the Federal Tort Claims Act which has a number of procedural restrictions imposed on plaintiffs.[18]

I. Lessor of Helicopter

Increasingly, helicopter operators are leasing their aircraft from various financing entities for cash flow and tax purposes. Aircraft lessor liability was thought to be extinguished by a specific federal statute which provides that the lessor of any civil aircraft, engine or propeller is liable for personal injury, death or property loss only when the aircraft "is in the actual possession or control of the lessor...."[19] However, recent court decisions have found that this federal statute does not preempt state law claims against financing companies which lease aircraft for operation.[20] In one case, the plaintiff claimed that the aircraft leased was in an "unreasonably dangerous condition" and that the crash was as a result of that dangerous condition. The court concluded that plaintiff properly stated a cause of action under Wisconsin law against the lessor for strict tort liability.[21]

Lessor liability is controversial in large part because of the claim that most lessors rely entirely on their lessees for proper maintenance and operation of the aircraft during the terms of the lease. Lessors often claim that their personnel are not equipped to evaluate such issues and are only knowledgeable about financing issues, basic delivery and return of the aircraft or lease defaults. However, imposing lessor liability would require that they at least take some minimal steps to determine how the helicopter lessee is maintaining and operating the aircraft during the lease term. This may require some affirmative action on the lessor's part to investigate such issues.

J. Owner or Lessee of Helicopter

An owner or lessee has the duty to provide proper maintenance support for the helicopter. However, if it can be shown that an owner or lessee entrusted a reputable and qualified FAA-certified repair station with these maintenance responsibilities, that is usually all that the standard of care requires.

Another potential basis for imposition of liability as against an owner or lessee would involve notice or knowledge of some mechanical deficiency or lack of airworthiness as to some aspect of the helicopter and failure to notify the pilot. If the owner or lessee entrusted the helicopter to a pilot who she knows or should have known is unfit, incompetent or even unlicensed to fly the helicopter, then liability may be predicated upon that negligent entrustment.

Several states have specific statutes which authorize a cause of action against the owner or lessee of the aircraft for the negligent conduct of those to whom the owner or lessee entrusts the aircraft.[22] These statutes depart from the typical common law by imposing liability on the aircraft's owner or lessee. The stated purpose of these statutory schemes is to impose liability on those who are presumed to be more financially responsible and thereby increase the certainty of recovery for those injured or killed by the negligent operation of aircraft. Some states have adopted aircraft owner liability by case law.[23] Absent such a statutory scheme or imposition of liability on the owner or a lessee by case decision, the majority of courts addressing the issue have held that an owner leasing an airworthy aircraft to a licensed pilot is not liable to third persons as a result of the pilot's negligence.

K. Fixed Base Operator

A fixed base operator (FBO) services the routine needs of general aviation aircraft including helicopters such as providing a safe and accessible landing area, re-fueling, routine maintenance and passenger boarding services. A FBO may be considered a target defendant if any of its maintenance personnel performed a routine repair on a suspect part or system of the helicopter. This may be as part of a mechanic's quick look while the helicopter was in the process of re-fueling. Alternatively, there may be an issue as to the quality of the fuel and whether it was contaminated. The FBO fuel attendant may have misunderstood the pilot's fueling directions resulting in less than expected reserves. All of these potential acts or omissions are grounds for liability of the FBO.

L. Pilots of Other Aircraft

Pilots of fixed-wing aircraft are not necessarily familiar with the flight capabilities and darting maneuvers of helicopters. In some instances the fixed-wing pilot will fly far too closely to a helicopter not realizing that it is actually flying close to if not in its intended flight path. Notwithstanding the pilot's familiar duty to "see and avoid" when flying in visual meteorological conditions, a fixed-wing airplane in the vicinity of a helicopter must provide a wide berth or margin of clearance. The recent Hudson crash occurred where a small plane flew directly into a tour helicopter. Other pilots may be at fault for creating a wake turbulence which triggered a loss of control of the helicopter.

M. Electrical or Utility Companies

In the vicinity of an airport or in known flight paths of aircraft, electrical or utility companies have a duty to mark their power lines so as to be visible to pilots. This is particularly important for helicopters given their common low-level flight altitude.

Helicopter wire strike incidents occur all too frequently. Rather than placing the total responsibility on the pilot the circumstances must be examined to assess whether a red marker ball on the line would have been visible and averted the mishap and whether the utility company acknowledged that this was a vicinity known to be frequented by aircraft.

N. Wire Strike Protection Manufacturers

Various devices have been marketed which purport to provide protection in the event the helicopter flies into utility wires or cables. Such equipment consists of an upper cutter or scissor-like blade placed along the front of the helicopter's nose in an upward angle and a lower cutter angled downward and affixed below the nose. These cutters are intended to guide any contacted wire to a jaw area which contains sharp saw-like blades. Unfortunately, such systems provide only limited protection as the helicopter must be flying straight and level upon contact and they provide potential protection only from frontal strikes against horizontally strung wires. Where such a system had been installed on a helicopter and fails to provide an appropriate measure of protection against a wire strike, the manufacturer of such devices has been sued on theories of misrepresentation, fraud and design defect. In such a scenario, counsel must assess the specific warranties and representations made by the seller to determine whether they overpromised the degree of protection to be afforded.

O. Film Production Companies

The motion picture industry has made extensive use of helicopters during film production, and the television and commercial advertising world has joined in. Helicopters now are used with increasing frequency in filming television commercials.

The inclusion of such companies as defendants in a lawsuit arising from a helicopter crash must be considered if those companies determined the location for the filming or limited the pilot from conducting any pre-filming area reconnaissance. In a recent case the author tried to verdict in Iowa, the jury imposed 25 percent of the fault for the helicopter crash upon the film production company for precisely these reasons.[24]

P. Hospitals or Regional Medical Centers

Many hospitals which use an air ambulance service for delivery of emergency patients enter into a joint operational agreement with the helicopter operator. These joint agreements typically provide that the operator shall provide the helicopter, pilot, and maintenance personnel, and the hospital will provide the on-board personnel, medical equipment, and hospital helipad. In that the hospital or the regional medical center would be considered a party to a joint venture with the operator, it would be subject to liability in the event of a helicopter accident and should be considered for possible inclusion in the lawsuit.

Q. Certification or Testing Laboratory

Some commonly used helicopter component parts are not amenable to on-site inspection or testing. Such parts include self-contained metal cylinders with rubber bladders used for hydraulic servo accumulators or certain flight instrumentation which requires electronic diagnostic equipment.

In such instances, these components require off-site certification or testing compliance by a laboratory certified to perform such airworthiness testing. Whether the part is even tested or tested improperly, liability can be attached to such an entity if it certifies the component as airworthy and permits it to be placed back in service on a helicopter. Any in-flight failure of a component which only recently had been certified as airworthy by a testing facility should land that facility an invitation to the lawsuit.

Courts have held that a duty of care attaches to organizations in the business of testing and certifying a particular product as being able to perform a certain task. When the product in fact cannot so perform the task certified that may impose liability on the certifying or testing organization for injuries suffered by those using that product.[25] That same theory would apply to testing equipment or devices which by improper calibration or other faulty measurement allow for improper or misaligned installation of helicopter equipment.

R. Flight Training Schools

The most frequent basis for suit against a helicopter flight school arises where a student helicopter pilot is injured or killed while on a training flight with one of the school's flight instructors. The prevailing view is that the relationship between a flight school and its pilot-trainee flying with the school's certified flight instructor is that of carrier and passenger. If not, then any claim for the trainee's injury or death must plead and prove a breach of the instructor's duty of care.

Suits by injured parties against the flight school based on negligent piloting by one of its graduates presents a different legal scenario. A flight school normally is not responsible for injuries caused by its student unless the principles of negligent entrustment apply. Some states expressly exempt flight schools from suit due to the negligence of the pilot who trained there disallowing any "educational malpractice" claim.[26] Under certain factual circumstances, one can envision a proper cause of action against a helicopter flight training school. For example, if an injured student-pilot or his passenger established that the flight training school omitted certain procedures such as emergency maneuvers from a helicopter pilot training program which proved causative to the helicopter accident, that may constitute a proper claim for negligence.

Where an operator runs its own flight school, those programs should be evaluated. Helicopter pilot training regimens require a minimum number of hands-on flight training hours in addition to classroom time. Any indication that these minimal standards have not been met is an additional ground for adding the operator as a defendant to the suit.

S. Airport, Heliport, or Helipad Operators

There exist well-recognized standards to which any airport operator must adhere. Numerous federal aviation regulations and circular advisories govern the appropriate location, design and other specifications for airports. Most airports are owned and operated by states or counties such that the state sovereign immunity statutes would need to be researched in order to assess the viability of such operators as a defendant.

One typical duty of any airport or helipad operator is to keep the landing area in a reasonably safe condition and free from any dangerous obstructions. An airport, heliport or helipad operator may be liable for not removing a foreign object in the intended landing area of the helicopter. This may be a wheelchair, medical cart or portable stretcher at a hospital helipad, or drilling equipment left unattended on the helipad of an oil platform in the Gulf of Mexico. Such obstructions may cause a tip-over of a helicopter which is potentially disastrous if the main rotor blade impacts the ground. Another basis for liability of an airport or heliport operation would be inadequate or not readily accessible medical facilities or equipment such as fire extinguishers.

Airport landing areas and helipads have certain lighting requirements at night and for weather-related visibility conditions such as severe fog or heavy rain. Any temporary but movable fixtures such as poles, towers, or wiring which could otherwise interfere with the safe take-off or landing of a helicopter at night or in difficult weather conditions should either be removed, well-lit or warned about.

T. Helmet, Seat or Seat Belt Manufacturer

Survivability of the crash is always a question in those cases where the ground impact was either controlled as in an autorotation or from low altitude. For those helicopter crashes involving controlled flight into terrain (CFIT) at cruise speed, survivability is not an issue as the helicopter will be completely demolished leaving only rubble. Occupant protection must be examined in terms of the availability and proper function of restraint systems. Where the autopsy report reveals blunt head trauma as a cause of injury or death and the pilot or passenger was wearing a helmet, its proper design and manufacture need to be assessed.

In instances where the helicopter lacked any passenger restraints whatsoever, that would be a potential liability issue for the aircraft manufacturer or, in some instances, maintenance personnel who either removed or failed to repair the restraint. However, if available seat belts were utilized and failed in the crash sequence, the manufacturer of that restraint system is a viable defendant.

Similarly, the seat design and attachment mechanism should be examined to assess its suitability and degree of occupant protection. If the seat did not withstand relatively moderate impact crash forces and is torn from its attachments, the occupant may be ejected and suffer severe injury or death as a result. The maker of the seat and seat attachments may in that instance be joined as a defendant in the suit.

U. Fire and Rescue Personnel

As in a motor vehicle accident, rescue workers may in their zeal fail to timely and properly immobilize a spinal cord injury patient with resultant permanent neurological damage. Failure to timely remove occupants from a helicopter thereby subjecting them to fire or explosion is another potential basis for liability against rescue personnel. Notwithstanding that fire, police and other rescue personnel are well-intentioned and courageous to engage in their line of work, they nevertheless are governed by minimal standards of care and should be defendants in the lawsuit if those standards are breached.

4.5 Jurisdictional and Choice of Laws Issues

Before drawing up the first draft of the petition or complaint for filing the lawsuit, counsel must engage in a most careful analysis of the jurisdictional and choice of laws issues. As there are so many entities involved in a helicopter's design, manufacture, distribution, sale, ownership, operation and maintenance in addition to the manufacturer of the multitude of various component parts and systems, some choice of jurisdictional options is usually available. The intent of this section is to point counsel to those factors considered most salient to the critical decision of where to file the lawsuit—which as to liability may be outcome determinative and as to damages may be monumental.

A. Selection of Lawful and Appropriate Forum

In any helicopter crash case, the selection of the appropriate forum without exaggeration may be the single most important judgment call that counsel makes. The choice of law and jurisdictional decision will govern how and which defendants are liable and the specific damages elements lawfully recoverable. This is one of those decisions where counsel truly earns the fee. The potential recovery and ultimate value of the claim will stand or fall on this critical early decision.

Notwithstanding the negative connotation attached to the term "forum shopping" by anti-consumer propagandists, counsel representing plaintiffs lawfully and ethically must select from among the various available options the court which is most favorable in terms of the applicable substantive and procedural law and the known propensities of the various judges and likely jury panels. The concept of forum shopping has been severely impugned by those favoring the corporate industrial interests, and the plaintiffs' bar has been subjected to harsh criticism for the practice of forum shopping. Forum shopping is nothing more than selecting the most favorable jurisdiction considering all of the appropriate and lawful parameters. It is precisely what defendants do when they remove a state court filing to federal court or seek a change of venue in state court to a more strategically advantageous locale from the defense perspective. The issue then is not whether plaintiff's counsel should forum shop but how to do so most effectively in furtherance of counsel's ethical obligation to zealously, effectively and competently represent the client.

In the context of helicopter crash litigation, the proper selection of forum is not only required but the selection of an improper forum may constitute clear legal malpractice. For example, if during the factual investigation counsel learns that the helicopter and suspect component parts at issue were purchased and placed into delivery eight years before the date of the helicopter crash and nevertheless proceeds to file in North Carolina, that lawsuit will be promptly dismissed on the merits as barred by the 6-year statute of repose in products liability actions.

Similarly, if given any other viable option, counsel should not file the lawsuit in North Dakota as against the helicopter manufacturer or component part maker. North Dakota has enacted some of the most severe anti-consumer products liability legislation in the country.[27] North Dakota law expressly utilizes the useful safe life concept providing that if a manufacturer can prove that the damages resulted after the useful safe life of the aircraft or aircraft component then it is not liable.[28] North Dakota also has a rebuttable presumption that after ten years an aircraft or aircraft part has passed its useful life unless there is an express warranty to the contrary.[29] Finally, the most unfair provision provides that aircraft manufacturers are entitled to a presumption that their product is defect-free if it was in compliance with FAA regulations when it was manufactured notwithstanding the inapplicability, minimal nature, or outdatedness of many of those regulations.[30] An important choice of law rule would be to stay out of North Dakota if any other forum is available.

Helicopter crash litigation normally does not present as widespread a choice of forums as in the fixed-wing or commercial aircraft lawsuit. Most helicopter operations are locally based and tend to operate within a single state or may occasionally cross a state line. A notable exception is where a helicopter may be ferried over a considerable distance either because of a recent purchase or to undergo overhaul or refurbishing. Choices may be available considering that there are potentially numerous defendants in any single case. The fortuitousness of the helicopter crash location is less important than the residence of the defendants, or where they and critical witnesses may be found. Although the options may not be as numerous as for a typical airplane crash case, the determination of forum may still be outcome-determinative on liability or value-determinative as to recoverable damages.

Lawyers handling helicopter crash litigation must become certified experts at selecting the proper and lawful forum for the case. If filing in one state versus another will avoid the application of some severe evidentiary burden (such as in North Dakota) or the application of a claim-killing statute of repose (as in North Carolina), the more favorable jurisdiction has to be selected. With the enactment of restrictive tort legislation in many states, the question is no longer whether counsel should engage in forum analysis and selection. Forum evaluation is mandatory in helicopter crash litigation as per the above examples. Beyond these critical liability-based considerations there are a number of other reasons to investigate the law of all possible forums for assessment of the relative advantages.

In a recent helicopter case handled by the author, the critical players hailed not only from across the U.S. but also literally from around the world:

- Place of Helicopter Crash—Meadview, Arizona
- Plaintiffs—Brooklyn, New York
- Helicopter Manufacturer—Marignane, Cedex, France
- Helicopter Operator—Las Vegas, Nevada
- Owner—Seattle, Washington

- Prior Owner Which Had Repaired Helicopter—Okinawa, Japan
- Assembler of Portion of Helicopter—Richmond, New Zealand
- Helicopter Pilot—Hendersonville, Nevada

Given such a panoply of forum choices, counsel's pre-filing analysis must involve substantial legal research to determine the most favorable forum given the liability, procedural, evidentiary and damages issues pertinent to that specific case.

1. Jurisdiction Over Essential Defendants

At the outset, counsel cannot consider any court which presents any significant obstacle to obtaining personal jurisdiction over critical defendants. All other considerations with respect to forum selection, choice of law, favorable liability or damages laws are irrelevant if the case is filed in a court in which the plaintiff is unable to obtain jurisdiction over the target defendants.

Plaintiff attorneys have to resist the tendency to play cute by filing the lawsuit in a peripheral jurisdiction where the laws are favorable but where jurisdiction over the target defendant is highly suspect if not outright unsupportable. Just such a scenario developed approximately ten years ago in a case involving a crash which killed a middle-aged married couple and another passenger. Notwithstanding some of the potential roadblocks of North Carolina law including the short statute of repose, the case was filed in North Carolina which was the location of the crash. No question existed as to obtaining proper jurisdiction over the culpable and solvent defendant.

The other passenger's counsel elected to file in Texas claiming jurisdiction on the basis of a component part manufacturer of the aircraft. The target defendant challenged and successfully won dismissal leaving the passenger with little remedy. The lesson from these experiences is simple: If in doubt, rule number one is to file in the court where the plaintiff is most likely to obtain jurisdiction over the target defendant.

In the often muddled factual scenarios attendant to much helicopter crash litigation, the safest harbor will be filing in the state where the crash occurred or where the principal defendant resides or does business. In most instances, the helicopter manufacturer or suspect component part supplier does not have offices in or other substantial contacts with the particular state. In such cases, the only basis for obtaining in personam jurisdiction is the exercise of that state's long-arm statute. Because most state courts have ruled that the long-arm statute reaches to the outer limits of constitutional due process, the only relevant inquiry becomes whether there are sufficient "minimum contacts" with the forum state to satisfy the due process clause.

To determine what are "the full constitutional limits of due process," one must look to cases decided by the United States Supreme Court on this issue. The seminal case on the issue of personal jurisdiction of a nonresident corporation is the 1945 decision of the U.S. Supreme Court in the famous case of *International Shoe Company v. Washington*.[31] There, the Court ruled that a nonresident must have certain minimum contacts with the state such that the maintenance of the suit does not offend "traditional notions of fair play and substantial justice."[32] In that case, the Supreme Court found the exercise of jurisdiction proper by a Washington state court over a Delaware corporation with its principal place of business in Missouri, despite it having no office, making no contracts, maintaining no stock of merchandise, and making no intrastate deliveries of merchandise in Washington.[33] The court found that the presence of International Shoe's salesmen in the state constituted sufficient contacts.[34]

The exercise of personal jurisdiction may be either specific or general. Specific jurisdiction is proper where the defendant purposely availed itself of the benefits of the forum and the controversy is related to or arises out of the defendant's contacts with the forum.[35] A court properly may assert general jurisdiction over a nonresident defendant whose contacts with the forum state are "substantial, continuous and systematic."[36] Unlike specific jurisdiction, the exercise of general jurisdiction does not require a connection between the specific controversy at issue and the forum state.[37]

Where the helicopter crash occurred in that state, a sufficient basis for exercising specific jurisdiction over its manufacturer or the manufacturer of a component part exists so long as it could have been reasonably anticipated that the actions of the manufacturer in supplying the helicopter or component part would subject it to the prospect of being hailed into court in that particular state. Where the defendant is the helicopter pilot, maintenance facility, or operator and the crash occurred in their state of residence or citizenship, no jurisdictional issue presents, as the court would exercise both specific and general jurisdiction over such a defendant.

In those cases where the helicopter component manufacturer is a U.S. resident and the crash took place in the forum state, the overwhelming majority of courts have found the component part manufacturer amenable to personal jurisdiction. Courts have found the "minimum contacts" requirement satisfied by either the "stream of commerce" or the "purposeful activity" approach. In the former, courts look to see whether the out-of-state defendant delivered its products into the national stream of commerce with the reasonable expectation that they would be purchased or used by helicopter owners or operators in the forum state. Under the "purposeful activity" test, the defendant must take some action which would purposefully avail itself of the privilege of conducting activities within the forum state. Under either approach, courts find that the "minimum contacts" required by constitutional due process analysis are met.

This analysis is similar among the states and follows a generic three-prong test set out by the U.S. Supreme Court:

1. Whether the non-resident defendant performed some act or consummated some transaction within the state or performed some act by which it purposely availed itself of the privilege of conducting activities in the forum, thereby invoking the benefits and protections of its laws;
2. Whether the claim is one that relates to or arises out of the defendant's forum-related activities; and
3. Whether the exercise of jurisdiction under the circumstances is "reasonable."[38]

A typical and illustrative factual scenario and disposition is where a foreign aircraft manufacturer challenged personal jurisdiction under New Hampshire's long-arm statute. The court found jurisdiction proper as it was "reasonably consistent with due process" to subject such a manufacturer to suit in any one of the fifty states in view of the nature of that business.[39] Similarly, the manufacturers of servo actuators which were components in the subject aircraft were held subject to personal jurisdiction in Oregon because those products were distributed in a national market as part of the completely assembled aircraft and it was reasonable to expect that the company might be subject to suit in the State of Oregon.[40]

Obtaining jurisdiction over out-of-state or foreign helicopter or component manufacturers under the general jurisdiction test based on those contacts other than the crash itself involves a careful and detailed factual analysis of the defendant's commercial contacts with the forum. The principal U.S. Supreme Court decision analyzing the sufficiency of a foreign corporation's "minimum contacts" with the forum state sufficient to obtain general jurisdiction arose out of a helicopter crash. On January 26, 1976, a helicopter owned by a Colombian corporation crashed in Peru. The four families of the U.S. citizens who were killed in the crash brought suit in Texas. In Helicopteros Nacionales de Colombia, S.A. v. Hall, the Court reviewed the decision of the Supreme Court of Texas which had determined that the foreign corporation's contacts with the state were sufficient to allow it to assert jurisdiction over the corporation in a helicopter crash action.[41] The corporation, Helicopteros Nacionales de Colombia, S.A., was engaged in the business of providing helicopter transportation for oil and construction companies in South America.

The Court's analysis was based on the extent of the Colombian corporation's business contacts with Texas. It noted critically that the helicopter crash occurred in Peru and was not related to the corporation's contacts with the state of Texas. The Court noted that the defendant did not maintain a place of business in Texas but merely purchased helicopter parts there and sent employees there for training. In an 8-1 decision, the Court ruled that these contacts were not sufficient to subject the corporation to the exercise of that state's in personam jurisdiction.[42]

To succeed in obtaining general jurisdiction, a plaintiff must plead and prove that the out-of-state defendant conducted significant business within the forum state, most of which involved activities that would be relating to those which gave rise to the same activity involved in the helicopter crash.[43] Most state courts hold that the plaintiff's choice of forum is to be given proper deference (although how much can vary) and is balanced against the undue burden to the defendant of being forced to defend the action in that locality.

The U.S. Supreme Court in Burger King explained that while it may be "somewhat burdensome" to defend a lawsuit away from a corporation's home state, it is not a burden that violates due process in every instance.[44] The Court observed that modern transportation and communications means that it is usually not unfair or too burdensome to require a company to defend itself in a state where it engages in economic activity.[45] That thinking has been taken up by the lower courts:

> Easy air transportation, the rapid transmission of documents, and the abundance of law firms with nationwide practices, make it easy these days for cases to be litigated with little extra burden in any of the major metropolitan areas.[46]

The general jurisdiction test also is satisfied if the defendant maintains any office for the purpose of conducting business in that state. Similarly, the "purposeful availment" requirement is met where the non-resident defendant has such a degree of conduct and connection with the forum state such that it should "reasonably anticipate being hailed into court there."[47] The "purposeful availment" aspect of this general jurisdiction test is satisfied where the non-resident defendant "has taken deliberate action" toward the forum state[48] or has performed "some type of affirmative conduct which allows or promotes the transaction of business within the forum state."[49] The element is clearly satisfied where the foreign non-resident corporation marketed and sold products within the state, as those acts support a finding of "purposeful availment."[50]

Jurisdiction is not to be trifled with under any circumstances, for to do so is potentially self-defeating and an invitation to disaster. The first and by far the most critical consideration in filing the lawsuit is that the particular court selected must be able to obtain and maintain jurisdiction over that defendant or those defendants considered to be the viable target defendants in the case.

2. Liability, Procedural and Evidentiary Considerations

Once it is determined that the viable defendants are subject to the jurisdiction of the selected forum, other considerations relating to liability, procedural and evidentiary matters have to be weighed in the process of properly and zealously representing the client. On the liability front, these matters include more favorable and less restrictive joint and several liability laws, inapplicability of certain complete defenses such as contributory negligence or assumption of risk, and in some instances whether liability may attach at all such as the existence of an owner or lessee liability statute. Another key consideration related to the state's joint and several liability laws is whether a defendant is permitted to argue the so-called "empty chair" liability, a notion that may prove problematic under the facts of the case. At the outset of any wrongful death case it behooves counsel to confirm that the laws of the jurisdiction under consideration permit the client or an acceptable surrogate to act as plaintiff given the specific relationship to the deceased as these rules vary widely.

Various evidentiary issues are potentially critical depending on the circumstances of the case. These include whether a widow or widower's subsequent re-marriage is admissible in the trial of the wrongful death of the spouse, various discounting methods to present value in assessing economic loss, taxability of any recovery and the admissibility of various collateral source payments.

3. Damages Issues

Once the liability and procedural concerns have been addressed and to the extent that there remains any option, the critical damages differential among the potential courts has to be considered. Damages considerations in these cases are paramount. States under consideration for filing may or may not bar punitive damages either in their entirety or in wrongful death cases. A number of states such as Kansas, Wisconsin, and Alaska have enacted severe limitations on the amount of money recoverable either in wrongful death cases or for non-economic damages in their entirety to as little as $250,000. This is a pitiful sum to be awarded to the 35-year-old accountant rendered paraplegic but still able to work.

Occupants of a helicopter are likely to know the aircraft is in serious trouble well prior to the actual crash. Where the helicopter suffered a disastrous in-flight failure of a critical flight control or the engine, the occupants will be thrashed about as the helicopter is spinning, and then descending and lifting rapidly. Those last life moments prior to impact with the ground where the occupants know that they will likely die in a crash are known as "pre-impact terror." Although horrific, such damages are not compensable in a number of states.[51] Some states allow such damages under the category of "apprehension of impending death"[52] or "pre-impact fright."[53]

Counsel should determine whether a damages recovery may be offset by collateral sources such as governmental assistance or medical or life insurance proceeds. Other potential damages issues critical to the case at hand and for which recovery may not be had or had in a limited way:

1. Manner in which lost earnings or income are calculated;
2. Requirement of reducing recovery to present value; and
3. Recoverability of loss of consortium as between a parent and child or vice versa.

4. Choice of Law Considerations

Choice of laws or conflicts of laws analysis is not as critical as it once was given the adoption by most states of the most significant contacts rule. A choice of laws analysis, unlike a forum-selection or jurisdictional issue, looks to which substantive law should be applied depending on the facts and circumstances of the case. On both liability and damage issues, the options range from the law of the forum state to the law of the state of the helicopter crash or, alternatively, the law of the defendant manufacturer's principal place of business. This is different from the jurisdictional determination as the court may determine that it has jurisdiction both over the subject matter and in personam jurisdiction over the named defendants but elect to apply the law of some different state to the facts of the case.

Most states now utilize the "most significant contacts" rule which uses the law of that state with the most significant contacts to the incident. Utilizing that test, a court reviews the facts of the helicopter crash to determine which state has the most significant contacts and in so doing will look at:

a. The place where the injury occurred;
b. The place where the conduct causing the injury occurred;
c. The domicile, residence, nationality, place of incorporation and place of business of the party; and
d. The place where the relationship, if any, between the parties is centered.[54]

A few states still use the antiquated lex loci or "place of the injury" rule to determine the applicable law. If the laws of the state where the helicopter crash occurred are onerous or in some cases even claim-prohibitive, other forums must be evaluated to avoid the oppressive application of that state's laws. The choice of law determination must be made relatively early in the litigation so that counsel will know the requisite elements of the prima facie case which need to be proved, the evidence rules to be used, and the specific defenses which must be met.

However, counsel must be forewarned that the choice of forum does not automatically equate to choice of that forum's law or avoidance of another forum's law. As such, in seeking to evade the unfavorable law of a particular state, counsel must avoid a forum that would apply that law pursuant to its own choice of law rules. Any decision on forum must include an analysis of that forum's choice of law rules lest the plaintiff be confronted with the application of the same unfavorable law sought to be avoided.

5. Venue

Venue is almost always proper where the tort occurs meaning the county or judicial district within which the helicopter crashed. Most states still permit filing in that county or judicial district where the defendant resides or does business, but that is strictly a function of state statute. Many states have limited venue options for plaintiffs, allowing for venue solely in the district where the incident or accident occurred. Venue rules in federal court are governed by local rules as to where the case is to be tried and federal system-wide by 28 U.S.C. § 1391.

Venue considerations include the court's amenability to plaintiff's claims and the knowing tendency of that venue's judges to permit full and fair discovery from aviation defendants. Once all of these other venue factors are considered, then other less significant matters come into play such as the proximity of the court to counsel's law office or the plaintiffs and accessibility to air travel and whether key witnesses would be subject to subpoena for trial attendance.

B. The Federal versus State Court Decision

In almost every case, the question arises whether the lawsuit should be filed in federal or state court even if both would use the same substantive law on liability and damages. The option to bring the action in federal court would not be available absent a complete diversity of citizenship of the parties,[55] the raising of a substantial federal question issue[56] or pursuant to the provisions of the Federal Tort Claims Act.

Some plaintiff's lawyers opt to file in federal court because the trial would occur in a large metropolitan city with a presumably more favorable jury pool whereas the state court filing would land the case in a small farming community: population 8,210. These practitioners also may opt for federal court believing that federal judges are more demanding of discovery from defendants and less forgiving of any dilatory tactics. Other potentially positive aspects of filing in federal court are the mandatory early Alternative Dispute Resolution (ADR) procedures in place in many federal judicial districts as well as the rocket docket which permits cases to move much more quickly than in many state courts.

Alas, notwithstanding these perceived advantages, most plaintiff's counsel handling complex aviation cases prefer to file the case and remain in state court wherever it is lawful and proper to do so. In the past 20 years the federal court system has taken a decided tilt in favor of corporate interests, a fact ignored at the plaintiff's peril. The unanimity requirement for federal court juries is a significant damages-reducing procedure. Most state court juries in civil cases require only two-thirds or three-fourths majority—not unanimity.

Many federal district court judges have opted for severe time limitations on argument and examination of witnesses in addition to disallowing any lawyer-conducted voir dire. Most state courts permit a full voir dire of the potential venirepersons so long as the questioning is relevant and not repetitive. The geographic scope of the federal jury pool may tend toward a more conservative composition. The likelihood of retaining any favorable verdict must be assessed by looking at the track record of the particular U.S. Circuit Court of Appeals within which the U.S. District Court sits. Many federal appeals courts have a poor record for affirming meaningful jury awards even in catastrophic injury or wrongful death actions.

Another potential drawback to filing in federal court is the inability to voluntarily dismiss the entire lawsuit one time without any showing of good cause or obtaining the court's or adversary's permission.[57] In most state courts, a plaintiff may voluntarily dismiss the action once as a matter of right without judicial authority or permission of the adversary. Another procedural difference as between federal and state court is the option to take a change of judge. In the federal court system that is not a preemptory right but must be upon a showing warranting disqualification and recusal. In many states, one change of judge is permitted as a matter of right.

A major factor in deciding between a federal or state court filing is the Daubert standard for admissibility of expert opinion testimony applicable in federal court.[58] Well-qualified helicopter crash experts should have no difficulty meeting the Daubert criteria. The potential for predatory use of that standard by some defendants and the opportunity to conduct additional merit-based discovery before a sitting U.S. district court judge weigh in favor of avoiding that prospect where possible.

This determination of filing in federal or state court may be localized in terms of the likely judges to be assigned to the case. These are strategic decisions which must be made in conjunction with local counsel who are well familiar with the various court personnel and trial practice customs and procedures.

Any defendant seeking to remove a lawsuit from state to federal court must meet all of those conditions for original jurisdiction which would include the diversity of citizenship requirement. The jurisdictional amount in controversy is not an issue given the extent of the damages in helicopter crash cases.

Where the decision is made to bring the action in state court, lawful, ethical and proper precautions should be taken to prevent defendants' removal to federal court. Where any of the plaintiffs or any of the defendants are residents of the same state there would be no diversity jurisdiction and no basis for removal. Where one of the defendants is a citizen of the state within which the action is brought that will also render the case non-removable. An important extension of that principle heretofore insufficiently utilized by the plaintiffs' bar is where the defendant corporation may not be incorporated in the state in which the action is filed but maintains its principal place of business there.[59] Where a defendant corporation has its principal place of business in a state it is a citizen of that state and no diversity of citizenship would exist to support removal to federal court.

An additional basis foreclosing federal jurisdiction is where certain claims arise under state workers' compensation law.[60] The removal of such cases is improper because such claims are creatures of state statute. Proper and lawful removal also requires that all of the defendants join in and consent to the notice of removal to federal court.[61]

Counsel must be prepared to promptly file a motion to remand the action to state court where removal has been improper. Federal judges should be repeatedly reminded that our highest court has long warned that the removal statutes must be strictly construed because they encroach on a state court's jurisdiction.[62]

Federal courts in the years 2010-2014 have not been reluctant to remand helicopter crash actions to state court which have been improvidently removed by helicopter manufacturers or component part makers.[63] In one case handled by the author, two defendants removed a state court filing to federal court alleging federal question and diversity jurisdiction. A prompt remand motion was filed. The federal district court adopted the magistrate's recommendation finding no federal question was presented in that the state law claim was based on the state's standard of care and that potential applicability of FAA regulations did not raise a federal question. The court further found that not all of the defendants had consented to removal and that one defendant, a Nebraska citizen, was still a party to the action despite a tentative agreement as to settlement.[64] The court ruled that "the plaintiff's motion to remand is granted pursuant to 28 U.S.C. § 1447(c)."[65]

C. Suing a Foreign Helicopter or Helicopter Component Manufacturer

Much of the same jurisdictional analysis applies to a foreign helicopter or component manufacturer as is applicable to a nonresident U.S. manufacturer. However, the likelihood of the foreign national company transacting "usual or customary business" in the forum state is unlikely. Hence, the ordinary and usual safe harbor for obtaining jurisdiction over such a foreign corporation is by means of the state's long-arm statute which normally requires filing the action within the state where the helicopter crash occurred. Such was the case in a 1982 decision involving an Agusta A-109 helicopter which crashed in Pennsylvania allegedly as a result of defective ball bearings manufactured by a French company. The court noted that the Pennsylvania long-arm statute permitted exercise of personal jurisdiction to the fullest extent allowed under the U.S. Constitution and that the cause of action specifically arose from defendant's tortious activity within the state: "Plaintiff's cause of action arises out of a specific forum-related act."[66]

In assessing the reasonableness and fundamental fairness of jurisdiction under these circumstances, the court concluded that:

> The final prong of the analysis focuses upon whether the exercise of jurisdiction was reasonable and fundamentally fair. [The defendant French corporation] designed and manufactured a component [ball bearings] that was incorporated into a product [helicopter] which was intended to be, and was, in

fact sold in both Europe and in the United States. Where that component allegedly fails and causes injury in the very market in which the product was expected to be sold, it is not unreasonable or unfair to require the defendant to be subject to suit in that forum.[67]

In a similar scenario the widow of a deceased pilot filed suit against the British manufacturer of an ejector seat used for military aircraft. The court found personal jurisdiction was proper over the British company which designed and manufactured the ejector seat despite the manufacturer's claim that it had never transacted business or even been present for any reason in the State of Arizona. The court concluded that the Arizona long-arm statute permitted the court to exercise jurisdiction to the maximum degree permitted by the U.S. constitution and because the injury-producing event occurred in Arizona, jurisdiction was proper.[68]

Long arm jurisdiction usually will be sufficient to obtain in personam jurisdiction over a foreign product manufacturer which put the product into the stream of commerce with a reasonable anticipation that it would be used in the forum state and potentially be the cause of injury or death to persons within that state. In the case of helicopter or helicopter engine manufacturers or those which supply various components and systems, such entities routinely market and promote their aircraft, engines and products in the U.S. market. As for any component manufacturer, the knowledge that its part is installed and incorporated into the completed aircraft is sufficient to subject it as well to the jurisdiction of a U.S. court.

The vast majority of courts entertaining these issues have held that where the foreign manufacturer injects its products into the international stream of commerce with the expectation that they will be used by persons in the U.S., there is no violation of due process for that state to exercise jurisdiction over that foreign corporation.[69] The prevailing view finds jurisdiction proper even where the foreign company utilizes various intermediaries for distribution.[70] An early and oft-cited case out of the Third Circuit U.S. Court of Appeals in holding personal jurisdiction proper over a Japanese corporation concluded:

> Underlying the assumption of jurisdiction in these cases is the belief that the fairness requirements of due process do not extend so far as to permit a manufacturer to insulate itself from the reach of the forum state's long-arm rule by using an intermediary or by professing ignorance of the ultimate destination of its products.[71]

In one such case plaintiffs brought wrongful death actions stemming from the crash of a helicopter during the process of landing on an offshore platform in the Gulf of Mexico.[72] The defendant filed a third-party action against AMPEP, the British designer and manufacturer of the ball bearings that allegedly failed and contributed to cause the crash. AMPEP filed a motion to dismiss for lack of personal jurisdiction on the basis that it was a foreign corporation with offices located in the United Kingdom. AMPEP claimed to have no offices, employees or representatives in Texas.[73] The court noted that AMPEP "sold its bearings for use in 'virtually all makes of European helicopters,'" and found that it was reasonably foreseeable that helicopters with the company's bearings would end up in Texas.[74] The court further found that "[m]ere foreseeability or awareness that a defendant's product may find its way into the forum state is a constitutionally sufficient basis for personal jurisdiction where the product reached the forum state while still within the stream of commerce."[75] The resultant exercise of personal jurisdiction over AMPEP did not "offend traditional notions of fair play and substantial justice" where helicopters are known to be used to transport people to and from offshore oil platforms. Finding the exercise of personal jurisdiction proper, the court denied AMPEP's motion to dismiss for want of personal jurisdiction.[76]

The transitory nature and inherent mobility of helicopters makes it difficult for any foreign manufacturing entity to seriously argue that it had no conceivable notion that its aircraft would be operated in any particular state. Outdated attempts by foreign manufacturers to sell their products on an FOB basis and blindly disclaim any knowledge as to how or where they are distributed have increasingly fallen on deaf judicial ears. Nevertheless, counsel in such cases must be prepared to thoroughly address such jurisdictional challenges as may be brought by a foreign manufacturer and, if necessary, conduct thorough discovery as to all of the possible contacts and distribution procedures utilized by the foreign company.

D. Filing Foreign Helicopter Crash Cases in U.S.

U.S. helicopter manufacturers supply much of the world with their aircraft as do their engine-manufacturing and component part U.S. colleagues. Despite the recent backlashes in the substantive tort and products law of many states, the tort compensation scheme in the United States remains the fairest system in the world for the lawful compensation of persons injured by the fault of others. In no other country is there a comparable means of compensating badly injured people or the families of those killed. Many countries have no comparable system for compensating product liability victims and may even permit companies to harass those who make claims such as in Japan.[77]

Using standard jurisdictional analysis, such actions are permissible in the United States in those states wherein the manufacturer and defendants reside or may be found. Most courts have ruled that jurisdiction properly lies in those circumstances. But obtaining personal jurisdiction is not the problem. The procedural hurdle in most of these instances is the invariable motion to dismiss for forum non conveniens wherein the U.S. defendant claims that the U.S. forum is not convenient because most of the witnesses are in the foreign country where the crash occurred. This is not necessarily where the claim is one of design or manufacturing defect and all of the applicable documentation is local and the corporate engineers and other defendant employees live and work within ten miles of the courthouse where the case was filed.

Given modern travel conveniences, defendants' claims of undue hardship should be firmly rejected. In one case, a helicopter crashed in Western Alberta, Canada during slinging operations after running out of fuel, severely injuring the pilot, a Canadian resident. The trial court denied the defendant's motion to dismiss on forum non conveniens grounds and the Fifth Circuit U.S. Court of Appeals affirmed.[78] The reviewing court determined that the trial court's analysis of the facts was proper where it determined that a large number of witnesses and much of the evidence was available in Texas and that Texas had a greater interest in enforcing its laws against the defendant, a Texas-based manufacturer. Of particular interest was the trial court's remark that "Defendant may cut costs by transporting its witnesses to Galveston on AEC helicopters, assuming it is confident that its helicopters won't crash."[79]

A similar scenario arose out of a helicopter crash in Sierra Leone, West Africa that plaintiffs filed in North Carolina.[80] All plaintiffs were citizens of Sierra Leone. Two defendants were agencies of the Polish government. The third defendant, Melex, was owned in part by one of the defendant Polish agencies, organized under the law of Delaware, and located in Raleigh, North Carolina.[81] In response to Melex's motion to dismiss on forum non conveniens grounds, the court ruled that the plaintiff's choice of forum was proper where the foreign plaintiffs were willing to come to North Carolina and Melex presented no countervailing reasons compelling enough to disturb the plaintiffs' choice of forum.[82]

While counsel in these cases may successfully leap over the jurisdictional hurdle, the forum non conveniens obstacle lurks menacingly. Unfortunately, some federal courts have closed the doors to foreign plaintiffs asserting personal injury products liability claims against U.S. corporations based on incidents occurring abroad. Even though jurisdiction properly exists many such cases are thrown out by U.S. District Court judges on forum non conveniens grounds.

A 2009 federal court case in Connecticut illustrates this disturbing tendency. The surviving family members of two Finnish pilots killed in a helicopter crash in the territorial waters of Estonia brought claims of product liability and wrongful death.[83] The defendants, including Sikorsky Aircraft Corporation which manufactured the helicopter, filed a motion to dismiss on forum non conveniens grounds. The court noted that "the accident at issue in this dispute took place in the Baltic Sea between Tallinn and Helsinki, involved a Finnish corporation operating a helicopter which had been serviced and maintained in Finland, and led to the deaths of six Finnish citizens, four Estonian citizens and two citizens of the United States."[84]

The court determined that much of the evidence, documents, and witnesses were located in Estonia while only the records and witnesses concerning the helicopter's design and manufacture were in Connecticut. While according some deference to the plaintiff's choice to initiate suit in the defendants' home forum, heightened deference was not called for due to the weak connection to the United States and no connection to the plaintiffs, particularly since the defendants agreed to submit to the jurisdiction of the courts in Finland. The court further noted that legal assistance was available in either place. Finding that a court in Finland was a suitable alternative forum and that public and private factors favored a Finnish forum, the court granted the defendants' motion to dismiss.[85] For further discussion of forum non conveniens, please see Section 6.2(B).

Similar circumstances led to a similar result involving the crash of a Sikorsky helicopter in Tenerife, Spain where suit was filed once again in Connecticut against Sikorsky.[86] Defendants moved to dismiss based on the forum non conveniens doctrine. While some documents and witnesses are located in Connecticut based on the helicopter's manufacture there, the trial court granted the motion dismiss based on the following factors favoring dismissal: the accident happened in Spain and killed six Spanish citizens, the Spanish authorities investigated the accident and issued or will issue the official reports, the presence of documents and witnesses regarding the accident and the maintenance of the subject helicopter in Spain, the availability of more witnesses in Spain, Spain as an adequate alternate forum, and public and private interest factors that favored trying the case in Spain.[87]

In another example, Russian passengers sued McDonnell Douglas Helicopters, Inc. in California for injuries resulting from a helicopter crash in Russia.[88] The defendant filed a motion to dismiss on the basis of forum non conveniens. Noting a decreased deference due a foreign plaintiff's choice of forum, the court granted the motion to dismiss, finding that Russia was an adequate alternate forum and the balancing of public and private interest factors favored dismissal.

The cases are sadly inconsistent. In one helicopter crash in Germany which killed the pilot, the subsequent product liability lawsuit was brought against the Connecticut companies that manufactured the helicopter, its engine and fuel control unit. The federal district court found that the doctrine of forum non conveniens required dismissal of the action so it could proceed in Germany.[89] Compare that outcome with precisely the same scenario where the crash occurred in Indonesia and plaintiff brought the claim against the defective aircraft engine manufacturer in the U.S. where the court rejected dismissal on forum non conveniens grounds.[90] Some courts have shown a reluctance to provide a forum to "alien" plaintiffs who would come to the U.S. solely for the purpose of bringing legal action against U.S. helicopter or component part manufacturers.

Sadly, the author has recent personal experience with a U.S. court's declining to provide just such a forum to foreign plaintiffs who would seek to hold U.S. companies accountable for the death of their loved one. In what even the Indiana Supreme Court described as "an almost unbelievable accident," a twenty year old college student and citizen of Kenya was walking along the sidewalk in Cranbrook, British Columbia, Canada for the purpose of mailing a letter to his parents in Kenya when a low-flying helicopter lost engine power and crashed to the ground.[91] The student was struck by the helicopter, dragged along for some distance and died at the scene.

Suit was instituted in 2010 by the deceased's parents, also residents of Kenya, against Rolls-Royce Corporation, Bell Helicopter Textron, and Honeywell International in Marion County, Indiana. The defendants promptly filed a motion to dismiss the lawsuit pursuant to Indiana Trial Rule 4.4(C) on the grounds of forum non conveniens claiming that Indiana was an "inconvenient forum" compared to British Columbia.

Notwithstanding the fact that Rolls-Royce headquarters was within seven miles of the Marion County Courthouse and the alternative judicial forum in British Columbia was over 2,000 miles away, the trial court granted the defendants' motion finding that British Columbia was the "more convenient forum."[92] The trial court further found that the law of British Columbia provided a proper alternative forum, even though the parents' only remedy was the recovery of funeral and burial expenses. In 2012, the Indiana Supreme Court unanimously upheld the trial court's ruling.[93]

4.6 Dealing With Specialized Statutes and Regulations Potentially Applicable to Helicopter Crash Lawsuits

Many different statutes and regulations are potentially applicable in any helicopter crash lawsuit. Counsel must have a firm grasp as to these laws and regulations and how they may impact the lawsuit.

A. General Aviation and Revitalization Act

The General Aviation and Revitalization Act (GARA) was enacted in 1994 to provide aircraft and aircraft component manufacturers with certain liability protections as a means of promoting the business of general aviation. The most important aspect of GARA from a litigation standpoint is its imposition of an 18-year statute of repose applicable to general aviation aircraft.[94] As defined, that includes virtually all helicopter operations in the U.S. Such aircraft are defined as any for which a Type Certificate or Airworthiness Certificate has been issued by the FAA and which have a maximum seating capacity of fewer that twenty (20) passengers. If the helicopter was used at the time for scheduled passenger carrying operations GARA would not be applicable.

GARA provides that no civil action for injury, death or property damage can be brought against any general aviation aircraft or any component manufacturer of that aircraft if the lawsuit would be brought greater than 18 years after that aircraft's or the component part's first delivery upon purchase. If applicable, GARA provides an absolute bar to the lawsuit:

> No civil action for damages for death or injury to persons or damage to property arising out of an accident involving a general aviation aircraft may be brought against the manufacturer of the aircraft or the manufacturer of any new component, system, subassembly, or other part of the aircraft, in its capacity as a manufacturer if the accident occurred… after the applicable limitation period beginning on (A) The date of delivery of the aircraft to its first purchaser or lessee, if delivered directly from the manufacturer; or (B) The date of first delivery of the aircraft to a person engaged in the business of selling such aircraft…[95]

Understanding and navigating around GARA is essential for handling helicopter crash litigation. Counsel must understand GARA's potential applicability, its various "retriggering" provisions and the statutorily enumerated exceptions to its application. A full discussion of the GARA exceptions and suggested approaches by plaintiff's counsel is set out in Section 6.1(B).

B. Federal Tort Claims Act

In any helicopter crash case where the actions or omissions of an employee of the U.S. were a causal factor, suit must be brought under the provisions of the Federal Tort Claims Act (FTCA).[96] The most common such claim would arise where an air traffic controller was negligent in the performance of her duties resulting in a crash. Other common FTCA claims arise where a U.S. government-owned or operated aircraft is involved in a crash such as where that aircraft has ferried governmental officials or even prisoners.

In those cases, suit under the FTCA is the exclusive means of recovery and the provisions require strict compliance. The Act mandates that an administrative claim first must be presented to the appropriate federal agency in writing and sent by certified or registered mail.[97] In the case of claimed negligence by an air traffic controller that agency would be the FAA. The FAA would have six months within which to seek to adjudicate the claim. After six months, or sooner if the claim is denied in writing, suit may then be filed in the appropriate U.S. district court. Unless the administrative claim procedure has been followed, the subsequent filing of any lawsuits against any agent or employee of the United States will be summarily dismissed.

The filing of the administrative claim is an absolute jurisdictional prerequisite to filing a helicopter crash or any other aviation lawsuit against the FAA. Such an administrative claim must be filed within two years of the crash.[98] Counsel must take care that the claim is properly filed with the "appropriate federal agency," as failure to do so will result in dismissal of the later federal lawsuit.[99] The claim should be filed on Standard Form 95 a current version of which is available at www.justice.gov/forms/dojform.php.

The notice of claim is required to include enough information for the federal agency to appropriately investigate the claim and it must specify a "sum certain" of the amount of damages claimed. This is proven to be a trap for the unwary on many an occasion resulting in substantial savings to the U.S. Treasury. Where the claimant fails to specify the sum certain for damages on the administrative claim or has set out an unreasonably low figure prior to contacting counsel, the U.S. Supreme Court has ruled that the plaintiff may not seek any sum in excess of that which was presented to the federal agency.[100] The only statutory exception would be where an additional amount is claimed "based upon newly discovered evidence not reasonably discoverable at the time of presenting the claim to the federal agency, or upon allegation and proof of intervening facts, relating to the amount of the claim."[101] The Act prohibits any claim against the U.S. for punitive damages.[102]

The complaint must be filed in federal court within six months of the date of the final denial of the administrative claim by the agency to which it was presented.[103] Venue in such actions is strictly limited to the judicial district where the plaintiff resides or where the "act or omission complained of occurred."[104] In addition to these procedural traps and other hurdles, lawsuits brought under the FTCA are not particularly favorable to claimants. All such cases are heard by the district court sitting without a jury.[105] And no prejudgment interest may be awarded as a matter of law.[106]

Finally, the act restricts attorneys' fees to 20 percent of any recovery for the administrative claim and 25 percent of any judgment or settlement once the case has been filed in federal court. The fee restrictions have had the effect of discouraging general practice lawyers from associating with experienced aviation counsel and attempting to handle such matters on their own. Most of the other federal court procedural hurdles for plaintiffs which would be present in a non-FTCA lawsuit remain, such as the *Daubert* requirement for admissibility of expert opinion testimony, the inability to effectuate a change of judge or the right to dismiss the lawsuit once as a matter of course. Given these various considerations, counsel should pursue the FTCA route where the actions of the air traffic controller were the major cause of the helicopter accident and no other viable theory of liability exists against other defendants.

C. Death on the High Seas Act and the Outer Continental Shelf Lands Act

Whenever a helicopter crash occurs over navigable waters, it must be determined whether any federal maritime law is applicable. The most frequently invoked such statutes are the Death on the High Seas Act (DOHSA) and the Outer Continental Shelf Lands Act (OCSLA). These statutes come into play most commonly where helicopters crash in the Gulf of Mexico while providing worker transport either between stationary oil platforms or back and forth from the mainland. DOHSA originally was intended to provide a maritime remedy for wrongful deaths "occurring on the high seas."[107] In any incident involving a helicopter crash in the Gulf of Mexico or off the territorial waters of the United States, counsel must be familiar with the basic application of the DOHSA provisions.

Prior to its amendment in 2000, DOHSA permitted the recovery of pecuniary or economic damages only and barred any claim for loss of consortium or loss of society. The amendments provide that non-pecuniary damages for wrongful death are recoverable but continue to prohibit any claim for punitive damages.[108]

The 2006 amendments clarified the applicability of DOHSA to aircrash litigation:

This chapter does not apply if the death resulted from a commercial aviation accident occurring on the high seas 12 nautical miles from the shore of the United States.[109]

The amendments further clarify that in place of DOHSA the rules or "other appropriate" laws shall apply, meaning those which would otherwise be applicable under federal or state jurisdiction. The amendments also clarify that DOHSA did not apply to aviation accidents occurring between three and twelve nautical miles from shore, but would apply to any aircrash incident occurring beyond twelve nautical miles. Within the three nautical miles closest to U.S. shore, courts will continue to apply that state's law that is most consistent with U.S. federal law and the usual conflict issues will prevail.

Although DOHSA may confer original jurisdiction in federal court, the U.S Supreme Court has held that jurisdiction is not exclusive and that DOHSA actions may be brought in state courts.[110] Subsequent court decisions have confirmed that the operation of an on-demand helicopter air taxi service ferrying workers between stationary oil platforms in the Gulf of Mexico constituted a "commercial aviation accident" within the amended version of DOHSA.[111] The provisions of DOHSA would remain applicable to any helicopter crash which occurred more than twelve nautical miles offshore. By definition, DOHSA would not apply to any incidents occurring on the Great Lakes or the "inland waterways," meaning lakes and rivers of any state.[112]

OCSLA substitutes state law for any claims of injuries or deaths on certain portions of the Outer Continental Shelf "to the extent that they are applicable and not inconsistent with this subchapter or with the other federal laws and regulations."[113] If OCSLA is applicable, then the wrongful death laws including the damages provisions of the closest state govern the case. Given the enactment of OCSLA, the provisions of DOHSA are not applicable to wrongful deaths occurring on fixed oil drilling platforms which would be located more than a marine league off the Louisiana coast. OCSLA would apply if an individual standing on the platform were injured by a helicopter in the process of taking off or landing.

In a recent decision out of the Fifth Circuit U.S. Court of Appeals, the court found that OCSLA rather than DOHSA would apply to those claims arising from a passenger's death in a helicopter crash.[114] The helicopter crashed into the Gulf of Mexico while attempting to land on an offshore oil platform.[115] The pilot landed the helicopter on the helipad but passengers were not able to exit the aircraft because of equipment which blocked the exit. As the pilot attempted to re-position the helicopter it collided with the equipment and skidded off the helipad and fell into the Gulf of Mexico.[116] The court concluded that because the crash "actually occurred" on the platform that OCSLA properly governed the case.[117]

D. Federal Aviation Regulations

To the extent applicable, Federal Aviation Regulations (FARs) are evidence bearing on a defendant's standard of care. The FARs particularly applicable to helicopters are Parts 27 and 29 addressing airworthiness standards for rotorcraft and rotorcraft engines. Part 27 prescribes airworthiness standards applicable to "normal category" helicopters with maximum weights of 7,000 pounds and nine or fewer passenger seats.[118] The Part 27 standards apply to everything from the proper configuration of safety belts and shoulder harnesses to autorotation performance. Part 29 addresses airworthiness standards of helicopters with a maximum weight greater than 20,000 pounds. Part 61 of the FARs addresses certification and general operating and flight rules. Part 27 addresses certification and operation of scheduled air carriers with helicopters and Part 33 addresses the airworthiness standards applicable to engines. Where the violation of any FAR played some causal role in the crash, its violation may constitute negligence per se.

If relevant to one of the disputed issues in the case, an FAR may establish the "impartial and authoritative criteria" for the relevant standard of care. This follows the well-settled rule holding that any applicable regulation sets out the minimum standard of care the violation of which constitutes negligence, if not actual negligence per se. It has even been held to be an abuse of discretion for a trial court not to instruct the jury regarding violation of pertinent FARs.[119] Counsel must exercise caution not to inadvertently reference the FARs in the initial petition or complaint as this may invite a prompt notice of removal to federal court presumably under the federal question doctrine. For additional discussion on use of FARs, please see Section 6.3(F) addressing compliance with government standards.

E. State Workers' Compensation Statutes

The typical provisions of state workers' compensation statutes apply to the helicopter industry as for any other employment relationship where the employee is injured or killed while in the course and scope of employment. These statutes most commonly come into play in helicopter crash cases in one of two ways. Such statutes either create a bar to suit against a particular defendant because of the employment relationship or the workers' compensation carrier files a lien on any third-party recovery for all past and future benefits paid or payable. It may seek to intervene in the lawsuit as a putative party plaintiff.

The applicability of the exclusive remedy provision arises often in the air ambulance context where all on-board are employees of the helicopter operator or the hospital. The flight nurses are co-employees of the helicopter pilot. Another frequent scenario is where the pilot and maintenance personnel are employed by the same operator. In that instance, any maintenance errors causally related to the crash would render the pilot claimant with only a workers' compensation remedy as against those responsible for the improper maintenance.

Prudent practice dictates that counsel determine the amount of any claimed workers' compensation lien and to the extent possible dissuade the carrier from becoming a party to the suit. Written confirmation of an intention to lawfully abide by the lien and to protect the carrier's interests will assist in that regard.

F. State Statutes Imposing Liability On Aircraft Owners and Lessees

Several states including California, Iowa, Minnesota, New York, and South Dakota have enacted statutes that expand liability for an aircraft accident to owners, operators and lessees.[120]

The stated purpose of such statutory schemes is similar:

> …to make an aircraft owner accountable for the negligence of pilots where no such liability would otherwise exist. In other words, by imposing liability on an owner, a presumed financially responsible individual, there will be a greater certainty of recovery for those injured by the negligent operation of an airplane. To this end, the statute must be liberally construed and any doubts be resolved in favor of the injured party.[121]

Typically these statutes provide for a two-part analysis. The statute first provides that it is negligent for anyone to "operate" aircraft in the state in a careless manner. For example, the Iowa statute provides that:

> It shall be unlawful for any person to operate an aircraft in the air space above this state or on the ground or water within this state, while under the influence of intoxicating liquor, narcotics, or other habit-forming drug, or to operate an aircraft in the air space above this state or on the ground or water within this state in a careless or reckless manner so as to endanger the life or property of another.[122]

Aircraft "operation" is then defined as including the aircraft owner, lessee, or otherwise:

> The use of aircraft for the purpose of air navigation, and includes the navigation or piloting of aircraft and shall embrace any person who causes or authorizes the operation of aircraft, whether with or without the right of legal control (in the capacity of owner, lessee, or otherwise).[123]

The importance of these statutes is that the burden on the plaintiff to establish any negligent entrustment or proof of notice or knowledge of the pilot's lack of skill or experience is extinguished as is any notice or knowledge that the helicopter is non-airworthy. These statutes create absolute liability on the owner or operator based solely on the careless or negligent operation of the aircraft within the state. In any helicopter crash accident counsel must determine whether one of the potential forums has such a statute, as it may be a critical issue for recovery in the case.

4.7 Finding and Working With Local Counsel

In these instances where the case is filed in an unfamiliar court, counsel will need to associate with knowledgeable local counsel in the chosen forum. This is necessary to learn the local custom and practice as well as the inclinations of the local judges and juries. Association with local counsel in a different state also is required for counsel to appear *pro hac vice* if not otherwise admitted to the bar of that state.

The selection and hiring of local counsel requires consideration of those attributes which are unnecessary. Local counsel need know nothing about helicopter crash litigation although an understanding of that state's products liability laws is important. Affiliate counsel and their respective staff should be readily available for quick procedural questions or to run to the local courthouse to file a pleading.

Finding the right local counsel who can serve these needs is not an exact science. Many years of experience in selecting local counsel has generated a couple of rules of thumb. First, the local counsel must be well familiar with the local "lay of the land" in terms of experience with the judges and defense lawyers as well as the specific local customs and practices of that legal community. Second, it is immensely helpful if local counsel has a degree of enthusiasm and excitement about working along with lead counsel on such an interesting and high profile matter as a helicopter crash lawsuit.

In making initial contacts with prospective local counsel, counsel may quickly assess his facility with the tort laws of that state and applicable procedural rules. Additional questions that have been proven useful in interviewing local counsel are as follows:

1. With whom would we be dealing at your firm: you, an associate or a staff person?
2. Is your workload and staffing such that you will be available on somewhat short notice for consultation and advice?
3. Are you comfortable in the role of a local counsel following our lead?

After narrowing the list to two or three lawyers it is suggested that counsel independently inquire as to the local reputation of each such lawyer. Lawyers in any legal community are more than happy to share their candid assessments in that regard. Finally, counsel should arrange a meeting with the local counsel for purposes of assessing that lawyer in person, viewing the office and office staff, and gauging that office's proximity to the courthouse where the case is to be filed.

The method of compensation is a judgment call of hiring counsel based on the expected extent of the local counsel's involvement in the case. Many aviation lawyers prefer to hire local counsel on an hourly basis and some affiliate counsel prefer that arrangement as they are not comfortable with the risk of a contingency fee case. The other option is to allocate a percentage of lead counsel's contingency fee for the services of local counsel. The thinking in that regard is that local counsel may have greater incentive to be more responsive and participatory if that law firm "has some skin in the game."

The division of responsibilities must be clearly delineated between lead and local counsel. On one occasion without knowledge of the lead lawyer, local counsel entered into several agreements with local defense counsel, one of which was to supply a copy of all liability experts' written reports within thirty days! That, among other things, led to a prompt parting of the ways. Counsel must insist that no agreements of any kind are entered into by local counsel nor are any pleadings filed or communications with the court or adverse counsel made without lead counsel's prior knowledge and consent.

An example of a letter agreement with local counsel in helicopter crash litigation is as follows:

Local Counsel, Esq.
LOCAL LAW FIRM
151 North Missouri Street
Suite 1000
Anytown, USA 10000

RE: WRONGFUL DEATH OF JANE SMITH IN HELICOPTER CRASH OF SEPTEMBER 30, 2009 AT ANYTOWN, STATE

Dear Local Counsel:

I am delighted to confirm our agreement with you and your law firm to act as our local counsel in the above-referenced helicopter crash case. I enjoyed meeting with you and look forward to our collaboration in bringing about a successful resolution for our clients.

I am pleased to set out the specifics of our agreement as follows:

LEAD TRIAL COUNSEL—Our law firm will be lead trial counsel for all purposes including responsibility for discovery and trial of the case, retention and preparation of all liability and damages experts, funding all litigation expenses in connection with the case, filing or defending against all dispositive motions, preparing and filing all discovery motions, client contact and reporting, contact with adverse counsel on substantive issues (local counsel may have some role in scheduling certain matters), deposing defendants' corporate representatives and experts, and otherwise addressing and handling those duties and responsibilities inherent in the role of lead trial counsel;

LOCAL COUNSEL LAW FIRM—Your law firm will act in the capacity as our local counsel in the state of _____ for all of those usual and ordinary purposes including providing advice and counsel on [that state's] law and procedure, attendance and assistance at various hearings relating to discovery, scheduling, and otherwise, assistance in jury selection and preparation of jury instructions, assistance in preparation of all pleadings for initial filing of the case including Complaint and Petition to Appoint Personal Representative and all of the usual and ordinary duties and responsibilities of local counsel consistent herewith.

As compensation for your firm's acting as our local counsel, we agree to pay to your firm (X%) of our law firm's fee if the matter is resolved within twelve (12) months and (Y%) of our firm's fee if the case is resolved thereafter. Of course, we request and expect that the terms of our agreement shall remain confidential, other than disclosure to our client.

In a nutshell, we view the essential role of local counsel in these helicopter crash cases to assist us in "avoiding the minefields." I have every confidence and expectation that you will be able to do that.

If the terms of our agreement are acceptable, I would appreciate your retaining a copy for your file and returning the executed original for our records.

Once again, we are looking forward to working with you, and the rest of your law firm in this significant matter.

Sincerely yours,

_____

LEAD TRIAL COUNSEL

On behalf of the LOCAL COUNSEL LAW FIRM, we agree to act as local counsel in this matter on the terms and conditions set forth herein.

Dated: _____

_____

LOCAL COUNSEL

4.8 Common Legal Theories in Helicopter Crash Lawsuits

Once the factual basis of liability for each defendant is established, counsel must examine all potentially applicable legal theories. It is not the intention of this section to provide a survey of each state's law. The basic legal theories set forth are applicable to common factual scenarios encountered in helicopter crash litigation. Every state has its own particular nuances in terms of its products liability laws and rules of negligence. In drafting the initial complaint, counsel should make certain that all of the elements of the cause of action are properly pled. Though many states still permit simple notice pleading, as opposed to fact pleading, an initial complaint which sets out the theories of liability with greater factual specificity is more likely to survive any defense motion to dismiss on the pleadings or, at least at the early stages, a motion to make more definite and certain.

In many helicopter crash lawsuits no one simple explanation or cause exists for the crash. Helicopter accidents are complex events and the actions or omissions of one party may commingle with another to produce the circumstances resulting in the crash. This results in a complaint containing a multitude of legal theories against several defendants. The appropriate legal theory must be alleged as to each defendant. A strict liability theory will not be a proper legal claim against the helicopter pilot but would be most appropriate against the manufacturer of a failed part.

The primary legal theories applicable in helicopter crash litigation are those applicable in the ordinary negligence context as well as the products liability laws applicable to manufacturers of the aircraft and component part makers. Appendix B contains examples of complaints involving theories of negligence for improper engine design, pilot error and strict liability for design defect and failure to warn.

A. Negligence

Under ordinary negligence principles, the defendant must owe a duty of care and that duty is defined as that degree of care that an ordinarily prudent or reasonably careful person or company would use under the same or similar circumstances. This would be the legal standard applicable to the pilot operating the helicopter as it would for those in charge of its routine maintenance. A helicopter pilot is not required to exercise the highest degree of care but only that required of other pilots under the same or similar circumstances.

It is never sufficient to plead and prove under a negligence theory that a defendant might have avoided the crash by taking some different action. No helicopter pilot, maintenance facility or other defendant is required to be perfect or omniscient. If a defendant has exercised the care which any other would have used under similar circumstances, there can be no finding of negligence.

An issue often arising in such cases is whether there should be separate standards of care for experienced as opposed to trainee or novice pilots. That is not the case as experience is merely a factor to be considered by a jury in determining the standard of care. However, in some instances where the pilot is operating for-hire in a transport context, the carrier liability standard would impose upon her a duty to exercise the highest degree of care.

Similarly, where a helicopter operator holds itself out to the public as a business undertaking to carry passengers for hire it would be considered a common carrier just as a scheduled airliner. That would include charter helicopter flights such as tour operations or shuttle services in some of the larger metropolitan areas. Characterizing the helicopter operator as a common carrier subjects that defendant to the highest degree of care for the safety of its passengers.

Almost all states have the same essential elements to recover on a theory of negligence:

1. Plead and prove a duty of care;
2. Plead and prove a breach of the applicable duty of care;
3. Plead and prove that the damages were proximately caused by the violation of the duty of care; and
4. Plead and prove damages.

A mechanic who failed to change out a helicopter system component on a timely basis where that component contributed to a crash may be found liable under these negligence principles. Product manufacturers as well must adhere to those standards of ordinary care in the design of their products.

The essential elements of any negligence action applicable in all respects to a helicopter crash lawsuit involve the establishment of a duty of care, the violation or breach of that legal duty, and the proximate cause of injury because of that breach. It may be undisputed that the pilot failed to perform any pre-flight inspection before the crash but unless this failure were somehow causally related to the crash, negligence would not attach.

An example of a pleading setting out pilot negligence is as follows:

1. On July 4, 2009, defendant Pilot was the pilot-in-command of a Bell Jet Ranger 206B helicopter.
2. Defendant Pilot held himself out as a person who could carefully and properly pilot that helicopter and provide safe air transportation.
3. Defendant Pilot had a duty to use that degree of care that an ordinarily careful and prudent pilot would use under the same or similar circumstances.
4. Defendant Pilot breached that duty and was negligent by failing to maintain control of the aircraft in flight, losing control of the helicopter in flight and crashing at the above-referenced location thereby causing the injuries and damages complained of and was further negligent for reasons including, but not limited to, the following:
   a. Defendant Pilot failed to maintain an adequate and safe altitude;
   b. Defendant Pilot failed to keep a proper lookout for aerial hazards;
   c. Defendant Pilot failed to recognize the existence of utility wires in the flight path of the helicopter;
   d. Defendant Pilot failed to maintain a safe and proper distance from utility power lines;
   e. Defendant Pilot improperly caused the helicopter to come into contact with utility power lines;

f. Defendant Pilot failed to obtain the intended flight path and/or location of the aerial filming prior to flight;

g. Defendant Pilot failed to properly follow the generally accepted standards of care in providing aerial cinematography services;

h. Defendant Pilot failed to properly survey by aerial reconnaissance or ground reconnaissance or both the intended scene in advance of the actual filming to determine the existence of any potential hazards, risks, or dangers;

i. Defendant Pilot failed to avoid impact of the helicopter into overhead power lines;

j. Defendant Pilot caused the aircraft to crash at said location; and

5. Plaintiffs as heretofore described, suffered damages as a direct and proximate result of said negligence resulting in the wrongful death of occupant.

Similarly, the manufacturer of a component part used in a helicopter has a duty of care to design and manufacture that part using that degree of care that an ordinarily careful and prudent component part manufacturer would use under the same or similar circumstances. An example of that pleading is as follows:

1. Defendant Helicopter Component Company failed to use that degree of care that an ordinarily careful and prudent designer, manufacturer, and seller of helicopter component parts would use under the same or similar circumstances; and

2. Defendant Helicopter Component Company knew or by using ordinary care should have known of the potential dangerous condition as was created by its failure to properly design, machine, manufacture, distribute, and sell a safe helicopter component part and taken such action as to correct the dangerous condition.

3. Defendant Helicopter Component Company breached its duty of due care in one or more of the following material ways:

a. The tail rotor load compensator accumulator bladder is made of a rubber material which is in direct contact with the rough-machined surface of the interior wall of the accumulator canister;

b. The condition of the rubber bladder within the accumulator canister is not subject to inspection in that the accumulator is a welded and sealed unit;

c. The rubber bladder within the accumulator is subject to a wear-induced perforation and loss of nitrogen charge into the hydraulic system without warning;

d. Wear of the accumulator rubber bladder is a known and recognized failure mode;

e. The subject tail rotor load compensator accumulator was not subject to any life limit as specified in the maintenance manual notwithstanding knowledge that the bladder was constructed of a rubber material that degraded over time;

f. The flight control system of the subject helicopter is unreasonably dangerous and difficult to control in the event that the hydraulic system is switched off especially at low speeds or at hover;

g. The combination of activating the hydraulic cut-off switch and the failed tail rotor accumulator renders the helicopter uncontrollable;

h. The pilot operating handbook or flight manual did not address a failure of the tail rotor accumulator or its symptoms or provide a proper and safe emergency maneuver;

i. The pilot operating handbook or flight manual did not address a binding of a tail rotor control pedal or provide any instruction or guidance for that occurrence;

j. The pilot of the subject model helicopter would have no in-flight warning that a tail rotor accumulator had failed;

k. The subject helicopter lacked a proper warning system to advise the pilot of an in-flight accumulator failure; and

l. The tail rotor accumulator lacked a pressure gauge to enable a pilot or mechanic to assess the pressure in the accumulator prior to or during flight.

4. The wrongful death of Joe Smith was proximately caused by Defendant's breach of the duty of care and negligence as further set out herein.

Absent enactment of some special statute, states will assess the liability of an owner or operator of a helicopter under ordinary rules of negligence. Without a special statute imposing liability on the owner or operator of the helicopter, plaintiff will need to plead and prove the elements of a standard negligence action. As such the owner or operator will be held only to that degree of care expected of the ordinarily careful owner or operator. As most owners or operators delegate maintenance responsibilities to FAA-certified repair facilities to perform the required maintenance, few would argue that they must have direct involvement in the maintenance process in order to meet that standard of care.

B. Strict Products Liability

Most states have adopted the Restatement (Second) of Torts, Section 402A, providing for the imposition of strict liability on manufacturers of defectively designed products. The most common elements of that cause of action are as follows:

1. Pleading and proof that the defendant was engaged in the business of selling the helicopter or component part at issue;
2. That the helicopter or component part was used in a manner reasonably anticipated;
3. That the helicopter or component part reached the ultimate user or consumer without a substantial or material change in its condition;
4. That the helicopter or component part was in a defective condition unreasonably dangerous at the time it was sold;
5. That the defective condition was a proximate cause of the injuries or death; and
6. Pleading and proof of damages.

The precise definition of defective design varies from state to state. Whereas some states use the risk utility analysis, others use the consumer expectations test. The most common test for design defect is the risk utility test which balances the risk or utility of the product against its potential risks of danger.

Warnings claims under strict liability most commonly allege that without adequate warning the helicopter component part is unsafe for its reasonably anticipated uses. Strict liability failure to warn claims frequently arise where a system or component part maker fails to provide safe and proper operating or maintenance instructions.

Twenty-one states and the District of Columbia presently require that a plaintiff plead and prove the existence of a reasonable alternative design under a strict liability theory. Four states have passed specific legislation requiring that a plaintiff prove a reasonable alternative design in strict products liability cases: Louisiana, Mississippi, Ohio, Texas, Washington and Wisconsin.[124]

For example, the Texas statute requires proof of a "safer alternative design" which is defined as:

> a product design other than the one actually used that in reasonable probability: (1) would have prevented or significantly reduced the risk of the

claimant's personal injury, property damage, or death without substantially impairing the product's utility; and (2) was economically and technologically feasible at the time the product left the control of the manufacturer or seller by the application of existing or reasonably achievable scientific knowledge.[125]

The other fifteen states plus the District of Columbia have adopted the reasonable alternative design requirement by court decision. These states are Alabama, Arizona, Arkansas, Florida, Idaho, Indiana, Iowa, Kentucky, Maryland, New Jersey, New Mexico, New York, Pennsylvania, South Carolina and Utah.[126] A typical formulation of the requirement as adopted by a New York court is as follows:

> To establish a prima facie case in a strict products liability action predicated on a design defect, plaintiff must show that the manufacturer marketed a product which was not reasonably safe in its design, that it was feasible to design the product in a safer manner, and that the defective design was a substantial factor in causing the plaintiff's injury.[127]

In such states it is no longer sufficient to criticize the design as defective or unreasonably dangerous. Expert opinion must be presented that there was in existence, at the time the product was sold, a reasonable alternative design which would have prevented the claimed injuries. In these jurisdictions, plaintiff's design experts will have to develop a safer product design or fix which would have averted the failure and the resulting accident. Presentation of a safer alternative design is good practice even if absolutely not required as part of a strict liability claim.

C. Breach of Warranty

In most jurisdictions, the evidence underlying warranty and strict liability claims are similar if not identical.[128] There are circumstances where warranty claims should be asserted in addition to allegations of negligence and strict products liability. Warranty claims most often come into play where the owner or operator of the helicopter has had direct contact with the aircraft or engine supplier or the helicopter component part distributor and purchased the aircraft, engine, or component part in reliance on particular claims or representations. The warranty theories potentially applicable are breach of express warranty, breach of implied warranty of fitness for a particular purpose and breach of implied warranty of merchantability.

1. Express Warranty

The claim for breach of express warranty requires that the defendant have warranted or represented that its product would perform or operate in a specified manner and that such warranty or representation be specifically presented to, understood by and relied upon by the purchaser. The express warranty claim must allege that the aircraft, system or component did not conform to the express warranty and that its breach was a proximate cause of the plaintiff's damages. This may apply in the case of certain safety equipment or other improvements to the helicopter. The breach of express warranty claim may be extended to third party beneficiaries who could reasonably have been expected to benefit from any warranties made or extended by the defendant.

In the context of any personal injury or wrongful death action, a breach of warranty is considered a separate and independent tort from any sales agreement or contract.[129] In addition, in those circumstances where an express warranty would exist as for some quality representation to a helicopter owner or pilot, a concurrent action for negligence would not be barred.[130] Counsel should include warranty claims if supported by the facts because most courts have held that verdicts in favor of the plaintiff on either negligence or warranty grounds are not inconsistent and may be upheld on appeal even if one finding is expressly for the defendant.[131]

2. Implied Warranty of Fitness for a Particular Purpose

The breach of implied warranty of fitness for a particular purpose requires that the defendant have reason to know of the particular purpose intended by the purchaser and that the purchaser was relying on the defendant's skill or judgment to select, furnish or install the particular system or component. The claim must allege that the system or component as selected and sold was not fit for the particular purpose and that its failure to do so was a proximate cause of the plaintiff's damages.

3. Implied Warranty of Merchantability

The final warranty claim is that of breach of implied warranty of merchantability. That claim is limited to a merchant which deals in the specific product or system in question and which held itself out as having knowledge or skills specific or particular to those products. The claim is that the component or system was not merchantable and that its lack of merchantability was a proximate cause of the plaintiff's damages. Merchantability is customarily defined as the expectation of the usual or ordinary quality of product in comparably sold goods.

State law varies as to the notice requirements in any breach of warranty claim. In some circumstances, a breach of warranty action may be the easiest to prove and for that reason should be explored and pled if applicable.

D. Fraud and Misrepresentation

The most common application of fraud and misrepresentation claims involves sales of helicopters involved in prior accidents or where specific maintenance or overhaul work was represented as being performed but was not in fact done at all. Such cases are fact specific but where a crash and injuries or death occur because of the fraud and misrepresentation, the claim should be made and is a predicate for the imposition of punitive liability.

As regards a products manufacturer, there are three types of misrepresentation: innocent misrepresentation, negligent misrepresentation, and fraudulent misrepresentation. Innocent misrepresentation subjects a product manufacturer to liability for the plaintiff's injuries where the defendant:

1. Publicly misrepresented a material fact as to the character or quality of the product;
2. Which representation is false and upon which that consumer was expected to justifiably rely; and
3. The representations are more than mere statements of opinion or so-called "puffing."[132]

Negligent misrepresentation as against a product manufacturer requires that:

1. The defendant made material misrepresentation of fact to the plaintiffs;
2. That the plaintiffs relied upon such representation;
3. That the defendant knew or should have known that representation was false at the time it was made;
4. That the defendant intended to induce plaintiffs to rely on such representation; and
5. That plaintiff's reliance proximately caused the injuries.[133]

A fraudulent misrepresentation claim requires plaintiff to plead and prove that the defendant:

1. Made a false representation or falsely concealed a material fact;
2. Defendant had knowledge of the falsity or made such statements with utter disregard and recklessness;
3. Defendant had an intent to mislead others into relying on the representation;

4. The plaintiff had a right to and did in fact rely on the defendant's statement; and

5. As a consequence of plaintiff's reliance injuries were suffered.[134]

The common formulation of the tort of misrepresentation is as stated in the Restatement of Torts 2d, Section 402B, which provides that one engaged in the business of selling products who by advertising or otherwise makes to the public a misrepresentation of a material fact concerning the character or quality of that product sold is subject to liability for physical harm to a consumer of that product caused by justifiable reliance upon the misrepresentation even though:

1. The representation is not fraudulent or negligently made; and

2. The consumer has not bought the product from or entered into a contractual relationship with the seller.[135]

Misrepresentation is akin to strict liability for harm resulting from the misrepresentation even though it may be innocent.[136] The restatement formulation of misrepresentation has been judicially adopted in several states.[137]

Fraudulent misrepresentation claims in the context of products liability litigation require the following elements:

1. Representation made by defendant;

2. Representation was false;

3. When representation was made, it was known to be false by defendant or was made recklessly without knowledge of its truth;

4. The representation was made with the intention that it would be relied upon by others;

5. There was reliance upon the representation; and

6. Damage occurred as a result of the fraudulent misrepresentation.[138]

Counsel should consider adding a count for misrepresentation wherever the facts are supportive of that theory. The claim does not require the plaintiff to prove that the product was defective at the time of sale or distribution but only the specific elements enumerated. Of significance in the helicopter crash context is that the justifiable reliance need not be of the party ultimately injured. If the helicopter owner or operator was the party to whom the misrepresentation was made, the passenger injured or killed as a result thereof may bring a proper claim for misrepresentation.[139]

In that context, counsel should inquire specifically about the purchase from the purchasing party, whether it was the client, the helicopter owner, operator or maintenance facility, as to the specific reasons why the specific helicopter component part was purchased and all discussions surrounding that purchase decision.

E. Liability for Punitive Damages

Two of the largest punitive damage awards in U.S. history have come in helicopter crash litigation. In 1995, a jury awarded $70 million to the family of a 20-year-old waitress being transported by a Life Flight air ambulance which crashed.[140] Later that same year another jury awarded $350 million, $175 million of which was punitive damages, to the family of the helicopter pilot who died in that same crash.[141] Plaintiffs claimed and the jury believed that the defendant helicopter engine manufacturer, Turbomeca France, continued to market and sell its Aerial 1 engine long after it had learned of a dangerous defect involving the nozzle guide vane.

The legal standard for imposition of punitive liability in the helicopter industry context is the same as for any other individual or corporate defendant. Counsel must ascertain the recoverability of punitive damages under applicable law as many states have severe limitations of pleading, burden of proof and monetary awards if not outright prohibition. This section focuses on the legal basis for submitting punitive damages. Chapter 8 addresses practical suggestions for presenting the most persuasive evidence in support of any punitive damages claim.

Under a strict liability theory, punitive damages are properly submitted where (1) defendant "introduced the offending product into commerce with actual knowledge of the product's defect," and (2) defendant showed complete indifference to or conscious disregard for safety.

Under a negligence theory, punitive damages are properly submitted where (1) defendant "knew or had information from which defendant, in the exercise of ordinary care, should have known that such conduct created a high degree of probability of injury," and (2) defendant showed complete indifference or conscious disregard for safety. The negligence standard does not require specific intent to injure but only that defendant's actions were "conscious" and that from his knowledge of the circumstances his conduct will naturally or probably result in injury.

The admissible evidence heard by the jury and the reasonable inferences derivable therefrom must support at minimum the factual findings that: (1) the defendant product manufacturer placed the product into the stream of commerce with actual knowledge of its defective condition; (2) defendant knew or had reason to know of the high probability of injuries due to product failures; and (3) defendant's actions in numerous respects showed a complete indifference to and conscious disregard for safety.

Punitive damages are justified and may be awarded "because of the defendant's evil motive or reckless indifference to the rights of others....Plaintiff must prove that the defendant's evil hand was guided by an evil mind."[142] The evidence of a defendant's evil state of mind must be captured on videotaped testimony shown to the jury in which the company's executives repeatedly affirm that it was a conscious business decision to subject innocent people to risk of serious injury and death from continued use of the dangerous product.

4.9 Pleading Issues

Even without the immediate time pressure of an impending statute of limitations or repose, the lawsuit should be filed promptly. Plaintiffs often cannot gain access to the wreckage absent compulsory process of a court. And the sooner the case is filed, the sooner counsel can begin discovery and chart the path to trial.

A. Drafting the Initial Complaint

Finally, after considering all of the pertinent legal theories, jurisdictional options, and known facts of the case, counsel is ready to draw up the initial complaint or petition for filing. The ordinary pleading rules prevailing in that jurisdiction will apply and this is a key reason for associating with knowledgeable local counsel. As in any complex legal action, the theories of liability should be plainly alleged and separately stated as to each defendant.

The pleading requirements of each jurisdiction whether in federal or state court must be complied with and include:

1. Signed request for jury trial;
2. Jurisdictional amount within the pleading;
3. Propriety of claiming pre-judgment interest in the initial complaint;
4. Propriety of claiming punitive damages in initial complaint;
5. Requirement of pre-filing appointment of personal representative or guardian;
6. Arrangements for private service of process and summons;
7. Appropriate payment of filing fee and service expenses (many a lawsuit has been delayed because court clerks have a policy of refusing out-of-state checks even drawn upon law firm accounts).

Most jurisdictions permit amendment of the initial complaint without leave of court prior to the filing of an answer by any defendant. This rule comes in handy for those cases where information has been rather scarce and new data is acquired shortly after filing that supports claims against an additional defendant or provides further grounds of liability against an already named defendant. During the course of every helicopter crash case, the initial complaint will be amended frequently as new parties are added or dismissed and additional factual bases emerge to support legal theories of liability or particular types or elements of damages.

A sample outline of the initial complaint is as follows:

1. Plaintiffs—Identification of the plaintiff by name, address and legal capacity to bring the action.
2. Plaintiff's Deceased—Identification of the party killed with address and other pertinent identifying information such as employer, pilot or passenger.
3. Defendant Helicopter Manufacturer—Full corporate name and business address of defendant alleging that it designed, manufactured, sold, marketed and distributed the subject helicopter.
4. Defendant Pilot—Full name and address of pilot of the subject helicopter alleging that he or she was the pilot-in-command of the helicopter at the time of the facts giving rise to the complaint; if pilot is deceased must serve administrator of estate or other proper entity under local procedure.
5. Listing of All Other Defendants—These parties should be separately listed and identified with business address and by general description of the entity and role in the crash.
6. Identification of Helicopter—This should include the make, year and model of the helicopter and registration number.
7. Identification of Defective Component Part or System—The allegedly defective component or system should be identified as precisely as possible using model and part numbers and years of manufacture, if available.
8. Jurisdiction—The basis for jurisdiction should be asserted including whether by long-arm statute or transaction of general business within that forum. Disclaimers as to the reliance or application of any federal law, regulation or statute may be inserted here as well.
9. Venue—The statutory basis for venue in that particular court citing the specific statute.
10. Dates and Acts of Conduct Complained Of—This section should set out the date, time, place and circumstances of the helicopter crash including the reason for the mission, identification of all occupants, and location of crash site. If known, some description of the crash sequence or crash dynam-

ics should be alleged such as "during which the helicopter was spinning" or "impacted the trees at a high rate of speed."

11. Plaintiff's Injuries and Damages—This section includes all of the recoverable economic and non-economic damages elements in that jurisdiction and should set these out with great specificity including the factual basis for any claim of pre-impact terror or post-impact physical pain and suffering.

12. Defendant's Conscious Disregard and Complete Indifference to Safety—This section sets out those known facts supporting a claim of punitive damages including defendant's sale of the subject system or component knowing of its dangerous condition or latent defect.

13. Request for Trial By Jury—Many states require the jury demand or request in the initial pleading and failure to do so may waive trial by jury. If the case is removed to federal court the jury demand will prevent waiver of a jury in that court as well.

Thereafter, all of the theories of liability should be set out in separate counts with each and every one of the elements of plaintiff's prima facie case enumerated. An example of a complaint filed in a recent helicopter crash lawsuit alleging negligence against the pilot and design defect is set out in Appendix B.

B. Challenging Sufficiency of Defendant's Answer

Many aviation defense firms have a standard or boilerplate answer to the complaint filed in any helicopter accident case without consideration of the specific facts of that crash. When served with such a standardized answer, counsel should force the defendant to plead any defense with sufficient particularity and to strike any defense that is immaterial or insufficient as a matter of law.

Under Federal Rule of Civil Procedure 12(f) and comparable state court rules, a plaintiff may move to strike "any insufficient defense" within twenty days after the service of that answer. Many times the affirmative defense raised by a defendant simply will not apply as a matter of law to the specific legal theories alleged in plaintiff's complaint. For example, many states prohibit a state of the art defense as against a strict products liability claim. If as against the helicopter or a component part manufacturer plaintiff has pled only in strict products liability and not negligence, counsel for plaintiff should not be burdened with the time and expense of litigating a state of the art issue where that would be irrelevant as a matter of law.

Similarly, a defendant manufacturer's answer often alleges the comparative or relative fault of other parties, most typically the pilot or some non-party such as an employer, prior aircraft owner, or governmental entity. If these allegations are generally framed and do not set forth any factual basis, plaintiff's counsel immediately should challenge them under Rule 12(e) of the Federal Rules and comparable state pleading rules with a motion to make more definite and certain. Many of the standard affirmative defenses are waived if not timely pled. All defense answer dates should be calendared and noted if the response is untimely.

For example, plaintiff's counsel should not permit an alleged defense of improper capacity to stand where it lacks any legal or factual basis. The defendant should be asked to withdraw that defense or respond frivolously to plaintiff's motion to strike it.

Failing to take advantage of either Rule 12(e) or Rule 12(f) and comparable state court rules only encourages a defendant to wiggle and obfuscate throughout discovery. A streamlined approach to discovery always benefits the plaintiff's cause. Counsel should use these pleading rules to forcibly compel a defendant to strike or withdraw collateral issues so that a clear framework of the legal issues to be litigated will emerge which also streamlines the discovery process.

Endnotes

1. This section draws upon previously published work in G. Robb, "Handling Helicopter Crash Litigation: The Ten Indispensable Steps," BNA Product Safety & Liability Reporter, p. 151, (February 12, 2007).

2. *The History of Helicopter Safety*, by Roy G. Fox as presented at the International Helicopter Safety Symposium at Montreal, Quebec (September 26-29, 2005).

3. *Flight Safety Australia*, "Wirestrike," p. 38 (July-August 1999).

4. Li and Baker, "Crash Risk in General Aviation," *Journal of the American Medical Association*, April 11, 2007, at p. 1596.

5. NTSB Accident Report, Adopted April 9, 2013 Crash of Eurocopter AS350 B2, N352LN Near Mosby, Missouri on August 26, 2011. Report No. PB2013-104866.

6. *Id.* Section 11.5. Prohibiting use of portable electronic devices by flight crew during aircraft operation. 7. NTSB Factual Report, p. 2 (January 14, 2009).

8. See Chapter 12.2 for specific recommendations for enhanced safety in helicopter news-gathering operations.

9. Robert D. McFadden, "9 Dead After Copter and Plane Collide over Hudson, The New York Times, August 9, 2009.

10. *Id.*

11. *McLennan v. American Eurocopter Corp., Inc., 245 F.3d 403 (5th Cir. 2001).*

12. *The History of Helicopter Safety, supra,* at 5.

13. *Southern Helicopter Service, Inc. v. Jones, 379 S.W.2d 10 (Ark. 1964).*

14. *Delaware: 2 Del.C. 305 (1995); Hawaii: HRS β 263-5 (1987); Minnesota: Minn.Stat. β 360.012 (1986); New Jersey: N.J.S.A. β 6:2-7 (1946); South Carolina: Code 1976 ββ 55-3-60 (1962); Tennessee: T.C.A. β 42-1-105 (1972); Vermont: 5 V.S.A. β 479 (1985)* (but owner or lessee liability is extinguished should the aircraft be flown without the owner's or lessee's knowledge or permission).

15. *Maryland: Md. Code Ann., Transp. β 5-1005 (1977)* ("Presumption of liability. The owner and lessee of an aircraft operated above the lands and waters of this State are each prima facie liable, jointly and severally, for any injury to persons or property on the land or water beneath them that is caused by the operation of the aircraft or by the falling of any object from the aircraft,..."); *Wisconsin: W.S.A. 114.05 (2005)* ("... there shall be a presumption of liability on the part of the owner, lessee or pilot, as the case may be, where injury or damage is caused by the dropping or falling of the **aircraft** or spacecraft or of any object or material therefrom,...").

16. *Motley v. Bell Helicopter Textron, Inc., 892 F.Supp. 249 (M.D. Ala. 1995).*

17. 14 C.F.R. Part 91.

18. See Section 4.6(B) of this Chapter 4.

19. *49 U.S.C. β 44112 (1994).*

20. *Retzler v. Pratt & Whitney Co., 723 N.E.2d 345, 352-53 (Ill. App. 1999); Layug v. AAR Parts Trading, Inc., No. 00 L9 599 (Ill. Cir. Ct, May 6, 2005).*

21. *George v. Tonjes, 414 F.Supp. 1199, 1201 (W.D. Wisc. 1976)* (applying Wisconsin law).

22. *A.C.A. β β 27-116-303 (1941) (Arkansas); Cal. Pub. Util. Code β 21404 (West 1973); Iowa Code β 328.41 (2010); ;MD Code, Transportation, β 5-1005 (1977); M.C.L.A. 259.180a (1989) (Michigan); Minn. Stat. β 360.012 (1986); N.R.S. 493.060 (1991) (Nevada); N.Y. Gen. Bus. Law β 251 (McKinney 1962); NDCC β β 2-03-05 (1971) (North Dakota); 74 Pa.C.S.A. β 5502 (1984) (Pennsylvania); SDCL β 50-13-6 (2014) (South Dakota); T.C.A. β 42-1-105 (1972) (Tennessee); 5 V.S.A. β β 479 (1985) (Vermont).*

23. *White v. Inbound Aviation, 82 Cal.Rptr.2d 71 (Cal. App. 1999); Sosa v. Young Flying Service, 277 F.Supp. 554 (S.D.Texas 1967).*

24. *Schlotzhauer v. The Final Season, Inc., et al.*, Case No. CL102824 (District Court of Polk County, Iowa).

25. *Hempstead v. General Fire Extinguisher Corp., 269 F.Supp. 109 (D.C. Del. 1967)* (applying Virginia law).

26. *Dallas Airmotive, Inc. v. FlightSafety Intern., Inc., 277 S.W.3d 696 (Mo. App. 2008).*

27. *N.D. Cent. C. ββ 28-01.4-01 to 28-01.4-04 (1999).*

28. *Id. at β 28-01.4-04(1).*

29. *Id. at β 28-01.4(2).*

30. *Id. at β 28-01.4-02.*

31. *International Shoe Co. v. State of Wash. Office of Unemployment Compensation and Placement*, 326 U.S. 310 (1945).

32. *Id.* at 316.

33. *Id. at 313, 320.*

34. *Id. at 320.*

35. *Burger King Corp. v. Rudzewicz*, 471 U.S. 462, 475-76 (1985).

36. *Id.*

37. *Id.*

38. *Id.* at 475-78; see also *Harris Rutsky & Co. Ins. Services, Inc. v. Bell & Clements Ltd., 328 F.3d 1122, 1129-30 (9th Cir. 2003).*

39. *Gill v. Fairchild Hiller Corp., 312 F.Supp. 916 (D.N.H. 1970).*

40. *State, ex rel. Hydraulic Servocontrols Corp. v. Dale, 657 P.2d 211 (Or. 1982).*

41. *Helicopteros Nacionales de Colombia, S.A., v. Hall, 466 U.S. 408 (1984).*

42. *Id.* at 416-17.

43. *Vibratech, Inc. v. Frost, 661 S.E.2d 185, 190 (Ga. App. 2008)* (finding jurisdiction proper over a component part manufacturer when it "shipped its products to [manufacturer] with the expectation that it would be installed in [its] engines for re-sale to other locales across the country, including Georgia" and benefitted from those sales); *Petroleum Helicopters, Inc. v. Avco Corp., 834 F.2d 510 (5th Cir. 1987)* (finding jurisdiction proper where a flotation device manufacturer had distributors in the state, visited the state for training and service, and advertised in the state despite never having sold a flotation device directly to a Louisiana resident); *State, ex rel. Hydraulic Servocontrols Corp. v. Dale, 657 P.2d 211, 215 (Or. 1982)* (finding jurisdiction over a foreign corporation was proper in that the corporation effectively "deliver[ed] its products into the stream of commerce with the expectation that they will be purchased by consumers" in the state, thereby benefitting from sales of products incorporated into Cessna aircraft sold in the state); *Rockwell Intern. Corp. v. Costruzioni Aeronautiche Giovanni Agusta, S.p.A., 553 F.Supp. 328, 334 (E.D. Pa. 1982)* (finding jurisdiction proper over a nonresident and ruling that "a manufacturer or major distributor should not be allowed to profit from the sale of its product in a state, while simultaneously insulating itself from liability by establishing an indirect and multi-faceted chain of distribution").

44. *Burger King, 471 U.S. at 474.*

45. *Id.*

46. *Board of Trustees, Sheet Metal Workersí Nat. Pension Fund v. Elite Erectors, Inc., 212 F.3d 1031, 1037 (7th Cir. 2000).*

47. *World-Wide Volkswagen Corp. v. Woodson, 444 U.S. 286, 297 (1980).*

48. *Ballard v. Savage, 65 F.3d 1495, 1498 (9th Cir. 1995).*

49. *Sher v. Johnson, 911 F.2d 1357, 1362 (9th Cir. 1990).*

50. *International Shoe Co., 326 U.S. at 313-14, 320* (held jurisdiction over a shoe company whose purposeful contacts with forum state were limited to salesmen exhibiting and marketing company's products).

51. For further discussion of pre-impact terror, see Chapter 8.

52. *Nelson v. Dolan, 434 N.W.2d 25, 30 (Neb. 1989).*

53. *Smallwood v. Bradford, 720 A.2d 586, 590 (Md. App. 1998).*

54. *Restatement (Second) of Conflicts of Laws ß 145*; see also *Foster v. United States, 768 F.2d 1278 (11th Cir. 1985).*

55. *28 U.S.C. ß 1332 (2005).*

56. *28 U.S.C. ß 1441(b) (2002).*

57. However, a plaintiff may voluntarily dismiss an action in federal court prior to any defendant's filing of an answer or a motion for summary judgment so long as the plaintiff has not previously dismissed any federal or state court action. *Fed. R. Civ. 41 (a)(1).*

58. *Daubert v. Merrill Dow Pharmaceuticals, Inc., 509 U.S. 579 (1993).*

59. *28 U.S.C. ß 1332(c)* ("A corporation shall be deemed to be a citizen of any State by which it has been incorporated and of the State where it has its principal place of business,…").

60. *28 U.S.C. ß 1445(c) (1976).*

61. *Wisconsin Dept. of Corrections v. Schacht, 524 U.S. 381, 393 (1998)* (Kennedy, J., concurring "Removal requires the consent of all of the defendants").

62. *Shamrock Oil & Gas Corp. v. Sheets, 313 U.S. 100, 108-09 (1941).*

63. *Estate of Hecker v. Robinson Helicopter Co., 2013 WL 5674982 (E.D.Wash. 2013); Laugelle v. Bell Helicopter Textron, Inc., 2012 WL 368220 (D.Del. 2012); Reger v. Mountain Lifeflight Inc., 2012 WL 1328128 (E.D.Cal. 2012); Ritz v. Mountain Lifeflight Inc., 2012 WL 1332407 (E.D.Cal. 2012); Lucas v. Dylan Aviation, LLC, 2010 WL 1135903 (E.D. Pa. 2010); Carey v. Dylan Aviation, LLC, 2010 WL 1141215 (E.D. Pa. 2010).*

64. *Scollard v. Rocky Mountain Holding Co., 2007 WL 119166 (D.Neb. 2007).*

65. *Id.*

66. *Rockwell Intern. Corp. v. Costruzioni Aeronautiche Giovanni Agusta, S.p.A, 553 F.Supp. 328, 334 (E.D. Pa. 1982)* (applying Pennsylvania law).

67. *Id. at 334.*

68. *Bach v. McDonnell Douglas, Inc., 468 F.Supp. 521 (D.Ariz. 1979)* (applying Arizona law).

69. *Carr v. Pouilloux, S.A., 947 F.Supp. 393 (C.D.Ill. 1996) (applying Illinois law); Barone v. Rich Bros. Interstate Display Fireworks Co., 25 F.3d 610 (C.A.8 (Neb.) 1994), cert. denied, 513 U.S. 948 (1994) (applying Nebraska law); Rockwell Intern. Corp. v. Costruzioni Aeronautiche Giovanni Agusta, S.p.A, 553 F.Supp. 328 (E.D. Pa. 1982)* (applying Pennsylvania law); *Bach v. McDonnell Douglas, Inc., 468 F.Supp. 521 (D.Ariz. 1979)* (applying Arizona law).

70. *DeJames v. Magnificance Carriers, Inc., 654 F.2d 280, 285 (3d Cir. 1981) cert. denied, 454 U.S. 1085 (1981).*

71. *Id. at 285.72.Williamson v. Petroleum Helicopters, Inc., 31 F.Supp. 2d 548 (S.D. Tex. 1998).*

73. *Id. at 551-52.*

74. *Id. at 552.*

75. *Id.*

76. *Id. at 553.*

77. Hiroko Tabuchi, "Little Help in Japan for Owners of Toyotas with Accelerator Problems" *The New York Times*, (March 5, 2010) (former head of Japanese Automobile Consumers Union labeled a "dangerous agitator" and charged with blackmail).

78. *McLennan v. American Eurocopter Corp., Inc., 245 F.3d 403 (5th Cir. 2001).*

79. *McLennan v. American Eurocopter Corp., Inc., 26 F.Supp. 2d 947, 951 (S.D. Tex. 1998), affirmed 245 F.3d 403 (5th Cir. 2001).*

80. *Bahsoon v. Pezetel, Ltd., 768 F.Supp. 507 (E.D.N.C. 1991).*

81. *Id. at 509.*

82. *Id. at 512-13.*

83. *Fredriksson v. Sikorsky Aircraft Corp., Inc., 2009 WL 2952225 (D.Conn. 2009).*

84. *Id. at 7.*

85. *Id. at 21.*

86. *Melgares v. Sikorsky Aircraft Corp., 613 F.Supp.2d 231 (D.Conn. 2009).*

87. *Id. at 242-47.*

88. *Vorbiev v. McDonnell Douglas Helicopters, Inc., 2009 WL 1765675 (N.D.Cal. 2009).*

89. *Helog Ag v. Kaman Aerospace Corp., 228 F.Supp.2d 91 (D.C. Conn. 2002).*

90. *McCafferty ex rel. Estate of Prant v. Raytheon Inc., 2004 WL 1858080 (E.D. Pa. 2004).*

91. *Anyango v. Rolls-Royce Corporation, 971 N.E.2d 654 (Ind. 2012).*

92. *Id. at 656.*

93. *Id. at 664.*

94. *49 U.S.C. ß 40101 (2000).*

95. *49 U.S.C. ß 40101, Section 2(a) (1997).*

96. *28 U.S.C. ß 1346 (2013).*

97. *28 U.S.C. ß 2675 (1966).*

98. *28 U.S.C. ß 2401 (2011).*

99. *28 U.S.C. ß 2675(a).*

100. *McNeil v. United States, 508 U.S. 106, 108 n.2 (1993).*

101. *28 U.S.C. ß 2675(b).*

102. *28 U.S.C. ß 2674 (1988).*

103. *28 U.S.C. ß 2401(b).*

104. *28 U.S.C. ß 1402(b) (1982).*

105. *28 U.S.C. ß 2402 (1996).*

106. *28 U.S.C. ß 2674 (1988).*

107. *46 U.S.C. ßß 30301-30308 (2006).*

108. *46 U.S.C. ßß 30301-30303, 30307.*

109. *46 U.S.C.§ 30307.*

110. *Offshore Logistics, Inc. v. Tallentire, 477 U.S. 207 (1986).*

111. *Brown v. Eurocopter S.A., 111 F.Supp.2d 859 (S.D. Tex. 2000).*

112. *46 U.S.C. ß 30308.*

113. *43 U.S.C. ß 1333(b) (1984).*

114. *Alleman v. Omni Energy Services Corp., 580 F.3d 280, 285-86 (5th Cir. 2009).*

115. *Id. at 282.*

116. *Id.*

117. *Id. at 286.*

118. *14 C.F.R. ß 27.1 (1999)* (applicability).

119. *Campbell v. Keystone Aerial Surveys, Inc., 138 F.3d 996, 1003 (5th Cir. 1998).*

120. *Cal. Pub. Util. Code ß 21404 (West 1973); Minn. Stat. ß 360.012 (1986); .Iowa Code ß 328.41 (2010); N.Y. Gen. Bus. Law ß 251 (McKinney 1962); S.D. Codified Laws Ann. ß 50-13-6 (2014).*

121. *Ewers v. Thunderbird Aviation, Inc., 289 N.W.2d 94, 97 (Minn. 1979).*

122. *Iowa Code ß 328.41 (2010).*

123. *Iowa Code ß 328.1(1)(u) (2010).*

124. *Louisiana: LSA-R.S. 9:2800.56 (1988)* (requiring proof of "an alternative design for the product that was capable of preventing the claimant's damage"); *Mississippi: Miss. Code Ann. ß 11-1-63(f)(ii) (2014)* (requiring proof of "a feasible design alternative that would have to a reasonable probability prevented the harm where a feasible design alternative is defined as "a design that would have to a reasonable probability prevented the harm without impairing the utility, usefulness, practicality or desirability of the product to users or consumers"); *Ohio: R.C. ß 2307.75(F) (2004)* (requiring proof of "a practical and technically feasible alternative design or formulation…that would have prevented the harm for which the claimant seeks to recover compensatory damages without substantially impairing the usefulness or intended purpose of the product"); *Texas: V.T.C.A., Civil Practice & Remedies Code ß 82.005 (1993)* (requiring proof of "safer alternative design" defined as "a product design other than the one actually used that in reasonable probability: (1) would have prevented or significantly reduced the risk of the claimant's personal injury, property damage, or death without substantially impairing the product's utility; and (2) was economically and technologically feasible at the time the product left the control of the manufacturer or seller by the application of existing or reasonably achievable scientific knowledge") ; *Washington: West's RCWA 7.72.030 (1988)* ("A product is not reasonably safe as designed, if, at the time of manufacture, the likelihood that the product would cause the claimant's harm or similar harms, and the seriousness of those harms, outweighed the burden on the manufacturer to design a product that would have prevented those harms and the adverse effect that an alternative design that was practical and feasible would have on the usefulness of the product . . ."); *Wisconsin: W.S.A. 895.047 (2011)* (A product is defective in design if the foreseeable risks of harm posed by the product could have been reduced or avoided by the adoption of a reasonable alternative design by the manufacturer and the omission of the alternative design renders the product not reasonably safe").

125. *V.T.C.A., Civil Practice & Remedies Code ß 82.005 (1993).*

126. *Alabama: General Motors Corp. v. Edwards, 482 So.2d 1176, 1189-90 (Ala. 1985)* (overruled on other grounds) (requiring proof that "a 'safer' practical, alternative design was available to the manufacturer" in crashworthiness cases); *Arizona: Gebhardt v. Mentor Corp., 191 F.R.D. 180, 185 n.2 (D.Ariz. 1999), affïd, 15 Fed.Appx. 540 (9th Cir. 2001)* (applying Restatement (Third) of Torts, § 2(b), to determine that summary judgment was proper were the plaintiff failed to show that the risk of harm could have been reduced by "a reasonable alternative design"); *Arkansas: Miller v. Baker Implement Co., 439 F.3d 407, 412 (8th Cir. 2006)* ("Arkansas law requires that a plaintiff who claims product defects must show that an alternative design was feasible"); *District of Columbia: Warner Fruehauf Trailer Co., Inc. v. Boston, 654 A.2d 1272, 1278 (D.C. 1995)* (requiring proof of a safer, feasible alternative design in a strict liability action); *Florida: Edic ex rel. Edic v. Century Products Co., 364 F.3d 1276, 1280 n.2 (11th Cir. 2004)* ("A product is defective in design, under Florida law [in a strict liability case] when the foreseeable risks of harm posed by the product could have been reduced or avoided by the adoption of a reasonable alternative design and its omission renders the product not reasonably safe"); *Idaho: Nepanuseno v. Hansen, 104 P.3d 984, 988 (Idaho App. 2004)* ("To succeed on a strict products liability claim, [the plaintiff] would have had

the burden of establishing, among other things, that the backhoe manufactured by John Deere was defective and unreasonably dangerous"); *Indiana: Whitted v. General Motors Corp., 58 F.3d 1200, 1206 (7th Cir. 1995)* ("To allege that a manufacturer breached its duty to design a safe product under strict liability, a claimant must offer a safer, more practicable product design than the design in question") *Iowa: Wright v. Brooke Group Ltd., 652 N.W.2d 159, 169 (Iowa 2002)* ("adopt[ing] Restatement (Third) of Torts: Product Liability sections 1 and 2 for product defect cases"); *Kentucky: Toyota Motor Corp. v. Gregory, 136 S.W.3d 35, 42 (Ky. 2004)* (stating that, in a strict liability case under Kentucky law, "defect liability requires proof of a feasible alternative design"); *Maryland: Nissan Motor Co. Ltd. v. Nave, 740 A.2d 102, 118 (Md. App. 1999), cert. denied, 745 A.2d 437 (Md. 2000)* (requiring a plaintiff in a design defect case under a strict liability theory to prove six elements in regard to the feasibility of a safer alternative design); *New Jersey: Simmons v. Ford Motor Co., 132 Fed.Appx. 950, 951 (3rd Cir. 2005)* (For a claim of product defect under a strict liability theory, a plaintiff must prove a reasonable alternative design); *New Mexico: Morales v. E.D. Etnyre & Co., 382 F.Supp.2d 1278, 1283-84 (D.N.M. 2005)* (stating that it "believes that the New Mexico law required the plaintiff to propose an alternative design"); *New York: Pierre-Louis v. DeLonghi America, Inc., 887 N.Y.S.2d 628, 631 (N.Y.A.D. 2009)* ("'To establish a prima facie case in a strict products liability action predicated on a design defect, a plaintiff must show that the manufacturer marketed a product which was not reasonably safe in its design, that it was feasible to design the product in a safer manner, and that the defective design was a substantial factor in causing the plaintiff's injury'"); *Pennsylvania: Martinez v. Triad Controls, Inc., 593 F.Supp.2d 741, 757 n.12 (E.D.Pa. 2009)* (requiring proof of a "feasible alternative design" only in crashworthiness cases); *South Carolina: Branham v. Ford Motor Co., 701 S.E.2d 5, 14 (S.C. 2010)* ("We hold today that the exclusive test in a products liability design case is the risk-utility test with its requirement of showing a feasible alternative design"); and *Utah: Allen v. Minnstar, Inc., 8 F.3d 1470, 1479 (10th Cir. 1993)* (holding that "a showing of an alternative, safer design, practicable under the circumstances and available at the time of defendants' placing [its product] in the stream of commerce,…was required").

127. *Pierre-Louis v. DeLonghi America, Inc., 887 N.Y.S 2d 628, 631 (N.Y. A.D. 2009).*

128. *See, e.g., Dawson v. Chrysler Corp., 630 F.2d 950 (3rd Cir. 1980); Touch v. Master Unit Die Products, Inc., 43 F.3d 754 (1st Cir. 1995).* New York provides that the theories of strict liability and breach of implied warranty of merchantability are virtually indistinguishable. *Jones by Jones v. Lederle Laboratories, a Div. of American Cyanamid Co., 695 F.Supp. 700 (E.D.N.Y. 1988).*

129. *Singer v. Walker, 331 N.Y.S.2d 823 (N.Y.A.D. 1972), order affd, 345 N.Y.S.2d 542 (N.Y. App. 1973).*

130. *Green v. City of Los Angeles, 115 Cal.Rptr. 685 (Cal. App. 1974).*

131. *Collins v. Uniroyal, Inc., 315 A.2d 16 (N.J. 1974).*

132. *Ladd By Ladd v. Honda Motor Co., Ltd, 939 S.W.2d 83 (Tenn. App. 1996).*

133. *Board of Educ. of City of Chicago v. A, C and S, Inc., 546 N.E.2d 580 (Ill. 1989).*

134. *Henley v. Phillip Morris, Inc., 9 Cal.Rptr.3d 29 (Cal. App. 2004), review granted and opinion superseded, 88 P.3d 497 (Cal. 2004); First Nat. Bank of Louisville v. Brooks Farms, 821 S.W.2d 925 (Tenn. 1991).*

135. *Restatement (Second) of Torts β 402B.*

136. *Id. at Comment A; see also Hauter v. Zogarts, 534 P.2d 377 (Cal. 1975).*

137. *California: Hauter v. Zogarts, 534 P.2d 377; Colorado: American Safety Equipment Corp. v. Winkler, 640 P.2d 216 (Colo. 1982); Illinois: Rozny v. Marnul, 250 N.E.2d 656 (Ill. 1969); Pennsylvania: Klages v. General Ordinance Equipment Corp., 367 A.2d 304 (Pa. Super. 1976); Tennessee: Ford Motor Co. v. London, 398 S.W.2d 240 (Tenn. 1966), overld in part on other grounds, First National Bank v. Brooks Farms, 821 S.W.2d 925 (Tenn. 1991).*

138. *In re Temporomandibular Joint (TMJ) Implants Products Liability Litigation, 113 F.3d 1484 (8th Cir. 1997)* (applying Minnesota law).

139. *See, e.g., Westlye v. Look Sports, Inc., 22 Cal.Rptr.2d 781 (Cal. App. 1993)* (product manufacturer misrepresented to retailer the safety of certain ski bindings and where retailer rented those skis and bindings to plaintiff who was subsequently injured, plaintiff may have direct action as against manufacturer under misrepresentation theory); *in accord Baughn v. Honda Motor Co., Ltd., 727 P.2d 655 (Wash. 1986).*

140. At the time of trial, Missouri law provided that punitive liability in wrongful death actions would be assessed

as "aggravating circumstances" and added to any compensatory award. The precise allocation as between compensatory and punitive-type damages was not delineated.

141. *Letz v. Turbomeca Engine Corporation, 975 S.W.2d 155, 164-65 (Mo. App. 1997); Barnett v. La Societe Anonyme Turbomeca France, 963 S.W.2d 639 (Mo. App. 1997), cert. denied, 525 U.S. 827 (1998).* On appeal, a total of $53 million in punitive damages, $26.5 million in each case, was upheld by the Missouri Court of Appeals, Western District, en banc. Subsequently, the Missouri Supreme Court denied transfer in the *Barnett* action and re-transferred *Letz* to the Missouri Court of Appeals and the U.S. Supreme Court denied certiorari. *Letz v. Turbomeca Engine Corporation, cert. denied, 119 S.Ct. 75 (1998).* Ultimately, the families received a total cash payment of $82 million for the two wrongful deaths in that helicopter crash.

142. *Burnett v. Griffith, 769 S.W.2d 780, 787 (Mo. 1989).*

Chapter 5

Discovery and Case Development

Introduction

Effective use of the tools of discovery is a required skill set in helicopter crash litigation. Plaintiff's counsel must fully utilize all of the permissible discovery rules and, as importantly, in the proper order to meet the primary discovery objectives. These discovery objectives in helicopter accident litigation are as follows:

1. Obtaining the requisite factual basis for the opinions of plaintiff's liability experts;
2. Locking in defendants and their experts into a theory or explanation for the helicopter crash;
3. Obtaining all possible discovery as to substantially similar incidents and accidents; and
4. Averting extensive delay and motion practice.

It is particularly true for helicopter crash litigation that "the case is won in discovery."

5.1 Sequence of Discovery

The depositions of defendants should not be taken before receiving each defendant's lawful and responsive answers both to interrogatories and document requests. If that discovery is not complete and improper objections are raised, counsel must insist that the defendant produce all relevant documents and answers to interrogatories and by court compulsion, if necessary. Plaintiff's liability experts will need time to study these materials before plaintiff's counsel deposes the defendant's employees and designated corporate representatives on specific subject matters. Further, it presents risks to depose one defendant while awaiting discovery responses from a co-defendant. Documents may be produced by a co-defendant which counsel will wish to use in questioning other defendants.

It may be tempting to avoid discovery disputes by playing nice and accepting the defendant's offer for minimal or scaled-down discovery responses. Although the far easier route, counsel must resist that temptation. Such an offer is made only to avoid disclosing information and documents damaging to defendants' position and that are most strongly supportive of plaintiff's claims.

Similarly, counsel must resist the defense offer to produce for deposition its employees or designated agents while awaiting resolution of any ongoing paper discovery disputes. Counsel must have the opportunity to carefully review all documents produced by the defendant and to consult with the plaintiff's liability experts about relevant points the documents contain well before these depositions.

During this initial paper phase of discovery, there is a lurking danger. During these early discovery scrimmages, defendants often will attempt to seize the initiative by objecting to plaintiff's lawful discovery while insisting on full discovery for the plaintiff's responses. These tactics must be resisted by the prompt filing of motions to compel adequate discovery and by the refusal to be bogged down in discovery disputes propounded on the plaintiff. Plaintiffs must maintain an open book posture as to all lawful and proper discovery so as to foreclose any motion to compel relating to plaintiff's alleged non-disclosure of discoverable information. Plaintiffs should resist defense efforts to obtain liability opinions via interrogatories prior to the deposition of plaintiff's experts. In most jurisdictions, the only means of discovering expert opinions is by deposition. Forthright responses to defendant's proper discovery requests for all lawful information accords plaintiffs an advantage. This clean hands approach puts plaintiffs in a favorable position should the court need to be approached to rule on frivolous objections made by the defendant.

Following the completion of the entire first wave of written discovery, particularly document production, plaintiffs may then embark on the second wave of discovery which includes the depositions of all defendants, both corporate and individual, as well as a defendant's designated agents. By this stage of the litigation, counsel should know the names of the various employees and engineers who were involved with designing, manufacturing and marketing the helicopter engine, system or component part implicated in causing the crash. Approaching the discovery in this order will maximize the potential benefit of these tools, create a more efficient development of the case and accomplish the critical early objective of preparing plaintiff's liability experts for their depositions.

5.2 Written Discovery

The first wave of written discovery seeks certain fundamental information some of which relates to the propriety of suit in the particular forum and the proper identification of the defendants. The effectiveness of interrogatories in seeking any meaningful information is limited because the responses are often designed by defense counsel to yield minimal information. Nevertheless, interrogatories remain an essential discovery tool for learning basic facts.

The most critical written discovery procedure by far are the formal document requests. Unlike interrogatories, these are not limited in number and typically will be the first critical discovery battlefield given the defendants' habitual unwillingness to part with damaging information. Where permissible, all of the initial written discovery comprised of interrogatories and document requests should be served along with the summons and complaint. Follow-up discovery can be tailored to specific issues.

A. Effective Use of Interrogatories

No general set of interrogatories will be usable in every case. The questions must be tailored to the facts and legal theories of the particular case. At minimum, plaintiff's initial set of interrogatories should include the following subject matters:

1. Jurisdiction and Venue
    a. Defendant sued in correct capacity.
    b. Defendant conducts business within the forum state.
    c. Defendant registered to or otherwise does business in the forum state.
    d. Defendant supplies products and services in the forum state.
    e. Defendant agrees that jurisdiction in forum state is proper.
    f. Defendant agrees that venue in forum state is proper.
    g. Defendant agrees that helicopter crash occurred in forum state.
    h. Defendant agrees that injuries or wrongful death occurred in forum state.
    i. Defendant agrees that [name of pilot] was pilot-in-command on the date and time of the subject helicopter accident.
2. Insurance Coverage
    a. Existence of any and all applicable policies of insurance.
    b. Existence of any excess policies of insurance.

c. Existence of any potential claims or previous payments depleting available insurance coverage.

d. Existence of any reservation of rights as to applicability of insurance.

e. Indemnity agreements between or among various defendants.

3. Information About Helicopter, Subsystem or Components

a. Identification of manufacturer of aircraft or component part at issue.

b. Identification of designer of helicopter or component part at issue.

c. Information as to certification history of helicopter or component part at issue.

d. Registration number and date of manufacture of subject helicopter.

e. Identification of any vendors or suppliers of component parts.

f. Identification of individuals within the company having the most knowledge of particular facets of helicopter or a component part including:

1. Certification history.
2. Development and design history.
3. In-house and field testing.
4. Issuance of pertinent service letters, safety bulletins, and airworthiness directives.

4. Information about other similar lawsuits and claims.

a. Information about other similar accidents, incidents, crashes or in-flight failures.

b. Information about warranty claims.

5. Identification of tests, studies, analyses performed on subject model helicopter or subject model component part.

6. Identification of all individuals within the company who participated in any way in the NTSB investigation of the subject aircraft.

7. Identification of all individuals within the company who conducted, performed or participated in any investigation, analysis, examination or review of the subject accident.

8. Dates of sales to operator at time of accident.

9. Identification of experts and the description of opinions as provided by applicable rule and local practice.

10. Identity of witnesses having knowledge of the subject helicopter accident.

Interrogatories about lawsuits alleging similar accidents or malfunctions should include the name of the court and date of filing and whether the lawsuit was disposed of prior to trial or proceeded to verdict. These interrogatories should include all types of tests performed on the aircraft or, if pertinent, the helicopter engine or component. A list of all such studies or tests should be requested along with their test dates. Interrogatories should request the identity of the head of engineering, chief of flight testing, project engineer, or designated engine representative.

Most helicopter or engine manufacturers are called in as party participants to the NTSB investigation. They will supply basic information about the specific aircraft, engine or component at issue to the investigator-in-charge as well as conduct inspections or testing concerning the area of inquiry. Interrogatories should require identification of all company personnel who participated in the investigation by the NTSB as well as their current job titles.

Sample first sets of interrogatories in a helicopter failure/design defect case, in a helicopter component part case and to a helicopter pilot are attached as sample pleadings in Appendix B.

B. Effective Use of Document Requests

The initial or first wave of document requests to the defendants are standard because at that point in the litigation the critical areas of inquiry may not be known. The responses to this initial set should be reviewed immediately, primarily to assess their sufficiency, but also to permit follow-up on any factual leads set forth in the answers. The initial request for production of documents should be filed simultaneously with the complaint. This initial request for documents should include the following.

1. Aircraft Type Certification

Any helicopter operated within the U.S. must have a Type Certification authorized by the FAA. The entire type certificate file should be requested and includes:

a. Date aircraft first received its Type Certificate (TC) issued by FAA or other countries' comparable aviation authority as well as early design development, flight tests, and application for type certification.

b. Relevant correspondence between FAA certification authorities and manufacturer.

The design development and history includes flight and ground test documentation used to obtain FAA type certification of the aircraft. Aircraft or component part design and development includes all original design drawings as well as engineering change orders. Helicopter manufacturers frequently are making significant design and manufacturing changes in their aircraft. The identification of this paperwork will reveal the dates and types of changes as well as the personnel involved who sign off on the engineering change orders.

2. Field Data and Customer Feedback

The document requests should seek written complaints and material setting out the company's program for retaining, organizing, and reviewing Service Difficulty Reports.

3. Reported Accidents or Incidents

Helicopter airframe and engine makers maintain extensive records of any accident involving their aircraft or engine, as do component part manufacturers. It is a manufacturer's duty to affirmatively acquire and review any reported malfunctions with respect to its helicopter, engine, or component part systems. Reporting of failures, malfunctions and defects to the FAA is mandatory pursuant to FAR 21.3. The federal regulations mandate that the Type Certificate holder or parts manufacturer approval (PMA) report any failure, malfunction or defect in their product which may have been contributory to an aircrash or which had been reported as an in-flight failure. These reports may later prove the foundation for proof of defect or notice of danger to the manufacturer.

4. Company Organization Chart

This chart is a valuable resource for identifying and deposing various personnel within the company.

5. Insurance Documentation

All applicable policies should be requested including the declaration sheets.

6. Airworthiness Directives, Service Letters and Service Bulletins

These documents will reveal the defendant's knowledge and response to particular airworthiness problems in the aircraft, engine or component part. Included within the request should be all of the defendant's correspondence with the FAA or memoranda of meetings with FAA personnel surrounding the ultimate issuance of the airworthiness directive. Invariably, the manufacturer seeks to dissuade the FAA from issuing an airworthiness directive given its mandatory and ominous implications, and these documents are worthy of review.

All helicopter aircraft and engine manufacturers as well as component part manufacturers publish and distribute service letters and service bulletins addressing ongoing safety issues. Interrogatories should seek to identify any service bulletins or service letters addressing the particular system or component suspected of failure. Although counsel can independently obtain airworthiness directives from the FAA, the underlying internal memoranda or correspondence with FAA with respect to a proposed airworthiness directive (AD) will provide very pointed reasons either in support of or against issuing the proposed AD. All files and documents relating to issuance of any of these informational matters should be identified.

7. Warranty Claims and Lawsuits

Copies of complaints filed against the defendant alleging similar types of malfunctions should be requested along with any paperwork or documentation of customer complaints.

8. Internal Engineering Meeting Minutes and Memoranda

All documentation relative to a particular airworthiness issue or concern should be requested. Helicopter and engine manufacturers maintain careful records on these matters as they may lead to an engineering change order or customer advisory notice in the form of a service letter or service bulletin.

9. Subject Accident Investigation File

The entire file relative to the manufacturer's investigation of the subject helicopter accident should be requested. Manufacturers participating in the NTSB investigation will resist such production on the grounds that these matters cannot be released pending issuance of the NTSB Report. Although that objection is questionable, there is no arguable basis for withholding that information once the NTSB has completed its work.

A sample first request for production of documents directed to a helicopter engine manufacturer, helicopter component part manufacturer, and helicopter pilot is attached in Appendix B.

In the document discovery battles with helicopter manufacturers and the manufacturers of the various engines and component parts and systems, a frequent source of contention is the location of the document production, as well as the method or manner of production. Counsel should request that the document production go forward at the defendant's place of business and that the documents be produced in their usual and ordinary manner. This document production procedure has proven to be extremely effective and expedient by reducing the number of needless copies of unwanted or unneeded documentation, the ease of access to particular documents given the company's own filing system, and either the defendant's inability or conscious decision to refrain from cherry picking some of the most damaging documents under the guise of some asserted privilege or claims of irrelevancy. Typically, the most vigorous discovery disputes address the breadth and scope of plaintiff's document requests. Documents from the defendant's files that support plaintiff's liability claim and provide notice to the defendant that a malfunction of its product or system was recurring with serious safety consequences are often the most persuasive evidence of liability in the case. For these reasons, counsel must file as many motions to compel as are necessary to obtain all lawfully discoverable documents. While this serves the defendant's desire to delay the case and drive up expenses, it is a necessary prerequisite for the further handling of the lawsuit.

It has proven useful to take a preliminary deposition from the defendant's corporate representative as to the existence, location and description of various documents. This procedure averts much of the usual and frivolous basis for objections that the documents do not exist as described or that the request is vague and ambiguous. Issuance of the deposition notice forces the defendant to identify a company representative knowledgeable about its various documentation thereby eliminating much of this squabbling.

The second set or follow-up document request is then specifically tailored to those documents which are known to be in existence. Counsel may cite to those portions of the deposition where the deponent agrees with the description of the category of documents or sets out what the company calls them and confirms that they are readily accessible.

An example of such a deposition notice for this specific purpose is as follows:

PLAINTIFF'S NOTICE OF DEPOSITION OF DEFENDANT HELICOPTER COMPONENT PART MAKER'S DESIGNATED AGENT AS TO THE IDENTIFICATION, DESCRIPTION, LOCATION AND CUSTODIAN OF VARIOUS DOCUMENTS

Plaintiffs hereby notice the deposition of the designated agent of defendant upon the subject matters designated below on Wednesday, the 20th day of May 2009 at 8:30 a.m. at the LAW OFFICES OF _ _____, Anytown, USA, and continuing from day to day and time to time until completed. Pursuant to Rule 57.03(b)(4) of the Missouri Supreme Court Rules, Plaintiff herein demand that defendant designate one or more of its officers, directors, or managing agents, or other persons who consent to testify on its behalf as each of the subject matters set forth below and please be advised that each person so designated shall testify as to matters known and reasonably available to the organization as follows:

NOTE 1: Note that the limited purpose of this deposition is to acquire information from this Defendant as to the identification, description, location and custodian of various documents and categories of documents described and referenced herein.
NOTE 2: All categories address defendant's design, manufacture, sale and distribution of the subject component part as installed on the subject helicopter.
NOTE 3: To the extent applicable, all categories address defendant's sales, field use and maintenance experience, and notice and claims issues for every U.S. State and Canada.
NOTE 4: The applicable time frame for all categories is 1990 to the present day.

1. The existence, identification, description, location and custodian of the following documents, files, reports, electronic mail, records and paperwork:

(a) All correspondence including written correspondence and electronic mail, between this defendant and NTSB.

The narrowed scope of this deposition permits counsel to identify precisely those documents which bear on the disputed issues. The deposition is then used to frame the second or follow-up request for production of documents. For example, Request No. 1:

1. All correspondence, including written correspondence, e-mails or other electronic communication between this defendant and the NTSB, including but not limited to drafts or partial drafts of NTSB reports, all as identified and referenced by the defendant's corporate representative in her deposition on pages 4-5.

The final advantage of this procedure is that it makes for a very simple and focused motion to compel. There is no doubt as to the existence, nomenclature or the location of the documents and the only issue is the extent of defendant's displeasure in producing the documents.

C. Effective Use of Request for Admissions
In most of these cases requests for admissions are of limited usefulness at the outset of the case. Any issues of controversy will be denied with an indication that defendant has no information at this point in time given the limited discovery to date. Certain essential information can be confirmed by use

of requests for admission. If not, counsel can inquire about such issues at the time of the corporate representatives' depositions. The basic issues which should be included in the initial request for admissions are as follows.

1. Jurisdictional and Venue Facts

Requests for admissions may go to jurisdictional and venue issues including the correct corporate name of the defendant and the location of its principal place of business.

2. Defendant's Relation to the Aircraft or Product at Issue

These would be admissions that the defendant manufactured, designed, and sold the helicopter or subject engine or component part. Included within these requests are admissions as to the specific registration number, and owner of record of the subject aircraft.

3. Accident Facts

Certain essential facts concerning the crash are properly the subject of requests for admissions and these include the date, location, and persons involved. If the requests are to a defendant operator or pilot they also may include the identity of the employer as well as the job title or description of the employee's duties.

5.3 Fact Depositions

Many fact witnesses can be deposed while the process of written discovery to the defendants is ongoing. While counsel should never take the pilot, a manufacturer's in-house engineers or other remaining defendants without first obtaining all appropriate document discovery, other potential witnesses including those on the scene or surviving passengers can and should be deposed. Many of these early fact depositions are as important on damages issues as on the liability or fault determination.

A. On-Scene Witnesses

The primary prerequisite for taking any of the scene witnesses is receipt and review of any governmental or agency interviews or statements taken of the witness. These would include police or fire department reports as well as any statement taken by NTSB investigators. These witnesses should describe in precise detail the movement and actions of the helicopter in-flight prior to the crash and the angle and direction of the helicopter at impact if that was observed. Just as for the initial interviewing of such witnesses, the use of a model helicopter to illustrate the movement witnessed has proven to be very effective. Given the unfamiliarity of helicopter flight movement to most lay people, holding the helicopter and demonstrating its movements as observed in-flight will generate the very best description. All of these depositions should be videotaped for this reason alone.

Too often, rescue and fire personnel are ignored as potential witnesses. These early responders may have information bearing on damages issues. They will bear witness to the survival struggles of those horribly injured or burned in a helicopter crash. They can either relay actual conversations with those crash victims or other indicia of consciousness such as eyes open, breathing with pulse and hand gestures for those unable to speak.

Counsel should be creative in locating and deposing other fact witnesses with potentially important information. In one recent case a dispute evolved as to the pilot's proper performance of the pre-flight inspection. By sheer luck, an airplane pilot came forward who was visiting with the deceased prior to takeoff and observed his careful and detailed pre-flight inspection. That pilot's subsequent deposition laid to rest any potential dispute about whether the pre-flight inspection had been performed.

Other fact witnesses include those along the flight path who would not necessarily have witnessed any loss of control of the helicopter nor observed or heard the actual crash. In a recent case, two fishermen located approximately two miles along the flight path preceding the crash came forward to report that the helicopter had been "seeming to lose altitude" and that the "engine sounded funny." Their depositions were corroborative of an in-flight engine power loss and helped to pinpoint the timing of the trigger event because, as is so often the case, all aboard perished in the crash.

B. Maintenance Personnel

The maintenance of the subject helicopter is often a disputed issue. For that reason deposing all maintenance personnel with any role to play on the accident aircraft is critical. The qualifications of all such personnel should explored as should their current standing as FAA-certified A&P mechanics.

The maintenance logbooks should be reviewed in advance to assess timely compliance with regularly scheduled maintenance and replacement intervals as well as annual inspections and major overhauls. The identity of any outside parts vendors or other overhaul or servicing providers must be inquired about. This includes simple instrument calibration all the way to major engine overhaul. One of the reasons for deposing such maintenance personnel early on is to discover the identity of any other potential defendants so that they may be timely added to the lawsuit.

C. NTSB Investigators

One discovery problem unique to these cases relates to obtaining information from the NTSB investigators. By federal regulation, they are not permitted to testify in court and may only testify as to "personally known facts...observed by the employee or uncovered during the employee's investigations of the accident."[1] The regulations also provide that investigators "shall not testify as an expert or opinion witness...arising out of the employee's official duties."[2]

There is a specific regulatory procedure for requesting testimony of NTSB employees in civil litigation.[3] The appropriate procedure for requesting the deposition of any NTSB personnel is for counsel to forward a letter to the NTSB Office of General Counsel who may approve or deny the request. The request must set forth the title of the civil action, the court, the type of accident (such as aviation, railroad, or school bus), the date and place of the accident and the "reasons for desiring the testimony" with a showing that the information requested is not "reasonably available from other sources." A sample letter requesting the deposition testimony of a helicopter crash investigator-in-charge is included in Appendix A.

The location of the deposition must be at the NTSB office of the testifying employee. Counsel seeking the employee's deposition is required to advise all interested parties so that they may have the opportunity to attend and participate so as to avoid the need for multiple depositions. Although the NTSB and its general counsel are normally accommodating in scheduling depositions, counsel must be familiar with the subject matter restrictions on such testimony. Also, experience dictates that depositions should be scheduled when the investigator is on leave. Otherwise, he may be on call and summoned to investigate an aircraft crash just when the deposition is scheduled to commence. Pursuant to the federal statute, a subpoena must not be served.

Any plaintiff lawyer who has tried an aviation case knows there are numerous legal and practical constraints to using the NTSB findings at trial, whether through the actual report or the investigator's testimony. Absent unusual circumstances, the NTSB's final or "probable cause" report is inadmissible under current law and numerous other investigative reports and materials have hearsay and other admissibility problems. However, with effective use of the rules of evidence and careful planning, counsel will in almost all circumstances be able to bring before the jury the factual underpinnings of the NTSB's findings either by testimony of the NTSB investigator or by introduction into evidence of the NTSB Factual Report. An alternative to presenting deposition testimony is using the NTSB Factual Report at trial.

For authentication purposes, counsel must obtain the "Blue Ribbon" copy, an original copy of the NTSB report upon which is affixed the official agency seal attached to a blue ribbon. In almost all states and in all federal courts, such an official government document is self-authenticating. It does not require testimony from a business records custodian.

D. FAA Personnel

The depositions of FAA personnel most commonly are taken in helicopter accident cases to obtain either ATC or radar information. The deposition testimony of an air traffic controller is critical whenever any material radio communications are exchanged between the controller and the pilot. For those cases where the actions of the air traffic controller are implicated in the crash, the deposition will not be subject to Part 9 of the FAA Regulations but will be with the U.S. as a defendant and accompanied by Department of Justice trial counsel defending under the Federal Tort Claims Act.

Where the deposition does involve communications with the pilot, counsel must make arrangements to have high quality audio equipment available to replay the audiocassette of the communications. The tape can be started and stopped at intervals permitting for questions as to the actions of the controller at specific moments in time.

Similar to the NTSB, the FAA has set out procedures for the depositions of its employees. Counsel desiring deposition testimony of any FAA employee must write to the regional counsel's office for that specific region in which the FAA employee is affiliated. As for NTSB, FAA regulations do not permit the employee to give any opinion testimony and FAA counsel are permitted to attend and participate in the deposition.

At present there are nine regional FAA offices with the main headquarters located in Washington, D.C. The specific inquiry should be directed as follows:

ALASKAN REGION
222 West 7th Avenue #14
Anchorage, Alaska 99513
(907-271-5645)
This region is responsible for Alaska.

CENTRAL REGION
901 Locust Street
Kansas City, Missouri 64106
(816-329-3050)
This region is responsible for governing Iowa, Kansas, Missouri, and Nebraska.

EASTERN REGION

1 Aviation Plaza

Jamaica, New York 11434

(718-553-3001)

This region is responsible for governing Delaware, the District of Columbia, Maryland, New Jersey, New York, Pennsylvania, Virginia, and West Virginia.

GREAT LAKES REGION

O'Hare Lake Office Center

2300 East Devon Avenue

Des Plaines, Illinois 60018

(847-294-7294)

This region is responsible for governing Illinois, Indiana, Michigan, Minnesota, North Dakota, Ohio, South Dakota and Wisconsin.

NEW ENGLAND REGION

12 New England Executive Park

Burlington, Massachusetts 01803

(781-238-7020)

This region is responsible for governing Connecticut, Maine, Massachusetts, New Hampshire, Rhode Island and Vermont.

NORTHWEST MOUNTAIN REGION

1601 Lind Avenue Southwest

Renton, Washington 98057

(425-227-2001)

This region is responsible for governing Idaho, Oregon, Washington, Colorado, Montana, Utah, and Wyoming.

SOUTHERN REGION

P.O. Box 20636

Atlanta, Georgia 30320

(404-305-5000)

This region is responsible for governing Alabama, Florida, Georgia, Kentucky, Mississippi, North Carolina, Puerto Rico, South Carolina, Tennessee, and U.S. Virgin Islands.

SOUTHWEST REGION

2601 Meacham Boulevard

Forth Worth, Texas 76137

(817-222-5000)

This region is responsible for governing Arkansas, Louisiana, New Mexico, Oklahoma, and Texas.

WESTERN PACIFIC REGION

P.O. Box 92007

Los Angeles, California 90009

(310-725-3550)

This region is responsible for governing Arizona, California, Nevada, and Hawaii.

E. Surviving Passengers

At the earliest opportunity counsel should depose any survivors of the helicopter crash. In some instances this may even include the plaintiff, counsel's own client. The first-hand accounts of what the passengers experienced in the moments leading up to the loss of helicopter control, and ultimately the crash, is information unattainable from any other source. Those accounts include the descriptions of the early phases of the flight and whether the initial flight was routine and otherwise without incident. Observations as to the movement and physical actions of the pilot also are useful. For example, an observation that she was struggling with the rudder pedals may be an indication of tail rotor control problems.

Surviving passengers may be able to pinpoint the first hint of a problem: whether it was actually communicated by the pilot or in the form of some erratic movement or loud noise. The experience of such passengers may lay the groundwork for a pre-impact terror claim on behalf of those who did not survive.

These witnesses should be deposed and their testimony preserved as early as is practicable because of the criticality of that testimony to both liability and damages issues as well as the fact that many helicopter crash victims are seriously injured and ultimately may not survive. The recovery rates of burn victims in particular are notoriously low given the risk of post-operative infections and other complications. Counsel must make every effort to obtain this critical testimony even if it requires setting up for the deposition in the witness's hospital room and taking breaks every 15-20 minutes under the bedside supervision of a physician.

F. Pilot and Co-Pilot

The pilot will be a party defendant in most cases. The pilot also may be the client bringing the action. Whether the pilot is the plaintiff, defendant or both as in some cases, the pilot's deposition must be taken. The testimony of the pilot should begin with a thorough exposition of qualifications and training especially in the subject helicopter type. Inquiry should be made about prior experience or problems with the subject helicopter. The same basic information should be elicited from the co-pilot , if one was involved.

The deposition testimony should include an in-depth step-by-step description of all of the pilot's actions from the moment she reported to duty on the day of the crash up to and through all post-crash activity. Where the pilot is the defendant it is useful to obtain agreement that as pilot-in-command of the helicopter she was at all times the individual with ultimate responsibility for maintaining operational control of the aircraft and providing for the safety of the crew and passengers.

G. Defendant Manufacturer's In-House Engineers and Employees

In aviation cases as well as products liability litigation generally, there is a debate about whether counsel should adopt a bottom up or top down approach to deposition discovery of the manufacturer. With a bottom-up approach, counsel begins with depositions of lower-level employees and ends with division or departmental supervisors or even officers. With a top down approach, counsel proceeds down the chain of command. The bottom-up approach in helicopter crash litigation is more effective and yields more compelling information. Counsel may inquire of these lower level employees not only what they know about the product but also if they know about internal memoranda or any other documents that were not produced in discovery. Counsel must pay particular attention to the directions and instructions given to such hands-on employees by their superiors and, particularly, what communications were relayed up the corporate ladder.

Following the completion of these depositions, counsel may move to the depositions of the corporation's designated agents or officers. These witnesses are official spokespersons for the corporate defendant and can bind the company by making admissions or statements against interest. These depositions are taken pursuant to Federal Rule 30(b)(6) or comparable state law procedure which require the defendant to designate the organization's designated agents on particular subject matters. The purpose of these depositions is to commit the helicopter aircraft, engine, system or component part manufacturer to what information that company knew about its product and when. Counsel can discover the existence of similar complaints and lawsuits, commit the defendant to particular safety policy directives and confirm knowledge of any design or manufacturing problems.

The only drawback of the designated witness deposition is that the defendants select and choose the witnesses. Defendants will call the most articulate, impressive and coachable witnesses. Hence, a helpful stratagem is to review the documents produced by defendant to pinpoint the names of particular employees who would appear from the content of the document to know about certain matters but who were not identified in defendant's answers to interrogatories. Defendants usually have good reason to keep these people hidden. Perhaps such witnesses resisted the routine coaching by defense counsel and were rejected for use as witnesses.

All discovery of fact witnesses and acquisition of all empirical records should be completed before undertaking the depositions of the defendant's personnel. Technical and crash-related data such as aircraft certification records, maintenance logbooks, and the basic engineering documentation must be secured, organized and analyzed before deposing any of these company employees. At that point there should be little guesswork remaining about the underlying facts of the crash, identity and use of the subject system or product and directions for use. Experience teaches that proceeding with these company depositions without first nailing down these specific facts relating to the crash is an invitation to disaster. If questions in these depositions are based on an inaccurate or ill-informed understanding of the helicopter or helicopter component part's use in a given circumstance, the depositions will be worthless. While there may be some disagreement about some of the underlying facts, these must be fully developed in the record so that counsel is not surprised later.

In advance of these depositions, if not prepared already, counsel should prepare a draft of the proposed jury instructions setting out the essential elements of liability as to each defendant. Defendants in these cases may dispute critical aspects of the plaintiff's prima facie case at trial unless these points are admitted by witnesses during deposition. Counsel may be so focused on obtaining proof of defect and otherwise establishing liability that lesser although important issues may be forgotten. This includes such matters as whether the defendant designed and manufactured the part, questions directed to the component part's "reasonably anticipated usage" or that the part reached the operator and was installed without substantial change in condition. These seemingly minor issues should be nailed down during these depositions to foreclose any evidentiary problem, or worse, a claimed submissibility challenge, at trial. The advantage of preparing these jury instructions and tracking their language with the defendant's witnesses is that counsel's focus will be on obtaining precise answers on the elements of required proof.

These depositions are often extremely technical and involve complex engineering principles such as hydraulics, metal fatigue or useful life calculations. It is beneficial in such cases to have an engineering consultant available to assist counsel during the deposition both with understanding responses and in suggesting formal questions. Such a consultant may be an assistant to one of counsel's primary testifying experts or one of the experts involved in the case who will not be testifying. Another objective of the depositions of defendant's in-house engineers is to explore the company's knowledge of safety-related concerns relative to the product, consideration of alternative and potentially safer designs, and notice of prior incidents or accidents where the company's product was implicated.

Sequentially, counsel should defer the designated agent depositions until all other individually named personnel and engineers are deposed. One of the reasons this is effective is because in any litigation there will be a learning curve and counsel will know much more about the defendant's product, the pertinent documentation and engineering procedures after completing the depositions of the individually named personnel. The golden opportunity presented by a designated agent's deposition should not be wasted as an educational experience.

Moreover, previously deposed engineers and employees of the company may be ignorant of basic information. One of the chief purposes of a designated agent deposition is to commit the defendant entity to certain knowledge about engineering and policy practices and to obtain a clear picture of what that defendant knew about the product and when.

In that these early depositions will be informational and true discovery depositions, counsel can be freer to seek explanatory answers not normally of the type presented to the jury. The depositions of the company's designated agents should be presented to the jury as evidence at trial. By saving this category of depositions for last, counsel also avoids a number of procedural objections or admissibility hurdles because that testimony is binding on the corporate defendant.

Following preliminary information about the witness and his employment background both prior to and with the defendant company, it is necessary to establish a common basis for communication. The best starting point is to agree on definitions of some basic helicopter aircraft terminology and the operation and function of the particular system or component under consideration. Counsel must directly confront witnesses with memoranda, engineering reports or correspondence generated by that witness or for whom the witness was identified as a recipient. The specific sequence of how these documents are presented to the witness is a matter of trial strategy. The most easily understood method is to use a chronological order starting with the early design, tracing through design modifications, showing early reports of incidents or field complaints and ultimately leading to considerations of product re-design or alteration of maintenance instructions. A key objective of these depositions is to

uncover knowledge that the company's engineers had safety or airworthiness concerns about the design or production of the component. That information can then be extrapolated and built upon by assessing the full extent of the defendant's knowledge of risk of an in-flight failure of the component and specifying those actions taken based on that knowledge. The inquiry may proceed along the following lines:

DEPOSITION OUTLINE OF DEFENDANT HELICOPTER COMPANY'S DESIGNATED CORPORATE REPRESENTATIVE

A. PRELIMINARY
1. Witness name and country, county and state of residence.
   a. By whom employed? Title and position?
   b. Understand that we represent the family of Jane Smith who was killed in the crash of a YOUR COMPANY helicopter on June 24, 2009 at Anytown, USA?
   c. Understand Mrs. Smith was a flight nurse aboard that helicopter?
2. Understand that you have been formally designated to speak on behalf of YOUR COMPANY on various subject matters?
   a. Are you reasonably knowledgeable about these subject matters?
   b. What steps have you taken to further inform yourself as to the subject matters set out in the deposition notice?
   c. What documents have you reviewed to prepare for this deposition?

B. WITNESS BACKGROUND
1. On how many occasions have you given testimony either in deposition or at trial on behalf of YOUR COMPANY?
   a. Current job duties and responsibilities?
   b. For how many years have you been the company's accident investigator?
2. I understand that you had previously occupied a similar role for another helicopter company?
   a. Were Senior Accident Investigator for Competition Helicopter?
   b. Graduated from Aviation University in 1984?
   c. You are not a trained A&P mechanic?
   d. How many aircrashes have you been involved in from an investigation standpoint?
   e. Training and experience in aircrash investigation?

C. YOUR COMPANY

1. Understand that you had a role in the investigation of this helicopter crash?
2. What is the business of YOUR COMPANY?
   a. Where is its principal place of business?
   b. How many employees does it have?
   c. Sell to every state in the U.S.?
3. Relationship to parent corporation of YOUR COMPANY?
4. Role of PARENT COMPANY?
   a. Designs and manufactures helicopters?
   b. Supply helicopters to YOUR COMPANY for sale within U.S.?
   c. Prepare maintenance manual?
   d. Prepare flight manual?

D. RESPONSIBILITY OF YOUR COMPANY
1. YOUR COMPANY sold the subject helicopter? (Title transferred from PARENT COMPANY?)
2. YOUR COMPANY supplied the subject helicopter?
3. Involvement in preparation and supply of maintenance manual?
   a. Supplied the very maintenance manual for the helicopter in this case?
   b. Input into proper maintenance?
   c. Input into particular parts to be examined and inspected?
   d. Input into appropriate language to be used?
   e. Rewriting or revising maintenance manual?
   f. Who reviews drafts of maintenance manual at YOUR COMPANY?
   g. Who supplies maintenance manual with aircraft sold by YOUR COMPANY?
   h. Who deals with FAA on regulatory and certification issues?
4. Involvement in flight manual or Pilot Operating Handbook or POH?
   a. What is a flight manual or POH?
   b. Supplied the very flight manual for the helicopter in this case?
   c. What is its significance with respect to operation of aircraft?
   d. What is role of YOUR COMPANY in supplying flight manual or POH with aircraft?
   e. Who prepares flight manual?
   f. Who supplies flight manual?
   g. Role of YOUR COMPANY in re-writing or revising flight manual?
5. As a matter of industry practice, does YOUR COMPANY accept responsibility for seeing that the helicopter is safe for its intended uses?

6. You would agree that YOUR COMPANY has more knowledge, information and experience as to the proper maintenance and inspection procedures of PARENT COMPANY aircraft than operators in this country to whom it sells the aircraft?
   a. More than mechanics? (Who cannot overhaul or look inside many of the systems and components.)
   b. More than aircraft owners?
   c. More than pilots?
7. Agree that it is important that YOUR COMPANY provide truthful and accurate information to owners, operators and pilots as to how to properly maintain and inspect the aircraft and its component parts?
   a. Agree that it is important to provide information to owners, operators, and pilots as to how to properly pilot that aircraft?—Especially under emergency conditions?
   b. Agree that it would be unsafe if YOUR COMPANY provided either inaccurate or insufficient information to aircraft operators, owners, or pilots as to how to operate a YOUR COMPANY helicopter in an emergency situation?
   c. Why would that be unsafe?

E. FAMILIAR WITH STATEMENT OF PARTY REPRESENTATIVE FORM
1. Sign a "party representative" form concerning the investigation of this particular crash?
2. How many of those do you suppose you have signed in your capacity as the "Accident Investigator" for an aircraft company?
   a. How many helicopter crash investigations have you been involved in where the system was examined as a possible factor?
   b. You are also an individual at YOUR COMPANY designated to coordinate and assist with respect to lawsuits, correct?
   c. Assist in providing documents, work with defense counsel, and give depositions?
3. Were you aware from early on in your investigation that there were lawsuits pending against your company alleging equipment and system malfunctions?
   a. Throughout this process while there were lawsuits pending you were the individual on behalf of YOUR COMPANY charged with dealing with the NTSB and also communicating with anyone inside your company with respect to providing information with respect to these lawsuits?

4. How many times been designated to testify on behalf of YOUR COMPANY?

5. Understand we did not ask for you, just give subjects we wanted a YOUR COMPANY witness to address?

6. You know that you were selected to testify by company or its counsel?

7. Consider that part of your job duties with company?

    a. Are you the "point person" for litigation involving helicopter crash lawsuits?

8. Gather information and documents for lawsuits?

9. Testify at trial?

10. Fair to say that in many of your investigations, you are aware that lawsuits either had been filed or would be filed with respect to the crash at issue?

    b. You also know that the factual findings of the NTSB are going to be important with respect to the lawsuit, don't you?

11. In all of your various crash investigations where YOUR COMPANY helicopters were suspected of either having equipment or systems failures which caused a helicopter crash, have you made an honest and diligent attempt to assess whether some aspect of the helicopter may have been faulty and caused the crash?

    a. Have you always made an honest effort to assess whether anything about a YOUR COMPANY helicopter played any role in killing someone as a result of a helicopter crash?

    b. The reason you would want to make any honest effort in this regard is that it would be extremely important that these companies would want to identify any recurrent problem, correct it, and hopefully prevent it from happening to other people, correct?

    c. And were taught that that is the sole purpose for investigating any aircraft accident to improve safety, correct?

12. Now in your other role as a "Liability Coordinator" for YOUR COMPANY, have you ever allowed your judgment to be swayed knowing that in all likelihood your company would be found liable if you concluded that a failed part or system contributed to a helicopter crash?

    a. To your knowledge, has YOUR COMPANY ever hired any outside expert for consulting purposes to evaluate the safety of this system?

13. Or propriety and accuracy of the flight manual?

14. Or propriety and accuracy of the maintenance manual?

    b. So then other than for lawsuits or litigation purposes, YOUR COMPANY to your knowledge has never retained any outside expert or consultant to conduct an independent safety evaluation?

    c. Would you agree with me that safety is something that should be independent of lawsuits and that you should not make safety decisions based solely upon whether a lawsuit is filed which might affect YOUR COMPANY?

    d. So are you aware of any prohibition in acting as a party representative to the NTSB investigation and also being involved on the legal side for your company?

15. Can you recall a single instance of a consultant on a safety issue being hired purely for reasons of safety and safety improvement that had absolutely nothing to do with a lawsuit in progress?

    a. The only reason YOUR COMPANY retains any consultants or experts is to assist in defending it once it sued, correct?

    b. Now in many of the accidents you investigate, if not all, the actions of the pilot are carefully scrutinized?

    c. Now what percentage of the time do you conclude that from a factual standpoint some action of the pilot caused or contributed to cause the crash?

    d. Do you take the position that every time a YOUR COMPANY'S helicopter crashes that that is necessarily the fault of the pilot?

16. Can you name one specific example where a YOUR COMPANY helicopter crashed which was not the fault of the pilot?

    a. Number of crashes involving YOUR COMPANY helicopter?

    b. How many times did you conclude that a part or system in a YOUR COMPANY helicopter failed?

F. SPECIFIC ROLE IN INVESTIGATION

1. What was nature of your involvement in the investigation of this helicopter crash?

    a. On scene?

    b. Work with the IIC in this case previously?

2. Provide information to NTSB?

G. SIMILAR LAWSUITS AND CRASHES

1. You are aware that this is not the first helicopter crash where some aspect of the [component or system] has been implicated as a cause of the crash?

2. You know that in the discovery process, we requested information on similar crashes?

3. Were you involved in the preparation of that response?

4. You agree that there would have to be a number of factors in order for another crash to be judged reasonably or substantially similar to this one?

5. What would be some of those factors?

H. ALTERNATIVE CAUSES

1. Purpose of your investigation was to assist in providing facts to NTSB for the investigation?

   a. Another purpose to point out facts which you think might absolve your company from any responsibility?

   b. If you frequently pointed out to NTSB facts which implicated company, how would you have this job?

2. Satisfied with accuracy and completeness of Final Factual Report prepared by NTSB?

   a. Ever express to IIC in writing that you did not agree with aspect of that factual report?

   b. Ever express in conversation?

A critical safety engineering function within the aviation industry is to identify any risk of an in-flight failure of an airframe, engine, or component part. As to any particular component part the precise failure mode may not be predictable by computer analysis, in-house testing or even pre-FAA certification testing. This is why the actual environment of use must be considered by the manufacturer; and documentation in the form of service difficulty reports, warranty claims, accidents or incidents, and even lawsuits constitute notice to the manufacturer of a suspect airworthiness problem.

Within the helicopter industry, a component part manufacturer is not permitted to stick its head in the sand and blindly ignore how its helicopters or parts function in the real world. The standard of care requires that there exists some mechanism for field feedback to assist ongoing developmental engineering. This includes company receipt and review of service difficulty reports and warranty claims. Responses range from a redesign of the particular component or system to issuance of a service letter or service bulletin all the way to the FAA-sanctioned airworthiness directive. Counsel should explore which of the alternatives were considered and why the particular course of action was selected.

In most instances, witnesses quibble as to the probability of product failure whether it be an engine, swashplate, or even avionics. Notwithstanding that common dispute, counsel must always seek to obtain agreement that the severity of an in-flight failure of that particular component or system under particular flight conditions creates a serious hazard resulting in a high prospect of helicopter loss of control or crash. Counsel should elicit testimony that the likely result of an in-flight failure of the subject component is loss of control of the helicopter with resultant uncontrolled impact and severe injuries or death to the occupants. The means by which the defendant company sought to acquire or document this type of information is illustrative. In-house engineering studies and their results may confirm that any failure of the part during the conditions faced by the pilot or similar conditions will result in a serious control problem.

Other examples of field use data about which these witnesses should be asked include customer complaints, warranty reports, lawsuits and claims. It is a violation of the Federal Aviation Regulations to ignore such field use feedback or to fail to timely report it.

In these depositions, counsel also should focus on alternative designs considered that may have eliminated the particular hazard at issue. If cost was a factor in the design or materials selection, the precise cost per item should be discovered and confirmed. If the component was given a longer time between overhaul (TBO) than competitor components, the reason may have been marketing attractiveness and false claims of efficiency. Counsel may examine the tradeoff of higher sales against lower safety which a jury normally reacts to with some degree of disfavor.

Communications between the FAA and the product manufacturer as to any ongoing safety issues are highly revealing. In most instances the manufacturer is resisting taking any corrective action even if it means issuance of a service letter to all owners or operators of the helicopter or component. Failure to take appropriate safety-related actions in the face of clear knowledge of a recurring problem may form the basis for the submission of a punitive damages claim to the jury.

These marketing and cost issues are often injected into the design process by corporate management. There exists an inherent tension and competition between the engineering, research and development arm of the company and the marketing and sales departments. Tapping into this tension and exposing that the true decision was based on marketing and cost considerations, and not customer safety, will be of immense interest to the jury who will find such decisions disdainful.

H. Remaining Defendants

The depositions of all defendants must be completed before presenting plaintiff's liability experts for deposition.

Whether that defendant is the helicopter operator or the U.S. subsidiary of a foreign helicopter manufacturer, permitting plaintiff's liability experts to be deposed ahead of them is a tactical error. In many respects, the expert's opinions will be based on assumptions as to what the defendant may testify to in deposition. Those depositions must be completed first to avoid the potential for the defense to discredit plaintiff's expert at trial by correcting her false assumptions.

I. Plaintiff's Deposition

In most cases the plaintiffs are those surviving family members of a relative killed in the helicopter accident. Defendants habitually will depose each such plaintiff and the focus will be on the amount of any financial dependency and the nature and extent of the familial relationship. In those instances where the plaintiff is the injured pilot or passenger, the same principles of preparation apply. Counsel can never meet with these clients on the morning of the deposition and give a perfunctory admonition to "just tell the truth." Defendants in these cases have a specific game plan. They will either seek to blame the victim who was foolhardy enough to climb into one of their helicopters or a helicopter equipped with one of its engines or component parts. Alternatively, they will inquire extensively of family members whether the deceased had any fears, misgivings, or other indicia of risk prior to the subject flight. Defendants will inquire of every plaintiff as to his criminal background, lawsuit history, and known future employment plans of the deceased or injured plaintiffs such as whether he contemplated early retirement.

Counsel must thoroughly and carefully prepare all plaintiffs for their deposition with at least one if not two preparatory conferences. Included within that preparation should be a hard-hitting practice session with counsel or a colleague playing the role of the defense lawyer. As part of that deposition preparation, the following points should be reviewed with the client.

1. The Defense Lawyer is Not Your Friend

No matter how pleasant or congenial the defense lawyers may be, remember that they are paid mercenaries with one goal in mind: to defeat the plaintiff's case and minimize any damages payable by the helicopter companies.

2. Never Volunteer

Answer only the question asked, never any more. Never try to be helpful. If the question can be answered with a simple yes or no, do so. Let the lawyer ask the follow-up question if she wants a more complete answer. That is the lawyer's job. However, do not be evasive. Just answer the question, and stop there.

3. Make Sure You Understand the Question

Wait to hear the entire question, and think it over in your mind to make absolutely sure you understand it. If you are not sure you heard the question or understood it thoroughly, ask the lawyer to repeat it or rephrase it. Make sure the question is precise enough so that your answer cannot later be twisted out of context.

4. Take Time to Think Before Answering

Never answer before the lawyer finishes the question. Take a moment to replay the question in your mind, and consider carefully the question and then your answer before you give your answer. Do not let a fast-paced lawyer's questioning speed up your answering process.

5. Never Guess

Never, never guess in giving an answer. If you don't know, say you don't know. If you think you may know, it is acceptable to give an answer but be sure that you qualify your answer by saying that you are not sure.

6. Remember That Sometimes You Can't Remember

No one can remember everything. There is nothing wrong with not remembering, although the other attorney might try to make you feel guilty or stupid for not remembering. If you do not remember, simply say that you do not remember and hold fast. It is dangerous to do otherwise.

7. Never Lose Your Temper

Some defense lawyers will intentionally try to make you lose your temper, in hopes that they will get you to say things favorable to their side. If you recognize that the other attorney may be trying to get you mad just for this purpose, you can avoid losing your temper.

8. Be Polite But Firm

Say "yes sir" or "yes ma'am" as much as possible. This will make for a good record. However, politeness and good manners should never mean backing away from the truth. Be polite but firm.

9. Speak Your Answers

The court reporter cannot pick up nodding, grunting, or gestures. Remember this throughout the deposition.

10. Never Exaggerate

Neither overdramatize nor downplay your answers. Communicate accurately and truthfully.

11. Always Finish Your Answer

Often, a defense lawyer will try to cut off your answer for strategic purposes. If opposing counsel interrupt you before you are finished, tell the opposing lawyer, politely but firmly, that you were not finished. Your attorney will help insure that you are allowed to finish. It is effective to begin the continuation of your answer with, "As I was saying before the interruption."

12. Feel Free To Correct Your Answer

If, during the deposition, you recall or realize that a previous answer was incorrect, say so. It is far better to correct your answer during the deposition than to be impeached with an incorrect answer later at trial.

13. Do Not Fall for the Opposing Lawyer's Act

If defense lawyers feel that they can obtain better answers from you by playing games, they will try. A lawyer may try to be mean, rude, demeaning, or insulting or, on the other hand, sweet, sympathetic, and concerned, or even flustered, disorganized, or confused. Ignore these tactics, and keep alert.

14. Never Assume False Events

Many a lawyer will attempt to lead you down a slippery slope by getting you to assume things that are not true. If a lawyer asks you to assume that day is night or that night is day, refuse to do so. Often, a lawyer may say, "Please assume with me just for the sake of argument." No matter what excuses are given or promises made, you may refuse to assume something which you know is not true or you are not sure is true. This can only lead to trouble. One option is to respond, "I'm sorry, I just can't assume anything unless I know it to be true."

15. Amount of Money in Prayer

Often, the opposing attorney will try to get you to justify or reject the amount of money plead in the petition. Refuse to play this game. One of our clients said it the best: "No amount of money can compensate for what I have been through."

16. Remember You Are Not a Doctor

Often, a defense attorney will try to induce non-medical witnesses to give medical explanations or opinions. Only describe how symptoms feel or appear. Otherwise, an available answer simply may be, "I'm sorry, I'm not a doctor, so I just can't say." There will be plenty of other medical doctors in the case to answer medical questions, and opposing counsel are aware of this.

17. Do Not Back Yourself Into a Corner

Often, a lawyer will try to have you compile a complete list of some aspect of the case such as physical symptoms or ways you miss the deceased. Doing so could put you in a bind should you think of other items before or during trial. When a lawyer asks the magic question "Is that all and can you think of anything else?," you may always qualify your answer. It is acceptable to say that this is all you can think of right now, but that you are confident there are other items.

18. Appearance

The usual attire for a deposition is as it would be at church when at your Sunday best. A plaintiff should not wear anything flashy, showy, or that could offend the jury. Conservative and neat are the catch words. Also, sit up straight throughout the deposition. Look your interrogator in the eye, but do not make it a staring contest.

19. Review Complaint

Before your deposition, review the complaint so that you are familiar with the basic allegations therein.

20. Do Not Be Afraid to Cast Blame

Typically, the opposing lawyer will indignantly assert that you simply could not be saying that X, Y, or Z was negligent. Do not back off. Feel free to place criticism where it belongs.

21. Do Not Blame Yourself

The opposing lawyer will typically try to get you to take part of the blame or responsibility yourself. Do not fall into this trap. This is not the time to be modest or gracious. Remember, you did nothing wrong.

22. Do Not Let Fast Questions Yield Fast Answers

The opposing attorney is used to asking questions. Often, they will ask their questions very quickly in an effort to get you to answer quickly, hoping that your mouth will move before your brain does. Be prepared for this. Do not let fast-paced questioning speed up your answering.

5.4 Expert Depositions

Most helicopter crash litigation will be governed by the terms of a court-imposed discovery scheduling order. That scheduling order should provide that plaintiff need not produce liability experts for deposition until the completion of all defendants' depositions. It is imperative that plaintiff's liability experts have the benefit of reviewing both the documents obtained from the defendant during discovery and the deposition transcripts of the defendant's employees and other agents before giving their final opinions on liability and causation.

Most jurisdictions require a fairly extensive disclosure as to the opinions to be expressed by the expert at trial either in response to interrogatories or as part of a case management order. For that reason, counsel must go over each and every opinion with that expert and make certain that the pre-deposition disclosure is timely filed and fully encompasses all opinions to be expressed at trial. An example of such a disclosure from an engineering expert in a recent helicopter action is as follows:

Dr. Jones will testify at trial as to the following opinions:

1. That the subject helicopter was in an unsafe and dangerous condition on the date of the crash for reasons which were known or should have been known to Defendants;

2. That there were technological and economically feasible design alternatives which would address the specific hazards and dangers which caused the helicopter to crash;

3. That the helicopter crash sequence was reasonably predictable and foreseeable to Defendants and that each failed to take proper action to address these known dangers;

4. Defendants failed to use reasonable care to see that the helicopter was safe for the use for which it was made;

5. That this failure to use reasonable care was a proximate cause of the helicopter crash and the damages to Plaintiffs;

6. That Defendants knew or had reason to know that their helicopter was likely to be dangerous when put to the use for which it was sold;

7. That Defendants failed to provide reasonably foreseeable users of their helicopter with adequate warnings of the danger and proper instructions for use;

8. That Defendants knew or should have known that the tail rotor accumulator would be used without inspection;

9. That Defendants, as the manufacturer of the subject helicopter, placed the helicopter on the market knowing that it was to be used without inspection for defects and proved to have a defect which caused the helicopter to crash resulting in the wrongful deaths and the subsequent damages to Plaintiffs;

10. That the defective and unreasonably dangerous condition of the tail rotor accumulator of the subject helicopter existed when the product left Defendants' control as well as the other defective and unreasonably dangerous matters as further set out in the attached report;

11. That the helicopter and its various components and systems as more fully delineated in the attached report was defective in design in that they failed to perform as safely as an ordinary consumer would expect when the helicopter and its components were used in the manner either intended by the manufacturer or reasonably foreseeable by the manufacturer;

12. That the helicopter including its various system and components as more fully delineated in the attached report, was accompanied by insufficient warnings and insufficient instructions on use in that these warnings and instructions did not properly inform of the risks of harm and were not readily recognizable by an ordinary user while using the helicopter or any of its components or systems in a manner reasonably foreseeable by the manufacturer and that these insufficient instructions and insufficient warnings expressly relate to the flight manual, instruction manual, and maintenance manual which accompanied the subject helicopter as more fully delineated in the attached report;

13. That the flight instructions for proper emergency procedures in the helicopter fight manual were insufficient for the reasons further delineated in the attached report, which had the effect of rendering the helicopter defective and unreasonably dangerous;

14. That the instructions on use and maintenance as delineated in the maintenance manual were insufficient as further delineated in the attached report which rendered the helicopter defective and unreasonably dangerous;

15. That the pilot was properly qualified and trained to operate the subject helicopter and, further, that the pilot operated the subject helicopter at all times in conformity with that degree of skill and learning ordinarily used by other pilots under same or similar circumstances including, to wit, that the pilot followed all applicable flight procedures and maneuvers set out in the flight manual and, otherwise, performed within the operating standard of care of an ordinarily careful and prudent helicopter pilot;

16. That all of the manufacturer's specified maintenance procedures and inspections were timely and properly performed in the maintenance facility and

that no maintenance discrepancies existed on the subject helicopter;

17. That the negligence, breach of duty, and omissions by Defendants, and each of them, as further delineated in the attached report, was a proximate cause of the helicopter crash and of the death of each occupant thereof;

18. That Defendants knew and should have known within the aviation industry standard of care of the exhaustive field reports in the form of service difficulty reports, field literature, and accident reports of the failure history of accumulators and the necessity of placing a life limit on these components as demonstrated, in part, by the publicly available documents addressing these issues which were equally and easily available to Defendants;

19. That Defendants knew or should have known of an inordinately high number of helicopter crashes with common factors which are substantially similar to the subject helicopter crash including, but not limited to NTSB ID numbers: LAX91LA034, CHI93FA249, MIA95LA131, FTW99LA048, IAD99GA056, LAX01LA083, LAX02FA281, FTW01LA121, and LAX00FA136;

20. That there are an extraordinarily high number of service difficulty reports (SDR's), Federal Administration Accident/Incident Reports, Canadian TSB reports, accident/incident reports from other countries, and NTSB accident/incident summaries which reference comparable component and system failure and of which Defendants knew or should have known as part of their responsibility as a seller and manufacturer of helicopter and helicopter products based on the standard of care within the aviation industry;

21. That there are a number of other helicopters, helicopter control systems, and related components which have been and are currently in the marketplace which are comparable in operation and function to the subject model of helicopter but which do not have the unsafe and dangerous design, characteristics and features associated with and found in the helicopter;

22. That there are a number of other maintenance manuals, instruction manuals, and helicopter flight manuals which have been and are currently in use with other helicopters which provide safe, sufficient, and adequate instructions and which render the helicopter safe for its intended usages;

23. That there exist technologically and economically feasible measures to address the safety hazards and risks described herein and in the attached report, which measures were known or reasonably available to Defendants at the time this particular helicopter was designed, manufactured, and sold;

24. That the Defendants have no reasonable justification or excuse for many of the design, manufacturing, instructional aspects whether in maintenance, instruction, or flight manual associated with the subject model helicopter for failing to address the specific hazards and dangers further identified herein;

25. That the quantum and quality of mistakes, errors and inadequacies reflect a structural and organizational recklessness and irresponsibility towards safety which can be presumed to be with full knowledge of the consequences and intentional;

26. That the quantum and seriousness of the lapses of judgment demonstrated by Defendants with respect to the lack of safety measures and known dangers in its AS350 helicopter demonstrate an utter disregard for the safety of operators, occupants, users, and others who would fly in this type of helicopter given the unacceptable degree of risk and danger;

27. That Defendants should take immediate steps in whatever manner necessary and appropriate to remedy the specific safety concerns and issues addressed herein so as to prevent precisely this type of accident sequence from transpiring in the future and causing further destruction of lives including the consideration of, but not limited to, the following: immediate grounding of the aircraft, immediate issuance of service advisories and service bulletins addressing the precise issues described herein, and the immediate revision of the maintenance, instruction, and flight manual to address those precise issues addressed herein; and

28. That the above and foregoing opinions are based upon his education, training, and experience, as further set out in his Curriculum Vitae (attached hereto as *"Exhibit X"*), which also contains a listing of all publications authored by Dr. Jones which contain any discussion of concepts which will be used in expressing the opinions reached in this case.

All of the information discovered during document production, pertinent interrogatories, and all deposition transcripts should be given to the liability experts before the deposition. If additional or different underlying facts reach experts after the deposition, the opinions given may be incomplete, or even worse, erroneous. This leads to complications, not the least of which is having to offer up the liability expert again to revise or bolster the earlier opinions. That is likely to be a discrediting factor for that expert's trial testimony.

The other sequential imperative is that all of the on-scene or crash witnesses' depositions must be completed before the depositions of plaintiff's liability experts. Otherwise, if there are versions of the helicopter crash sequence testified to by on-scene witnesses which differ materially from those either assumed by or concluded by the expert, the expert's opinion is rendered suspect.

A. Preparing Plaintiff's Experts

The depositions of plaintiff's experts in all respects should be considered literally a trial run in preparation for the main event which is the trial. The expert must be fully prepared, familiar with the critical documents, and able to present final and complete opinions. In those jurisdictions where a written report in some form is required, the scope and contents of that report should be discussed well in advance of the deposition. The report should include a full listing of all opinions and the factual bases in arriving at those opinions in addition to a complete listing of all materials reviewed upon which the opinions are based.

Even in those jurisdictions which do not require the preparation and exchange of an expert report, counsel should ask the liability expert to prepare a summary list of every opinion in the case. That list should be made available to defendants at the time of the deposition. The expert should be asked to bring to the deposition all materials reviewed and which otherwise support the opinions to be expressed even though these may not have been requested by defendant. The list of opinions may be as simply set forth as an outline form.

Many well-experienced aviation experts prepare an opinion notebook. That notebook has a listing of all opinions separately stated and number tabbed. Behind each tab are specific documents, deposition excerpts, photographs or testing which support that opinion. As there tends to be voluminous documents and depositions in these cases, organizing the opinions and supporting data in that fashion is useful as well as time efficient.

All of the ordinary rules for presenting the expert at deposition in complex personal injury or products liability cases are squarely applicable in helicopter crash lawsuits. These include the time-valued axioms such as be truthful in every respect and be certain to understand the question. Counsel should take great care during the deposition not to permit the defense to stretch or otherwise induce the expert to wade into areas for which he is not qualified to render an opinion. In many helicopter crashes, the liability experts are interrogated at great length as to alternative crash scenarios and explanations for the in-flight loss of control of the aircraft. These inquiries are intended to depict the expert as indecisive. The expert should be reminded that any aviation accident reconstruction requires a full development of alternative causal factors and the systematic ruling out of each.

B. Deposing Defendant's Experts

There is a school of thought that says counsel should forego deposing defense liability experts either because they have been deposed countless times before or because the line of questions are intended to be a surprise at the time of trial. In virtually all jurisdictions where expert depositions are permitted, neither of these factors warrants dispensing with the opportunity to discover the defense expert's opinions prior to trial. This is also an opportunity to confirm that the defense experts have not received any documentation or data from any source not previously disclosed to the plaintiff and made available to the plaintiff's own experts.

While every experienced helicopter crash lawyer has developed a comprehensive outline for taking a defense expert's deposition, they all have identical objectives:

1. Commit the defense expert to whatever opinions are expressed and are final at the time of the deposition;
2. Obtain those admissions and concessions concerning plaintiff's theory of the case as are obtainable;
3. Highlight undisputed facts supportive of plaintiff's theory of the case and which are inconsistent with the defense expert's opinions; and
4. Obtain from the defense expert an alternative explanation of the helicopter crash.

While some aviation lawyers preach holding back on some avenues of inquiry and saving certain matters for trial, defense experts as a rule are savvy enough that no true surprise or tactical advantage emerges from that approach. It may backfire if counsel are not fully apprised of the scope of opinions or grounds for certain opinions to be presented by the defense expert. For this reason, objective one remains to delineate all of the specific opinions and basis for those opinions which the defense expert intends to present at trial.

A sample outline of subjects to be covered in the deposition of a defense liability expert is as follows:

SAMPLE DEPOSITION OUTLINE OF HELICOPTER MANUFACTURER'S DEFENSE LIABILITY EXPERT

A. Witness Name and General Background Information
1. Start out by briefly reviewing your background and some of the things you have looked at in forming your expert opinions in this case?
2. Bring a current curriculum vitae with you?
    a. Current and up to date to the best of your knowledge?
    b. Accurate and truthful to the best of your knowledge?
    c. When was last time you revised your CV?
    d. Rely on anyone other than yourself for preparing the CV?
    e. This CV has been presented to courts and juries for purposes of evaluating your professional qualifications?
    f. How many times in last 5 years?
3. Accurately set forth your education, work experience, professional associations and memberships?
B. Basic Engineering Principles
1. The selection of materials is an important aspect of design engineering.
    a. A product manufacturer should know and understand the environment of use of its product.
    b. The extent of degradation of any material directly impacts its safe useful life.
    c. The manufacturer of any product should select a design criteria which minimizes the risk of harm for the ordinarily foreseeable user.
    d. A product is unreasonably dangerous if it creates a risk of harm beyond that which would be contemplated by the ordinary foreseeable user.
    e. A product is defective in its design if it fails to perform as safely as an ordinary consumer would expect when it is used in a manner either intended by the manufacturer or reasonably foreseeable by the manufacturer.
2. Manufacturer Guidelines
    a. Understand what is meant by "shelf life" of a product?
    b. What is meant by "useful safe life" of a product?
    c. Does any aircraft component have longer "useful safe life" than a "shelf life?"
    d. Agree that at least for aircraft components, "useful safe life" or time the product safely functions in actual use will be less than the safe storage or "shelf life"?
    e. Know who manufacturers the subject product?
    f. Ever consulted with any aircraft manufacturer other than for lawsuit or litigation-related purposes?
    g. Ever serve as an employee for any helicopter manufacturer?
    h. Ever work for any helicopter operator?
    i. Have you testified as an expert in lawsuits concerning products outside the aviation field?
3. Within the last ten years how many times have you testified that a product was unreasonably dangerous and unsafe in its design?
4. Identify product and incident.
C. Talk specifically about your experience within aviation field?
1. Are you or have you ever been a helicopter pilot?
    a. Ever received any flight training in a helicopter?
    b. Ever been a pilot of an airplane?
    c. Ever received any flight training in an airplane?
    d. Do you hold yourself out as an expert on how to fly a helicopter?
2. Ever received any training as an aircraft mechanic?
    a. Ever been licensed or certified as an aircraft mechanic?
    b. Ever hold an aircraft and power plant license?
    c. Ever been authorized by FAA to maintain any aircraft?
    d. Have you ever maintained any aircraft of any type?
    e. You do not hold yourself out as an expert or one having any expertise in maintenance on an aircraft, true?
3. Ever work for any governmental agency as an aircrash accident investigator?
    a. Ever attended any classes or coursework on aircrash accident investigation?
    b. Ever attended any seminars or programs on aircrash accident investigation?
    c. Currently a member of any aircrash accident investigation organizations or associations?
    d. Consider yourself to be an aeronautical and mechanical engineer and not an accident investigator per say?
    e. Familiar with any aircrash accident investigation treatises or textbooks?

f.   Own any?

g.   Studied any of them?

h.   Agree that there are many possible contributing factors to a helicopter crash?

4.   Can you identify what some of the most common contributing factors of a helicopter crash are?

5.   List the most common contributing factors (e.g., maintenance, weather, ATC, pilot error, component or system failure, engine failure).

6.   Any indication of engine failure in this case?

7.   Not an ATC-type matter is it, sir?

8.   Agree that a helicopter crash accident investigation, conducted properly, assesses all relevant factors in determining the cause of an aircrash?

a.   Ever worked on any helicopter crash case where some malfunctioning component or control system was a contributing factor to the helicopter crash?

9.   Ever worked on any aviation case where a malfunctioning component or a malfunctioning control system or even an engine problem contributed to the aircrash as a factor?

10. Fair to say you reviewed some of the factors which may or may not have been involved in this helicopter crash?

a.   Looked at maintenance?

b.   Looked at the pilot's actions?

c.   Looked at the overall design of the tail rotor control system?

d.   What are some of the contributing causal factors to this helicopter crash?

e.   Any other potential factors from your perspective?

D.   Review portions of NTSB report?

E.   Prior experience with this helicopter defendant?

1.   How many times help defend this company?

2.   How many current helicopter matters handling?

3.   Ever testify that any component or system of any type was improperly designed in a helicopter?

F.   Opinions to be presented at trial

1.   Review each and every opinion listed in expert's designation.

2.   What are the factual bases for each opinion?

3.   Performed any testing or analysis to support any opinion?

4.   What other specific steps taken to prepare for deposition testimony?

5.   Ever worked on any aircrash case where there was a confirmed malfunction of any component or system?

6.   Agree that in assessing any pilot's performance, would need to know whether that pilot experienced an in-flight malfunction or failure of a critical control system?

5.5 Common Discovery Issues

There are frequently encountered in helicopter crash litigation some unique discovery challenges, whether that involves deposing witnesses in other countries or obtaining information from the U.S. military where one of their aircraft has been involved in an accident.

A. Conducting Discovery in Foreign Countries

Given that fully one-half of all helicopters in this country are foreign-made as are most of the helicopter engines and various component parts and systems, counsel must become adept at performing discovery in foreign lands. Discovery involving foreign defendants requires special considerations. Counsel must determine whether that foreign defendant or product manufacturer is a necessary defendant in the lawsuit. In view of the time, expense and effort involved in pursuing discovery against a foreign defendant, counsel must consider whether essential discovery may be obtained from U.S. defendants alone.

If the foreign manufacturer is a peripheral or nominal defendant or if it has a design and manufacturing presence in the United States as does virtually every helicopter aircraft manufacturer or component part maker, counsel must consider whether that discovery is truly essential to the case. In those instances where the helicopter crash was clearly caused by a product or action of the foreign defendant and there are no other defendants, then discovery must proceed against the foreign manufacturer. Even those instances where the U.S. subsidiary is named as a defendant, prudent practice dictates that the foreign parent company be named where its product is implicated. If the product's primary design and engineering specifications were formulated at the company's foreign headquarters then that information will not be easily accessible at the offices of the U.S. subsidiary. Most U.S. subsidiaries will not have access to or possess developmental engineering, early design drawings or other technical manufacturing data. All of the original testing, whether computer-simulated or actual flight testing, will remain with the foreign parent company. Also, the U.S. subsidiaries rarely will have access to field data or reports of other substantially similar incidents or accidents involving use of the helicopter or helicopter component outside the United States.

The formal method of taking evidence abroad is under the terms of the Hague Convention on the Taking of Evidence

Abroad in Civil or Commercial Matters (Evidence Convention).[4] Terms of the Evidence Convention are complicated, cumbersome and essentially require that all requests for evidence go through the foreign country's state department. Fortunately, once a U.S. court has established that it has personal jurisdiction over the foreign defendant, the overwhelming majority of courts have ruled that the defendant must comply with U.S. discovery procedures irrespective of whether the documents or witnesses are located in a foreign country.

Many countries, including Japan and Germany, consider discovery an interference with their sovereign powers. In several countries, it is a crime to be involved in "voluntary disclosure" of information in aid of the U.S. civil litigation process.[5] Consequently, discovery proceedings including document productions or depositions should be initiated only after securing an order from the U.S. court. The best course of action is to arrange for the depositions on U.S. soil, if at all possible.

If the foreign helicopter defendant provides the requested documents, usually only by court order, these are often in the language of the foreign country. This is so even if the defendant has translated the documents into English for its U.S. defense counsel. Plaintiff's counsel should ask the defendant whether the documents have been translated into English and, with the court's assistance if necessary, acquire the translated versions. But some word of caution is needed. These translations may strongly favor the defendant's liability position and should be independently reviewed by plaintiff counsel's own translator. If the documents are not already translated, plaintiff's counsel must of necessity hire a translator.

Often, plaintiff's counsel will have to go to the foreign country to review the documents because there are so many in number that it would be too burdensome to ship them to the United States or so the defendant claims. To assist in the document review process, counsel must bring along at least one if not several proficient translators. A good source for these translators is engineering schools which often enroll students who are native to foreign countries and who understand the engineering terminology.

All documents used during depositions should be translated well ahead of the deposition date. There is nothing that can unravel a deposition more quickly than disagreement over the meaning of particular words in a translated document. Plaintiff's lawyers should forward these translated documents to defense counsel with the request to bring to plaintiff counsel's attention any objections to or discrepancies found in the translations for possible resolution by the court. Defense counsel then will be hard pressed later to argue that a document's offered translation was incorrect.

Key documents should be shown to the person who will translate the deposition testimony in advance. This allows the translator to become familiar with engineering or other technical terms that may be used during the deposition which can help to avoid disagreement about the proper translation of those terms.

Courts are increasingly requiring foreign defendants to produce key witnesses in the United States especially if the plaintiff agrees to share in the expense. This is good news given how expensive and difficult it is to transport the entire legal staff, documents and materials, court reporter, video technician and translator needed for deposing witnesses in a foreign country. Even when the deposition is conducted in the U.S. and the translator is competent and accurate, the prospects of obtaining useful information from a witness are hampered by the translation procedure. The plaintiff's lawyer asks the question in English which the translator repeats in the witness's native language.

The defense lawyer raises any objection to the question in English. The objection must then also be translated into the witness's language, a step which really should not be necessary because it is intended only to coach the witness. The witness answers the question in the foreign language and the translator translates that answer into English. It often takes ten to fifteen minutes to get an answer to a simple question.

Consequently, plaintiff's counsel must keep questions short and to the point. A long and rambling question especially with these translation difficulties often yields a like response. Some ground rules should be established before the deposition. First and foremost, the parties should agree that only one translator will be present. This will avoid a battle of the translators during the deposition. Anyone who has experienced this frustrating exercise knows these battles can be interminable.

If the parties cannot agree on an official translator for the deposition, the court should be asked to select one for them. Allowing the defendant to choose a translator creates a great risk that the witness's answers will be translated in a form that is either favorable to the defendant's position or wholly indecipherable and nonsensical. Another alternative is to use a translator selected by the defendant and have another translator present to ensure that the official translations are accurate. If plaintiff's counsel has to use a translator selected by the defendant, then a backup translator is essential to ensure that the translations are accurate. In that case, avoiding the battle of the translators may be impossible. It is a mistake to rely solely on the defendant's translator.

For example, during the deposition of a French executive in one helicopter crash lawsuit, an issue arose regarding the English translation of the French word *defaut*. The word had been used frequently in the French company's internal documents to describe the helicopter engine's failure mechanism. The witness testified that a defaut was simply a "problem." An official French-English language dictionary was produced that indicated the word was synonymous with the English word "defect."

Given the difficulty of securing the attendance of witnesses, it is established practice to videotape the depositions of all foreign witnesses whether taken in the U.S. or abroad. This preserves the option at trial of either reading the deposition transcript or playing edited videotape deposition testimony. Sometimes costs can be minimized by videoconferencing by stipulation. If counsel are comfortable and experienced with that procedure, then by all means. In all such cases using videoconference for the deposition, plaintiff's counsel should have an observer present in the room where the deposition is being taken.

An issue that arises with great frequency is whether an executive or an engineering witness of a foreign defendant should be compelled to give testimony in English if the witness is fluent in English. Some courts have so held. Any objections to the translation of deposition testimony must be addressed well in advance of trial. The witness's signing of the deposition should be taken as a waiver of any translation disputes. Plaintiff's counsel simply cannot permit any aspect of the trial to degenerate into an unseemly dispute concerning the correct translation of certain words in either a document or a deposition.

The process of obtaining discovery from foreign product manufacturers although tedious and cumbersome is critical in these cases and often yields positive results. If the foreign helicopter or component part manufacturer is the only entity that can produce all relevant engineering and field data by either documentation or testimony of evidence then it must be named as a party defendant, and that requires following through on the essential discovery.

B. Utilizing Freedom of Information Act Requests

The helicopter industry is a federally regulated activity, so discovery from the federal government ranging from original aircraft certification documentation to current aircraft registration records are obtainable only by means of a Freedom of Information Act (FOIA) request. A wealth of material may be obtained by use of a FOIA request much of which may not voluntarily be produced by defendants in helicopter crash lawsuits.

FOIA is the federal law that sets out the public's right to receive certain information from federal government agencies.[6] Under the provision of the Act "any person" can file a FOIA request and the procedure is relatively simple and straightforward. The letter must be written to the particular agency responsible for collecting and maintaining the information and should include:

1. A declaration that this request is made under the provisions of the Freedom of Information Act (FOIA). The subject line should also include that this matter involves a "Freedom of Information Act Request";
2. A description of the documentation requested;
3. A request that a response be forthcoming promptly but no later than the customary twenty-day statutory time period; and
4. That should any material be withheld for any reason a request is made to provide "reasonably segregable portions" of such documents which may be extensively redacted and an indication that a timely administrative appeal would be filed.

Given the time expended and the customary cooperativeness of the FAA and related agencies, it is recommended that fee waivers in such instances not be requested and that counsel indicate a willingness to pay for the reasonable fees associated with the request. A sample FOIA request is attached in Appendix A.

Under the terms of FOIA, records obtainable which may bear on any helicopter crash include the following:

1. Official U.S. weather reports for the time and location of the crash;
2. Radar tracking information for the time and location of the crash;
3. FAA airworthiness and certification documents;
4. FAA certification of the helicopter model at issue;
5. FAA airworthiness directives for that model helicopter;
6. FAA Service Difficulty Reports (SDRs) for that model of helicopter;
7. FAA pilot medical records;
8. FAA pilot certification records;
9. FAA aircraft registration and title records; and
10. Air Traffic Control (ATC) package that includes transcript of ATC audiotape, reports, and witness statements. Actual audiocassette must be specifically requested.

There are certain categories of information that are not provided and these include national security material, governmental trade secrets or the results of ongoing law enforcement investigations. Another advantage of utilizing the FOIA for discovery is that it is a means to obtain information without having to disclose to the defendant that the material has been requested and obtained. In terms of discovery procedures, it is one of the most efficient and effective means of obtaining basic information in any helicopter accident litigation.

Counsel should not dispense with a FOIA request simply because the helicopter or part manufacturer is foreign. Foreign helicopter manufacturers are required to apply for U.S. airworthiness certificates for helicopters operated in the U.S. The FAA maintains a certification branch in Europe (currently in Brussels), and inquiries as to aircraft design and certification by any foreign manufacturer are directed to that foreign branch. Knowledge of the availability of this procedure is very useful in obtaining discovery in cases involving foreign helicopter manufacturers.

C. Discovery in U.S. Military Helicopter Accidents

The extensive use of helicopters by the U.S. military in all phases of operations both domestic and foreign results in an unfortunately high number of military helicopter accidents. The accident rate for military helicopters is substantially higher than for comparable civilian aircraft. Many military personnel are badly injured and killed every year in non-active-combat-related helicopter crashes. These military helicopter cases present far greater challenges than the comparable civilian cases which are difficult enough.[7] One of the primary obstacles is the difficulty of obtaining full discovery in these cases. The other primary roadblock is the limited pool of defendants available to military personnel suffering serious or fatal injuries in military helicopters. Members of the United States armed forces who suffer injuries incident to their military service may not utilize the Federal Tort Claims Act.[8] In instances where nonmilitary personnel or civilians would be permitted to sue the U.S. in tort for damages suffered, military personnel are barred from so doing.[9] The current state of federal law is to essentially immunize the United States from liability to any claim by military personnel for damages suffered in a helicopter crash.[10] The U.S. Supreme Court has ruled that a manufacturer's claims for indemnity against the U.S. should be denied.[11] These judicial barriers to recovery against the U.S. compel military personnel or their survivors to look to the helicopter manufacturer, engine manufacturer, or the manufacturer of the helicopter component part for recovery of damages.

The existence of the military industrial complex is a reality. Unfortunately, that symbiotic relationship between the U.S. military and helicopter manufacturers has the effect of rendering discovery doubly difficult. Military helicopter cases should be pursued only where there is clear evidence of some in-flight mechanical malfunction which is the primary causal factor in the crash. Any indication that actions of the military pilot or military maintenance personnel played a critical role in the crash render the lawsuit non-recoverable.

Fortunately, in such instances where a design or manufacturing defect can be identified discovery can move forward against the helicopter or component manufacturer in much the same manner as for a civilian helicopter crash. The difficulty is where the manufacturer seeks to hide behind the government contractor defense, or otherwise claims that "military secrets" are at issue. Discovery in such cases should focus on the types of maintenance manuals or other specific maintenance instructions provided to the military and how these vary from the comparable civilian directives. In many instances there is no variation whatsoever between either the product as designed and supplied or the accompanying maintenance and replacement instructions.

To obtain the military accident reports and attachments, counsel must use a FOIA request sent directly to the particular military branch at issue. The current addresses for obtaining all military investigative reports are set forth in Chapter 3, Section 3.5. By use of FOIA requests, plaintiff's counsel have been provided with a wealth of material above and beyond the military report, including military specifications and contract documentation. Such contract documentation includes developmental design and testing of the helicopter or component at issue as well as design parameters for the component. As always, the FOIA request should include all maintenance manuals and follow-up service bulletins and revisions.

A common roadblock in the pursuit of discovery in military helicopter cases is the "state secrets" doctrine. This is a claim of privilege assertible by and unique to the United States to protect military operations and any military secrets.[12] Once the privilege is raised and held to be valid "even the most compelling necessity cannot overcome the claim of privilege if the court is ultimately satisfied that military secrets are at stake."[13] The state secrets privilege has been routinely upheld as a means to block discovery in military aircrash cases.

The other substantial deterrent in such cases is the government contractor defense which provides a qualified immunity to aircraft and component part manufacturers who supply military aircraft.[14] That defense provides that government contractors such as helicopter manufacturers are immune from state court liability for improper design or failure to warn where:

1. The U.S. approved the reasonably precise specifications;
2. The equipment provided to the military conformed to those requested specifications; and
3. The government contractor warned the U.S. about dangers in use of the equipment known to the contractor but not known to the U.S.[15]

Where applicable, the government contractor defense has stopped many a lawsuit in its tracks. Given the difficulty of record acquisition from the military, the FOIA request should be sent immediately. The adequacy and completeness of the response can then be assessed and any decision on an appeal can be promptly made.

D. Protective Orders

Manufacturers will insist on entry of a protective order prior to the production of any requested documents or other discovery. A protective order that properly seeks to protect from public dissemination a company's legitimate trade secret, proprietary or financial information should be routinely agreeable. But plaintiff's counsel must resist the entry of overly broad protective orders seeking to cover all information produced in the case. Otherwise, defendants will seek to stamp every single document as protected. The author recalls one case where the helicopter manufacturer marked a Hertz map as "CONFIDENTIAL—PROTECTED DOCUMENT" where it had been used by its aircrash investigator to drive to the crash site.

The order also should provide that any such records lose all protection once admitted as exhibits at trial, and there is authority for that proposition.[16] The protective order should be drafted to protect plaintiff's confidential information such as medical and tax records. The order must provide for some method of objecting to a party's overly broad claim of confidentiality. A sample protective order used in many aircrash cases is as follows:

STIPULATED PROTECTIVE ORDER RE: CONFIDENTIAL INFORMATION

This matter having come before the Court upon the Stipulated Motion for Entry of Protective Order and the Court being duly advised of the premises herein,

IT IS HEREBY ORDERED as follows:

1. The parties to this helicopter accident litigation agree that given the likely volume of documents to be produced and exchanged in this case, each party will bate-stamp, in serial consecutive form along with identifying letter(s) for the producing party each page of documents, records or items (including electronic records) that are made available for inspection or otherwise produced to opposing counsel.

2. The parties anticipate that some of the documents and information requested during the discovery process will likely contain confidential information, including proprietary information, trade secrets, copyrighted information, financial data or privacy protected medical information [hereinafter "Confidential Information"]. Any documents produced or information provided by a party in response to any discovery request may be designated as "confidential" by either party in the following manner:

    a. By identifying by bate-stamp number those documents which it claims are Confidential Information and will disclose those bate-stamp numbers to opposing counsel along with a description and/or justification for why such documents or things should be regarded as Confidential Information;

    b. By imprinting the word "confidential" next to or above any answer to any Interrogatory; and

    c. With respect to portions of a deposition transcript, by making arrangements with the attending court reporter to bind the confidential portion(s) of such transcripts separately and labeling them as "confidential."

2. All documents and information provided by a party in compliance with a discovery rule or in response to a discovery request or deposition testimony which is designated as Confidential Information shall be subject to the following restrictions:

    a. Such Confidential Information shall be used only for the purpose of this litigation and not for any business or other purposes whatsoever;

    b. Such Confidential Information shall not be communicated or disclosed in any manner, either directly or indirectly, to anyone other than:

        (1) The attorneys of record and persons employed by them;

        (2) The parties involved herein or their representatives having responsibilities related to the subject matter of this litigation (including in-house counsel actively involved in the prosecution or defense of this action):

        (3) This Court and Court personnel;

        (4) Experts or consultants who have, prior to disclosure, signed a Nondisclosure Agreement in the form attached as Exhibit "A," attached hereto, certifying that they have read this Protective Order and agree to be bound by its terms;

        (5) Witness for depositions or trial, who prior to disclosure signed a Nondisclosure Agreement

in the form attached as Exhibit "'A," attached hereto, certifying that they have read this Protective Order and agree to be bound by its terms; and

(6) Such other persons as the Court may specifically approve after notice and hearing.

c. That all information designated as "Confidential Information" shall neither be used nor disclosed except for purpose of this litigation, and solely in accordance with this Protective Order or subsequent order of the Court upon motion.

d. Individuals authorized to review Confidential Information pursuant to this Protective Order shall hold such information in the strictest confidence and shall not divulge the information, either verbally or in writing, to any other person, entity or government agency unless authorized by the party claiming that the information is Confidential Information or order of a Court. The identity of those individuals signing the Nondisclosure Agreement need not be disclosed absent any dispute arising hereunder and such disclosures shall be only to the court in camera.

e. In the event a Defendant learns of information which causes any of them to have a good faith concern that a signatory to a Nondisclosure Agreement is employed by or affiliated with any business or enterprise that is in a competitive position to the Defendant and otherwise poses a threat that disclosure of Confidential Information to the signatory will create a reasonable risk that the information could be used in a manner that could harm Defendant's business interests, Defendant may file an objection to disclosure of Confidential Information to such signatory with the Court. In such an event, no Confidential Information will be provided to such signatory until the Court determines whether disclosure will be permitted.

f. A party may refer to Confidential Information at any hearing or pretrial conference before the Court or any special Magistrate or any other assistant the Court may appoint as well as evidentiary hearings and at trial. Before trial, counsel for the parties shall agree to the appropriate means to protect the confidentiality of the Confidential Information that counsel desire to present at trial. If counsel cannot reach an agreement, they shall apply to the Court for resolution of the issue. Nothing herein is intended to impair or limit the manner or method of presenting evidence to the jury by any party.

g. All documents or information identified as Confidential Information, including all copies, excerpts and summaries, must be retained in the custody of counsel or other persons authorized by this Protective Order during the pendency of this litigation.

3. Acceptance by a party of any information, document or thing identified as Confidential Information hereunder shall not constitute a concession that the information, document or thing is confidential. If, subsequent to the receipt of information or documents identified as Confidential Information, a party wishes this Court to rule upon the other party's claim of confidentiality, that party may move this Court for such determination. In the resolution of such motion, the burden of establishing the confidentiality of the information or document shall be on the party who made the claim of confidentiality. However, materials designated as confidential shall be treated as such pending resolution of the motion by the Court. It is acknowledged by the parties that, without limitation, the following information may be claimed as being "Confidential Information":

a. "Trade Secret" or Proprietary Information;

b. Financial/net worth and investor information; and

c. Medical records, reports and medical expense invoices.

Provided that nothing herein shall preclude either party from challenging in court the confidential status of any document.

4. In the event that a party shall desire to provide access to information or documents identified as Confidential Information hereunder to any person or category of persons not identified above, it shall move this Court for an order that such a person or category of persons may be given access to the information. In the event that the motion is granted, such person or category of persons may have access to the information, provided that such person or persons have agreed in writing before such access is given to be bound by the terms of this Protective Order, or other conditions as the Court may order.

5. Inadvertent disclosure of Confidential Information does not waive the protections otherwise attaching to the Confidential Information. Upon a party's discovery that information was not properly designated as Confidential Information, that party shall serve notice to the other litigants that the information was not properly designated. The party shall then have seven business days in which to designate the information as Confidential Information. In the interim, once written notices have been served, the alleged Confidential Information may not be used in a manner inconsistent with the terms of this Protective Order protecting such Confiden-

tial Information from disclosure until such time the Court orders otherwise.

6.   Any Confidential Information that is attached to or contained within motions, pleadings, briefs, memoranda or other filings shall be filed under seal with the Court. Any exhibit subject to this Order that is admitted as an exhibit at trial loses any protection as a confidential document.

7.   This Order shall survive the termination of this litigation. Within ninety (90) days from the date of final termination of this action, including all appeals, all Confidential Information provided and/or exchanged in this matter, including any copies, excerpts, or summaries thereof that have been prepared by Plaintiff or any Defendant, their counsel, experts, consultants and other persons or entities retained to assist Plaintiff in this litigation, shall be returned to counsel which had originally designated information as Confidential Information. No copies shall be retained by a party, his counsel, experts, consultants or other individuals retained to assist in this litigation. In lieu of returning confidential documents, counsel may elect to destroy all such documents and shall so certify said destruction to the producing party within thirty (30) days thereof. Counsel shall keep an accurate record of all copies, excerpts or summaries made by counsel, the parties, experts, consultants and any other person retained to assist in this litigation. The language contained in this paragraph shall not preclude counsel from retaining documents constituting their attorney work product as defined by applicable law. In the event copies of Confidential Information provided in discovery, including any copies or excerpts or summaries thereof, contain counsel's work product, counsel shall obliterate its work product and return such documents to opposing counsel in accordance with the provisions of this paragraph.

Dated this _____ day of _____, 2009

By the Court:

_____

JUDGE OF THE FIRST JUDICIAL DISTRICT

5.6 Case Development Matters

Counsel should utilize all available means of enhancing the efficiency of the discovery process. Two such techniques involve consolidation for purposes of discovery or for trial and the court's entry of a discovery schedule or case management order.

A. Consolidation for Discovery or Trial

Most helicopter crashes involve multiple injuries or deaths. This leads to a comparable number of potential claims and lawsuits. Various circumstances dictate whether it would be advantageous to consolidate the filed lawsuits for discovery or possibly for trial. Where filed in the same court system, courts invariably will consolidate helicopter lawsuits arising out of the same crash for discovery purposes at the very least. Due to budgetary and judicial time constraints, counsel may have no choice as to whether the cases are consolidated for trial because the court may determine that they should be.

The initial consideration in determining whether consolidation would be advantageous is simply whether counsel has been hired to represent the multiple claimants or whether there are known to be other claimants represented by other counsel. It is always in the client's best interest to coordinate the prosecution of such cases for efficiency purposes as well as to avoid competing or even inconsistent theories of liability. The advantage of sharing liability-related litigation expenses is apparent.

In cases where one law firm represents all of the potential claimants, consolidation for discovery purposes is obvious. Most state courts have rules comparable to *Federal Rule 42(a)* according them authority to consolidate for discovery those cases involving a common question of law or fact. Invariably a motion to consolidate at least for discovery purposes will be granted and that is so even where multiple claimants would be represented by different counsel with different sets of liability experts and potentially differing theories of liability.

In the multiple claimant-multiple counsel scenario, every step should be taken to coordinate the use of liability experts and that means utilizing the same team of experts. A formal expert-sharing agreement is advisable where one counsel would take the lead in selecting, retaining and preparing the experts while in return co-counsel would cooperate with all discovery scheduling deadlines, participate as desired and pay a pro-rata share of the expert charges. Recent experiences have demonstrated the disadvantage of proceeding in a consolidated jury trial with different liability experts.

Consolidation of helicopter cases for trial presents an entirely different issue irrespective of whether all clients are represented by the same counsel. In most cases, plaintiff's counsel will find it advantageous to try each case separately. In that way the jury can focus on providing full and fair compensation to the claimants in that case only. Defendants often seek to consolidate multiple cases for trial believing that a single jury is capable of awarding only so much in damages irrespective of whether it is one claim or many. Defendants also espouse the belief that the jury will compromise the value of each case in order to minimize the financial burden on the defendants. The contrary considerations are the cost and time efficiency of trying all cases at once and that is especially so given the usual complexities of this litigation. Once again that decision may not be counsel's to make as some courts decide on their own, due to budgetary and judicial time constraints, that all lawsuits arising out of the same helicopter crash are to be consolidated for trial.[17]

B. Discovery Schedule and Trial Setting

As soon as all defendants have answered, it is prudent practice to arrange a conference with the court and opposing counsel to prepare a discovery scheduling order. At minimum, that order should set out deadlines for amendment of the pleadings, joinder of additional parties, identification of expert witnesses, filing of dispositive motions and conclusion or close of discovery. The primary advantage to a discovery schedule early in the case is that it discourages stonewalling and delay tactics by defendants.

As with any other complex litigation, it behooves plaintiff's counsel to request a discovery schedule to provide for the orderly process of discovery and to keep the lawsuit on a steady advance toward trial. Entry of a discovery schedule has the added advantage of forcing the defendants to produce all corporate representatives for deposition prior to plaintiffs having to identify and produce liability experts for deposition. Unfortunately, if no discovery schedule or trial setting is entered defendants have little if any incentive to push the case along and will employ a number of dilatory tactics to prevent the case from making any considerable progress.

The trial setting should be requested at the outset so that all experts as well as all counsel and their respective parties can hold the dates well in advance. The vast majority of judges will honor a request for a trial setting in these cases given the multitude of experts involved and the need to address their scheduling well in advance.

An example of such a discovery schedule routinely used in helicopter crash litigation is as follows:

DISCOVERY SCHEDULE AND TRIAL SETTING

I. Discovery Deadlines

    A. Preliminary witness and exhibit lists will be exchanged forty-five (45) days from the Court's approval of this Case Management Order.

    B. Plaintiffs shall identify all corporate representatives to be deposed by April 12, 2010.

    C. Plaintiffs shall complete the depositions of all identified corporate representatives by June 4, 2010.

    D. Plaintiff shall identify all expert witnesses on or before July 12, 2010 and shall make expert witnesses

available for depositions, and have depositions completed, no later than September 10, 2010.

    E. Defendants shall identify all expert witnesses on or before October 25, 2010 and shall make expert witnesses available for depositions, and have depositions completed, no later than January 10, 2011.

    F. Plaintiff shall identify rebuttal expert witnesses on or before January 24, 2011 and shall make rebuttal expert witnesses available for deposition, and have depositions completed, no later than February 21, 2011.

    G. Final witness and exhibit lists will be exchanged by February 1, 2011, other than those exhibits which relate to Plaintiff's rebuttal expert witnesses.

    H. All motions to enforce discovery by any party shall be filed on or before January 31, 2011.

    I. Discovery will be completed by February 28, 2011. All written discovery shall be submitted so that responses will be due on or before this date. Depositions of parties and fact witnesses shall be completed by this date.

II. Additional Parties

    A. The parties do not contemplate joining additional parties.

III. Pre-Trial Motions

    A. All dispositive motions by any party as to any issue shall be filed on or before February 7, 2011.

    B. All responsive briefs to dispositive motions shall be filed on or before March 9, 2011.

    C. Additional pre-trial motions will be filed no later than March 28, 2011.

    D. Any party wishing to present deposition testimony at trial, whether to be read or shown by videotape, must designate by page and line number all such offered testimony by March 15, 2011. Any party wishing to counter-designate portions from the same deposition testimony or enter objections to another party's initial deposition transcript designations shall do so by March 25, 2011. Objections to counter-designated testimony shall be served no later than April 2, 2011.

IV. Settlement Position

    A. No settlement discussions have taken place.

V. Trial

    A. Pre-Trial Conference: April 11, 2011 at 9:30 a.m.

    B. Jury Trial: All parties in this matter anticipate this case will be ready for trial beginning April 25, 2011. All dates within this Order are assuming an April 25, 2011 jury trial is scheduled.

C. The parties anticipate that a trial of this case will take fifteen (15) trial days.

NOTE: The Court will allow any discovery deadline to be altered by agreement of all the parties, except for the discovery deadline.

By the time the complaint is filed, plaintiff's counsel already will have retained the liability and damages experts. A critical objective of early discovery is to equip those liability experts with additional factual bases for their opinions. Under no circumstances should they be identified or deposed until those opinions are final. Imposition of a court-imposed discovery schedule allows for the completion of critical discovery upon which the liability experts will rely. The progressive nature of plaintiff's discovery means that the defendants' various corporate representatives will not be taken until all requested document discovery has been completed either by agreement among counsel or by order of the court. Plaintiff's counsel will not begin the depositions of the corporate representatives without such documents. Plaintiffs will not agree to have the various liability experts deposed until the corporate representative depositions have been completed which is part of the discovery schedule.

Defendants should be required to identify their liability experts within thirty or sixty days after plaintiff's disclosure, although some courts require that the deadline should be the same for both. The discovery schedule should always include a specific date for identification of the defendant's liability experts. Without a court-imposed date, defense counsel will delay identification of defense expert witnesses for as long as possible up to and including the eve of trial. Defense lawyers routinely request an expert disclosure deadline of thirty or sixty days following the completion of all of plaintiff's liability experts' depositions. Such an arrangement should be resisted because it allows defense counsel to depose plaintiff's experts piecemeal while delaying the identification of the defense experts indefinitely.

A firm deadline for amending the pleadings also works to the plaintiff's advantage. Any affirmative defense not raised by this deadline should be waived. Such a deadline also avoids the last-minute third-party claim or cross claim desperate manufacturers in these cases often resort to.

Finally, at the earliest possible juncture in the lawsuit counsel should obtain a firm or special trial setting. Depending on local practice a special or "first out" trial date turns over the hourglass and starts the flow of sand against the defendant meaning the day of reckoning will soon be close at hand. For reasons of efficiency and effectiveness, counsel for plaintiffs should prepare for trial once and only once.

5.7 In-Depth Examination and Testing

A visual inspection of the subject wreckage, engine or component part is normally insufficient to yield definitive conclusions as to failure mode. For this reason, more in-depth examination and even some form of destructive testing is essential on either the subject helicopter or component and, in many cases, exemplar parts or systems.

A. Of Subject Helicopter, Engine and Component Part or System

Once counsel and the appropriate liability experts have zeroed in on the particular component suspected of in-flight failure that played a causal role in the accident, further examination and testing may be in order. In most cases, a metallurgical or materials failure expert will need to engage in some type of destructive testing on specific sections of the engine or some other critical flight component. It is customary for that expert to prepare a testing protocol of the components which will be subjected to the testing and the specific tests and equipment used. Ordinarily plaintiff's counsel circulates that protocol to all counsel for any feedback or possible objection. Even if defense counsel are agreeable to the protocol, counsel should prepare and file an unopposed motion to conduct destructive testing to avert any conceivable claim of spoliation at a later date.

Under no circumstances should any destructive testing of the helicopter, helicopter engine or any component part be undertaken without an appropriate protocol which has been reviewed by all defense counsel and then subsequently authorized by the court. Included in any such protocol are appropriate agreements as to the time and place of the destructive testing, the allowance of all counsel and their respective representatives and consultants to be present, the requirement of a sign-in sheet, and provisions for the exchange of any data generated.

An example of such a protocol in helicopter crash litigation is as follows:

TESTING AND INSPECTION PROTOCOL OF HELICOPTER WRECKAGE

A. Component Shipment and Arrangements:
Wreckage components will remain sealed and stored in the as-received condition until the start of the examination. The following components will be shipped in addition to others, as requested by any party:
1. Tail boom assembly
2. Tail rotor control rods
3. Tail rotor hydraulic unit
4. Tail rotor assembly including tail rotor gearbox

5. Teleflex cable components including housing and cable

6. Rudder control system components

7. Pilot's seat and mating floorboard sections

B. Laboratory Analysis:

1. Reconstruct the wreckage components as applicable, and photo document.

2. Perform visual examination of the wreckage components and photo document.

3. Perform laboratory analysis of selected wreckage components to include visual examination, dimensional analysis, sampling for deposits and particulates to be labeled and photo documented, stereomicroscopic examination, variable pressure scanning electron microscopic examination (SEM), x-ray energy dispersive spectroscopy (EDS) and FTIR chemical analysis, as required. It is anticipated that plastic components will be analyzed using the SEM.

4. Clean selected components with acetone and/or aqueous Alconox soap solution, as required.

5. Perform additional laboratory analysis of the cleaned components to include visual examination, dimensional analysis, stereomicroscopic examination variable pressure scanning electron microscopic examination (SEM), x-ray energy dispersive spectroscopy (EDS) and FTIR chemical analysis, as required. It is anticipated that plastic components will be analyzed using the SEM.

6. Perform laboratory analysis and disassembly of components/assemblies as required for detailed examination, including as follows:

   (a) Perform visual examination of the wreckage components and photo document.

   (b) Remove control rod above the tail boom and photodocument.

   (c) Analyze internal and external cable for tail rotor servo. Perform borescopic examination of cable if possible and photodocument.

   (d) Section the control cable sheath and photodocument.

   (e) Perform laboratory analysis of sectioned control cable sheath to include dimensional analysis and sampling for deposits/particulates. Label all debris removed from sheath and photodocument.

   (f) Remove plastic sheath from control cable and photodocument.

   (g) Perform stereomicroscopic examination, variable pressure scanning electron microscopic

examination (SEM), x-ray energy dispersive spectroscopy (EDS) and FTIR chemical analysis, as required. It is anticipated that plastic components will be analyzed using the SEM.

   (h) Clean selected components with acetone and/or aqueous Alconox soap solution, as required.

7. Perform additional laboratory analysis of the cleaned components to include visual examination, dimensional analysis, stereomicroscopic examination, variable pressure scanning electron microscopic examination (SEM), x-ray energy dispersive spectroscopy (EDS) and FTIR chemical analysis, as required. It is anticipated that plastic components will be analyzed using the SEM.

8. Test, disassemble and examine the following:

   (a) Entire yaw load compensator system

   (b) All system check valves

   (c) T/R hydraulic pressure relief valve to cracking pressure (approx. 55 BAR)

   (d) Solenoid valves

   (e) Servo actuator

   (f) System filter and clogging indicator

   (g) Filter bypass system

   (h) Solenoid shut-off valves

   (i) T/R and M/R system hydraulic bypass relays

   (j) M/R servos

9. Additional Inspection Techniques

   (a) Examine and analyze push/pull link control linkage and brackets.

   (b) Use borescope for inspection if possible. Cut external sheath for examination.

   (c) Analyze internal and external cable for T/R servo.

10. All parties present shall make every effort to complete non-destructive examination and testing prior to destructive examination and testing.

Note: Disassembly of components will be done non-destructively, whenever possible, otherwise minimum amount of sectioning will be accomplished.

C. Conditions of Inspection:

As with any investigation of this type, findings at one stage of the protocol may suggest changes in the later steps or the need for additional steps. Such changes or additions are acceptable upon mutual agreement of all parties present. Every attempt will be made to honor requests for specific analyses during the inspection.

The methods and procedures utilized will be consistent with good material engineering practices commonly used in forensic engineering investigations. Every effort will be made to preserve forensic evidence. A video and photographic record will be made of any cleaning and/or sectioning of components. Photographic and video documentation shall be by film and/or digital techniques.

No audio recording will be permitted during the inspection without the consent of all participants.

D.   Resolution of disputes:

Any disputes relative to this Protocol will be resolved by teleconference hearing with the Court at the time the dispute is determined to reach impasse at the testing. The Court will be available to entertain any hearings necessary to resolve disputes on the three (3) days of inspection between 8:00 a.m. and 5:00 p.m. (Pacific Time).

Part of the protocol should provide that all destructive testing must be photodocumented and such photodocumentation should be extensive prior to any material destruction or disassembly of an engine or system. One of the primary reasons to conduct such microscopic examination of metal components is to ascertain the reason for the part's failure. The dispute in many cases will be that the component broke because it was in a helicopter accident and it failed upon impact with the ground. Experienced failure analysts can readily determine whether the part broke because of some pre-existing structural deficiency or loading or combination of the two. Component parts can break in various ways. By use of sophisticated visual enhancement techniques, engineering experts can specify with high degrees of certainty the particular cause of the break as being impact, fatigue, excess loading, compression, or even corrosion. In a recent case involving separation of main rotor blade in-flight, metallurgical analysis of the blade revealed portions where epoxy had not been applied to bond portions of the blade together.

Such analysis requires extensive understanding and study of the properties of particular metals and alloys and the operational function in order to assess the particular failure mode and what would cause that failure mode. Helicopters utilize high-strength aluminum alloys which are extremely brittle and prone to shatter. Such materials would break without evidence of outside forces providing strong evidence that the failure occurred in-flight prior to ground impact. This type of precision analysis normally requires sectioning or cutting a transverse portion of the metal or other alloy for purposes of inspection under scanning electron microscope. The use of scanning electron microscopy allows for a determination of the type of fracture and whether it was of a failure mode which could only have occurred while the helicopter was in-flight and prior to the crash. A practiced metallurgist can also determine whether the materials selection process was appropriate by assessing whether

the part failed due to design stresses or was simply a type of metal which could not withstand the ordinarily expected stress and temperature forces.

Metallurgical examination of various engine components may also allow the expert to assess if the engine was producing power at impact. Such in-depth examination and testing will also reveal whether the turbine blades were rotating at the time of impact, whether the engine suffered any foreign object damage or whether there was any explosive force on the engine shroud evidencing an in-flight separation of a component. This type of in-depth examination and testing cannot ordinarily or even comfortably be performed at a storage facility where the helicopter wreckage may be kept. The engine or various component parts at issue and even the airframe itself may need to be transported to an appropriate facility which has the laboratory equipment customarily utilized for such extensive failure analysis. Due to the heightened stresses and vibration inherent in helicopter flight as opposed to fixed-wing aircraft, fatigue failure of any critical component must be considered. If any component part of a helicopter fails in-flight, that is likely to trigger a sequence of events causing the destruction of proximal flight control systems resulting in an inability to control the aircraft.

Fatigue failure in metal is a standard and predictable failure mode. Fatigue failure routinely propagates or extends from an initial failure area over a well-defined space. As the crack grows and progresses the particular component will weaken and ultimately come apart. Helicopter component manufacturers must design that part to withstand fatigue failures. That includes knowledge of the strength of the metal itself and its predicted or useful safe life. Given the heat and number of cycles sustained by most helicopter component parts a lower useful safe life will attach then to a comparable airplane part requiring a much more frequent replacement of that part.

With respect to the helicopter engine a qualified metallurgist can easily determine whether it was producing power at impact. The direction and extent of internal rotation provides a clear picture of what was occurring at the time of impact. The way that certain turbine blades are broken or bent also will assist in determining the direction of rotation which will tell the story.

Many helicopters use cables as a means of activating and controlling flight controls. These cables are often a suspect component in any helicopter accident. While they may break apart and fail as a result of the helicopter crash itself, they also fail in-flight in one of two ways: either tensile overload or cutting. Tensile overload is where the cable is stretched until it comes apart. The appearance of the cable will be vastly different as to whether it is stretched or cut. A cut will normally be a clean break with a flat surface. A cable which stresses to separation or failure will have the appearance of a small brush or "broomstick." Depending on the position of the cable and the circumstances of the crash, one failure mode may dictate an in-flight failure while the other will necessarily indicate that the cable failed at the moment of impact.

B. Of Exemplar Helicopter, Engine and Component Part or System

Usually the helicopter, engine, and all critical component parts are not subject to any type of performance testing because of impact-related damage. Exceptions include certain avionics which may survive intact, as well as internal system components such as servos or actuators within the main rotor or tail rotor control system. As a result, in most instances it will be necessary to acquire exemplar component parts for purposes of performing operational or failure mode testing. It has proven helpful to gain access to a similar model helicopter to conduct actual in-flight testing in support of some portion of an expert's opinion. The purpose may be to assess certain operational or flight characteristics or more simply to assess the angle of attack or forward pitch of the helicopter at a certain speed. All possible safety precautions should be taken for in-flight testing of a model helicopter and no tests should be performed which would place the pilot or occupant in any danger.

One of the advantages to such exemplar or similar component part testing is that it can be performed in the absence of other counsel and their respective company representatives and expert consultants. This testing may reveal that the component part in question failed under similar conditions as were thought to be experienced by the subject component. Such testing is an essential element of plaintiff's case development because it corroborates plaintiff's theory of the case by utilizing a component part as precisely similar to the subject part as is available.

In many cases it is advisable to conduct certain limited in-flight testing on a comparable model helicopter.

5.8 Alternative or Informal Discovery Methods

Counsel should explore ways of acquiring information other than using the traditional methods of discovery which the rules provide. No court limits admissibility of evidence to documents or other information obtained exclusively through the discovery process. All of these methods may be employed without permission by the court or notice to defense counsel.

A. Networking with Other Aviation Counsel

No group has more information about potential defendants and theories of liability than other plaintiff lawyers. The single greatest impediment to sharing that information is the insistence by most helicopter and component part manufacturers to a protective order governing all discovery whether documents or deposition testimony. That all-encompassing protective order should be resisted as being against public policy and as restricting claimants with similar claims from access and cross-checking confirmability.

The networking process may include the types of defenses likely to be raised by certain defendants as well as available insurance coverage and discovery tactics employed. Many plaintiff aviation groups such as the Aviation Law Section of the American Association for Justice (AAJ) have well-maintained websites and listservs which can be used for networking and information sharing. Various state trial lawyer associations also are active in maintaining listservs for its members and these are fruitful avenues for non-formal discovery.

B. Patent and Trademark Searches

Most every helicopter component will have been patented by the engineer employed by the company at the time of the product development. These patents can be obtained and the original application data scrutinized. These original patent applications invariably will include the design intent and functional parameters of the component part including specific design factors such as useful safe life and heat tolerances. The patent application may also reveal such useful information as any limitations to the component or system design and the specifications for materials to be included in the final manufacturing process.

C. Defendant's Litigation History

Given the availability of such legal search engines such as Westlaw and Lexis-Nexis it is inexcusable for counsel not to conduct a thorough search of every defendant's lawsuit history. For most major helicopter manufacturers and component part makers an extensive record of litigation is accessible not only in the reported appellate decisions but also in federal and state court filings as well. In accessing a defendant's lawsuit history, PACER is an excellent database for federal filings. It is remarkable how often a defendant will deny ever having been sued in connection with its product. Having this lawsuit information permits plaintiff's counsel to conduct effective impeachment of the corporate representative who denies knowledge of any prior lawsuits. Other means of accessing this information are through deposition libraries kept by many aviation law firms which contain the depositions of many employees of habitual defendants.

D. Defendant's Website

A virtual treasure-trove of useful information can be gleaned from a defendant's own website. Advertising and marketing claims often exceed the reality of the product's capabilities. Representations made in the marketing arm of that company may not necessarily coincide with the engineering and customer support realities. Various websites such as http://web.archive.org/collections/web.html permit anyone to go back in time to search any website content that had ever been posted on that address.

E. Technical and Trade Literature

The Internet is a modern indispensable tool in any litigation, especially that involving helicopters. Technical papers addressing certain component parts or the airworthiness of various systems are all over the Internet and easily accessible.

Endnotes

1. *49 C.F.R. §§ 835.3 (1999)* and *835.5 (1998)*.

2. *49 C.F.R. § 835.3*.

3. *49 C.F.R. § 835.6 (1998)*.

4. *23 U.S.T. 2555, 847 U.N.T.S. 231* (entered into force for the United States on October 7, 1972)*; see also 28 U.S.C.A. § 1781 (1964)*.

5. *U.S. Dept. of State, Obtaining Evidence Abroad (1987)*.

6. *5 U.S.C. § 552 (2009)*.

7. See Section 3.5 for a discussion of Factual Investigation of Military Helicopter Crashes.

8. *Feres v. United States, 340 U.S. 135 (1950)*.

9. *Id. at 143*.

10. *Stencel Aero Engineering Corp. v. United States, 431 U.S. 666 (1977)*.

11. *Id*.

12. *United States v. Reynolds, 345 U.S. 1, 7-8 (1953)*.

13. *Id. at 11*.

14. *Boyle v. United Technologies Corporation, 487 U.S. 500 (1988)*.

15. *Id. at 512*.

16. *Littlejohn v. BIC Corporation*, 851 F.2d 673, 680 (3d Cir. 1988); *In re National Consumer Mortg., LLC*, 512 B.R. 639, 641 (D.Nev. 2014); *Cottone v. Reno*, 193 F.3d 550, 554-55 (D.C. 1999); *Glaxo, Inc. v. Novopharm Limited*, 931 F.Supp. 1280, 1300 (E.D.N.C. 1996).

17. *Schlotzhauer v. The Final Season, No. CL102824 (Iowa District Court 2008)*.

Chapter 6

Common Defenses in Helicopter Crash Cases

Introduction

There are as many available defenses in a helicopter crash case as in any other field of litigation. In addition to the factual, legal, and regulatory complexities, defendants will raise every potential time-based, jurisdictional and substantive defense. And there is always the ever-popular smokescreen defense. As the potential damages awards in helicopter accident litigation are substantial as well as the potential harm to a defendant manufacturer's commercial reputation, counsel will encounter the very best defense counsel. Defense lawyers in helicopter crash cases routinely raise every possible legal defense. Much of plaintiff counsel's efforts must be expended in anticipating and countering the many defenses which will commonly be raised in these cases.

If the primary defendant is the pilot or operator based on a theory of pilot negligence, the defense will point to extenuating circumstances such as weather or alternative causes such as component malfunction. Where the pilot is killed in the crash along with other passengers, the defense will point out that the pilot was exercising the best possible care so as to avoid injury to herself. These various defenses make for intriguing alliances as where the plaintiff and the defendant pilot claim fault against a co-defendant, most likely the helicopter airframe manufacturer or a component part maker. In such cases, a product defendant typically must decide on one of two trial defenses. One is a straightforward defense of the product. The defendant will claim that it is a safe and reliable product and did not fail on the occasion in question. The other trial approach is to raise every conceivable alternative cause for the helicopter crash, focus on the pilot error, and hold plaintiff to a strict burden of proof as to one particular liability theory. Experience has demonstrated that a defendant's efforts to have it both ways inures to the plaintiff's advantage. It is not a credible defense position to claim the product was safely designed and did not fail, but that if it did fail the crash was not due to that product malfunction.

This chapter sets forth suggestions for meeting and defeating these commonly raised defenses. In general, an effective stratagem for meeting these defenses is to isolate one particular negligent act or product failure and pursue a streamlined theory of recovery against as few target defendants as possible. The defendant's corporate representatives and liability experts should be thoroughly examined about all claimed defenses, especially the factual basis therefore. And the defendants should be compelled to come up with some alternative theory or explanation for the helicopter crash. Otherwise, defendants will attack plaintiff's theory of the case and attempt to prove it wrong without having to defend their own case theory.

6.1 Time-Based Defenses

Time-based defenses must be plaintiff counsel's immediate concern. The absolute nature of such statutes renders them the best defense where applicable. Counsel must either avoid those forums with claim-barring statutes or find proper and lawful exceptions to their applicability.

A. State Statutes of Limitations and Repose

The most critical concern facing any practitioner is the dreaded one year statute of limitations and there are presently three such states with this extremely short statute: Kentucky, Louisiana and Tennessee. Even if the lawsuit is brought within the applicable statute of limitations of a certain state, counsel must be wary of that state's borrowing statute under which the defendant may seek the benefit of some other jurisdiction's shorter limitations period. Inadvertence, excusable neglect, even severe disability or incapacity in most cases will be insufficient to overcome the harshness of these time bars. Section 3.1(A) in Chapter 3 contains a chart setting out the statutes of limitations and repose for all fifty states.

State statutes of repose vary from as little as five years from the date of sale (such as in Kentucky) to fifteen years from the sale date (such as in Texas) to no statute of repose at all in more than half the states. Counsel must determine as soon as possible the trigger dates in whichever jurisdiction's statute of repose may be applicable. In several states the end date is the date the lawsuit is filed, so the quicker the case is filed the better.

In the face of an impending statute of repose, counsel must determine quickly whether product failure was involved and specify the part that was defective and contributed to the crash of the helicopter. For example, the engine itself may be subject to the statute of repose as having been sold or delivered outside the statutory safe harbor. But if a replacement component such as a turbine disk or blades were defective and these were installed within the statutory period of time then the lawsuit survives as against the manufacturer of those parts. Counsel must take great care to define the component part as that which would not be subject to that state's statute of repose as having been replaced or sold within the viable time period.

B. General Aviation and Revitalization Act

The General Aviation and Revitalization Act (GARA) 18-year statute of repose frequently comes into play because of the large number of 18-year-old and older helicopters in active operation in this country. Accordingly, the practitioner must become familiar with and adept at using all of the known lawful exceptions to applicability of the GARA repose statute.

The GARA statutory scheme sets out four specific exceptions to its applicability. These are (1) the knowing misrepresentation exception, (2) the air ambulance exception, (3) on-ground injury or death and (4) the warranty exception. A fifth exception to GARA applicability while technically an avoidance rather than an exception is the GARA re-triggering provision. In considering pursuit of the lawsuit which would otherwise be GARA-barred, counsel must assess the potential applicability of these exceptions.

1. Knowing Misrepresentation Exception

The knowing misrepresentation exception applies where the aircraft or component part manufacturer "knowingly misrepresented, concealed or withheld" required information from the FAA which is relevant to the performance of the aircraft and which was causally related to the harm, meaning that it was a factor in the crash.[1] To utilize this exception, counsel will have to confer with experts on FAA-required documents. The pleading requirements for this knowing misrepresentation exception are set out in the terms of the statute and are not insurmountable from a proof standpoint. Plaintiff must plead "with specificity the facts necessary to prove" that the defendant manufacturer: (1) knowingly, (2) misrepresented, concealed or withheld required information from the FAA, (3) which was material and relevant and (4) which was causally related to the crash.

An example of pleading the knowing misrepresentation exception is set out below:

> 1. At all material times herewith, defendant knowingly misrepresented to the Federal Aviation Administration and/or concealed or withheld from the Federal Aviation Administration required information that is material and relevant to the performance or the maintenance or operation of such aircraft, or the component, system, subassembly, or other part that is causally related to the harm that Plaintiffs have suffered as further detailed herein including, but not limited to, warranty and claim reports of malfunctions and difficulties, in-flight failures and reports of defects and power losses as to the system and [product] used in its aircraft as referenced in Service Bulletin XXX issued on October 2, 2008 specifically regarding the [product].

But pleading is not proof. Counsel will need to conduct extensive discovery on this issue and, ultimately, adduce prima facie evidence in support of the allegations. Otherwise, the attempt to circumvent the GARA time bar will fail.

Defendant manufacturers frequently file motions to dismiss on the pleadings in cases of potential GARA applicability. That is why plaintiff's petition or complaint carefully must track the statutory exception and plead specific facts which, if proven, would bring the case within that statutory exception. A sample brief in a case handled by the author which resulted in the overruling of the motion to dismiss and permitting plaintiff to proceed with discovery on the alleged GARA exception is set out in Appendix B.

2. Air Ambulance Exception

The second GARA exception has particular application to crashes of air ambulance helicopters. This exception renders GARA inapplicable in all respects if the individual injured or killed was a passenger aboard the helicopter for purposes of receiving "medical or emergency treatment." This has been referred to as the air ambulance exception to GARA and would apply to the patient picked up at the scene of a motor vehicle accident or other trauma-related event. The phrase "other emergency" may refer to a helicopter search and rescue operation which finds a lost snowboarder after an avalanche but would not strictly speaking involve any medical treatment.

3. Out of Aircraft Exception

The third GARA exception applies where the party injured or killed was not on the aircraft at the time of the crash. This would involve those cases where the helicopter causes injury or death to persons on the ground and the exception also may be asserted for any mid-air collision involving a helicopter for a claim against the other aircraft.

4. Written Warranty Exception

The fourth exception is for any legal actions brought under a manufacturer's written warranty. Alas, no one has ever seen a 20 year written warranty for any helicopter, helicopter component part, system, or structure.

5. Re-triggering Provision for New Part or System

Another means of avoiding GARA's applicability to the lawsuit is by use of the statute's re-triggering provision. GARA provides that for any new replacement part or system:

> [No action may be initiated] with respect to any new component, system, subassembly or other part which replaced another component, system, subassembly, or other part originally in, or which was added to, the aircraft, which is alleged to have caused such death, injury, or damage, after the applicable limitation period beginning on the date of completion of the replacement or addition.[2]

As the vast majority of helicopter component parts and even systems are replaced long before the expiration of 18 years, the positive applicability of this provision is apparent.

If any helicopter component part, system or subassembly is implicated in the crash, GARA would not apply if that component, system or subassembly were installed less than 18 years prior to filing suit.

The language of the provision is important in that it dates from installation of the new component part and not purchase. The component part actually may have been purchased by the pilot, helicopter operator, maintenance facility or other end user several years previously and remained in storage sitting on some shelf. The GARA time clock would not begin to run until that part "replaced another" part on the helicopter. The effect of that re-triggering provision is that as to any new component part claimed to have caused the crash, the limitation period begins anew on the date when that new component part was physically installed for service on the helicopter.

Considerable litigation has ensued over what constitutes a "replacement part" so as to escape dismissal by application of GARA's 18-year statute of repose. In one of the early cases, a Texas federal court found that a helicopter's maintenance manual which had been revised and replaced was not a "component part" of the helicopter and would not serve to trigger the running of a new 18-year limitation period. However, other courts since then have ruled that changes in an aircraft's maintenance manual which were relevant and material to those factors responsible to the crash should re-trigger the 18-year clock.[3]

A California decision handed down in June 2010 is in accord with these decisions.[4] In this case, the plaintiff was injured when a Bell 47D1 helicopter she was piloting crashed. She sued the manufacturer, Bell Helicopter Textron, for negligence based on an allegedly defective maintenance manual that improperly instructed on balancing the helicopter's tail rotor blades. The helicopter itself had been in operation since 1951. The maintenance manual was issued in 1969 and last revised in 1975.

Defendant Bell argued that the plaintiff's claim was barred by the GARA 18-year federal statute of repose. The trial court granted Bell's motion finding that the maintenance manual was a "part" of the helicopter and was last revised in 1975. The appellate court reversed concluding that the maintenance manual was not a "part" of the helicopter which then provided for a re-triggering of the 18-year limitations period and permitted the lawsuit to go forward.[5] The court analyzed other similar decisions and found persuasive the fact that federal regulations do not require a maintenance manual to be on board a helicopter. GARA requires that a replacement part must replace a part "originally in" or "added to the aircraft." A maintenance manual was not a "part" of the original aircraft and "unlike a flight manual that is unique to the aircraft, used by the pilot, and necessary to operate the aircraft, a maintenance manual applies to different aircraft models, is used by the mechanic, and only for trouble shooting and repairing the aircraft."[6]

Absent applicability of one of these statutory or other exceptions to GARA or the viability of proceeding against a non-GARA defendant, counsel must advise the client that the claim is time-barred and decline the representation. Where the helicopter, engine, or other critical components are clearly sold, delivered and in use longer than 18 years, then the GARA repose statute is squarely applicable and to press forward against those defendants under those circumstances is quixotic.

6.2 Jurisdictional Defenses

Defendants often will raise challenges to the jurisdiction of the court selected by plaintiffs on various grounds. Alternatively, defendants will utilize any lawful basis available to remove plaintiff's state court action to federal court. Plaintiff's counsel must be well familiar with the ins and outs of all of these jurisdictional issues.

A. Federal Preemption

Defendant manufacturers often seek to remove an action to federal court claiming federal preemption or federal question jurisdiction. This issue is referred to as federal preemption because the federal law would preempt the field. The federal district courts have federal jurisdiction over all cases "arising under the Constitution, treaties or laws of the United States."[7] Preemption results where the federal law or regulation is "so pervasive as to make reasonable the inference that Congress left no room for the states to supplant it."[8]

Plaintiffs need to exercise particular care in drafting the initial complaint or petition so as not to raise any federal question potentially triggering the prospect of removal to federal court if that is not desired. If any claim in the complaint is based on a federal cause of action the entire case is removable. The federal courts will look to the plaintiff's complaint to assess whether any federal question arises.

The removal issue in federal question cases is governed by the "well-pleaded complaint" rule which provides for federal jurisdiction where a federal question is presented on the face of the plaintiff's properly pleaded complaint.[9] If on examination of plaintiff's "well-pleaded complaint," no federal question appears, then federal removal jurisdiction is not present.[10] As the U.S. Supreme Court has noted:

> Only state-court actions that originally could have been filed in federal court may be removed to federal court by the defendant. Absent diversity of citizen-

ship, federal question jurisdiction is required. The presence or absence of federal question jurisdiction is governed by the "well-pleaded complaint rule," which provides that federal jurisdiction exists only when a federal question is presented on the face of the plaintiff's properly pleaded complaint...The rule makes the plaintiff the master of the claim; he or she may avoid federal jurisdiction by exclusive reliance on state law.[11]

When the federal district court examines whether any claim raises a federal question, it must examine the contents of the complaint only and ignore any potential defenses.[12]

The U.S. Supreme Court found that federal question jurisdiction may be present, even in the absence of a federal remedy, where "a state-law claim necessarily raises a stated federal issue, actually disputed and substantial, which a federal forum may entertain without disturbing any congressionally approved balance of federal and state judicial responsibilities."[13] On that basis defendant helicopter and component manufacturers frequently attempt to remove these cases to federal court claiming that they necessarily involve federal question jurisdiction because of the applicability of the Federal Aviation Regulations.

In one helicopter crash case, the court found that federal law preempted the state law failure to warn claim against the gyroscope manufacturer brought by the wife of a helicopter pilot who was killed in a crash. Plaintiff claimed that the manufacturer violated its duty to warn and the court found preemption because federal law established the standard of care in the field.[14] For this reason it is advisable that plaintiff's complaint in no way refers to or references the Federal Aviation Regulations or federally required record-keeping. So doing will eliminate any question as to whether a federal question is presented and foreclose an improvident and time-wasting removal and remand process.

Counsel also must refrain from pleading any federal statute as the basis for a state law claim of negligence per se. Some federal courts will construe the mere citation of federal law as constituting a federal claim though it clearly is and remains a claim under state law using only a federal regulation as evidence. To avert any potential confusion and ultimate removal the complaint should not allege negligence per se and certainly not cite to any federal law, rule or regulation.

Even without a citation to any federal law or regulation and plaintiff's meticulous avoidance of any federal reference in the complaint, some federal courts will find that a federal cause of action has been pled under the "artful pleading doctrine." In those jurisdictions which are particularly preemption-happy it may even be prudent to include the following disclaimer in the jurisdictional section of the complaint: "Plaintiffs herein do not now nor do they plan to assert any federal claim and any attempt to remove this lawsuit by defendants on the basis of any alleged federal question jurisdiction is indisputably without merit."

B. Forum Non Conveniens

Forum non conveniens is the common law doctrine permitting a court otherwise vested with jurisdiction of the case to dismiss a lawsuit on the basis that it may be tried more conveniently elsewhere. The doctrine is not solely one of federal law, although the state standards enumerated closely resemble those which the federal courts routinely apply. There exists a striking divergence between the use and applicability of the doctrine as between federal and state courts. Whereas the federal courts apply forum non conveniens aggressively to dismiss cases, some state courts have abolished the doctrine altogether and most give far greater deference to the plaintiff's choice of forum.[15] Many times the courts will impose conditions to their dismissal of the case pursuant to forum non conveniens where the action accrued in a foreign country, allowing for the suit to be brought back to the U.S. court should the foreign court be unwilling or unable to hear the case.

Forum non conviens must be distinguished from a change of venue to another federal district court or division under 28 U.S.C. 1404. Application of the former results in dismissal of the case whereas a Section 1404 transfer is a mere change of federal venue. As a tactical matter, one of the reasons defendants seek to remove cases to federal court is the availability of Section 1404 to transfer the case to an even more desirable federal venue.

Under the federal standard, the U.S. district court first determines whether there exists an adequate alternative forum. If one exists, the court then decides which forum would best serve both the private interests of the litigants involved and the public interests of both forums.[16] The private interest factors to be considered on such a motion are as follows:

- Relative ease of access to proof and witnesses
- Availability of compulsory process to obtain the attendance of unwilling witnesses
- Possibility of view of necessary premises
- Enforceability of a judgment
- "All other practical problems that make trial of a case easy, expeditious and inexpensive"[17]

The public interest considerations are:

- Administrative ease

- Reasonableness of imposing jury duty on citizens where the forum has no relation to the litigation
- Propriety of having the trial of any diversity case in a forum accustomed to applying relevant state law
- "A local interest in having localized controversies decided at home"[18]

Unless the balance of convenience factors is strongly in favor of the defendant, the U.S. Supreme Court cautioned that the plaintiff's choice of forum should not be disturbed. Over the next sixty years, that caution has largely been ignored. Such dismissals are rarely overturned because in reviewing such matters on appeal, the most deferential "clear abuse of discretion" standard is utilized.

The stark differences in federal and state usage and application of forum non conveniens render that doctrine outcome determinative in many instances. Whereas some states like Louisiana and Texas do not recognize the doctrine, federal courts aggressively apply it. The U.S. Circuit Court of Appeals for the Fifth Circuit quite candidly acknowledged that distinction. The court noted that applying federal versus Louisiana rules for forum non conveniens would result in diametrically opposed outcomes as "one case will proceed to judgment [in Louisiana] and the other will be dismissed to a foreign land [from federal court]."[19]

In any action where a foreign plaintiff is seeking jurisdiction in any U.S. court for a helicopter crash which occurred outside the U.S., the doctrine of forum non conveniens will come into play. Some states either by statute or case law will refuse to dismiss any lawsuit on forum non conveniens grounds unless all properly joined defendants stipulate that they will submit to the jurisdiction of the court in the alternative forum and waive any defense based on the statute of limitations potentially applicable in that other forum.[20] Plaintiff's counsel must be conscious of its potential applicability in any case where the lawsuit is being filed in a forum other than where the helicopter accident occurred.

Successful challenges to a forum non conveniens motion will point out the lack of undue burden to the defendant in having to litigate the action in plaintiff's chosen forum. A defendant often is put in the position of arguing that even though the plaintiff has elected to bring suit outside of its home forum, the defendant is prejudiced and severely inconvenienced by being forced to defend the claim in its home forum on its own turf. Plaintiff's counsel also should point to the discovery advantages in leaving the case where filed. Among these are ease of access to the defendant's own engineering and other personnel as well as all of the relevant documentation concerning design, development and marketing of the subject component or system. Counsel's stipulated willingness to defer to the scheduling needs of any and all such witnesses also will be considered positively by the court in ruling on this motion.

C. Foreign Sovereign Immunities Act

The Foreign Sovereign Immunities Act (FSIA) confers federal subject matter jurisdiction over any action brought against a foreign entity or "foreign state."[21] As many helicopter airframe and component part manufacturers are based in and partially or entirely owned by foreign countries, FSIA may be invoked as a basis for removal of a state court action to federal court because the statute grants federal subject matter jurisdiction over any case brought against a "foreign state." The premise of FSIA is that a foreign government is immune to suit unless there is a specific exception within the statute. The exception applicable in any case involving a foreign helicopter manufacturer or manufacturer of a component part is the "commercial activities" exception.[22] As defined by the statute, a foreign state includes any "political subdivision" or "agency or instrumentality of a foreign state."[23] An "agency or instrumentality of a foreign state" is then defined as any entity:

1. Which is a separate legal person, corporate or otherwise,
2. Which is an organ of a foreign state or political subdivision thereof, or a majority of whose shares or other ownership interest is owned by a foreign state or political subdivision thereof, and
3. Which is neither a citizen of a state of the United States as defined in Section 1332(c) and (d) of [Title 28, United States Code], nor created under the laws of any third country.[24]

Accordingly, any helicopter or engine manufacturer that is majority-owned by a foreign government may remove the action to federal court. There is, however, one exception. The U.S. Supreme Court has recently ruled that FSIA applies only if the company is majority-owned by a foreign government at the time that the lawsuit was filed against it.[25] The author was fortunate to obtain remand in one Nevada helicopter crash case on precisely this basis.[26] Counsel should not take any manufacturer's representation at face value but must be willing to conduct discovery on the ownership issue. Given the various ownership structures and interlocking corporate relationships of many European companies this often requires some untangling.

However, the U.S. subsidiary of a foreign-owned helicopter or component part manufacturer is not entitled to a bench trial under the provisions of FSIA. The Ninth Circuit ruled as follows:

The foreign sovereign immunities act grants no right to a bench trial to a domestic subsidiary of a foreign corporation, at least when the district court would have had jurisdiction over a separate action against the subsidiary alone and the liability of the principal and subsidiary do not depend on another under the governing substantive law.[27]

In that case, the plaintiff brought an action against the French corporation, Societe Nationale Industrielle Aerospatiale, which manufactured the helicopter and also against the American distributor, Aerospatiale Helicopter Corp., a Delaware Corporation which was wholly owned by the French manufacturer.[28] At the time suit was brought, the French concern was owned by the French government. Damages were determined for the French manufacturer in a bench trial while a jury determined damages for the American distributor. On appeal the court affirmed the district court's denial of the U.S. distributor's demand for a bench trial.[29]

D. Outside of Maximum Reach of Long-Arm Statute

Helicopter manufacturers and the manufacturers of various helicopter component parts and systems may challenge jurisdiction where the action is filed in a state where they claim to transact no business. Given the inherent mobility of helicopters, that claim is being made with decreasing frequency and success. Nevertheless, counsel must be prepared to extensively brief all of the defendant's contacts with the forum jurisdiction which render it both foreseeable and reasonable to exercise jurisdiction over the out-of-state defendant.

6.3 Substantive Defenses

Where no product or system malfunction is claimed to have contributed to the crash, the substantive defenses are limited to negligence principles. For example, in a claim of pilot error for flying too closely to a landmark, the defendant may claim comparative negligence of the landmark's owner for failing to properly highlight the landmark.

In those cases where product or system malfunction is alleged, then all of those familiar product liability defenses are equally available to the defendant in helicopter crash litigation. Most of these product-related defenses are a function of the specific state products liability statutes and applicable case law. Whether specific defenses such as product misuse, component part alteration, the government contractor defense or comparative fault are utilized depends on the facts of the case, the defense strategy and the opinions of the various defense experts. Plaintiff's counsel must carefully plan and structure the lawsuit to defeat or minimize the impact of any applicable defenses.

A. Product Misuse or Alteration of Component Part

The premise underlying strict products liability is that the product is defective for its normal, intended or anticipated usage. A product would not be considered in a defective condition if it failed as a result of misuse or unintended or unforeseeable alteration. Within the context of helicopter crash litigation, that defense often is raised where maintenance personnel use a critical component part to replace another critical component part not designed or intended to fulfill that function. This scenario occurs where a replacement part is not one recommended for use by the original equipment manufacturer or is not compatible with the other parts or system in the helicopter. A mechanic either intentionally or inadvertently may install an improperly sized blade or disk into the engine with catastrophic results. Inappropriate length tubing or rods frequently are used as part of a main or tail rotor control system. In all such instances, the product manufacturer may claim that the product's failure or malfunction was due to the misuse or alteration and not its design.

In a negligence context, product misuse may vitiate the ordinary duty of care owed by the manufacturer. Product misuse or alteration may serve to bar or substantially diminish recovery where the manufacturer can prove that someone else was responsible for the product's malfunction. In many factual contexts, the key issue is the foreseeability of any misuse or alteration of the product. If the plaintiff can show that the manufacturer knew of these uses, intended or not, then the product misuse will not necessarily bar the claim.

In one helicopter crash case out of Texas, the court found that there was sufficient evidence concerning the helicopter manufacturer's notice or knowledge of unauthorized maintenance practices such as to overcome the manufacturer's claim that the improper maintenance constituted misuse.[30] Mechanics were not routinely inspecting or replacing the tail rotor blade on the helicopter. The court found this was a foreseeable misuse which would not form the basis of a product misuse defense because the manufacturer had knowledge of this practice and was aware that owners and operators were not adequately inspecting and maintaining the tail rotor.

Instances where misuse or a product alteration come into play are fact intensive and counsel must take steps to combat any inference or claim that the helicopter component at issue was the subject of misuse or abuse either by plaintiff or some third party. Some courts view product misuse as going to the issue of proximate cause. The focus of the inquiry is whether the crash occurred because of the design and function of the subject component or by the acts of some third party in altering or abusing the product. Evidence of substantially similar incidents is particularly useful in these cases to negate the impact of the misuse or alteration defense and highlight that the failure is related to the product design.

B. Contributory or Comparative Negligence

Comparative negligence or comparative fault is a statutorily adopted affirmative defense to reduce the salutary effect of contributory negligence which had been an absolute bar to a plaintiff's recovery. In most statutory schemes, the defense permits a comparison of the percentages of negligence of all defendants or alleged tortfeasors including that of the plaintiff. There still exist various state formulae which may bar recovery to the plaintiff if his percentage is greater than any of the individual or combined percentages of the defendants.

Helicopter defendants raise the defenses of contributory or comparative negligence and comparative fault to diminish their percentage of liability for plaintiff's damages. In those jurisdictions providing for relative fault, without pure joint and several or some modified form of joint and several liability, a defendant is only responsible for its percentage of liability as determined by the finder of fact. In such jurisdictions, the defense of comparative fault is an affirmative defense which must be pled and proved. In some states the entity to whom a percentage of fault may be allocated need not even be a party to the lawsuit, potentially generating the non-party fault defense.

There are six jurisdictions where contributory negligence is a complete bar to recovery. In Alabama,[31] the District of Columbia,[32] Maryland,[33] North Carolina,[34] South Carolina,[35] and Virginia,[36] the claimant's contributory negligence acts as a complete defense to the defendant's liability for negligence, no matter how slight. A particularly brutal formulation absolving product manufacturers or sellers from liability is the North Carolina statutory scheme:

No manufacturer or seller shall be held liable in any product liability action if:

(1) The use of the product giving rise to the product liability action was contrary to any express and adequate instructions or warnings delivered with, appearing on, or attached to the product or on its original container or wrapping, if the user knew or with the exercise of reasonable and diligent care should have known of such instructions or warnings; or

(2) The user knew of o discovered a defect or dangerous condition of the product that was incon-

sistent with the safe use of the product, and then unreasonably and voluntarily exposed himself or herself to the danger, and was injured by or caused injury with that product; or

(3) The claimant failed to exercise reasonable care under the circumstances in the use of the product, and such failure was a proximate cause of the occurrence that caused the injury or damage complained of.[37]

Where the claimant is the pilot or pilot's family and some basis exists for impugning fault, counsel must in this case look to file in some other jurisdiction rather than risk a potential total bar to recovery. A handful of states have statutorily enacted a total bar to recovery in any products liability action where the plaintiff's contributory negligence is found to be a "substantial cause" of the occurrence which causes the injury.

Most states provide that contributory negligence serves as a total bar to recovery only where the claimant's negligence is greater than the aggregate of the defendants' negligence. These states are Arkansas,[38] Colorado,[39] Delaware,[40] Georgia,[41] Guam,[42] Hawaii,[43] Idaho,[44] Indiana,[45] Iowa,[46] Kansas,[47] Maine,[48] Massachusetts,[49] Minnesota,[50] Montana,[51] Nebraska,[52] Nevada,[53] New Hampshire,[54] New Jersey,[55] North Dakota,[56] Ohio,[57] Oklahoma,[58] Oregon,[59] Tennessee,[60] Texas,[61] Utah,[62] Vermont,[63] Virgin Islands,[64] West Virginia,[65] Wisconsin,[66] and Wyoming.[67] Courts in Illinois and Pennsylvania have declared that statutes apportioning liability in this manner are unconstitutional for reasons other than this provision.[68]

A variant of this rule is found in South Dakota, where a plaintiff "guilty of contributory negligence" may recover if "the contributory negligence of the plaintiff was slight in comparison with the negligence of the defendant, but in such case, the damages shall be reduced in proportion to the amount of plaintiff's contributory negligence." [69] Michigan, too, offers a twist on recovery for claimants who are contributorily negligent to a degree greater than the aggregate fault of other persons, providing for a reduction of economic damages by the percentage of fault assessed to the claimant and barring recovery for noneconomic damages.[70]

Many states have a form of comparative negligence which would not bar the pilot's claim where a pilot may have some minimal degree of fault but will instead reduce the recovery by the percentage of negligence found by the pilot. Those states where contributory negligence merely diminishes recovery are Alaska,[71] Arizona,[72] California,[73] Connecticut,[74] Florida,[75] Kentucky,[76] Louisiana,[77] Mississippi,[78] Missouri,[79] New Mexico,[80] New York,[81] Rhode Island,[82] and Washington.[83] Since most jurisdictions apply some variation of comparative negligence or fault, a pilot plaintiff will suffer a percentage reduction of damages if she is found comparatively negligent. But there would be no automatic bar to recovery for the jury's finding of pilot error so long as that negligence is not greater than the total of all defendant's negligence. This defense places the burden on the defendant to plead and prove the comparative negligence to claim a reduction of recovery.

Comparative fault in strict products liability actions, especially involving conduct of the plaintiff, varies greatly among the states. Courts have struggled with the apportionment of fault in strict liability actions.[84] Recognizing that a strict liability claim focuses on the existence of a product defect and not on the manufacturer's lack of care in producing it, courts have hesitated to introduce negligence principles in a strict liability case to apportion liability among the parties.[85] Moreover, some consider that the apportionment of liability defeats the purpose of strict liability which is to "encourage the manufacturer to take greater care in designing and manufacturing his products" and apportioning liability to one who can "more easily absorb the loss by spreading the risk among its products."[86] Many states, however, have determined that liability should be borne by those responsible for it and assess liability according to the share of each in contributing to the damages.[87]

Comparative fault systems, also called comparative causation, contributory negligence, comparative responsibility, and comparative blameworthiness,[88] can be "modified" or "pure."[89] In modified comparative fault systems, a plaintiff is barred from recovery if the plaintiff's "share of causation is found to be greater than the total causation attributed to the defendants."[90] In pure contributory negligence systems, a plaintiff "can recover the percentage of damages caused by the defendants, regardless of the extent of [the plaintiff's] own causation."[91]

In addition, the types of fault for which a plaintiff may be assessed a proportionate share differ by state. Of those types of fault that state courts or statutes determine must be considered in apportioning fault in a strict liability actions, the most common are ordinary negligence, Assumption of risk, and product misuse. All three types of fault, as "variants of contributory negligence,…focus on the reasonableness of a plaintiff's conduct."[92]

Table 6.1 is a chart of the jurisdictions that have adopted a comparative fault system, indicating whether the system is pure or modified, and listing the types of fault which may be assessed against a plaintiff.

Table 6.1
Chart of Comparative Fault Systems

Jurisdiction	Type of System	Type of Fault Assessable to Plaintiff
Alaska[93]	Pure	Assumption of risk Product Misuse Ordinary negligence Unreasonable failure to avoid injury Unreasonable failure to mitigate damages
Arizona[94]	Pure	Assumption of risk Product misuse Product modification Product abuse
Arkansas[95]	Modified	Ordinary negligence Assumption of risk Unforeseeable alteration, change, improper maintenance, or abnormal use
California[96]	Pure	Ordinary negligence Assumption of risk Product misuse
Colorado[97]	Pure	Ordinary negligence Assumption of risk
Connecticut[98]	Pure	Ordinary negligence Product misuse Assumption of risk Product alteration or modification
Delaware[99]	Modified	Ordinary negligence
Federal admiralty[100]	Pure	Ordinary negligence and "all of plaintiff's conduct contributing to the cause of his loss or injury"
Florida[101]	Pure	Ordinary negligence other than the failure of the user to discover the defect in the product or the failure of the user to guard against the possibility of its existence. Product misuse
Hawaii[102]	Pure	Ordinary negligence
Idaho[103]	Modified	Assumption of risk Product misuse Product alteration or modification Claimant's failure to observe an obvious defective condition
Illinois[104]	Modified	Ordinary negligence Assumption of risk Product misuse
Indiana[105]	Modified	Assumption of risk Product misuse Product alteration or modification
Iowa[106]	Modified	Ordinary negligence Recklessness Product misuse Assumption of risk Unreasonable failure to avoid injury Unreasonable failure to mitigate damages

continued on next page…

Table 6.1 (continued)
Chart of Comparative Fault Systems

Jurisdiction	Type of System	Type of Fault Assessable to Plaintiff
Kansas[107]	Modified	Ordinary negligence Product misuse Assumption of risk
Kentucky[108]	Pure	Ordinary negligence Product misuse Breach of warranty Unreasonable assumption of risk Unreasonable failure to avoid injury Unreasonable failure to mitigate damages
Louisiana[109]	Pure	Ordinary negligence Product misuse Assumption of risk
Maine[110]	Pure	Negligence, breach of statutory duty or other act or omission that gives rise to a liability in tort or would, apart from this section, give rise to the defense of contributory negligence Assumption of risk
Michigan[111]	Pure	An act, an omission, conduct, including intentional conduct, . . . or a breach of a legal duty . . . that is a proximate cause of damage sustained by a party.
Minnesota[112]	Modified	Ordinary negligence other than failure to inspect a product or to guard against defects Assumption of risk Product misuse Unreasonable failure to avoid an injury Unreasonable failure to mitigate damages
Mississippi[113]	Pure	Ordinary negligence
Missouri[114]	Pure	Assumption of risk Product misuse Unreasonable failure to appreciate the danger involved in use of the product or the consequences thereof and the unreasonable exposure to said danger The failure to undertake the precautions a reasonably careful user of the product would take to protect himself against dangers which he would reasonably appreciate under the same or similar circumstances The failure to mitigate damages
Montana[115]	Modified	Assumption of risk Product misuse
New Hampshire[116]	Modified	Ordinary negligence Product misuse or abnormal use Assumption of risk
New Jersey[117]	Pure	Assumption of risk
New Mexico[118]	Pure	Ordinary negligence Assumption of the risk Product misuse
New York[119]	Pure	Ordinary negligence Assumption of risk
North Dakota[120]	Pure	Assumption of risk Product misuse

continued on next page...

Table 6.1 (continued)
Chart of Comparative Fault Systems

Jurisdiction	Type of System	Type of Fault Assessable to Plaintiff
Oregon[121]	Modified	Negligence other than failure to discover or to guard against the defect causing danger Assumption of risk Product misuse
Rhode Island[122]	Pure	Ordinary negligence
Tennessee[123]	Modified	Assumption of risk Last clear chance doctrine Sudden emergency doctrine Rescue doctrine Remote contributory negligence
Texas[124]	Modified	Ordinary negligence Assumption of risk Conduct other than the mere failure to discover or guard against a product defect
Utah[125]	Modified	Ordinary negligence Product misuse Product alteration or modification Assumption of risk Product abuse
Virgin Islands[126]	Pure	Ordinary negligence
Washington[127]	Pure	Ordinary negligence Recklessness Product misuse Unreasonable assumption of risk Unreasonable failure to avoid injury Unreasonable failure to mitigate damages
West Virginia[128]	Modified	Ordinary negligence other than the failure to discover a defect or to guard against it Assumption of risk Product misuse or abuse Product alteration
Wisconsin[129]	Modified	Ordinary negligence Product misuse Product alteration or modification Assumption of risk
Wyoming[130]	Modified	Assumption of risk Product misuse Product alteration

States that reject the application of comparative fault principles in strict products liability actions are Alabama,[131] District of Columbia,[132] Georgia,[133] Maryland,[134] Massachusetts,[135] Nebraska,[136] Nevada,[137] North Carolina,[138] Ohio,[139] Oklahoma,[140] Pennsylvania,[141] South Carolina,[142] and South Dakota.[143] Vermont has not yet ruled on whether comparative negligence generally applies in strict liability actions.[144] Virginia is silent on the issue.

C. Assumption of Risk

Assumption of risk is an affirmative defense raised within the context of a strict products liability claim. It requires the defendant to plead and prove that the plaintiff had specific knowledge of a risk, knew and appreciated the extent of the risk and voluntarily proceeded to encounter that known risk. The assumption of risk defense often is raised where a pilot knows that there is an outstanding maintenance discrepancy but yet decides to fly the helicopter anyway. The defense also comes into play in those instances where a pilot knows that a particular flight instrument is carded or known to be inoperative but makes the decision to take on the mission anyway.

In some jurisdictions, the plaintiff's assumption of risk is a complete defense and a total bar to recovery in a strict products liability claim. Four states, Mississippi, North Carolina, Ohio and South Carolina, have enacted statutes providing that the plaintiff's assumption of risk is a complete defense barring recovery.[145 6] For example, the South Carolina statutes provides:

> If the user or consumer discovers the defect and is aware of the danger, and nevertheless proceeds unreasonably, to make use of the product and is injured by it, he is barred from recovery.[146]

Most states by statute have placed assumption of risk in the same category as comparative negligence and it would not create a complete bar to plaintiff's recovery.[147] Typical of the latter is the Alaska statute:

> In an action based on fault seeking to recover damages for injury or death to a person or harm to property, contributory fault chargeable to the claimant diminishes proportionately the amount awarded as compensatory damages for the injury attributable to the claimant's contributory fault, but does not bar recovery.[148]

A few states by case decision have established that assumption of risk is a complete bar to recovery in a strict liability action.[149] Finally, a few states have by court decision determined that the assumption of risk defense would not create a complete bar to recovery.[150]

In a Pennsylvania case involving the death of a pilot in a helicopter crash, the court affirmed a jury instruction to consider the pilot's failure to determine the amount of fuel required for the flight.[151] Noting that a plaintiff's own negligence will not bar a strict liability claim, the court held that assumption of risk bars recovery where a plaintiff "knows of the specific defect eventually causing injury and voluntarily proceeds to use the product with knowledge of the danger caused by the defect."[152] And here, where the defendant introduced evidence "that the decedent knew of the specific defect causing his death and appreciated the danger it involved before using the aircraft," the jury would be allowed to consider whether this constituted assumption of risk.[153]

In some cases defendants have raised an assumption of risk defense simply for a plaintiff's voluntarily boarding a helicopter. Just such an affirmative defense was raised by a film production company with respect to a cameraman in a recent helicopter crash case tried by the author. The defendant argued that as an experienced helicopter cameraman, plaintiff's deceased was aware of the risks and proceeded aboard the helicopter with full knowledge of those risks. Plaintiff filed a summary judgment motion on the grounds that simply boarding a helicopter without any specific knowledge of mechanical deficiencies or pilot incapacity or inexperience was an insufficient basis for applicability of the defense. The district court judge struck the defense as a matter of law and at trial the plaintiff did not have any allocation of fault attributed to any actions of the deceased.[154]

D. Government Contractor Defense

The government contractor defense provides a qualified immunity to any aircraft or component part manufacturer which supplies aircraft to the U.S. military. Government contractors such as helicopter or engine manufacturers are immune from any state court liability for improper design where:

1. The U.S. approved the reasonably precise specifications;
2. The equipment provided to the military conformed to those requested specifications; and
3. The government contractor warned the U.S. about dangers in use of the equipment known to the contractor but not known to the U.S.

If applicable, the government contractor defense is an absolute bar and results in dismissal of the entire lawsuit. The U.S. Supreme Court decision in Bo*yle v. United Technologies Corporation* which established the government contractor defense involved a marine helicopter.[155] In a five to four decision, the Court in Boyle ruled that the defense barred a plaintiff's state law design defect claim as a matter of law.

The first factor dealing with "reasonably precise specifications" is the primary battleground for application of the government contractor defense. The product manufacturer must establish some degree of collaboration where the government had some role in the actual design of the aircraft or aircraft component. This means that the product manufacturer must establish that the U.S. government had some meaningful evaluation of the product design and ultimately approved it in order to establish the requisite governmental discretion for the defense. Absent proof of some hands-on involvement by the government during the design or testing phase of the product then the defense is unlikely to prevail.

In recent years, federal courts increasingly have applied the government contractor defense set out in *Boyle* to bar a plaintiff's state law failure to warn claims. An instructive set of cases on this issue starts with *Tate v. Boeing Helicopters (Tate I - 1995)*. In July 1990, five Army soldiers were on a training mission on board a CH-47D Chinook helicopter at Fort Campbell, Kentucky.[156] The training mission was to teach the crew members how to attach heavy equipment to a hook and sling system on the underbelly of the helicopter. While moving a 15,760 pound concrete block toward a pre-designated drop site, the block became lodged into the side of a hill in the helicopter's flight path. One of the crew tried to free the load by releasing the hook but to no avail and the helicopter crashed. Chief Warrant Officer Tate was killed and his family brought the wrongful death action against the helicopter manufacturer for, among other theories, "that the defendants failed to adequately warn the crew members of the dangers associated with use of the tandem hook system."[157]

Plaintiffs also brought a design defect claim. After affirming a grant of summary judgment as to the design defect claim based on the government contractor defense, the court found that the Army engaged in an interactive design development process with the contractor. It approved detailed specifications for the defective part at issue, namely the tandem hook. The tandem hook conformed to these specifications and the contractor had warned the Army of the danger of the hook failing to open if the line was slack which were the circumstances contributing to the subject helicopter crash.

The court reversed the trial court's grant of summary judgment in defendant's favor on the plaintiff's failure to warn claim under Kentucky state law. That claim was remanded for a determination of whether (1) the Army approved the warnings that were provided with the helicopter, (2) the warnings conformed to the specifications and (3) the contractor warned the Army of any dangers known to it of which the Army was not aware. The court ruled that the government contractor defense would apply to bar the failure to warn claim if the trial court found that sufficient evidence supported these elements.

Following the court's remand to the district court for further proceedings, that court granted the manufacturer's motion for summary judgment on the plaintiff's failure to warn claim based on the government contractor defense. In *Tate v. Boeing Helicopters (Tate II - 1998)*,[158] the appellate court noted that "the government contractor defense to failure to warn claims is not necessarily established merely by satisfying the government contractor defense as to design defect claims." But in this case, "the undisputed cause of the action was a failure of the tandem cargo hook system to release the cargo, and the only relevant inquiry was whether Boeing and Breeze Eastern warned of the situation of which

the hooks could fail to release." The court concluded that the Army's review of the operator's manual was extensive specifically including field testing by Army personnel. Second, the Army's acceptance of the manual demonstrated the contractor's conformance with its specifications. Third, the contractor warned the Army about the exact problem that caused the subject crash. And lastly, the court found a conflict between the warnings specified and the state law failure to warn claim once the government discussion was satisfied. Upon review of that information the court concluded that "no reasonable jury could have found that Boeing failed to warn the United States of the relevant danger."[159]

Plaintiffs have been successful in arguing that the defense imposes upon the manufacturer the obligation to have express governmental approval of the specific design feature at issue.[160] If the military branch simply leaves the design specifications for the aircraft up to the manufacturer, then the government contractor defense does not apply.[161] In recent years, the defense has been construed narrowly and unless the manufacturer can establish that the military approved the specific design feature at issue as part of a "meaningful review process," then the defense will not be successful.[162] The defendant must prove a "continuous back and forth" review process between the government and the contractor to satisfy the test.[163]

The government contractor defense is not a free pass for any manufacturer supplying helicopters or helicopter equipment to the military. The *Boyle* opinion was not intended to give complete immunity for defective product design but only if the defect was precisely attributable to the governmentally approved specifications.

In these cases, plaintiffs must emphasize that the burden of proof rests squarely with the manufacturer claiming the defense. Its mere assertion in a responsive pleading does not permit the manufacturer to go free. In handling military helicopter crash cases, plaintiffs must uncover precisely what documents and evidence are relied upon by the defendant manufacturer. This results in a turning of the tables in that the defendant manufacturer may be the victim of military stonewalling where the military secrets privilege could thwart the defendant's acquisition of the necessary proof in support of the defense. Plaintiff must hold the defendant to its proof and even rely upon en camera review by the court of certain evidence. Unless defendants in these cases can establish sufficient proof that the military branch at issue exercised its discretionary function to approve the reasonably precise design specifications then the defense should fail. In that instance, plaintiffs may pursue the action against the manufacturer in much the same fashion as any other type of helicopter crash litigation.

E. Useful Safe Life Presumptions

Six states, Arkansas, Connecticut, Idaho, Kansas, Kentucky, Twelve states, Arkansas, Connecticut, Florida, Idaho, Kansas, Kentucky, Minnesota, North Dakota, South Dakota, Tennessee, Texas and Washington, have enacted statutes providing for a presumption that a product manufacturer or seller is not liable for injuries caused after expiration of its product's "useful safe life."[164] Most of these jurisdictions treat the useful safe life as a complete defense to a products liability claim while other states permit evidence of the use of the product after its useful safe life as evidence of plaintiff's fault.

The North Dakota statute applies specifically to aircraft and aircraft components. It harshly defines the useful safe life as ten years from the date of first delivery to the first user, purchaser or lessee.[165] The presumption is only rebuttable by clear and convincing evidence.[166] However, as to aircraft components as distinguished from the actual aircraft:

> No claim for damages may be made after the useful safe life of the component, the period stated in the warranty, or ten years after manufacture of the component, whichever is later.[167]

A more typical formulation of the useful safe life presumption is the Kansas Statute:

> (a)(1) Except as provided in paragraph (2) of this subsection, a product seller shall not be subject to liability in a product liability claim if the product seller proves by a preponderance of the evidence that the harm was caused after the product's "us safe life" had expired. "Useful safe life" begins at the time of delivery of the product and extends for the time during which the product would normally be likely to perform or be stored in a safe manner. For the purposes of this section, "time of delivery" means the time of delivery of a product to its first purchaser or lessee who was not engaged in the business of either selling such products or using them as component parts of another product to be sold.[168]

The statute then provides examples of evidence probative of the expiration of a useful safe life and notes a rebuttable presumption that the useful life expired after ten years with certain exceptions.

This useful safe life defense is particularly troublesome in the context of helicopter accident litigation because many components and systems installed in the helicopter remain functioning long after the particular useful safe life period

prescribed. Although most of these statutes provide for a ten-year presumption, Kentucky's statute is the shortest. It provides for a presumption of product non-defect where the injury or death occurred more than five years from the date of sale to the first consumer or more than eight years after the date of manufacture.[169]

Many components in a system and helicopter are designed to function for the life of the helicopter such as control rods, cables, electrical wiring and various brackets. Application of this statutory defense may result in unjust results especially in Kentucky and North Dakota. In those jurisdictions where the defense is rebuttable, it is incumbent on counsel to show that the helicopter or helicopter component manufacturer had actual knowledge or notice that its aircraft or various component parts were being operated beyond their so-called useful safe life and that the defendant took no action to limit the continued use beyond that time period. Discovery from large helicopter operators and the nature of their interaction with the manufacturer's technical support and sales representatives also may yield critical evidence in seeking to rebut the statutory presumption.

Counsel must carefully examine the particular statutory language to determine if the presumption applies to non-purchasers of the product. Based on the definitions used in several of the statutes, counsel may be able to make a persuasive argument that the presumption is inapplicable to claimants who did not purchase, lease or consume the allegedly defective product. Such an argument clearly would exempt any on-ground injury victims from the presumption as they assuredly did not purchase, lease or use the helicopter.

F. Compliance with Government Standards

The evidentiary impact of a defendant's compliance with government standards varies significantly among the states. The way this evidence most frequently arises in helicopter crash litigation is where a defendant helicopter airframe or component part manufacturer claims compliance with an FAA standard, rule or regulation. The inverse scenario where the plaintiff introduces evidence of a defendant's violation of a government standard or regulation normally results in a negligence per se finding and is, at minimum, probative as to defendant's violation of the applicable standard of care.

Many states including Arkansas, California, Colorado, Florida, Indiana, Kansas, Kentucky, Massachusetts, Michigan, North Dakota, Ohio, Oklahoma, South Dakota, Tennessee, Texas, Utah, Washington and Wisconsin, have enacted specific statutes providing for a rebuttable presumption that a manufactured product or a component is not defective if it complied with governmental standards or regulations at the time it was sold.[170] A typical formulation is the Tennessee statute which provides:

Compliance by a manufacturer or seller with any federal or state statute or administrative regulation existing at the time a product was manufactured and prescribing standards for design, inspection, testing, manufacture, labeling, warning or instructions for use of a product, shall raise a rebuttable presumption that the product is not in an unreasonably dangerous condition in regard to matters covered by these standards.[171]

In two states, the statutory scheme provides for a near absolute defense if at the time the component or product was manufactured it was in compliance with some government standard or regulation relating either to designs, warnings, or instructions. For example, under the Kansas product liability statute, if any product was in compliance with any legislative or administrative regulatory safety standard at the time of its manufacture relating to design or performance "the product shall be deemed not defective by reason of design or performance,…unless the claimant proves by a preponderance of the evidence that a reasonably prudent product seller could and would have taken additional precautions."[172] Kentucky has a similar statutory scheme which provides for a near ironclad presumption unless plaintiff is somehow able to rebut it "by a preponderance of evidence to the contrary."[173] South Dakota, on the other hand, provides that compliance with legislative or administrative regulatory safety standards as to design, performance, warnings or instructions is a complete defense.[174] Once again the North Dakota statutory scheme singles out aviation manufacturers for special treatment providing that:

1. There is a disputable presumption that a product is free from any defect or defective condition if the product was in compliance with:

a. Government standards established for that product; or

b. If no government standards exist, applicable industry standards that were in existence at the time of manufacture.

2. An aviation manufacturer or a seller of aircraft or aircraft components may utilize the presumption provided by subsection 1 if the manufacture, design, formulation, inspection, testing, packaging, labeling, or warning complied with:

a. Federal Aviation Administration or Department of Transportation regulations that relate to the safety or establish safety standards for the aircraft or aircraft component and which

existed at the time the aircraft or aircraft component was produced;

b. Any premarket approval or certification by the federal aviation administration or any other federal agency; and

c. Applicable industry standards that were in existence at the time the plans, designs, warnings, or instructions for the aircraft or aircraft component or the methods and techniques of manufacturing, inspecting, and testing the product were adopted.

3. The presumption under subsection 1 is not available if the plaintiff proves by clear and convincing evidence that the aviation manufacturer or product seller knowingly and in violation of applicable agency regulations made misrepresentations, made illegal payments to an official for the purpose of securing approval, committed fraud, or concealed evidence.

4. There is an absolute defense to any product liability action brought against an aviation manufacturer when a claimant, in violation of federal aviation administration regulations, has used alcohol or illicit drugs while operating or using an aircraft or aircraft component.

5. This chapter does not affect the authority of the federal aviation administration or any other federal agency with regard to the regulation of aircraft and aircraft components.[175]

In most other states, the courts have ruled that, although no presumption applies, evidence of compliance with government regulations may be considered by the trier of fact in determining liability for negligence as those bear on the applicable standard of care.[176] Some courts have admitted evidence of the defendant's compliance with a government regulation in a strict liability context but that is a minority view. If standard of care is not at issue in the case such as where plaintiffs dismiss their negligent design count, then compliance with a governmental regulation should be irrelevant.[177] An example of this minority view arose in the context of helicopter crash litigation. In a Pennsylvania case, the plaintiff alleged a strict products liability claim for design defect after a rotor blade snapped causing the helicopter to crash.[178] The court observed that while compliance with a Federal Aviation Regulation negates a claim of negligence per se, "it does not establish as a matter of law that due care was exercised."[179] Further:

Compliance with the statute or regulation is admissible as evidence of the actor's exercise of due care, but such compliance "does not prevent a finding of negligence where a reasonable man would take additional precautions."[180]

Although noting that the plaintiff did not allege negligence in this case, the court nevertheless admitted evidence of the defendant's compliance with the FAA regulation "to show that the helicopter was not unreasonably dangerous."[181]

In dealing with those state statutes providing for a rebuttable presumption that a product is not defective where it is designed in compliance with government standards, plaintiff's counsel must seek to rebut the presumption vigorously. That process starts with a careful analysis of the particular jurisdiction's statutory scheme.

By way of example, the Texas statute expressly outlines the types of proof by which plaintiff may rebut the presumption:

1. the mandatory federal safety standards or regulations applicable to the product were inadequate to protect the public from unreasonable risks of injury or damage; or
2. the manufacturer, before or after marketing the product, withheld or misrepresented information or material relevant to the federal government's or agency's determination of adequacy of the safety standards or regulations at issue in the action.[182]

Counsel must retain early on an expert as to the FAA regulatory scheme to assist with drafting discovery and in marshalling appropriate and sufficient evidence in rebuttal of the presumption. One common tact is to assess whether any regulation is specifically applicable to the failure alleged. Counsel's expert must be prepared to testify about the minimal nature of the Federal Aviation Regulations as establishing merely a floor for airworthiness and not the standard of care. For example, evidence of a competing product manufacture's safer design is useful evidence to rebut the presumption.

G. State of the Art Defense

The term state of the art generally refers to the technical and scientific knowledge which was in existence and reasonably feasible at the time that product was manufactured.[183] It is also variously defined as the "best technology reasonably available" at the time the specific product was first sold to anyone not engaged in the business of selling such a product. Courts disagree on what constitutes state of the

art evidence.[184] While some courts have defined the term as industry custom,[185] others reject that definition, finding that custom may lag behind technological development.[186] The majority of courts as well as statutes define state of the art evidence as "the level of relevant scientific, technological and safety knowledge existing and reasonably feasible at the time of design."[187]

Courts have disagreed on the claims for which state of the art evidence is admissible. In negligence actions, it may be admitted to rebut "the existence or feasibility of safer designs to support [the plaintiff's] allegations that the product in question is unreasonably dangerous."[188] But more often, it is admitted as a factor to be considered in determining if a defendant manufacturer failed to use ordinary care.[189]

By statute some states provide that conformance with the state of the art at the time the product was manufactured is an affirmative defense.[190] Other statutory schemes provide that the finder of fact may consider the state of the art available to the manufacturer or seller at the time the product was placed on the market in determining whether a product is in a defective condition or unreasonably dangerous.[191]

Several states have enacted legislation referring to state of the art evidence but not providing that it may be raised as an affirmative defense. These statutes vary considerably in how this evidence is applied and its effect once admitted. Some states either explicitly provide for a state of the art defense or refuse to admit evidence of changes to state of the art since the product's sale. In other states, state of the art evidence creates a rebuttable presumption that the product was not defective or the manufacturer or seller was not negligent.[192] Still others consider state of the art evidence as merely one factor in determining the standard of care or whether a product is defective.

Most states admit state of the art evidence in design defect cases. Others restrict its admission to only negligence or strict liability failure-to-warn cases.[193] The law becomes more complicated for strict liability claims of design defect. Some find the application of this evidence to strict liability cases inappropriate because it applies negligence principles in a strict liability claim, shifting attention from the product's condition to the manufacturer's conduct.[194] Other courts not only admit state of the art evidence in strict liability actions, they admit it as a complete defense.[195] And some admit it merely as a factor to be considered in determining if the product is defective[196] Although courts differ on how it is used, most admit state of the art evidence in design defect cases.[197]

In regard to strict liability claims for failure to warn, the differences in opinion converge on the issue of knowledge.[198] Relying on a comment to Restatement (Second) Torts § 402A, many courts require a seller "to give warning against [the danger], if he has knowledge, or by the application of reasonable, developed human skill and foresight should have knowledge, of the...danger."[199] The knowledge required of a manufacturer in failure-to-warn claims under a strict liability theory refers to "the knowledge of an expert in the field" who has kept "reasonably abreast of scientific knowledge and discoveries" in regard to the product at issue.[200] Or, as described by another court, state of the art in these cases is "evidence that the particular risk was neither known nor knowable by the application of scientific knowledge available at the time of manufacture and/or distribution."[201] Other courts attribute even unknowable risks to the manufacturer, rejecting state of the art evidence because the defendant's actual or constructive knowledge, as a negligence concept, is irrelevant to a strict liability claim.[202]

As for manufacturing defect claims, "courts have excluded evidence of the state of the art because the plaintiff need only show the product does not conform to the manufacturer's specifications to prove it is defective."[203] With the enactment of statutes that specifically provide that state of the art evidence applies to manufacturing defect claims, more cases may be admitting such evidence.[204]

Although most helicopter airframe and component part manufacturers plead state of the art as a defense, it rarely arises as a contested issue in these cases. By definition, the state of the art has no application to any manufacturing defect claim. And in design defect cases the issue is typically not whether the safer alternative design was technologically available but whether practical considerations such as cost, function, ease of mass production or difficulty of maintenance render it commercially feasible

Endnotes

1. 49 U.S.C. § 40101, Section 2(b)(1) (1997).

2. 49 U.S.C. § 40101, Section 2(a)(2).

3. *Caldwell v. Enstrom Helicopter Corp.*, 230 F.3d 1155 (9th Cir. 2000) (ruling that an aircraft's flight manual was a component part of the aircraft); *Colgan Air, Inc. v. Raytheon Aircraft Co.,* 507 F.3d 270, 278 (4th Cir. 2007) (district court erred in concluding as a matter of law that a maintenance manual was part of an aircraft); *Alter v. Bell Helicopter Textron, Inc.*, 944 F.Supp. 531, 538 (S.D. Tex. 1996) (a maintenance manual was not a part originally in or added to the aircraft and a revision to a manual was not a replacement part that started a new limitations period under the act); *Moyer v. Teledyne Continental Motors, Inc.*, 979 A.2d 336, 344 (Pa. Super. Ct. 2009) (a service bulletin that instructed on revised maintenance procedures was not the equivalent of a flight manual for purposes of the Act).

4. *Rogers v. Bell Helicopter Textron, Inc.*, 112 Cal.Rptr.3d 1 (Cal.App. 2010).

5. *Id.*

6. *Id.*

7. 28 U.S.C. § 1331 (1980).

8. *Rice v. Sante Fe Elevator Corp.*, 331 U.S. 218, 230 (1947).

9. *Krispin v. May Department Stores Co.*, 218 F.3d 919, 922 (8th Cir. 2000).

10. *Caterpillar, Inc. v. Williams*, 482 U.S. 386, 392 (1987).

11. *Id.* at 392, 399.

12. *Beneficial National Bank v. Anderson*, 539 U.S. 1, 6 (2003).

13. *Grable & Sons Metal Products, Inc. v. Darue Engineering & Manufacturing*, 545 U.S. 308, 125 S.Ct. 2363 (2005).

14. *Greene v. B.F. Goodrich Avionics Systems, Inc.*, 409 F.3d 784, (6th Cir. 2005), cert. denied 547 U.S. 1003 (2006).

15. Federal cases dismissing cases on forum non conveniens grounds though jurisdiction proper: *Seguros Universales, S.A. v. Microsoft Corp.*, 32 F.Supp.3d. 1242 (S.D.Fla. 2014); *In re Optimal U.S. Litigation*, 886 F.Supp.2d 298 (S.D.N.Y. 2012); *In re Union Carbide Corp. Gas Plant Disaster at Bhopal, India in December 1984*, 634 F.Supp. 842 (S.D.N.Y. 1986), aff'd in part, 809 F.2d 195 (2nd Cir. 1987); *Sibaja v. Dow Chemical Co.*, 757 F.2d 1215 (11th Cir. 1985). State courts abolishing forum non conveniens or holding it inapplicable to wrongful death or personal injury suits: *Dow Chemical Co. v. Castro Alfaro*, 786 S.W.2d 674 (Tex. 1990), *cert. denied*, 498 U.S. 1024 (1991); *Kassapas v. Arkon Shipping Agency, Inc.*, 485 So.2d 565 (La. App. 1986) *writ denied*, 488 So.2d 203 (La. 1986), *cert. denied*, 479 U.S. 940 (1986) (Forum non conveniens doctrine does not exist under Louisiana law); *Smith v. Board of Regents of the University System of Georgia*, 302 S.E.2d 124, 126 (Ga. App. 1983) (Forum non conveniens doctrine "has never been expressly sanctioned in Georgia courts").
In response to the Texas Supreme Court's abolition of the common law doctrine of forum non conveniens, the Texas legislature adopted it by statute in 1993 although the law specifically exempts wrongful death or injury

actions arising from air transportation so long as there is some factual basis in support of sufficient contacts with the State of Texas.

16. The primary federal court case is *Gulf Oil Corp. v. Gilbert*, 330 U.S. 501, 509 (1947), superseded by 28 U.S.C. § 1404(a) (1996) (applying similar factors).

17. *Id.* at 508.

18. *Id.* 508-09.

19. *In re Aircrash Disaster Near New Orleans*, 821 F.2d 1147, 1157 (5th Cir. 1987), *judgment vacated on other grounds, sub nom. Pan American Airways, Inc. v. Lopez World*, 490 U.S. 1032 (1989).

20. *See, e.g.*, In. St. Trial P. Rule 4.4(D).

21. 28 U.S.C. § 1602 (1976).

22. 28 U.S.C. § 1605(a)(2) (2008).

23. 28 U.S.C. § 1603(a) (2005).

24. 28 U.S.C. § 1603(b).

25. *Dole Food Co. v. Patrickson*, 538 U.S. 468 (2003).

26. *Daskal v. Eurocopter, S.A., et al.*, Case No: CV-S-04-0506 (D.Nev. 2004).

27. *Gould v. Aerospatiale Helicopter Corp.*, 40 F.3d 1033 (9th Cir. 1994).

28. *Id.* at 1034.

29. *Id.* at 1036.

30. *Bell Helicopter Co. v. Bradshaw*, 594 S.W.2d 519 (Tex. Civ. App. 1979), disapproved on other grounds, *Torrington Co. v. Stutzman*, 465 S.W.3d 829 (Tex. 2000).

31. *Norfolk Southern Ry. Co. v. Johnson*, 75 So.3d 624, 639 (Ala. 2011).

32. *Jarrett v. Woodward Bros., Inc.*, 751 A.2d 972, 985 (D.C. 2000).

33. *Doe v. Board of Educ. of Prince George's County*, 982 F.Supp.2d 641, 663 (D.Md. 2013).

34. N.C. Stat. § 99B-4 (1996).

35. *Wallace v. Owens-Illinois, Inc.*, 389 S.E.2d 155, 157 (S.C. App. 1989).

36. *Jones v. Ford Motor Co.*, 559 S.E.2d 592, 604-05 (Va. 2002).

37. NC St Section 99B-4 (1996).

38. A.C.A. § 16-64-122 (1991).

39. C.R.S.A. § 13-21-111 (1986).

40. 10 Del.C. § 8132 (1995).

41. *Union Camp Corp. v. Helmy*, 367 S.E.2d 796, 800 (Ga. 1988).

42. Gu St. T. 18, § 90108 (1973).

43. HRS § 663-31 (1984).

44. I.C. § 6-801 (1987).

45. IC 34-51-2-5 (1998); IC 34-51-2-6 (1998).

46. I.C.A. § 668.3 (1997).

47. K.S.A. 60-258(a), (2010).

48. 14 M.R.S.A. § 156 (1999).

49. M.G.L.A. 231 § 85 (1973).

50. M.S.A. § 604.01 (1990).

51. MCA 27-1-702 (1997).

52. Neb. Rev. St. § 25-21,185.09 (1992).

53. N.R.S. 41.141 (1989).

54. N.H. Rev. Stat. § 507:7-d (1986).

55. N.J.S.A. 2A:15-5.1 (1982).

56. NDCC, 32-03.2-02 (1993).

57. R.C. § 2315.33 (2005).

58. 23 Okl.St.Ann. § 13 (1979).

590.O.R.S. § 31.600 (1995).

60. *McIntyre v. Balentine*, 833 S.W.2d 52, 57 (Tenn. 1992).

61. V.T.C.A., Civil Practice & Remedies Code § 33.001 (1995).

62. U.C.A. 1953 § 78B-5-818 (2008).

63. 12 V.S.A. § 1036 (1979).

64. 5 V.I.C. § 1451 (1986).

65. *Star Furniture Co. v. Pulaski Furniture Co.*, 297 S.E.2d 854, 861 (W.Va. 1982).

66. W.S.A. 895.045 (2011).

67. W.S. 1977 § 1-1-109 (1994).

68. *Best v. Taylor Mach. Works*, 689 N.E.2d 1057 (Ill. 1997) (declaring 735 ILCS 5/2-1116 unconstitutional); *DeWeese v. Weaver*, 880 A.2d 54 (Pa.Cmwlth. 2005) *order affd sub nom. Deweese v. Cortes*, 906 A.2d 1193 (Pa. 2006) (declaring 42 Pa. C.S.A. § 7102 unconstitutional).

69. SDCL § 20-9-2 (1998).

70. M.C.L.A. 600.2959 (2013).

71. AS § 09.17.060 (1986).

72. A.R.S. § 12-2505 (1984).

73. *Li v. Yellow Cab Co.*, 532 P.2d 1226, 1242-43 (Cal. 1975).

74. C.G.S.A. § 52-572o (1984).

756. West's F.S.A. § 768.81 (201106).

76. KRS § 411.182 (1988).

77. LSA-C.C. Art. 2323 (1996).

78. Miss. Code Ann. § 11-7-15 (1942).

79. V.A.M.S. 537.765 (1987).

80. NMRA, Civ. UJI 13-2218 (2005); NMRA, Civ. UJI 13-2219 (2005).

81. McKinney's CPLR § 1411 (1975).

82. RI ST § 9-20-4 (1972).

83. West's RCWA 4.22.005 (1981).

84. *Duncan v. Cessna Aircraft Co.*, 665 S.W.2d 414, 424-26 (Tex. 1984).

85. *Whitehead v. Toyota Motor Corp.*, 897 S.W.2d 684, 688-693 (Tenn. 1995); *Daly v. General Motors Corp.*, 575 P.2d 1162, 1167-68 (Cal. 1978).

86. *Whitehead*, 897 S.W.2d at 688-89; *see also Duncan*, 665 S.W.2d at 424-25; *Daly*, 575 P.2d at 1166-69.

87. *Whitehead*, 897 S.W.2d at 690-91; *Pan-Alaska Fisheries, Inc. v. Marine Const. & Design Co.*, 565 F.2d 1129, 1139 (9th Cir. 1977); *Daly*, 575 P.2d at 1172.

88. *Pan-Alaska Fisheries*, 565 F.2d at 1139.

89. *Duncan*, 665 S.W.2d at 428.

90. *Id.*

91. *Id.*

92. *Id.* at 423.

93. AS § 09.17.900 (1997); AS § 09.17.060 (1986); *Smith v. Ingersoll-Rand Co.*, 14 P.3d 990, 994-96 (Alaska 2000).

94. A.R.S. § 12-2505 (1984); A.R.S. § 12-2506 (2001); A.R.S. § 12-2509 (1984); *Jimenez v. Sears, Roebuck and Co.*, 904 P.2d 861, 86-70 (Ariz. 1995).

95. A.C.A. § 16-55-216 (2003); A.C.A. § 16-64-122 (1991); A.C.A. § 16-116-106 (1979).

96. *Daly*, 575 P.2d at 1168-73; *Milwaukee Electric Tool Corp. v. Superior Court*, 19 Cal.Rptr.2d 24, 32 (Cal. App. 1993).

97. C.R.S.A. § 13-21-406 (1986); *Huffman v. Caterpillar Tractor Co.*, 908 F.2d 1470, 1473-77 (C.A.10 (Colo.) 1990); *States v. R.D. Werner Co., Inc.*, 799 P.2d 427, 429-30 (Colo. App. 1990).

98. C.G.S.A. §§ 52-572n and 52-572o (1984); C.G.S.A. § 52-572l (1977); C.G.S.A. § 52-572p (1979); *Elliot v. Sears, Roebuck and Co.*, 621 A.2d 1371, 1375 (Conn. App. 1993), aff'd, 642 A.2d 709 (1994).

99. 10 Del.C. § 8132 (1995); *Meekins v. Ford Motor Co.*, 699 A.2d 339, 344-46 (Del. Super. 1997).

100. *Pan-Alaska Fisheries*, 565 F.2d at 1137-39; *Lewis v. Timco, Inc.*, 716 F.2d 1425, 1428 (5th Cir. 1983).

101. West's F.S.A. § 768.81 (2011); *West v. Caterpillar Tractor Co., Inc.*, 336 So.2d 80, 90 (Fla. 1976); *Hoffman v. Jones*, 280 So.2d 431, 438 (Fla. 1973).

102. *Kaneko v. Hilo Coast Processing*, 654 P.2d 343, 353-54 (Hawaii 1982); *Hao v. Owens-Illinois, Inc.*, 738 P.2d 416, 418-19 (Hawaii 1987).

103. I.C. § 6-1405 (2005); *Vannoy v. Uniroyal Tire Co.*, 726 P.2d 648, 654-56 (Idaho 1985).

104. *Malen v. MTD Products, Inc.*, 628 F.3d 296, 313 (C.A.7 (Ill.) 2010).

105. IC 34-20-6-3, IC 34-20-6-4, IC 34-20-6-5, IC 34-20-8-1, IC 34-51-2-7, IC 34-51-2-8 (1998)

106. I.C.A. § 668.3 (1997); I.C.A. § 668.1 (1984).

107. *Kennedy v. City of Sawyer*, 618 P.2d 788, 798 (Kan. 1980); *Forsythe v. Coats Co., Inc.*, 639 P.2d 43, 43 (Kan. 1982).

108. KRS § 411.182 (1988); *Owens Corning Fiberglas Corp. v. Parrish*, 58 S.W.3d 467, 474-75 (Ky. 2001).

109. LSA-CC Art. 2323 (1996); *Bell v. Jet Wheel Blast, Div. of Ervin Industries*, 462 So.2d 166, 170-73 (La. 1985) (applied only in cases where the policies goals of comparative fault would be furthered, refusing to assess negligence against a worker where "the application of comparative fault would not serve to provide any greater incentive to an employee to guard against momentary neglect or inattention so as to prevent his hand from being mangled by machinery").

110. 14 M.R.S.A. § 156 (1999); *Austin v. Raybestos-Manhattan, Inc.*, 471 A.2d 280, 282-87 (Me. 1984).

111. M.C.L.A. 600.2957 (1996); M.C.L.A. 600.2958 (1996); M.C.L.A. 600.2959 (2013); M.C.L.A. 600.6304 (1996).

112. M.S.A. § 604.01 (1990); *Busch v. Busch Const., Inc.*, 262 N.W.2d 377, 393-94 (Minn. 1977).

113. Miss. Code Ann. § 11-7-15 (1942); *Horton v. American Tobacco Co.*, 667 So.2d 1289, 1292-93 (Miss. 1995).

114. Mo. Rev. Stat. § 537.765 (1987).

115. MCA 27-1-702 (1997); MCA 27-1-719 (2009); *Hart-Albin Co. v. McLees, Inc.*, 870 P.2d 51, 53 (Mont. 1994).

116. *Thibault v. Sears, Roebuck & Co.*, 395 A.2d 843, 850 (N.H. 1978).

117. NJ ST 2A:15-5.2 (1995); *Cartel Capital Corp. v. Fireco of New Jersey*, 410 A.2d 674, 681-82 (N.J. 1980).

118. NMRA, Civ. UJI 13-1427 (2005); *Marchese v. Warner Communications, Inc.*, 670 P.2d 113, 117-18 (N.M.App. 1983), *cert. denied*, 100 N.M. 259 (1983).

119. McKinney's CPLR § 1411 (1975).

120. *Day v. General Motors Corp.*, 345 N.W.2d 349, 357 (N.D. 1984); *Mauch v. Manufacturers Sales & Service, Inc.*, 345 N.W.2d 338, 344-48 (N.D. 1984).

121. O.R.S. § 31.600 (1995); *Jett v. Ford Motor Co.*, 84 P.3d 219, 222 (Or.App. 2004), *review denied*, 94 P.3d 876 (2004) (Table); *Sandford v. Chevrolet Division of General Motors*, 642 P.2d 624, 626-36 (Or. 1982).

122. Gen.Laws 1956, § 9-20-4 (1972); *Fiske v. MacGregor, Div. of Brunswick*, 464 A.2d 719, 726-29 (R.I. 1983).

123. *Whitehead*, 897 S.W.2d at 686-93; *Eaton v. McLain*, 891 S.W.2d 587, 590 (Tenn. 1994).

124. V.T.C.A., Civil Practice & Remedies Code § 33.001 (1995); V.T.C.A., Civil Practice & Remedies Code §§ 33.002, 33.003 (2003); *JCW Electronics, Inc. v. Garza*, 257 S.W.3d 701, 705 (Texas 2008); *General Motors Corp. v. Sanchez*, 997 S.W.2d 584, 594 (Texas 1999).

125. U.C.A. 1953 § 78B-5-817 (2008); U.C.A. 1953 § 78B-5-818 (2008).

126. *Murray v. Fairbanks Morse*, 610 F.2d 149, 162 (3rd Cir. 1979).

127. West's RCWA 4.22.005, 4.22.015 (1981); *Lundberg v. All-Pure Chemical Co.*, 777 P.2d 15, 17-19 (Wash.App. 1989), *review denied*, 784 P.2d 530 (1989).

128. *Star Furniture Co. v. Pulaski Furniture Co.*, 297 S.E.2d 854, 861-63 (W.Va. 1982).

129. W.S.A. 895.045, 895.047 (2011); *Dippel v. Sciano*, 155 N.W.2d 55, 62-64 (Wis. 1967).

130. W.S.1977 § 1-1-109 (1994).

131. *Ex parte Goldsen*, 783 So.2d 53, 56 (Ala. 2000).

132. *Warner Fruehauf Trailer Co., Inc. v. Boston*, 654 A.2d 1272, 1275 n.7 (D.C. 1995).

133. *Deere & Co. v. Brooks*, 299 S.E.2d 704, 706 (Ga. 1983).

134. *Mayor and City Council of Baltimore v. Utica Mut. Ins. Co.*, 802 A.2d 1070, 1089 (Md. App. 2002), *cert. denied sub nom. Baltimore v. Utica Mutual*, 810 A.2d 961 (Md. 2002), *appeal dismissed*, 821 A.2d 369 (Md. 2003).

135. *Correia v. Firestone Tire & Rubber Co.*, 446 N.E.2d 1033, 1039-41 (Mass. 1983).

136. *Shipler v. General Motors Corp.*, 710 N.W.2d 807, 831-32 (Neb. 2006).

137. *Young's Mach. Co. v. Long*, 692 P.2d 24, 24-25 (Nev. 1984).

138. *Wilson Bros. v. Mobil Oil*, 305 S.E.2d 40, 45 (N.C. App. 1983), *review denied*, 308 S.E.2d 718 (N.C. 1983) and 308 S.E.2d 719 (N.C. 1983).

139. *Bowling v. Heil Co.*, 511 N.E.2d 373, 380 (Ohio 1987).

140. *Kirkland v. General Motors Corp.*, 521 P.2d 1353, 1367 (Okl. 1974).

141. *Kimco Development Corp. v. Michael Dís Carpet Outlets*, 637 A.2d 603, 607 (Pa. 1993) (ruling that "comparative negligence may not be asserted as a defense in § 402A strict product liability actions"); *Clark v. Bil-Jax, Inc.*, 763 A.2d 920, 923 (Pa. Super. 2000) *appeal denied*, 782 A.2d 541 (Pa. 2001) (ruling that "[e]vidence of plaintiff's voluntary assumption of the risk, misuse of product, or highly reckless conduct is admissible in strict products liability action insofar as it relates to element of causation; [h]owever, evidence of plaintiff's ordinary negligence may not be admitted in strict products liability action…unless it is shown that accident was solely the result of user's conduct and not related in any way with the alleged defect in the product").

142. *Bragg v. Hi-Ranger, Inc.*, 462 S.E.2d 321, 326 (S.C. App. 1995).

143. *Smith v. Smith*, 278 N.W.2d 155, 160-61 (S.D. 1979).

144. *Webb v. Navistar Intern. Transp. Corp.*, 692 A.2d 343, 346 (Vt. 1996).

145. Mississippi: "Subject to the provisions of Section 11-1-64 [repealed], in any action for damages caused by a product except for commercial damage to the product itself:…

(d) In any action alleging that a product is defective pursuant to paragraph (a) of this section, the manufacturer or seller shall not be liable if the claimant (i) had knowledge of a condition of the product that was inconsistent with his safety; (ii) appreciated the danger in the condition; and (iii) deliberately and voluntarily chose to expose himself to the danger in such a manner to register assent on the continuance of the dangerous condition." Miss. Code Ann. § 11-1-63 (2004);

North Carolina: "No manufacturer or seller shall be held liable in any product liability action if: . . . (2) The user knew of or discovered a defect or dangerous condition of the product that was inconsistent with the safe use of the product, and then unreasonably and voluntarily exposed himself or herself to the danger, and was injured by or caused injury with that product . . . .". N.C.G.S.A. § 99B-4 (1996);

Ohio: "(A) Subject to divisions (B)(1), (2), and (3) of this section, sections 2315.32 to 2315.36 of the Revised Code [statutes relating to contributory fault] apply to a product liability claim that is asserted pursuant to sections 2307.71 to 2307.80 of the Revised Code [product liability actions].

(B)(1) Express or implied assumption of the risk may be asserted as an affirmative defense to a product liability claim under sections 2307.71 to 2307.80 of the Revised Code, except that express or implied assumption of the risk may not be asserted as an affirmative defense to an intentional tort claim.

(2) Subject to division (B)(3) of this section, if express or implied assumption of the risk is asserted as an affirmative defense to a product liability claim under sections 2307.71 to 2307.80 of the Revised Code and if it is determined that the claimant expressly or impliedly assumed a risk and that the express or implied assumption of the risk was a direct and proximate cause of harm for which the claimant seeks to recover damages, the express or implied assumption of the risk is a complete bar to the recovery of those damages.

(3) If implied assumption of the risk is asserted as an affirmative defense to a product liability claim against a supplier under division (A)(1) of section 2307.78 of the Revised Code, sections 2315.32 to 2315.36 of the Revised Code are applicable to that affirmative defense and shall be used to determine whether the claimant is entitled to recover compensatory damages based on that claim and the amount of any recoverable compensatory damages." R.C. § 2307.711 (2004);

South Carolina: "If the user or consumer discovers the defect and is aware of the danger, and nevertheless proceeds unreasonably to make use of the product and is injured by it, he is barred from recovery." South Carolina Code 1976 § 15-73-20 (1974).

146. South Carolina Code 1976 § 15-73-20 (1974).

147. Alaska: Definitions. "In this chapter, 'fault' includes acts or omissions that are in any measure negligent, reckless, or intentional toward the person or property of the actor or others, or that subject a person to strict tort liability. The term also includes breach of warranty, unreasonable assumption of risk not constituting an enforceable express consent, misuse of a product for which the defendant otherwise would be liable, and unreasonable failure to avoid an injury or to mitigate damages. Legal requirements of causal relation apply both to fault as the basis for liability and to contributory fault." AS § 09.17.900 (1997).

Effect of contributory fault. "In an action based on fault seeking to recover damages for injury or death to a person or harm to property, contributory fault chargeable to the claimant diminishes proportionately the amount awarded as compensatory damages for the injury attributable to the claimant's contributory fault, but does not bar recovery." AS § 09.17.060 (1986).

Arizona: Definitions. "2. 'Fault' means an actionable breach of legal duty, act or omission proximately causing or contributing to injury or damages sustained by a person seeking recovery, including negligence in all of its degrees, contributory negligence, assumption of risk, strict liability, breach of express or implied warranty of a product, products liability and misuse, modification or abuse of a product." A.R.S. § 12-2506(F) (2001).

Comparative negligence; definition. "A. The defense of contributory negligence or of assumption of risk is in all cases a question of fact and shall at all times be left to the jury. If the jury applies either defense, the claimant's action is not barred, but the full damages shall be reduced in proportion to the relative degree of the claimant's fault which is a proximate cause of the injury or death, if any. There is no right to comparative negligence in favor of any claimant who has intentionally, willfully or wantonly caused or contributed to the injury or wrongful death.

B. In this section, 'claimant's fault' includes the fault imputed or attributed to a claimant by operation of law, if any." A.R.S. § 12-2505 (1984);

Arkansas: "(a) In all actions for damages for personal injuries or wrongful death or injury to property in which recovery is predicated upon fault, liability shall be determined by comparing the fault chargeable to a claiming party with the fault chargeable to the party or parties from whom the claiming party seeks to recover damages.

(b)(1) If the fault chargeable to a party claiming damages is of a lesser degree than the fault chargeable to the party or parties from whom the claiming party seeks to recover damages, then the claiming party is entitled to recover the amount of his or her damages after they have been diminished in proportion to the degree of his or her own fault.

(2) If the fault chargeable to a party claiming damages is equal to or greater in degree than any fault chargeable to the party or parties from whom the claiming party seeks to recover damages, then the claiming party is not entitled to recover such damages.

(c) The word 'fault' as used in this section includes any act, omission, conduct, risk assumed, breach of warranty, or breach of any legal duty which is a proximate cause of any damages sustained by any party." A.C.A. § 16-64-122 (1991);

Colorado: Assumption of risk—consideration by trier of fact. "Assumption of a risk by a person shall be considered by the trier of fact in apportioning negligence pursuant to section 13-21-111. For the purposes of this section, a person assumes the risk of injury or damage if he voluntarily or unreasonably exposes himself to injury or damage with knowledge or appreciation of the danger and risk involved. In any trial to a jury in which the defense of assumption of risk is an issue for determination by the jury, the court shall instruct the jury on the elements as described in this section." C.R.S.A. § 13-21-111.7 (1986).

Negligence cases—comparative negligence as measure of damages. "(1) Contributory negligence shall not bar recovery in any action by any person or his legal representative to recover damages for negligence resulting in death or in injury to person or property, if such negligence was not as great as the negligence of the person against whom recovery is sought, but any damages allowed shall be diminished in proportion to the amount of negligence attributable to the person for whose injury, damage, or death recovery is made." C.R.S.A. § 13-21-111 (1986);

Idaho: "(1) Failure to discover a defective condition.

…

(2) Use of a product with a known defective condition.

(a) By a claimant. When the product seller proves, by a preponderance of the evidence, that the claimant knew about the product's defective condition, and voluntarily used the product or voluntarily assumed the risk of harm from the product, the claimant's damages shall be subject to reduction to the extent that the claimant did not act as an ordinary reasonably prudent person under the circumstances.

(b) By a nonclaimant product user. If the product seller proves by a preponderance of the evidence that a product user, other than the claimant, knew about a product's defective condition, but voluntarily and unreasonably used or stored the product and thereby proximately caused claimant's harm, the claimant's damages shall be subject to apportionment." I.C. § 6-1405 (2005);

Iowa: Fault defined. "1. As used in this chapter, "fault" means one or more acts or omissions that are in any measure negligent or reckless toward the person or property of the actor or others, or that subject a person to strict tort liability. The term also includes breach of warranty, unreasonable assumption of risk not constituting an enforceable express consent, misuse of a product for which the defendant otherwise would be liable, and unreasonable failure to avoid an injury or to mitigate damages." I.C.A. § 668.1 (1984).

Comparative Fault. "1. a. Contributory fault shall not bar recovery in an action by a claimant to recover damages for fault resulting in death or in injury to person or property unless the claimant bears a greater percentage of fault than the combined percentage of fault attributed to the defendants, third-party defendants and persons who have been released pursuant to section 668.7, but any damages allowed shall be diminished in proportion to the amount of fault attributable to the claimant." I.C.A. § 668.3 (1997);

Minnesota: "Subdivision 1. Scope of application. Contributory fault does not bar recovery in an action by any person or the person's legal representative to recover damages for fault resulting in death, in injury to person or property, or in economic loss, if the contributory fault was not greater than the fault of the person against whom recovery is sought, but any damages allowed must be diminished in proportion to the amount of fault attributable to the person recovering. The court may, and when requested by any party shall, direct the jury to find separate special verdicts determining the amount of damages and the percentage of fault attributable to each party and the court shall then reduce the amount of damages in proportion to the amount of fault attributable to the person recovering.

Subd. 1a. Fault. 'Fault' includes acts or omissions that are in any measure negligent or reckless toward the person or property of the actor or others, or that subject a person to strict tort liability. The term also includes breach of warranty, unreasonable assumption of risk not constituting an express consent or primary assumption of risk, misuse of a product and unreasonable failure to avoid an injury or to mitigate damages, and the defense of complicity under section 340A.801. Legal requirements of causal relation apply both to fault as the basis for liability and to contributory fault. The doctrine of last clear chance is abolished." M.S.A. § 604.01 (1990);

Missouri: "2. Defendant may plead and prove the fault of the plaintiff as an affirmative defense. Any fault chargeable to the plaintiff shall diminish proportionately the amount awarded as compensatory damages but shall not bar recovery.

3. For purposes of this section, "fault" is limited to:

(1) The failure to use the product as reasonably anticipated by the manufacturer;

(2) Use of the product for a purpose not intended by the manufacturer;

(3) Use of the product with knowledge of a danger involved in such use with reasonable appreciation of the consequences and the voluntary and unreasonable exposure to said danger;

(4) Unreasonable failure to appreciate the danger involved in use of the product or the consequences thereof and the unreasonable exposure to said danger;

(5) The failure to undertake the precautions a reasonably careful user of the product would take to protect himself against dangers which he would reasonably appreciate under the same or similar circumstances;..." V.A.M.S. 537.765 (1987);

New York: "In any action to recover damages for personal injury, injury to property, or wrongful death, the culpable conduct attributable to the claimant or to the decedent, including contributory negligence or assumption of risk, shall not bar recovery, but the amount of damages otherwise recoverable shall be diminished in the proportion which the culpable conduct attributable to the claimant or decedent bears to the culpable conduct which caused the damages." McKinney's CPLR § 1411 (1975);

North Dakota: Definition. "As used in this chapter, 'fault' includes acts or omissions that are in any measure negligent or reckless towards the person or property of the actor or others, or that subject a person to tort liability or dram shop liability. The term also includes strict liability for product defect, breach of warranty, negligence or assumption of risk, misuse of a product for which the defendant otherwise would be liable, and failure to exercise reasonable care to avoid an injury or to mitigate damages. Legal requirements of causal relation apply both to fault as the basis for liability and to contributory fault." NDCC, 32-03.2-01 (1987).

Modified comparative fault. "Contributory fault does not bar recovery in an action by any person to recover damages for death or injury to person or property unless the fault was as great as the combined fault of all other persons who contribute to the injury, but any damages allowed must be diminished in proportion to the amount of contributing fault attributable to the person recovering. The court may, and when requested by any party, shall direct the jury to find separate special verdicts determining the amount of damages and the percentage of fault attributable to each person, whether or not a party, who contributed to the injury. The court shall then reduce the amount of such damages in proportion to the amount of fault attributable to the person recovering. When two or more parties are found to have contributed to the injury, the liability of each party is several only, and is not joint, and each party is liable only for the amount of damages attributable to the percentage of fault of that party, except that any persons who act in concert in committing a tortious act or aid or encourage the act, or ratifies or adopts the act for their benefit, are jointly liable for all damages attributable to their combined percentage of fault. Under this section, fault includes negligence, malpractice, absolute liability, dram shop liability, failure to warn, reckless or willful conduct, assumption of risk, misuse of product, failure to avoid injury, and product liability, including product liability involving negligence or strict liability or breach of warranty for product defect." NDCC, 32-03.2-02 (1993);

Utah: Definitions. "(2) 'Fault' means any actionable breach of legal duty, act, or omission proximately causing or contributing to injury or damages sustained by a person seeking recovery, including negligence in all its degrees, comparative negligence, assumption of risk, strict liability, breach of express or implied warranty of a product, products liability, and misuse, modification, or abuse of a product." U.C.A. 1953 § 78B-5-817 (2008).

Comparative negligence. "(1) The fault of a person seeking recovery may not alone bar recovery by that person.

(2) A person seeking recovery may recover from any defendant or group of defendants whose fault, combined with the fault of persons immune from suit and nonparties to whom fault is allocated, exceeds the fault of the person seeking recovery prior to any reallocation of fault made under Subsection 78B-5-819(2)." U.C.A. 1953 § 78B-5-818 (2008);

Washington: "Fault" defined. "'Fault' includes acts or omissions, including misuse of a product, that are in any measure negligent or reckless toward the person or property of the actor or others, or that subject a person to strict tort liability or liability on a product liability claim. The term also includes breach of warranty, unreasonable assumption of risk, and unreasonable failure to avoid an injury or to mitigate damages. Legal requirements of causal relation apply both to fault as the basis for liability and to contributory fault.

A comparison of fault for any purpose under RCW 4.22.005 through 4.22.060 shall involve consideration of both the nature of the conduct of the parties to the action and the extent of the causal relation between such conduct and the damages." West's RCWA 4.22.015 (1981).

Effect of contributory fault. "In an action based on fault seeking to recover damages for injury or death to person or harm to property, any contributory fault chargeable to the claimant diminishes proportionately the amount awarded as compensatory damages for an injury attributable to the claimant's contributory fault, but does not bar recovery. This rule applies whether or not under prior law the claimant's contributory fault constituted a defense or was disregarded under applicable legal doctrines, such as last clear chance." West's RCWA 4.22.005 (1981);

Wyoming: "iv) 'Fault' includes acts or omissions, determined to be a proximate cause of death or injury to person or property, that are in any measure negligent, or that subject an actor to strict tort or strict products liability, and includes breach of warranty, assumption of risk and misuse or alteration of a product;

(b) Contributory fault shall not bar a recovery in an action by any claimant or the claimant's legal representative to recover damages for wrongful death or injury to person or property, if the contributory fault of the claimant is not more than fifty percent (50%) of the total fault of all actors. Any damages allowed shall be diminished in proportion to the amount of fault attributed to the claimant." W.S. 1977 § 1-1-109 (1994).

148. AS § 09.17.060 (1986) (Effect of contributory fault).

149. Alabama: "The essential elements that a defendant must show to establish a defense of assumption of the risk are: (1) knowledge by the plaintiff of the dangerous condition, (2) appreciation of the danger under the surrounding conditions and circumstances, and (3) that the plaintiff acted unreasonably by placing himself into the way of the known danger…[T]o bar recovery it is not enough that the plaintiff knew of a general danger connected with the use of the product. Instead, to prevail with an assumption-of-the-risk defense, the defendant must show that the plaintiff actually appreciated the specific danger which caused his injuries." *Campbell v. Robert Bosch Power Tool Corp.*, 795 F.Supp. 1093, 1099-1100 (M.D.Ala. 1992) (citations omitted, noting that "evidence which at most demonstrates that Mr. Campbell was aware of a generalized danger of eye injury when using power tools, or evidence that he assumed the risk of having small particles of wood or metal striking his eye, is insufficient to raise an issue of material fact concerning assumption of the risk of harm from a shattering grinding disc" in regard to a strict liability failure-to-warn claim);

District of Columbia: "In the District of Columbia, assumption of risk by the injured party, if established, is a complete bar to recovery in a strict liability action. To establish assumption of risk in a negligence action, " 'the plaintiff must subjectively know of the existence of the risk and appreciate its unreasonable character.'…To establish an assumption of risk defense in a strict liability action, the defendant must show that the plaintiff knew of the specific defect in the product and was aware of the danger arising from it, but nevertheless voluntarily and unreasonably proceeded to use the product." *Warner Fruehauf Trailer Co., Inc. v. Boston*, 654 A.2d 1272, 1274-75 (D.C. 1995) (citations omitted, affirming a directed verdict for the plaintiff on their design defect strict liability claim in the second trial after the trial court ruled that it erred in the first trial by instructing the jury on assumption of the risk based on a truck liftgate falling on plaintiff);

Florida: A flight attendant sued the aircraft and engine manufacturers under negligence and strict liability theories, alleging that she contracted multiple sclerosis from being exposed to "the trauma occasioned by the noise and jet fuel emission" when she opened the aft door to permit a late passenger to enter the aircraft. *Clark v. Boeing Co.*, 395 So.2d 1226, 1228 (Fla. App. 1981). Affirming the trial court's dismissal of the case, the court ruled that "[u]nreasonable exposure to a known and appreciated risk bars recovery in an action based upon implied warranty as well as in an action for negligence." *Id.* at 1230;

Georgia: "The affirmative defense of assumption of the risk bars recovery when it is established that a plaintiff, without coercion of circumstances, chooses a course of action with full knowledge of its danger and while exercising a free choice as to whether to engage in the act or not. In Georgia, a defendant asserting an assumption of the risk defense must establish that the plaintiff (1) had actual knowledge of the danger; (2) understood and appreciated the risks associated with such danger; and (3) voluntarily exposed himself to those risks." *Dixie Group, Inc. v. Shaw Industries Group*, Inc.,693 S.E.2d 888, 893 (Ga. App. 2010);

Maryland: Where a test pilot died in a plane crash as a result of a malfunctioning actuator assembly, the defendant pleaded assumption of risk as a complete bar to recovery in a negligence case. *Cincotta v. U.S.*, 362 F.Supp. 386, 389, 406 (D.C.Md. 1973). In Maryland, "[w]hen the plaintiff enters voluntarily into a relation or situation involving obvious danger, he may be taken to assume the risk, and to relieve the defendant of responsibility. Such implied assumption of risk requires knowledge and appreciation of the risk, and a voluntary choice to encounter it." *Id.* at 406. Applying an objective standard, the plaintiff is only imputed with appreciation of "risks reasonably expected to exist, and not *unusual* dangers." *Id.* at 406-07. Noting that a defective actuator assembly could only be an unusual risk in that it was unrelated to the maneuver performed by the test pilot, the court ruled that the assumption of the risk defense was not available to the defendant. *Id.* at 407;

Massachusetts: Recovery is barred in a breach of warranty claim for design defect when "[a] defendant claiming unreasonable use [ ] prove[s] that the plaintiff knew of the product's defect and its danger, that she proceeded voluntarily and unreasonably to use the product, and she was injured as a result." *Chapman ex rel. Chapman Estate v. Bernardís Inc.*, 167 F.Supp.2d 406, 416 (D.Mass. 2001);

Mississippi: "Assumption of the risk is a valid defense under Mississippi law...and [has] actually extended to apply to products liability cases." *Little v. Liquid Air Corp.*, 37 F.3d 1069, 1079 n.26 (5th Cir. 1994). Recovery is barred by proving the elements of assumption of risk: "(1) Knowledge on the part of the injured party of a condition inconsistent with his safety; (2) appreciation by the injured party of the danger of the condition; and (3) a deliberate and voluntary choice on the part of the injured party to expose his person to that danger in such a manner as to register assent on the continuance of the dangerous condition." *Id.* (ruling that assumption of risk barred recovery from welding torch manufacturer where welders died in an explosion after discovering a leak in a welding hose);

Nebraska: "[A]]ssumption of risk, when imposed to defeat recovery, is . . . an affirmative defense." *Hancock v. Paccar*, 283 N.W.2d 25, 37-38 (Neb. 1979);

Nevada: "[A] manufacturer may not be held liable for injury resulting from...a plaintiff's assumption of the risk" in a strict liability case. *Rowell v. Powerscreen Intern., Ltd.*, 808 F.Supp. 1459, 1462-63 (D.Nev. 1992);

Oklahoma: Recovery is barred in a strict liability case if "the defendant...prove[s] that the plaintiff was subjectively aware of and appreciated the specific dangers in using the specific product in the specific manner he was using it when the accident occurred." *Holt v. Deere & Co.*, 24 F.3d 1289, 1293 (10th Cir. 1994);

Pennsylvania: "Under Pennsylvania law, assumption of risk is a complete defense to strict liability and negligence claims. In order to prevail on this defense, Defendants must show that Plaintiff 'knew of the defect and voluntarily and unreasonably proceeded to use the product or encounter a known danger.'" *Martinez v. Triad Controls, Inc.*, 593 F.Supp.2d 741, 765 (E.D.Pa. 2009) (citations omitted);

Rhode Island: "In Rhode Island, the doctrine of assumption of the risk is an affirmative defense which operates to absolve a defendant of liability for creating a risk of harm to a plaintiff [in regard to both strict liability and negligence claims]. To establish this defense, a defendant must show that plaintiff knew of the existence of a danger, appreciated its unreasonable character, and then voluntarily exposed himself to it. The standard for determining whether a plaintiff knew of and voluntarily encountered a risk is subjective, and is keyed to what the particular plaintiff in fact saw, knew, understood and appreciated." *Colantuoni v. Alfred Calcagni & Sons, Inc.*, 44 F.3d 1, 2-5 (1st Cir. 1994) (citations omitted, finding that plaintiff assumed the risk of using "a ladder in an altered condition," barring recovery for plaintiff's negligence and strict liability claims);

South Dakota: A defendant may assert an assumption-of-risk defense to bar recovery in a strict liability case against a plaintiff "who "is aware the product is defective, knows the defect makes the product unreasonably dangerous, has a reasonable opportunity to elect whether to expose himself to the danger, and nevertheless proceeds to make use of the product." *Smith v. Smith*, 278 N.W.2d 155, 161 (S.D. 1979);

Virgin Islands: Although the Virgin Islands had enacted a comparative fault statute, the court ruled that assumption of the risk nonetheless barred recovery where "a plaintiff who 'discovers the defect and is aware of the danger, and nevertheless proceeds unreasonably to make use of the product and is injured by it,' thereby releasing a manufacturer from the consequences of otherwise tortious conduct." *Chelcher v. Spider Staging Corp.*, 892 F.Supp. 710, 717 (D.Virgin Islands 1995) (applying assumption of the risk to both strict liability and negligence claims where a misrigged scaffolding caused injury);

Virginia: Assumption of the risk "bar[s] recovery on claims of both negligence and breach of warranty, even if a defect is proved." *Hoban v. Grumann Corp.*, 717 F.Supp. 1129, 1138 (E.D.Va. 1989), *aff'd*, 907 F.2d 1138 (4th Cir. 1990) (ruling that a pilot flying a plane contrary to IFR flight rules and failing to follow Navy procedures in response to an aircraft fire assumed the risk of injury and directed a verdict for the manufacturer);

150. California: Where a trier of fact finds secondary assumption of the risk, the type occupying the field of product liability, it "is merged into the comparative fault scheme so that a trier of fact may consider the relative responsibility of the parties in apportioning the loss and damage resulting from the injury." *Milwaukee Electric Tool Corp. v. Superior Court*, 19 Cal.Rptr.2d 24, 27 (Cal. App. 1993);

Hawaii: Reasonable ("primary") assumption of risk serves as a complete bar to recovery in negligence cases and express assumption of risk undertaken in a contract also serves as a complete bar in any action. On the other hand, unreasonable ("secondary") assumption of risk, "where plaintiff knows of the danger presented by a defendant's negligence and proceeds voluntarily and unreasonably to encounter it," operates under comparative fault principles, reducing a plaintiff's recovery by degree of his fault in negligence, strict liability, and implied warranty actions. *Larsen v. Pacesetter Systems, Inc.*, 837 P.2d 1273, 1289-92 (Hawaii 1992);

Illinois: "In the context of a wrongful death case based on strict products liability, the affirmative defense of assumption of the risk requires proof of a deliberate decision by the decedent to encounter a known risk, or a willingness on the part of the decedent to take a chance. The courts apply a subjective standard rather than a reasonable person standard to determine whether the decedent was aware of the known risk. However, a showing of the decedent's awareness is not limited to direct evidence but may also include circumstantial factors like the decedent's age, experience and knowledge; whether a decedent was aware of the known risk is to be deduced from the totality of the evidence. In light of this, a determination of whether a decedent assumed the risk is ordinarily a question for the jury. Finally, the affirmative defense of assumption of the risk no longer completely bars recovery; instead, the misconduct will be compared in the apportionment of damages." *Hanlon v. Airco Indus. Gases*, 579 N.E.2d 1136, 1141 (Ill. App. 1991) *appeal denied* 587 N.E. 2d 1014 (Ill 1992) (citations omitted, ruling the trial court erred by issuing a directed verdict on assumption of risk as it is a question for the jury and ordering that the defendant could present evidence on assumption of risk);

Kansas: "In both strict liability and implied warranty claims the defense of "assumption of risk" is recognized. In such a context assumption of risk is a contributory negligence concept." *Kennedy v. City of Sawyer*, 618 P.2d 788, 796 (Ks. 1980) (citations omitted).

Louisiana: "[T]he common law doctrine of assumption of risk no longer has a place in Louisiana tort law" and "can no longer bar recovery." *Murray v. Ramada Inns, Inc.*, 521 So.2d 1123, 1132-33 (La. 1988). Instead, "in any case where the defendant would otherwise be liable to the plaintiff under a negligence or strict liability theory, the fact that the plaintiff may have been aware of the risk created by the defendant's conduct should not operate as a total bar to recovery. [Rather,] "comparative fault principles should apply, and the victim's 'awareness of the danger' is among the factors to be considered in assessing percentages of fault." *Id.* at 1134. The only exceptions to this rule are express assumption of risk and implied primary assumption of risk cases where the "plaintiff has made no express agreement to release the defendant from future liability, but he is presumed to have consented to such a release because he has voluntarily participated in a 'particular activity or situation' which involves inherent and well known risks." *Id.* at 1129, 1134;

Maine: "[A]ssumption of the risk" is a defense to a strict liability claim and so counts as 'fault' . . . under section 156" (comparative negligence statute). *Austin v. Raybestos-Manhattan, Inc.*, 471 A.2d 280, 285-86 (Maine 1984);

New Hampshire: Assumption of the risk is a defense in a strict liability case in cases of "plaintiff's misconduct" where a plaintiff "voluntarily and unreasonably proceed[s] to encounter a known danger. *Thibault v. Sears, Roebuck & Co.*, 395 A.2d 843, 849 (N.H. 1978). In those cases, recovery is allocated according to "plaintiff's misconduct" and the defendant's fault, with the plaintiff receiving nothing if the plaintiff's misconduct caused greater than one-half of the injury or damage. *Id.* at 850;

New Jersey: Where "a plaintiff with actual knowledge of the danger presented by a defective product knowingly and voluntarily encounters that risk, a trial court should submit the comparative-negligence defense to a jury" in a strict liability case. *Johansen v. Makita U.S.A., Inc.*, 607 A.2d 637, 641-42 (N.J. 1992);

New Mexico: The court ruled that assumption of the risk applied to strict liability claims as well as negligence claims. *Marchese v. Warner Communications, Inc.*, 670 P.2d 113, 116-17 (N.M.App. 1993);

North Dakota: "[W]e hold that where an unreasonably dangerous defect of a product and the plaintiff's assumption of risk or unforeseeable misuse of the product are concurring proximate causes of the injury suffered, the trier of fact must compare those concurring causes to determine the respective percentages by which each contributed." *Mauch v. Manufacturers Sales & Service, Inc.*, 345 N.W.2d 338, 348 (N.D. 1984);

Oregon: "Unreasonable use despite knowledge of the dangerous defect in the product and awareness of the risk posed by that defect" is an accurate statement of the voluntary assumption of risk defense available in a products liability action in Oregon. Taken as a whole, the trial court's instruction indicating the sort of negligent conduct by plaintiff that the jury could—and could not—consider in assessing her fault is, therefore, a correct statement of the law." *Jett v. Ford Motor Co.*, 84 P.3d 219, 222 (Or. 2004), *review denied*, 84 P.3d 219 (Or. 2004);

Tennessee: Under an assumption-of-risk defense, "[a] plaintiff's conduct...bar[s] recovery when the plaintiff assumes a risk by means of express contract, when the defendant has no duty to protect the plaintiff from a risk, or, under comparative fault, when the fault attributable to the plaintiff's conduct is equal to or greater than the fault attributable to the defendant. In other circumstances, the plaintiff's conduct [ ] serves to merely reduce the plaintiff's recovery." *McKinnie v. Lundell Mfg. Co., Inc.*, 825 F.Supp. 834, 842 (W.D.Tenn. 1993) (ruling that Tennessee courts would extend the application of the assumption-of-the-risk defense to strict liability claims);

Texas: Texas courts apply "a comparative causation" system in strict liability cases and a contributory negligence scheme in negligence cases, resulting in a comparison of plaintiff's "faults" of misuse or assumption of risk to the fault of defendants in regard to all claims. In regard to the effect of these comparative systems in product liability cases, if "at least one defendant is found liable on a theory other than negligence, the plaintiff's

damages shall be reduced only by the percentage of causation attributed to the plaintiff, regardless of how large or small that percentage may be. A plaintiff may recover the percentage of damages caused by the defendants, even though his own share of causation is greater than that attributed to the defendants individually or combined." *Duncan v. Cessna Aircraft Co.*, 665 S.W.2d 414, 423-29 (Tex. 1984) (where decedent's survivors sued the manufacturer of the aircraft, alleging defective design of the seats in that they failed and caused fatal injuries);

Washington: "In a strict liability case, assumption of the risk, [where the plaintiff knew of the specific defect causing his injury,] operates as a damage-reducing factor rather than a complete bar to recovery." *Campbell v. ITE Imperial Corp.*, 733 P.2d 969, 976 (Wash. 1987);

West Virginia: "[T]he defense of assumption of risk is available against a plaintiff in a product liability case where it is shown that the plaintiff had actual knowledge of the defective or dangerous condition, fully appreciated the risks involved, and continued to use the product. However, the plaintiff is not barred from recovery unless his degree of fault under assumption of risk equals or exceeds the combined fault of the other parties to the accident." Nonetheless, "the defense of assumption of risk is not available where the defendant's conduct is willful, malicious, or grossly negligent. *King v. Kayak Mfg. Corp.*, 387 S.E.2d 511, 518 (W.Va. 1989);

Wisconsin: "At this juncture we find no reason why acts or failure on the part of the user or consumer of defective products which constitute a failure to exercise reasonable care for one's own safety and might ordinarily be designated assumption of risk cannot be considered contributory negligence." *Dippel v. Sciano*, 155 N.W.2d 55, 64 (Wis. 1967).

11 *Berkebile v. Brantly Helicopter Corp.*, 337 A.2d 893, 897, 901-02 (Pa. 1975), *abrogated on other grounds, Reott v. Asia Trend, Inc.*, 55 A.3d 1088, 1099 (Pa. 2012).

152. *Id.* at 901.

153. *Id.* at 902.

154. *Schlotzhauer v. The Final Season, Inc., et al.*, Case No. CL102824 (Iowa District Court), Order of May 6, 2009.

155. *Boyle v. United Technologies Corp.*, 487 U.S. 500 (1988).

156. *Tate v. Boeing Helicopters*, 55 F.3d 1150 (6th Cir. 1995).

157. *Id.* at 1156.

158. *Tate v. Boeing Helicopters*, 140 F.3d 654 (6th Cir. 1998).

159. *Id.* at 660.

160. *See Snell v. Bell Helicopter Textron, Inc.*, 107 F.3d 744 (9th Cir. 1997).

161. *Id.* at 748.

162. *Hill v. Raytheon Aircraft Co.*, 470 F.Supp.2d 1214, 1223-24 (D.Kan. 2006) (citations omitted):
The 'reasonably precise' standard is satisfied as long as the specifications address, in reasonable detail, the product design feature alleged to be defective. This element of the test is met if the government and the contractor engaged in a 'continuous back and forth' review process regarding the design in question. Nor is it a requirement that the government specifications focus explicitly on all features of the product, including that later in question; it is sufficient if the government evaluate and approve the design feature in question.
Kerstetter v. Pacific Scientific Co., 210 F.3d 431, 435 (5th Cir. 2000), *cert. denied*, 531 U.S. 919 (2000) (citations omitted):
The government need not prepare the specifications to be considered to have approved them. To determine whether 'substantive review' occurred, a court must take into consideration a number of factors. The factors involve examining drawings, evaluation from time to time, criticism and extensive government testing-a 'continuous back and forth' between the contractor and the government. The specifications need not address the specific defect alleged; the government need only evaluate the design feature in question.

163. *Hill*, 470 F.Supp.2d at 1224.

164. The states that have enacted statutes providing for a "useful safe life" presumption are:
Arkansas: "Use of a product beyond its anticipated life by a consumer where the consumer knew or should have known the anticipated life of the product may be considered as evidence of fault on the part of the consumer." A.C.A. § 16-116-105 (1979). "'Anticipated life' means the period over which the product may reasonably be expected to be useful to the user as determined by the trier of facts." A.C.A. § 16-116-102(1) (2007);
Connecticut: "(a) No product liability claim, as defined in section 52-572m, shall be brought but within three years from the date when the injury, death or property damage is first sustained or discovered or in the exercise of reasonable care should have been discovered,

except that, subject to the provisions of subsections (c), (d) and (e) of this section, no such action may be brought against any party nor may any party be impleaded pursuant to subsection (b) of this section later than ten years from the date that the party last parted with possession or control of the product.
…
(c) The ten-year limitation provided for in subsection (a) of this section shall not apply to any product liability claim brought by a claimant who is not entitled to compensation under chapter 568 [workers' compensation] provided the claimant can prove that the harm occurred during the useful safe life of the product." C.G.S.A. § 52-577a (2005). The statute then names factors to be considered in determining the length of a product's useful safe life and circumstances that will extend a product's useful safe life;
Florida: "[For products other than commercial aircraft and other products not related to aviation] which the manufacturer specifically warranted, through express representation or labeling, as having an expected useful life exceeding 10 years, has an expected useful life commensurate with the time period indicated by the warranty or label. Under such circumstances, no action for products liability may be brought after the expected useful life of the product, or more than 12 years after delivery of the product to its first purchaser or lessee who was not engaged in the business of selling or leasing the product or of using the product as a component in the manufacture of another product, whichever is later." West's F.S.A. § 95.031(2)(b) (2003);
Idaho: "(1) Useful safe life.
(a) Except as provided in subsection (1)(b) hereof, a product seller shall not be subject to liability to a claimant for harm under this chapter if the product seller proves by a preponderance of the evidence that the harm was caused after the product's "useful safe life" had expired.
'Useful safe life' begins at the time of delivery of the product and extends for the time during which the product would normally be likely to perform or be stored in a safe manner. For the purposes of this chapter, 'time of delivery' means the time of delivery of a product to its first purchaser or lessee who was not engaged in the business of either selling such products or using them as component parts of another product to be sold.
(b) A product seller may be subject to liability for harm caused by a product used beyond its useful safe life to the extent that the product seller has expressly warranted the product for a longer period." I.C. § 6-1403 (20050). Paragraph 2 of this statute contains a statute of repose that provides that harm occurring from the use of a product more than ten years after delivery to the first consumer is considered to be past its useful safe life with certain limitations;

Kansas: "(a)(1) Except as provided in paragraph (2) of this subsection, a product seller shall not be subject to liability in a product liability claim if the product seller proves by a preponderance of the evidence that the harm was caused after the product's "useful safe life" had expired. "Useful safe life" begins at the time of delivery of the product and extends for the time during which the product would normally be likely to perform or be stored in a safe manner. For the purposes of this section, "time of delivery" means the time of delivery of a product to its first purchaser or lessee who was not engaged in the business of either selling such products or using them as component parts of another product to be sold." K.S.A. 60-3303 (1992). The statute also lists examples of evidence "that is especially probative in determining whether a product's useful safe life had expired." Paragraph (b) contains a statute of repose that provides that harm occurring from the use of a product more than ten years after delivery to the first consumer is considered to be past its useful safe life with certain limitations;

Kentucky: "(1) In any product liability action, it shall be presumed, until rebutted by a preponderance of the evidence to the contrary, that the subject product was not defective if the injury, death or property damage occurred either more than five (5) years after the date of sale to the first consumer or more than eight (8) years after the date of manufacture." K.R.S. § 411.310 (1978);

Minnesota: "In any action for the recovery of damages for personal injury, death or property damage arising out of the manufacture, sale, use or consumption of a product, it is a defense to a claim against a designer, manufacturer, distributor or seller of the product or a part thereof, that the injury was sustained following the expiration of the ordinary useful life of the product. . . . The useful life of a product is not necessarily the life inherent in the product, but is the period during which with reasonable safety the product should be useful to the user," which would be determined by certain evidence outlined in the statute." M.S.A. § 604.03 (1978).

North Dakota: "1. An aviation manufacturer may not be held liable in a product liability action if the defendant establishes that the harm was caused after the period of useful safe life of the aircraft or aircraft component had expired. The useful safe life of an aircraft or aircraft component may be measured in units of time or in other units that accurately gauge the useful safe life of a product.

2. In a claim for relief that involves injury more than ten years after the date of first delivery of the aircraft or aircraft component to the first user, purchaser, or lessee, a disputable presumption arises that the harm was caused after the useful safe life had expired. The presumption may only be rebutted by clear and convincing evidence. If the aviation manufacturer or seller expressly warrants that its product can be utilized safely for a period longer than ten years, the period of repose is extended according to the promise." NDCC, 28-01.4-04 (1995). For aircraft components, "no claim for damages may be made after the useful safe life of the component, the period stated in the warranty, or ten years after manufacture of the component, whichever is later." NDCC, 28-01.4-04(3);

South Dakota: "Except [if a warranty provides for a longer period], no aviation product seller is liable in an aviation product liability claim if the product seller proves by a preponderance of the evidence that the harm was caused after the aviation product's useful safe life had expired. Useful safe life begins at the time of delivery of the aviation product and extends for the time during which the product would normally perform." SDCL §§ 21-63-2 (2011). Other statutes provide that a warranty may extend a product's useful safe life and the factors to be considered in determining whether an aviation product's useful safe life has expired. SDCL §§ 21-63-3, 21-63-4 (2011);

Tennessee: "Any action against a manufacturer or seller of a product for injury to person or property caused by its defective or unreasonably dangerous condition must be brought within the period fixed by §§ 28-3-104, 28-3-105, 28-3-202 and 47-2-725, but notwithstanding any exceptions to these provisions, it must be brought within six (6) years of the date of injury, in any event, the action must be brought within ten (10) years from the date on which the product was first purchased for use or consumption, or within one (1) year after the expiration of the anticipated life of the product, whichever is the shorter, except in the case of injury to minors whose action must be brought within a period of one (1) year after attaining the age of majority, whichever occurs sooner." T.C.A. § 29-28-103(a) (1993). "The anticipated life of a product shall be determined by the expiration date placed on the product by the manufacturer when required by law but shall not commence until the date the product was first purchased for use or consumption." T.C.A. § 29-28-102 (1978);

Texas: "If a manufacturer or seller expressly warrants in writing that the product has a useful safe life of longer than 15 years, a claimant must commence a products liability action against that manufacturer or seller of the product before the end of the number of years warranted after the date of the sale of the product by that seller," but "[t]his section does not extend the limitations period within which a products liability action involving the product may be commenced under any other law." V.T.C.A., Civil Practice & Remedies Code § 16.012(c) and (e) (2003);

Washington: "(1) Useful safe life. (a) Except as provided in subsection (1)(b) hereof, a product seller shall not be subject to liability to a claimant for harm under this chapter if the product seller proves by a preponderance of the evidence that the harm was caused after the product's 'useful safe life' had expired.

'Useful safe life' begins at the time of delivery of the product and extends for the time during which the product would normally be likely to perform or be stored in a safe manner. For the purposes of this chapter, 'time of delivery' means the time of delivery of a product to its first purchaser or lessee who was not engaged in the business of either selling such products or using them as component parts of another product to be sold. In the case of a product which has been remanufactured by a manufacturer, 'time of delivery' means the time of delivery of the remanufactured product to its first purchaser or lessee who was not engaged in the business of either selling such products or using them as component parts of another product to be sold." West's RCWA 7.72.060 (1981). The statute lists exceptions and provides a rebuttal presumption of a useful safe life of 12 years.

165. NDCC, 28-01.4-04 (1995).

166. Id.

167. NDCC, 28-01.4-04(3).

168. Kansas: K.S.A. 60-3303 (1992).

169. KRS § 411.310 (1978).

170. Arkansas: "(a) Compliance by a manufacturer or supplier with any federal or state statute or administrative regulation existing at the time a product was manufactured and prescribing standards of design, inspection, testing, manufacture, labeling, warning, or instructions for use of a product shall be considered as evidence that the product is not in an unreasonably dangerous condition in regard to matters covered by these standards… A.C.A. § 16-116-105 (1979);

California: "(a) The failure of a person to exercise due care is presumed if:
(1) He violated a statute, ordinance, or regulation of a public entity;
(2) The violation proximately caused death or injury to person or property;
(3) The death or injury resulted from an occurrence of the nature which the statute, ordinance, or regulation was designed to prevent; and
(4) The person suffering the death or the injury to his person or property was one of the class of persons for whose protection the statute, ordinance, or regulation was adopted.

(b) This presumption may be rebutted by proof that:
(1) The person violating the statute, ordinance, or regulation did what might reasonably be expected of a person of ordinary prudence, acting under similar circumstances, who desired to comply with the law; or
(2) The person violating the statute, ordinance, or regulation was a child and exercised the degree of care ordinarily exercised by persons of his maturity, intelligence, and capacity under similar circumstances, but the presumption may not be rebutted by such proof if the violation occurred in the course of an activity normally engaged in only by adults and requiring adult qualifications." West's Ann.Cal.Evid.Code § 669 (2004);

Colorado: "1) In any product liability action, it shall be rebuttably presumed that the product which caused the injury, death, or property damage was not defective and that the manufacturer or seller thereof was not negligent if the product:
…
(b) Complied with, at the time of sale by the manufacturer, any applicable code, standard, or regulation adopted or promulgated by the United States or by this state, or by any agency of the United States or of this state.
(2) In like manner, noncompliance with a government code, standard, or regulation existing and in effect at the time of sale of the product by the manufacturer which contributed to the claim or injury shall create a rebuttable presumption that the product was defective or negligently manufactured." C.R.S.A. § 13-21-403 (2003);

Florida: "(1) In a product liability action brought against a manufacturer or seller for harm allegedly caused by a product, there is a rebuttable presumption that the product is not defective or unreasonably dangerous and the manufacturer or seller is not liable if, at the time the specific unit of the product was sold or delivered to the initial purchaser or user, the aspect of the product that allegedly caused the harm:
(a) Complied with federal or state codes, statutes, rules, regulations, or standards relevant to the event causing the death or injury;
(b) The codes, statutes, rules, regulations, or standards are designed to prevent the type of harm that allegedly occurred; and
(c) Compliance with the codes, statutes, rules, regulations, or standards is required as a condition for selling or distributing the product.
(2) In a product liability action as described in subsection (1), there is a rebuttable presumption that the product is defective or unreasonably dangerous and the manufacturer or seller is liable if the manufacturer or seller did not comply with the federal or state codes, statutes, rules, regulations, or standards which:

(a) Were relevant to the event causing the death or injury;

(b) Are designed to prevent the type of harm that allegedly occurred; and

(c) Require compliance as a condition for selling or distributing the product..." West's F.S.A. § 768.1256 (1999);

Indiana: "Sec. 1. In a product liability action, there is a rebuttable presumption that the product that caused the physical harm was not defective and that the manufacturer or seller of the product was not negligent if, before the sale by the manufacturer, the product:

(1) was in conformity with the generally recognized state of the art applicable to the safety of the product at the time the product was designed, manufactured, packaged, and labeled; or (2) complied with applicable codes, standards, regulations, or specifications established, adopted, promulgated, or approved by the United States or by Indiana, or by an agency of the United States or Indiana." IC 34-20-5-1 (1998);

Kansas: "(a) When the injury-causing aspect of the product was, at the time of manufacture, in compliance with legislative regulatory standards or administrative regulatory safety standards relating to design or performance, the product shall be deemed not defective by reason of design or performance, or, if the standard addressed warnings or instructions, the product shall be deemed not defective by reason of warnings or instructions, unless the claimant proves by a preponderance of the evidence that a reasonably prudent product seller could and would have taken additional precautions.

(b) When the injury-causing aspect of the product was not, at the time of manufacture, in compliance with legislative regulatory standards or administrative regulatory safety standards relating to design, performance, warnings or instructions, the product shall be deemed defective unless the product seller proves by a preponderance of the evidence that its failure to comply was a reasonably prudent course of conduct under the circumstances.(c) When the injury-causing aspect of the product was, at the time of manufacture, in compliance with a mandatory government contract specification relating to design, this shall be an absolute defense and the product shall be deemed not defective for that reason, or, if the specification related to warnings or instructions, then the product shall be deemed not defective for that reason.

(d) When the injury-causing aspect of the product was not, at the time of manufacture, in compliance with a mandatory government contract specification relating to design, the product shall be deemed defective for that reason, or if the specification related to warnings or instructions, the product shall be deemed defective for that reason." Kan.Stat.Ann. 60-3304(a) (1981);

Kentucky: "(1) In any product liability action, it shall be presumed, until rebutted by a preponderance of the evidence to the contrary, that the subject product was not defective if the injury, death or property damage occurred either more than five (5) years after the date of sale to the first consumer or more than eight (8) years after the date of manufacture.

(2) In any product liability action, it shall be presumed, until rebutted by a preponderance of the evidence to the contrary, that the product was not defective if the design, methods of manufacture, and testing conformed to the generally recognized and prevailing standard or the state of the art in existence at the time the design was prepared, and the product was manufactured." KRS § 411.310 (1978);

Massachusetts: "The violation of a criminal statute, ordinance or regulation by a plaintiff which contributed to said injury, death or damage, shall be considered as evidence of negligence of that plaintiff, but the violation of said statute, ordinance or regulation shall not as a matter of law and for that reason alone, serve to bar a plaintiff from recovery." M.G.L.A. 231 § 85 (1973);

Michigan: "(4) In a product liability action brought against a manufacturer or seller for harm allegedly caused by a product, there is a rebuttable presumption that the manufacturer or seller is not liable if, at the time the specific unit of the product was sold or delivered to the initial purchaser or user, the aspect of the product that allegedly caused the harm was in compliance with standards relevant to the event causing the death or injury set forth in a federal or state statute or was approved by, or was in compliance with regulations or standards relevant to the event causing the death or injury promulgated by, a federal or state agency responsible for reviewing the safety of the product. Noncompliance with a standard relevant to the event causing the death or injury set forth in a federal or state statute or lack of approval by, or noncompliance with regulations or standards relevant to the event causing the death or injury promulgated by, a federal or state agency does not raise a presumption of negligence on the part of a manufacturer or seller. Evidence of compliance or noncompliance with a regulation or standard not relevant to the event causing the death or injury is not admissible." M.C.L.A. 600.2946 (1996) (ruled unconstitutional on other grounds and severable under *White v. SmithKline Beecham Corp.*, 538 F.Supp.2d 1023 (W.D.Mich. 2008));

North Dakota: Rebuttable Presumption Against Defects

"There is a rebuttable presumption that a product is free from any defect or defective condition if the plans, designs, warnings, or instructions for the product or the methods and techniques of manufacturing, inspecting, and testing the product were in conformity with government standards established for that industry or if no government standards exist then with applicable industry standards, which were in existence at the time the plans, designs, warnings, or instructions for the product or the methods and techniques of manufacturing, inspecting, and testing the product were adopted." NDCC, 28-01.3-09 (1995).

Compliance with Federal Standards—Presumptions and Defense

"1. There is a disputable presumption that a product is free from any defect or defective condition if the product was in compliance with:

a. Government standards established for that product; or

b. If no government standards exist, applicable industry standards that were in existence at the time of manufacture.

2. An aviation manufacturer or a seller of aircraft or aircraft components may utilize the presumption provided by subsection 1 if the manufacture, design, formulation, inspection, testing, packaging, labeling, or warning complied with:

a. Federal aviation administration or department of transportation regulations that relate to the safety or establish safety standards for the aircraft or aircraft component and which existed at the time the aircraft or aircraft component was produced;

b. Any premarket approval or certification by the federal aviation administration or any other federal agency; and

c. Applicable industry standards that were in existence at the time the plans, designs, warnings, or instructions for the aircraft or aircraft component or the methods and techniques of manufacturing, inspecting, and testing the product were adopted.

3. The presumption under subsection 1 is not available if the plaintiff proves by clear and convincing evidence that the aviation manufacturer or product seller knowingly and in violation of applicable agency regulations made misrepresentations, made illegal payments to an official for the purpose of securing approval, committed fraud, or concealed evidence.

4. There is an absolute defense to any product liability action brought against an aviation manufacturer when a claimant, in violation of federal aviation administration regulations, has used alcohol or illicit drugs while operating or using an aircraft or aircraft component.

5. This chapter does not affect the authority of the federal aviation administration or any other federal agency with regard to the regulation of aircraft and aircraft components." NDCC, 28-01.4-02 (1995);

Ohio: Products Defective In Design Or Formulation; Foreseeable Risks; Benefits; Drug Or Medical Device.

"(A) Subject to divisions (D), (E), and (F) of this section, a product is defective in design or formulation if, at the time it left the control of its manufacturer, the foreseeable risks associated with its design or formulation as determined pursuant to division (B) of this section exceeded the benefits associated with that design or formulation as determined pursuant to division (C) of this section.

(B) The foreseeable risks associated with the design or formulation of a product shall be determined by considering factors including, but not limited to, the following:

…

(4) The extent to which that design or formulation conformed to any applicable public or private product standard that was in effect when the product left the control of its manufacturer;

…

(C) The benefits associated with the design or formulation of a product shall be determined by considering factors including, but not limited to, the following:

(1) The intended or actual utility of the product, including any performance or safety advantages associated with that design or formulation;

(2) The technical and economic feasibility, when the product left the control of its manufacturer, of using an alternative design or formulation;

(3) The nature and magnitude of any foreseeable risks associated with an alternative design or formulation.

…

(E) A product is not defective in design or formulation if the harm for which the claimant seeks to recover compensatory damages was caused by an inherent characteristic of the product which is a generic aspect of the product that cannot be eliminated without substantially compromising the product's usefulness or desirability and which is recognized by the ordinary person with the ordinary knowledge common to the community.

(F) A product is not defective in design or formulation if, at the time the product left the control of its manufacturer, a practical and technically feasible alternative design or formulation was not available that would have prevented the harm for which the claimant seeks to recover compensatory damages without substantially impairing the usefulness or intended purpose of the product." R.C. § 2307.75 (2004) (emphasis added).

Punitive or Exemplary Damages

(A) Subject to divisions (C) and (D) of this section, punitive or exemplary damages shall not be awarded against a manufacturer or supplier in question in connection with a product liability claim unless the claimant establishes, by clear and convincing evidence, that harm for which the claimant is entitled to recover compensatory damages in accordance with section 2307.73 or 2307.78 of the Revised Code was the result of misconduct of the manufacturer or supplier in question that manifested a flagrant disregard of the safety of persons who might be harmed by the product in question. The fact by itself that a product is defective does not establish a flagrant disregard of the safety of persons who might be harmed by that product.

…

(D)(1) If a claimant alleges in a product liability claim that a product other than a drug or device caused harm to the claimant, the manufacturer or supplier of the product shall not be liable for punitive or exemplary damages in connection with the claim if the manufacturer or supplier fully complied with all applicable government safety and performance standards, whether or not designated as such by the government, relative to the product's manufacture or construction, the product's design or formulation, adequate warnings or instructions, and representations when the product left the control of the manufacturer or supplier, and the claimant's injury results from an alleged defect of a product's manufacture or construction, the product's design or formulation, adequate warnings or instructions, and representations for which there is an applicable government safety or performance standard.

(2) Division (D)(1) of this section does not apply if the claimant establishes, by a preponderance of the evidence, that the manufacturer or supplier of the product other than a drug or device fraudulently and in violation of applicable government safety and performance standards, whether or not designated as such by the government, withheld from an applicable government agency information known to be material and relevant to the harm that the claimant allegedly suffered or misrepresented to an applicable government agency information of that type." R.C. § 2307.80 (2004);

Oklahoma: "A. In a product liability action brought against a product manufacturer or seller, there is a rebuttable presumption that the product manufacturer or seller is not liable for any injury to a claimant caused by some aspect of the formulation, labeling, or design of a product if the product manufacturer or seller establishes that the formula, labeling, or design for the product complied with or exceeded mandatory safety standards or regulations adopted, promulgated, and required by the federal government, or an agency of the federal government, that were applicable to the product at the time of manufacture and that governed the product risk that allegedly caused harm.

B. The claimant may rebut the presumption in subsection A of this section by establishing that:

1. The mandatory federal safety standards or regulations applicable to the product and asserted by the defendant as its basis for rebuttable presumption were inadequate to protect the public from unreasonable risks of injury or damage; or

2. The manufacturer, before or after marketing the product, withheld or misrepresented information or material relevant to the federal government's or agency's determination of adequacy of the safety standards or regulations at issue in the action.

C. In a product liability action brought against a product manufacturer or seller, there is a rebuttable presumption that the product manufacturer or seller is not liable for any injury to a claimant allegedly caused by some aspect of the formulation, labeling, or design of a product if the product manufacturer or seller establishes by a preponderance of the evidence that the product was subject to premarket licensing or approval by the federal government, or an agency of the federal government, that the manufacturer complied with all of the government's or agency's procedures and requirements with respect to premarket licensing or approval, and that after full consideration of the product's risks and benefits the product was approved or licensed for sale by the government or agency. The claimant may rebut this presumption by establishing that:

1. The standards or procedures used in the particular premarket approval or licensing process were inadequate to protect the public from unreasonable risks of injury or damage; or

2. The manufacturer, before or after premarket approval or licensing of the product, withheld from or misrepresented to the government or agency information that was material and relevant to the performance of the product and was causally related to the claimant's injury.

D. This section does not extend to manufacturing flaws or defects even though the product manufacturer has complied with all quality control and manufacturing practices mandated by the federal government or an agency of the federal government, or if the product becomes the subject of a recall, or is no longer marketed, pursuant to any order, consent decree, or agreement between the manufacturer and any federal agency." 76 Okla.St.Ann. § 57.2 (2014);

Tennessee: "(a) Compliance by a manufacturer or seller with any federal or state statute or administrative regulation existing at the time a product was manufactured and prescribing standards for design, inspection, testing, manufacture, labeling, warning or instructions for use of a product, shall raise a rebuttable presumption that the product is not in an unreasonably dangerous condition in regard to matters covered by these standards."

(b) A manufacturer or seller, other than a manufacturer of a drug or device, shall not be liable for exemplary or punitive damages if:

(1) The product alleged to have caused the harm was designed, manufactured, packaged, labeled, sold, or represented in relevant and material respects in accor-

dance with the terms of approval, license or similar determination of a government agency; or

(2) The product was in compliance with a statute of the state or the United States, or a standard, rule, regulation, order, or other action of a government agency pursuant to statutory authority, when such statute or agency action is relevant to the event or risk allegedly causing the harm and the product was in compliance at the time the product left the control of the manufacturer or seller.

(c) Subsection (b) shall not apply if the claimant establishes that the manufacturer or seller:

(1) At any time before the event that allegedly caused the harm, sold the product after the effective date of an order of a government agency that ordered the removal of the product from the market or withdrew the agency's approval of the product; or

(2) In violation of applicable regulations, withheld or misrepresented to the government agency information material to the approval and such information is relevant to the harm which the claimant allegedly suffered. T. C. A. § 29-28-104 (2011);

Texas: "(a) In a products liability action brought against a product manufacturer or seller, there is a rebuttable presumption that the product manufacturer or seller is not liable for any injury to a claimant caused by some aspect of the formulation, labeling, or design of a product if the product manufacturer or seller establishes that the product's formula, labeling, or design complied with mandatory safety standards or regulations adopted and promulgated by the federal government, or an agency of the federal government, that were applicable to the product at the time of manufacture and that governed the product risk that allegedly caused harm.

(b) The claimant may rebut the presumption in Subsection (a) by establishing that:

(1) the mandatory federal safety standards or regulations applicable to the product were inadequate to protect the public from unreasonable risks of injury or damage; or

(2) the manufacturer, before or after marketing the product, withheld or misrepresented information or material relevant to the federal government's or agency's determination of adequacy of the safety standards or regulations at issue in the action.

(c) In a products liability action brought against a product manufacturer or seller, there is a rebuttable presumption that the product manufacturer or seller is not liable for any injury to a claimant allegedly caused by some aspect of the formulation, labeling, or design of a product if the product manufacturer or seller establishes that the product was subject to pre-market licensing or approval by the federal government, or an agency of the federal government, that the manufacturer complied with all of the government's or agency's procedures and requirements with respect to pre-market licensing or approval, and that after full consideration of the product's risks and benefits the product was approved or licensed for sale by the government or agency. The claimant may rebut this presumption by establishing that:

(1) the standards or procedures used in the particular pre-market approval or licensing process were inadequate to protect the public from unreasonable risks of injury or damage; or

(2) the manufacturer, before or after pre-market approval or licensing of the product, withheld from or misrepresented to the government or agency information that was material and relevant to the performance of the product and was causally related to the claimant's injury.

(d) This section does not extend to manufacturing flaws or defects even though the product manufacturer has complied with all quality control and manufacturing practices mandated by the federal government or an agency of the federal government." V.T.C.A., Civil Practice and Remedies Code § 82.008 (2003);

Utah: "(1) In any action for damages for personal injury, death, or property damage allegedly caused by a defect in a product, a product may not be considered to have a defect or to be in a defective condition, unless at the time the product was sold by the manufacturer or other initial seller, there was a defect or defective condition in the product which made the product unreasonably dangerous to the user or consumer.

(2) There is a rebuttable presumption that a product is free from any defect or defective condition where the alleged defect in the plans or designs for the product or the methods and techniques of manufacturing, inspecting and testing the product were in conformity with government standards established for that industry which were in existence at the time the plans or designs for the product or the methods and techniques of manufacturing, inspecting and testing the product were adopted." U.C.A. 1953 § 78B-6-703 (2008);

Washington: "(1) Evidence of custom in the product seller's industry, technological feasibility or that the product was or was not, in compliance with nongovernmental standards or with legislative regulatory standards or administrative regulatory standards, whether relating to design, construction or performance of the product or to warnings or instructions as to its use may be considered by the trier of fact.

(2) When the injury-causing aspect of the product was, at the time of manufacture, in compliance with a specific mandatory government contract specification relating to design or warnings, this compliance shall be an absolute defense. When the injury-causing aspect of the product was not, at the time of manufacture, in compliance with a specific mandatory government specification relating to design or warnings, the product shall be deemed not reasonably safe under RCW 7.72.030(1) [statute regarding the liability of a manufacturer]." West's RCWA 7.72.050 (1981);

Wisconsin: "(4) Prohibited acts; enforcement. No person may manufacture, sell or distribute for sale any consumer product which is not in compliance with applicable consumer product safety standards under the federal act or rules of the department, or which has been banned as a hazardous product or ordered from sale by the department. No person may fail or refuse to comply with an order under sub. (3)(b) or any other rule or order under this section. In addition to other penalties and enforcement procedures, the department may apply to any court of competent jurisdiction for a temporary or permanent injunction restraining any person from violating this section or rules adopted under this section." W.S.A. 100.42 (1986).

171. Tenn.Code.Ann. § 29-28-104 (2011).

172. Kan.Stat.Ann. § 60-3304(a) (1981).

173. KRS § 411.310 (1978).

174. "If the injury-causing aspect of the aviation product was, at the time of manufacture, in compliance with legislative or administrative regulatory safety standards relating to design or performance, the aviation product is deemed not defective by reason of design or performance. If the standard addressed warnings or instructions, the aviation product is deemed not defective by reason of warnings or instructions." SDCL § 21-63-6 (2011).

175. NDCC, 28-01.4-02 (1995).

176. *Estep v. Mike Ferrell Ford Lincoln-Mercury, Inc.*, 672 S.E.2d 345, 356-57 (W.Va. 2008) (ruling that compliance with national standards does not raise a rebuttal presumption "that this vehicle was reasonably safe and not defective" but is admissible evidence to be considered in regard to ordinary care in the design or manufacture of the vehicle); *Hofer v. Mack Trucks, Inc.*, 981 F.2d 377, 383 (8th Cir. 1992) (ruling that "the jury may consider Mack's compliance with standards in determining whether it failed to use reasonable care in connection with the performance of its duties, and was thus negligent"); *Wagner v. Clark Equipment Co., Inc.*, 700 A.2d 38, 50 (Conn. 1997) (holding that "where the OSHA regulation at issue relates to the safety of a product, evidence that the product is in compliance with that regulation may be considered by the jury as a factor in determining whether the product is defectively designed and whether the manufacturer exercised due care in designing the product"); *Banko v. Continental Motors Corp.*, 373 F.2d 314, 315-16 (4th Cir. 1966) (ruling that compliance with Federal Aviation Admin-

istration safety regulations are "relevant and useful evidence on the standard-of-care issue").

177. Alabama: After a 14-year-old girl was struck by a propeller and severely injured, she sued the boat motor manufacturer under negligence and product liability theories, alleging that a guard should have been constructed around the propeller. *Elliott v. Brunswick Corp.*, 903 F.2d 1505, 1506 (11th Cir. (Ala.) 1990), *cert. denied sub nom. Elliott v. Mercury Marine*, 498 U.S. 1048 (1991). After a mistrial, the jury in the second trial returned a verdict for the plaintiff. Id. at 1506. Although the court on appeal acknowledged that "a manufacturer's proof of compliance with either industry-wide practices, or even federal regulations, fails to eliminate conclusively its liability for its design of allegedly defective products," it reversed the judgment of the district court. *Id.* at 1508-10;

Arizona: In a product liability case involving an airplane crash, the court ruled that "[t]he fact that the design of the Centurion [airplane] was specifically approved by the Federal Aviation Administration (FAA), while admissible evidence, does not provide a complete defense to a charge of design defect." *Ferguson v. Cessna Aircraft Co.*, 643 P.2d 1017, 1019 (Ariz.App. 1981) (overruled on other grounds).

Connecticut: In a case involving a forklift accident, the trial court rejected the defendant's request for a jury instruction that compliance with OSHA regulations should be considered to determine if the manufacturer acted with due care and the product was reasonably safe. *Wagner v. Clark Equipment Co. Inc.*, 700 A.2d 38, 49-50 (Conn. 1997). Ruling that the jury instruction should have been given, the court on appeal held that "where the OSHA regulation at issue relates to the safety of a product, evidence that the product is in compliance with that regulation may be considered by the jury as a factor in determining whether the product is defectively designed and whether the manufacturer exercised due care in designing the product." *Id.* at 50-51;

District of Columbia: An 87-year-old woman, who was injured when she fell on a bus while reaching for the stop cord, sued the bus manufacturer for negligent design. *Turner v. American Motors General Corp.*, 392 A.2d 1005, 1006 (D.C. 1978). After summary judgment was granted for the defendants, the plaintiff appealed. *Id.* Reversing the trial court, the court noted that "it is settled that compliance with a statute or regulation neither establishes due care, nor precludes a finding of negligence" and that negligence may be found where a reasonable person "would take additional precautions" beyond that required by a government standard. *Id.* at 1007;

Georgia: In a case involving serious injury resulting from the absence of a lap belt causing excessive force to the chest from a shoulder belt, the plaintiff brought negligence, strict liability, and breach of implied warranty of fitness claims. *Doyle v. Volkswagenwerk Aktiengesellschaft*, 481 S.E.2d 518, 519-20 (Ga. 1997). In answer to a certified question from the United States Court of Appeals for the Eleventh Circuit, the Georgia Supreme Court ruled that "proof of compliance with federal standards or regulations will not bar manufacturer liability for design defect." *Id.* at 521;

Illinois: Where rear passengers were killed or seriously injured in a car accident, suit was brought against the manufacturer, alleging that the rear-seat-anchoring system was dangerously defective. *Moehle v. Chrysler Motors Corp.*, 443 N.E.2d 575, 576 (Ill. 1982). On appeal, the court affirmed the trial court's admission of the defendant's compliance with federal safety standards, ruling that a jury may "weigh it with all the other evidence in the record," and even "conclude that a product is in an unreasonably dangerous defective condition notwithstanding its conformity to Federal standards." *Id.* at 578;

Iowa: After a man was injured by contact with an electrical line, he brought negligence and failure-to-warn claims against the power company. *Johnson v. Interstate Power Co.*, 481 N.W.2d 310, 313-15 (Iowa 1992). Ruling that the power company is "held to the highest degree of care consistent with the conduct and operation of its business," the court held that "such a company may be negligent even though it has complied with the minimum requirements of safety codes and regulations." *Id.* at 322;

Louisiana: Where a man was injured when he was thrown from a forklift in a collision, he brought suit for negligence and failure to warn. *Hopper v. Crown*, 646 So.2d 933, 935-36 (La. App. 1994), *writ denied*, 651 So.2d 275 (La. 1995). Based on the evidence showing that "[the manufacturer] installed doors for its larger customers, knew that its competitors offered doors to their warehouse customers as safety options, and admitted that forklifts with doors could be a safer usage in warehouse environments," the court ruled that "[c]ompliance with industry regulations does not excuse unreasonable behavior." *Id.* at 946;

Maryland: In a suit involving allegations of design defect of airplane seats, the court ruled that "[c]ompliance with governmental air-safety regulations is admissible, but not conclusive, evidence in a suit arising out of an airplane crash."
Bruce v. Martin-Marietta Corp., 544 F.2d 442, 446 (10th Cir. 1976) (applying Maryland law);

Michigan: A wing of a commercial airliner hit a pole on takeoff, resulting in 156 deaths and injuries to others. *In re Air Crash at Detroit Metropolitan Airport, Detroit, Mich. On August 16, 1987*, 791 F.Supp. 1204, 1208-09 (E.D.Mich. 1992), *affid*, 86 F.3d 498 (6th Cir. 1996). The evidence submitted at trial showed that a car rental company's placement of the pole was in violation of Federal Aviation Administration development standards. *Id.* at 1223-25. Noting that "[u]nder Michigan law, the violation of a federal regulation constitutes mere evidence of negligence," the court ruled that the suit against the car rental company would continue, denying its motion that for partial summary judgment based on compliance with federal regulations. *Id.* at 1219-1225;

Minnesota: In a suit where farmers sued a feed producer after its feed caused illnesses in livestock, the court ruled on appeal that "although statutory regulation in a field may supply the standard of care, compliance with such regulations does not protect a party from common law actions. *Duxbury v. Spex Feeds, Inc.*, 681 N.W.2d 380, 386 (Minn. App. 2004);

New Jersey: In a case involving a forklift accident, the court noted that "the OSHA regulation could potentially be admitted in evidence to shed light on the manufacturer's standard of care." *Gonzalez v. Ideal Tile Importing Co. Inc.*, 853 A.2d 298, 304 n. 3 (N.J.Super. A.D. 2004) *cert. denied*, 866 A.2d 984 (N.J. 2005);

New Mexico: Where a plaintiff alleged that the absence of a shoulder harness was a design defect that resulted in her husband's death in an airplane crash, the court ruled that "[r]egulations, codes, or standards [are] not determinative in design-defect cases." *Brooks v. Beech Aircraft Corp.*, 902 P.2d 54, 63 (N.M. 1995). The court held that government regulations, "while probative of what a reasonably prudent manufacturer would do" as to ordinary care in negligence actions or acceptable risk in strict liability actions, are not conclusive. *Id.* at 64;

New York: A plaintiff alleged that a truck was defectively designed because the installation of the fuel tank outside the frame rails allowed it to be ruptured and catch on fire when the truck hit a tree, killing her husband. *Ake v. General Motors Corp.*, 942 F.Supp. 869, 873 (W.D.N.Y. 1996). In denying the plaintiff's motion to exclude evidence of compliance with a federal regulation, the court noted that "compliance with a statute may constitute some evidence of due care…," though it does not preclude a finding that the product was defective." *Id.* (applying New York law). In addition to the negligence claim, the court extended the admissibility of compliance with regulations to the plaintiff's strict liability claims because the two theories in design defect cases are "virtually identical." *Id.* at 874;

North Carolina: In a case involving OSHA regulations in handling asbestos, the court ruled that "OSHA regulations are evidence of custom and can be used to establish the standard of care required in the industry." *Schenk v. HNA Holdings, Inc.*, 613 S.E.2d 503, 508 (N.C. App. 2005), *review denied*, 626 S.E.2d 649 (N.C. 2005);

Oregon: Where a car under rode a tractor-trailer from behind, the estate of the man killed brought an action alleging negligence and product liability claims. *Hagan v. Gemstate Mfg., Inc.*, 982 P.2d 1108, 1110 (Or. 1999). After a defense verdict and appeal, the court reversed the trial court, ruling that the meaning of a relevant regulation should have been explained to the jury for it "to consider in determining whether defendant met the standard of care in designing and manufacturing the trailer." *Id.* at 1110-13;

Pennsylvania: Where a helicopter crashed after a rotor blade snapped, the plaintiff alleged a strict liability claim for a design defect. *Berkebile v. Brantly Helicopter Corp.*, 281 A.2d 707, 708 (Pa. Super. 1971). While compliance with a federal aviation regulation disposes of a claim for negligence per se, "it does not establish as a matter of law that due care was exercised." *Id.* at 710. Rather, "[c]ompliance with the statute or regulation is admissible as evidence of the actor's exercise of due care, but such compliance 'does not prevent a finding of negligence where a reasonable man would take additional precautions.'" *Id.* Noting that plaintiff did not allege negligence in this case, the court admitted evidence of compliance with an FAA regulation "to show that the helicopter was not unreasonably dangerous." *Id.*;

South Dakota: A man, who was rendered a paraplegic while in the sleeping compartment of a truck when it rolled over, sued the truck manufacturer for negligence and strict liability. *Hofer v. Mack Trucks, Inc.*, 981 F.2d 377, 379 (8th Cir. 1992). After a defense verdict the plaintiff appealed, arguing that the trial court erred when it refused his jury instruction: "[c]ompliance with federal motor vehicle safety standards is not, in and of itself, sufficient to exempt a manufacturer from liability." *Id.* at 383. The court affirmed the trial court's refusal of the instruction, noting that had the court accepted the proposed instruction, a further instruction would have been necessary, as a complete statement of substantive South Dakota law, "that the jury may consider [the manufacturer's] compliance with standards in determining whether it failed to use reasonable care in connection with the performance of its duties, and was thus negligent." *Id.*;

Virginia: Where ice was found after an engine failure caused the crash landing of an airplane, the pilot and his insurer sued, alleging a design defect in that no heat was provided to the throttle, allowing ice to form. *Banko v. Continental Motors Corp.*, 373 F.2d 314, 314 (4th Cir. 1966). The court ruled that Federal Aviation Agency regulations were admissible on the standard of care in a negligence case as "relevant and useful evidence" under federal practice and Virginia law. *Id.* at 315-16.

178. *Berkebile v. Brantly Helicopter Corp.*, 281 A.2d 707, 708 (Pa. Super. 1971).

179. *Id.* at 710.

180. *Id.*

181. *Id.*

182. V.T.C.A., Civil Practice and Remedies Code § 82.008 (2003).

183. *See* G.Robb, "A Practical Approach to Use of State of the Art Evidence in Strict Products Liability Cases," 77 *Nw.U.L.Rev. 1*, 9-19 (1982) (addressing the theoretical underpinnings for use of state of the art as a defense along with divergent views).

184. *Potter v. Chicago Pneumatic Tool Co.*, 694 A.2d 1319, 1347 (Conn. 1997).

185. *Livingston v. Isuzu Motors, Ltd.*, 910 F.Supp. 1473, 1498 (D. Mont. 1995) (ruling that courts may consider, as evidence of state of the art, "the customary methods, standards, and techniques of manufacturing, inspecting, and testing employed by other manufacturers or sellers of similar products").

186. *Potter*, 694 A.2d at 1347; *Morden v. Continental AG*, 611 N.W.2d 659, 675 (Wis. 2000) (describing custom in the industry as "what the industry was doing" and the state of the art as "what the industry feasibly could have done"); *Hughes v. Massey-Ferguson, Inc.*, 522 N.W.2d 294, 295-96 (Iowa 1994) ("The question…'is not whether anyone else was doing more, although that may be considered, but whether the evidence disclosed that anything more could reasonably and economically be done'"); *Frantz v. Brunswick Corp.*, 866 F.Supp. 527, 534 (S.D.Ala. 1994) (holding that "compliance with industry standards is not, and should not be, a complete defense to a products liability cause" where a feasible alternative design is proven; "it may indicate a failure on the part of an entire industry"); *George v. Celotex Corp.*, 914 F.2d 26, 29 (2nd Cir. 1990) ("there are precautions so imperative that even their universal disregard will not excuse their omission").

187. *Potter*, 694 A.2d at 1346 (citations omitted); *see also Shreve v. Sears, Roebuck & Co.*, 166 F.Supp.2d 378, 413-14 (D.Md. 2001) (defining state-of-the-art evidence as "the evidence concerning the presence or absence of knowledge in the expert community"); *Horne v. Owens-Corning Fiberglas Corp.*, 4 F.3d 276, 281 (4th Cir. 1993) (defining state-of-the-art evidence as "all of

the available knowledge on a subject at a given time, and this includes scientific, medical, engineering, and any other knowledge that may be available").

188. *Murphy v. Chestnut Mountain Lodge, Inc.*, 464 N.E.2d 818, 823 (Ill. App. 1984).

189. *Morden*, 611 N.W.2d at 675-76; *OíBanion v. Owens-Corning Fiberglas Corp.*, 968 F.2d 1011, 1015-17 (10th Cir. 1992); *Lancaster Silo & Block Co. v. Northern Propane Gas Co.*, 427 N.Y.S.2d 1009, 1016 (N.Y.A.D. 1980) (noting that "a plaintiff can argue that a deviation from th[e standard of the state of the art] is negligence").

190. Arizona: A.R.S. § 12-683(1) (2009); Iowa: Iowa Code § 668.12 (2004) which provides product liability defendants in strict liability cases a complete defense if their product conformed to the state of the art which was in existence at the time the product was manufactured; Louisiana: LSA-R.S. 9:2800.59 (1988); Nebraska: Neb. Rev.St. § 25-21,182 (1978); New Hampshire: N.H. Rev. Stat. § 507:8-g (1989); New Jersey: N.J.S.A. 2A:58C-3 (1987); North Carolina: N.C.G.S.A. § 99B-6 (1996); North Dakota: NDCC, 28-01.4-03 (1995); Ohio: R.C. § 2307.75 (2004)

191. *See, e.g.*, Arkansas: A.C.A. § 16-116-104 (1979) (State of the art may be considered by trier of fact on manufacturer's strict products liability); Florida: West's F.S.A. § 768.1257 (1999) (State of the art at the time of manufacture may be considered in defective-design cases); South Dakota: SDCL § 20-9-10.1 (1995) (State of the art may be considered in negligence or strict-liability actions to determine the standard of care or whether the product was unreasonably dangerous); Tennessee: T.C.A. § 29-28-105(b) (1978). The statute provides: In making this determination, the state of scientific and technological knowledge available to the manufacturer or seller at the time the product was placed on the market, rather than at the time of injury, is applicable. Washington: West's RCWA 7.72.050 (1981) (State of the art may be considered in strict liability or negligence actions).

192. Colorado: C.R.S.A. § 13-21-403 (2003); Indiana: IC 34-20-5-1 (1998); Kentucky: KRS § 411.310 (1978).

193. Connecticut: "(b) In determining whether instructions or warnings were required and, if required, whether they were adequate, the trier of fact may consider: (1) The likelihood that the product would cause the harm suffered by the claimant; (2) the ability of the product seller to anticipate at the time of manufacture that the expected product user would be aware of the product risk, and the nature of the potential harm; and (3) the technological feasibility and cost of warnings and instructions." C.G.S.A. § 52-572q (1990); Michigan: "(3) In a product liability action brought against a manufacturer or seller for harm allegedly caused by a failure to provide adequate warnings or instructions, a manufacturer or seller is not liable unless the plaintiff proves that the manufacturer knew or should have known about the risk of harm based on the scientific, technical, or medical information reasonably available at the time the specific unit of the product left the control of the manufacturer." M.C.L.A. 600.2948 (1996); Missouri: "1. As used in this section, "state of the art" means that the dangerous nature of the product was not known and could not reasonably be discovered at the time the product was placed into the stream of commerce.
2. The state of the art shall be a complete defense and relevant evidence only in an action based upon strict liability for failure to warn of the dangerous condition of a product. This defense shall be pleaded as an affirmative defense and the party asserting it shall have the burden of proof.
3. Nothing in this section shall be construed as limiting the rights of an injured party to maintain an action for negligence whenever such a cause of action would otherwise exist.
4. This section shall not be construed to permit or prohibit evidence of feasibility in products liability claims." V.A.M.S. 537.764 (1987);

194. *Potter*, 694 A.2d at 1346 (citations omitted); *Sternhagen v. Dow Co.*, 935 P.2d 1139, 1143-44 (Mont. 1997); *Connelly v. General Motors Corp.*, 540 N.E.2d 370, 376 (Ill. App. 1989) *appeal denied*, 545 N.E.2d 196 (Ill. 1989) (ruling that state-of-the-art is not a defense but "the defendant may introduce state of the art type evidence" to rebut the plaintiff's claim of feasible alternative design); *Santiago v. Johnson Mach. and Press Corp.*, 834 F.2d 84, 84-86 (3rd Cir. 1987).

195. *Potter*, 694 A.2d at 1346 (citations omitted).

196. *Potter*, 694 A.2d at 1347-48 (as a factor under the ordinary consumer expectation standard, state-of-the-art evidence helps the jury determine the safety features an ordinary consumer would expect at the time the product was manufactured; for the risk-utility analysis, it provides an objective standard to aid the jury in determining whether a product is unreasonably dangerous); *Bragg v. Hi-Ranger, Inc.*, 462 S.E.2d 321, 328 (S.C. App. 1995) ("The state of the art and industry standards are relevant

to show both the reasonableness of the design and that the product is dangerous beyond the expectations of the ordinary consumer"); *Robinson v. G.G.C., Inc.*, 808 P.2d 522, 525 (Nev. 1991) (ruling that "when commercial feasibility is in dispute, the court must permit the plaintiff to impeach the defense expert with evidence of alternative design"); *Patterson v. Ravens-Metal Prod., Inc.*, 594 N.E.2d 153, 162 (Ohio App. 1991) (affirming the trial court's admission of state-of-the-art evidence "since state of the art is a factor which a jury may properly consider in determining the issue of whether a product is defective under the risk/benefit standard"); *Norton v. Snapper Power Equipment, Div. of Fuqua Industries, Inc.*, 806 F.2d 1545, 1549 (11th Cir. 1987) (noting "that the feasibility of alternative designs is only one factor in the analysis); *Rainbow v. Albert Elia Bldg. Co., Inc.*, 436 N.Y.S.2d 480, 485 (N.Y.A.D. 1981), *appeal denied*, 54 N.Y.S.2d 602 and 54 N.Y.S.2d 718 (1981) ("In short, the state of the art is an important and relevant inquiry, not only defensively as a qualitative limitation on . . . but also in determining the admissibility of plaintiff's evidence of post-accident test studies"); *Boatland of Houston, Inc. v. Bailey*, 609 S.W.2d 743, 749 (Texas 1980) ("Evidence offered under these circumstances is offered to rebut plaintiff's evidence that a safer alternative was feasible and is relevant to defectiveness"); *Bruce v. Martin-Marietta Corp.*, 544 F.2d 442, 446-47 (10th Cir. 1976) (admitting state-of-the-art evidence under the ordinary-consumer-expectation test to show that the "[p]laintiffs have not shown that the ordinary consumer would expect a plane made in 1952 to have the safety features of one made in 1970").

197.*Potter*, 694 A.2d at 1346-47 (citations omitted).

198.*Anderson v. Owens-Corning Fiberglas Corp.*, 810 P.2d 549, 553-60 (Cal. 1991).

199.*Owens-Illinois, Inc. v. Zenobia*, 601 A.2d 633, 639 (Md. 1992) (citing Comment j), *reconsideration denied*, 602 A.2d 1182 (1992).

200.*Id.* at 641.

201.*Anderson*, 810 P.2d at 555-56, 559; *see also Bernier v. Raymark Industries, Inc.*, 516 A.2d 534, 537 (Me. 1986).

202.*Sternhagen*, 935 P.2d at 1144-47 (imputing "knowledge of any undiscovered or undiscoverable dangers to manufacturers in strict liability actions); *In re Asbestos Cases*, 829 F.2d 907, 909 (9th Cir. 1987) (ruling that state-of-the-art evidence is not admissible in a strict liability failure-to-warn claim based on the Hawaii Supreme Court's answer to its certified question); *Carrecter v. Colson Equipment Co.*, 499 A.2d 326, 328-31 (Pa. Super. 1985).

203.*Reed v. Tiffin Motor Homes, Inc.*, 697 F.2d 1192, 1196 (4th Cir. 1982); but *see Candela v. City of New York*, 886 N.Y.S.2d 66 (Table) at 4 (N.Y.Sup. 2009) (noting that the defendant failed to show that the product was designed and manufactured in "state of the art conditions" as well as the rigorous testing and inspection process applied to each individual product prior to leaving the plant; all of which could lead an expert "to conclude that it was "virtually impossible" for the product to have left the plant in a defective state").

204.*McGuire v. Davidson Mfg. Co.*, 398 F.3d 1005, 1009-11 (8th Cir. 2005); *Indianapolis Athletic Club, Inc. v. Alco Standard Corp.*, 709 N.E.2d 1070, 1074-75 (Ind. App. 1999) *transfer denied*, 726 N.E.2d 304 (Ind. 1999) (Table).

Chapter 7

Common Evidentiary Issues

Introduction

Certain evidentiary issues recur in almost every helicopter accident trial. The same types of records and governmental reports are admitted in evidence by both sides in these cases. The same admissibility battles are carried on as to substantially similar crashes or incidents and subsequent remedial measures. Perhaps in no other litigation is the potential for actual creation of demonstrative evidence more unlimited and even as beneficial as for helicopter crash trials. These range from the simple model of the subject helicopter to extremely technical and expensive computer-generated animations of the crash sequence. This section highlights the typical evidentiary issues faced by the practitioner with suggestions for their proper legal handling and their effective use.

7.1 Preparation and Effective Use of Demonstrative Evidence

The use of effective demonstrative exhibits in these cases can spell the difference between the jury understanding the issues and delivering a verdict based on an accurate picture of the events and details in question, or jury confusion resulting in a flawed and unjust verdict. The technical nature of helicopter crash litigation not only calls for demonstrative evidence, but our visually oriented culture demands it. Visual media, such as Facebook, YouTube, movies, television, and video games all have contributed to a society that has become accustomed to and comfortable with sophisticated visual imagery. In lengthy and complex helicopter crash trials, counsel needs to engage the jury to ensure their attention and interest, increasing the likelihood that they will recall the critical facts in deliberations that were presented weeks earlier.

This section discusses the legal foundation required for the admission of demonstrative evidence and gives examples of the admission or exclusion of evidence in helicopter crash litigation. That discussion is followed by practical recommendations for the creation and use of demonstrative evidence in aircraft litigation.

To present demonstrative evidence to a jury, a proper foundation must be established for its admission. Foundational requirements differ for demonstrative and substantive evidence, so it is important to distinguish between the two. Demonstrative evidence is "[p]hysical evidence that one can see and inspect (i.e., an explanatory aid, such as a chart, map, and some computer simulations) and that, while of probative value and usually offered to clarify testimony, does not play a direct part in the incident in question."[1] Substantive evidence, on the other hand, is evidence that is offered to "prov[e] a fact in issue" or "establish the truth of a matter to be determined by the trier of fact."[2] The foundation required for the admission of substantive evidence is more stringent than that required for the admission of demonstrative evidence which is offered merely to illustrate or clarify a witness's testimony.

Appellate courts review these evidentiary rulings on an abuse-of-discretion standard,[3] and rarely rule that a trial court erred in admitting or excluding demonstrative evidence. So once the trial court's decision is made, the parties will likely live with that ruling through the trial and appeal. As a result, special care must be taken in laying the lawful and proper foundation before the trial court prior to seeking permission to present or display any demonstrative exhibit to the jury.

Generally, a demonstrative exhibit will be allowed to be used before the jury if it meets three criteria. First, a witness with personal knowledge must lay a proper foundation for its admission.[4] Second, it must be relevant.[5] Last, its probative value must substantially outweigh the danger of unfair prejudice, confusion of the issues, or misleading the jury.

The preparation of demonstrative evidence exhibits in these cases cannot wait until the eve of trial. This evidence requires a great deal of advance planning. When counsel considers the type of demonstrative evidence to present at trial, it is not the occasion to be frugal. Demonstrative evidence must be of sufficient quality and similarity so as to accurately depict what it purports to show, and do so in a manner that facilitates its admission. That process requires the expenditure of appropriate time and funds. Evidence has been rejected by the trial judge because it was of such poor quality that the court could not discern its contents.[6] The lesson is that demonstrative aids must accurately depict the subject matter in terms of both quality and likeness.

To ensure that demonstrative exhibits such as helicopter models or scale models of accident topography are properly authenticated and admitted, a near identical likeness should be the objective. If that is not possible, then any differences should be minimal, and counsel should be prepared to address the variations with the judge for their admission and with the jury to minimize the effect of the differences. If the judge finds that the probative value outweighs the danger of misleading the jury, the differences will go to the weight, not admissibility, of the exhibit.[7]

A. Model of the Subject Helicopter or System

Scale models of aircraft are admissible if they are substantially similar to-scale replicas of the subject aircraft. Such scale models are not controversial and routinely are used by both sides throughout trial.[8] Such aircraft models almost always are admitted by stipulation of the parties.

More disputes go to the admissibility of scale mock-ups of an aircraft system or control panel. In a Virginia case, the defendant sought permission to use a mock-up of a portion of the aircraft in trial.[9] The court granted permission after finding that its admission would satisfy Federal Rules of Evidence 611, 401, and 403.[10] Under Rule 611, the court found that the admission of the mock-up would aid in the "ascertainment of truth" and "'avoid needless consumption of time' that might otherwise be required to ensure jury comprehension."[11] Under Rule 401, the court determined that the mock-up was relevant because it would aid the jury in understanding "the highly technical aspects of the trim tabs and electronic controls of an aircraft [that] are foreign to the average juror."[12] Under Rule 403, the court determined that the probative value of the mock-up in assisting the jury in understanding the issues outweighed any "potentially misleading features" that could be explored in cross-examination.[13]

Similarly, the Tenth Circuit considered the admission of a model of an airplane's fuel system in an airplane crash case.[14] After a defense verdict, the plaintiffs appealed based, in part, on the admission of the fuel system model. The court affirmed the trial court's admission of the model as demonstrative evidence finding "nothing in the record to indicate that the model was flawed so as to present any serious problems" and further noting that the plaintiffs failed to cross-examine the witness about any inaccuracies at the trial.

B. Topographical Model or Map of Crash Site

The topography of the crash site is frequently useful to explain the crash dynamics of the helicopter and to demonstrate the final flight path leading to impact. As is true for the proper admission of other types of demonstrative evidence, a qualified witness must testify that the topographical model sought to be admitted is "reasonably accurate and correct."[15] Like a topographical model, a topographical map can be authenticated by the preparer or a witness who has personal knowledge of the terrain in question and can attest to its accuracy.[16] As is true for all demonstrative exhibits, the proponent must timely disclose a topographical model to the other side.[17]

C. Computer-Generated Animation or Simulation of Crash Sequence

Plaintiff's counsel should consider creating a computer-generated reconstruction of the helicopter crash sequence for several reasons. First and foremost, it is relevant to the liability theory advanced by plaintiff's experts. The in-flight movement of the helicopter as determined by the accident reconstruction expert should correlate precisely with the precipitating cause of the crash.

Second, given the outstanding quality of this potential evidence, the jury's visualization of the reconstruction is vastly superior to the most eloquent verbal description, even if accompanied by use of a helicopter model. And third, these accident reconstructions may impart to the jury some sense of what the occupants experienced in those final moments of flight prior to impact.

Computer-generated accident reconstructions "convert witnesses' verbal testimony into dynamic, visual demonstrations capable of mentally transporting jurors to the scene," observed one court, and explains why such evidence is so extremely forceful and persuasive.[18] They also have "the potential to mislead by an inaccurate portrayal of the facts, the potential to create lasting impressions that unduly override other testimony or evidence, and the need for heightened guarantees of trustworthiness due to the possibility of editorial distortion by the party preparing the animation."[19] To ensure the use of computer animations, the proponent must allay these concerns. "A computer-generated video animation is admissible as demonstrative evidence when the proponent shows that the animation is authentic, relevant, a fair and accurate representation of the evidence to which it relates," and its probative value substantially outweighs the danger of unfair prejudice, confusing the issues, or misleading the jury.[20]

Proper authentication depends upon the purpose for which the computer animation is offered. If used only to illustrate or "demonstrate" a witness's testimony by recreating a scene or process, it is classic demonstrative evidence and its admission is conditioned upon the testimony of a witness with knowledge that the animation depicts what its proponent claims.[21] If a computer animation is regarded as a "simulation" or actual reconstruction of the accident as it happened or where data is "entered into a computer, which is programmed to analyze the data and draw a conclusion from it" "based on scientific or physical principles and data," it is considered substantive evidence and must meet the more rigorous standard for admission of scientific evidence.[22]

A court that wrestled with this distinction admitted a computer animation showing how a fire started and spread in an airplane engine.[23] The defendant argued that the animation was a recreation of the accident and was therefore unduly prejudicial. The court rejected this argument because it had taken precautions to ensure that the jury did not perceive the animation as a recreation of the accident. The court had cautioned the jury that the animation was an illustration of the expert's theory and not a recreation of the accident.

Animations are used to aid the jury in understanding a witness's testimony. An expert can explain her theory of how the accident happened or the system in question performed during the accident, or an eyewitness can show to the jury what he saw, rather than describe the observations during the event.[24] In one helicopter crash case, the court denied the plaintiff's motion in limine seeking to exclude defense animations illustrating an expert's theory about the motions of a helicopter when its engine failed in flight.[25] The court permitted defendant to use an animation of an eyewitness account of the accident.[26] The court noted the relevance of both exhibits and conditioned admissibility upon proper authentication and the presence of both witnesses at trial.[27] In response to the plaintiff's argument that the jury would be misled into believing that the animations depicted the actual helicopter accident, the court noted that it would caution the jury in that regard.

For the admission of animations, the conditions depicted must be "substantially similar" to the conditions at issue.[28] Even where an animation depicts details that conflict with the testimony and facts in evidence, the animation may be admitted where the differences are discussed in trial.[29] The proponent must timely disclose the computer animation to allow the opposing party sufficient time to analyze the animation and the underlying data.[30] If a party fails to disclose the animation on a timely basis, the court may exclude the animation on that basis alone.[31]

For computer-generated reconstructions or animations, the simpler the exhibit, the more likely it will be admitted. Added bells and whistles in the form of color and sound may spell exclusion for an expensive exhibit. Sounds that may add an unduly prejudicial effect also should be left out. Efforts to replicate sounds of screaming victims have been squarely rebuffed.[32] While adding color to computer-generated evidence may elicit more attention and increase understanding and retention, it should be used only to objectively portray the item or event. Otherwise, this may expose the exhibit to an objection that the animation is not substantially similar to the item or event depicted or that unfair prejudice outweighs its probative value. For example, the color red representing blood is particularly risky as part of a computer animation. As is true of photographs, extensive displays of blood should not be depicted in animations as it increases the danger of unfair prejudice precluding the exhibit's admission.[33]

Counsel should seek to present challenged demonstrative evidence to the court for an admissibility ruling at the earliest opportunity.[34] This is particularly true of computer animations that elicit greater scrutiny. An objectionable aspect of an animation may be revised before trial and re-offered. If seeking to admit a computer-generated animation of an eyewitness's observations of the accident or of an expert's theory of how the accident happened, it can be submitted only for demonstrative purposes and not as substantive evidence. The standard for admission for demonstrative evidence is not as rigorous as that required under *Frye* or *Daubert* for simulations intended to reconstruct the accident.

When an animation of the accident is admitted as demonstrative evidence, a limiting instruction to the jury may persuade a court reviewing its admission on appeal to affirm the trial court.[35] The limiting instruction should contain the following elements: "the animation is not evidence but is intended only as a visual aid to the jury in understanding certain testimony or evidence presented at trial by illustrating and explaining that testimony or evidence;"[36] "the animation represents only a re-creation of the proponent's version of the event;"[37] "it should in no way be viewed as the absolute truth;"[38] and, "like all evidence, it may be accepted or rejected in whole or in part."[39] In addition, the trial court should "call attention to any assumptions upon which the animation is based, as well as any other particular facts that warrant a cautionary instruction."[40] Although evidentiary matters are overturned only if the trial court abuses its discretion, the potential to mislead the jury in these cases may lead to a finding on appeal that the trial court erred if it fails to caution the jury about the nature of the exhibit as demonstrative evidence. If the court fails to give a limiting instruction of its own initiative, counsel should provide one containing the elements noted above.

Showing the animation repeatedly to the jury members can increase their memory of it but may again make it subject to an objection of unfair prejudice.[41] Likewise, playing an animation in slow motion or playing the animation in segments can extend the event beyond the time frame of the actual event. As is true for all demonstrative evidence, its presentation to the jury should be smooth and seamless. The video technician running the equipment should be trained and proficient in its operation and have the exhibit ready at the right time. Fumbling with the presentation may diminish the jury's confidence in counsel and the exhibit. The equipment operator should be unobtrusive, as the attention of the jury should be on the demonstrative evidence. And, most important, the jury must be able to see it directly in clear view and without a lot of body-shifting and neck-craning.

D. Computer Animation of Helicopter Component or System Function

A computer animation need not be used solely for demonstrating an expert's view of the dynamics of the crash sequence. Counsel should consider creating an animation showing the operation of the component or system at issue so that the jury has a vivid picture of its proper and intended function.

In a case involving the crash of Northwest Flight 255 on August 16, 1987, it was alleged that a circuit breaker failed, causing the failure of the warning system that would have alerted the crew to the improper settings of the plane's wing flaps and slats.[42] The improper settings resulted in the aircraft not achieving lift on take-off and, ultimately, crashing. On appeal, the Sixth Circuit considered the admission of a six-minute computer animated videotape that depicted the general operation of the model of the circuit breaker at issue during the testimony of the circuit breaker expert.[43] A defendant objected to its admission arguing that it violated the Brumby Rule, which barred experts from testifying at trial about subjects and opinions not formed at the time of deposition. The court found, however, that the animation illustrated the expert's deposition testimony and that information about the animation was simply not drawn out by counsel.[44]

The same defendant also objected to the animation claiming that its prejudicial effect outweighed its probative value in that it appeared to simulate the actual event.[45] The court disagreed, noting that the trial court instructed the jury that the animation was limited to demonstrative purposes only. The court observed that the defendant did not object to the testimony of the expert and six other witnesses that testified about the circuit breaker's operation and that the expert "could have drawn the same information on a sketch pad in front of the jury."[46]

Although the jury may understand little about the operation or flight of an aircraft, a computer animation should reflect common-sense principles, or the jury is likely to question its validity. If an expert is on the stand explaining her version of the crash with the aid of an animation, and something about that explanation strikes the jury as unrealistic, counsel should be prepared to direct a question at that issue, expressing skepticism at the opinion perceived as nonsensical and asking for a clarification.

E. In-Court Demonstrations or Experiments

In-court demonstrations or experiments may illustrate how an accident happened or explain scientific principles involved in the accident. If a demonstration or experiment is intended to reconstruct an accident, its conditions and that of the accident must be the same or substantially similar.[47] Where it is difficult, if not impossible, to reproduce substantially similar circumstances, courts will not permit the demonstration.[48]

Regardless of a high degree of similarity, an in-court demonstration is improper where it exposes the jury to possible injury, particularly where protective equipment is provided to the jury that was not used at the time of the accident.[49] If such a demonstration is allowed, opposing counsel may use it to emphasize the dangerous nature of the product.[50]

On the other hand, if the purpose of the experiment or demonstration is not to reconstruct the accident but to demonstrate scientific principles, the court allows more latitude with respect to similarity. In fact, the likelihood for admission increases with the dissimilarity of the demonstration since jury confusion is less likely.[51] Appropriate limiting instructions are required to be given to the jury in regard to the admission of this evidence.[52]

Experiments created prior to trial face the same evidentiary hurdle. In a helicopter crash case, the defendant sought to prove that a loose labyrinth screw did not cause the seizure of the engine.[53] As proof, the defendant conducted an experiment where a labyrinth screw was placed in contact with a rotating titanium disc on a lathe, which the defendant maintained was similar to the turning compressor impeller on the helicopter, and showed that the screw failed to damage the lathe.[54] The plaintiffs filed a motion in limine to exclude the experiment. The trial court granted the motion in limine and the Tenth Circuit agreed, finding that "a substantial dissimilarity prevented a fair comparison."[55]

7.2 Photographs of Crash Scene and Helicopter Wreckage

Just as in any other accident case, admission of photographs of a helicopter crash scene requires that a witness with personal knowledge testifies that the images are a fair and accurate representation of the scene at the time of the accident.[56] A proper foundation for the admission of photographs in air-

craft litigation "is established when it is shown that the photograph has some probative value and that it is an accurate portrayal of what it purports to show."[57] The court affirmed the admission of a photograph taken 30-45 minutes after an airplane crash where it was made clear that the photograph was not offered to show the weather conditions at the time of the accident but billowing fog present at the time the photograph was taken and the judge admonished the jury to so regard the photograph.[58]

The photograph need not depict the scene exactly as it existed at the time of the accident if the differences are explained by a witness familiar with the scene at that time.[59] The witness testifying that the photographs or videotapes accurately depict the scene need not be the photographer or videographer of the materials in question but merely someone familiar with the scene.[60]

In addition to authentication, the photographs and videotapes must be relevant to be admitted.[61] In a Missouri case, a helicopter flew into unmarked power lines over a river and crashed, killing three people.[62] The court ruled that photographs depicting a helicopter flying at a low altitude the afternoon before the accident were inadmissible due, in part, to remoteness in time and were therefore irrelevant.

If photographs or videotapes are taken of the crash scene and the bodies are in view, then either that film must have been shot at a distance or in a way to avoid perspectives that emphasize the injuries or any other graphic details. These actions will prevent the exclusion of the exhibit due to unfair prejudice outweighing the film's probative value.

In addition to relevance, the probative value of the photograph or videotape must substantially outweigh the danger of unfair prejudice, confusion of the issues, or misleading the jury.[63] An objection of unfair prejudice often arises in accident cases in which bodies are photographed. In a case involving an airplane crash, the court affirmed the trial court's ruling that unfair prejudice substantially outweighed the probative value of inflammatory close-up photographs of bodies at the crash scene.[64] The court also affirmed the admission of a photograph that pictured the scene and the bodies from a distance because it did not overemphasize the gruesome nature of the injuries. The likelihood that photographs depicting the deceased victim of an accident will be admitted is greater if a defendant contests damages or liability, as the court is more apt to find that the probative value of the photographs substantially outweighs any unfair prejudice.[65]

Just as photographs of the scene must fairly and accurately depict what they purport to show, so too must photographs of the wreckage itself.[66] To accurately depict the wreckage, photographs must be of sufficient quality to allow the court to determine what they show.[67] In a Nevada air crash case, the plaintiff offered photographs showing "a piece of foam taken from the mishap aircraft after impact and depicts the defective nature of the foam adhesive used in that aircraft."[68] The court excluded the photocopies of the photographs due to their poor quality making it impossible to distinguish between "what is alleged to be foam adhesive and what is not."[69] Also excluded were black-and-white photographs of foam segments due to the court's inability to determine "what these photographs actually depict," despite the plaintiff's assurances that color photographs would make the objects clear. The court also excluded these photographs on the basis that no explanation was offered as to where on the aircraft the foam segments came from and what caused their separation.[70]

If photographs of the wreckage are not taken at the scene and instead are later taken after the removal of the wreckage to another location, testimony will be required to establish that the wreckage is in the same condition as it was before removal.[71] The lesson learned from these cases is that admissibility of photographs of either the scene or wreckage are not pro forma matters. Counsel must secure attendance of the witnesses with first hand knowledge of the scene or condition of the wreckage and offer these photographs through such witnesses. The author has had the best success in calling as a witness the photographer who was on the scene who can authenticate the photographs as those taken by her at the time.

7.3 Jury View of Helicopter Wreckage

Whenever possible counsel should arrange for an actual jury viewing of the helicopter wreckage as photographs or videotape footage are simply not comparable. In those cases where the wreckage is too large to bring into the courtroom, counsel should request that the jury be permitted to view the helicopter wreckage outside the courtroom. Nothing brings home to a jury the horror and tragic nature of a helicopter crash more than viewing the devastation and aftermath of what used to be a helicopter. What passes for helicopter wreckage ranges from a fairly intact airframe with little to moderate damage to thousands of pieces of mere rubble and worse if following a post-impact fire. Those critical pieces which played a role in the loss of control and subsequent crash should be brought into the courtroom.

Most defense counsel routinely object to plaintiff's request for a jury view of the helicopter wreckage. But plaintiff's counsel must press the issue. As one court observed, "the size of the courtroom should not necessarily limit the evidence to be presented to the jury."[72] Or to put it another way, the size of the evidence should not determine wheth-

er the jury sees it. A "courtroom without walls"[73] enables a jury to evaluate evidence without the filter of a witness or counsel. In determining whether to grant a request for a jury view, "a trial court considers such factors as the issues involved, the status of the evidence and its inferences, and whether a view will aid the jury in understanding the issues and appraising the evidence."[74] Courts have allowed a jury view to determine the operator's field of vision,[75] the visibility of the object,[76] and the value of a car before and after an accident.[77]

A jury view is more likely if the condition of the wreckage is unchanged in relevant aspects.[78] Where the condition has changed since the accident, a jury view is permissible if the court describes the changes before the jury view takes place. For example, a jury view of a police car took place seven months after the collision when rust spots had appeared, the trunk lid was open, the tires were flat, and the police radio had been removed.[79] On appeal, the court affirmed the authorization of the jury view, noting with approval the trial court's description of the changes to the jury before the view.[80]

Certain procedures must be followed during the jury view. The jury and counsel should be instructed not to comment on the evidence.[81] The jury should be escorted by the court or someone appointed by the court.[82] The jury should not be permitted to touch the wreckage or discuss it among themselves at that time. Usually, the judge and bailiff accompany the jury to the viewing of the wreckage with all counsel and their clients in tow. The most convenient location is normally the parking lot or side street adjacent to the courthouse with the wreckage located on a flatbed truck with a tarp which may easily and quickly be removed at the time of the jury's viewing.

The trial court's decision to permit a jury view is reviewed under an abuse of discretion standard.[83] Consequently, the decision is unlikely to be overturned on appeal,[84] even those that appear not to aid the jury in understanding the issues.[85] To obtain a ruling on appeal that a court erred by allowing a jury view, the opponent of the jury view must show undue prejudice to the opponent's rights.[86] A jury view is not prejudicial, however, "simply because [the evidence] may have undue weight with the jury."[87]

The helicopter wreckage is relevant evidence for several reasons. First, a jury viewing of the wreckage in its entirety is the best evidence of the speed and force of impact. Photographs cannot capture the full three-dimensional perspective or scale of the damage. There may be features about the airframe which should be highlighted in advance which bear on the final crash sequence. The size of the wreckage should not in and of itself exclude its admissibility into evidence as with the jury viewing. If the injury-producing vehicle were a bicycle, a motorcycle, or a riding lawn mower there would be no question as to its admissibility into evidence and "viewing" by the jury. Plaintiffs should not be prejudiced merely because the defendant's product would not easily fit into the courtroom.

Several states have a specific jury instruction applicable to a jury viewing that should be referenced where appropriate. An example of a pre-trial request for jury view of helicopter wreckage is the following:

PLAINTIFF'S REQUEST FOR JURY VIEW OF SUBJECT HELICOPTER WRECKAGE

Plaintiff respectfully requests that the Court allow the jury to view the helicopter that is the subject of this litigation. This action is authorized by Iowa law:
Pursuant to I.C.A. Rule 1.922, Plaintiff respectfully requests that this Court allow the jury to view the helicopter wreckage that is the subject of this litigation. If permitted, Plaintiff would make arrangements for the helicopter wreckage to be viewed under procedures approved by the Court at a specific date and time.
Counsel for Plaintiff has been in contact with [owner of wreckage] on this matter. Upon entry of an appropriate Order, [owner of wreckage] will cooperate in permitting the helicopter wreckage to be transported to the Court.

Most courts permit the jury view. The trial judge wants to see what the wreckage looks like up close and understands that the jury will be very interested in viewing the helicopter wreckage as well.

7.4 NTSB Reports
By operation of federal statute, the NTSB Factual Report may be admissible at trial but the Probable Cause Report is not.[88] The express purpose of the statute is to prevent evidence of the NTSB's opinions regarding the probable cause of a crash for purposes of private civil litigation. Admitting into evidence the NTSB Factual Report and highlighting those factual findings which are supportive of and consistent with plaintiff's theory of the crash will add credibility to plaintiff's case as bearing the stamp of approval of the federal government. Where possible to do so, plaintiffs aligning their claims with the factual findings of the NTSB can persuade the jury that plaintiff's theories are more likely to be based on the true facts.

The public records exception to the hearsay rule for investigation results, however, will not apply to admit an NTSB probable cause report. By statute, its admission is forbidden:

[n]o part of a report of the Board, related to an accident or an investigation of an accident, may be admitted into evidence or used in a civil action for damages resulting from a matter mentioned in the report.[89]

NTSB accident reports consist of two portions:[90] the factual findings and the Board's determinations of probable cause. While the Board's probable cause determinations are not admissible under any circumstances,[91] the factual findings are admissible as a public record.[92] Portions of the factual report may be excluded if they contain hearsay that fails to fall under one of the hearsay exceptions.[93] NTSB employees may testify about "the factual information they obtained during the course of an investigation."[94] They may not testify in regard to the probable cause of the accident.[95] The prohibition against the admission of the NTSB report on the probable cause of the subject accident does not foreclose the admission of such reports as evidence of substantially similar accidents[96] or aircraft inspections.[97]

As for all governmental reports, the safe practice is to obtain a certified copy which in the case of an NTSB Report is called the "Blue Ribbon" copy. Under any state's laws, that is a self-authenticating piece of evidence and need not require the testimony of any business records custodian. The report is used most effectively as a foundation for plaintiff's own expert witness's testimony or to impeach the defendant's expert witness who arrives at a contrary factual conclusion at trial. Using the NTSB Report in these ways is considerably more effective than simply reading isolated portions to the jury which cannot be extrapolated upon or explained. Another alternative for presenting some of the factual findings in an NTSB report is through deposition testimony of the NTSB investigator himself. When used with plaintiff's expert witness, a common line of questioning might be as follows:

Counsel: Did you review the factual findings in the course of preparing to testify?
Expert : Yes, I did.

Here the expert may be asked to explain the NTSB's role in investigating aviation crashes and the agency's resources and thoroughness in performing its tasks.

Counsel: Did the NTSB factually determine whether there had been a fuel spill at the time of impact?

Expert: Yes, interviews performed by the NTSB investigators revealed that a number of witnesses detected a puddle of fuel off the main fuselage and the odors were evident.

Counsel: Did you find this particular fact significant in formulating your opinions in this case?

Expert: Yes, it was particularly significant because…

Use of the NTSB report in this manner is also much more effective than simply reading isolated portions to the jury, because such a recitation would lack any context and would be particularly vulnerable to the aforementioned objections.

The NTSB report also may be used in cross-examining the adversary's experts. For example:

Counsel: Did you review the NTSB's factual findings with respect to this air crash?

Adverse Expert: Yes.

Counsel: You know the NTSB to be thorough and complete with respect to its investigations?

Adverse Expert: Yes.

Counsel: And you just testified, your opinion or theory as to how this crash occurred is based on one of the main rotor blades striking the ground at impact causing the overturn?

Adverse Expert: Yes, that's correct.

Counsel: Now, having read the factual findings of the NTSB, you know that they found no ground strikes or markings to indicate such an occurrence?

Adverse Expert: I don't recall that.

Counsel: Let me show you Page 8 of the NTSB's report…

Yet another method of bringing the NTSB's factual findings before the jury is in questioning the defendant manufacturer's engineers. Where aircraft integrity or engine failure is at issue, plaintiff's counsel may use the factual findings report with great effectiveness. It is astonishing how often a defendant's own engineers claim not to have read the NTSB report or simply to have dismissed it:

Counsel: Sir, you were interested to know precisely the facts concerning the crash of your company's helicopter?

Defendant's Engineer: Most definitely.

Counsel: And you wanted to have available to you all the information concerning that matter?

Defendant's Engineer: Yes.

Counsel: So you have carefully reviewed the NTSB's factual findings report that was issued last May?

Defendant's Engineer: Actually, I haven't.

Counsel: Why not?…

Counsel can use this failure to review the NTSB's findings in several ways. First, it can suggest that the corporate representative's failure to read the report was a litigation strategy or that the representative was given express instructions not to review the report. Sometimes it is possible to show that the individual was given a copy of the report and did read it.

In sum, the function of bringing the NTSB's factual findings before the jury is twofold: (1) to enhance the basis for the plaintiff's theory of the helicopter crash and (2) to bring the imprimatur of the federal government into the process. Because these cases are so vigorously litigated and close on the facts, where one party is seen to align itself with the NTSB's findings, the jury may be persuaded that that party's theories are more worthy of belief.

7.5 FAA Records

In every helicopter accident case both sides will seek to admit a number of FAA records. Such records include the ATC package as well as various aircraft registry records, pilot information as well as aircraft certification records.

To avert any potential admissibility problem counsel should always obtain certified copies of all FAA records sought to be admitted at trial. Many a judge has inquired, "Counsel, do you have a certified copy of that document?" It is always better to be able to respond "Yes, Your Honor, we certainly do."

For any FAA records to be admitted in evidence, they must be admissible under the applicable rules of evidence. As official government documents, FAA records must be certified to be admissible.[98] This requires that the document be either an official publication of the record or a copy accompanied by a certificate made under seal in which the officer with legal custody of the record attests to custody and the official nature of the document.[99] This requirement may be avoided if the opposing party admits to the document's accuracy.[100]

A. Air Traffic Control Communications

Transcripts and recordings of air traffic control communications are admissible as business records. In federal courts, they are admissible under the Federal Business Records Act.[101] In state courts, they are admissible under state rules of evidence, some of which are modeled after the Federal Business Records Act.[102]

Under state or federal rules, however, a business record is still subject to evidentiary objections. The most common objection to the admission of these documents is that they contain hearsay. For example, in one case the party opposing the admission of air traffic control communications objected that the following portions were hearsay: a report from another plane confirming that a beacon was operational, notations on the transcript about speakers and times, and the comments of the pilot.[103] The court found that the beacon report, although hearsay, was not prejudicial and the notations about speakers and times could be independently confirmed through the recording.[104] As to the pilot's comments, although acknowledging that they were hearsay as well, the court found them admissible as admissions of a party-opponent in that it was "highly unlikely, to say the least" that the transmissions came from a plane other than the subject aircraft.[105] Accordingly, the court affirmed the admission of the transcript.[106]

Likewise, the admission of an ATC transcript was affirmed on appeal where a hearsay objection was overruled based on a third party relaying some of the communications where the transcript showed no indication of relay transmissions.[107] An air traffic controller repeating other pilots' comments about the weather also did not prevent an appellate court from affirming the admission of a transcript where the court, while recognizing them as hearsay, noted the comments also were made in the regular course of business. [108]

B. Governmental Investigative Reports

In addition to the NTSB, a number of other federal, state and local governmental entities may investigate the circumstances of a helicopter crash and prepare reports on its findings. These may include municipal fire departments, state highway patrol offices or local police authorities.

Investigative reports by governmental agencies of air-crashes are admissible under the public record exception to the hearsay rule.[109] This rule provides that the following documents are not excluded by the hearsay rule:

> Public Records. A record or statement of a public office if:
>
> (A) it sets out:
> (i) the office's activities;

(ii) a matter observed while under a legal duty to report, but not including, in a criminal case, a matter observed by law-enforcement personnel; or
(iii) in a civil case or against the government in a criminal case, factual findings from a legally authorized investigation; and
(B) the opponent does not show that the source of information or other circumstances indicate a lack of trustworthiness.[110]

In determining the trustworthiness of government reports, the Tenth Circuit has identified four factors:

> (1) timeliness of the investigation, (2) special skill or experience of the investigator, (3) whether a hearing was held and the level at which it was conducted, and (4) any possible motivation or bias problems in the preparation of the report.[111]

Any interest an agency has in the report, bearing on the fourth factor, goes to the weight, not the admissibility, where specific evidence of bias is absent.[112] While " the [i]nclusion of uncorroborated statements and unauthenticated documents in a report," indicate untrustworthiness, "corroboration of the statements memorialized in the public record" indicate trustworthiness.[113] The opponent to admissibility bears the burden of showing untrustworthiness.[114]

Untrustworthiness is also indicated by the inclusion of double hearsay (hearsay recorded by the maker of the report) and reliance on double-hearsay.[115] Any portions of the report that contain hearsay that do not fall within one of the exceptions to the hearsay rule must be excluded.[116]

In a civil suit for breach of contract for failure to restore an airplane to an airworthy condition, the court ruled that the decision of an administrative law judge (ALJ) for the NTSB was admissible where the judge affirmed the Federal Aviation Administration's Emergency Order suspending the airplane's certificate of airworthiness.[117] On appeal, the defendant argued that the ALJ's "decision was the result of a quasi-judicial proceeding."[118] The court disagreed, affirming the admission of the decision under the public record exception of the hearsay rule. It found that the ALJ's "extensive factual inquiry" of the aircraft's airworthiness qualified as the factual findings of an investigation.[119]

C. Non-Accident Specific FAA Documents and Materials

Courts have admitted general FAA publications and productions if properly certified. In one case, an FAA videotape depicting a scenario nearly identical to one party's version of the accident was admitted under the Arizona Rules of Evidence permitting the admission of learned treatises.[120] The foundation for its admission was based on the "tape's being produced under the auspices of an agency which one would expect to have expert knowledge of the subject" and the sufficiency of an expert's testimony as a production from an authoritative source.[121] Likewise, courts have admitted FAA directives that "describe unsafe conditions and set forth mandatory precautions that must be taken in order to operate the affected aircraft."[122]

7.6 Service Difficulty Reports, Airworthiness Directives, Service Bulletins and Service Letters, and Malfunction and Defect Reports

Various documents are created that record airworthiness concerns or operational problems of a helicopter, a component or system. Plaintiff's counsel must take steps to assess the admissibility of these documents supportive of the liability case.

A. Service Difficulty Reports

Service Difficulty Reports (SDRs) are the voluntary reports sent to the FAA by maintenance personnel highlighting any service or performance issues with an aircraft, aircraft system or aircraft component part. The FAA maintains computer records and compilations of these reports and the overwhelming majority of aircraft and component manufacturers receive and review them on a regular basis.

Service and operation reports (SORs) are similar to SDRs. SORs are reports of mechanical problems from helicopter operators to the manufacturer.[123] In an action for rescission and products liability, the manufacturer sought the exclusion of 36 of these reports in its motion in limine.[124] The court ruled that they would be admitted if the proper foundation was laid.[125] When the plaintiff did not offer the SORs through its expert, counsel for the defendant manufacturer questioned the plaintiff's expert about each one to distinguish them from the subject incident, thus opening the door for their admission.[126] The court found them admissible as business records in that the incidents were sufficiently similar to the one at issue.[127]

SDRs are useful in establishing that the defendant manufacturer was aware of an ongoing airworthiness problem with its product. Service difficulty reports also have been used to oppose summary judgment motions under the General Aviation Revitalization Act by asserting the knowing concealment exception where the defendant either failed to disclose or misrepresented the defect or malfunction.[128]

Defendants routinely object to the admissibility of SDRs on various grounds such as hearsay, lack of evidence of substantial similarity of condition, remoteness in time or place, and general irrelevancy. All of these objections normally can be overcome where counsel can represent to the court that the defendant manufacturer receives and reviews these records in the usual course of its business, hence overcoming the lack of trustworthiness argument. If offered solely to show notice by the defendant of a recurring problem or the extent of a hazard, this is in many jurisdictions a less stringent admissibility threshold. For that reason, counsel must inquire of the defendant's corporate representatives whether SDRs are received and reviewed and, if so, for what purpose. If the defendant manufacturer is of the small minority which does not regularly review such field data about its products, that can be pointed out as a violation of the proper standard of care by plaintiff's experts.

B. Airworthiness Directives

Airworthiness directives (ADs) are documents issued by the Federal Aviation Administration that "describe unsafe conditions and set forth mandatory precautions that must be taken in order to operate the affected aircraft."[129] If they are properly certified,[130] these documents are admissible under the public records exception to the hearsay rule.[131] To defeat admission under this rule, the opponent of the evidence must show that the document is untrustworthy.[132] Untrustworthiness is indicated by the following factors:

> (1) the timeliness of the investigation; (2) the special skill or experience of the investigating officials; (3) whether hearings were held and at what level; and (4) possible motivation problems underlying the investigation.[133]

Airworthiness directives are relevant on the issues of design defect, availability, cost, practicality,[134] and causation.[135] In addition, those issued before the crash may establish negligence where a defendant's failure to comply with the airworthiness directive would have prevented the crash.[136] In those cases, the owner—as well as the party who failed to comply with the airworthiness directive[137]—is liable, having primary responsibility to comply with the FAA's mandatory directive.[138]

Attachments to airworthiness directives are admissible as well. In one case, a defendant argued that a chart of icing accidents issued with an airworthiness directive should be excluded because it was untrustworthy.[139] The defendant claimed that untrustworthiness was indicated by the omission of the underlying data, the unknown methodology in selecting the data, and the misleading nature of the graph.[140] In denying the defendant's motion in limine with respect to this issue, the court ruled that it would admit the chart if introduced through a competent witness.[141]

Airworthiness directives are essentially service bulletins but with the distinction that they are issued normally as mandatory changes or practice procedures by the FAA. From an evidentiary standpoint, these should not be excluded by defendants as a subsequent remedial measure because they are government-issued. It is surprising how frequently an airworthiness directive is issued precisely because of the malfunction or defect involved in the case at hand. Courts routinely have admitted evidence of airworthiness directives pursuant to the evidentiary rule allowing admissibility of evaluative reports as part of an official governmental investigation.[142]

Courts have held that the rule against the admission of subsequent remedial measures does not apply to airworthiness directives. This rule was enacted to "encourage tortfeasors to take steps to remedy a hazardous condition in their control" by assuring them that admissions in "a recall letter" would not be used as evidence of their negligence.[143] Because airworthiness directives require a manufacturer to perform a subsequent remedial measure, it is an action not voluntarily taken and therefore cannot violate the policy underlying the evidentiary rule against subsequent remedial measures.[144]

C. Service Bulletins and Service Letters

A service bulletin has been compared to "an automobile manufacturer's recall letter."[145] Manufacturers issue these documents to owners describing maintenance that should be performed within a specified time limit, noting a degree of urgency reflecting the seriousness of the problem.[146]

Service bulletins or service letters are universally admissible when the issuer is the party defendant in the lawsuit.[147] These are admissible as business records and are generated by the defendant manufacturer as part of its business. To the extent additional grounds are even necessary, they also may be admissible as an admission against interest. They similarly may be admissible to provide notice of a difficulty upon receipt and evidence acknowledged by the manufacturer of some safety issue worthy of formal contact with the helicopter owner or operator.

A service bulletin was admitted to establish that the defendant, a successor corporation to the manufacturer, satisfied its post-sale duty to warn.[148] Although the plaintiff denied receiving the service bulletin, the manufacturer provided an affidavit attesting to the delivery and an invoice containing a charge that included the service bulletin.[149]

Similar to the argument made with regard to airworthiness directives, a plaintiff sought the admission of a service bulletin in an action involving a products liability claim.[150] The plaintiff argued that Rule 407 did not apply in that the FAA required the issuance of the service bulletin and the manufacturer's action in issuing it was, therefore, not voluntary.[151] The court found otherwise, based on a letter from the manufacturer seeking approval of the service bulletin from the FAA that indicated that the manufacturer initiated the issuance of the bulletin.[152]

Where a wing separation of an airplane was alleged to have caused a crash, a court similarly excluded a service bulletin as a subsequent remedial measure where negligence and strict liability claims were asserted.[153] Because the service bulletin at issue called for a wing spar inspection to determine the presence of cracks that could result in wing separation, the court found that its admission was sought to prove the manufacturer's culpable conduct and ruled that the trial court erred in admitting it.[154]

Service bulletins and letters issued by the engine manufacturer were relied on by the author in one helicopter crash case to establish the requisite showing for punitive damages in that the defendant had actual knowledge of the engine defect and its danger at the time the helicopter engine was sold.[155] A timeline was presented that included the issuance of three service letters and two service bulletins that consistently underrepresented the seriousness of the defect.[156] In that case, the jury returned a substantial verdict for punitive damages.[157]

In an unusual case, at issue was a bulletin issued by the U.S. Forestry Service warning pilots of particular models of airplanes not to fly into icing conditions and the procedure to be followed if they encountered icing.[158] The plaintiffs offered this bulletin on the manufacturer's knowledge of the danger posed by the aircraft at issue and the manufacturer's failure to warn.[159] The court affirmed its exclusion because the author was unknown and the bulletin was therefore untrustworthy.[160]

D. Malfunction and Defect Reports

By federal regulation, "the holder of a Type Certificate (including amended or a Supplemental Type Certificate), a Parts Manufacturer Approval (PMA), or a TSO authorization, or the licensee of a Type Certificate must report any failure, malfunction, or defect in any product or article manufactured by it that it determines has resulted in any of the occurrences listed in paragraph (c) of this section."[161] In addition, the same parties must report "any defect in any product or article manufactured by it that has left its quality system and that it determines could result in any of the occurrences listed in paragraph (c) of this section."[162]

The list of occurrences listed in paragraph (c) include the failures of aircraft systems, excessive vibration, flammable fluid leakage, the presence of toxic or noxious gases, a structural defect, fires, and other indications of a defect.[163] Although some exceptions to the general reporting rule exist, if a report is required, it must be accomplished within 24 hours of the incident indicating the presence of a defect.[164] If the problem stems from a manufacturing or design defect, the manufacturer must investigate the defect and report to the FAA the results of that investigation.[165] If corrective action is required, the manufacturer must submit the data necessary for the FAA to issue an airworthiness directive.[166]

Malfunction and defect reports (MDRs) are admissible to show notice to the manufacturer.[167] These reports, however, are generated by the manufacturer itself and are required to be submitted to the FAA as part of the continuing certification requirements of the aircraft or airworthiness of the component part.

7.7 Internal Company Documents

A manufacturer's internal documents that discuss an alleged defect are admissible. In one helicopter accident case, the documents were admitted "to show the danger of the product and to establish that the defendant had actual knowledge of the danger."[168] In another case, a manufacturer's internal memorandum was admitted over a hearsay objection as it was not offered for its truth but as a rebuttal to plaintiff's evidence from the FAA that the manufacturer knew about the design defects and did nothing to cure them.[169] In affirming the admission of the internal memorandum, the court noted that the memorandum, "true or false, is evidence that the FAA allegations were not ignored."[170]

7.8 *Daubert* Motions to Exclude Expert Testimony

Perhaps the single greatest reason for plaintiff's counsel to avoid federal court wherever possible is the defendants' common predatory use and the court's potentially dispositive application of the *Daubert* standard for admitting expert testimony.[171] Where much has been written on the applicability and interpretation of *Daubert*, there is but one certainty: its potentially dispositive impact on the plaintiff's lawsuit is ignored at peril. The standard imparts an unfair burden on an injured plaintiff or the family of a deceased victim in seeking to hold accountable a multi-national corporation which may have ignored basic safety design principles.

The cases are legion where well-qualified experts are deemed to have an insufficient basis for their testimony which sends the whole case out the proverbial window. *Daubert* gives defendants a free shot at plaintiff's key liability experts with no adverse consequences to failure and drives up the costs of what is already hugely expensive litigation. There are numerous reported cases where the standard postulated by the federal district court judge is simply impossible because no such expert exists. And given the almost universal deference which the U.S. Circuit Courts of Appeals give to the district court judges in excluding an expert under *Daubert*, relief at that next level cannot be expected.

Counsel handling these cases must be adept at working with the *Daubert* standard whether encountered in federal court or in those states adopting a comparable standard for the admission of expert testimony. The court in *Daubert* set forth a list of factors which the trial court must examine to establish the reliability of the expert's underlying methodology:

1. Is the technique or theory published and peer reviewed?;
2. Does the methodology test the theory to determine if it can be falsified?;
3. What is the known rate of error of the proposed methodology?; and
4. Has the technique or theory been generally accepted in the relevant scientific community?[172]

The second aspect of the *Daubert* test is relevance. That requires an examination whether the testimony would "assist the trier of fact to understand the evidence or to determine the fact in issue."[173]

The *Daubert* standard is not limited to liability experts but applies to damages experts as well. If the lawsuit is in a *Daubert* jurisdiction, counsel must ensure that the economist retained uses reliable economic methodology and avoids "unexplained assumptions" which surely will result in that economist's exclusion.

A. Meeting the *Daubert* Challenge

Despite these rigorous standards, there are several measures counsel should take which can help overcome a *Daubert* challenge, as explained below.

1. Retain the Most Qualified Expert Possible for that Particular and Narrow Subject Matter

Although this should be the operating principle even without potential applicability of *Daubert*, it is critical where *Daubert* comes into play. Counsel must have an expert who is widely recognized as being an imminent authority in the field. Given the *Daubert* emphasis on peer review and publication, it is helpful if that expert has published in peer-review journals on the specific area of expertise called upon in the case. Listing not only publications but also lectures and presentations will help to convince the judge that the expert is not engaging in so-called "junk science" but has a well-accepted methodology and basis for the opinions to be expressed. Counsel must be certain that the particular opinions to be expressed in the case are those type upon which the expert has published or presented papers.

It is crucial to investigate the expert's "*Daubert* history." A potential expert who has been stricken half a dozen times in a *Daubert* hearing should be avoided at all costs. Conversely, an expert who has successfully withstood *Daubert* scrutiny on a number of occasions is particularly attractive.

2. The Expert's Report Must Be Comprehensive and All Facts Must Be Supported by Reference to the Record

Counsel must insist that all experts prepare a detailed, point-by-point narrative of all opinions to be expressed with careful citation to all reference works relied on. The report should follow to a great extent the *Daubert* factors: reliability of methodology, general acceptance in the field and straightforward application of the methodology to the established facts of record. Any actual or computer-simulated testing should be described in detail with a focus on how that testing applies to the opinions expressed.

The report should detail how the expert's qualifications and background qualify him to express opinions in the matter. Some courts will not take the time to separately review an expert's curriculum vitae. Specific experience relevant to the opinions in the case needs to be laid out in the report, especially publications in peer-reviewed journals. If there are any published standards or regulations applicable, those need to be set out and explained.

3. Learn the Judge's Specific *Daubert* Approach

Once the judge or assigned magistrate is known, counsel must collect all known *Daubert* decisions reached by that judge, and, where available, transcripts of *Daubert* hearings must be scrutinized. Conferring with other counsel who have successfully withstood a *Daubert* challenge before that judge is especially instructive.

4. Schedule *Daubert* Hearing as Early as Possible

The timing of the *Daubert* challenge is also critical. Defendants habitually like to wait until the last possible moment for any *Daubert* challenge so that plaintiff is unable to present any alternative testimony or rehabilitate the expert in some way. All federal courts and most of those

state courts applying *Daubert* set a deadline for any *Daubert* challenges in the case management or scheduling order. If defendants fail to timely raise a *Daubert* challenge, it is deemed waived.

Where *Daubert* is applicable, it has proven useful to identify at least two experts on any given subject matter. Arranging for an early *Daubert* hearing will permit counsel to learn of the court's precise standards and concerns so that the second expert may be specifically prepared on those matters.

5. Never Rely on an Expert's Affidavit but Present Live Testimony

In perusing successful *Daubert* challenges, a substantial number involves instances where plaintiffs submitted the expert's response by affidavit rather than calling the expert live at a hearing. Calling the expert live provides a far greater chance of overcoming the *Daubert* motion because the judge can assess the expert's credibility directly and may ask pointed questions which may allay any particular concern as to methodology, qualifications or other basis for the opinions to be expressed.

6. Compare and Contrast with Defense Expert Qualifications

Point out that the defense expert in that field is no more qualified than plaintiff's expert by specific reference to their level of education, experience and published work. Defendants must claim that their own experts pass *Daubert* muster. In the depositions of the defense experts, obtain clear concessions that the methods and approach which they use are grounded in generally accepted principles. Obtain admissions as to the authoritativeness of various scientific and technical literature relied on by plaintiff's experts.

7. Have All Trial Demonstrative Aids Ready

The *Daubert* hearing must be approached with the same degree of preparedness and intensity as the expert's trial testimony. Charts, models, computer animations and other helpful demonstrative aids are as useful for the judge hearing a *Daubert* challenge as for any jury hearing the substantive testimony. All such exhibits in aid of the expert's testimony should be fully prepared and available at the time of the *Daubert* hearing.

8. Retain More Experts and Narrow Field of Expertise

Many times counsel are tempted to proceed with the all-purpose liability expert in complex helicopter crash litigation. When faced with a potential *Daubert* challenge, that is a critical mistake. The various areas of expertise must be addressed by experts with specific and total mastery of that area. Collateral, incidental or side opinions will be jettisoned by almost any court applying the *Daubert* standard. Counsel must consider hiring more experts and narrowing the specific opinions so that no experts can be charged with testifying outside of their field of expertise.

9. Discretely Handle the "Testing" Issue

One of the most difficult issues in addressing a *Daubert* challenge in the context of any aviation litigation is the "testing" of the expert's theory or opinion. Such testing may not only be downright dangerous to perform by plaintiff but it may be prohibitively expensive. In such instances, there is no easy answer, but some useful alternatives are conducting computer simulated testing or analogizing comparable testing in other contexts. A frequent basis for a defendant's liability is the failure to conduct testing on a particular helicopter component or system. In that case it would seem untenable to require plaintiff to conduct testing on a scale required for helicopter design safety.

Finally, if counsel are not experienced or are uncomfortable in facing the prospect of a *Daubert* challenge, then it would behoove her to associate counsel who are experienced with *Daubert* challenges. Notwithstanding the most intensive and careful preparations, there are cases where the judge found that the particular methodology was not "reliable" or that the opinions were not necessarily helpful or relevant for the jury's consideration. All that counsel can do at that point is to re-configure the focus of the case as against any remaining defendants and be prepared to file a timely appeal, however fruitless, of the court's ruling if advisable.

B. Challenging Defense Experts

Daubert is a two-edged sword. After successfully parrying a *Daubert* challenge, plaintiff's counsel should give serious consideration to bringing a *Daubert* challenge against one or more defense experts. From a timing standpoint, there is an advantage to waiting until after withstanding defendant's challenge, so long as any time deadlines are complied with. The court will have been well-educated in the particular field, whether flight aerodynamics or some helicopter system design issue, and hopefully will require the same *Daubert* criteria for the defense as was required of the plaintiff.

Plaintiff's counsel should not be shy in aggressively seeking to exclude opinions of any defense expert with suspect *Daubert* qualifications. All defense experts should be asked about their prior relevant education, peer-reviewed publications and work experience which relate precisely to the opinions to be expressed. These experts must be called upon to explain the specific methodology utilized in arriving at their expert opinions for the defense. This often will yield precisely the same methodology as described by plaintiffs and may be of assistance in successfully fending off a *Daubert* challenge to plaintiff's experts.

If a defense expert fails to properly describe the methodology upon which the opinions are based, that is normally a sufficient basis to have those opinions stricken under *Daubert*. A qualifications and methodology chart can then be prepared comparing and contrasting one of the plaintiff's experts on a particular point with the counterveiling defense expert. Items to be compared include number of articles published in peer-reviewed journals, years of experience, years in the relevant industry, number of times approved to testify in *Daubert*-criteria courts, number of times inspected subject helicopter wreckage or key components and whether the expert visited helicopter crash site or not. In a few cases, defendants have forgone a challenge to plaintiff's expert for fear of a counter-*Daubert* attack. Absent agreement, that would be no reason for plaintiff's counsel to hesitate in moving forward with a *Daubert* challenge of any of the defendant's experts.

7.9 Substantially Similar Incidents and Crashes

Some of the most powerful evidence of liability in any helicopter crash trial involves the admissibility of other crashes or incidents due to the same or substantially similar defective part or malfunctioning system design. That explains why defendants routinely file their stock motions in limine seeking to exclude such evidence well knowing of its persuasive appeal. Counsel should take a number of pro-active measures to maximize the prospect that all or most of such offered evidence will be admitted by the trial court and considered by the jury.

A. Legal Standard for Admissibility

The legal standard for admissibility of any similar act evidence depends on the specific issue for which that evidence is being offered. When similar act evidence is offered as proof that the subject product or system was defective and unreasonably dangerous, then there must be some showing of substantial similarity as between the proffered similar evidence and the relevant facts established in the underlying helicopter crash. Most commonly, courts require a showing of "substantial similarity" if the similar accident evidence is offered as proof of defect and causation. The emphasis then is on the similarity between the specific defect at issue and the specific defect which was involved in the other similar accident. On appeal, the trial court's ruling on the admission of evidence of similar accidents is reviewed under an abuse of discretion standard.[174]

Evidence of similar crashes can be used to prove causation, the existence, dangerousness, or notice of a defect, or the existence of a duty in proving a negligence or failure-to-warn claim. It can also be used to refute a defendant's contentions. To be admissible, evidence of similar incidents must be substantially similar to the subject accident.[175] The degree of similarity depends upon the purpose for which the evidence is offered.[176] If it is offered to prove that the product was unreasonably dangerous[177] or to prove causation,[178] the plaintiff must show a high degree of similarity. For other purposes, the standard is less stringent and less similarity is required.[179]

Evidence of similar helicopter crashes and incidents is especially critical in these cases because the helicopter is most often totally destroyed and all that remains is circumstantial evidence to establish the defect or causation. As one court noted in a helicopter crash case, evidence of "similar accidents or failures involving the same product has great impact on a jury, as it tends to make the [purpose for which it was admitted] more probable than it would be without the evidence."[180]

In *Four Corners Helicopters, Inc. v. Turbomeca, S.A.*, plaintiffs sought the admission of similar helicopter crashes for multiple purposes. The case is instructive on the degree of similarity required to admit reports of other incidents in helicopter crash lawsuits. The Artouste IIIB turbine engine which powered the helicopter failed in-flight after a loose labyrinth screw backed out of position, contacted the compressor impeller, and rubbed against the diffuser holder plate, causing a squealing sound just before the crash.[181] The plaintiff offered sixteen reports of other incidents to prove "design defect, notice of design defect, duty to warn, negligence, causation, and to refute [the manufacturer's] claim that the accident was caused by a maintenance problem due to excessive vibration."[182] In admitting the reports, the trial court observed that while no two cases were identical, "any differences between the other incidents and the engine failure in this case affected the weight of the evidence and not its admissibility."[183]

The defendants noted the following differences between the subject accident and the other incidents: "none of the reports records an in-flight failure of an Artouste IIIB engine; some of the reports concerned Artouste II rather than Artouste IIIB engines; none of the incidents reported involved accidents, but instead concerned mechanical problems identified on the ground; in some of the reports the compressor impeller was made of aluminum, a softer material than the titanium used on other impellers; with one exception, the reports concerned engines which were not under power when problems occurred; and the screw in the instant case was fixed in place by a method described in [the manufacturer's] Service Bulletin TU133, whereas in other Artouste

IIIB engines, a different, less secure fixation method was utilized."[184]

In rebuttal, the plaintiffs countered with testimony that: "all incidents involved Artouste II or Artouste IIIB engines, the same generic engine; the screws and seals, and the retention of the screws were the same, as were the manufactured tolerances; and in virtually all incidents a squeaking or grinding noise was identified during engine coastdown, engine lockup or stiff stoppage occurred during shutdown, and a wear and rub pattern appeared on the head of the screw and the aft of the impeller."[185]

The U.S. Circuit Court of Appeals for the 10th Circuit affirmed the trial court's admission of the reports to prove the existence of a defect where the referenced accidents, although not identical, were substantially similar.[186] By meeting this higher standard, "[t]hey further met any relaxed requirement of similarity and were therefore admissible for all purposes offered by plaintiffs."[187]

1. Offered as Proof of Causation

Where similar incidents are offered to prove causation, the greatest degree of similarity is required. In one such case, the court found that the plaintiff failed to carry its burden of proof to warrant the admission of other-accident evidence.[188] The court ruled that the plaintiff should have shown the following elements: "(1) a similar product; (2) a similar defect; (3) causation related to the defect in other accidents and (4) exclusion of all reasonable secondary explanations as to the cause of this crash."[189]

Where an airworthiness directive is offered regarding other incidents to prove causation, no showing of similarity is required.[190] An airworthiness directive is issued by the Federal Aviation Administration and "describes unsafe conditions existing in an aircraft and the fact that such a condition is likely to exist or develop in other products of the same type design."[191] Because it is necessarily limited to similar classes of aircraft and excludes those relevantly different, it satisfies the requirement of substantial similarity with no need for additional proof.[192]

The trial court was found to have properly excluded evidence of another accident where the only similarity was a crash after encountering icing in-flight.[193] While a frozen elevator was alleged to have caused the subject crash, there was no evidence of the same dangerous condition in the other case.[194]

2. Offered as Proof of Design or Manufacturing Defect

Where a defendant sought the admission of an FAA report involving significantly different models than the subject model aircraft and despite its earlier objection that these models were irrelevant in discovery due to their differences, the court admitted the report.[195] In so ruling, the court noted that "plaintiffs are adequately equipped to impeach the FAA report, and denial of their motion will not unduly prejudice them."[196]

Another case involved an emergency landing in a sea near Russia where the plane sank and was never recovered.[197] Although other accidents involved engine in-flight shutdowns, they did not involve the same potential causes of the subject accident: "a power turbine blade failure, the misuse of the manual override lever, or the shutdown of an overheated engine."[198] Their admission to prove design defect was, therefore, error.[199]

In a case where the plaintiffs sought to prove defective condition, the court considered the following factors in determining whether other helicopter crashes were substantially similar to the subject crash: "changes in place, remoteness of time, changes in circumstances, and/or changes in the product or area itself."[200] The court found other accidents substantially similar and therefore admissible because they and the subject accident shared the same circumstances: the same model of "helicopter experiences a switchover, the collective control is forcibly pulled or jolted from the pilot's hand, the helicopter loses altitude, goes nose down and the pilot loses control of the helicopter."[201]

Another case involved the crash of a commercial airplane short of the runway.[202] There, the plaintiffs sought the admission of 25 of 37 similar accidents involving the identical malfunctioning altimeters as those involved in the subject accident.[203] The court ruled, however, that their admission would be cumulative and time-consuming where the malfunctions of the 12 admitted to prove notice were substantially of the same nature as the other 25 altimeters.[204]

In a case demonstrating the importance of pleading the facts in a complaint to facilitate the admission of similar accidents, the court ruled that the trial court erred when it limited the admission of similar accidents to one incident involving the same defective part, a gas cap with a broken hinge.[205] On appeal, the court found that all 25 prior incidents were admissible because the complaint alleged that "[t]he design of…(the) fuel system and gas cap was defective in using a single gas intake to supply two engines and five separate tanks, leaving the systems without any backup safety features permitting one engine to operate independently in case of loss of fuel."[206] Therefore, the court ruled that "[p]rior accidents in which all of [the airplane model's] fuel was siphoned through a single gas intake are relevant to this issue and evidence of them should have been admitted."[207] The court reversed and remanded the case based on the exclusion of this evidence.[208]

The plaintiff was not required to show similarity where the defendant opened the door to the admission of Service and Operation Reports (SORs), which are reports to the manufacturer of mechanical problems encountered by operators of its helicopters.[209] In response to a motion in limine, the court had ruled that they would be admitted if the plaintiff proved that they were substantially similar to the subject accident.[210] After the plaintiff's expert mentioned the SORs as a basis for his opinion during his direct examination, the defendant questioned him about each one in an attempt to distinguish them from the subject accident, opening the door for their admission.[211] The court admitted the SORs as business records, finding that they were "sufficiently similar to the incident here to justify their admission into evidence."[212]

In another case, although similar incidents involved broken ballistic foam as did the subject accident, the court ruled that the evidence was untrustworthy in that it was unclear if the foam was broken during maintenance or improperly glued during manufacture.[213] Even if the plaintiffs could prove a manufacturing defect, they would have to also show "how many pieces were broken, how many came unglued and where the pieces were discovered" where the subject accident involved foam jamming the flight controls.[214]

3. Offered as Notice of Defect

While the court acknowledged that evidence of similar accidents involving the same allegedly defective part before the subject crash was admissible to prove notice, their admission was unnecessary because two of the defendant's service bulletins in evidence showed that it was aware of the defect and notice was not an issue in the case.[215] The court observed, however, that evidence of the defendant's knowledge of other accidents would have been admissible if the plaintiff had sought punitive damages, noting that there was evidence that the defendant was "aware of the dangers inherent in [the part at issue] during the design stage of the helicopter in 1969, but they did not act because of the cost of redesigning the module and the resulting delay in production of the helicopter."[216]

The court affirmed the admission of three prior incidents involving the same defective part where the plaintiff's expert could not distinguish metallurgically between the parts in those incidents and the subject accident.[217] The court allowed their admission for the limited purpose that "the defendant had notice of defects or physical conditions which are dangerous" where "the prior accidents involve substantially the same circumstances or conditions which caused the accident at issue."[218]

A court determined that accidents involving a different model were substantially similar in that both it and the subject plane shared the same defect in the wing design, "which caused the aircraft to spin unduly in a single engine stall."[219]

The court noted that the circumstances need not be identical to show notice, merely that "the prior accidents should have alerted [the manufacturer] to the faulty spinning characteristics" of the subject plane.[220]

The court in another case admitted only seven of 45 reports of similar accidents in a case involving a pilot who was not qualified to fly under instrument conditions but flew into inclement weather requiring instrument flight and crashed when a wing separated from his plane.[221] On appeal the court ruled that the trial court properly excluded incidents involving models with greater structural strength and those not involving the same circumstances as those in this case.[222] The court affirmed the admission of seven reports of accidents where "pilots unqualified to fly under instrument conditions who nonetheless were in such conditions," the same circumstances as those in the present case, for the limited purpose of showing notice of defects to the defendant.[223]

Reports of other incidents were also excluded in another case involving the crash of an airplane spinning in tight circles just before impact, where the "[d]escriptions of flight attitude, trim settings, engine power, loading, weather conditions, altitudes, feathering, etc., were widely varied."[224] While the court acknowledged that reports of stall or spins of the same model of aircraft were admissible to show that the defendant had notice of a dangerous condition, the court nonetheless affirmed the trial court's exclusion based on the risk of prejudice from undue consumption of time where notice was not an issue.[225]

Where a malfunctioning altimeter was alleged to cause the crash of the subject aircraft, the court ruled that 12 incidents involving identical altimeters that malfunctioned before the date of the subject crash would be admitted but the 25 that malfunctioned after the date of the crash would be excluded.[226] In so ruling, the court reasoned that limiting the admission to those before the crash would be relevant as to notice to the defendants.[227]

To prove that an operator knew or should have known that the subject helicopter was negligently maintained, the plaintiffs sought the admission of another accident where spark plug problems caused engine problems, resulting in a forced landing.[228] The court ruled that two accidents were dissimilar in that the subject accident involving fouled spark plugs while the other accident involved eroded spark plugs; the subject plane had fewer spark plugs than the other; the subject plane spent greater time idling, increasing the potential for fouling of the spark plugs; and the weather conditions were different.[229] Finding that the two accidents were not caused by the same danger or defect, the court affirmed the exclusion of evidence of the other accident.[230]

4. Offered as Proof of Negligence or Failure to Warn

In a case involving a helicopter striking power lines across a river, evidence of prior substantially similar incidents was admitted to establish the existence of a duty in the plaintiff's action for negligence.[231] The court ruled that the defendant "knew or should have known of a risk of harm to pilots sufficiently probable to create a duty."[232] This conclusion was based on prior incidents of near-misses and an accident resulting in three deaths, the low visibility of the power lines, and the failure of the defendant to act in accordance with the industry norm of marking the lines after an accident or requesting an FAA study to determine if the lines should be marked.[233]

Where negligent repairs of an aircraft seat belt were at issue, the court ruled that the "occurrences must be numerous enough to base an inference of systematic conduct" to show "a party's habit or custom."[234] The court found that a single instance was insufficient and should not have been admitted.[235] The court affirmed, however, the admission of 191 instances of frayed cables in the seatbelt assembly, including eight in the subject aircraft, finding this "a sufficiently large number of instances on which the jury might base an inference of systematic conduct."[236]

In a case claiming negligent maintenance, the court ruled that the trial court erred when it admitted testimony of defendant's expert with regard to ball bearings removed from other helicopters showing the same pattern of wear.[237] The expert could not testify as to "the type of aircraft from which any of the bearings he examined came, the hours of service to which the bearings had been put prior to showing signs of fatigue, and the type of rotor blades that were on the helicopters from which the bearings came."[238] The expert's ignorance about the rotor blades was significant because the defendant contended that the stress level on ball bearings depended upon the type of rotor blade.[239] Because the defendant failed to show that the bearing failures "occurred under reasonably similar, but not necessarily identical, circumstances," the court ruled that their admission was error, although harmless as such evidence was cumulative.[240]

In a failure to warn case, the defendant's course of conduct in issuing warnings and recommendations about corrective measures after an accident was established by evidence of other accidents and the defendant's subsequent conduct with regard to those accidents.[241] The court affirmed the admission of this evidence based on the defendant's issuance of warnings, rather than the similarity of the accidents.[242]

5. Offered as Impeachment of Defendant's Experts

In a product liability case, when a defense expert testifies that a product is safe, a plaintiff may counter with evidence of other accidents to impeach the expert. Courts vary in their requirements for this evidence. For example, in one case a defense expert testified that the product in question "is a safe design," it "functions very well," and he had "tested it extensively" and had "no problems with it at all."[243] The trial court allowed the plaintiff to question the expert about other dissimilar accidents, which the defendant contended on appeal was error.[244] Affirming, the U.S. Court of Appeals for the Eighth Circuit ruled that "[t]his evidence was proper for impeachment purposes under the facts of this case where this expert delivered vast and comprehensive testimony as to the safety of [the] design."[245]

Following its sister Circuit, the U.S. Court of Appeals for the Ninth Circuit also affirmed the admission of evidence of dissimilar accidents to impeach an expert who testified that the product design was "safe and competent."[246] While acknowledging "[a] showing of substantial similarity is required when a plaintiff attempts to introduce evidence of other accidents as direct proof of negligence, a design defect, or notice of the defect, the court ruled that "evidence of other accidents, whether similar or not, tends to show the witness's claims of product safety are overstated and the witness therefore may not be reliable."[247]

Six years after the its initial opinion was issued, the Eighth Circuit narrowed its reach somewhat. Based on testimony that a product is "not defective...suitable and proper... [and] reasonably safe," with an affirmative response to a leading question about the product's general safety, the court held that the expert's testimony did not "rise[] to the level of 'vast and comprehensive' necessary to permit non-similar accident evidence for impeachment purposes."[248] The court ruled that it was error to admit evidence of other accidents, reasoning that "[t]o hold that an expert who simply offers his opinion that a product is 'generally safe' opens the door to all other accident evidence would create an exception which would swallow the general rule."[249]

In contrast, the U.S. Court of Appeals for the Tenth Circuit ruled that, even if only for the impeachment of an expert who attests to the safety of a product, evidence of other accidents, to be admissible, must be substantially similar.[250] There, the court ruled that the trial court erred when it admitted evidence of 23 accidents without a showing of substantial similarity.[251]

6. Rebuttal of Defendant's Contentions

In *Joy v. Bell Helicopter Textron, Inc.*, the defective part in the subject case was alleged to have failed due to a metallurgical defect while the same part in similar accidents failed due to severe wear.[252] The plaintiffs offered the other-accident evidence to refute the defendant's contention that the subject helicopter could not be defective because it was manufactured according to specifications.[253] Although the plaintiffs offered to withdraw the evidence if the defendant would stipulate that "parts can fail despite meeting manufacturing specifications," the defendant refused.[254] The court found that, despite the difference in the mode of failure weighing against admission, the failure of the parts in exactly the same location in all of the cases well before the end of their useful life was sufficient for their admission. The appellate court agreed, noting that the incidents were sufficiently similar when not offered to prove dangerousness.[255]

7. Offered as Proof of Punitive Liability

Where offered only to prove notice or to support a claim for punitive damages, the standard for establishing similarity is much less stringent. As one court has stated:

> The degree of similarity required for evidence that constitutes notice to the defendant of prior similar accidents is less demanding than the similarity required to show that the same accident occurred on the occasion in issue.[256]

The reason that the standard for admissibility of other similar act evidence for the purposes of establishing notice is less stringent is because such evidence is offered to show negligent conduct on the part of the product manufacturer. Where that manufacturer has actual notice of either confirmed or potentially defect aspects of its product it must exercise ordinary care by either investigating or taking appropriate steps to address the danger.

The least stringent standard for admitting evidence of other similar accidents is with respect to allegations of punitive conduct. The sole issue here is whether the manufacturer acted with complete indifference or conscious disregard of the safety of others. Proof that the manufacturer ignored or delayed efforts to correct the defective condition of its product when it knew of serious and recurring reports of defect is admissible in any jurisdiction authorizing the imposition of punitive damages. For example, the punitive damage award against a helicopter manufacturer in a Pennsylvania case was affirmed where Hughes Helicopter conducted a "woefully insufficient investigation" when it knew of over fifty similar incidents.[257]

The legal standard for admissibility of other helicopter crash evidence may be summarized as follows:

(a) Offered as proof of defective condition and causation

The evidence of other similar helicopter crashes or incidents must be "substantially similar" to the subject helicopter accident with particular emphasis on the specific type of defect, malfunction or negligence; and

(b) Offered to show notice to the manufacturer or as evidence of punitive conduct

The evidence must be "sufficiently similar" to the incident in question so as to trigger either a duty to investigate by the manufacturer or to take some other actions in keeping with its duty to exercise ordinary care.

B. Meeting the Challenge to Similar Incident Evidence

Under Fed. R. Evid. 402 or the equivalent state evidentiary rule, defendants opposing the admission of similar incidents may object on the basis of relevance if the accidents are not substantially similar.[258] Or a defendant may claim that another incident is too remote in time to be relevant.[259] Where the prior accident happened twenty years before, the court affirmed the trial court's admission of evidence of the accident, finding that a remote accident is material if it meets the similarity requirements for admission, observing that remoteness in time goes to weight not admissibility.[260] Ruling similarly, another court noted that "[w]hile only earlier accidents can be relevant to the issue of notice, causation is an issue affected only by the circumstances and the equipment, and is not related to the date of the occurrence."[261]

Even if the prior incidents are substantially similar to the subject accident, an opponent may object that their probative value is substantially outweighed by the danger of unfair prejudice under Fed. R. Evid. 403 or the equivalent state rule. An appellate court is likely to practice judicial restraint in overturning a trial judge's rulings in this respect, deferring instead to the court's balancing of probative value and prejudice.[262] In one case, the court ruled that the probative value substantially outweighed the prejudicial impact of evidence of substantially similar accidents where extensive testimony was presented at trial contesting causation and admitted evidence of those accidents.[263] Ruling in the reverse, another court affirmed the exclusion of evidence of another accident where its probative value would be substantially outweighed by the delay in trial required to debate the similarity of the accident, a collateral issue.[264]

Another possible objection is hearsay. A court overruled this objection when an airworthiness directive from the FAA was offered under the public record exception to the hearsay rule and no untrustworthiness was shown.[265] Likewise, a hearsay objection was overruled where experts relied on the evidence of similar incidents as a basis for their opinion.[266] Because they testified about the incidents as facts upon which they relied in forming their opinion, evidence that need not be admissible under the federal rules and equivalent state rules, the admission of documents about similar incidents was cumulative and their admission was harmless.[267]

In proffering such evidence counsel must emphasize that the emphasis is not on the specific details of the similar crash sought to be admitted but whether the nature of the defect being alleged in the other incident is "substantially similar" to the nature of the defect at issue in the present lawsuit. In responding to any motion to exclude such evidence, counsel should be prepared to address the following issues:

1. Underlying reliability and trustworthiness of the source material or other incident reports;
2. Sufficient detail for comparison;
3. Expert testimony that they are similar in a number of specific respects in terms of the failure mode, crash sequence, pilot reaction; and
4. Offering substantially similar incident evidence for notice rather than as probative on issues of causation or defect.

The preferred approach by trial courts in assessing such similar incident evidence is by means of a pre-trial hearing.[268] Prior to such a hearing the plaintiff must inform the defendant as to the specific incidents which will be offered at trial.[269]

Given the persuasive value of such evidence, counsel must dig deep during the discovery process. Either through pointed document requests to the defendants or by other means of alternative or informal discovery counsel must discover the existence of similar incidents before the admissibility question ever arises. Assuming that such similar accident evidence is located in the discovery process, there are no guarantees to its admissibility, but experience teaches that the safest and best prospects for success are as follows. Plaintiff's engineering liability experts must be supplied with all of the underlying data concerning the similar accidents and be prepared to address all such information in their depositions. Admissibility prospects are maximized where the engineering experts testify in deposition that such helicopter crashes were as a result of a similar in-flight malfunction to the case at bar and rely on them as additional bases for their opinions. That deposition testimony then can be cited to the trial court in opposition to the forthcoming motion to exclude such evidence.

One excellent documentary source for such similar act evidence are the "Blue Ribbon" copies of NTSB Reports of these other helicopter crashes. Plaintiffs should have all of these factual reports available for defendants at the time of the depositions of plaintiff's experts. Prior to the experts' depositions, plaintiffs should advise defendants that certain experts will testify on similar accident evidence and specify the documentation upon which the similar accident evidence is based. In comparing the similarity of the subject crash to the various incidents, it is useful to create a chart of the common factual elements which may include pilot experience, weather conditions, specific component or part number, age of part, age of aircraft, type of mission, quality of maintenance, and even the various similarities of the crash dynamics or in-flight behavior of the helicopter.

Other common factual bases for such evidence include Service Difficulty Reports or Malfunction and Defect Reports. Although often scant in the basic information, these reports often will provide some notice to the defendant with respect to a particular type of product defect or malfunction. Customer complaint letters have been excluded as proof of similar incidents as generally unreliable "accusations and self-serving."[270]

In combating a motion to exclude such evidence, plaintiffs should file a thorough trial brief setting out the method and manner of proof and the specific disputed issues for which the helicopter accident evidence will be admitted:

SAMPLE OUTLINE OF PROOF OPPOSING DEFENDANT'S MOTION TO EXCLUDE PLAINTIFF'S EVIDENCE OF ALLEGEDLY SIMILAR HELICOPTER ACCIDENTS

1. Fatal helicopter crashes due to in-flight failure of [component part].
A. Method of proof.
   1. Sixteen "Blue Ribbon" copies of NTSB Factual Reports.
   2. 75 Service Difficulty Reports (SDRs) of defendant component part manufacturer's failed part.
   3. Defendant's list of potential component part failure incidents.
   4. Excerpts of deposition of defendant employees.
   5. Excerpts of deposition of plaintiff's liability expert.
B. Issues to which prior similar helicopter crashes are relevant and probative.
   1. Strict liability—defect and causation.
   2. Negligence—notice and knowledge.
   3. Punitive liability.

4. Rebut defendant helicopter component part manufacturer's contention that:
   (a) Component part is safe.
   (b) Component part rarely fails.
   (c) Component part does not cause a helicopter to crash.
5. Impeachment of defendant component part's liability experts—No notice or knowledge of component part-related helicopter crashes.

Counsel should attempt to schedule this pre-trial hearing sufficiently in advance of trial to allow time for securing any additional factual support for a particular similar incident as may be required by the trial court.

7.10 Subsequent Remedial Measures

The general rule in negligence is that the admissibility of any evidence that the defendant made repairs or improvements to the product after the accident were deemed inadmissible with the limited exception of whether there is any dispute as to ownership or feasibility of those repairs. The logic underlying the exclusion of such evidence is that it does not bear on the defendant's duty of care or breach of care leading up to the incident and would discourage defendants from making safety improvements or repairs.

Admission of subsequent remedial measures may help prove notice of a defect, demonstrate negligence, or establish a basis for punitive damages. Under Fed. R. Evid. 407 and equivalent state evidentiary rules, evidence of subsequent remedial measures is inadmissible to prove negligence or culpable conduct.[271] Subsequent remedial measures are admissible, however, "when offered for another purpose, such as proving ownership, control, or feasibility of precautionary measures, if controverted, or impeachment."[272] In many jurisdictions, they may be admitted in strict liability cases.[273] In others, this rule bars the admission of subsequent remedial measures even in strict liability cases.[274]

In helicopter crash litigation, such evidence may involve either the design improvement of a particular control or power component, modified maintenance instructions or even shorter replacement intervals. The rules applicable to ordinary products liability cases apply in full force to helicopter crash litigation. And where the majority rule would exclude any such remedial repair evidence when offered solely for the purpose of establishing negligence, if the defendant component manufacturer denies that the fix was feasible or that an alternative design was possible then the evidence should properly be admitted.

The exclusionary rule has been held not to apply in strict products liability cases since the manufacturer's negligence is not at issue. Various jurisdictions have enacted different standards and exceptions to the general rules, especially in products liability cases, and counsel must look to the specific jurisdiction for the nuances in that regard. As a matter of trial tactics, considerations should be given to submitting the action solely on a strict products liability theory in order to assure the admissibility of such post-remedial conduct. Its persuasive value is summarized by the maxim: "If it ain't broke, why fix it?" In fact, where the defect is fairly simple to repair and evidence established that the defendant manufacturer took no steps to correct the danger, this has proven to be a powerful basis for imposition of punitive damages.

In strict liability actions, most courts have found that evidence of subsequent remedial measures serves as "circumstantial evidence of a dangerous defect in a similar product and therefore is relevant to prove that the product involved in this accident was defective." [275] A minority of courts bar such evidence, viewing subsequent remedial measures as "an implied admission that a product was defective."[276]

Under Fed. R. Evid. 407, evidence of subsequent remedial measures is generally not admissible:

> When measures are taken that would have made an earlier injury or harm less likely to occur, evidence of the subsequent measures is not admissible to prove:
> • negligence;
> • culpable conduct;
> • a defect in a product or its design; or
> • a need for a warning or instruction.
> But the court may admit this evidence for another purpose, such as impeachment or--if disputed--proving ownership, control, or the feasibility of precautionary measures.[277]

The purpose of the exclusionary rule is to "encourage tortfeasors to take steps to remedy a hazardous condition in their control."[278] This is accomplished by assuring manufacturers that the corrective steps they take after an accident "will not be used as evidence of their negligence by plaintiffs with claims arising from circumstances before the corrective steps were taken."[279]

This public policy has been fiercely criticized:[280]

> There is only skimpy evidence that tort defendants behave in the way that this argument supposes.... Moreover, the fear of further tort liability or other sanctions provides a substantial incentive for defendants to make repairs even if this will increase the likelihood of their being found liable for past

accidents. Finally, in cases where the only probative evidence of negligence is the taking of subsequent remedial measures, the rule of evidence undermines the policy of the law of torts by subsidizing the safety of others through a denial of compensation to the injured plaintiff.[281]

On the other hand, the policy behind a strict liability action is based not on the effect on a defendant's subsequent conduct but a determination that manufacturers are better able to bear the burden of injuries caused by a defective product.[282] Yet, the rationale for the exclusionary rule is to prevent "the [devastating] potential prejudicial effect [on defendants] as the act will most certainly be viewed as an admission of guilt or fault."[283] The rationale for the exclusionary rule, then, hardly advances the public policy underlying a strict liability action.

While negligence actions focus on the conduct of the defendant, strict liability actions focus only on the product.[284] In other words, "[t]he shift so wrought is from fault to defect."[285] In a negligence action, acting with due care "will exonerate [a defendant] from liability to the most seriously injured plaintiff."[286] In a strict products liability action, "it is no longer any answer that the defendant injured the plaintiff carefully."[287] Based on this distinction, some jurisdictions have ruled that Rule 407, or the equivalent state rule, does not apply in strict liability actions.[288]

The following jurisdictions hold that subsequent remedial measures are admissible in strict liability actions:

- **Eighth Circuit Court of Appeals**. The court admitted an airworthiness directive issued by the French aviation authority after the accident, cautioning owners about the "worsening" of the subject defect and warning that it could cause in-flight shut-downs.[289] The Eighth Circuit held that "where negligence and strict liability were both submitted, the post-accident evidence was relevant for one count, and, as long as it was not unduly prejudicial to [the defendant], being relevant for one purpose but not another, the evidence was admissible."[290]
- **Tenth Circuit Court of Appeals**. The court ruled that an airworthiness directive issued over a year after the accident should have been admitted that described a defect and required corrective action. It ruled that "where there is any reason for use of the evidence other than to establish the defendant's negligence, Rule 407 should not apply."[291]
- **California**. Reasoning that the exclusionary rule [against the admission of subsequent remedial

measures] does not affect the primary conduct of the mass producer of goods, but serves merely as a shield against potential liability," the court ruled that subsequent remedial measures are admissible in strict liability actions.[292]

- **Colorado**. Noting that "the manufacturer's conduct, whether culpable or negligent, is not germane in a strict liability action" while "the nature of the manufactured product itself" is germane, the court ruled that "any attempt to stretch the meaning of 'culpable conduct' or negligence to include design defect products liability claims would be disingenuous at best."[293] This opinion, however, was limited to design defect cases; and the court did not rule on a strict liability claim for failure to warn.[294]

- **Connecticut**. In admitting evidence of subsequent remedial measures in a strict liability action, the court concluded that such evidence "may be relevant without being prejudicial because the manufacturer's culpability is not an issue."[295]

- **Georgia**. Based on the numerous exceptions to the rule against the admission of subsequent remedial measures, the court ruled that such evidence was admissible in a strict liability action.[296]

- **Illinois**. Some Courts of Appeals in Illinois admit evidence of subsequent remedial measures[297] while others do not.[298]

- **Iowa**. Iowa rules of evidence specifically allow for the admission of subsequent remedial measures in strict liability claims.[299]

- **Louisiana**. "In a strict product liability case, evidence of such remedial measures should be allowed insofar as they are relevant in establishing what the manufacturer knew or should have known at the time of the injury."[300]

- **Missouri**. Reversing the trial court's exclusion of subsequent remedial measures, the court ruled that the rule against their admission "is inapplicable in strict liability cases because (1) the culpability of the defendant is irrelevant in such actions and (2) the purposes of the rule would not be served."[301]

- **Nebraska**. The Nebraska Supreme Court admitted evidence of subsequent remedial measures in an action where both negligence and strict liability claims were asserted without an express ruling that subsequent remedial measures were admissible in strict liability actions.[302]

- **Nevada**. Noting that a manufacturer "will not forego making improvements if failing to do so will subject it to additional lawsuits," the court admitted evidence of subsequent remedial measures in a strict liability action.[303]

- **New York**. The court approved the admission of subsequent remedial actions in a case involving a claim of "manufacturing and assembly" defect.[304]

- **Ohio**. After considering "the distinct policy and goals for applying strict liability involving defective products," the Ohio Supreme Court ruled that evidence of subsequent remedial measures was admissible in strict liability actions.[305]

- **Texas**. The court ruled that evidence of subsequent remedial measures is admissible if no rule of evidence bars its admission.[306]

- **Wisconsin**. Ruling that evidence of subsequent remedial measures is admissible in a strict liability action, the court found that the policy behind exclusion would not be violated where "[e]conomic realities will set the course and these realities are that the sooner remedial measures are taken, the less costly the defect will be to the manufacturer."[307]

- **Wyoming**. In admitting evidence of subsequent remedial measures, the court agreed with the committee note to the Wyoming exclusionary rule in regard to its interpretation of "'culpable conduct' as not encompassing breach of warranty or strict liability."[308]

The remaining jurisdictions have either held that subsequent remedial measures are not admissible in strict liability actions or have not ruled on the issue.

As the courts continue to debate the wisdom of admitting or excluding evidence of subsequent remedial actions, cases are being won and lost based, at least in part, on these decisions. Perhaps the Ohio Supreme Court has the best solution to the dilemma of admitting subsequent remedial measures:

Finally, we are aware of the contention by some that the introduction of evidence of subsequent remedial measures in a strict products liability case could be highly prejudicial to a defendant-manufacturer. While this contention may have some validity, an equally plausible assertion can be made on behalf of an injured plaintiff if such evidence is excluded. Without question, all evidence going to the heart of an issue is, to some extent, "prejudicial" to someone. That is the very essence of "evidence" and our adversary system. Let the jury decide![309]

7.11 Prior Lawsuits and Claims

Courts have routinely found that prior lawsuits against a product manufacturer involving similar allegations to those in the present case are admissible as having some tendency to show that the defendant was on notice concerning possible defects in its product.[310] In such instances where prior lawsuits are admitted, almost all courts will exclude evidence of the verdict or resolution of the lawsuit.[311]

Virtually all helicopter aircraft, engine and component manufacturers maintain comprehensive lists of all lawsuits and claims involving particular component failures. Most manufacturers have these categorized by model, whether lawsuits were involved, whether the failure was accompanied by a crash, and whether the crash involved fatalities or serious injuries. Where such lawsuits are discovered, the challenge is to admit these as evidence on any number of legal theories. The hornbook law as to admissibility of prior lawsuits is as follows:

> Evidence of substantially similar prior lawsuits against defendant are admissible to show that defendant had notice of the defect before plaintiff was injured.[312]

The primary basis upon which such evidence is held admissible is that the lawsuits put the defendant on notice of a potentially dangerous condition and trigger a duty to either investigate or to take some actions to address the problem.

In laying a proper foundation for admissibility of such evidence, counsel must inquire of the defendant's corporate representatives as to reasons why these lawsuit lists are kept. After establishing some basis for similarity of these lawsuits to the helicopter crash at incident, counsel should specifically inquire, "And the lawsuits or claims provide your company with notice of [that particular in-flight problem], correct?" The fact that defendant had been sued on prior occasions demonstrates to the jury that this is a recurring problem and defendant's continuing failure to address it is an aggravating liability factor.

7.12 Federal Aviation Regulations

By statute, the FAA is responsible for "assigning, maintaining, and enhancing safety and security as the highest priorities in air commerce."[313] To accomplish this, "the FAA is required by the Federal Aviation Act of 1958 to adopt minimum standards governing the design, construction and performance of aircraft."[314] Federal Aviation Regulations (FARs) may be admitted to prove a minimal duty of care in a negligence action, to set minimum standards for defectively designed products in strict liability actions, as evidence in

failure-to-warn and punitive damages claims, or to establish an exception under the General Aviation Revitalization Act. Plaintiff's counsel must note that FARs, by definition, are only "minimum standards" and are not intended to be the standard of care applicable in every instance.

FARs may be admitted in two ways. They are admissible as official government records so long as they are certified.[315] Or an expert witness may read the regulation into the record.[316] Admissibility of FARs is frequently a two-edged sword. Given the sheer volume of such regulations, most any defendant can find at least a few with which it was in full and proper compliance. Such evidence is troublesome especially in those jurisdictions which provide for a prima facie showing of non-defect where a product manufacturer is in compliance with applicable governmental regulations. Fortunately, the vast majority of states hold that compliance with any governmental regulation is simply evidence of the due care to be accorded under the circumstances and is not conclusive. The governing principle in most states is that violation of a Federal Aviation Regulation is a factor which the jury may consider in determining the issue of negligence.

Similarly, in many cases it may turn out that the pilot, helicopter manufacturer, maintenance facility or some other defendant violated a FAR. In a few states, that may form the basis for a negligent per se submission although counsel is cautioned about making any such claims in plaintiff's complaint. Pleading violation of a FAR may trigger removal to federal court based on the federal preemption doctrine.

Courts have ruled that the violation of regulations constitutes negligence as a matter of law.[317] In a case claiming "the crash was caused by the stall of the airplane with the left engine feathered, and an inadequate stall warning system," the court read five FARs that the plaintiffs alleged the manufacturer had violated.[318] The court instructed the jury members to "find [the manufacturer] negligent if they found that the regulations were violated and that the violations proximately caused decedents' injuries, unless [the manufacturer] justified its failure to comply."[319] The jury returned a general verdict for the plaintiffs.[320] On appeal, the court affirmed the negligence per se instruction.[321]

Another case involved the emergency landing of an airplane where two occupants rescued an unconscious third occupant but were unable to rescue the pilot, also unconscious, before her legs caught on fire when flames spread quickly from the engine compartment.[322] Both her legs were later amputated.[323] After the second jury verdict for the manufacturer, the plaintiff again appealed, arguing that the jury should have been instructed to shift the burden of proof on causation to the manufacturer if it violated two FARs.[324]

One regulation required the installation of firewalls separating the engine from the rest of plane that "must resist flame penetration for at least fifteen minutes;" the other required occupant protection in the event of an emergency landing.[325] The plaintiff presented evidence that the firewall "fittings could only resist flame penetration for 10 to 40 seconds."[326] Reversing the trial court, the court ruled that the instruction shifting the burden of causation to the manufacturer should have been submitted to the jury.[327]

In a case where the plaintiff alleged defective design of a fuel control unit. The court ruled that "the regulations promulgated by the FAA are merely minimum safety standards" and do not preclude a finding of negligence where a reasonable person would take additional precautions.[328] Some regulations, however, are "far too general to support a negligence per se instruction."[329] In one case, the regulations at issue prohibited the careless or reckless operation of an aircraft and required flight at an altitude sufficient for an emergency landing without undue hazard to persons or property below.[330] The court found that the standard of behavior required by the regulations at issue equated to "due care" and affirmed the trial court's refusal to submit a negligence per se instruction based on their violation.[331]

In a similar case, the court considered the same regulations that prohibited the careless or reckless operation of an aircraft as well as one that provided that the pilot is directly responsible for, and is the final authority as to, the operation of the aircraft.[332] Affirming the trial court, the court ruled that the subject regulations "do not impose a particular duty upon a pilot, rather, they provide for general standards of conduct," and affirmed the trial court's refusal to give a negligence instruction for their violation.[333]

In the defective firewall case, the plaintiff sought a jury instruction shifting the burden to the defendant after she established that the manufacturer violated two FARs.[334] In addition to proving negligence, she maintained that the violation of the regulations at issue proved the existence of an unreasonably dangerous design defect.[335] Reversing the trial court, the court agreed, noting that "federal safety regulations may set the minimum standards applicable under strict liability for defectively design products in a crashworthiness case."[336]

The knowing misrepresentation exception to GARA applies where a manufacturer "knowingly misrepresented to the Federal Aviation Administration, or concealed or withheld from the Federal Aviation Administration, required information that is material and relevant to the performance or the maintenance or operation of such aircraft, or the component, system, subassembly, or other part, that is causally related to the harm which the claimant allegedly suffered."[337]

FARs may be asked as evidence to back this GARA exception.[338] In two cases plaintiffs asserted the fraud exception based on a regulation that required a type certificate holder to report "any failure, malfunction, or defect in any product, part, process, or article manufactured by it...." Based on this regulation, the plaintiffs in those cases proved that the defendants knowingly concealed information from the FAA that they were required to disclose.[339]

7.13 Use of Accident Statistics

Based on past rulings, statistical reports summarizing accidents are unlikely to be admitted by either plaintiff or defendant. Plaintiff's counsel will wish to admit such evidence as probative of defendant's knowledge that its helicopter or component was involved in more incidents or crashes than similar or comparable helicopter types or components. From that, the argument is that the defendant should have known its product was unsafe and defective. However, defense counsel will seek to use accident data to establish precisely the opposite point. A lower accident rate supports the contention that defendant's aircraft is comparatively safer than other types.

One case involved government statistics known to the defendant, showing that the defendant's planes "had a rate of structural failure in flight approximately fifteen times the rate for all single engine civil aircraft."[340] The court affirmed the exclusion of this information, finding that it had "no relevance as notice to [the manufacturer] of the existence of a defect" where the accidents on which the statistic was based involved other circumstances and other models than the subject accident.[341] In so ruling, the court noted that "[i]t is extremely dubious, in fact, whether statistics involving probabilities as to causation have any significance at all when applied to a particular incident."[342]

Courts routinely exclude a defendant's proffered accident data purporting to show the relative safety of its product.[343] One court excluded a statistical analysis of National Transportation Safety Board data in which accident rates were compared for the model of aircraft with rates for other aircraft, on a per-flight-hour basis.[344] The trial court ruled that it was "hearsay upon hearsay, unreliable, speculative [and] conjectural" and, on appeal, the court affirmed.[345]

Endnotes

1. *Eckelkamp v. Burlington Northern Santa Fe Ry. Co., 298 S.W.3d 546, 550 n.2 (Mo. App. 2009)* (quoting *Black's Law Dictionary* 636 (9th ed. 2009)).

2. *Newsome v. Penske Truck Leasing Corp., 437 F.Supp.2d 431, 434-35 (D.Md. 2006)* (citations omitted).

3. *Delaney & Co. v. City of Bozeman, 222 P.3d 618, 622 (Mont. 2009); Whirlpool Corp. v. Camacho, 298 S.W.3d 631, 638 (Tex. 2009); Ferebee v. Hobart, 776 N.W.2d 58, 62 (S.D. 2009); Karpacs-Brown v. Murthy, 686 S.E.2d 746, 751 (W.Va. 2009); Vaughn v. Mississippi Baptist Medical Center, 20 So.3d 645, 654 (Miss. 2009); Scott v. Dutton-Lainson Co., 774 N.W.2d 501, 503 (Iowa 2009); Vreeken v. Lockwood Engineering, B.V., 218 P.3d 1150, 1167 (Idaho 2009); Parker v. Melican, 684 S.E.2d 654, 658 (Ga. 2009); Buchanna v. Diehl Mach., Inc., 98 F.3d 366, 371 (8th Cir. 1996).*

4. *Clark v. Cantrell, 529 S.E.2d 528, 536 (S.C. 2000).*

5. *Id.*

6. *Walker v. Fairchild Industries, Inc., 554 F.Supp. 650, 657-58 (D. Nev. 1982).*

7. *Datskow v. Teledyne Continental Motors Aircraft Products, a Div. of Teledyne Industries, Inc., 826 F.Supp. 677, 686 (W.D.N.Y. 1993).*

8. *Colgan Air, Inc. v. Raytheon Aircraft Co., 535 F.Supp.2d 580, 585-86 (E.D.Va. 2008).*

9. *Id. at 583.*

10. *Id. at 584-85.*

11. *Id. at 584.*

12. *Id. at 584-85.*

13. *Id. at 585.*

14. *Glenn v. Cessna Aircraft Co., 32 F.3d 1462, 1466 (10th Cir. 1994).*

15. *Martinez v. W.R. Grace Co., 782 P.2d 827, 830 (Colo. App. 1989)* (affirming the admission of the model of a speed bump on the testimony of a witness who confirmed that the model fairly and accurately depicted the speed bump on the date of the accident).

16. *Lake County Forest Preserve Dist. v. Larsen, 371 N.E.2d 306, 310 (Ill. App. 1977)* (affirming the admission of a topographical map prepared by the United States Department of Agriculture Soil Conservation Service where the engineer confirmed the topographic data through a field inspection and testified as to its accuracy); *Crawford v. City of Meridian, 186 So.2d 250, 252 (Miss. 1966)* (affirming the admission of a topographical map where the witness testified that he had verified various points on the map and was satisfied that it was correct, although the witness had not prepared the map).

17. *Dement v. State, 2009 WL 737786, at *5 n.3 (Ariz. App. 2009)* (affirming the exclusion of a three-dimensional model of the accident scene, "the single most demonstrative item of what actually happened that the jury might ever [have] see[n]" when it was not disclosed to opposing counsel until the first day of trial).

18. *Clark v. Cantrell, 529 S.E.2d 528, 536 (S.C. 2000).*

19. *Id.*

20. *Id. at 536.*

21. *Id. at 535 n.2 (S.C. 2000).*

22. *Id.* For a discussion of a simulation admitted as substantive evidence under *Daubert*, see *Livingston v. Isuzu Motors, Ltd., 910 F.Supp. 1473, 1494-95 (D.Mont. 1995).*

23. *Datskow, 826 F.Supp. at 685.*

24. *Jones v. Kearfott Guidance and Navigation Corp., 1998 WL 1184107 (D.N.J. 1998).*

25. *Id. at *1-*2.*

26. *Id.*

27. *Id. at *3.*

28. *Richardson v. State Highway & Transp. Com'n, 863 S.W.2d 876, 882 (Mo. 1993)* (ruling that too many facts were unknown to determine if the animation was substantially similar to the accident it purported to depict where the defendant sought to use a computer animation of vehicle at issue to demonstrate that it could not have hydroplaned as the plaintiff alleged). To be substantially similar to the conditions at issue, the animation must depict the conditions consistent with the facts and testimony in evidence. *Black v. U-Haul Co. of Missouri, 204 S.W.3d 260, 265 (Mo. App. 2006)* (affirming the admission of a computer animation of a car accident where the testifying expert had a sufficient evidentiary basis for the facts at issue depicted in the animation); *Tate v. Statco Engineering and Fabricators, Inc., 2014 WL 509521 at 5-6 (E.D.Okla. 2014)* (ruling that an animation was inadmissible where it failed to accurately depict the sounds at the time of the injury); *Clark v. Cantrell, 529 S.E.2d 528, 535 (S.C. 2000)* (affirming the

exclusion of a computer animation because it "did not accurately reflect the testimony of the witnesses or the experts who had reconstructed the accident," including the proponent's own expert); *Sommervold v. Grevlos, 518 N.W.2d 733, 737 (S.D. 1994)* (affirming the exclusion of a computer animation depicting an expert's reconstruction of a bicycle accident where the animation failed to reflect testimony about speed, the illumination of the street light, the location of the accident, and the injuries).

29. *Webb v. CSX Transp., Inc., 615 S.E.2d 440, 448-49 (S.C. 2005)* (where the conflict between the driver's testimony that she stopped for ten seconds at the railroad crossing and the video depicting a stop time of 4.8 seconds was explored in trial and several witnesses testified about the amount of vegetation at the scene on the day of the accident where the vegetation appeared enhanced in the video); *Tull v. Federal Express Corp., 197 P.3d 495, 499 (Okla. Civ. App. 2008)* (affirming the admission of a computer animation of an accident used to aid the jury in understanding an expert's testimony where the expert explained why his animation differed from the testimony of a driver involved in the accident); *Cleveland v. Bryant, 512 S.E.2d 360, 362 (Ga. App. 1999)* (affirming the admission of the defendant's computer animation where it accurately represented the opinion of defendant's expert, despite the plaintiff's complaint that the animation was inaccurate and unsupported by evidence in that "it showed her car leaving the intersection at an angle, her car going backwards rather than counterclockwise, the truck traveling down the lane before the collision, and damage to certain parts of her car").

30. *Clark v. Cantrell, 529 S.E.2d 528, 536 (S.C. 2000).*

31. *Richardson v. State Highway & Transp. Com'n, 863 S.W.2d 876, 882 (Mo. 1993)* (affirming the exclusion of an animation reconstructing an accident when the proponent disclosed it to the opposing party one business day before trial); *Tull v. Federal Express Corp., 197 P.3d 495, 501 (Okla. Civ. App. 2008)* (finding that the opposing party had ample time to examine a computer animation where the proponent provided it to the party on the day set by the trial court to exchange exhibits, even though the animation was only to be used to aid the jury in understanding expert testimony); *Dement v. State, 2009 WL 737786, at *5 (Ariz. 2009)* (affirming the exclusion of a three-dimensional model of the accident scene disclosed for the first time to opposing counsel on the first day of trial); *Buchanan v. Moreno, 980 A.2d 358, 360 (Conn. App. 2009)* (affirming the exclusion of a photograph based on late disclosure).

32. *Pierce v. State, 718 So.2d 806, 809-10 (Fla. App. 1997)* (affirming the admission of an animation where it did not replicate the sound of screaming victims).

33. *Com. v. Serge, 896 A.2d 1170, 1183 (Pa. 2006)*, cert. denied, *549 U.S. 920 (2006)* (approving a computer-generated animation as "neither inflammatory nor unduly prejudicial" in that it did not include "evidence of injury such as blood or other wounds"); *Pierce, 718 So.2d at 809-10* (affirming the admission of an animation that did not replicate the bloody scene of the crime).

34. *Serge, 896 A.2d at 1175 n.2.*

35. *Clark v. Cantrell, 529 S.E.2d 528, 537 (S.C. 2000); Tull v. Federal Express Corp., 197 P.3d 495, 502 (Okla. App. 2008); Bullock v. Daimler Trucks North America, LLC, 819 F.Supp.2d 1172, 1176 (D.Colo. 2011).*

36. *Tull, 197 P.3d at 502.*

37. *Clark, 529 S.E.2d at 537.*

38. *Tull, 197 P.3d at 502.*

39. *Clark, 529 S.E.2d at 537.*

40. *Clark, 529 S.E.2d at 537.*

41. *State v. Farner, 66 S.W.3d 188, 210 (Tenn. 2001)* (finding that the trial court erred when it allowed an animation based on inaccurate and incomplete information to be shown to the jury 15 times, noting that "animations generally have a substantial impact upon jurors, and that impact is no doubt increased where jurors are allowed to view the animated visualization not once or twice, but fifteen separate times"); *Pierce v. State, 718 So.2d 806, 810 (Fla. App. 1997)* (finding no undue emphasis on a computer animation that was "shown to the jury for a total of approximately six minutes during the course of an eleven-day trial").

42. *In re Air Crash Disaster, 86 F.3d 498, 511 (6th Cir. 1996)* (superseded by statute on other grounds).

43. *Id. at 538-39.*

44. *Id. at 539.*

45. *Id.*

46. *Id. at 540.*

47. *Timsah v. General Motors Corp., 591 P.2d 154, 164-65 (Kan. 1979)* (refusing to permit an in-court experiment where the plaintiff offered no proof that the conditions of the experiment were substantially similar to that of the accident); *Moldovan v. Allis Chalmers Mfg. Co., 268 N.W.2d 656, 660 (Mich. App. 1978), cert. denied, 444 U.S. 1034 (1980)* (refusing to permit an in-court experiment where "the conditions were not sufficiently similar to the allegedly defective valve on the date of the accident"); *Ryan v. Blakey, 389 N.E.2d 604, 614 (Ill. App. 1979)* (ruling that the trial court erred by admitting a complicated demonstration of a simple principle without a showing of substantial similarity).

48. *National Pressure Cooker Co. v. Stroeter, 50 F.2d 642, 644 (7th Cir. 1931), cert. denied, 284 U.S. 674 (1931)* (finding it difficult to replicate a demonstration to prove that tomato seeds could not clog the openings of a pressure cooker); *Naughton v. Bankier, 691 A.2d 712, 719 (Md. App. 1997)* (finding that a demonstration of how a sling-shot was used to propel a water balloon through a window, requiring three operators, difficult to replicate).

49. *Orwick v. Belshan, 231 N.W.2d 90, 96-7 (Minn. 1975)* (providing safety glasses to the jury where a plaintiff sought to recreate the accident in the courtroom and alleged that the action "entailed an unreasonable risk of harm to those in the vicinity of the operation).

50. *Hale v. Firestone Tire & Rubber Co., 820 F.2d 928, 932-33 (8th Cir. 1987)* (ruling that defense counsel created the "spectacle" by bringing the tires into the courtroom where plaintiff's counsel admonished him to "aim" the tires and rims, alleged to explode, away from the jury and moved his clients around the courtroom to avoid the line of fire).

51. *Guild v. General Motors Corp., 53 F.Supp.2d 363, 365, 370 (W.D.N.Y. 1999)* (admitting a test to demonstrate the scientific principles involved with inertial release that differed from the accident at issue to such a degree that the court found "little danger that the jury would confuse the demonstration as a simulation of the actual crash at issue; *Campbell v. The Daimler Group, Inc., 686 N.E.2d 337, 342-43 (Ohio App. 1996)* (affirming the admission of a model to demonstrate a "theory that a properly cross-braced structure that is not secured to its base will withstand greater vertical forces than an identical structure which is securely anchored" where the model was so dissimilar from the subject building that "the trial court was satisfied that there was little risk that the jury would mistakenly believe that the models were meant to represent the actual conditions which existed at the time of the collapse");

52. *Guild, 53 F.Supp.2d at 370; Campbell, 686 N.E.2d at 343.*

53. *Four Corners Helicopters, Inc. v. Turbomeca, S.A., 979 F.2d 1434, 1440-41 (10th Cir. 1992).*

54. *Id. at 1441.*

55. *Id. at 1442.* Courts have reached the same result in other types of cases. *McElhiney v. Mossman, 850 S.W.2d 369, 371 (Mo. App. 1993)* (affirming the admission of the defendant's exemplar vehicle with minor differences from the subject vehicle where the plaintiff's expert testified that the differences were of "no importance" to the issue in the case); *Hoffman v. Niagra Mach. & Tool Works Co., 683 F.Supp. 489, 492-93 (E.D.Pa. 1988)* (affirming the admission of a model of a foot pedal for a punch press where it was used for the limited purpose of demonstrating how high the operator would have to raise his foot and the distance that it would have to be depressed to achieve one full revolution of the press and counsel did not attempt to mislead the jury about the model); *Seward v. Griffin, 452 N.E.2d 558, 568-69 (Ill. App. 1983)* (affirming the exclusion of the front portion of a Volkswagen van similar to the subject van on which plaintiff's experts had run crashworthiness tests, even though a Volkswagen van was admitted as a defense exhibit, where plaintiffs offered no testimony as to structural similarity between the exhibit and the subject van).

56. *In re L.S., 11 N.E.3d 349, 356-57 (Ill. App. 2014)* (affirming the admission of still images from a webcam where a witness testified that the images were from the webcam archive that he had viewed earlier and accurately depicted the people, including the witness, and place depicted in the images at the relevant time); *Dillon v. Reid, 717 S.E.2d 542, 549 (Ga. App. 2011)* (affirming the admission of photographs from websites where a witness who had personally observed the docks in question testified that the photographs truly and accurately depicted the location of the docks at the relevant time periods); *Kartychak v. Consolidated Edison of New York, Inc., 758 N.Y.S.2d 644, 645 (N.Y.A.D. 2003)* (affirming the admission of a photograph where three workers testified that a photograph of a re-created work site was a fair and accurate representation of the work site on the day of the accident); *Wilson v. Kaufmann, 847 S.W.2d 840, 849 (Mo. App. 1992)* (affirming the admission of a photograph where a police officer who was present on the scene of a motorcycle accident testified that the photographs taken four years later were a fair and accurate representation of the scene on the night of the accident); *Tumey v. Richardson, 437*

S.W.2d 201, 203-04 (Ky. 1969) (affirming the admission of photographs of a vehicle that was replaced in its crash scene position after having been moved where a defendant and a witness at the scene testified that photographs were fair and accurate representations of the accident scene despite the disagreement of the tow truck driver who moved the vehicle).

57. *Levenson v. Lake-to-Lake Dairy Co-op., 394 N.E.2d 1359, 1367 (Ill. App. 1979).*

58. *Id. at 1367-68.*

59. *Stehn v. Cody, — F.Supp.3d —, 2014 WL 6478644 at 10 (D.D.C. 2014) (affirming the admission of photographs of a traffic signal at an accident scene taken over three years later where the court ruled that the photographs would be admitted if the jury was informed that a flashing orange hand replaced a flashing orange person); Lowery v. Illinois Cent. Gulf R.R., 356 So.2d 584, 585 (Miss. 1978) (affirming the admission of photographs taken some time after the accident where witnesses familiar with the scene at the time of the accident testified that grass and bushes were shorter in the photographs); Knight v. Gulf & Western Properties, Inc., 492 N.W.2d 761, 769-70 (Mich. App. 1992) (affirming the admission of photographs taken some time after a real estate agent fell off a loading dock where the witness who found the injured man described the loading dock as not as well lit on the night of the accident as shown in the photographs); Leven v. Tallis Department Store, Inc., 577 N.Y.S.2d 132, 133 (N.Y.A.D. 1991) (finding that the trial court erred when it admitted photographs taken two years after the accident where the witness was not present at the scene at the time of the accident); Allemand v. Zip's Trucking Co., Inc., 552 So.2d 1023, 1029 (La. App. 1989) (affirming the exclusion of photographs taken two years after an accident where no explanation of differences between the photographs and the scene at the time of the accident was offered).*

60. *Rutledge v. NCL (Bahamas), Ltd., 464 Fed.Appx 825, 830 (11th Cir. 2012); McLemore v. Alabama Power Co., 228 So.2d 780, 790-91 (Ala. 1969); Corsi v. Town of Bedford, 868 N.Y.S.2d 258, 261 (N.Y.A.D. 2008); Kessler v. Fanning, 953 S.W.2d 515, 522 (Tex. App. 1997); Department of Transp. v. Millen, 474 S.E.2d 687, 688-89 (Ga. App. 1996); Clauson v. Lake Forest Imp. Trust, 275 N.E.2d 441, 445 (Ill. App. 1971).*

61. *Lopez v. Three Rivers Elec. Co-op., Inc., 92 S.W.3d 165, 174 (Mo. App. 2002) (overruled on other grounds by Joy v. Morrison, 254 S.W.3d 885, 888-89 (Mo. 2008)).*

62. *Id. at 167-68.*

63. *Fed. R.Evid. 403.*

64. *Anderson Aviation Sales Co., Inc. v. Perez, 508 P.2d 87, 93 (Ariz. App. 1973). Other cases are in accord. Citrus County v. McQuillin, 840 So.2d 343, 345 (Fla. App. 2003) (affirming the admission of a photograph of a pedestrian that had been struck by a car being placed in a body bag where "[t]he photo was not enlarged nor did it unduly exaggerate [the victim]'s obvious lethal injuries"); Ryan v. United Parcel Service, 205 F.2d 362, 364 (2nd Cir. 1953) (finding that the trial court erred when it admitted a photograph of the victim who died in an intersection collision in which his body was pictured "hanging out of the doorway of the car, with his head below the running board and almost on the ground, and a condition of the head which was either blood or an opening in the skull").*

65. *Conlon v. Trans Nat. Trucking, LLC, 506 Fed.Appx. 185, 191-92 (3rd Cir. 2012) (affirming the admission of photographs of the deceased's body because it was the plaintiff's burden to prove that the incident was the cause of death and to impeach a witness who testified that the deceased was not bloody immediately following the incident); Castro v. Cammerino, 186 S.W.3d 671, 681-82 (Tex. App. 2006) (affirming the admission of photographs of a pedestrian struck by a bus that showed her position in the crosswalk at impact where the defendant blamed the victim for her injuries and the admission of photographs of the pedestrian's mangled leg that was later amputated where the defendant denied the extent of her damages); Strawder v. Zapata Haynie Corp., 649 So.2d 554, 559-60 (La. App. 1994) (affirming the admission of enlarged color photographs of victims' bodies that showed blistering of the skin due to the heat of an explosion when a ship struck a submerged gas line where defendant denied that victims had suffered burns); Harris v. Damron, 594 S.W.2d 256, 258 (Ark. App. 1980) (affirming the trial court's exclusion of photographs of the body and severed limb of a pedestrian struck by car where evidence had been admitted of the victim's injuries and the defendant admitted liability); Alcorn v. Erasmus, 484 P.2d 813, 819 (Colo. App. 1971) (affirming the admission of photographs to show a vehicle damaged in crash but ruling that the trial court erred when it admitted a photograph that showed the vehicle and "the disfigured body of the deceased" where the defendant admitted the death and manner of death of the deceased).*

66. *Gibbs v. Abiose, 508 S.E.2d 690, 694-95 (Ga. App. 1998) (affirming the admission of photographs where*

testimony confirmed that they depicted the condition of the vehicle accurately); *Annin v. Bi-State Development Agency, 657 S.W.2d 382, 385-86 (Mo. App. 1983)* (affirming the admission of photographs where the plaintiff testified that the car depicted in the photographs was his and that they showed the damage to his car fairly and accurately); *Isler v. Starke, 239 N.Y.S.2d 51, 52 (N.Y.A.D. 1963)* (finding that the trial court erred when it excluded a photograph taken of a vehicle one hour and forty-five minutes after it struck a pedestrian was "a fair and accurate representation of the car immediately after the accident" when no proof was offered that the condition of the car had changed).

67. *Walker v. Fairchild Industries, Inc., 554 F.Supp. 650, 657-58 (D.C.Nev. 1982).*

68. *Id. at 657.*

69. *Id.*

70. *Id. at 657-58.*

71. *Casson v. Nash, 384 N.E.2d 365, 368 (Ill. 1978)* (affirming the exclusion of a photograph of a damaged automobile where the witness could not confirm that "the photographs accurately depicted the condition of the automobile at the scene of the collision"); *Gleson v. Thompson, 154 N.W.2d 780, 789 (N.D. 1967)* (affirming the admission of photographs of a vehicle damaged in a collision on the testimony of the operator of the wrecker who moved it that its condition was unchanged); *Lohmeier v. Hammer, 148 P.3d 101, 104-05 (Ariz. App. 2006)* (affirming the admissions of photographs of a car damaged in a rear-end collision where the defendant testified that the condition was unchanged after it was removed by a body shop after looking at the photographs through a magnifier due to her poor eyesight while plaintiffs testified that the vehicle in the photograph had been repaired but failed to challenge the defendant's testimony on cross-examination).

72. *Williams v. Bethany Volunteer Fire Dept., 298 S.E.2d 352, 356 (N.C. 1983).*

73. *Id.* (quoting 1 Brandis on North Carolina Evidence § 94 (1982)).

74. *Parker v. Randolph County, 475 So.2d 1193, 1194 (Ala. Civ. App. 1985).*

75. *W. M. & A. Transit Co. v. Radecka, 302 F.2d 921, 922 (C.A.D.C. 1962)* (determining the ability of a bus driver to see a child that walked in front of the bus causing the driver to stop suddenly, injuring a passenger who was thrown out of her seat); *Larsen v. Omaha Transit Co., 95 N.W.2d 554, 563 (Neb. 1959)* (determining the ability of the bus driver to see a pedestrian who was struck by the bus); *But see Skyway Aviation Corp. v. Minneapolis, N & S. Ry. Co., 326 F.2d 701, 708 (8th Cir. 1964)* (refusing to allow a jury view of two airplanes that collided in order to determine the pilots' fields of vision).

76. *Williams, 298 S.E.2d at 356* (viewing the same fire truck to see the lights and hear the siren in a case where a car failed to yield to the fire truck); *Schnabel v. Waters, 549 P.2d 795, 799 (Colo. App. 1976)* (viewing a similar truck where the truck, while backing out of a driveway, struck a car).

77. *Parker, 475 So.2d at 1194* (where a truck struck a police car, badly damaging it).

78. *Hyler v. Garner, 548 N.W.2d 864, 869 (Iowa 1996)* (naming repairs to a mobile home as a reason not to view it where the mobile home was alleged to be defectively constructed); *Williams, 298 S.E.2d at 356* (observing that the same fire truck was viewed and that the lights and siren were unchanged from their condition on the day of the accident); *Radecka, 302 F.2d at 922* (noting that the bus was unchanged); *Larsen, 95 N.W.2d at 563* (commenting on the unaltered condition of the bus).

79. *Parker, 475 So.2d at 1194.*

80. *Id.*

81. *Williams, 298 S.E.2d at 354; Radecka, 302 F.2d at 925; Larsen., 95 N.W.2d at 563.*

82. *Williams, 298 S.E.2d at 354; Larsen, 95 N.W.2d at 563.*

83. *Hyler, 548 N.W.2d at 869; Parker, 475 So.2d at 1195; Williams, 298 S.E.2d at 356; Schnabel, 549 P.2d at 799; Skyway Aviation Corp., 326 F.2d at 708; Radecka, 302 F.2d at 925.*

84. *Williams, 298 S.E.2d at 356* (reversed court of appeals' holding that the trial court erred by allowing the jury view).

85. *Schnabel, 549 P.2d at 799* (permitting a jury view of a truck in the daylight where an accident occurred at night and the visibility of the truck with its running lights on was at issue).

86. *Larsen, 95 N.W.2d at 563.*

87. *Williams, 298 S.E.2d at 355-56.*

88. G. Robb, Using NTSB Factual Reports in Aviation Lawsuits, 13 No. 12 *Products Liability Law & Strategy* 4 (June 1995).

89. *49 U.S.C. § 1154(b) (1994).*

90. *Daniels v. Tew Mac Aero Services, Inc., 675 A.2d 984, 987 (Me. 1996)* (citing *49 CFR § 835.2*); *Chiron Corp. and PerSeptive Biosystems, Inc. v. National Transp. Safety Board, 198 F.3d 935, 941 (C.A.D.C. 1999)* (noting the FAA's definition of the Board report as only the portion of the report containing its determinations, including probable cause, under *49 C.F.R. § 835.2*).

91. *Davis v. Cessna Aircraft Corp., 893 P.2d 26, 33-34 (Ariz. App. 1994)* (superseded by statute on other grounds) (finding the trial court's admission of the Board's conclusions as reversible error); *Curry v. Chevron, USA, 779 F.2d 272, 274-75 (5th Cir. 1985)* (ruling that an opponent cannot "open the door" to evidence that is statutorily prohibited from admission); *Travelers Ins. Co. v. Riggs, 671 F.2d 810, 816 (4th Cir. 1982)* (affirming the admission of only the factual portion of the report).

92. *Riggs, 671 F.2d at 816* (excluding from evidence the conclusory section of the report); *Daniels., 675 A.2d at 989-90*; *Bolick v. Sunbird Airlines, Inc., 386 S.E.2d 76, 77-78 (N.C. App. 1989)* (finding that the trial court properly excluded hearsay portions of the report of witnesses who were not present at trial).

93. *Bolick, 386 S.E.2d at 77.*

94. *49 C.F.R. § 835.3(b) (1990).*

95. *Keen v. Detroit Diesel Allison, 569 F.2d 547, 551 (10th Cir. 1978).*

96. *Held v. Mitsubishi Aircraft Intern. Inc., 672 F.Supp. 369, 390-91 (D.Minn. 1987)* (admitting NTSB report concerning models of defendant manufacturer dissimilar to the one at issue, noting that the opponents of the evidence were "adequately equipped to impeach the FAA report"); *Brake v. Beech Aircraft Corp., 229 Cal. Rptr. 336, 339 (Cal. App. 1986)* (excluding NTSB reports of other accidents where no foundation was laid regarding their similarity to the subject accident, noting that it could have been admitted to show notice but affirming the trial court's exclusion based on the risk of prejudice from undue consumption of time); *Kast-*

ner v. Beech Aircraft Corp., 650 S.W.2d 312, 318-319 (Mo. App. 1983) (affirming the admission of properly authenticated FAA report on stall/spin accidents for the years 1967-69); *Piper Aircraft Corp. v. Evans, 424 So.2d 586, 588-89 (Ala. 1982)* (affirming the admission of five FAA reports published from 1964-1970 about exhaust system failures in general aviation aircraft to show that Piper had notice that "321 stainless steel (AISI 321) was a questionable muffler material").

97. *Omni Holding and Development Corp. v 3D.S.A., Inc., 156 S.W.3d 228, 241-42 (Ark. 2004)* (affirming the admission of the FAA aircraft inspection reports under the public reports exception of the Arkansas rule against hearsay).

98. *Fed. R.Civ. P. 44.*

99. *Id.*

100. *LeRoy v. Sabena Belgian World Airlines, 344 F.2d 266, 271 (2nd Cir. 1965), cert. denied, 382 U.S. 878 (1965).*

101. *LeRoy, 344 F.2d at 271-74* (citing *28 U.S.C. § 1732*); *Solomon v. Warren, 540 F.2d 777, 782-83 (5th Cir. 1976), cert. dismissed sub nom. Warren v. Serody, 434 U.S. 801 (1977)* (citing *28 U.S.C. § 1732*).

102. *Van Steemburg v. General Aviation, Inc., 611 N.E.2d 1144, 1165 (Ill. App. 1993), appeal denied, 616 N.E.2d 348 (Ill. 1993)* (citing the business records exception to the Illinois hearsay rule modeled after *28 U.S.C. § 1732*).

103. *LeRoy, 344 F.2d at 271-73.*

104. *Id. at 272-274.*

105. *Id.*

106. *Id.*

107. *Solomon v. Warren, 540 F.2d at 782-83.*

108. *Van Steemburg, 611 N.E.2d at 1165-66.*

109. *Id.*

110. *Fed. R. Evid. 803(8).*

111. *In re Air Crash Disaster at Stapleton Intern. Airport, Denver, Colo. On November 15, 1987, 720 F.Supp. 1493, 1498 (D.Colo. 1989).*

112. *Id.*

113. *Id.*

114. *Id. at 1497.*

115. *Id. at 1498.*

116. *Id. at 1497-98.*

117. *Zeus Enterprises, Inc. v. Alphin Aircraft, Inc., 190 F.3d 238, 239 (4th Cir. 1999).*

118. *Id. at 241.*

119. *Id. (citing Fed. R.Evid. 803(8)(C)).*

120. *Schneider v. Cessna Aircraft Co., 722 P.2d 321, 327 (Ariz. App. 1985).*

121. *Id. at 329-30.*

122. *Herndon v. Seven Bar Flying Service, Inc., 716 F.2d 1322, 1331 (10th Cir. 1983), cert. denied sub nom. Piper Aircraft Corporation v. Seven Bar Flying Service, Inc., 466 U.S. 958 (1984); Schneider, 722 P.2d at 330; Melville v. American Home Assur. Co., 584 F.2d 1306, 1315-16 (3rd Cir. 1978); Berkebile v. Brantly Helicopter Corp., 337 A.2d 893, 903 n.9 (Pa. 1975) (abrogated on other grounds).*

123. *Bemer Aviation, Inc. v. Hughes Helicopter, Inc., 621 F.Supp. 290, 301-02 (E.D.Pa. 1985), aff'd, 802 F.2d 445 (3rd Cir. 1986).*

124. *Id.*

125. *Id.*

126. *Id.*

127. *Id. at 302.*

128. *Robinson v. Hartzell Propeller Inc., 2007 WL 2007969, at *3 (E.D.Pa. 2007) (finding "genuine issues of material fact as to whether Hartzell's concealing or withholding the actual cause of propeller failures involved "required information" and was "causally related" to plaintiff's accident…based on expert testimony, letters sent by Hartzell to the FAA, and service difficulty reports ("SDRs"), which described propeller failures involving the same type of propeller and engine as those on plaintiff's aircraft"); Butler v. Bell Helicopter Tex-*

tron, Inc., 135 Cal.Rptr.2d 762, 774 (Cal. App. 2003) (finding that the defendant had notice of the defect in military helicopters and should have reported "the catastrophic in-flight failures of a yoke it manufactures and installs on both civil and military helicopters); *Hetzer-Young v. Precision Airmotive Corp., 921 N.E.2d 683, 695-700 (Ohio App. 2009)* (finding that, although the plaintiff proved that the defendant misrepresented the source of the subject problem to the FAA and that the reporting of this information was required by regulation, the plaintiffs failed to prove that the misrepresentation caused the subject accident).

129. *Herndon, 716 F.2d at 1331* (citing *49 CFR § 39.1*).

130. *Fed. R.Civ. P. 44; Berkebile v. Brantly Helicopter Corp., 337 A.2d 893, 903 n.9 (Pa. 1975)* (abrogated on other grounds) (ruling that on remand "[a]ny certified copies of FAA records and documents such as airworthiness directives, if relevant, are not inadmissible on the basis of hearsay if a foundation is also laid").

131. *Melville v. American Home Assur. Co., 584 F.2d 1306, 1315-16 (3rd Cir. 1978)* (citing *Fed. R.Evid. 803(8)(C)*).

132. *Melville, 584 F.2d at 1316.*

133. *Melville, 584 F.2d at 1316* (citing the Advisory Committee Comments to Rule 803(C)).

134. *Herndon, 716 F.2d at 1324-25* (noting the purpose for which service bulletins were admitted where they covered the same ground as two airworthiness directives, which were excluded based on their prejudicial effect as repetitive evidence outweighing their probative value).

135. *Melville, 584 F.2d at 1315-16* (affirming the admission of airworthiness directives where no untrustworthiness was shown).

136. *Fisher v. Bell Helicopter Co., 403 F.Supp. 1165, 1172-74 (D.D.C. 1975).*

137. *Id. at 1172-73* (ruling that, in addition to the owner, the engine manufacturer was liable for failing to approve the correct parts for an overhaul before the accident).

138. *Id. at 1173.*

139. *In re Cessna 208 Series Aircraft Products Liability Litigation, 2009 WL 2780223 at *5-*6 (D.Kan. 2009).*

140. *Id. at *6.*

141.*Id.*

142.See, e.g., *Melville v. American Home Assure Co., 584 F.2d 1306 (3d Cir. 1978)* (airworthiness directive admissible under *Rule 803(8)(C)* of the *Federal Rules of Evidence*).

143.*Herndon, 716 F.2d at 1327.*

144.*Herndon, 716 F.2d at 1331.*

145.*Herndon, 716 F.2d at 1326.*

146.*Barnett v. La Societe Anonyme Turbomeca France, 963 S.W.2d 639, 647-48 (Mo. App. 1997) cert denied, 525 U.S. 827 (1998).*

147.See, e.g., *Herndon v. Seven Bar Flying Service, Inc., 716 F.2d 1322 (10th Cir. 1983)* (Trial court's admission into evidence of service bulletin issued by aircraft manufacturer after plane crash relevant to show a manufacturer's negligence).

148.*Dalrymple ex rel. Dalrymple v. Fairchild Aircraft, Inc., 575 F.Supp.2d 790, 796-97 (S.D.Tex. 2008)* (where the court ruled that a successor corporation, holder of the type certificate holder but not the manufacturer of the product at issue, had no post-sale duty to warn).

149.*Id.*

150.*HDM Flugservice GmbH v. Parker Hannifin Corp., 332 F.3d 1025, 1034 (6th Cir. 2003).*

151.*Id.*

152.*Id.*

153.*Lawhon v. Ayres Corp., 992 S.W.2d 162, 166-67 (Ark. App. 1999)* (citing Ark. R.Evid. 407, similar in relevant respects to *Fed. R.Evid. 407*).

154.*Id.*

155.*Barnett, 963 S.W.2d at 651.*

156.*Id. at 647-51.*

157.*Id. at 645-46.*

158.*Nachtsheim v. Beech Aircraft Corp., 847 F.2d 1261, 1273-74 (7th Cir. 1988).*

159.*Id.*

160.*Id. at 1274.*

161.*14 C.F.R. § 21.3(a) (1989).*

162. *14 C.F.R. §§ 21.3(b).*

163.*14 C.F.R. § 21.3(c).*

164.*14 C.F.R. § 21.3(d) and (e).*

165.*14 C.F.R. § 21.3(f).*

166.*Id.*

167.*Butler v. Bell Helicopter, Textron, Inc., 135 Cal.Rptr.2d 762 (Cal. App. 2003); Hetzer-Young v. Precision Automotive Corporation, 921 N.E.2d 683 (Ohio App. 2009).*

168.*Barnett v. La Societe Anonyme Turbomeca France, 963 S.W.2d at 645-51.*

169.*John McShain, Inc. v. Cessna Aircraft Co., 563 F.2d 632, 637 (3rd Cir. (Pa.) 1977).*

170.*Id.*

171.*Daubert v. Merrill Dow Pharmaceuticals, Inc., 509 U.S. 579 (1993).*

172.*Id. at 592-94.*

173.*Fed.R.Evid. 702.*

174.*Nachtscheim, 847 F.2d at 1270; Joy v. Bell Helicopter Textron, Inc., 999 F.2d 549, 554 (D.C. Cir. 1993); Four Corners Helicopters, 979 F.2d at 1441-42.*

175.*Nachtsheim v. Beech Aircraft Corp., 847 F.2d 1261, 1268-69 (7th Cir. (Wis.) 1988); Joy v. Bell Helicopter Textron, Inc., 999 F.2d 549, 555 (D.C. Cir. 1993); Four Corners Helicopters, 979 F.2d at 1440; John E. Christ v. International Business Machines Corporation, 1989 WL 817176, 20 Phila.Co.Rptr. 610, 630 (Pa.Com.Pl. 1989).*

176.*Id.*

177.*Four Corners Helicopters, 979 F.2d at 1440; Joy, 999 F.2d at 555; Nachtsheim, 847 F.2d at 1268-69.*

178.*Nachtsheim, 847 F.2d at 1268-69; John E. Christ, 1989 WL 817176, 20 Phila.Co.Rptr. at 630.*

179.*Nachtsheim, 847 F.2d at 1268-69; John E. Christ, 1989 WL 817176, 20 Phila.Co.Rptr. at 630* (noting a sliding scale from minimal differences to prove causation to the toleration of greater differences for notice with the existence of a defect between the two); *Four Corners Helicopters, 979 F.2d at 1440; Joy, 999 F.2d at 555.*

180.*Four Corners Helicopters, 979 F.2d at 1440.*

181.*Id. at 1435-36.*

182.*Id. at 1439.*

183.*Id.*

184.*Id. at 1439-40.*

185.*Id. at 1440.*

186.*Id.*

187.*Id.*

188.*John E. Christ, 1989 WL 817176, 20 Phila.Co.Rptr. at 629-30.*

189.*Id. at 629.*

190.*Melville v. American Home Assur. Co., 584 F.2d 1306, 1315 (3rd Cir. 1978).*

191.*Id.*

192.*Id.*

193.*Nachtsheim, 847 F.2d at 1269-70.*

194.*Id.*

195.*Held v. Mitsubishi Aircraft Intern., Inc., 672 F.Supp. 369, 390-91 (D.Minn. 1987)* (while not noting the purpose for which the report was admitted, the court cited a case in support of its requirement of substantial similarity where the purpose of admission was to prove a design defect and the defendant's knowledge of the defect).

196.*Id.*

197.*U.S. Aviation Underwriters, Inc. v. Pilatus Business Aircraft, Ltd., 582 F.3d 1131, 1137-38 (10th Cir. 2009).*

198.*Id. at 1149.*

199.*Id.*

200.*John E. Christ, 1989 WL 817176, 20 Phila.Co.Rptr. at 611, 632.*

201.*Id. at 634.*

202.*Becker v. American Airlines, Inc., 200 F.Supp. 243, 244 (D.C.N.Y. 1961).*

203.*Id. at 244-46.*

204.*Id. at 245-46.*

205.*Rimer v. Rockwell Intern. Corp., 641 F.2d 450, 456 (6th Cir. 1981).*

206.*Id.*

207.*Id.*

208.*Id.*

209.*Bemer Aviation, Inc. v. Hughes Helicopter, Inc., 621 F.Supp. 290, 301 (D.C.Pa. 1985), aff'd, 802 F.2d 445 (3rd Cir. 1986).*

210.*Id.*

211.*Id.*

212.*Id. at 302.*

213.*Walker v. Fairchild Industries, Inc., 554 F.Supp. 650, 655-56 (D. Nev. 1982).*

214.*Id. at 654, 656.*

215.*John E. Christ, 1989 WL 817176, 20 Phila.Co.Rptr. at 629.*

216.*Id. at 629 n.14.*

217.*Bertrand v. Air Logistics, Inc., 820 So.2d 1228, 1239 (La. App. 2002).*

218.*Id. at 1238.*

219.*Elsworth v. Beech Aircraft Corp., 691 P.2d 630, 639 (Cal. 1984), cert. denied, 471 U.S. 1110 (1985).*

220.*Id. at 640.*

221.*Prashker v. Beech Aircraft Corp., 258 F.2d 602, 608-09 (3rd Cir. 1958), cert. denied, 358 U.S. 910 (1958).*

222.*Id.*

223. *Id.* at 609.

224. *Brake v. Beech Aircraft Corp.*, 229 Cal.Rptr. 336, 339 (Cal. App. 1986).

225. *Id.* at 339-340.

226. *Becker*, 200 F.Supp. at 245.

227. *Id.*

228. *Van Steemburg v. General Aviation, Inc.*, 611 N.E.2d 1144, 1162 (Ill. App. 1993), appeal denied, 616 N.E.2d 348 (Ill. 1993).

229. *Id.* at 1162-63.

230. *Id.* at 1163-64.

231. *Lopez v. Three Rivers Elec. Co-op, Inc.*, 26 S.W.3d 151, 155-56 (Mo. 2000).

232. *Id.* at 157.

233. *Id.*

234. *Strauss v. Douglas Aircraft Co.*, 404 F.2d 1152, 1158 (2nd Cir. 1968).

235. *Id.*

236. *Id.* at 1158 n.10.

237. *Beavers on Behalf of Beavers v. Northrup Worldwide Aircraft Services, Inc.*, 821 S.W.2d 669, 677 (Tex. App. 1991).

238. *Id.* at 677-78.

239. *Id.* at 678.

240. *Id.* at 677-78.

241. *Lawhon v. Ayres Corp.*, 992 S.W.2d 162, 165-66 (Ark. App. 1999).

242. *Id.*

243. *Hale v. Firestone Tire & Rubber Co.*, 820 F.2d 928, 934-35 (8th Cir. 1987).

244. *Id.*

245. *Id.*

246. *Cooper v. Firestone Tire & Rubber Co.*, 945 F.2d 1103, 1105 (9th Cir. 1991).

247. *Id.*

248. *Drabik v. Stanley-Bostitch, Inc.*, 997 F.2d 496, 509 (8th Cir. 1993).

249. *Id.*

250. *Wheeler v. John Deere Co.*, 862 F.2d 1404, 1409 (10th Cir. 1988).

251. *Id.* at 1408-09.

252. *Joy*, 999 F.2d at 554.

253. *Id.* at 555.

254. *Id.*

255. *Id.*

256. *Govreau v. Nu-Way Concrete Forms, Inc.*, 73 S.W.3d 737, 741 (Mo. App. 2002).

257. *Bemer Aviation*, 621 F. Supp. at 299.

258. *Joy*, 999 F.2d at 554; *Held*, 672 F.Supp. at 390.

259. *Lopez*, 26 S.W.3d at 159-160.

260. *Id.*

261. *Nachtsheim*, 847 F.2d at 1268.

262. *Joy*, 999 F.2d at 555.

263. *Melville*, 584 F.2d at 1315.

264. *Nachtsheim*, 847 F.2d at 1269; *Brake*, 229 Cal.Rptr. at 339.

265. *Melville*, 584 F.2d at 1315-16 (citing *Fed. R.Evid. 803(8)*).

266. *Lawhon*, 992 S.W.2d at 166.

267. *Id.* (citing *Rule 703* under the Arkansas Rules of Evidence).

268. *Wheeler v. John Deere Co.*, 862 F.2d 1404, 1407 (10th Cir. 1988).

269. *Olson v. Ford Motor Co., 410 F.Supp.2d 855, 868 (D.N.D. 2006).*

270. *Nissan Motors Co. Ltd. v. Armstrong, 145 S.W.3d 131, 139-40 (Tex. 2004).*

271. *Fed. R.Evid. 407* (including proof of a defect in a product, a defect in a product's design, or a need for a warning or instruction among the prohibited reasons for admission of subsequent remedial measures).

272. *Id.*

273. *Herndon, 716 F.2d at 1331; Barnett, 963 S.W.2d at 651-52* (ruling that evidence of subsequent remedial measures was admissible as to strict liability claim but inadmissible as to negligence claim).

274. *Krause v. American Aerolights, Inc., 762 P.2d 1011, 1013 (Or. 1988)* (applying *Or. R. Rev. Rule 407*); *see also Herndon, 716 F.2d at 1333* (summarizing the applicability of the rule against admitting subsequent remedial measures in strict liability cases in other jurisdictions).

275. *Krause, 762 P.2d at 1014.*

276. *Id. at 1013-14.*

277. *Fed. R.Evid. 407* (with equivalent state rules identical or nearly so).

278. *Herndon, 716 F.2d at 1327; see also, Krause, 762 P.2d at 1014-15.*

279. *Herndon, 716 F.2d at 1327.*

280. *Krause, 762 P.2d at 1015; Wagner v. Clark Equipment Co., Inc., 700 A.2d 38, 52 (Conn. 1997); Ault v. International Harvester Co., 528 P.2d 1148, 1151-52 (Cal. 1974).*

281. *Krause, 762 P.2d at 1015* (quoting 23 Wright & Graham, Federal Practice and Procedure, 93-94, § 5282 (internal citations omitted)).

282. *Wagner, 700 A.2d at 52.*

283. *Freeman v. Beech Aircraft Corporation, 1983 WL 4495, at *21 (Ohio App. 1983).*

284. *Id.; Krause, 762 P.2d at 1015; Ault, 528 P.2d at 1152.*

285. *Caprara v. Chrysler Corp., 417 N.E.2d 545, 549 (N.Y.1981).*

286. *Id. at 550.*

287. *Id.*

288. *Herndon, 716 F.2d at 1333.*

289. *Barnett, 963 S.W.2d at 651.*

290. *Id. at 651-52.*

291. *Herndon, 716 F.2d at 1331.*

292. *Ault, 528 P.2d at 1151-52.*

293. *Forma Scientific, Inc. v. BioSera, Inc., 960 P.2d 108, 115 (Colo. 1998).*

294. *Id. at 118.*

295. *Wagner, 700 A.2d at 52.*

296. *General Motors Corp. v. Moseley, 447 S.E.2d 302, 310 (Ga. App. 1994)* (overruled on other grounds).

297. *Burke v. Illinois Power Co., 373 N.E.2d 1354, 1369 (Ill. App. 1978)* (overruled on other grounds); *Holmes v. Sahara Coal Co., 475 N.E.2d 1383, 1388 (Ill. App. 1985)* (overruled on other grounds).

298. *Davis v. International Harvester Co., 521 N.E.2d 1282 (Ill. App. 1988), appeal denied, 530 N.E.2d 242 (Ill. 1988) and 545 N.E.2d 107 (Ill. 1989).*

299. *Scott v. Dutton-Lainson Co., 774 N.W.2d 501, 503-04 (Iowa 2009)* (citing *Iowa Rule of Evidence 5.407*).

300. *Toups v. Sears, Roebuck and Co., Inc., 507 So.2d 809, 816-17 (La. 1987)* (citing proposed law, later enacted as *LSA-C.E. Art. 407*).

301. *Stinson v. E.I. DuPont De Nemours and Co., 904 S.W.2d 428, 431-32 (Mo. App. 1995).*

302. *Hancock v. Paccar, Inc., 283 N.W.2d 25, 39 (Neb. 1979).*

303. *Robinson v. G.G.C., Inc., 808 P.2d 522, 526 (Nev. 1991).*

304. *Caprara, 417 N.E.2d at 549-551.*

305. *McFarland v. Bruno Mach. Corp., 626 N.E.2d 659, 664 (Ohio 1994).*

306.*Federal Pacific Elec. Co. v. Woodend, 735 S.W.2d 887, 892 (Tex. App. 1987).*

307.*Chart v. General Motors Corp., 258 N.W.2d 680, 683-84 (Wis. 1977).*

308.*Caldwell v. Yamaha Motor Co., Ltd., 648 P.2d 519, 523-25 (Wyo. 1982).*

309.*McFarland, 626 N.E.2d at 664.*

310.See, e.g., *Worsham v. A.H. Robins Co., 734 F.2d 676, 688-89 (11th Cir. 1984); Karns v. Emerson Electric Co., 817 F.2d 1452, 1460 (10th Cir. 1987).*

311.*Karns, 817 F.2d at 1460.*

312.*Collins v. Interroyal Corp., 466 N.E.2d 1191 (Ill. App. 1984); Rucker v. Norfolk & Western Railway Co., 396 N.E.2d 534 (Ill. 1979); Carney v. Bic, 1999 Mo. App. Lexis 941 (Mo. App. 1999); Foster v. American Motors Corp., 423 N.W.2d 881 (Wis. App. 1988)* ("It is within the trial court's discretion to determine whether prior accidents and resulting lawsuits are relevant and admissible").

313.*49 U.S.C. § 40101(d) (2000)).*

314.*Elsworth v. Beech Aircraft Corp., 691 P.2d 630, 634 (Cal. 1984), cert. denied, 471 U.S. 1110 (1985)* (citing *49 U.S.C. § 1421(a)(1)).*

315.*Fed. R.Civ. P. 44.*

316.*Ameristar Jet Charter, Inc. v. Dodson Intern. Parts, Inc., 2004 WL 76342, at *12 (Mo. App. 2004)* (reversed in part on other grounds).

317.*Elsworth, 691 P.2d at 637-38; McGee v. Cessna Aircraft Co., 188 Cal.Rptr. 542, 547-51 (Cal. App. 1983).*

318.*Elsworth, 691 P.2d at 633.*

319.*Id.*

320.*Id.*

321.*Id. at 637-38.*

322.*McGee, 188 Cal.Rptr. at 544-45.*

323.*Id. at 545.*

324.*Id.* at 547 (based on a state statute that the failure to exercise due care will be presumed where there is a violation of a regulation that caused the harm to one the statute was designed to protect and an occurrence that the statute was designed to prevent).

325.*Id. at 547 n.4 and n.5.*

326.*Id. at 547.*

327.*Id. at 550.*

328.*Sunbird Air Service, Inc. v. Beech Aircraft Corp., 789 F.Supp. 360, 362-63 (D.Kan. 1992).*

329.*Joy, 999 F.2d at 558.*

330.*Id.* (citing *14 C.F.R. §§ 91.13* and *91.119).*

331.*Id. at 558-59.*

332.*Ridge v. Cessna Aircraft Co., 117 F.3d 126, 130-31 (4th Cir. 1997)* (citing *14 C.F.R. §§ 91.13* and *91.3).*

333.*Id.*

334.*McGee, 188 Cal.Rptr. at 547.*

335.*Id. at 549.*

336.*Id.*

337.*49 U.S.C.A. § 40101, Section 2(b).*

338.*Hetzer-Young v. Precision Airmotive Corp., 921 N.E.2d 683, 697-98 (Ohio App. 2009); Butler v. Bell Helicopter Textron, Inc., 135 Cal.Rptr.2d 762, 764-65 (Cal. App. 2003).* (citing *14 C.F.R. § 21.3).*

339.*Id.*

340.*Prashker, 258 F.2d at 608.*

341.*Id. at 609.*

342.*Id.*

343.*Jaramillo v. Ford Motor Co., 116 Fed. Appx. 76, 78-79 (9th Cir. 2004).*

344.*Brake, 229 Cal.Rptr. at 339.*

345.*Id.*

Chapter 8

Damages In Helicopter Crash Cases[1]

Introduction

Juries in helicopter crash cases have awarded substantial compensatory and punitive damages awards including sums of $13 million,[2] $16 million,[3] $22 million,[4] $35 million,[5] $70 million,[6] and $350 million.[7] While damages in helicopter crash litigation have features in common with other serious injury and wrongful death cases, there are some unique features concerning damages in these cases about which the practitioner must be aware. This section addresses both sets of issues: those damages similar to other catastrophic injury and wrongful death litigation and those damage categories entirely or principally unique to helicopter crash cases.

While the liability issues are critical in these cases, counsel should not ignore the duty to maximize recovery on behalf of the client where it is legally and factually possible to do so. Helicopter crash victims and their families deserve nothing less.

8.1 Non-Unique Damages Issues in Helicopter Crash Cases

Certain damages issues associated with death and horrific injury frequently recur in almost any negligence or prod-ucts lawsuit and are not unique to helicopter crash litigation. Counsel must address those damages issues and lay the proper foundation for admitting that evidence at trial.

A. Wrongful Death

All of the legal and factual considerations associated with assessing damages in other wrongful death cases are squarely applicable to helicopter crash damages. In every state, statutes have been enacted to provide some form of compensatory damages to either the estate or family members of a deceased.

1. Economic Loss

In some states, the plaintiffs are statutorily determined based on a specific relationship to the deceased while in other states the loss is calculated to the decedent's estate or to beneficiaries of that estate. Counsel must determine the particular mechanism by which the surviving parties are able to recover in whichever state jurisdiction they seek to file. The most typical claims for compensatory damages are on behalf of the surviving spouse and children for loss of economic support as well as loss of consortium and society.

The permissible elements of compensation in an aviation death case as for other wrongful death cases include the economic loss occasioned by the death including lost income and loss of services provided by the deceased. Economic loss also may include the funeral and burial expenses, or medical costs associated with treatment of the deceased following impact and up to the moment of death.

Counsel must determine the precise basis for the calculation of lost wages and associated employee benefits in wrongful death actions. Many states follow the simple "loss to the estate" rule. Others, such as Indiana, tie the calculation of permissible lost earnings to the financial dependence of the survivors. That applies most harshly in the single parent scenario. The economic loss would terminate once the children would be deemed financially independent.

A qualified forensic economist must be retained to establish a present value of the deceased's lost income. In those instances where the deceased's employment had not stabilized, a vocational expert also may be required. As in all cases, counsel must determine whether the particular jurisdiction authorizes defendants to require a reduction of economic loss to account for taxation.

2. Non-Economic Loss

The common non-economic elements of compensation include the familiar loss of comfort, society and companionship and, increasingly, in some jurisdictions the deceased's loss of enjoyment of life. In many jurisdictions there are impermissible damages elements such as grief, sorrow, and sympathy, for which compensation is not to be accorded.

Another non-unique element of compensatory damages in wrongful death cases is the deceased's post-impact physical pain and suffering. This element frequently emerges in aircrash litigation. A medical expert's review of the autopsy report and other impact factors may establish that the deceased died of smoke inhalation or severe burns. In either case, expert testimony must be utilized in order to lay the groundwork for admissibility of a conscious pain and suffering claim.

B. Debilitating Physical Injury

Unfortunately, helicopter crash cases produce their share of catastrophic injuries as well as deaths. The economic damages associated with such injuries are familiar and include the rehabilitative and medical care costs as well as the injury victim's future lost income.

For those crash survivors who have suffered horrendous physical injury including paralysis, loss of limb, or head trauma, a well-considered life care plan is essential. That plan should include all future medical care which is reasonable and necessary through the plaintiff's life expectancy. For severe trauma, around the clock care often is essential and those costs must be part of the plan. Because defendants' only avenue of attack as to damages is often the plaintiff's life care plan, that expert should be well-qualified and experienced in severe trauma and rehabilitative care.

The non-economic factors associated with the survival of a helicopter crash include disfigurement, loss of enjoyment of life, inability to participate in one's avocational activities, and inability to perform the usual and ordinary functions of everyday life. As in any such case, counsel should spend as much time at trial addressing these non-economic factors as the economic ones.

8.2 Typical Damages Issues in Helicopter Crash Litigation

Unlike most routine tort cases, the helicopter crash case presents particular choice of law and jurisdictional options which early on must be addressed. In choosing the appropriate forum to litigate the case, counsel should analyze the recoverable damages in whichever state is being considered. Some states have enacted draconian limits on plaintiff's ability to recover non-economic damages.

In every helicopter crash case, counsel must survey the potential damages factors and assess the legal and evidentiary basis separately for each one. Determining where to file the lawsuit ultimately may be based on whether the law of that jurisdiction permits or refuses a major damages element of that case. Given a choice, counsel should seek to bring the lawsuit in a state which would permit full non-economic recovery as well as recovery for economic damages. Choice of law issues also may affect the ability to obtain punitive damages as well as such other issues as pre-impact terror and the breadth of elements in a non-economic recovery.

A. Pre-Impact Terror

Pre-impact terror refers to the mental and psychological anguish suffered by passengers from the time an aircrash is imminent until the crash impact itself. Probably the most well-publicized instance of pre-impact terror was the disastrous explosion of the space shuttle Challenger on January 28, 1986. At just over one minute after take off—73 seconds precisely—the space shuttle exploded. News reports confirmed that the astronauts had attempted to utilize emergency breathing supplies and were otherwise doing everything possible to stay alive following the explosion. All aboard the spacecraft knew that they were helplessly falling to their certain death.

1. The Legal Framework

Pre-impact terror has been described as "the mental anguish a decedent consciously suffers by the apprehension and fear of impending death prior to sustaining fatal injury."[8] It has been variously referred to by courts and commentators as pre-impact or pre-accident terror, pre-impact fright, pre-crash mental anguish or emotional distress, apprehension of impending death or fear of imminent death.

Pre-impact terror damages are recoverable in Alabama,[9] Georgia,[10] Louisiana,[11] Maine,[12] Maryland,[13] Missouri,[14] Nebraska,[15] New Hampshire,[16] New York,[17] Texas,[18] Washington,[19] and Wisconsin.[20] Those states that limit or do not permit the recovery of damages for pre-impact terror are Arizona,[21] Arkansas,[22] California,[23] Kansas,[24] Massachusetts,[25] and Pensylvania.[26] The courts in the remaining states have not ruled on whether damages for pre-impact fright may be recovered. Courts have noted the absence of a ruling on this issue in Illinois,[27] Michigan,[28] Ohio,[29] Pennsylvania,[30] and South Carolina.[31]

Damages for pre-impact terror are recoverable in an action brought on behalf of the deceased, commonly referred to as a survival action.[32] Such a claim "permit[s] a decedent's estate to bring an action that the decedent could have instituted had he or she lived."[33]

As would be expected, the vast majority of those cases addressing the recoverability of damages for pre-impact terror arise out of airplane and helicopter crashes. In a 1983 case analyzing the propriety of such damages arising out of a plane crash, a New York federal district court observed:

> New York provides a cause of action for the pain and suffering of a decedent before his death. In several cases it has been held that a decedent's estate may recover for the decedent's pain and suffering endured after the injury that led to his death. From this proposition, it is only a short to the step to the allowing of damages for a decedent's pain and suffering before the mortal blow and resulting from the apprehension of impending death.[34]

In affirming the trial court's analysis, the Second Circuit U.S. Court of Appeals concluded:

> A decedent's representative unquestionably may recover for pain and suffering experienced in a brief interval between injury and death. We see no intrinsic or logical barrier to recovery for the fear experienced during a period in which the decedent is uninjured but aware of an impending death.[35]

Other courts have reached the same result reasoning that the mental anguish need not await physical injury in order for it to be compensable:

> While in the garden variety of claims under survival statutes,…fatal injuries sustained in automobile accidents and the like the usual sequence is impact followed by pain and suffering, we are unable to discern any reason based on either law or logic for rejecting a claim because in this case as to at least part of the suffering, this sequence was reversed. We will not disallow the claims for this item of damages on that ground.[36]

Defendants often argue that the time period for experiencing the pre-impact terror was so brief that damages for that element should not be recoverable. The courts have rejected that argument and have allowed recovery for pre-impact terror which in many cases has been extremely brief in duration.[37] One Texas court in rejecting the defense argument that pre-impact terror damages were not recoverable because of their brevity observed:

> Such an argument fails to consider the terror and consequent mental anguish [deceased] suffered for the six to eight seconds while he faced imminent death.[38]

Under Illinois law, for example, the court held that conscious pain and suffering was compensable where it occurred in "an extremely short interval" between "the wing of the plane [striking] the ground first, followed almost immediately by the nose of the aircraft."[39] A federal court, applying Hawaii law, affirmed an award of $15,000 for pain and suffering where death was "almost instantaneous" in a plane crash.[40] In Michigan, the court ruled that a plaintiff could recover for pain and suffering experienced by the decedent where "the plane descended through a dense cloud cover, struck several trees, and crashed into the ground, killing all three occupants" within seconds.[41]

A Nebraska court held that even a five second apprehension of death is sufficient for recovery of damages:

> While it is true that in the present case there is no evidence that decedent said anything prior to his death revealing an awareness of his impending death, the personal representative's offers of proof nonetheless provide a basis upon which the jury certainly need not, but could, if it wished, find that decedent apprehended and feared his impending death during the five seconds his motorcycle traveled 268 feet locked with [defendant's] automobile before he was crushed and thus killed.[42]

2. Sufficiency of Pre-Impact Terror Evidence

In an early and prescient article on pre-impact terror, famed trial attorney Abraham Fuchsberg observed that aviation counsel typically encounter three major proof hurdles: "brevity of time, brevity of damages, and brevity of proof."[43] In some instances, there may be only a matter of seconds before the knowledge of impact is known to the aircraft passenger and this is especially so where a crash occurs during takeoff or landing.

No matter how short that time period—even it is only a matter of seconds—those courts allowing recovery for pre-impact terror routinely rely upon the jury to determine whether and to what extent that matter is compensable. As Fuchsberg observed, "It is the intensity of feeling rather than its duration that explains the size of recovery. It is the compression of fear within a few fleeting seconds of horror and panic."[44]

Recovery for pre-impact terror requires proof that the decedent was "consciously aware of and feared his impending death."[45] Because the victim is unable to provide testimony as to the nature and extent of any terror or fear, any recovery for pre-impact terror must by necessity be based on forensic, medical and circumstantial evidence. Evidence that is speculative and conjectural is insufficient.[46] Rather, the evidence must "provide some basis for the jury to make a reasonable inference that the decedent suffered conscious mental anguish."[47] In fact, "even a scintilla of evidence showing any pain or suffering by a victim prior to his death" may be sufficient to recover damages.[48] Pre-impact fear may also be inferred from evidence immediately prior to or following the injury.[49] In other words, circumstantial evidence may support a claim for pre-impact terror.[50] Certainly, "eyewitness testimony is not necessary to support an award for conscious pain and suffering."[51]

In helicopter crash cases, damages for pre-impact terror may be awarded from the point the decedent is or should be aware that a crash is imminent until the point of impact. The decisions upholding awards for pre-impact terror in both helicopters and fixed-wing airplane crashes are notable for their graphic descriptions of the evidence presented:

- Texas court finding that the survivor of a helicopter crash suffered mental anguish where "he feared the aircraft's impending impact with the water."[52]
- Michigan ruling that damages for pre-impact fright were recoverable where a plane "[w]hile on an instrument approach to Romeo Airport,…descended through a dense cloud cover, struck several trees, and crashed into the ground, killing all three occupants."[53]
- New York court reserving a ruling on whether the plaintiff presented sufficient evidence of pre-impact terror for trial but noting that it "is inclined to believe that the evidence as described by plaintiff's counsel would support an inference that [the decedent] knew she was in immediate danger of injury when the aircraft turned nose-up and rolled over due to the loss of an engine".[54]

- Florida court determining that "both of the deceased knew of the impending crash landing at sea, knew of the immediate dangers involved and are certain to have experienced the most excruciating type of pain and suffering (the knowledge that one is about to die, leaving three cherished children alone)" at the time of the pilot's last transmission when he notified the tower that he was out of gas.[55]
- Louisiana court affirming a finding that damages for pre-impact pain and suffering may be recovered where a witness testified that "he saw the plane lose altitude, clip power lines and trees, roll to one side, and finally explode several blocks from where he stood" and another witness "heard the plane blow up and the screams of people inside the plane."[56]
- Missouri court finding that "substantial evidence was introduced to show that Decedents suffered from pre-impact terror prior to the crash of the Twin Otter. [Plaintiffs' expert] described pre-impact terror as a set of sensations, feelings, and emotions a person experiences when that person feels that death is imminent."[57]

The import of these various decisions is that plaintiff's counsel may establish sufficient proof of pre-impact terror without the victim's testimony, other eyewitness testimony as to what the victim experienced, helicopter crash on-scene witnesses or first-responders or any medical or forensic evidence whatsoever, such as where the deceased's body is burned beyond recognition. So long as the circumstances of the flight are such that it may be fairly and reasonably surmised from the helicopter's flight path, pre-crash uncontrolled flight, and any objects it strikes before the final impact, that evidence should be sufficient to support a verdict.

For example, in a case where there were no eyewitnesses or survivors, the court relied on expert testimony and a videotape simulation of the takeoff and crash of a commercial plane.[58] The simulation showed that "the Pan Am plane took off and rose to an altitude of 163 feet,…rolled to its left…[when its] wing struck a tree fifty-three feet above ground, rolled, impacted and disintegrated some four to six seconds later."[59] The expert opined that "'most of the people [aboard Flight 759], if not all, would be in an absolute state of pandemonium, panic and extreme state of stress,' at least from the time the plane hit the tree, if not from the beginning of its descent and roll, until impact seconds later."[60] Based on this evidence, the court ruled that it was reasonable to infer that the decedent "apprehended his death at least from the time the plane's wing hit the tree [and that he] experienced the mental anguish commonly associated with anticipation of one's own death."[61]

Courts have found the evidence of pre-impact terror insufficient to award damages in those cases where the events leading to the crash failed to communicate the seriousness of the situation.[62] For example, a survivor of a plane crash testified that "when the plane took off, it shook so abnormally that he knew almost immediately that something was wrong," as did other passengers who were looking around after take-off.[63] Continuing to describe the crash of a commercial plane into the Potomac River, he testified that "he observed that the plane was not ascending after take-off[; and s]ince he knew the layout of the runway, he realized within ten seconds after take-off that the plane would crash."[64] The court ruled that the evidence did not support an award for pre-impact terror because: (1) this witness did not know the decedent and could not testify as to his "probable knowledge of, reaction to, and condition after the crash;" and (2) the evidence failed to show that the decedent "was in a position to see, as the witness was, that the airplane was about to crash,...that [the decedent] was sitting in a place in which it was likely that he would have survived and been conscious after the first impact."[65]

Damages for pre-impact terror, like other damage categories that are hard to quantify, vary from case to case. Courts appear to consider the duration of the period when a decedent becomes aware of an impending crash and the circumstances of the events communicating the seriousness of the situation.[66]

Pre-impact terror is more readily found for those with more experience with aircraft and flight. One court found that the decedent's status "as an experienced pilot [made him] uniquely aware of the impending crash and its probable result to him." [67] Likewise, another court observed that "the decedent, [as] a former flight attendant and [ ] an experienced flier would be expected to detect danger sooner than the average passenger," particularly here where "a quick, unexplained descent on take-off can be nothing less than a panic-inducing event."[68] A witness in another case who survived the crash testified that he, as an experienced traveler, "realized within ten seconds after take-off that the plane would crash."[69]

3. Proving Pre-Impact Terror

Over the years, a great body of medical and scientific research has confirmed that there is a very real mental trauma and physiological response of an individual threatened with imminent death.[70] Psychological and related scientific research has evolved over the last fifty years and references six stress-related phenomena: (1) Homeostasis—That is the usual physiological state of a person prior to exposure to severe stressors and almost certain death; (2) Alarm—Ini-

tial reaction to threat, it is the initial "fight or run" response and includes elevated blood pressure and cold sweat; (3) Reaction—Elevation of the initial physiologic response and including hypertension, palpitations, nausea, vomiting, and even loss of bowel and bladder control; (4) Resignation—Physiological acceptance that victim has little or no control over threat to survival often accompanied by intense longing for loved ones and fear and realization that they will never be seen again; (5) Anticipated Annihilation—Acceptance that death is near and realization that life is ending and often accompanied by the "life review phenomenon" where an individual's entire life passes before her eyes immediately prior to expected death; and (6) Death—The actual process of the victim's succumbing whether from toxic fumes, burn injury or trauma from the aircrash.[71]

Where an individual has a firm and realistic expectation of death there is the realization of never seeing their families and loved ones again which is a devastating prospect. There is sufficient medical and psychiatric research to confirm that there is a physiological component to pre-impact terror.[72] That physiological response includes palpitations and tachycardia, nausea, vomiting and loss of bowel and bladder sphincter control. Part of this response is the manifestation of the survival mechanism known as "fright-flight-fight" response.[73]

A number of aircrash survivors who believed they were going to die have later described the aircrash incident as occurring in "slow motion" and that they "saw their lives pass in front of their eyes." This is so even when it is subsequently confirmed that the entire incident may have lasted only a matter of seconds.[74] This medical research has and should continue to be helpful in overcoming the judicial reluctance in recognizing pre-impact terror as a "non-physical" factor—it is anything but that.

A claim for pre-impact terror cannot be based on pure speculation. The evidentiary foundation is based on a comprehensive review of the facts and circumstances leading to the crash. In order to establish pre-impact terror there should be some circumstantial evidence that the deceased knew on the basis of the circumstances that a crash was imminent.

Counsel will need to rely on circumstantial evidence that the deceased was conscious and aware prior to death in order to proceed with a claim for pre-impact terror. This could include an in-flight explosion, a rapid descent of the aircraft, or a communication from the pilot or crew that the aircraft is no longer airworthy or that an aircrash is unavoidable. The cockpit voice recorder may be critical evidence on this issue. Use of an aircraft reconstruction expert as well as an experienced psychologist in this field are normally essential to reaching a jury on this issue.

Where the law of the jurisdiction supports a claim for pre-impact terror, counsel must retain the services of an expert in that field. For many decades prior to his retirement, Dr. Richard A. Levy was this country's preeminent expert in the field of pre-impact terror. Dr. Levy is a Board-Certified psychiatrist and aviation medicine specialist who had studied the phenomenon of pre-impact terror with U.S. Air Force pilots who had ejected from an aircraft believing that they would be subject to certain death. Dr. Levy also studied the psychological trauma of prisoners of war captured and detained in Vietnam.

In conjunction with Dr. Levy's testimony, the author obtained from the aircrash reconstruction expert an estimated time that elapsed from an occupant's first sensation that something had gone terribly wrong or the helicopter exhibited a loss of control, through final descent and ground impact. In one case involving an air ambulance helicopter crash in Nebraska, that estimated time was a minimum of 30-45 seconds. The accident reconstruction expert also supplied to Dr. Levy the reconstructed flight path which at various moments was either a "spiral" or a "spin." On the basis of the accident reconstruction and medical information supplied to Dr. Levy, his opinions, offered to a reasonable degree of medical certainty, were as follows:

- The crew of the helicopter were alerted to a problem shortly after takeoff resulting in an early stress response often referred to as the "fright-fight-flight" syndrome or "alarm response;"
- With increasing erratic flight this alarm response would have ramped up with an increasing physiological response (i.e., tachycardia, hypertension, sweating, and loss of bowel and bladder control);
- During the course of the 30-45 seconds of spiral descent the crew of the helicopter realized that the aircraft could not be controlled and that they would certainly die of traumatic injuries sustained in the crash;
- With expectation of impending death and the misperception of passing time ("time distortion," i.e., seconds seem like minutes), the victims of this helicopter crash realized they would never see their loved ones again, they would be finally and forever separated from family and friends, never complete their life's goals, and that their lives would be finished; and
- Two of the crew died shortly after ground impact. The paramedic did not sustain significant brain injury or any other injury which would have been capable of causing instantaneous death. Given that

a number of individual witnesses heard him moaning "help me," the pain and disability of his injuries prior to his eventual death, prolonged his awareness of imminent death.

Given the expanding medical and psychiatric research, pre-impact terror should continue to gain judicial acceptance. In any aircrash case where evidence supports it, pre-impact terror is a powerful and significant element of the overall damages picture.

4. Sample Direct Examination of Pre-Impact Terror Expert

Some of the most dramatic damages testimony in any helicopter crash trial may be that elicited from the Plaintiffs' pre-impact terror expert. In a case tried by the author in August 2014 in Las Vegas, the passengers were aware of the impending crash for over one minute as the helicopter was spiraling out of control. The following are excerpts from that direct examination presented to the jury at trial. The witness is Dr. Carlos Diaz who is one of this country's foremost authorities on the subject of pre-impact terror experienced by those in airplane and helicopter crashes:

BY MR. ROBB:
Q. Good morning, Dr. Diaz.
A. Good morning.
Q. Are you a medical doctor —
A. I am.
Q. — an MD?
A. I am an MD.
Q. As well as a pilot?
A. Yes.
Q. How long have you been a medical doctor?
A. Over 40 years.
Q. How long have you been a pilot?
A. Over 35 years.
Q. Dr. Diaz, have I asked you to come to Las Vegas to testify to this jury about a particular field of expertise that you have studied for many years, called pre-impact terror, in connection with this case?
A. You did.
Q. Is that a field of which you have some considerable study, familiarity, knowledge, and expertise?
A. It is.
Q. Have you for many years professionally investigated and studied the concept of what is called aircraft pre-impact terror?

A. I have.

Q. Also called the apprehension of impending death in some circles?

A. Yes.

Q. Doctor, generally speaking, and I mean generally, what do these concepts refer to?

A. They refer — concepts you spoke about refer to the both psychologic and physical consequences of a person who is met with the certainty of an impending violent death.

Q. And are these fears and concepts and this medical condition well recognized, well documented within the medical community, Dr. Diaz?

A. They are.

Q. Well, what I'd like to do before we get into this in more detail, sir, with your permission, is to trace through your medical education, your background, your specific aviation experience in this subject which would permit you in this court of law to give your medical opinions to the ladies and gentlemen of the jury, fair?

[Lengthy exposition of the witness's medical and aeronautical education and experience.]

Q. Dr. Diaz, we talked about that since 1982 you have studied and been seriously interested in this field of pre-impact terror?

A. Uh-huh.

Q. How many years have you formally studied this medical phenomenon?

A. It's been over 15 to 20 years. Because I became very interested in it because of my interest in aviation. And I was seeing the effects of trauma in the emergency room, maybe not aviation related, but it was still significant trauma and significant — and I was seeing those patients. And so I became interested in the aviation aspect of it.

Q. Doctor, have you from time to time been asked to come into court and testify about this field of expertise, this precise issue?

A. I have.

Q. And I'm going to ask you this, are you, Dr. Diaz, one of only a handful of pilot physicians in this country with this particular expertise?

A. I believe I am.

Q. Doctor, would you tell the jury what are the primary characteristics of aircraft pre-impact terror? Primary characteristics.

A. The primary characteristics are, as I mentioned before, twofold. One are — one is the — the effects psychologically, the mental effects. And the — the overwhelming and crippling fear that — and — and feeling of hopelessness and terror that occupies your mind in those seconds. But there's also the physical aspects of it, because your body will react physically to terrible fear with various responses that initially are meant to help the body cope with a serious situation, but actually overwhelm the body physically as much as the mental aspects overwhelms your mind mentally.

Q. Dr. Diaz, have both the psychological and physical reactions of human beings caught in that situation been physically observed by you and documented by you in your personal practice, as well as documented in generally accepted medical literature?

A. I have. Obviously, I have not been present during the actual occurrence of an accident. But I have, in my career as an emergency room physician, I have — I have been there immediately after things have happened, and I have seen, spoken with, and handled patients. Also during my career as a flight surgeon, I have had occasion to listen to actual tapes of aircraft accidents where the pilots were talking in the seconds just before impact.

Q. Before they died?

A. Before they died.

Q. And is that by reason of the increasing use of flight data recorders on aircraft?

A. Flight data recorders and recording of two-way transmissions from the aircraft, yes.

Q. Did that experience that you had in listening to those further corroborate what you had known and what the medical literature has taught you?

A. It did.

Q. Doctor, I want to talk about what you have reviewed in connection with your work in this case, and let me ask you, have you reviewed the medical examiner's report for each of the four decedents?

A. I have.

Q. And have you reviewed the one-page death certificate for each of the decedents?

A. I have.

. . .

Q. Doctor, are these the types of materials that you have reviewed in this case that are ordinarily relied upon by other medical experts in your field in reaching medical conclusions and determinations on pre-impact terror or apprehension of impending death?

A. Yes, they are.

Q. Are they sufficient for you to express your opinions to a reasonable degree of medical certainty—

A. Yes.

Q. — in your judgment?

A. Excuse me. Yes.

Q. Dr. Diaz, based upon your long-time study of this field, your years of medical experience and training within the aviation area, do you have an opinion to express to the ladies and gentlemen of this jury to a reasonable degree of medical certainty whether the four passengers aboard this helicopter that crashed on December 7, 2011, Lovish Bhanot, Anupama Bhola, Delwin Chapman, and Tamara Chapman, each experienced pre-impact terror from the moment the helicopter lost control and up through and including the time of crash impact with the ground, Doctor?

A. Yes.

Q. Would you tell the jury your opinion?

A. In my opinion, these four individuals suffered horribly from the time that the aircraft abruptly became uncontrollable until the time of impact. And in — in cases such as these of sudden overwhelming terror, as I mentioned before, there's the physical aspect. The body suffers numerous symptoms related to sudden terror. There's a – a nervous discharge that increases the heart rate tremendously, it makes it difficult to breathe. You develop chest pain, you develop tremors. You sweat profusely. It — you may even lose control of your bowel and bladder. It's — it's a — an overwhelming physical incapacitation.

But in addition to that, and I think even — even much more cruel, is that the — the mental state of this overwhelming feeling of hopelessness, as soon as they realized this aircraft is going to crash and there's nothing that I can do about it. All they could do is just ride it down to the ground. And when — when this — these kinds of situations occur, there's an — many

effects, but one of the effects is called tokipsia. Just a fancy word that means time slows down. And what you see is that — and — and people who have been in these situations and may have survived will say, My goodness, I thought it — it lasted for an hour, and it might have lasted for a few seconds. You know.

But in — in this instance we know that from the time that the aircraft became uncontrollable until impact was over a minute and seven seconds, or about a minute and seven seconds. And that is an eternity to feel an overwhelming sensation of hopelessness and impending death.

They may have suffered for a minute and seven seconds, but in their minds it was a very, very prolonged torture, in my opinion. And the only thing that brought them the final closure is that they ultimately had the impact and — and died. But until that time, their — their minds were filled not only with terror, but thoughts of their loved ones, which they're leaving behind, which is a very common, actually, part and parcel of this kind of sensation. And often you hear, and I've heard in recordings, that most last words are references to wives, sons, daughters, because they — the person who is in this situation knows that not only are they being — seeing an end to their existence, but what their loved ones are going to see.

And to compound this misery, these individuals in the helicopter actually were two couples. One was a young couple, newlywed. The other one — couple, they — they had been married for 25 years and they were in a — in a celebratory mood when they started this. And now here they were dying with their loved one next to them. And we always have a — an impetus to protect loved ones. And yet in this case they knew that there was nothing they could do. They were — they were all going to finish out in a terribly mangled wreck.

And I think that's — that's a very, very difficult thing to live with for their relatives who survive, and it was a terrible thing for them to have gone through until their impact deaths.

Q. Dr. Diaz, in your study of this medical phenomenon, what is meant by the term "total and unconditional panic"?

A. Total and unconditional panic means that you have — not only are you overwhelmed by — by sensations that you're feeling, but you are no longer capable of doing anything useful. Because sometimes you may think, Well, I was really scared at this time and — and — but you managed to do something, close the valve, stand on the brakes, or do something. But we have total panic, your body is incapacitated. It is — it is unable to perform useful activity, it is unable to — even to think. Your mind almost becomes cognitively incapable of even having any useful thought. You're completely consumed by the fear.

Q. Dr. Diaz, did you understand, from your study of that one minute and seven seconds, that there were two Sundance pilots on the same radio frequency who heard a scream approximately halfway through the uncontrolled flight during the time of the steep descent?

A. I did. I knew that.

Q. What is the significance of that, in your professional opinion, Dr. Diaz?

A. In my opinion, that would even compound the — the — the terror further. Because when you're in an airplane and you're not a pilot yourself, you put all your trust and your life in the hands of the pilot. And you have confidence that the pilot can always do something.

But when your pilot is screaming, you know it's over. The pilot is feeling the same sensations you are. He's as scared as you are. And he — now you realize you are all in the same boat.

Q. Dr. Diaz, the time that you understand that this total occurrence took place over one minute and seven seconds, is that a significant amount of time to suffer pre-impact terror, in your professional opinion?

A. It's an eternity.

Q. You touched on this, but is it significant to what each of the decedents suffered, that each of them was with the person they loved the most in the world?

A. I think that's extremely significant, yes.

Q. Why?

A. Because it — it makes you, in essence, be suffering for two.

Q. Can you describe the extent of the conscious suffering that these individuals would have in reality experienced and the thoughts that normally to those in that situation precisely?

A. Well, the — the thoughts in this case, as you mentioned, because there were two couples, and the thoughts are compounded by the fact that not only are you thinking of your own death, first of all, your — your own impending destruction and ending of your life, you're also thinking of the impact that has on your loved ones. They — they know that their loved ones were waiting for them. That's uppermost in their mind. And now you have those same feelings for the loved one who's with you. And you know that they are going to suffer the same fate. And I think that's very — very difficult to deal with under any circumstances.

On the basis of this testimony, the jury awarded the sum of $500,000 to each of the four passenger decedents for their one minute and seven seconds of pre-impact suffering—one of the largest such awards in any aviation litigation.[75]

B. Post-Impact Conscious Pain and Suffering

Many helicopter crash victims survive the initial impact only to succumb minutes or some hours later. Although not strictly unique to helicopter or other aviation lawsuits, because similar damages can occur in motor vehicle or train accidents, the frequency of their occurrence warrants expanded treatment. As opposed to the patchwork of states expressly authorizing pre-impact terror, every jurisdiction provides for conscious pain and suffering of the deceased as a recoverable element of plaintiff's damages where sufficient proof exists.

In 1915, the United States Supreme Court affirmed an award for post-injury conscious pain and suffering where the decedent lived for little more than thirty minutes.[76] The court noted that "the question here is…whether there was evidence from which the jury reasonably could find that while he lived he endured conscious pain and suffering as a result of his injuries."[77] As a result, evidence of consciousness between the time of the injury and the time of death is critical in cases where pain and suffering is "short-lived."

In any helicopter crash case, the interval between injury on impact and death can be extremely short due to the severity of injuries. Because this period can be brief, sometimes as little as a few seconds, defendants often argue that it is not compensable. Several courts have held, however, that recovery for pain and suffering is permitted even if death is nearly instantaneous.

In a case arising from the crash of a helicopter in Missouri that resulted in the pilot's death, one of the issues on appeal was whether the award of compensatory damages was excessive.[78] The court evaluated the non-economic categories of loss to determine if the award was reasonable, including the post-impact conscious pain and suffering experienced by the decedent before his death.[79] "Any pain and suffering the decedent may have endured shall also be considered in determining damages."[80] The testimony of the Chief Medical Examiner who performed the autopsy established that the decedent "consciously suffered pain for three to five minutes as he bled to death after his thoracic aorta was severed upon impact."[81] The court considered this evidence of post-crash conscious pain and suffering in concluding that the plaintiffs "demonstrated significant non-economic losses stemming from the death of [the decedent]."[82]

That same appellate court observed that there may be an enormous range "between an inadequate award and an excessive award for pain and suffering" and "each case depends on its own particular facts."[83] The court set no arbitrary limit on a jury's determination of damages for post-crash conscious pain and suffering even of short duration:

> Substantial disparity among juries as to what constitutes pain and suffering must be expected.[84]

New York law, on the other hand, requires that other factors be considered in calculating damages for pain and suffering when the duration of conscious pain is short.[85] As examples, the court named "the degree of consciousness, severity of pain, [and] apprehension of impending death..."[86] In that case, four people survived the plane crash but were burned to death when the fire spread from the engine to the passenger compartment.[87] An expert estimated that the decedents' pain and suffering lasted anywhere from one or two seconds to several minutes.[88] Although the court acknowledged that "the jury could reasonably have found that decedents suffered unbearable pain, as well as extreme mental anguish both from fear of their own deaths and out of concern for each other," the court ordered remittitur of the $107,000,000 award to $1,000,000 to the four plaintiffs.[89]

Another court reversed a jury award for pain and suffering for a woman killed when an airplane crashed into her home and she was found in a crawling position.[90] The testimony of a pathologist established that she died from 100 percent third-degree burns that would have resulted in death between five to thirty seconds.[91] The court found no evidence that she was conscious after impact, reasoning that "[b]ecause the house was destroyed around [the decedent], it is impossible to attribute any significance to the fact that her body was found in a position which could be characterized as a "crawling-type" position."[92] On the other hand, a court on appeal affirmed the trial court's denial of damages for pain and suffering where "[a]ll indications are that the pilot and passengers were killed instantly in the crash[, and t]he record contain[ed] no evidence as to what happened inside the plane before its crash."[93] Similarly, a court awarded no damages for pain and suffering where the court found that the decedents' deaths were "for all practical purposes instantaneous."[94] Another court on appeal affirmed the trial court's remittitur of an award for pain and suffering to the survivors of two passengers who died in a plane crash "where there was no direct evidence as to decedents' conscious pain and suffering and where any suffering that might have occurred could not have lasted more than seconds anyway."[95]

Proof of post-crash conscious pain and suffering often will come from the testimony of on-site eyewitnesses who are first to the scene or early emergency responders whether ambulance, fire or police personnel. Because the NTSB is not focused on any aspect of damages, counsel must re-visit all on-site witness interviews to determine whether there is any evidence that any of the crash victims survived initial impact.

The best evidence of post-impact conscious pain and suffering is testimony from on-scene witnesses arriving shortly after the crash such as the nurse in one helicopter crash case who heard the surviving passenger moan repeatedly for help. Such direct evidence is not always available and counsel must gather sufficient circumstantial evidence in order to present such a damages claim to the jury. Only a few court decisions have carefully analyzed the types and sufficiency of circumstantial evidence which would support conscious pain and suffering.

The Sixth Circuit U.S. Court of Appeals did conduct such an analysis in the context of Korean Airlines Flight 007. In that case 269 persons were on board a commercial plane when it was hit by a Soviet missile and crashed into the sea. The court analyzed evidence that the passengers were conscious for an estimated 10 or 11 minutes in which they experienced the effects of the initial explosion and decompression. In so doing, the court affirmed the basic premise that such damages evidence must be viewed in the light most favorable to the plaintiffs and that a jury could infer from the evidence that each passenger:

> (1) Survived the initial explosion which caused a hole in the rear section of the fuselage, (2) donned an emergency oxygen mask, and (3) remained conscious during the twelve minute descent into the sea of Japan, suffering the physical effects of decompression and recompression along the way, as well as the horror of knowing that death was imminent.[96]

The medical examiner who performed the autopsy may be able to provide basic medical information to support the claim of post-impact physical pain and suffering. Most medical examiners have extensive experience in forensic pathology as part of their training and experience in determining the cause of death by way of anatomic examination and diagnosis. Where the medical examiner concludes from the anatomic examination that death was not instantaneous, this provides very strong support for the claim of post-impact physical pain and suffering.

Defendants will seek to establish that the cause of death was instantaneous when the helicopter crashed. By establishing precisely what the medical examiner found to be the cause of death and eliminating causes of death which are most likely instantaneous, the medical basis for the claim can be established. In one recent helicopter crash case, the medical examiner had the following opinions to a reasonable degree of medical certainty:

1. The deceased died by reason of blunt trauma to the chest and abdomen;

2. There was no evidence of trauma to the head of the deceased;

3. The internal organs of the deceased were unremarkable and in their usual position within the anatomy of the deceased;

4. There was no evidence of cerebellar or cerebral herniation and the basilar circulation of the deceased's brain appeared unremarkable;

5. The brain of the deceased contained no subcutaneous hemorrhaging and the calvarium was intact with no evidence of fracture;

6. The brain of the deceased evidenced no subdural, epidural, or subarachnoid hemorrhage;

7. There were no identifiable disease processes located in any of the organs of the body of the deceased;

8. The body of the deceased appeared to be in excellent health prior to the time of his death;

9. The aortic valve was not severed or separated and there was no evidence of valve herniation; and

10. The medical examiner's opinion based on the anatomic examination of the deceased was that the sole and only cause of death was attributable to the helicopter crash from which he sustained blunt trauma to the chest and abdomen.

That medical testimony established that the deceased would not have lost consciousness due to any head injury at the time of impact nor would he have sustained such extensive internal bleeding as to have caused an immediate loss of consciousness. That medical testimony in combination with an eyewitness reporting that the deceased exclaimed "help me, help me" repeatedly was sufficient to establish a submissible claim of post-impact physical pain and suffering as a legally compensable item.

C. Severe Burn Injuries

Severe burn injuries are not unique to helicopter crashes but occur with great frequency. Although there have been many advances in the design and materials selection of helicopter airframes to minimize post-impact fire and explosion, the necessary placement of the fuel tank along the bottom of the airframe and the typical high impact forces are sufficient to cause cabin-invasive fires in a substantial number of helicopter crashes. The inability of the passengers to escape from the cabin at impact due either to loss of consciousness or being physically trapped in the wreckage leaves them vulnerable to fuel-fed flames surrounding and intruding into the passenger compartment of the aircraft. Most occupants do not survive such trauma. For those who do the injuries are horrific and utterly beyond description.

In a case involving a crash in the Grand Canyon, one passenger survived, a 24 year old woman. She was burned over 85 percent of her body and underwent 70 surgeries under general anesthesia. Her left leg and right foot were lost. Burn injuries require the most intensive round-the-clock medical and rehabilitative care by far of any other medical condition due to the constant risks of infection. Though they valiantly carry on for weeks and even months, a number of horrifically injured burn victims will not survive in the long run.

The medical and rehabilitative needs of a severely burned helicopter crash victim are extensive as illustrated by the following report:

Summary of Patient's Condition
The patient is permanently disabled due to injuries following burns and multiple trauma in a helicopter crash. He has cognitive dysfunction, bilateral lower extremity amputations, upper extremity contractures and dysphagia. His skin requires special care and protection due to scarring and he will require specialized beds for the remainder of his life. His condition is permanent. He requires 24-hour assistance of a licensed practical nurse or a registered nurse if an L.P.N. is not available. This plan outlines his minimal care needs to return home with his family. Additional costs will be incurred for the treatment of complications or hospitalizations. Among the complications he is at risk for are

skin breakdown, pneumonia, urinary tract infections, urosepsis and bowel impactions. He is not employable. His life expectancy is normal to near normal with proper care.

The medical care plan for this patient prescribed various medications, disposable supplies, daily therapy, medical equipment, home nursing care and wheelchair transportation. Reduced to present value and given the age of the young woman, the medical and life care plan totaled in excess of $19 million.

D. Death on the High Seas Act (DOHSA)

The Death on the High Seas Act (DOHSA) was enacted on March 30, 1920. In cases prior to April 5, 2000, the Act disallowed a deceased's family from recovering pre-death pain and suffering as well as punitive damages. By its terms, the provisions of DOHSA have not applied to the Great Lakes or to any body of water within any state or to any water in the Panama Canal Zone.

On April 5, 2000 President Clinton signed into law the Wendell H. Ford Aviation Investment and Reform Act ("Ford Act") which provides that DOHSA did not apply to aviation accidents occurring between 3 and 12 nautical miles from shore. The Ford Act allowed recovery for non-pecuniary damages if the aircrash accident occurred beyond 12 nautical miles.

Non-pecuniary damages are defined as loss of care, comfort and companionship. Punitive damages continue to be prohibited. While the Ford Act arguably overturned DOHSA, conflicts of law issues remain. Within the 3 nautical miles closest to U.S. shore, courts may continue to apply that state's law that is most consistent with U.S. federal law and the usual conflicts issues prevail. However, between three and twelve nautical miles from the U.S. coastline, maritime law continues to be applicable and some courts may even apply state law.

E. Ground Impact Damages

Aircraft litigation may on occasion involve claims of personal injury or wrongful death due to aircrash impact into homes or businesses. For these purposes, it is important for counsel to note that under the provisions of the General Aviation and Revitalization Act (GARA), persons injured or killed on the ground are exempt from the 18-year Statute of Repose.[97]

F. Hull Damage

The aircraft's certificated owner may have a claim for the fair market value of the aircraft to the extent it was declared a total loss. In these instances, the insurance carrier will of-ten seek to join a plaintiff's personal injury claim in order to seek that reimbursement for insurance monies paid out.

From plaintiff's perspective a mutually beneficial arrangement often evolves where plaintiffs and their experts are given access to the aircraft wreckage in exchange for a "piggy back" on plaintiffs' liability claims against the parties responsible. The advantage to plaintiffs of full and unfettered access to the wreckage are numerous. Ownership ensures complete and timely inspection and testing as well as use of any desired parts as evidence at trial.

A substantial body of law has developed concerning the "economic loss doctrine." This doctrine prohibits a contracting party seeking only business losses defined as loss of use of the helicopter, the value of the helicopter, and loss of revenues from recovering in tort contrary to the terms of any express warranties and disclaimers. This defense is often an issue in commercial and subrogated claims and is subject to varying interpretations and exceptions in different jurisdictions.[98] In most cases involving serious injuries, deaths or damages to "other property," the economic loss doctrine is not likely to be an issue.

8.3 Punitive Damages in Helicopter Crash Cases

Substantial punitive damage awards have been levied in helicopter crash cases.[99] Where the helicopter or helicopter parts manufacturer knew or should have known that its product was defective and had a high probability of failure so as to cause human injury or death, that manufacturer may be responsible for punitive damages just as any other product manufacturer. Section 4.8(E) in Chapter 4 addresses the legal standard for submission of a punitive damages claim.

There are a number of factors which raise the potential for imposition of punitive damages in these cases. Where the aircraft or component has been the cause of repeated in-flight failure and resultant crashes, that manufacturer has a legal duty to recall, replace, or repair the known defective or malfunctioning component or aspect of the aircraft.

Where the manufacturer continues to supply the defective or malfunctioning helicopter or component part with full knowledge of its dangerous propensities, the groundwork is laid for a punitive damages claim. In many jurisdictions, the threshold standards are where the manufacturer had a "complete indifference" or "conscious or reckless disregard" for human safety. Providing false information to governmental or regulatory authorities and concealing or covering up safety data are also common grounds for imposing punitive damages.

It is simply not possible to create out of whole cloth a punitive damages case unless there presents a factual basis for such a case to begin with. Given a thoroughly compelling and factually extensive record, a significant punitive damages award can be assessed against a helicopter aircraft, engine or component part manufacturer. However, such cases are truly rare. Assuming such a case presents with overwhelming facts of reckless disregard, counsel should consider the following suggestions. Throughout discovery, constant emphasis must be placed on the defendant's "conscious" and "knowledge based" decision-making. In fact, the terms should be integrated throughout the numerous videotaped depositions presented at trial.

For example, there are instances where a defendant plainly admitted that it gave no warning whatsoever as to the known dangers of its defective helicopter engine. Despite the knowledge that there were several "persons injured in crashes due to engine failures," it "was a conscious business decision made by defendant not to disclose that information."

Such admissions are critical to the punitives case and, as importantly, they must come from the highest executives within the company. In such cases counsel obtains discovery from the lower ranking engineers and executives; counsel obtains admissions from the top officers and the chief engineer.

The Turbomeca cases provide a legal roadmap and evidentiary framework for submitting, obtaining and affirming punitive damages awards in helicopter crash cases.[100] Substantial punitive damages were imposed on Turbomeca, S.A., a French helicopter engine manufacturer, as well as its U.S. subsidiary and distributor, Turbomeca Engine Corporation. The French entity made critical safety changes in the helicopter engines sold in its native country but not in the United States. Subsequent appellate opinions confirmed that this was a critical factor in affirming the punitive damages award against that company.[101]

According to the Turbomeca Chief Engineer, the company disclaimed any responsibility for how the helicopter and the pilot and passengers inside safely get to the ground when the engine stopped in flight due to a manufacturing defect. The decision was to simply wait and replace the defective part at routine overhaul and this was a "conscious decision" made by the company:

> MR. ROBB: And that was a conscious decision made by the company, wasn't it?
>
> ANSWER: Yes.
>
> MR. ROBB: With knowledge of the facts that engineering had, true?
>
> ANSWER: Yes.
>
> MR. ROBB: And with knowledge of the facts that the technical support department had, true?

> ANSWER: True.
>
> MR. ROBB: Conscious decision?
>
> ANSWER: Yes.

By using the precise language of the punitive elements, the testimony is rendered more incriminating and supportive of the punitives claim.

In seeking to submit a punitive damages claim, the underlying product defect must be clear and not seriously disputed. In the Turbomeca cases, the actual product defect was not seriously in dispute. The defective product in question was a helicopter engine which contained an improperly manufactured and poorly designed nozzle guide vane, called a TU 76. The evidentiary foundation for the punitive conduct stemmed from the company's internal acknowledgment that the TU 76 parts were dangerous and defective.

The reviewing court expressly referenced such testimony in the context of establishing that Turbomeca had "actual knowledge" of the defect in quoting from the trial record as follows:

> MR. ROBB: Well, do you know, as President of the corporation, whether it's true or not that the TU 76 nozzle guide vane is a defective component?
>
> ANSWER: Would you state the question again, please?
>
> MR. ROBB: Do you know as President of Turbomeca Engine Corporation whether the TU 76 nozzle guide vane is a defective component?
>
> ANSWER: Yes.
>
> MR. ROBB: And did you know that it was defective before May 27, 1993?
>
> ANSWER: I-I can't say.[102]

In addition to the existence of clear product defect, it is further evidence of conscious disregard for safety when the defendants readily acknowledge that their actions violate known industry standards, which these defendants did:

> MR. ROBB: Sir, as the President of Turbomeca Engine Corporation, how would you evaluate an aircraft engine company that would stand by and permit its customers to continue to use a dangerous engine which they know to be defective?
>
> ANSWER: I would evaluate that situation as being not in accordance with normal industry standards.

Turbomeca knew the standards of care required of the company. It concluded as early as June 1986 that it should redesign TU 76 because it is part of the safety responsibility of a company like Turbomeca to eliminate a bad design from a product "at the earliest practical time." Such testimony should be the point of departure for the opinion testimony of plaintiff's experts:

> MR. ROBB: Is it appropriate industry practice to install a part in an engine which a company knows is dangerous and defective and breaks apart in the air?
>
> EXPERT: Absolutely not.
>
> MR. ROBB: Why not?
>
> EXPERT: We're talking about peoples' lives here. You are talking about a part which not only do you know does not last as long as it is supposed to but when it does fail, it doesn't fail in a benign way. It is a malignant failure that results in the engine shut down and usually through a crash…It is extremely serious and it's been demonstrated that it can cause crashes, cause in-flight shut downs, and they know what the safe life is and this would be a very urgent matter to fix.

Plaintiff's counsel can prove corporate recklessness by showing that the product manufacturer had actual knowledge of the dangerous consequences of its actions. Plaintiffs must establish that the product manufacturer "knew or had reason to know" by exercising ordinary care that continued use of the product created a "high degree of probability" of injury.

One of the known consequences to Turbomeca of an in-flight helicopter engine shut-down with subsequent loss of power due to the TU 76 part failure had been injuries. When the TU 76 part fails, the company's experience before May 27, 1993 (the date of the crash of Life Flight 2) was that crashes occurred and people were injured.

To support a substantial punitives award, the evidence adduced at trial must clearly support a finding that the manufacturer itself, at least internally, regarded the product defect to be a major, widespread, and serious safety problem. The number of TU 76 cracks found during routine overhaul and the number of in-flight failures alone established the inevitability of a crash.

This type of evidence supports a jury finding that although the manufacturer may not have known precisely when and where such a product failure would occur, on the basis of their extensive engineering knowledge and field experience, they knew or had reason to know that incidents

with serious injuries would inevitably continue to occur. Prior similar product failures are essential to proving this element of the punitives case.

The evidence of a defendant's evil state of mind must be captured on videotaped testimony shown to the jury in which the company's executives repeatedly affirm that it was a "conscious business decision" to subject innocent people to risk of serious injury and death from continued use of the dangerous product. In the Turbomeca cases, despite the internal documentation and knowledge of the TU 76 defect, the defendants continued "sending out hundreds of those defective engines into the stream of commerce." Though recognizing a serious problem with TU 76, they continued to manufacture engines with that part without making any changes and "literally hundreds and hundreds" of the TU 76-equipped engines with the defective design and weak metal were manufactured and sold after June 9, 1986. This evidence was squarely probative to their "reckless disregard for safety."

It is useful to establish a substantial economic and profit motive for the defendant's reckless conduct. Rather than recall or retrofit the TU 76 component, Turbomeca's company-wide policy was to wait until the engine came back to a repair facility for routine overhaul at which time the TU 76 part would be systematically replaced at the customer's cost. The company chose to wait and make this modification at overhaul because the customer had to bring the engine in for overhaul anyway and the customer would then pay for the parts and labor involved in replacing TU 76. However, if Turbomeca were to recall the engines before overhaul this would be at its own expense, not the customer's.

According to the company's President, the reason for this policy was clear:

> Q. Now the reason that Turbomeca, S.A. took the position that we're going to wait until overhaul and take the chance of failure in the interim of some of these parts is one of cost, isn't it?
>
> A. I agree with that statement.

Testimony of this nature was essential to upholding the punitives finding. As set forth by the court: "The Letzes' premise was that the failure to immediately recall and replace the known defective TU 76 within helicopter engines manufactured by [Turbomeca] and operating throughout the world was the consequence of a deliberate decision and was motivated by the desire to save the company $48 million."[103]

During discovery, the Turbomeca President testified that the cost of replacing one of the dangerous engine parts was $17,000 and that there were approximately 2,850 in existence around the world of which approximately one-third were in the U.S. According to the court: "Mr. Dennis Nichols, the President of Turbomeca Engine Corporation, acknowledged that the companies saved up to $48 million by not immediately recalling all helicopter engines equipped with the known defective part."[104] Such testimony addressing the cost savings not only was critical in establishing the economic motive of the defendant but also to set forth the total punitive amount as requested of the jury and, ultimately, endorsed on appeal.[105]

Counsel should seek to identify customers or markets for which the manufacturer supplied the same product but with a safe design. Product manufacturers will often perform a "selective recall." Turbomeca did warn the French military that there were problems with this engine type in December 1985. In early 1991, they retrofitted all French military helicopter engines with the safe design.

The effects were startling in that there has never been a report of a TU 76 causing in-flight failure or crash in any French military helicopter. The evidence supported an inference that the defendant gave notice of the TU 76 problem to the French military in 1986 because it clearly had preferentially informed a certain customer and left all of its other customers in the dark. That Turbomeca would selectively recall and retrofit all defective engines in use by the French military and no one else demonstrated its insouciance for the safety of any other worldwide user of its engine product.

Counsel must uncover any false or fraudulent representations made to customers or regulatory authorities. There was considerable evidence that Turbomeca had misrepresented material facts to regulatory authorities and misrepresented the product's safety history to worldwide users.[106] This evidence was admissible as to the defendant's motive to save the cost of a recall.

Where it exists, such evidence in a products liability case goes to the heart of the manufacturer's egregious actions. Not only is the company willing to subject innocent people to risk of serious injury or death, but in the process they are also willing to lie about it whenever convenient to promote their own economic benefit. By squarely holding such evidence of misrepresentation admissible on the issue of punitive damages, the *Letz* and *Barnett* courts confirmed the proper use of such evidence in these cases. Withholding critical safety information from customers was expressly referenced by the court in the *Barnett* opinion as an example of such devious conduct:

MR. ROBB: Did Turbomeca ever notify its customers about a potential problem with the TU 76 design, sir?

ANSWER: I am still confused by the question.

MR. ROBB: Well, did you or did you not send out any information or alert your customers that these things were cracking and had the potential to kill and seriously injure people?

ANSWER: No.[107]

As the Court stated in *Barnett*: "Turbomeca's post-accident under-reporting of prior failures of the modified TU-76, however, pales in comparison to the lack of forthrightness to its customers."[108]

Counsel also should show that the product manufacturer has continued to produce and market the same dangerous and defective design even following the injury-producing event at bar. Unfortunately, some product manufacturers show little remorse when it is established that their defective product is out in the marketplace injuring and killing innocent people. In such circumstances, careful and persistent inquiry into the decision-making processes which underlie continued marketing of such products is very likely to yield strong proof of reprehensible misconduct as it did in the *Letz* and *Barnett* cases.

Turbomeca France has had it within its power to order a retrofit of all existing TU 76 parts since 1991. Long after the subject helicopter crash, TU 76 remained in engines powering helicopters around the world and at least one-third of all these TU 76 equipped engines were in use in the U.S. Turbomeca continued to expose innocent passengers, crew, and pilots around the world to the known, predictable, and ever-increasing failure rate of TU 76. Turbomeca continued to represent to the FAA and to worldwide operators that TU 76 is a safe and airworthy part and they have no current or future plans for recalling TU 76. At the then rate of overhaul and replacement, TU 76 remained in helicopter engines in the U.S. and around the world for seven years after the helicopter crash.

In so many instances, the safety and well being of the users of its products are totally and inexplicably ignored by the manufacturer. The real "crisis" from the company's standpoint is the concomitant loss of sales and customer "complaints" which arise from the injury-producing product failures. Such was precisely the evidence in these cases. Also important are a defendant's efforts to point to other parties for the product failure and evidence of such "diversionary tactics" was considered in these cases.[109]

Given the extensive evidence of corporate recklessness, the Missouri Court of Appeals, Western District, en banc, determined that an appropriate total punitive amount for both cases was $53 million, divided equally between the cases.[110] It can be presumed that this sum represents the $48 million in costs savings to Turbomeca plus an additional $5 million penalty.

The trial record in these cases presents a high bar for the affirmance of substantial punitive damages awards in aviation products liability cases. Nevertheless, the true lesson of the *Letz* and *Barnett* decisions is that where the evidence so clearly and convincingly supports a finding of reprehensible corporate misconduct which endangers the lives of innocent people, the appellate courts will fairly and justly affirm a substantial punitive damages award.

Endnotes

1. Portions of this section are derived from G. Robb, Damages in Aviation Cases, printed in AAJ Annual Convention Materials, Vol. II, at 828 (July 2007).

2. *Arno v. Helinet Corp., 30 Cal. Rptr. 3d 669 (Cal. App. 2005).*

3. *Riggs v. Sundance Helicopters, Inc.*, Case No. A-11-653149-C (Dist. Ct. Clark County, Nevada, October 9, 2014).

4. *Densberger v. United Technologies Corp., 297 F.3d 66 (2d Cir. 2002), cert. denied, 537 U.S. 1147 (2003).*

5. *Torrington Co. v. Stutzman, 46 S.W.3d 829 (Tex. 2000).*

6. *Letz v. Turbomeca Engine Corporation, 975 S.W.2d 155, 164-65 (Mo. App. 1997).*

7. *Barnett v. La Societe Anonyme Turbomeca France, 963 S.W.2d 639 (Mo. App. 1997), cert. denied, 525 U.S. 827 (1998).*

8. *Nelson v. Dolan, 434 N.W.2d 25, 30 (Neb. 1989).*

9. *Winn Dixie of Montgomery, Inc. v. Colburn, 709 So.2d 1222, 1225 (Ala. 1998)* (in a case where a pharmacist failed to accurately dispense the plaintiff's prescription causing her to go into anaphylactic shock, "conclud[ing] that it was well within the right of the jury to award Colburn $130,000 because she experienced the natural terror associated with what she believed to be imminent death").

10. *Monk v. Dial, 441 S.E.2d 857, 859 (Ga. App. 1994).*

11. *Smith v. Louisiana Farm Bureau Cas. Ins. Co.*, 35 So.3d 463, 472-73 (La. App. 2010), writ denied, 45 So.3d 1052 (La. 2010).

12. *Phillips v. Eastern Maine Medical Center, 565 A.2d 306, 309 (Me. 1989)* (recognizing that the decedent suffered mental anguish caused by his impending death and reversing a damages award on other grounds).

13. *Beynon v. Montgomery Cablevision Ltd. Partnership, 718 A.2d 1161, 1183 (Md. App. 1998)* (holding that "damages for emotional distress or mental anguish are recoverable in Maryland, provided that it is proximately caused by the wrongful act of the defendant and it results in a physical injury…or is capable of objective determination").

14. *Blum v. Airport Terminal Services, Inc., 762 S.W.2d 67, 75-76 (Mo. App. 1988)* (ruling that "[the decedent]'s pre-impact awareness of the impending disaster can also be considered"); *Delacroix v. Doncasters, Inc., 407 S.W.3d 13, 23-24 (Mo. App. 2013)* (affirming the trial court's instructing the jury that it could award damages sustained as a result of the plaintiffs' fatal injuries, including pre-impact terror experienced during the 52 seconds before the plane crashed).

15. *Nelson, 434 N.W.2d at 30-32.*

16. *Thibeault v. Campbell, 622 A.2d 212, 215 (N.H. 1993)* (allowing for recovery of "pre-accident fright" under New Hampshire's wrongful death statute).

17. *Phiri v. Joseph, 822 N.Y.S.2d 573, 574 (N.Y.A.D. 2006)* (permitting recovery for pre-impact terror where the evidence establishes "that the decedent perceived grave injury or death").

18. *Green v. Hale, 590 S.W.2d 231, 238 (Tex. Civ. App. 1979)* (affirming an award of damages for mental anguish where a truck backed up over a 13-year-old boy who tried to maintain his grip on the tailgate, ruling that "[r]egardless of how brief in duration, a tremendous amount of fear can be inferred from the surrounding circumstances").

19. *Chapple v. Granger, 851 F.Supp. 1481, 1487 (E.D.Wash. 1994)* (finding "as credible evidence that both mother and son were aware of and did appreciate the impending impact at least several seconds before it happened where, during his hospital stay, [the son], on one occasion when he was not fully cognizant, screamed "Watch out, Mom! Watch out, Mom!") *Bingaman v. Grays Harbor Community Hosp., 699 P.2d 1230, 1234 (Wash. 1985)* that permitted the jury to consider "the decedent's fear that she was dying" in a medical malpractice case).

20. *Bowen v. Lumbermenís Mut. Cas. Co., 517 N.W.2d 432, 446 (Wis. 1994)* (although not directly ruling on the ability to recover damages for pre-impact fright, denying recovery after determining that the evidence was insufficient to establish the authenticity of the claim).

21. *A.R.S. ß 14-3110 (1974)* (providing that damages for pain and suffering are not recoverable in a survival action).

22. *Chicago, R.I. & P. Ry. Co. v. Caple, 179 S.W.2d 151, 153-55 (Ark. 1944)* (ruling that the trial court erred by submitting a jury instruction permitting the jury to consider "mental anguish preceding the injury" as an element of damages where a seven-year-old girl was struck by a train when she caught her foot in a cattle guard).

23. *Westís Ann.Cal.C.C.P. ß 377.34 (1992)* (providing that damages for pain and suffering are not recoverable in a survival action).

24. *Stephenson v. Honeywell Intern, Inc., 669 F.Supp.2d 1259, 1261 (D.Kan. 2009)* (concluding "that the rapid heart rate and difficulty breathing suffered by decedents [in the 21 seconds that elapsed between the failure of an engine and the impact] in the present action do not constitute 'physical injury,' but instead represent the kind of generalized symptoms of emotional distress for which recovery has been denied under Kansas law"). This ruling was reached notwithstanding that the Kansas Supreme Court neglected to address the issue of whether plaintiffs may recover for pre-impact emotional distress in *St. Clair v. Denny, 781 P.2d 1043, 1049-50 (Kan. 1989)*.

25. *Gage v. City of Westfield, 532 N.E.2d 62, 70-71 (Mass. App. 1988), review denied, 536 N.E.2d 1093 (Mass. 1989)* (noting that "the relevant period for purposes of measuring compensation for conscious pain and suffering has consistently been defined in our appellate decisions as commencing with the impact of the fatal injury, refusing "to extend the right to recover for conscious pain and suffering to pre-impact fright").

26. *Stecyk v. Bell Helicopter Textron, Inc., 53 F.Supp.2d 794, 797 n.4 (E.D.Pa. 1999)* (ruling that "under Pennsylvania law, there can be no recovery for pre-impact fear, pain and suffering").

27. *In re Air Crash Disaster Near Chicago, Ill. on May 25, 1979, 507 F.Supp. 21, 24 (N.D.Ill. 1980)* (recognizing that no Illinois court has addressed the issue of recovering damages for pre-impact suffering but predicting that they would not permit it).

28. *Platt v. McDonnell Douglas Corp., 554 F.Supp. 360, 363-364 (E.D.Mich. 1983)* (noting that a Michigan court had not yet ruled on whether damages for pre-impact fright may be recovered but predicting an affirmative answer).

29. *Case v. Norfolk and Western Ry. Co., 570 N.E.2d 1132, 1136-37 (Ohio App. 1988) cause dismissed, 534 N.E.2d 1202 (Ohio 1989)* ("Our research discloses no Ohio cases permitting a cause to proceed . . . for 'pre-impact terror'").

30. *Nye v. Com., Dept. of Transp., 480 A.2d 318, 321-22 (Pa. Super. 1984)* (not reaching the issue of whether damages for pre-impact fright may be recovered in Pennsylvania but implying that it would not be permitted).

31. *Rutland v. South Carolina Dept. of Transp., 734 S.E.2d 142, 144 (S.C. 2012)* ("reserv[ing] the novel question3 of whether South Carolina should allow recovery for pre-impact fear for another day").

32. *Smith, 35 So.3d at 472 ; Beynon, 718 A.2d at 1168.*

33. *Beynon, 718 A.2d at 1185; see also Nelson, 434 N.W.2d at 30-31; Phiri, 822 N.Y.S.2d at 574.*

34. *Shu-Tao Lin v. McDonnell Douglas Corp., 742 F.2d 45, 52-53 (2d Cir. 1984)* (quoting with approval the trial court's analysis at *574 F.Supp. 1407, 1416 (S.D.N.Y. 1983)*).

35. *Id. at 53.*

36. *Solomon v. Warren, 540 F.2d 777 (5th Cir. 1976) (applying Florida law) cert. denied, 434 U.S. 801 (1977).*

37. *Green v. Hale, 590 S.W.2d 231 (Tex. App. 1979); Missouri Pacific R. Co. v. Lane, 720 S.W. 2d 830 (Tex. App. 1986).*

38. *Lane, 720 S.W. 2d at 833.*

39. *In re Air Crash Disaster Near Chicago, Ill. on May 25, 1979, 507 F.Supp. at 24.*

40. *U.S. v. Furumizo, 381 F.2d 965, 970 (9th Cir. 1967).*

41. *Brereton v. U.S., 973 F.Supp. 752, 757 (E.D.Mich. 1997).*

42. *Nelson, 434 N.W.2d at 32.*

43. Abraham Fuchsberg, "Damages for Pre-Impact Terror," *16 Trial Law Quarterly 29, 31-32* (1984).

44. Fuchsberg, *supra, at 33.*

45. *Nelson, 434 N.W.2d at 31; see also Haley v. Pan American World Airways, Inc., 746 F.2d 311, 315 (5th Cir. 1984).*

46. *Nelson, 434 N.W.2d at 32.*

47. *Nelson, 434 N.W.2d at 32* (ruling that "the personal representative's offers of proof nonetheless provide a basis upon which the jury certainly need not, but could, if it wished, find that decedent Nelson apprehended and feared his impending death during the 5 seconds his motorcycle traveled 268 feet locked with Dolan's automobile before he was crushed and thus killed").

48. *Smith, 35 So.3d at 472*, (affirming an award of $250,000 where the decedent was "placed in great fear" when he saw the runaway trailer coming across the center line at him and attempted to pull over on the right shoulder before being struck and dying "in a horrific manner").

49. *Monk, 441 S.E.2d at 859* (affirming an award for pre-impact pain and suffering where the decedent's truck veered shortly before the collision with the tractor-trailer and death was instantaneous); *Department of Transportation v. Dupree, 570 S.E.2d 1, 11 (Ga. App. 2002)* (affirming an award for pre-impact pain and suffering where a pedestrian was struck by a car while crossing an intersection and "[the decedent] would have been able to see the approaching headlights rounding the curve over 350 feet away and up to 14 seconds away"); *Beynon, 718 A.2d at 1185* (holding that 71-1/2 feet of skid marks before the decedent struck the rear of a tractor-trailer was sufficient to infer pre-impact fear, affirming an award of $350,000 for pre-impact fear that had been reduced from the jury's award of $1,000,000).

50. *Moorhead v. Mitsubishi Aircraft Intern., Inc., 828 F.2d 278, 288 n.43 (5th Cir. 1987).*

51. *Haley, 746 F.2d at 317.*

52. *Hetrick v. Air Logistics, Inc., 55 F.Supp.2d 663, 669 (S.D.Tex. 1999).*

53. *Brereton, 973 F.Supp. at 754 and 757.*

54. *Malacynski v. McDonnell Douglas Corp., 565 F.Supp. 105, 107 (D.C.N.Y. 1983).*

55. *Solomon, 540 F.2d at 792-93.*

56. *In re Air Crash at New Orleans, La., 795 F.2d 1230, 1237 (5th Cir. 1986).*

57. *Delacroix, 407 S.W.3d at 23.*

58. *Haley, 746 F.2d at 315.*

59. *Id. at 315-16.*

60. *Id. at 316.*

61. *Id. at 317.*

62. *Larsen v. Delta Air Lines, Inc., 692 F.Supp. 714, 721 (S.D.Tex. 1988)* (finding that conflicting evidence "coupled with a lack of testimony relating directly to [the decedent] precludes an award for his pre-impact mental anguish" where two survivors testified that they experienced "trepidation" upon landing while two others testified that the landing was the same as any other in stormy weather); *Moorhead, 828 F.2d at 288 n.43* (ruling that a trial court could refuse to speculate "how much, if at all, [the decedents] were aware and fearful of their plight" when it appears that those on board were killed instantly and "[t]he record contains no evidence as to what happened inside the plane before its crash"); *Shatkin v. McDonnell Douglas Corp., 727 F.2d 202, 206-07 (2d Cir. 1984)* (holding that a jury's award of $87,500 for pre-impact mental anguish "was wholly unsupported" where the plane "took off normally, was able to correct a slight bank to the left, and did not go into its 90-degree left plunge until only 3 seconds before it crashed").

63. *Air Florida, Inc. v. Zondler, 683 S.W.2d 769, 774-75 (Tex. App. 1984).*

64. *Id. at 774.*

65. *Id. at 774-75.*

66. *In re Air Crash at New Orleans, La., 795 F.2d at 1237* (ruling that "the maximum allowable recovery was $7,500 per decedent," where a witness testified that "he saw the plane lose altitude, clip power lines and trees, roll to one side, and finally explode several blocks from where he stood" and another witness "heard the plane blow up and the screams of people inside the plane); *Pregeant v. Pan American World Airways, Inc., 762 F.2d 1245, 1249 (5th Cir. 1985)* (affirming an award of $16,000 for pre-impact mental suffering where when the left wing of the plane struck a tree at an altitude

of 53 feet and rolled to the left before it crashed 20 seconds later); *DíAngelo v. U.S., 456 F.Supp. 127, 142 (D.C.Del. 1978), affd, 605 F.2d 1194 (3rd Cir. 1979), affd, sub nom. U.S. v. Atlantic Aviation Corp., 605 F.2d 1197 (3rd Cir. 1979)* and *Driscoll v. U.S., 456 F.Supp. 143, 154 (D.C.Del. 1978), affd, 605 F.2d 1195 (3rd Cir. 1979)* (affirming an award of $25,000 where a jeep struck a plane on take-off, the plane climbed steeply in a nearly vertical ascent to avoid the collision, leveled off at which time the nose fell off the plane, and the plane crashed onto the runway); *Solomon, 540 F.2d at 793* (viewing an award of $10,000 to each of decedents' estates for pre-impact terror as "on the very low side" where a plane ran out of fuel and it and its occupants were lost at sea); *Griffin v. Air South, Inc., 324 F.Supp. 1284, 1291 (D.C.Ga. 1971)* (answering affirmatively the question: "Does a decedent suffer a compensable agony in an airplane in a death plunge?").

67. *Blum v. Airport Terminal Services, Inc., 762 S.W.2d 67, 76 (Mo. App. 1988).*

68. *Pregeant, 762 F.2d at 1249.*

69. *Zondler, 683 S.W.2d at 774.*

70. See, e.g., Richard A. Levy, "Mental Stress and Physical Factors in the Terminal Phase of Fatal Aircraft Accidents: A Review of the Related Scientific Literature, the Significance of Recovered Voice Recorder Tapes, & the Victim's Perception of Injury in the Last Nanoseconds of Life," *65 J. Air L. & Com. 45,* (Winter 1999).

71. *Id.*

72. See, e.g., Kastenbaum and Eisenberg, *The Psychology of Death* (1976); Stevens and Cook, "Evaluation and Memories During Severe Physical Illness and Injuries," *Journal of Nervous and Mental Diseases*, Vol. 1855, (July 1995) Sabom, *Recollections of Death, a Medical Investigation*, (1982).

73. Kastenbaum and Eisenberg, *The Psychology of Death* (1976).

74. Richard A. Levy, "Mental Stress and Physical Factors in the Terminal Phase of Fatal Aircraft Accidents: A Review of the Related Scientific Literature, the Significance of Recovered Voice Recorder Tapes, & the Victim's Perception of Injury in the Last Nanoseconds of Life," *65 J. Air L. & Com. 45,* (Winter 1999).

75. *Riggs v. Sundance Helicopters, Inc., Entry of Judgment, Case No. A-11-653149-C (Dist. Ct. Clark County, Nevada, October 9, 2014).*

76. *St. Louis I.M. & S. Ry. Co. v. Craft, 237 U.S. 648, 654-660 (1915).*

77. *Id. at 655.*

78. *Barnett v. La Societe Anonyme Turbomeca France, 963 S.W.2d 639, 657-58 (Mo. Ct. App. 1997), cert. denied, 525 U.S. 827 (1998)* (overruled on other grounds).

79. *Id. at 658.*

80. *Id.*

81. *Id.*

82. *Id.*

83. *Barnett, 963 S.W.2d at 658; see also Delacroix, 407 S.W.3d at 37.*

84. *Barnett, 963 S.W.2d at 658.*

85. *Datskow v. Teledyne Continental Aircraft Products, a Div. of Teledyne Industries, Inc., 826 F.Supp. 677, 693 (W.D.N.Y. 1993).*

86. *Id.*

87. *Id. at 682.*

88. *Id. at 692 n.7.*

89. *Id. at 681, 694.*

90. *In re Air Crash Disaster Near New Orleans, La. on July 9, 1982, 767 F.2d 1151, 1157 (5th Cir. 1985).*

91. *Id.*

92. *Id.*

93. *Moorhead v. Mitsubishi Aircraft Intern., Inc., 828 F.2d 278 (5th Cir. 1987).*

94. *Higginbotham v. Mobil Oil Corp., 360 F.Supp. 1140, 1142-43, 1146 (W.D.La. 1973).*

95. *Bonn v. Puerto Rico Intern. Airlines, Inc., 518 F.2d 89, 94 (1st Cir. 1975).*

96. *Bickel v. Korean Airlines Company, Ltd., 96 F.3d 151, 155 (6th Cir. 1996), cert. denied, 519 U.S. 1093 (1997).*

97. *49 U.S.C. ß 40101, Section 2(b)(3) (1997).*

98. See, e.g., *Bocre Leasing Corp. v. General Motors Corp., 621 N.Y.S. 2d 497 (N.Y. 1995)* (New York's adoption of the ELD); *Mountain West Helicopter, LLC v. Kaman Aerospace Corp., 310 F.Supp.2d 459 (D. Conn. 2004)* (ELD applied to bar various claims); *Robinson Helicopter Company, Inc. v. Dana Corporation, 102 P.3d 268 (Cal. 2004)* (applying fraud and misrepresentation exception to ELD).

99. *See, e.g., Barnett, 963 S.W.2d at 659.*

100. *Letz v. Turbomeca Engine Corporation, 975 S.W.2d 155, (Mo. App. 1997); Barnett v. La Societe Anonyme Turbomeca France, 963 S.W.2d 639 (Mo. App. 1997), cert. denied, 525 U.S. 827 (1998)* (overruled on other grounds).

101. *Barnett, 963 S.W.2d at 661.*

102. *Id. at 664.*

103. *Letz 975 S.W.2d at 172.*

104. *Id. at 165.*

105. *Letz, 975 S.W.2d at 180; Barnett, 963 S.W.2d at 669.*

106. *Letz, 975 S.W.2d at 174.*

107. *Barnett, 963 S.W.2d at 665.*

108. *Id. at 666.*

109. *Id. at 667.*

110. *Id. at 668-69.*

Chapter 9

Pre-Trial Matters

Introduction

Many experienced trial lawyers claim to prepare for the trial of a case from the moment the client walks through the door. While all of the intensive factual and legal investigation as well as the process of formal discovery is in a sense trial preparation, several specific preparatory tasks should be undertaken toward the close of discovery and in the 30-60 days leading up to the start of trial. The focus of this chapter is to address those general pre-trial issues in the 30-60 days preceding trial as well as those which arise specifically in the context of helicopter crash litigation.

While all of these other matters require attention, the single most critical use of counsel's time should be taken up by the final preparation of the fact and expert witnesses for their trial testimony. As to that there is one inviolable rule: the lawyer presenting the witness at trial must prepare that witness.

9.1 Final Trial Preparation

Final trial preparation encompasses practical matters such as witness and expert scheduling, transport and storage of exhibits and transport and setup of courtroom video equipment. For advanced scheduling purposes it is always beneficial to have a firm trial date, but many jurisdictions either by practice or necessity cannot accommodate that and will sometimes provide notice of a trial date as little as 30-60 days in advance.

A. Logistics and Witness Scheduling

As soon as the trial date is set, the best practice is to advise all fact and expert witnesses in writing of the trial date and the approximate day or days when their testimony will be needed. Should any problem arise as to the availability of a fact witness for trial, prompt arrangements should be made for videotaping that witness's testimony for presentation at trial even if the discovery deadline has passed. Almost any court will recognize that counsel has little or no control over the schedule of most fact witnesses. Upon learning of their unavailability due to a long-planned trip or a scheduled surgery, the request to conduct the videotaped deposition of that witness out of time ordinarily will be permitted.

Travel and hotel accommodations should be made for all experts as soon as the trial date is known. Sad stories abound where such arrangements are made too late and a major convention in the town of the trial books all available hotel rooms. It does little for the preparedness or enthusiasm of one's primary experts to be lodged ninety minutes from the courthouse.

Advance thought must be given to when exhibits are delivered to the courtroom given the need for access to such exhibits in the trial preparation process. Many courts will permit advance delivery of exhibits on the Friday prior to trial and will keep those exhibits secure under lock and key prior to and during trial.

The author is a strong proponent of using an electronic courtroom support system with an on-site video operator. Such a system allows counsel to present all exhibits at trial on a large screen easily viewed by the court and jury including photographs, documents, video depositions, computer animations, and charts. This system eliminates the usual fumbling with old-fashioned enlarged exhibits or "blow-ups." The system's ability to highlight or enlarge certain parts of a photograph or text of a document promotes greater jury follow-along and interest. Counsel may display a particular exhibit only on the trial court's monitor where an admissibility ruling is required.

The setup of equipment necessary for that process requires advance measuring of the courtroom to assess the particular type and size of equipment needed and the optimum location for a projector screen if the courtroom is not already outfitted with one. It is prudent to conduct a run-through with the equipment as set up in the courtroom before its first use, usually in the opening statement. Seemingly minor details such as lighting, sound, placement of the equipment or use of a microphone may enhance or detract from the jury's ease of comprehension and such details need to be addressed.

Where particular transcripts of testimony or argument are desired, the court reporter should be advised as early as possible. Such requests may include the transcripts of testimony of key witnesses or one of the defendant's opening statements.

B. Dismissal of Non-Essential Defendants and Claims

As part of the final trial preparation process, counsel must take a hard look at all defendants and all claims for the purpose of winnowing out those which are non-essential, confusing, conflicting, or otherwise non-meritorious. Part of that process depends on the laws of the jurisdiction. In those states permitting an assignment of fault to non-parties at trial, counsel will need to strongly consider leaving such defendants in the case so that they will defend themselves and minimize the fault allocation vis-a-vis those primary defendants. Similarly, for those states with "vanishing venue" rules, the dismissal of a particular defendant may cost plaintiff the venue of choice. Absent these considerations, considering the inherent complexity of helicopter crash litigation the rule of thumb is simple: The fewer the defendants and claims, the better for plaintiff.

Final trial preparation is also the appropriate time to dismiss those theories of liability which are redundant, unnecessary or that allow for a potentially harmful affirmative defense. For example, where the pilot or the pilot's estate is a plaintiff and there are serious claims of pilot error in connection with some alleged airframe or component part failure, counsel should consider dismissing plaintiff's negligence count, as in many states that negates the comparative negligence defense in strict products liability actions. Claims against helicopter component part distributors or maintenance personnel that are thinner than old paint should be dismissed so as not to clog up the works for the main event.

But counsel must be wary of accepting minimal or insignificant settlement sums from any dismissed parties. This is another trap for the unwary as many states allow settling parties to remain on the verdict form for an allocation of fault whereas a party dismissed for no consideration would not appear on the verdict form. Having reviewed the case progression and the current liability posture it is now time to abandon those claims which were pleaded at the outset "just for safety's sake." It is also that time when counsel must elect to go with one of several factually inconsistent or mutually exclusive claims and jettison the rest. Nothing will alienate, much less confuse, a jury more than a plaintiff's factually inconsistent theories of a helicopter crash.

C. Witness Selection

The approaching trial date is also the time to think about culling the Plaintiffs' Witness List to those who actually will come and testify at the trial. It is one of the cardinal sins of trial lawyers that we tend to call far too many witnesses on the same issue. This is because of our inherent insecurity and desire to hammer home and "win" every single point. Over the course of many trials, jurors have routinely commented as to "why were so many witnesses called on the same subject?" The list should be ratcheted back and counsel should pick the best witness on a matter and leave it at that. The jury will appreciate it and they will be much more attentive realizing that this will be the only witness on that issue.

D. Editing Videotaped Deposition Testimony

If the case is developed using the methods outlined in this book, significant portions of videotaped deposition testimony will be presented to the jury. These edited depositions are comprised primarily of the various defendants' designated corporate representatives and employees but also include fact witnesses outside of the subpoena power of the court or who are otherwise unavailable at the time of trial.

The process of preparing and editing the deposition transcripts for presentation at trial is lengthy. Counsel for plaintiffs initially must designate by page and line number the specific transcript portions sought to be presented. Defendants then have an opportunity to counter-designate additional portions of the deposition transcript and to interpose objections to specific areas offered by the plaintiff. Plaintiff's counsel then has an opportunity to object to any of defendant's offered material. Finally, the court must rule on any objections to designated deposition transcripts which the parties are unable to resolve.

Counsel must request firm deadlines for all of these matters in the initial discovery scheduling or case management order. It is important to reserve sufficient time with the trial court in advance of trial to resolve any objections or other disputes relative to the presentation of these depositions. Counsel should try to avoid having to address these matters during trial as that can interfere with the orderly and persuasive witness presentation plan as well as consume valuable trial team time needed to prepare for the next day's witnesses. Some time must also be allotted to the video technician who will prepare the edited videotape on the basis of the parties' respective designations and court rulings.

9.2 Final Witness Preparation

Most of counsel's trial time in the days leading up to trial will be spent in outlining witness direct and cross-examinations as well as selecting which exhibits to be offered with what witness. Either in person or by telephone it is imperative to confer with all of counsel's witnesses who will testify live at trial.

A. Client Preparation for Trial

With all the hubbub of activity in the 30-60 days preceding a helicopter crash trial, counsel must not ignore the client. It is a stressful and uncertain time for those folks who have waited literally years for their day in court and now it is almost upon them. Clients must be reassured that counsel has everything under control and is fully prepared to take this matter to trial. Utmost trust and confidence in their counsel's preparedness helps avert the occasional "cold feet" clients feel as the trial date finally approaches. As most plaintiffs never will have stepped inside of a full courtroom it is the author's experience that the simple expedient of taking the client to the particular courtroom where the case will be tried allays much of the mystery and uncertainty. "That doesn't look so bad," most say after leaving the courtroom after having sat in the witness chair, the jury box and (if court is not in session and permission is granted) in the judge's chair with a view of all below.

Whatever frequency of contact counsel may have had with the clients up until that juncture, that contact should be increased in the days leading up to trial. The plaintiff's testimony is deserving of the same degree of preparedness as any other fact witness. Counsel should carefully go over each area of intended questions along with all photographs or other exhibits. The plaintiff also will be prepared as to defendant's cross-examination questions, if any. The client should receive regular updates as to the progress of trial preparation as well as any ongoing settlement negotiations.

B. Fact Witness Preparation for Trial

In the days leading up to trial, someone from the law firm should be in touch with each fact witness whom counsel intends to call live at trial. Many fact witnesses require a subpoena for their attendance in order to secure their absence from employment, and those should be served well in advance of trial. The witness should be provided with a copy of his deposition to refresh recollection of prior testimony. It may have been three to four years or longer since the helicopter crash and almost that long since their deposition testimony. Essential details may be forgotten. That is the last thing plaintiff's counsel needs when presenting fact witness testimony to the jury.

Counsel must exercise caution in preparing fact witnesses for their testimony, as whatever discussion takes place with such witnesses is not protected by work product or attorney client privileges. Counsel should advise all such witnesses that the single most important aspect of their testimony is simply to tell the truth.

Any photographs, maps, or models to be used with any fact witness must be reviewed before the courtroom event itself. The presence of a court and jury and a mostly full gallery jangles the nerves of most lay witnesses. It is simple to become disoriented by a simple topographical model or map that may have been seen only once previously and for which the witness was not comfortably oriented ahead of time.

C. Expert Witness Preparation for Trial

The arrival date for each of the expert witnesses will be planned and coordinated. In addition to one or more telephone conference calls with the experts, counsel will want a final run through on the evening before that expert's testimony to bring the expert up to date about any ongoing issues before the jury or particular concerns by the court. Any and all demonstrative aids or exhibits intended to be used with that expert must be shown to and reviewed by the expert ahead of time. During these final preparatory sessions counsel should pay particular attention to any portions of the expert's deposition that may potentially be taken out of context or otherwise used as fodder for defense impeachment.

9.3 Final Briefing Preparation
A. Motions in Limine

Plaintiffs must take full advantage of the opportunity to file extensive motions in limine as to any and all matters that should lawfully and properly be excluded from evidence at the trial. These include such routine matters as the improper mention of collateral sources, any insurance benefits received by plaintiff, or any specific opinions advanced by defense experts which are factually or legally unsupportable.

Other areas for which plaintiff's counsel should file a motion in limine to exclude any evidence, inference or argument are as follows.

1. Settlement Negotiations or Offers to Settle

In every state, any evidence of the parties attempting to settle or compromise a claim is not admissible.[1] The motion should be made to exclude that evidence directly or "hints or suggestions" by defense counsel to the effect that "obviously someone here is not being reasonable or we would not have to go through this" as those comments indirectly reference failed settlement negotiations.

2. Reference to the NTSB Probable Cause Report

Pursuant to federal statute, no part of the Probable Cause Report of the NTSB "may be admitted into evidence or used in a civil action for damages resulting from a matter mentioned in the report."[2] Counsel must make certain that the motion includes not only the content of the NTSB Probable Cause Report but any reference to its very existence as to do so would be prejudicial to plaintiffs who presumably

would have admitted it if it were helpful to plaintiff's cause. As addressed elsewhere, the NTSB Factual Report is commonly admissible.[3]

3. Potential Financial Burden of An Adverse Verdict On Any Defendants or Reference to Limited Assets or Wealth

Defendants should be prohibited from making any reference or comment to the effect that a judgment would burden them or that they have limited assets with which to satisfy any judgment. This is especially so where defendants have sizeable insurance coverage which would insulate them from any financial obligation. Any comment or inference by defense counsel to the contrary should trigger a request for immediate retaliatory evidence disclosing the insurance coverage amounts to the jury by plaintiff's counsel. Courts have universally ruled that defense counsel may not argue that a substantial award of compensatory damages against the defendant would cause a financial hardship.[4]

4. Plaintiff's Attorney's Fees or That Plaintiff's Attorneys Have a Contingency in the Recovery

Defendants should not be permitted to argue or imply that plaintiff's attorneys have any contingency or interest in the recovery of the case. The vast majority of courts will hold such argument to be improper as it is irrelevant and would only tend to prejudice the plaintiff and serve no purpose in advancing any of the issues in dispute.

5. That Any Damages Awarded Would Not Be Subject to Taxes

In the vast majority of jurisdictions any evidence or argument to the effect that a damages award to plaintiffs would or would not be subject to taxes is properly excluded.[5] Plaintiff's counsel must move to exclude any argument, evidence or inference to the effect that a damages award would not be taxable under the laws of the forum jurisdiction. As punitive damages are taxable, requesting the court to exclude any reference one way or the other is the preferred approach.

6. Expressions of Sorrow, Remorse or Apology By Helicopter Crash Defendants

In most jurisdictions, expressions or evidence of a defendant's regret are recognized as intending to only elicit sympathy of the jury and are improper.[6] Plaintiff's counsel must make sure that that includes not only an expression of sorrow by the defendants but also by defense counsel themselves. Such expressions of personal opinions or counsel's feelings also are barred by the Rules of Professional Conduct in most states.[7]

7. That the Trial or Civil Justice System is a "Lottery" or "Crapshoot" or "Monopoly Game" or Similar Language Intended to Impart Unflattering Intentions to Plaintiffs

Increasingly it has been the practice for defense counsel in wrongful death and serious personal injury lawsuits to argue to the jury that the trial is simply a "lottery" implying that the process is solely one of gamesmanship or money-seeking. Such commentary is universally denounced as unlawful and improper as it demeans and degrades the trial process and is prejudicial to the plaintiff. Many courts have found such defense statements comparing the lawsuit to "playing the lottery" as grossly improper. These include references to plaintiffs "playing lotto" or "power ball" or "rolling the dice."[8] Courts have held that such arguments demean "not only the plaintiff but also the judicial system itself" and denigrate "the fairness, integrity and public perception of the judicial system."[9]

Other courts have ruled that "counsel's characterization of the plaintiffs' case as cashing in on a lottery ticket" are similarly unlawful and improper.[10] Similarly, a Louisiana court found that the defense lawyer's suggestion that the trial "is not the lottery" was "improper and did appeal to passion and prejudice."[11] These types of defense arguments are intended to imply that the justice system is a game of chance and that the plaintiff is a gambler. They improperly appealed to the passion and prejudice of the jury and, for these reasons, they are universally excoriated by courts.

8. Argument By Defense Counsel That We Live in a "Litigious Society" or "Sue Happy Society"

Implications, statements, or assertions by defense lawyers that we live in a "litigious society" or words to that effect have no place in a helicopter crash trial or any other trial and should be excluded. Courts have found that comments derogatory and demeaning about a plaintiff's lawful use of the civil justice system are grossly improper and are essentially defense efforts to seek "impermissible jury nullification."[12] Defense counsel's remarks that people are "looking for an excuse to sue someone at the drop of a hat" and that "Americans have become a society of blamers" were improper because:

> [Defendant's] arguments suggested to the jurors that, regardless of the evidence, if the jury found in the defendants' favors, the jury could remedy the social ills of frivolous lawsuits. Essentially, [defendant] asked the jury to "send a message" about frivolous lawsuits. His arguments were directed at

causing the jurors to harbor disdain for the civil jury process—a defining, foundational characteristic of our legal system—and at perpetuating a misconception that most personal injury cases are unfounded and brought in bad faith by unscrupulous lawyers. These arguments were irrelevant to the cases at hand and improper in a court of law and constitute a clear attempt at jury nullification.[13]

Similarly, defense lawyers referring to America as an "over-lawyered litigious, sue-happy country" and referring to a "litigation industry" were found to be "unprofessional, offensive, and exceeded the proper bounds of trial advocacy."[14] A Connecticut court recently condemned a defense lawyer's remarks that the plaintiff was "sue happy" and was looking for a "handout" and that the jury should "send a message to the public by not granting or rewarding dollars to this plaintiff so that we won't have this type of activity."[15] In similar fashion, a Florida court held that defense counsel "played on general fears and prejudices of the jury by evoking images of runaway verdicts and frivolous lawsuits and their effect on the American system of justice."[16]

Such comments have no place in this type of litigation and counsel must file a careful motion to exclude such inflammatory remarks. At any point in the trial, a defense lawyer commenting on the litigious nature of society implies that plaintiff's case is just one of many and has no merit. Such arguments also attack the integrity of the justice system implying that it promotes frivolous lawsuits. Counsel must zealously be on guard for any comments during the trial which remotely hint of such a comment and immediately approach the bench and seek appropriate relief from the court.

9. Defense Expert Opinions for Which That Expert is Not Qualified

Prior to trial, plaintiff's counsel must carefully review the opinions expressed by defense experts in their deposition and determine which are unsupported by that witness's education, training or experience. In a recent case, one helicopter defendant called to trial an accident reconstruction expert who was not qualified in the field of helicopter aerodynamics. At his deposition, the witness testified as follows:

Q. (By Mr. Robb): But you're not considered, and don't consider yourself an expert on helicopter aerodynamics, do you sir?

A. I would say probably not.

Q. You don't consider yourself an expert in the principles of helicopter flight, do you sir?

A. No sir.

On the basis of the above testimony, the court ruled that the defense expert was not qualified to give opinions either on helicopter aerodynamics or the principles of helicopter flight.

Other than the above subject matters which are commonly anticipated and encountered, counsel should consider all potential evidence and seek to exclude that specific evidence or defense lawyer arguments which are either outside of the evidence or specifically to be excluded as unlawful and improper.

B. Trial Brief

Counsel should recognize that the lawsuit probably will be the court's first trial of a helicopter crash case and maybe the first aviation case of any kind. A well-organized and carefully researched trial brief will be particularly helpful to the trial judge hearing her first aviation lawsuit. The function of the trial brief should be to apprise the trial court of the specific theories of liability upon which plaintiff intends to submit the case to the jury as against each defendant and a summary of the admissible evidence supporting each element of that theory.

At this point in time on literally the eve of trial, counsel should not be concerned with alerting or tipping off the defense as to any particular evidence or legal theory. It is a safe bet that defense counsel will at that juncture know plaintiff's case as well as plaintiff's counsel. Although some lawyers prefer not to divulge such information to the adversary, it has been the author's experience that laying out in summary fashion the expected evidence for the trial court is beneficial. The days of Perry Mason surprise witnesses or evidence are long gone. By setting out plaintiff's legal and evidentiary roadmap for the trial court, counsel demonstrates a high degree of confidence and trust in the merits of the action.

That brief also must address and itemize all of the damages elements and specify all economic losses where applicable. In this context a trial brief is a pleading specially drafted for submission to the court just prior to trial. It is not to be confused with the type of trial brief prepared on an anticipated legal issue such as the admissibility of particular evidence which counsel has in readiness to present to the court during trial. Most judges greatly appreciate a simple and non-argumentative trial brief which succinctly sets out the applicable law and anticipated evidence.

Many courts require the parties to submit proposed jury instructions in advance of trial. Those instructions will set out the various elements within each legal theory and provide a convenient organizing platform for the trial brief. For example, as to the element that the defendant component manufacturer designed and manufactured the subject prod-

uct, plaintiff may reference excerpts from the deposition of that defendant's corporate representative wherein he confirmed that the company specifically designed and manufactured the component which had been installed on the subject helicopter. Setting out the elements in the trial brief provides a convenient submissible case checklist for the court to reference when ruling on the defendant's motions for directed verdict at the close of plaintiff's case.

On a practical note, the trial brief should not be so lengthy and detailed that the trial court would not have sufficient time to read it. A suggested length for a fully adequate trial brief is anywhere from 10-20 pages. Where the trial court is given a contextual framework with reference to particular disputed evidence, the court may be more inclined to comprehend the persuasive value of that proof where attached to its probative point.

The purpose of the trial brief is twofold. It is to educate the court as to the basic factual record and legal theory, and, secondly, is a persuasive tool to induce the court to rule favorably on disputed submissibility or evidentiary matters. It is as important to advise the trial court of those factual legal matters as to which there is no dispute as it is to outline those matters which are contested. Usually the court's case management order will include some deadline for submission of a pre-trial memorandum or trial brief to the court. However, in those instances where there is no court order or local rule for the filing of trial briefs, the ordinary complexity and novelty of helicopter crash cases demand it.

Counsel can be assured that defendants will file a trial brief to the court as to their theories and defenses and the court's reference to that one-sided document must be counteracted. This is particularly important where the trial court has little or no involvement in any of the discovery or other pre-trial proceedings such as where a magistrate or motion judge supervises and manages pre-trial litigation and resolves discovery disputes. Or where the trial judge is only assigned after the close of discovery. The trial brief may then be the trial court's first detailed introduction to the lawsuit other than knowing that it involves a helicopter crash with attendant wrongful deaths.

The trial brief must be written with knowledge of who the trial judge will be. If the trial judge is well versed on the ordinary products liability law of that jurisdiction, there is no need to reference that law in detail, and counsel's so doing may alienate the court. On the other hand, counsel may assume that the trial judge is not intimately familiar with the facts of the case and those may be discussed in the context of the applicable legal theories. It has been useful to provide headings in the trial brief so that the trial judge can pick and choose those areas she wishes to reference. A common organization of a trial brief utilized in these cases is as follows:

1. General Statement of the Case
2. Uncontested or Admitted Issues of Fact
3. Plaintiff's Theories of Liability
4. Affirmative Defenses
5. Anticipated Legal Theory Disputes
6. Anticipated Evidentiary Disputes
7. Summary of Facts in Support of Legal Theory
8. Applicability of Certain Statutes or Regulations
9. Matters for Judicial Notice
10. Applicable Presumptions and Burden of Proof
11. Elements of Plaintiff's Damages

A concise and well-written trial brief will provide a factual and legal framework for the trial court's various decision-making and apprise the court of any matters for which either the court or a clerk would desire additional research.

C. Trial Memoranda

Although arbitrary, most lawyers and judges recognize the difference between a trial brief and trial memoranda. Trial memoranda are those one-page briefs covering one discreet issue of law that may be expected to be disputed and which counsel predict will arise at some point during the trial. When the issue comes up, counsel presents the one-page trial memorandum to the trial judge on that disputed issue.

It is commonplace that a trial memorandum succinctly sets out the legal issue with no more than one or two cases directly on point and, preferably, decided by a controlling court within that jurisdiction. There is no limit other than counsel's imagination to the number of these single issue memoranda which may be prepared in advance of trial. The author maintains a tab in a pre-trial notebook for such trial memoranda and throughout pre-trial discovery proceedings jots down ideas for which later legal research is performed. It not uncommon to have 50 or more trial memoranda "at the ready" in these cases.

Examples of some trial memoranda used in recent air-crash trials are as follows:

1. PLAINTIFF'S TRIAL MEMORANDUM ON ADMISSIBILITY OF NTSB FACTUAL REPORTS

The NTSB Factual Report is a self-authenticating document pursuant to V.A.M.S. § 490.220. This is a specific statute in Missouri that encompasses public records for official documents of the United States. The section provides that:

> All records and exemplifications of office books, kept in any public office of the United States, or of a sister state, not appertaining to a court, shall be evidence in this state, if attested by the keeper of said record or books, and the seal of his office, if there be a seal.

V.A.M.S. 490.220 (R.S.Mo. 1994)

The Missouri Supreme Court has held that § 490.220 eliminates the foundational requirements of authentication, best evidence, and hearsay with respect to certain public documents. *Hancock v. Director of Revenue*, 860 S.W.2d 335, 337 (Mo. 1983). In *Hancock*, the Court held that "so long as the requirements of the statute are met and the records are relevant, they are admissible" *Id.*

In that all of the NTSB factual reports are official government documents bearing the seal of the United States government, they should be considered by this Court. Accordingly, a report of a U.S. government agency under seal is regarded as genuine and admissible for all purposes.

WHEREFORE, for the above-stated reasons, the NTSB factual findings should be admitted by this Court for the purposes intended and for such other uses as are just and proper.

2. PLAINTIFF'S TRIAL MEMORANDUM ON ADMISSIBILITY OF DEFENDANT'S WITHDRAWAL OF ALLEGEDLY DEFECTIVE COMPONENT PARTS FROM HELICOPTER MARKET

In Missouri, evidence about subsequent remedial events is relevant and admissible in strict liability cases. *Barnett v. La Societe Anonyme Turbomeca*, 963 S.W.2d 639, 651 (Mo. App. 1997). Such evidence bears directly on whether the product is "unreasonably dangerous." *Stinson v. E.I. dupont de Nemours & Co.*, 904 S.W.2d 428, 432 (Mo. App. 1995). The Court of Appeals for the Western District has held that it is reversible error to exclude such evidence in a strict liability case. *Id.* at 432-33.

Logic dictates that a manufacturer's recall of its product or withdrawal from the market is one kind of subsequent remedial measure covered by the Missouri rule. The jury can certainly infer that the withdrawal of a profitable product from the market is an acknowledgment that there is something wrong with that product—i.e., that it is defective.

Two cases involving tampons that caused toxic shock syndrome illustrate the rule. In *Wolf by Wolf v. Proctor & Gamble Co.*, 555 F.Supp. 613 (D.N.J. 1982), defendant voluntarily withdrew the product from the market. The Court found that this constituted a "subsequent remedial measure." *Id.* at 623. The law in the Third Circuit at that time excluded such evidence, even in strict liability cases, so the Court excluded evidence of the recall.

But the opinion clearly acknowledged that other jurisdictions, like the Eighth Circuit (and Missouri) admit such evidence in strict liability cases. When the Eighth Circuit considered the same issue involving the same manufacturer, therefore, it reached the opposite result. *Kehm v. Proctor & Gamble Mfg. Co.*, 724 F.2d 613 (8th Cir. 1983), held that such evidence was admissible and the manufacturer was not entitled to a limiting instruction:

> The withdrawal of Rely from the market is inextricably bound up with Proctor & Gamble's credibility and its portrait of itself as a corporation concerned only for the public's welfare. It would only obscure the issues to instruct the jury to regard the fact of withdrawal as mere "background," when Proctor & Gamble itself made the voluntariness of its withdrawal a part of its attempt to show that it acted responsibly during the TSS crisis.

> 724 F.2d at 622.

Complete withdrawal from the market is simply a more extreme form of product recall. Cases in jurisdictions that allow evidence of subsequent remedial measures in strict liability cases allow evidence of recalls. *E.g.*, *Farnar v. Paccar, Inc.*, 562 F.2d 518, 527 (8th Cir. 1977) (recall letter was "probative both of the existence of a design defect in the Farnar vehicle and of the negligent failure to warn of known dangers"); *Longenecker v. General Motors Corp.*, 594 F.2d 1283, 1286 (9th Cir. 1979) (recall "letter was relevant evidence that there was a flaw in the mounts"). The same is true of Defendant's withdrawal of this product from the market. That is circumstantial evidence that it was defective and the jury is entitled to consider it as such.

WHEREFORE, for the above-stated reasons, evidence that the defendant has subsequently withdrawn its products from the aviation marketplace should be admitted by this Court for all proper purposes.

The effectiveness of trial memoranda is the result of their focus and brevity. When the evidentiary dispute arises in the middle of trial and counsel are able to immediately provide to the trial court a simple and straightforward trial memorandum on the precise issue of law, it is comforting to the trial court, and the resultant ruling should be comfortable to plaintiff's counsel as well.

9.4 Request for Sequestration of Witnesses

Plaintiff's counsel also should file a timely request for sequestration of witnesses with the court to exclude all witnesses from the courtroom during the testimony of any other witnesses. Most states provide that such a request will be granted upon the request of any party. For example under the Arkansas Rules of Evidence:

> At the request of a party the court shall order witnesses excluded so that they cannot hear the testimony of other witnesses, and it may make the order of its own motion.[17]

Allowing experts to sit in the courtroom is particularly prejudicial to plaintiffs given the fact that plaintiff's presentation of evidence goes first. It is a major advantage for the defense to have its experts present in the courtroom for the testimony of plaintiff's experts because they will be able to comment directly on that expert's testimony and also provide assistance to defense counsel for cross-examination of plaintiff's experts. Plaintiff will have no opportunity to question these defense experts as to what criticisms they may have of plaintiff's expert's trial testimony. Allowing defense experts in the courtroom to hear testimony of other defense experts presents an opportunity to coordinate the defense testimony, which should not be permitted. Plaintiff's counsel can often point out the inconsistencies of the various defense expert opinions to discredit that testimony.

9.5 Use of Jury Focus Group and Jury Consultants

In helicopter crash litigation as for any complex litigation the use of jury focus groups and jury consultants has become a must. Counsel have been working on these cases for years and the jargon comes swimmingly off the tongue. Use of jury focus groups will pinpoint areas of the case where the jury becomes hopelessly lost and confused. Areas where the proof is thought to be unconvincing or unpersuasive can be shored up in advance of trial.

Jury focus groups are particularly useful in criticizing incomprehensible exhibits whether they are confusing documents, helicopter maintenance manual diagrams or photographs. So many of the visual aids we lawyers like to use at trial actually cause, rather than lessen, jury confusion. Whereas many lawyers take the position that if the money and time were spent to create the exhibit they are going to use it, that is obviously not the proper reference point. Any particular exhibit that passes muster with a jury focus group and is one that they first understand and second appreciate its persuasive value as part of plaintiff's case should be kept and, preferably, given a greater role in the proceedings.

In today's world of jury focus groups, a highly sophisticated selection process assures that a demographic of 30-35 people will be a representative and predictive population of the actual constituted jury panel. This is a study unto itself, but unless the focus group is properly selected and shares the socioeconomic and other critical demographic factors with the community's jury pool, the resultant feedback and other information will be worthless.

Most focus group coordinators will videotape all of the sessions. That is enormously helpful for counsel to study and analyze the juror's reactions to different arguments and evidence presented. As to the content of the case material presented, there is no value in presenting plaintiff's strongest case and "winning" the jury focus group trial. In this respect, evidence must intentionally be altered in the following respects. Plaintiff's evidence should be presented in an understated way with the principal and most persuasive evidence outlined but not beaten to death. The defendant's absolute best case and even more so should be constructed. In that manner, plaintiff will obtain the most usable information possible which is how to defeat and overcome the defendant's best possible case.

It is highly recommended that jury focus groups be conducted toward the end of discovery but not after the close of discovery for one reason: any potential factual black holes in plaintiff's proof are still potentially fillable prior to the close of discovery. Whether that is a particular liability or fact witness who had heretofore been thought either unnecessary or redundant, the result of the focus group may convince counsel otherwise.

Most focus group coordinators also will work as jury consultants during jury selection. That has proved immensely helpful as they already have an excellent understanding of the case issues and can use that knowledge to better assist in actual juror evaluation.

9.6 Development of Case Theme for Trial

As is true in any trial, evidence wins helicopter crash cases. And the plaintiff's best evidence should be highlighted. Whether that is a critical admission from the helicopter pilot or a key memorandum from the airframe manufacturer, that best evidence should be tied in to the key issue in the case. The best case theme sets out the key issue and answers it with the plaintiff's best evidence. The development of a case theme for trial on behalf of the plaintiff requires a proactive determination of what the key issue in the case is and highlights plaintiff's most powerful proof in support of that issue. This approach of developing an evidence-specific case theme for trial involves a global litigation philosophy on behalf of the plaintiff which relates to and impacts all aspects of the trial, from voir dire to and through closing argument.

A. Case Theme Examples

Within the context of helicopter accident litigation there are numerous potential case themes but this is not a situation where "one size fits all." The case theme must be precisely molded to fit the particular facts and, most importantly, the admissible evidence in that case. Some examples are as follows.

1. "If It Ain't Broke, Don't Fix It."

The author has used this case theme in helicopter cases where the component part manufacturer has made a significant alteration in the design of the component or system post crash which renders it safer. In that most jurisdictions allow

evidence of subsequent remedial measures especially within the context of a strict products liability theory, that evidence is by itself powerful and incriminating. But counsel cannot simply introduce the evidence and walk away. That evidence must fit within the context of a story or theme. The theme and the take-away message is that the manufacturer would not have gone to the time, trouble and expense of a design improvement if it had not needed the safer design to begin with.

2. "The Helicopter Manufacturer Ran a Red Light."

In many cases this is and should be the plaintiff's case theme where there is evidence that a helicopter manufacturer or component part maker violated recognized industry standards, as those standards are set forth either in published regulations or by expert testimony. The theme is powerful because of its simplicity: all jurors will understand what it means to run a traffic light. Counsel must carry through this theme throughout the trial and hammer home that the consequences of violating the industry standard are the same as running a red light.

3. "You Break It, You Pay For It."

This is the case theme in helicopter crash cases where a key component such as a main or tail rotor blade or other critical safety component is returned to service in a non-airworthy condition. For example, in a recent case a helicopter maintenance facility purported to repair a main rotor blade. That MRB was re-installed on a helicopter containing cracks along the leading edge. It disintegrated in flight killing all aboard.

This easily understandable case theme also brings into play the adequacy of the damage award. The helicopter maintenance facility's negligence should result in their obligation to fully account for the losses.

4. "When You Point To Someone Else, Three Fingers Point Back At You."

This is often the case theme where a defendant in a helicopter crash case seeks to avert responsibility by shifting the blame to co-defendants. It is most effective where the liability proof as against the target defendant is strong such that defendant's efforts to "shift the blame" appear desperate and unavailing. This case theme is not advisable where that defendant alleges negligence of the plaintiff. The defendant may make the same charge about plaintiff's finger-pointing.

5. "Do As I Say, Not As I Do."

This theme has been used where the defendant fails to follow its own internal policies and procedures or those set forth in its own maintenance manual. It is an available theme where a helicopter operator has an FAA-approved inspection program that it expects everyone else to follow, except it.

6. "Don't Bother Me With The Facts."

Evidence that the helicopter component manufacturer had actual knowledge of numerous incidents prior to the injury-producing accident in question will support this case theme. Counsel may point out as a corollary that there is no more impactful information that a manufacturer could receive than that its product in the marketplace was failing and injuring people. Failure to act upon that information is inexcusable. Such a defendant literally closes its ears to this information and fails to act upon it.

7. "Johnny Didn't Break The Lamp, But…"

This is a case theme based on the well-known story of Johnny's explanation to his parents about why their favorite lamp was broken while they were away. "I know nothing about how the lamp broke," Johnny told his parents. "But even if I did break it, I didn't damage it that bad." That is often the defendant's position. They did not cause the helicopter crash, but if they did and if it killed or injured somebody, then the damages are not really that bad.

Trying a helicopter crash case without a case theme is akin to erecting a building without architectural drawings. The case must have some thread weaving through all of the evidence which explains its relevance in the overall scheme. Simply presenting the case in a linear and predictable fashion to the jury is a mistake. The case theme is a simple and common sense declaration of the key dispute in the case. The case theme sets forth the plaintiff's view as to that precise issue as compellingly as possible. In this respect, the central purpose of the case theme is to define the critical issue in the case and to highlight the plaintiff's most compelling proof as to why plaintiff should prevail on that issue.

Even though the case theme should be carefully crafted and tailored for the particular case, a number of common categories of case themes tend to emerge where a critical issue is identified and plaintiff's proof on that issue is highlighted. Some categories of this type of case theme are as follows.

B. Case Theme Reversing Principle Weakness in Case

In many cases, the defendant may perceive a critical weakness or void in plaintiff's case. Naturally, the defendant will seek to exploit that weakness and seek to undermine plaintiff's entire case in the process. One example is where a defendant seeks to blame the helicopter pilot for failing to effectuate a safe landing after experiencing an in-flight mal-

function of some sort such as engine failure. This defense tactic commonly occurs and the author has pushed back in this respect: which party was in the better position and had the most time to address this situation as between the helicopter component manufacturer and the helicopter pilot? In one case the author pointed out that the defendant manufacturer had been designing the component at issue for 8 years. The pilot had a total reaction and response time of about 20 seconds. The following excerpt from an actual closing argument delivered by the author demonstrates this principle:

> So what did Mr. Tavourou say? He gave you the party line about how to handle that situation. And he said, it's not our responsibility. We expect the pilot to handle it. That's what he said in a video.
>
> But, you know, in this case there is no issue concerning whether or not Mr. Bales did or did not do anything he's supposed to do concerning the autorotation. So what are we really talking about here? You know what we're talking about. We're talking about a company that did nothing for 8 years with full knowledge of the facts of the dangerous defective part, and how much time did they give Jim Bales to solve the problem?
>
> You know, I did this the other night. It was kind of interesting. If some of you have a second hand, I invite you to follow along with me because let's just see what happens in 20 seconds. Starting with engine failure and there's engine failure and he's looking around, there's some trees, 5 seconds. Looking for a place to land, operating the cyclic and collective, 10 seconds. Getting close to the trees, operating as carefully as he can, the engine going down, the helicopter is decelerating, 15 seconds. Going down over the trees, finally, impact. That's the amount of time they gave Jim Bales. That's it. 20 seconds. They had 8 years to sit around a table and do nothing and if that's not conscious disregard, nothing is.

One particularly effective use of an evidence-specific case theme is to lure the defendant into that position. The technique is so effective because both the plaintiff and defendant agree that this particular issue is the key issue in the case. Use of this method renders it imperative that plaintiff's evidence as to this issue be impressive and overwhelming.

C. Case Theme Focusing on Specific Impact of Injury

This technique is extremely effective in presenting a helicopter crash case where the nature of the injury is a direct result of the specific negligence or design defect at issue.

For example, in cases of severe burn injury due either to improper placement or inadequate lining and protection of the helicopter fuel tank, the best exhibit for the inadequacy of the design is the condition of the plaintiff himself. In such cases, it is remarkable how little time the defendants wish to address or even reference the plaintiff or his injuries. They would rather have the jury forget that this is a severe burn injury case because that only highlights and focuses the jury's attention on the defective fuel tank.

D. Case Theme Directly Contrary to the Main Defense

This is one of the author's favorite approaches to developing case themes. It is based on the principle that "defendant doth protest too much." There are two aspects in the development of this case theme that render it unique. First, the plaintiff takes the cue from the defendant as to what the primary defense will be and thoroughly investigates and explores all avenues throughout the informal and formal discovery process to find evidence contrary to that position. Second, the approach involves plaintiff's committing the defendant to that position in the testimony of its employees, principals, experts, and other witnesses in addition to taking that position in answers to formal discovery and court pleadings.

For example, in many cases the helicopter manufacturer will point out that "we tested and we tested." The problem typically lies in the fact that while the defendant tested they did not do the appropriate tests and did not learn from the tests that were conducted. Plaintiff's most effective response is to point out, "why do they test?" Was it only to provide an excuse that would insulate them from liability in a lawsuit or to genuinely and sincerely improve the product?

For example, plaintiff's case theme in a lawsuit claiming inadequate or improper testing is: "the purpose of product testing is to enhance safety." Admissions to that effect may be obtained from defendant's engineering witnesses as well as defendant's liability experts. Where defendant conducted extensive testing for litigation purposes only, it may be pointed out that such testing is not for purposes of enhancing public safety but for protecting the financial and legal interests of the company.

The case theme in any helicopter crash case should highlight evidence that has the greatest potential to independently determine the outcome of the case. The specificity of the evidence-based case theme enhances the credibility of the plaintiff's case. The true measure of a powerful case theme is that it serves to unravel the defense, by thoroughly discrediting the defendant's own theory of the case in a simple and easily understandable way. The particular evidence that should be highlighted in the plaintiff's case theme may

consist of witness testimony, a particularly incriminating document, or physical evidence such as the defective helicopter part, or any combination thereof. One of the chief advantages of the recommended approach is to convince the court and jury that this helicopter trial is a special case deserving of special attention and interest and, ultimately, a special result.

9.7 Jury Instructions
A. General Considerations

The single most important feature of the jury instructions, especially as to those setting out the essential elements for recovery on any claim, is that they must be clear and understandable. Confusion and complexity are the defendant's best friends. Any liability-directing instruction which has the potential for permitting a jury to "trip up" and deliver either an unintended or inconsistent verdict must be averted at all costs. Key terms must be well defined. Cases are legion where a jury is unable to understand a term and improperly seeks clarification by impermissible means such as looking up the term in a dictionary or on a website. Such calamities will result in the loss of the entire trial time and effort, as a new trial would be forthcoming. Counsel may never assume that juries will use the common or standard definition of any particular word or phrase.

Many courts require the parties to file and exchange proposed jury instructions prior to the start of trial. This should present little challenge to plaintiff's counsel who will have been working with a full set of jury instructions throughout the case. The verdict directing instructions or list of elements required for each submitted legal theory also form a convenient submissible case checklist in advance of trial. Counsel must use the instructions as a check on presenting sufficient admissible evidence as to each required element of the case.

Most states have generated court-approved pattern jury instructions. The liability instructions on theories of negligence, strict products liability, warranty or misrepresentation will apply in straightforward fashion to the circumstances of almost any helicopter crash lawsuit. A frequent basis for appeal and even reversal of trial court judgments is some alleged error or impropriety with the jury instructions. That warrants taking particular care in the framing of the instructions so as to be in accordance with applicable law, and any extensions or extrapolations should be considered with great caution. For that reason counsel should carefully consider the offered or alternative defense instructions and should give careful thought to specific objections to jury instructions raised by the defense.

As with other aspects of trial, simplicity of the jury instructions is the preferred approach and that means winnowing down defendants and claims. Due to the length and complexity of these trials, some courts will give several "mini-instructions" at the outset of the trial so that the jury will have some notion of the legal claims to be submitted to them at the close of all of the evidence.

B. Standard Jury Instructions

Most jurisdictions follow a standardized order of jury instructions along the following:

1. General Jury Instructions

These set out the respective duties of the court and jury, describe the appropriate burden of proof in a civil case along with how the jury is to consider certain evidence such as opinion evidence, credibility of witnesses or deposition testimony.

2. Elements of Recovery

These instructions detail the essential factual findings to recover on each theory of liability.

3. Affirmative Defenses

Any defenses for which the defendant has the burden of proof are normally set out directly after the plaintiff's liability recoverable elements.

4. Punitive Damages Liability

Where the trial court elects to submit the issue of punitive damages liability to the jury those instructions normally will fall after affirmative defenses and prior to the compensatory damages elements. More and more jurisdictions are bifurcating the issue of punitive liability from the determination of damages. The primary reason is to preclude the jury's hearing evidence of the financial condition or net worth of the defendant which is admitted solely on the issue of punitive damages.

5. Damages Elements

Most civil jury instructions will have fairly detailed descriptions of the recoverable elements of damages normally given in one instruction for economic damages and a separate one for non-economic damages.

6. Procedure and Manner of Deliberations Instructions

The next set of instructions apply to the manner of organization and deliberations and include the duty to elect a foreperson, the ability to review exhibits which were admitted during the trial, and the number of jurors required to constitute a verdict.

7. Form of Verdict

The jury will be given the verdict sheet, which is the document where the verdict is recorded and signatures of the requisite number of jurors entered.

C. Examples of Jury Instructions

An example of jury instructions used in a recent helicopter crash case tried to verdict by the author include the following.

1. Instruction as to Statement of Case

Members of the jury: In this case, plaintiff claims that her husband was killed in a helicopter accident as a result of the fault of the defendants. Her specific claims as to each defendant are as follows:

As to defendants Smith, Jones and Wilson, plaintiff claims that they used improper and unsafe practices for the use of the helicopter in aerial cinematography. Specifically, plaintiff claims that defendants failed to require the pilot to conduct an aerial or ground surveillance of the intended flight path, failed to advise him prior to the flight of the intended flight path, failed to provide a qualified air safety coordinator, failed to advise the pilot that there were utility wires in the intended flight path, and selected an unsafe location for the aerial cinematography.

As to defendant Pilot, plaintiff claims that he was negligent in the operation of the helicopter. Specifically, plaintiff claims that the pilot flew the helicopter into horizontal utility wires.

The defendants and each of them deny plaintiff's claims.

Do not consider this summary as proof of any claim. Decide the facts from the evidence and apply the law which I will give you in the case.

2. Instruction as to Film Company Negligence

An example from that same trial of a jury instruction setting out the essential elements for recovery as against a film production company is as follows:

In order to recover on her claim of negligence as against defendant film production company, the plaintiff must prove all of the following propositions:

1. Defendant was negligence in one or more of the following ways:
    a. Defendant failed to inform the pilot of the presence of the utility wires in the intended flight path of the helicopter; or
    b. Defendant failed to require the pilot to conduct either a ground or aerial surveillance of the intended flight path; or
    c. Defendant selected an unsafe location for the aerial filming

2.   The negligence was a proximate cause of damage to the plaintiff.

3.   The amount of damage.

If the plaintiff has failed to prove any of these propositions, the plaintiff is not entitled to damages. If the plaintiff has proved all of these propositions, the plaintiff is entitled to damages in some amount.

3. Instruction as to Pilot Negligence

The instruction used on plaintiff's claim of negligence as against the helicopter pilot was as follows:

In order to recover on her claim of negligence as against defendant Pilot, plaintiff must prove all of the following propositions:

1.   The defendant Pilot was negligent in one or more of the following ways:

  a.   Defendant flew the helicopter into horizontal utility wires; or

  b.   Defendant failed to see and observe horizontal utility lines in his intended flight path.

2.   The negligence was a proximate cause of damage to the plaintiff.

3.   The amount of damage.

If the plaintiff has failed to prove any of these propositions, the plaintiff is not entitled to damages. If the plaintiff has proved all of these propositions, the plaintiff is entitled to damages in some amount.

In those cases where claims of pilot error survive various directed verdict motions and are presented to the jury in combination with an in-flight mechanical malfunction, counsel for the plaintiff pilot or the pilot's decedents may wish to consider submission of a sudden emergency instruction. Just as in any other situation, a pilot is held to the standard of care of others "in the same or similar circumstances." That standard of care means that the actions of pilots in emergency conditions should not be judged in comparison with those pilots facing non-emergency situations. Even in those jurisdictions which do not provide for such an instruction, the argument can and should be made that the jury should assess the conduct of the pilot within the full context of the circumstances present at that time.

As in any lawsuit, counsel should frame many of the questions to the experts in terms of the specific language of the jury instruction. That is important so that the first time the jury reads these terms and phrases within the instructions they are not totally foreign and the jury will be well familiar with the concepts.

9.8 Settlement Considerations

Not until the case discovery is drawing to a close are the major legal disputes in the typical helicopter accident lawsuit known or resolved sufficiently to evaluate the case, although some may not be decided until the eve of or during trial itself. Although some preliminary settlement talks may have occurred unproductively early in the case, the close of discovery represents the best time to realistically evaluate the liability risks and potential jury verdict now that the day to day focus on discovery and motion practice is gone.

Defendants in aviation cases as in any other personal injury or wrongful death litigation often adhere to the belief that financial pressure in addition to the plaintiff's fear of going to trial will induce settlement of a case for far less than its true value. Once the discovery process is complete and plaintiff is literally at the courthouse steps, defendant's tune will have changed markedly. For it is then clear that plaintiff is ready, willing, able and prepared to proceed to trial.

As with any other case, the first rule of thumb to consider is that the lawsuit belongs to the client and not counsel. The decision to settle the lawsuit belongs to the client with the advice of counsel.[18] Whereas the client has been kept up to date about the progress of discovery and other significant developments the client will share an appreciation of some of the potential risks involved in proceeding to trial. By so doing, the client will also be aware of the strengths of the case and be buoyed to go to trial where the case is sound on the merits. The author's experience in many such instances is that the client, following years of heated discovery battles, is not only willing to proceed to trial but also most desirous of doing so.

It is during these settlement evaluation discussions that all of the confidence and trust between lawyer and client are most manifested. One of the tools in assessing case value are the results of the jury focus groups in comparable socio-demographic populations. Counsel also must consider the risks of any potentially dispositive motions if potentially applicable. In that respect, notwithstanding counsel's desire to proceed to trial for professional or other reasons, the client's interest is paramount and a reasonable and appropriate settlement is normally in the client's best interests.

There are as many approaches to settling a lawsuit as there are plaintiff's lawyers. The constant which plaintiff's counsel must address is that the relatively small size of the aviation defense bar means that counsel will repeatedly run into the same defense lawyers. Unrealistic or extravagant settlement proposals or positions taken in one case may impair the credibility of counsel down the road and are discouraged. Within the aviation bar there is a high degree of mutual respect and civility, given that the lawyers and insurance representatives are well familiar with one another. One of the other unique aspects of this litigation which promotes more civil dealings is that a defendant opposing plaintiff's position in one case may be taking the same position as plaintiff in another.

Another common aviation defense tactic with respect to settlement is to obtain a settlement proposal at the very outset of the case and view that as "continuing" throughout the case notwithstanding the substantial sums of time, effort, and money expended by counsel from that point in time. For that reason, plaintiff's counsel who do agree to extend an early settlement proposal must do so with the understanding that the proposal is withdrawn on a date certain and that the case will be fully re-evaluated at a later time presumably at or near the close of discovery.

Various pressures can be brought to bear against the defendants in a helicopter crash case. For example, in any case where insurance coverage is minimal a certified letter offering to accept the insurance policy limits will exert pressure on that insurance carrier from its insured to accept the proposal. Otherwise, a potential insurance bad faith action may follow against the insurance company in those cases where the policy limits were not tendered.

In cases against component part or engine manufacturers where defective design allegations are made, the manufacturer must cope with the prospect of an adverse verdict that will be widely publicized and result in more product liability lawsuits with higher potential exposure to the defendant. Regardless of the settlement amount, a defendant may always disclaim liability and claim that the settlement was solely "to avert the inherent risks of litigation." Not so with a jury verdict squarely imposing liability for defective design on that defendant manufacturer. Although not necessarily admissible in pending or subsequent actions, a jury verdict and court judgment entered on that verdict may persuade future courts that other similar plaintiffs' cases are meritorious.

Consequently, plaintiff's counsel must take control of the appropriate time window for exploring settlement and must never allow such discussions to interfere or distract from case preparation or, even worse, handling of the trial itself. For these reasons, many aviation plaintiff attorneys have a policy of not engaging in settlement discussions during trial and for some period of time, such as two to three weeks, prior to trial. The advantages to that approach are that counsel know that the case will proceed to trial and can prepare with full confidence, vigor and energy. The client must be fully consulted in advance with respect to such an approach and counsel should obtain direction and authorization in writing to forego any further settlement discussions and proceed to trial.

The most difficult aspect of the settlement process is arriving at some appropriate measure of the value of the case. The single most important criteria for case evaluation by far is the relative merits of the case meaning the strength of the liability evidence and the quantum of recoverable damages. Other case evaluation considerations include the demographics and jury verdict history of the particular venue, the known tendencies of the trial judge, comparable verdicts and settlements in similar helicopter crash cases in similar venue demographics, and an evaluation of the relative skill and experience of plaintiff and defense counsel.

Another issue that must enter into the evaluation is evidence of any aggravating factors in either the liability or damages phase of the case. If sufficient evidence exists for the potential submission to the jury of a punitive damages claim, defendants will integrate that factor into the case evaluation. The mere threat of a substantial punitive damages award will bring many defendants to the table and will have the tendency to enhance the settlement value of the case.

Aggravating damages factors such as any evidence of pre-impact terror or post-impact conscious pain and suffering are also matters that will enhance the settlement value of the case. Counsel should determine the procedure for imposition of pre-judgment interest in the jurisdiction. Several states allow for pre-judgment interest as triggered by defendant's rejection of a pre-trial settlement offer.[19]

The settlement evaluation of any case is a direct function of the anticipated or potential jury verdict range. Most lawyers and experienced mediators employ as an evaluative tool statistical bell curve analysis in assessing the most likely range of jury verdicts. Once the "end points" are established counsel can theoretically predict that a certain percentage of trials taken to verdict in that venue will be in between these end points. Many lawyers follow the rule of thumb that they will not recommend settlement of the case to the client unless or until the offer is at least equal to or greater than the statistically significant lower endpoint.

In the majority of cases, helicopter companies fight tooth and nail. These defendants and their insurers defend their aircraft and component parts vigorously in the face of spurious claims. But there are astute and experienced business people who will strive to settle meritorious crash lawsuits where they are genuinely at fault. There are those instances where strong liability and profound damages may produce an early and appropriate settlement. *Pearson v. Bell Helicopter Textron* is one such case.[20]

In August 2008, a Bell 206 L-1 helicopter operated by an air ambulance service was returning to its home base in Rushville, Indiana. Shortly after lift-off, witnesses saw components flying off of the helicopter. It crashed to the ground and was consumed by fire. The aircraft was completely destroyed and all three occupants were killed. Plaintiff's deceased was Sandra Pearson, age 38, who was single mother of two children, ages 7 and 9.

Liability was not seriously disputed. The main rotor blade disintegrated in flight as a result of a fatigue crack which had propagated to separation. Shortly after filing the lawsuit, Bell's counsel contacted the author and graciously requested a mediation. After plaintiff's experts were permitted to examine the helicopter wreckage and the failed main rotor blade, a mediation was scheduled and conducted. Because all parties were in good faith and operating with the best interests of their clients in mind, the case was resolved prior to the taking of a single deposition for the sum of $5.6 million.

Where appropriate within the context of a mediation or otherwise, counsel may wish to prepare a settlement proposal letter that outlines all of the pertinent factors involved in a thorough case evaluation. A sample outline of such a settlement letter is as follows:

SAMPLE OUTLINE OF SETTLEMENT PROPOSAL

A. Facts of the Helicopter Crash

This section should detail the essential circumstances surrounding the crash including a description of the mission, date and location of the crash, identification of those aboard, identification of aircraft and a simplified explanation for the crash.

B. Plaintiff's Liability Experts and Opinions

Plaintiff should identify by name those experts retained and give a brief summary of their likely opinions at deposition (if not already deposed) and if deposed, a summary of those opinions likely to be elicited at trial.

C. Damages Calculations

Plaintiff should here identify the forensic economist and reference the specific opinions and economic loss calculations arrived at by the economist.

D. Description and Extent of Injuries/Extent of Loss to Survivors

This section describes the nature and full extent of the injuries suffered by the occupant of the helicopter crash with some emphasis on the impact on his or her daily functioning and quality of life. In a wrongful death case, a description of the relationship that existed between the survivors and the deceased should be described with specific examples of activities conducted together.

E. Case Evaluation and Settlement Proposal

This section should provide a thorough case evaluation based on the liability and expected damages evidence. Comparable helicopter crash verdicts from similar demographic communities may be used to establish case value. Similarity of circumstances in terms of age and family circumstances of the deceased will also form a basis for a comparison.

In assessing the jury verdict or settlement value of helicopter crash cases, defendants often point to verdicts or settlements reached in motor vehicle, medical malpractice, slip and fall or nursing home litigation. A review of helicopter crash verdicts and settlements confirms that these cases are evaluated far differently and the awards are routinely higher. Especially in those communities which have not had a jury verdict in an aviation case, defendants will point to the lack of any precedent for a substantial settlement. As with any settlement proposal, the relative certainty of liability must enter into the equation and the settlement range appropriately discounted by reason of genuinely disputed liability. As for any settlement offer, plaintiff's counsel must provide an appropriate time for consideration of their proposal and set out a certain date after which that proposal is withdrawn.

Attachments to any such settlement proposal may include photographs of the crash site as well as the injured plaintiff or plaintiff's deceased, the NTSB Factual Report, and pertinent deposition excerpts from on-scene witnesses and plaintiff's experts as well as from the depositions of corporate representatives. An analysis of comparable verdicts and settlements in similar helicopter crash cases should also be attached.

Placing a dollar value range on these cases is essential for reasons other than settlement. Counsel need to ask the jury for a specific damages number. Clients want and deserve counsel's judgment of the potential jury verdict range. Ultimately, the value determination of any given case is a judgment call based on counsel's experience.

It is important to emphasize that the value of any case is always a matter of perspective. In 1995, following trial of the second *Turbomeca* helicopter crash case, the author called his young son to report the jury's verdict of $350 million. Hosting a roomful of fellow 6-year olds, he proudly announced: "Hey everybody, my daddy just won $350!"

Given the complexity and inordinate length of helicopter crash trials, many trial courts will order a mediation among all parties prior to trial. A number of states require pre-trial mediation as part of their rules of civil procedure.[21] Where mediation is ordered by the court or otherwise agreed to by counsel, proper preparation includes a preliminary meeting with the client and a candid assessment of the settlement value of the case. Most mediators will request some materials in advance of the session. Those materials should include

a) counsel's case evaluation as well as supporting material such as the economist's report, b) photographs of the crash scene and plaintiff or plaintiff's deceased and c) excerpts from deposition testimony of plaintiff's liability experts. Counsel, in consultation with the plaintiff, should have a pre-determined settlement range for the case which governs the typical back and forth of the mediation. If the parties are able to reach an agreement on a settlement amount, that should be committed to writing and witnessed by the mediator along with all other material terms and conditions of the settlement.

Throughout the entire case from the initial discovery to and through pre-trial matters, counsel must always evince a willingness to proceed to trial. Should the defendants become convinced at any point in time that plaintiff's counsel has either lost the nerve or is otherwise unwilling to proceed to trial, it is quite literally "blood in the water" time and defendants will have little incentive to reach a fair value settlement. One of the best defense attorneys of all time, former ABA president the late John Shepherd of St. Louis, advocated that very little time be spent with settlement considerations. "The best way to get a case settled is to be fully prepared and willing to proceed to trial," he would often say. That approach is ever so true in the context of helicopter crash litigation.

Endnotes

1. See I.C.A. Rule 5.408.

2. 49 U.S.C. § 1154 (2000).

3. See Chapter 7.4 addressing evidence of NTSB reports.

4. *Samuels v. Torres*, 29 So.3d 1193, 1196-97 (Fla. App. 2010) (ruling that "[i]t is clear that counsel for Torres employed a defense stratagem in his opening statement to curry sympathy from the jury and it is obvious from this record that he succeeded" where defense counsel discussed his client's meager income); *Hoekstra v. Farm Bureau Mutual Insurance Co.*, 382 N.W.2d 100, 109 (Iowa 1986) ("evidence of net worth is admissible on the issue of punitive damages, but not on the issue of compensatory damages") (internal citation omitted).

5. *Stover v. Lakeland Square Owners Assín*, 434 N.W.2d 866, 868-71 (Iowa 1989).

6. *Waits v. United Fire & Cas. Co.*, 572 N.W.2d 565, 569 (Iowa 1997); *Smith v. Belterra Resort Indiana, LLC*, 2007 WL 4238959 at *1 (S.D. Ind. 2007) (refusing to admit evidence of expressions of "sympathy, apology, or a sense of benevolence").

7. See, e.g., ABA Model Rule of Professional Conduct 3.4(e).

8. *In re Estate of Smallman*, 398 S.W.3d 134, 153-54 (Tenn. 2013); *Schoon v. Looby*, 670 N.W.2d 885, 890-91 (S.D. 2003).

9. *Schoon*, 670 N.W.2d at 891.

10. *Murphy v. International Robotic Systems, Inc.*, 766 So.2d 1010, 1028 (Fla. 2000).

11. *Kelly v. Riles*, 751 So.2d 302, 307 (La. App. 1999).

12. *Lioce v. Cohen*, 174 P.3d 970, 983 (Nev. 2008).

13. *Id.* at 983.

14. *Anderson v. Johnson*, 441 N.W.2d 675, 677 (S.D. 1989).

15. *McKee v. Erikson*, 654 A.2d 1263, 1267 (Conn. App. 1995), *cert denied* 658 A.2d 980 (Conn. 1995).

16. *Norman v. Gloria Farms, Inc.*, 668 So.2d 1016, 1022 (Fla. App. 1996), *review denied*, 680 So.2d 422 (Fla 1996).

17. A.R.E. Rule 615. The Arkansas Rule does not apply to parties or the designated representative of a party.

18. ABA Model Rule of Professional Conduct 1.2.

19. Mo.Rev.Stat. 408.040 (2015).

20. *National Bank of Indianapolis (Pearson) v. Bell Helicopter Textron, Inc.*, Marion County Superior Court (Indiana), No. 49D01-09-05-CT-022863.

21. Indiana ADR Rule 2.2.

Chapter 10

Trial

Introduction

Finally, after years of extensive factual investigation, legal research and analysis and formal discovery including dozens of depositions, court hearings, expert conference calls and countless meetings, the jury trial is at hand. All of the effective and time-tested trial techniques ordinarily used by plaintiff's lawyers in trying any type of serious injury or wrongful death lawsuit should be employed in helicopter crash trials. Plaintiff counsel's trial skill and experience will be put to the test because well-experienced aviation defense counsel will be on the other side. After all of the years of discovery and case preparation, now it is counsel's privilege and opportunity to present plaintiff's case to a group of unbiased and unaffiliated arbiters. In the trial of a helicopter crash lawsuit, the following general suggestions may prove helpful.

1. Simplify the Technical Evidence and Empower the Jury with Knowledge

Counsel cannot allow the presentation of evidence at trial to become so overly technical and complex that even an all-engineer jury could not follow it. At the first mention of any new helicopter or flight system terminology, counsel needs to stop and carefully define and explain that term. Extensive use of the helicopter model is a must to show the location of various components and systems. In the opening statement or with one of the plaintiff's first liability experts, counsel should utilize a chart of technical and engineering terms with understandable definitions to help acclimate the jury to the terminology to be used throughout the trial.

Counsel must not relinquish the task of educating the jury and demonstrating technical expertise to the opposition. Juries appreciate learning new and interesting things and will feel empowered by that new knowledge. After the trial, a juror will have the rapt attention of her children when she says, "Mommy learned how a helicopter flies. Want me to tell you?"

2. Avoid the Overemphasis on Liability to the Detriment of Damages
There is an unfortunate tendency in these cases for plaintiff's lawyers to forego a thorough presentation of the damages suffered because of a fascination for or attachment to the liability side of the case. The lawsuit is not primarily about the helicopter crash but more so about the impact of that crash on the human beings present in the courtroom and the appropriate measure of relief to be accorded to them.

3. This Crash Was No "Accident"
Counsel should be wary of the "helicopter accidents happen" defense that may be a subtle or, in some instances, not so subtle undercurrent of the defense case. That mentality must be forcefully addressed during the jury selection process and any jurors ascribing to such deterministic beliefs should be excluded for cause.

The techniques suggested here are illustrated by trial transcript excerpts from actual helicopter crash trials. The names of witnesses and venirepersons have been changed for privacy reasons as have the identities of some plaintiffs and defendants. All cases were handled by the author and were tried to jury verdict.

10.1 Jury Selection
The opportunity and concomitant advantage to conduct a thorough voir dire of the jury panel is one of the reasons why plaintiff's counsel elected to bring the action in state court several years earlier. Given the benefit of that marvelous tool, counsel should maximize its benefit in every respect. The author's experience with state court trial judges hearing helicopter crash cases is that they will give a fair amount of latitude to counsel for both sides so long as the questions are relevant, not duplicative and counsel does not, as one North Carolina judge called it, "speechify." Jury selection is proceeding as intended if the lawyer does far less talking than the venirepersons.

If counsel is in an unfamiliar jurisdiction, there must be more reliance on the local counsel who knows the lay of the land in terms of knowledge about the large local employers, neighborhood politics and other local idiosyncrasies. Counsel should consider using a jury consultant experienced in aviation matters. The author has found the use of such consultants to be important in two respects. First, they may either corroborate or challenge counsel's instincts and judgment as to a particular juror's attitudes, beliefs or opinions. Second, a consultant may single out potential jurors for whom there is some concern and provide pointed questions to elicit information from that juror sufficient to make a judgment on exercise of a for cause challenge or preemptory strike.

A. Objectives
The specifics of the jury selection or voir dire process vary greatly from one jurisdiction to the next. This is one area where the experience and assistance of good local counsel is invaluable. But the lead trial counsel must pick the jury and not leave this critical trial task to the local lawyer. This means that the local jury selection procedure in all respects must be learned stone-cold. Counsel must learn not only the process but also the particular strategies and court idiosyncrasies for the order of questioning, the standard for striking jurors for cause, and the sequence for exercising preemptory jury strikes.

There are all manner of styles and techniques for conducting jury selection. Whichever approach or style is used is a function of the trial lawyer's experience, temperament, and personality. Not many can copy the particular voir dire style of the late Johnnie Cochran or the marvelous Gerry Spence. Jurors will spot a fake or feigned technique faster than a bad penny. So long as counsel has experienced success with his own style of jury selection, there is no reason to depart from that in trying a helicopter crash case. The two essential objectives of jury selection must be accomplished by whichever technique or style is utilized:

1. Elicit sufficient and accurate feedback from each panel member so as to form the basis for intelligent evaluation and use of for cause and preemptory strikes; and
2. Establish a trustworthy connection and rapport with the jury panel.

The first objective allows counsel to eliminate from the jury pool as many biased or attitudinally prejudiced jurors as possible by a combination of for cause and peremptory strikes. The second objective is applicable to those who remain on the jury. Counsel must come across to the jury as honest, sincere, and credible. One of the time-tested ways of establishing an honest rapport whether in the context of jury selection or otherwise is to listen and appropriately respond to specific points raised by jury panel members. Counsel's response can demonstrate that "this lawyer gets it." That means sensitively acknowledging and responding to a potential juror who has spilled her guts in describing how difficult it was to lose a brother in a plane crash ten years ago. That type of candid juror disclosure must be encouraged and a simple but sincerely spoken "I am sorry for your loss" is appropriate and all that is required.

Failing to respond in an appropriate way may have cost Governor Michael Dukakis his bid for the Presidency in 1988. Most will recall the televised debate where Moderator Bernard Shaw asked the following question: "Governor, if your wife Kitty Dukakis were raped and murdered would you favor an irrevocable death penalty for the killer?" The Governor's rapid "No, I don't" response was cold and inappropriate in stating his analytical objections to the death penalty. A natural response such as "My goodness, Bernard, that's a horrible prospect for me to consider because I love my wife so dearly, but let me tell you some of the reasons why I'm against the death penalty." The lesson is that counsel must follow a simple rule during jury selection: listen carefully to what the jurors say and respond appropriately. It is important that potential jurors disclose personal and even private feelings, attitudes and beliefs. That cannot be accomplished unless counsel creates an environment in which the panel members feel comfortable in sharing very personal and emotional details of their private lives. Counsel should express appreciation for all candid responses whether they are favorable or not.

Another important aspect of jury selection is to identify and fully disclose any troublesome facts or issues and to assess the jury's attitudes and reaction to the facts disclosed. Although many lawyers prefer not to disclose so-called "bad facts" early on either in jury selection or opening statement, many trial lawyers including this author believe that the benefits far outweigh the risks. It is human nature to forgive as well as to reward candor and honesty. It makes a world of difference if the jury hears the bad fact first from counsel for plaintiff than from counsel for defendant. At minimum, the client will not be penalized for "hiding anything" as the warts are there for all to see. If the plaintiff's motion in limine to exclude the bad fact is overruled then that fact initially should be disclosed to the jury by the plaintiff's lawyer.

Some trial lawyers and jury consultants advance another purpose of voir dire which is for counsel to argue his case or set out the primary case themes to be presented. In the author's opinion and experience that is not a proper or valid objective of the voir dire process. Notwithstanding the court's likely sustaining objections to such tactics, potential jurors may recognize argument at that early stage and resent it. Focusing on the two primary objectives outlined earlier

will be a sufficient challenge as is. Counsel will have the remainder of the trial to set forth the themes of the case and to argue, but at the appropriate designated times.

Because the jury selection process can be tedious and boring many lawyers either rush through it or fail to ask all significant and permissible questions. The purported objective of jury selection is to achieve a fair and impartial jury panel to decide the case solely on the evidence and applicable law; however, that is more of an ideal than reality. Men and women enter the courthouse as potential jurors with a lifetime of experiences, attitudes, opinions, biases and prejudices which unalterably affect their view of the world and their view of any kind of personal injury or wrongful death case. Notwithstanding this utopian ideal, the obligation of counsel to her client is to lawfully and ethically empanel a jury composed of men and women who will be fair and receptive to the plaintiff's position and bring in a just verdict based on the law. Anything less is a dereliction of that duty.

Counsel's first interaction with and statement to the jury is important. Counsel should answer the foremost question on the jury's mind which is, "What is this case about?" A simple explanation of the case at the outset of the jury selection process will give some background to the jury and, due to the novelty of a helicopter crash case, may just create a bit more interest and attention during that process than would otherwise be the case:

> MR. ROBB: Thank you Your Honor, may it please the Court:
>
> THE COURT: Mr. Robb.
>
> MR. ROBB: Good afternoon ladies and gentlemen. My name is Gary Robb and I am one of the lawyers for the plaintiffs here who are bringing this case which is a civil action. This involves the crash of a helicopter that killed a twenty year old woman by the name of Sally Peters. The people I'm representing are the deceased's mother who is Jane Peters. Jane, would you stand.
>
> I also represent the surviving minor children of Sally Peters. She left two little boys who were four and one at the time she was killed in the helicopter crash.

The extent of detail about the case imparted at the outset of jury selection depends on what the trial court informs the jury beforehand. Some courts provide a brief presentation of the case setting out the claims and defenses prior to the lawyers' questioning. Others say almost nothing about the facts of the case and leave that up to the lawyers as occurred below:

MR. ROBB: Thank you Your Honor. Good morning, ladies and gentlemen and welcome back. My name is Gary Robb and it is my privilege to represent the plaintiffs in this particular case which is a civil action. This is a civil case. I don't think before this moment any of you knew that. It is not a criminal case. You knew how long the case would be but you didn't know what it involved. Kind of a backwards procedure a little bit.

Let me tell you in a brief synopsis what this case is about. This case involves the crash of a Life Flight helicopter that occurred just over two years ago which killed two people. On the basis of that information alone, I think you can see that if any of you at any time in your past had been a Life Flight helicopter pilot, for that reason alone it probably would not be a good idea for you to be on this jury. You would know too many things one way or another.

B. Suggested Voir Dire Questions, Trial Excerpts and Commentary

The following trial transcript excerpts are from actual helicopter crash trials handled by the author. The names of the venirepersons have been changed for privacy reasons, as have the identities of some plaintiffs and defendants. All were cases tried to verdict. A summary of the recommended voir dire topics utilized in helicopter crash lawsuits is as follows.

1. Previous Experience with the Court System
a. Prior jury service

A good early topic of discussion is to identify those jurors who have had prior jury service. The specifics of a case are not important so long as the case is not an airplane or helicopter crash, in which case more in-depth questioning is essential, as outlined further on. What should be drawn from each panel member with prior jury service is whether they considered it a good or bad experience and why. Many jurors find it to be inspiring and come away with a renewed confidence and trust in the justice system. Others are completely soured by the system, consider jury service a waste of time and would just as soon be home peeling potatoes. Such people make poor plaintiff's jurors because they tend to blame the plaintiff and plaintiff's counsel for putting them through this worthless ordeal. Counsel should inquire as to which jurors previously served as foreperson of a jury. Many juries will elect a foreperson in part based on prior jury experience and especially so if one had prior experience as a foreperson. Accordingly, plaintiff's trial team must scrutinize such jurors carefully given the increased probability that a juror previously serving as a foreperson will be elected to that position once again.

The following exchange revealed this potential juror's attitude about the court system:

MR. ROBB: Ms. McMaster, what was your experience, ma'am?

VENIREPERSON MCMASTER: I served on a jury under Judge Gant in the county seat in Independence. It was a burglary. And about two hours—it's been about 12 years ago. A couple of hours into the trial the defense requested a recess. When they came back, he changed his plea to guilty. I think that a deal had been offered and at first he said no, and this is speculation.

MR. ROBB: Let me interrupt you one second. The real thrust of this question is whether there is anything at all about that experience which would cause you to perhaps question the validity of what we are about, and that is the deciding dispute by means of the jury system. That is really the heart of it.

VENIREPERSON MCMASTER: No. If anything it gave me a taste or gave me an insight just as to how serious and really how well I think our justice system does work.

MR. ROBB: I appreciate your sharing the thought with us.

This juror had a positive experience as a juror and would take that job seriously if selected again which is a plus for a plaintiff. Not all people have that view:

MR. ROBB: I think I saw another hand on that row. Mr. Reeves?

VENIREPERSON REEVES: I served on a couple civil cases.

MR. ROBB: And did you reach a verdict in both of them, sir?

VENIREPERSON REEVES: Yes, we did.

MR. ROBB: How long ago was it, sir?

VENIREPERSON REEVES: It seems to me probably at least ten years ago.

MR. ROBB: Did you feel that it was an appropriate mechanism for resolving this particular civil dispute?

VENIREPERSON REEVES: No.

MR. ROBB: Did you bring some negative feeling, a view of the system, to your task in this particular case given that particular experience?

VENIREPERSON REEVES: I would not want to but it's very possible that I would.

MR. ROBB: Could you not with any degree of certainty guarantee us that that would not influence your decision making—

VENIREPERSON REEVES: I couldn't guarantee it.
MR. ROBB: Thank you sir.

Mr. Reeves would not appear to be a favorable plaintiff's juror.

b. Burden of proof

Determining whether any panel members had prior jury experience with either a criminal or civil trial provides a springboard for a discussion of the burden of proof as being vastly different between criminal and civil cases. Almost every hand in the room will shoot up when counsel asks "Who here can tell us the legal burden of proof in a criminal case?"

The author has found it useful early on in voir dire to establish clearly what the plaintiff's burden of proof is in a civil case such as this helicopter crash case. That burden is commonly described in most jurisdictions as "more probably than not," "preponderance of the evidence," or "the greater weight of the evidence." Each of these formulations lends itself to counsel's illustrating that principle with upward palms depicting the scales of justice and demonstrating that, "if the weight of plaintiff's evidence tips the scales ever so slightly in her favor, she is entitled to your verdict as a matter of law." Counsel must delve into this issue thoroughly with the panel. Many people are not comfortable with this simple burden of proof and will disclose that they would hold plaintiff to a higher burden of "at least 75 percent or so," for example. Counsel then may embark on a for cause challenge to establish that this panel member would be unable to commit to following the court's instruction on the proper burden of proof and should be stricken for cause.

> MR. ROBB: Now, with respect to those of you who have been on the criminal—had experience on a criminal jury, would you raise your hand once again? Okay. One of the critical distinctions between a civil, which is this case, and a criminal case is the burden of proof. Because we know from watching television and media that the burden of proof in a criminal case is much more stringent and severe than in a civil case which is between private parties. Who can tell me what the burden of proof is in a criminal case? Ms. McMaster?
>
> VENIREPERSON MCMASTER: Beyond a reasonable doubt.
>
> MR. ROBB: Precisely. Beyond a reasonable doubt. That is the burden and it should be the burden when we are looking to seek the full power of the State against an individual.

In this case there is a completely different and much less stringent standard. That simply is more probable than not. We like to, as lawyers, and the Court talks about it, think of it as greater than a 50 percent probability, 51 percent. That is the burden that we as plaintiffs have in this court which is different from the criminal burden which is much more stringent.

My question to each and every one of you who have raised your hand with the experience having served on a criminal jury, is there any one of you who would not be able to with 100 percent certainty set aside your prior experience in working on a case that required proof beyond a reasonable doubt and applying the standard which his Honor is going to be instructing the jury on in this case which is simply more probably than not? Anything? There is a possibility that they could be confused or somehow influenced by that prior experience?
(No response.)

> MR. ROBB: Because, ladies and gentlemen, the standard of more probable than not envisions the scales of justice and they come into this court—we parties come into this court and those scales are balanced equally. That is one of the prime functions of this entire proceeding to see to it that all parties do start out on that scale equally, with no evidence at all. When after the evidence is in and after you have seen the evidence, if the evidence on behalf of the plaintiffs causes that scale to tip ever so slightly, that is sufficient proof in civil law.
>
> Is there anyone here who as a matter of personal belief or option or attitude feels that that should not be the law and that they would have difficulty following Judge Wells' instructions on the law with respect to that issue? Anyone here in this courtroom couldn't follow that law as to how to weigh the evidence because it is a critical instruction, one which this Court will give to the jury prior to their deliberations in the case?
> (No response.)
>
> MR. ROBB: Seeing no hands, I presume that all of you would be able to follow the Court's instruction as to the burden of proof.

The extensive discussion of burden of proof also is intended to apply some peer pressure to any juror expressing a contrary view during deliberations. Jurors may remind that juror that she should have responded to a question on this issue had there been any concern.

This questioning as to burden of proof is difficult as well as monotonous and tedious but it is absolutely essential to rid the panel of jurors who would impose upon Plaintiffs a higher burden of proof than the law requires. In a helicopter crash trial handled by the author in Las Vegas in August 2014, a venireperson revealed the classic mindset often expressed as "super proof" or "black and white" beliefs:

MR. ROBB: Let me ask the panel as a whole because we've all seen the TV shows and criminal shows and some people are just wired differently, and they want beyond a reasonable doubt on anything. They want that 99 percent proof, and that's what I'm getting at. Are there any among you who say, you know, I'd have problems with that. My mind is wired a little bit different. I want a little higher standard of proof, especially given what's at stake here, and we're saying this helicopter company had bad maintenance. 51, 55, whatever it is percent ain't good enough for me. I want 80 or 90. Who would agree with that?

And tell us about your thoughts on that, Mr. Sego, No. 277. It's just the way you're used to thinking?

PROSPECTIVE JUROR NO. 277: Yes, sir. You know, I don't know anything about this, but in this case, to me, it's, like, unless there's overwhelming proof, it could've just been an accident.

MR. ROBB: I understand. How long have you had this belief or mindset that something in your life, in your world, really, really for you to believe it has to be proven — you used the word overwhelmingly. How long have you believed that?

PROSPECTIVE JUROR NO. 277: Pretty much since I was a kid. I used to argue with my dad about a lot of different things, you know, and I'm just a black-and-white guy. It's either there or it's not there.

MR. ROBB: Mr. Sego, I am the last person to be judgmental of your belief. I applaud you for bringing it to our attention because we need to know now because by the time you all get back and decide the case, if you don't answer these questions and suppose you went back in the jury room and you're back there and they're saying, okay, well, here's the burden of proof. You say, oh, no, not for me, not for me. I want 99 percent and the other jurors would look at you and say, why didn't you tell Mr. Robb?

He did the right thing. And I applaud you and appreciate it, but I need to ask you, is it true that all your adult life, sir, you have had the belief that something needs to be proved to you to your satisfaction in overwhelming fashion, correct?

PROSPECTIVE JUROR NO. 277: Yes, sir.

Counsel then must be sure to elicit the strength of this long-held belief:

MR. ROBB: And I'm gathering from the strength and fervor of your belief, Mr. Sego, that this is something you feel pretty strongly about, fair?

PROSPECTIVE JUROR NO. 277: Yes.

MR. ROBB: Maybe a 9 or even 9-plus on a scale of 1 to 10 with 10 being the most strong?

PROSPECTIVE JUROR NO. 277: It's up there.

MR. ROBB: 9?

PROSPECTIVE JUROR NO. 277: 9 at least.

MR. ROBB: 9 at least. So it could be 9-plus?

PROSPECTIVE JUROR NO. 277: Sure.

MR. ROBB: Okay.

Be attentive to other jurors who often will voice the same dangerous belief:

PROSPECTIVE JUROR NO. 325: I'd have to agree.

MR. ROBB: We are going to get to you in a minute, but let me go with Mr. Sego, and please, just — I appreciate that.

PROSPECTIVE JUROR NO. 325: Okay.

MR. ROBB: But let me go with Mr. Sego first.

PROSPECTIVE JUROR NO. 325: Okay.

MR. ROBB: All right. Mr. Sego, I respectfully suggest that the burden of proof is not going to be overwhelming as a requirement. It's not going to be 90 percent. It's not going to be 85 percent. . . . the preponderance of the evidence, which is evidence with more convincing force to be proved more probably true than not true. If you put your evidence on the scales of justice, it would be — commonly we say over 50 percent.

And you essentially said you're a black-and-white guy?

PROSPECTIVE JUROR NO. 277: Yes, sir.

MR. ROBB: And that's fine. Lots of people think that way, but I think you said it was a 9 or a 9-plus that you're one of those people who believe things have to be super proved to them, right?

PROSPECTIVE JUROR NO. 277: Yes, sir.

MR. ROBB: Mr. Sego, understanding that this is a civil case, would you understand that the parties I represent could potentially have a concern with your mindset and belief in this?

PROSPECTIVE JUROR NO. 277: I can understand that.

MR. ROBB: And you understand that in a criminal case your mindset would be perfect? You got to prove it, got to prove the guilt. In fact, many people would say that you'd be an excellent criminal juror, and, you know, there's a lot of criminal trials in this courthouse.

PROSPECTIVE JUROR NO. 277: Uh-huh.

MR. ROBB: Recognizing that, Mr. Sego, would you accept the possibility that you or someone like you who has felt this way about having to have super proof all their adult life and I think feels over 9 on a scale from 1 to 9 in terms of the proof that that mindset could possibly come into play and affect your ability to be a fair and impartial juror? Would you recognize that possibility?

PROSPECTIVE JUROR NO. 277: Yes, sir.

MR. ROBB: And, Mr. Sego, having accepted the possibility, you're saying this because it's how you really feel, right?

PROSPECTIVE JUROR NO. 277: Yes, sir.

MR. ROBB: You're not saying this because you're wanting to get out of jury service?

PROSPECTIVE JUROR NO. 277: No.

MR. ROBB: Okay. We already had that drill. You're willing to be a juror, right?

PROSPECTIVE JUROR NO. 277: Yes.

MR. ROBB: And you recognize that sometimes based on peoples' mindset or belief, they might not be the correct juror for a particular kind of case; would you accept that?

PROSPECTIVE JUROR NO. 277: Yes, sir.

Counsel then must utilize the precise language in that jurisdiction for striking potential jurors for cause:

MR. ROBB: And having recognized honestly and candidly in front of your fellow panel members and His Honor that you would recognize the possibility that your mindset could interfere with and prevent your ability to be a fair and impartial juror, would you search in your conscience and heart and soul, recognize the probability that it would affect your ability to be fair, Mr. Sego?

PROSPECTIVE JUROR NO. 277: Yes, sir.

MR. ROBB: And that's your honest answer based on how you believe?

PROSPECTIVE JUROR NO. 277: Yes, sir.

And then it is good practice to "lock in" those responses ahead of rehabilitation efforts by defense counsel or even the trial court:

MR. ROBB: And there's nothing I or these lawyers or the Judge could say this afternoon or tomorrow or Thursday or Friday that's going to convince you to change your mind; am I right about that?

PROSPECTIVE JUROR NO. 277: Yes, you'd have to really say that it happened.

MR. ROBB: And that would affect your ability also to fairly follow the Court's instruction on the law, wouldn't it, if it varied from that?

PROSPECTIVE JUROR NO. 277: Yes, sir.

MR. ROBB: And just jumping to it, your long-held, all-your-life, strongly held, 9-plus on a scale of 1 to 10 belief that things need to be super proved to you would absolutely, definitively, beyond the shadow of a doubt prevent you and substantially impair your ability to be a fair and impartial juror in this type of case, agreed, sir? Agreed?

PROSPECTIVE JUROR NO. 277: Yes, sir.

MR. ROBB: No doubt about it, is there?

PROSPECTIVE JUROR NO. 277: Yes.

MR. ROBB: And if the Judge asked you whether you could set aside that belief and follow the instructions, you would be honest with him as you would with me and say, sir, I couldn't do it; wouldn't you say that?

PROSPECTIVE JUROR NO. 277: Yes, sir.

MR. ROBB: Or if [defense counsel] asked you or whoever's conducting voir dire for the defendant, you'd say, I told Mr. Robb the truth, right?

PROSPECTIVE JUROR NO. 277: Yes, sir.

MR. ROBB: I want to thank you. There's no question in my mind that you are an honest person, that you've told us the truth, and as the Judge said, that's what this process is called. Remember he said, Voir dire. Anybody remember what it stands for, what it means?

PROSPECTIVE JURORS: The truth.

The trial court promptly struck Mr. Sego for cause based on the foregoing answers.

c. Experience as party to case

A number of panel members will have had experience in some court proceeding whether as the party bringing the action or against whom the action is brought. Attitudes, feelings and opinions may run very strong where a plaintiff did not obtain the justice being sought or a defendant was improperly "railroaded." Counsel must explore each of these situations carefully and assess whether grounds exist to excuse that juror for cause. No matter the cause, jurors with negative feelings about the jury system are unlikely to be strong jurors for the plaintiff.

d. Experience as a witness

Counsel must not forget to inquire as to the experience of panel members as a witness in court proceedings. Some people come away from that experience disgruntled either because they believed that the verdict was a miscarriage of justice or because they had to wait around to testify so long. Other people think of it as part of their civic duty and will vouch that it was a satisfying experience.

Venirepersons with experience as witnesses on behalf of some manufacturing entity may have strong feelings in association with the defendants:

MR. ROBB: What was your experience as a witness in a jury trial Mr. Fisher?

VENIREPERSON FISHER: I was called as a witness in a case. The company I work for we sell parts for machines and stuff like that and we had a machine fall apart one day. I got called in as a witness and so was the owner of the business. But the experience and stuff everything, everything got drug out, it was like politics. I've gotten to the point where I don't know how I could view sitting in here because I've been on both sides and, you know, see the millions and millions of dollars roll through or whatever.

MR. ROBB: Mr. Fisher, I can understand your experience. No one here is being judgmental. That's not our function. There is no right or wrong answer. There is just an answer. And I wish to thank you for coming forward with that answer because there are people who have had experiences with the court system that are not favorable and no one, least of all myself, believes that anyone would claim that this is a perfect system.

VENIREPERSON FISHER: Right.

MR. ROBB: I think you can understand, however, how someone who expresses your thoughts might be viewed as perhaps having an inability to be a fair and impartial juror in a case like this?

VENIREPERSON FISHER: Right.

MR. ROBB: You can understand that?

VENIREPERSON FISHER: Yes.

MR. ROBB: Obviously you are willing to be a juror. You wouldn't have come Monday in response to the summons and you sure wouldn't have shown up again this morning if you weren't willing to do service in a jury case, but maybe this is not the case for you.

VENIREPERSON FISHER: Right.

MR. ROBB: Would you believe on the basis of what you know about this case and having the recent experience you related as witness would interfere with your ability to fairly and impartially be fair to both sides?

VENIREPERSON FISHER: Yes, I do.

MR. ROBB: There is no question in your mind about it?

VENIREPERSON FISHER: No.

MR. ROBB: I want to thank you for your candor.

Mr. Fisher would have been a scary juror for the plaintiff in a helicopter products liability action given his identity with a company that "makes parts for machines and stuff like that" in addition to his comments about "the millions and millions of dollars." The trial court sustained plaintiff's motion to strike Mr. Fisher for cause on the basis of the above exchange.

2. Prior Knowledge of the Helicopter Crash
a. Specific or special non-media knowledge of the case

In smaller communities especially, the circumstances of a helicopter crash creates big news and is the subject of much local chatter and gossip. However, counsel must exercise caution because the basis of some of this knowledge may be erroneous or otherwise inadmissible information from an eyewitness, someone at the hospital, or a deputy sheriff who "knows what really happened" from on-site conversations with NTSB personnel or some local official. Anyone with special knowledge should not be permitted to express that information before the entire panel as, true or not, the information may poison the panel. Those individuals should be noted and requested to approach the court to answer the question at a break without the other panel members present.

b. Recollection of media coverage of helicopter crash

As can be seen in some of the following trial excerpts, many people will have specific memories about the helicopter crash from newspaper, television or radio coverage. Once again those panel members should not reveal the extent of their knowledge before the panel as a whole but should be asked to approach the bench at a break to describe what they recall. In some instances, panel members have stated in such a break before the court and counsel that they specifically recall the NTSB Probable Cause Report and can accurately relay its findings. Given the inadmissibility of those findings, one side or another will have a valid basis for striking that panel member for cause. A generalized recollection or non-specific memory that the helicopter crash was reported in the newspaper is ordinarily not sufficient to strike such a juror for cause.

The extent to which a potential juror will recall media coverage about the helicopter crash can be particularly revealing of that person's attitudes about the case:

VENIREPERSON CASEY: I am a newsaholic.

MR. ROBB: You said newsaholic?

VENIREPERSON CASEY: I can watch CNN for hours. I read the newspaper cover to cover. I read the articles. I've read the follow-up investigations regarding this case.

MR. ROBB: Let me interrupt you one second. Other than what you've read in the newspaper, did you go out and investigate anything about this case other than that?

VENIREPERSON CASEY: No, but I'm afraid I may have already preformed an opinion in this case.

MR. ROBB: Mr. Casey, with respect to the evidence that would come into this court should it differ at all from any of your understanding, you would naturally I presume defer to the evidence that is admitted by the court?

VENIREPERSON CASEY: Yes I would. But there was another instance similar to this—

DEFENSE COUNSEL: Objection. May we approach the bench.

Based on the content of the prior media coverage of this helicopter crash, this juror most probably knew that mechanical failure was determined to be the cause. Defendants would have had an uphill battle divesting this juror of this knowledge. The juror was successful challenged for cause by defense counsel.

3. Experience of Accidental or Sudden Death of Relative or Close Friend

The prior series of questions are the getting acquainted phase. That series is primarily factual, not too personal or likely to elicit uncomfortable emotional responses. The following sequence of questions is the time to become more specific and to inquire about matters for which jurors may become emotional or even distraught.

It is the author's experience that virtually every jury panel will contain at least one person who has lost a family member or close friend in an airplane crash but rarely so in a helicopter. Counsel must address these issues sensitively especially where a panel member does become emotional in recounting the incident such as where it involved a parent, child or sibling. Some people were so impacted by the experience that they would have a difficult time setting it aside and fairly and impartially assessing the evidence in the instant case. Other panel members view the prior experience as an entirely separate matter or so remote in time that it would have no bearing on their ability to serve as a fair and impartial juror. These are instances where counsel must exercise immediate and accurate judgment. If the juror appears desirable as one who could be fair and open to plaintiff's position, then that juror should be saved. If as a result of previous responses, the juror does not appear as one who would be fair or open to plaintiff's position then this may be an appropriate opportunity to develop facts upon which a lawful for cause strike may be exercised.

a. Family member or friend injured or killed in an airplane or helicopter crash

Counsel will obtain responses about family members or close friends killed in an airplane crash, if not a helicopter crash itself, and those jurors demand careful scrutiny:

MR. ROBB: Yes Mr. Skaggs.

VENIREPERSON SKAGGS: I don't know if this is the time to bring it up. I had a good friend killed in an airplane crash.

MR. ROBB: I am so sorry to hear of that. How long ago was that?

VENIREPERSON SKAGGS: Two years. It was an airplane, not helicopter, but it brings up a lot of memories. His wife was pregnant at the time.

MR. ROBB: You said it was a good friend and died in an airplane crash, not helicopter but airplane crash. This was not a family member?

VENIREPERSON SKAGGS: No.

MR. ROBB: But people with whom you felt a close personal bond?

VENIREPERSON SKAGGS: Yes, very.

Assuming no negative attitudes or beliefs about the civil justice system are expressed by Mr. Skaggs, he would appear to be a fine plaintiff's juror. Unfortunately, most defendants would develop a basis for a for cause strike.

Normally venirepersons who have had relatives or close friends killed in plane or helicopter crashes are more inclined to be fair and open to the plaintiff's position, having had a similar experience to plaintiff. Absent some countervailing consideration, plaintiff's counsel would not want to exclude such a juror. For example, a negative consideration would be if anyone were not compensated for the death of a family member. But that question will be asked in another context involving experience with the judicial system. Counsel not only must identify them but insulate such jurors from potential for cause attacks by the defense:

MR. ROBB: Anyone else? Mr. Moseley?

VENIREPERSON MOSELEY: I had a second cousin, I believe it was. He had a pilot's license. He was killed in a crash in New Mexico but I don't know any details.

MR. ROBB: How long ago?

VENIREPERSON MOSELEY: Probably twenty-nine, thirty years ago.

MR. ROBB: Is that remote enough in time that it would influence in any way your ability to be an impartial juror in this case Mr. Moseley?

VENIREPERSON MOSELEY: It would not.

MR. ROBB: You say it would not?

VENIREPERSON MOSELEY: Yes.

b. Family member or friend killed in any kind of traumatic accident such as a car crash

Sadly, there will be many more responses to this personal question than to the last which was limited to aircraft. Almost everyone has known someone killed in a motor vehicle accident. Similar considerations apply to this inquiry as apply to those who had family members or friends killed in an aircrash, and the same cautionary note applies as to counsel's sensitivity. Counsel should be sincere and genuine in expressing sorrow for the loss as described but must delve into the experiences as is necessary to fully explore the attitudes and potential biases of that particular venireperson. Retaining such a juror who is perceived as being unbiased and fair to plaintiff's position in the face of a defense challenge may be somewhat easier because the prior event did not involve an aircraft crash.

MR. ROBB: Anybody else have that experience? And I'm not asking now whether it would affect you. I just want to know the fact—I want you to bring it out for us to evaluate it. Does anybody here have that experience of a family member, close friend who has been—Mr. Johnson?

VENIREPERSON JOHNSON: I had a cousin and his wife was killed in a car accident. Two girls survived.

MR. ROBB: How long ago was it?

VENIREPERSON JOHNSON: 1984.

MR. ROBB: Fourteen years ago. It was remote enough in time that you can move on and put that out of your mind and be fair to all parties in this case?

VENIREPERSON JOHNSON: Yes, I can.

MR. ROBB: Thank you, Mr. Johnson.

c. Experience of sudden loss of spouse or other family member or close friend

The final leg of this trilogy addresses the prior experience vernirepersons have had with the sudden loss for any reason of a spouse or other family member. This may be due to sudden heart attack, aneurysm, stroke or even a rapidly progressive disease such as pancreatic cancer. Jurors responding to this question also must be sensitively handled. The danger with such jurors is that they could be hesitant in awarding monetary damages to a widow who lost her husband because the venireperson suffered a similar loss with no compensation whatever. Alternatively, some panel members may volunteer statements making it clear that they are unduly sympathetic to the plaintiff's position stating "I can understand what she's going through" or "I'm afraid I would be leaning to Mrs. Plaintiff at the outset." The author has found from experience that where such jurors clearly have "for caused" themselves based on such statements that it promotes an atmosphere of trust and fair-dealing for plaintiff's counsel to establish their inability to be fair and reasonable and, where local practice calls for it, promptly ask that the juror be excused for cause.

4. Aviation Experiences and Beliefs

Any potential jurors with experience in the helicopter industry or aviation generally, especially pilots, must be stricken. Such individuals generally have strong views and tend to identify with and be protective of that industry. Moreover they will be viewed as an expert to whom the jury turns for any disputed piloting, technical or engineering matters. Many old-time aviation trial lawyers speak of juries that included a pilot or aircraft mechanic that turned out well. They were lucky. A jury trial is not the time to gamble three to four years of hard work on a single wild-card juror.

a. Experience as an airplane or helicopter pilot

Any fixed-wing or helicopter pilot on the jury is a wild card and plaintiff's lawyers should seek to strike pilot venirepersons for cause. Part of the mindset is that the pilot may think that even under the circumstances faced by the pilot at issue the pilot juror would most likely have been able to effectuate a safe landing. Alternatively, there may have been some basis for not embarking on the mission and this pilot juror might believe that under those circumstances he would never have made that flight. Where the risks are high the venireperson must go and this is an example of that.

Many pilots tend to be rather opinionated and this pilot was not going to be stricken easily:

MR. ROBB: Mr. Contice, you have been a pilot for fifty years?

VENIREPERSON CONTICE: Yes I have.

MR. ROBB: And that is part of your life's experience and I would imagine that you could not cut it out like you would a bad portion of an apple or anything?

VENIREPERSON CONTICE: I think I could.

MR. ROBB: You think you could?

VENIREPERSON CONTICE: Yes. In fact, I'm sure I could.

MR. ROBB: Is it something that you would feel comfortable with in serving on this jury?

VENIREPERSON CONTICE: I would be perfectly comfortable, yes.

This was a venireperson for whom a peremptory strike was exercised.

b. Helicopter flight experience

Counsel must explore the experiences, attitudes and opinions the potential jurors have with respect to helicopters and those who would fly on helicopters. Over the years, the author has found that typically four or five potential jurors will have flown on a helicopter. In many cases this will be many years ago while the juror was in the service. Others will speak fondly of their thrilling experience taking a helicopter ride in Hawaii, over the Grand Canyon, or some other special occasion. These potential jurors must be thoroughly questioned about the experience and the opinions or attitudes formed thereby. Their helicopter experience was safe and enjoyable, and they may view this crash as nothing but an unfortunate accident. Other jurors with comparable experiences were "scared out of their wits" and might impute some fault whether permitted by the instructions or not to the unfortunate souls who voluntarily boarded this dangerous flying machine.

As some of the following trial excerpts demonstrate, answers to this question yield extreme results ranging from "Yes I loved it" to "I would never do it again." The judgment call here centers on whether a particular panel member may have been so enthralled with the helicopter flight and experience that she may give some edge to the defendants because of their association with that industry. Jurors who had a very bad experience flying a helicopter, whether it was on a military mission or aerial tour, will likely be challenged by the defense. Due credit from everyone in the courtroom, including the trial judge and other jurors, will be accorded counsel for eliciting information making it clear that such a juror could not fairly and impartially hear the evidence and decide this case, with the exception of defense counsel who would have preferred to challenge such jurors themselves.

Occasionally, a prospective juror will immediately volunteer information indicating that she identifies so thoroughly with one of the defendants, here the helicopter operator and hospital, that the bias is evident:

MR. ROBB: Yes Mrs. Boying?

VENIREPERSON BOYING: Six years ago I was transported by Research Hospital helicopter after a bad car accident. I felt like I wouldn't be here today if not for them.

MR. ROBB: I'm sorry to hear about your accident. You say that you wouldn't be here today because of the ambulance?

VENIREPERSON BOYING: Because of the quick transportation to the hospital.

Mrs. Boying would identify far too closely with the defendants in the case. She needed no prompting with this disclosure. She was stricken for cause.

Sometimes the potential juror's past experience in an air ambulance helicopter is somewhat innocuous and, without anything more, would provide no reason or basis to challenge that juror either for cause or peremptorily:

MR. ROBB: Who else has any experience riding in a helicopter? Yes? Mr. Ross?

VENIREPERSON ROSS: Yes, I worked at the University of Missouri Medical Center in Columbia, and it was at that job that I was a nurse and I worked on the transport team for a while and we did fly.

MR. ROBB: So you were actually a flight nurse for a time being?

VENIREPERSON ROSS: Well mostly we did ground transports.

MR. ROBB: On occasion you would act as a flight nurse?

VENIREPERSON ROSS: Yes.

MR. ROBB: You know what the duties and responsibilities are of a flight nurse?

VENIREPERSON ROSS: Yes. Although I was not technically a flight nurse I was on the neonatal transport team. It's slightly different but we worked with infants and flew them.

MR. ROBB: Mr. Ross, based upon what you've heard so far is there anything about your experience that would affect your ability to fairly and impartially hear the evidence, apply the instructions and the law and decide this case sir?

VENIREPERSON ROSS: I don't think so.

One of plaintiff's primary fact witnesses was a flight nurse and this venireperson likely would give her testimony additional weight. Defense counsel requested and obtained a for cause strike of venireperson Ross.

Experience flying in a helicopter may yield extreme reactions. The potential juror may have loved the experience and had no safety concerns whatsoever. Others may have been terrified and would never climb aboard a helicopter again. One of the purposes of this question is to assess whether the venireperson may be inclined to impose any fault on the plaintiff merely for riding in the helicopter.

> MR. ROBB: This case involves a young woman who was flying in a helicopter. Have any among you ever had the experience in your lives of flying in a helicopter? Yes Mr. Wheeler.
> VENIREPERSON WHEELER: Oh, many years ago when I took a helicopter from Midway to O'Hare Airport in Chicago.
> MR. ROBB: Is that the only time?
> VENIREPERSON WHEELER: Only time I've been in a helicopter, thank goodness.

The following juror's experience would be fairly neutral:

> VENIREPERSON JOHNSON: Yes, just a helicopter ride over Table Rock Lake.
> MR. ROBB: Was it a small—
> VENIREPERSON JOHNSON: Just a small helicopter.
> MR. ROBB: Four or five-seat helicopter?
> VENIREPERSON JOHNSON: I think there were three of us.
> MR. ROBB: Was this what we call a touring helicopter?
> VENIREPERSON JOHNSON: Yes.
> MR. ROBB: Anything at all about the experience that would affect your ability to be a fair and impartial juror and hear the evidence impartially in this case?
> VENIREPERSON JOHNSON: No.

The following exchange reveals some concern and anxiety about helicopter flight:

> MR. ROBB: Mr. Neal what's been your experience?
> VENIREPERSON NEAL: Just an excursion over Mount Rushmore. My daughter and I flew on one, a small one.
> MR. ROBB: Without incident I presume?
> VENIREPERSON NEAL: Luckily. I mean, we had a cowboy pilot. I would have to be medicated before I get on another one (laughter).

> MR. ROBB: Well now we all chuckle. Did you find it to be an unpleasant experience?
> VENIREPERSON NEAL: Very much so.
> MR. ROBB: Terrifying for you personally?
> VENIREPERSON NEAL: Right.
> MR. ROBB: Your daughter was with you.
> VENIREPERSON NEAL: Yes.

The reference to the "cowboy pilot" would suggest this venireperson might be a desirable juror where the case involves risky actions by a defendant pilot leading to the helicopter crash.

Occasionally counsel will find potential jurors who are true helicopter aficionados:

> MR. ROBB: Who on this side of the room has had experience flying in a helicopter? Mr. Farmer?
> VENIREPERSON FARMER: Commercial and travel and stuff and they're easier to get in and out of, quicker and easier to get and around in.
> MR. ROBB: Any experiences that would cause you concern?
> VENIREPERSON FARMER: I prefer them more than airplanes.

The author was not about to permit Venireperson Farmer to be a member of that jury.

c. Experience with homemade helicopters

Those who have experience with home-built helicopters are not desirable plaintiff jurors. These individuals who build helicopters as a hobby would naturally identify with and admire a "real" helicopter manufacturer and they must be stricken for cause:

> MR. ROBB: Thank you. Mr. Barry what was your experience sir riding in a helicopter?
> VENIREPERSON BARRY: Me and my father years ago built a two-man helicopter.
> MR. ROBB: You built a helicopter?
> VENIREPERSON BARRY: Yes.
> MR. ROBB: Now how long ago was that?
> VENIREPERSON BARRY: Fifteen years ago.
> MR. ROBB: How long did you fly in the helicopter that you and your father built?
> VENIREPERSON BARRY: Two years.
> MR. ROBB: Did you build the engine?
> VENIREPERSON BARRY: Yes, we built everything, not by hand. We bought it in pieces and built it.
> MR. ROBB: Did you assemble the engine as well?
> VENIREPERSON BARRY: Yes.

MR. ROBB: Anything about your experience sir having been involved in building a helicopter engine that would cause you any difficulty in being fair and impartial in this case?

VENIREPERSON BARRY: Not really. I can't judge it because I don't know.

The trial court struck helicopter maker Barry for cause. The following juror readily admitted his home-built helicopter experience disqualified him:

MR. ROBB: Mr. Kerr, I think you'd understand why we are concerned about somebody who would not only build helicopters, but also build helicopter engines. And in view of all that experience which we have enumerated, and in searching your own mind and conscience you can understand that someone who has all of that experience may have a very, very difficult time in divorcing themselves from that knowledge and special experience and be able to decide the case solely on the evidence? Would you agree?

VENIREPERSON KERR: Yes, I think I would have a very difficult time.

MR. ROBB: Naturally, you would agree that it would likely interfere with your ability to serve as a fair and impartial juror on this case, would you not, sir?

VENIREPERSON KERR: Yes, I agree.

MR. ROBB: I appreciate your candor, Mr. Kerr. I think you probably bring more knowledge here than anyone else and I appreciate your sharing with us your views and attitudes.

VENIREPERSON KERR: You're welcome.

d. Experience in or association with the aviation industry

One will occasionally encounter panel members who although not pilots or mechanics have a direct business association with or were longtime employees of commercial air carriers, travel agencies or manufacturers of components supplied to the aeronautical industry. Such jurors may have inside knowledge of corner-cutting due to costs and time constraints. The risks of their associating too closely with similarly situated companies such as the defendants in the case at bar are too high. Sufficient factual bases should be established to exercise a for cause strike if possible.

i. Helicopter industry

The types of experiences and opinions potential jurors have of helicopters and helicopter flight are varied but counsel must be able to elicit that experience and opinions for all of the purposes mentioned earlier. Many times it is instructive when a potential juror recalls an incident and chooses to raise her hand. On the second day of jury selection in one helicopter crash case the first question out of the box is typically as follows:

MR. ROBB: …and having said that, the way I would like to start this morning the first thing is to ask you, having gone home and perhaps thought about some of the questions and matters that we discussed yesterday afternoon, did it occur to anyone with respect to any of those questions that I put to you that perhaps maybe something occurred to you that you should have answered yesterday?

VENIREPERSON JONES: Yes.

MR. ROBB: What was it that you thought of?

VENIREPERSON JONES: My father-in-law was on the committee to get air ambulances for St. Joseph Hospital and, of course, they have Life Flight.

Given that the hospital had been a defendant in the case at one time, counsel elected to develop grounds for support of a for cause challenge which was granted.

MR. ROBB: And Mr. Drasier what was your experience in flying on a helicopter, sir?

VENIREPERSON DRASIER: I flew in one. We worked on jet engines and we worked on some jet engines for helicopters. I only flew in one once in the Philippines. If you asked me would I fly in another one today? No. Jets don't bother me. I just don't like helicopters.

Venirepersons with mechanical experience and especially any experience as an aircraft mechanic must be identified. Those with specific experience with helicopters need to be challenged for cause for reasons stated earlier, in that they will be viewed as the "expert" on the jury.

VENIREPERSON LISTER: I had over ten years of experience in actual aircraft mechanics, engine mechanics. I actually flew next to the pilot as a flight mechanic on engines. My specialty was jet engines.

That developed into a for cause challenge which was granted by the trial court:

MR. ROBB: The next one we have, Your Honor, is No. 54, Mr. Lister. Mr. Lister also had an experience which could interfere with his ability to be fair and impartial sitting on this jury. He said he works as a mechanic on jet engines, and would not be able to set his experiences aside and sever them and that they would impact and color his ability to serve as a fair and impartial juror.

THE COURT: Mr. Lister did so indicate and challenge for cause as to Mr. Lister is sustained.

ii. General Aviation

In addition to identifying all potential jurors who are affiliated with the helicopter industry, counsel must explore whether anyone on the panel has any relation to or past experience with commercial and general aviation or piloting:

MR. ROBB: You have people in your family who have done both commercial and general aviation?

VENIREPERSON DIAMOND: Right.

MR. ROBB: To your knowledge did they ever fly in a helicopter?

VENIREPERSON DIAMOND: I don't believe so. My uncle worked for American Airlines. He is retired now. But my aunt and uncle both fly small planes.

Potential jurors like Mrs. Diamond must be questioned thoroughly about whether their relative's experience in the aviation industry would cause them to identify with any of the defendants.

The last important connection would be anyone on a jury panel who is acquainted with or has close friends as opposed to relatives in the airplane industry. Such individuals may have more of a business orientation because of that affiliation as follows:

MR. ROBB: Yes Mrs. Smith.

VENIREPERSON SMITH: I have lots of friends in the aviation field.

MR. ROBB: Naturally because of your business and your experience?

VENIREPERSON SMITH: Right.

MR. ROBB: I am glad you brought that to our attention.

Mrs. Smith would not be a desirable juror because she would identify with the defendants.

Some people have experiences which would make it risky for counsel to keep them on a jury:

MR. ROBB: Would you tell us about your experience?

VENIREPERSON BELT: My ex-husband was a crew chief in the military, in the Air Force so I've heard countless stories of crashes and talk about wheth-

er it was pilot error or mechanical and their fault. There were countless stories. Just part of being an Air Force wife.

MR. ROBB: Would any of those experiences that you have had effect your ability to be a fair and impartial juror in this case?

VENIREPERSON BELT: I'm not sure it could.

MR. ROBB: You think perhaps knowing what you do know that you would be more comfortable on a case where aviation crashes were not involved?

VENIREPERSON BELT: Yes.

MR. ROBB: Do you feel that it would be difficult for you to set aside that experience and fairly and impartially decide this case?

VENIREPERSON BELT: Yes.

MR. ROBB: I appreciate your candor.

It is difficult to know whether Ms. Belt's husband's prior experience with military air crashes were mostly pilot error or mostly mechanical, and the risks of further inquiry are too great. Counsel may elicit some statement such as "All were pilot error" which may not be helpful in that case. Prudence dictates that such a venireperson be stricken for cause if possible.

e. Belief that deceased assumed risk of helicopter flight

Over the last several years the author has added a question about whether anyone on the panel might believe that the plaintiff's deceased [by name] is even partially to blame for getting aboard the helicopter. Even though no legal issue may exist in the case as to assumption of risk or comparative fault by the occupant who was flying in the helicopter, some people may think some fault should be assessed. There have been panel members who have responded positively to this question and have concluded that the plaintiff got what was coming. Another approach to eliciting this same bias or attitude is to inquire whether any on the panel believe that the plaintiff or plaintiff's deceased bears even the smallest iota of fault because she chose to go on that helicopter tour. It may take some prodding, but one or two panel members will normally volunteer some concerns along these lines. Those concerns should be explored and those folks stricken for cause if the concerns demonstrably interfere with their ability to be fair to plaintiff's position.

A recent voir dire from a case the author tried in Las Vegas illustrates this issue:

MR. ROBB: Any of you — we've had some potential panel members talk about the fact that they think it's maybe inherently, and I may not be saying it correctly, but I'm going to do my best, risky to go on a helicopter and that they wouldn't do it.

Do any of you feel that way, that it's risky to go on a helicopter and that their loved ones perhaps to some extent took a risk? Any of you feel that way?

PROSPECTIVE JUROR NO. 412: I personally wouldn't go on a helicopter —

MR. ROBB: And we have to for the record, Mr. Minnow, 412.

PROSPECTIVE JUROR NO. 412: Four, twelve.

MR. ROBB: 412. Did you have a — is there a particular reason? Talk to me about why that is.

PROSPECTIVE JUROR NO. 412: I just — I just personally wouldn't do it. I just don't feel it's safe.

MR. ROBB: How long have you had that opinion?

PROSPECTIVE JUROR NO. 412: I just wouldn't do it. You know, now that I'm here having to discuss it, I just personally wouldn't do it.

MR. ROBB: I understand. And —

PROSPECTIVE JUROR NO. 412: Planes are enough.

MR. ROBB: You know why I'm asking the question, because of my concern that in the back of somebody's mind they'd say they had it coming. They took the risk, they went on that helicopter, they're all over 21, you know what, things happen. Do you feel that way?

PROSPECTIVE JUROR NO. 412: I believe that anybody that does anything, it's their business, you know. I have no control over that, but that's my personal opinion.

MR. ROBB: And I understand that. But I guess my question is how strongly, and I'm sensing that you feel pretty strongly in your mind, I mean, if somebody said, Mr. Fred Minnow, you won a free helicopter ride, would you turn it down?

PROSPECTIVE JUROR NO. 412: Probably.

MR. ROBB: So you feel pretty strongly about this issue, that it — it's a risk that you would not expose yourself to?

PROSPECTIVE JUROR NO. 412: Right. Right. Or my family.

MR. ROBB: Or your family. How long have you felt that way?

PROSPECTIVE JUROR NO. 412: It's just my thought, you know. It's not a particular time, time frame.

MR. ROBB: But I mean, it's not something you just thought of yesterday, with all due respect?

PROSPECTIVE JUROR NO. 412: Right. Right.

MR. ROBB: You've had this thought long before you came into the courtroom —

PROSPECTIVE JUROR NO. 412: Right. I wouldn't bungee jump. I wouldn't do stuff like that. I wouldn't go up on Stratosphere, stuff like that. It's, you know, just a thought.

MR. ROBB: I understand.

PROSPECTIVE JUROR NO. 412: If you're asking me a question, I'm giving you an answer.

MR. ROBB: And you've been here since Monday and you know that that's exactly what this Court expects and that's what I appreciate, because that's what this system is all about. Everybody knows by now what this process is called. It's called voir dire and you're doing it. So let's keep talking. You mentioned bungee jumping.

PROSPECTIVE JUROR NO. 412: Right.

MR. ROBB: If somebody bungee jumps and the cord breaks, would you say they did take a little bit of a risk?

PROSPECTIVE JUROR NO. 412: Absolutely.

MR. ROBB: By the same token, since you kind of put them in the same category, sir, would you feel to any way, shape or form that people who voluntarily do get on a helicopter, no one forces them, they're all adults, that to some degree they're taking a risk? Do you agree with that statement?

PROSPECTIVE JUROR NO. 412: I do.

[Finally, the unequivocal answers demonstrating the bias:]

MR. ROBB: And I imagine, Mr. Minnow, just having spoken with you for 27 minutes now, I don't know what it is, that you're the kind of gentleman that if I tried to talk you out of it or the judge tried to talk you out of that particular attitude, it ain't going to be successful?

PROSPECTIVE JUROR NO. 412: No.

MR. ROBB: Not this week, not next week, not next month?

PROSPECTIVE JUROR NO. 412: No.

MR. ROBB: Would it be fair that you couldn't assure these families that that thought process would not come into play as you enter into this case; fair and true and accurate?

PROSPECTIVE JUROR NO. 412: Yes.

MR. ROBB: Would you agree that you are telling me these things, Mr. Minnow, because they are how you honestly and sincerely feel and for no other reason?

PROSPECTIVE JUROR NO. 412: Yes.

MR. ROBB: Mr. Minnow, you did not — I don't recall your trying to get out of jury service by hardship, did you, sir?

PROSPECTIVE JUROR NO. 412: No.

MR. ROBB: Respectfully, would you understand and recognize that if you were in another type of case that's not a helicopter case, that your opinion or attitude would not come into play and potentially impair your decision or the way you receive the evidence?

PROSPECTIVE JUROR NO. 412: Right.

MR. ROBB: Are we tracking?

PROSPECTIVE JUROR NO. 412: Yes.

MR. ROBB: So here's my question. Would you recognize, sir, that at least it's more probably true than not true that this opinion you have that those folks over there, their relatives, family members, to some extent, to some extent took a risk by getting on that chopper that day, true?

PROSPECTIVE JUROR NO. 412: Yes.

Now, counsel is prepared to take the next step:

MR. ROBB: And you would agree, sir, searching your heart and your conscience, that that attitude and opinion and belief that you sincerely and honestly hold would prevent and substantially impair your ability to be a fair and impartial juror in this case to those folks based on what their relatives did, true?

PROSPECTIVE JUROR NO. 412: Yes.

MR. ROBB: And you're saying it because it is true and it's how you honestly feel?

PROSPECTIVE JUROR NO. 412: Yes.

MR. ROBB: And you understand that it's a serious issue that would seek to impart fault or risk to the deceased because that's a very serious aspect of the case; you understand that?

PROSPECTIVE JUROR NO. 412: Yes.

MR. ROBB: And I would put it to you one more time. There's no question in your mind as you sit here today, on Wednesday, August 27, 2014, that within the next four weeks that you would be hearing this case, that particular attitude that you hold honestly, Mr. Minnow, would no doubt in your mind interfere with your ability to be a fair and impartial juror in this case, true?

PROSPECTIVE JUROR NO. 412: My own thoughts, yes.

MR. ROBB: And if the other lawyer asked you these exact same questions, your answers would be pre-

cisely the same because they are honest and that's how you feel, correct?

PROSPECTIVE JUROR NO. 412: Yes.

MR. ROBB: And you're not saying them just to get out of jury service, are you?

PROSPECTIVE JUROR NO. 412: No.

MR. ROBB: If the judge asked you these questions, your answers would be the same because they are true?

PROSPECTIVE JUROR NO. 412: Yes.

MR. ROBB: Thank you, Mr. Minnow. And I again, it's not — you know, if you think it's easy, and you know it's not easy to bare your heart in front — you didn't know any of these people before here, did you, sir?

PROSPECTIVE JUROR NO. 412: No.

MR. ROBB: Thank you very much for your candor and your honesty. And you are why this system works and why I believe we obtain fair and impartial juries in this country, and I thank you.

PROSPECTIVE JUROR NO. 412: Thank you.

The trial court excused Mr. Minnow for cause based on his answers to these questions. If prospective jurors make it to the jury room with the belief that "the helicopter passengers took the risk," not only are damages potentially compromised but also liability itself will be jeopardized.

5. Other Relevant Experiences
a. Self-employment
Self-employed jurors tend to identify very closely with defendants because they know first-hand the costs of liability insurance and are normally conservative in their thinking. Absent some strong predilection that the particular juror examined could be completely fair to plaintiff's position, such persons should be stricken either for cause or by peremptory challenge.

b. Mechanical experience
The danger in mechanically trained jurors is that they will be for all intents and purposes the expert to whom the jury turns for any mechanical issues. In almost every helicopter crash case where the issue is broader than pilot error, there will be some mechanical or technical issue. It is too risky to base the entire liability determination on the singular judgment of one juror notwithstanding his ability to understand the issue at hand and communicate it accurately to fellow jurors. Gambling is for the casinos and not for voir dire:

MR. ROBB: Anyone else have that experience? Mr. Williams?

VENIREPERSON WILLIAMS: I had over three years experience in actual aircraft mechanics, engine mechanics. I actually flew next to the pilot as a flight mechanic on engines. My specialty was engines. They were not helicopter engines.

MR. ROBB: Were they turbine engines?

VENIREPERSON WILLIAMS: No, sir, piston.

MR. ROBB: This is a turbo shaft, turbo engine. That is not something you are familiar with?

VENIREPERSON WILLIAMS: I've had courses in their operation but we did not have any at that time.

MR. ROBB: Okay. Mr. Williams, if the Court asked you to be on this jury, is there anything about your experience which would cause you to have difficulty in evaluating the evidence fairly and impartially as to both sides?

VENIREPERSON WILLIAMS: Well, my understanding of mechanics might interfere.

MR. ROBB: Do you feel in your mind that if there is evidence in this case which differs from your own opinion or belief as to how something is done, that your own opinion or belief could possibly override the evidence in this case?

VENIREPERSON WILLIAMS: I could listen to the evidence.

MR. ROBB: Now, my question is: You can listen to the evidence but is it a possibility, Mr. Williams, that your experience could—and I'm not saying even which way this plays out whether this would be for the plaintiff or defendant because that is not the important point. The point is, is it a possibility that your experience that you bring to bear having worked on these aircraft engines could override what the Court permits in as evidence for the consideration of the jury in this case? Is that a possibility? Can you say one way or another?

VENIREPERSON WILLIAMS: No, sir I can't.

MR. ROBB: Is it a possibility it could influence?

VENIREPERSON WILLIAMS: It could influence.

MR. ROBB: You couldn't guarantee us, Mr. Williams, as you decide this case that your own experience wouldn't sway you one way or other?

VENIREPERSON WILLIAMS: I couldn't say that.

MR. ROBB: Mr. Williams, I appreciate your candor and your answer because it's important to us to have this jury—pick this jury.

Mr. Williams was stricken for cause.

c. Personal experience with dangerous or unsafe products

This is a critical area for exploration in any case involving a claim of design defect of a helicopter component part or system. The answers to look for here involve a push back to the user or operator of the equipment. Some responses along those lines will be "Yes I injured myself but it was my own darn fault" or "Products don't hurt people, people do." Responses detailing an experience with a home appliance, tool or vehicle that malfunctioned and critically injured the venireperson or family member will yield a defense challenge. Plaintiff's counsel should demonstrate how fair and even handed they are by making the for cause challenge themselves.

6. Philosophical, Religious or Moral Beliefs Interfering with Ability to Serve as Juror

This is a highly personal and intrusive series of questions. These should not be undertaken until later in the session after jurors can trust that they will not be humiliated or ridiculed for expressing intimate beliefs.

a. Determinism

Determinism is the philosophy or belief that destiny pre-determines when events will happen and specifically when people die. There are people who ascribe to the deterministic point of view whether in the context of some religious belief or otherwise. It is a point of view inconsistent with the purposes of the civil justice system because it would not ascribe fault to defendants for the wrongful death. Simply, but respectfully stated, the philosophy is that "stuff happens" whether we intend it or not. In every instance in the author's experience where a prospective panel member has described an adherence to deterministic beliefs, the trial court has stricken that panel member for cause.

Almost every jury panel will include one or two individuals who have a personal or religious belief that "accidents happen" and that this is a pre-determined matter based on destiny:

MR. ROBB: Is there any adherence to or believers of the philosophy of determinism among this panel? That it is a matter of destiny regarding when it is your time to die. When it is your time to die, no matter how young, it is your time to go. Is there anyone who adheres to this particular philosophy?

VENIREPERSON SMITH: Yes, I do.

MR. ROBB: That would be something that would be difficult for you to set aside under any circumstances I would imagine, wouldn't it?

VENIREPERSON SMITH: Yes, I think it would be. I've lost a lot of family through natural causes and through accidents and it would be very difficult.

MR. ROBB: Knowing how you feel about that, searching your conscience and soul, you believe it would affect your ability to be a juror in this case?

VENIREPERSON SMITH: I would think so. When it is your time, it's your time. There is nothing you can do about it.

Venireperson Smith was stricken from the panel for cause.

b. Difficulty sitting in judgment

There are religious sects and moral philosophies adhering to the belief that one human being should not sit in judgment of another human being. That, however, is precisely what a civil jury is being asked to do with respect to the conduct of the defendants in allegedly causing a death or serious injury as a result of a helicopter crash. This hesitancy is a difficult hurdle for counsel to overcome and a sensitive but thorough exposition of the belief should lay the appropriate foundation for a successful for cause challenge.

7. Relevant Beliefs about Court System
a. Opinions about frivolous lawsuits

Much has been written about the criticality of exploring venirepersons' beliefs and attitudes about tort reform. The most effective and open-ended question to launch into that discussion is, "What are your thoughts and feelings about what has been called 'the lawsuit crises' or 'tort reform'?" The question is neutral and the responses will reveal much about prospective jurors' mindset about lawsuits.

Some on the panel may express the belief that people should not be able to come into court to seek money damages in injury or death cases because of the insurance costs and other society ills as a result. The function of this and the remaining series of questions is to identify any such biases, opinions or attitudes among the panel and variations or permutations thereof.

MR. ROBB: Mr. Oliver, I made a note that you had a concern in this area; is that true?

VENIREPERSON OLIVER: My concern in this particular area was more along the lines of frivolous lawsuits, not in a cap.

MR. ROBB: You believe there are frivolous lawsuits?

VENIREPERSON OLIVER: I believe there are.

MR. ROBB: Do you believe there are too many lawsuits?

VENIREPERSON OLIVER: Too many lawsuits.

MR. ROBB: Is that a yes or no?

VENIREPERSON OLIVER: Lawsuits, yeah, there's too many lawsuits, but what makes them too many are the ones that are frivolous.

MR. ROBB: Would you be able with that attitude or opinion to apply the specific instructions in the law that the Court is going to give in this case without influencing—being influenced by the fact you think some lawsuits are too frivolous? Would that cause you a problem in some way? If it is, I would appreciate your candor in hearing about it so we can explore it.

Let me put it to you this way, Mr. Oliver, because I think I understand what you are saying. Is it possible, is it possible that your concern or attitude about the frivolity of suits, is it possible that that is something that is ingrained and part of your overall attitude and framework and web of attitudes and beliefs; is that correct?

VENIREPERSON OLIVER: That is correct.

MR. ROBB: Is this an opinion and philosophy that you have expressed to others on more than one occasion?

VENIREPERSON OLIVER: Numerous occasions.

MR. ROBB: Would it be difficult for Mr. Oliver to extract in any circumstances that attitude or opinion from his being, from your attitudinal framework?

Let me put it to you this way: If a person, not you, but if a person had this firmly entrenched attitude or belief, would you agree that such a person couldn't guarantee us that attitude or belief wouldn't color even remotely their ability to assess the evidence in this case where that could be an issue? Would you agree with that? Not you but a person who has your attitude?

VENIREPERSON OLIVER: A person with a similar attitude I can see where it could cloud.

MR. ROBB: Obviously, you are willing to be a juror. You sat through all these hours. You are willing—

VENIREPERSON OLIVER: I've been a juror before.

MR. ROBB: You are willing to serve on a jury?

VENIREPERSON OLIVER: Yes, sir.

MR. ROBB: There are cases where that isn't even an issue; criminal cases, other cases, trespass where frivolous is not an issue or it couldn't conceivably be an issue. You recognize that.

VENIREPERSON OLIVER: I recognize that.

MR. ROBB: You can naturally assume that could create to others outside this courthouse the appearance, just the appearance of impartiality to have somebody, not you, but like you on a jury deciding cases such as this given the magnitude? Would you agree with that?

VENIREPERSON OLIVER: I can see that, yes.

MR. ROBB: Naturally, sir, given your soul searching you've done on this point, Mr. Oliver, and asking you in all candor if instead of being this hypothetical person, if we talked specifically and only about David Oliver, you couldn't guarantee us or this Court with 100 percent certainty you could set aside this point of view and fairly and impartially decide the case? Removing that, you couldn't do it, could you, sir?

VENIREPERSON OLIVER: One hundred percent honestly, no, I could not.

MR. ROBB: Because there is a likelihood or probability that these things, because you can't separate your own attitudes, could creep into the way you view the evidence; agreed?

VENIREPERSON OLIVER: I would like to think not but I understand.

MR. ROBB: In all candor you would agree with me wouldn't you, sir?

VENIREPERSON OLIVER: I would agree.

MR. ROBB: Mr. Oliver, I thank you for your candor because it is citizens like you that make this process work.

Mr. Oliver was stricken for cause.

b. Belief that there are too many lawsuits

This is another variant of the tort reform line of questions and should generate the same show of hands although counsel must spot the new ones. Another variant that should be put to the panel includes "Is too much money being awarded?" All of these are designed to insure that any prospective juror's attitudes or biases reflecting on any aspect of the civil justice system are identified and can be further explored by counsel.

c. Belief that court system should restrict amounts of money in injury or death cases

Most jurors will understand what it means to put "caps on damages." Whereas one potential juror will respond to a question about "caps on damages," another may raise her hand only when asked to express a belief whether a court system should restrict the amounts of money awarded. That is why these questions must be asked in a number of different ways. Any jurors who believe that there should be artificial damages caps are dangerous for the plaintiff. The

preferred approach is to confirm the duration and strength of that conviction prior to asking whether that conviction would in all likelihood interfere with the potential juror's ability to assess fair damages pursuant to the court's instructions on the law:

MR. ROBB: That is my point. Anybody here who feels there should be some arbitrary or predetermined limit on any kind of damages before the evidence is even heard? In other words, it should be set and that is the maximum, or would people be more inclined to believe that every case should be judged on its own merits and based on the evidence? May I see a show of hands who believe you should assess the damages in every case based on the evidence in that case rather than an arbitrary amount?

And who would have an attitude or belief to the contrary, that we should cap or, for example—I'll throw out an example. Whatever the damages would be for a dead person, $50 and that—or whatever $500, a $1,000. Is there anybody who believes there should be some kind of a monetary ceiling to any type of damages which would be awarded for the death of a human being? Anyone at all?

Yes, ma'am. I apologize because I saw that you had your hand up before. And you are Ms. Roberts, Ms. Karen Roberts?

VENIREPERSON ROBERTS: Yes.

MR. ROBB: Would you share your thought with us.

VENIREPERSON ROBERTS: Well, you are saying we can put a price on a death. I don't think that we can come in and say that this person's life was worth more than this person's. Yes, I think you should put a cap on someone's death so the damage should be allowed this much. I think the family or anyone should be compensated, but I do believe that the numbers are so high. I don't understand—I have a three-year old son. I don't understand how that much money would make it okay that he was gone no matter how much I was compensated. So it seems a little bit ridiculous when you are talking huge amounts, stuff I heard in the media. So I don't have—always have all the detail.

MR. ROBB: Is this a point of view you had for some time now, Ms. Roberts?

VENIREPERSON ROBERTS: Yes.

MR. ROBB: You expressed your point of views to others?

VENIREPERSON ROBERTS: Here today? I mean—

MR. ROBB: Before today.

VENIREPERSON ROBERTS: Yes.

MR. ROBB: And you had—you've had this point of view, this opinion for some time?

VENIREPERSON ROBERTS: I think so.

MR. ROBB: Would I be correct in suggesting that this would be perhaps part of your own internal mature set of beliefs and attitudes that you as an adult have?

VENIREPERSON ROBERTS: Yes.

MR. ROBB: That would be ingrained in you?

VENIREPERSON ROBERTS: Yes.

MR. ROBB: Obviously, as we have discussed, you are willing to be a juror and do your civic duty? You are here.

VENIREPERSON ROBERTS: Yes.

MR. ROBB: I would presume that and I think you understand that there may be other cases in this courthouse where your services as a juror are required and necessary which wouldn't involve assessing damages in a death case or that potentiality? You would acknowledge that?

VENIREPERSON ROBERTS: Yes, I would.

MR. ROBB: Ms. Roberts, would you agree that from appearance standpoint, that a person such as yourself who has that firmly ingrained belief couldn't exclude with 100 percent certainty the possibility that they could deliberate in this case without having their own attitude or opinion influenced how they arrive at a verdict?

VENIREPERSON ROBERTS: I would like to think—

MR. ROBB: We are not talking about you, yet we are talking about from appearances standpoint. If someone such as yourself has that attitude, that it would be very difficult for such a person to exclude 100 percent to guarantee this Court and the parties and the lawyers that they would not permit that attitude, point of view to influence their own evaluation of the case. Now, that would be difficult for such a person, wouldn't it?

VENIREPERSON ROBERTS: Yes.

MR. ROBB: Naturally, in that you have that type of attitude or belief that is ingrained in you, ma'am, in all candor and knowing the importance of this, would you agree that your attitude would make it difficult for you to assess how to put a dollar figure on the loss of a human being in this case? Would you acknowledge that?

VENIREPERSON ROBERTS: Probably.

MR. ROBB: I appreciate your candor. There may be other cases—there may be other matters in this courthouse which don't involve this sensitive matter for you, and I appreciate your honesty in dealing with us.

Of course, the "tort reformers" are ever present:

MR. ROBB: Mr. Dowd, would you share your thoughts with us?

VENIREPERSON DOWD: I would like to see tort reform put caps on liability. Personally I think there's misuse of it, and it's raising costs for the medical professionals and others and for the insured also.

All jurors with such beliefs should be stricken for cause as their negative beliefs about the civil justice system will poison the deliberations of the jury.

d. Opinions about wrongful death damages

The panel members should be advised that should there be a finding of liability the trial court will provide to them the law for properly assessing damages. That damages finding contains two elements: one for economic loss, the other for non-economic loss. Non-economic elements in a jurisdiction may consist of spousal consortium, fellowship, company, affection, aid, usefulness, industry and attention.

A surprising number of prospective jurors firmly believe that surviving family members in a wrongful death case should be compensated only for their economic or financial loss and not for these other factors referred to variously as "fluff," "gold digger money," or even "blood money." It is often the case that widows who have lost a husband early due to accident or a health condition and were uncompensated do not believe that others should be compensated for their own husband's death. The strong and longly held conviction by such potential jurors is inconsistent with the law of damages in most jurisdictions. Prospective jurors who hold to the belief that a surviving family member's recovery should be limited to economic loss without consideration of other elements such as consortium, companionship and fellowship must be identified and stricken for cause:

MR. ROBB: Anybody have that thought or belief, opinion, attitude? Is there anyone here who would feel that they could not follow the court's instruction about considering spousal consortium issues such as the loss of companionship, the loss of fellowship, the normal benefits of a spouse and not just the lost wages?

VENIREPERSON PARSONS: I don't know. I kind of feel like a death is kind of normal process whether by accident or purpose or whatever. I can see the monetary support for any sort of financial loss that the person was bringing into the family unit. But emotional distress and everything, I have a problem with that.

MR. ROBB: Is that a feeling or belief that you had prior to today?

VENIREPERSON PARSONS: Yes.

MR. ROBB: That you have had for some time?

VENIREPERSON PARSONS: Yes.

MR. ROBB: Is it a strongly held belief?

VENIREPERSON PARSONS: Yes.

MR. ROBB: One that probably is not going to be going away in the next month?

VENIREPERSON PARSONS: No.

MR. ROBB: You will have that belief going into your jury deliberations?

VENIREPERSON PARSONS: Yes.

MR. ROBB: You can see from our point of view why I'm asking this.

VENIREPERSON PARSONS: Yes.

MR. ROBB: Do you think if you were asked to follow that law that you're long held very strong beliefs could run head-on into the court's instructions and maybe you would have a problem with that?

VENIREPERSON PARSONS: Yes.

MR. ROBB: Would that ma'am in all fairness affect your ability on this damages issue to be a fair and impartial juror?

VENIREPERSON PARSONS: Yes.

Venireperson Parsons was stricken by the court for cause.

Similar are those venirepersons who are reluctant to give any recovery to family members who have lost a loved one. That attitude is often difficult to elicit but can be deduced by addressing accidental deaths of family members.

VENIREPERSON ORR: I agree that money is not going to replace her husband. It isn't going to replace any one of our loved ones. They're gone.

MR. ROBB: You are so right about that. And if she could go to some court and get her husband back, she would go there.

VENIREPERSON ORR: Right.

MR. ROBB: But, Ms. Orr, my question to you is: Given that that's the only thing she can do, there is no other court that she could go to other than this one. Is that an opinion that you had for some time?

VENIREPERSON ORR: Yes.

MR. ROBB: Pretty strongly held?

VENIREPERSON ORR: Yes.

MR. ROBB: Could you just leave it at the foot of the jury room when you go in there, or does that opinion go with you?

VENIREPERSON ORR: That's a part of me, so I guess it goes with me.

MR. ROBB: Of course. Fair to say that searching your conscience and thinking about it as only you can look into your conscience, Ms. Orr, that it would be difficult for you to be fair and impartial on that issue in this case?

VENIREPERSON ORR: Money is not going to replace the person.

MR. ROBB: Let me put it to you a different way. More probably than not as to this issue, you would find it difficult to be fair and impartial to our client on this issue agreed?

VENIREPERSON ORR: Agreed.

MR. ROBB: Thank you Ms. Orr, for your candor and for your honesty. It's not easy to be in a room full of strangers and express these opinions, and I appreciate it very much.

Venireperson Orr was stricken for cause by the court.

e. Opinions about punitive damages

Counsel must determine the law of the jurisdiction to assess what leeway may be had on questions concerning punitive damages. In some jurisdictions the question may be asked only by prior approval of the trial court while in others there is a specified form for that question. In any case where a punitive submission is likely, counsel must assess the willingness of jurors to follow the law in that regard without hesitation.

f. Belief that people should not be able to sue a corporation for money

Although unlikely that this would generate any new responses counsel cannot take that chance and need to inquire whether any member of the jury panel believe that people should not be able to sue a corporation for money. That question will on occasion generate a separate response that must be addressed and explored. Any venireperson with a strongly held opinion or belief in this regard assuredly will be stricken for cause.

g. Personal, religious or moral belief that one should not sue for a wrongful death

Somewhat related to the deterministic belief is the opinion that lawsuits should not be brought for a wrongful death. Many panel members explain their belief as based on the premise that "money won't bring the person back" or "people should not profit from someone's death." Whatever the reason, these are dangerous potential jurors and the sufficient factual basis should be elicited in terms of the length of time the venireperson has maintained this belief as well as the strength and conviction of that belief in laying the groundwork for the successful for cause strike.

10.2 Opening Statement

Early social science studies on juries confirmed what most trial lawyers knew by instinct and experience: an overwhelming majority of jurors, some studies report 80-85 percent, make up their mind about the outcome of the case based on the opening statements. In no other aspect of trial does the principle of primacy account for more. The jurors are interested, receptive and anxious to learn what is expected of them. The opening statement is counsel's first chance to set out for the jury the facts of the case and to do so in the most persuasive and understandable manner possible laying the foundation for a favorable verdict.

A. Objectives and Suggested Techniques

There are some general principles which apply in full force to all helicopter crash case opening statements:

1. Do Not Argue the Case

The opening statement should be in the form of what counsel expects the evidence to show. The jury will resent counsel's arguing or drawing inferences from the facts and counsel is likely to draw an objection that is likely to be sustained. Properly presented, counsel need not argue in the opening statement, but may present the evidence in such a way that there is only one appropriate verdict.

2. Do Not Use Notes

Suppose one is at dinner with friends and a fellow lawyer says "I've been working on this case for three years let me tell you a little bit about it." The friend brings out a yellow legal pad with pages of notes to read to those munching on their salads. Several thoughts come to mind. First, and most telling, after years of preparation, the lawyer does not know the case. Second, the lawyer is afraid to speak without the crutch of notes. Third, and most importantly, those assembled will quickly lose interest because the lawyer will make no eye contact. Who wants to listen to someone reading anyway?

Precisely the same responses will be forthcoming from members of a jury. If counsel has been involved in the case through pre-trial investigation, filing and the extensive discovery, there will be no need to take notes to the lectern for opening statement. The confidence displayed by counsel in striding to a spot comfortably in front of the jury box also inspires the jury to believe that lawyer. The impact of maintaining eye contact throughout the opening is irretrievably lost by the use of notes.

3. Be Yourself

This is self-explanatory. A lawyer must present the opening statement in a natural and conversational manner. Any attempt to engage in hyperbole or other dramatics will quickly turn off the jury.

4. Make Extensive Use of Exhibits and Demonstrative Aids

No one on the jury will know a swashplate from a servo or a rod from a rudder pedal. Descriptive words alone will be woefully insufficient. Counsel has an opportunity in the opening to introduce and show the jury exhibits that will assist them in understanding the evidence. This is not optional in helicopter crash trials.

Following these four general rules for the opening statement will start the trial off positively and permit an efficient and persuasive presentation of plaintiff's evidence. Opening statement will be counsel's first opportunity to explain to the jury how and why this helicopter crash occurred and to set out the impact in terms of the harms, losses and other damages suffered by the plaintiffs as a result of that crash. The critical points of that opening should include:

a. Helicopter Flight Purpose

Counsel must provide a sufficient explanation of helicopter flight to enable the jury to understand the precise mission of the aircraft. Use of an enlarged map or a topographical model at this juncture helps convey to the jury the nature of the flight and the surrounding circumstances.

b. Standards of Care

Counsel must explain the proper and ordinary standards of care in terms of the appropriate practices that should be followed before talking about any negligent conduct by any of the defendants. Counsel must point out that these standards of conduct are not in dispute, that all agree as to what the appropriate rules and standards within the industry are and that they must be followed.

c. Description of Specific Component or System

Where specific components or helicopter systems are alleged to be defective and played a causal role in the crash, counsel must engage in a basic "show and tell" and carefully describe the purpose and function of those component parts or systems. Only thereafter should counsel proceed to describe the precise way in which the component part or system failed and the impact of that failure on overall control and operation of the helicopter.

B. Sample Outline of Opening Statement

A sample outline of an opening statement used in recent helicopter crash trials is as follows:

1. Capsule

These are the first words out of counsel's mouth following recognition from the court. This opportunity should not be wasted. Rather than explaining the purpose of opening statement or the role of counsel at this point, it is far more effective to lay out the essential premise or case theme at the outset. As an example:

> Ladies and gentlemen, this case is about a simple rule: If it's not broke, don't fix it. This defendant company made parts for use on helicopters. The company had a product that worked—no complaints, no problems, no accidents. But it undertook a major re-design of the product. It eliminated the most critical safety feature of the system which made it ineffective and defective and the company did so for one reason—to save money.
>
> As a result of these actions, a good and innocent man was killed in a helicopter crash. The name of that man was Mr. Jonathan Jones.

2. Civics

Here counsel may explain the role of the opening statement, the basic order of witnesses to be called to the stand, and the methods and types of proof to be expected.

3. Rules and Standards of Conduct

Juries want to know the "rules of the game." This applies to rules of conduct for all of the parties, principally the defendants but also the plaintiff. If there is any potential theory of comparative fault against the plaintiff, the rule of conduct applicable to his conduct must be set out and the conduct scrutinized within that framework.

It is most effective for counsel to point out that the helicopter industry rules of conduct are not subject to dispute by anyone in the case. Counsel may then tell the jury that these standards are well known and have been well known to all entities within the industry for a long time. The rules may be stated simply:

- "A component part on a helicopter must have a useful safe life at least as long as that certified or represented by the manufacturer."
- "A pilot faced with the prospect of severe weather conditions that compromise the safety of the mission must not undertake that flight."
- "A helicopter airframe manufacturer must provide proper, safe and understandable instructions for the maintenance of the aircraft."

It is more effective not to tell the jury whether the rules were violated at this juncture; in hearing what happened the jury will be able to determine that for themselves.

4. Identification of Helicopter and Component Part or System at Issue

"Ladies and gentlemen this is a scale model of the helicopter that crashed on August 4, 2006. Every one of you has seen a helicopter but let me point out some of its basic features and explain what they do."

Counsel should then focus on those particular systems which are implicated in the crash. For example, in a case involving in-flight disintegration of the main rotor blade (MRB), counsel should focus the explanation on the criticality of the main rotor blade:

> "This is the main rotor blade. It is the horizontal propeller affixed to the top of the airframe. The main rotor blade provides the sole means of lift and powered flight for any helicopter. Without that main rotor blade working properly, the helicopter will fall out of the sky like a rock."

Where a particular component part is alleged to be the cause of the crash, its purpose and function must be carefully explained. Counsel may wish to consider creating and using a computer-generated animation in the opening statement to depict the workings of the component or system that may not be otherwise visible. Only after a thorough explanation of the proper functioning of the component or system should counsel move to an explanation of precisely what went wrong in the design or manufacturing of that component.

5. Story of the Helicopter Crash

This is the answer to the simple question: "How did this helicopter crash happen?" Here counsel will be able to detail for the jury the specifics of the flight mission, the occupants, location of the flight and, ultimately, the circumstances leading to the crash.

6. Liability and Fault

Here counsel answers in simple and understandable terms the question, "Who is plaintiff suing and why?" Counsel should set out in non-argumentative fashion the specific actions undertaken by the various defendants and leave the basic processing of the information for the jury. It should be obvious to the jury that each defendant violated those rules which the lawyer just outlined. Counsel should address the foreseeable consequences of breaking the rules which may be pilot loss of control of the aircraft, system malfunction, or any other malady which triggered the sequence of events leading to the crash.

7. Damages Caused By Defendants' Conduct

Use of buzzwords during the damages portion of opening statement such as "good provider" or "loyal friend" are ineffective. Jurors want specific facts. Counsel must specify the economic losses sustained and explain how these figures were determined. Though preferably introduced during jury selection, the non-economic elements should be enumerated with specific examples of how plaintiff's loss fits within those categories.

8. Defenses

Given that defenses require evidence, plaintiffs are entitled to preview the evidence of any anticipated defenses. Counsel should not sell any defenses short but must lay them out for the jury and carefully set forth the facts showing why that defense is not persuasive or applicable in this case.

9. Wrap Up

As the late, great Bob Hanley used to say, "When you're done, sit down." Since there are rarely strict time limits on opening statements, there is a temptation for counsel to ramble long after the essentials of the opening have been presented. That is not starting off on a good foot, and when the above points have been covered, counsel should thank the court and jury and be seated.

C. Trial Excerpts and Commentary

1. The first few moments of the opening statement should provide the essential theme of the case:

MR. ROBB: May it please the court?

THE COURT: Yes.

MR. ROBB: Ladies and gentlemen of the jury, eight years ago the highest ranking officers, engineers and executives of this helicopter engine manufacturer, Turbomeca France, eight years before the crash of Life Flight 2 that killed Richard Hartman, knew that they had a very serious problem on their hands with respect to a critical engine component. They knew that there was a part in the helicopter engine that would crack, rupture, come apart without any warning and cause that engine to stop instantaneously while the engine was powering the helicopter in flight. They knew this. And to a person every single one of these executives, officers and engineers knew what a serious danger and life-threatening problem it was.

Once they had notice about it, they set about to investigate. They did full, complete engineering analysis and they were soon able to locate exactly what the part was because that is important to be able to identify what the problem is and they identified exactly what the part was, the name of the part, and where it was in the engine that was failing.

Secondly, they were able to identify exactly, exactly why it was failing, why it was cracking, and why it was breaking apart. But, thirdly, they immediately were able to determine how to fix it, how to retrofit it, or what was needed to make a correct part, a safe part such that the engine wouldn't fail in flight.

And yet once they knew this information, once they had performed their internal engineering analysis, they didn't tell anybody. They didn't tell users, pilots, operators around the world that we've got a dangerous part in the engine and that it can fail and bring the chopper down. They didn't tell Richard Hartman. They didn't tell his employer who operated and maintained the aircraft and they didn't tell any other U.S. aviation authorities nor any of the other civil aviation authorities in the over 100 countries around the world, around the world that use this engine.

There will be a reason that you will determine from the evidence, a single reason why they didn't recall or retrofit which would have been so very easy for them to do. The evidence will establish in this case that the reason they failed to recall or retrofit and fix this dangerous part was cost. It was the cost to the company. For that reason the evidence in this case will show that they did not inform anyone about the danger. The evidence will be that they did not warn anyone using this engine, relying on this engine to maintain powered flight of the helicopter. They didn't know where, they didn't know when, and they didn't know who but they knew. They knew that these engines would fail and engines did fail. Some twenty all around the world from Africa to Guyana to Australia to Portugal to Bolivia, engines failed in flight. People hurt, gravely injured people. We are here in court because this company denies any responsibility for what happened. We are here in court to seek justice.

From this excerpt, the jury knows plaintiff's essential contentions, the anticipated proof, and has an overall framework of what the case is about.

2. In the opening statement of any helicopter crash case, identification of the helicopter and the functioning of the critical components is a must:

MR. ROBB: It will be important in this case to understand a little bit about helicopters, helicopter engines, and this particular part, the nozzle guide vane, and everything you need to know will be explained in the trial. I would like to briefly go over some of the basics concerning this industry so that you will have an overview of what it is exactly we are talking about.

I would like to start with the helicopter itself. This particular aircraft is called an Aerospatiale AS-350B because it was manufactured by a company called Aerospatiale which is now called Eurocopter. Its designation is AS-350B. The B designation is the type of engine used in a helicopter. The B in this case designates it was an Arriel 1B engine which is the engine manufactured and designed by Turbomeca France.

This particular type of helicopter is a very widely used helicopter for a number of different functions all over the world, for business transport, for touring, many police departments use this particular type of helicopter. It's used by the United States Border Patrol. It's also very popular for news-gathering operations for eye-in-the-sky type things, for traffic because it is fairly light.

But one of the major uses of this particular helicopter was for EMS programs because it was just about the right size to carry a pilot, a crew of two which is what they need for an emergency medical services helicopter and enough room for a stretcher such that a patient could be loaded in and strapped down. And that indeed was the use that Turbomeca knew was going to be made of this particular helicopter and this particular engine.

The Arriel 1B engine manufactured by Turbomeca France is what is known as a modular engine. It is a turbine engine or what's called a turbo shaft engine and I'll explain that as we go along. But by a modular design of the engine what that means is that if there's something wrong with one of the modules they are interchangeable, kind of like a blocks set.

I would like to show you the module which we are going to be paying the most attention to in this case. That is Module 3 of the Turbomeca Arriel 1B engine. Just to orient you a little bit, this would be the front of the engine on the left. This would be the back. Airflow comes into the entire engine from a porthole at the top of the engine and the airflow has two critical purposes.

3. Critical liability testimony should be highlighted at the earliest opportunity and that is normally during the opening statement:

Ladies and gentlemen, either tomorrow morning or early tomorrow afternoon you will hear and see the videotaped deposition testimony of Daniel Nesbit who is the highest ranking executive. He is the President of Turbomeca Engine Corporation here in the United States and he says clearly, unequivocally and plainly that the most effective and quickest approach to remedy the TU76 problem would have been to have recalled the engine and retrofitted it with the safe part at the company's expense. He says in no uncertain terms, and you will see it yourself, the reason Turbomeca took the position that it was going to wait until customary overhaul time and take the chance of failure in the interim was one of cost.

One of my last questions to Mr. Nesbit, and you will see and hear it, I asked him, "Mr. Nesbit, as the President of Turbomeca, how would you evaluate an aircraft engine company that would stand by and permit its customers to continue to use a defective engine which they knew to be defective?" His answer, under oath, was, "I would evaluate that situation as being not in accordance with normal industry standards."

Truly powerful evidence cannot be repeated and highlighted enough. In this case, this evidence was foreshadowed in the opening, presented by videotape, further addressed by plaintiff's experts, inquired about in examination of defendant's experts, and then hammered home during closing argument.

10.3 Plaintiff's Case-In-Chief

The order of the plaintiff's case-in-chief in these and other complex litigation trials is important. Counsel should front-load the case with liability witnesses and start with relatively non-controversial fact witnesses. On-scene witnesses or early responders are excellent early witnesses because their testimony is compelling and not seriously disputed by the defense. Counsel then may intersperse some of the videotaped depositions of various defendants and their corporate representatives to be followed by live testimony of plaintiff's liability experts.

A sample outline of the sequence of witnesses presented in a recent helicopter crash case is as follows:

A. On Scene Fact Witnesses (Bystanders and Emergency Responders)
B. Helicopter Maintenance Personnel
C. Owner Operator
D. Defendant's Corporate Representatives
E. Plaintiff's Liability Experts
F. Damages Witnesses (Relatives, Co-Workers, and Friends of Family)
G. Damages Expert
H. Medical and Rehabilitative Witnesses
I. Plaintiffs

Due to the availability and travel schedules of witnesses, there invariably will be exceptions to this sequencing.

A. Direct Examination of On-Scene Witnesses

The most dramatic testimony in the entire trial usually will come from on-scene witnesses of a helicopter crash. It is the author's experience that many such witnesses become emotional in re-telling the event even many years after. These are people who by shear happenstance were in the vicinity of the helicopter accident and the honest, genuine, and unconditional credibility of their testimony can be riveting. Of all helicopter crash trials, perhaps the most compelling on-scene witness the author has ever presented to a jury was that of a flight nurse who survived a horrific helicopter crash. An excerpt from that dramatic trial testimony is as follows:

MR. ROBB: Good afternoon, ma'am. Would you state your full name for our record, please.
A. Sally Ann Ross.
Q. Mrs. Ross, were you the flight nurse aboard Life Flight 2, N34TA on May 27, 2003 at the time it crashed?
A. Yes, I was.
…
Q. I want to return to that date May 27, 2003. Were you on duty as the flight nurse for the crew of Life Flight 1 on that date?
A. Yes I was.
Q. Did you receive a call in the early morning hours to go to pick up a patient at Carthage, Missouri.
A. Yes we did.…
Q. Now, after you had proceeded to your cruising altitude, did you hear the pilot call in a position report?

A. Yes I did.
Q. And would you tell this jury approximately what time he called in that position report?
A. The closest that I can come to is around 6:25.
Q. And at that time was the helicopter operating and cruising normally in every respect based on your experience?
A. As best as I can tell, yes.
Q. Mrs. Ross, would you please tell this jury precisely what you recall happening shortly after the pilot's last position report?
A. I had just finished doing a secondary exam on the patient and taking another set of vitals, and I had reached down to pick up my clipboard to start doing some charting, and it couldn't have been more than a couple minutes after the ground report was called in. I was sitting in the seat behind the pilot and my paramedic was sitting next to me and he was bagging our patient, and all of a sudden we just heard this big, loud pop. It was just so loud. I could almost feel it behind me at my back.

I remember I looked at my paramedic and neither one of us said a word. I just was kind of wanting some sort of indication as to what was going on and he merely just reached over and grabbed the tail of my seat belt and pulled it tighter. About that time I started hearing clatter like something was caught in a fan or kind of like when I was a kid you put baseball cards in the spokes of your bicycle and you would ride it and it would make the clatter noise (sobbing).

MR. ROBB: Could we have a moment, Your Honor?
THE COURT: Yes.
A. And I remember I looked up and I looked through the front of the helicopter trying to zero my focus in on what was making this sound and then I heard this horn go off and the horn is an indicator the pilot's right hand or his right shoulder basically doing something with the cyclic which is the joystick in front of him and I remember seeing his left hand on the collective.

I remember kind of looking back and forth in the cabin trying to figure out what was going on and I remember looking out my side of the helicopter out of my window and I could see the ground coming up.

I remember it felt like we came in tail first. I remember hitting and then the front of the helicopter came down. And then I remember just a lot of dirt and debris going through my face and my arms and my legs just kind of shot out. I don't know how long that took but the next thing I remember—I remember being taught that in these situations the first thing you do is get yourself out of the helicopter and then come back and help the others if you can.

I remember pushing out to my right and I fell out of the helicopter. I was still in my seat belt. I was hanging to my left. My feet were on the ground and I had to hold my upper body up with my hands, and a few minutes later, I would say probably about two minutes, it was just like total silence. There was nothing.

…

Q. Were you contacted by the NTSB concerning this helicopter crash?

A. Yes, I was.

Q. And did the record of that telephone interview become an official part of the Factual Report of the NTSB?

A. Yes.

Q. And did you find that report to be accurate and correct in every respect?

A. Yes.

MR. ROBB: Nothing further, Your Honor.

The testimony of Mrs. Ross humanized the helicopter crash. The jury was placed on board that helicopter at the very moment when the engine failed. That first-hand testimony early on laid the groundwork for much of the liability and damages evidence which followed.

B. Direct Examination of Defendant's Corporate Representatives

Much of this testimony will be presented in plaintiff's case-in-chief in the form of videotaped depositions taken earlier in the discovery phase of the case. Lacking subpoena power over employees of helicopter companies in other states or even in foreign countries, perpetuation and presentation of this testimony by videotaped deposition is a must.

The following is an excerpt from the testimony of the Vice President of Engineering for a major helicopter aircraft company which was presented to the jury by videotaped deposition:

MR. ROBB: Good afternoon, sir.

…

Q. You understand that the Court and jury will have an opportunity to view this videotape at the time of trial?

A. You tell me.

…

Q. Was the TU76 nozzle guide vane defective?

A. For me what is defective is the fact that certain parts are allowed to remain in operation until they have developed a deterioration such that they will induce an engine stoppage.

Q. And using your definition, it is true, isn't it, that with the TU76 hub that such a failure can occur well within the service life limit for these engines set by Turbomeca?

A. It is true that such failures have taken place within the agreed time between overhaul set by our company.

Q. What does the term time between overhaul or TBO mean?

A. It means the time which when it has been used requires that the engine of module to which the TBO refers has to return the repair organization to undertake an overhaul.

Q. That's the time set by you the manufacturer based on the specified number of operating hours correct?

A. Yes.

Q. Is it one of the engineering goals in the design and manufacture of any of these engines to provide the engine with as long a time between overhaul interval as is practical?

A. Yes, and within certain limits.

…

Q. One of the marketing tools that the company used to sell its engines was that it makes an engine that has a longer TBO than one of its competitors, true?…Well, isn't that correct?

A. Certainly TBO is an argument that is a parameter that is used in discussion with our customers to compare the engine with other competing engines but that is not the only one.

Q. Isn't it advantageous to tell your customer that the engine you sell has a longer TBO than one of your competitor's engines?

A. I would say, yes, it is an advantage if we can show we got TBOs.

Q. As of May 1990, the engineering department had done several things with respect to this problem, hadn't it sir.

A. Yes.

Q. They had identified the nature of the defect right?

A. Yes.

Q. They developed a fix, true?

A. Yes.

Q. Developed a second fix, correct?

A. Yes.

Q. And had done some testing on both fixes, the 197 and 202?

A. Yes.

…

Q. At that point in time in-flight failures or problems as we have discovered continued to occur, did they not?

A. Yes.

Q. And before May of 1990, give or take one or two, we have the in-flight failures or problems that we have identified in the Congo and Paris, one, two, three, four, five, Hong Kong, one, two, three, four, five, six, seven. We have seven before May of 1990, correct?

A. I can see on this chart seven, yes seven statements, yes.

Q. Okay before May of 1990?

A. Correct.

Q. Sir, with respect to each of the incidents that occurred prior to May of 1990, through and including the crash of this helicopter, it was known to the engineering department the precise nature of the modifications that were necessary to prevent the cracking of that part, true?

A. Yes.

The factual admissions by the defendant's Chief Engineer as to what the company knew and when it knew it were the keys to this case. Upon that testimony, the case theme was established that this company cared nothing about safety and everything about saving money.

In many aviation companies, the same individual occupies the roles of air accident investigator and in-house litigation coordinator for the company. This "dual role" of the so-called objective air safety investigator can be revealed and exposed to the jury. Although the following excerpt is from one of the author's airplane crash trials and not a helicopter crash case, it illustrates the conflicting demands of this "dual role" of the defendant's aircrash accident investigator:

Q. You are what is called an accident investigator for the company, true?

A. That's an Air Safety Investigator.

Q. And you are serving in that role currently?

A. That's correct.

Q. When there is a crash, the NTSB will call your company and then you'll get the call to assist in the investigation, correct?

A. We can be contacted by the NTSB, the FAA or airframe manufacturer. Or sometimes when we re-

view various accidents on the FAA database, we will contact the local authorities and ask to participate.

Q. And that is a role which you have functioned in continuously from 1996 through the present date?

A. Yes, whenever an issue arises, I would get involved.

…

Q. So we have on this one side, as I understand it, the role that you play for the company which is the Air Safety Investigator. And for that you cooperate with and assist the NTSB and the FAA in providing them information about crashes presumably involving your company's products, right?

A. Yes. Again, also, airframe manufacturers.

Q. In your capacity as Air Safety Investigator, you provide information to the NTSB when it's investigating a crash where your company's components are involved?

A. That's correct.

Q. And in that capacity you need to be independent and impartial in providing the information.

A. Well, actually, at that point, when you become a party or the corporation becomes a party of the investigation, in essence they are working for the NTSB.

Q. And you are expected to be independent and impartial.

A. That's correct.

Q. In fact, the rules require that.

A. Yes.

Q. And in supplying information in your capacity as the Air Safety Investigator, it is expected that you will be independent and impartial.

A. Yes.

Q. As a matter of fact, there is another role that you play for the company in that your are also the Liability Coordinator correct?

A. That's an old terminology, but, yes, I also work with our attorneys.

Q. And basically, that would be lawsuit or defense coordination, correct?

A. Again, I'm an Air Safety Investigator and besides dealing with the NTSB, FAA and airframe manufacturers, I deal with attorneys relative to gathering information for requests for production, depositions and so forth.

Q. Now, just so I'm clear, perhaps it's not a formal title, but within the company, you are the "Liability Coordinator" with respect to lawsuits that may be brought against the company, correct?

A. I mean, if you want to term it that way, but again, it's not a formal title.

…

Q. Irrespective of the title, you serve in that capacity in that function?

A. Basically.

Q. Yes?

A. Yes.

Q. Which means that on behalf of the company you assist in gathering information to defend the company against liability lawsuits such as this, true?

A. That happens.

Q. And that's what you do in that role, true?

A. Yes.

…

Q. In all of these various crash investigations where your company's components were suspected of having failed in-flight and contributed to the crash, you were to have made an honest and diligent attempt to assess whether your company's products may, indeed, have failed, correct?

A. Again, my job was to, again, review various components and identify if there's any safety issues, and you know, present them to the NTSB and of course, organizations, so if there are safety issues, they could be fixed.

Q. But you don't disagree that you were supposed to be and intended by the NTSB to make an honest and diligent effort to assess whether your company's products may, indeed, have failed, agreed?

A. I would agree that the NTSB expects us to examine and be up front and honest, which we are.

Q. And you certainly knew that you were supposed to be honest and diligent in assessing whether your company's products caused the crash, agree?

A. We are.

Q. Well, do you agree with the statement?

A. We are honest and diligent.

…

Q. And for many years now you've acted as the Liability Coordinator for all of these lawsuits true?

A. Along with other products, yes.

Q. And as part of that process, part of that role, you gather or produce facts to help the defense of the company in product liability lawsuits, true?

A. These facts aren't any different than the facts I give to the NTSB or the FAA.

Q. As the Liability Coordinator for the company you gather or produce facts to help the company defend itself in products liability lawsuits, true or not true?

A. It's true.

…

Q. And you are not allowed to have your judgment swayed because of your role in defending the company, knowing it would be sued if there was a failure which caused a fatal crash?

A. No.

…

Q. Now, sir, as the Liability Coordinator with responsibilities to gather or produce facts to help to defend the company in these lawsuits, don't you have an inherent conflict?

A. No.

Q. Is it proper in the aviation industry, sir, for an Air Safety Investigator who works with the NTSB on behalf of a company to at the same time be the person in the company charged with gathering information to help defend the company in lawsuits brought by people injured by that company's products?

A. Our job is to gather facts.

…

Q. So whether you knew that a lawsuit in this case had been filed or not, at the time you were writing and drafting that report for the NTSB, you knew that there would be a lawsuit, true?

A. Possibly.

…

Q. Well, let's talk about today, sir, are you wearing your Liability Coordinator hat or your Air Safety Investigator hat as you sit here today or both, or neither.

A. If you ask me about my reports, I'd tell you from my air safety perspective. If you're asking me for production material information or whatever happens I—maybe I'm doing the coordinator. Again, I'm here to tell the truth.

…

Q. Did you ever tell the NTSB investigator of this crash that you also had the position of being the Liability Defense Coordinator for the company?

A. No. I was working as a safety investigator.

Following the presentation of this deposition testimony, the jury had a clear understanding of this witness's inherently conflicted role in the aircrash investigation and severely discounted the trustworthiness of his factual findings and report.

C. Direct Examination of Plaintiff's Expert Witnesses

By the time plaintiffs are ready to call their first liability expert, the jury should have a sufficient factual basis for understanding why the defendants are at fault and are being sued. Naturally, the opinion testimony of plaintiff's liability experts must provide the necessary and sufficient evidentiary support on each of the essential elements of recovery. The second and equally important task of the experts' testimony is to provide compelling reasons for the jury to find fault with the defendant's actions.

1. Sample Direct Examination Outline: Plaintiff's Aircrash Accident Reconstruction Expert

A simple but time-tested outline of a plaintiff's accident reconstruction expert is as follows:

1. Would you tell the jury your name and where you are from?

This is a simple introduction and since everyone has to be from somewhere, it is usually a nice way to start.

2. Did I ask you to perform an accident reconstruction as to what happened in this helicopter crash?

The jury should know at the outset precisely who this witness is and why she is being called to testify.

3. Prior to giving any opinions you have in the area of aircrash accident reconstruction, would you mind if we trace through your education, training, experience and other qualifications which allow you to present these opinions to this jury?

This is a common transition to the qualifications and puts that usually lengthy exposition in a context for the jury. Counsel should highlight the specific helicopter experience of the witness as well as any specific articles or industry positions relevant to the opinions to be expressed. Counsel should elicit from the witness the number of years within the aviation field, how many aircrash accident reconstructions had been performed and personally investigated by the expert, and an identification of the major commercial aircrash disasters with which the witness has been involved.

4. What is the field of aircrash accident reconstruction?

Prior to launching into an exposition of what happened, it is helpful for the jury to understand the expert's field of expertise and what it involves. The jury must understand that there are generally accepted techniques and methods in any field and, especially, the field of aircrash accident reconstruction.

5. Would you tell us all the materials you specifically have reviewed in connection with this case?

This forms the factual predicate for application of the expert's opinions. It may also be impressive in terms of the quantum of work usually performed by these experts which include multiple visits to the crash scene, exemplar in addition to subject component part testing, and a review of all depositions taken in the case.

6. On the basis of the information you have reviewed and applying your expertise in the field of aircrash accident reconstruction, do you have any opinion to a reasonable degree of certainty as to how this helicopter crash occurred?

This is where the expert may be called down from the stand to use a topographical model in conjunction with a small helicopter that the author's trial team lovingly refers to as "helicopter on a stick." This is an approximate two-foot long rod with a small helicopter affixed to the end. By using that tiny helicopter in conjunction with a topographical model of the crash scene, the expert can bring the accident sequence alive for the jury and repeat or back up as may be necessary to gain their nods of comprehension.

7. Have you considered alternative causes to that scenario?

This is the pre-rebuttal to defendant's counter-veiling explanations for the crash. It should be explained that as a matter of aircrash accident reconstruction it is standard practice to consider and rule out alternative causes.

2. Trial Excerpts and Commentary

1. The presentation of plaintiff's engineering expert in a helicopter crash trial should be one of the highlights. Plaintiff's expert in the trial excerpt below was particularly well-qualified to address failures of helicopter gas turbine engines. Despite the complex subject matter, the answers were short and easily understood:

Q. Would you tell us your name, please and where you are from?
A. My name is Adam Anderson and I'm from the Boston area.

Q. What is your profession, sir?

A. I'm a Professor of Aeronautics and Astronautics at the Massachusetts Institute of Technology and Associate Director of the Gas Turbine Lab there.

Q. Dr. Anderson, did I ask you to travel here to Chicago, Illinois, to give your professional engineering opinions to this jury concerning a component part manufactured by these defendants?

A. Yes, sir.

Q. And are you prepared at this time, on the basis of the things which you have reviewed, to state your professional engineering opinions to the ladies and gentlemen of this jury?

A. Yes, I am.

Q. Before we do that doctor, what I would like to do is trace through some of your education, your training, and your experience in your field so that the ladies and gentlemen of the jury would have a little bit of an idea of the nature of your qualifications to render the opinions. May we do that?

A. Yes, sir.

…

Q. Doctor, on the basis of all of the information that you have reviewed, do you believe that these materials are sufficient to enable you to state your opinions to this Court and to this jury with a reasonable degree of aeronautical engineering certainty?

A. I do.

Q. Now, for the last two and a half weeks this jury has heard about something called a gas turbine engine and you, doctor, would seem to be a pretty good person to ask about that. Would you mind explaining to us the very basic essentials as to how a gas turbine engine works?

A. That's my business.

…

Q. Dr. Anderson, what I would like to do at this point is to start by asking you your most basic opinions concerning the findings that you have made in this case. I would like to have your opinion for our record then we'll explain the basis for your aeronautical engineering opinion. Would that be satisfactory with you, sir?

A. Yes, sir.

Q. I would like you to state each of your opinions to a reasonable degree of aeronautical engineering certainty, and if you cannot so state your opinion with that degree of certainty would you advise the Court or myself?

A. Yes.

Q. On the basis of your education and experience and training and applying that training and that experience to the specific facts that you have studied in this case, do you have an opinion to a reasonable degree of aeronautical engineering certainty whether the engine was in a defective condition unreasonably dangerous when it was sold by these defendants. Do you have such an opinion?

A. I do.

Q. What is your opinion?

A. That is was so defective.

Q. Do you have an opinion to whether the defective condition of the engine caused or contributed to cause the helicopter crash?

A. I do.

Q. And your opinion?

A. That it did.

…

Q. Now, for the next series of questions what I would like to do when I use the term "ordinary care" or "standard industry practice," can we agree that that term means that degree of care, skill, and learning that an ordinarily careful and prudent expert in the defendant's business would use under the same or similar circumstances?

A. Yes.

Q. Do you have an opinion whether the defendant failed to use ordinary care in the design or manufacture of the engine?

A. I do.

Q. And your opinion?

A. It so failed.

…

Q. Now, let's get into some of the bases for the opinions you have expressed to this jury, doctor. With respect to your opinion that the engine is defective, what is a defect in the field of aeronautical engineering?

A. A defect is a problem with the part that causes either the engine to cease operating or not to deliver the power that it's supposed to or not to last for as long as the manufacturer claims.

Q. Why is this engine defective?

A. There are two answers to that question. It's defective because it breaks and causes the engine to stop producing power and helicopters to crash. There is no doubt in my mind that this helicopter crash was caused by this part failing, freezing up, seizing the engine, and the engine stopped operating in-flight.

One of the defendant engine manufacturer's primary contentions was that it had previously warned helicopter owners, operators and pilots to be on the alert for a "rubbing noise" from the vicinity of the engine. No defense contention can go unrebutted. Plaintiff by and through the engineering expert had to confront this defense contention head-on:

Q. Based upon industry practice whether in the field of aeronautical engineering, what is the importance or relevance of operator experience and field experience concerning feedback to the manufacturer?

A. It's critical because you may have something in the factor that seems like a good idea and then when you actually get them out in the real world, things don't operate that way, and so prudent manufacturers are always updating and changing their procedures based upon the feedback they have from their customers.

Q. Based upon your own personal and professional experience in setting up tests, testing parts and working with parts, do you have an opinion concerning the adequacy of this listening for rubbing noise procedure, doctor?

A. I think it is totally inadequate.

Q. Why?

A. There are several reasons. One is in terms of listening. Things are rubbing as the engine slows down anyway. The engine is connected to the gear box. The gear box is connected to the generator. The generator has brushes that rub so it is making noise. What they are telling you to listen for is an abnormal noise. Since you haven't been listening, you don't necessarily know what an abnormal noise is. The other thing is there is no reason why this part has to rub before it fails.

Q. Why is that?

A. Because it's still connected to the rest of the vane. It may rub, part of it may fracture and clatter around and certainly if you hear a rub that means you have a problem. You may not know what the source of the problem is. You know the engine isn't supposed to sound like a mix master. It is supposed to make a whining sound like engines do. The other thing is, how long does it take between when the part starts to rub and when it actually fails? It only tells you to test it once a day.

Q. Is that adequate?

A. They have customers who are making sixty to eighty flights a day.

…

Q. Now, doctor, do you have a judgment, based on your review of all of the internal documents, whether at any time the company itself suspected the inadequacy of this procedure?

A. Yes.

…

Q. They are talking about the AD note, are they not, doctor?

A. Yes.

Q. And the first indication is that "we are concerned by the problem arising with the AD" which tracks the words in the service bulletin, correct?

A. Yes.

Q. And it indicates that "We suspect that the words used in our service bulletin are not adequate. We want to revise our intentions." Doctor does the next sentence have reference to this rubbing noise procedure?

A. Yes. It simply says "We think that the check for unusual noise during the engine shutdown is not sufficient."

Q. "We think that the check for unusual noise during the engine shutdown is not sufficient." Did they ever, to your knowledge, inform any operator that they thought that the check for unusual noise was not sufficient, doctor?

A. Not at this time, no.

…

Q. Based on all of these materials, do you have an opinion to a reasonable degree of aeronautical engineering certainty, whether those checks for unusual rubbing noise were sufficient in order to catch any problem with the engine?

A. I'm convinced they are insufficient.

…

Q. To your knowledge, sir in the field of aeronautical engineering as of today has either company recalled or retrofitted that engine?

A. To my knowledge, they have not.

Q. Thank you, doctor. Your Honor I have no further questions.

D. Direct Examination of Damages Witnesses

Many times, the fewer damages witnesses the better. As to non-plaintiff family members, counsel should select those who are or were the closest to the plaintiff or plaintiff's deceased. It is the quality of the witnesses rather than their quantity which most impresses a jury. It is often extremely effective to select only two or three lay non-family witnesses who knew the plaintiff or knew the deceased best. Of course, there are always the essential damages witnesses such as the first on-scene responders including ambulance, fire or police personnel, in addition to nurses, health care providers, doctors, rehabilitation providers, medical examiners, and forensic economists.

1. Objectives and Suggested Techniques

Damages witnesses will include family and close friends of the plaintiff or the plaintiff's deceased in addition to employers and a forensic economist. In eliciting testimony from those who know the plaintiff or who knew the deceased, juries want to hear stories about what the deceased did or descriptions of his routine. Usual descriptors such as kind, generous and caring fall flat. But witnesses who can recount a particular episode, joyful pursuits or types of activity engaged in by the injured plaintiff or plaintiff's deceased prior to the helicopter crash reveal much more about the person. The objective in presenting any damages witness is to reveal some unique qualities of the plaintiff or plaintiff's deceased.

2. Trial Excerpts and Commentary

Rather than to describe the deceased as simply having an interest in poetry, the author's questioning of a close friend of the young woman who died in the helicopter crash proceeded as follows:

BY MR. ROBB: Now did she ever author anything that you are aware of?

A. Yes. She wrote poetry and she had a poem already published and submitted another one to a publishing company that they were going to print.

Q. When did she tell you about this?

A. It was about two weeks before the helicopter crash.

Q. Was it something that she shared with a lot of people?

A. No. No. This was something more private that she did for herself and really didn't want people to know.

Q. Did she actually share some of the writing with you, Mr. Turner?

A. Yes. We were riding around one night and she had a set of books on her lap, and I looked at her and I said what are you doing with all those books? She said they're just some things I have been doing. I said what are they? And she looked me and said poems I've been writing.

This testimony about the deceased's poetry writing elevated her from a mere high school graduate working as a waitress to someone with high ambition and deeper intelligence. The jury was moved by knowledge of the deceased's literary efforts.

***

Another witness in that same trial described the deceased's relationship with her son:

MR. ROBB: Good morning. Would you tell us your full name?

A. Debra Ann Caldwell.

Q. And did you know Mary Campbell?

A. Yes, I did.

Q. What was your relationship with her?

A. We were best friends and roommates.

Q. I would like to talk with you a little about Mary, but before we do that, could we take just a moment and have you share with us a little bit about your background?

...

Q. What type of mother was she?

A. She was a very caring mother. If she had to go without something so Edward would have, she would. She was playful with him. They always were playing together, having a good time and she was very caring. If friends wanted to see her, they would have to go over there because she did not like to leave Edward.

Q. How did you find out that Mary had died?

A. I was taking my son up to the babysitter and I was in our car and I turned the corner to go up to my sister's and I heard it over the radio that the helicopter had crashed and that she was killed.

Everyone on a jury can either relate to or understand that most horrific of phone calls informing one of a family member or close friend's death. A recounting of that experience may engage that dreaded feeling among the jury.

***

The following direct examination of a damages witness by the author's law partner focused on his long-time relationship with the deceased helicopter pilot who had been his best friend since childhood.

DIRECT EXAMINATION BY MRS. ROBB:

Q. State your full name for the record if you would please, sir?

A. John Robert Howard.

Q. Where do you live, sir?

A. I live in Macon, Missouri.

Q. Did you know Richard Hartman, Jr.?

A. Yes.

Q. At what point in time, sir did you become acquainted with him?

A. I met him when I was in eighth grade.

Q. Was he also in eighth grade?

A. I believe he was in seventh grade at the time.

Q. Did you consider yourself, sir, up until the time of his death to be his best friend?

A. I would say so.

Q. What is your employment?

A. I work for the City of Macon. I'm the Director of Public Works.

Q. Now from the time you became acquainted with Mr. Hartman, when you were in the eighth grade, did you maintain personal contact with him throughout that point up until the time of his death?

A. Yes. We were friends through high school and then after high school, we ran around together. We both moved away but we kept in touch, and when we would come back to Macon over holidays or something we would keep in touch with each other.

...

Q. Was he, based on your observation and your personal time that you spent with, much of a family man?

A. Yes, I would say so. Once he was married and had a family, his whole existence was around his family.

Q. Why do you say that? In what way?

A. Well, it's how he spent his time. When he was off work, he was with his family and doing things around the house and doing home improvements or taking the kids out, things like that.

Q. Since the time of his death, have you continued to maintain close ties with his family?

A. Yes, I keep in touch with his family.

Q. Do you see his widow and his two children on a regular basis?

A. Yes, I would say so.

Q. Can you tell us, sir, personally have you observed changes in his children since his death?

A. Probably, if anything, they have become a little more quiet and reserved, a little bit more withdrawn I guess you could say.

Q. And what about Mrs. Hartman, Jane? Have you observed changes in her generally in terms of her personality and demeanor since the death of her husband?

A. Probably. I'd say she's been, she seems a little depressed.

E. Direct Examination of Plaintiffs

1. Objectives, Suggested Techniques and Sample Outline

By the time counsel are ready to call the plaintiff to the witness stand the jury should be comfortably at ease with the virtue of plaintiff's claims and with the clarity of defen-

dants' fault. At that point, the jury is wanting to hear plaintiff's testimony. The surefire way to turn off an otherwise favorably disposed jury is to be overlong with the plaintiff or permit the plaintiff to become too weepy and emotional.

A common order for the questioning of the plaintiff who is a surviving family member of the deceased is as follows:

a. Witness Identification and Relationship to the Deceased

Jurors want to know who the individual is in terms of background and education and how long they have known the deceased. The length of the marriage and wedding date should come from the witness.

b. Life with the Deceased Prior to the Date of the Crash

Testimony should be elicited about the life and times with the deceased including special trips, memorable activities, and the ordinary day-to-day routine. Photographs, keepsakes and mementos can be admitted and passed to the jury throughout this phase of the testimony.

c. Day of the Crash

"Mrs. Jones, if it is all right with you, could we now talk to the jury about May 27, 2004?"

The transition from a discussion of happier times to the helicopter crash date must be done sensitively. A change in the mood and demeanor of the witness will be apparent. A discussion of the events leading up to the helicopter flight to the extent known by the witness and not previously addressed should be recounted. The time, place and circumstances by which the plaintiff first learned of the crash and fatal injuries suffered by the deceased should also be recounted.

d. Days and Weeks Following the Crash

This is an intensely difficult time period for any family member who has lost a loved one. They may be alternating between moments of shock, grief and disbelief. Whichever coping mechanisms are utilized, the process of planning for and attending a funeral fills the time and it is not until afterwards that the true impact of the loss is felt. These issues should be thoroughly addressed in order for the jury to assess the impact of the loss.

e. Impact of Loss of the Deceased

Counsel should elicit the change in life routine and the circumstances undergone by the plaintiff. Specific things or routines missed about the deceased should be elicited. This entire direct examination should take no longer than 10-15 minutes.

2. Trial Excerpts and Commentary

An example of such testimony from a woman who lost her husband in a helicopter crash is as follows:

MR. ROBB: I think we all know who you are, but can we hear you say your name?

A. Rachel Ann Hartman.

Q. And you go by Shelly?

A. Yes.

Q. Were you married to Richard Hartman, Jr.?

A. Yes I was.

Q. As of June 17, 1999, were you married to Mr. Hartman?

A. Yes.

Q. Are you the mother of Missy Hartman sitting at counsel table?

A. Yes.

Q. Are you also the mother of James Hartman sitting there with her?

A. Yes.

…

Q. And I want to ask you if you have gathered some family photographs and whether these photographs are of your family and your husband and your children doing certain things?

A. Yes.

Q. Let me show you a board with some of these photographs on it and are these the photographs that you gathered at my request, Mrs. Hartman?

A. Yes.

Q. And plaintiffs' Exhibit 21 depicts you and your husband and your family engaged in a variety of simple family-type things?

A. Yes.

At this point in the examination the comfort and familiarity of Mrs. Hartman with family photographs permits her to overcome her natural nervousness and open up and communicate fully with the jury.

Q. Did you have occasion to fly in the helicopter with your husband piloting?

A. Yes, I did.

Q. Did you like that?

A. Yes, very much.

Q. And the next two are also photographs taken at that same time inside the helicopter and then one with Richard standing by it?

A. Yes.

Q. And that is him standing by the Life Flight helicopter?

A. Yes it is.

…

Q. Mrs. Hartman, how did you learn that the helicopter had crashed?

A. Someone…phone call. Just someone called. I was in the kitchen that morning. It was 8:20 and I had called my mother-in-law and I really—I didn't know what I was going to do.

…

Q. Let me ask you, what do you miss most about your husband?

A. I miss everything. I miss everything.

DEFENSE COUNSEL: I have no questions, Your Honor.

***

Children can be particularly challenging witnesses because of the unpredictability of their demeanor and their responses. Nonetheless, where young children lose a parent in a helicopter accident and they can pass qualification by the court, they should testify. In many states there is a rebuttable presumption that a child under a certain age is not competent to testify. For example, in Missouri that age is ten years old. Counsel must present to the court sufficient evidence of the child's confidence in terms of his ability to tell the truth and understanding of the oath:

THE COURT: Edward I'm Judge Mills. I need to ask you some questions. Edward, how old are you?

THE WITNESS: Six.

THE COURT: What's your birth date?

THE WITNESS: October 21st.

THE COURT: Edward are you in school?

THE WITNESS: Yes.

THE COURT: What grade are you in?

THE WITNESS: Kindergarten.

THE COURT: Are you doing well in your classes?

THE WITNESS: Yes.

THE COURT: Do you feel comfortable testifying and being in court today?

THE WITNESS: Yes.

THE COURT: Do you know what it is to tell a lie?

THE WITNESS: Yes.

THE COURT: What happens if you tell a lie?

THE WITNESS: You get in trouble.

THE COURT: You won't do that when you are testifying, will you?

THE WITNESS: No.

THE COURT: That's good enough for me I think based on the responses of Edward, that he would be competent to testify.

The testimony of young Edward proceeded as follows:

MRS. ROBB: Good morning. Could you please say your name into the microphone.
A. Edward.
Q. What's your last name?
A. Hartman.
Q. And how old are you Edward?
A. Six.
Q. Now did you bring some friends here with you today?
A. Yes.
Q. Who do you have?
A. Batman, Joker, and Mr. Bear.
Q. Now Edward, do you go to school?
A. Yes.
Q. What grade are you in?
A. Kindergarten.
Q. Do you know the name of your school?
A. No.
…
Q. Do you have a best friend?
A. Yes.
Q. Who's that?
A. Lance.

At this point, the author's partner showed Edward a number of photographs depicting his mother and him engaged in several activities including cooking, playing on a playground, and swimming.

Q. Do you remember making any food or sandwiches with mommy?
A. Yes.
Q. What was that all about? Do you remember? Did mommy like to make peanut butter and jelly?
A. Yes.
Q. Did she have a special way of making that with you?
A. Yes.
Q. What was it?
A. Throwing it at each other.
…
Q. Did you watch movies with Mommy?
A. Yes.
Q. Do you remember being sick and having Mommy taking care of you?

A. Yes.
Q. Do you miss Mommy?
A. Yes.
Q. Did you love Mommy?
A. Yes.
Q. Did Mommy love you?
A. Yes.
Q. How do you know?
A. Because I loved her so much I couldn't doubt it.
MRS. ROBB: I have nothing further.
DEFENSE COUNSEL: No questions, Your Honor.

10.4 Defendant's Case-in-Chief

Defendants in these cases normally will not call additional on-site witnesses in their case because it serves only to emphasize the traumatic and horrific nature of the helicopter crash. Most manufacturing entities, whether of the airframe, component part or systems, will not call an engineer at trial to defend the product but a management-type who will seek to defend the company's actions. If that witness has not previously been deposed, counsel must exercise caution in delving into unfamiliar areas. Focusing on key documents or confining questions to the principle facts at issue is a relatively safe harbor.

Defendant's case and presentation of evidence in most personal injury or wrongful death litigation is far shorter than the plaintiff's case. Normally the defense will call a representative of the airframe manufacturer if it is a party to the litigation. If the primary defendant is a component part or system manufacturer, most defense lawyers will ask an articulate managerial type to testify for the company. Because they are in management they entrust all technical and engineering decisions to the engineering department and cannot give much technical testimony in those areas.

Finally, defendants will present their own liability experts. All of the standard rules for cross-examination of these defense experts at trial apply. A sample cross-examination of a defense liability expert is set out in the next section.

A. Cross-Examination of Defendant's Corporate Representative

Counsel for defendant airframe or component part manufacturers face a difficult decision in bringing a top level engineer to trial. Failure to do so risks a severe backlash as plaintiff's counsel invariably may point out in closing argument that the defendant brought not a single knowledgeable employee from the company to take the stand and defend the product to the jury. That is a strong argument. The other defense risk is to bring such an engineering type to testify at trial and subject her to cross-examination by plaintiff's counsel. Where the evidence of defect is manifest, that defense tactic poses some risks as well:

CROSS-EXAMINATION BY MR. ROBB:
Q. You are the Vice-President of Engineering for Turbomeca France?
A. Yes.
Q. You are the number one engineering person within the entire organization, correct?
A. Yes.
Q. You appeared here today as the number one engineer for Turbomeca France?
A. Yes.
Q. You are today?
A. Yes.
Q. And in terms of engineering matters and discussions and situations on engineering, there is no one who would speak with more authority than you, true?
A. No.

The purpose for this early questioning was to point out to the jury that this witness had ultimate engineering responsibility for the helicopter engine manufacturer and that as to all such decisions "the buck stops with him." The next series of questions stemmed from the French company's position that it was ignorant about U.S. sales of its helicopters.

Q. Now, in other words, within the North American region, the selling of the product is done by Turbomeca Engine Corporation, true?
A. I don't know.
Q. Turbomeca France ships parts to Turbomeca Engine Corporation, correct?
A. Yes.
Q. And Turbomeca Engine Corporation in turn sells those within the United States, right?
A. I don't know.
Q. You don't know that?
A. No.
Q. You have no knowledge about who sells your product in the United States and that is what you are telling this jury as chief engineer to the company?
A. Correct.
Q. You just think they appear on K-Mart or Sears store shelves, sir?
DEFENSE COUNSEL: Objection, Your Honor, that is argumentative.
THE COURT: Sustained.
Q. You don't have any knowledge about how these products are sold in this country and that's your testimony?

A. Yes.
Q. Well let me show you what we have marked as Plaintiffs' Exhibit 377 and if I may approach again, Your Honor.
THE COURT: You may.
Q. And do you recognize this as a failed TU76 nozzle guide vane?
A. Yes.
Q. You wouldn't put that into a Module 3 and expect it to run in that condition, would you sir?
A. I don't know.
Q. You think that the engine could run with this part in this condition without the labyrinth ring, without the labyrinth seal and with the gash on the left?
A. Maybe.
Q. You think it would run real well?
A. Not very well.
…
Q. Tell this jury, when is the first time anyone showed you the failed TU76 or the failed rings from the Life Flight 2 helicopter which crashed on May 27, 1993?
A. The actual parts?
Q. The actual parts is what I'm talking about that's the question.
A. It is the first time.
Q. Right now, Thursday, July 13, 1995 is the first time that you have physically examined these parts out of this helicopter engine, true?
A. Yes.

As this was the highest-ranking engineer for the company, the author later would argue that if he had truly been concerned or interested in the reasons for this helicopter crash he would have made arrangements to examine the engine parts at some earlier point in time. The jury was visibly surprised that the first time he looked at the parts was when they were presented to him by plaintiff's counsel during trial.

Q. In any event, sir, getting back to these two photos, what we have here is a portion of the lab ring sticking out from the second stage turbine, kind of almost exactly like that, true?
A. Yes.
Q. And the engine won't run very well with this part sticking out from the blades of the second stage turbine wheel, will it?
A. Correct.
Q. In fact, it won't run at all, will it?
A. In this case that was the case.

Q. Because you know that what happened in this case was the TU76 failed, true?

A. Yes.

Q. And with respect to the Life Flight helicopter crash of May 27, 1993, it was the failure of the TU76 which caused the engine to shut down in-flight, true?

A. Yes.

…

Q. Now you recall when you and I visited back in January in Kansas City we created a chart?

A. Yes.

Q. And on that chart you and I plotted the known TU76 failures and in-flight problems and the city or identification where they occurred, true?

A. Yes.

Q. And we plotted some in 1985, 1986 and we plotted them all the way through to the date of this crash, 1993, did we not?

A. Yes.

Q. And this is that chart, right?

A. Yes.

The critical issue in plaintiff's punitive liability claim was the company's continued marketing of the engine with actual knowledge that it contained a defective component that had failed on a number of prior occasions causing in-flight engine failure and crashes. That issue was developed as follows:

Q. But yet after mid-1990, we continued to have failure after failure after failure leading up to the crash that killed Mr. Barnett in May 1993, true?

A. We continued to have failure after mid-1990, yes.

Q. In each of these it was determined the TU76 caused an in-flight failure, true?

A. Yes.

Q. And the decision was made prior to May 27, 1993 on the basis of seven years of experience with this part not to recall the part, true?

A. Yes.

Q. Because what the decision was, was to simply replace the TU76 at routine overhaul or the engine had come back for some other purpose, true?

A. Correct.

Q. And that was a conscious decision made by the company, wasn't it?

A. Yes.

Q. With knowledge of the facts that engineering had, true?

A. Yes.

Q. And with knowledge of the facts that the Technical Support Department had, true?

A. True.

Q. Conscious decision?

A. Yes.

MR. ROBB: Nothing further.

B. Cross-Examination of Defense Expert Witnesses

Defendant's liability experts normally are called to testify in support of one or more of the following three defense contentions. First, the crash did not occur in the manner presented by the plaintiff. Second, the crash could not have been the fault of or caused by the defendant. Third, the defendant's aircraft or specific component part was safely and properly designed and did not fail as claimed by plaintiff's experts.

For each of these defense positions, the engineering analysis is crucial. Juries should be able to follow the key technical issues if appropriately explained by counsel and plaintiff's liability experts. Nevertheless, the comparative credibility as between plaintiff's set of experts and those experts retained by the defense will play a key role in determining what the jury ultimately decides. In some liability situations, defendants are unable to obtain first-rate experts and counsel must make very clear to the jury the inadequacies of defendant's experts.

All of plaintiff's liability experts will have reviewed all of the pertinent documents in the case as well as the depositions of on-scene witnesses, of any FAA or NTSB employees and of defendants' corporate representatives. In some difficult liability cases, defense counsel may identify and present a liability expert but attempt to "carve out" a specific and limited opinion without providing that expert with the full picture. An example of that occurred in the trial excerpt below:

CROSS-EXAMINATION BY MR. ROBB:

Q. You are appearing here as a witness on behalf of the helicopter engine manufacturer?

A. I didn't read the complete legal description.

Q. Counsel for the company has asked you to come into court and give testimony to this jury, true?

A. I'm sorry?

Q. Counsel for the defendants has asked you to come into court and give sworn testimony under oath to members of this jury, true?

A. Yes, sir. I'm testifying about the results of the examination I did.

Q. I'm asking if they were the ones that called you to court. True, sir?

A. Yes. They employed me in the case, yes.

…

Q. Now did defense counsel tell you, sir, about the testimony that was presented to this jury the first two weeks of trial?

A. Did he tell me about that?

Q. Yes.

A. No, sir.

Q. Did he tell you about certain company employees who testified via deposition to the members of this jury?

A. He did not go over that with me.

Q. Surely in order to form your opinions in this case you were supplied with a lot of the materials, weren't you?

A. Yes.

Q. It's important to have all the materials and information in the case, isn't it, sir?

A. I would like to have as much as possible.

Q. Otherwise, your testimony or your opinions might be incomplete for that lack of knowledge, right?

A. Well, I'm basing my testimony on my present knowledge.

Q. That's what I'm saying. You want the full picture, don't you?

A. You would always like to have the full picture, yes sir.

Q. And you weren't presented with the deposition of the testimony of the Chief of Engineering of the company, were you, sir?

A. No, I wasn't. That would have nothing to do with my opinions.

Q. We'll get to your opinions.

A. No, I wasn't.

Q. You weren't presented with the testimony in any form of the Customer Support Director, were you, sir?

A. Nothing.

Q. Prior to your deposition, you weren't given any information about these depositions true?

A. That's true.

Q. Do you know who the Chief of the Airworthiness Department is for the helicopter manufacturer?

A. No.

Q. Do you know what he had to say about what caused this helicopter to crash, sir?

A. Obviously not.

…

Q. You were not provided with any of the depositions of any of the engineers who testified for the helicopter aircraft manufacturer, correct?

A. No, I was not.

…

Q. Let me ask you this question: Is this engine as designed defective?

A. No, it is not defective as designed.

Q. And you're stating that without the benefit of the deposition testimony of any of the witnesses that I've told you about, correct? Is that true?

A. That's true.

…

Q. Well, using your definition of defect then, it is your testimony to the folks on this jury that the engine was not defective as designed, true?

A. As designed.

Q. I understand that is your opinion to this jury. Well, now, have you ever heard the expression "If it ain't broke, don't fit it?" Is that something you are familiar with down in Alabama?

A. In Missouri also.

Q. Why sure. Did you know that there were two design modifications made for this engine? Did you know that?

A. Yes.

During the direct examination, the witness expressed opinions about turbine gas engines on less than exemplary experience. That should be highlighted in cross:

Q. You've given this jury opinions and hold yourself out as having knowledge and special expertise with respect to gas turbine engines, true?

A. I don't believe I have done that.

Q. The fact is, you are not an expert in gas turbine engines are you? Is that true?

A. I would not say so, although I've had a lot of experience with gas turbine engine manufacturers and I've tested many components from gas turbines.

Q. My question is very simple, sir. You have no prior experience, other than this case, in failure analysis regarding gas turbine engines, true or not true?

A. No, that's not true.

Q. Let's see what you said back when your deposition was taken to that very same question. Would you turn to page 6, line 1?

A. Page 6?

Q. Did you find it?

A. All right.

Q. You were under oath when you gave this deposition testimony, weren't you?

A. Yes.

Q. Do you know what it means to be under oath?

A. I certainly do.

Q. It's happened several times in your career hasn't it sir?

A. Yes, it has.

Q. At that time was it your sworn answer to this question under oath: "Is it true that your failure analysis experience with jet engines is well, what is your failure analysis experience with gas turbine engines?" Answer: "This is really the first instance of that type." Is that the sworn answer you gave under oath then, sir?

A. Yes sir. And that is not in conflict with what I just said a minute ago either.

Q. That's for the jury to determine. That is not for you to determine. You have absolutely no experience whatsoever with a second stage nozzle guide vane and module 3 of a turbine engine, is that true?

A. That's true before this case.

Q. Right.

A. Yes.

…

Q. You are not a turbine engine expert, are you?

A. No. I'm a metallurgist.

Q. You've never participated in the design of a turbine engine, true?

A. That's true.

This expert's true vocation as a hired gun for products liability defendants had to be exposed:

Q. When you are not talking about gas turbine engines or second stage nozzle guide vanes, there are some areas that you are a little more comfortable testifying to juries about, aren't there sir, correct?

A. No. I feel very comfortable testifying about what I've done in this case.

Q. Over the period from 1967 to 1991 you completed approximately 600 assignments relating to product liability litigation?

A. Yes, sir.

Q. Of these 600 cases you've done no industrial consulting at all, correct?

A. That's correct.

Q. In fact, there is a whole group of types of products where you claim to be an expert, right?

A. A large number of different products. I'm a metallurgical expert and metallurgy is applied to a whole range of products.

Q. Such as lightbulbs?

A. Yes.

Q. You've testified on lightbulbs, particularly automobile lightbulbs?

A. Whether they were in an on or off condition. That's one of the things I have done a great deal of.

Q. That is one of your specialties, in fact, is determining or deciding whether a lightbulb was in an on or off condition?

A. I've done quite a few examinations on lightbulbs.

Q. You've testified a lot about bar stools?

A. I remember a bar stool case but—

Q. Why sure. Chairs and sofas, right, sir?

A. Well, if there was a metallurgical question—

Q. Right.

A. —Then I probably could have or would.

Q. Six chair cases right?

A. I don't know. I have examined many household products where there was a metallurgical question involved.

Q. Sign supports?

A. Yes sir I have examined sign supports.

The trial court usually can be counted on to keep the expert from crossing inappropriate lines:

Q. It is important for an engine manufacturer to get information from the customer to know if a particular procedure is working, right?

A. Well, that's true. That is—you're taking me now into an area where it seems to me you objected to me answering the question before.

MR. ROBB: Now I object to this, Your Honor. He's being a lawyer again. I move to strike it.

THE COURT: Motion sustained. It is stricken.

Q. There is no question pending, sir. You've been in the courtroom. I think that you understand that the lawyer asks the questions and it is the witness who answers. Can we have that understanding please?

A. I try to not be pushed around too much. I'm sorry.

Q. Well, I certainly don't mean to push you around.

A. All right.

Q. Now in answer to my question: It is important for the aircraft engine manufacturer to be able to have feedback and to rely on that feedback from the customer, right?

A. That's important. There's no doubt about that.

Now, after the preliminary fencing, the time is ripe for the critical issue:

Q. Now in how many of these, sir, was it reported to the manufacturer that there had been any sound of a rubbing noise before the breakage of the part? How many of them?

A. I don't know.

Q. You can't tell us because you weren't given the information, were you, correct?

A. Well, the information was not available to me.

Q. Did you ever ask counsel for the company about that, gee, have there been any other in-flight engine failures? Have there been any other in-flight problems associated with this engine because I need to have this information so that I can give a full and complete picture to the jury? Did you ask him?

A. Oh, yes, and we've talked about two where there were reports and I can't relate those two particular ones but there are two that we discussed in my deposition where noises were heard and those are very important.

Q. But he didn't give you information about the engine failures and crashes from Guyana, Virginia, Phoenix, Hong Kong or Bolivia?

A. I can't identify them that way. Not that I know of.

...

Q. And isn't it true that in this scenario that you and I are discussing, if an engine manufacturer knows that it has a dangerous and critical component on its hands, it must take steps to get it out of the engine and retrofit it, agreed?

A. No, I don't agree with that.

10.5 Plaintiff's Rebuttal Evidence

In most jurisdictions, plaintiff may not offer as rebuttal evidence matters that properly should have been part of plaintiff's case-in-chief. Many courts are highly scrutinous of rebuttal evidence especially after a long and complicated trial. Many lawyers wisely seek to avoid plaintiff's rebuttal because of the unhappy glaze that comes over jurors' eyes when they hear that more testimony is about to be presented.

For these reasons, plaintiff's counsel must exercise some restraint in deciding to present rebuttal evidence. Where some rebuttal evidence is called for such as when an unexpected development occurs or some unanticipated evidence is presented by defendants, then counsel must make the leap. When the decision to present rebuttal evidence has been made, that evidence should be framed in such a way that it is clear that it is being offered to rebut particular points raised first by the defendant.

In one helicopter crash trial, during the defendant helicopter manufacturer's case-in-chief, defendant's liability experts took the position that the recommended procedure for listening to engine noise during engine shutdown was a sufficient warning. Plaintiff represented to the trial court that this would be one of the issues addressed by the rebuttal evidence if the court were to admit it. The court admitted the following rebuttal evidence from one of the defendant's engineering corporate representatives who was present in the courtroom and had earlier been subpoenaed by plaintiffs:

DIRECT EXAMINATION OF MR. ROBB:

Q. You are Henri Souciet?

A. Yes.

Q. You are still the Vice President of Engineering for Turbomeca France?

A. Yes.

Q. And you are the top engineer still, I imagine there haven't been any changes in the last couple of days worldwide for Turbomeca France, true?

A. Yes.

...

Q. Turbomeca France, for which you are the top engineer, reached its own conclusions with respect to the adequacy of this listening for noise procedure in December 1993 true?

A. I don't know.

...

Q. And that document clearly means that the checking for the unusual noise during engine shutdown alone is not sufficient, true?

A. Yes.

Q. You acknowledge that that is the fact, agreed?

A. Yes.

...

Q. And as I understand it, according to Turbomeca France's own definition, that was in existence at the time, the in-flight engine shutdown that occurred on this very case would be characterized by Turbomeca France as safe, true?

A. Yes.

Rebuttal evidence should be short and to the point. Anything longer runs the risk of alienating the jury.

10.6 Closing Argument

Many trial lawyers view closing argument as the high point of the trial. All roads lead to closing. In helicopter accident litigation, as in any complex lawsuit, the finality of closing creates a heightened degree of jury attention. Counsel must not squander that attention.

A. Objectives and Suggested Techniques

Closing argument is not the time for presenting evidence: it is a time for arguing. Too many lawyers use too many exhibits in their closing argument. The time for presenting evidence and showing documents to the jury ended at the close of plaintiff's case-in-chief. The primary documents that should be referenced in the closing argument are the jury instructions and counsel should only sparingly refer to and exploit the most incriminating liability documents in the case. By the time of closing argument, the jury should well know the critical documents because counsel has fully described and referenced them in questioning the defendant's corporate representatives and plaintiff's own liability experts, and even in the cross-examination of defendant's liability experts.

Counsel must track the court's jury instructions in presenting closing argument to the jury. In the time allotted by the court for closing, counsel must sufficiently address any outstanding liability issues while also presenting a full summary of the damages claimed.

B. Sample Outline of Closing Argument
The outline of closing argument the author used in a recent helicopter crash case is as follows.

1. Closing Capsule
Counsel should summarize the principle themes of the case as supported by the evidence admitted during the trial. This is a big picture presentation and in a sense mirrors that evidence predicted by counsel in the opening statement. Reminding the jury that certain evidence was promised and delivered enhances counsel's credibility and reinforces the proposition that this lawyer is to be believed and trusted. Similarly, counsel's reminding the jury that defense counsel made certain promises as to what evidence would be produced but did not deliver can diminish the defendant's credibility.

2. Jury's Role
The sworn duty of the jury is to apply the law and decide all fact questions. Counsel may use this opportunity to thank the jurors for their time and attention in serving on the jury, but this should not be overdone.

3. Preliminary Jury Instructions
Counsel should go over some of the procedural aspects of the jury's deliberations. In most jurisdictions the instructions will have been read to the jury only moments before the start of closing argument. Counsel may wish to further present and explain the burden of proof instruction, procedures for selecting a foreperson and other particular instructions as to how to consider circumstantial and opinion evidence.

4. What Happened?
Now that the jury has heard all the evidence they will have to answer a series of specific factual propositions as to who was at fault and in many instances assign a percentage of fault to each party. Counsel should point out to the jury that by answering the question "what happened," the jury easily will be able to answer the court's questions in the verdict form with respect to who is at fault, who caused the crash, and their relative percentage of fault. If there are serious disputes as to the crash sequence or mechanics, counsel should remind the jury of the evidence including the physical evidence that supports plaintiff's position. Brief references to photographs and testimony may be made, but the time should be spent arguing evidence and not presenting evidence.

Counsel may weave particular evidence references into an argument based on physical observations, experience, and common sense. Normally under the category of physical observations, counsel may reference documents, photographs and other materials viewed by the jury and available during deliberations. Experience refers to the opinions of the experts whose expertise has been applied to the facts of the case. Finally, counsel should appeal to the common sense and every day wisdom of the jury in deciding what happened to cause the crash. Along the way, it is useful to compare the qualifications of the experts and to remind the jury of any lack of objectivity on the part of in-house experts called to the stand by the defendants.

5. Review of the Required Elements for a Finding of Liability as to Each Defendant
Counsel must never assume that the jury will be able to work their way through even the simplest of charge instructions. Those instructions should be displayed to the jury on the overhead screen and each element should be addressed and explained and the pertinent evidence in support of each element reviewed.

6. Measuring the Harms and Losses to the Plaintiff
Jurors do not understand the word or concept "damages" which is a legal term lawyers easily bandy about. Juries do understand the impact of a crash victim's death on family members and a measure of the harms and losses sustained by the plaintiffs. Counsel must explain the elements of recovery as permitted and summarize the evidence in support of those elements.

7. Suggesting a Verdict Range
It is counsel's obligation to suggest to the jury a range for the monetary amount to be filled in on the jury verdict form. There are any number of techniques for arriving at a

dollar figure some of which are based on a multiple of the economic damages. Others take into consideration the period of time over which the loss will be sustained such as the deceased's life expectancy or the life expectancy of the injured plaintiff. Whichever method is selected counsel must advance reasoned arguments why the plaintiff is deserving of full justice in the amount requested.

C. Trial Excerpts of Liability Argument and Commentary

Before launching into a discussion of the specific elements required for the liability findings, counsel should summarize the basic liability case by answering, "What were the actions and circumstances leading up to and causing this helicopter crash?" The discussion of the jury instructions follows logically.

***

An example of a liability argument used in a helicopter crash trial is as follows:

MR. ROBB: May it please the court?

THE COURT: Mr. Robb.

MR. ROBB: Counsel. And may it please you, ladies and gentleman of the jury. Three and a half weeks ago I stood before you in this very spot and I told you that this case was about a helicopter engine manufacturer that discovered in 1986 that they had a serious problem with a critical component in their engine. I stood here and told you they went about the task of analyzing it, figuring out what was the part that went wrong, and I told you at that time that they figured out very quickly which part it was, how precisely it failed, what caused it to fail, where in the part it failed, and I told you that they knew that it would have to be modified.

I told you that each engineer and executive and officer of this helicopter engine company knew what a dangerous, what a dangerous situation this presented, not only to people riding in the helicopter with this engine but to folks on the ground below. And I told you at that time, ladies and gentlemen, that they went about the task of creating modifications, but I told you in the interim they didn't tell any United States operator about the defect that they knew about. They told you they didn't tell any operators around the world that in-flight failures and crashes continued to occur year after year, and I told you early on that there was a reason why this company didn't tell operators in the U.S. or around

the world, and there is a reason why they didn't do what they should have done which was to retrofit or recall this dangerous part which you all know about so well by now.

I told you the reason was that it would have cost them 48 million dollars. I told you it had nothing to do with the fact that they couldn't track the operators or didn't know where they were because the evidence would be, I promised you, that they would know where the operators are.

I also told you before you heard any evidence that at all times they had the power to issue a recall or retrofit of this part, and they didn't know when and they didn't know where and they didn't know who but they knew. They knew what would happen. That was before you heard any evidence, any testimony, any videos, seen any exhibits; and, ladies and gentlemen of this jury, I saw it in your eyes. You had to have, had to have thought this just can't be. What he's telling us can't be true. It mustn't be true. It shouldn't be true.

But we're on the other side of it now. You have sat through and watched all of the videos. You've seen all the documents. You've heard all of the testimony that was appropriate, which His Honor admitted for your consideration; and, ladies and gentlemen, you know what I told you three and a half weeks ago is true. It's true. And what I told you led to the death of James S. Barnett, Jr.

This initial phase of the argument was a mirror image of the first portion of the opening statement. The jury is told what they will hear, they see and hear that evidence, and then they are reminded of the accuracy of counsel's words several weeks beforehand.

***

Many lawyers skip the traditional jury thank you believing that it is no longer appropriate. Helicopter crash trials are lengthy ordeals and jurors make enormous personal sacrifices both at home and on the job. A sincere and genuine expression of appreciation for that sacrifice is appropriate:

It's been a long trial. It's been a longer trial by three days then you even bargained for when you first arrived. You know, you didn't have much of a choice when you got that summons in the mail and you reported to the jury room on that Thursday morning and you showed up there. And you didn't bail out.

You could have. You could have gotten in that long line on the left. You saw how it was going because when someone wanted a deferral, they did and you didn't. You stuck it out. And then you served.

Once you were drafted, you didn't have much of a choice about that, but you did have a choice about what type of juror you were going to be and to a person, each and every one of you, have taken oaths. During the most boring, long videos you were all attentive and alert. That was your choice to do that. And it is for that that on behalf of my clients, I thank you. I thank you.

But you know, being on a jury, in my judgment, is part of the rent you pay for living in a free and democratic society; and if that's true, you folks are paid in full. And I think you know why it is having participated in such a long trial and seen how it is going why the lawyers and judges feel so protective, so loyal about this system because it is so right. It's so true. If any of you had said anything during the first part when we gathered here about some attitude or opinion you had, had that interfered with your ability to be fair, the Judge wouldn't have permitted you to be on this jury. Ladies and gentlemen of the jury, each of you is an absolutely appropriate, fair, and impartial juror in this case.

***

It is useful to remind the jury how they were chosen and that their purpose is to do justice. Many lawyers recite the juror's oath at this point which commonly compels each juror to "render a true and just verdict upon the evidence and law." The message must be that their desires to do justice must be channeled through the court's instructions on the law:

> MR. ROBB: Now, you've heard all of the evidence. You are going to be embarking on the task for which it was you were really drafted because it just wasn't to hear the evidence. It was to decide this case, to do justice, to do justice. How do you do that? How can you possibly do justice in this case? I submit to each and every one of you there is only one way and that is to strictly and faithfully follow the instructions of Judge Andrew on the law. There is no other way. And if you do that, if you follow the law, you will do justice. No question about it.
>
> Your Honor, may I borrow the Court's official copy of the instructions for a moment?

THE COURT: You may.

> MR. ROBB: Ladies and gentlemen, this is your road map for accomplishing a just verdict in this case. These instructions that are binding upon you which you all have agreed to follow and which I, on behalf of my clients, know that you will follow. They contain each and every one of the instructions that the Court has read to you, but the one I would like to show you is the one at the very end, which the Court doesn't read, and it's called the verdict form, Verdict A, and it is the form by which you record your verdict.
>
> And with the Court's permission, if I may show Verdict A?

THE COURT: You may.

> MR. ROBB: Ladies and gentlemen, this is Verdict A and it is where you actually record your verdict. My thought, and just a thought, and suggestion to you is that you are your own masters of deliberations. You control how you do that; and when you get up to the jury room after you've heard all the evidence and heard the argument—you've been told not to discuss the case. Now when you go back up after you've heard the argument, you are told to discuss the case, to deliberate, to decide the case. That's a different story.

***

The purpose of this opening section is to not only review the evidence but also to give the jury some reassurance that their task is not insurmountable. The jury will not have had an opportunity to review all of these instructions and counsel's careful and patient explanation of their relevance will be appreciated. A careful review of the elements of fault is essential:

> Ladies and gentlemen, let me run through one of them for you because I think with respect to this first verdict director against Turbomeca France, I'll respectfully submit to you that against that defendant you need not go any further because each of these paragraphs represent a proposition; and once you've found the proposition, you can check it off or however you like to do it, but the first one is TSA sold it. That's not disputed. Second one—
>
> ...
>
> Ladies and gentlemen, in terms of whether or not Turbomeca, S.A. sold the TU76 nozzle guide vane, there is very little question from this evidence that this was a TU76 part designed and manufactured by Turbomeca, S.A.

Second, the TU76 nozzle guide vane was then in a defective condition unreasonably dangerous when put to a reasonably anticipated use. And how much more evidence could we have adduced on that point, that this particular part, this particular part which you have seen over and over again was defective? Because you know, if I had just handed it to you without any evidence and I said what do you think about this, your common sense alone would tell you by looking at this it's taken out of an aircraft engine that failed, in conjunction with the photographs, that this messed up, this malfunctioned. But we have so much more than that.

We have all of the testimony by these defendants where they say that it was a defaut, was a flaw, was a malfunction; and if you will recall the testimony of Mr. Simpson, because Mr. Simpson specifically stated that he agrees that it was a defect. "Let me clarify an answer you gave earlier. Do you now know that the TU76 second stage nozzle guide vane is defective?" "Answer, yes."

The factual findings of the National Transportation Safety Board were referenced over and over again, and you know what they find: inner portion of labyrinth seal separated from the hub. That's a defect. They had to create modifications to avoid the safety problem. If it ain't broke, don't fit it. It was a defect.

***

In reviewing testimony for the jury, any evident bias of defendant's experts can and should be pointed out:

And what was their evidence to the contrary? Well, you remember Mr. Davidson. Remember Mr. Davidson, the gentlemen they brought out of retirement who was well acquainted, has known Tom Peters for a long time, officed right next to TEC for, I don't know how long, but he was right next door to these people. He told you on the stand when I first asked him the question, he said, I am independent, I am unbiased, I am impartial, and I am objective. But is that what he said in his deposition? It's 180 degrees opposite because he admitted that he was not being independent and impartial.

And what did Mr. Davidson say? He said, well, it's the fault of the operator. And who told him that he should shift the responsibility to the operator? Plaintiffs' Exhibit 389, that yellow pad, in the very first phone call, "D.G. wants engine maintenance

expert to shift responsibility to RMH."

…

And so from the initial git-go Mr. Davidson knew what he was supposed to do. He was supposed to shift responsibility away from these people to Rocky Mountain Helicopters, and the only thing he could find was that the engine operating time, if you refigure it contrary to what the FARs provide in the beginning, that maybe they were a couple hundred hours over. NTSB didn't see it that way. Mr. Favre took the stand this morning—

…

He took the stand this morning and he told you that nobody, to his knowledge, contacted him in the engineering department to express any safety concern about this revision. So what's the point? I suggest to you that there is none.

You heard from Mr. Sam Tasker and, you know, I objected a lot last night, yesterday evening to some of the things that came up; primarily, to be real frank with you, because, in my judgment, based upon his expertise and experience, he is not qualified to state the opinions he was giving, and the Court told you that he is not a gas turbine engine expert. He can't testify as to the operation of a gas turbine engine.

DEFENSE COUNSEL: Objection, Your Honor. The Court didn't tell the jury that. That is not the statement of the evidence.

MR. ROBB: The jury will recall he could not testify outside that area.

THE COURT: I did not allow him to testify as a gas turbine expert, that's correct.

MR. ROBB: And the reason that you have to have expertise is when you come into court and give testimony to a jury, you have got to have some background that permits you to give your opinions. And this morning it occurred to me, you know, let's just hear it. Let's get on with it. Let's hear what he has to say. And he came up with this opinion about the number of hours that you could have heard the rubbing noise in the operation of the components within the engine without any education or training or experience whatsoever with gas turbine engines. I submit to you, how much credibility does that testimony have?

And he denied to each and every one of you that he had testified for 24 years on a variety of products, 600 of them. He denied it. And I passed out to you his earlier resume and he said it right in there. He denied that he promoted himself or his ability to testify rather than his expertise, and you saw that that was right in there, too.

And, ladies and gentlemen, I'll submit to you that Mr. Tasker never met a product he didn't like. He's testified on a lot of them, 600 of them, 675, I think it was. From barstools to lightbulbs to aerosol cans. And where is he going to be next week or the week after and what product is he going to be defending then?

Finally, Mr. Olive. You remember Mr. Olive, pilot, the chief pilot. He said he was the chief pilot for Eurocopter. Then the buyout material came out about why he was let go, and he denied to you that he was fired but he admitted that he was fired in his deposition; and, you know, based upon the kind of philosophy of safety and helicopter operation that he has, it's not hard to understand why.

What did he tell you? He told you that the cause of this accident, and I sincerely believe this is what he said, was misadjustment by—I don't know how many threads it was—of the collective stop bolt. He of the collective stop bolt theory. Well, you know, it was real interesting because I inquired about that a little bit. I said, you didn't know that these trees and the 96 feet from the point of impact were these trees? No, I never knew—

***

In contrast to the qualifications and bias of the defendant's liability experts, plaintiff was able to point out in contrast the superior qualifications of plaintiff's primary liability expert:

Professor Anderson came to you, came to you and told you what he did, told you of his experience in aeronautical engineering with helicopter engines specifically, and I think you can understand exactly why it is that the largest single user of helicopters in the world, the United States Army, has consulted with Dr. Anderson for 20 years, why NASA consults with Dr. Anderson. Because I will submit to you he is a brilliant engineer with integrity, and this is his third time ever being involved with this process.

He doesn't seek it out. I sought him out and I'll tell you why. I'll tell you why. I wanted to bring the best person I could find to sit in this witness box on behalf of this family to explain what it was that caused this crash. I don't think I could have done much better than Dr. Anderson. And he told you it was defective. He told you it didn't adequately

warn. He told you about the industry practices that they failed to comply with.

And with respect to that whole issue if what the company should have done once they knew about the defect, they didn't bring any contrary testimony. All of it stands unrebutted, uncontested, and undisputed for your consideration.

…

When you get right down to it, the only thing you need to consider is that it was—is that the TU76 nozzle guide vane was in a defective condition unreasonably dangerous. It caused the shutdown, it caused the crash; and as a direct result of such defective condition, James S. Barnett died, and I submit to you that there is no competent contrary evidence.

***

Counsel must remind the jury of particularly incriminating testimony or admissions by defendant's corporate representatives:

I suppose the most telling fact in this entire scenario is that you know our crash where two people died and two people horribly injured would have been reported by their own definition? If was a safe incident. It was a safe shutdown. Unbelievable.

And what I asked him was, "Does your company have a responsibility for how the helicopter and the pilot or passenger safely get to the ground, Mr. Souciet?" And the answer that we have on this transcript is "No." And then I asked him, "And you claimed that it is somebody else's responsibility to safely get the helicopter to ground once your engine, your engine fails in flight, true?" Answer, "Yes." Boy, those people will install the engine and that engine will get you up in the air but if it fails because a defective part, boy, that's not their problem.

***

In closing argument in a 2009 helicopter crash trial in Des Moines, Iowa, the author compared the qualifications and experience of plaintiff's experts with that of the defendants:

We tried to bring you experts in the aviation field for one reason, and for one focus, and that is to help you, guide you, in making a decision. That's all they're there for. For your assistance in reaching a verdict in this case. And there's a specific instruction as to exactly how you are to be governed by expert witness testimony. It's Instruction No. 8. Brian, if you would put it up.

Instruction No. 8 talks about experts. And why are they experts? Because of their education and experience. That's why they're coming in. You can't just come in off the street, not knowing anything and say, "Folks on the jury, I'm an expert in aviation, and you should believe me because you should." No. Experience and education matters. It matters and you need to be able to look at the experience in aviation of each and every one of the experts. Do they have experience with helicopters? What is their experience? And it's something you need to look at. And what I would like you to do is go to a comparison chart, and you and you alone, decide who you're going to believe.

At this point, the author referred to a comparative chart which set out as for all plaintiffs and defendants liability experts their field of expertise, years of experience, number of published papers and educational background.

D. Trial Excerpts of Damages Argument and Commentary

Perhaps the most difficult thing a plaintiff's lawyer does is stand before the jury and place a monetary figure on the case. Plaintiff's counsel never should "demand" a damages amount, but the suggestion of a damages figure or range of figures is almost always appropriate. It is possible to do this in such a way that the jury does not feel that some monetary figure is being crammed down their throats.

1. Deference to jury on damages

And, you know, if it were up to me, I would just as soon defer to you because we brought in an aeronautical engineering expert and brought in a helicopter pilot expert and economist expert; but, you know, we don't need experts for the value of this man. You are the experts. With the experience of all of your lives you know the deepness of this loss and value of this man to this family. It is my suggestion to you what would be fair and just compensation under all of the facts and circumstances in this case, and there is a legal reason for that. That's because defense counsel has to be able to come up and respond to my suggested figure, and I invite him to do so. Absolutely he may respond.

It is always a good idea to specifically invite defense counsel to address the damages figure because if it does have a logical and reasonable basis, defense counsel will be hard-pressed to attack it successfully. This then forms a successful basis for rebuttal argument. Indeed, in most every jurisdiction, one of the reasons why plaintiff's counsel are prohibited from stating a damages figure in rebuttal if one is not stated in the principle argument is because the defendant is then deprived of the opportunity to address and argue as against the stated damages figure.

Counsel should never pull a damages figure out of the air. In fact, experience teaches that it usually works best to itemize the economic losses first and then address the non-economic elements of compensation. While it is relatively easy to provide some rational basis for the economic loss, it is a greater challenge to provide that basis for a non-economic loss and stay within the lawful boundaries of closing argument. Available options are tying the non-economic loss to the monthly or annual wage of the plaintiff, or making a comparison as between the plaintiff's participation in the sport and the extraordinary income others derive from professional playing of that sport.

2. Emphasizing the elements of loss in wrongful death

And, ladies and gentlemen of the jury, I will follow the order of the Court and I will suggest figures which I deem are appropriate and fair and just under this case. And the first three, we talked about an example of that, services and support. Who is there to be with Jane? Who is there to understand her? Who will replace that? That is a loss to her. How do you value just the joy of dancing in an empty store? And for all these plaintiffs, for all five of them, for that loss, those first three, I submit to you that a sum of 50 million dollars for those elements, those statutory elements would be fair and just and proper under the facts and circumstances of this case.

And then the next three are commonly taken together: guidance, instruction, and training. As an example of that, John had every right to expect that his father would be there to help him make this difficult transition from being a teenager to a man; and, you know, the hard thing about this is that it's going to be the proudest moments of their lives, the happiest days in their lives when John and Jackie are going to miss their father the most. On the happiest day of her life who is going to walk down the aisle and give his movie star away? And that is going to hurt more than what we can possibly imagine, and for that loss, the loss to all of these people of guidance, instruction, and training, I submit to you that no less a sum would be fair and just than what we have for the first.

That leads us to the final element; comfort, companionship, and counsel. Those are all taken together. And, you know, how do you value, how do you possibly value that morning phone call that Joe would make to his mother, and she looked forward to that. What does it say about Joe that he would call her every morning? And that's a loss to this family. And his father, he had every right to be fiercely proud of his son and he was. And how do you compensate that?

Counsel's damages argument should track the court's jury instruction as to permissible damage elements. In most jurisdictions, juries are told that they should "fairly and justly compensate" plaintiffs for the damages sustained. It is prudent to remind the jury that to "compensate" means to replace with that of equal value. This presents the challenge to the jury of equating the plaintiff's injury with some dollar sum and not within the context of a reward or some award.

3. Damages argument for the wrongful death of a 20-year old single mother of two children

But, you know, you also heard testimony in this case that this is simply the economic, this is the aspect of their earning capacity. It doesn't apply to the other elements of loss which would be love, companionship, the society—all of those things which make up the relationship which you're entitled to consider.

And, you know, we can bring the economist and he can go through the calculations, but there's no computer as to how to get to that figure. And, we defer to your judgment totally. You've heard all the evidence—there will never be a jury better suited to hear this than you, because you've heard all of the evidence.

But, what I would like to do is in accordance with our procedure, it is my obligation if I'm going to make a suggestion, to make a suggestion at this point of the proceedings so that counsel may comment upon it if he wishes to do so, because it would not be appropriate for me to suggest a figure in the second half when he would not have an opportunity. And, I will fulfill that obligation."

Counsel should remind the jury of the damages testimony:

You had an opportunity to get to know a little bit about what Sally was like, to see people with whom she associated; Sergeant McCain who came in and told you about her industriousness. You met her good friend, Elen Jennings, so close because they did each other's labor coaching for their children. Labor coach is what you call it. You met Les Turner who got to know her pretty darn well in the last year of her life. These are people with whom she associated, whom she liked, and who liked her.

Ladies and gentlemen, I could have had witnesses paraded through here. We had to select three and we selected three about Sally to talk to you. No number of witnesses, no number of witnesses could have better told you about the relationship between Sally and her mom, the relationship between Sally and those two boys. All we had to do was show you that video.

No testimony needed because you saw something, you felt something on that video, and it's real simple. It's called love. The unabashed, unashamed, unqualified love of a mother for her children. The total and complete love at that time of a four-year-old boy for his mommy who comes off the ride, where's mommy? No better evidence than that, than the tape.

4. Helicopter crash argument addressing the wrongful death of the pilot, leaving a wife and two young children

What does that leave? That leaves the loss to this family of Richard Hartman, Jr. and you know, we brought in some friends and family who spoke about him. But you didn't need to hear a word of it because you saw and you heard and you felt in twelve short minutes the essence of Richard Hartman, Jr., because in that twelve-minute video you saw and you heard and you felt something special and it's love and happiness and joy of a family. I didn't need to bring you any other evidence than that.

You know, he worked so hard to get to that point in this life, forty years old, a wonderful marriage, a wonderful career. He loved it. He was so good at it. He dedicated his life to saving people. He was an accomplished helicopter pilot. He was a loving husband. He was a devoted father figure. He was a loyal son. And how do you compensate the family for that loss, ladies and gentlemen. Again, the law helps. It doesn't solve it completely, not without your help, but it helps because there are statutory elements that you may consider. There are nine of them.

5. Damages argument from a recent helicopter crash case involving the wrongful death of a fifty-year old cameraman who was shooting a movie when the helicopter struck power lines and crashed. He left a wife to whom he had been married for over 25 years.

You know in life you've recognized when there are marriages that are truly beautiful and wonderful. And for almost twenty-six years, this was a beautiful marriage and if you say that that would be worth at least twice the other elements and that's $4 million, well that would get you to $20 million. And so I ask you to consider that range, ladies and gentlemen of $15-20 million. And looking up on the board, it seems like a big number but it's not. It's not when you consider the magnitude, the duration, and the impact of this loss. Just consider the magnitude. Death is so final. It is so irreversible. It is so complete.

You consider the duration of this loss. It's not for a year or two or five. She'll suffer this loss for thirty years. And, finally, the impact. Other than horrific physical injury or death to her, could there have been anything in her life that would have impacted her more than the death of her beloved husband? No. In these instructions, Her Honor tells you that you should fully compensate her for the death of her husband. Fully compensate. To compensate means to replace with that of equal value.

In our society, $15 to $20 million is not that much. You couldn't get a starting pitcher in the rotation in major league baseball for one year for that amount of money. Oprah makes that in a month. You have an opportunity to do something very, very special and that is to right a horrific wrong, to do justice in this case under the law based on the evidence that you have heard.

Nothing will affect the ultimate damages verdict as much as the evidence adduced at trial. But plaintiff counsel's closing argument is a tremendous opportunity for maximizing those damages. The final analysis by which plaintiff's counsel arrives at the requested damages figures are a result of counsel's comfort level with the jury, the economic and non-economic impact of the injuries and the nature of the liability. Ultimately, if the client is satisfied with the jury's verdict, counsel will have done all that can be asked.

10.7 Plaintiff's Rebuttal Argument

Plaintiff's rebuttal argument is truly the last word at the trial. Because defense counsel have no further opportunity to ad-

dress the jury, rebuttal argument is a powerful tool in plaintiff's arsenal that can bolster the liability case and re-direct the jury's focus on damages.

1. During the concluding portion of plaintiff's closing argument, the jury can be alerted to expect a short rebuttal argument by plaintiff's counsel. The author does this as follows:

You've extended to me not only now but over the last three and a half weeks every possible courtesy and attention and I thank you. I'll have a brief opportunity to make some short remarks after remarks of counsel.

An effective rebuttal argument does precisely that: it rebuts points and contentions raised by defense counsel in their closing argument. It is good practice to anticipate as many of the defense arguments as is possible so that the rebuttal points already will be outlined and at the ready.

2. An example of plaintiff's rebuttal argument used in one helicopter crash trial is as follows.

MR. ROBB: Ladies and gentlemen, you heard the response from the Turbomeca lawyer as to the figure which I had discussed with you pursuant to the court's instruction. I gave specific, cogent reasons for the figure of full justice in this case, and the sole comment by counsel for Turbomeca is that that figure is inconceivable. Turbomeca cannot conceive of such a figure. I submit to you I did not pull that figure out of a hat.

The evidence in this record which under the law I am permitted to argue came from Mr. Beacher. That is the testimony that there were 2,850 engines out in the world that needed to eventually be changed and the cost was $17,000.00 to make the change. If the mathematics is correct, it would cost the manufacturer Turbomeca, S.A., some $48 million for the replacement of the defectively designed part and Mr. Beacher agreed with that arithmetic. Is this an inconceivable figure? Of course not.

3. One of the points defense counsel made in closing argument was that the company did address these concerns by issuing service letters and service bulletins. This was the author's rebuttal:

And Dr. Harper explained that these engineering companies are paper intensive. There's standards, objectives, and guidelines. They want to promote things. And in that entire period of time knowing the significance of this problem, do you believe that Mr. Fasteux did not generate one single solitary piece of paper?

That's not my job to decide the facts. It's yours but I point that out. They did generate some paper, the service letters, and I submit to you that those were pretensive, false, knowing vehicles in view of the circumstances to send out paper instead of fixing the problem. Send out paper. Let's just send out some paper. Listen. The first service letter, listen, listen a little harder. Second service letter, listen real hard. It doesn't work.

Ladies and gentlemen of this jury, there was a time that Mr. Fasteux had power. When Mr. Fasteux had the power to save lives, and at that time he and all these nine people involved they had the power and they didn't use it.

You now have the power, a different kind of power. You have the power to do a full measure of justice, not 60%, not 80%. You took an oath to do 100% justice. I stand before you and I look each of you in the eye and you give me that courtesy for which I am grateful and you say we are going to do 100% justice. We're not going to do 60%. 60% justice is 40% injustice. Hasn't there been enough injustice in this situation already?

...

I'll tell you, ladies and gentlemen, you will never forget as long as you live, this experience when you were on the jury for the Life Flight Helicopter case for four weeks. What an experience that was. You will have your own observations and experiences about it, and you will never forget about it and I urge you not to forget it. If you feel it in your heart, if you know it in your mind, argue for it.

...

We'll be waiting for your verdict and we know and trust that you will do full justice.

And then comes the most difficult time in any jury trial, waiting for the jury's verdict. Hopefully, that verdict will be a fair and just award for the plaintiff.

Part III:
Safety Recommendations for the Helicopter Industry

The vast majority of helicopter accidents are preventable events. The causal analysis for almost every helicopter crash reveals some critical safety lapse and often several which directly led to the fatal crash. An inordinately high number of helicopter accidents are attributable to fatigue fracture of a safety critical component. The enhanced vibrational forces experienced by helicopter components should require a far shorter time between overhaul (TBO) than for comparable parts in fixed-wing aircraft. So many crashes occur at night where the aircraft impacts a fixed obstacle that the use of night vision goggles (NVGs) should be mandatory equipment on all helicopters.

The purpose of this Part III is to set out a series of generic safety improvements for the helicopter industry as well as mission-specific recommendations. Adoption of even a few of these recommendations would prevent a significant number of helicopter accidents each year. Many of these safety recommendations arise from specific knowledge gained from litigating helicopter crash lawsuits. Some of these same measures have been recommended by groups which have carefully studied and analyzed helicopter accidents such as the International Helicopter Safety Team (IHST) as well as the FAA and NTSB, the Professional Helicopter Pilots Association International (PHPA), the National Press Photographers Association, Helicopter Association International (HAI), the newly formed National Electronic News-Gathering Helicopter Association (NEHA), and the Helicopter Safety Advisory Committee (HSAC).

This author has seen first-hand the devastation to human lives caused by helicopter crashes. The helicopter industry itself candidly recognizes that the current accident rate is unacceptable and "excessive." When the presidents of the four major helicopter manufacturers author and sign a joint "Call to Action by Helicopter Owners" to "improve the entire industry's safety practices," that is the sign of an industry in crisis.[1] Far too often the pilot is the easy scapegoat for any helicopter accident whereas the true fault lies with either the helicopter or component manufacturer for improper design or the operator for failing to install essential safety equipment or to promote safer practices. Implementation of only a few of the suggested safety improvements set out here would significantly reduce the number of accidents in this industry. A long-time credo of the plaintiffs' bar is "It is far better to place a fence at the top of the cliff then an ambulance in the valley below." The helicopter industry needs far more fences and far fewer ambulances.

---

1. "A Call to Action by Helicopter Owners," "Helicopter Safety Recommendation Summary for Small Operators," September 2009, prepared by International Helicopter Safety Team (IHST).

Chapter 11

Generic Safety Improvements for the Helicopter Industry

Introduction

Across the board there are a number of measures which can be undertaken by helicopter and helicopter component part manufacturers as well as helicopter operators to dramatically reduce the unacceptably high helicopter accident rate. While certain of these recommended safety improvements involve helicopter design and manufacturing changes as well as installation of additional equipment, others encompass simple policy changes in operator management systems, helicopter pilot training, and flight restrictions.

A comprehensive study undertaken by the Transportation Safety Board of Canada determined that over one-half of all reported helicopter crashes had some mechanical explanation and that improper maintenance was implicated in one-quarter to one-third of those.[1] The pilot's loss of visual reference accounted for 15 percent of the reported crashes. The study further found that loss of engine power was responsible for 35 percent of all helicopter crashes and that airframe or rotor system problems together accounted for 18 percent of the crashes, for a combined total of 53 percent

of all occurrences. Positively addressing these specific design and maintenance-related issues alone would result in an enormous reduction of helicopter accidents, fatalities and injuries.

11.1 Safer Design and Manufacturing Processes

The helicopter accident rate has skyrocketed so rapidly that various players within the helicopter industry recently formed a study group to analyze the causes of helicopter accidents and to make safety recommendations. In 2006, a varied group of leaders within the helicopter community came together to form the International Helicopter Safety Team (IHST). The findings and recommendations of that group were published in September 2009.[2] These recommendations are based on accident analyses of U.S. helicopter crashes but are believed by the team to have universal applicability to worldwide helicopter operations. The highest executives of the four largest helicopter manufacturers strongly endorsed the findings and recommendations of the IHST. But while those recommendations are excellent, the IHST conspicuously omitted any reference to helicopter design and manufacturing errors which some studies suggest account for at least one-third of all reported helicopter accidents. The IHST recommendations were developed primarily for small helicopter fleet operators which generally operate from one to two helicopters although the recommendations are applicable to larger operations. The IHST recommendations are grouped into five areas:

1. Safety Management Systems (SMS)
2. Training
3. Helicopter Systems and Equipment
4. Enhanced Accident Feedback
5. Maintenance

The sale of helicopters is a highly competitive business. Operators in a position to purchase multiple helicopters such as police departments, air ambulance operators, or aerial tour companies are price sensitive and will seek out the most competitive bid without a full consideration or realization of the comparative safety implications. For this reason, helicopter airframe, engine and component part manufacturers frequently engage in impermissible cost-cutting measures at the expense of safety.

A. Addressing Known Design and Manufacturing Deficiencies

There is no uniform level of design and manufacturing criteria implemented by the FAA. The FARs do not represent the industry standard of care but merely the lowest practices tolerable below which minimal fines may potentially be levied or FAA certification denied. At minimum, helicopter design criteria should include a minimum hour requirement for the testing and field use of any re-configured airframe, system or component. In many cases critical design modifications are grandfathered in by the manufacturer with no additional testing or field usage documentation whatsoever. So long as the in-house Designated Engineering Representative (DER) reports to the FAA that these are non-controversial and safe design modifications, no current requirement exists for additional testing.

The peculiar aerodynamics in combination with the extensive vibration, mechanical wear and heat generated by helicopter operation imposes significantly more maintenance per hour of operation than fixed-wing aircraft. For example, helicopter engine components are known to deteriorate rapidly due to the enhanced vibratory and thermal stresses imposed when the helicopter is utilized in a heavy lifting operation or in high temperature conditions. That is why many engineers refer to helicopters as "flying fatigue machines" due to the enhanced wear and part failure due to excessive frequency and amplitude vibration. Nevertheless, the current FAA regulatory scheme for approving new models, systems or components, insuring reliability of backup systems and even collecting data about in-service performance problems is insufficient.

Helicopter flight missions typically result in more operational stresses and vibrational spectra than are encountered by their fixed-wing brethren. Helicopter engines, rotors, bearings, freewheel units or clutches, rotor systems including the gear box, and trunnions fail frequently because the load or force spectra had not been evaluated properly from a design standpoint. Much more emphasis by these manufacturers needs to be placed on assuring that the tools of reliability-based design are applied within the industry along with all known quality assurance programs. Manufacturers

must take responsibility for maintaining airworthiness of their engines, systems, and various components within the known and anticipated number of hours of use or cycles.

Helicopter manufacturers must continue to engage in research to improve the fundamental operational and performance characteristics of their helicopters. Many of the helicopter design deficiencies which contribute to loss of control accidents have been analyzed by the U.S. military. For many years, the U.S. Army flight engineers in conjunction with NASA at the Ames Research Center have studied ways to make helicopters safer for both military and civil use. These design issues have focused among other things on:

- Cockpit Controls: Various layout and design alternatives for the cockpit configuration have been studied which may substantially ease the difficulty and workload of piloting a helicopter.
- Handling and Performance Issues: Army engineers have experimented with helicopter flight control systems which allow for easier operational control.
- Noise Reduction: As most helicopter noise is as a result of vibrating parts as well as the interaction of air vortices shed from the tips of rotors, Army researchers are using wind tunnels in an effort to reduce vibrational amplitudes with resultant reduction in noise.

Extremely promising research is currently being undertaken by NASA engineers on helicopters to cushion the impact of crash landings.[3] NASA research engineers have tested deployable energy absorbers (DEA) which function similarly to standard automotive airbags. These DEAs are made of a rigid, honey-combed Kevlar material which is affixed to the underside of a helicopter. When expanded, the material resembles a manila-colored accordion and deforms during a crash providing a substantial cushioning.

NASA researchers have tested DEA-equipped helicopters with crash test dummies and concluded that the dummies would have survived an otherwise non-survivable crash. The DEA softened the impact of the crash to such an extent that one helicopter needed only minor repairs before another test crash.[4] This type of simple and relatively inexpensive safety device should be standard equipment on every single helicopter. Given the number of high impact, undercarriage-first helicopter accidents, the beneficial effect of DEAs is self-evident and would save many lives and prevent numerous serious injuries.

B. Enhanced Reporting of Helicopter Accidents or Incidents and Component or System Malfunction

Reporting obligations of manufacturers and operators should extend to any known incidents, failures or mishaps regardless of whether an accident or crash ensues. These reporting duties must include failures or malfunctions of safety critical components and systems. Such incidents or malfunctions may occur prior to helicopter takeoff or during maintenance procedures. The fault here does not lie totally at the feet of the manufacturer as maintenance facilities are overworked and operate on deadline; and many times the last thing a mechanic wishes to do is to stop and fill out an SDR. Regulatory authorities must take far more seriously any reported incident which may potentially cause an in-flight component or system failure. Until the underlying basis for that failure is identified and addressed, helicopters containing the subject component or system should be grounded. To date the FAA and comparable regulatory authorities have hesitated to impose such a severe requirement on the helicopter industry, but it can and will result in the saving of lives.

C. Reducing Post-Impact Fires

Post-impact fires and explosions continue to remain an unacceptably high risk in helicopter crashes. Enhanced fuel containment measures should be undertaken as a means of averting post-impact fires. Such measures include constructing fuels tanks that are more impact resistant and either positioning or insulating them from ignition sources or structures capable of penetrating the fuel tank. A number of helicopters are currently being constructed with self-sealing fuel tanks as well as break-away fuel line connection valves. The containment of fuel during impact significantly decreases the risk of fire and significantly slows its entry into the cabin which has the critical benefit of allowing passengers and crew some brief period of time to escape the wreckage.

11.2 Enhanced Management Oversight

Many helicopter accidents are directly attributable to the operator's failure to have and to follow specific flight risk profiles. Lack of a safety culture abounds among many helicopter operators and management facilities. A lax concern with safety manifests in different ways. These may be routine untimely reporting and correction of maintenance concerns. Reporting of on-ground or in-flight concerns may be discouraged or the operation may not foster a pilot-supportive environment. Helicopter accident studies have confirmed that a documented safety management system (SMS) with specific written standards as to flight operations, training

and maintenance results in significantly fewer accidents and incidents. Maintaining a non-punitive reporting environment for both maintenance personnel as well as pilots and crew fosters a heightened safety environment which seeks to correct identified safety issues rather than to ignore or hide them.

Helicopter operators must take ultimate responsibility for the exercise of sound judgment by their pilots. In order to assess ongoing pilot competence, management must periodically assess the piloting skills of each pilot to insure that they are continuing to demonstrate sound judgment and decision-making capabilities. All operators should insist that pilots conduct their in-flight activity in a professional manner and that all comply with designated reporting points on a common radio frequency. Ultimately, helicopter management must take responsibility for the recurrent training needs of pilots and address any mission-specific issues which arise. Such simple procedures as periodic pilot meetings may foster this shared concern on safety issues as well as alert all fleet pilots of any particular safety issues.

All operators should require their pilots to engage in frequent recurrent training. In that regard, the IHST study found that small helicopter operators in particular benefited when their pilots underwent more frequent simulator training as well as other specialized training in aeronautical decision making, crew resource and management (CRM), and instrument meteorological conditions (IMC) recognition and avoidance. Although many operators utilize the same make and model of helicopter for ease of training purposes as well as maintenance considerations, many operators mix and match. Not all helicopters operate in the same way. For that reason, operators must insure that their pilots have specific helicopter make and model transition training which should include factory training on the particular helicopter type. Every major helicopter manufacturer offers specific ground and flight training for each make and model of helicopter manufactured and that is by far the most preferred industry training for safety purposes.

Pilot error is cited by the NTSB as the predominant cause of helicopter accidents. In many of those instances, the more appropriate probable cause of the accident would have been fleet operator error or failed management oversight. As set forth recently by the Professional Helicopter Pilots Association International (PHPA):

> It is easy and perhaps correct to blame the pilot, operating a single engine aircraft at its maximum allowable weight, at night, with no vision enhancing system, no terrain warning system, no co-pilot or autopilot, attempting to transition from the glare of

lights to an accident scene to the pitch darkness of an overcast sky who hits wires or gets disoriented and plows back into the ground. Yet placing such blame does not make the next flight safer.[5]

11.3 Improved Maintenance Procedures

Too many helicopter accidents are the direct result of a critical error committed by a mechanic. The training and experience of helicopter mechanics must be helicopter-specific as there are aspects which render such maintenance work entirely different from comparable work on fixed-wing aircraft.

A. Strict Compliance with Manufacturer's Maintenance Program

Many maintenance-related errors have been attributed to the operator's intentional or benign indifference to the manufacturer's maintenance program. All operators of whatever size would contribute substantially to overall helicopter accident reduction by requiring strict adherence to the published maintenance program for that manufacturer and by implementing oversight of maintenance activity to insure that compliance. This was one of the four major recommendations endorsed by the four helicopter company chief executives in their joint "Call for Action" by helicopter owners.

B. Helicopter-Specific Training for Mechanics

Helicopter mechanics should be required to undergo at least 100 hours of specialized training or apprenticeship devoted exclusively to helicopters. At present, the training requirements and experience for a full-time A&P mechanic devoted to helicopters is far too minimal. The FAA must completely revamp these training requirements given the existence of so many systems and operational differences between helicopters and fixed-wing aircraft. Transport Canada requires specific in-type certifications for mechanics to be eligible to perform work on a specific aircraft. The FAA must change its policies and procedures to adopt a system that differentiates between fixed-wing and helicopter mechanics. Currently, the FAA has no distinct differentiation or requirement.

C. Implementation of Health and Usage Monitoring Systems

One of the most significant technical developments in recent years for improving helicopter safety is the design and commercial availability of health and usage monitoring systems (HUMS) for helicopters. While component and system monitoring programs long have been available for fixed-wing aircraft, HUMS was developed specifically for helicopters. Such helicopter monitoring systems were first used for large twin-engine helicopters flown to offshore rigs in the North Sea.[6] HUMS is a helicopter component monitoring system which provides an analysis and diagnostics of mechanical operation of certain components, rotor track and balance and other systems within the helicopter. HUMS is accomplished by a series of strategically placed sensors in addition to other ancillary systems which provide real-time on-demand information allowing diagnostics of the condition of the helicopter's key components and function.

HUMS may replace the now typical time-based maintenance regimen which requires periodic examination and inspection of helicopter critical components. Almost all helicopter maintenance operations are driven by specific maintenance schedules. Following specific time intervals as short as 20-25 flight hours, certain critical components must be removed and inspected. Not only is that maintenance activity costly and time-consuming but also the lost flight hours result in decreased revenue for the operator.

A HUMS system which is capable of monitoring the vibrational characteristics of the helicopter's safety critical components is capable of giving an early indication of an incipient mechanical defect.[7] Temperature and vibration may be measured by HUMS and these two factors are capable of giving an early indication of some brewing mechanical defect which may be growing over time. While a HUMS system is capable of detecting a component failure before that failure causes an accident, the system may also result in significant maintenance savings for operators freed from the rigors of periodic removal and inspection of key components. The additional advantage is that the aircraft may be required to be out of service far less often, resulting in additional savings.

Such systems are becoming more affordable and more frequently utilized in the helicopter industry.[8] A fully operational HUMS program records engine and helicopter gearbox performance while also providing rotor track and balance feedback.[9] The system also monitors auxiliary power unit usage and can store data from various sensors and accelerometers that monitor safety critical components. The compiled data may be analyzed so as to allow helicopter operators to target specific types of pilot training as well as to implement flight operations and quality assurance programs (FOQA) all in an effort to enhance safety in helicopter operations.

11.4 Pilot Training and Flight Restrictions

The overwhelming majority of men and women flying helicopters are professional pilots. This is the inverse for those pilots flying general aviation fixed-wing aircraft who are predominantly amateur pilots. For this reason, the sheer number of helicopter crashes attributable to pilot error is astounding. Much of that may be explained by the inordinate demands operators and other employers place on their helicopter pilots including simultaneous service as a tour guide, news reporter, or even utility wire inspector. A pilot's first and only obligation should be to operate the helicopter without any additional or collateral demands on the workload. As for the aviation industry generally, pilot fatigue is a recurrent concern. Operators must establish specific rest and off duty periods so that pilots are not subject to continuous or back-to-back flight responsibilities.

Helicopters are predominantly oriented toward VFR flying. There are many pilots holding valid rotorcraft certification but without a valid instrument rating. Without pilots trained in helicopters equipped with sufficient avionics to enter instrument meteorological conditions (IMC) or other types of problematic visual or weather conditions, absolute flight restriction to visual flight rules (VFR) conditions is critical to safety.

Helicopter flight certification should be stair-stepped relative to a pilot's experience. No helicopter pilot should be permitted to transport paying passengers without a minimum of 500 hours of flight time as pilot-in-command. Currently, the FAA only requires 150 hours of flight experience for a commercial helicopter pilot certificate, whereas fixed-wing pilots are required to have a minimum of 250 hours of flight experience for a commercial license. All too often, pilots of minimal experience are hired who have barely passed their FAA flight tests and training. Enhanced pilot training also would involve better training for specific flight missions or over specific types of terrain. For example, helicopter pilots should be far better trained in flying over mountainous regions. Generic pilot training improvement would include such basic items as avoiding inadvertent entry into instrument meteorological condition (IMC) flight conditions, increased pilot awareness of obstacles and pre-flight notation of obstacles. Many helicopter accidents occur as a result of improperly executed autorotations. That being the case, helicopter pilots must receive far more extensive training and practice in performing autorotations. Because not all helicopters follow the same flight parameters for autorotations, pilots should engage in type-specific training and practice for autorotations. It is common industry knowledge that operators of twin engine helicopters very rarely require recurrent autorotation training due to the unlikely occurrence of a dual engine failure.

One of the chief reasons the accident rate for helicopters is so much higher than all other types of aircraft is that almost all helicopter pilots train only in the aircraft. Greater use of flight simulation and scenario-based training already is having a marked effect on reducing crashes due to pilot error.[10] As that type of training becomes more cost-effective and more readily available, it should be standard operating practice for all helicopter pilots to train and improve their piloting skills by use of flight simulators.

Regulatory authorities should impose strict flight rules on the use of helicopters in congested or crowded areas. The failure of just such a flight restriction resulted in the crash of a helicopter with a small plane on August 8, 2009 over the Hudson River. Only thereafter did the FAA consider flight restrictions within that corridor. But nine people died before any such regulation went into effect.

11.5 Mandatory Equipment

One of the chief reasons commercial aircraft have a substantially higher safety record than general aviation helicopters is the routine installation of necessary safety equipment. Operators and managers of helicopter services continue to expect accident-free operation from their pilots but are loath to provide them with the necessary tools to achieve that result. The Professional Helicopter Pilots Association (PHPA) has over 4,000 helicopter pilot members across the U.S. and Canada of which over 1,300 are active emergency medical services (EMS) helicopter pilots. The PHPA recommends the addition of several types of safety equipment specifically for use in emergency medical services helicopters.[11]

A. Night Vision Goggles

The single most important piece of equipment which would serve to prevent the most helicopter accidents would be the use of night vision goggles (NVGs). The routine low-altitude flight of most helicopters renders them particularly vulnerable in the dark to contact with fixed obstacles such as radio towers, telephone poles, horizontal utility wires, and even unexpected hills and small buildings. Thus far the industry has resisted mandatory issuance and use of NVGs by reason of their cost. A current set of goggles of sufficient quality runs approximately $10,000. That is a small price to pay for the dozens of lives lost each year due to a helicopter pilot's CFIT (controlled flight into terrain or other object).

B. Terrain Awareness and Warning System

Where the flight mission would involve flying into poor weather conditions or at night and require landing in unfamiliar locations, the installation of a Terrain Awareness and Warning System (TAWS) should be mandatory. The equipment costs about $100,000 per helicopter. TAWS has been standard equipment on jets for some time and has been cited as preventing numerous aircrashes. The use of improved helicopter cockpit technology to provide accurate altitude and ground clearance information to the pilot would be vastly safer in all flight conditions. The safety device commonly sets off an alarm based on a computerized tracking device which can give a pilot sufficient warning so as to avoid the danger. Recent industry statistics show that more than 40 percent of air ambulance operators have voluntarily installed TAWS safety devices on their air ambulance helicopters. That figure is derived in large part from information provided by Honeywell which is the leading manufacturer of TAWS safety devices. Honeywell has reported selling approximately 200 TAWS systems to air ambulance operators.

C. Global Positioning System Technology

Global Positioning System Technology (GPS) is similar to Terrain Awareness and Warning Systems. GPS units are now capable of displaying maps of potential obstacles and obstructions and will provide data on terrain such as unseen mountains, trees or other obstructions.[12] So many helicopter crashes are due to impact with unexpected terrain or obstacles that helicopter pilots need some means of obtaining critical data on the location of such obstructions and terrain. New GPS technology contains a global terrain database and an obstruction database for North America which can provide sufficient warnings to pilots about the presence of towers, trees or any other obstructions. Given the minimal expense of such units, it is imperative that all helicopters be provided with GPS units if they are not otherwise equipped with TAWS and, preferably, both. Some of the new units such as the Garmin GNS-530AWT also provide weather information, helicopter radio communication and navigational capabilities.

D. Multi-Engine Helicopters

This is one area where the substantial additional cost would result in immediate substantial benefit. Regrettably, engine power failure in a single engine helicopter is all too often fatal because of the flight environment in which helicopters are being operated that renders autorotation impossible. Helicopters which typically operate over mountainous or forest regions or congested urban areas would not permit even the most capable pilots of executing an autorotation. On a practical note, a high percentage of professional helicopter pilots gain their training and experience in the U.S. military which operates virtually all multi-engine helicopters. These pilots then have minimal power-off experience or training other than the minimal transition training they receive before they begin their duties as a single engine helicopter pilot. The obvious engine redundancy for a multi-engine helicopter

and ability to maintain powered flight with one engine out would save many lives and prevent numerous devastating injuries.

E. Flotation and Locator Devices

Many deaths and serious injuries resulting from helicopter crashes could have been avoided had the operator equipped the helicopter with such basic safety equipment as flotation devices for missions over water or locator devices to assure more rapid rescue and response time in dealing with remote helicopter usage.

F. Flight Data Recorder

All too often there exists scant information concerning the operational profile of a helicopter immediately prior to a crash. The lack of such information strikes at the heart of helicopter accident prevention in that without a verifiable cause there can be no preventative measures taken.

Some helicopter manufacturers recently have developed so-called simple flight data recorders (FDRs) that record the primary operating parameters of the helicopter immediately prior to a helicopter accident such as altitude, attitude, airspeed, and rotor speed. Some of these FDRs also have cockpit image and voice recording capability. These instruments are easy to install and are relatively inexpensive. The installation of FDRs as standard equipment on all helicopters would permit crash investigators a far more complete analysis of accidents which has the salutory effect of implementing targeted safety enhancements for the helicopter industry.

11.6 Enhanced FAA Regulatory Oversight

Many of the foregoing generic safety recommendations for the helicopter industry set forth herein require no additional equipment and come at relatively minimal cost. The most important of these are to establish risk assessment programs for the flight mission with a particular focus on adverse weather conditions, enhanced pilot training, and pre-planned route analysis before departure to identify potentially dangerous obstacles along the flight path.

Finally, after ten years of proposed initiatives, the FAA has adopted a final rule requiring helicopter operators, specifically including air ambulances, to implement stricter flight rules and procedures, adopt improved communications and pilot training, and to add safety-critical equipment to the helicopter.[13]

Under the new rule, all Part 135 helicopter operators are required to:

(a) Equip the helicopter with radio altimeters;

(b) Require occupants to wear life preservers and to equip helicopters with an emergency locater transmitter (ELT);

(c) Use higher weather minimums; and

(d) Require enhanced training of pilots to enable them to handle adverse weather conditions and especially so from an inadvertent entry into instrument meteorological conditions.

Under this new FAA rule, all air ambulance operators have additional requirements:

(a) Equip the aircraft with helicopter terrain awareness and warning systems (HTAWS);

(b) Equip the helicopter with a flight data monitoring system within four (4) years;

(c) Establish operations control centers if operating ten or more air ambulance helicopters;

(d) Institute pre-flight risk analysis programs;

(e) Ensure that its pilots hold an instrument rating and that they identify and document the highest obstacle along the planned flight path prior to departure;

(f) That the operator comply with visual flight rules (VFR) weather minimums;

(g) That flight crew time limitations and rest requirements are followed when medical personnel are on board; and

(h) Conduct safety briefings and training for medical personnel.[14]

These procedures are a step in the right direction. But, unfortunately, they do not address some of the most important potential safety improvements for this industry. For example, one of the most important pieces of equipment which certainly would prevent the greatest number of helicopter accidents would be the standard utilization of night vision goggles (NVGs). While the FAA continues to support and encourage their use, its failure to mandate their use is disappointing and, indeed, will be fatal in the years to come. It is the author's fervent hope that many more of the generic safety recommendations set forth in this Chapter are adopted either voluntarily by the industry or mandated by FAA regulation as well as the mission-specific safety measures addressed in Chapter 12.

Endnotes

1. Lessons Learned from Transportation Safety Board Investigations of Helicopter Accidents, 1994-2003, presented at International Helicopter Safety Symposium, September 26-29, 2005, American Helicopter Society International, Inc., at p. 1.

2. "Helicopter Safety Recommendation Summary for Small Operators," September 2009, prepared by International Helicopter Safety Team (IHST).

3. A. Hadhazy, "NASA Crashes Helicopters to Improve Safety," *TechNewsDaily*, http://www.technewsdaily.com/nasa-crashes-helicopters-to-improve-safety-0318/, March 16, 2010.

4. *Id.*

5. Helicopter EMS Issues, March 5, 2009, Professional Helicopter Pilots Association Website.

6. *Aviation Maintenance Magazine*, "HUMS: Health and Usage Monitoring Systems," February 1, 2006.

7. *Rotor & Wing*, "Helicopter Hums Update 2K10," February 1, 2010.

8. *Id.*

9. *Id.*

10. Greenyer, "Progress with Helicopter Sims is Cutting High Accident Rate," *Airline*, May 13, 2010.

11. Helicopter EMS Issues, March 5, 2009, Professional Helicopter Pilots Association Website.

12. Graham, "Global Positioning Systems Improve Helicopter Safety," *U.S. Department of Defense*, November 30, 2009.

13. 79 Federal Register No. 35 (February 21, 2014, Helicopter Air Ambulance, Commercial Helicopter and Part 91 Helicopter Operations; Final Rule).

14. *Id.*

Chapter 12

Mission-Specific Recommendations for Enhanced Safety

Introduction

Within the helicopter industry, there exist a wide variety of flight missions potentially exposing the helicopter and its crew to variant risks. The purpose of this section is to set out specific recommendations to eliminate or substantially reduce the risks of operating a helicopter within specific flight mission profiles.

12.1 Helicopter Touring Industry

There has been a disturbingly high rate of fatal helicopter crashes involving sightseeing tours. During 2000-10, the NTSB has recorded more than 140 sightseeing flight accidents nationally, 19 of which resulted in 86 fatalities. Helicopter flights cause more than half of the fatal crashes and 24 of these fatalities occurred in Hawaii alone.

Intense lobbying by the helicopter aerial tour industry, including threats of operator bankruptcy, have resulted in an almost hands-off regulatory role from the FAA. For example, in response to complaints from Hawaiian helicopter air tour operators that present flight restrictions made their tours less appealing to tourists resulting in decreased industry revenue, the FAA issued exemptions permitting helicopter tour pilots to fly lower and lower.[1] The FAA granted exemptions to several helicopter tour operators to fly as low as 1,000 feet and some as low as 500 feet. Given the rash of fatal helicopter crashes in Hawaii these exemptions are not only unadvisable but they are irresponsible. Low altitude flight poses additional risks including increased crowding of aircraft at certain altitudes especially in low visibility conditions when fixed-wing aircraft may be flying at low altitude to get below the clouds. These exemptions are ill-advised and should be cancelled thereby reverting to the general limitation on helicopter flights to 2,000 feet above the surface for mountainous terrain except for takeoff and landing.

While various helicopter tour companies adhere to a high standard of operation, others simply adhere to FAA minimum requirements. Those operators with operating procedures higher than the FAA minimum standards will often display certificates so indicating.

The primary causes of crashes within the helicopter tour industry are as follows:

1. Inadequate management or operator supervision
2. Inadequate maintenance practices
3. Inadequate risk assessment of weather or environmental conditions
4. Compromising pilot workload by imposing tour guide responsibilities
5. Incentives to fly too close to fixed obstacles
6. Operating in crowded airspace

Virtually all of the crashes within the helicopter tour industry have been as a result of one of the foregoing risk factors, other than where the helicopter suffered an in-flight failure of a safety critical control or system. Such was the case for the 1999 helicopter crash in Herbert Glacier in Alaska resulting in the death of seven people. The helicopter impacted the glacier at a 90 degrees nose down position at 135 KTS. Later examination of the wreckage revealed that the helicopter had suffered a failure of the pitch servo which drove the helicopter into a rapid descent. The pitch attitude servo had a manufacturing plug come out of place which jammed the selector valve in the full nose down position. The aircraft went from a level attitude to 90 degrees nose down in 200 feet of altitude at 135 KTS.

The following mission specific recommendations would result in substantially enhanced safety of helicopter tour flights without compromising to any great degree their attractiveness.

A. Greater Scrutiny and Monitoring of Tour Operator Management and Maintenance Practices

Helicopter tour operators should be required to adhere to higher maintenance standards than those current FAA minimal requirements. For those missions where the aircraft are used for common carrier purposes, the mechanics should have top-flight training and be highly experienced with a minimum of five (5) years of primary maintenance of rotorcraft. Waivers of any extended use or past regularly scheduled or annual inspections should be the exception rather than the rule. Any helicopter which is not fully in compliance with all regularly scheduled maintenance and component part replacement should be considered non-airworthy and grounded until such time as any maintenance or component part discrepancies are rectified.

At present, helicopter touring operations come under Part 135 for on-demand flights or Part 91 sightseeing flights. Part 135 applies to aircraft with ten or more seats. It requires that such operators establish and maintain a program referred to as a continuing analysis and surveillance system or CASS as applicable to its maintenance program as well. Unfortunately, most helicopters tour operators fly much smaller helicopters and are exempt from these requirements to have the high-quality maintenance assurance program provided for under the federal regulations.

The NTSB issued a number of safety recommendations arising out of two separate helicopter crashes involving Heli-USA Airways. According to the NTSB, the operator's general operating manual showed that 20 safety critical maintenance items were signed off by mechanics other than the ones providing the maintenance.[2] According to the NTSB:

Because there was no effective quality assurance program in place at Heli-USA, maintenance errors were not detected, which led to accidents.[3]

It is self-evident but the NTSB concluded that "[e]ffective quality assurance programs can identify and prevent maintenance issues...."[4]

Given the high number of maintenance-related crashes, maintenance practices would be substantially upgraded were there more frequent and consistent on-site surveillance of maintenance practices by FAA principal maintenance inspectors (PMIs). PMIs should review maintenance records on a surprise or spot check basis to insure that all required maintenance activity is properly and timely performed.

Far too many helicopter touring operations leave it to their mechanics to determine when any additional or recurrent training is needed. This is not satisfactory. Helicopter mechanics' routine training requirements should include airframe, power plant, and specialized equipment training courses for the make and model of helicopter routinely maintained. In many instances, helicopter mechanics have no specialized training in the specific model to which they are assigned.

In the Princeville helicopter crash of an Aerospatiale AS-350BA in March 2007 that killed four people and seriously injured three others, the NTSB determined that the mechanic who performed maintenance on that helicopter had never attended a formal AS-350 maintenance training class. It was also determined by training records that none of the mechanics for Heli-USA's Hawaiian facility had ever attended a model-specific maintenance training course. These deficiencies must be corrected: responsible helicopter tour operators should comply voluntarily and those who do not should be compelled by regulation.

B. Enhanced Pilot Training and Experience

Pilots hired to operate tour helicopters should have a minimum of 500 hours of flight experience exclusively in a helicopter with a significant amount in the model or type utilized in the touring operations. Management should insure that all active pilots demonstrate sound judgment and decision-making capabilities that includes verification that pilots are following the designated routes and are complying with all designated reporting points on a common frequency.

C. Pre-Determined Flight Path

Most tour operators give their pilots too much latitude as to flight path. Touring helicopters that follow a pre-determined flight path also can render some familiarity to the pilot should adverse weather conditions be encountered. The helicopter touring operator should plot its routes in advance so that all potential obstacles can be noted and avoided by the helicopter pilots.

D. Independent Risk Assessment of Weather Conditions

Revenue considerations often add pressure to the helicopter operator to depart in marginal weather. Tourists already have bought tickets and will demand a refund if the flight does not depart as scheduled. Both the FAA and NTSB have recognized the need for independent risk-assessment of weather and environmental conditions. In connection with that assessment, there must be no adverse consequences to the pilot or risk assessment manager for the cancellation or re-scheduling of flights due to weather or other environmental conditions such as volcanic ash, military aircraft exercises or major glacier break-up. The pilot has ultimate responsibility whether to launch the flight and to conduct or continue to conduct the flight in view of any adverse weather conditions.

E. Dedicated Non-Pilot Tour Guide or Recorded Commentary

Given the workload demands faced by helicopter pilots, it is unreasonable to impose the additional duties of tour guide upon them. Pilots should be able to concentrate only on providing a safe flight. In too many instances a scenic tour helicopter pilot is asked to devote much of his attention to providing the passengers with continuous narration of the tour area as well as answering questions. This is a serious distraction. Operators do not want to carry a separate tour guide because this would deprive them of revenue from that attractive front left seat. In lieu of a separate tour guide, recorded commentary would serve much the same purpose by relieving the pilot of these additional duties without a significant reduction of ride attractiveness.

F. Minimize Crowded Airspace

In some locations there are too many aircraft and not enough space. The recent crash between a helicopter and small plane over the Hudson River illustrates the dangers of too many aircraft flying in a narrow flight corridor. Much the same problem occurs over major scenic areas such as the Grand Canyon or the waterfalls of Kauai where no regulatory minimums or separation are required. Without voluntary self-restrictions, local, state or federal authorities need to step in and regulate the number of aircraft within or over a scenic landmark at any given time. This type of regulation may require careful scheduling in order to monitor the number of aircraft in any designated area at a given time.

G. Minimum Hover and Flight Distances

The job of a scenic helicopter pilot is to provide a thrilling experience, within reason and safely, to the passengers. For that reason, pilots far too often fly dangerously close to mountains, volcanoes, buildings and the edges of cliffs and waterfalls and operate the helicopters as if performing an acrobatic flight. This is precisely the opposite of what helicopter pilots are trained to do and is inconsistent with safe practice. The proper standard requires pilots to fly the helicopter at a safe distance from any obstacle that could create a crash hazard. Too many helicopter crashes have occurred because the tour pilot attempted to give tourists an up-close view that simply got too close. Such were the causes of the March 1994 crash in Hawaii where the helicopter hovered just 40 feet over a volcano vent and the August 1999 crash of a pilot maneuvering the helicopter for a photo opportunity near Mount Rushmore which crashed into the rocks killing two people.

Many scenic helicopter pilots seek to scare their passengers by flying as close to fixed objects as possible before suddenly veering away. Unfortunately, such acrobatic antics have resulted in far too many crashes and needless loss of life. If the industry does not voluntarily impose a minimum distance, governmental authorities must step in to require a 1500 foot minimum separation from any fixed obstacle, the violation of which must be dealt with harshly.

12.2 News-Gathering Operations

In July 2007, two news helicopters collided midair over Phoenix, Arizona, killing both pilots and two photojournalists onboard. These were just two of five helicopters covering a police chase in downtown Phoenix. Although the helicopter pilots reported observing each other and talking on the radio, they all were clearly intent on following and covering the police chase. These pilots failed to maintain proper visual contact with each other.

Voice transcripts from both helicopters demonstrate that the crews were intensely focused on covering the police chase taking place on the ground beneath them. Both helicopter pilots were on the air and reporting live to their respective news stations at the time of the collision.[5] The voice transmissions further indicate that neither helicopter pilot realized that they were in imminent danger or had any indication that they were about to collide. Recommendations to improve the safety of helicopter news-gathering operations are as follows.

A. Eliminate Reporting Duties for Pilots of News-Gathering Helicopters

The Phoenix midair collision between two helicopters illustrates the recurring safety problem of having numerous helicopters involved in a police chase or other on-ground event while simultaneously having the pilots report live. In October 2007, the National Press Photographers Association recommended that news helicopter pilots no longer report live while they are flying the helicopter. The NPPA rightly determined that the practice puts the helicopter and its passengers, not to mention those on the ground beneath them, an unnecessary risk.

B. Enhanced Visibility of Aircraft

Other safety precautions which should be taken by news helicopters include painting a highly visible stripe pattern on the helicopters' rotors so that they may more easily be seen from above, and adding bright strobe lights which may be positioned for maximum visibility so as to avoid a collision with other aircraft.

C. Enhanced Air and Ground Communications Among News-Gathering Pilots

Simple and inexpensive procedures such as requiring helicopter pilots within each market to communicate with each other, report their positions and meet periodically to discuss safety issues, are all simple and inexpensive measures designed to eliminate these risks.

12.3 Air Ambulance Services

The number of people seriously injured and killed in helicopter air ambulance crashes has been well documented. In one 10-month period alone between December 2007 and October 2008, there were 13 helicopter air ambulance crashes which resulted in 35 deaths.[6] At present, there are 75 air ambulance companies operating more than 1500 helicopters in the U.S.[7] Citing cost factors, many air ambulance services have resisted both industry-wide and FAA proposals calling for enhanced use of safety equipment and other regulatory measures. Of the 27 fatal medical air ambulance helicopter crashes between 1998 and 2004, 21 were at night and often in bad weather conditions.[8] Much of the mission incentive has an economic basis. A typical medical air ambulance transport costs $5,000-$8,000 which is five or more times that of a traditional ground ambulance.[9] Private health insurance plans and even some public ones such as Medicare cover at least part of these costs.[10] Given that there are about 400,000 medical helicopter flights annually, that amounts to a great deal of funding both for the helicopter operator and the hospital.[11] A number of mission-specific measures should be taken to address the serious risks inherent in helicopter air ambulance operations.

A. Implementation of Flight Risk Assessment Program

The NTSB has long proposed a flight risk evaluation program for air ambulance operators specifically including consideration of weather, visibility and the prospect of unfamiliar or unsafe landing sites. The NTSB convened a public meeting on September 1, 2009 to further advance its safety recommendations concerning helicopter emergency medical services. In laying out these proposals, the NTSB noted that there was pressure to conduct these operations in less than ideal weather conditions. As a result, many of the NTSB's safety recommendations address enhanced pilot training and risk assessment measures to reduce the number of flight missions undertaken in dangerous operational environments. This push by the NTSB was precisely responsible for the stricter flight rules finally implemented by the FAA in late 2014[12]

As part of the risk assessment procedure, the NTSB recommended using a more formal dispatch approach which would include an evaluation of the current weather information and assistance to the pilot in assessing some of the other flight risk decisions. Many studies have determined that helicopter air ambulances are not always the best means of transporting patients and in many cases are not even necessary. In many instances the patient's injuries are relatively minor and ground transportation would have resulted in arrival at the hospital faster than via helicopter transport.

On far too many occasions helicopter air ambulances have taken on a mission in weather conditions not suitable for flight. Many traffic-related accidents and resultant trauma are caused by poor weather conditions such as fog, heavy snow or rain or thunderstorm and lightning conditions. These conditions are potentially as hazardous for helicopters as for on-ground vehicles. In such a scenario, the hospital facility must elect to send the on-ground ambulance rather than to risk the safety of the pilot, crew and potentially the patient to a helicopter crash.

B. Installation of Terrain Awareness and Warning System

The recommended use of terrain awareness and warning systems (TAWS) for air ambulance helicopters is not a novel idea. Such equipment provides a warning to helicopter pilots when they come close to the ground or other obstacles such as radio control towers or buildings. In April 2009 the FAA announced that it would seek to persuade all helicopter air ambulance operators in the U.S. to voluntarily add TAWS devices to their aircraft. But the proposal is strictly voluntary. NTSB has recommended terrain awareness and warning systems on all air ambulance helicopters.

C. Mandatory Use of Night Vision Goggles

Given the number of night missions routinely flown by air ambulance helicopters, the TAWS system should not be the only additional safety device required. All air ambulance operators should be required to equip their helicopters with night vision goggles (NVGs) which substantially enhance the pilot's ability to visualize obstacles and maneuver around them in low light and dark conditions.

Night vision technology has long been used by military helicopter pilots and is capable of providing pilots with the equivalence of 20/20 vision in the dark. The use of NVGs would not require any modification of the aircraft structure but would require some additional pilot training as to their appropriate use. A recent survey conducted by the National EMS Pilots Association found overwhelming support for use of NVGs.[13] The addition of NVGs for all air ambulance helicopters in this country would have a marked impact on reducing helicopter crashes for these types of flight missions. The NTSB has been at the forefront of recommending safety improvements for air ambulance helicopters for many years.

D. Enhanced Pilot Training

Enhanced helicopter pilot training would have immediate impact on reduction of accidents. The FAA has considered and should now implement far more rigorous testing for air ambulance helicopter pilots to make sure that these pilots can operate the aircraft in sub-par weather conditions which have led to many helicopter accidents. This should be interconnected with the flight risk assessment program before each and every flight. If the flight risks are too high such as where the potential landing zone poses undue risks or the weather is of poor visibility, the flight should not be undertaken. There is a great disparity in the required pilot experience among air ambulance operations. The Mayo Clinic requires helicopter pilots to have 5,000 hours of experience while other operators require only a minimum of 1,500 hours of flight time.[14]

12.4 Utility Wire Inspection

Helicopters are being used increasingly in the utilities industry for the inspection and maintenance of their transmission lines. That industry is also using helicopter crews to collect data for system quality and for transmission line maintenance planning. These utilities also use helicopters for line inspections, stringing wire, setting poles and for placing crews and equipment in areas otherwise inaccessible.

This flight mission brings the helicopter in close proximity to horizontally strung utility lines or telephone wires. These are typically difficult for helicopter pilots to see and are especially hazardous to a helicopter. Many crashes have resulted from the helicopter pilot's inadvertent flight into wires. Utility companies routinely hire private helicopter operators to inspect these lines or wires. Some utilities have begun purchasing and operating their own helicopters. For example, the Tennessee Valley Authority currently owns and operates seven helicopters.

Flying a helicopter in a low altitude environment where wires are present requires a degree of skill which is more complex and demanding than other types of helicopter flying. Nothing about the common helicopter flight mission experience prepares pilots for operating in that wire environment. There is no FAA examination of a helicopter pilot for proficiency or competency flying a helicopter in a wire environment such as in the course of conducting utility line inspections. A number of specific safety precautions can be undertaken to dramatically reduce the incidents of helicopter wire strike. Wire Strike Protection Systems (WSPS) provide some measure of protection from inadvertent flight into horizontally strung wires but only where the helicopter strikes the wires while flying on a straight and level path. Pilots must know and understand the limitations of any WSPS installed on their helicopter.

A. Advance Ground or Aerial Reconnaissance

For those known flight missions where the pilot has advance knowledge of the flight path, either an aerial or ground reconnaissance can pinpoint the location of all horizontally strung power lines so that they can be noted and avoided by the helicopter in-flight. Although there are missions for which the pilot would not know the flight path in advance such as air ambulance or some news-gathering operations, flights for the purpose of utility wire inspection would lend themselves to such advance planning.

B. Separate Spotter or Observer

For any utility wire inspection mission the helicopter pilot should not take on the added workload of flying the helicopter and inspecting wires. A separate spotter or observer should be tasked solely with the responsibility of inspecting wires leaving the pilot devoted to flight responsibilities.

C. Mandatory Attendance at Wire Strike Avoidance Training

Helicopter safety organizations such as Helicopter Association International (HAI) offer specific training sessions on wire strike avoidance. These sessions are taught by highly experienced helicopter pilots and provide tips and strategies for spotting and avoiding horizontally strung wires. These sessions include such lessons as understanding the configuration of utility poles and being aware of residential dwellings and other buildings which may be presumed to be supplied with electricity and, hence, connected by wire.

D. Greater Use of Marker Devices on Utility Wires

Stricter guidelines should be imposed on utility companies which operate in the vicinity of airports or known aircraft flight paths. These utility companies should be required to place marker balls on all utility wires in known flight paths so that they may be visible to helicopters routinely flying at low altitude.

12.5 Search and Rescue Operations

Helicopters are the aircraft of choice in seeking to rescue stranded snow skiers, adventurers lost in the wilderness or people trapped on disabled sailing vessels. Many of the same considerations for air ambulance operations apply to search and rescue operations. A formalized method of risk assessment must be utilized to avoid ad hoc and hurried risk evaluations. It is useful to have a dispatch operator independent of the pilot to participate in the risk assessment of the flight. In addition, the aforementioned safety devices including TAWS and NVGs should be standard equipment on any search and rescue helicopter.

12.6 Law Enforcement and Border Patrol Usage

Police use of helicopters is increasingly common in most urban areas. From the famous O.J. Simpson vehicle tracking by the Los Angeles Police Department helicopter these helicopter usages are increasingly common. Given the uncertain and unanticipated flight path upon which such helicopters may embark a separate spotter or observer is a must. If these helicopters are to be utilized for nighttime operations, and most are, they should be equipped with both TAWS and NVGs.

In 2005, the U.S. Customs and Border Patrol (CBP) aircraft operations merged creating the largest aviation law enforcement service in the world.[15] The CBP uses helicopters to monitor immigrant crossing points which requires low altitude flight in often unfamiliar terrain. For such operations, CBP aircraft should be equipped with both NVGs and TAWS to maximize safety for the pilots and crew.

12.7 Military Training Exercises

Too many servicemen and women are killed and seriously injured while flying a helicopter as part of a military training exercise. The predominant cause of such accidents is the commanding officer's lack of knowledge and understanding of the operational limitations on a helicopter and unrealistic demands on the helicopter pilot. Any training mission that utilizes helicopters must be designed and managed by officers with specific helicopter training.

12.8 Private Transportation

Use of helicopters for private transportation has increased in recent years given the congested nature of many urban areas. It has become common for many downtown office buildings to install a helipad for use by regular tenants or visiting dignitaries. Landing a helicopter on a helipad on the roof of a tall building requires a pilot who is knowledgeable, experienced and proficient in executing this type of operation. Such things as the velocity and direction of wind across the helipad can place the helicopter in an extremist situation which requires a high degree of skill by the pilot. Obstacles that are not readily a problem or consideration may rapidly become a problem. Although it is prudent to restrict such private travel to daylight hours only, that is a difficult proposition to enforce. Given that daylight ends during some periods of the year as early as 4:30-5:00 p.m., some low light or nighttime operation is inevitable. For that reason, NVGs should be standard equipment in all helicopters used for private transportation.

12.9 Transport to Offshore Oil Platforms

More than 600 helicopters currently operate in the Gulf of Mexico offshore fleet taking almost 1.3 million flights and carrying almost three million passengers per year.[16] These helicopters provide transport service to the approximately 4,000 oil production platforms in the gulf's outer continental shelf which stretch from western Texas to southwestern Florida.[17] The use of helicopters to transport workers and other personnel to offshore platforms, primarily in the petroleum industry, has resulted in far too many crashes. In the five years from 2004 to 2009, there were 33 helicopter accidents in Gulf offshore operations, resulting in 30 deaths.[18] A substantial number of these crashes have occurred in the process of landing the helicopter on the offshore platform. Many proposals have been advanced to reduce the risks of landing on offshore platforms, the most useful of which is to design a larger landing area which would be free of vertical obstacles. A more careful monitoring of prevailing weather conditions should be incorporated into any operator's safety program. Where weather conditions pose an undue risk to safe landing, the mission should be aborted.

In 2005, the Helicopter Safety Advisory Conference (HSAC) addressed the high incidents of helicopter accidents in the Gulf of Mexico.[19] That report was devoted to the correction of known hazards encountered by helidecks on the offshore oil platform. Platform helideck hazards include difficult to see obstacles as well as conditions which could snag the helicopter landing gear. In addition to recommending regular helideck inspections, the HSAC encouraged pilots not to attempt a landing on an offshore helideck if it appeared that any obstacle had been added to the deck which might present a hazard to flight.[20]

12.10 Fire-Fighting Operations

Uncontained wildfires notably in southern California and massive forest fires are devastating events which can destroy thousands of acres of timber and force people to evacuate their homes and businesses. Helicopters were first utilized to combat wildfires in southern California in 1947 and have been utilized extensively ever since.[21] The U.S. Forest Service makes extensive use of helicopters for water or fire retardant dropping purposes. Some helicopters are capable of carrying almost 3,000 gallons of water for use in fire-fighting operations.[22] Large helicopters are frequently used for firefighting operations both to carry water and other heavy equipment as well as firefighting personnel. A recent helicopter crash during firefighting operations in Northern California illustrates the high risk of such operations.

Such operations should be required to more appropriately assess the weight and balance restrictions imposed on the aircraft by the manufacturer. Some means must be present to assure that the weight calculations not become overly aggressive but have some margin for error. The risks of a mistake are too great. A standardized methodology for assessing weight for water, equipment and personnel would dramatically reduce the number of weight-related helicopter crashes for this flight mission. The Helicopter Association of Canada (HAC) recently published a useful guide for pilot training and evaluation for helicopter wildfire operations.[23] Among the recommended pilot training criteria are advanced level training in mountain flying, precision load placement and low visibility flight.

Endnotes

1. John H. Cushman, Jr., "Travel Advisory: Tourist Helicopters in Hawaii Can Fly Lower," *The New York Times*, May 19, 1996.

2. NTSB Safety Recommendation, June 12, 2008 at p. 3-4.

3. *Id.* at 4.

4. *Id.* at 4.

5. National Press Photographers Association, "NTSB Releases Reports on Phoenix News Helicopters Crash," August 29, 2008.

6. Alan Levin, "FAA plan would require alarms on air ambulances," *USA Today*, April 23, 2009.

7. FAA Fact Sheet - Initiatives to Improve Helicopter Air Ambulance Safety, February 20, 2014.

8. Barry Meier, "Crashes Start Debate on Safety of Sky Ambulances," *The New York Times*, February 28, 2005.

9. *Id.*

10. *Id.*

11. R.L. Sumwalt, "Update on NTSB's HEMS-Related Activities," National Transportation Safety Board, www.ntsb.gov/Speeches/sumwalt/AAMS-update-March-2010.pdf, March 17, 2010.

12. 79 Federal Register No. 35 (February 21, 2014, Helicopter Air Ambulance Commercial Helicopter and Part 91 Helicopter Operations; Final Rule).

13. Garry Meier, "Crashes Start Debate on Safety of Sky Ambulances," *The New York Times*, February 28, 2005.

14. Alan Levin, "Air Ambulance Pilots Push for Night Goggles," *USA Today*, July 17, 2008.

15. Pinkerton, "Border Patrol Air Crashes Raise Concern: Agency Defends its Practices after Recent Fatalities," *Houston Chronicle*, May 31, 2007.

16. "Fatal Crash Reminders of Dangers of Offshore Work," *Daily Comet*, January 11, 2009.

17. *Id.*

18. "Gulf of Mexico Risk Reduction Work Group Progress Report—2004," Helicopter Safety Advisory Conference (HSAC), January 13, 2005.

19. "Gulf of Mexico Risk Reduction Work Group Progress Report—2004," Helicopter Safety Advisory Conference (HSAC), January 13, 2005.

20. *Id.*

21. "Helicopters: Stopping the Blaze," Rotor, Winter 2007-08 at p. 64.

22. *Id.*

23. "Pilot Competencies for Helicopter Wildfire Operations: Best Practices Training and Evaluation," *Pilot Qualifications Working Group of Helicopter Association of Canada*, March 11, 2010.

Appendix A

Sample Pleadings in Helicopter Crash Cases

A.1 Sample Complaint 1: Helicopter Engine Design (Nozzle Guide Vane Failure)

IN THE CIRCUIT COURT OF JACKSON COUNTY,
MISSOURI AT KANSAS CITY

JODIE A. LETZ, ET AL,)	CASE NO.: CV93-19156
PLAINTIFFS,)	CIVIL DOCKET: M
v.)	DIVISION: 9
LA SOCIÉTÉ ANONYME TURBOMECA)	
FRANCÉ A/K/A TURBOMECA, S.A., or)	
SOCIÉTÉ TURBOMECA FRANCÉ,)	
)	
TURBOMECA ENGINE CORPORATION,)	
)	
LABINAL, S.A.,)	
A/K/A GROUPÉ LABINAL or)	
SOCIÉTÉ LABINAL)	
A French Corporation)	
5 Avenue Newton)	
BP 218)	
F-78051 Saint Quentin)	
Yvelines Cedex, France,)	

Serve:	)	
Designated French	)	
Central Authority,	)	
Pursuant to Hague Convention,	)	
	)	
ROCKY MOUNTAIN HELICOPTERS, INC.,	)	COUNSEL FOR PLAINTIFFS:
	)	
SPIRIT OF KANSAS CITY LIFE FLIGHT	)	Gary C. Robb
A JOINT VENTURE BETWEEN	)	Anita Porte Robb
ST. LUKE'S HOSPITAL	)	ROBB & ROBB LLC
OF KANSAS CITY and	)	One Kansas City Place
ST. JOSEPH HEALTH CENTER	)	Suite 3900
OF JACKSON COUNTY, MISSOURI	)	1200 Main Street
ST. LUKE'S HOSPITAL OF KANSAS CITY	)	Kansas City, Missouri 64105
A Missouri Corporation	)	Telephone: (816) 474-8080
4400 Wornall	)	Facsimile: (816) 474-8081
Kansas City, Missouri 64111,	)	
Serve:	)	
Registered Agent (for St. Luke's)	)	
BSMWL, INC.	)	
2300 Main	)	
Suite 1100	)	
Kansas City, Missouri 64108,	)	
	)	
ST. JOSEPH HEALTH CENTER OF	)	
JACKSON COUNTY, MISSOURI	)	
A Missouri Corporation	)	
1000 Cardonelet Drive	)	
Kansas City, Missouri 64114,	)	
Serve:	)	
Registered Agent (for St. Joseph)	)	
EUGENE P. MITCHELL	)	
1220 Washington Street	)	
3rd Floor	)	
Kansas City, Missouri 64105,	)	
	)	
_____DEFENDANTS.	)	

SECOND AMENDED PETITION FOR DAMAGES IN WRONGFUL DEATH
(PRODUCTS LIABILITY/AIRCRAFT)

COME NOW Plaintiffs, Jodie A. Letz, individually, and Eric David Letz and Christopher Scott Letz, minor children, by and through their duly-appointed Guardian Ad Litem and Next Friend, Jodie A. Letz, and Jodie A. Letz, as Representative and Administratrix of the Estate of Sherry Ann Letz, deceased, and for their causes of action against defendants Turbomeca, S.A., Turbomeca Engine Corporation, Labinal, S.A., Rocky Mountain Helicopters, Inc., and Spirit of Kansas City Life Flight, state and allege as follows:

INTRODUCTION PERTAINING TO ALL COUNTS

PLAINTIFFS

1.   Plaintiff Jodie A. Letz is an individual residing at 1307 Harrison, Des Moines, Iowa. Plaintiff Jodie A. Letz is the natural mother of the deceased, Sherry Ann Letz, and is the court-appointed Guardian Ad Litem and Next Friend of the minor children of the deceased, Eric David Letz and Christopher Scott Letz. Jodie A. Letz is the Representative and Administratrix of the Estate of Sherry Ann Letz, deceased, 1215 S. 12th, Bethany, Missouri 64424.

LA SOCIÉTÉ ANONYME TURBOMECA FRANCÉ A/K/A TURBOMECA, S.A., OR SOCIÉTÉ TURBOMECA FRANCÉ

2.   Defendant La Société Anonyme Turbomeca Francé A/K/A Turbomeca, S.A., or Société Turbomeca Francé (hereinafter' "defendant Turbomeca France") is a French Corporation doing business in these United States. Service may be had at its place of business at 64320 Bordes, Bizanos, France, under the terms of the 1969 Hague Convention for the service of process abroad of judicial and extrajudicial documents.

3.   Defendant Turbomeca France is engaged in the design, manufacture, testing, inspection, assembly, labeling, advertising, sale, promotion, exportation, and/or distribution of helicopters and jet engines for ultimate sale and/or use in the State of Missouri.

4.   At all times material hereto, defendant Turbomeca France has sold, delivered, and/or distributed such products for ultimate sale and/or use in the forty-eight (48) continental states of these United States of America, including the State of Missouri, to be used by a foreseeable class of persons, of whom Sherry Ann Letz was a member, consisting of those persons who may be passengers of air ambulance helicopters.

5.   At all times material hereto defendant Turbomeca France was acting by and through its agents, servants and/or employees, each of whom were acting within the course and scope of their employment with defendant.

DEFENDANT TURBOMECA ENGINE CORPORATION

6.   Defendant Turbomeca Engine Corporation (hereinafter "defendant Turbomeca U.S.") is a Texas Corporation doing business in the State of Missouri. Service may be had on its Registered Agent by serving U.S. Corporation Co., 807 Brazos, Suite 102, Austin, Texas 78701.

7.   Defendant Turbomeca is engaged in the design, manufacture, testing, inspection, assembly, repair, service, labeling, advertising, sale, promotion, and/or distribution of helicopter jet engines for ultimate sale and/or use in the State of Missouri.

8.   At all times material hereto, defendant Turbomeca has sold, delivered, and/or distributed such products for ultimate sale and/or use in the forty-eight (48) continental states of these United States of America, including the State of Missouri, to be used by a foreseeable class of persons, of whom Sherry Ann Letz was a member, consisting of those persons who may be passengers of aircraft using Turbomeca engines.

9.   At all times material hereto, defendant Turbomeca was acting by and through its agents, servants and/or employees, each of whom were acting within the course and scope of their employment with defendant.

DEFENDANT LABINAL, S.A., A/K/A GROUPÉ LABINAL OR SOCIÉTÉ LABINAL

10. Defendant Labinal, S.A., A/K/A Groupé Labinal or Société Labinal (hereinafter "defendant Labinal") is a French corporation doing business in these United States. Service may be had at its place of business at 5 Avenue Newton, BP 218, F-78051 Saint Quentin, Yvelines Cedex, France, under the terms of 1969 Hague Convention for the service of process abroad of judicial and extrajudicial documents.

11. Defendant Labinal is engaged in the design, manufacture, testing, inspection, assembly, labeling, advertising, sale, promotion, exportation, and/or distribution of small and medium gas turbine engines for the aviation industry particularly the Arriel 1B turbine engine which was installed in the A-Star 350-B helicopter which is the subject of this litigation. Defendant Labinal engaged in the development and distribution of turbine engines for the purpose and expectation of ultimate sale and/or use in the State of Missouri.

12. At all times material hereto, defendant Labinal has sold, delivered, or distributed such turbine engines for use in helicopters for ultimate or expected sale or use in the forty-eight (48) continental states of these United States of America,

including the state of Missouri, to be used by a foreseeable class of persons, of whom Sherry Ann Letz was a member, consisting of those persons who may be passengers of air ambulance helicopters.

13. Defendant Labinal engaged in a careful and continuous practice of supervision, monitoring, control and direction over its wholly-owned subsidiary, Turbomeca, S.A. and, at all times material hereto, had a continuing non-delegable duty of supervision and control over the activities of Turbomeca, S.A. Defendant Labinal maintained an almost total interlocking Board of Directors as with Turbomeca, S.A., so as to negate any true separate corporate identity or interest and to create direct responsibility for the actions of Turbomeca, S.A.

14. At all times material hereto defendant Labinal was acting by and through its agents, servants or employees, each of whom were acting within the course and scope of their employment with defendant Labinal.

DEFENDANT ROCKY MOUNTAIN HELICOPTERS, INC.

15. Defendant Rocky Mountain Helicopters, Inc. (hereinafter "defendant Rocky Mountain Helicopters") is a Utah corporation doing business in the State of Missouri. Service may be had on its Registered Agent, Thomas Spriggs, Route 3, Box 362D, Eldon, Missouri 65026.

16. Defendant Rocky Mountain Helicopters is engaged in the business of leasing, operating, maintaining, servicing, and distributing air ambulances for uses including, but not limited to, air evacuation and air rescue operations such as that provided for by Life Flight.

17. At all times material hereto, defendant Rocky Mountain Helicopters leased, operated, maintained, and distributed air ambulance helicopters and particularly, the air ambulance helicopter which is the subject of this lawsuit throughout these United States, including the state of Missouri, to be used by a foreseeable class of person, of whom Sherry Ann Letz was a member, consisting of those persons who may be passengers on air ambulances.

18. At all times material hereto, defendant Rocky Mountain Helicopters was acting by and through its agents, servants, and/or employees, each of whom were acting in the course and scope of their employment with this defendant.

DEFENDANT SPIRIT OF KANSAS CITY LIFE FLIGHT, A JOINT VENTURE BETWEEN ST. LUKE'S HOSPITAL AND ST. JOSEPH HEALTH CENTER

19. Defendant Spirit of Kansas City Life Flight (hereinafter "defendant Life Flight") is a joint venture between St. Luke's Hospital of Kansas City and St. Joseph Health Center of Jackson County, Missouri which is doing business in the State of Missouri. Service may be had on the Registered Agent for St. Luke's Hospital of Kansas City, BSMWL, Inc., 2300 Main, Suite 1100, Kansas City, Missouri 64108 and the Registered Agent for St. Joseph Health Center of Jackson County, Missouri, Eugene P. Mitchell, 1220 Washington Street, 3rd Floor, Kansas City, Missouri 64105.

20. Defendant Life Flight is engaged in the operation of an air rescue ambulance service within approximately a 100-mile radius of Kansas City and serving St. Luke's Hospital and St. Joseph Health Center. Life Flight responds to calls from regional and community health centers and transports patients in need of care to the aforesaid medical institutions.

21. At all times material hereto, defendant Life Flight administered, operated, maintained, and serviced air ambulance helicopters and administered its air transport service within the State of Missouri, to be used and operated by a foreseeable class of persons, of whom Sherry Ann Letz was a member, consisting of those persons who may be passengers of air ambulance aircraft.

22. At all times material hereto, defendant Life Flight was acting by and through its agents, servants, and/or employees each of whom were acting within the course and scope of their employment with defendant.

IDENTIFICATION OF AIRCRAFT AND DEFECTIVE COMPONENTS

23. This aircrash involves a 1982 Model A-Star 350-B air ambulance helicopter. The air ambulance helicopter which is the subject of this lawsuit was designed, manufactured, assembled, distributed, and sold for use as an air ambulance, and known to be used as an air ambulance.

24. A component part of the air ambulance was a jet engine unit designed, manufactured, distributed and sold by defendants Turbomeca and Labinal, particularly, an Arriel 1B helicopter jet engine. Defendants Turbomeca and Labinal knew that said engine unit was being incorporated into and assembled as part of the air ambulance helicopter and knew of the uses for which said engine was intended.

JURISDICTION

25. Defendants Turbomeca France, Turbomeca U.S., Labinal and Rocky Mountain Helicopters sell and distribute their products and services throughout the United States, including, but not limited to various wholesalers and leasing agents knowing that these air ambulances will be sold, used, leased, operated and flown in states of the United States, including the State of Missouri.

26. Defendants had a reasonable expectation that they would be hailed into any Court within these United States, including a Court in the State of Missouri, by reason of their injecting their products and services into a stream of commerce.

27. It does not offend "traditional notions of fair play and substantial justice" to require defendants to defend themselves in this forum. The contacts, ties and relations of defendants, and each of them, are sufficient to the exercise of personal jurisdiction within the Courts of the State of Missouri. Defendants engaged in a persistent course of conduct such that subjecting them to jurisdiction within the Circuit Court of Jackson County, Missouri is lawful, appropriate, and fair.

VENUE

28. Venue in the Circuit Court of Jackson County, Missouri is proper pursuant to V.A.M.S. Sec. 508.010 in that defendants St. Luke's Hospital and St. Joseph's Health Center are resident corporations of Jackson County, Missouri and for the reason that all defendants are "doing business" in this county. Defendants, and each of them, initiated a flow of commerce into the State of Missouri by their knowing and intended distribution of air ambulance helicopters, air ambulance engines, and related products, components, and services to entities located within this county.

29. Defendants Rocky Mountain Helicopters and Life Flight maintain offices within Jackson County, Missouri for the conduct of their usual and ordinary business. In that these offices are maintained within the boundaries of Jackson County, Missouri, venue as to all defendants for this cause of action is proper in the Circuit Court of Jackson County, Missouri.

DATES OF ACTS AND CONDUCT COMPLAINED OF

30. On or about May 27, 1993, Sherry Ann Letz, the deceased, then twenty (20) years of age, was a passenger in a motor vehicle being driven in Harrison County, Missouri. As a result of a motor vehicle accident, the deceased, Sherry Ann Letz, suffered personal injuries, and was in need of medical care and treatment.

31. Sherry Ann Letz was transferred by ground ambulance to Harrison County Community Hospital where she was diagnosed with a broken left arm and chest contusions, but no other fractures. She was responding well and becoming alert. The injuries sustained in the motor vehicle accident were not life-threatening nor would they have resulted in any permanent disability, impairment, or disfigurement. Her condition was stabilized and improving.

32. At 6:10 a.m. on May 27, 1993, Sherry Ann Letz was air evacuated from Harrison County Community Hospital with an intended destination of St. Luke's Hospital in Kansas City, Missouri. According to the Emergency Room records at Harrison County Community Hospital, "patient was stable at the time she left the hospital by Life Flight. Blood pressure, pulse and everything was good." (Emergency Room records, Harrison County Community Hospital).

33. The air ambulance helicopter which picked-up Sherry Ann Letz from the Harrison County Community Hospital was a 1982 Model A-Star 350-B air ambulance helicopter which was equipped and powered by an Arriel 1B turbine jet engine manufactured and sold by the Turbomeca defendants.

34. At 6:26 a.m. the Life Flight Helicopter crashed near Cameron, Missouri in DeKalb County, approximately forty (40) miles northwest of Kansas City, Missouri. Sherry Ann Letz was pronounced dead at the scene.

35. Plaintiff's deceased, Sherry Ann Letz, was killed as a direct result of the foregoing crash of the 1982 Model A-Star 350-B air ambulance helicopter.

PLAINTIFF'S INJURIES AND DAMAGES

36. As a direct and proximate result of the defendants' design, manufacture, sale, shipment, distribution, maintenance, operation, ownership, leasing, and transfer of the subject air ambulance helicopter engine in a dangerous and defective condition, improperly maintained, inspected, and serviced and improperly certified, Sherry Ann Letz, daughter of Plaintiff Jodie

A. Letz, and mother of minor children, Eric David Letz and Christopher Scott Letz, was killed. By virtue of her untimely death, Plaintiffs are lawfully entitled to such damages as are fair and just for the death and loss thus occasioned, including but not limited to the pecuniary losses suffered by reason of the death, funeral expenses, and the reasonable value of the services, consortium, companionship, comfort, instruction, guidance, counsel, training, and support of which Plaintiffs have been deprived by reason of such death, further including the past and future lost income, household services, and other value of benefits which would have been provided by the deceased.

37. Plaintiffs further claim such damages as the deceased may have suffered between the time of injury and the time of death and for the recovery of which the deceased might have maintained an action had death not ensued including, but not limited to, mental anguish, physical disability, conscious pain and suffering, pre-impact terror, and further considering the aggravating circumstances attendant upon the fatal injury. Such aggravating circumstances include, but are not limited to, the wanton, willful, callous, reckless, and depraved conduct of defendants which entitle Plaintiffs to punitive damages to punish the defendants and to deter future wrongdoing in that the acts and omissions of defendants have manifested such reckless and complete indifference to and conscious disregard for the safety of others that the decedent would have been entitled to punitive damages had she lived.

COUNT I

(STRICT LIABILITY—DEFECTIVE DESIGN AND MANUFACTURE BY DEFENDANT TURBOMECA FRANCE)

COME NOW Plaintiffs, as heretofore set out, and for Count I of their causes of action against these defendants allege and state as follows:

38. Plaintiffs hereby incorporate by reference, as though fully set out herein, paragraphs 1 through 37, inclusive of this Second Amended Petition for Damages.

39. Defendant Turbomeca France designed, manufactured, assembled, supplied, distributed, or sold the aforementioned helicopter jet engine and/or related component parts used therein in the course of its business referred to as an Arriel 1B helicopter jet engine.

40. The aforesaid helicopter jet engine and/or related component parts used therein were then in a defective condition, unreasonably dangerous when put to their reasonably anticipated uses for reasons including, but not limited to, the following:

(A) The labyrinth seal was designed with insufficient strength and utilized materials incapable of withstanding heat, pressure, and other dynamic forces reasonably anticipated in the combustion chamber of a helicopter jet engine;

(B) The guide vanes in the combustion chamber of the jet engine utilized insufficient materials and were designed in such a way that properly maintained airflow could not reach a stalled engine;

(C) Improper material was utilized around the labyrinth seal permitting the seal to break and fly apart;

(D) The guide vane of the second stage gas producer corroded causing a partial loss of power in the engine;

(E) Metal portions of the guide vane broke off destroying the moving turbine blades;

(F) The guide vanes were mismatched and mis-assembled component parts within the jet engine assembly structure;

(G) The guide vanes within the engine utilized an improper light duty metal;

(H) The engine was designed with no backup support mechanism in the event of corroded and/or defective guide vanes;

(I) The engine assembly used defective and unreasonably dangerous guide vanes which were prone to fracture and burst;

(J) The helicopter jet engine used a defective and unreasonably dangerous seal design; and

(K) For some unknown reason and common experience is such that the death resulting from the deceased's transport within the subject air ambulance helicopter would not have occurred absence the existence of defect.

41. The aforesaid air ambulance jet engine and the air ambulance itself were used in a manner reasonably anticipated by this defendant and others.

42. Plaintiffs as heretofore set forth suffered damages as a direct and proximate result of said defective condition as existed when the air ambulance jet engine was sold by this defendant resulting in the death of Sherry Ann Letz.

WHEREFORE, Plaintiffs Jodie A. Letz, individually, as Guardian Ad Litem and Next Friend for the minor children Eric David Letz and Christopher Scott Letz, and as Representative and Administratrix of the Estate of Sherry Ann Letz, deceased, pray judgment against defendant Turbomeca, S.A. for damages as follows:

(A) For all lawful damages such as are fair and reasonable for the wrongful death of Sherry Ann Letz considering the aggravating circumstances attendant upon the fatal injury;

(B) For pre-judgment interest at the rate of nine percent (9%) per annum pursuant to Plaintiffs' compliance with V.A.M.S. 408.040(2);

(C) For Plaintiffs' costs herein expended; and

(D) For such other and further relief as this Court deems just and proper.

COUNT II

(STRICT LIABILITY—DEFECTIVE DESIGN AND MANUFACTURE BY DEFENDANT TURBOMECA U.S.)

COME NOW Plaintiffs, as heretofore set out, and for Count II of their causes of action against these defendants allege and state as follows:

43. Plaintiffs hereby incorporate by reference, as though fully set out herein, paragraphs 1 through 42, inclusive of this Second Amended Petition for Damages.

44. Defendant Turbomeca U.S. designed, manufactured, assembled, supplied, distributed, or sold the aforementioned helicopter jet engine and/or related component parts used therein in the course of its business referred to as an Arriel 1B helicopter jet engine.

45. The aforesaid helicopter jet engine and/or related component parts used therein were then in a defective condition, unreasonably dangerous when put to their reasonably anticipated uses for reasons including, but not limited to, the following:

(A) The labyrinth seal was designed with insufficient strength and utilized materials incapable of withstanding heat, pressure, and other dynamic forces reasonably anticipated in the combustion chamber of a helicopter jet engine;

(B) The guide vanes in the combustion chamber of the jet engine utilized insufficient materials and were designed in such a way that properly maintained airflow could not reach a stalled engine;

(C) Improper material was utilized around the labyrinth seal permitting the seal to break and fly apart;

(D) The guide vane of the second stage gas producer corroded causing a partial loss of power in the engine;

(E) Metal portions of the guide vane broke off destroying the moving turbine blades;

(F) The guide vanes were mismatched and mis-assembled component parts within the jet engine assembly structure;

(G) The guide vanes within the engine utilized an improper light duty metal;

(H) The engine was designed with no backup support mechanism in the event of corroded and/or defective guide vanes;

(I) The engine assembly used defective and unreasonably dangerous guide vanes which were prone to fracture and burst;

(J) The helicopter jet engine used a defective and unreasonably dangerous seal design; and

(K) For some unknown reason and common experience is such that the death resulting from the deceased's transport within the subject air ambulance helicopter would not have occurred absence the existence of defect.

46. The aforesaid air ambulance jet engine and the air ambulance itself were used in a manner reasonably anticipated by this defendant and others.

47. Plaintiffs as heretofore set forth suffered damages as a direct and proximate result of said defective condition as existed when the air ambulance jet engine was sold by this defendant resulting in the death of Sherry Ann Letz.

WHEREFORE, Plaintiffs Jodie A. Letz, individually, as Guardian Ad Litem and Next Friend for the minor children Eric David Letz and Christopher Scott Letz, and as Representative and Administratrix of the Estate of Sherry Ann Letz, deceased, pray judgment against defendant Turbomeca Engine Corporation for damages as follows:

(A) For all lawful damages such as are fair and reasonable for the wrongful death of Sherry Ann Letz considering the aggravating circumstances attendant upon the fatal injury;

(B) For pre-judgment interest at the rate of nine percent (9%) per annum pursuant to Plaintiffs' compliance with V.A.M.S. 408.040(2);

(C) For Plaintiffs' costs herein expended; and

(D) For such other and further relief as this Court deems just and proper.

COUNT III

(STRICT LIABILITY—DEFECTIVE DESIGN AND MANUFACTURE BY DEFENDANT LABINAL)

COME NOW Plaintiffs, as heretofore set out, and for Count III of their causes of action against these defendants allege and state as follows:

48. Plaintiffs hereby incorporate by reference, as though fully set out herein, paragraphs 1 through 47, inclusive of this Second Amended Petition for Damages.

49. Defendant Labinal designed, manufactured, assembled, supplied, distributed, or sold the aforementioned helicopter jet engine and/or related component parts used therein in the course of its business referred to as an Arriel 1B helicopter jet engine.

50. The aforesaid helicopter jet engine and/or related component parts used therein were then in a defective condition, unreasonably dangerous when put to their reasonably anticipated uses for reasons including, but not limited to, the following:

(A) The labyrinth seal was designed with insufficient strength and utilized materials incapable of withstanding heat, pressure, and other dynamic forces reasonably anticipated in the combustion chamber of a helicopter jet engine;

(B) The guide vanes in the combustion chamber of the jet engine utilized insufficient materials and were designed in such a way that properly maintained airflow could not reach a stalled engine;

(C) Improper material was utilized around the labyrinth seal permitting the seal to break and fly apart;

(D) The guide vane of the second stage gas producer corroded causing a partial loss of power in the engine;

(E) Metal portions of the guide vane broke off destroying the moving turbine blades;

(F) The guide vanes were mismatched and mis-assembled component parts within the jet engine assembly structure;

(G) The guide vanes within the engine utilized an improper light duty metal;

(H) The engine was designed with no backup support mechanism in the event of corroded and/or defective guide vanes;

(I) The engine assembly used defective and unreasonably dangerous guide vanes which were prone to fracture and burst;

(J) The helicopter jet engine used a defective and unreasonably dangerous seal design; and

(K) For some unknown reason and common experience is such that the death resulting from the deceased's transport within the subject air ambulance helicopter would not have occurred absence the existence of defect.

51. The aforesaid air ambulance jet engine and the air ambulance itself were used in a manner reasonably anticipated by this defendant and others.

52. Plaintiffs as heretofore set forth suffered damages as a direct and proximate result of said defective condition as existed when the air ambulance jet engine was sold by this defendant resulting in the death of Sherry Ann Letz.

WHEREFORE, Plaintiffs Jodie A. Letz, individually, as Guardian Ad Litem and Next Friend for the minor children Eric David Letz and Christopher Scott Letz, and as Representative and Administratrix of the Estate of Sherry Ann Letz, deceased, pray judgment against defendant Labinal for damages as follows:

(A) For all lawful damages such as are fair and reasonable for the wrongful death of Sherry Ann Letz considering the aggravating circumstances attendant upon the fatal injury;

(B) For pre-judgment interest at the rate of nine percent (9%) per annum pursuant to Plaintiffs' compliance with V.A.M.S. 408.040(2);

(C) For Plaintiffs' costs herein expended; and

(D) For such other and further relief as this Court deems just and proper.

COUNT IV

(STRICT LIABILITY—SALE, SUPPLY, AND DISTRIBUTION OF DEFECTIVE AIRCRAFT ENGINE BY DEFENDANTS ROCKY MOUNTAIN HELICOPTERS AND LIFE FLIGHT)

COME NOW Plaintiffs, as heretofore set out, and for Count IV of their causes of action against these defendants allege and state as follows:

53. Plaintiffs hereby incorporate by reference, as though fully set out herein, paragraphs 1 through 52, inclusive of this Second Amended Petition for Damages.

54. Defendants Rocky Mountain Helicopters and Life Flight designed, manufactured, assembled, supplied, imported, distributed, operated, or sold the aforementioned air ambulance with the subject Arriel 1B turbine jet engine in the course of their business.

55. The subject air ambulance with the subject Arriel 1B turbine jet engine was then in a defective condition unreasonably dangerous when put to a reasonably anticipated use.

56. Defendants Rocky Mountain Helicopters and Life Flight did incorporate a jet engine designed, manufactured, supplied, tested, and sold by Turbomeca Engine Corporation and Turbomeca, S.A., as further set out in heretofore and expressly incorporated herein by reference.

57. Defendants Rocky Mountain Helicopters and Life Flight did place the Arriel 1B jet turbine engine into the stream of commerce by their service, maintenance, and operation of an air ambulance taxi service.

58. The aforesaid air ambulance was used in a manner reasonably anticipated by this defendant and others.

59. Plaintiffs as heretofore set forth were damaged as a direct result of the subject air ambulance being sold in a defective condition unreasonably dangerous which resulted in the death of Sherry Ann Letz.

WHEREFORE, Plaintiffs Jodie A. Letz, individually, as Guardian Ad Litem and Next Friend for the minor children Eric David Letz and Christopher Scott Letz, and as Representative and Administratrix of the Estate of Sherry Ann Letz, deceased, pray judgment against defendants Rocky Mountain Helicopters and Life Flight for damages as follows:

(A) For all lawful damages such as are fair and reasonable for the wrongful death of Sherry Ann Letz considering the aggravating circumstances attendant upon the fatal injury;

(B) For pre-judgment interest at the rate of nine percent (9%) per annum pursuant to Plaintiffs' compliance with V.A.M.S. 408.040(2);

(C) For Plaintiffs' costs herein expended; and

(D) For such other and further relief as this Court deems just and proper.

COUNT V

(STRICT LIABILITY—FAILURE TO WARN BY DEFENDANTS TURBOMECA FRANCE, TURBOMECA U.S., LABINAL, ROCKY MOUNTAIN HELICOPTERS AND LIFE FLIGHT)

COMES NOW Plaintiffs, as heretofore set out, and for Count V of their causes of action against these defendants allege and state as follows:

60. Plaintiffs hereby incorporate by reference, as though fully set out herein, paragraphs 1 through 59, inclusive of this Second Amended Petition for Damages.

61. Defendants Turbomeca France, Turbomeca U.S., Labinal, Rocky Mountain Helicopters, and Life Flight designed, manufactured, assembled, supplied, distributed, operated, or sold the aforementioned helicopter jet engine and/or related component parts used therein in the course of their business referred to specifically as an Arriel 1B helicopter jet turbine engine.

62. The Arriel 1B turbine engine used in the AS 350 B helicopter which crashed on May 27, 1993 was then unreasonably dangerous when put to a reasonably anticipated use without knowledge of its characteristics.

63. Defendants, and each of them, failed to provide an adequate warning as to the danger of use of said helicopter which was then and there equipped with an unreasonably dangerous turbine engine.

64. Both the Arriel 1B turbine engine and the helicopter within which it was installed were used in a manner reasonably anticipated.

65. Defendants had both an original and continuing duty to monitor the airworthiness of helicopter engines used both in the course of their business and by other operators using the same type of engine and to make such repair and maintenance modifications and recommendations and warnings as necessary to assure the reasonable safety of persons utilizing helicopters with Arriel 1B turbine engines.

66. Defendants breached their continuing duty in that:

(A) The Arriel 1B engine had a confirmed malfunction problem and defect with the TU 76 second stage nozzle guide vane assembly and hub in the area of the labyrinth seal;

(B) Defendants knew that replacement of the TU 76 modified nozzle guide vane assembly and labyrinth seal with either the TU 197 or TU 202 modification eliminated the safety hazard; and

(C) Defendants failed to take the appropriate steps to repair, replace, circumstances and warn or inform operators of the full circumstances and field experience regarding the TU 76 assembly and the safety-modified replacements.

67. Defendants, and each of them, failed to properly and timely report known and suspected aircraft component defects and thereby breached their duty to repair, replace, recall, inform and warn operators, users, passengers, and others of the known malfunctions and defects associated with the Arriel 1B engine with the TU 76 modification.

68. Plaintiffs' deceased, Sherry Ann Letz, was killed as a direct result of the sale, use, operation, and service of the Arriel 1B engine with the TU 76 modification without an adequate warning as to its replacement, repair, servicing, hazards, and conditions.

WHEREFORE, Plaintiffs Jodie A. Letz, individually, as Guardian Ad Litem and Next Friend for the minor children Eric David Letz and Christopher Scott Letz, and as Representative and Administratrix of the Estate of Sherry Ann Letz, deceased, pray judgment against defendants Turbomeca France, Turbomeca U.S., Labinal, Rocky Mountain Helicopters, and Life Flight for damages as follows:

(A) For all lawful damages such as are fair and reasonable for the wrongful death of Sherry Ann Letz considering the aggravating circumstances attendant upon the fatal injury;

(B) For pre-judgment interest at the rate of nine percent (9%) per annum pursuant to Plaintiffs' compliance with V.A.M.S. 408.040(2);

(C) For Plaintiffs' costs herein expended; and

(D) For such other and further relief as this Court deems just and proper.

COUNT VI

(NEGLIGENCE—FAILURE OF DEFENDANT TURBOMECA FRANCE TO USE ORDINARY CARE TO DESIGN AND MANUFACTURE TURBINE ENGINE)

COME NOW Plaintiffs, as heretofore set out, and for Count VI of their causes of action against these defendants allege and state as follows:

69. Plaintiffs hereby incorporate by reference, as though fully set out herein, paragraphs 1 through 68, inclusive of this Second Amended Petition for Damages.

70. Defendant Turbomeca France designed, manufactured, assembled, supplied, distributed, exported or sold the aforementioned helicopter jet engine and/or related component parts used therein in the course of its business referred to as an Arriel 1B helicopter jet engine.

71. Defendant Turbomeca France held itself out as an entity which could carefully and competently design, manufacture, select materials for, design maintenance programs for, inspect, supply, distribute, and sell helicopter jet engines for use in air ambulances.

72. Defendant Turbomeca France had a duty to use that degree of care that an ordinarily careful and prudent designer, manufacturer, and seller of helicopter jet engines and component parts would use under the same or similar circumstances.

73. The jet engine assembly unit and related component parts designed, manufactured, and sold by defendant Turbomeca France were defective and otherwise flawed which had the effect, of creating a blockage of air flow to the jet engine under normal usage.

74. Defendant Turbomeca France knew or by or by using ordinary care should have known of the potential of such dangerous condition as was created by its failure to properly design, test, manufacture, sell, monitor field performance, accumulate field data, recall, and distribute safe helicopter jet engines.

75. Defendant Turbomeca France violated known and applicable industry standards in that it failed to conduct itself as a reasonable and prudent helicopter manufacturer under the same or similar circumstances.

76. Defendant Turbomeca France was negligent in the following respects:

(A) The labyrinth seal was designed with insufficient strength and utilized materials incapable of withstanding heat, pressure, and other dynamic forces reasonably anticipated in the combustion chamber of a helicopter jet engine;

(B) The guide vanes in the combustion chamber of the jet engine utilized insufficient materials and were designed in such a way that properly maintained airflow could not reach a stalled engine;

(C) Improper material was utilized around the labyrinth seal permitting the seal to break and fly apart;

(D) The guide vane of the second stage gas producer corroded causing a partial loss of power in the engine;

(E) Metal portions of the guide vane broke off destroying the moving turbine blades;

(F) The guide vanes were mismatched and mis-assembled component parts within the jet engine assembly structure;

(G) The guide vanes within the engine utilized an improper light duty metal;

(H) The TU 76 second stage nozzle guide vane assembly and related components were not properly tested, developed, analyzed or evaluated prior to sale, distribution, or installation as a component within the Arriel 1B engine;

(I) The engine was designed with no backup support mechanism in the event of corroded and/or defective guide vanes;

(J) The engine assembly used defective and unreasonably dangerous guide vanes which were prone to fracture and burst;

(K) The helicopter jet engine used a defective and unreasonably dangerous seal design; and

(L) For some unknown reason and common experience is such that the death resulting from the deceased's transport within the subject air ambulance helicopter would not have occurred absence the existence of defect.

77. Plaintiffs' deceased was killed as a direct and proximate result of the negligence and carelessness of defendant Turbomeca France as further set out above.

WHEREFORE, Plaintiffs Jodie A. Letz, individually, as Guardian Ad Litem and Next Friend for the minor children Eric David Letz and Christopher Scott Letz, and as Representative and Administratrix of the Estate of Sherry Ann Letz, deceased, pray judgment against defendant Turbomeca France for damages as follows:

(A) For all lawful damages such as are fair and reasonable for the wrongful death of Sherry Ann Letz considering the aggravating circumstances attendant upon the fatal injury;

(B) For pre-judgment interest at the rate of nine percent (9%) per annum pursuant to Plaintiffs' compliance with V.A.M.S. 408.040(2);

(C) For Plaintiffs' costs herein expended; and

(D) For such other and further relief as this Court deems just and proper.

COUNT VII

(NEGLIGENCE—FAILURE OF DEFENDANT TURBOMECA U.S. TO USE ORDINARY CARE TO DESIGN AND MANUFACTURE TURBINE ENGINE)

COMES NOW Plaintiffs, as heretofore set out, and for Count VII of their causes of action against these defendants allege and state as follows:

78. Plaintiffs hereby incorporate by reference, as though fully set out herein, paragraphs 1 through 77, inclusive of this Second Amended Petition for Damages.

79. Defendant Turbomeca U.S. designed, manufactured, assembled, supplied, distributed, or sold the aforementioned helicopter jet engine and/or related component parts used therein in the course of its business referred to as an Arriel 1B helicopter jet engine.

80. Defendant Turbomeca U.S. held itself out as an entity which could carefully and competently design, manufacture, select materials for, design maintenance programs for, inspect, supply, distribute, and sell helicopter jet engines for use in air ambulances.

81. Defendant Turbomeca U.S. had a duty to use that degree of care that an ordinarily careful and prudent designer, manufacturer, importer, distributor, and seller of helicopter jet engines and component parts would use under the same or similar circumstances.

82. The jet engine assembly unit and related component parts designed, manufactured, and sold by defendant Turbomeca U.S. were defective and otherwise flawed which had the effect, of creating a blockage of air flow to the jet engine under normal usage.

83. Defendant Turbomeca U.S. knew or by or by using ordinary care should have known of the potential of such dangerous condition as was created by its failure to properly design, test, manufacture, sell, monitor field performance, accumulate field data, recall, and distribute safe helicopter jet engines.

84. Defendant Turbomeca U.S. violated known and applicable industry standards in that it failed to conduct itself as a reasonable and prudent helicopter manufacturer under the same or similar circumstances.

85. Defendant Turbomeca U.S. was negligent in the following respects:

(A) The labyrinth seal was designed with insufficient strength and utilized materials incapable of withstanding heat, pressure, and other dynamic forces reasonably anticipated in the combustion chamber of a helicopter jet engine;

(B) The guide vanes in the combustion chamber of the jet engine utilized insufficient materials and were designed in such a way that properly maintained airflow could not reach a stalled engine;

(C) Improper material was utilized around the labyrinth seal permitting the seal to break and fly apart;

(D) The guide vane of the second stage gas producer corroded causing a partial loss of power in the engine;

(E) Metal portions of the guide vane broke off destroying the moving turbine blades;

(F) The guide vanes were mismatched and mis-assembled component parts within the jet engine assembly structure;

(G) The guide vanes within the engine utilized an improper light duty metal;

(H) The TU 76 second stage nozzle guide vane assembly and related components were not properly tested, developed, analyzed or evaluated prior to sale, distribution, or installation as a component within the Arriel 1B engine;

(I) The engine was designed with no backup support mechanism in the event of corroded and/or defective guide vanes;

(J) The engine assembly used defective and unreasonably dangerous guide vanes which were prone to fracture and burst;

(K) The helicopter jet engine used a defective and unreasonably dangerous seal design; and

(L) For some unknown reason and common experience is such that the death resulting from the deceased's transport within the subject air ambulance helicopter would not have occurred absence the existence of defect.

86. Plaintiffs' deceased was killed as a direct and proximate result of the negligence and carelessness of defendant Turbomeca U.S. as further set out above.

WHEREFORE, Plaintiffs Jodie A. Letz, individually, as Guardian Ad Litem and Next Friend for the minor children Eric David Letz and Christopher Scott Letz, and as Representative and Administratrix of the Estate of Sherry Ann Letz, deceased, pray judgment against defendant Turbomeca U.S. for damages as follows:

(A) For all lawful damages such as are fair and reasonable for the wrongful death of Sherry Ann Letz considering the aggravating circumstances attendant upon the fatal injury;

(B) For pre-judgment interest at the rate of nine percent (9%) per annum pursuant to Plaintiffs' compliance with V.A.M.S. 408.040(2);

(C) For Plaintiffs' costs herein expended; and

(D) For such other and further relief as this Court deems just and proper.

COUNT VIII

(NEGLIGENCE—FAILURE OF DEFENDANT LABINAL TO USE ORDINARY CARE TO DESIGN AND MANUFACTURE TURBINE ENGINE)

COME NOW Plaintiffs, as heretofore set out, and for Count VIII of their causes of action against these defendants allege and state as follows:

87. Plaintiffs hereby incorporate by reference, as though fully set out herein, paragraphs 1 through 86, inclusive of this Second Amended Petition for Damages.

88. Defendant Labinal designed, manufactured, assembled, supplied, distributed, exported or sold the aforementioned helicopter jet engine and/or related component parts used therein in the course of its business referred to as an Arriel 1B helicopter jet engine.

89. Defendant Labinal held itself out as an entity which could carefully and competently design, manufacture, select materials for, design maintenance programs for, inspect, supply, distribute, and sell helicopter jet engines for use in air ambulances.

90. Defendant Labinal had a duty to use that degree of care that an ordinarily careful and prudent designer, manufacturer, and seller of helicopter jet engines and component parts would use under the same or similar circumstances.

91. The jet engine assembly unit and related component parts designed, manufactured, and sold by defendant Labinal were defective and otherwise flawed which had the effect, of creating a blockage of air flow to the jet engine under normal usage.

92. Defendant Labinal knew or by or by using ordinary care should have known of the potential of such dangerous condition as was created by its failure to properly design, test, manufacture, sell, monitor field performance, accumulate field data, recall, and distribute safe helicopter jet engines.

93. Defendant Labinal violated known and applicable industry standards in that it failed to conduct itself as a reasonable and prudent helicopter manufacturer under the same or similar circumstances.

94. Defendant Labinal was negligent in the following respects:

(A) The labyrinth seal was designed with insufficient strength and utilized materials incapable of withstanding heat, pressure, and other dynamic forces reasonably anticipated in the combustion chamber of a helicopter jet engine;

(B) The guide vanes in the combustion chamber of the jet engine utilized insufficient materials and were designed in such a way that properly maintained airflow could not reach a stalled engine;

(C) Improper material was utilized around the labyrinth seal permitting the seal to break and fly apart;

(D) The guide vane of the second stage gas producer corroded causing a partial loss of power in the engine;

(E) Metal portions of the guide vane broke off destroying the moving turbine blades;

(F) The guide vanes were mismatched and mis-assembled component parts within the jet engine assembly structure;

(G) The guide vanes within the engine utilized an improper light duty metal;

(H) The TU 76 second stage nozzle guide vane assembly and related components were not properly tested, developed, analyzed or evaluated prior to sale, distribution, or installation as a component within the Arriel 1B engine;

(I) The engine was designed with no backup support mechanism in the event of corroded and/or defective guide vanes;

(J) The engine assembly used defective and unreasonably dangerous guide vanes which were prone to fracture and burst;

(K) The helicopter jet engine used a defective and unreasonably dangerous seal design; and

(L) For some unknown reason and common experience is such that the death resulting from the deceased's transport within the subject air ambulance helicopter would not have occurred absence the existence of defect.

95. Plaintiffs' deceased was killed as a direct and proximate result of the negligence and carelessness of defendant Labinal as further set out above.

WHEREFORE, Plaintiffs Jodie A. Letz, individually, as Guardian Ad Litem and Next Friend for the minor children Eric David Letz and Christopher Scott Letz, and as Representative and Administratrix of the Estate of Sherry Ann Letz, deceased, pray judgment against defendant Labinal for damages as follows:

(A) For all lawful damages such as are fair and reasonable for the wrongful death of Sherry Ann Letz considering the aggravating circumstances attendant upon the fatal injury;

(B) For pre-judgment interest at the rate of nine percent (9%) per annum pursuant to Plaintiffs' compliance with V.A.M.S. 408.040(2);

(C) For Plaintiffs' costs herein expended; and

(D) For such other and further relief as this Court deems just and proper.

COUNT IX

(NEGLIGENCE—FAILURE OF DEFENDANTS TURBOMECA FRANCE, TURBOMECA U.S., LABINAL, ROCKY MOUNTAIN HELICOPTERS, AND LIFE FLIGHT TO WARN OF KNOWN HAZARD)

COME NOW Plaintiffs, as heretofore set out, and for Count IX of their causes of action against these defendants allege and state as follows:

96. Plaintiffs hereby incorporate by reference, as though fully set out herein, paragraphs 1 through 95, inclusive of this Second Amended Petition for Damages.

97. Defendants Turbomeca France, Turbomeca U.S. Labinal, Rocky Mountain Helicopters, and Life Flight and each of them, designed, manufactured, sold, used, and operated the Arriel lB engine utilized in the subject helicopter which crashed on May 27, 1993 resulting in the death of Plaintiffs' deceased Sherry Ann Letz.

98. The Arriel lB engine was in a defective condition and unreasonably dangerous because the second stage nozzle guide vane assembly utilized material of insufficient strength to withstand the forces and heat generated within in addition to all those reasons set forth heretofore incorporated herein by reference.

99. Defendants, and each of them, failed to use ordinary care to adequately warn of the risk of harm from use of the Arriel lB turbine engine in that said engine contained a hazard of such magnitude as to create massive and instantaneous in flight engine failure. Defendants, and each of them, failed to report, warn, instruct, recall, replace, repair, inspect, test, investigate and monitor the safety of the Arriel lB engine with the TU 76 modification where they had an initial and continuing duty and obligation to do so.

100. As a direct result of the failure of the defendants to adequately warn of the risk of harm from the heretofore enumerated defects or hazards, Plaintiffs' deceased, Sherry Ann Letz, was killed.

WHEREFORE, Plaintiffs Jodie A. Letz, individually, as Guardian Ad Litem and Next Friend for the minor children Eric David Letz and Christopher Scott Letz, and as Representative and Administratrix of the Estate of Sherry Ann Letz, deceased, pray judgment against defendants for damages as follows:

(A) For all lawful damages such as are fair and reasonable for the wrongful death of Sherry Ann Letz considering the aggravating circumstances attendant upon the fatal injury;

(B) For pre-judgment interest at the rate of nine percent (9%) per annum pursuant to Plaintiffs' compliance with V.A.M.S. 408.040(2);

(C) For Plaintiffs' costs herein expended; and

(D) For such other and further relief as this Court deems just and proper.

COUNT X

(NEGLIGENCE—FAILURE OF DEFENDANT ROCKY MOUNTAIN HELICOPTERS TO USE ORDINARY CARE TO MAINTAIN, SERVICE, AND INSPECT TURBINE ENGINE)

COME NOW Plaintiffs, as heretofore set out, and for Count X of their causes of action against these defendants allege and state as follows:

101. Plaintiffs hereby incorporate by reference, as though fully set out herein, paragraphs 1 through 100, inclusive of this Second Amended Petition for Damages.

102. Defendant Rocky Mountain Helicopters held itself out as an entity which could carefully and competently repair, re-tool, service, inspect, machine or otherwise provide and maintain safe engine components for air ambulances it utilized in the course of its operations.

103. Defendant Rocky Mountain Helicopters had a duty to use that degree of care that an ordinarily careful and prudent helicopter repair and maintenance operations facility or mechanic would use under the same or similar circumstances.

104. The engine assembly unit and related component parts repaired, serviced, provided, or supplied by defendant Rocky Mountain Helicopters were defective and otherwise flawed which had the effect, of creating a blockage of air flow to the jet engine under normal usage.

105. Defendant Rocky Mountain Helicopters knew or by using ordinary care should have known of the potential of such dangerous condition as was created by its failure to properly maintain and service said jet engine.

106. Defendant Rocky Mountain Helicopters violated known and applicable industry standards in that it failed to conduct itself as a reasonable and prudent helicopter manufacturer under the same or similar circumstances.

107. Defendant Rocky Mountain Helicopters was negligent in the following respects:

(A) Defendant Rocky Mountain Helicopters provided an improperly maintained and flawed jet assembly unit and component parts thereof;

(B) Defendant Rocky Mountain Helicopters failed to properly repair and maintain the jet engine assembly unit and related component parts;

(C) Defendant Rocky Mountain Helicopters failed to properly machine, retool, service, repair or replace the jet engine assembly unit or component parts thereof comprising the jet engine of the air ambulance helicopter at issue herein;

(D) Defendant Rocky Mountain Helicopters failed to properly install or assemble the jet engine assembly unit and component parts as heretofore described;

(E) Defendant Rocky Mountain Helicopters failed to properly train, educate, and inform its mechanics and others as to appropriate maintenance procedures;

(F) Defendant Rocky Mountain Helicopters failed to maintain proper records as to the life limits of engine parts;

(G) Defendant Rocky Mountain Helicopters failed to properly inspect and examine any new or replaced parts or its repaired work product with respect to the subject jet engine assembly unit and component parts thereof; and

(H) Defendant Rocky Mountain Helicopters was negligent in further particulars presently unknown to Plaintiffs, but which will become known during the course of discovery.

108. Plaintiffs' deceased was killed as a direct and proximate result of the negligence and carelessness of defendant Rocky Mountain Helicopters as further set out above.

WHEREFORE, Plaintiffs Jodie A. Letz, individually, as Guardian Ad Litem and Next Friend for the minor children Eric David Letz and Christopher Scott Letz, and as Representative and Administratrix of the Estate of Sherry Ann Letz, deceased, pray judgment against defendant Rocky Mountain Helicopters for damages as follows:

(A) For all lawful damages such as are fair and reasonable for the wrongful death of Sherry Ann Letz considering the aggravating circumstances attendant upon the fatal injury;

(B) For pre-judgment interest at the rate of nine percent (9%) per annum pursuant to Plaintiffs' compliance with V.A.M.S. 408.040(2);

(C) For Plaintiffs' costs herein expended; and

(D) For such other and further relief as this Court deems just and proper.

COUNT XI

(NEGLIGENCE—FAILURE OF DEFENDANT LIFE FLIGHT TO USE ORDINARY CARE TO SERVICE, MAINTAIN, AND INSPECT AIRCRAFT ENGINE; NON-DELEGABLE DUTY)

COME NOW Plaintiffs, as heretofore set out, and for Count XI of their causes of action against these defendants allege and state as follows:

109.   Plaintiffs hereby incorporate by reference, as though fully set out herein, paragraphs 1 through 108, inclusive of this Second Amended Petition for Damages.

110.   Defendant Life Flight held itself out as an entity which could carefully and competently repair, retool, service, inspect, machine or otherwise provide safe air ambulances it utilized in the course of its operations.

111.   Defendant Life Flight had a duty to use that degree of care that an ordinarily careful and prudent helicopter repair and maintenance operations facility or mechanic would use under the same or similar circumstances.

112.   The air ambulance, engine assembly unit and related component parts repaired, serviced, provided, or supplied by defendant Life Flight were defective and otherwise flawed which had the effect of creating a blockage of air flow to the jet engine under normal usage.

113.   Defendant Life Flight knew or by using ordinary care should have known of the potential of such dangerous condition as was created by its failure to properly maintain and service said jet engine.

114.   Defendant Life Flight violated known and applicable industry standards in that it failed to conduct itself as a reasonable and prudent helicopter manufacturer under the same or similar circumstances.

115.   Defendant Life Flight by and through its agents, servants and employees had a continuing non-delegable duty to persons, specifically including Plaintiffs' deceased, to safely operate, manage, and maintain its air ambulance operations and this defendant failed in this duty to assure the safe operation, management and maintenance of its air ambulance operations including, but not limited to:

(A) Defendant Life Flight failed to supervise or review maintenance procedures of aircraft engines;

(B) Defendant Life Flight failed to require briefing from Rocky Mountain Helicopters, the operator of its service, or others, as to safety requirements for proper operation, maintenance or management of its air taxi operations;

(C) Defendant Life Flight failed to enforce safe practices of its air taxi operators;

(D) Defendant Life Flight failed to maintain sufficient knowledge of the safety and operating procedures of its air taxi service;

(E) Defendant Life Flight failed to review or inspect safety operations and procedures relating to aircraft maintenance and overhaul; and

(F) Defendant Life Flight was further negligent in breaching other continuing and non-delegable duties in particulars presently unknown to Plaintiffs but which will become further known during the course of discovery.

116.   Defendant Life Flight was further negligent in the following respects:

(A) Defendant Life Flight provided and operated an improperly maintained and flawed jet engine assembly unit and component parts thereof;

(B) Defendant Life Flight failed to properly repair, inspect, and maintain the jet engine assembly unit and related component parts;

(C) Defendant Life Flight failed to properly machine, retool, service, repair or replace the jet engine assembly unit or component parts thereof comprising the jet engine of the air ambulance helicopter at issue herein;

(D) Defendant Life Light failed to properly install or assemble the jet engine assembly unit and component parts as heretofore described;

(E) Defendant Life Flight failed to properly inspect and examine any new or replaced parts or its repaired work product with respect to the subject jet engine assembly unit and component parts thereof; and

(F) Defendant Life Flight was negligent in further particulars presently unknown to Plaintiff, but which will become known during the course of discovery.

117.   Plaintiffs' deceased was killed as a direct and proximate result of the negligence and carelessness of defendant Life Flight as further set out above.

WHEREFORE, Plaintiffs Jodie A. Letz, individually, as Guardian Ad Litem and Next Friend for the minor children Eric David Letz and Christopher Scott Letz, and as Representative and Administratrix of the Estate of Sherry Ann Letz, deceased, pray judgment against defendant Life Flight for damages as follows:

(A) For all lawful damages such as are fair and reasonable for the wrongful death of Sherry Ann Letz considering the aggravating circumstances attendant upon the fatal injury;

(B) For pre-judgment interest at the rate of nine percent (9%) per annum pursuant to Plaintiffs' compliance with V.A.M.S. 408.040(2);

(C) For Plaintiffs' costs herein expended; and

(D) For such other and further relief as this Court deems just and proper.

COUNT XII

(COMMON CARRIER LIABILITY—FAILURE OF DEFENDANT ROCKY MOUNTAIN HELICOPTERS TO PROVIDE HIGHEST DEGREE OF CARE IN SUPPLYING SAFE AND AIRWORTHY HELICOPTER)

COME NOW Plaintiffs, as heretofore set out, and for Count XII of their causes of action against these defendants allege and state as follows:

118.   Plaintiffs hereby incorporate by reference, as though fully set out herein, paragraphs 1 through 117, inclusive of this Second Amended Petition for Damages.

119.   Plaintiffs' deceased, Sherry Ann Letz, was a passenger for hire of an air ambulance service controlled, operated, dispatched, and supervised by defendant Rocky Mountain Helicopters.

120.   Defendant Rocky Mountain Helicopters held itself out as an entity which could safely and competently transport persons in need of medical care by emergency air ambulance services utilizing helicopter transport.

121.   At all times material hereto, defendant Rocky Mountain Helicopters was and is a commercial air taxi service carrying passengers in need of medical care and treatment and doing so for hire and for profit as a common carrier.

122.   Defendant Rocky Mountain Helicopters had a duty to Plaintiffs' deceased to exercise the highest degree of care and diligence in the operation, management, maintenance, and service of its air ambulance program to be provided to persons within the general public such as Sherry Ann Letz and, specifically, the highest degree of care and diligence to provide a safe and airworthy aircraft.

123.   Defendant Rocky Mountain Helicopters failed to provide a reasonably safe aircraft for the use and transport of Plaintiffs' deceased thereby breaching its duty to exercise the highest degree of care.

124.   Plaintiffs' deceased was killed as a direct and proximate result of defendant Rocky Mountain Helicopters' failure to exercise the highest degree of care in providing a safe helicopter for her use and transport.

WHEREFORE, Plaintiffs Jodie A. Letz, individually, as Guardian Ad Litem and Next Friend for the minor children Eric David Letz and Christopher Scott Letz, and as Representative and Administratrix of the Estate of Sherry Ann Letz, deceased, pray judgment against defendant Rocky Mountain Helicopters for damages as follows:

(A) For all lawful damages such as are fair and reasonable for the wrongful death of Sherry Ann Letz considering the aggravating circumstances attendant upon the fatal injury;

(B) For pre-judgment interest at the rate of nine percent (9%) per annum pursuant to Plaintiffs' compliance with V.A.M.S. 408.040(2);

(C) For Plaintiffs' costs herein expended; and

(D) For such other and further relief as this Court deems just and proper.

COUNT XIII

**(COMMON CARRIER LIABILITY—FAILURE OF DEFENDANT LIFE FLIGHT
TO PROVIDE HIGHEST DEGREE OF CARE IN SUPPLYING SAFE AND AIRWORTHY HELICOPTER)**

COME NOW Plaintiffs, as heretofore set out, and for Count XIII of their causes of action against these defendants allege and state as follows:

125.   Plaintiffs hereby incorporate by reference, as though fully set out herein, paragraphs 1 through 124, inclusive of this Second Amended Petition for Damages.

126.   Plaintiffs' deceased, Sherry Ann Letz, was a passenger for hire of an air ambulance service controlled, operated, dispatched, and supervised by defendant Life Flight.

127.   Defendant Life Flight held itself out as an entity which could safely and competently transport persons in need of medical care by emergency air ambulance services utilizing helicopter transport.

128.   At all times material hereto, defendant Life Flight was and is a commercial air taxi service carrying passengers in need of medical care and treatment and doing so for hire and for profit as a common carrier.

129.   Defendant Life Flight had a duty to Plaintiffs' deceased to exercise the highest degree of care and diligence in the operation, management, maintenance, and service of its air ambulance program to be provided to persons within the general public such as Sherry Ann Letz and, specifically, the highest degree of care and diligence to provide a safe and airworthy aircraft.

130.   Defendant Life Flight failed to provide a reasonably safe aircraft for the use and transport of Plaintiffs' deceased thereby breaching its duty to exercise the highest degree of care.

131.   Plaintiffs' deceased was killed as a direct and proximate result of defendant Life Flight's failure to exercise the highest degree of care in providing a safe helicopter for her use and transport.

WHEREFORE, Plaintiffs Jodie A. Letz, individually, as Guardian Ad Litem and Next Friend for the minor children Eric David Letz and Christopher Scott Letz, and as Representative and Administratrix of the Estate of Sherry Ann Letz, deceased, pray judgment against defendant Life Flight for damages as follows:

(A) For all lawful damages such as are fair and reasonable for the wrongful death of Sherry Ann Letz considering the aggravating circumstances attendant upon the fatal injury;

(B) For pre-judgment interest at the rate of nine percent (9%) per annum pursuant to Plaintiffs' compliance with V.A.M.S. 408.040(2);

(C) For Plaintiffs' costs herein expended; and

(D) For such other and further relief as this Court deems just and proper.

COUNT XIV

(APPARENT AUTHORITY AND ESTOPPEL; CORPORATE REPRESENTATION AND OSTENSIBLE AGENCY—LIABILITY OF DEFENDANT LIFE FLIGHT FOR REPRESENTING TO PUBLIC AND HOLDING ITSELF OUT AS OWNER/OPERATOR OF AIRCRAFT)

COME NOW Plaintiffs, as heretofore set out, and for Count XIV of their causes of action against these defendants allege and state as follows:

132.   Plaintiffs hereby incorporate by reference, as though fully set out herein, paragraphs 1 through 131, inclusive of this Second Amended Petition for Damages.

133.   Plaintiffs' deceased, Sherry Ann Letz, was a passenger of an air ambulance helicopter controlled, operated, dispatched and supervised by defendant Life Flight, Registration Number N782LF, on the outside of which was prominently labeled and displayed the notation "Spirit of Kansas City Life Flight."

134.   By placing its name on the subject air ambulance helicopter and holding itself out as the owner/operator of said aircraft, defendant Life Flight is estopped from denying liability or responsibility for any defective conditions or for the negligent acts of others creating a defective condition within said aircraft, notwithstanding any exculpatory agreement which may exist between and among any of the parties.

135.   At all times material hereto, defendant Life Flight held itself out and represented itself to the public as a commercial air taxi service carrying passengers in need of medical care and treatment and expressly and impliedly represented that it had authority to so operate, control, dispatch and function as a federally certified air taxi service.

136.   By so labeling and prominently displaying its name upon the subject air ambulance helicopter, defendant Life Flight has voluntarily inserted itself into the position of owner/operator of said aircraft with the effect of binding itself and attaching any liability for any defects therein or negligent acts of others creating said defects onto itself.

137.   The apparent authority and corporate representation by defendant Life Flight in representing to the public and holding itself out as the owner/operator of the subject helicopter estops it from denying liability in that defendant created a reliance by others upon the representation that defendant Life Flight does control, operate, manage and dispatch the helicopter at issue herein.

138.   As a direct and proximate result of the aforementioned actions of defendant Life, defendant Life Flight is vicariously liable for the actions of others in creating a defective condition and Plaintiffs' deceased was killed as a result of said defective condition or negligent actions.

WHEREFORE, Plaintiffs Jodie A. Letz, individually, as Guardian Ad Litem and Next Friend for the minor children Eric David Letz and Christopher Scott Letz, and as Representative and Administratrix of the Estate of Sherry Ann Letz, deceased, pray judgment against defendant Life Flight for damages as follows:

(A) For all lawful damages such as are fair and reasonable for the wrongful death of Sherry Ann Letz considering the aggravating circumstances attendant upon the fatal injury;

(B) For pre-judgment interest at the rate of nine percent (9%) per annum pursuant to Plaintiffs' compliance with V.A.M.S. 408.040(2);

(C) For Plaintiffs' costs herein expended; and

(D) For such other and further relief as this Court deems just and proper.

Respectfully submitted,

ROBB & ROBB

_____

GARY C. ROBB #29618
ANITA PORTE ROBB #30318
One Kansas City Place - Suite 3900

1200 Main Street
Kansas City, Missouri 64105
Telephone: (816) 474-8080
Facsimile: (816) 474-8081

ATTORNEYS FOR PLAINTIFFS

DEMAND FOR JURY TRIAL

Plaintiff Jodie A. Letz, individually, and as Guardian Ad Litem and Next Friend for the minor children Eric David Letz and Christopher Scott Letz, demand trial by jury of the issues herein.

_____

GARY C. ROBB

A.2 Sample Complaint 2: Helicopter Mechanical System Malfunction Due to Manufacturing Defect (Tail Rotor System)

IN THE DISTRICT COURT OF LANCASTER
COUNTY, NEBRASKA

TAMMY SCOLLARD,	)	
Executor of the Estate of	)	
PATRICK SCOLLARD,	)	**CASE ID. CI-02-2621**
	)	
and	)	SEVENTH AMENDED
	)	PETITION
WAUSAU INSURANCE COMPANY, INC.,	)	AND PRAECIPE
	)	
PLAINTIFF,	)	
	)	
v.	)	
	)	
EUROCOPTER, S.A.S.	)	
	)	
and	)	
	)	
AMERICAN EUROCOPTER CORPORATION,	)	
	)	
DEFENDANTS.	)	

SEVENTH AMENDED PETITION

COMES NOW Tammy Scollard, Executor of the Estate of Patrick Scollard, and for her causes of action against the defendants states and alleges as follows:

1.   Tammy Scollard is a resident of Woodbury County, Iowa and is the duly-appointed executor of the Estate of Patrick Scollard. Plaintiff brings this action both on behalf of the deceased's next of kin as well as on behalf of the estate for the decedent's damages.

2.   At all relevant times, the decedent, Patrick Scollard, was a resident of Woodbury County, Iowa.

3.   Plaintiff Wausau Insurance Company, Inc. is the Workers' Compensation carrier for Rocky Mountain Holding Company.

4.   That at all relevant times the defendant Eurocopter, S.A.S. was a French Corporation authorized to do business in Nebraska.

5.   That at all relevant times the defendant American Eurocopter Corporation was a Delaware Corporation authorized to do business in Nebraska.

6.   That Tammy Scollard was the wife of Patrick Scollard and is the duly appointed Executor for his estate, having been so appointed by the District Court of Woodbury County, Iowa.

7.   That at all relevant times the decedent was employed as a paramedic for LifeNet of the Heartland in Norfolk, Nebraska.

8.   Rocky Mountain Holding Company, Inc. was the employer of the deceased Patrick Scollard and Wausau Insurance Company was the Worker's Compensation insurance carrier for Rocky Mountain Holding Company.

9.   That at all relevant times, defendant Eurocopter, S.A.S. designed, machined, manufactured, assembled, supplied, imported, distributed and/or sold the subject helicopter, an AS350B2 Eurocopter, in the course of its business.

10. That at all relevant times, defendant American Eurocopter designed, machined, manufactured, assembled, supplied, imported, distributed and/or sold the subject helicopter, an AS350B2 Eurocopter, in the course of its business.

11. The aforesaid helicopter was used in a manner reasonably anticipated by these defendants and others.

12. That the causes of action herein arose out of a helicopter crash which occurred on June 21, 2002 while the pilot, Phillip Herring, was trying to make an emergency landing at Karl Stefan Memorial Airport near Norfolk, Nebraska. Patrick Scollard, paramedic on the subject helicopter died along with the pilot and one other passenger.

13. Just prior to the crash, the pilot, Phillip Herring, had reported problems with the right rudder pedal stating that it was binding.

14. Mr. Scollard's death was proximately caused by the negligence and strict liability of defendant Eurocopter, S.A.S. including, but not limited to, the following:

(a) The subject helicopter, at the time of its design, manufacture, assembly and sale, was then placed in the market in a defective condition unreasonably dangerous for its intended use, or for any use the defendant could have reasonably foreseen;

(b) Defendant Eurocopter, S.A.S. failed to use reasonable care to see that the helicopter was safe for the use for which it was made, supplied, and sold;

(c) Defendant Eurocopter, S.A.S. failed to use that degree of care that an ordinarily careful and prudent designer, manufacturer, and seller of helicopters would use under the same or similar circumstances;

(d) Defendant Eurocopter, S.A.S. knew or by using ordinary care should have known of the potential dangerous condition as was created by its failure to properly design, machine, manufacture, distribute, and sell a safe helicopter and taken such action as to correct the dangerous condition; and

(e) Defendant Eurocopter, S.A.S. failed to warn sellers, owners, operators and maintenance facilities of the potential dangerous condition and knew, or should have known, that the helicopter or components within it would be used without inspection for defects, in that:

1.   Defendant knew or had reason to know that those for whose use the helicopter was made, sold, supplied, and distributed would not realize the danger; and

2.   Defendant failed to provide reasonably foreseeable users of the product with adequate warning of the danger and/or sufficient and proper instructions for safe use and operation.

(f) At the time the helicopter left the possession of Eurocopter S.A.S., it was in a defective condition unreasonably dangerous for reasons including, but not limited to, the following:

1.   The tail rotor load compensator accumulator bladder is made of a rubber material which is in direct contact with the rough-machined surface of the interior wall of the accumulator canister;

2.   The condition of the rubber bladder within the accumulator canister is not subject to inspection in that the accumulator is a welded and sealed unit;

3.   The rubber bladder within the accumulator is subject to a wear-induced perforation and loss of nitrogen charge into the hydraulic system without warning;

4.   Wear of the accumulator rubber bladder is a known and recognized failure mode;

5.   The subject tail rotor load compensator accumulator was not subject to any life limit notwithstanding knowledge that the bladder was constructed of a rubber material that degraded over time;

6.   The flight control system of the subject helicopter is unreasonably dangerous and difficult to control in the event that the hydraulic system is switched off especially at low speeds or at hover;

7.   The combination of activating the hydraulic isolation switch in the "off" position and the failed accumulator bladder rendered the helicopter uncontrollable;

8.   The pilot operating handbook or flight manual did not address a failure of the tail rotor accumulator or its symptoms or provide a proper and safe emergency maneuver;

9.   The pilot of the subject model helicopter would have no in-flight warning that a tail rotor accumulator had failed;

10.   The subject helicopter lacked a proper warning system to advise the pilot of an in-flight accumulator failure; and

11.   Accumulators within the subject helicopter lacked pressure gages to enable a pilot or mechanic to assess the pressure in the accumulators prior to or during flight.

27. Mr. Scollard's death was proximately caused by the negligence and strict liability of defendant American Eurocopter Corporation including, but not limited to, the following:

(a) The subject helicopter, at the time of its design, manufacture, assembly and sale, was then placed in the market in a defective condition unreasonably dangerous for its intended use, or for any use the defendant could have reasonably foreseen;

(b) Defendant American Eurocopter Corporation failed to use reasonable care to see that the helicopter was safe for the use for which it was made, supplied, and sold;

(c) Defendant American Eurocopter failed to use that degree of care that an ordinarily careful and prudent designer, manufacturer, and seller of helicopters would use under the same or similar circumstances;

(d) Defendant American Eurocopter knew or by using ordinary care should have known of the potential dangerous condition as was created by its failure to properly design, machine, manufacture, distribute, and sell a safe helicopter and taken such action as to correct the dangerous condition; and

(e) Defendant American Eurocopter failed to warn sellers, owners, operators and maintenance facilities of the potential dangerous condition and knew, or should have known, that the helicopter or components within it would be used without inspection for defects, in that:

  1.   Defendant knew or had reason to know that those for whose use the helicopter was made, sold, supplied, and distributed would not realize the danger; and

  2.   Defendant failed to provide reasonably foreseeable users of the product with adequate warning of the danger and/or sufficient and proper instructions for safe use and operation.

(f) At the time the helicopter left the possession of American Eurocopter, it was in a defective condition unreasonably dangerous for reasons including, but not limited to, the following:

  1.   The tail rotor load compensator accumulator bladder is made of a rubber material which is in direct contact with the rough-machined surface of the interior wall of the accumulator canister;

  2.   The condition of the rubber bladder within the accumulator canister is not subject to inspection in that the accumulator is a welded and sealed unit;

  3.   The rubber bladder within the accumulator is subject to a wear-induced perforation and loss of nitrogen charge into the hydraulic system without warning;

  4.   Wear of the accumulator rubber bladder is a known and recognized failure mode;

  5.   The subject tail rotor load compensator accumulator was not subject to any life limit notwithstanding knowledge that the bladder was constructed of a rubber material that degraded over time;

  6.   The flight control system of the subject helicopter is unreasonably dangerous and difficult to control in the event that the hydraulic system is switched off;

  7.   The combination of activating the hydraulic isolation switch in the "off" position and the failed accumulator bladder rendered the helicopter uncontrollable;

  8.   The pilot operating handbook or flight manual did not address a failure of the tail rotor accumulator or its symptoms or provide a proper and safe emergency maneuver;

  9.   The pilot of the subject model helicopter would have no in-flight warning that a tail rotor accumulator had failed;

  10.   The subject helicopter lacked a proper warning system to advise the pilot of an in-flight accumulator failure; and

  11.   Accumulators within the subject helicopter lacked pressure gages to enable a pilot or mechanic to assess the pressure in the accumulators prior to or during flight and/or as to the apportionment of damages as to various defendants.

First Cause of Action

34. Plaintiff incorporates paragraphs 1-33 herein.

35. As a proximate result of the negligence and/or strict liability of the defendants, and each of them, Patrick Scollard was caused to incur burial and funeral expenses and expenses for medical services including emergency care, hospital services, and physician charges.

Second Cause of Action

36. Plaintiff incorporates paragraphs 1-35 as is fully set forth herein.

37. As a direct and proximate result of the aforesaid negligence and/or strict liability of the defendants, and each of them, Patrick Scollard sustained serious personal injury which resulted in his death. He left as heirs and next of kin the following:

    a. Tammy Scollard, wife of decedent;

    b. Tyler Cleveland, step-son of decedent;

    c. Matthew Cleveland, step-son of decedent;

    d. Michael Scollard, son of decedent; and

    e. Meghan Scollard, daughter of decedent.

38. That he provided support, society, comfort and companionship to his wife and next of kin, and his spouse sustained damages for loss of consortium in that she has been deprived of rights to which she is entitled because of the marriage relationship, namely, the deceased's affection, companionship, comfort, assistance, and conjugal society. By reason of this wrongful death, the wife and next of kin have been deprived of his present and future contributions to their care, support, maintenance, counseling, advice and companionship, and have sustained past, present and future pecuniary loss, to their damage, including past and future lost earnings, lost earning capacity, and the monetary value of the deceased's services, comfort, and companionship.

Third Cause of Action

39. The Plaintiff incorporates paragraphs 1-38 as if fully set forth herein.

40. That as a proximate cause of the defendants' negligence and/or strict liability, and each of them, the decedent suffered severe and excruciating physical pain and mental suffering including pre-impact terror, conscious prefatal-injury fear and apprehension of impending death, and post-crash conscious physical, mental, and emotional pain and suffering, and that the decedent, Patrick Scollard, was deprived of his lawful right to his life and did thereby suffer from the loss of enjoyment of that life for which his estate should be fully compensated.

Fourth Cause of Action

41. Plaintiffs Wausau Insurance Company, Inc. incorporates paragraphs 1-30, and 33-39 as if fully set forth herein.

42. That as a proximate cause of the defendants' negligence and/or strict liability, and each of them, Plaintiff Wausau Insurance Company, Inc. expended significant amounts of compensation to Plaintiff Tammy Scollard for Workers' Compensation benefits and other employee benefits payable due to the death of Patrick Scollard.

Fifth Cause Of Action

48. The Plaintiff incorporates Paragraphs 1-47 as if fully set forth herein.

49. Plaintiff hereby seeks pre-judgment interest in the amount to be imposed by law and by further Order of the Court should she prevail in these actions and obtain a judgment in an amount greater than that which was claimed in her certified letter of March 15, 2005, all in accordance with Section 45-103.02 R.R.S.Neb.

WHEREFORE, the Plaintiffs request that this Court enter judgment against the defendants, and each of them:

A. On Plaintiff Scollard's first cause of action, for special damages for burial and funeral expenses and for the value of all medical and emergency care services incurred;

B. On Plaintiff Scollard's second cause of action for general damages as determined by law;

C. On the Estate's third cause of action for general damages as determined by law together with costs of this action and for such other and further relief as the Court deems just;

D. On Plaintiffs' fourth cause of action Plaintiffs ask this Court pursuant to Nebraska law to determine what money and/or damages that Wausau Insurance Company, Inc. should receive as a result of the negligence and/or strict liability of the defendants;

E.   On Plaintiffs' fifth cause of action, Plaintiffs ask this Court, pursuant to Nebraska law, to determine the appropriate amount of pre-judgment interest to be assessed as against Defendants Eurocopter S.A.S. and American Eurocopter Corporation pursuant to the provisions of Section 45-103.02 R.R.S.Neb.; and

F.   Plaintiffs further seek such other and further relief pursuant to the actions as stated herein as are consistent with Nebraska law and in furtherance of justice given the wrongful death of Patrick Scollard.

Respectfully submitted,

ROBB & ROBB LLC

_____

GARY C. ROBB
One Kansas City Place
Suite 3900
1200 Main Street
Kansas City, Missouri 64105
Telephone: (816) 474-8080
Facsimile: (816) 474-8081

ATTORNEY FOR PLAINTIFF

DEMAND FOR JURY TRIAL

Plaintiff Tammy Scollard demands trial by jury of the issues herein.

_____

GARY C. ROBB

A.3 Sample Complaint 3: Helicopter Pilot Error (wire strike)

IN THE IOWA DISTRICT COURT FOR
POLK COUNTY, IOWA

KATHRYN L. SLOTZHAUER, Administrator of the Estate of ROLAND SCHLOTZHAUER, PLAINTIFF, v. BRISTOL AEROSPACE LIMITED A Canada Corporation, and THE FINAL SEASON, INC. A California Corporation, and RITEL COPTER SERVICE INC. An Iowa Corporation, and RICHARD GREEN An Iowa Resident, DEFENDANTS.	))	LAW NO.: CL102824 FOURTH AMENDED PETITION AT LAW (WRONGFUL DEATH/AIRCRAFT) COUNSEL FOR PLAINTIFF: Gary C. Robb Anita Porte Robb ROBB & ROBB LLC One Kansas City Place Suite 3900 1200 Main Street Kansas City, Missouri 64105 Telephone: (816) 474-8080 Facsimile: (816) 474-8081

FOURTH AMENDED PETITION AT LAW
(WRONGFUL DEATH/AIRCRAFT)

   COMES NOW Kathryn L. Schlotzhauer, Administrator of the Estate of Roland Schlotzhauer, and for her cause of action against the defendants Bristol Aerospace Limited, The Final Season, Inc., Ritel Copter Service Inc., and Richard Green states and alleges as follows:

PLAINTIFF

   1.   Kathryn L. Schlotzhauer brings this action individually and/or in her capacity as Administrator of the Estate of Roland Schlotzhauer as appointed by the District Court of Polk County, Iowa.
   2.   Plaintiff Kathryn L. Schlotzhauer was lawfully married to the deceased at the time of his death.
PLAINTIFF'S DECEASED
   3.   Plaintiff's deceased, Roland Schlotzhauer, age 50, died from injuries sustained in the helicopter crash.

DEFENDANTS
DEFENDANT BRISTOL AEROSPACE LTD.

4.   That at all relevant times the defendant Bristol Aerospace Limited was a Canada corporation, located in Winnipeg, Manitoba, Canada.

5.   Defendant Bristol Aerospace designs, develops, manufacturers, markets, houses, distributes, installs, and/or sells helicopter products and accessories. Bristol Aerospace supplies and installs these products and accessories to helicopter manufacturers and operators world-wide for installation on new or existing aircraft.

6.   That at all relevant times, defendant Bristol Aerospace designed, developed, manufactured, housed, distributed, installed, serviced and/or sold the subject Wire Strike Protection System (WSPS) on the subject helicopter in the course of its business.

DEFENDANT THE FINAL SEASON, INC.

7.   That at all relevant times, defendant The Final Season, Inc. was a California corporation licensed to do business in the State of Iowa and formed for the purpose of producing and filming the subject motion picture entitled "The Final Season." At all relevant times, defendant The Final Season, Inc. maintained its primary Iowa office in Des Moines, Polk County, Iowa.

8.   That at all relevant times, defendant The Final Season, Inc. operated in Iowa by and through its various employees and agents including Tony C. Wilson, Kenny Burke, Steven B. Schott, Michael Wasserman, Herschel Weingrod, Parker Widemire, Carl Borack, Sean Astin, Terry Trimpe, and David M. Evans.

9.   That at all times relevant hereto, Plaintiff's deceased, Roland Schlotzhauer, was an independent contractor retained by defendant The Final Season, Inc. This defendant provided general direction as to the course of his work and the deceased determined for himself as a professional cameraman the specific and exact means and methods for accomplishing the desired result. The deceased's work involved performance of a specific task on a short term basis for which he had a distinct ability as it was his trade and occupation by experience, training and education and, further, the deceased supplied the necessary tools and camera equipment required to perform the desired tasks.

DEFENDANT RITEL COPTER SERVICE INC.

10.   That at all relevant times the defendant Ritel Copter Service Inc. (hereinafter referred to as "defendant Ritel") was an Iowa Corporation owned by defendant Richard Green located in Hudson, Iowa.

11.   Defendant Ritel is in the business of aircraft charter rental, leasing, servicing and providing piloting services. It owned, operated, maintained and serviced the subject Bell helicopter.

12.   At all times material hereto, defendant Ritel was acting by and through its agents, servants and/or employees, each of whom were acting within the course and scope of their employment with defendant.

DEFENDANT RICHARD GREEN

13.   That at all relevant times defendant Richard Green (hereinafter referred to as "defendant Green") was an Iowa resident.

14.   Defendant Green is the owner of Ritel Copter Services, Inc. and of the subject helicopter. He was a licensed pilot who flew, maintained and serviced the subject helicopter. Defendant Green was piloting the subject helicopter at the time of the crash.

IDENTIFICATION OF AIRCRAFT AND DEFECTIVE EQUIPMENT

15.   This aircrash involves a 1980 Bell "Jet Ranger" 206B helicopter, serial number 2971, registration (tail) no. N2877F.

16.   The subject helicopter was equipped with a Wire Strike Protection System (WSPS) installed by defendant Edwards & Associates, Inc. and sold by defendant AAI.

17. The WSPS was designed and manufactured by defendant Bristol Aerospace and is to provide protection for the helicopter in the event of inadvertent flight into horizontally strung electrical transmission wires. Defendants knew of the uses for which said equipment and parts were intended.

18. The aforesaid helicopter was used in a manner reasonably anticipated by these defendants and others.

JURISDICTION

19. Defendants, and each of them, had a reasonable expectation that they would be hailed into a Court in the State of Iowa, by reason of their injecting products and services into a stream of commerce which caused or contributed to cause this fatal helicopter crash within the State of Iowa.

20. It does not offend "traditional notions of fair play and substantial justice" to require these defendants to defend themselves in this forum. The contacts, ties and relations of defendants, and each of them, are sufficient to the exercise of personal jurisdiction within the Courts of the State of Iowa and by reason of their making and producing a motion picture that takes place in and is filmed in the State of Iowa, Defendants are engaged in a persistent course of conduct within this State such that subjecting them to jurisdiction within the District Court of Iowa is lawful, appropriate, and fair.

VENUE

21. Venue in the Circuit Court of Polk County, Iowa is proper in that defendants The Final Season, Inc., is a resident of, located in, and doing or transacting business in Polk County in the State of Iowa.

DATES AND ACTS OF CONDUCT COMPLAINED OF

22. On or about June 30, 2006, Roland Schlotzhauer, decedent herein, was a passenger on a 1980 Bell "Jet Ranger" 206B helicopter, serial number 2971, registration (tail) no. N2877F which was being flown approximately one mile west of Walford, Iowa westbound along Highway 151 and 33rd Avenue while filming a route to be used for a parade scene for the motion picture film entitled "The Final Season." The aircraft was operating in visual meteorological conditions without a flight plan.

23. At approximately 12:51 p.m. central daylight time, the helicopter impacted the north-south power lines that ran perpendicular to Highway 151 and crashed in a cornfield in the southeast corner of Benton County, Iowa.

24. Plaintiff's deceased, Roland Schlotzhauer, was fatally wounded in the crash.

PLAINTIFF'S INJURIES AND DAMAGES

25. As a direct and proximate result of the defendants' negligence, Roland Schlotzhauer was killed. By virtue of his untimely death, the Estate of Ronald Schlotzhauer is lawfully entitled to such damages as are fair and just for the death and loss thus occasioned, including but not limited to the pecuniary losses suffered by reason of the death, the present value of the additional amounts the decedent would reasonably be expected to have accumulated as a result of his own effort if he had lived out the term of his natural life, loss of enjoyment of life, burial expenses, and the reasonable present value of the services, spousal consortium, the lost fellowship as is befitting a husband and wife and the right to the benefits of company, cooperation, affection, aid, general usefulness, industry, and attention within the home and family, in addition to the companionship, comfort, instruction, guidance, counsel, training, and support of which Kathryn Schlotzhauer has been deprived by reason of such death, further including the past and future lost support, household services, and other value of benefits which would have been provided by the decedent. All claims for post-death loss of spousal consortium are brought by Plaintiff in her capacity as Administrator of the Estate.

26. Plaintiff Kathryn Schlotzhauer further claims such damages as the decedent may have suffered between the time or just prior to the helicopter's impact with the utility lines and the time of his death and for the recovery of which the decedent might have maintained an action had death not ensued including, but not limited to, mental anguish, physical disability, conscious pain and suffering, pre-impact terror, awareness of imminent death, and further considering the aggravating circumstances attendant upon the fatal injury.

DEFENDANTS' CONSCIOUS DISREGARD FOR SAFETY

27. The wanton, willful, callous, reckless and depraved conduct of defendants, and each of them, entitle Plaintiff to punitive damages to punish defendants, and each of them and to deter future wrongdoing by these defendants and others in that the acts and omissions of defendants have manifested such reckless and complete indifference to and a conscious disregard for the safety of others that the decedent would have been entitled to punitive damages had he lived in that defendants, and each of them knew or should have known of the high probability of injury or death associated with the use of the subject helicopter in the manner so intended and know or should have known of the hazards and risks associated with that use and recklessly failed to adequately consider or guard against them including, but not limited to, the knowledge that utility power lines were located in the vicinity of intended travel and that such lines posed a danger to any aircraft in flight.

COUNT I

(STRICT LIABILITY—SALE, SUPPLY, AND DISTRIBUTION OF DEFECTIVE AIRCRAFT PARTS BY DEFENDANT BRISTOL AEROSPACE LIMITED)

COMES NOW Plaintiff, as heretofore set out, and for Count I of her cause of action against defendant Bristol Aerospace Limited alleges and states as follows:

28. Plaintiff hereby incorporates by reference, as though fully set out herein, paragraphs 1 through 27, inclusive of this Petition at Law.

29. Defendant Bristol Aerospace designs, develops, manufacturers, markets, houses, distributes, installs, and/or sells helicopter products and accessories. Bristol supplies and installs these products and accessories to helicopter operators world-wide for installation on new or existing aircraft.

30. Defendant Bristol Aerospace sold or distributed the Wire Strike Protection System which was installed on the subject Bell 206B helicopter.

31. Bristol Aerospace was engaged in the business of selling or distributing the Wire Strike Protection System.

32. The product was in a defective condition at the time it left defendant's control in one or more of the following ways:

(a) The Wire Strike Protection System lacked a serrated hacksaw blade embedded along the length of the windshield center guide bar which was designed to cut small, weak and brittle utility wires such as those struck by the subject helicopter on June 30, 2006;

(b) The Wire Strike Protection System failed to protect the helicopter from crashing upon impact with relatively small, weak, and brittle utility wires;

(c) The Wire Strike Protection System permitted wires to be severed due to tensile load which could affect the pitch of the helicopter and not due to any cutting action of the system itself;

(d) The Wire Strike Protection System failed to protect the main rotor mast and helicopter flight controls from contact with utility wires;

(e) The Wire Strike Protection System was not appropriate for use on the subject aircraft;

(f) The Wire Strike Protection System was re-designed and modified so as to be less safe, less effective, and less able to provide protection from foreseeable contact with horizontally strung wires;

(g) The Wire Strike Protection System failed to conform to the original patent of said system which incorporated a serrated cutting edge on the windshield center bar;

(h) The Wire Strike Protection System failed to utilize any cutting surface or edge along the length of the windshield center guide bar for the purpose of cutting or weakening impacted utility wires;

(i) The Wire Strike Protection System lacked a method to guide wire into the cutter jaws without creating high forces on the forward flight of the helicopter such as to deflect the helicopter downward and further exposing non-protected areas of the helicopter to wire strike;

(j) The Wire Strike Protection System failed to protect a critical area of the helicopter between the top of the upper guide bar and the rotating main rotors such that wires were permitted to enter a highly sensitive and vulnerable location of the helicopter;

(k) The Wire Strike Protection System as designed had an improper guide system on top of the windshield;

(l)   The Wire Strike Protection System failed to protect an unreasonably large area and left exposed critical components for helicopter flight;

(m)   The Wire Strike Protection System failed to utilize a specific and separate protective device which was technologically feasible and safer for the express purpose of protecting the main rotor mast and flight controls from inadvertent wire strike;

(n)   The Wire Strike Protection System was placed in the U.S. marketplace without proper testing or in-field usage; and

(o)   The Wire Strike Protection System provided a false sense of security to pilots operating helicopters with that system to the extent that it induced risky and unsafe flight operation.

33.   A reasonable alternative safer design could have been practically adopted at the time of sale or distribution as follows:

(a)   The reasonable alternative design would have been including the embedded hacksaw blade along the windshield center guide bar which was part of the original design of the Wire Strike Protection System and that design would have reduced or prevented the Plaintiff's harm, could have been practically adopted at the time of sale or distribution of the Wire Strike Protection System and was a reasonable alternative safer design;

(b)   An additional or alternative reasonable safer design would have been to retain the length of the original upper cutter or upper deflector; and

(c)   There are reasonable alternative safe designs which could have been practically adopted at the time or sale or distribution of the subject Wire Strike Protection System which would specifically have protected the main rotor mast and flight controls in the event of contact with horizontally strung cables or wires including but not limited to:

(i)   A Wire Strike Protection System designed to more readily deflect the horizontally strung wires into a cutting area and which would protect the main rotor mast from wire contact;

(ii)   A circular protective Wire Strike Protection System dedicated to preventing contact with the main rotor mast and helicopter flight controls which has been patented; and

(iii)   A separate smaller wire strike unit containing deflectors and a cutting jaw area for the express purpose of protecting the main rotor mast and helicopter flight controls.

34.   The alternative designs for the Wire Strike Protection System are reasonable and their omission rendered the Wire Strike Protection System not reasonably safe in considering:

(a)   The magnitude and probability of foreseeable risks of harm;

(b)   The instructions and warnings accompanying the Wire Strike Protection System;

(c)   Consumer expectations about product performance and the dangers attendant to use of the Wire Strike Protection System including expectations arising from product portrayal and marketing;

(d)   Whether the risk presented by the Wire Strike Protection System is open and obvious to or generally known by foreseeable users;

(e)   The technological feasibility and practicality of the alternative design;

(f)   Whether the alternative design could be implemented at a reasonable cost;

(g)   The relative advantages and disadvantages of the Wire Strike Protection System as designed and as it alternatively could have been designed;

(h)   The likely effects of the alternative design on product longevity, maintenance, repair, aesthetics and on the efficiency and utility of the Wire Strike Protection System;

(i)   The range of consumer choice among similar products with and without the alternative design;

(j)   The overall safety of the Wire Strike Protection System with and without the alternative design and whether the alternative design would introduce other dangers of equal or greater magnitude;

(k)   Custom and practice in the industry and how defendant's design compares with other competing products and actual use; and

(l)   Any other factors shown by the evidence bearing on this question.

35.   The alternative designs would have reduced or avoided the foreseeable risks of harm posed by the Wire Strike Protection System as was designed, manufactured, and installed on the subject helicopter at the time of the crash.

36.   The omission of the alternative designs, separately or together, rendered the Wire Strike Protection System not reasonably safe.

37.   The alternative designs would have reduced or prevented the Plaintiff's harm.

38. The design defect was a proximate cause of Plaintiff's damages.

39. The aforesaid helicopter's WSPS was used in a manner reasonably anticipated by this defendant and others.

40. The Wire Strike Protection System was expected to and did reach the ultimate user or consumer without substantial change in condition such that the defect complained of existed at the time of sale.

41. Plaintiff as heretofore set forth was damaged as a direct result of the subject helicopter's wire strike protection equipment being sold, assembled, and installed in a defective condition unreasonably dangerous which resulted in the death of Roland Schlotzhauer.

42. The amount in controversy exceeds the minimum jurisdictional amount required by this Court.

43. Plaintiff suffered damages by reason of the death of her husband as more fully set out herein.

WHEREFORE, Plaintiff Kathryn L. Schlotzhauer, Administrator of the Estate of Roland Schlotzhauer, prays judgment against defendant Bristol Aerospace Limited for damages as follows:

(A) For actual damages such as are fair and reasonable for the wrongful death of Roland Schlotzhauer;

(B) For punitive damages in such sum as will punish and deter this defendant and deter others from similar conduct in the future;

(C) For Plaintiff's costs herein expended; and

(D) For such other and further relief as this Court deems just and proper.

COUNT II
(STRICT LIABILITY DESIGN DEFECT—SALE AND DISTRIBUTION OF DEFECTIVE AIRCRAFT DEVICE BY DEFENDANT BRISTOL AEROSPACE LIMITED)

COMES NOW Plaintiff, as heretofore set out, and for Count II of her cause of action against defendant Bristol Aerospace alleges and states as follows:

44. Plaintiff hereby incorporates by reference, as though fully set out herein, paragraphs 1 through 43, inclusive of this Petition at Law.

45. Defendant Bristol Aerospace sold or distributed the Wire Strike Protection System as further described herein.

46. Defendant Bristol Aerospace was engaged in the business of selling, promoting, advertising, installing, and distributing the Wire Strike Protection System.

47. The Wire Strike Protection System was in a defective condition at the time it left Bristol Aerospace's control in one or more of the following ways:

(a) The Wire Strike Protection System lacked a serrated hacksaw blade embedded along the length of the windshield center guide bar which was designed to cut small, weak and brittle utility wires such as those struck by the subject helicopter on June 30, 2006;

(b) The Wire Strike Protection System failed to protect the helicopter from crashing upon impact with relatively small, weak, and brittle utility wires;

(c) The Wire Strike Protection System permitted wires to be severed due to tensile load which could affect the pitch of the helicopter and not due to any cutting action of the system itself;

(d) The Wire Strike Protection System failed to protect the main rotor mast and helicopter flight controls from contact with utility wires;

(e) The Wire Strike Protection System was not appropriate for use on the subject aircraft;

(f) The Wire Strike Protection System was re-designed and modified so as to be less safe, less effective, and less able to provide protection from foreseeable contact with horizontally strung wires;

(g) The Wire Strike Protection System failed to conform to the original patent of said system which incorporated a serrated cutting edge on the windshield center bar;

(h) The Wire Strike Protection System failed to utilize any cutting surface or edge along the length of the windshield center guide bar for the purpose of cutting or weakening impacted utility wires;

(i) The Wire Strike Protection System lacked a method to guide wire into the cutter jaws without creating high forces on the forward flight of the helicopter such as to deflect the helicopter downward and further exposing non-protected areas of the helicopter to wire strike;

(j) The Wire Strike Protection System failed to protect a critical area of the helicopter between the top of the upper guide bar and the rotating main rotors such that wires were permitted to enter a highly sensitive and vulnerable location of the helicopter;

(k) The Wire Strike Protection System as designed had an improper guide system on top of the windshield;

(l) The Wire Strike Protection System failed to protect an unreasonably large area and left exposed critical components for helicopter flight;

(m) The Wire Strike Protection System failed to utilize a specific and separate protective device which was technologically feasible and safer for the express purpose of protecting the main rotor mast and flight controls from inadvertent wire strike;

(n) The Wire Strike Protection System was placed in the U.S. marketplace without proper testing or in-field usage; and

(o) The Wire Strike Protection System provided a false sense of security to pilots operating helicopters with that system to the extent that it induced risky and unsafe flight operation.

48. A reasonable alternative safer design could have been practically adopted at the time of sale or distribution as follows:

(a) The reasonable alternative design would have been including the embedded hacksaw blade along the windshield center guide bar which was part of the original design of the Wire Strike Protection System and that design would have reduced or prevented the Plaintiff's harm, could have been practically adopted at the time of sale or distribution of the Wire Strike Protection System and was a reasonable alternative safer design;

(b) An additional or alternative reasonable safer design would have been to retain the length of the original upper cutter or upper deflector; and

(c) There are reasonable alternative safe designs which could have been practically adopted at the time or sale or distribution of the subject Wire Strike Protection System which would specifically have protected the main rotor mast and flight controls in the event of contact with horizontally strung cables or wires including but not limited to:

(i)   A Wire Strike Protection System designed to more readily deflect the horizontally strung wires into a cutting area and which would protect the main rotor mast from wire contact;

(ii)   A circular protective Wire Strike Protection System dedicated to preventing contact with the main rotor mast and helicopter flight controls which has been patented; and

(iii)   A separate smaller wire strike unit containing deflectors and a cutting jaw area for the express purpose of protecting the main rotor mast and helicopter flight controls.

49. The alternative design would have reduced or avoided the foreseeable risks of harm posed by the Wire Strike Protection System.

50. The alternative designs for the Wire Strike Protection System are reasonable and their omission rendered the Wire Strike Protection System not reasonably safe in considering:

(a) The magnitude and probability of foreseeable risks of harm;

(b) The instructions and warnings accompanying the Wire Strike Protection System;

(c) Consumer expectations about product performance and the dangers attendant to use of the Wire Strike Protection System including expectations arising from product portrayal and marketing;

(d) Whether the risk presented by the Wire Strike Protection System is open and obvious to or generally known by foreseeable users;

(e) The technological feasibility and practicality of the alternative design;

(f) Whether the alternative design could be implemented at a reasonable cost;

(g) The relative advantages and disadvantages of the Wire Strike Protection System as designed and as it alternatively could have been designed;

(h) The likely effects of the alternative design on product longevity, maintenance, repair, aesthetics and on the efficiency and utility of the Wire Strike Protection System;

(i) The range of consumer choice among similar products with and without the alternative design;

(j) The overall safety of the Wire Strike Protection System with and without the alternative design and whether the alternative design would introduce other dangers of equal or greater magnitude;

(k) Custom and practice in the industry and how defendant's design compares with other competing products and actual use; and

(l) Any other factors shown by the evidence bearing on this question.

51. The alternative design would have reduced or prevented the Plaintiff's harm.

52. The design defect was a proximate cause of Plaintiff's damages.

53. The subject helicopter was flown and the WSPS was used in a manner reasonably anticipated by this defendant and others.

54. The Wire Strike Protection System was expected to and did reach the ultimate user or consumer without substantial change in condition such that the defect complained of existed at the time of sale.

55. Plaintiff as heretofore set forth was damaged as a direct result of the subject helicopter's wire strike protection equipment being sold, assembled, and installed in a defective condition unreasonably dangerous which resulted in the death of Roland Schlotzhauer.

56. The amount in controversy exceeds the minimum jurisdictional amount required by this Court.

57. Plaintiff suffered damages by reason of the death of her husband as more fully set out herein.

WHEREFORE, Plaintiff Kathryn L. Schlotzhauer, Administrator of the Estate of Roland Schlotzhauer, prays judgment against defendant Bristol Aerospace for damages as follows:

(A) For actual damages such as are fair and reasonable for the wrongful death of Roland Schlotzhauer;

(B) For punitive damages in such sum as will punish and deter this defendant and deter others from similar conduct in the future;

(C) Plaintiff's costs herein expended; and

(D) For such other and further relief as this Court deems just and proper.

COUNT III
(WARRANTY—BREACH OF EXPRESS WARRANTY BY DEFENDANT BRISTOL AEROSPACE LIMITED)

COMES NOW Plaintiff, as heretofore set out, and for Count III of her cause of action against defendant Bristol Aerospace alleges and states as follows:

58. Plaintiff hereby incorporates by reference, as though fully set out herein, paragraphs 1 through 57, inclusive of this Petition at Law.

59. Defendant Bristol Aerospace sold the Wire Strike Protection System and/or provided or installed that product and expressly warranted that it would protect the helicopter and its occupants from inadvertent wire contact during flight.

60. Plaintiff's deceased, Roland Schlotzhauer, as a passenger in the subject helicopter, was an individual who could reasonably have been expected to use or be affected by the use of the Wire Strike Protection System and was injured by breach of the warranty.

61. Defendant Bristol Aerospace warranted, among other things, that the subject Wire Strike Protection System would provide a "measure of protection" to the helicopter in the event of an inadvertent contact with horizontally strung wires or cables and warranted and/or represented that the windshield center guide bar of the system contained an embedded or hacksaw blade, which were matters represented to, understood by and relied upon by the purchaser.

62. Defendant Bristol Aerospace knew or reasonably should have known that the subject helicopter would carry passengers who would reasonably expect that any and all safety devices would be installed and warranted for their benefit. Moreover, Plaintiff's deceased was intended by the contracting party to benefit from the warranty and were expressly third-party beneficiaries of any and all such warranties made, represented, or extended by defendant Bristol Aerospace.

63. The Wire Strike Protection System did not conform to the express warranty.

64. The breach of the express warranty was a proximate cause of the Plaintiff's damages.

65. The Wire Strike Protection System was expected to and did reach the ultimate user or consumer without substantial change in condition such that the defect complained of existed at the time of sale.

66. Plaintiff's deceased was killed as a direct and proximate result of the breach of express warranty as set forth herein.

67. The amount in controversy exceeds the minimum jurisdictional amount required by this Court.

68. Plaintiff suffered damages by reason of the death of her husband as more fully set out herein.

WHEREFORE, Plaintiff Kathryn L. Schlotzhauer, Administrator of the Estate of Roland Schlotzhauer, prays judgment against defendant Bristol Aerospace for damages as follows:

(A) For actual damages such as are fair and reasonable for the wrongful death of Roland Schlotzhauer;

(B) For Plaintiff's costs herein expended; and

(C) For such other and further relief as this Court deems just and proper.

COUNT IV
(WARRANTY—BREACH OF IMPLIED WARRANTY OF FITNESS FOR PARTICULAR PURPOSE BY DEFENDANT BRISTOL AEROSPACE LIMITED)

COMES NOW Plaintiff, as heretofore set out, and for Count IV of her cause of action against defendant Bristol Aerospace alleges and states as follows:

69. Plaintiff hereby incorporates by reference, as though fully set out herein, paragraphs 1 through 68, inclusive of this Petition at Law.

70. At the time of the sale, defendant Bristol Aerospace had reason to know the particular purpose of the Wire Strike Protection System as installed on the subject helicopter.

71. Defendant Bristol Aerospace had reason to know that occupants of the helicopter were relying on the defendant's skill or judgment to select, furnish, or install the subject Wire Strike Protection System.

72. Defendant Bristol Aerospace warranted, among other things, that the subject Wire Strike Protection System would provide a "measure of protection" to the helicopter in the event of an inadvertent contact with horizontally strung wires or cables and warranted and/or represented that the windshield center guide bar of the system contained an embedded or hacksaw blade, which were matters represented to, understood by and relied upon by the purchaser.

73. The purchaser of the Wire Strike Protection System relied upon the defendant's skill or judgment in selecting, furnishing, and installing the subject device.

74. Plaintiff's deceased, as a passenger in the subject helicopter, was a person whom defendant should expect or may reasonably be expected to use, consume or be affected by the product in question and was injured by breach of the warranty.

75. The Wire Strike Protection System as selected, furnished, supplied, sold, or installed by defendant Bristol Aerospace was not fit for the particular purpose.

76. The failure of the Wire Strike Protection System to fit the particular purpose was a proximate cause of the Plaintiff's damages.

77. Defendant Bristol Aerospace was given appropriate notice and/or obtained knowledge of the breach within a reasonable time.

78. The Wire Strike Protection System was expected to and did reach the ultimate user or consumer without substantial change in condition such that the defect complained of existed at the time of sale.

79. Plaintiff's deceased was killed as a proximate cause of the subject device not being fit for the particular purpose.

80. Plaintiff's deceased was killed as a direct and proximate result of the breach of the implied warranty of fitness for particular purpose by defendant Bristol Aerospace.

81. The amount in controversy exceeds the minimum jurisdictional amount required by this Court.

82. Plaintiff suffered damages by reason of the death of her husband as more fully set out herein.

WHEREFORE, Plaintiff Kathryn L. Schlotzhauer, Administrator of the Estate of Roland Schlotzhauer, prays judgment against defendant Bristol Aerospace for damages as follows:

(A) For actual damages such as are fair and reasonable for the wrongful death of Roland Schlotzhauer;

(B) For Plaintiff's costs herein expended; and

(C) For such other and further relief as this Court deems just and proper.

COUNT V
(WARRANTY—BREACH OF IMPLIED WARRANTY OF MERCHANTABILITY BY DEFENDANT BRISTOL AEROSPACE LIMITED)

COMES NOW Plaintiff, as heretofore set out, and for Count V of her cause of action against defendant Bristol Aerospace alleges and states as follows:

83. Plaintiff hereby incorporates by reference, as though fully set out herein, paragraphs 1 through 82, inclusive of this Petition at Law.

84. Defendant Bristol Aerospace at all relevant times was a merchant which dealt in the specific products or services of the kind in question and who held itself out as having knowledge or skills specific or particular to the practices or products or services in question whose knowledge or skill specific to the practices, products or services in question may be attributed

to them by their employment of an agent or other intermediary who by their occupation held themselves out as having such knowledge or skill.

85. Defendant Bristol Aerospace at the time of the sale, supply, or installation of the subject Wire Strike Protection System was a merchant.

86. Defendant Bristol Aerospace warranted, among other things, that the subject Wire Strike Protection System would provide a "measure of protection" to the helicopter in the event of an inadvertent contact with horizontally strung wires or cables and warranted and/or represented that the windshield center guide bar of the system contained an embedded or hacksaw blade, which were matters represented to, understood by and relied upon by the purchaser.

87. The Wire Strike Protection System as provided and/or installed was not merchantable.

88. Appropriate notice was given to Bristol Aerospace and/or defendant obtained sufficient knowledge within a reasonable time of the event.

89. The lack of merchantability of the subject Wire Strike Protection System was a proximate cause of the Plaintiff's damages.

90. Plaintiff's deceased, Roland Schlotzhauer, as a passenger in the subject helicopter, was an individual who could reasonably have been expected to use or be affected by the use of the Wire Strike Protection System and was injured by breach of the warranty.

91. The Wire Strike Protection System was expected to and did reach the ultimate user or consumer without substantial change in condition such that the defect complained of existed at the time of sale.

92. Plaintiff's deceased was killed as a proximate result of the lack of merchantability of the subject product.

93. The amount in controversy exceeds the minimum jurisdictional amount required by this Court.

94. Plaintiff suffered damages by reason of the death of her husband as more fully set out herein.

WHEREFORE, Plaintiff Kathryn L. Schlotzhauer, Administrator of the Estate of Roland Schlotzhauer, prays judgment against defendant Bristol Aerospace for damages as follows:

(A) For actual damages such as are fair and reasonable for the wrongful death of Roland Schlotzhauer;

(B) For Plaintiff's costs herein expended; and

(C) For such other and further relief as this Court deems just and proper.

COUNT VI

(NEGLIGENCE—FAILURE OF DEFENDANT BRISTOL AEROSPACE LIMITED TO USE ORDINARY CARE TO DESIGN AND MANUFACTURE AIRCRAFT PARTS)

COMES NOW Plaintiff, as heretofore set out, and for Count VI of her cause of action against defendant Bristol Aerospace Limited alleges and states as follows:

95. Plaintiff hereby incorporates by reference, as though fully set out herein, paragraphs 1 through 94, inclusive of this Petition at Law.

96. Defendant Bristol Aerospace designed, manufactured, assembled, supplied, distributed, or sold the aforementioned Wire Strike Protection System (WSPS) and/or related component parts used therein in the course of its business.

97. Defendant Bristol Aerospace held itself out as an entity which could carefully and competently design, manufacture, select materials for, design maintenance programs for, inspect, supply, distribute, and sell its WSPS for use in helicopters.

98. Defendant Bristol Aerospace had a duty to use that degree of care that an ordinarily careful and prudent designer, manufacturer, and seller of helicopter parts would use under the same or similar circumstances.

99. Defendant Bristol Aerospace knew or by using ordinary care should have known of the potential of such dangerous condition as was created by its failure to properly design, manufacture, and sell safe helicopter parts in the following particulars:

(a) The Wire Strike Protection System lacked a serrated hacksaw blade embedded along the length of the windshield center guide bar which was designed to cut small, weak and brittle utility wires such as those struck by the subject helicopter on June 30, 2006;

(b) The Wire Strike Protection System failed to protect the helicopter from crashing upon impact with relatively small, weak, and brittle utility wires;

(c) The Wire Strike Protection System permitted wires to be severed due to tensile load which could affect the pitch of the helicopter and not due to any cutting action of the system itself;

(d) The Wire Strike Protection System failed to protect the main rotor mast and helicopter flight controls from contact with utility wires;

(e) The Wire Strike Protection System was not appropriate for use on the subject aircraft;

(f) The Wire Strike Protection System was re-designed and modified so as to be less safe, less effective, and less able to provide protection from foreseeable contact with horizontally strung wires;

(g) The Wire Strike Protection System failed to conform to the original patent of said system which incorporated a serrated cutting edge on the windshield center bar;

(h) The Wire Strike Protection System failed to utilize any cutting surface or edge along the length of the windshield center guide bar for the purpose of cutting or weakening impacted utility wires;

(i) The Wire Strike Protection System lacked a method to guide wire into the cutter jaws without creating high forces on the forward flight of the helicopter such as to deflect the helicopter downward and further exposing non-protected areas of the helicopter to wire strike;

(j) The Wire Strike Protection System failed to protect a critical area of the helicopter between the top of the upper guide bar and the rotating main rotors such that wires were permitted to enter a highly sensitive and vulnerable location of the helicopter;

(k) The Wire Strike Protection System as designed had an improper guide system on top of the windshield;

(l) The Wire Strike Protection System failed to protect an unreasonably large area and left exposed critical components for helicopter flight;

(m) The Wire Strike Protection System failed to utilize a specific and separate protective device which was technologically feasible and safer for the express purpose of protecting the main rotor mast and flight controls from inadvertent wire strike;

(n) The Wire Strike Protection System was placed in the U.S. marketplace without proper testing or in-field usage; and

(o) The Wire Strike Protection System provided a false sense of security to pilots operating helicopters with that system to the extent that it induced risky and unsafe flight operation.

100. Plaintiff's decedent was killed as a direct and proximate result of the negligence and carelessness of defendant Bristol Aerospace as further set out above.

101. The amount in controversy exceeds the minimum jurisdictional amount required by this Court.

102. Plaintiff suffered damages by reason of the death of her husband as more fully set out herein.

WHEREFORE, Plaintiff Kathryn L. Schlotzhauer, Administrator of the Estate of Roland Schlotzhauer, prays judgment against defendant Bristol Aerospace for damages as follows:

(A) For actual damages such as are fair and reasonable for the wrongful death of Roland Schlotzhauer;

(B) For punitive damages in such sum as will punish and deter this defendant and deter others from similar conduct in the future;

(C) For Plaintiff's costs herein expended; and

(D) For such other and further relief as this Court deems just and proper.

COUNT VII
(NEGLIGENCE—DEFENDANT THE FINAL SEASON, INC.'S FAILURE TO USE ORDINARY CARE IN UTILIZING AERIAL CINEMATOGRAPHY)

COMES NOW Plaintiff, as heretofore set out, and for Count VII of her cause of action against defendant alleges and states as follows:

103. Plaintiff hereby incorporates by reference, as though fully set out herein, paragraphs 1 through 102, inclusive of this Petition at Law.

104. Defendant The Final Season, Inc., by and through its agents and employees, had a duty to use that degree of care that an ordinarily careful and prudent motion picture production company would use under the same or similar circumstances in using aerial cinematography.

105.Defendant The Final Season, Inc. was negligent and in breach of its duties of due care as follows:

(a) The Final Season, Inc. failed to ensure the safety of Plaintiff's deceased during the filming of the scenes of the subject motion picture "The Final Season;"

(b) The Final Season, Inc. used unsafe, improper, and hazardous methods and procedures in the manner of filming the scenes for the subject motion picture, including the scenes for which Plaintiff's deceased, Roland Schlotzhauer, was to film;

(c) The Final Season, Inc. failed to hire a competent, professional pilot to operate aircraft in the filming of the aerial scenes for the subject motion picture;

(d) The Final Season, Inc. failed to evaluate the flight training, experience, and ability of defendant Green;

(e) The Final Season, Inc. instructed the pilot, Richard Green, to operate the aircraft in an unsafe manner;

(f) The Final Season, Inc. instructed the pilot, Richard Green to fly too closely to utility wires and to the ground;

(g) The Final Season, Inc. selected a dangerous and unsafe location for the intended aerial filming;

(h) The Final Season, Inc. failed to provide a ground safety contact or observer;

(i) The Final Season, Inc. failed to provide for or insist on a ground or aerial survey or reconnaissance of the intended scene of filming;

(j) The Final Season, Inc. permitted the aerial filming to proceed without prior confirmation that an aerial or ground reconnaissance of the flight path had been performed;

(k) The Final Season, Inc. failed to inform the pilot as to the presence of utility wires in the flight path for the intended filming wherein its employees had actual knowledge of their presence;

(l) The Final Season, Inc. failed to provide the pilot in advance with the proper flight path, film plan, film location and/or shot list;

(m) The Final Season, Inc. failed to require and administer complete and appropriate safety meetings and briefings prior to the subject helicopter flight;

(n) The Final Season, Inc. should have realized their inexperience and lack of qualifications for coordinating, producing, conducting or coordinating aerial cinematography and should not have engaged in the subject filming;

(o) The Final Season, Inc. failed to provide for a safety director or safety coordinator on site for purposes of assessing the safety conditions and hazards as to the uses of aircraft for aerial cinematography;

(p) The Final Season, Inc. failed to hire a location manager to properly plan, scout, photograph, and obtain all necessary governmental permits for the aerial photography sequence; and

(q) The Final Season, Inc. failed to survey the intended scene in advance of filming to determine the existence of any potential hazards, risks, or dangers.

106. Defendant The Final Season, Inc.'s breach of its duty and negligence caused the injuries and damages complained of herein.

107.The amount in controversy exceeds the minimum jurisdictional amount required by this Court.

108.Plaintiff suffered damages by reason of the death of her husband as more fully set out herein.

WHEREFORE, Plaintiff Kathryn L. Schlotzhauer, Administrator of the Estate of Roland Schlotzhauer, prays judgment against defendant The Final Season, Inc. for damages as follows:

(A) For actual damages such as are fair and reasonable for the wrongful death of Roland Schlotzhauer;

(B) For punitive damages in such sum as will punish and deter this defendant and deter others from similar conduct in the future;

(C) For Plaintiff's costs herein expended; and

(D) For such other and further relief as this Court deems just and proper.

COUNT VIII
(NEGLIGENCE—DEFENDANT THE FINAL SEASON INC.'S CAUSING OR AUTHORIZING THE OPERATION OF AIRCRAFT IN A CARELESS OR RECKLESS MANNER)

COMES NOW Plaintiff, as heretofore set out, and for Count VIII of her cause of action against defendant alleges and states as follows:

109.Plaintiff hereby incorporates by reference, as though fully set out herein, paragraphs 1 through 108, inclusive of this Petition at Law.

110. Defendant The Final Season, Inc., by and through its agents and employees, caused or authorized the operation of the subject aircraft by pilot Richard Green for the flight mission which ultimately led to the crash at issue.

111. The subject aircraft was at all times operated with defendant The Final Season, Inc.'s express or implied knowledge and consent for those purposes and objectives held by defendant The Final Season, Inc.

112. The pilot of the subject aircraft operated the aircraft in a careless or reckless manner, to wit, in that:

(a) Defendant Green failed to maintain an adequate and safe altitude;

(b) Defendant Green failed to keep a proper lookout for aerial hazards;

(c) Defendant Green failed to recognize the existence of utility wires in the flight path of the helicopter;

(d) Defendant Green failed to maintain a safe and proper distance from utility power lines;

(e) Defendant Green improperly caused the helicopter to come into contact with utility power lines;

(f) Defendant Green failed to obtain the intended flight path and/or location of the aerial filming prior to flight;

(g) Defendant Green failed to properly follow the generally accepted standards of care in providing aerial cinematography services;

(h) Defendant Green failed to properly survey by aerial reconnaissance or ground reconnaissance or both the intended scene in advance of the actual filming to determine the existence of any potential hazards, risks, or dangers;

(i) Defendant Green failed to avoid impact of the helicopter into overhead power lines;

(j) Defendant Green caused the aircraft to crash at said location; and

(k) Defendant Green supplied, furnished and equipped his helicopter with an unsafe, ineffective and dangerous Wire Strike Protection System.

113. By operation of Iowa law, defendant The Final Season, Inc. is responsible for damages caused by the negligence, carelessness, or recklessness of the aircraft pilot in that on the occasion in question the subject aircraft and/or pilot Richard Green were hired or chartered by defendant The Final Season, Inc. and the aircraft was operated and used with its knowledge and consent.

114. Defendant The Final Season, Inc. caused or authorized defendant Richard Green to pilot the subject helicopter.

115. Plaintiff's decedent Roland Schlotzhauer was killed as a direct and proximate result of The Final Season, Inc.'s causing or authorizing the operation of the aircraft in a careless or reckless manner as further set out above.

116. The amount in controversy exceeds the minimum jurisdictional amount required by this Court.

117. Plaintiff suffered damages by reason of the death of her husband as more fully set out herein.

WHEREFORE, Plaintiff Kathryn L. Schlotzhauer, as Administrator of the Estate of Roland Schlotzhauer, prays judgment against defendant The Final Season, Inc. for damages as follows:

(A) For actual damages such as are fair and reasonable for the wrongful death of Roland Schlotzhauer;

(B) For punitive damages in such sum as will punish and deter this defendant and deter others from similar conduct in the future;

(C) For Plaintiff's costs herein expended; and

(D) For such other and further relief as this Court deems just and proper.

COUNT IX
(NEGLIGENCE—VICARIOUS LIABILITY OF DEFENDANT THE FINAL SEASON, INC. FOR DEFENDANT RICHARD GREEN'S FAILURE TO USE ORDINARY CARE)

COMES NOW Plaintiff, as heretofore set out, and for Count IX of her cause of action against defendant alleges and states as follows:

118. Plaintiff hereby incorporates by reference, as though fully set out herein, paragraphs 1 through 117, inclusive of this Petition at Law.

119. Defendant The Final Season, Inc. had a duty to possess and use that degree of care that an ordinarily careful and prudent company in defendant's business would use under the same or similar circumstances.

120. Defendant Richard Green had a duty to possess and use that degree of care that an ordinarily careful and prudent pilot would use under the same or similar circumstances while piloting the subject helicopter.

121. Defendant The Final Season, Inc. is vicariously liable for any and all actions of defendant Richard Green in his negligent and careless piloting of the subject helicopter by reason of its principal and agent relationship with defendant Richard Green and further:

(a) Defendant The Final Season, Inc. selected defendant Richard Green for the particular task of providing aircraft services for its film production;

(b) Defendant The Final Season, Inc. expressly authorized use of the subject helicopter for carrying out business on its behalf; and

(c) Defendant The Final Season, Inc. expressly authorized defendant Richard Green to pilot the subject helicopter for carrying out business on its behalf.

122. Accordingly, defendant The Final Season, Inc. is vicariously liable for the negligence and carelessness of defendant Richard Green as follows:

(a) Defendant Green failed to maintain an adequate and safe altitude;

(b) Defendant Green failed to keep a proper lookout for aerial hazards;

(c) Defendant Green failed to recognize the existence of utility wires in the flight path of the helicopter;

(d) Defendant Green failed to maintain a safe and proper distance from utility power lines;

(e) Defendant Green improperly caused the helicopter to come into contact with utility power lines;

(f) Defendant Green failed to obtain the intended flight path and/or location of the aerial filming prior to flight;

(g) Defendant Green failed to properly follow the generally accepted standards of care in providing aerial cinematography services;

(h) Defendant Green failed to properly survey by aerial reconnaissance or ground reconnaissance or both the intended scene in advance of the actual filming to determine the existence of any potential hazards, risks, or dangers;

(i) Defendant Green failed to avoid impact of the helicopter into overhead power lines;

(j) Defendant Green caused the aircraft to crash at said location; and

(k) Defendant Green supplied, furnished and equipped his helicopter with an unsafe, ineffective and dangerous Wire Strike Protection System.

123. Defendant The Final Season, Inc. was further negligent in failing to evaluate the flight training, specific experience and ability of defendant Green.

124. Plaintiff's decedent Roland Schlotzhauer was killed as a direct and proximate result of the negligence and carelessness of defendant The Final Season, Inc. as further set out above.

125. The amount in controversy exceeds the minimum jurisdictional amount required by this Court.

126. Plaintiff suffered damages by reason of the death of her husband as more fully set out herein.

WHEREFORE, Plaintiff Kathryn L. Schlotzhauer, Administrator of the Estate of Roland Schlotzhauer, prays judgment against defendant The Final Season, Inc. for damages as follows:

(A) For actual damages such as are fair and reasonable for the wrongful death of Roland Schlotzhauer;

(B) For punitive damages in such sum as will punish and deter this defendant and deter others from similar conduct in the future;

(C) For Plaintiff's costs herein expended; and

(D) For such other and further relief as this Court deems just and proper.

COUNT X

(NEGLIGENCE—DEFENDANT RITEL COPTER SERVICE'S VICARIOUS LIABILITY FOR RICHARD GREEN'S FAILURE TO USE ORDINARY CARE IN PILOTING THE SUBJECT AIRCRAFT)

COMES NOW Plaintiff, as heretofore set out, and for Count X of her cause of action against defendant alleges and states as follows:

127. Plaintiff hereby incorporates by reference, as though fully set out herein, paragraphs 1 through 126, inclusive of this Petition at Law.

128. Defendant Ritel owned, operated, maintained, and serviced the subject Bell helicopter and employed Richard Green as a pilot for the subject flight.

129. On June 30, 2006, defendant Green was a licensed pilot who flew, maintained and serviced the subject helicopter. Defendant Green was piloting the subject helicopter at the time of the crash.

130. Defendant Richard Green held himself out as a person who could carefully and competently pilot or otherwise provide safe air transportation.

131. Defendant Richard Green had a duty to use that degree of care that an ordinarily careful and prudent pilot would use under the same or similar circumstances.

132. Defendant Richard Green breached that duty and was negligent by failing to maintain control of the aircraft in flight, causing the helicopter to strike overhead power lines and crash at said location, thereby causing the injuries and damages complained of herein, and was further negligent for reasons including, but not limited, to the following:

(a) Defendant Green failed to maintain an adequate and safe altitude;

(b) Defendant Green failed to keep a proper lookout for aerial hazards;

(c) Defendant Green failed to recognize the existence of utility wires in the flight path of the helicopter;

(d) Defendant Green failed to maintain a safe and proper distance from utility power lines;

(e) Defendant Green improperly caused the helicopter to come into contact with utility power lines;

(f) Defendant Green failed to obtain the intended flight path and/or location of the aerial filming prior to flight;

(g) Defendant Green supplied, furnished and equipped his helicopter with an unsafe, ineffective and dangerous Wire Strike Protection System;

(h) Defendant Green failed to properly follow the generally accepted standards of care in providing aerial cinematography services;

(i) Defendant Green failed to properly survey by aerial reconnaissance or ground reconnaissance or both the intended scene in advance of the actual filming to determine the existence of any potential hazards, risks, or dangers;

(j) Defendant Green failed to avoid impact of the helicopter into overhead power lines; and

(k) Defendant Green caused the aircraft to crash at said location.

133. Defendant Ritel Copter Services is responsible for defendant Green's conduct under the doctrine of respondent superior and as the operator of the aircraft pursuant to Iowa law.

134. Plaintiff, as heretofore set forth, suffered damages as a direct and proximate result of said negligence resulting in the death of Roland Schlotzhauer.

135. The amount in controversy exceeds the minimum jurisdictional amount required by this Court.

136. Plaintiff suffered damages by reason of the death of her husband as more fully set out herein.

WHEREFORE, Plaintiff Kathryn L. Schlotzhauer, Administrator of the Estate of Roland Schlotzhauer, prays judgment against defendant Ritel Copter Services for damages as follows:

(A) For actual damages such as are fair and reasonable for the wrongful death of Roland Schlotzhauer;

(B) For punitive damages in such sum as will punish and deter this defendant and deter others from similar conduct in the future;

(C) For Plaintiff's costs herein expended; and

(D) For such other and further relief as this Court deems just and proper.

COUNT XI
(NEGLIGENCE—DEFENDANT RICHARD GREEN'S FAILURE TO USE ORDINARY CARE IN PROVIDING AIRCRAFT SERVICES AND IN PILOTING THE SUBJECT AIRCRAFT)

COMES NOW Plaintiff, as heretofore set out, and for Count XI of her cause of action against defendant alleges and states as follows:

137. Plaintiff hereby incorporates by reference, as though fully set out herein, paragraphs 1 through 136, inclusive of this Petition at Law.

138. On June 30, 2006, defendant Green was the pilot who flew the subject helicopter. Defendant Green was piloting the subject helicopter at the time of the crash.

139. Defendant Richard Green held himself out as a person who could carefully and competently pilot or otherwise provide safe air transportation.

140. Defendant Richard Green had a duty to use that degree of care that an ordinarily careful and prudent pilot would use under the same or similar circumstances.

141. Defendant Richard Green breached that duty and was negligent by failing to maintain control of the aircraft in flight, causing the helicopter to strike overhead power lines and crash at said location, thereby causing the injuries and damages complained of herein, and was further negligent for reasons including, but not limited, to the following:

(a) Defendant Green failed to maintain an adequate and safe altitude;

(b) Defendant Green failed to keep a proper lookout for aerial hazards;

(c) Defendant Green failed to recognize the existence of utility wires in the flight path of the helicopter;

(d) Defendant Green failed to maintain a safe and proper distance from utility power lines;

(e) Defendant Green improperly caused the helicopter to come into contact with utility power lines;

(f) Defendant Green failed to obtain the intended flight path and/or location of the aerial filming prior to flight;

(g) Defendant Green failed to properly follow the generally accepted standards of care in providing aerial cinematography services;

(h) Defendant Green failed to properly survey by aerial reconnaissance or ground reconnaissance or both the intended scene in advance of the actual filming to determine the existence of any potential hazards, risks, or dangers;

(i) Defendant Green failed to avoid impact of the helicopter into overhead power lines;

(j) Defendant Green caused the aircraft to crash at said location; and

(k) Defendant Green supplied, furnished and equipped his helicopter with an unsafe, ineffective and dangerous Wire Strike Protection System.

142. Plaintiff, as heretofore set forth, suffered damages as a direct and proximate result of said negligence resulting in the death of Roland Schlotzhauer.

143. The amount in controversy exceeds the minimum jurisdictional amount required by this Court.

144. Plaintiff suffered damages by reason of the death of her husband as more fully set out herein.

WHEREFORE, Plaintiff Kathryn L. Schlotzhauer, Administrator of the Estate of Roland Schlotzhauer, prays judgment against defendant Richard Green for damages as follows:

(A) For actual damages such as are fair and reasonable for the wrongful death of Roland Schlotzhauer;

(B) For punitive damages in such sum as will punish and deter this defendant and deter others from similar conduct in the future;

(C) For Plaintiff's costs herein expended; and

(D) For such other and further relief as this Court deems just and proper.

DEMAND FOR JURY TRIAL

Plaintiff Kathryn L. Schlotzhauer demands trial by jury of the issues herein.

Respectfully submitted,

ROBB & ROBB LLC

BY: _____

GARY C. ROBB
One Kansas City Place
Suite 3900
1200 Main Street
Kansas City, Missouri 64105
Telephone: (816) 474-8080
Facsimile: (816) 474-8081
ATTORNEYS FOR PLAINTIFF

A.4 Sample Complaint 4: Helicopter Mechanic Negligence (Failure to Properly Install and Secure Connection Hardware for Fore/Aft Servo Assembly)

DISTRICT COURT

CLARK COUNTY, NEVADA

* * *

MARY RIGGS, as Personal Representative of the ESTATES OF LOVISH BHANOT and ANUPAMA BHOLA, for the benefit of the ESTATES OF LOVISH BHANOT and ANU-PAMA BHOLA; SUMAN BHANOT, as Next of Kin and Natural Mother of LOVISH BHANOT, deceased, MEERA BHOLA, as Next of Kin and Natural Mother of ANUPAMA BHOLA, deceased, and BALRAJ BHOLA as Next of Kin and Natural Father of ANUPAMA BHOLA, deceased. Plaintiffs, vs. SUNDANCE HELICOPTERS, INC., A Nevada Corporation, Defendant.	CASE NO. A-11-653149-C DEPT. NO. XXVIII **SECOND AMENDED COMPLAINT FOR WRONGFUL DEATH; DEMAND FOR JURY TRIAL AND CONSENT TO SERVICE VIA ELECTRONIC MEANS AND FACSIMILE** **ARBITRATION EXEMPTION CLAIMED: EXTRAORDINARY RELIEF**

Plaintiffs MARY RIGGS, as Personal Representative of the ESTATES OF LOVISH BHANOT and ANUPAMA BHOLA, for the benefit of the ESTATES OF LOVISH BHANOT and ANUPAMA BHOLA; SUMAN BHANOT, as Next of Kin and Natural Mother of LOVISH BHANOT, deceased, and MEERA BHOLA, as Next of Kin and Natural Mother of ANUPAMA BHOLA, deceased, for their causes of action against the above-captioned Defendant, state and allege as follows:

INTRODUCTION PERTAINING TO ALL CAUSES OF ACTION

PLAINTIFFS

1. Plaintiff MARY RIGGS is a resident of and domiciled in the State of Nevada and is the duly appointed Personal Representative of the ESTATES OF LOVISH BHANOT and ANUPAMA BHOLA, and is entitled to maintain this action.

2. Plaintiff Suman Bhanot is a resident of Gurgaon, India. Suman Bhanot is next of kin and the natural mother of Lovish Bhanot who was killed in a helicopter crash which occurred on December 7, 2011, near Lake Mead. Her son, Lovish Bhanot, died from injuries sustained in the helicopter crash.

3. Plaintiff Meera Bhola is a resident of New Delhi, India. Meera Bhola is next of kin and the natural mother of Anupama Bhola who was killed in a helicopter crash which occurred on December 7, 2011, near Lake Mead. Her daughter, Anupama Bhola, died from injuries sustained in the helicopter crash.

4. Plaintiff Balraj Bhola is a resident of New Delhi, India. Balraj Bhola is next of kin and the natural father of Anupama Bhola who was killed in a helicopter crash which occurred on December 7, 2011, near Lake Mead. His daughter, Anupama Bhola, died from injuries sustained in the helicopter crash.

DEFENDANT

DEFENDANT SUNDANCE HELICOPTERS, INC.

5.   Defendant Sundance Helicopters, Inc. (hereinafter referred to as Defendant Sundance) is a Nevada Corporation doing business in the State of Nevada.

6.   Defendant Sundance is engaged in the business of operating, maintaining, servicing and distributing helicopters for uses including, but not limited to, sightseeing and touring activities.

7.   At all times material hereto, Defendant Sundance operated, maintained, serviced, and distributed touring helicopters, in particular the subject helicopter, throughout these United States, including the State of Nevada, to be used by a foreseeable class of persons, consisting of those persons who may be passengers on touring helicopters, of which Lovish Bhanot and Anupama Bhola were members.

8.   At all times material hereto, Defendant Sundance was acting by and through its agents, servants, and/or employees, each of whom were acting in the course and scope of their employment with this defendant.

IDENTIFICATION OF AIRCRAFT

9.   This air crash involves a 1989 Eurocopter AS350 B2 helicopter, Registration Number N37SH, serial number 2300. The said helicopter was owned by Defendant Sundance, and operated in the course of a sightseeing business.

GENERAL ALLEGATIONS

10.   On or about December 6, 2011, a mechanic for Sundance Helicopters, Inc. performed a replacement of the fore/aft servo of the Sundance helicopter, Registration Number N37SH.

11.   The next day, December 7, 2011, Lovish Bhanot and Anupama Bhola were passengers in the 1989 Eurocopter AS350 B2 helicopter on a "Twilight tour" sightseeing trip of Hoover Dam and the Lake Mead reservoir on the Colorado River.

12.   At approximately 4:30 p.m., the subject helicopter crashed in mountainous terrain approximately 14 miles east of Las Vegas between Lake Mead and Henderson, burned, and killed all on board, including Lovish Bhanot and Anupama Bhola.

13.   Lovish Bhanot and Anupama Bhola died from thermal injuries and blunt force trauma which they received from the helicopter crash.

14.   Pursuant to N.R.S. 41.085., damages of the heirs and the Estate are the following:

a.   SUMAN BHANOT, as Next of Kin and Natural Mother of LOVISH BHANOT has suffered related grief, sorrow, loss of probable support, companionship, society, comfort and consortium. All of these damages have been incurred in the past and will continue in the future.

b.   MEERA BHOLA as Next of Kin and Natural Mother of ANUPAMA BHOLA has suffered related grief, sorrow, loss of probable support, companionship, society, comfort and consortium. All of these damages have been incurred in the past and will continue in the future.

c.   BALRAJ BHOLA as Next of Kin and Natural Father of ANUPAMA BHOLA has suffered related grief, sorrow, loss of probable support, companionship, society, comfort and consortium. All of these damages have been incurred in the past and will continue in the future.

d.   The ESTATE OF LOVISH BHANOT has incurred funeral expenses.

e.   The ESTATE OF ANUPAMA BHOLA has incurred funeral expenses.

FIRST CAUSE OF ACTION
(NEGLIGENCE OF DEFENDANT SUNDANCE – VICARIOUS LIABILITY FOR LANDON NIELD'S FAILURE TO USE ORDINARY CARE IN PILOTING THE SUBJECT HELICOPTER - WRONGFUL DEATH OF LOVISH BHANOT AND ANUPAMA BHOLA)

15.   Plaintiffs hereby incorporate by reference, as though fully set out herein, each and every allegation of the preceding paragraphs.

16. Defendant Sundance held itself out as an entity, which could carefully and competently provide and maintain safe helicopter tours which were utilized in the course of its operations.

17. That Defendant Sundance had a duty to use that degree of care that ordinarily careful and prudent owners, supervisors, and operators of a helicopter tour business would use under the same or similar circumstances.

18. Defendant Sundance had a duty to use that degree of care that an ordinarily careful and prudent pilot would use under the same or similar circumstances.

19. Defendant Sundance is vicariously liable for any and all actions of Landon Nield as to his negligent and careless piloting, pre-flight inspection and operation of the subject helicopter by reason of its principal and agent relationship with defendant Sundance.

20. Landon Nield was negligent in the following respects:

a. Pilot Nield failed to perform a proper pre-flight inspection;

b. Pilot Nield failed to maintain proper control of the helicopter in-flight;

c. Pilot Nield failed to properly avoid natural obstacles in the flight path;

d. Pilot Nield failed keep a safe distance between the helicopter and natural obstacles;

e. Pilot Nield failed to operate the helicopter in a safe manner;

f. Pilot Nield failed to follow the designated flight path; and

g. Pilot Nield failed to properly respond to an in-flight loss of control.

21. Defendant Sundance's breach of its duty and negligence caused the injuries and damages complained of herein and Plaintiffs' deceased, Lovish Bhanot and Anupama Bhola were killed as a direct result of the conduct of Landon Nield for which defendant Sundance is vicariously liable in all respects.

22. That said Defendant breached that duty and was negligent by, but not limited to, failing to properly and adequately monitor and supervise the conduct and activities of their business and/or related employee, causing the helicopter to crash at said location, thereby causing the injuries and damages complained of herein.

23. That as a direct and proximate result of the aforesaid negligence and carelessness on the part of said defendant, Lovish Bhanot and Anupama Bhola were killed.

24. By virtue of Lovish Bhanot"s and Anupama Bhola's untimely death, Plaintiffs are lawfully entitled to such damages as are fair and just for the death and loss thus occasioned, including but not limited to the pecuniary losses suffered by reason of the death, grief, sorrow, funeral expenses, and the reasonable value of the services, consortium, companionship, comfort, society, instruction, guidance, counsel, training, and support of which Plaintiffs have been deprived by reason of such death, further including, loss of probable support, past and future lost income, household services, and other value of benefits which would have been provided by the deceased.

25. Plaintiffs further claim such damages as the decedents may have suffered between the time of injury and the time of death and for the recovery of which the decedents might have maintained an action had death not ensued including, but not limited to, mental anguish, physical disability, conscious pain and suffering, pre-impact terror, disfigurement, and further considering the aggravating circumstances attendant upon the fatal injury.

SECOND CAUSE OF ACTION
(NEGLIGENCE OF DEFENDANT SUNDANCE – FAILURE TO USE ORDINARY CARE IN PROVIDING PROPER AND SAFE AIRCRAFT AND AIRCRAFT SERVICES - WRONGFUL DEATH OF LOVISH BHANOT AND ANUPAMA BHOLA)

26. Plaintiffs hereby incorporate by reference, as though fully set out herein, each and every allegation of the preceding paragraphs.

27. Defendant Sundance held itself out as an entity, which could carefully and competently provide and maintain safe helicopter tours which were utilized in the course of its operations.

28. That Defendant Sundance had a duty to use that degree of care that ordinarily careful and prudent owners, supervisors, and operators of a helicopter tour business would use under the same or similar circumstances.

29. Defendant Sundance had a duty to use that degree of care that an ordinarily careful and prudent company would use under the same or similar circumstances.

30. Defendant Sundance was negligent in its duties as follows:

a. Defendant Sundance failed to have in place a policy for keeping a safe distance between the helicopter and natural obstacles;

b. Defendant Sundance failed to provide proper training to its pilots;

c. Defendant Sundance failed to properly and adequately monitor and supervise the contact and activities of their business and/or employee;

d. Defendant Sundance failed to properly maintain the subject aircraft;

e. Defendant Sundance failed to follow the manufacturer's reuse guidelines relating to self-locking nuts which led to the repeated improper reuse of degraded nuts on its helicopters;

f. Defendant Sundance failed to properly inspect the fore/aft servo hardware prior to installation;

g. Defendant Sundance failed to properly install the split pin;

h. Defendant Sundance failed to hire and train a qualified mechanic to perform the work on the fore/aft servo;

i. Defendant Sundance failed to have in place policies and procedures regarding maintenance personnel fatigue;

j. Defendant Sundance failed to have in place policies and procedures regarding personnel duty-time limitations; and

k. Defendant Sundance failed to provide human factors training for maintenance personnel.

31. That as a direct and proximate result of the aforesaid negligence and carelessness on the part of said defendant, Lovish Bhanot and Anupama Bhola were killed.

32. By virtue of Lovish Bhanot's and Anupama Bhola's untimely death, Plaintiffs are lawfully entitled to such damages as are fair and just for the death and loss thus occasioned, including but not limited to the pecuniary losses suffered by reason of the death, grief, sorrow, funeral expenses, and the reasonable value of the services, consortium, companionship, comfort, society, instruction, guidance, counsel, training, and support of which Plaintiffs have been deprived by reason of such death, further including, loss of probable support, past and future lost income, household services, and other value of benefits which would have been provided by the deceased.

33. Plaintiffs further claim such damages as the decedents may have suffered between the time of injury and the time of death and for the recovery of which the decedents might have maintained an action had death not ensued including, but not limited to, mental anguish, physical disability, conscious pain and suffering, pre-impact terror, disfigurement, and further considering the aggravating circumstances attendant upon the fatal injury.

THIRD CAUSE OF ACTION
(NEGLIGENCE OF DEFENDANT SUNDANCE – CAUSING OR AUTHORIZING THE OPERATION OF HELICOPTER IN A CARELESS OR RECKLESS MANNER- WRONGFUL DEATH OF LOVISH BHANOT AND ANUPAMA BHOLA)

34. Plaintiffs hereby incorporate by reference, as though fully set out herein, each and every allegation of the preceding paragraphs.

35. Defendant Sundance held itself out as an entity, which could carefully and competently provide and maintain safe helicopter tours which were utilized in the course of its operations.

36. That Defendant Sundance had a duty to use that degree of care that ordinarily careful and prudent owners, supervisors, and operators of a helicopter tour business would use under the same or similar circumstances.

37. Defendant Sundance operated the aircraft in a negligent, careless or reckless manner to wit, in that:

a. Defendant Sundance failed to have in place a policy for keeping a safe distance between the helicopter and natural obstacles;

b. Defendant Sundance failed to provide proper training to its pilots; and

c. Defendant Sundance failed to properly and adequately monitor and supervise the contact and activities of their business and/or employee;

d. Defendant Sundance failed to properly maintain the subject aircraft;

e. Defendant Sundance failed to follow the manufacturer's reuse guidelines relating to self-locking nuts which led to the repeated improper reuse of degraded nuts on its helicopters;

f. Defendant Sundance failed to properly inspect the fore/aft servo hardware prior to installation;

g. Defendant Sundance failed to properly install the split pin;

h. Defendant Sundance failed to hire and train a qualified mechanic to perform the work on the fore/aft servo;

i. Defendant Sundance failed to have in place policies and procedures regarding maintenance personnel fatigue;

j. Defendant Sundance failed to have in place policies and procedures regarding personnel duty-time limitations; and

k. Defendant Sundance failed to provide human factors training for maintenance personnel.

38. That as a direct and proximate result of the aforesaid negligence and carelessness on the part of said defendant, Lovish Bhanot and Anupama Bhola were killed.

39. By virtue of Lovish Bhanot's and Anupama Bhola's untimely death, Plaintiffs are lawfully entitled to such damages as are fair and just for the death and loss thus occasioned, including but not limited to the pecuniary losses suffered by reason of the death, grief, sorrow, funeral expenses, and the reasonable value of the services, consortium, companionship, comfort, society, instruction, guidance, counsel, training, and support of which Plaintiffs have been deprived by reason of such death, further including, loss of probable support, past and future lost income, household services, and other value of benefits which would have been provided by the deceased.

40. Plaintiffs further claim such damages as the decedents may have suffered between the time of injury and the time of death and for the recovery of which the decedents might have maintained an action had death not ensued including, but not limited to, mental anguish, physical disability, conscious pain and suffering, pre-impact terror, disfigurement, and further considering the aggravating circumstances attendant upon the fatal injury.

FOURTH CAUSE OF ACTION
(AS TO ALL DEFENDANT SUNDANCE - WRONGFUL DEATHS OF LOVISH BHANOT AND ANUPAMA BHOLA)

41. Plaintiffs reallege and replead each and every allegation of the preceding paragraphs as though fully set forth hereunder.

42. That on or about December 7, 2011, Lovish Bhanot and Anupama Bhola died from injuries sustained as a direct and proximate result of the aforesaid negligence of Defendant. That prior to their death, as a direct and proximate result of said negligence, Decedents Lovish Bhanot and Anupama Bhola suffered severe pain and physical and emotional injury, all to their general damages in an amount in excess of TEN THOUSAND DOLLARS ($10,000.00).

43. At the time of the Decedents' death, the Decedents were loving and caring children to their mothers. As a direct and proximate result of the aforementioned negligence of the Defendant, Suman Bhanot and Meera Bhola have suffered severe grief, sorrow, and loss of comfort, society, companionship, and probable support from the Decedents, and have thereby suffered damages in an amount in excess of TEN THOUSAND DOLLARS ($10,000.00).

FIFTH CAUSE OF ACTION
(COMMON CARRIER LIABILITY – FAILURE OF DEFENDANT SUNDANCE HELICOPTERS, INC. TO PROVIDE HIGHEST DEGREE OF CARE IN SUPPLYING SAFE AND AIRWORTHY HELICOPTER)

44. Plaintiffs reallege and replead each and every allegation of the preceding paragraphs as though fully set forth hereunder.

45. Plaintiffs' deceaseds, Lovish Bhanot and Anupama Bhola, were passengers for hire of a helicopter sightseeing tour service controlled, operated, dispatched, and supervised by Defendant Sundance Helicopters, Inc.

46. Defendant Sundance Helicopters, Inc. held itself out as an entity which could safely and competently transport persons purchasing helicopter sightseeing tours.

47. At all times material hereto, Defendant Sundance Helicopters, Inc. was and is a commercial air taxi service carrying passengers who have purchased helicopter sightseeing tours and doing so for hire and for profit as a common carrier.

48. Defendant Sundance Helicopters, Inc. had a duty to Plaintiffs' deceaseds to exercise the highest degree of care and diligence in the operation, management, maintenance, and service of its helicopter tours to be provided to persons within the general public such as Lovish Bhanot and Anupama Bhola and, specifically, the highest degree of care and diligence to provide a safe and airworthy aircraft.

49. Defendant Sundance Helicopters, Inc. failed to provide a reasonably safe aircraft for the use and transport of Plaintiffs' deceaseds thereby breaching its duty to exercise the highest degree of care.

50. Plaintiffs' deceaseds were killed as a direct result and proximate result of Defendant Sundance Helicopters' failure to exercise the highest degree of care in providing a safe helicopter for their use and transport.

SIXTH CAUSE OF ACTION
(APPARENT AUTHORITY AND ESTOPPEL; CORPORATE REPRESENTATION AND OSTENSIBLE AGENCY - - LIABILITY OF DEFENDANT SUNDANCE HELICOPTERS, INC. FOR REPRESENTING TO PUBLIC AND HOLDING ITSELF OUT AS OWNER/OPERATOR OF AIRCRAFT)

51. Plaintiffs reallege and replead each and every allegation of the preceding paragraphs as though fully set forth hereunder.

52. Plaintiffs' deceaseds, Lovish Bhanot and Anupama Bhola, were passengers of a sightseeing tour helicopter controlled, operated, dispatched and supervised by Defendant Sundance Helicopters, Inc., Registration Number N37SH, on the outside of which was prominently labeled and displayed the notation "SUNDANCE."

53. By placing its name on the subject sightseeing tour helicopter and holding itself out as the owner/operator of said aircraft, Defendant Sundance Helicopters is estopped from denying liability or responsibility for any defective conditions or for the negligent acts of others creating a defective condition within said aircraft, notwithstanding any exculpatory agreement which may exist between and among any of the parties.

54. At all times material hereto, Defendant Sundance Helicopters held itself out and represented itself to the public as a commercial air taxi service carrying passengers who purchased sightseeing tours and expressly and impliedly represented that it had authority to so operate, control, dispatch and function as a federally certified air taxi service.

55. By so labeling and prominently displaying its name upon the subject helicopter, Defendant Sundance Helicopters has voluntarily inserted itself into the position of owner/operator of said aircraft with the effect of binding itself and attaching any liability for any defects therein or negligent acts of others creating said defects onto itself.

56. The apparent authority and corporate representation by Defendant Sundance Helicopters representing to the public and holding itself out as the owner/operator of the subject helicopter estops it from denying liability in that defendant created a reliance by others upon the representation that Defendant Sundance Helicopters does control, operate, manage and dispatch the helicopter at issue herein.

57. As a direct and proximate result of the aforementioned actions of Defendant Sundance Helicopters, Inc., Defendant Sundance Helicopters, Inc. is vicariously liable for the actions of others in creating a defective condition and Plaintiffs' deceased was killed as a result of said defective condition of negligent actions.

SEVENTH CAUSE OF ACTION
(PUNITIVE DAMAGES)

58. Plaintiffs reallege and replead each and every allegation of the preceding paragraphs as though fully set forth hereunder.

59. That the aforesaid acts and omissions on the part of Defendant Sundance Helicopters, Inc. constitute malice, oppression, and a conscious disregard of known safety procedures, practices, and policies, thereby entitling Plaintiffs to punitive damages against Defendant Sundance Helicopters, Inc. in an amount to be proven at trial.

WHEREFORE, Plaintiffs MARY RIGGS, as Personal Representative of the ESTATES OF LOVISH BHANOT and ANUPAMA BHOLA, for the benefit of the ESTATES OF LOVISH BHANOT and ANUPAMA BHOLA; SUMAN BHANOT, as Next of Kin and Natural Mother of LOVISH BHANOT, deceased, and MEERA BHOLA, as Next of Kin and Natural Mother of ANUPAMA BHOLA, deceased pray judgment against Defendant Sundance Helicopters, Inc. as follows:

FIRST CAUSE OF ACTION

1. For general damages and loss in an amount in excess of TEN THOUSAND DOLLARS ($10,000.00);

2. For special damages in an amount to be determined at time of trial;
3. For attorney's fees, costs, and pre and post judgment interest; and
4. For such other and further relief as the Court may deem just and proper.

SECOND CAUSE OF ACTION

1. For general damages and loss in an amount in excess of TEN THOUSAND DOLLARS ($10,000.00);
2. For special damages in an amount to be determined at time of trial;
3. For attorney's fees, costs, and pre and post judgment interest; and
4. For such other and further relief as the Court may deem just and proper.

THIRD CAUSE OF ACTION

1. For general damages and loss in an amount in excess of TEN THOUSAND DOLLARS ($10,000.00);
2. For special damages in an amount to be determined at time of trial;
3. For attorney's fees, costs, and pre and post judgment interest; and
4. For such other and further relief as the Court may deem just and proper.

FOURTH CAUSE OF ACTION

1. For general damages and loss in an amount in excess of TEN THOUSAND DOLLARS ($10,000.00);
2. For special damages in an amount to be determined at time of trial;
3. For attorney's fees, costs, and pre and post judgment interest; and
4. For such other and further relief as the Court may deem just and proper.

FIFTH CAUSE OF ACTION

1. For general damages and loss in an amount in excess of TEN THOUSAND DOLLARS ($10,000.00);
2. For special damages in an amount to be determined at time of trial;
3. For attorney's fees, costs, and pre and post judgment interest; and
4. For such other and further relief as the Court may deem just and proper.

SIXTH CAUSE OF ACTION

1. For general damages and loss in an amount in excess of TEN THOUSAND DOLLARS ($10,000.00);
2. For special damages in an amount to be determined at time of trial;
3. For attorney's fees, costs, and pre and post judgment interest; and
4. For such other and further relief as the Court may deem just and proper.

SEVENTH CAUSE OF ACTION

1. For general damages and loss in an amount in excess of TEN THOUSAND DOLLARS ($10,000.00);
2. For special damages in an amount to be determined at time of trial;
3. For attorney's fees, costs, and pre and post judgment interest;
4. For punitive damages in an amount to be determined at trial; and
5. For such other and further relief as the Court may deem just and proper.

DATED: March 14, 2014   ROBB & ROBB LLC

By: _____

GARY C. ROBB

ANITA PORTE ROBB

One Kansas City Place

Suite 3900

1200 Main Street

Kansas City, Missouri 64105

Telephone: (816) 474-8080

Facsimile: (816) 474-8081

E-Mail: gcr@robbrobb.com

E-Mail: apr@robbrobb.com

LAWRENCE J. SMITH

BENSON, BERTOLDO,

BAKER & CARTER

Nevada Bar No. 6505

7408 W. Sahara Avenue

Las Vegas, Nevada 89117

Telephone: (702) 228-2600

Facsimile: (702) 228-2333

E-mail: lawre3@bensonlawyers.com

Attorneys for Plaintiffs

DEMAND FOR JURY TRIAL

Plaintiffs demand trial by jury of the issues herein.

DATED: March 14, 2014   ROBB & ROBB LLC

By: _____

GARY C. ROBB

ANITA PORTE ROBB

One Kansas City Place

Suite 3900

1200 Main Street

Kansas City, Missouri 64105

Telephone: (816) 474-8080

Facsimile: (816) 474-8081

E-Mail: gcr@robbrobb.com

E-Mail: apr@robbrobb.com

A.5 Sample First Set of Interrogatories: Helicopter Engine Failure/Design Defect

IN THE CIRCUIT COURT OF JACKSON COUNTY, MISSOURI
AT KANSAS CITY

JODIE A. LETZ, Individually, and)	
as Guardian Ad Litem and)	
Next Friend of)	
ERIC SCOTT LETZ and)	
CHRISTOPHER SCOTT LETZ,)	
Minor Children,)	
and as Representative and)	
Administratrix of the Estate of)	
SHERRY ANN LETZ, Deceased,)	
)	CASE NO.: _____
PLAINTIFFS,)	
)	CIVIL DOCKET: _____
v.)	
)	DIVISION: _____
TURBOMECA ENGINE CORPORATION,)	
)	
EUROCOPTER INTERNATIONAL)	
(Formerly AEROSPATIALE),)	
)	
AMERICAN EUROCOPTER CORPORATION,)	
)	
ROCKY MOUNTAIN HELICOPTERS, INC.,)	
)	
LIFE FLIGHT SERVICES, INC.,)	
A JOINT VENTURE BETWEEN)	
ST. LUKE'S HOSPITAL and)	
ST. JOSEPH'S HEALTH CENTER)	
ST. LUKE'S HOSPITAL OF KANSAS,)	
)	
ST. JOSEPH HEALTH CENTER OF)	
JACKSON COUNTY, MISSOURI ,)	
)	
_____DEFENDANTS.)	

PLAINTIFFS' FIRST SET OF INTERROGATORIES TO
DEFENDANT TURBOMECA ENGINE CORPORATION

COME NOW Plaintiffs, Jodie A. Letz, individually, and Eric Scott Letz and Christopher Scott Letz, by and through their Guardian Ad Litem and Next Friend, Jodie A. Letz pursuant to Missouri Rules of Civil Procedure, and propound the following First Set of Interrogatories to be answered by an appropriate officer or agent of defendant Turbomeca and not its attorneys, in writing, under oath and according to law.

The interrogatories and requests for production which are included pursuant to Missouri Rules of civil Procedures are to be regarded as continuing, and you are requested to provide, by way of supplementary answers thereto, such additional information or material as you, your counsel, or any other person in your behalf, or subject to your control, may hereafter obtain which will augment or otherwise modify the answers now given to those interrogatories or requests to produce, which has reference to names and addresses of persons having knowledge of discoverable facts, which has reference to the names and addresses of expert witnesses expected to be called at trial, or which corrects those interrogatories or requests to produce the responses to which were incorrect when made or which are now incorrect because of a change in circumstances.

Such supplemental responses are to be filed and served upon the Plaintiffs within fourteen (14) days after receipt of such information, but not later than three (3) weeks preceding the date of trial.

"Identify," when referring to an individual person, means to state his or her full name, present or last-known address and telephone number, present or last-known position and business affiliation, and title of position held and by whom employed at the time of each event, transaction or occurrence hereinafter referred to.

"Identify," when referring to a document, shall mean the date and author, type of document (e.g., letter, memorandum, etc.) or some other means of identifying it. Further, a request for the "description" or "identification" of any document should be understood to include as well a request for the following information:

(a) The name and address of each and every person, as defined below, by whom such "document" was received, to whom it was sent or circulated, or by whom it was received;

(b) The nature and substance of the "document" with sufficient particularity to enable the same to be identified;

(c) The date of the document and the date the document was executed (if different from the date it bears);

(d) Whether you claim any privilege as to such "document," and if so, a precise statement of the facts on which such claim of privilege is based;

(e) The name and address of each and every person who participated in the drafting or creation of the "document;"

(f) The present location and the name and address of the present custodian of the "document;" and

(g) If a "document" was, but no longer is, in your control, the disposition that was made of it, the circumstances surrounding, the authorization for such disposition, and the date or approximate date thereof.

INTERROGATORY NO. 1:

Please state the full name, current complete address, telephone number, and position, capacity, or job title of each person who assisted in answering these interrogatories on behalf of defendant.

ANSWER:

INTERROGATORY NO. 2:

Have you been correctly designated as a party defendant in this cause insofar as the legal description and correct spelling is concerned?

(a) If not, then state how you should properly be designated in an action at law as of May 27, 1993 and at present; and

(b) Is defendant currently a Texas Corporation?

ANSWER:

INTERROGATORY NO. 3:

With respect to the subject 1982 Model A-Star 350-B Air Ambulance Helicopter described in the Petition for Damages and which is at issue in this action, did you provide any component parts including, but not limited to the jet engine and engine assembly of that air ambulance? If your answer is "yes," please provide the following information:

(a) A complete description including part numbers, model numbers, assembly unit, and trade name of any and all components which were incorporated into and part of the subject helicopter on the date of its crash; and

(b) Identify all suppliers of component parts from whom you have purchased, in whole or in part, parts to be incorporated into units or any parts thereof which you supplied.

ANSWER:

INTERROGATORY NO. 4:

Please state which of the named defendants in this action with which you at any time have conducted business and in connection therewith, please state:

(a) The first and last (if not a present business relationship) date of any ongoing business transactions between you and any of the other named defendants;

(b) Please state the nature of the business relationship as between the parties and identify which was your relationship (e.g., vendor/purchaser, lessor/lessee, etc.); and

(c) Identify those individuals in your company with knowledge of the business relationship between you and any of the aforementioned named defendants.

ANSWER:

INTERROGATORY NO. 5:

With respect to the subject helicopter jet engine at issue in this case, please provide the following information:

(a) The original date of design and manufacturer; and

(b) Any and all names by which such engine is known either to you or in the aviation industry.

ANSWER:

INTERROGATORY NO. 6:

Please identify the current custodian and whereabouts of all studies or tests made with respect to the subject jet engine including but not limited to safety and fatigue analysis and consideration of various alternative designs.

ANSWER:

INTERROGATORY NO. 7:

Please set forth a description including identification of equipment, date, crash site, and fatality/injury information, of any and all malfunctions, incidents, accidents, or complaints regardless of whether injury or death ensued associated with use of any helicopter jet engines manufactured, designed, or sold by defendant Turbomeca which are substantially similar to the incidents set forth in this lawsuit.

(a) Please state all of the ways in which this defendant attempts to ascertain the existence of any malfunctions or complaints associated with its engines other than the receipt of legal action; and

(b) Please describe any and all documents reflecting the above and indicate their present location.

ANSWER:

INTERROGATORY NO. 8:

Please identify any and all documents in your possession, custody or control describing any changes to or the reasons for such changes in the design or materials used of the helicopter jet engine design at issue herein, including any component parts therein, subsequent to its original manufacturer and design.

ANSWER:

INTERROGATORY NO. 9:

Please identify any and all documents in your possession, custody, or control relating to any notices directed to you, claims made against you, or lawsuits filed against you wherein it was claimed or alleged that one of your jet engines failed because of any malfunction, maintenance problem, manufacture, inspection, metallurgical problem or corrosion of the guide vanes within one of your jet engines intended for use in any model helicopter and in connection therewith, please state:

    (a) The custodian of any and all such documents in your possession referring or reflecting any such notice, claims, or lawsuits; and

    (b) Set forth and identify any and all such notices, claims, and lawsuits by date, aircraft description, engine part number, location of malfunction, and aircraft owner.

ANSWER:

INTERROGATORY NO. 10:

Please describe any and all bulletins, manuals, written instructions, warnings, procedures, or the like that were:

    (a) Provided with the promotion or sale of the subject jet engine; and

    (b) Subsequently supplied to any owner, operator, or lessor of any of your jet engines such as that used in the subject air ambulance forming the basis for this lawsuit.

ANSWER:

INTERROGATORY NO. 11:

Please detail every lawsuit that has been filed against you (regardless of whether injury or death ensued) wherein it was claimed or alleged that any jet engine supplied by you for use in an air ambulance helicopter malfunctioned, failed, lost power, or contributed to a reportable aviation mishap between 1973 and present, specifically identifying:

    (a) The name, court, docket number of each lawsuit as well as identifying in which lawsuits this defendant gave interrogatories, oral depositions; and

    (b) The identity including name, address, and telephone number of the attorneys representing Plaintiffs in each such matter, as well as whether the case was or has been resolved or settled.

ANSWER:

INTERROGATORY NO. 12:

Please identify each and every person whom you expect to call as an expert witness at trial, stating the general nature of the subject matter upon which he or she is expected to testify.

ANSWER:

INTERROGATORY NO. 13:

For any liability insurance coverage which this defendant held and which will cover the occurrence out of which this loss arises, please state:

    (a) The name and address of each such carrier;

    (b) The policy numbers of each such policy;

    (c) Whether any reservation of the insurer's rights has been declared with respect to a potential dispute in coverage for this loss; and

    (d) Whether the defendant must approve of any settlement entered into by its insurance carrier.

ANSWER:

INTERROGATORY NO. 14:

Please identify any and all engineering change orders made with respect to the jet engine and substantially similar engines as that which was in operation in the subject helicopter. In connection therewith, please set forth the effective date and serial number of any such engineering change order.

ANSWER:

INTERROGATORY NO. 15:

Please set forth the certification history of the helicopter jet engine at issue herein including but not limited to the dates and test results of all developmental ground tests, developmental flight tests, and in connection therewith:

    (a) Please identify the current location of all applications for type certification, ground and flight tests, and all documents related thereto; and

    (b) Please identify the custodian of all such files.

ANSWER:

INTERROGATORY NO. 16:

Please set forth the custodian and current whereabouts of all flight and ground test documentation including, but not limited to, test protocol, field test results, and any videotapes or photographs.

ANSWER:

INTERROGATORY. NO 17:

Please identify the current custodian and whereabouts of all correspondence, communications, or safety notices or bulletins generated by you and forwarded to the National Transportation Safety Board and any such responses, directives, notices, or requests imparted by NTSB to this defendant involving the subject model jet engine at issue in this lawsuit.
ANSWER:

INTERROGATORY NO. 18:

Has this defendant caused to be issued any mechanical reliability reports to the FAA with respect to the jet engine model at issue herein. If the answer is "yes," please state as follows:

(a) The current custodian and whereabouts of any such reports; and

(b) The dates and subject matter of any such reports.

ANSWER:

INTERROGATORY NO. 19:

Has the model jet engine used in the air ambulance which is the subject of this lawsuit at any time been the subject of a service letter or service bulletin generated by this defendant referring or relating to safety, maintenance, use, operation, replacement, inspection, and the like. Please provide the following: If your answer is "yes,"

(a) State the current custodian and whereabouts of any and all such service letters and service bulletins; and

(b) Set forth the dates of all such service letters and service bulletins and the general nature of the subject matter of each.

ANSWER:

INTERROGATORY NO. 20:

Has the FAA or NTSB ever directed you to issue an airworthiness directive with respect to any aspect of the design, manufacture, operation, maintenance, or use of the model jet engine used in the air ambulance at issue in this lawsuit. If your answer is "yes," please set forth the following:

(a) The current custodian and whereabouts of any such airworthiness directives; and

(b) The dates of any such directives including the general subject matter of each.

ANSWER:

INTERROGATORY NO. 21:

Has the FAA or NTSB ever conducted an inquiry into the manufacturer, design, operation, maintenance, or use of the model jet engine used in the subject air ambulance? If your answer is "yes," please set forth the following:

(a) The current custodian and whereabouts of any such inquiries; and

(b) The dates of any such inquiries including the general subject matter of each.

ANSWER:

INTERROGATORY NO. 22:

Has the jet engine model used in the subject air ambulance ever been sold to or utilized by United States military operations? If so, please provide the following information:

(a) The branches of armed services purchasing or utilizing said jet engine and the particular types of helicopters in which it was used; and

(b) Has this defendant ever received from the military any inquiry notice, or complaint related to or concerning design safety, appropriate maintenance, inspection, or use of the jet engine?

ANSWER:

INTERROGATORY NO. 23:

Please identify the following persons with responsibility for the design, testing, and certification of the subject jet engine both originally and at the present time:

(a) Head of engineering;

(b) Project engineer;

(c) Chief of flight operations and testing;

(d) Governmental liaison between defendant and FAA/NTSB; and

(e) Investigating officer for malfunction notices.

ANSWER:

INTERROGATORY NO. 24:

With respect to the jet engine used by the air ambulance at issue in this case, please provide the following information:

(a) To whom was the jet engine originally sold and the date of such sale;

(b) The number of jet engines of this model which have been sold to anyone from its inception;

(c) The number of this model of jet engine which continued to be in operation (to the best extent known by this defendant); and

(d) State the purchase price of the particular helicopter jet engine used in the air ambulance at issue in this action.

ANSWER:

INTERROGATORY NO. 25:

Please state whether there have been any predecessor corporations to this corporation and in connection therewith identify any and all other names by which this defendant has been or is presently known.

ANSWER:

INTERROGATORY NO. 26:

Please identify all of the individuals who have or have had any responsibilities whether administrative, investigative, or engineering, arising out of the aircrash giving rise to this action. In connection therewith, please state the name of each and every such individual and set forth their current positions with the company, date hired, and current employment.

ANSWER:

INTERROGATORY NO. 27:

Please identify all employees of this defendant who were present for the "tear down" of the helicopter jet engine which took place on defendant's premises in Grand Prairie, Texas and in connection therewith, please state:

    (a) The job title or position of every such company employee; and

    (b) The reasons for their presence including their responsibilities and assignments in connection therewith.

ANSWER:

INTERROGATORY NO. 28:

Please identify all non-employees of this defendant who were present for the "tear down" of the helicopter engine which took place on defendant's premises in Grand Prairie, Texas and in connection therewith, please state:

    (a) The job title or governmental position of every such individual; and

    (b) The reasons for their presence including their responsibilities and assignments in connection therewith.

ANSWER:

INTERROGATORY NO. 29:

With respect to the Arriel 1-Bl helicopter jet engine at issue in this case, please state:

    (a) Whether any other company supplied the labyrinth seal between the combustion chamber and power turbine and in connection therewith, please state the complete name of said company and its address; and

    (b) Whether any companies supplied any of the guide vanes lining the inside of the engine and setting forth the name and address of any such companies.

ANSWER:

ROBB & ROBB LLC

_____

GARY C. ROBB #29618
ANITA PORTE ROBB #30318
One Kansas City Place - Suite 3900
1200 Main Street
Kansas City, Missouri 64105
Telephone: (816) 474-8080
Facsimile: (816) 474-8081

FILED SIMULTANEOUSLY WITH PETITION

A.6 Sample First Set of Interrogatories: Helicopter Component Part Manufacturer

IN THE DISTRICT COURT OF LANCASTER
COUNTY, NEBRASKA

PAMELA MANSKE, Special	)	
Administrator of the Estate of	)	
PHILLIP HERRING,	)	
	)	CASE ID: CI-02-2620
PLAINTIFF,	)	
	)	
v.	)	
	)	
DUNCAN AVIATION, et al,	)	
	)	
DEFENDANTS.	)	
	)	
TAMMY SCOLLARD	)	
Executor of the Estate of	)	
PATRICK SCOLLARD,	)	
	)	CASE ID: CI-02-2621
PLAINTIFF,	)	
	)	
v.	)	
	)	
DUNCAN AVIATION, et al,	)	
	)	
DEFENDANTS.	)	
	)	
JEFFREY SCHREMPP, Personal	)	
Representative of the Estate of	)	
LORI SCHREMPP,	)	
	)	CASE ID: CI-02-2622
PLAINTIFF,	)	
	)	
v.	)	
	)	
DUNCAN AVIATION, et al,	)	
	)	
DEFENDANTS.	)	

PLAINTIFFS' FIRST SET OF INTERROGATORIES TO DEFENDANT EUROCOPTER, S.A.

COME NOW Plaintiffs, and pursuant to Nebraska Rules of Civil Procedure, and propound the following First Set of Interrogatories to be answered by an appropriate officer or agent of defendant Eurocopter, S.A. and not its attorneys, in writing, under oath and according to law.

The interrogatories and requests for production which are included pursuant to Nebraska Rules of Civil Procedures are to be regarded as continuing, and you are requested to provide, by way of supplementary answers thereto, such additional information or material as you, your counsel, or any other person in your behalf, or subject to your control, may hereafter obtain which will augment or otherwise modify the answers now given to those interrogatories or requests to produce, which has reference to names and addresses of persons having knowledge of discoverable facts, which has reference to the names and addresses of expert witnesses expected to be called at trial, or which corrects those interrogatories or requests to produce the responses to which were incorrect when made or which are now incorrect because of a change in circumstances.

Such supplemental responses are to be filed and served upon the Plaintiffs within fourteen (14) days after receipt of such information, but not later than three (3) weeks preceding the date of trial.

"Identify," when referring to an individual person, means to state his or her full name, present or last-known address and telephone number, present or last-known position and business affiliation, and title of position held and by whom employed at the time of each event, transaction or occurrence hereinafter referred to.

"Identify," when referring to a document, shall mean the date and author, type of document (e.g., letter, memorandum, etc.) or some other means of identifying it. Further, a request for the "description" or "identification" of any document should be understood to include as well a request for the following information:

(a) The name and address of each and every person, as defined below, by whom such "document" was received, to whom it was sent or circulated, or by whom it was received;

(b) The nature and substance of the "document" with sufficient particularity to enable the same to be identified;

(c) The date of the document and the date the document was executed (if different from the date it bears);

(d) Whether you claim any privilege as to such "document," and if so, a precise statement of the facts on which such claim of privilege is based;

(e) The name and address of each and every person who participated in the drafting or creation of the "document;"

(f) The present location and the name and address of the present custodian of the "document;" and

(g) If a "document" was, but no longer is, in your control, the disposition that was made of it, the circumstances surrounding, the authorization for such disposition, and the date or approximate date thereof.

INTERROGATORY NO. 1

Please state the full name, current complete address, telephone number, and position, capacity, or job title of each person who assisted in answering these interrogatories on behalf of defendant.

ANSWER:

INTERROGATORY NO. 2

Have you been correctly designated as a party defendant in this cause insofar as the legal description and correct spelling is concerned?

(a) If not, then state how you should properly be designated in an action at law as of June 21, 2002 and at present; and

(b) Is defendant currently a French corporation?

ANSWER:

INTERROGATORY NO. 3

With respect to the subject AS350B Eurocopter helicopter described in the Petition for Damages and which is at issue in this action, did you design, manufacture, assemble or sell that helicopter including , but not limited to the servos to the main and tail rotors, actuators, hydraulic pumps, tail rotor load compensator, or any related component parts? If your answer is "yes," please provide the following information:

(a) Please describe precisely the helicopter which is the subject of this action;

(b) Identify all suppliers of component parts from whom you have purchased, in whole or in part, parts to be incorporated into the helicopter.

ANSWER:

INTERROGATORY NO. 4

Please state which of the named defendants in this action with which you at any time have conducted business and in connection therewith, please state:

(a) The first and last (if not a present business relationship) date of any ongoing business transactions between you and any of the other named defendants;

(b) Please state the nature of the business relationship as between the parties and identify which was your relationship (e.g., vendor/purchaser, lessor/lessee, etc.); and

(c) Identify those individuals in your company with knowledge of the business relationship between you and any of the aforementioned named defendants.

ANSWER:

INTERROGATORY NO. 5

Please identify the business of defendant Eurocopter, S.A. and Eurocopter S.A.S.

ANSWER:

INTERROGATORY NO. 6

With respect to the subject helicopter at issue in this case, please provide the following information:

(a) The original date of design and manufacture; and

(b) Any and all names by which such helicopter is known either to you or in the aviation industry.

ANSWER:

INTERROGATORY NO. 7

Please identify the current custodian and whereabouts of all studies or tests made with respect to the subject helicopters' servos, or pitch control rods, to the main and tail rotors, actuators, hydraulic pumps, tail rotor load compensator, and any related component parts including but not limited to safety and fatigue analysis and consideration of various alternative designs.

ANSWER:

INTERROGATORY NO. 8

How long have you been doing business with Dunlop Limited and state the total number of servo parts or related component parts you have purchased from them.

ANSWER:

INTERROGATORY NO. 9

How long have you been doing business with Societe D' Applications Des Machines Motrices (A/K/A SAMM) and state the total number of servo parts or related component parts you have purchased from them.

ANSWER:

INTERROGATORY NO. 10

Please identify any and all documents in your possession, custody, or control relating to any notices directed to you, claims made against you, or lawsuits filed against you wherein issues involving the servos to the main and tail rotors, actuators, hydraulic pumps, tail rotor load compensator, or any related component parts were claimed or alleged, regardless of whether injury or death ensued which are substantially similar to the incident set forth in this lawsuit and in connection therewith, please state:

(a) The custodian of any and all such documents in your possession referring or reflecting any such notice, claims, or lawsuits; and

(b) Set forth and identify any and all such notices, claims, and lawsuits by date, aircraft description, location of malfunction, and aircraft owner.

ANSWER:

INTERROGATORY NO. 11

Please describe any and all bulletins, manuals, written instructions, warnings, procedures, or the like that you are aware were:

(a) Provided with the promotion or sale of the subject helicopter servos to the main and/or tail rotors, actuators, hydraulic pumps, tail rotor load compensator, or any and all related component parts.

(b) Subsequently supplied to any owner, operator, lessor, or maintenance facility.

ANSWER:

INTERROGATORY NO. 12

Please identify each and every person whom you expect to call as an expert witness at trial, stating the general nature of the subject matter upon which he or she is expected to testify.

ANSWER:

INTERROGATORY NO. 13

Please identify any and all documents in your possession, custody or control describing any engineering change orders, and the reasons for such changes, to the servos to the main and/or tail rotors, actuators, hydraulic pumps, tail rotor load compensator, or any and all related component parts, which were the same or substantially similar to the ones in the subject helicopter ,subsequent to its original manufacture and design.

ANSWER:

INTERROGATORY NO. 14

For any liability insurance coverage which this defendant held and which will cover the occurrence out of which this loss arises, please state:

    (a) The name and address of each such carrier;

    (b) The policy numbers of each such policy;

    (c) Whether any reservation of the insurer's rights has been declared with respect to a potential dispute in coverage for this loss; and

    (d) Whether the defendant must approve of any settlement entered into by its insurance carrier.

ANSWER:

INTERROGATORY NO. 15

Please set forth the certification history of the helicopter at issue herein including but not limited to the dates and test results of all developmental ground tests, developmental flight tests, and in connection therewith:

    (a) Please identify the current location of all applications for type certification, and all ground and flight tests, including, but not limited to, test protocol, field results, and any videotapes or photographs, and all documents related thereto.

ANSWER:

INTERROGATORY NO. 16

Has the servos to the main and tail rotors, actuators, hydraulic pumps, tail rotor load compensator, or any related component parts, which are the subject of this lawsuit, at any time been the subject of a service letter or service bulletin referring or relating to safety, maintenance, use, operation, replacement, inspection, and the like. If your answer is "yes," please provide the following:

    (a) State the current custodian and whereabouts of any and all such service letters and service bulletins; and

    (b) Set forth the dates of all such service letters and service bulletins and the general nature of the subject matter of each.

ANSWER:

INTERROGATORY NO. 17

Has the FAA or DGAC ever issued an air-worthiness directive with respect to any aspect of the design, manufacture, operation, maintenance, or use of the servos to the main and tail rotors, actuators, hydraulic pumps, tail rotor load compensator, or any related component parts at issue in this lawsuit? If your answer is "yes," please set forth the following:

    (a) The current custodian and whereabouts of any such airworthiness directives; and

    (b) The dates of any such directives including the general subject matter of each.

ANSWER:

INTERROGATORY NO. 18

Has the FAA or DGAC, NTSB or BEA ever conducted an inquiry into the manufacture, design, operation, maintenance, or use of the subject servos to the main and tail rotors, actuators, hydraulic pumps, tail rotor load compensator, or any related component parts? If your answer is "yes," please set forth the following:

    (a) The current custodian and whereabouts of any such inquiries; and

    (b) The dates of any such inquiries including the general subject matter of each.

ANSWER:

INTERROGATORY NO. 19

Please identify the current custodian and whereabouts of all correspondence, and communications, between you and the National Transportation Safety Board or the Bureau Enquetes Accidents (BEA) involving the subject helicopter.

ANSWER:

INTERROGATORY NO. 20

Has this defendant caused to be issued any mechanical reliability reports to the FAA or DGAC with respect to the subject servos to the main and tail rotors, actuators, hydraulic pumps, tail rotor load compensator, or any related component parts at issue herein. If the answer is "yes", please state as follows:

    (a) The current custodian and whereabouts of any such reports; and

    (b) The dates and subject matter of any such reports.

ANSWER:

INTERROGATORY NO. 21

Please state whether there have been any predecessor corporations to this corporation and in connection therewith identify any and all other names by which this defendant has been or is presently known.

ANSWER:

INTERROGATORY NO. 22

Please identify all of the individuals who have or have had any responsibilities whether administrative, investigative, or engineering, arising out of the aircrash giving rise to this action. In connection therewith, please state the name of each and every such individual and set forth their current positions with the company, date hired, and current employment.

ANSWER:

INTERROGATORY NO. 23

Please identify all employees and non-employees of this defendant who were present at the crash site and in connection therewith, please state:

    (a) The job title or position of every such company employee;

    (b) The reasons for their presence including their responsibilities and assignments in connection therewith; and

    (c) Did they take photographs and/or videotapes?

ANSWER:

INTERROGATORY NO. 24

Please identify all employees and non-employees of this defendant who were present at the "tear down" of the helicopter and in connection therewith, please state:

    (a) The job title or position of every such company employee;

    (b) The reasons for their presence including their responsibilities and assignments in connection therewith; and

    (c) Did they take photographs and/or videotapes?

ANSWER:

INTERROGATORY NO. 25

Please identify the following persons with responsibility for the design, testing, selection, assembly, use, and certification of the subject servos to the main and tail rotors, actuators, hydraulic pumps, tail rotor load compensator, or any related component parts used in your helicopters both originally and at the present time:

    (a) Head of engineering;

    (b) Project engineer;

    (c) Chief of flight operations and testing;

    (d) Governmental liaison between defendant and the FAA, DGAC, NTSB and BEA; and

    (e) Investigating officer for malfunction notices.

ANSWER:

INTERROGATORY NO. 26

With respect to the subject servos to the main and tail rotors, actuators, hydraulic pumps, tail rotor load compensators, and any related component parts at issue herein please state:

(a) Whether any other company supplied any related or connecting parts and in connection therewith, please state the complete name of said company and its address.

ANSWER:

INTERROGATORY NO. 27

Please identify all maintenance, repairs, overhauls, flight tests, and/or service performed on the subject aircraft prior to and including June 21, 2002 and in connection therewith state:

(a) Dates and location of any such maintenance, repairs, overhauls, flight tests and/or service;

(b) Names of persons performing such services; and

(c) Location of records of all maintenance, repairs, overhauls, flight tests and/or service.

ANSWER:

INTERROGATORY NO. 28

Please identify anyone who has taken ground or aerial photographs or videos of the accident as it was occurring, and/or of the wreckage site both immediately after the accident herein and after the wreckage was removed.

ANSWER:

INTERROGATORY NO. 29

How long have you been doing business with Turbomeca Engine Corporation and state the total number of fuel control units or related component parts you have purchased from them.

ANSWER:

Respectfully submitted,

ROBB & ROBB LLC

_____

GARY C. ROBB
One Kansas City Place
Suite 3900
1200 Main Street
Kansas City, Missouri 64105
Telephone: (816) 474-8080
Facsimile: (816) 474-8081

ATTORNEYS FOR PLAINTIFFS

A.7 Sample First Set of Interrogatories: Helicopter Pilot Error

IN THE DISTRICT COURT OF POLK COUNTY, IOWA

KATHRYN L. SCHLOTZHAUER,	)	LAW NO.: CL102824
Administrator of the Estate of	)	
ROLAND SCHLOTZHAUER,	)	
	)	
PLAINTIFF,	)	
	)	PLAINTIFF'S FIRST SET OF
v.	)	INTERROGATORIES TO
	)	DEFENDANT RICHARD GREEN
RITEL COPTER SERVICE INC.	)	
An Iowa Corporation,	)	
	)	
and	)	
	)	COUNSEL FOR PLAINTIFF:
RICHARD GREEN	)	
An Iowa Resident,	)	GARY C. ROBB
	)	ANITA PORTE ROBB
and	)	ROBB & ROBB LLC
	)	One Kansas City Place
THE FINAL SEASON, INC.	)	Suite 3900
A California Corporation,	)	1200 Main Street
	)	Telephone: (816) 474-8080
DEFENDANTS.	)	Facsimile: (816) 474-8081

PLAINTIFF'S FIRST SET OF INTERROGATORIES TO DEFENDANT RICHARD GREEN

COMES NOW Plaintiff, pursuant to Iowa Rules of Civil Procedure, and propounds the following First Set of Interrogatories to be answered by an appropriate officer or agent of defendant and not its attorneys, in writing, under oath and according to law.

DEFINITIONS

"Identify," when referring to an individual person, means to state his or her full name, present or last-known address and telephone number, present or last-known position and business affiliation, and title of position held and by whom employed at the time of each event, transaction or occurrence hereinafter referred to.

"Identify," when referring to a document, shall mean the date and author, type of document (e.g., letter, memorandum, etc.) or some other means of identifying it. Further, a request for the "description" or "identification" of any document should be understood to include as well a request for the following information:

(a) The name and address of each and every person, as defined below, by whom such "document" was received, to whom it was sent or circulated, or by whom it was received;

(b) The nature and substance of the "document" with sufficient particularity to enable the same to be identified;

(c) The date of the document and the date the document was executed (if different from the date it bears);

(d) Whether you claim any privilege as to such "document," and if so, a precise statement of the facts on which such claim of privilege is based;

(e) The name and address of each and every person who participated in the drafting or creation of the "document;"

(f) The present location and the name and address of the present custodian of the "document;" and

(g) If a "document" was, but no longer is, in your control, the disposition that was made of it, the circumstances surrounding, the authorization for such disposition, and the date or approximate date thereof.

As used herein, the term the "Aircraft" refers to, unless otherwise specified, 1980 Bell "Jet Ranger" 206B helicopter, serial number 2971, registration (tail) number N2877F.

As used herein, unless otherwise specified, the term the "Accident" refers to the accident involving the 1980 Bell "Jet Ranger" 206B helicopter, serial number 2971, registration (tail) number N2877, which occurred on June 30, 2006, in the vicinity of Walford, Iowa.

As used herein, the term the "WSPS" refers to, unless otherwise specified, the Wire Strike Protection System installed on the subject helicopter.

SCOPE OF INTERROGATORIES

These Interrogatories seek all information encompassed thereby known to you or your principals, employees, agents, representatives, insurers, or attorneys.

OBJECTIONS

If you claim that information responsive to an Interrogatory is privileged or work product, please provide sufficient detail about the information, the manner in which it was created, collected, or discovered, and the persons in possession of it, to allow an evaluation of your claim of privilege or work product. A party is entitled to adequate information about the existence of documents or witnesses, or the occurrence of communications or statements, to independently determine whether an asserted privilege or protective doctrine applies to prohibit detailed discovery of the content or knowledge of the document, witness, communication, or statement. See, e.g., *Robbins v. Iowa-Illinois Gas and Electric Co.,* 160 N.W.2d 847, 853 (Iowa 1968) (discovery of a preliminary nature designed to determine whether information is protected is available).

If you object to an Interrogatory and then answer "notwithstanding the objection", please include in your answer a statement as to whether there is any information currently known to you which you are withholding on the basis of the objection and , if "yes", please provide sufficient detail as requested above to allow independent assessment of your objection. Oftentimes objections are posed because an Interrogatory could, conceivably encompass privileged, confidential, or otherwise non-discoverable information even though, at the time of response, no such privileged, confidential, or non-discoverable information is known to the responder. If such is the case, please so state. Clarification as to whether any information is being withheld pursuant to such an objection will eliminate or reduce the necessity of follow-up inquiries regarding the existence of information being withheld.

INTERROGATORY NO. 1

Please state the full name, current complete address, telephone number, and position, capacity, or job title of each person who assisted in answering these interrogatories on behalf of defendant.

ANSWER:

INTERROGATORY NO. 2

Have you been correctly designated as a party defendant in this cause insofar as the legal description and correct spelling is concerned?

(a) If not, then state how you should properly be designated in an action at law as of June 30, 2006 and at present.

ANSWER:

INTERROGATORY NO. 3

With respect to the subject 1980 Bell "Jet Ranger" 206B helicopter, serial number 2971, registration (tail) number N2877F described in Plaintiff's Petition At Law and which is at issue in this action, did you provide any component parts? If your answer is "yes", please provide the following information:

(a)   A complete description including part numbers, model numbers, assembly unit, and trade name of any and all components which were incorporated into and part of the subject helicopter; and

(b)   Identify all suppliers of component parts from whom you have purchased, in whole or in part, parts to be incorporated into the subject helicopter.

ANSWER:

INTERROGATORY NO. 4

Please state which of the named defendants in this action with which you at any time have conducted business and in connection therewith, please state:

(a)   The first and last (if not a present business relationship) date of any ongoing business transactions between you and any of the other named defendants;

(b)   Please state the nature of the business relationship as between the parties and identify which was your relationship (e.g., vendor/purchaser, lessor/lessee, etc.); and

(c)   Identify those individuals in your company with knowledge of the business relationship between you and any of the aforementioned named defendants.

ANSWER:

INTERROGATORY NO. 5

Please identify your current business/profession.
ANSWER:

INTERROGATORY NO. 6

Please state whether or not any of the individuals aboard the "Aircraft" on the flight that terminated in the accident had cell phones, video cameras, or other electronic devices with them on that flight.
ANSWER:

INTERROGATORY NO. 7

If your answer to Interrogatory No. 8 is in the affirmative, please identify the individual or individuals who had the electronic device(s) on that flight.
ANSWER:

INTERROGATORY NO. 8

Please identify any and all documents in your possession, custody, or control relating to any notices directed to you, claims made against you, or lawsuits filed against you wherein piloting or maintenance issues were claimed or alleged and in connection therewith, please state:

(a) The custodian of any and all such documents in your possession referring or reflecting any such notice, claims, or lawsuits; and

(b) Set forth and identify any and all such notices, claims, and lawsuits by date, and aircraft description.

ANSWER:

INTERROGATORY NO. 9

Please describe any and all bulletins, manuals, written instructions, warnings, procedures, or the like that you are aware were provided with the promotion or sale of the subject aircraft's WSPS (Wire Strike Protection System).

ANSWER:

INTERROGATORY NO. 10

Please identify each and every person whom you expect to call as an expert witness at trial, stating the general nature of the subject matter upon which he or she is expected to testify.

ANSWER:

INTERROGATORY NO. 11

For any liability insurance coverage which this defendant held and which will cover the occurrence out of which this loss arises, please state:

(a) The name and address of each such carrier;

(b) The policy numbers of each such policy;

(c) Whether any reservation of the insurer's rights has been declared with respect to a potential dispute in coverage for this loss; and

(d) Whether the defendant must approve of any settlement entered into by its insurance carrier.

ANSWER:

INTERROGATORY NO. 12

For any liability insurance coverage which this defendant held at the time of the installation of the subject aircraft's WSPS and which will cover the occurrence out of which this loss arises, please state:

(a) The name and address of each such carrier;

(b) The policy numbers of each such policy;

(c) Whether any reservation of the insurer's rights has been declared with respect to a potential dispute in coverage for this loss; and

(d) Whether the defendant must approve of any settlement entered into by its insurance carrier.

ANSWER:

INTERROGATORY NO. 13

Has the subject WSPS at any time been the subject of a service letter or service bulletin referring or relating to safety, maintenance, use, operation, replacement, inspection, and the like? If your answer is "yes", please provide the following:

(a) State the current custodian and whereabouts of any and all such service letters and service bulletins; and

(b) Set forth the dates of all such service letters and service bulletins and the general nature of the subject matter of each.

ANSWER:

INTERROGATORY NO. 14

Please identify all of the individuals who have or have had any responsibilities whether administrative or investigative, arising out of the aircrash giving rise to this action. In connection therewith, please state the name of each and every such individual and current employer.

ANSWER:

INTERROGATORY NO. 15

Has the FAA ever issued an air-worthiness directive with respect to any aspect of the design, manufacture, operation, maintenance, or use of the subject WSPS at issue in this lawsuit? If your answer is "yes", please set forth the following:

(a) The current custodian and whereabouts of any such airworthiness directives; and

(b) The dates of any such directives including the general subject matter of each.

ANSWER:

INTERROGATORY NO. 16

Has the FAA or the NTSB ever conducted an inquiry into the manufacture, design, operation, maintenance, or use of the subject WSPS? If your answer is "yes", please set forth the following:

(a) The current custodian and whereabouts of any such inquiries; and

(b) The dates of any such inquiries including the general subject matter of each.

ANSWER:

INTERROGATORY NO. 17

Please identify all employees of this defendant who were present at the crash site and in connection therewith, please state:

    (a) The job title or position of every such employee;

    (b) The reasons for their presence including their responsibilities and assignments in connection therewith; and

    (c) Did they take photographs and/or videotapes?

ANSWER:

INTERROGATORY NO. 18

Please identify all non-employees of this defendant who were present at the crash site and in connection therewith, please state:

    (a) The job title or governmental position of every such individual;

    (b) The reasons for their presence including their responsibilities and assignments in connection therewith; and

    (c) Did they take photographs and/or videotapes?

ANSWER:

INTERROGATORY NO. 19

With respect to the WSPS at issue herein please state whether any other company supplied any related or connecting parts and in connection therewith, please state the complete name of said company and its address.

ANSWER:

INTERROGATORY NO. 20

Please identify all maintenance, repairs, overhauls, flight tests, and/or service performed on the subject aircraft prior to and including June 30, 2006 and in connection therewith state:

    (a) Dates and location of any such maintenance, repairs, overhauls, flight tests and/or service;

    (b) Names of persons performing such services; and

    (c) Location of records of all maintenance, repairs, overhauls, flight tests and/or service.

ANSWER:

INTERROGATORY NO. 21

Please identify anyone who has taken ground or aerial photographs or videos of the wreckage site both immediately after the accident herein and after the wreckage was removed.

ANSWER:

INTERROGATORY NO. 22

State the name, employer, address and telephone number of each and every one of your flight instructors, flight schools, and each other entity that provided you with formal or informal flight training for the five years prior to and including the date of the incident and identify all documents that support and/or were reviewed in answering this Interrogatory.
ANSWER:

INTERROGATORY NO. 23

Were any photographs, movies, and/or videotapes being taken at the time of the occurrence from inside the subject helicopter? If so, identify the person or persons taking such photographs, movies, and/or videotapes, and state who now has custody of them, and their name and address.
ANSWER:

Respectfully submitted,

ROBB & ROBB LLC

BY: _____

GARY C. ROBB
One Kansas City Place
Suite 3900
1200 Main Street
Kansas City, Missouri 64105
Telephone: (816) 474-8080
Facsimile: (816) 474-8081

ATTORNEYS FOR PLAINTIFF

FILED SIMULTANEOUSLY WITH PETITION

A.8 Sample First Set of Interrogatories: Helicopter Mechanic Negligence
DISTRICT COURT

CLARK COUNTY, NEVADA

* * *

MARY RIGGS, as Personal Representative of the ESTATES OF LOVISH BHANOT and ANUPAMA BHOLA, for the benefit of the ESTATES OF LOVISH BHANOT and ANUPAMA BHOLA; SUMAN BHANOT, as Next of Kin and Natural Mother of LOVISH BHANOT, deceased, MEERA BHOLA, as Next of Kin and Natural Mother of ANUPAMA BHOLA, deceased, and BALRAJ BHOLA as Next of Kin and Natural Father of ANUPAMA BHOLA, deceased.
 	
     Plaintiffs,
 	
vs.
 	
SUNDANCE HELICOPTERS, INC., A Nevada Corporation,
 	
     Defendant.
	CASE NO. A-11-653149-C
	DEPT. NO. XXVIII
	
	PLAINTIFFS' FIRST SET OF INTERROGATORIES TO DEFENDANT SUNDANCE HELICOPTERS, INC.

PLAINTIFFS' FIRST SET OF INTERROGATORIES
TO DEFENDANT SUNDANCE HELICOPTERS, INC.

COME NOW Plaintiffs, pursuant to Nevada Rules of Civil Procedure, and propounds the following First Set of Interrogatories to be answered by an appropriate officer or agent of defendant Sundance Helicopters, Inc. and not its attorneys, in writing, under oath and according to law.

The interrogatories and requests for production which are included are to be regarded as continuing, and you are requested to provide, by way of supplementary answers thereto, such additional information or material as you, your counsel, or any other person in your behalf, or subject to your control, may hereafter obtain which will augment or otherwise modify the answers now given to those interrogatories or requests to produce, which has reference to names and addresses of persons having knowledge of discoverable facts, which has reference to the names and addresses of expert witnesses expected to be called at trial, or which corrects those interrogatories or requests to produce the responses to which were incorrect when made or which are now incorrect because of a change in circumstances.

Such supplemental responses are to be filed and served upon the Plaintiffs within thirty (30) days after receipt of such information.

DEFINITIONS

1. "Identify," when referring to an individual person, means to state his or her full name, present or last-known address and telephone number, present or last-known position and business affiliation, and title of position held and by whom employed at the time of each event, transaction or occurrence hereinafter referred to.

2. "Identify," when referring to a document, shall mean the date and author, type of document (e.g., letter, memorandum, etc.) or some other means of identifying it. Further, a request for the "description" or "identification" of any document should be understood to include as well a request for the following information:

(a) The name and address of each and every person, as defined below, by whom such "document" was received, to whom it was sent or circulated, or by whom it was received;

(b) The nature and substance of the "document" with sufficient particularity to enable the same to be identified;

(c) The date of the document and the date the document was executed (if different from the date it bears);

(d) Whether you claim any privilege as to such "document," and if so, a precise statement of the facts on which such claim of privilege is based;

(e) The name and address of each and every person who participated in the drafting or creation of the "document;"

(f) The present location and the name and address of the present custodian of the "document;" and

(g) If a "document" was, but no longer is, in your control, the disposition that was made of it, the circumstances surrounding, the authorization for such disposition, and the date or approximate date thereof.

As used herein, the term the "aircraft" refers to, unless otherwise specified, 1989 Eurocopter AS 350 B2 helicopter, serial number 2300, registration (tail) number N357SH.

As used herein, unless otherwise specified, the term the "accident" refers to the accident involving the 1989 (Eurocopter AS 350 B2) helicopter, serial number 2300, registration (tail) number N37SH, which occurred on December 7, 2011, in the vicinity of Las Vegas, Nevada.

INTERROGATORY NO. 1

Please state the full name, current complete address, telephone number, and position, capacity, or job title of each person who assisted in answering these interrogatories on behalf of Sundance Helicopters, Inc.

ANSWER:

INTERROGATORY NO. 2

Does the defendant do business as a corporation, a professional corporation, partnership, or other business organization? If so, please state with regard thereto:

(a) The nature of the business organization. Please set forth the entire name of the organization, and also produce a copy of the Articles or other documents by which this business organization came into existence.

(b) The identity of any insurance that pertains to this business organization or professional corporation, stating whether the individual is an insured within the scope of such insurance. Produce a copy of the policy covering said business organization or corporation at the time of the acts alleged in the Complaint.

ANSWER:

INTERROGATORY NO. 3

Please state the name, complete residential and business addresses, telephone numbers, date of birth, Social Security Number, and occupation of the Sundance Helicopters, Inc.'s personnel that responded to the scene of the events referenced in Plaintiffs' Complaint.

ANSWER:

INTERROGATORY NO. 4

Please state the name, complete residential and business addresses, telephone numbers, date of birth, Social Security Number, of all persons known to you who have spoken to any of the Bhanot and Bhola's families and/or witnesses of the events referenced in Plaintiffs' Complaint. Please also list the date of the conversation and/or meeting, all persons who were present and a detailed description of the subject matter discussed.

ANSWER:

INTERROGATORY NO. 5

Identify any and all insurance and/or indemnifying agreements which may indemnify you, in whole or in part, to satisfy a judgment which may be obtained against you in this action, or to indemnify or reimburse for payments made to satisfy the judgment, including any excess coverage or umbrella insurance, and with respect to each, please state:

(a) The name of the carrier, and the policy number;

(b) The face amount and/or limits of liability of coverage;

(c) The effective policy period;

(d) The insured's identity;

(e) The insurer's identity; and

(f) Whether there are any secondary carriers involved who have received or sent any reservation of rights letters with regard to each such policy or policies.

ANSWER:

INTERROGATORY NO. 6

Please state the name, complete residential and business addresses, telephone numbers, date of birth, social security number, and occupation of each person known to you to be present at the scene of the event referenced in Plaintiffs' Complaint within one (1) hour of such event.

ANSWER:

INTERROGATORY NO. 7

Please state the name, complete residential and business addresses, telephone numbers, date of birth, social security number, and occupation of all persons known to you who witnessed the events referenced in Plaintiffs' Complaint.

ANSWER:

INTERROGATORY NO. 8

Identify each incident that you have been made aware of from 1996 through present where defendant was a named party in a lawsuit or claim arising out of the fault or alleged fault of any Sundance Helicopters, Inc. personnel resulting in injuries or wrongful deaths of persons, and state whether the case was filed, what jurisdiction it was filed in, if it was dismissed, or if it settled prior to litigation being filed.

ANSWER:

INTERROGATORY NO. 9

Please state whether any statements, either written, recorded, stenographic, or otherwise, have been obtained by you or anyone acting on your behalf in connection with the occurrence described in Plaintiffs' Complaint from any party. If so, with respect to each statement, please state:

(a) The date the statement was obtained;

(b) Full name, residential and business address and telephone numbers of the person(s) whose statement was taken;

(c) The full name, residential and business address and telephone number of the person obtaining the statement;

(d) The method by which the statement was taken; and

(e) The full names and complete residential and business addresses and telephone numbers of the present custodians of each statement.

ANSWER:

INTERROGATORY NO. 10

Please state whether you or anyone acting on your behalf have any photographs, videotapes or audiotapes that were taken or obtained since the occurrence which may relate to the occurrence described in Plaintiffs' Complaint. If so, please state:

(a) The number of photographs, videotapes, or audiotapes in your possession;

(b) The subject matter of each such photograph, videotape, or audiotape;

(c) The photographs, videotapes, or audiotapes were taken;

(d) The full name and complete address and telephone number of each photographer or recorder taking such photographs, videotapes, or audiotapes; and

(e) The full names and complete residential and business addresses and telephone numbers of the custodians of the photographs, videotapes, or audiotapes.

ANSWER:

INTERROGATORY NO. 11

Please state whether you claim some other person or entity caused or contributed to cause the deaths of Lovish Bhanot and Meera Bhola. If so, please state and identify in detail:

(a) The full names and complete addresses of each such person, firm, corporation, or entity;

(b) The facts upon which you base such claim;

(c) The full names, complete addresses and telephone numbers of any person or persons who have knowledge, or claim to have knowledge, regarding that claim;

(d) For each such witness, please state that you understand to be that person's knowledge or information;

(e) The identity of any documents, photographs, publications, regulations, statutes, laws or other writings upon which you rely in making your claim; and

(f) The full names, complete addresses and telephone numbers of the custodians of those items enumerated in the above paragraph.

ANSWER:

INTERROGATORY NO. 12

Please state whether you expect to call any expert witnesses at trial, and for each expected expert witness, please state and identify with particularity:

(a) The full name, complete residential and business addresses, telephone numbers, occupation, and job title for each expert witness;

(b) The subject matter upon which each expert witness is expected to testify;

(c) The substance of the facts and opinions as to which each expert is expected to testify; and

(d) A summary for the grounds for each expert witness' opinions.

ANSWER:

INTERROGATORY NO. 13

Please state the name, complete residential and business addresses, telephone numbers, dates of birth, Social Security number, title and occupation of the defendant's personnel that were responsible for setting and enforcing helicopter tour policies for the years 1996 to the present.

ANSWER:

INTERROGATORY NO. 14

Did you or anyone to your knowledge receive any notice or information prior to the accident of any defect, malfunction, or non-function of said helicopter or any part or mechanisms thereof which might have caused or contributed to the alleged accident?

If your answer to the preceding interrogatory is yes, please state:

(a) The date and place information was received;

(b) A description of each defect, malfunction, or non-function of which you or anyone acting on your behalf received notice;

(c) The name, address and telephone number of each person from whom notice was received.

ANSWER:

INTERROGATORY NO. 15

Please describe any and all bulletins, manuals, written instructions, memorandums, e-mails, warnings, procedures, or the like with respect to helicopter tours issued to pilots.

ANSWER:

DATED: August 27, 2012   ROBB & ROBB LLC

                        By: _____
                                 GARY C. ROBB
                                 ANITA PORTE ROBB
                                 One Kansas City Place - Suite 3900

1200 Main Street
Kansas City, Missouri 64105
Telephone: (816) 474-8080
Facsimile: (816) 474-8081
e-mail: gcr@robbrobb.com
         apr@robbrobb.com

                                 LAWRENCE J. SMITH

BENSON, BERTOLDO, BAKER
& CARTER
                                 Nevada Bar No. 6505
                                 7408 W. Sahara Avenue
                                 Las Vegas, Nevada 89117
                                          Telephone: (702) 228-2600
                                          Facsimile: (702) 228-2333
                                          e-mail: lawre3@bensonlawyers.com

Attorneys for Plaintiffs

DEFENDANT'S SWORN SIGNATURE

STATE OF _____)
)
COUNTY OF _____)

    The below named person, being duly sworn on oath states that he or she read the foregoing Interrogatories and the answers given are true to the best of affiant's knowledge and belief.

                                 _____
                                 Signature of Party
                                 (NOT TO BE SIGNED BY

ATTORNEY)

The foregoing answers to Interrogatories were subscribed and sworn to before me this _____ day of _____ _____, 2012.

_____
NOTARY PUBLIC

My commission expires:

A.9 Sample First Request for Production of Documents: Helicopter Engine Failure/ Design Defect

IN THE CIRCUIT COURT OF JACKSON COUNTY, MISSOURI
AT KANSAS CITY

JODIE A. LETZ, Individually, and	)	
as Guardian Ad Litem and	)	
Next Friend of	)	
ERIC SCOTT LETZ and	)	
CHRISTOPHER SCOTT LETZ,	)	
Minor Children,	)	
and as Representative and	)	
Administratrix of the Estate of	)	
SHERRY ANN LETZ, Deceased,	)	
	)	CASE NO.: _____
PLAINTIFFS,	)	
	)	CIVIL DOCKET: _____
v.	)	
	)	DIVISION: _____
TURBOMECA ENGINE CORPORATION,	)	
	)	
EUROCOPTER INTERNATIONAL	)	
(Formerly AEROSPATIALE),	)	
	)	
AMERICAN EUROCOPTER CORPORATION,	)	
	)	
ROCKY MOUNTAIN HELICOPTERS, INC.,	)	
	)	
BERGERON COMPANY, INC.,	)	
	)	
LIFE FLIGHT SERVICES, INC.,	)	
A JOINT VENTURE BETWEEN	)	
ST. LUKE'S HOSPITAL and	)	
ST. JOSEPH'S HEALTH CENTER	)	
ST. LUKE'S HOSPITAL OF KANSAS,	)	
	)	
ST. JOSEPH HEALTH CENTER OF	)	
JACKSON COUNTY, MISSOURI,	)	
	)	
_____DEFENDANTS.	)	

**PLAINTIFFS' FIRST REQUEST FOR PRODUCTION OF DOCUMENTS TO
DEFENDANT TURBOMECA ENGINE CORPORATION**

COME NOW Plaintiffs, by and through Rule 58.01, and hereby request defendant Turbomeca Engine Corporation to produce and permit inspection and copying of the following documents, objects and tangible things on October 22, 1993, at the law office of ROBB & ROBB, One Kansas City Place, Suite 3900, 1200 Main, Kansas City, Missouri 64105:

1. Original and any and all subsequent design drawings and/or blue prints relating to the Arriel 1-B1 jet helicopter engine which is the subject of this lawsuit.

2. Any and all documents referring or reflecting any operational malfunction, testing malfunction, or operational failure or defect of any type with the Arriel 1-B1 jet helicopter engine manufactured and sold by defendant.

3. Any and all documents referring or reflecting any changes, alterations, or modifications in the design instructions or service bulletins of the Arriel 1-B1 jet helicopter engine manufactured by this defendant.

4. Any and all advertising brochures, service bulletins, service advisories, promotional literature and the like relating to the Arriel 1-B1 jet helicopter engine manufactured by this defendant.

5. Copies of any and all articles, evaluations, reports, case studies, and the like appearing in aviation or general mechanical engineering periodicals, industry or aviation trade journals, or governmental or aviation groups relative to or concerning any alleged operational or testing malfunction or failure in connection with the Arriel l-Bl jet helicopter engine manufactured by the defendant.

6. Copies of any and all contracts or policies of insurance which might afford coverage to the defendant in the event of a verdict for Plaintiffs in the above-styled cause, whether primary, secondary or excess coverage.

7. Any and all correspondence between Turbomeca Engine Corporation and either American Eurocopter Corporation and Eurocopter International regarding the use, experience, anticipated use, flight use, operational concerns, or otherwise specifically pertaining to or governing the maintenance, inspection, or operation of the Arriel l-Bl jet helicopter engine manufactured by this defendant incorporated into air ambulance helicopters manufactured or assembled by Eurocopter International or American Eurocopter Corporation.

8. Copies of any and all petitions for damages or complaints filed in any court or comparable administrative tribunal in connection with any lawsuits against this defendant in which it is alleged or acclaimed that the Arriel l-Bl jet helicopter engine failed due to a malfunction or defect in design or materials of the labyrinth seal or guide vanes.

9. Any and all copies of the maintenance manual prepared by the defendant and sent to distributors, dealers, or repair facilities with respect to appropriate maintenance, inspection, and testing of the Arriel 1-Bl jet helicopter engine.

10. Any and all service difficulty reports generated by this defendant and submitted to any field operatives, dealers, maintenance facilities and distributors with respect to the Arriel 1-B1 jet helicopter engine.

11. Any and all notice of malfunction or defect reports reported to the Federal Aviation or National Transportation Safety Board which in any way relate to the design failure or operational malfunction of the labyrinth seal or guide vanes used within the Arriel 1-B1 jet helicopter engine.

12. Any and all internal memoranda including, but not limited to letters, bulletins, reports, test results, investigative evaluations, and the like generated within and by employees of this defendant or at the behest of this defendant relating to any alleged or perceived malfunction, materials problem, operational or maintenance failure or alleged failure with either the labyrinth

seal or guide vanes of the Arriel 1-Bl jet helicopter engine manufactured by this defendant.

13. Copies of any accident investigation report or memoranda prepared by or at the behest of this defendant including reports of all in-house investigations, diagrams, photographs, witness statements, engineering or test reports and memoranda and the like.

14. All documents, materials, reports, or memoranda contained within the FAA or NTSB file concerning operation or testing deficiencies or failures either actual or alleged, relating to the Arriel 1-B1 jet helicopter engine.

15. Any and all metallurgical evaluations whether conducted internally or externally at the behest of this defendant upon the guide vanes of the Arriel 1-B1 jet helicopter engine including but not limited to testing as to the material strength, plasticity, tensile strength, compressive strength, and fatigue strength.

16. Any and all documents referring or reflective of any testing whether operation or field testing or component, experimental or laboratory testing concerning the metallurgical evaluation of the guide vanes of the Arriel 1-B1 engine including, but not limited to the results of any and all such testing and documents reflecting the appropriate selection of metals.

17. Any and all correspondence between this defendant and Rocky Mountain Helicopters, Inc. referring or relating to the proper inspection, maintenance, and operation of the Arriel 1-B1 jet helicopter engine.

18. Any and all correspondence referring or reflecting proper maintenance, operation, and flight use of the Arriel 1-B1 engine manufactured by this defendant.

19. Any and all documents referring or reflecting any design input, suggestions, or recommendations to this defendant made by any representatives or employees of Eurocopter International or American Eurocopter Corporation relating to the safe flight use, maintenance, or operation of the Arriel 1-B1 jet helicopter engine.

Respectfully submitted,

ROBB & ROBB LLC

_____

GARY C. ROBB #29618
ANITA PORTE ROBB #30318
One Kansas City Place - Suite 3900
1200 Main Street
Kansas City, Missouri 64105
Telephone: (816) 474-8080
Facsimile: (816) 474-8081

ATTORNEYS FOR PLAINTIFFS

FILED SIMULTANEOUSLY WITH PETITION

A.10 Sample First Request for Production of Documents: Helicopter Component Part Manufacturer

IN THE DISTRICT COURT OF LANCASTER
COUNTY, NEBRASKA

PAMELA MANSKE, Special	)	
Administrator of the Estate of	)	
PHILLIP HERRING,	)	
	)	CASE ID: CI-02-2620
PLAINTIFF,	)	
	)	
v.	)	
	)	
DUNCAN AVIATION, et al,	)	
	)	
DEFENDANTS.	)	
	)	
TAMMY SCOLLARD	)	
Executor of the Estate of	)	
PATRICK SCOLLARD,	)	
	)	CASE ID: CI-02-2621
PLAINTIFF,	)	
	)	
v.	)	
	)	
DUNCAN AVIATION, et al,	)	
	)	
DEFENDANTS.	)	
	)	
JEFFREY SCHREMPP, Personal	)	
Representative of the Estate of	)	
LORI SCHREMPP,	)	
	)	CASE ID: CI-02-2622
PLAINTIFF,	)	
	)	
v.	)	
	)	
DUNCAN AVIATION, et al,	)	
	)	
DEFENDANTS.	)	

PLAINTIFFS' FIRST REQUEST FOR PRODUCTION OF DOCUMENTS TO DEFENDANT EUROCOPTER, S.A.

COME NOW Plaintiffs, by and through Nebraska Rules of Civil Procedure, and hereby request defendant Eurocopter, S.A. to produce and permit inspection and copying of the following documents, objects and tangible things on July 23, 2004, at 9:00 a.m., at the law office of ROBB & ROBB LLC, One Kansas City Place, Suite 3900, 1200 Main, Kansas City, Missouri 64105:

1.   Original and any and all subsequent design drawings and/or blue prints relating to the AS350B helicopter which is the subject of this lawsuit.

2.   Any and all documents referring to or reflecting any operational malfunction, testing malfunction, or operational failure or defect of any type with the AS350B helicopter servos to the main and tail rotors, actuators, hydraulic pumps, tail rotor load compensators, or any related component parts.

3.   Any and all documents referring to or reflecting any changes, alterations, or modifications in the design instructions or service bulletins of the AS350B helicopter servo parts, actuators, hydraulic pumps, tail rotor load compensators, and related component parts as referenced herein.

4.   Any and all advertising brochures, service bulletins, service advisories, promotional literature and the like relating to the AS350B helicopter servo parts, actuators, hydraulic pumps, tail rotor load compensators and related component parts referenced herein.

5.   Copies of any and all articles, evaluations, reports, case studies, and the like appearing in aviation or general mechanical engineering periodicals, industry or aviation trade journals, or governmental or aviation groups relative to or concerning any alleged operational or testing malfunction or failure in connection with the AS350B helicopter servo parts, actuators, hydraulic pumps, tail rotor load compensators, and related component parts as referenced herein.

6.   Copies of any and all contracts or policies of insurance which might afford coverage to the defendant in the event of a verdict for Plaintiffs in the above-styled cause, whether primary, secondary or excess coverage.

7.   Any and all correspondence between Eurocopter, S.A. and any other defendants in this case regarding the use, experience, anticipated use, flight use, operational concerns, or otherwise specifically pertaining to or governing the maintenance, inspection, or operation of the AS350 B helicopter servo parts, actuators, hydraulic pumps, tail rotor load compensators and related component parts as referenced herein manufactured by Dunlop Limited or SAMM incorporated into helicopters manufactured or assembled by Eurocopter, S.A. and American Eurocopter Corporation.

8.   Copies of any and all petitions for damages or complaints filed in any court or comparable administrative tribunal in connection with any lawsuits against this defendant in which it is alleged or claimed that an AS350B helicopter's servos to the main and tail rotors, actuators hydraulic pumps, tail rotor load compensators failed or any related component parts failed.

9.   Any and all copies of the maintenance manual prepared by this defendant and sent to distributors, dealers, or repair facilities with respect to appropriate maintenance, inspection, and testing of the AS350B helicopter's servos, actuators, hydraulic pumps, tail rotor load compensators and any related component parts.

10. Any and all service difficulty reports generated by this defendant and submitted to any field operatives, dealers, maintenance facilities and distributors with respect to the AS350B helicopter's servos, actuators, hydraulic pumps, tail rotor load compensators and related component parts.

11. Any and all notice of malfunction or defect reports reported to the FAA, National Transportation Safety Board, BEA or DGAC which in any way relate to the design failures or operational malfunctions of the AS350B helicopter servos, actuators, hydraulic pumps, tail rotor load compensators and related component parts.

12. Any and all internal memoranda including, but not limited to letters, bulletins, reports, test results, investigative evaluations, and the like generated within and by employees of this defendant or at the behest of this defendant relating to any alleged or perceived malfunction, materials problems, operational or maintenance failures of the AS350B helicopter servos, actuators, hydraulic pumps, tail rotor load compensators and related component parts.

13. Copies of any accident investigation reports or memoranda prepared by or at the behest of this defendant including reports of all in-house investigations, diagrams, photographs, witness statements, engineering or test reports and memoranda and the like involving claims of an AS350B helicopter's failure of its servos, actuators, hydraulic pumps, tail rotor load compensators and related component parts.

14. All documents, materials, reports, or memoranda contained within the FAA, NTSB, BEA or DGAC file concerning operation or testing deficiencies or failures either actual or alleged, relating to the AS350B helicopter's servos, actuators, hydraulic pumps, tail rotor load compensators and related component parts.

15. Any and all metallurgical evaluations whether conducted internally or externally at the behest of this defendant upon the AS350B helicopter's servos, actuators, hydraulic pumps, tail rotor load compensators and related component parts, including but not limited to testing as to the material strength, plasticity, tensile strength, compressive strength, and fatigue strength.

16. Any and all documents referring to or reflective of any testing whether operation or field testing or component, experimental or laboratory testing concerning the metallurgical evaluation of the AS350B helicopter servos, actuators, hydraulic pumps, tail rotor load compensators and related component parts, including, but not limited to the results of any and all such testing and documents reflecting the appropriate selection of metals.

17. Any and all correspondence between this defendant and Duncan Aviation and CIT Leasing Corporation referring to or relating to the proper inspection, maintenance, and operation of the AS350B helicopter servos, actuators, hydraulic pumps, tail rotor load compensators and/or related component parts.

18. Any and all correspondence referring to or reflecting proper maintenance, operation, and flight use of the AS350B helicopter servos, actuators, hydraulic pumps, tail rotor load compensators and/or related component parts.

19. Any and all documents referring to or reflecting any design input, suggestions, or recommendations made by any representatives or employees of Eurocopter, S.A. or American Eurocopter Corporation relating to the safe flight use, maintenance, or operation of the AS350B helicopter servos, actuators, hydraulic pumps, tail rotor load compensators and/or related component parts.

20. Any and all photographs, videos or maps of the subject crash scene.

Respectfully submitted,

ROBB & ROBB LLC

_____

GARY C. ROBB
One Kansas City Place
Suite 3900
1200 Main Street
Kansas City, Missouri 64105
Telephone: (816) 474-8080
Facsimile: (816) 474-8081

ATTORNEYS FOR PLAINTIFFS

FILED SIMULTANEOUSLY WITH PETITION

A.11 Sample First Request for Production of Documents: Helicopter Pilot Error

IN THE DISTRICT COURT OF POLK COUNTY, IOWA

KATHRYN L. SCHLOTZHAUER,	)	LAW NO.: CL102824
Administrator of the Estate of	)	
ROLAND SCHLOTZHAUER,	)	
	)	
PLAINTIFF,	)	
	)	PLAINTIFF'S FIRST REQUEST
v.	)	FOR PRODUCTION OF
	)	DOCUMENTS TO DEFENDANT
RITEL COPTER SERVICE INC.	)	RICHARD GREEN
An Iowa Corporation,	)	
	)	
and	)	
	)	COUNSEL FOR PLAINTIFF:
RICHARD GREEN	)	
An Iowa Resident,	)	GARY C. ROBB
	)	ANITA PORTE ROBB
and	)	ROBB & ROBB LLC
	)	One Kansas City Place
THE FINAL SEASON, INC.	)	Suite 3900
A California Corporation,	)	1200 Main Street
	)	Telephone: (816) 474-8080
DEFENDANTS.	)	Facsimile: (816) 474-8081

PLAINTIFF'S FIRST REQUEST FOR PRODUCTION OF DOCUMENTS TO
DEFENDANT RICHARD GREEN

COMES NOW Plaintiff, pursuant to Iowa Rules of Civil Procedure, and propounds the following First Request for Production of Documents to be answered by an appropriate officer or agent of defendant and not its attorneys, in writing, under oath and according to law.

DEFINITIONS

The terms "you" or "your" shall refer to each Defendant to whom this discovery is directed and shall include the knowledge of, and actions on that Defendant's behalf by that Defendant's principals, employees, agents, representatives, and attorneys.

The term "predecessor persons" shall refer to any prior persons, including non-natural persons, from which there was a total or substantial transfer of business assets to you or another such prior person for the purpose of continuing the same or similar business enterprise.

The term "person" shall refer to all entities permitted by law to bring or answer to legal action, whether directly or through a representative, including natural persons (whether or not legally incapacitated), corporations, partnerships, and associations.

The term "individual" shall refer to a natural person.

The term "document" shall refer to all writings, drawings, graphs, charts, photographs, audio recordings, visual recordings, computer data, or any other recording medium or data compilation from which information that pertains in any way to the subject matter indicated can be obtained. The term shall include any and all reproductions of the foregoing where originals are not available, and whether or not the original is produced, all copies of such documents upon which appear any initialing, notation, imaging, printing, or handwriting of any kind not appearing on the original, which are in the custody, control or possession of you, unless privilege or work product is claimed. If you claim privilege or work product, please refer to and comply with the "claim of privilege or work product" statement below.

Without limitation of the term "control" as used in the preceding paragraph, a document is deemed to be in your control if you have the right to secure the documents or a copy thereof from another person or public or private entity having actual possession thereof. If a document is responsive to a request for identification or production and is in your control, but is not in your possession or custody, identify the person with possession or custody. If any document was, but is no longer, in your possession or subject to your control, state what disposition was made of it, by whom, and the date or dates or approximate date or dates on which such disposition was made and why.

The term "statement" shall refer to a document signed or otherwise adopted or approved by the person making it, or a stenographic, mechanical, audio, visual, or other recording, or a transcription thereof, which is a substantially verbatim recital of an oral statement by the person making it and contemporaneously recorded.

The term "employee" shall include current and former employees.

The singular and plural and the masculine and feminine should be construed in a manner consistent with the full disclosure of information.

As used herein, the term the " Aircraft or Helicopter" refers to, unless otherwise specified, 1980 Bell "Jet Ranger" 206B helicopter, serial number 2971, registration (tail) number N2877F.

As used herein, unless otherwise specified, the term the "Accident or Crash" refers to the accident involving the 1980 Bell "Jet Ranger" 206B helicopter, serial number 2971, registration (tail) number N2877, which occurred on June 30, 2006, in the vicinity of Walford, Iowa.

As used herein, the term the " WSPS" refers to, unless otherwise specified, the Wire Strike Protection System installed on the subject helicopter.

As used herein, the term "The Final Season" refers to, unless otherwise specified, the motion picture production being filmed on the date of the subject crash.

SCOPE OF REQUEST

These requests seek all documents or tangible items described below in the care, custody, or control of you or your principals, employees, agents, representatives, insurers, or attorneys.

DOCUMENTS REQUESTED

1. Documents concerning all agreements (including contracts, leases, promissory notes, financing agreements, joint production agreements, joint venture agreements, or consulting agreements) between or among Defendant Green and any of the named Defendants of the subject lawsuit.
2. Documents concerning all promotional, advertising, or marketing materials concerning the subject Wire Strike Protection System.
3. All filings made by or on behalf of Defendant Richard Green with any Iowa governmental, aviation, or administrative agency, concerning the subject helicopter, crash, or crash litigation.
4. Documents sufficient to identify all actions in the state of Iowa in which Defendant Richard Green is or has been a party, including the name of the action, the name of the parties, the name of the forum in which the action was or is pending, and any identifying docket numbers for the action.
5. Documents sufficient to identify all agreements (including contracts, leases, promissory notes, financing agreements, joint production agreements, joint venture agreements, or consulting agreements) entered into by or on behalf of Defendant Richard Green with persons located in Iowa or California, including documents showing the date, parties, subject matter, consideration, and place of performance of such agreements.
6. Documents sufficient to identify (by name, address, telephone number, and fax number) all employees of Defendant Richard Green.
7. Documents sufficient to identify the owners, lessors, lessees, and users of the subject aircraft owned by Defendant Richard Green, including their names, addresses, telephone numbers, and dates of ownership, lease or use.

8.   For the subject aircraft's WSPS, or any component part thereof that was purchased, leased, or otherwise transferred to Defendant Richard Green, documents sufficient to identify each component part, including its date and place of manufacture, and all order forms, specifications, invoices, agreements, warranties, product descriptions, brochures, or other documents concerning such aircraft part, and any related correspondence.

9.   Documents concerning any advertising by or on behalf of any Defendant, or their related entities conducted in Iowa or targeting persons located in Iowa.

10. Documents concerning any aircraft, mechanic, or pilot training of Defendant Richard Green.

11. Documents concerning any communications between Defendant Richard Green and any other defendant, or their related entities, concerning the use of the subject helicopter.

12. Documents identifying by date, name, address, telephone number and fax number, each person that owned, leased, or otherwise used the subject helicopter at any time since it was manufactured.

13. Documents concerning communications with any prior owners or leasees concerning the subject helicopter, crash, or crash litigation.

14. Manuals, guidebooks, training materials, or brochures prepared by or on behalf of any Defendant herein.

15. Documents concerning the subject helicopter and crash, including any documents concerning maintenance, repair, overhaul, training, or support services concerning the helicopter including Aircraft Log Books.

16. Any and all videotapes, audio tapes, or photographs that were confiscated from the electronic devices that were onboard the subject helicopter at the time of the crash.

17. All policies of primary and/or excess insurance which were in full force and effect for defendant and provide coverage for the subject incident.

Respectfully submitted,

ROBB & ROBB LLC

BY: _____

GARY C. ROBB
One Kansas City Place
Suite 3900
1200 Main Street
Kansas City, Missouri 64105
Telephone: (816) 474-8080
Facsimile: (816) 474-8081

ATTORNEYS FOR PLAINTIFF
KATHRYN L. SCHLOTZHAUER,
ADMINISTRATOR OF THE ESTATE OF
ROLAND SCHLOTZHAUER

FILED SIMULTANEOUSLY WITH PETITION

A.12 Sample First Request for Production of Documents: Helicopter Mechanic Negligence

DISTRICT COURT

CLARK COUNTY, NEVADA

*** * ***

MARY RIGGS, as Personal Representative of the ESTATES OF LOVISH BHANOT and ANUPAMA BHOLA, for the benefit of the ESTATES OF LOVISH BHANOT and ANUPAMA BHOLA; SUMAN BHANOT, as Next of Kin and Natural Mother of LOVISH BHANOT, deceased, MEERA BHOLA, as Next of Kin and Natural Mother of ANUPAMA BHOLA, deceased, and BALRAJ BHOLA as Next of Kin and Natural Father of ANUPAMA BHOLA, deceased.	CASE NO. A-11-653149-C DEPT. NO. XXVIII PLAINTIFFS' FIRST REQUEST FOR PRODUCTION OF DOCUMENTS TO DEFENDANT SUNDANCE HELICOPTERS, INC.
Plaintiffs,	
vs.	
SUNDANCE HELICOPTERS, INC., A Nevada Corporation,	
Defendant.	

PLAINTIFFS' FIRST REQUEST FOR PRODUCTION OF DOCUMENTS TO DEFENDANT SUNDANCE HELICOPTERS, INC.

COME NOW Plaintiffs, by and through the Nevada Rules of Civil Procedure, and hereby requests defendant to produce and permit inspection and copying of the following documents objects, and tangible things on Friday, September 28, 2012, at the law offices of ROBB & ROBB, One Kansas City Place, Suite 3900, 1200 Main, Kansas City, Missouri 64105:

1.   Any and all documents requested in Plaintiffs' opening interrogatories to defendant.

2.   Written, recorded or transcribed testimony or statements made by any persons relating to the occurrence described in Plaintiffs' Complaint.

3.   Any photographs, negatives, slides, prints, videotapes, or audiotapes relating to the occurrence referenced in Plaintiffs' Complaint for the wrongful death to Lovish Bhanot and Anupama Bhola.

4.   Notes, memoranda, letters or documents prepared by any personnel of defendant or eyewitnesses regarding the occurrence described in Plaintiffs' Complaint.

5.   Any accident reports, NTSB reports, FAA reports, fire reports, paramedic reports, police reports, supplemental reports, records or field notes prepared in connection with the occurrence described in Plaintiffs' Complaint.

6.   Letters, correspondence, memoranda, notes, reports or other documents received by defendant from any investigative or law enforcement agency which investigated the occurrence described in Plaintiffs' Complaint.

7.   Certified insurance agreements, policies, certificates, face sheets, indemnity bonds or other insurance documents obtained or carried by you in connection with any liability insurance coverage for personal injury or death which will provide Sundance Helicopters, Inc. with coverage for the damages and loss claimed by Plaintiffs in this action.

8.   Any documents, writings, or other things which defendant intends to offer as exhibits for trial.

9.   Any correspondence, statements, photographs, slides, prints, films, videotapes, reports, diagrams, sketches, drawings, treatises, books, regulations, authoritative reports, test results, or other documents, things or items used by or relied

upon by defendant's trial expert witnesses in connection with this case.

10. Memoranda, notes, reports or letters from any trial expert who investigated, reported, or rendered any opinion relating to the occurrence described in Plaintiffs' Complaint.

11. Copies of all incident reports or documents from 1996 to present regarding any incidents or occurrences of accidents involving injuries or death to persons due to the fault or alleged fault of Sundance Helicopters, Inc.

12. All policies, manuals, amendments, addendums, correspondence, memoranda and documents regarding policies with respect to helicopter tours.

13. The complete employment file maintained by defendant Sundance Helicopters, Inc. on Landon Nield along with any other documents contained therein, in its precise state of existence on December 7, 2011. This should include, but is not limited to, the following:

(a) Pre-employment Questionnaire and investigation/notes;

(b) Application for Employment;

(c) All medical examinations and certification of medical examination cards;

(d) FAA Airmen's file;

(e) Training; and

(f) Any and all other contents of the file, regardless of form or purpose.

14. Any documents added to Landon Nield's employment file from December 7, 2011, to present, as presently maintained by defendant Sundance Helicopters, Inc.

15. The results of any and all pre-employment, random, for cause, or post-accident drug and/or alcohol testing results related to Landon Nield

16. Any and all Sundance Helicopter, Inc.'s Operations Manuals and flight manuals for the period 2002 to present.

17. Any and all correspondence to or from Sundance Helicopters, Inc. regarding the subject helicopter crash.

18. Annual Reports of defendant Sundance Helicopters, Inc. for the years 2002 to the present.

19. Any and all promotional literature, advertising brochures, and the like for Sundance Helicopters, Inc. tours.

20. Any and all maintenance records for the subject helicopter including service letters, service bulletins, and airworthiness directives.

21. Any and all air tour flight routes for Sundance Helicopter, Inc. tours.

22. Any and all documents, including correspondence, memoranda, inter-office safety memoranda, and reports, relating to any post-accident changes in Sundance Helicopter, Inc.'s flight operations.

23. Any and all documents, including correspondence, memoranda, inter-office safety memoranda, and reports, relating to any changes implemented to Sundance Helicopter, Inc.'s operating procedures.

24. All Sundance Helicopters AS350B2 Flight Manual Expanded External Checks Checklists for the years 2002 to the present.

DATED: August 27, 2012   ROBB & ROBB LLC

By: _____

GARY C. ROBB
ANITA PORTE ROBB
One Kansas City Place - Suite 3900

1200 Main Street
Kansas City, Missouri 64105
Telephone: (816) 474-8080
Facsimile: (816) 474-8081
e-mail: gcr@robbrobb.com
        apr@robbrobb.com

LAWRENCE J. SMITH

BENSON, BERTOLDO, BAKER
& CARTER

Nevada Bar No. 6505
7408 W. Sahara Avenue
Las Vegas, Nevada 89117

Telephone: (702) 228-2600
Facsimile: (702) 228-2333
e-mail: lawre3@bensonlawyers.com

Attorneys for Plaintiffs

A.13 Sample Plaintiffs' Brief in Opposition to Defendants' Motion to Dismiss Based on GARA

PLAINTIFFS' OPPOSITION TO DEFENDANT'S MOTION TO DISMISS BASED ON THE GARA 18 YEAR STATUTE OF REPOSE

Defendant filed an identical motion in all three lawsuits seeking to dismiss each and every count against it claiming that Plaintiffs have failed to state a lawful claim upon which relief can be granted. As further set out below, Defendant's Motion to Dismiss should be overruled because:

(a) Under Missouri law, a petition cannot be dismissed for failure to state a claim if it asserts any set of facts which, if proved, would entitle Plaintiff to recover;

(b) Defendant's dismissal motion is based solely on the eighteen-year statute of repose set forth in the General Aviation Revitalization Act (GARA). The statute itself contains several exceptions and Plaintiffs have pled facts clearly bringing them within the first exception of a manufacturer's "knowingly misrepresenting" material facts to the FAA;

(c) Plaintiffs properly alleged that improper and inadequate revisions of Defendant's Maintenance Manuel caused or contributed to cause the crash which states a lawful claim under Missouri law and overrides the GARA statute of repose; and

(d) In utter contravention of Missouri law, Defendant seeks to dismiss Plaintiffs' claims because they have not been pled "with specificity." Plaintiffs filed 60-page Petitions with 5 appendices, containing 21 counts with 5 counts asserted against Defendant. It is absurd for Defendant to argue to this Court that Plaintiffs' Petition "lacks sufficient detail to allow a defendant to prepare a responsive pleading."

Plaintiffs respectfully remind the Court that in a dismissal motion the Court need only look at Plaintiffs' well-pleaded allegations and must deem all such allegations to be true and derive all reasonable inferences favorable to Plaintiffs from those allegations. Under this standard and applying the proper substantive law, Defendant's motion must fail.

I. FACTUAL BACKGROUND AND PROCEDURAL CONTEXT OF DEFENDANT'S MOTION TO DISMISS BASED ON GARA

These three lawsuits were filed on December 21, 2005 arising out of the crash of a helicopter near St. Louis, Missouri. It is undisputed that the helicopter was designed, manufactured and sold by Defendant.

In lieu of an answer, Defendant has challenged the sufficiency of Plaintiffs' allegations claiming that they fail to state a claim for which relief can be granted. Under the applicable substantive law, Plaintiffs have properly pled allegations which, if proven, would clearly entitle a recovery against Defendant. It is further undisputed that the component parts at issue were designed, manufactured and sold by Defendant. These component parts were installed in the helicopter well after its initial delivery date, thereby rendering the entire GARA statute inapplicable to this case.

In ruling on Defendant's motion this Court need only review the Petition itself and need not refer to any other matters:

At the trial court level, when considering a motion to dismiss for failure to state a cause of action, the trial court can only look to the pleadings.

Industrial Testing Laboratories, Inc. v. Thermo Science, Inc., 953 S.W.2d 144, 146 (Mo. App. 1977).

II. LEGAL AUTHORITY AND ANALYSIS

Defendant is correct that the General Aviation Revitalization Act (GARA) provides for an 18-year statute of repose applicable to general aviation aircraft and that the helicopter in this case was a general aviation aircraft. Defendant, however, gives short shrift to a well-recognized exception to this statute of repose which the Plaintiffs carefully pled and Plaintiffs should be permitted to conduct full and fair discovery on this issue.

Further, Plaintiffs have properly pled that Defendant's inadequate and untimely revision of its Maintenance Manual squarely brings Plaintiffs within this eighteen-year time period under the "rolling" limitation provision because this revision took place two (2) weeks before this tragic aircrash. These allegations independently serve to defeat Defendant's dismissal motion.

A. Plaintiffs Have Fully and Properly Pled Defendant's Knowing Misrepresentation to the FAA in Conformance with Missouri Pleading Practice.

A well-recognized exception to the application of the GARA statute of repose—in fact, the very first exception—is where plaintiffs allege that a manufacturer "knowingly misrepresented to the FAA, or concealed or withheld from the FAA" certain material information relevant to the safety of the aircraft. GARA, 49 U.S.C. § 40101, Sec. 2(b)(1). This GARA exception provides that the 18-year time limitation on civil actions against aircraft manufacturers simply "does not apply" under the following circumstance:

> (1) if the claimant pleads with specificity the facts necessary to prove, and proves, that the manufacturer with respect to a type certificate or airworthiness certificate for, or obligations with respect to continuing airworthiness of an aircraft or a component, system, subassembly, or other part of an aircraft knowingly misrepresented to the Federal Aviation Administration, or concealed or withheld from the Federal Aviation Administration, required information that is material and relevant to the performance or the maintenance or operation of such an aircraft, or the component system, subassembly, or other part, that is causally related to the harm which the claimant allegedly suffered.

Id. Plaintiffs in the case at bar did precisely that which is called for in this exception in that they "pled with specificity the facts necessary to prove" the referenced allegations. In fact, the Plaintiffs specifically pled that Defendant both "misrepresented" and "concealed or withheld" material and relevant "required information" from the FAA.

All of these allegations and the facts in support thereof were set forth in each of the three sets of Plaintiffs' Petitions for Damages as follows:

> At all material times herewith, defendant knowingly misrepresented to the Federal Aviation Administration and/or concealed or withheld from the Federal Aviation Administration required information that is material and relevant to the performance or the maintenance or operation of such helicopter, or the component, system, subassembly, or other part that is causally related to the harm that Plaintiffs have suffered as further detailed herein including, but not limited to, warranty and claim reports of malfunctions and difficulties, in-flight failures and reports of defects and power losses as to parts referenced in Service Bulletin JV878 issued on October 2, 2005.
>
> In that Defendant affirmatively undertook to issue said Service Bulletin, Defendant was obligated to do so utilizing the standard of care to be exercised by other helicopter manufacturers of the same or similar circumstances and did fail to comport with said standard of care for all of the reasons set forth herein.

(Petitions, pars. 10-11, p. 7).

Without any authority or support, Defendant claims to this Court that the GARA exception is "narrow." (Defendant's Brief, p. 4). There is nothing in the legislative history to support this view and, to the contrary, Congress intended GARA itself as a "narrow and considered response to the 'perceived' liability crisis in the general aviation industry" 1994 H.R. Rep.

The "knowing misrepresentation" exception is a critical aspect of the GARA scheme—where such allegations are made and later proved, GARA is out the window. *Rickert v. Mitsubishi Heavy Industries, Ltd*., 929 F.Supp. 380 (D. Wyo. 1996). Indeed, according to one court:

> GARA erects a formidable first hurdle to a plaintiff bringing a product liability lawsuit against a general aviation aircraft manufacturer, but once a plaintiff "leaps GARA's knowing misrepresentation exception," the case goes forward and plaintiff "then faces the usual product liability obstacles."

Id. This is perfectly consistent with the Congressional intent of the exception.

It was the unambiguous legislative intent of Section (2)(b) to carve out an exception for a manufacturer's misrepresentation of safety information to the FAA. As set forth in the legislative history contained in the House Report:

> Section 2(b) sets forth a number of exceptions to the Statute of Repose. Section 2(b)(1) contains an exception for cases in which the manufacturer has misrepresented certain safety information to the Federal Aviation Administration.

103 H.Rpt. 525, part 2 (June 24, 1994) (emphasis added). Plaintiffs in the case at bar have every expectation that they will be able to "leap GARA's knowing misrepresentation exception."

Indeed, courts looking at this precise issue have observed that GARA is "narrowly drafted" and recognize that there are instances where the exceptions would permit lawsuits beyond its 18-year statute of repose time limitation. In *Wright v. Bond-Air, Ltd.*, 930 F.Supp. 300, 304 (E.D. Mich., 1996) the court expressly found that:

> GARA is narrowly drafted to preempt only state law statutes of limitation of repose that would permit lawsuits beyond GARA's 18-year limitation period in circumstances where its exceptions do not apply.

Id. (emphasis added). Plaintiffs respectfully submit that the exception is properly pled in the case at bar so as to permit full and fair discovery on the issue.

Moreover, and with all due respect, Defendant is not being forthright with this Honorable Court. Defendant cites the decision of a federal district court judge from Michigan in support of its proposition that Plaintiffs herein have failed to plead with specificity the GARA "misrepresentation" exception (Defendant's Brief, p. 15, citing *to Cartman v. Textron Lycoming Reciprocating Engine Division*, 1996 U.S. Dist. LEXIS 20189 (E.D. Mich. 1996)). This is not correct. The Cartman decision supports precisely the opposite conclusion.

Defendant fails to point out to the Court that the *Cartman* case was decided in the context of a motion for summary judgment. That is, of course, a much different procedural creature than that which we are addressing here—i.e., a simple motion to dismiss based on allegations in the pleadings which must be taken as true.

In *Cartman*, the defendant moved for summary judgment based on GARA. In reviewing that motion under Federal Rule 56(c), the Court looks to evidence presented by both parties in the record and the Court "tests the sufficiency of the evidence against the substantive standard of proof that would control at trial." *Id.* This is a far cry from the standard and basis of review applicable in the case at bar.

The Court, in fact, expressly concluded that Plaintiff in that case had properly pled the GARA exception. Defendant omitted the critical footnote from the case citation (Defendant's brief, p. 16), which provides as follows:

> Footnote 2 - Defendant also has argued that plaintiff cannot satisfy the exception at issue because he failed to plead with specificity that defendant concealed information from the FAA. First, the Court simply disagrees with defendant that plaintiff's pleadings were insufficiently specific.

Cartman, *supra*, Footnote 2 (emphasis added). The court went on to point out that defendant was not even permitted to argue the sufficiency of the allegations "because this is a motion for summary judgment, defendant must constrain itself to arguing only that the facts failed to support plaintiff's claims." *Id.*

Defendant's motion herein is not one for summary judgment. *Cartman* supports the Plaintiffs' position that they have pled with requisite specificity that Defendant has misrepresented and concealed material information from the FAA.

In viewing Plaintiffs' allegations in the pleadings in the light most favorable to the Plaintiffs and, further, granting to Plaintiffs all favorable inferences therefrom, it simply cannot be credibly argued that they have failed to even allege a recoverable cause of action as against Defendant.

B. Defendant's Dismissal Motion Also Should Fail Because Plaintiffs Properly Allege Negligent and Untimely Revision of the Defendant's Maintenance Manual.

Plaintiffs' allegations involving the Maintenance Manual, if true, squarely take GARA out of the picture. As to this issue, Defendant appears to demand a level of pleading never before required under Missouri law.

Plaintiffs attached to their Petitions as "Exhibit A" the "Owner Advisory" sent out by Defendant to all applicable helicopter owners and operators including the pilot in this very case. On its face, this advisory states that it "shall be considered an amendment to the manufacturer's maintenance manual..." The document states in pertinent part that:

> The information contained in the referenced Service Bulletin shall be considered an amendment to the manufacturer's maintenance manual or instructions for continued airworthiness, and must be accomplished for ongoing airworthiness compliance as required per FAR 43.13.

("Exhibit A," attached hereto, emphasis added).

The U.S. Court of Appeals for the Ninth Circuit very recently held that revisions of a manufacturer's manual constitute a new "part" of the aircraft within the meaning of GARA and begin GARA's statute of repose running from the date of any such revision. *Caldwell v. Enstrom Helicopter Corp.*, 230 F.3d 1155, 1157-58 (9th Cir. 2000).

The *Caldwell* Court based this decision on GARA's so-called "rolling" statute of limitation feature which expressly extends the limitation period "with respect to any new component, system, subassembly, or other part which replaced another component, system, subassembly, or other part originally in, or which was added to, the aircraft and which is alleged to have caused such death, injury or damage." *Id.* (citing to GARA Sec. 2(a)(2)). The Court held that the aircraft's flight manual, which had been revised within the past 18 years was a new "system…or other part" of the aircraft within the meaning of GARA's "rolling" statute of repose provision. *Id.*

The Ninth Circuit's conclusion makes sense and is consistent with the underlying intent of GARA. The *Caldwell* case is squarely applicable to the circumstances of the case at bar. In that case, as here, plaintiffs contended under theories of both strict liability and negligence that the revised manual itself was the defective product that caused or contributed to cause the accident. *Id.* at 1156-57. The Court ruled that the flight manual at issue was not a separate product but was an integral part of the aircraft pointing out that federal regulations require that helicopter manufacturers include such a flight manual with each helicopter.

Similarly, federal regulations require that aircraft manufacturers provide and update a Maintenance Manual which provides information for airworthy and safe operation and handling of the aircraft. The Court concluded that:

> In other words, a flight manual is an integral part of the general aviation aircraft product that a manufacturer sells. It is not a separate, general instructional guide (like a book on how to ski), but instead is detailed and particular to the aircraft to which it pertains. The manual is the "part" of the aircraft that contains the instructions that are necessary to operate the aircraft and is not separate from it. It fits comfortably within the terminology and scope of GARA's rolling provision.

Id. at 1157.

This case is particularly instructive because in the case at bar Plaintiffs allege that Defendant's revision to its Maintenance Manual is deficient and negligent and even attached that inadequate revision as "Exhibit A" to their Petition. How could Plaintiffs be any more clear in providing to Defendant clear notice of their claims other than by attaching one of the primary advisories they claim is deficient?

Indeed, within their Petitions, Plaintiffs, and each of them, alleged that:

> Further, defendant improperly, inadequately, and in an untimely manner revised its flight manual or pilot's operating handbook, or maintenance manual, which did not adequately warn users of its helicopter of the malfunctions, deficiencies, in-flight failures, and potential hazards associated with continued use of the subject component parts rendering that flight manual defective in that a flight manual or maintenance manual is an integral part of a general aviation aircraft product that a manufacturer sells and is not a separate, general instruction guide, but instead is detailed and particular to the helicopter to which it pertains as the manual is the "part" of the helicopter that contains the instructions which are necessary to operate the helicopter and is not separate from it.

> Further, the inadequate warning in the various manuals caused or contributed to cause the helicopter crash and subsequent damages alleged herein and defendant substantively altered or deleted the warning about the subject parts from the flight or maintenance manuals within relevant time periods.

(Petitions, pars. 12-13, p. 8). Plaintiffs submit that the allegation as set out above complies in every respect with proper Missouri pleading practice.

The *Caldwell* Court went on to address the causative element which is necessary in order to come within this "rolling provision" extension of the GARA Statute of Repose:

> A revision to the manual does not implicate GARA's rolling provision, however, unless the revised part "is alleged to have caused the death, injury or damages."

Id. at 1158 (citing to GARA § 2(a)(2)).

The *Caldwell* court concluded that GARA does not bar a cause of action based on the 18-year statute of repose if the defendant substantively alters or deletes its manual within the last eighteen years and "it is alleged that the revision or omission is the proximate cause of the accident…" *Id.* at 1158.

In the case at bar, Plaintiffs set out precisely this causative element in a separate and distinct paragraph as follows:

> Further, the inadequate warning in the various manuals caused or contributed to cause the aircrash and subsequent damages alleged herein and defendant substantively altered or deleted the warning about the subject part from the flight or maintenance manuals within relevant time periods.

(Petition, p. 8, par. 13). Defendant is hard pressed to argue that Plaintiffs herein fail to properly allege that the manual at issue failed to cause or contribute to cause the aircrash and subsequent damages in that these precise words are set forth in the Petitions. Plaintiffs in these cases well pled the liability of Defendant based on its improper, inadequate, and negligent revision of its Maintenance Manual and the causal relationship of this conduct to the three deaths in this aircrash.

C. If All of the Facts Which Plaintiffs Allege Are True, Plaintiffs Are Entitled to Recover Against Defendant Such That Its Motion to Dismiss for Failure to State a Claim for Relief Should Be Overruled.

Under Missouri law, Plaintiffs have never been required to allege evidentiary facts which form the basis for allegations in pleadings. *M & H Enterprises v. Tri-State Delta Chemicals, Inc.*, 984 S.W.2d 175, 181 (Mo. App. 1998). Indeed, under Supreme Court Rule 55.05, all that a Plaintiff is required to do in his or her pleading is to set forth "a short and plain statement of the facts showing that the pleader is entitled to relief." Missouri is not an evidence-pleading state but is and always has been a "fact-pleading state." *Gibson v. Brewer*, 952 S.W.2d 239, 245 (Mo. Banc 1997); *ITT Commercial Finance v. Mid-America Marine*, 854 S.W.2d 371, 377-79 (Mo. Banc 1993).

The Missouri Supreme Court in *Gibson v. Brewer*, *supra*, set forth that:

Fact-pleading presents, limits, defines and isolates the contested issues for the trial court and the parties in order to expedite a trial on the merits.

Id. at 245. The sole purpose of fact pleading under Missouri practice reveals that its intended purpose is "to enable a person of common understanding to know what is intended." *ITT Commercial Finance v. Mid-America Marine*, *supra*, at 377. This means that a claimant need not allege evidentiary facts but must merely allege the "ultimate facts" upon which the cause of action is based. *M & H Enterprises v. Tri-State*, *supra*, at 181; *City of Fenton v. Executive International Inn, Inc.*, 740 S.W.2d 338-339 (Mo. App. 1987).

The Missouri Supreme Court has set forth the clear standard for ruling on a motion to dismiss for failure to state a cause of action. In *Nazeri v. Missouri Valley College*, 860 S.W.2d 303, 306 (Mo. Banc 1993), the Court held that such a motion was "solely" a test of the adequacy of the plaintiff's petition and for purposes of that motion all of plaintiffs' allegations were deemed to be true and the motion the Court should liberally grant to plaintiff all reasonable inferences based on said allegations. A petition cannot be dismissed under Missouri law for failure to state a claim if it asserts any set of facts which, if proved, would entitle plaintiff to relief. *Sullivan v. Carlisle*, 851 S.W.2d 510, 512 (Mo. Banc 1993).

Our own Missouri Court of Appeals for the Western District has carefully followed the dictates of the Missouri Supreme Court. In *Pranger v. Baumhoer*, 914 S.W.2d 413, 415 (Mo. App. 1996), Judge Lowenstein wrote:

If the facts and the reasonable inferences therefrom establish any ground for relief, the petition should not be dismissed.

Id. The allegations pled in the lawsuits as well as the reasonable inferences flowing therefrom squarely establish a clear right to recovery against this Defendant.

III. CONCLUSION

Based on the above and foregoing, Defendant's Motion to Dismiss based on Plaintiffs' well-pled allegations in their Petitions should be denied. Plaintiffs should be permitted full and fair opportunity to conduct discovery on all of these well-pleaded allegations.

WHEREFORE, for the above-stated reasons, Plaintiffs jointly request that this Court enter its Order as follows:

(A) Overruling Defendant's Motion to Dismiss Based on the GARA 18 year Statute of Repose; and

(B) For such other and further relief as this Court deems just and proper under the circumstances presented.

Appendix B

Significant Helicopter Crash Case Decisions

Synopsis

B.1 *Barnett v. La Societe Anonyme Turbomeca France*, 963 S.W.2d 639 (Mo. App. 1997), cert. denied, 525 U.S. 827 (1998)

Missouri Court of Appeals,
Western District.
Kyong Ju BARNETT, et al., Respondent-Appellant,
James S. Barnett, Sr., and Wanda Barnett, Respondents-Appellants,
v.
LA SOCIETE ANONYME TURBOMECA FRANCE a/k/a Turbomeca, S.A., Appellant-Respondent,
Turbomeca Engine Corporation, Appellant-Respondent.
Nos. WD 51980, WD 52016.

Nov. 25, 1997.
Motion for Rehearing and/or Transfer to Supreme Court Denied Jan. 27, 1998.
Application for Transfer Denied March 24, 1998.

Administrator of estate of helicopter pilot who had died in crash sued corporation which had manufactured helicopter and its subsidiary, which distributed helicopter. After jury returned verdict for plaintiffs, the Circuit Court, Jackson County, Lee E. Wells, J., remitted verdicts to $25 million in actual damages and $87.5 million in punitive damages, and issued statutory credit for punitive damages awarded in separate action against defendants arising from same crash. Appeals were taken, and the Court of Appeals, Lowenstein, J., held that: (1) any error in punitive damage instruction was harmless; (2) use of pattern instructions was not reversible error; (3) evidence of defendants' yearly gross sales was admissible with respect to punitive damages; (4) damage awards were excessive, and would be remitted to $3.5 million in compensatory damages and $26.5 million in punitive damages; and (5) statutory credit was not warranted, as statute does not apply where two actions are pending in same court at same time and total amount of punitive damages imposed was not excessive.

Affirmed upon remittitur; otherwise reversed and remanded for new trial.

For space considerations, all headnotes have been deleted.

Gary C. Robb, Kansas City, for Kyong Ju Barnett, et al.

Douglas N. Ghertner, Kansas City, for La Societe Anonyme Turbomeca France.

Before ULRICH, C.J., and LOWENSTEIN, BRECKENRIDGE, HANNA, SPINDEN, SMART, ELLIS, LAURA DENVIR STITH, EDWIN H. SMITH and HOWARD, JJ., and BERREY, Senior Judge.

LOWENSTEIN, Judge.

This case, brought by survivors of the pilot in the same Life Flight helicopter accident which underlies the companion opinion handed down this day in *Letz v. Turbomeca Engine Corporation, et al.,* No. WD 51446, 975S.W.2d —, 1997 WL 727544 (Mo.App.W.D. 1997)., was tried after the *Letz* case. The defendants have appealed on numerous grounds-the plaintiffs cross-appeal on one point. The case was submitted to the jury on the theories of strict liability, negligence and failure to warn. *Letz* is being handed down simultaneously with this, the *Barnett* case, because the cases contain the same facts, similar and overlapping points and because the amount of punitive damages in the previous case bears on the net amount of this award. This is an appeal by the same defendants in *Letz,* from the jury verdicts of $175 million actual damages and $175 million punitive damages which resulted in a trial court judgment, after remittitur, of $25 million actual and $87.5 million punitive arising from the wrongful death suit brought by the family of the pilot.[FN1] Therefore, this opinion will only briefly recite the relevant facts of the incident including factual and procedural details**645** specific to this appeal. Additional facts will be included in the points to which they are relevant. This opinion will address only the points raised which are not resolved by this court's opinion in *Letz.*

> FN1. There is a cross-appeal by the plaintiffs Barnett which relates to the amounts of the credit to be allowed on this judgment for the punitive damages assessed in *Letz.*

GENERAL FACTS

On May 27, 1993, a single engine helicopter piloted by James Barnett, Life Flight 2, was transporting trauma victim, Sherry Ann Letz, from Maryville, Missouri to St. Luke's Hospital in Kansas City. En route, the helicopter engine suddenly failed and within ten to fifteen seconds crashed near Cameron. After the engine failed, Barnett maneuvered the aircraft some seventy feet beyond a stand of sixty foot trees, and crash-landed in a field. Four individuals were aboard the helicopter at the time of the crash: James Barnett, Jr., ("Barnett") the pilot; Sherry Letz, the trauma victim; Sheila Roth, a flight nurse; and Philip Hedrick, a respiratory therapist. Letz and Barnett were killed in the crash and the other two passengers were seriously injured. The crash was attributed to the failure of the TU-76 nozzle guide vane, in fact, Turbomeca finally admitted in their brief: "…there is no question in this case that the engine involved sustained an inflight shutdown as a result of the failure of the TU-76 nozzle vane due to low stress thermal fatigue." [FN2]

> FN2. For specific details explaining the TU-76 nozzle guide vane, the cause of the crash, and the reports generated by this accident, refer to *Letz v. Turbomeca Engine Corporation,* (slip opinion at pages 3-7).

The crash resulted in four separate lawsuits: the flight nurse and the respiratory therapist reached settlement agreements with Turbomeca, S.A., which designed and manufactured the helicopter, and Turbomeca Engine Corporation, a wholly owned subsidiary and distributor of the helicopter (hereinafter, the two defendant companies will be collectively referred to as "Turbomeca" and the American subsidiary, when standing alone, will be referred to as "Turbomeca Engine"). Letz's family filed a wrongful death action, and Barnett's family filed the wrongful death action here appealed. Again, in an effort to simplify the facts, Turbomeca shall mean *both* the defendant companies, and previous individual verdicts and judgments rendered against each of the two defendants shall be combined into one figure to represent the total judgment against "Turbomeca."

Barnett's immediate surviving family members who joined in the wrongful death action were: his wife of fifteen years, Kyong Ju ("Julia") Barnett; his fourteen-year-old son, Jessie; his twelve-year-old daughter Mia; and his parents, Wanda and James Barnett, Sr.

James Barnett died as a result of a transected thoracic aorta-he bled to death in the helicopter within 3 to 5 minutes after the crash. On the date of his death, Barnett was forty years old and in generally good health. He was an experienced military and civilian pilot having completed Army flight school and helicopter training. He was also certified for commercial flights. Barnett was employed as a full-time Life Flight pilot for eight years prior to the accident and earned a salary of $34,000.00 annually. His life expectancy was an additional thirty-five years. Trial testimony indicated the purely economic damages suffered by Barnett's wife and children was $649,080.00. The amount of those damages is not contested.

Because this case was tried after *Letz,* the procedural aspects of the case are distinct. Specifically, the *Letz* trial was not bifurcated and the verdict on damages (originally $70 million) was rendered in one lump sum which did not distinguish the amounts attributable to actual damages and punitive damages. This case was bifurcated as outlined in § 510.263, RSMo 1994, [FN3] to distinguish the actual and punitive damages. A more detailed discussion of the statute is contained in Point 3, *infra.*

> FN3. All further statutory references are to the 1994 Revised Statutes of Missouri.

After a seventeen day jury trial, the jury returned a verdict of $175 million actual damages and $175 million punitive damages ($350 million total) in favor of Barnett's family. The verdicts were remitted by the trial court ***646** to $25 million actual damages and $87.5 million punitive damages ($112.5 million total). The trial court then issued a credit under § 510.263.5 for the amount of punitive damages previously imposed by the trial court in *Letz.* Since the *Letz* verdict was not bifurcated, the court determined one half of the $70 million total judgment was punitive and, accordingly, issued a $35 million credit. The Barnetts accepted the remitted award and the Second Amended and Final Judgment was entered awarding $25 million in actual damages and $52.5 million in punitive damages ($77.5 million total) allocated among the two named defendants.[FN4] Turbomeca appeals from this judgment and the Barnetts cross-appeal only on the matter of the credit based on the *Letz* punitive judgment.

> FN4. The Appendix to this opinion presents a graphic summary of the dollar amounts awarded in the trial court and this court.

Among the points raised in this appeal are several that are addressed and answered in this court's opinion in *Letz* [FN5]. Those points will not be directly dealt with in this opinion. The six points to be dealt with in this opinion are as follows:

> FN5. Both, (1) the relevance of documents sent by Turbomeca to the FAA after the date of the accident, and (2) challenges to admission of deposition testimony of Dennis Nichols, president of Turbomeca Engine, regarding $48 million in cost savings for Turbomeca in not fixing the TU-76, were addressed in *Letz.*

1. Evidentiary questions involving: (A) pre-accident defects, and (B) whether Exhibit 111, an airworthiness directive, and Exhibit 177, an in-house letter on Turbomecca Engine letterhead suggesting the service bulletin was inadequate, should not have been admitted in evidence as they were evidence of post-accident subsequent remedial measures.

2. The trial court improperly instructed the jury in that: Instructions # 25 and # 27 did not instruct on proper mental state; Instruction # 5 improperly defined "ordinary care"; and, Instruction # 19 improperly withdrew an issue from the jury's consideration.

3. The trial court erred in refusing to allow the bifurcation process to be explained to the jury, and as a result, the jury was confused and misled.

4. The trial court erred in overruling defendants' objections to plaintiffs' admission of evidence of defendants' gross sales figures to support plaintiffs' claim for aggravating circumstances damages.

5. The trial court erred in denying defendants' motion for a new trial and refusing to enter a further remittitur of compensatory damages because the judgment as remitted, is grossly excessive, unsupported by the evidence, the product of counsel's misconduct and the jurors' bias, passion and prejudice, and bears no relation to damages authorized by § 537.090.

6. The trial court erred in failing to grant a directed verdict (not preserved in *Letz),* and denying defendants' motion for a new trial and refusing to further remit punitive damages because the judgment remains grossly excessive, the product of counsel's misconduct, constitutes an excessive fine under the Eighth Amendment, denies defendants' due process and shocks the conscience of the court. Points 5 and 6 will be treated together as the final point on the Turbomeca appeal.

Finally, this opinion will address the Barnett cross-appeal on the proper net judgment amount for aggravating damages after calculation of the credit due from *Letz.*

SPECIFIC FACTS

The following is a timeline indicating the number and dates of all crash incidents involving the modified TU-76 and related Service Bulletins and Letters. It is presented to better acquaint the reader with the issues pertinent to this appeal. Legend:

1. The chronology includes only incidents involving the *modified* TU-76 second stage nozzle-the same defective product on the aircraft in this case. The original TU-76 was replaced by the modified TU-76 in the early 1980s, in order to gain a cost savings in production. The original component had not, prior to the modification, been *647 implicated in any cracking problems or in-flight failures.[FN6] The later developed TU-202 ("Replacement") and TU-197 ("New") nozzles have not been implicated in any aircraft power failures.

> FN6. This opinion will refer to the defective *modified* TU-76 as simply the TU-76, since the original TU-76 has never been implicated in any in-flight engine failures.

2. Entries under "Information" are taken from internal Turbomeca reports or from testimony of its officials.

3. Entries involving this Life Flight helicopter are printed in bold.

Year	Specific Date	Information
1985	June-July	Cracking problem discovered in TU-76 following accident, due to in-flight engine stoppage, in Congo. (1374 hours)(hereafter, where a number appears in parenthesis, that number indicates the number of flight hours between overhauls logged on that particular engine. **There were 2482 hours on the Life Flight helicopter in this case).** Turbomeca examines and determines the second stage problem came after cracking.
	September	Helicopter engine was returned by the owner to Turbomeca because of cracking found on the TU-76.
	October	Cracking incident involving TU-76 (940).
1986	January	1985 Congo accident involving a defective TU-76 reported to French DGAC and to French Military. DGAC is the French equivalent of the United States' F.A.A. This information of a TU-76 problem was not given to the F.A.A., or other owners.
	January	Engine failure (1998)
		Engine failure (682)
	April	In-flight failure of engine (1148) in France, landed with some power. Turbomeca engineering report concludes a nozzle redesign is necessary and suggests overhaul of engine.
	June	Turbomeca conducts in-house testing of twelve second stage nozzles for cracking. The engineering report (Saviot) sent to the Executive Vice President, Chief of Engineering and ten others within Turbomeca, suggests the need to correct the cracking problem with TU-76, "caused by a low cycle fatigue stress of thermal origin...." Preliminary conclusions point to poor design and poor manufacturing, and state that poor "machining process has been an aggravating factor." Research begins to correct problem.

1986	July	Follow-up to the June engineering report (Saviot) is sent to all high ranking Turbomeca officials, concluding modifications are needed to solve cracking problems which stemmed in part from "poor manufacturing quality of certain parts, and their improper stress level." Two 2nd stage nozzles were used in this test, one from a unit sold in January 1986 to Heli Union which had cracked after (682) hours and was described in the report as "...earliest cracked nozzle we have identified..." Turbomeca continues to manufacture engines with the modified TU-76 module.
	Year-end	In 1986 there were at least sixteen engines returned to Turbomeca because of cracking. Hours ranged from (682) to (2005).
1987		Testing for modifications to TU-76 continues.
	Year-end	In 1987 ten engines were returned to the manufacturer for cracking. Hours between overhaul were from (1156) to (2057).
1988		Testing for modifications continues, results yield "Replacement" (TU-202) (metal change) and "New" (TU-197) (change in shape).
	May	Turbomeca increases time between overhauls from 2000 to 2500 hours.
	Year-end	In 1988, fifteen engines were returned because of cracking, two were from the French police. Hours ranged from (455) to (2745).
	1989	April Turbomeca examines unit (865) from Germany which was returned because it suffered "seizing of axial compressor," with torn vanes and broken central hub on 2nd stage assembly. Conclusion: "We have registered up to now 3 cases of ruptures...."
	June	Engine (1015) failure, resulting in grave injuries to four individuals in Bolivia. Turbomeca exam by engineer Delbert finds rupture in 2nd stage turbine blades with deterioration of central hub and rupture of outer ring. Report sent to top executives.
	June	**TU-76 installed in this helicopter during overhaul by Turbomeca Engine.**
	October	Engineering Department of Turbomeca (Delbert) seeks approval of New (TU-197) part but a November notation states it is being "blocked by the Turbomeca's Commercial Department." After examining wreckage from the Bolivian crash, Delbert felt there was an urgent need to correct the TU-76.
	November	Loss of power in a Phoenix TV station's helicopter caused an in-flight shutdown. The engine (1607) was examined and it was apparent the helicopter had a complete power failure over a busy freeway. Pilot successfully autorotated and landed in a field-no injuries. Crack around 2nd stage of nozzle guide vane central box-Turbomeca initially advises the owner that the warranty will not cover damage. Turbomeca relents and sends station another engine with the same TU-76 module.
	December	Engine failure in flight-Hong Kong.
1990	January	Engineering memo to Commercial Department seeking "very urgent" approval of Replacement (TU-202) part.
	February	A helicopter engine (1639.7) suffers momentary deceleration in Oakland, as pilot hovered, prior to landing, after a round-trip flight. The pilot heard a loud, muffled explosion, power failure occurred, the aircraft yawed, pilot set up hovering autorotation, then engine power returned in 2-3 seconds, and the helicopter safely landed.
	May	Replacement and New parts completed and tested by Turbomeca.

1990	October	A confidential Turbomeca technical note (Delbert) on cracking nozzles listed three in-flight shutdowns (1015, 865, and 1602), and that twelve helicopters had been returned by owners because of cracking (all had between 500 and 2000 hours). At the time of the report, 427 engines had *not* been modified with the cheaper TU-76-of these engines with the *original* TU-76, none had been returned nor had been subject to an in-flight shut-down. 2105 of the modified variety existed, including those units that were sent back to Turbomeca or had shut-down in flight. This report was sent directly to the DGAC, but never supplied, even after the 1993 accident, to the FAA. This report stated the Replacement and New parts "…were developed to remedy this (cracking) problem."
	November	Turbomeca receives certification of New and Replacement parts from DGAC.
1991	January	Engine deceleration occurs in Oakland-no injuries sustained.
	February	Replacement and New parts available to the 2,850 worldwide owners with TU-76, but no general recall is announced. Turbomeca never sent a notice to owners of aircraft with the modified TU-76 part that the New or Replacement components were available. French military were offered New and Replacement nozzles. Turbomeca makes a decision to replace TU-76 during the regular overhaul. (See May 1988).
	March	First Service Letter sent to Owners who do not have Replacement, discusses checking for "abnormal noise during engine stop" to check. If owner hears a rubbing noise, it "may be due to a rubbing between the internal hub of the 2nd stage turbine nozzle guide vane and the rotating assembly." The owner was told if the rubbing noise has been loud, the part was to be removed. This was the first notice given to non-French owners of a TU-76 problem. It does not include in-flight failures of TU-76 to date, does not mention the cracking problem and does not mention that Replacement (TU-202) was to be installed at Turbomeca's cost.
	June	In-flight shutdown in Portugal. Pilot and two passengers injured. (1354).
	June	French military gives approval of New and Replacement parts.
1992	March	DGAC approval of Replacement part.
	April	Service bulletin to American owners announcing availability of Replacement and New parts and recommending installation of either Replacement or New parts at time of regular overhaul. The degree of urgency of the Bulletin was listed as "optional." Levels go from most important, "urgent," down to "mandatory," "recommended," and finally, "optional."
	November	In-flight shutdown during take-off in Australia. Engine (1455) examined by Turbomeca-indicates the cracks are due to friction and disconnection of TU-76 second stage nozzle guide vane.
	December	Second Service Letter, to Owners who do not have New or Replacement parts, similar to March 1991 Letter (listen for noises).
1993	January	"Guyana" incident-an in-flight engine shutdown (1401), after explosive noise. DGAC approval of New part.
	February	Second service bulletin, similar to April 1992. The degree of urgency was "recommended." It stated the change to the Replacement part would take one mechanic two hours to install.
	February 15	Turbomeca inspects aircraft (1966) with 2nd stage nozzle guide vane damage, after in-flight failure preceded by several loud bangs and rapid loss of power (49 percent). Occurrence takes place on return portion of a round trip in Virginia. No injuries.
	February 15	Customer in Brazil sends helicopter engine (1669) to Turbomeca after in-flight stoppage.

1993	April 13	Third Service Letter. Turbomeca sends "Alert Information" service letter to Owners, "following an engine in-flight shut-down which occurred recently," warning to be aware of rubbing sounds. The word "mandatory" is used for all Owners who do not have the New or Replacement part. This is first reference in any correspondence by Turbomeca to an in-flight shut down.
	May 22	Turbomeca Engine finds 2nd stage problem (2011.5) after a pilot in Houston, Texas heard loud bang, no power loss occurred but while landing, the pilot heard a rubbing noise on coastdown.
	May 26	Phoenix TV station (see November 1989) helicopter engine (1894.9 hours on the replacement engine equipped with the TU-76) explodes five minutes after takeoff, yaws to right, pilot makes emergency landing with three passengers after a loss of power. Turbomeca Engine attempts to settle, but in letter sent to Turbomeca, says "I have tried to negotiate with this customer based on repairing his damaged engine which prices out at $178,000 for overhauls which I pro-rated to $134,000 based on the time of 1800 hours on the engine. He stated to me he did not want this engine back and wanted an offer on a new engine. I then offerred (sic) him a new 1B engine for $165,000 plus his old engine. He was insulted. He expects that based on his history of two engine problems for the same reason, we should be willing to show better faith and expects a new engine for free."
	May 27	**The Life Flight accident followed a "big, loud pop," then a clattering sound, then a horn indicating an engine failure which would not sustain the helicopter staying airborne.** Also on this date, a Turbomecca technical note distributed in-house concerned cracking on the TU-76 nozzle listed six previous in-flight shutdowns as of December 1992. An increase in "crack rate" over 1990 study. No cracks or shutdowns attributable to the Replacement or New parts.
	May 27	Turbomeca Technical Report (Delbert) saying, the crack occurrence may happen at any time along the TU-76 nozzle's lifetime, and may well never happen. 75 of 98 nozzles with cracks examined by Turbo have 2000 hours, or less.
	June	Turbomeca letter to FAA stating this accident was the seventh incident/accident relating to the TU-76 nozzle. Reported numerous incidents of cracks found during repairs and overhauls, due to a design and manufacture defect that caused rubbing and stress. Appended Service Bulletins which disclosed to Owners that a visual inspection will not disclose cracks but deterioration may be indicated by listening for the rubbing noise while helicopter is on ground.
	June	**FAA report on this accident. (2482) hours on engine. Barnett had 4,970 flight hours of which 1,400 were from military. He had averaged 100 to 120 Life Flights a year for preceding 3 years. Pilot had not been trained in autorotation without power. Nurse on board was interviewed: Her statement indicated that 10-15 seconds from loud pop, then clattering noise, white light went on left side cockpit, pilot maneuvered "cyclic and collective," and pulled the nose up, then rear of copter struck earth.** A witness reported seeing the helicopter just before the accident at 400-500 foot altitude. Report also states "the crack may develop to a complete opening (failure), even if rubbing not detectable.
	July	Turbomeca reports to DGAC. In July and August the DGAC issues Airworthiness Directive stating "Deteriorations…have resulted…in engine shutdowns." It makes mandatory the check of the module for rubbing noises.
	December	Portugal, power loss, emergency landing during take-off.
1994	February	Accident, following in-flight shutdown, Australia. Turbomeca tells FAA this was accident number 8 involving TU-76.
	July	In-flight failure in Italy.

*651 Other specific facts will be presented in the relevant Point Relied On. Again, the issues now presented are those not raised nor decided upon in *Letz.*

1. EVIDENTIARY QUESTIONS INVOLVING:

A) PRE-ACCIDENT DEFECTS AND B) POST-ACCIDENT REMEDIAL MEASURES.

A.

[1][2] Turbomeca now asserts that many of the memos and reports shown in the chronology of the facts should have been excluded on relevancy grounds. This case was submitted, in part, for recovery of actual damages in a product liability case, where the plaintiffs were required to show the product was defective and dangerous when put to a use reasonably anticipated by the manufacturer, and plaintiffs sustained damage as a direct result of the defect. For punitive damages, there had to be a showing that the defendant had actual knowledge of the defect and danger at the time the product was sold. *Angotti v. Celotex Corp.,* 812 S.W.2d 742, 751-52 (Mo.App.1991). Turbomeca internal reports and the evidence of other crash information relating to this defective part went to show the danger of the product and to establish the defendant had actual knowledge of the danger. *Angotti,* 812 S.W.2d at 751-52.

B.

This point is a variation on Point V in *Letz,* the reasoning there is applicable here, so it will not be repeated. There is an additional reason for denial.

[3] Exhibit 111 was an Airworthiness Directive issued in the summer of 1993 (see timeline) by the French DGAC and referred to the potential "worsening of this defect," and resulted in a more profound warning to owners of a defect that might cause in-flight shutdowns. Exhibit 177 was an internal Turbomeca memo in December 1993 in which the previous procedure to detect, listening for rubbing noises, was deemed not sufficient. Turbomeca correctly points out that evidence of subsequent remedial measures is inadmissible in negligence actions. *Pollard v. Ashby,* 793 S.W.2d 394, 401 (Mo.App.1990). Turbomeca grudgingly admits, in a footnote at the end of it's Point Relied On, the existence of this court's opinion in *Stinson v. E.I. DuPont De Nemours and Company,* 904 S.W.2d 428 (Mo.App.1995). In *Stinson,* under a strict product liability theory the plaintiff sought to introduce evidence showing the pre-injury warning label on the defendant's product said the product "could cause an allergic respiratory reaction," while the post-accident label "warned of the possibility of permanent lung injury." *Stinson,* 904 S.W.2d at 432. At page 432 this court said the post-accident rule in negligence cases did not apply "…in strict liability cases because: (1) the culpability of the defendant is irrelevant in such actions; and (2) the purposes of the rule would not be served."

[4][5][6] In this case, where negligence and strict liability were both submitted, the post-accident evidence was relevant for one count, ***652** and, as long as it was not unduly prejudicial to Turbomeca, being relevant for one purpose but not another, the evidence was admissible. *Rodriguez v. Suzuki Motor Corporation,* 936 S.W.2d 104, 109 (Mo. banc 1996); *Tune v. Synergy Gas Corp.,* 883 S.W.2d 10, 15 (Mo. banc 1994). If a defendant wishes to emphasize the limited purpose of the evidence, a limiting instruction may be requested. *Id.* A broad or blanket objection will not suffice when an exhibit is admissible for one purpose and not another. *Crockett by Crockett v. Schlingman,* 741 S.W.2d 717, 718 (Mo.App.1987).

The point is denied.

2. INSTRUCTIONAL ERRORS:

A) IN PROPERLY DEFINING DEFENDANT'S MENTAL STATE, B) IMPROPERLY DEFINING THE TERM ORDINARY CARE, AND C) WITHDRAWING AN ISSUE FROM THE JURY

[7][8] A) Turbomeca asserts the exemplary damage instructions given by the trial court were improper as they did not adequately define, nor require a jury to find that "the defendant knew or should have known its conduct created a high probability of injury." The trial court utilized MAI 10.06 which is to be used in cases where exemplary damages are sought where both negligence and strict liability are submitted. MAI 10.06 states that if the jury finds that the acts set out in the plaintiff's negligence and strict liability verdict directors, "showed a complete indifference to or conscious disregard for the safety of others," then the jury could award punitive damages. Turbomeca here contends MAI instructions 10.02 (negligence) and 10.04 (strict liability) should have instead been given. There are several problems with this point. First, both MAI 10.02 and 10.04 contain the language "showed a complete disregard for the safety of others." While this is not exactly the same as the damage instruction given to the jury, the damage instruction given was so sufficiently similar to imply the same direction to the jury that any prejudice would be utterly minimal. Second, Turbomeca's point on appeal regarding the lack of definition as to scienter or conduct was not properly preserved. The objections at the instruction conference make no mention of this objection now raised on appeal. Turbomeca, in its reply brief, candidly admits any review would be under plain error. The admonition in *Fowler v. Park,* 673 S.W.2d 749, 757 (Mo. banc 1984) as to making the proper objection at the instruction conference, and the reluctance of appellate courts to reverse for errors in instruction without a substantial indication of prejudice, apply here. In addition, Rule 70.03 is clear-"No party may assign as error the giving or failure to give instructions unless that party objects thereto before the jury retires to consider its verdict, stating distinctly the matter objected to and the grounds for the objection." Therefore, the court will not grant plain error relief.

[9] B) The next assignment of instructional error concerns the definition of ordinary care. Turbomeca argued for MAI 11.05 which defines the degree of care required of a defendant as what "an ordinarily careful person would use...." The court gave 11.10 II which "...means the degree of care, skill and learning that an ordinarily careful expert in defendant's business would use under the same or similar circumstances." Turbomeca states that all cases cited in the Committee Comment for use of this instruction for "Manufacturers of Certain Products," involve defendants who manufactured drugs. The argument is not persuasive. There was extended evidence offered from both sides as to the sophisticated nature of the engineering, dynamics, and production of helicopter engines. The trial court was justified in giving 11.10 II under these facts. Further, Turbomeca puts forth no showing of prejudice. This argument is denied.

[10][11][12][13] C) Finally, Turbomeca disputes the trial court, pursuant to MAI 34.01, for giving a withdrawal instruction on evidence presented by Turbomeca that Rocky Mountain Helicopters had not performed so-called power checks or engine condition checks every 25 flying hours on the Life Flight's engine. These checks appear to be in the order of regularly scheduled maintenance on all aircraft as compared to the checks for **653** rubbing noises as described in the service letters and bulletins. The trial court determined from the evidence that the performing of these particular checks would not have divulged anything relevant to the owner of impending power failure based on the *admitted* cause of this accident-the defective TU-76. The purpose and use of withdrawal instructions is to avoid misleading a jury on a specious issue and the giving or refusing of these instructions is up to the discretion of the judge. *Bradley v. Browning-Ferris Industries,* 779 S.W.2d 760, 765 (Mo.App.1989). An abuse of the trial court's discretion is reviewed to determine whether the ruling is clearly against the logic of the circumstances and so arbitrary and unreasonable to shock a sense of justice, thus indicating a lack of careful consideration. *Shady Valley Park & Pool, Inc. v. Weber, Inc.* 913 S.W.2d 28, 37 (Mo.App.1995).

This point is denied.

3. TRIAL COURT FAILED TO ALLOW TURBOMECA IN ARGUMENT AND THROUGH INSTRUCTIONS TO ADEQUATELY EXPLAIN TO JURY THE TRIAL WOULD BE BIFURCATED.

Under the auspices of § 510.263, Turbomeca invoked the option for a bifurcated trial.

1. All actions tried before a jury involving punitive damages shall be conducted in a bifurcated trial before the same jury if requested by any party.

2. In the first stage of a bifurcated trial, in which the issue of punitive damages is submissible, the jury shall determine liability for compensatory damages, the amount of compensatory damages, including nominal damages, and the liability of a defendant for punitive damages. Evidence of defendant's financial condition shall not be admissible in the first stage of such trial unless admissible for a proper purpose other than the amount of punitive damages.

3. If during the first stage of a bifurcated trial the jury determines that a defendant is liable for punitive damages, that jury shall determine, in a second stage of trial, the amount of punitive damages to be awarded against such defendant. Evidence of such defendant's net worth shall be admissible during the second stage of such trial.

[14] When this statutory scheme is utilized in a suit involving punitive damages, the first phase of the trial calls for the jury to first determine liability and the amount of compensatory damages, then liability for punitive damages. The second phase, if necessary, allows the jury to determine the amount of punitive damages.

Turbomeca does not claim instructional error such as a failure to use mandatory jury instructions or an improper amendment of jury instructions. Turbomeca here levels two complaints at the trial court for failure to heed the *suggestions* under MAI 35.19. MAI 35.19 contains a sample package of instructions for a trial involving punitive damages, and is contained in the "Illustrations" portion of MAI.

First, Turbomeca points to the following language in the Committee Comment to MAI 35.19: "The trial judge should exercise sound discretion in affording attorneys appropriate leeway during the various stages of trial to describe to the jury the proceedings contemplated by Section 510.263." Turbomeca's claim is that the quoted language is mandatory and should have been the authority to require the court to allow it to explain during voir dire, and in opening statement and closing argument that there would be a phase two and to emphasize the jury was not to award punitive style damages in phase one. The trial court did not allow Turbomeca to pursue this course.

Second, Turbomeca states the judge failed to include the proper and "mandatory" language contained in MAI 35.19: "If you find that defendant is liable for punitive damages in this stage of the trial, you will be given further instructions for assessing the amount of punitive damages in the second stage of the trial."

[15][16] Turbomeca argues that both these errors constitute an abuse of discretion. The prejudice it claims is the $175 million verdict for compensatory damages. Turbomeca stresses that the jury failed to understand that the punitive damage portion *654 of the trial was separate, and that it covered different damages. Appellate courts hesitate to overturn an order of a trial court on matters resting within the discretion of trial court. *Forester v. Roddy,* 418 S.W.2d 67 (Mo.1967). The decision to inform the jury of the technical workings of a bifurcated trial was an exercise of judicial discretion and will not be disturbed on appeal in absence of evidence of abuse thereof. *Arno v. St. Louis Public Service Co.,* 356 Mo. 584, 202 S.W.2d 787, (1947).

[17][18] The court can hardly be faulted for having given MAI instructions. It can not amount to reversible error in this case to fail to heed language in an illustrative instruction. *Northeast Missouri Electric Power Cooperative, v. Fulkerson,* 542 S.W.2d 26, 31-32 (Mo.App.1976). Committee Comments are advisory not mandatory, and prejudice does not follow from a neglect to use them. *Sall v. Ellfeldt,* 662 S.W.2d 517, 524 (Mo.App.1983). Although the court does not recognize reversible error here, certainly the better practice would be to more fully instruct the jury as to the bifurcated proceedings. Even if the jury was misled by the two-phase aspect of the trial, any prejudice is corrected by this court's action taken in point 5 on remittitur.

Turbomeca's claim that the compensatory damages were polluted with punitive damage evidence, is, however, worthy of further mention. Without unduly extending this opinion, a question may remain for legislative consideration. How much should the jury know, and at what stage in the trial should the defendant's conduct and the defendant's wealth be presented? Missouri's bifurcation process where punitive or aggravating damages are sought, is employed, with variations, in California, Georgia, Kansas, Montana, Nevada, New York, Tennessee, Utah and Wyoming.

What our system does is initially shield the evidence of the defendant's wealth from the jury, until there has been a determination that the defendant's conduct merits punitive damages. One commentator has mused, "It is a good guess that rich men do not fare well before juries, and the more emphasis placed on their riches, the less well they fare." Morris, Punitive Damages in Tort Cases, 44 Harvard Law Review. 1173, 1191 (1931). Though evidence of wealth is delayed, our system allows the jury, in the first phase, to hear evidence on both the issues of liability and punitive damages. *Angotti v. Celotex Corp.,* 812 S.W.2d at 751. As earlier noted, it is only after hearing this evidence that the jury decides liability for compensatory damages, and renders a verdict as to whether to proceed to phase two to determine the amount of punitive damages. Combining a jury's determination of actual damages with liability for punitive damages, after hearing all the evidence on the elements of defendant's conduct, could lead to an inflated amount of compensatory damages. Some states, including Minnesota and North Dakota, have attempted to handle this situation by allowing only purely compensatory evidence at the first stage, then combining punitive damage type evidence and net worth in the second stage. This method does allow the jury to hear the wealth of the defendant along with examples of its conduct. Another alternative, which New Jersey used for a time, calls for a trifurcated proceeding, where compensatory damages are dealt with in the first phase, punitive type conduct is presented in the second phase to determine liability for punitive damages, and, then in the third stage, the defendant's net worth is presented and the amount of punitive damages is determined. Needless to say, the other methods are not without pitfalls and problems such as unduly prolonging a trial.

4. NET WORTH EVIDENCE

Turbomeca's next point asserts trial court error in the admission of evidence of its net worth in the second portion of the bifurcated trial where the jury was to consider the amount of punitive damages. Specifically, Turbomeca says Missouri law permits only evidence of the defendant's net worth, and allowing evidence before the jury of gross yearly sales is unrelated to "punitive-type damages."

Section 510.263, which deals with the procedure of a bifurcated trial where punitive damages are sought, first states in subsection two, "[E]vidence of defendant's *financial *655 condition* shall not be admissible in the first stage....," and then in subsection three, "If during the first stage of a bifurcated trial the jury determines that a defendant is liable for punitive damages, that jury shall determine, in a second stage of trial, the amount of punitive damages to be awarded against such defendant. Evidence of such defendant's *net worth* shall be admissible during the second stage of such trial." (Emphasis added). Turbomeca insists the reference to net worth evokes a legislative intent to limit evidence solely to a net worth figure, and use of any other financial evidence during this stage, is prejudicial error requiring reversal. The trial court allowed the Barnett plaintiffs to introduce two prior years' sales figures of the Turbomeca.

During discovery, Turbomeca submitted a financial report prepared for it showing a 1993 net worth of 591,255,863 francs which translated into $122,565,470. There was additional evidence of $200,369,360 as the net worth figure (assets minus liabilities) which was given to the jury and, over objection the reports 1992 and 1993 sales figures of $498,373,130 and $474,967,030 were allowed in evidence. Admission of the sales figures is at the heart of this point on appeal.

To support this point, Turbomeca relies primarily on *Gollwitzer v. Theodoro,* 675 S.W.2d 109, 111-112 (Mo.App.1984). In *Gollwitzer* the Eastern District noted the *only* evidence offered by the plaintiff as to determining the proper measures of "affluence and wealth" of the defendant, consisted of gross sales and inventory taken from the defendant's prior tax returns. The opinion noted that admission of gross sales figures does not demonstrate that a profit was had, "and standing alone means nothing." *Id.* Similarly, the court noted inventory figures mean nothing without knowing whether goods on hand were mortgaged, or even if a large inventory equated to a lack of business.

[19][20] Turbomeca's point that the only evidence relevant here is the net worth figure, is not well taken. This language from this court's decision in *Green v. Miller,* 851 S.W.2d 553, 555 (Mo.App.1993) shows the law allows additional evidence other than the assets minus liabilities figure: "When determining the amount of punitive damages to be awarded, the worth or financial condition of the tortfeasor is a relevant consideration." *See also (Call v. Heard,* 925 S.W.2d 840, 849 (Mo. banc 1996), where the Court referred to the "financial status," of the defendant as being relevant in determination of puni-

tive damages); *Moore v. Missouri-Nebraska Express, Inc.* 892 S.W.2d 696, 714 (Mo.App.1994). The law does not make irrelevant and inadmissible any evidence of the defendant's "financial status" other than the net worth figure. Under the proscription of Gollwitzer, there was sufficient evidence, including net worth, to support a jury determination of the extent of punitive damages necessary to punish and deter this defendant. The evidence here of sales was admissible, its weight was to be determined by the jury. The point is denied.

5. SUBMISSIBILITY AND AMOUNT OF COMPENSATORY AND PUNITIVE DAMAGES

The court now recites the standards for remittitur and determining excessiveness of damages under § 537.090, Missouri's wrongful death act. This section shall apply to Turbomeca's request for new trial and further remittitur of the compensatory and punitive awards.

[21] In Missouri, there are generally two situations in which an appeal of an excessive verdict arises: (1) where the verdict is simply disproportionate to the proof of injury and results from an honest mistake by the jury in assessment of the evidence and, (2) where the verdict's excessiveness is engendered by trial misconduct and thus results from the bias and prejudice of the jury. A verdict in the first instance may be corrected by an enforced remittitur and does not require a retrial. A verdict of the second variety is prejudiced and can only be remedied with a new trial. *Young v. Jack Boring's, Inc.,* 540 S.W.2d 887, 897 (Mo.App.1976) (citation omitted); *Coulter v. Michelin Tire Corp.,* 622 S.W.2d 421, 436 (Mo.App.1981), *cert. denied,* 456 U.S. 906, 102 S.Ct. 1752, 72 L.Ed.2d 162 (1982).

*656 Turbomeca argues that both the compensatory damages award and the punitive damages award were the product of trial misconduct and, thus, justify ordering a new trial. The points raised by Turbomeca to support its claims of misconduct are as follows: (1) plaintiffs improperly referred to cost-savings figure and the FAA reports; (2) plaintiffs employed improper videotaping techniques in depositions; (3) counsel's closing argument for plaintiffs was inflammatory and overly emotional; and (4) plaintiffs' counsel indicated to the jury that Turbomeca executives' deposition testimony was inferior to a personal appearance in court. Turbomeca's first claim of misconduct-the referral to the cost-savings figure and the FAA reports-was resolved in Letz, where this court held such evidence was relevant and admissible to show aggravating circumstances. The second, third, and fourth points raised, even assuming they amount to error or misconduct, are not, on appeal, so significant as to require a new trial.

[22][23] Whether trial misconduct exists such that it engendered passion and prejudice on the part of the jury is left largely to the discretion of the trial court. *Walton v. U.S. Steel Corp.,* 362 S.W.2d 617, 627 (Mo.1962); *Skadal v. Brown,* 351 S.W.2d 684, 690-91 (Mo.1961). The trial court had every opportunity to see and observe the conduct of plaintiffs' counsel, and was aware of the circumstances surrounding counsels' actions as well as the general atmosphere of the trial. Based on its observations, the trial court ordered a remittitur of the verdicts, effectively ruling that any alleged trial misconduct did not warrant a new trial. This court sees nothing in this record to indicate that the trial court abused its discretion in failing to grant defendants a new trial because of the aforementioned incidents, whether such are considered separately or cumulatively. Accordingly, with no trial misconduct by plaintiffs' counsel warranting a new trial, remittitur is an appropriate remedy.

[24] The doctrine of remittitur has long been grounded in our common law. Although the Supreme Court of Missouri abrogated the doctrine in *Firestone v. Crown Center Redevelopment Corp.,* 693 S.W.2d 99, 110 (Mo. banc 1985), Missouri's legislature reinstated remittitur soon thereafter. The remittitur statute, § 537.068, was designed to establish equitable compensation and to eliminate, to the extent possible, the retrial of lawsuits. *Bishop v. Cummines,* 870 S.W.2d 922, 924 (Mo. App.1994). Under § 537.068, remittitur is proper only where, "after reviewing the evidence in support of the jury's verdict, the court finds that the jury's verdict...exceeds fair and reasonable compensation for plaintiff's injuries and damages...."

[25][26] The trial court has broad discretion in ordering remittitur because the ruling is based upon the weight of the evidence, and the trial court is in the best position to weigh the evidence. *Magnuson by Mabe v. Kelsey-Hayes Co.,* 844 S.W.2d 448, 457 (Mo.App.1992); *Fust v. Francois,* 913 S.W.2d 38, 49 (Mo.App.1995). This court will interfere with an order of remittitur only upon a finding that both the jury's verdict and the trial court's ruling constituted an arbitrary abuse of discre-

tion. *Hall v. Superior Chemical & Fertilizer, Inc.,* 819 S.W.2d 422, 425 (Mo.App.1991); *See also Bishop v. Cummines,* 870 S.W.2d at 923. The trial court will be deemed to have abused its discretion where the remitted judgment is still so excessive as to shock the conscience of the appellate court. *Larabee v. Washington,* 793 S.W.2d 357, 360 (Mo.App.1990); *See also Fust v. Francois,* 913 S.W.2d at 49 (Mo.App.1995).

[27][28][29] Missouri courts have consistently adhered to the rule that a verdict of a jury in assessing damages will not be disturbed unless it is grossly excessive or inadequate. *Sandifer v. Thompson,* 280 S.W.2d 412, 415 (Mo.1955). In determining whether a verdict is grossly excessive, the appellate court reviews the evidence in the light most favorable to the plaintiff. *Sandifer v. Thompson,* 280 S.W.2d 412, 416 (Mo.1955). *See also Triplett v. Beeler,* 268 S.W.2d 814, 819 (Mo.1954). The ultimate test is what fairly and reasonably compensates the plaintiff for the injuries sustained. *Coulter v. Michelin Tire Corp.,* 622 S.W.2d 421, 436 (Mo.App.1981), *cert. denied,* ***657**456 U.S. 906, 102 S.Ct. 1752, 72 L.Ed.2d 162 (1982); *Morrissey v. Welsh Co.,* 821 F.2d 1294, 1299 (8th Cir.1987).

A. COMPENSATORY DAMAGES

The jury awarded plaintiffs $175 million in compensatory damages, which the trial court remitted to $25 million. Turbomeca appeals the remitted compensatory award claiming that the trial court erred in denying defendant's motion for a new trial and refusing to further remit the compensatory verdict. Turbomeca claims that the verdict, even as remitted is: (1) grossly excessive, (2) the product of misconduct by plaintiffs' counsel thus demonstrating bias, passion and prejudice of the jury; (3) shocks the conscience of the court, (4) exceeds fair and reasonable compensation, and (5) is unsupported by the evidence.

[30] Turbomeca first requests that this court order a new trial arguing that such relief is warranted by the excessiveness of the verdict. Entitlement to a new trial based on the excessiveness of the verdict requires a showing of trial court error. *Callahan v. Cardinal Glennon Hosp.,* 863 S.W.2d 852, 872 (Mo. banc.1993); *Larabee,* 793 S.W.2d at 359. The size of the verdict alone will not establish bias, passion, and prejudice of the jury. *Id.* The complaining party must show that the verdict, viewed in the light most favorable to the prevailing party, was glaringly unwarranted and that some trial error or misconduct of the prevailing party was responsible for prejudicing the jury.[FN7] *Id.*

> FN7. See discussion *supra* for analysis of Turbomeca's claim of trial misconduct by plaintiffs' counsel.

[31][32] There is no exact formula to determine whether a verdict for compensatory damages is excessive and, of course, each case must be considered on it own merits. *Larabee v. Washington,* 793 S.W.2d at 360, a personal injury case, indicates that in evaluating the excessiveness of an award, the reviewing court should consider the evidence in the case and the verdict in light of the following factors: (1) loss of income, present and future, (2) medical expenses, (3) [decedent's] age, (4) the nature and extent of the injuries, (5) economic factors, (6) awards given and approved in comparable cases, and (7) the superior opportunity for the jury and trial court to appraise [decedent's] injuries and other damages.

Guidance may also be taken from the Wrongful Death Act. The persons entitled to recover under the wrongful death statute are identified in § 537.080.1(1) as the spouse, children, and parents of the deceased-all of whom were plaintiffs below. Wrongful death damages are governed by § 537.090 which provides:

[T]he trier of facts may give to the party or parties entitled thereto such damages as the trier of the facts may deem fair and just for the death and loss thus occasioned, having regard to the pecuniary losses suffered by reason of the death, funeral expenses, and the reasonable value of services, consortium, companionship, comfort, instruction, guidance, counsel training, and support of which those on whose behalf suit may be brought have been deprived by reason of such death...In addition, the trier of the facts may award such damages as the deceased may have suffered between the time of injury and the time of death and for the recovery of which the deceased might have maintained an action had death not ensued. The mitigating or aggravating circumstances attending the death may be considered by the trier of facts, but damages for grief and bereavement by reason of death shall not be recoverable.

[33][34] A factor to be considered in evaluating damages under the Wrongful Death Act is potential financial aid by the decedent, which can be shown through evidence of the decedent's health, character, talents, earning capacity, life expectancy, age and habits. *Kilmer v. Browning,* 806 S.W.2d 75, 81 (Mo.App.1991). In computing the loss of consortium for the loss of a parent for a child, or the loss of a child for a parent, factors such as the physical, emotional, and psychological relationship between the parent and child must be considered. *Kilmer,* 806 S.W.2d at 81.

*658 [35] Any pain and suffering the decedent may have endured shall also be considered in determining damages. § 537.090. The range between an inadequate award and an excessive award for pain and suffering can be enormous, each case depends upon its own particular facts. *Morrissey v. Welsh Co.,* 821 F.2d 1294, 1301 (8th Cir.1987). Substantial disparity among juries as to what constitutes pain and suffering must be expected. As the Eighth Circuit Court of Appeals stated,

This is a litigious fact of life of which counsel, clients, and insurance carriers are fully aware. Once they place their fate in the hands of a jury, then they should be prepared for the result....They cannot expect the [c]ourt to extricate them in all cases where the award is higher or lower than hoped for or anticipated.

Morrissey v. Welsh Co., 821 F.2d at 1301(citations omitted).

[36] In light of these general principles of law, a review of the evidence favorable to the compensatory damage award is in order. The purely economic damages attributable to Barnett's death are undisputed, both sides agree that $649,080.00 represents the lost past and future earnings, benefits and household services related to James Barnett's death. As a result, the non-economic losses, when applying the trial court's remittitur of compensatory damages to $25 million, amount to $24,350,920.00 in non-economic damages. The non-economic losses for wrongful death require this court to properly consider the reasonable value of services, consortium, companionship, comfort, instruction, guidance, counsel, training and support, as well as any pain and suffering which the deceased may have suffered. § 537.090.

At the time of his death, James Barnett, Jr., was forty years old and was in good health. His life expectancy was an additional thirty-six years to age seventy six. His salary was approximately $34,000.00 annually. He was an excellent pilot by all accounts and had been employed as a full-time Life Flight pilot for eight years prior to his death. He received flight training in the military and was licensed for commercial flights. He had been married for fifteen years to Julia Barnett, whom he met during overseas military service. The couple had two young children, Jessie (14) and Mia (12), both of whom enjoyed a close relationship with their father. In addition, he had a close relationship with his parents James and Wanda Barnett. A videotape demonstrating the closeness and intimacy of interactions between James Barnett and his family was admitted into evidence.

Additional factors to consider include the pain and suffering of the deceased prior to death and the number of plaintiffs suffering a loss. § 537.090. Testimony of the Chief Medical Examiner of Jackson County who performed the autopsy demonstrated that James Barnett consciously suffered pain for three to five minutes as he bled to death after his thoracic aorta was severed upon impact.

Plaintiffs properly point out that the compensatory verdict considers the economic and non-economic losses to five individual plaintiffs. "[A]n element of the total damages is based upon the relationship between the deceased and each individual party to the action." *Call v. Heard,* 925 S.W.2d 840, 851 (Mo. banc 1996). The fact that each of five individuals who were proper plaintiffs under the Wrongful Death Act demonstrated significant non-economic losses stemming from the death of James Barnett would work to increase the total compensatory award. Under the authority of § 537.068, and having reviewed and weighed the evidence of economic and non-economic compensatory damage and considering the number of plaintiffs, this court finds that the 25 million compensatory award remains excessive and finds that 3.5 million dollars is an appropriate compensatory damage award and orders remittitur accordingly, providing the plaintiffs accept this figure, otherwise a new trial will be ordered.

B. PUNITIVE DAMAGES

1) Refusal to Grant Directed Verdict

Turbomeca also alleges the trial court erred in refusing to grant a directed verdict on the issue of aggravating circumstances and in submitting the issue to the jury because plaintiffs failed to make a submissible case that: (1) Turbomeca knew of the defective condition of the TU-76 nozzle guide vane ***659** at the time the TU-76 left Turbomeca's possession; (2) Turbomeca knew or had reason to know of the high probability that its actions would result in injury; and (3) Turbomeca showed complete indifference to or conscious disregard for the safety of others when they sold or installed the TU-76 nozzle guide vane.

[37][38] In reviewing the denial of a motion for directed verdict, the evidence presented at trial is viewed in the light most favorable to the non-moving party in order to determine whether or not substantial evidence was introduced which tended to prove facts essential to plaintiff's recovery. *Gamble v. Bost,* 901 S.W.2d 182, 185 (Mo.App.1995); *Lindsey Masonry Co. v. Jenkins & Assoc.,* 897 S.W.2d 6, 15 (Mo.App.1995). A case should not be withdrawn from the jury unless the facts in evidence and the inferences fairly deductible therefrom are so strongly against plaintiffs that reasonable minds could not differ. *Bridgeforth v. Proffitt,* 490 S.W.2d 416, 423 (Mo.App.1973).

Section 537.090 provides that in wrongful death cases "[t]he mitigating or aggravating circumstances attending the death may be considered by the trier of facts" in assessing damages. In *Bennett v. Owens-Corning Fiberglas Corp.,* 896 S.W.2d 464, 466 (Mo. banc 1995), the Supreme Court of Missouri held that aggravating circumstances damages in wrongful death cases are punitive in nature. Subsequently, in *Call v. Heard,* 925 S.W.2d at 847-849, Missouri's highest court applied a punitive damages analysis in reviewing an award of aggravating circumstances damages under § 537.090, Missouri's wrongful death statute.[FN8]

> FN8. In *Call v. Heard,* the Supreme Court jettisoned the term "aggravating circumstances damages" for "punitive damages," thereby solidifying its holding in *Bennett* that aggravating circumstances damages are the equivalent of punitive damages. *Baker v. General Motors Corp.,* 86 F.3d 811, 817 (8th Cir.1996). Hence, this opinion, following the Supreme Court of Missouri's opinion in Call, refers to the Wrongful Death Act's aggravating circumstances damages as punitive damages.

[39][40] The well-established purpose of punitive damages is to inflict punishment and to serve as an example and a deterrent to similar conduct. *Vaughan v. Taft Broadcasting Co.,* 708 S.W.2d 656, 660 (Mo. banc 1986). Submission of punitive damages in a wrongful death case is proper when the defendant could have reasonably been charged with knowledge of a potentially dangerous situation but failed to act to prevent or reduce the danger. *Kilmer v. Browning,* 806 S.W.2d 75, 80 (Mo.App.1991).[FN9]

FN9. In *Kilmer v. Browning,* a wrongful death case brought against the landlord and gas company when a tenant died of carbon monoxide asphyxiation, the court held that failing to adequately examine a carbon monoxide venting system, or ignoring the system's defective condition, was indicative of indifference to the safety of others, and justified submitting punitive damages to the jury. *Kilmer v. Browning,* 806 S.W.2d at 80.

[41][42] In the context of products liability actions, the legal standard for submitting punitive damages depends on whether the underlying theory is in strict liability or in negligence. The trial court submitted both theories to the jury. Under a negligence theory, punitive damages may be awarded if the defendant showed complete indifference to or a conscious disregard for the safety of others. *Stojkovic v. Weller,* 802 S.W.2d 152, 155 (Mo. banc 1991) (citing *Menaugh v. Resler Optometry, Inc.,* 799 S.W.2d 71, 73 (Mo. banc 1990)). Missouri cases have interpreted "complete indifference to or a conscious disregard for the safety of others" to mean if the defendant knew or had reason to know that there was a high degree of probability that the action would result in injury. *Hoover's Dairy, Inc. v. Mid-America Dairymen,* 700 S.W.2d 426, 436 (Mo. banc 1985); *Sharp v. Robberson,* 495 S.W.2d 394, 397 (Mo. banc 1973). In a strict liability case, punitive damages are properly

submitted where (1) the defendant showed complete indifference to or a conscious disregard for the safety of others, and (2) the defendant introduced the offending product into commerce with actual knowledge of the product's defect. *Angotti v. Celotex Corp.,* 812 S.W.2d 742, 746 (Mo.App.1991).

[43] A review of the evidence presented at trial reveals that substantial evidence existed from which the trial court could determine***660** that plaintiffs had made a submissible case for punitive damages. Testimony by Turbomeca's own officers indicates complete indifference to, and a conscious disregard for, the safety of others. Jean Meliet, a mechanical engineer who has been Turbomeca's Customer Technical Support Manager since 1989, testified at trial that he knew in 1986 or 1987 that a problem caused by moving parts rubbing on non-moving parts were causing a deterioration that resulted in engine shutdowns. (See timeline, June 1986, Saviot report). He agreed that, in 1986, the Saviot report revealed a serious TU-76 problem. At trial, the following dialogue followed:

Q. Now, notwithstanding the fact you know you have a serious problem with the TU-76, you still keep manufacturing ARRIEL engines with the TU-76 modifications in them without making changes; isn't that true, in design?

A. Yes.

Q. And you keep manufacturing them and selling them without changing the metal, correct?

A. Yes.

Q. And literally hundreds and hundreds of these engines with the weak metal get manufactured and sold after June 9 of 1986, correct?

A. Yes.

Q. And that goes out on new aircraft and when people bring their engines back for overhaul, TU-76 with this weak metal gets put right back in them correct?

A. Yes.

Q. And during that period of time the number of these cracks and the ruptures and the incidents and the accidents starts mount in, doesn't it?

A. Yes.

* * * * * *

Q. So, we know a third of these engines with this part in it with a bad metal are coming here to this country, correct?

A. Yes

* * * * * *

Q. You know anybody within your company, Turbomeca, whoever expressed a concern that due to the TU-76 experience that we'd better recall this because someone is going to get hurt or maybe killed?

A. No.

Meliet was in charge of the first two service letters (See timeline March, 1991 and December, 1992) sent to Turbomeca's customers. He made a conscious decision not to include information of in-flight shutdowns and failures in the letters, nor to advise helicopter owners of the safety situation involved with the modified TU-76 part. Safety, as far as Turbomeca was concerned, was not directly related to the cracks in the TU-76. "The in-flight deterioration of a TU 76 leads only to an in-flight shutdown of the engine. That's all." According to Turbomeca officers, an in-flight loss of engine power did not constitute an emergency, rather they simply stated "the pilot must be in a position to land this helicopter in safety."

At trial, Meliet agreed it would have been a large expense to have the TU-76 replaced, at Turbomeca's cost, in all Turbomeca helicopters worldwide. [FN10] In addition, Meliet admitted the impetus to extend the time between overhauls (See timeline May 1988) was for better sales, and that it would have been possibly bad for sales to have included the safety concerns connected with the TU-76. The Life Flight helicopter in this case had 2482 flight hours at the time of the accident, thus, had Turbomeca not extended the time between overhauls from 2000 to 2500, the accident in this case would have never occurred.

FN10. Turbomeca officers, Dennis Nichols and Steven Ives both testified that a retrofit of the Replacement (TU-202) during a recall would have cost Turbomeca $17,000 per helicopter, with approximately 2850 helicopters worldwide using the defective TU-76.

Alain Calamard, the vice-president for engineering and the technical manager of 670+ persons, including 150 engineers at Turbomeca, admitted the problem of cracking and disintegration around the hub was known to Turbomeca in June 1986, and that this problem led to in-flight failures of engines. He **661** admitted that the cracking in the TU-76 developed after relatively few hours of usage, and often occurred prior to "Turbomeca's prescribed limits" for overhaul service. He also said that in 1991, Turbomeca made mandatory for a customer to change another part of the engine-but not this part. Only the French military was advised of the existence of the Replacement part.

The testimony at trial established that a manufacturer has a sales advantage if it can lengthen the time between overhauls, because not only does the helicopter owner pay for overhauls FN11, but the helicopter is out of service during that time. Calamard agreed that the May 1988 Turbomeca extension for overhaul from 2000 to 2500 hours (some two years after the 1986 Saviot report), was "significant", and came after "…we already knew of a number of failures of the TU 76 standard nozzle guide vane."

FN11. Dennis Nichols, president of Turbomeca Engine Corp., testified that an overhaul costs a helicopter owner, on average, between $90,000 and $140,000.

Based on Meliet and Calamard's testimony at trial, as well as the testimony of several other Turbomeca officers (see Point B *infra*), there was ample evidence from which the trial court could determine the submission of punitive damages was proper. Denial of the directed verdict and submission of punitive damages was not error. Point denied.

2) Remittitur of Damages

Turbomeca next alleges the trial court erred in denying its motion for a new trial and refusing to further remit punitive damages because the judgment: (1) remains grossly excessive, the product of misconduct by plaintiff's counsel; (2) constitutes an excessive fine under the Eighth Amendment; (3) denies the defendants due process; and (4) shocks the conscience of the court and demonstrates bias, passion and prejudice.

[44][45][46][47] Generally, the decision to award punitive damages is peculiarly committed to the jury and trial court's discretion, and the appellate court will only interfere in extreme cases. *Fust v. Francois,* 913 S.W.2d 38, 50 (Mo.App.1995); *Young v. Jack Boring's, Inc.,* 540 S.W.2d 887, 898 (Mo.App.1976). When a jury awards punitive damages, "both the trial court…and the appellate court review the award to ensure that it is not an abuse of discretion." *Call v. Heard,* 925 S.W.2d at 849. On appellate review, an abuse of discretion is established when the size of the punitive award is so disproportionate to the relevant factors that it reveals improper motives or a clear absence of the honest exercise of judgment. *Id.* at 849 (citing *Beggs v. Universal C.I.T. Credit Corp.,* 409 S.W.2d 719, 724 (Mo.1966)). Only when the amount is manifestly unjust will appellate courts interfere with or reduce the size of a verdict. *Ball v. Burlington Northern R. Co.,* 672 S.W.2d 358, 363 (Mo. App.1984).

[48][49][50] Unfortunately no "punctilious prescription", no brightline test, exists to determine if a punitive damage award is excessive. *Hodges v. Johnson,* 417 S.W.2d 685, 690 (Mo.App.1967). While an appellate court can look to other decided cases for guidance, they are often not determinative, for each case presents its own peculiar facts and circumstances which must be evaluated. *Id.* at 689; see also *Huffman v. Young,* 478 S.W.2d 332, 333 (Mo.1972). It is because of the unique facts and circumstances of each case that no fixed mathematical relation, between the amount of actual damages and the amount of punitive damages, can exist. However, the amount of the punitive award must somehow be related to the wrongful act and the actual or potential injury resulting therefrom. *Call v. Heard,* 925 S.W.2d at 849. If the jury's verdict appears to be grossly excessive, outrageous, or the result of an honest mistake, so as to be obviously disproportionate to the injury shown, it is the duty of the court to modify the verdict. *Cates v. Eddy,* 669 P.2d 912, 920-21 (Wyo.1983); 52 Am.Jur.2d 251.

[51][52] Fortunately, juries, even in the most complicated cases, generally achieve good results. It is true, however, that no system is perfect and on occasion a jury will reach an incorrect result in the eyes of all reasonable persons. "[A] jury is not free to award any sum it might choose, however ***662** large or small, whether from anger, sorrow, prejudice, mistake, or other improper cause." *Cates v. Eddy,* 669 P.2d at 920, 50 A.L.R.4th 821. Although considerable latitude is afforded the jury in arriving at a punitive award, the award must fall within a range, however large, that is acceptable under the Due Process Clause of the 14th Amendment. *Honda Motor Co. v. Oberg,* 512 U.S. 415, 420, 114 S.Ct. 2331, 2334-35, 129 L.Ed.2d 336 (1994).

[53][54][55][56] The Supreme Court of Missouri has held that aggravating circumstances damages in wrongful death cases are the equivalent of punitive damages and that due process safeguards are required. *Bennett v. Owens-Corning Fiberglas Corp.* 896 S.W.2d 464, 466 (Mo. banc 1995). Procedurally, the Due Process Clause of the 14th Amendment requires that adequate standards and controls be in place to prevent a punitive damage award from becoming an arbitrary deprivation of property.[FN12] *Pacific Mutual Life Ins. Co. v. Haslip,* 499 U.S. 1, 18-19, 111 S.Ct. 1032, 1043-44, 113 L.Ed.2d 1 (1991). Substantively, a punitive award cannot be so "grossly excessive" in relation to the state's interests in punishment and deterrence that it enters into the "zone of arbitrariness" that violates the Due Process Clause. *BMW v. Gore,* 517 U.S. 559, 568, 116 S.Ct. 1589, 1595, 134 L.Ed.2d 809 (1996). In *BMW,* the United States Supreme Court set out three guideposts for determining when a punitive damages award is so excessive as to violate a defendant's due process rights: (1) the degree of reprehensibility of the defendant's conduct, (2) whether there is a reasonable relationship between the punitive damages award and the harm that has either occurred or is likely to result from the defendant's conduct, and (3) the difference between this remedy and the civil or criminal penalties authorized or imposed in comparable cases. *Id.* at 574-75, 116 S.Ct. at 1598-99, 1602. *See also TXO Production Corp. v. Alliance Resources Corp.,* 509 U.S. 443, 459-460, 113 S.Ct. 2711, 2721-22, 125 L.Ed.2d 366 (1993).

> FN12. Because Turbomeca does not argue on appeal that Missouri's standards and controls are so inadequate as to violate due process, this issue is outside the scope of this opinion.

[57] With these cases in mind, this court must both: (1) review the court's remittitur under the guideposts set forth in *BMW,* to determine if the punitive award remains grossly excessive so as to violate due process; and (2) review the remitted amount under the factors set out in Missouri's case law, to determine if the trial court's remittitur constitutes an abuse of discretion so as to require further remittitur or a new trial.

[58] The constitutional inquiry begins by looking at the reprehensibility of the defendants' conduct. *BMW v. Gore,* 517 U.S. at 574, 116 S.Ct. at 1599. Reprehensibility is perhaps the most important indicium of the reasonableness of a punitive damage award. *Id.* A review of the trial testimony of Turbomeca's own officers reveals the degree of reprehensibility of the defendants.

Albert Ducrocq, the vice president of Turbomeca's "Airworthiness Department," [FN13] admitted, like Meliet and Calamard, that the cracks in the TU-76 were due to "thermal fatigue," and that the rubbing of the hub against the turbine could cause an engine to sustain a power loss or shutdown in flight. He further admitted that "[t]he TU-76 doesn't achieve what we would want as a goal for [a] reliable part." In spite of this admission, Ducrocq then testified that an in-flight engine shutdown, caused by a defective TU-76, would not render the engine "unairworthy," but rather *might* create a "potential[ly] dangerous situation."

> FN13. Turbomeca's Airworthiness Department manages the "airworthiness" of all engines in service and reports to the FAA and its French equivalent, the DGAC.

This obvious failure by Turbomeca's officers to recognize the severity of the situation was further illustrated by its repeated decision to not report in-flight engine failures to the helicopter owners, or the FAA, even though the in-flight failures warranted critical internal reports. In response to questions about incidents not reported to the FAA or the DGAC, Ducrocq replied in one such case, where Turbomeca's internal report stated that a locking engine caused "a brutal whiplash in power," that the occurrence was merely "a malfunction," but "...not necessarily***663** what we call an incident." Ducrocq was later asked about the May 26, 1993, Phoenix TV station incident (see timeline-this was the second failure of this particular engine), and could not give a reason why this event, though causing an internal Turbomeca report, would not merit its listing in answer to the FAA inquiry.[FN14]

> FN14. A third event not reported was the May 22, 1993 incident in Houston where the pilot heard a "loud bang," and made a precautionary landing. The fourth event not reported was the February 15, 1993 Virginia incident where, on the return flight, after the pilot heard a loud bang, power fell to 83 percent, and after another bang power went to 51 percent, prior to a forced landing. Again, this event was the subject of an internal report, but not included in the June report to the FAA. The same holds true for the very first accident involving the modified TU-76 where there was an in-flight failure in the Congo. (see timeline June-July 1985).

The following questions and answers are illustrative of Turbomeca's senior safety person's forthrightness, engineering acumen, and attitude toward the situation created by the modified part:

> Q. And would you agree that if the pilot hears a loud bang coming from the engine compartment, it is prudent to make a precautionary landing?
> A. This is left to his own judgment.
> Q. Well, a loud bang from the engine compartment is not something that a pilot would normally hear within the normal flight parameters of the aircraft, correct?
> A. I-I have no idea what is a loud bang.
> Q. ...these engines are not supposed to create a loud bang in flight, are they?
> A. I-I know this engine running in test status, not on helicopter. So, I can't make any judgment about the noise it can produce once they're installed.
> Q. Yes, sir, but you've never heard in the test situation a normal engine make a loud bang as described here, have you?
> A. A loud bang in the test cell would be judged unnormal.

After several more questions Ducrocq then admitted the failure was due to the same problem that caused the accident in this case. Ducrocq also testified that many of the occurrences not reported to the FAA were reported to the French DGAC.

The reprehensibility of Turbomeca's conduct is unparalleled, considering that Turbomeca knew the TU-76 was defective and had discussed incidents resulting from the TU-76's failure internally, but did not find it necessary to either: inform the helicopter owners of the in-flight failures, notify the FAA of such incidents, or conduct a recall of the defective TU-76 part.

From the evidence it can easily be inferred that Turbomeca's decision-making was motivated solely by economics. The crash in this case, plus the two failures in February and July of 1994, prompted a Turbomeca meeting, in the summer of 1994, at the home office "...to ask ourselves, why does this keep happening." The following colloquy about the meeting is now recounted:

> "Q. And Mr. Ducrocq, in evaluating the situation, certainly you all discussed what other options had been in the past available to the company and what options were still available, true?
> A. True.
> Q. One of the options that had been available from the beginning with respect to [the] TU-76 was something we had discussed before and that is to plainly and simply remove it at the earliest opportunity, right?
> A. That's a possible action.
> Q. Did anyone at that committee express any regret or concern that that particular remedial action had not been taken before hand, sir?
> A. Not that I remember."

In fact, according to the head of Customer Support, the decision was made in 1991 to offer the Replacement part only to certain owners, but no replacement would be installed in U.S. helicopters, "until the engine [was] taken to a repair facility."

With knowledge that there were 1300 to 1400 TU 76's in use worldwide, of which 200 were in use in the United States, the meeting of the executives resulted in a decision to not **664** recall the parts and to wait until the scheduled overhaul to change the defective part. During overhaul the helicopter owner, rather than Turbomeca, is responsible for paying for any replacement parts. As a result, Turbomeca could avoid the cost of replacing the defective TU-76's during a recall, and instead could charge the owner for the replacement nozzle guide vane while overhauling the engine.[FN15]

> FN15. As discussed, *supra,* another indication that Turbomeca was motivated solely by economics was Turbomeca's decision, in spite of Nichols testimony that increasing the time between overhauls would increase the chance of TU-76 failures, to extend the length of time between overhauls in order to gain a sales advantage over competitors.

> Steven Ives stated that the owner would pay for the retrofit of the New or Replacement part, unless Turbomeca of France consented. Somewhat contrary to who bore the cost of replacing the modified TU-76s, Ives then said that if the customer brought in a defective nozzle guide vane, Turbomeca had a policy by which it would pay for the retrofit. However, Ives knew of no service letter or of any correspondence sent by Turbomeca or Turbomeca Engine to any of its customers explaining that this policy existed.

In an attempt to justify the decision to not recall the TU-76, Ducrocq testified that a mandatory recall and replacement, was "…not necessary because the other actions which were put in place have proven efficient." However, he then admitted that had the replacement part been on the life flight helicopter in this case, Barnett would have been alive. The "other actions" that Ducrocq found to be "efficient" consisted of a series of service letters and bulletins sent to the helicopter owners to suggest that the owners listen for "rubbing noises" before and after shutdown of the engine. In reality, these service letters did little to inform the owners of the seriousness of the situation and nothing to inform them that the TU-76 was defective or that it could result in an in-flight engine failure.

Steven Ives, the manager of Technical Services for Turbomeca Engine, as well as several others who testified, have never personally heard the "rubbing" noises mentioned in the service letters and bulletins. In addition, none of Turbomeca's officers could state that any pilot, mechanic, owner, or accident report had ever mentioned hearing a rubbing noise.

Dennis Nichols, president of Turbomeca Engine,[FN16] testified that he became aware of the problem in 1991, the date of the first service letters, and that prior to May 27, 1993, North American customers were advised of the problems with the TU-76 through the service letters and bulletins. His testimony was as follows:

> FN16. Turbomeca Engine supports and maintains all Turbomeca aircraft in North America, about one third of the worldwide fleet.

> Q   Well sir we can go through the service letters and service bulletins as much as you like, and I invite you to look at them. They're right in front of you. But did they ever tell the customer that the TU-76 nozzle guide vane is defective and dangerous and could result in in-flight power failure?
> A.   I don't believe that I have read words of that nature in any of the documents.
> Q.   But that's true isn't it?
> A.   It's inappropriate for me to-I'm not a technical expert. I-I can't say that.

> * * * * * *

> Q.   Well, do you know, as president of the corporation, whether it's true or not that the TU-76 nozzle guide vane is a-defective component?

A. Would you state the question again, please?

Q. Do you know as president of Turbomeca Engine Corporation whether the TU 76 nozzle guide vane is a defective component?

A. Yes.

Q. And did you know that it was defective before May 27, 1993?

A. I-I can't say.

Nichols agreed that one possibility to have corrected the problem as quickly as possible would have been for the company to recall the engines and retrofit them with the Replacement (TU-202) at Turbomeca's expense. He also admitted that waiting for an overhaul, or increasing the time between overhauls,**665** would increase the chance of TU-76 failures.

Q. ...[N]ow the reason that...Turbomeca...took the position that we're going to wait until overhaul time and take the chance of failure in the interim of some of these part, is one of cost, isn't it?

A. I agree with that statement.

In July, 1994, the time of the Nichols deposition, he was asked if any decision had been made on the remaining aircraft for a recall, and he answered,..."there's been no decision."

Steven Ives investigated the crash in this case, as well as the one the day before in Phoenix and gathered the documents for the National Transportation Safety Board, ("NTSB") which had requested the number of previous failures. Like Nichols, he testified there were still engines "out there" flying with the defective TU-76 part. According to the service bulletins, it would take but two hours of a mechanic's time to install the Replacement on the Life Flight helicopter. Neither Ives nor anyone else at Turbomeca Engine told any owner or operator, including Rocky Mountain, that there was a defective part in these engines that created a potentially deadly situation.

Neither Ives, nor anyone else at Turbomeca Engine, questioned Turbomeca about TU-76 problems world wide. It was only after the accident in this case, coupled with the requests of the two U.S. agencies, that a comprehensive compilation was prepared. Ives admits to thirteen worldwide accidents or forced landings, all caused by the TU-76 part, occurring prior to the accident in the case at bar. He admitted this was an important number, and that it did not correspond with the figure of six priors as reported by Turbomeca to the FAA and NTSB.

Carey Brown, Turbomeca Engine's director of customer support, and Ives' superior, testified as follows,

"Q. Mr. Brown, when did you first become aware of any...problems...associated with the...TU-76?

A. I don't know when I first became aware...

Q. Was it before the crash of Life Flight?

A. I was not aware of any ongoing problems...

* * * * * *

I still do not myself know that the nozzle was the-problem."

Then when asked what he did when problems were discovered, he said, "I did-basically, when the various service letters came out, we simply administered those service letters."

* * * * * *

Q. And you did not have any knowledge as to either the severity or widespread nature of the TU-76 problem; is that correct, sir?

A. That's correct.

Q. Do you have a mechanical background, Mr. Brown?

A. Yes, I do.

Q. Do you have enough mechanical background to know that a failure of the TU-76 nozzle guide vane could lead to a catastrophic crash?

A. No, I don't.

Q. That's not something within your knowledge as the director of the customer support department?

A. No, it's not.

* * * * * *

Q. Did Turbomeca Engine Corporation ever notify its customers about a potential problem with the TU-76 design, sir?

A. I am still confused by the question.

Q. Well, did you or did you not send out any information or alert to your customers that these things were cracking and had the potential to kill or seriously injure people?

A. No.

Brown had not read the NTSB report, nor was he familiar with anything specific pertaining to the TU-76 problem.

Q. Well, with all of that in mind, Mr. Brown, I'm wondering as the director of technical support for this entire corporation, what is it that you do?

A. I manage the department.

*666 Given the testimony of Turbomeca's own officers, it is not difficult to understand why a large punitive damage amount was awarded. Turbomeca's conduct was unquestionably reprehensible.

The second indicium of a grossly excessive punitive award is its ratio to the actual and potential harm to the plaintiff. *Id.* at 580, 116 S.Ct. at 1601. The trial court's remittitur of $87.5 million in punitive damages, and to $25 million in compensatory damages exhibits a ratio of just over 3:1. For only illustrative purposes, it is noted the Supreme Court of the United States previously approved a ratio of 526:1 as not being in violation of the Due Process Clause of the 14th Amendment in *TXO Prod. Corp. v. Alliance Resources Corp.,* 509 U.S. 443, 462, 113 S.Ct. 2711, 2722-23, 125 L.Ed.2d 366 (1993). While such a ratio might not be proper here, it is evident there is no pre-set or magic ratio of actual to punitive damages. This court concludes that the trial court's remittitur evinces a "reasonable relationship" between actual and punitive damages given the nature of Turbomeca's conduct. *BMW v. Gore,* 517 U.S. 559, 580, 116 S.Ct. 1589, 1601, 134 L.Ed.2d 809 (1996).

Finally the third factor in determining whether a punitive damage award violates the Due Process Clause is the difference between this remedy and the civil or criminal penalties authorized or imposed in comparable cases. *BMW v. Gore,* 517 U.S. at 575, 116 S.Ct. at 1599. Given the testimony of Turbomeca's officers and the other evidence presented at trial, it appears that the punitive damage award given was the only real way to deter the conduct of Turbomeca. The evidence has demonstrated that Turbomeca's decisions were solely based on economics. In addition, it could not reasonably be said that Turbomeca did not have adequate "notice" of the severity of the sanction that might befall them as a result of their conduct. The aforementioned testimony reveals this fact.

[59] To supplement the requirements set out above for the imposition of punitive damages, the courts of this state have identified a variety of factors, a nonexclusive list, that should be considered in determining whether the trial court abused its discretion in not further remitting the jury's punitive award. Several factors may be considered, including: (1) the degree of malice or outrageousness of the defendant's conduct, *State ex rel. St. Joseph Belt Ry. Co. v. Shain,* 341 Mo. 733, 108 S.W.2d 351, 356 (1937); (2) aggravating and mitigating circumstances, *Beggs v. Universal C.I.T. Credit Corp.,* 409 S.W.2d 719, 724 (Mo.1966); (3) the defendant's financial status, *Id.* at 724.; (4) the character of both parties, *Maugh v. Chrysler Corp.,* 818 S.W.2d 658, 662 (Mo.App.1991); *Holcroft v. Missouri-Kansas-Texas RR Co.,* 607 S.W.2d 158, 164 (Mo.App.1980);

(5) the injury suffered; *Moore v. Missouri-Nebraska Exp., Inc.,* 892 S.W.2d 696, 714 (Mo.App.1994); (6) the defendant's standing or intelligence, *Id.*; (7) the age of the injured party, *State ex rel. St. Joseph Belt Ry. Co.,* 108 S.W.2d at 356; and (8) the relationship between the two parties. *Call v. Heard,* 925 S.W.2d at 849 (citing *Moore v. Missouri-Nebraska Exp., Inc.,* 892 S.W.2d 696, 714 (Mo.App.1994)). Each of these factors has been addressed in the discussion above.

It is a fact, a sad fact gleaned from *all* witnesses, that this accident resulted from the defect in the modified TU-76. Had the replacement TU-202 been installed, the module that used a different metal, there would have been no "metal fatigue" leading to the failure. What Turbomeca's own records, and indeed the early conclusions of their engineers show, is the fatigue or stress was brought on by a flight, followed by a short wait, and then a return trip (see time line incident February, 1990)- exactly the scenario for air rescue or air transport of fragile patients in need of emergency care. Turbomeca advertised the use of this helicopter for emergency medical transport. Turbomeca's reliance on experienced pilots being able to autorotate to a forced landing in such unexpected emergency situations as loss of power, with such a cargo, is void of any support and totally unrealistic.

Turbomeca's post-accident under-reporting of prior failures of the modified TU-76, however, pales in comparison to the lack of forthrightness to its customers. Turbomeca's failure to be candid with owners about the well-***667** documented dangers of their product, was evidenced by the diversionary tactic of directing persons to listen for rubbing sounds. The company always seemed to be motivated by cutting costs, saving money and increasing sales-all at the expense of the unlucky owners. The TU-76 was modified to save money. The New and Replacement parts took longer to implement for some customers than to build the entire original engine because of "being blocked" by its Commercial Sales Department. Its laissez-faire attitude of never notifying, even post- *Letz* and *Barnett,* owners of the lethal, undetectable dangers inherent in the modified TU-76, along with its net worth and financial ability justifies the imposition here of substantial punitive damages.

While this court concludes that the remitted judgment of $87.5 million entered by the trial court is excessive, the court finds in light of the relevant factors and considering all the evidence, and giving deference to this court's unanimous opinion this day in *Letz,* that $26.5 million is the amount to be rendered against Turbomeca as punitive damages in this case. Considering the extreme reprehensibility of Turbomeca's conduct and the other relevant factors, this court does not believe this punitive award, as now remitted, is grossly excessive as to violate the Due Process Clause of the 14th Amendment.

THE BARNETTS' CROSS APPEAL—THE STATUTORY CREDIT

The relationship between this case and Letz, and the reason both decisions are being handed down the same day, is exemplified by the cross-appeal of the plaintiffs. The over-arching question here is whether, under § 510.263.4, a trial court may grant a punitive damage credit in a second case, for punitive damages awarded, but not yet paid, in a prior case, that arise out of the same incident, when the prior case is on appeal?

The facts vis-a-vis a credit are as follows. The Barnett trial started in June of 1995. In *Letz,* which was tried first, an amended judgment was entered in August 1995. Turbomeca subsequently appealed and the case was heard by this court en banc. As the reader will remember, there was no bifurcation of compensatory and punitive damage awards in *Letz.* After the verdicts in Barnett, Turbomeca timely filed for a punitive damage credit under 510.263.4. Since the *Letz* verdict was not bifurcated, the Barnett trial court determined one-half of the $70 million judgment was punitive, and accordingly, applied a $35 million credit to the remitted Barnett punitive damage award. The Barnetts' primary basis for appealing Turbomeca's punitive damage credit is that no punitive damages award has been paid by Turbomeca in *Letz.*

The confusion caused by this point is due to the language of the statute, which simply does not envision the situation in this case-where there are separate trials, one soon after the other, with the same facts and the same aggravating circumstances, and both cases pend on appeal. Section 510.263.4 states in pertinent part:

> Within the time for filing a motion for new trial, a defendant may file a post-trial motion requesting the amount awarded by the jury as punitive damages be credited by the court with *amounts previously paid* by the defendant

for punitive damages arising out of the same conduct on which the imposition of punitive damages is based. At any hearing, the burden on all issues relating to such a credit shall be on the defendant and either party may introduce relevant evidence on such motion. Such a motion shall be determined by the trial court within the time and according to procedures applicable to motions for new trial. If the trial court sustains such a motion the trial court shall credit the jury award of punitive damages by the *amount* found by the trial court to have been *previously paid* by the defendant arising out of the same conduct and enter judgment accordingly. (Emphasis Added).

Paraphrased, the other pertinent portions of this subsection require the trial court to deny the credit if it finds: 1) that the defendant failed to establish entitlement to a credit or, 2) the conduct in the second case was not the same conduct on which the imposition of punitives was based on in the prior case, or 3) that the defendant unreasonably continued [its] conduct after acquiring actual ***668** knowledge "of the dangerous nature of such conduct...[FN17] § 510.263.4.

> FN17. It appears that Missouri's statutory credit mechanism is unique. Georgia at one time had a credit legislation. Offering a credit is an alternative to caps on punitive or aggravating awards. The Missouri General Assembly should not be criticized for allowing, but not mandating, a credit to avoid redundant punishment.

The Barnetts ask for a strict construction of the statutory language, and argue that the statute requires that after thirty days following entry of judgment if the prior judgment has not been paid, then no credit may be allowed in the second suit.[FN18]

> FN18. Section 510.263.4 requires the post-trial motions to be filed within the time for filing a motion for new trial. Rule 78.04 states that such time will not exceed 30 days after entry of judgment.

Somewhat surprisingly, there are very few cases that have interpreted § 510.263.4. This may, in part, be due to the numerous pitfalls and snarls encountered with implementation of the statutory credit. For example, consider what happens if no appeal is taken in *Barnett,* and *Letz* is appealed and results in a punitive award other than $26.5 million. Such a situation, when interpreted under § 510.263.4, would result in confusion because Barnett would then become the first judgment paid. As a result, *Letz,* which then becomes the second judgment, could not receive a credit for Barnett since the defendant in *Letz* did not apply for a credit as required by the statute-within 30 days after entry of judgment. The defendant in *Letz* never applied for a credit because it was the first case tried and there was no reason to ask for a credit at that time. This possible scenario would unwittingly force a defendant to illogically apply for a credit that does not exist at the time it is sought, and may never come into existence. In addition, even if Letz resulted in a higher punitive award than Barnett, the defendant could not, under the statute, obtain a credit for the amount paid in Barnett.

As has been stated earlier in this opinion, the purpose of punitive damages is to inflict punishment and deter similar misconduct and not to allow punishment over and over again for the same previous conduct. Punitive damages are not to reward plaintiffs, but to punish and deter defendants. *Menaugh v. Resler Optometry, Inc.,* 799 S.W.2d 71, 75 (Mo.banc 1990). To allow excessive financial punishment invites a constitutional due process violation. In *Elam v. Alcolac, Inc.,* 765 S.W.2d 42, 231 (Mo.App.1988), a case involving numerous plaintiffs who were damaged by the defendant's noxious emissions, the court upheld the defendant's liability for actual and punitive damages, but reversed only for the purpose of adjudicating the proper amount of damages. The court in *Elam* said: "It is a desideratum of the statute [S. 510.262.4] that a defendant not be required to pay redundant punitive damages based on the same conduct."

[60] The long and short is that the statutory credit under § 510.263.4 just won't adjust to these facts where two cases pend and are ripe for adjudication in one court at the same time. The statute's language allows a credit to be given only for "amounts previously paid." Rather than attempt to make the statute fit by allowing a larger judgment in Barnett and a "conditional" credit when and if *Letz* is paid, the court feels the overall effect of both cases and the remitted amounts of punitive damages in *each* case, when combined, reach the proper result and supply the relief that the credit statute envisions and the United State's Supreme Court has enunciated: that total punitive damages, where there are successive suits, will not go beyond due process limits in punishment and deterrence. As the Appendix shows, Turbomeca will have to pay a total of $26.5 million in punitive damages in each for *Letz* and Barnett. These amounts, when considered together are deemed sufficient to

judicially accomplish a total result that is not excessive, nor unduly harsh by repeated punishment. The trial court's granting of a credit on the cross-appeal is reversed.

[61] The wrongful death statute allows the jury to consider both aggravating and mitigating circumstances. § 537.090. Missouri courts have long held that mitigating circumstances are a factor appellate courts must consider when remitting the trial court's judgment. *Moore v. Missouri-Nebraska, Inc.* 892 S.W.2d at 714 (Mo.App.1994); *Beggs v. Universal CIT Credit Corp.* 409 S.W.2d at 724 (Mo.1966). In reviewing ***669** the jury's verdict, the trial court, as well as the appellate court, must consider both previous and pending judgments against the defendant as mitigating circumstances when the prior judgment was for the same conduct as the conduct at issue before them. The burden is on the defendant to establish that previous or pending punitive damage judgments against the defendant result from the same conduct at issue in the present case. The defendant is certainly in the best position to know of previous or pending judgments against them. By giving consideration to other judgments upon a request for remittitur, the appellate court can in the spirit of § 510.263.4, effectuate the goal of the credit statute-to prevent repetitive punitive awards for the same conduct.

The court realizes trial judges may be put in an unenviable position where a credit is timely requested by a defendant and other cases involving judgments against the same defendant are still pending. However, under these types of circumstances, where the statute does not apply, judges should attempt to use discretion in affording relief to keep punitive awards within due process limits. The legislature is encouraged to immediately revisit § 510.263.4.

Except for the points on the excessive amounts of compensatory and punitive damages, all of Turbomeca's points are denied. The trial court's grant of a $35 million credit is reversed. If the Barnetts agree, within fifteen days of this court's mandate, to remit the total judgment against both defendants for compensatory damages to $3.5 million, and of punitive damages to $26.5 million, this judgment shall stand as of the date of the original date of judgment. Otherwise, that judgment is reversed and remanded for a new trial on damages.

All concur.

APPENDIX

TRIAL COURT	Letz		Barnett	
	Actual	Punitive	Actual	Punitive
Jury's verdict	combined	$70 m	$175 m	$175 m
Judgment after *Barnett* trial court's remittitur	—	—	$25 m	$87.5 m
Barnett trial ct's damages allocation to determine credit[19]	$35 m	$35 m	—	—
Trial court's punitive damage credit	—	—	—	$35 m credit
Net judgment after trial court's credit	—	—	$25 m	$52.5 m
Appellate action	—	—	—	—
Mandate amount after the court's remittitur	$2.5 m	$26.5 m	$3.5 m	$26.5 m

Total Payment by Turbomeca under Letz and Barnett decisions: **$59 million**

FN19. Because the *Letz* trial occurred prior to the Supreme Court's decision in *Barnett,* the *Letz* jury did not render separate compensatory and punitive damage verdicts. As a result, the *Barnett* trial court, in order to determine the punitive damage credit under § 510.263, attempted to determine the portion of the combined $70 million verdict in *Letz* that constituted punitive damages.

B.2 *Boyle v. United Technologies Corporation*, 108 S.Ct. 2510 (1988)

Supreme Court of the United States

Delbert BOYLE, Personal Representative of the Heirs and Estate of David A. Boyle, Deceased, Petitioner,

v.

UNITED TECHNOLOGIES CORPORATION.
No. 86-492.

Argued Oct. 13, 1987.
Reargued April 27, 1988.
Decided June 27, 1988.

Wrongful death action was brought against independent contractor who supplied military helicopter to United States after helicopter crashed. The United States District Court for the Eastern District of Virginia, Richard L. Williams, J., found in favor of plaintiff, and manufacturer appealed. The United States Court of Appeals for the Fourth Circuit, 792 F.2d 413, reversed. Plaintiff's petition for certiorari was granted. The Supreme Court, Justice Scalia, held that: (1) liability of independent contractors performing work for federal government is area of uniquely federal concern, despite absence of legislation specifically immunizing government contractor from liability for design defects; (2) state law holding government contractors liable for design defects in military equipment may present significant conflict with federal policy, thereby requiring its displacement; but (3) Court of Appeals failed to clearly indicate whether reasonable jury could have found for plaintiff on facts presented under properly formulated defense.

Vacated and remanded.

Justice Brennan dissented and filed opinion in which Justice Marshall and Justice Blackmun joined.

Justice Stevens dissented and filed opinion.

For space considerations, all headnotes have been deleted.

**2512 *Syllabus*[FN*]

> FN* The syllabus constitutes no part of the opinion of the Court but has been prepared by the Reporter of Decisions for the convenience of the reader. See *United States v. Detroit Lumber Co.,* 200 U.S. 321, 337, 26 S.Ct. 282, 287, 50 L.Ed. 499.

*500 David A. Boyle, a United States Marine helicopter copilot, drowned when his helicopter crashed off the Virginia coast. Petitioner, the personal representative of the heirs and estate of Boyle, brought this diversity action in Federal District Court against the Sikorsky Division of respondent corporation (Sikorsky), alleging, *inter alia,* under Virginia tort law, that Sikorsky had defectively designed the helicopter's copilot emergency escape-hatch system. The jury returned a general verdict for petitioner, and the court denied Sikorsky's motion for judgment notwithstanding the verdict. The Court of Appeals reversed and remanded with directions that judgment be entered for Sikorsky. It found that, as a matter of federal law, Sikorsky could not be held liable for the allegedly defective design because Sikorsky satisfied the requirements of the "military contractor defense."

Held:

1. There is no merit to petitioner's contention that, in the absence of federal legislation specifically immunizing Government contractors, federal law cannot shield contractors from liability for design defects in military equipment. In a few areas involving "uniquely federal interests," state law is pre-empted and replaced, where necessary, by federal law of a content

prescribed (absent explicit statutory directive) by the courts. The procurement of equipment by the United States is an area of uniquely federal interest. A dispute such as the present one, even though between private parties, implicates the interests of the United States in this area. Once it is determined that an area of uniquely federal interest is implicated, state law will be displaced only where a "significant conflict" exists between an identifiable federal policy or interest and the operation of state law, or the application of state law would frustrate specific objectives of federal legislation. Here, the state-imposed duty of care that is the asserted basis of the contractor's liability is precisely contrary to the duty imposed by the Government contract. But even in this situation, it would be unreasonable to say that there is always a "significant conflict" between state law and a federal policy or interest. In search of a limiting principle to identify when a significant ***501** conflict is present, the Court of Appeals relied on the rationale of *Feres v. United States,* 340 U.S. 135, 71 S.Ct. 153, 95 L.Ed. 152. This produces results that are in some respects too broad and in some respects too narrow. However, the discretionary function exception to the Federal Tort Claims Act does demonstrate the potential for, and suggest the outlines of, "significant conflict" between federal interest and state law in this area. State law is displaced where judgment against the contractor would threaten a discretionary function of the Government. In sum, state law which imposes liability for design defects in military equipment is displaced where (a) the United States approved reasonably precise specifications; (b) the equipment conformed to those specifications; and (c) the supplier warned the United States about dangers in the use of the equipment known to the supplier but not to the United States. Pp. 2513-2518.

2. Also without merit is petitioner's contention that since the Government contractor defense formulated by the Court of Appeals differed from the instructions given ****2513** by the District Court to the jury, the Seventh Amendment guarantee of jury trial requires a remand for trial on the new theory. If the evidence presented in the first trial would not suffice, as a matter of law, to support a jury verdict under the properly formulated defense, judgment could properly be entered for respondent at once, without a new trial. It is unclear from the Court of Appeals' opinion, however, whether it was in fact deciding that no reasonable jury could, under the properly formulated defense, have found the petitioner on the facts presented, or rather was assessing on its own whether the defense had been established. The latter would be error, since whether the facts established the conditions for the defense is a question for the jury. The case is remanded for clarification of this point. Pp. 2518-2519.

792 F.2d 413 (CA4 1986), vacated and remanded.

SCALIA, J., delivered the opinion of the Court, in which REHNQUIST, C.J., and WHITE, O'CONNOR, and KENNEDY, JJ., joined. BRENNAN, J., filed a dissenting opinion, in which MARSHALL and BLACKMUN, JJ., joined, *post*, p. —.
STEVENS, J., filed a dissenting opinion, *post*, p. —.
Louis S. Franecke reargued the cause for petitioner. With him on the briefs was *John O. Mack.*

Philip A. Lacovara reargued the cause for respondent. With him on the briefs were *Lewis T. Booker, W. Stanfield Johnson,* and *William R. Stein.*

Deputy Solicitor General Ayer reargued the cause for the United States as *amicus curiae* urging affirmance. With him on the brief were *Solicitor General Fried, Assistant* ***502** *Attorney General Willard, Deputy Assistant Attorneys General Spears* and *Willmore,* and *Christopher J. Wright.**

* Briefs of *amici curiae* urging reversal were filed for Edwin Lees Shaw by *Joel D. Eaton* and *Robert L. Parks;* and for Joan S. Tozer et al. by *Michael J. Pangia.*

Briefs of *amici curiae* urging affirmance were filed for the Chamber of Commerce of the United States by *Herbert L. Fenster, Raymond B. Biagini,* and *Robin S. Conrad;* for the Defense Research Institute, Inc., by *James W. Morris III, Ann Adams Webster,* and *Donald F. Pierce;* for Grumman Aerospace Corp. by *James M. FitzSimons, Frank J. Chiarchiaro, Charles M. Shaffer, Jr., L. Joseph Loveland,* and *Gary J. Toman;* for the National Security Industrial Association et al. by *Kenneth S. Geller* and *Andrew L. Frey;* and for the Product Liability Advisory Council, Inc., et al. by *Michael Hoenig, David B. Hamm, William H. Crabtree,* and *Edward P. Good.*

Briefs of *amici curiae* were filed for the Association of Trial Lawyers of America by *Robert L. Habush, Dale Haralson,* and *Denneen L. Peterson;* for Bell Helicopter Textron Inc. by *R. David Broiles, George Galerstein,* and *James W. Hunt;* and for UNR Industries, Inc., by *Joe G. Hollingsworth.*

Justice SCALIA delivered the opinion of the Court.

This case requires us to decide when a contractor providing military equipment to the Federal Government can be held liable under state tort law for injury caused by a design defect.

I

On April 27, 1983, David A. Boyle, a United States Marine helicopter copilot, was killed when the CH-53D helicopter in which he was flying crashed off the coast of Virginia Beach, Virginia, during a training exercise. Although Boyle survived the impact of the crash, he was unable to escape from the helicopter and drowned. Boyle's father, petitioner here, brought this diversity action in Federal District Court against the Sikorsky Division of United Technologies Corporation (Sikorsky), which built the helicopter for the United States.

*503 At trial, petitioner presented two theories of liability under Virginia tort law that were submitted to the jury. First, petitioner alleged that Sikorsky had defectively repaired a device called the servo in the helicopter's automatic flight control system, which allegedly malfunctioned and caused the crash. Second, petitioner alleged that Sikorsky had defectively designed the copilot's emergency escape system: the escape hatch opened out instead of in (and was therefore ineffective in a submerged craft because of water pressure), and access to the escape hatch handle was obstructed by other equipment. The jury returned a general verdict in favor of petitioner and awarded him $725,000. The District Court denied Sikorsky's motion for judgment notwithstanding the verdict.

The Court of Appeals reversed and remanded with directions that judgment be entered for Sikorsky. 792 F.2d 413 (CA4 1986). It found, as a matter of Virginia law, that Boyle had failed to meet his burden of demonstrating that the repair work performed by Sikorsky, as opposed to work that had been done by the Navy, was responsible for the alleged malfunction of the flight control system. *Id.,* at 415-416. It also found, as a matter of federal law, that ****2514** Sikorsky could not be held liable for the allegedly defective design of the escape hatch because, on the evidence presented, it satisfied the requirements of the "military contractor defense," which the court had recognized the same day in *Tozer v. LTV Corp.,* 792 F.2d 403 (CA4 1986). 792 F.2d, at 414-415.

Petitioner sought review here, challenging the Court of Appeals' decision on three levels: First, petitioner contends that there is no justification in federal law for shielding Government contractors from liability for design defects in military equipment. Second, he argues in the alternative that even if such a defense should exist, the Court of Appeals' formulation of the conditions for its application is inappropriate. Finally, petitioner contends that the Court of Appeals erred in not remanding for a jury determination of whether the elements***504** of the defense were met in this case. We granted certiorari, 479 U.S. 1029, 107 S.Ct. 872, 93 L.Ed.2d 827 (1986).

II

[1] Petitioner's broadest contention is that, in the absence of legislation specifically immunizing Government contractors from liability for design defects, there is no basis for judicial recognition of such a defense. We disagree. In most fields of activity, to be sure, this Court has refused to find federal pre-emption of state law in the absence of either a clear statutory prescription, see, *e.g., Jones v. Rath Packing Co.,* 430 U.S. 519, 525, 97 S.Ct. 1305, 1309, 51 L.Ed.2d 604 (1977); *Rice v. Santa Fe Elevator Corp.,* 331 U.S. 218, 230, 67 S.Ct. 1146, 1152, 91 L.Ed. 1447 (1947), or a direct conflict between federal and state law, see, *e.g., Florida Lime & Avocado Growers, Inc. v. Paul,* 373 U.S. 132, 142-143, 83 S.Ct. 1210, 1217-1218, 10 L.Ed.2d 248 (1963); *Hines v. Davidowitz,* 312 U.S. 52, 67, 61 S.Ct. 399, 404, 85 L.Ed. 581 (1941). But we have held that a few areas, involving "uniquely federal interests," *Texas Industries, Inc. v. Radcliff Materials, Inc.,* 451 U.S. 630, 640,

101 S.Ct. 2061, 2067, 68 L.Ed.2d 500 (1981), are so committed by the Constitution and laws of the United States to federal control that state law is pre-empted and replaced, where necessary, by federal law of a content prescribed (absent explicit statutory directive) by the courts-so-called "federal common law." See, *e.g., United States v. Kimbell Foods, Inc.,* 440 U.S. 715, 726-729, 99 S.Ct. 1448, 1457-1459, 59 L.Ed.2d 711 (1979); *Banco Nacional v. Sabbatino,* 376 U.S. 398, 426-427, 84 S.Ct. 923, 939-940, 11 L.Ed.2d 804 (1964); *Howard v. Lyons,* 360 U.S. 593, 597, 79 S.Ct. 1331, 1333, 3 L.Ed.2d 1454 (1959); *Clearfield Trust Co. v. United States,* 318 U.S. 363, 366-367, 63 S.Ct. 573, 574-575, 87 L.Ed. 838 (1943); *D'Oench, Duhme & Co. v. FDIC,* 315 U.S. 447, 457-458, 62 S.Ct. 676, 679-680, 86 L.Ed. 956 (1942).

The dispute in the present case borders upon two areas that we have found to involve such "uniquely federal interests." We have held that obligations to and rights of the United States under its contracts are governed exclusively by federal law. See, *e.g., United States v. Little Lake Misere Land Co.,* 412 U.S. 580, 592-594, 93 S.Ct. 2389, 2396-2397, 37 L.Ed.2d 187 (1973); *Priebe & Sons, Inc. v. United States,* 332 U.S. 407, 411, 68 S.Ct. 123, 125, 92 L.Ed. 32 (1947); ***505** *National Metropolitan Bank v. United States,* 323 U.S. 454, 456, 65 S.Ct. 354, 355, 89 L.Ed. 383 (1945); *Clearfield Trust, supra.* The present case does not involve an obligation to the United States under its contract, but rather liability to third persons. That liability may be styled one in tort, but it arises out of performance of the contract-and traditionally has been regarded as sufficiently related to the contract that until 1962 Virginia would generally allow design defect suits only by the purchaser and those in privity with the seller. See *General Bronze Corp. v. Kostopulos,* 203 Va. 66, 69-70, 122 S.E.2d 548, 551 (1961); see also Va. Code § 8.2-318 (1965) (eliminating privity requirement).

Another area that we have found to be of peculiarly federal concern, warranting the ****2515** displacement of state law, is the civil liability of federal officials for actions taken in the course of their duty. We have held in many contexts that the scope of that liability is controlled by federal law. See, *e.g., Westfall v. Erwin,* 484 U.S. 292, 295, 108 S.Ct. 580, ---, 98 L.Ed.2d 619 (1988); *Howard v. Lyons, supra,* 360 U.S., at 597, 79 S.Ct., at 1333; *Barr v. Matteo,* 360 U.S. 564, 569-574, 79 S.Ct. 1335, 1338-1341, 3 L.Ed.2d 1434 (1959) (plurality opinion); *id.,* at 577, 79 S.Ct., at 1342 (Black, J., concurring); see also *Yaselli v. Goff,* 12 F.2d 396 (CA2 1926), aff'd, 275 U.S. 503, 48 S.Ct. 155, 72 L.Ed. 395 (1927) (*per curiam*); *Spalding v. Vilas,* 161 U.S. 483, 16 S.Ct. 631, 40 L.Ed. 780 (1896); *Bradley v. Fisher,* 13 Wall. 335, 20 L.Ed. 646 (1872). The present case involves an independent contractor performing its obligation under a procurement contract, rather than an official performing his duty as a federal employee, but there is obviously implicated the same interest in getting the Government's work done.[FN1]

> FN1. Justice Brennan's dissent misreads our discussion here to "intimat[e] that the immunity [of federal officials]...might extend...[to] nongovernment employees" such as a Government contractor. *Post,* at 2524. But we do not address this issue, as it is not before us. We cite these cases merely to demonstrate that the liability of independent contractors performing work for the Federal Government, like the liability of federal officials, is an area of uniquely federal interest.

We think the reasons for considering these closely related areas to be of "uniquely federal" interest apply as well to ***506** the civil liabilities arising out of the performance of federal procurement contracts. We have come close to holding as much. In *Yearsley v. W.A. Ross Construction Co.,* 309 U.S. 18, 60 S.Ct. 413, 84 L.Ed. 554 (1940), we rejected an attempt by a landowner to hold a construction contractor liable under state law for the erosion of 95 acres caused by the contractor's work in constructing dikes for the Government. We said that "if [the] authority to carry out the project was validly conferred, that is, if what was done was within the constitutional power of Congress, there is no liability on the part of the contractor for executing its will." *Id.,* at 20-21, 60 S.Ct., at 414. The federal interest justifying this holding surely exists as much in procurement contracts as in performance contracts; we see no basis for a distinction.

[2] Moreover, it is plain that the Federal Government's interest in the procurement of equipment is implicated by suits such as the present one-even though the dispute is one between private parties. It is true that where "litigation is purely between private parties and does not touch the rights and duties of the United States," *Bank of America Nat. Trust & Sav. Assn. v. Parnell,* 352 U.S. 29, 33, 77 S.Ct. 119, 121, 1 L.Ed.2d 93 (1956), federal law does not govern. Thus, for example, in *Miree v. DeKalb County,* 433 U.S. 25, 30, 97 S.Ct. 2490, 2494, 53 L.Ed.2d 557 (1977), which involved the question whether cer-

tain private parties could sue as third-party beneficiaries to an agreement between a municipality and the Federal Aviation Administration, we found that state law was not displaced because "the operations of the United States in connection with FAA grants such as these…would [not] be burdened" by allowing state law to determine whether third-party beneficiaries could sue, *id.,* at 30, 97 S.Ct., at 2494, and because "any federal interest in the outcome of the [dispute] before us '[was] far too speculative, far too remote a possibility to justify the application of federal law to transactions essentially of local concern.' " *Id.,* at 32-33, 97 S.Ct., at 2495, quoting *Parnell, supra,* 352 U.S., at 33-34, 77 S.Ct., at 121; see also ***507** *Wallis v. Pan American Petroleum Corp.,* 384 U.S. 63, 69, 86 S.Ct. 1301, 1304, 16 L.Ed.2d 369 (1966).[FN2] But the same is not true here. The imposition of liability on Government contractors will directly****2516** affect the terms of Government contracts: either the contractor will decline to manufacture the design specified by the Government, or it will raise its price. Either way, the interests of the United States will be directly affected.

> FN2. As this language shows, Justice Brennan's dissent is simply incorrect to describe *Miree* and other cases as declining to apply federal law despite the assertion of interests "comparable" to those before us here. *Post,* at 2523.

[3][4][5] That the procurement of equipment by the United States is an area of uniquely federal interest does not, however, end the inquiry. That merely establishes a necessary, not a sufficient, condition for the displacement of state law.[FN3] Displacement will occur only where, as we have variously described, a "significant conflict" exists between an identifiable "federal policy or interest and the [operation] of state law," *Wallis, supra,* at 68, 86 S.Ct., at 1304, or the application of state law would "frustrate specific objectives" of federal legislation, *Kimbell Foods,* 440 U.S., at 728, 99 S.Ct., at 1458. The conflict with federal policy need not be as sharp as that which must exist for ordinary pre-emption when Congress legislates "in a field which the States have traditionally occupied." *Rice v. Santa Fe Elevator Corp.,* 331 U.S., at 230, 67 S.Ct., at 1152. Or to put the point differently, the ***508** fact that the area in question *is* one of unique federal concern changes what would otherwise be a conflict that cannot produce pre-emption into one that can.[FN4] But conflict there must be. In some cases, for example where the federal interest requires a uniform rule, the entire body of state law applicable to the area conflicts and is replaced by federal rules. See, *e.g., Clearfield Trust,* 318 U.S., at 366-367, 63 S.Ct., at 574-575 (rights and obligations of United States with respect to commercial paper must be governed by uniform federal rule). In others, the conflict is more narrow, and only particular elements of state law are superseded. See, *e.g., Little Lake Misere Land Co.,* 412 U.S., at 595, 93 S.Ct., at 2398 (even assuming state law should generally govern federal land acquisitions, particular state law at issue may not); *Howard v. Lyons,* 360 U.S., at 597, 79 S.Ct., at 1333 (state defamation law generally applicable to federal official, but federal privilege governs for statements made in the course of federal official's duties).

> FN3. We refer here to the displacement of state law, although it is possible to analyze it as the displacement of federal-law reference to state law for the rule of decision. Some of our cases appear to regard the area in which a uniquely federal interest exists as being entirely governed by federal law, with federal law deigning to "borro[w]," *United States v. Little Lake Misere Land Co.,* 412 U.S. 580, 594, 93 S.Ct. 2389, 2398, 37 L.Ed.2d 187 (1973), or "incorporat[e]" or "adopt" *United States v. Kimbell Foods, Inc.,* 440 U.S. 715, 728, 729, 730, 99 S.Ct. 1448, 1458, 1459, 1459, 59 L.Ed.2d 711 (1979), state law except where a significant conflict with federal policy exists. We see nothing to be gained by expanding the theoretical scope of the federal pre-emption beyond its practical effect, and so adopt the more modest terminology. If the distinction between displacement of state law and displacement of federal law's incorporation of state law ever makes a practical difference, it at least does not do so in the present case.

> FN4. Even before our landmark decision in *Clearfield Trust Co. v. United States,* 318 U.S. 363, 63 S.Ct. 573, 87 L.Ed. 838 (1943), the distinctive federal interest in a particular field was used as a significant factor giving broad pre-emptive effect to federal legislation in that field:

> "It cannot be doubted that both the state and the federal [alien] registration laws belong 'to that class of laws which concern the exterior relation of this whole nation with other nations and governments.' Consequently the regulation of aliens is…intimately blended and intertwined with responsibilities of the national government.…And where the federal government, in the exercise of its superior authority in this field, has enacted a complete scheme

of regulation and has therein provided a standard for the registration of aliens, states cannot, inconsistently with the purpose of Congress, conflict or interfere with, curtail or complement, the federal law, or enforce additional or auxiliary regulations." *Hines v. Davidowitz,* 312 U.S. 52, 66-67, 61 S.Ct. 399, 403-404, 85 L.Ed. 581 (1941) (citation omitted).

In *Miree, supra,* the suit was not seeking to impose upon the person contracting with the Government a duty contrary to the duty imposed by the Government contract. Rather, it was the contractual duty *itself* that the private plaintiff (as third-party beneficiary) sought to enforce. Between *Miree* ***509** and the present case, it is ****2517** easy to conceive of an intermediate situation, in which the duty sought to be imposed on the contractor is not identical to one assumed under the contract, but is also not contrary to any assumed. If, for example, the United States contracts for the purchase and installation of an air conditioning-unit, specifying the cooling capacity but not the precise manner of construction, a state law imposing upon the manufacturer of such units a duty of care to include a certain safety feature would not be a duty identical to anything promised the Government, but neither would it be contrary. The contractor could comply with both its contractual obligations and the state-prescribed duty of care. No one suggests that state law would generally be pre-empted in this context.

The present case, however, is at the opposite extreme from *Miree.* Here the state-imposed duty of care that is the asserted basis of the contractor's liability (specifically, the duty to equip helicopters with the sort of escape-hatch mechanism petitioner claims was necessary) is precisely contrary to the duty imposed by the Government contract (the duty to manufacture and deliver helicopters with the sort of escape-hatch mechanism shown by the specifications). Even in this sort of situation, it would be unreasonable to say that there is always a "significant conflict" between the state law and a federal policy or interest. If, for example, a federal procurement officer orders, by model number, a quantity of stock helicopters that happen to be equipped with escape hatches opening outward, it is impossible to say that the Government has a significant interest in that particular feature. That would be scarcely more reasonable than saying that a private individual who orders such a craft by model number cannot sue for the manufacturer's negligence because he got precisely what he ordered.

In its search for the limiting principle to identify those situations in which a "significant conflict" with federal policy or interests does arise, the Court of Appeals, in the lead case ***510** upon which its opinion here relied, identified as the source of the conflict the *Feres* doctrine, under which the Federal Tort Claims Act (FTCA) does not cover injuries to Armed Services personnel in the course of military service. See *Feres v. United States,* 340 U.S. 135, 71 S.Ct. 153, 95 L.Ed. 152 (1950). Military contractor liability would conflict with this doctrine, the Fourth Circuit reasoned, since the increased cost of the contractor's tort liability would be added to the price of the contract, and "[s]uch pass-through costs would...defeat the purpose of the immunity for military accidents conferred upon the government itself." *Tozer,* 792 F.2d, at 408. Other courts upholding the defense have embraced similar reasoning. See, *e.g., Bynum v. FMC Corp.,* 770 F.2d 556, 565-566 (CA5 1985); *Tillett v. J.I. Case Co.,* 756 F.2d 591, 596-597 (CA7 1985); *McKay v. Rockwell Int'l Corp.,* 704 F.2d 444, 449 (CA9 1983), cert. denied, 464 U.S. 1043, 104 S.Ct. 711, 79 L.Ed.2d 175 (1984). We do not adopt this analysis because it seems to us that the *Feres* doctrine, in its application to the present problem, logically produces results that are in some respects too broad and in some respects too narrow. Too broad, because if the Government contractor defense is to prohibit suit against the manufacturer whenever *Feres* would prevent suit against the Government, then even injuries caused to military personnel by a helicopter purchased from stock (in our example above), or by any standard equipment purchased by the Government, would be covered. Since *Feres* prohibits all service-related tort claims against the Government, a contractor defense that rests upon it should prohibit all service-related tort claims against the manufacturer-making inexplicable the three limiting criteria for contractor immunity (which we will discuss presently) that the Court of Appeals adopted. On the other hand, reliance on *Feres* produces (or logically should produce) results that are in another respect too narrow. Since that doctrine covers only service-related injuries, and not ****2518** injuries caused by the military to civilians, it could not be invoked to prevent, for example, a civilian's suit against the manufacturer of fighter planes, based on a state ***511** tort theory, claiming harm from what is alleged to be needlessly high levels of noise produced by the jet engines. Yet we think that the character of the jet engines the Government orders for its fighter planes cannot be regulated by state tort law, no more in suits by civilians than in suits by members of the Armed Services.

[6][7] There is, however, a statutory provision that demonstrates the potential for, and suggests the outlines of, "significant conflict" between federal interests and state law in the context of Government procurement. In the FTCA, Congress autho-

rized damages to be recovered against the United States for harm caused by the negligent or wrongful conduct of Government employees, to the extent that a private person would be liable under the law of the place where the conduct occurred. 28 U.S.C. § 1346(b). It excepted from this consent to suit, however,

> "[a]ny claim…based upon the exercise or performance or the failure to exercise or perform a discretionary function or duty on the part of a federal agency or an employee of the Government, whether or not the discretion involved be abused." 28 U.S.C. § 2680(a).

We think that the selection of the appropriate design for military equipment to be used by our Armed Forces is assuredly a discretionary function within the meaning of this provision. It often involves not merely engineering analysis but judgment as to the balancing of many technical, military, and even social considerations, including specifically the trade-off between greater safety and greater combat effectiveness. And we are further of the view that permitting "second-guessing" of these judgments, see *United States v. Varig Airlines,* 467 U.S. 797, 814, 104 S.Ct. 2755, 2765, 81 L.Ed.2d 660 (1984), through state tort suits against contractors would produce the same effect sought to be avoided by the FTCA exemption. The financial burden of judgments against the contractors would ultimately be passed through, substantially if not totally, to the ***512** United States itself, since defense contractors will predictably raise their prices to cover, or to insure against, contingent liability for the Government-ordered designs. To put the point differently: It makes little sense to insulate the Government against financial liability for the judgment that a particular feature of military equipment is necessary when the Government produces the equipment itself, but not when it contracts for the production. In sum, we are of the view that state law which holds Government contractors liable for design defects in military equipment does in some circumstances present a "significant conflict" with federal policy and must be displaced.[FN5]

> FN5. Justice Brennan's assumption that the outcome of this case would be different if it were brought under the Death on the High Seas Act, Act of Mar. 30, 1920, ch. 111, § 1 *et seq.* (1982 ed., Supp. IV), 41 Stat. 537, codified at 46 U.S.C.App. § 761 *et seq.* is not necessarily correct. That issue is not before us, and we think it inappropriate to decide it in order to refute (or, for that matter, to construct) an alleged inconsistency.

[8] We agree with the scope of displacement adopted by the Fourth Circuit here, which is also that adopted by the Ninth Circuit, see *McKay v. Rockwell Int'l Corp., supra,* at 451. Liability for design defects in military equipment cannot be imposed, pursuant to state law, when (1) the United States approved reasonably precise specifications; (2) the equipment conformed to those specifications; and (3) the supplier warned the United States about the dangers in the use of the equipment that were known to the supplier but not to the United States. The first two of these conditions assure that the suit is within the area where the policy of the "discretionary function" would be frustrated-*i.e.,* they assure that the design feature in question was considered by a Government officer, and not merely by the contractor itself. The ****2519** third condition is necessary because, in its absence, the displacement of state tort law would create some incentive for the manufacturer to withhold knowledge of risks, since conveying that knowledge might disrupt the contract but withholding it would produce no liability. We adopt this provision lest our effort to protect***513** discretionary functions perversely impede them by cutting off information highly relevant to the discretionary decision.

We have considered the alternative formulation of the Government contractor defense, urged upon us by petitioner, which was adopted by the Eleventh Circuit in *Shaw v. Grumman Aerospace Corp.,* 778 F.2d 736, 746 (1985), cert. pending, No. 85-1529. That would preclude suit only if (1) the contractor did not participate, or participated only minimally, in the design of the defective equipment; *or* (2) the contractor timely warned the Government of the risks of the design and notified it of alternative designs reasonably known by it, *and* the Government, although forewarned, clearly authorized the contractor to proceed with the dangerous design. While this formulation may represent a perfectly reasonable tort rule, it is not a rule designed to protect the federal interest embodied in the "discretionary function" exemption. The design ultimately selected may well reflect a significant policy judgment by Government officials whether or not the contractor rather than those officials developed the design. In addition, it does not seem to us sound policy to penalize, and thus deter, active contractor participation in the design process, placing the contractor at risk unless it identifies all design defects.

III

[9] Petitioner raises two arguments regarding the Court of Appeals' application of the Government contractor defense to the facts of this case. First, he argues that since the formulation of the defense adopted by the Court of Appeals differed from the instructions given by the District Court to the jury, the Seventh Amendment guarantee of jury trial required a remand for trial on the new theory. We disagree. If the evidence presented in the first trial would not suffice, as a matter of law, to support a jury verdict under the properly formulated defense, judgment could properly be entered for the respondent at once, without a new trial. And that is so even though (as petitioner claims) respondent failed to *514 object to jury instructions that expressed the defense differently, and in a fashion that would support a verdict. See *St. Louis v. Praprotnik,* 485 U.S. 112, 118-120, 108 S.Ct. 915, 918, 99 L.Ed.2d 107 (1988) (plurality opinion of O'CONNOR, J., joined by REHNQUIST, C.J., WHITE, and SCALIA, JJ.); *Ebker v. Tan Jay Int'l, Ltd.,* 739 F.2d 812, 825-826, n. 17 (CA2 1984) (Friendly, J.); 9 C. Wright & A. Miller, Federal Practice and Procedure § 2537, pp. 599-600 (1971).

It is somewhat unclear from the Court of Appeals' opinion, however, whether it was in fact deciding that no reasonable jury could, under the properly formulated defense, have found for the petitioner on the facts presented, or rather was assessing on its own whether the defense had been established. The latter, which is what petitioner asserts occurred, would be error, since whether the facts establish the conditions for the defense is a question for the jury. The critical language in the Court of Appeals' opinion was that "[b]ecause Sikorsky has satisfied the requirements of the military contractor defense, it can incur no liability for...the allegedly defective design of the escape hatch." 792 F.2d, at 415. Although it seems to us doubtful that the Court of Appeals was conducting the factual evaluation that petitioner suggests, we cannot be certain from this language, and so we remand for clarification of this point. If the Court of Appeals was saying that no reasonable jury could find, under the principles it had announced and on the basis of the evidence presented, that the Government contractor defense was inapplicable, its judgment shall stand, since petitioner did not seek from us, nor did we **2520 grant, review of the sufficiency-of-the-evidence determination. If the Court of Appeals was not saying that, it should now undertake the proper sufficiency inquiry.

Accordingly, the judgment is vacated and the case is remanded.

So ordered.

*515 Justice BRENNAN, with whom Justice MARSHALL and Justice BLACKMUN join, dissenting.
Lieutenant David A. Boyle died when the CH-53D helicopter he was copiloting spun out of control and plunged into the ocean. We may assume, for purposes of this case, that Lt. Boyle was trapped under water and drowned because respondent United Technologies negligently designed the helicopter's escape hatch. We may further assume that any competent engineer would have discovered and cured the defects, but that they inexplicably escaped respondent's notice. Had respondent designed such a death trap for a commercial firm, Lt. Boyle's family could sue under Virginia tort law and be compensated for his tragic and unnecessary death. But respondent designed the helicopter for the Federal Government, and that, the Court tells us today, makes all the difference: Respondent is immune from liability so long as it obtained approval of "reasonably precise specifications"-perhaps no more than a rubber stamp from a federal procurement officer who might or might not have noticed or cared about the defects, or even had the expertise to discover them.

If respondent's immunity "bore the legitimacy of having been prescribed by the people's elected representatives," we would be duty bound to implement their will, whether or not we approved. *United States v. Johnson,* 481 U.S. 681, 703, 107 S.Ct. 2063, 2076, 95 L.Ed.2d 648 (1987) (dissenting opinion of SCALIA, J.). Congress, however, has remained silent-and conspicuously so, having resisted a sustained campaign by Government contractors to legislate for them some defense.[FN1] The Court-unelected and unaccountable to the people-has unabashedly stepped into *516 the breach to legislate a rule denying Lt. Boyle's family the compensation that state law assures them. This time the injustice is of this Court's own making.

FN1. See, *e.g.,* H.R. 4765, 99th Cong., 2d Sess. (1986) (limitations on civil liability of Government contractors); S. 2441, 99th Cong., 2d Sess. (1986) (same). See also H.R. 2378, 100th Cong., 1st Sess. (1987) (indemnification of civil liability for Government contractors); H.R. 5883, 98th Cong., 2d Sess. (1984) (same); H.R. 1504, 97th Cong., 1st Sess. (1981) (same); H.R. 5351, 96th Cong., 1st Sess. (1979) (same).

Worse yet, the injustice will extend far beyond the facts of this case, for the Court's newly discovered Government contractor defense is breathtakingly sweeping. It applies not only to military equipment like the CH-53D helicopter, but (so far as I can tell) to any made-to-order gadget that the Federal Government might purchase after previewing plans-from NASA's Challenger space shuttle to the Postal Service's old mail cars. The contractor may invoke the defense in suits brought not only by military personnel like Lt. Boyle, or Government employees, but by anyone injured by a Government contractor's negligent design, including, for example, the children who might have died had respondent's helicopter crashed on the beach. It applies even if the Government has not intentionally sacrificed safety for other interests like speed or efficiency, and, indeed, even if the equipment is not of a type that is typically considered dangerous; thus, the contractor who designs a Government building can invoke the defense when the elevator cable snaps or the walls collapse. And the defense is invocable regardless of how blatant or easily remedied the defect, so long as the contractor missed it and the specifications approved by the Government, however unreasonably dangerous, were "reasonably precise." *Ante,* at 2518.

In my view, this Court lacks both authority and expertise to fashion such a rule, whether to protect the Treasury of the **2521 United States or the coffers of industry. Because I would leave that exercise of legislative power to Congress, where our Constitution places it, I would reverse the Court of Appeals and reinstate petitioner's jury award.

I

Before our decision in *Erie R. Co. v. Tompkins,* 304 U.S. 64, 58 S.Ct. 817, 82 L.Ed. 1188 (1938), federal courts sitting in diversity were generally free, in the absence of a controlling state statute, to fashion *517 rules of "general" federal common law. See, *e.g., Swift v. Tyson,* 16 Pet. 1, 10 L.Ed. 865 (1842). *Erie* renounced the prevailing scheme: "Except in matters governed by the Federal Constitution or by Acts of Congress, the law to be applied in any case is the law of the State." 304 U.S., at 78, 58 S.Ct., at 822. The Court explained that the expansive power that federal courts had theretofore exercised was an unconstitutional " 'invasion of the authority of the State and, to that extent, a denial of its independence.' " *Id.,* at 79, 58 S.Ct., at 823 (citation omitted). Thus, *Erie* was deeply rooted in notions of federalism, and is most seriously implicated when, as here, federal judges displace the state law that would ordinarily govern with their own rules of federal common law. See, *e.g., United States v. Standard Oil Co.,* 332 U.S. 301, 307, 67 S.Ct. 1604, 1607, 91 L.Ed. 2067 (1947).FN2

> FN2. Not all exercises of our power to fashion federal common law displace state law in the same way. For example, our recognition of federal causes of action based upon either the Constitution, see, *e.g., Bivens v. Six Unknown Fed. Narcotics Agents,* 403 U.S. 388, 91 S.Ct. 1999, 29 L.Ed.2d 619 (1971), or a federal statute, see *Cort v. Ash,* 422 U.S. 66, 95 S.Ct. 2080, 45 L.Ed.2d 26 (1975), supplements whatever rights state law might provide, and therefore does not implicate federalism concerns in the same way as does pre-emption of a state-law rule of decision or cause of action. Throughout this opinion I use the word "displace" in the latter sense.

In pronouncing that "[t]here is no federal general common law," 304 U.S., at 78, 58 S.Ct., at 822, *Erie* put to rest the notion that the grant of diversity jurisdiction to federal courts is itself authority to fashion rules of substantive law. See *United States v. Little Lake Misere Land Co.,* 412 U.S. 580, 591, 93 S.Ct. 2389, 2396, 37 L.Ed.2d 187 (1973). As the author of today's opinion for the Court pronounced for a unanimous Court just two months ago, " ' " 'we start with the assumption that the historic police powers of the States were not to be superseded...unless that was the clear and manifest purpose of Congress.' " ' " *Puerto Rico Dept. of Consumer Affairs v. Isla Petroleum Corp.,* 485 U.S. 495, 500, 108 S.Ct. 1350, 1353, 99 L.Ed.2d 582 (1988) (citations omitted). Just as "[t]here is no federal pre-emption *in vacuo,* without a constitutional text or a federal statute to assert it," *id.,* at 503, 108 S.Ct., at 1355, federal common law cannot supersede state law *in vacuo* out of no *518 more than an idiosyncratic determination by five Justices that a particular area is "uniquely federal."

Accordingly, we have emphasized that federal common law can displace state law in "few and restricted" instances. *Wheeldin v. Wheeler,* 373 U.S. 647, 651, 83 S.Ct. 1441, 1444, 10 L.Ed.2d 605 (1963). "[A]bsent some congressional authorization to formulate substantive rules of decision, federal common law exists only in such narrow areas as those concerned with the rights and obligations of the United States, interstate and international disputes implicating conflicting rights of States or our relations with foreign nations, and admiralty cases." *Texas Industries, Inc. v. Radcliff Materials, Inc.,* 451 U.S. 630, 641, 101 S.Ct. 2061, 2067, 68 L.Ed.2d 500 (1981) (footnotes omitted). "The enactment of a federal rule in an area of national concern, and the decision whether to displace state law in doing so, is generally made not by the federal judiciary, purposefully insulated from democratic pressures, but by the people through their elected representatives in Congress." *Milwaukee v. Illinois,* 451 U.S. 304, 312-313, 101 S.Ct. 1784, 1790, 68 L.Ed.2d 114 (1981). See also ****2522** *Wallis v. Pan American Petroleum Corp.,* 384 U.S. 63, 68, 86 S.Ct. 1301, 1304, 16 L.Ed.2d 369 (1966); *Miree v. DeKalb County,* 433 U.S. 25, 32, 97 S.Ct. 2490, 2495, 53 L.Ed.2d 557 (1977). State laws "should be overridden by the federal courts only where clear and substantial interests of the National Government, which cannot be served consistently with respect for such state interests, will suffer major damage if the state law is applied." *United States v. Yazell,* 382 U.S. 341, 352, 86 S.Ct. 500, 507, 15 L.Ed.2d 404 (1966).

II

Congress has not decided to supersede state law here (if anything, it has decided not to, see n. 1, *supra*) and the Court does not pretend that its newly manufactured "Government contractor defense" fits within any of the handful of "narrow areas," *Texas Industries, supra,* 451 U.S., at 641, 101 S.Ct., at 2067, of "uniquely federal interests" in which we have heretofore done so, 451 U.S., at 640, 101 S.Ct., at 2067. Rather, the Court creates a new category of "uniquely federal interests" out of a synthesis of two whose origins predate *Erie* itself: the interest in administering the "obligations to and rights of the United States under its contracts," *ante,* ***519** at 2514, and the interest in regulating the "civil liability of federal officials for actions taken in the course of their duty," *ante,* at 2514. This case is, however, simply a suit between two private parties. We have steadfastly declined to impose federal contract law on relationships that are collateral to a federal contract, or to extend the federal employee's immunity beyond federal employees. And the Court's ability to list 2, or 10, inapplicable areas of "uniquely federal interest" does not support its conclusion that the liability of Government contractors is so "clear and substantial" an interest that this Court must step in lest state law does "major damage." *Yazell, supra,* 382 U.S., at 352, 86 S.Ct., at 507.

A

The proposition that federal common law continues to govern the "obligations to and rights of the United States under its contracts" is nearly as old as *Erie* itself. Federal law typically controls when the Federal Government is a party to a suit involving its rights or obligations under a contract, whether the contract entails procurement, see *Priebe & Sons v. United States,* 332 U.S. 407, 68 S.Ct. 123, 92 L.Ed. 32 (1947), a loan, see *United States v. Kimbell Foods, Inc.,* 440 U.S. 715, 726, 99 S.Ct. 1448, 1457, 59 L.Ed.2d 711 (1979), a conveyance of property, see *Little Lake Misere, supra,* 412 U.S., at 591-594, 93 S.Ct., at 2396-2397, or a commercial instrument issued by the Government, see *Clearfield Trust Co. v. United States,* 318 U.S. 363, 366, 63 S.Ct. 573, 574, 87 L.Ed. 838 (1943), or assigned to it, see *D'Oench, Duhme & Co. v. FDIC,* 315 U.S. 447, 457, 62 S.Ct. 676, 679, 86 L.Ed. 956 (1942). Any such transaction necessarily "radiate[s] interests in transactions between private parties." *Bank of America Nat. Trust & Sav. Assn. v. Parnell,* 352 U.S. 29, 33, 77 S.Ct. 119, 121, 1 L.Ed.2d 93 (1956). But it is by now established that our power to create federal common law controlling the *Federal Government's* contractual rights and obligations does not translate into a power to prescribe rules that cover all transactions or contractual relationships collateral to Government contracts.

In *Miree v. DeKalb County, supra,* for example, the county was contractually obligated under a grant agreement with the Federal Aviation Administration (FAA) to " 'restrict ***520** the use of land adjacent to…the Airport to activities and purposes compatible with normal airport operations including landing and takeoff of aircraft.' " *Id.,* 433 U.S., at 27, 97 S.Ct., at 2492 (citation omitted). At issue was whether the county breached its contractual obligation by operating a garbage dump adjacent to the airport, which allegedly attracted the swarm of birds that caused a plane crash. Federal common law would undoubtedly ****2523** have controlled in any suit by the Federal Government to enforce the provision against the county or to collect damages for its violation. The diversity suit, however, was brought not by the Government, but by assorted private parties injured in some way by the accident. We observed that "the operations of the United States in connection with FAA grants such as these are undoubtedly of considerable magnitude," *id.,* at 30, 97 S.Ct., at 2494, and that "the United States has a substantial interest in regulating aircraft travel and promoting air travel safety," *id.,* at 31, 97 S.Ct., at 2495. Nevertheless, we held that state law should govern the claim because "only the rights of private litigants are at issue here," *id.,* at 30, 97 S.Ct., at 2494, and the claim against the county "will have *no direct effect upon the United States or its Treasury,*" *id.,* at 29, 97 S.Ct., at 2494 (emphasis added).

Miree relied heavily on *Parnell, supra,* and *Wallis v. Pan American Petroleum Corp., supra,* the former involving commercial paper issued by the United States and the latter involving property rights in federal land. In the former case, Parnell cashed certain bonds guaranteed by the Government that had been stolen from their owner, a bank. It is beyond dispute that federal law would have governed the United States' duty to pay the value bonds upon presentation; we held as much in *Clearfield Trust, supra.* Cf. *Parnell, supra,* 352 U.S., at 34, 77 S.Ct., at 121. But the central issue in *Parnell,* a diversity suit, was whether the victim of the theft could recover the money paid to Parnell. That issue, we held, was governed by state law, because the "litigation [was] purely between private parties and [did] *not touch the rights and duties of the United States.*" 352 U.S., at 33, 77 S.Ct., at 121 (emphasis added).

*521 The same was true in *Wallis,* which also involved a Government contract-a lease issued by the United States to a private party under the Mineral Leasing Act of 1920, 30 U.S.C. § 181 *et seq.* (1982 ed. and Supp. IV)-governed entirely by federal law. See 384 U.S., at 69, 86 S.Ct., at 1304. Again, the relationship at issue in this diversity case was collateral to the Government contract: It involved the validity of contractual arrangements between the lessee and other private parties, not between the lessee and the Federal Government. Even though a federal statute authorized certain assignments of lease rights, see *id.,* at 69, 70, and n. 8, 86 S.Ct., at 1304, 1305, and n. 8, and imposed certain conditions on their validity, see *id.,* at 70, 86 S.Ct., at 1305, we held that state law, not federal common law, governed their validity because application of state law would present "no significant threat to any identifiable federal policy or interest," *id.,* at 68, 86 S.Ct., at 1304.

Here, as in *Miree, Parnell,* and *Wallis,* a Government contract governed by federal common law looms in the background. But here, too, the United States is not a party to the suit and the suit neither "touch[es] the rights and duties of the United States," *Parnell, supra,* 352 U.S., at 33, 77 S.Ct., at 121, nor has a "direct effect upon the United States or its Treasury," *Miree,* 433 U.S., at 29, 97 S.Ct., at 2494. The relationship at issue is at best collateral to the Government contract.[FN3] We have no greater power to displace state law governing the collateral relationship in the Government procurement realm than we had to dictate federal rules governing equally collateral relationships in the areas of aviation, Government-issued commercial paper, or federal lands.

> FN3. True, in this case the collateral relationship is the relationship between victim and tortfeasor, rather than between contractors, but that distinction makes no difference. We long ago established that the principles governing application of federal common law in "contractual relations of the Government...are equally applicable...where the relations affected are noncontractual or tortious in character." *United States v. Standard Oil Co.,* 332 U.S. 301, 305, 67 S.Ct. 1604, 1607, 91 L.Ed. 2067 (1947).

2524 That the Government might have to pay higher prices for what it orders if delivery in accordance with the contract exposes*522** the seller to potential liability, see *ante,* at 2514-2515, does not distinguish this case. Each of the cases just discussed declined to extend the reach of federal common law despite the assertion of comparable interests that would have affected the terms of the Government contract-whether its price or its substance-just as "directly" (or indirectly). *Ibid.* Third-party beneficiaries can sue under a county's contract with the FAA, for example, even though-as the Court's focus on the absence of "*direct* effect on the United States or its Treasury," 433 U.S., at 29, 97 S.Ct., at 2494 (emphasis added), suggests-counties will likely pass on the costs to the Government in future contract negotiations. Similarly, we held that state law may govern the circumstances under which stolen federal bonds can be recovered, notwithstanding Parnell's argument that "the value of bonds to the first purchaser and hence their salability by the Government would be materially affected." Brief for Respondent Parnell in *Bank of America Nat'l Trust & Sav. Assn. v. Parnell,* O.T. 1956, No. 21, pp. 10-11. As in each of the cases declining to extend the traditional reach of federal law of contracts beyond the rights and duties of the

Federal Government, "any federal interest in the outcome of the question before us 'is far too speculative, far too remote a possibility to justify the application of federal law to transactions essentially of local concern.' " *Miree, supra,* 433 U.S., at 32-33, 97 S.Ct., at 2495-2496, quoting *Parnell,* 352 U.S., at 33-34, 77 S.Ct., at 121-122.

B

Our "uniquely federal interest" in the tort liability of affiliates of the Federal Government is equally narrow. The immunity we have recognized has extended no further than a subset of "officials of the Federal Government" and has covered only "discretionary" functions within the scope of their legal authority. See, *e.g., Westfall v. Erwin,* 484 U.S. 292, 108 S.Ct. 580, 98 L.Ed.2d 619 (1988); *Howard v. Lyons,* 360 U.S. 593, 79 S.Ct. 1331, 3 L.Ed.2d 1454 (1959); *Barr v. Matteo,* 360 U.S. 564, 571, 79 S.Ct. 1335, 1339, 3 L.Ed.2d 1434 (1959) (plurality); *Yaselli v. Goff,* 12 F.2d 396 (CA2 1926), aff'd, 275 U.S. 503, 48 S.Ct. 155, 72 L.Ed. 395 (1927) (*per curiam*); *Spalding v. Vilas,* 161 U.S. 483, 16 S.Ct. 631, 40 L.Ed. 780 (1896). Never before**523 have we so much as intimated that the immunity (or the "uniquely federal interest" that justifies it) might extend beyond that narrow class to cover also nongovernment employees whose authority to act is independent of any source of federal law and that are as far removed from the "functioning of the Federal Government" as is a Government contractor, *Howard, supra,* 360 U.S., at 597, 79 S.Ct., at 1334.

The historical narrowness of the federal interest and the immunity is hardly accidental. A federal officer exercises statutory authority, which not only provides the necessary basis for the immunity in positive law, but also permits us confidently to presume that interference with the exercise of discretion undermines congressional will. In contrast, a Government contractor acts independently of any congressional enactment. Thus, immunity for a contractor lacks both the positive law basis and the presumption that it furthers congressional will.

Moreover, even within the category of congressionally authorized tasks, we have deliberately restricted the scope of immunity to circumstances in which "the contributions of immunity to effective government in particular contexts outweigh the perhaps recurring harm to individual citizens," *Doe v. McMillan,* 412 U.S. 306, 320, 93 S.Ct. 2018, 2028, 36 L.Ed.2d 912 (1973); see *Barr, supra,* 360 U.S., at 572-573, 79 S.Ct., at 1340, because immunity "contravenes the basic tenet that individuals be held accountable for their wrongful conduct," *Westfall, supra,* 484 U.S., at 295, 108 S.Ct., at 583. The extension of immunity to Government contractors skews the balance we have historically struck. On the one hand, whatever marginal effect contractor **2525 immunity might have on the "effective administration of policies of government," its "harm to individual citizens" is more severe than in the Government-employee context. Our observation that "there are…other sanctions than civil tort suits available to deter the executive official who may be prone to exercise his functions in an unworthy and irresponsible manner," *Barr,* 360 U.S., at 576, 79 S.Ct., at 1342; see also *id.,* at 571, 79 S.Ct., at 1339, offers little deterrence to the Government contractor. On the other hand, a grant of immunity to Government*524 contractors could not advance "the fearless, vigorous, and effective administration of policies of government" nearly as much as does the current immunity for Government employees. *Ibid.* In the first place, the threat of a tort suit is less likely to influence the conduct of an industrial giant than that of a lone civil servant, particularly since the work of a civil servant is significantly less profitable, and significantly more likely to be the subject of a vindictive lawsuit. In fact, were we to take seriously the Court's assertion that contractors pass their costs-including presumably litigation costs-through, "substantially if not totally, to the United States," *ante,* at 2518, the threat of a tort suit should have only marginal impact on the conduct of Government contractors. More importantly, inhibition of the Government official who actually sets Government policy presents a greater threat to the "administration of policies of government," than does inhibition of a private contractor, whose role is devoted largely to assessing the technological feasibility and cost of satisfying the Government's predetermined needs. Similarly, unlike tort suits against Government officials, tort suits against Government contractors would rarely "consume time and energies" that "would otherwise be devoted to governmental service." 360 U.S., at 571, 79 S.Ct., at 1339.

In short, because the essential justifications for official immunity do not support an extension to the Government contractor, it is no surprise that we have never extended it that far.

C

Yearsley v. W. A. Ross Construction Co., 309 U.S. 18, 60 S.Ct. 413, 84 L.Ed. 554 (1940), the sole case cited by the Court immunizing a Government contractor, is a slender reed on which to base so drastic a departure from precedent. In *Yearsley* we barred the suit of landowners against a private Government contractor alleging that its construction of a dam eroded their land without just compensation in violation of the Takings Clause of the Fifth Amendment. We relied in part on the observation that the plaintiffs failed to state a Fifth Amendment claim ***525** since just compensation had never been requested, much less denied) and at any rate the cause of action lay against the Government, not the contractor. See *id.,* at 21, 60 S.Ct., at 415 ("[T]he Government has impliedly promised to pay [the plaintiffs] compensation and has afforded a remedy for its recovery by a suit in the Court of Claims") (citations omitted). It is therefore unlikely that the Court intended *Yearsley* to extend anywhere beyond the takings context, and we have never applied it elsewhere.

Even if *Yearsley* were applicable beyond the unique context in which it arose, it would have little relevance here. The contractor's work "was done pursuant to a contract with the United States Government, and under the direction of the Secretary of War and the supervision of the Chief of Engineers of the United States,…as authorized by an Act of Congress." *Id.,* at 19, 60 S.Ct., at 414. See also *W.A. Ross Construction Co. v. Yearsley,* 103 F.2d 589, 591 (CA8 1939) (undisputed allegation that contractor implemented "stabilized bank lines as set and defined by the Government Engineers in charge of this work for the Government"). In other words, unlike respondent here, the contractor in *Yearsley* was following, not formulating, the Government's specifications, and (so far as is relevant here) followed them correctly. Had respondent merely manufactured****2526** the CH-53D helicopter, following minutely the Government's own in-house specifications, it would be analogous to the contractor in *Yearsley,* although still not analytically identical since *Yearsley* depended upon an actual agency relationship with the Government, see 309 U.S., at 22, 60 S.Ct., at 415 ("The action of the agent is 'the act of the government' ") (citation omitted), which plainly was never established here. See, *e.g., Bynum v. FMC Corp.,* 770 F.2d 556, 564 (CA5 1985). Cf. *United States v. New Mexico,* 455 U.S. 720, 735, 102 S.Ct. 1373, 1383, 71 L.Ed.2d 580 (1982). But respondent's participation in the helicopter's design distinguishes this case from *Yearsley,* which has never been read to immunize the discretionary acts of those who perform service contracts for the Government.

**526* III

In a valiant attempt to bridge the analytical canyon between what *Yearsley* said and what the Court wishes it had said, the Court invokes the discretionary function exception of the Federal Tort Claims Act (FTCA), 28 U.S.C. § 2680(a). The Court does not suggest that the exception has any direct bearing here, for petitioner has sued a private manufacturer (not the Federal Government) under Virginia law (not the FTCA). Perhaps that is why respondent has three times disavowed any reliance on the discretionary function exception, even after coaching by the Court,[FN4] as has the Government.[FN5]

FN4. "QUESTION: [Would it be] a proper judicial function to craft the contours of the military contractor defense…even if there were no discretionary function exemption in the Federal Tort Claims Act?

"MR. LACOVARA: I think, yes.…[I]t ought not to make a difference to the contractor, or to the courts, I would submit, whether or not the Government has a discretionary function exception under the Federal Tort Claims Act.…

"QUESTION: I think your position would be the same if Congress had never waived its sovereign immunity in the Federal Tort Claims Act.…

"MR. LACOVARA: That's correct.…

"QUESTION: Now wait. I really don't understand that. It seems to me you can make the argument that there should be preemption if Congress wanted it, but how are we to perceive that's what Congress wanted if in the Tort Claims Act, Congress had said the Government itself should be liable for an ill designed helicopter? Why would we have any reason to think that Congress wanted to preempt liability of a private contractor for an ill designed helicopter?

"QUESTION:…[Y]our preemption argument, I want to be sure I understand it-does not depend at all on the Federal Tort Claims Act, as I understand it.…

"MR. LACOVARA: That's correct." Tr. of Oral Arg. 33-35 (reargument Apr. 27, 1988).

FN5. "QUESTION: Does the Government's position depend at all on the discretionary function exemption in the Federal Tort Claims Act?

"MR. AYER: Well, that's a hard question to answer....I think my answer to you is, no, ultimately it should not." *Id.,* at 40-41.

*527 Notwithstanding these disclaimers, the Court invokes the exception, reasoning that federal common law must immunize Government contractors from state tort law to prevent erosion of the discretionary function exception's *policy* of foreclosing judicial " 'second-guessing' " of discretionary governmental decisions. *Ante,* at 2517, quoting *United States v. Varig Airlines,* 467 U.S. 797, 814, 104 S.Ct. 2755, 2764, 81 L.Ed.2d 660 (1984). The erosion the Court fears apparently is rooted not in a concern that suits against Government contractors will prevent them from designing, or the Government from commissioning the design of, precisely the product the Government wants, but in the concern that such suits might preclude the Government from purchasing the desired product at the price it wants: "The financial burden of judgments against the contractors," the Court fears, "would ultimately be passed through, substantially if not totally, to the United States itself." *Ante,* at 2518.

Even granting the Court's factual premise, which is by no means self-evident, the Court cites no authority for the proposition that burdens imposed on Government contractors, but passed on to the Government, burden the Government in a way that justifies extension of its immunity. However substantial such indirect burdens may be, ****2527** we have held in other contexts that they are legally irrelevant. See, *e.g.,* at 2522-2523; *South Carolina v. Baker,* 485 U.S. 505, 521, 108 S.Ct. 1355, ---, 99 L.Ed.2d 592 (1988) (our cases have "completely foreclosed any claim that the nondiscriminatory imposition of costs on private entities that pass them on to...the Federal Government unconstitutionally burdens...federal functions").

Moreover, the statutory basis on which the Court's rule of federal common law totters is more unstable than any we have ever adopted. In the first place, we rejected an analytically similar attempt to construct federal common law out of the FTCA when we held that the Government's waiver ***528** of sovereign immunity for the torts of its employees does not give the Government an implied right of indemnity from them, even though the "[t]he financial burden placed on the United States by the Tort Claims Act [could conceivably be] so great that government employees should be required to carry part of the burden." *United States v. Gilman,* 347 U.S. 507, 510, 74 S.Ct. 695, 697, 98 L.Ed. 898 (1954). So too here, the FTCA's retention of sovereign immunity for the Government's discretionary acts does not imply a defense for the benefit of contractors who participate in those acts, even though they might pass on the financial burden to the United States. In either case, the most that can be said is that the position "asserted, though the product of a law Congress passed, is a matter on which Congress has not taken a position." *Id.,* at 511, 74 S.Ct., at 697 (footnote omitted).

Here, even that much is an overstatement, for the Government's immunity for discretionary functions is not even "a product of" the FTCA. Before Congress enacted the FTCA (when sovereign immunity barred any tort suit against the Federal Government) we perceived no need for a rule of federal common law to reinforce the Government's immunity by shielding also parties who might contractually pass costs on to it. Nor did we (or any other court of which I am aware) identify a special category of "discretionary" functions for which sovereign immunity was so crucial that a Government contractor who exercised discretion should share the Government's immunity from state tort law.[FN6]

FN6. Some States, of course, would not have permitted a stranger to the contract to bring such a tort suit at all, but no one suggested that this rule of state tort law was compelled by federal law.

Now, as before the FTCA's enactment, the Federal Government is immune from "[a]ny claim...based upon the exercise or performance [of] a discretionary function," including presumably any claim that petitioner might have brought against the Federal Government based upon respondent's negligent design of the helicopter in which Lt. Boyle died. ***529** There is no more reason for federal common law to shield contractors now that the Government is liable for some torts than there was when the Government was liable for none. The discretionary function exception does not support an immunity for the discretionary acts of Government *contractors* any more than the exception for "[a]ny claim [against the Government] arising out of assault," § 2680(h), supports a personal immunity for Government employees who commit assaults. Cf. *Sheridan v. United States,* 487 U.S. 392, 400, 108 S.Ct. 2449, 2453, 101 L.Ed.2d 352 (1988). In short, while the Court purports to divine whether Congress would object to this suit, it inexplicably begins and ends its sortilege with an exception to a statute that is itself inapplicable and whose repeal would leave unchanged every relationship remotely relevant to the accident underlying this suit.

Far more indicative of Congress' views on the subject is the wrongful-death cause of action that Congress itself has provided under the Death on the High Seas Act (DOHSA), Act of Mar. 30, 1920, ch. 111, § 1 *et seq.,* 41 Stat. 537, codified at 46 U.S.C. App. § 761 *et seq.* (1982 ed., Supp. IV)-a cause of action that could have been asserted against United Technologies had Lt. Boyle's helicopter crashed a mere three ****2528** miles further off the coast of Virginia Beach. It is beyond me how a state-law tort suit against the designer of a military helicopter could be said to present any conflict, much less a " 'significant conflict,' " with "federal interests…in the context of Government procurement," *ante,* at 2518, when federal law itself would provide a tort suit, but no (at least no explicit) Government-contractor defense,[FN7] against the same ***530** designer for an accident involving the same equipment. See Pet. for Cert. in *Sikorsky Aircraft Division, United Technologies Corp. v. Kloss,* O.T. 1987, No. 87-1633, pp. 3-6 (trial court holds that family of marine can bring a wrongful-death cause of action under the DOHSA against United Technologies for the negligent design of a United States Marine Corps CH-53D helicopter in which he was killed when it crashed 21 miles offshore), cert. denied, 486 U.S. 1008, 108 S.Ct. 1736, 100 L.Ed.2d 200 (1988).

> FN7. But cf. *Tozer v. LTV Corp.,* 792 F.2d 403 (CA4 1986) (applying defense in DOHSA case), cert. pending, No. 86-674; *Shaw v. Grumman Aerospace Corp.,* 778 F.2d 736 (CA11 1985) (same), cert. pending, No. 85-1529; *Koutsoubos v. Boeing Vertol, Division of Boeing Co.,* 755 F.2d 352 (CA3) (same), cert. denied, 474 U.S. 821, 106 S.Ct. 72, 88 L.Ed.2d 59 (1985); *McKay v. Rockwell Int'l Corp.,* 704 F.2d 444 (CA9 1983) (same), cert. denied, 464 U.S. 1043, 104 S.Ct. 711, 79 L.Ed.2d 175 (1984).

IV

At bottom, the Court's analysis is premised on the proposition that any tort liability indirectly absorbed by the Government so burdens governmental functions as to compel us to act when Congress has not. That proposition is by no means uncontroversial. The tort system is premised on the assumption that the imposition of liability encourages actors to prevent any injury whose expected cost exceeds the cost of prevention. If the system is working as it should, Government contractors will design equipment to avoid certain injuries (like the deaths of soldiers or Government employees), which would be certain to burden the Government. The Court therefore has no basis for its assumption that tort liability will result in a net burden on the Government (let alone a clearly excessive net burden) rather than a net gain.

Perhaps tort liability is an inefficient means of ensuring the quality of design efforts, but "[w]hatever the merits of the policy" the Court wishes to implement, "its conversion into law is a proper subject for congressional action, not for any creative power of ours." *Standard Oil,* 332 U.S., at 314-315, 67 S.Ct., at 1611. It is, after all, "Congress, not this Court or the other federal courts, [that] is the custodian of the national purse. By the same token [Congress] is the primary and most often the exclusive arbiter of federal fiscal affairs. And these comprehend, as we have said, securing the treasury or the Government against financial losses *however inflicted…." Ibid.* (emphasis added). See also ***531***Gilman, supra,* 347 U.S., at 510-512, 74 S.Ct., at 697-698. If Congress shared the Court's assumptions and conclusion it could readily enact "A BILL [t]o place limitations on the civil liability of government contractors to ensure that such liability does not impede the ability of the United States to procure necessary goods and services," H.R. 4765, 99th Cong., 2d Sess. (1986); see also S. 2441, 99th Cong., 2d Sess. (1986). It has not.

Were I a legislator, I would probably vote against any law absolving multibillion dollar private enterprises from answering for their tragic mistakes, at least if that law were justified by no more than the unsupported speculation that their liability might ultimately burden the United States Treasury. Some of my colleagues here would evidently vote otherwise (as they have here), but that should not matter here. We are judges not legislators, and the vote is not ours to cast.

I respectfully dissent.

Justice STEVENS, dissenting.

When judges are asked to embark on a lawmaking venture, I believe they should carefully consider whether they, or a legislative body, are better equipped to perform the task at hand. There are instances of **2529 so-called interstitial lawmaking that inevitably become part of the judicial process. [FN1] But when we are asked to create an entirely new doctrine-to answer "questions of policy on which Congress has not spoken," *United States v. Gilman,* 347 U.S. 507, 511, 74 S.Ct. 695, 697, 98 L.Ed. 898 (1954)-we have a special duty to identify the proper decisionmaker before trying to make the proper decision.

> FN1. "I recognize without hesitation that judges do and must legislate, but they can do so only interstitially; they are confined from molar to molecular motions. A common-law judge could not say I think the doctrine of consideration a bit of historical nonsense and shall not enforce it in my court. No more could a judge exercising the limited jurisdiction of admiralty say I think well of the common-law rules of master and servant and propose to introduce them here *en bloc.*" *Southern Pacific Co. v. Jensen,* 244 U.S. 205, 221, 37 S.Ct. 524, 531, 61 L.Ed. 1086 (1917) (Holmes, J., dissenting).

*532 When the novel question of policy involves a balancing of the conflicting interests in the efficient operation of a massive governmental program and the protection of the rights of the individual-whether in the social welfare context, the civil service context, or the military procurement context-I feel very deeply that we should defer to the expertise of the Congress. That is the central message of the unanimous decision in *Bush v. Lucas,* 462 U.S. 367, 103 S.Ct. 2404, 76 L.Ed.2d 648 (1983); [FN2] that is why I joined the majority in *Schweiker v. Chilicky,* 487 U.S. 412, 108 S.Ct. 2460, 101 L.Ed.2d 370 (1988), [FN3] a case decided only three days ago; and that is why I am so distressed by the majority's decision today. For in this case, as in *United States v. Gilman, supra:* "The selection of that policy which is most advantageous to the whole involves a host of considerations that must be weighed and appraised. That function is more appropriately for those who write the laws, rather than for those who interpret them." *Id.,* 347 U.S., at 511-513, 74 S.Ct., at 697-698.

> FN2. "[W]e decline to create a new substantive legal liability without legislative aid and as at the common law, because we are convinced that Congress is in a better position to decide whether or not the public interest would be served by creating it." 462 U.S., at 390, 103 S.Ct., at 2417 (internal quotation omitted).

> FN3. "Congressional competence at 'balancing governmental efficiency and the rights of [individuals],' *Bush,* 462 U.S., at 389 [103 S.Ct., at 2417], is no more questionable in the social welfare context than it is in the civil service context. Cf. *Forrester v. White,* 484 U.S. 219, 223-224 [108 S.Ct. 538, 542, 98 L.Ed.2d 555] (1988)." 487 U.S., at 425, 108 S.Ct., at 2469.

I respectfully dissent.

B.3 *Four Corners Helicopters, Inc. v. Turbomeca, S.A.,* **979 F.2d 1434 (10th Cir. 1992)**

United States Court of Appeals,
Tenth Circuit.

FOUR CORNERS HELICOPTERS, INC., a Colorado corporation; Jenny R. Paton, as surviving spouse and as personal
representative of the Estate of William Paton, deceased, Plaintiffs-Appellees,
v.
TURBOMECA, S.A., a French corporation, Defendant-Appellant,
and
Societe Nationale Industrielle Aerospatiale, a French corporation; Aerospatiale Helicopter Corporation, a Delaware corporation; Avialle, Inc., a Delaware corporation; Roberts Aircraft, Inc., an Arizona corporation, Defendants.
No. 91-1295.

Nov. 17, 1992.

Helicopter owner and pilot's surviving spouse brought action against helicopter and engine manufacturers to recover for
damages resulting from fatal crash. The United States District Court for the District of Colorado, Jim R. Carrigan, J., entered
judgment on jury verdict in favor of spouse and owner. Engine manufacturer appealed. The Court of Appeals, Barrett, Senior Circuit Judge, held that: (1) evidence of similar incidents of labyrinth screw backing out was admissible; (2) evidence
of experiment conducted on lathe was inadmissible; (3) helicopter owner was entitled to recover from engine manufacturer
for loss of helicopter and compressor being transported; and (4) Colorado law permitted award of prejudgment interest on
entire jury verdict discounted to date of trial.

Affirmed.

For space considerations, all headnotes have been deleted.

Mary A. Wells (J. Mark Smith and Stephen J. Baity, with her on the briefs), of Weller, Friedrich, Ward & Andrew, Denver,
Colo., for appellant.

James A. Cederberg (Douglas E. Bragg, with him on the brief), of Bragg, Baker & Cederberg, P.C., and Chris A. Mattison
(Alan Epstein, with him on the brief), of Hall & Evans, Denver, Colo. for plaintiffs-appellees.

Before LOGAN, HOLLOWAY and BARRETT, Circuit Judges.

BARRETT, Senior Circuit Judge.

Turbomeca, S.A. (Turbomeca) appeals from a judgment entered in favor of plaintiffs Jenny Paton and Four Corners Helicopters, Inc. (Four Corners).

Factual Background

This case arises from a helicopter crash which resulted in the death of pilot William Paton (Paton), husband of Jenny Paton.
At the time of the accident, Paton was operating an Aerospatiale SA 315 B "Lama" helicopter for his employer, Four Corners.
The helicopter was powered by an Artouste IIIB turbine engine, designed and manufactured by defendant Turbomeca.

*1436 The Artouste IIIB is a constant-speed engine which maintains the same revolutions per minute (RPMs) during op-
erational maneuvers by sensing deviations in RPMs and adjusting the amount of fuel delivered to the engine. This process
produces additional heat, and if the engine temperature limits are exceeded, the engine will burn itself up.

At the time of the accident, Paton was using the helicopter to transport a compressor by long-line. Although this maneuver placed substantial demands on the engine, it was within the engine's limits. Prior to the accident, this helicopter had been used extensively for this type of mission and, in fact, following the accident, was replaced by a similar aircraft. In the instant case, it is undisputed that the helicopter engine overheated, causing the aircraft to crash. The issue at trial was the cause of overheating.

The National Transportation Safety Board (NTSB) investigated the accident at the scene, during engine dismantling, and at Turbomeca's facility in France. The NTSB discovered that a loose labyrinth screw had backed out of position and contacted the compressor impeller. In its report, the NTSB noted that an abnormal squeal, caused by the screw rubbing the diffuser-holder plate, had been witnessed prior to the crash of the aircraft. The NTSB's report also documented twenty-one previously reported instances where, during the course of engine repair or maintenance, it was discovered that the labyrinth screw had rubbed the impeller. In each instance, the engine was removed either because of abnormal noise which occurred during engine rundown, later discovered to be the screeching of the screw on the impeller, or because of a slightly slower rundown time.

Turbomeca also participated in the investigation, conducting loose screw tests upon a similar engine and then transmitting the results to the NTSB and the Federal Aviation Administration (FAA). In its report, Turbomeca reviewed the same twenty-one prior loose screw incidents but concluded that the friction between the screw and the impeller was a minor anomaly which had no effect on the correct operation of the engine. Turbomeca had previously issued Service Bulletin TU133, labelled "URGENT," which outlined a modification procedure to "improve locking of front labyrinth fastening screws on diffuser cover." The company recommended that the modification be performed as soon as possible on both the production line and when repairing engines. The modification consisted of "staking" the screw heads to the surrounding metal, and was performed on the subject engine in 1979 at Turbomeca's factory in France. During Turbomeca's final testing of the engine in question, the engine "seized" during rundown. This seizure was the subject of a second report by Turbomeca which was never provided to the NTSB, the FAA, or Four Corners.

Plaintiffs proceeded to trial on strict liability in tort and negligence theories. They asserted that the helicopter engine failed when a loose labyrinth housing screw backed out of position and contacted the rear face of the compressor impeller. They claimed that this contact reduced the engine's RPMs, causing additional amounts of fuel to be injected into the engine. The additional fuel produced an increase in temperature beyond the engine's limits, resulting in the engine's destruction.

Turbomeca asserted that the loose labyrinth screw could not have caused the engine failure. Turbomeca presented evidence that when a helicopter is required to hover and place a load in a confined area, a collective pitch change results, increasing the engine's temperature, over which the pilot has control. Turbomeca argued that in the instant case, the pilot's demands on the aircraft, namely pulling up too much on the collective pitch control, caused the engine to overheat and ultimately fail. Although Turbomeca's accident reconstructionist opined that no mechanical failure caused the accident, he nevertheless conceded that if there had been a mechanical problem, his theory on pilot error would not be appropriate.

The jury found Turbomeca liable under strict liability only. The district court entered*1437 judgment on the jury's verdict, including interest and costs, in favor of Paton in the amount of $959,926.20 and in favor of Four Corners in the amount of $306,204.37.

On appeal, Turbomeca contends that the district court erred in: (1) instructing the jury on a rebuttable presumption that the decedent acted with reasonable care at the time of the accident which caused his death; (2) admitting evidence of sixteen incidents involving labyrinth seal screw backouts; (3) excluding evidence of an experiment conducted by Turbomeca's expert; (4) permitting recovery of economic damages under a strict liability theory; and (5) awarding prejudgment interest on future damages, discounted to the date of trial rather than the date of the decedent's death.

Discussion

I. PRESUMPTION OF REASONABLE CARE INSTRUCTION

[1] Turbomeca contends that the district court erred in instructing the jury on a rebuttable presumption that the decedent acted with reasonable care at the time of the accident which caused his death.

In instructing the jury, the district court directed the jurors to "consider only evidence admitted in the trial," which included, among other things, "all presumptions stated in [the] instructions." The court indicated that "[p]resumptions are rules based on experience or public policy and are established om [sic] the law to assist the jury in ascertaining the truth." Then, over Turbomeca's objection, the court instructed that "[w]hen a person is dead and cannot testify concerning his actions, the law presumes, unless there is evidence to the contrary, that the decedent acted with reasonable care."

A.

Citing *Simpson v. Anderson*, 33 Colo.App. 134, 517 P.2d 416, 417 (1973), *rev'd on other grounds*, 186 Colo. 163, 526 P.2d 298 (1974), Turbomeca asserts that under Colorado's comparative fault law, the decedent in a wrongful death action is not presumed to have acted with reasonable care. In *Simpson*, the Colorado Court of Appeals noted that the presumption of due care was "created primarily to ameliorate the harsh effect of a complete denial of recovery resulting from a finding of contributory negligence...." *Id.* Because under comparative negligence a plaintiff's fault will not entirely defeat his recovery, "the rationale behind [the] presumption is therefore no longer persuasive." *Simpson*, 517 P.2d at 417. The *Simpson* court concluded "that a rule that presumes exercise of due care by a decedent is inapplicable in wrongful death actions tried under [the] comparative negligence statute." *Id.*

Simpson is determinative on this issue, even though the presumption of due care was later reaffirmed by the Colorado Supreme Court in *City and County of Denver v. DeLong*, 190 Colo. 219, 545 P.2d 154 (Colo.1976). *DeLong* indicates that an instruction on the rebuttable presumption of due care is appropriate in a personal injury action where a party's injury results in amnesia. The court in *DeLong* intended that the reader compare the presumption discussed in *DeLong* with its discussion in *Simpson*. The *DeLong* court cited five cases supporting the presumption, followed by this reference: "cf., *Simpson v. Anderson*," (citation omitted), "which prohibits the use of the presumption in a wrongful death action when comparative negligence is the issue." *DeLong*, 545 P.2d at 156-57. *DeLong* cites *Simpson* as authority which supports a proposition different from that espoused in *DeLong*.

The instant case is brought under Colorado's comparative fault statute. As such, decedent's fault, if any, will not completely bar recovery. Therefore, the rationale behind application of the presumption does not exist. Following *Simpson*, we hold that the presumption is inapplicable in a wrongful death action where comparative negligence is at issue. Though the district court gave an erroneous jury instruction, this does not end our inquiry.

*1438 B.

[2] "[A]n error in jury instructions will mandate reversal of a judgment only if the error is determined to have been prejudicial, based on a review of the record as a whole." *Street v. Parham*, 929 F.2d 537, 539-40 (10th Cir.1991) (citations omitted). Turbomeca claims that the giving of a jury instruction on a presumption which is not available under state law is prejudicial error requiring a new trial. "When reviewing a claim of error relating to jury instructions, the instructions must be read and evaluated in their entirety." *United States v. Denny*, 939 F.2d 1449, 1454 (10th Cir.1991) (citing *Cupp v. Naughten*, 414 U.S. 141, 146-47, 94 S.Ct. 396, 400, 38 L.Ed.2d 368 (1973)). The reviewing court "will consider from the jury's standpoint whether what the jury heard, even though not faultless, misled it in any way." *United States v. Agnew*, 931 F.2d 1397, 1410 (10th Cir.1991) (citing *Durflinger v. Artiles*, 727 F.2d 888, 895 (10th Cir.1984)), *cert denied*, 502 U.S. 884, 112 S.Ct. 237, 116 L.Ed.2d 193 (1991).

Turbomeca raises three arguments asserting that this erroneous jury instruction was prejudicial. Citing *Union Ins. Co. v. RCA Corp.*, 724 P.2d 80 (Colo.Ct.App.1986), Turbomeca initially contends that the instruction impermissibly aided the plaintiff by influencing the jury's determination of whether Turbomeca met its burden of proving comparative fault. In *Union Insurance*, a products liability action, the court held that while the presumption of nondefectiveness instruction did not shift or alter the plaintiff's burden of persuasion, it affected that burden by aiding the defendant in supplementing his burden of going forward. Because the defendant's evidence was confusing, precluding the court from determining whether the jury was influenced by the instruction, the instruction provided the jury with "affirmative evidence to which defendant was not entitled." *Id.* at 83-84.

For the same proposition, Turbomeca also relies on *Telecky v. Yampa Valley Elec. Assn.*, 837 P.2d 253 (Colo.Ct.App.1992), *cert. granted* (Oct. 13, 1992), where the district court gave a jury instruction on a proper rebuttable presumption but nevertheless held that that instruction alone was "incomplete and possibly confusing to the jury, in that it [did] not instruct the jury concerning what circumstances [were] sufficient to rebut the presumption." The court indicated that reversal was required where the instruction may have impermissibly influenced the jury's determination of whether plaintiff met her burden.

The instant case is distinguishable from the cases upon which Turbomeca relies. Unlike *Union Insurance*, the presumption instruction in the instant case included limiting language. Clearly, with evidence to the contrary, the presumption was rebutted and Turbomeca's burden was thereby unaffected. While the instruction alone in *Telecky* may have been incomplete and possibly confusing, in the instant case, the substance of the instructions given was not confusing to the jury. Taken together, the instructions fairly, adequately, and correctly stated the law, providing the jury with an ample understanding of the principles of law confronting them. *United States v. Denny*, 939 F.2d 1449 (10th Cir.1991).

Second, Turbomeca asserts that the court did not state that the presumption of due care was rebuttable, thereby providing no guidance on the amount of proof required to overcome the presumption. This court has indicated that "[r]ebuttable presumptions in the civil law are normally overcome by a preponderance of the evidence," though there are "no universal rules" governing the amount of evidence required. *Tafoya v. Sears Roebuck and Co.*, 884 F.2d 1330, 1337 (10th Cir.1989).

In the instant case, the court instructed the jury that the plaintiff bears the burden to prove, by a preponderance of the evidence, every element of the claim it asserts. And, the court instructed that the defendant bears the same burden to prove its affirmative defense. The court defined a preponderance as "such evidence as, when considered and compared with that opposed to it, has more convincing force and produces in [the jurors'] minds a belief that what is sought to be proved is more ***1439** likely true than not true," indicating that this does not require proof to an absolute certainty. Furthermore, prior to giving the instruction on the presumption of due care, the court gave a presumption instruction on the defectiveness of the helicopter engine, where it concluded that the presumption could be "rebutted by evidence to the contrary."

The parties' burdens of proof were clearly set forth in the jury instructions. The court similarly made it clear that presumptions could be rebutted by contrary evidence. The instruction in question, on its face, stated in part that "the law presumes, *unless there is evidence to the contrary,* that the decedent acted with reasonable care." (Emphasis added). Furthermore, during oral argument before this court, counsel for Turbomeca acknowledged that in her closing arguments to the jury she contended that the presumption could not apply because Turbomeca had presented evidence of the decedent's fault. Counsel's argument indicated that "evidence to the contrary" had been presented, thereby rebutting the presumption and dissipating any potentially reversible error.

Finally, Turbomeca asserts that when a general verdict is returned and it cannot be determined with absolute certainty that the jury was not influenced by the erroneous instruction, reversal and remand for a new trial are required. *See Farrell v. Klein Tools, Inc.*, 866 F.2d 1294, 1298-1301 (10th Cir.1989). In the instant case, a general verdict form was not used. Jurors answered Special Verdict Form B, indicating that both plaintiffs were entitled to recover damages on their claims of product liability but not on their claims of negligence, and that neither the decedent nor Four Corners was at fault. The completion of this Special Verdict does not frustrate a determination of the basis of the jury's decision.

Though the district court erroneously instructed the jury on a rebuttable presumption of due care which does not exist in wrongful death actions brought under the comparative negligence statute, such error did not prejudice Turbomeca. The jury instructions, taken as a whole, constituted a fair and adequate statement of the law upon which the jury could base its decision.

II. EVIDENCE OF SIMILAR INCIDENTS

[3] Turbomeca contends that the district court erred in admitting evidence of other incidents of labyrinth seal screw back-outs.

At trial, plaintiffs introduced, from various repair facilities, sixteen reports of loose labyrinth screws and a computer print-out listing those reports. These documents were offered on the issues of design defect, notice of design defect, duty to warn, negligence, causation, and to refute Turbomeca's claim that the accident was caused by a maintenance problem due to excessive vibration.

The district court concluded that plaintiffs showed substantial similarity between the other incidents and the engine failure in this case. Indicating that there are never two exactly identical cases, the district court ruled that "slightly different factors don't render any of the proffered incidents not substantially similar for the purpose for which they are offered...." The court found that the incidents were relevant for all purposes offered by plaintiffs and that any differences between the other incidents and the engine failure in this case affected the weight of the evidence and not its admissibility. Furthermore, Turbomeca was free to cross-examine on the distinctions, and it subsequently failed to request a limiting instruction.

Citing *Wheeler v. John Deere Co.,* 862 F.2d 1404 (10th Cir.1988), Turbomeca asserts that the incidents were not other accidents caused by inflight engine failure and, accordingly, were not substantially similar to the accident in question. It contends that significant distinctions exist between the incidents and the accident in question, which reflect a lack of substantial similarity between the occurrences. Specifically, Turbomeca notes the following differences: none of the reports records an inflight failure of an Artouste IIIB engine; some of the reports concerned Artouste II rather than Artouste IIIB engines; none of the *1440 incidents reported involved accidents, but instead concerned mechanical problems identified on the ground; in some of the reports the compressor impeller was made of aluminum, a softer material than the titanium used on other impellers; with one exception, the reports concerned engines which were not under power [FN1] when problems occurred; and the screw in the instant case was fixed in place by a method described in Turbomeca Service Bulletin TU133, whereas in other Artouste IIIB engines, a different, less secure fixation method was utilized. Further, Turbomeca claims that none of the reports established proof that the labyrinth screw could cause a catastrophic engine failure such as occurred in the instant case.

> FN1. An engine is "under power" when fuel is being delivered to it and it is producing 550 horsepower. An engine is not "under power" if it has been shut off and is winding down or is just being started with its electric starter motor.

Plaintiffs introduced testimony that: all incidents involved Artouste II or Artouste IIIB engines, the same generic engine; the screws and seals, and the retention of the screws were the same, as were the manufactured tolerances; and in virtually all incidents a squeaking or grinding noise was identified during engine coastdown, engine lockup or stiff stoppage occurred during shutdown, and a wear and rub pattern appeared on the head of the screw and the aft of the impeller. Plaintiffs' expert also indicated that Turbomeca's use of these very incidents to support its own position, in its report submitted to the NTSB and the FAA, demonstrated Turbomeca's belief that the incidents were sufficiently similar.

The district court's ruling regarding the admission of similar incidents will not be reversed absent a clear abuse of discretion. *C.A. Assocs. v. Dow Chemical Co.,* 918 F.2d 1485, 1489 (10th Cir.1990). In product liability actions, the occurrence of similar accidents or failures involving the same product has great impact on a jury, as it tends to make the existence of the defect more probable than it would be without the evidence. *Id.* In such actions, courts routinely permit the introduction of substantially similar acts to demonstrate notice, the existence of a defect, or to refute testimony given by defense witnesses. *Id.*

"Before introducing such evidence, the party seeking its admission must show the circumstances surrounding the other accidents were substantially similar to the accident involved in the present case." *Wheeler,* 862 F.2d at 1407. Substantial similarity depends upon the underlying theory of the case. "Evidence proffered to illustrate the existence of a dangerous condition necessitates a high degree of similarity because it weighs directly on the ultimate issue to be decided by the jury." *Id.* The requirement of substantial similarity is relaxed, however, when the evidence of other incidents is used to demonstrate notice or awareness of a potential defect. *Id.* "Any differences in the accidents not affecting a finding of substantial similarity go to the weight of the evidence." *Id. See also Jackson v. Firestone Tire & Rubber Co.,* 788 F.2d 1070, 1083 (5th Cir.1986).

In the instant case, plaintiffs offered evidence of these similar incidents to prove, among other things, a design defect and notice thereof, and to refute Turbomeca's assertion that there was no mechanical failure. The incidents, though not identical, were substantially similar and were therefore admissible to indicate the existence of a defect. They further met any relaxed requirement of similarity and were therefore admissible for all purposes offered by plaintiffs. We hold that the district court did not abuse its discretion in admitting these prior incidents which showed substantial similarity with the engine failure in the instant case.

III. VIDEOTAPED EVIDENCE OF EXPERIMENT

[4] Turbomeca contends that the district court erred in excluding evidence of an experiment conducted by Turbomeca's expert, Dr. Manning.

Turbomeca undertook two experiments in support of its argument that the loose labyrinth screw could not have caused the ***1441** seizure of the helicopter engine. The first experiment, an attempted recreation of the accident under controlled conditions at Turbomeca's plant, is not at issue. Rather, at issue is the second experiment which was conducted by Manning. For his experiment, Manning attached a titanium disc to a lathe which, according to Turbomeca, rotated the disc "in a manner representative of the turning compressor impeller." Manning observed the results when a screw, identical to the labyrinth screw in issue, was mounted in a holder and was placed in contact with the rotating disc. According to Manning's report, the screw head was worn similar to the one in question, but the lathe was not affected and continued to operate without a reduction in RPMs. Manning concluded that since the three horsepower lathe was unaffected by the contact, an eight-hundred horsepower engine would likewise be unaffected.

According to Turbomeca, the purpose of the experiment was three-fold: (1) to determine the coefficient of friction and demonstrate why the screw contacting the titanium impeller could not have caused the engine to overheat; (2) to show what happens to a screw which comes into contact with a rotating titanium impeller, in terms of thermal damage and physical deformation (Turbomeca noted that this gave Manning a basis upon which to form his expert opinion); and (3) to show the reduction in RPMs which might be expected to occur (Turbomeca asserted that the force required to cause the engine to overheat as plaintiffs suggested would have caused considerably different and more extensive damage to the screw than actually occurred). Overall, Turbomeca argues that the experiment was offered to illustrate general physical and scientific principles.

Plaintiffs filed a Motion in Limine to exclude evidence of the experiment which they challenged as being substantially dissimilar to the accident. In support thereof, plaintiffs attached the affidavit of their expert, Robert Phillips, who described the dissimilarities between Manning's experiment and the conditions operating in the Artouste IIIB engine at the time of the accident. The distinctions included the following: the lathe is a high-torque device while the helicopter engine is low-torque; the lathe operated at approximately 1000 RPMs while the engine functioned at 35,500 RPMs; and in the lathe experiment, 100% of the torque was applied to the screw, while in the engine only a small percentage of torque handled the resistance of the screw; plaintiffs assert that the jamming of the screw and subsequent impact on RPMs occurred in less than two seconds while the lathe tests lasted between 45 and 54 seconds; and in the lathe experiment, there was no support for the screw head and thus no wedging or jamming occurred, whereas wedging occurred in the engine. Phillips concluded that Manning's experiment did not accurately depict events occurring inside of the engine at the time of the accident.

The district court excluded the videotape of Manning's experiment, finding such evidence irrelevant due to lack of substantial similarity. Further, the court excluded the information because, under Rule 403 of the Federal Rules of Evidence, its probative value was far outweighed by its unfairly prejudicial effect on the jury.

Turbomeca submits that where, as here, an experiment is offered to illustrate physical principles and not to simulate the actual event, the experiment results should be admitted into evidence. It claims that the information contained in the videotape is neither confusing nor prejudicial, and that the court could have given a limiting instruction to overcome any potential confusion. Turbomeca asserts that the exclusion of this evidence constituted an abuse of discretion by the district court. *Harvey v. General Motors Corp.,* 873 F.2d 1343, 1355 (10th Cir.1989); *Bannister v. Town of Noble, Okla.,* 812 F.2d 1265, 1270-72 (10th Cir.1987).

[5][6] "A trial court's evidentiary rulings are reviewed for an abuse of discretion, (citation omitted), as are its decisions on instructing the jury (citation omitted)." *Durtsche v. American Colloid Co.,* 958 F.2d 1007, 1011 (10th Cir.1992). The admissibility of experiments is discretionary, and *1442 a ruling on admissibility will only be disturbed on appeal if it is clearly erroneous-a clear abuse of discretion. *Jackson v. Fletcher,* 647 F.2d 1020, 1026 (10th Cir.1981); *Bannister,* 812 F.2d at 1270. Admissibility of experimental evidence does not depend on identical actual and experimental conditions. Typically, dissimilarities go to the weight of the evidence rather than its admissibility. *Champeau v. Fruehauf Corp.,* 814 F.2d 1271, 1278 (8th Cir.1987) (citing *Randall v. Warnaco, Inc.,* 677 F.2d 1226, 1233-34 (8th Cir.1982)). When ruling under Fed.R.Evid. 403, the task of balancing the probative value of evidence against the harm likely to result from its admission is well-suited for the trial judge who is familiar with the full scope of the evidence. *C.A. Assocs. v. Dow Chemical Co.,* 918 F.2d 1485, 1489 (10th Cir.1990).

[7] Experiments purporting to simulate actual events may be admissible if made under conditions which are substantially similar to those which are the subject of the litigation. While the conditions need not be identical, they must be sufficiently similar to provide a fair comparison. *Jackson v. Fletcher,* 647 F.2d 1020, 1027 (10th Cir.1981). In *Jackson,* the experiment was designed as a reenactment. We held that since a substantial dissimilarity in conditions prevented a fair comparison and could have misled the jury on a critical element of the case, the admission of the evidence was prejudicial. *Id.* at 1028.

[8][9][10][11] On the other hand, filmed evidence which is not meant to depict the actual event may be admitted to show mechanical principles, "upon a showing that 'the experiment [was] conducted under conditions that were at least similar to those which existed at the time of the accident.'" *Bannister,* 812 F.2d at 1270 (citing *Brandt v. French,* 638 F.2d 209, 212 (10th Cir.1981)). However, if the evidence is offered to merely show physical principles, the experiment should be conducted without suggesting that it simulates actual events. *Jackson,* 647 F.2d at 1027. Experiments used to simply demonstrate the principles used in forming expert opinion need not strictly adhere to the facts. *Brandt,* 638 F.2d at 212. It is important then that the jury be instructed that the evidence is admitted for a limited purpose only. *Id.; see also Millers' Natl. Ins. Co. v. Wichita Flour Mills Co.,* 257 F.2d 93, 97 (10th Cir.1958).

At trial, Turbomeca attempted to maintain both positions, arguing that the experiment had sufficient similarity to pass the substantial similarity test, and that it could also be admitted to show physical principles. The district court disagreed, finding that the experiment could not pass the substantial similarity test because it did not "come close enough to the elements of what happened in this situation." The court also noted that the experiment attempted to mock engine conditions to an extent that its admission would have confused the jury into thinking it was a reenactment, thereby precluding its admission. According to the court, Turbomeca's attempted recreation of the incident under controlled conditions at its own plant was "far better than the out-of-court experiment" conducted by Manning.

In the instant case, Manning's experiment was not being offered simply to show physical principles such as coefficient of friction. Instead, it was being offered to demonstrate what Manning believed occurred in the helicopter engine. Manning used the experiment to counter plaintiffs' theory by asserting that an 800 horsepower engine would not be affected by the screw-impeller contact when a three horsepower lathe was unaffected. Taken together, we hold that the district court did not abuse its discretion in excluding the experiment after determining that the conditions present in the out-of-court experiment were not substantially similar to those present at the time of the accident.

IV. PROPERTY VERSUS ECONOMIC LOSSES

[12] Turbomeca contends that the district court erred in permitting recovery of economic damages under the plaintiffs' strict liability theory.

*1443 In returning a verdict for Four Corners on its strict liability claim only, the jury awarded Four Corners $226,500 for the loss of the helicopter and $17,500 for the loss of the air compressor. The jury did not award damages for Four Corners' loss of use of the helicopter, loss of business income, loss of business opportunity, or other direct and consequential damages.

Turbomeca asserts that Four Corners' loss of the aircraft is a business loss and that the jury improperly awarded purely economic damages under Four Corners' strict liability theory. It claims that because Four Corners is a commercial user which lost the value of its product, Four Corners should be limited to a cause of action under warranty rather than strict liability.

Turbomeca cites *East River S. Corp. v. Transamerica Delaval, Inc.,* 476 U.S. 858, 106 S.Ct. 2295, 90 L.Ed.2d 865 (1986) for the proposition that a commercial plaintiff's damages for economic losses are not recoverable in a strict liability action. The Court in *East River* emphasized the need to keep products liability and contract law separate, and indicated that "loss due to repair costs, decreased value, and lost profits is essentially the failure of the purchaser to receive the benefit of its bargain-traditionally the core concern of contract law." *Id.* 476 U.S. at 870, 106 S.Ct. at 2302. Turbomeca contends that Colorado follows the *East River* rationale in that "a commercial buyer seeking damages for economic losses resulting from the purchase of defective goods may recover under the U.C.C., but not in strict liability." *Richard O'Brien Cos. v. Challenge-Cook Bros., Inc.,* 672 F.Supp. 466, 472 (D.Colo.1987).

As a federal court sitting in diversity, we are required to apply Colorado law. *Adams-Arapahoe School Dist. No. 28-J v. GAF Corp.,* 959 F.2d 868, 870 (10th Cir.1992). Contrary to Turbomeca's contention, Colorado law does not support the *East River* decision. In *Richard O'Brien Cos.,* the federal district court simply attempted to interpret Colorado's application of Restatement § 402A.

In *Hiigel v. General Motors Corp.,* 190 Colo. 57, 544 P.2d 983 (1975), the Colorado Supreme Court adopted § 402A of the Restatement (Second) of Torts. Section 402A provides that damage to a product itself is covered under the doctrine of strict liability. The court in *Hiigel,* however, "decline[d] to extend the doctrine of 402A to commercial or business loss," and thereby limited application of the Restatement to " 'physical harm…caused to the ultimate user or consumer, or to his property….' " *Hiigel,* 544 P.2d at 989 (citing *Seely v. Shite Motor Co.,* 45 Cal.Rptr. 17, 403 P.2d 145 (1965)). Relying on *Hiigel,* the Colorado Court of Appeals then "inferred that 'commercial or business losses' [meant] lost profits or loss of the benefit of a bargain." *Aetna Casualty & Surety Co. v. Crissy Fowler Lumber Co.,* 687 P.2d 514 (Colo.Ct.App.1984).

In an effort to square Colorado's *Hiigel* decision with *East River,* the court in *Richard O'Brien Cos.* restricted *Hiigel* to its particular facts. The court distinguished between commercial and noncommercial cases, indicating that *Hiigel* involved a noncommercial plaintiff, and it subsequently held that "[p]laintiffs may not claim damages for injury to a product itself in tort pursuant to a commercial transaction." *Richard O'Brien Cos.,* 672 F.Supp. at 472.

The instant case does not fall within the purview of the *East River* decision. As the Ninth Circuit has indicated, *East River* holds "that a cause of action for breach of warranty, not a products liability claim, lies for damage to a defective product, unless damage is caused to persons or property other than the product itself." *Bancorp Leasing & Fin. Corp. v. Agusta Aviation Corp.,* 813 F.2d 272, 277 (9th Cir.1987) (emphasis added) (citing *East River,* 476 U.S. 858, 866-74, 106 S.Ct. 2295,

2300-04 (1986)). This court has similarly discussed *East River*, indicating that "the Supreme Court stated that whether an action is couched in terms of negligence or strict liability, no products liability claim lies in admiralty when a commercial party alleges *injury only to the product itself* resulting in *purely economic loss.*" *Lutz Farms v. Asgrow Seed Co.,* 948 F.2d 638, 643 (10th Cir.1991) (emphasis added).

Here, the defective engine was not purchased by Four Corners in a commercial *1444 transaction, and Four Corners is not seeking recovery for pure economic loss. Four Corners is a noncommercial plaintiff alleging injury to the product itself and the compressor being transported. We hold that, under applicable Colorado law, Four Corners is entitled to recover under strict liability for loss of the helicopter.

V. PREJUDGMENT INTEREST

[13] Turbomeca asserts that the district court erred in awarding prejudgment interest on future damages which were valued as of the date of trial, resulting in a duplication of damages.

Plaintiff Paton's economist, in evaluating Paton's net pecuniary loss, discounted the future damages to their present value as of the date of trial. The jury returned a verdict for $692,100, and the district court, under Colo.Rev.Stat. § 13-21-101(1), applied prejudgment interest to the entire award. Turbomeca agrees that the statute allows prejudgment interest on future damages; however, it asserts that the district court erred in awarding prejudgment interest to future losses which were discounted back only to the date of trial. Turbomeca argues that future damages must be *properly* discounted to the time at which the cause of action arose, in this case, the date of decedent's death.

Turbomeca claims that to award prejudgment interest on future damages discounted only to the date of trial permits a duplication of interest. Turbomeca relies on *Woodling v. Garrett Corp.,* 813 F.2d 543 (2d Cir.1987), in which the court held that "[i]f the award of damages for losses that have yet to occur is not discounted for that earlier period from the date of death to date of decision, then an award of interest for that earlier period would not compensate any loss but would give plaintiff a windfall." *Id.* at 560.

Section 13-21-101 provides that for actions brought after July 1, 1979, "it is lawful for the plaintiff in the complaint to claim interest on the damages claimed from the date the action accrued." The Colorado Court of Appeals has "interpret[ed] this statute to mean that if interest is claimed from the date the action accrued, the trial court *must* calculate interest from that date." *Smith v. JBJ, Ltd.,* 694 P.2d 352, 354 (Colo.Ct.App.1984) (emphasis added). The statute is ministerial in nature, providing that "[w]hen such interest is so claimed, it is the *duty* of the court in entering judgment for the plaintiff…to add to the amount of damages assessed by the verdict of the jury…interest on such amount…." (Emphasis added).

In the instant case, plaintiffs claimed interest from the date the action accrued. The district court, in accordance with its duty under section 13-21-101, awarded interest "to the amount of damages assessed by the verdict of the jury."

Turbomeca's only challenge concerns the discounting of future damages back to the date of trial instead of back to the date the action accrued. However, Turbomeca has referenced no Colorado case law supportive of this position. Moreover, nothing in section 13-21-101 dictates the date to which future losses must be discounted. Under these circumstances, we hold that plaintiffs are entitled to prejudgment interest on the entire jury verdict.

We AFFIRM.

B.4 *Helicopteros Nacionales de Colombia, S.A. v. Hall*, 466 U.S. 408 (1984)

Supreme Court of the United States
HELICOPTEROS NACIONALES DE COLOMBIA, S.A., Petitioner,
v.
Elizabeth HALL et al.
No. 82-1127.

Argued Nov. 8, 1983.
Decided April 24, 1984.

Wrongful death action was instituted in a Texas state court against a Colombian corporation and others. Denying Colombian corporation's motion to dismiss actions for lack of in personam jurisdiction over it, the District Court, Harris County, Wyatt H. Heard, J., entered judgment against corporation on a jury verdict in favor of plaintiffs. Corporation appealed. The Texas Court of Civil Appeals, 616 S.W.2d 247, reversed and dismissed case for lack of jurisdiction, and plaintiffs appealed. The Texas Supreme Court, 638 S.W.2d 870, reversed. Certiorari was granted. The Supreme Court, Justice Blackmun, held that Colombian corporation's contacts with Texas, which consisted of one trip to Texas by corporation's chief executive officer for purpose of negotiating transportation services contract, acceptance of checks drawn on Texas bank, and purchases of helicopters and equipment from Texas manufacturer and related training trips, were insufficient to satisfy requirements of due process clause of the Fourteenth Amendment and hence to allow Texas court to assert in personam jurisdiction over corporation in wrongful death action.

Texas Supreme Court judgment reversed.

Justice Brennan dissented and filed an opinion.

For space considerations, all headnotes have been deleted.

Syllabus [FNa1]

FNa1. The syllabus constitutes no part of the opinion of the Court but has been prepared by the Reporter of Decisions for the convenience of the reader. See *United States v. Detroit Lumber Co.*, 200 U.S. 321, 337, 26 S.Ct. 282, 287, 50 L.Ed. 499.

Petitioner, a Colombian corporation, entered into a contract to provide helicopter transportation for a Peruvian consortium, the alter ego of a joint venture that had its headquarters in Houston, Tex., during the consortium's construction of a pipeline in Peru for a Peruvian state-owned oil company. Petitioner has no place of business in Texas and never has been licensed to do business there. Its only contacts with the State consisted of sending its chief executive officer to Houston to negotiate the contract with the consortium, accepting into its New York bank account checks drawn by the consortium on a Texas bank, purchasing helicopters, equipment, and training services from a Texas manufacturer, and sending personnel to that manufacturer's facilities for training. After a helicopter owned by petitioner crashed in Peru, resulting in the death of respondents' decedents-United States citizens who were employed by the consortium-respondents instituted wrongful-death actions in a Texas state court against the consortium, the Texas manufacturer, and petitioner. Denying petitioner's motion to dismiss the actions for lack of in personam jurisdiction over it, the trial court entered judgment against petitioner on a jury verdict in favor of respondents. The Texas Court of Civil Appeals reversed, holding that in personam jurisdiction over petitioner was lacking, but in turn was reversed by the Texas Supreme Court.

Held: Petitioner's contacts with Texas were insufficient to satisfy the requirements of the Due Process Clause of the Fourteenth Amendment and hence to allow the Texas court to assert in personam jurisdiction over petitioner. The one trip to Houston by petitioner's chief executive officer for the purpose of negotiating the transportation services contract cannot be regarded as a contact of a "continuous and systematic" nature, and thus cannot support an assertion of general jurisdiction. Similarly, petitioner's acceptance of checks drawn on a Texas bank is of negligible significance for purposes of determining whether petitioner had sufficient contacts in Texas. Nor were petitioner's purchases of helicopters and equipment from the Texas manufacturer and the related training trips a sufficient basis for the Texas court's assertion of jurisdiction. *Rosenberg Bros. & Co. v. Curtis Brown Co.*, 260 U.S. 516, 43 S.Ct. 170, 67 L.Ed. 372. Mere purchases, even if occurring at regular intervals, are not enough to warrant ***409** a State's assertion of in personam jurisdiction over a nonresident corporation in a cause of action not related to the purchases. And the fact that petitioner sent personnel to Texas for training in connection with the purchases did not enhance the nature of petitioner's contacts with Texas. Pp. 1872-1874.

638 S.W.2d 870 (Tex.1982), reversed.

Thomas J. Whalen argued the cause for petitioner. With him on the briefs were *Austin P. Magner, Cynthia J. Larsen, James E. Ingram,* and *Barry A. Chasnoff.*

George E. Pletcher argued the cause and filed a brief for respondents.*

* *Robert L. Stern, Stephen M. Shapiro, William H. Crabtree,* and *Edward P. Good* filed a brief for the Motor Vehicle Manufacturers Association as *amicus curiae* urging reversal.

Solicitor General Lee, Assistant Attorney General McGrath, Deputy Solicitor General Geller, Kathryn A. Oberly, Michael F. Hertz, and *Howard S. Scher* filed a brief for the United States as *amicus curiae.*

Justice BLACKMUN delivered the opinion of the Court.

We granted certiorari in this case, 460 U.S. 1021, 103 S.Ct. 1270, 75 L.Ed.2d 493 (1983), to decide whether the Supreme Court of Texas correctly ruled that the contacts of a foreign corporation with the State of Texas were sufficient to allow a Texas state court to assert jurisdiction over the corporation in a cause of action not ****1870** arising out of or related to the corporation's activities within the State.

I

Petitioner Helicopteros Nacionales de Colombia, S.A. (Helicol), is a Colombian corporation with its principal place of business in the city of Bogota in that country. It is engaged in the business of providing helicopter transportation for oil and construction companies in South America. On ***410** January 26, 1976, a helicopter owned by Helicol crashed in Peru. Four United States citizens were among those who lost their lives in the accident. Respondents are the survivors and representatives of the four decedents.

At the time of the crash, respondents' decedents were employed by Consorcio, a Peruvian consortium, and were working on a pipeline in Peru. Consorcio is the alter ego of a joint venture named Williams-Sedco-Horn (WSH).[FN1] The venture had its headquarters in Houston, Tex. Consorcio had been formed to enable the venturers to enter into a contract with Petro Peru, the Peruvian state-owned oil company. Consorcio was to construct a pipeline for Petro Peru running from the interior of Peru westward to the Pacific Ocean. Peruvian law forbade construction of the pipeline by any non-Peruvian entity.

> FN1. The participants in the joint venture were Williams International Sudamericana, Ltd., a Delaware corporation; Sedco Construction Corporation, a Texas corporation; and Horn International, Inc., a Texas corporation.

Consorcio/WSH [FN2] needed helicopters to move personnel, materials, and equipment into and out of the construction area. In 1974, upon request of Consorcio/WSH, the chief executive officer of Helicol, Francisco Restrepo, flew to the United States and conferred in Houston with representatives of the three joint venturers. At that meeting, there was a discussion of prices, availability, working conditions, fuel, supplies, and housing. Restrepo represented that Helicol could have the first helicopter on the job in 15 days. The Consorcio/WSH representatives decided to accept the contract proposed by Restrepo.

Helicol began performing before the agreement was formally signed in Peru on November 11, 1974.[FN3] The contract was written in Spanish on **411** official government stationery and provided that the residence of all the parties would be Lima, Peru. It further stated that controversies arising out of the contract would be submitted to the jurisdiction of Peruvian courts. In addition, it provided that Consorcio/WSH would make payments to Helicol's account with the Bank of America in New York City. App. 12a.

> FN2. Throughout the record in this case the entity is referred to both as Consorcio and as WSH. We refer to it hereinafter as Consorcio/WSH.

> FN3. Respondents acknowledge that the contract was executed in Peru and not in the United States. Tr. of Oral Arg. 22-23. See App. 79a; Brief for Respondents 3.

Aside from the negotiation session in Houston between Restrepo and the representatives of Consorcio/WSH, Helicol had other contacts with Texas. During the years 1970-1977, it purchased helicopters (approximately 80% of its fleet), spare parts, and accessories for more than $4 million from Bell Helicopter Company in Fort Worth. In that period, Helicol sent prospective pilots to Fort Worth for training and to ferry the aircraft to South America. It also sent management and maintenance personnel to visit Bell Helicopter in Fort Worth during the same period in order to receive "plant familiarization" and for technical consultation. Helicol received into its New York City and Panama City, Fla., bank accounts over $5 million in payments from Consorcio/WSH drawn upon First City National Bank of Houston.

[1] Beyond the foregoing, there have been no other business contacts between Helicol and the State of Texas. Helicol never has been authorized to do business in Texas and never has had an agent for the **1871** service of process within the State. It never has performed helicopter operations in Texas or sold any product that reached Texas, never solicited business in Texas, never signed any contract in Texas, never had any employee based there, and never recruited an employee in Texas. In addition, Helicol never has owned real or personal property in Texas and never has maintained an office or establishment there. Helicol has maintained no records in Texas and has no shareholders in that State.[FN4] None of the **412** respondents or their decedents were domiciled in Texas, Tr. of Oral Arg. 17, 18,[FN5] but all of the decedents were hired in Houston by Consorcio/WSH to work on the Petro Peru pipeline project.

> FN4. The Colombian national airline, Aerovias Nacionales de Colombia, owns approximately 94% of Helicol's capital stock. The remainder is held by Aerovias Corporacion de Viajes and four South American individuals. See Brief for Petitioner 2, n. 2.

> FN5. Respondents' lack of residential or other contacts with Texas of itself does not defeat otherwise proper jurisdiction. *Keeton v. Hustler Magazine, Inc.*, 465 U.S. 770, 780, 104 S.Ct. 1473, 1481, 79 L.Ed.2d 790 (1984); *Calder v. Jones*, 465 U.S. 783, 788, 104 S.Ct. 1482, 1486, 79 L.Ed.2d 804 (1984). We mention respondents' lack of contacts merely to show that nothing in the nature of the relationship between respondents and Helicol could possibly enhance Helicol's contacts with Texas. The harm suffered by respondents did not occur in Texas. Nor is it alleged that any negligence on the part of Helicol took place in Texas.

Respondents instituted wrongful-death actions in the District Court of Harris County, Tex., against Consorcio/WSH, Bell Helicopter Company, and Helicol. Helicol filed special appearances and moved to dismiss the actions for lack of in personam jurisdiction over it. The motion was denied. After a consolidated jury trial, judgment was entered against Helicol on a jury verdict of $1,141,200 in favor of respondents.[FN6] App. 174a.

> FN6. Defendants Consorcio/WSH and Bell Helicopter Company were granted directed verdicts with respect to respondents' claims against them. Bell Helicopter was granted a directed verdict on Helicol's cross-claim against it. App. 167a. Consorcio/WSH, as cross-plaintiff in a claim against Helicol, obtained a judgment in the amount of $70,000. Id., at 174a.

The Texas Court of Civil Appeals, Houston, First District, reversed the judgment of the District Court, holding that in personam jurisdiction over Helicol was lacking. 616 S.W.2d 247 (Tex.1981). The Supreme Court of Texas, with three justices dissenting, initially affirmed the judgment of the Court of Civil Appeals. App. to Pet. for Cert. 46a-62a. Seven months later, however, on motion for rehearing, the court withdrew its prior opinions and, again with three justices dissenting, reversed the judgment of the intermediate court. 638 S.W.2d 870 (Tex.1982). In ruling that the Texas courts had **413** in personam jurisdiction, the Texas Supreme Court first held that the State's long-arm statute reaches as far as the Due Process Clause of the Fourteenth Amendment permits. Id., at 872.[FN7] Thus, the only question remaining **1872** for the court to decide was whether it was consistent with the Due Process Clause for Texas courts to assert in personam jurisdiction over Helicol. Ibid.

FN7. The State's long-arm statute is Tex.Rev.Civ.Stat.Ann., Art. 2031b (Vernon 1964 and Supp.1982-1983). It reads in relevant part:

"Sec. 3. Any foreign corporation…that engages in business in this State, irrespective of any Statute or law respecting designation or maintenance of resident agents, and does not maintain a place of regular business in this State or a designated agent upon whom service may be made upon causes of action arising out of such business done in this State, the act or acts of engaging in such business within this State shall be deemed equivalent to an appointment by such foreign corporation…of the Secretary of State of Texas as agent upon whom service of process may be made in any action, suit or proceedings arising out of such business done in this State, wherein such corporation…is a party or is to be made a party.

"Sec. 4. For the purpose of this Act, and without including other acts that may constitute doing business, any foreign corporation…shall be deemed doing business in this State by entering into contract by mail or otherwise with a resident of Texas to be performed in whole or in part by either party in this State, or the committing of any tort in whole or in part in this State. The act of recruiting Texas residents, directly or through an intermediary located in Texas, for employment inside or outside of Texas shall be deemed doing business in this State." The last sentence of § 4 was added by 1979 Tex.Gen.Laws, ch. 245, § 1, and became effective August 27, 1979.

The Supreme Court of Texas in its principal opinion relied upon rulings in *U-Anchor Advertising, Inc. v. Burt*, 553 S.W.2d 760 (Tex.1977); *Hoppenfeld v. Crook*, 498 S.W.2d 52 (Tex.Civ.App.1973); and *O'Brien v. Lanpar Co.*, 399 S.W.2d 340 (Tex.1966). It is not within our province, of course, to determine whether the Texas Supreme Court correctly interpreted the State's long-arm statute. We therefore accept that court's holding that the limits of the Texas statute are coextensive with those of the Due Process Clause.

II

[2][3] The Due Process Clause of the Fourteenth Amendment operates to limit the power of a State to assert in personam **414** jurisdiction over a nonresident defendant. *Pennoyer v. Neff*, 95 U.S. 714, 24 L.Ed. 565 (1878). Due process requirements are satisfied when in personam jurisdiction is asserted over a nonresident corporate defendant that has "certain minimum contacts with [the forum] such that the maintenance of the suit does not offend 'traditional notions of fair play and substantial justice.'" *International Shoe Co. v. Washington*, 326 U.S. 310, 316, 66 S.Ct. 154, 158, 90 L.Ed. 95 (1945), quoting *Milliken v. Meyer*, 311 U.S. 457, 463, 61 S.Ct. 339, 342, 85 L.Ed. 278 (1940). When a controversy is related to or "arises out of" a defendant's contacts with the forum, the Court has said that a "relationship among the defendant, the forum, and the litigation" is the essential foundation of in personam jurisdiction. *Shaffer v. Heitner*, 433 U.S. 186, 204, 97 S.Ct. 2569, 2579, 53 L.Ed.2d 683 (1977).[FN8]

FN8. It has been said that when a State exercises personal jurisdiction over a defendant in a suit arising out of or related to the defendant's contacts with the forum, the State is exercising "specific jurisdiction" over the defendant. See Von Mehren & Trautman, Jurisdiction to Adjudicate: A Suggested Analysis, 79 Harv.L.Rev. 1121, 1144-1164 (1966).

Even when the cause of action does not arise out of or relate to the foreign corporation's activities in the forum State,[FN9] due process is not offended by a State's subjecting the corporation to its in personam jurisdiction when there are sufficient contacts between the State and the foreign corporation. *Perkins v. Benguet Consolidated Mining Co.*, 342 U.S. 437, 72 S.Ct. 413, 96 L.Ed. 485 (1952); see *Keeton v. Hustler Magazine, Inc.*, 465 U.S. 770, 779-780, 104 S.Ct. 1473, 1480-1481, 79 L.Ed.2d 790 (1984). In Perkins, the Court addressed a situation in which state courts had asserted general jurisdiction over a defendant foreign corporation. During the Japanese*415 occupation of the Philippine Islands, the president and general manager of a Philippine mining corporation maintained an office in Ohio from which he conducted activities on behalf of the company. He kept company files and held directors' meetings in the office, carried on correspondence relating to the business, distributed salary checks drawn on two active Ohio bank accounts, engaged an Ohio bank to act as transfer agent, and supervised policies dealing with the rehabilitation of the corporation's properties in the Philippines. In short, the foreign corporation, through its president, "ha[d] been carrying on in Ohio a continuous and systematic, but limited, part of its general business," and the exercise of general jurisdiction over the Philippine corporation by an Ohio court was "reasonable and just." 342 U.S., at 438, 445, 72 S.Ct., at 414, 418.

> FN9. When a State exercises personal jurisdiction over a defendant in a suit not arising out of or related to the defendant's contacts with the forum, the State has been said to be exercising "general jurisdiction" over the defendant. See Brilmayer, How Contacts Count: Due Process Limitations on State Court Jurisdiction, 1980 S.Ct.Rev. 77, 80-81; Von Mehren & Trautman, 79 Harv.L.Rev., at 1136-1144; *Calder v. Jones*, 465 U.S., at 786, 104 S.Ct., at 1485.

[4] All parties to the present case concede that respondents' claims against Helicol did not "arise out of," and are not related to, Helicol's activities within Texas.[FN10] We thus must *416 explore the nature **1873 of Helicol's contacts with the State of Texas to determine whether they constitute the kind of continuous and systematic general business contacts the Court found to exist in Perkins. We hold that they do not.

> FN10. See Brief for Respondents 14; Tr. of Oral Arg. 26-27, 30-31. Because the parties have not argued any relationship between the cause of action and Helicol's contacts with the State of Texas, we, contrary to the dissent's implication, post, at 1875, assert no "view" with respect to that issue.

The dissent suggests that we have erred in drawing no distinction between controversies that "relate to" a defendant's contacts with a forum and those that "arise out of" such contacts. Post, at 1875. This criticism is somewhat puzzling, for the dissent goes on to urge that, for purposes of determining the constitutional validity of an assertion of specific jurisdiction, there really should be no distinction between the two. Post, at 1879.

We do not address the validity or consequences of such a distinction because the issue has not been presented in this case. Respondents have made no argument that their cause of action either arose out of or is related to Helicol's contacts with the State of Texas. Absent any briefing on the issue, we decline to reach the questions (1) whether the terms "arising out of" and "related to" describe different connections between a cause of action and a defendant's contacts with a forum, and (2) what sort of tie between a cause of action and a defendant's contacts with a forum is necessary to a determination that either connection exists. Nor do we reach the question whether, if the two types of relationship differ, a forum's exercise of personal jurisdiction in a situation where the cause of action "relates to," but does not "arise out of," the defendant's contacts with the forum should be analyzed as an assertion of specific jurisdiction.

It is undisputed that Helicol does not have a place of business in Texas and never has been licensed to do business in the State. Basically, Helicol's contacts with Texas consisted of sending its chief executive officer to Houston for a contract-negotiation session; accepting into its New York bank account checks drawn on a Houston bank; purchasing helicopters, equipment, and training services from Bell Helicopter for substantial sums; and sending personnel to Bell's facilities in Fort Worth for training.

[5] The one trip to Houston by Helicol's chief executive officer for the purpose of negotiating the transportation-services contract with Consorcio/WSH cannot be described or regarded as a contact of a "continuous and systematic" nature, as Perkins described it, see also *International Shoe Co. v. Washington*, 326 U.S., at 320, 66 S.Ct., at 160, and thus cannot support an assertion of in personam jurisdiction over Helicol by a Texas court. Similarly, Helicol's acceptance from Consorcio/WSH of checks drawn on a Texas bank is of negligible significance for purposes of determining whether Helicol had sufficient contacts in Texas. There is no indication that Helicol ever requested that the checks be drawn on a Texas bank or that there was any negotiation between Helicol and Consorcio/WSH with respect to the location or identity of the bank on which checks would be drawn. Common sense and everyday experience suggest that, absent unusual circumstances,[FN11] the bank on which a check is drawn is generally of little ***417** consequence to the payee and is a matter left to the discretion of the drawer. Such unilateral activity of another party or a third person is not an appropriate consideration when determining whether a defendant has sufficient contacts with a forum State to justify an assertion of jurisdiction. See *Kulko v. California Superior Court*, 436 U.S. 84, 93, 98 S.Ct. 1690, 1697, 56 L.Ed.2d 132 (1978) (arbitrary to subject one parent to suit in any State where other parent chooses to spend time while having custody of child pursuant to separation agreement); *Hanson v. Denckla*, 357 U.S. 235, 253, 78 S.Ct. 1228, 1239, 2 L.Ed.2d 1283 (1958) ("The unilateral activity of those who claim some relationship with a nonresident defendant cannot satisfy the requirement of contact with the forum State"); see also Lilly, Jurisdiction Over Domestic and Alien Defendants, 69 Va.L.Rev. 85, 99 (1983).

> FN11. For example, if the financial health and continued ability of the bank to honor the draft are questionable, the payee might request that the check be drawn on an account at some other institution.

The Texas Supreme Court focused on the purchases and the related training trips in ****1874** finding contacts sufficient to support an assertion of jurisdiction. We do not agree with that assessment, for the Court's opinion in *Rosenberg Bros. & Co. v. Curtis Brown Co.*, 260 U.S. 516, 43 S.Ct. 170, 67 L.Ed. 372 (1923) (Brandeis, J., for a unanimous tribunal), makes clear that purchases and related trips, standing alone, are not a sufficient basis for a State's assertion of jurisdiction.

The defendant in Rosenberg was a small retailer in Tulsa, Okla., who dealt in men's clothing and furnishings. It never had applied for a license to do business in New York, nor had it at any time authorized suit to be brought against it there. It never had an established place of business in New York and never regularly carried on business in that State. Its only connection with New York was that it purchased from New York wholesalers a large portion of the merchandise sold in its Tulsa store. The purchases sometimes were made by correspondence and sometimes through visits to New York by an officer of the defendant. The Court concluded: "Visits on such business, even if occurring at regular intervals, would not warrant the inference that the corporation was present within the jurisdiction of [New York]." Id., at 518, 43 S.Ct., at 171.

[6] ***418** This Court in International Shoe acknowledged and did not repudiate its holding in Rosenberg. See 326 U.S., at 318, 66 S.Ct., at 159. In accordance with Rosenberg, we hold that mere purchases, even if occurring at regular intervals, are not enough to warrant a State's assertion of in personam jurisdiction over a nonresident corporation in a cause of action not related to those purchase transactions.[FN12] Nor can we conclude that the fact that Helicol sent personnel into Texas for training in connection with the purchase of helicopters and equipment in that State in any way enhanced the nature of Helicol's contacts with Texas. The training was a part of the package of goods and services purchased by Helicol from Bell Helicopter. The brief presence of Helicol employees in Texas for the purpose of attending the training sessions is no more a significant contact than were the trips to New York made by the buyer for the retail store in Rosenberg. See also *Kulko v. California Superior Court*, 436 U.S., at 93, 98 S.Ct., at 1697 (basing California jurisdiction on 3-day and 1-day stopovers in that State "would make a mockery of" due process limitations on assertion of personal jurisdiction).

> FN12. This Court in International Shoe cited Rosenberg for the proposition that "the commission of some single or occasional acts of the corporate agent in a state sufficient to impose an obligation or liability on the corporation has not been thought to confer upon the state authority to enforce it." 326 U.S., at 318, 66 S.Ct., at 159. Arguably, therefore, Rosenberg also stands for the proposition that mere purchases are not a sufficient basis for either general or specific jurisdiction. Because the case before us is one in which there has been an assertion of general jurisdiction over a foreign defendant, we need not decide the continuing validity of Rosenberg with respect to an assertion

of specific jurisdiction, i.e., where the cause of action arises out of or relates to the purchases by the defendant in the forum State.

III

We hold that Helicol's contacts with the State of Texas were insufficient to satisfy the requirements of the Due Process**419** Clause of the Fourteenth Amendment.[FN13] Accordingly, we reverse the judgment of the Supreme Court of Texas.

> FN13. As an alternative to traditional minimum-contacts analysis, respondents suggest that the Court hold that the State of Texas had personal jurisdiction over Helicol under a doctrine of "jurisdiction by necessity." See *Shaffer v. Heitner*, 433 U.S. 186, 211, n. 37, 97 S.Ct. 2569, 2583, n. 37, 53 L.Ed.2d 683 (1977). We conclude, however, that respondents failed to carry their burden of showing that all three defendants could not be sued together in a single forum. It is not clear from the record, for example, whether suit could have been brought against all three defendants in either Colombia or Peru. We decline to consider adoption of a doctrine of jurisdiction by necessity-a potentially far-reaching modification of existing law-in the absence of a more complete record.

It is so ordered.

1875 Justice BRENNAN, dissenting.

Decisions applying the Due Process Clause of the Fourteenth Amendment to determine whether a State may constitutionally assert in personam jurisdiction over a particular defendant for a particular cause of action most often turn on a weighing of facts. See, e.g., *Kulko v. California Superior Court*, 436 U.S. 84, 92, 98 S.Ct. 1690, 1697, 56 L.Ed.2d 132 (1978); id., at 101-102, 98 S.Ct., at 1701-1702 (BRENNAN, J., dissenting). To a large extent, today's decision follows the usual pattern. Based on essentially undisputed facts, the Court concludes that petitioner Helicol's contacts with the State of Texas were insufficient to allow the Texas state courts constitutionally to assert "general jurisdiction" over all claims filed against this foreign corporation. Although my independent weighing of the facts leads me to a different conclusion, see infra, at 1877, the Court's holding on this issue is neither implausible nor unexpected.

What is troubling about the Court's opinion, however, are the implications that might be drawn from the way in which the Court approaches the constitutional issue it addresses. First, the Court limits its discussion to an assertion of general jurisdiction of the Texas courts because, in its view, the **420** underlying cause of action does "not aris[e] out of or relat[e] to the corporation's activities within the State." Ante, at 1870. Then, the Court relies on a 1923 decision in *Rosenberg Bros. & Co. v. Curtis Brown Co.*, 260 U.S. 516, 43 S.Ct. 170, 67 L.Ed. 372, without considering whether that case retains any validity after our more recent pronouncements concerning the permissible reach of a State's jurisdiction. By posing and deciding the question presented in this manner, I fear that the Court is saying more than it realizes about constitutional limitations on the potential reach of in personam jurisdiction. In particular, by relying on a precedent whose premises have long been discarded, and by refusing to consider any distinction between controversies that "relate to" a defendant's contacts with the forum and causes of action that "arise out of" such contacts, the Court may be placing severe limitations on the type and amount of contacts that will satisfy the constitutional minimum.

In contrast, I believe that the undisputed contacts in this case between petitioner Helicol and the State of Texas are sufficiently important, and sufficiently related to the underlying cause of action, to make it fair and reasonable for the State to assert personal jurisdiction over Helicol for the wrongful-death actions filed by the respondents. Given that Helicol has purposefully availed itself of the benefits and obligations of the forum, and given the direct relationship between the underlying cause of action and Helicol's contacts with the forum, maintenance of this suit in the Texas courts "does not offend [the] 'traditional notions of fair play and substantial justice,'" *International Shoe Co. v. Washington,* 326 U.S. 310, 316, 66 S.Ct. 154, 90 L.Ed. 95 (1945) (quoting *Milliken v. Meyer*, 311 U.S. 457, 463, 61 S.Ct. 339, 342, 85 L.Ed. 278 (1940)), that are the touchstone of jurisdictional analysis under the Due Process Clause. I therefore dissent.

I

The Court expressly limits its decision in this case to "an assertion of general jurisdiction over a foreign defendant." ***421** Ante, at 1874, n. 12. See ante, at 1873, and n. 10. Having framed the question in this way, the Court is obliged to address our prior holdings in *Perkins v. Benguet Consolidated Mining Co.,* 342 U.S. 437, 72 S.Ct. 413, 96 L.Ed. 485 (1952), and *Rosenberg Bros. & Co. v. Curtis Brown Co.,* supra. In Perkins, the Court considered a State's assertion of general jurisdiction over a foreign corporation that "ha[d] been carrying on…a continuous and systematic, but limited, part of its general business" in the forum. 342 U.S., at 438, 72 S.Ct., at 414. Under the circumstances of that case, we held that such contacts were constitutionally sufficient "to make it reasonable and just to subject the corporation ****1876** to the jurisdiction" of that State. Id., at 445, 72 S.Ct., at 418 (citing International Shoe, supra, 326 U.S., at 317-320, 66 S.Ct., at 158-160). Nothing in Perkins suggests, however, that such "continuous and systematic" contacts are a necessary minimum before a State may constitutionally assert general jurisdiction over a foreign corporation.

The Court therefore looks for guidance to our 1923 decision in Rosenberg, supra, which until today was of dubious validity given the subsequent expansion of personal jurisdiction that began with International Shoe, supra, in 1945. In Rosenberg, the Court held that a company's purchases within a State, even when combined with related trips to the State by company officials, would not allow the courts of that State to assert general jurisdiction over all claims against the nonresident corporate defendant making those purchases.[FN1] ***422** Reasoning by analogy, the Court in this case concludes that Helicol's contacts with the State of Texas are no more significant than the purchases made by the defendant in Rosenberg. The Court makes no attempt, however, to ascertain whether the narrow view of in personam jurisdiction adopted by the Court in Rosenberg comports with "the fundamental transformation of our national economy" that has occurred since 1923. *McGee v. International Life Ins. Co.,* 355 U.S. 220, 222-223, 78 S.Ct. 199, 200-201, 2 L.Ed.2d 223 (1957). See also *World-Wide Volkswagen Corp. v. Woodson,* 444 U.S. 286, 292-293, 100 S.Ct. 559, 564-565, 62 L.Ed.2d 490 (1980); id., at 308-309, 100 S.Ct., at 585-586 (BRENNAN, J., dissenting); *Hanson v. Denckla,* 357 U.S. 235, 250-251, 78 S.Ct. 1228, 1237-1238, 2 L.Ed.2d 1283 (1958); id., at 260, 78 S.Ct., at 1243 (Black, J., dissenting). This failure, in my view, is fatal to the Court's analysis.

> FN1. The Court leaves open the question whether the decision in Rosenberg was intended to address any constitutional limits on an assertion of "specific jurisdiction." Ante, at 1874, n. 12 (citing International Shoe, 326 U.S., at 318, 66 S.Ct., at 159). If anything is clear from Justice Brandeis' opinion for the Court in Rosenberg, however, it is that the Court was concerned only with general jurisdiction over the corporate defendant. See 260 U.S., at 517, 43 S.Ct., at 171 ("The sole question for decision is whether…defendant was doing business within the State of New York in such manner and to such extent as to warrant the inference that it was present there"); id., at 518, 43 S.Ct., at 171 (the corporation's contacts with the forum "would not warrant the inference that the corporation was present within the jurisdiction of the State"); ante, at 1874. The Court's resuscitation of Rosenberg, therefore, should have no bearing upon any forum's assertion of jurisdiction over claims that arise out of or relate to a defendant's contacts with the State.

The vast expansion of our national economy during the past several decades has provided the primary rationale for expanding the permissible reach of a State's jurisdiction under the Due Process Clause. By broadening the type and amount of business opportunities available to participants in interstate and foreign commerce, our economy has increased the frequency with which foreign corporations actively pursue commercial transactions throughout the various States. In turn, it has become both necessary and, in my view, desirable to allow the States more leeway in bringing the activities of these nonresident corporations within the scope of their respective jurisdictions.

This is neither a unique nor a novel idea. As the Court first noted in 1957:

"[M]any commercial transactions touch two or more States and may involve parties separated by the full continent. With this increasing nationalization of commerce has come a great increase in the amount of business conducted by mail across state lines. At the ***423** same time modern transportation and communication have made it much less burdensome for a party sued to defend himself in a State where he engages in economic activity." McGee, supra, at 222-223, 78 S.Ct., at 200-201.

See also World-Wide Volkswagen, supra, 444 U.S., at 293, 100 S.Ct., at 565 (reaffirming that "[t]he historical developments noted in McGee...have only accelerated in the generation since that case was decided"**1877); Hanson v. Denckla, supra, 357 U.S., at 250-251, 78 S.Ct., at 1237-1238.

Moreover, this "trend...toward expanding the permissible scope of state jurisdiction over foreign corporations and other nonresidents," McGee, supra, 355 U.S., at 222, 78 S.Ct., at 200, is entirely consistent with the "traditional notions of fair play and substantial justice," International Shoe, 326 U.S., at 316, 66 S.Ct., at 158, that control our inquiry under the Due Process Clause. As active participants in interstate and foreign commerce take advantage of the economic benefits and opportunities offered by the various States, it is only fair and reasonable to subject them to the obligations that may be imposed by those jurisdictions. And chief among the obligations that a nonresident corporation should expect to fulfill is amenability to suit in any forum that is significantly affected by the corporation's commercial activities.

As a foreign corporation that has actively and purposefully engaged in numerous and frequent commercial transactions in the State of Texas, Helicol clearly falls within the category of nonresident defendants that may be subject to that forum's general jurisdiction. Helicol not only purchased helicopters and other equipment in the State for many years, but also sent pilots and management personnel into Texas to be trained in the use of this equipment and to consult with the seller on technical matters.[FN2] Moreover, negotiations for the **424** contract under which Helicol provided transportation services to the joint venture that employed the respondents' decedents also took place in the State of Texas. Taken together, these contacts demonstrate that Helicol obtained numerous benefits from its transaction of business in Texas. In turn, it is eminently fair and reasonable to expect Helicol to face the obligations that attach to its participation in such commercial transactions. Accordingly, on the basis of continuous commercial contacts with the forum, I would conclude that the Due Process Clause allows the State of Texas to assert general jurisdiction over petitioner Helicol.

> FN2. Although the Court takes note of these contacts, it concludes that they did not "enhanc[e] the nature of Helicol's contacts with Texas [[[because the] training was a part of the package of goods and services purchased by Helicol." Ante, at 1874. Presumably, the Court's statement simply recognizes that participation in today's interdependent markets often necessitates the use of complicated purchase contracts that provide for numerous contacts between representatives of the buyer and seller, as well as training for related personnel. Ironically, however, while relying on these modern-day realities to denigrate the significance of Helicol's contacts with the forum, the Court refuses to acknowledge that these same realities require a concomitant expansion in a forum's jurisdictional reach. See supra, at 1876 - 1877. As a result, when deciding that the balance in this case must be struck against jurisdiction, the Court loses sight of the ultimate inquiry: whether it is fair and reasonable to subject a nonresident corporate defendant to the jurisdiction of a State when that defendant has purposefully availed itself of the benefits and obligations of that particular forum. Cf. Hanson v. Denckla, 357 U.S. 235, 253, 78 S.Ct. 1228, 1239, 2 L.Ed.2d 1283 (1958).

II

The Court also fails to distinguish the legal principles that controlled our prior decisions in Perkins and Rosenberg. In particular, the contacts between petitioner Helicol and the State of Texas, unlike the contacts between the defendant and the forum in each of those cases, are significantly related to the cause of action alleged in the original suit filed by the respondents. Accordingly, in my view, it is both fair and reasonable for the Texas courts to assert specific jurisdiction over Helicol in this case.

By asserting that the present case does not implicate the specific jurisdiction of the Texas courts, see ante, at 1872-1873, and nn. 10 and 12, the Court necessarily removes its decision **425** from the reality of the actual facts presented for our consideration.[FN3] Moreover, the Court refuses to consider**1878 any distinction between contacts that are "related to" the underlying cause of action and contacts that "give rise" to the underlying cause of action. In my view, however, there is a substantial difference between these two standards for asserting specific jurisdiction. Thus, although I agree that the respondents' cause of action did not formally "arise out of" specific activities initiated by Helicol in the State of Texas, I believe that the wrongful-death claim filed by the respondents is significantly related to the undisputed contacts between Helicol and the forum. On that basis, I would conclude that the Due Process Clause allows the Texas courts to assert specific jurisdiction over this particular action.

FN3. Nor do I agree with the Court that the respondents have conceded that their claims are not related to Helicol's activities within the State of Texas. Although parts of their written and oral arguments before the Court proceed on the assumption that no such relationship exists, other portions suggest just the opposite:

"If it is the concern of the Solicitor General [appearing for the United States as amicus curiae] that a holding for Respondents here will cause foreign companies to refrain from purchasing in the United States for fear of exposure to general jurisdiction on unrelated causes of action, such concern is not well founded.

"Respondents' cause is not dependent on a ruling that mere purchases in a state, together with incidental training for operating and maintaining the merchandise purchased can constitute the ties, contacts and relations necessary to justify jurisdiction over an unrelated cause of action. However, regular purchases and training coupled with other contacts, ties and relations may form the basis for jurisdiction." Brief for Respondents 13-14. Thus, while the respondents' position before this Court is admittedly less than clear, I believe it is preferable to address the specific jurisdiction of the Texas courts because Helicol's contacts with Texas are in fact related to the underlying cause of action.

The wrongful-death actions filed by the respondents were premised on a fatal helicopter crash that occurred in Peru. Helicol was joined as a defendant in the lawsuits because it provided transportation services, including the particular helicopter and pilot involved in the crash, to the joint venture *426 that employed the decedents. Specifically, the respondent Hall claimed in her original complaint that "Helicol is...legally responsible for its own negligence through its pilot employee." App. 6a. Viewed in light of these allegations, the contacts between Helicol and the State of Texas are directly and significantly related to the underlying claim filed by the respondents. The negotiations that took place in Texas led to the contract in which Helicol agreed to provide the precise transportation services that were being used at the time of the crash. Moreover, the helicopter involved in the crash was purchased by Helicol in Texas, and the pilot whose negligence was alleged to have caused the crash was actually trained in Texas. See Tr. of Oral Arg. 5, 22. This is simply not a case, therefore, in which a state court has asserted jurisdiction over a nonresident defendant on the basis of wholly unrelated contacts with the forum. Rather, the contacts between Helicol and the forum are directly related to the negligence that was alleged in the respondent Hall's original complaint.[FN4] Because Helicol should have expected to be amenable to suit in the Texas courts for claims directly related to these contacts, it is fair and reasonable to allow the assertion of jurisdiction in this case.

FN4. The jury specifically found that "the pilot failed to keep the helicopter under proper control," that "the helicopter was flown into a treetop fog condition, whereby the vision of the pilot was impaired," that "such flying was negligence," and that "such negligence...was a proximate cause of the crash." See App. 167a-168a. On the basis of these findings, Helicol was ordered to pay over $1 million in damages to the respondents.

Despite this substantial relationship between the contacts and the cause of action, the Court declines to consider whether the courts of Texas may assert specific jurisdiction over this suit. Apparently, this simply reflects a narrow interpretation of the question presented for review. See ante, at 1873, n. 10. It is nonetheless possible that the Court's opinion may be read to imply that the specific jurisdiction of the Texas courts is inapplicable because the cause of action *427 did not formally "arise out of" the contacts between Helicol and the forum. In my view, however, such a rule would place unjustifiable limits on the **1879 bases under which Texas may assert its jurisdictional power.[FN5]

FN5. Compare Von Mehren & Trautman, Jurisdiction to Adjudicate: A Suggested Analysis, 79 Harv.L.Rev. 1121, 1144-1163 (1966), with Brilmayer, How Contacts Count: Due Process Limitations on State Court Jurisdiction, 1980 S.Ct.Rev. 77, 80-88. See also Lilly, Jurisdiction Over Domestic and Alien Defendants, 69 Va.L.Rev. 85, 100-101, and n. 66 (1983).

Limiting the specific jurisdiction of a forum to cases in which the cause of action formally arose out of the defendant's contacts with the State would subject constitutional standards under the Due Process Clause to the vagaries of the substantive law or pleading requirements of each State. For example, the complaint filed against Helicol in this case alleged negligence based on pilot error. Even though the pilot was trained in Texas, the Court assumes that the Texas courts may not assert jurisdiction over the suit because the cause of action "did not 'arise out of,' and [is] not related to," that training. See ante, at 1872. If, however, the applicable substantive law required that negligent training of the pilot was a necessary element of a cause of action for pilot error, or if the respondents had simply added an allegation of negligence in the training provided for the Helicol pilot, then presumably the Court would concede that the specific jurisdiction of the Texas courts was applicable.

Our interpretation of the Due Process Clause has never been so dependent upon the applicable substantive law or the State's formal pleading requirements. At least since *International Shoe Co. v. Washington*, 326 U.S. 310, 66 S.Ct. 154, 90 L.Ed. 95 (1945), the principal focus when determining whether a forum may constitutionally assert jurisdiction over a nonresident defendant has been on fairness and reasonableness to the defendant. To this extent, a court's specific jurisdiction should be applicable whenever the cause of action arises out of or relates to the contacts between the defendant and the forum. It is eminently*428 fair and reasonable, in my view, to subject a defendant to suit in a forum with which it has significant contacts directly related to the underlying cause of action. Because Helicol's contacts with the State of Texas meet this standard, I would affirm the judgment of the Supreme Court of Texas.

B.5 *Letz v. Turbomeca Engine Corporation*, 975 S.W.2d 155 (Mo. App. 1997)

Missouri Court of Appeals,
Western District.
Jodie A. LETZ, et al., Respondent,
v.
TURBOMECA ENGINE CORPORATION, et al., Appellant.
No. WD 51446.

Nov. 25, 1997.
Motion for Rehearing and/or Transfer to Supreme Court Denied Jan. 27, 1998.
Application for Transfer Sustained March 24, 1998.
Case Retransferred Sept. 22, 1998.
Court of Appeals Opinion Readopted Sept. 29, 1998.

Mother and sons of helicopter crash victim brought wrongful death action against manufacturer and installer of helicopter engine and owner and operator of helicopter. The Circuit Court, Jackson County, Lee E. Wells, J., entered judgment against manufacturer and installer on jury verdict awarding compensatory and punitive damages. Manufacturer and installer appealed. The Court of Appeals, Ulrich, C.J., P.J., held that: (1) manifest injustice did not result from submission to jury of issue of aggravating circumstances; (2) trial court did not abuse its discretion in denying motion for mistrial based on admission of irrelevant picture of passenger's gravestone; (3) evidence of cost savings realized by decision not to recall and retrofit helicopters with defective part was relevant to issue of aggravating circumstances; (4) compensatory award, if separately delineated from punitive damages, could not have exceeded $2.5 million; and (5) punitive verdict of $67.5 million was excessive in amount of $41 million.

Affirmed on condition of remittitur.

For space considerations, all headnotes have been deleted.

Douglas N. Ghertner, Kansas City, for appellants.

Gary Charles Robb, Kansas City, for respondent.

Before ULRICH, C.J., P.J., and LOWENSTEIN, BRECKENRIDGE, HANNA, SPINDEN, SMART, ELLIS, LAURA DENVIR STITH, EDWIN H. SMITH and HOWARD, JJ., and BERREY, Senior Judge.

ULRICH, Chief Judge, Presiding Judge.

Turbomeca, S.A. and Turbomeca Engine Corporation appeal the judgment of the trial court following a jury trial awarding Jodie, Eric, and Christopher Letz $70 million in a wrongful death action. The award included compensatory and punitive damages. The Letzes sued Turbomeca, S.A. (TSA), Turbomeca Engine Corporation (TEC), and Rocky Mountain Helicopters for the death of Sherry Ann Letz, the daughter of Jodie and mother of Eric and Christopher, resulting from a helicopter crash.[FN1] TSA, a French company, manufactured the helicopter engine on the helicopter, allegedly defective and the cause of the crash, and TEC, a wholly owned subsidiary of TSA located in Texas, installed it. Rocky Mountain Helicopters owned and operated the helicopter.

> FN1. The helicopter crash also formed the basis of the lawsuit in the companion case, *Barnett v. Turbomeca Engine Corporation*, 963 S.W.2d 639, which is also decided this day.

TSA and TEC allege several errors on appeal. They claim the trial court erred in (1) submitting the issue of "aggravating circumstances" to the jury, (2) submitting Instruction No. 25 and Verdict Form A regarding aggravating circumstances, (3) failing to declare a mistrial after introduction into evidence of a photograph of the decedent's gravemarker, (4) admitting evidence of the cost to recall a defective engine part and allowing plaintiffs to reference the "cost savings" of not recalling the part in arguing damages, (5) admitting evidence of facsimiles sent to the FAA after the helicopter accident regarding prior in-flight engine stoppages, and (6) denying their motion for a new trial or remittitur. The judgment of the trial court is affirmed on condition of remittitur.[FN2]

> FN2. Appellants' motion to strike portions of Respondents' supplemental legal file is denied. Appellants' motion to strike portions of Respondents' brief is denied.

FACTS

In the early morning of May 27, 1993, Sherry Letz was involved in a motor vehicle accident and was taken by ambulance to the Harrison County Community Hospital in Bethany, Missouri. She was successfully resuscitated, treated for a collapsed lung, a broken left arm, and concussion, and was stabilized. She suffered a severe trauma; and because *162 the local hospital was not equipped with a CT scan, an MRI, a cardiothoracic surgeon, a neurosurgeon, or a radiologist, her treating physician ordered her transfer by helicopter to St. Luke's Hospital in Kansas City.

The Life Flight 2 helicopter departed for Kansas City just after 6:00 a.m. with Sherry, the pilot, a nurse, and a medical technician on board. Soon after the pilot gave his position report at 6:25 a.m. over Cameron, Missouri, the nurse heard a loud "pop" or "bang" in the engine. Within 15 seconds, the helicopter crashed. Sherry and the pilot were killed. The other two passengers sustained serious injuries.

The Life Flight 2 helicopter was powered by an Arriel 1B gas turbine engine manufactured by TSA. The Arriel 1B engine consisted of five modules. In June 1989, TEC installed a TU 76 modified nozzle guide vane in Module 3 of the engine.

A nozzle guide vane directs the flow of air between the first and second stage turbine disc blades. The hub, or internal envelope, is in the center of the nozzle guide vane. A crack along the front or rear flange of the hub will cause a failure in the module and a partial to complete loss of power in the engine.

TSA became aware of a cracking problem in the TU 76 nozzle guide vane in June 1985 after an in-flight failure in the Congo. In January 1986, TSA reported the failure to the French Director General of Civil Aviation, the DGAC. A second in-flight failure involving the TU 76 nozzle guide vane occurred in France in April 1986. In June and July 1986, a TSA metallurgist outlined the cracking problems with the TU 76 as a result of evaluations of in-flight failures and cracks identified during overhaul in two reports. By the summer of 1986, the highest ranking officers of TSA knew that the TU 76 cracking problems had the potential to cause in-flight engine shutdowns. They also recognized the need for modifications of the nozzle guide vane to eliminate the cracking problems.

After the 1986 reports, TSA began research for a replacement nozzle guide vane. At least three possible modifications were tested between 1987 and 1988 without success. In 1988, two new designs, the TU 202 [FN3] and the TU 197 [FN4], were developed and tested. Eventually, the two nozzle guide vanes were certified by French authorities.

> FN3. This modification was to be used as a replacement part in existing engines.

> FN4. This modification was an entirely new design to be used in newly manufactured engines.

During the development of a substitute nozzle guide vane, in-flight engine failures or problems involving the TU 76 nozzle guide vane continued to occur in the United States and worldwide. In the spring of 1989, an in-flight engine failure resulted in serious injury to four passengers in Bolivia. In November of 1989, the TU 76 caused an in-flight loss of power in a helicopter in Phoenix, Arizona. Two months later, another incident of engine deceleration while landing occurred in Oakland, California. In Portugal in December 1991, breakage of the second stage nozzle guide vane caused loss of power in takeoff forcing an emergency landing. TSA records reflect that six prior in-flight engine stoppages were attributable to the TU 76 nozzle guide vane beginning in 1989.

By early 1991, the substitute TU 202 and TU 197 were in production and available. TSA management, however, decided not to immediately recall helicopters equipped with the defective TU 76 nozzle guide vane for fitting with the replacements. Instead, the TU 76 was to be replaced during the regularly scheduled overhaul of the engine.

On March 11, 1991, TSA sent a service letter to all customers advising them to perform a compulsory check at least once a day for a rubbing noise in the gas generator rotating assembly of any engine containing a TU 76 nozzle guide vane. Removal of Modules 2 and 3 was recommended to customers if a continuous or loud intermittent rubbing noise was noticed. In April 1992 and February 1993, two service bulletins were issued by TSA advising customers whose helicopters were equipped with an Arriel 1 engine of the approval and availability of the TU 202 and TU 197 nozzle guide vanes and recommending their installation during a repair*163 procedure on the nozzle guide vane or during overhaul. A second service letter that resembled the March 11, 1991 letter was sent to customers on December 18, 1992. It again reminded customers to be attentive to an abnormal noise during engine stop. The service letters and bulletins, however, did not inform customers that the TU 76 nozzle guide vane had caused in-flight engine stoppages.

Since the certification of the TU 202 and TU 197 replacement nozzle guide vanes in 1991, at least six additional incidents of in-flight engine stoppage or loss of power in engines containing the defective TU 76 nozzle guide vane have occurred around the world. These incidents happened in Guyane, Virginia, Brazil, Arizona, Texas, and Australia.

At trial, the Letzes argued that the helicopter engine manufactured and sold by TSA and installed by TEC in the Life Flight 2 helicopter that crashed, killing Sherry, contained a defective nozzle guide vane, the TU 76, which had caused many engines to fail in flight; that TSA and TEC knew the nozzle guide vane was defective when it was installed in the Life Flight 2 helicopter in June 1989; and that TSA and TEC failed to recall the engine prior to the regularly scheduled overhaul. They asserted that TSA and TEC made a fully informed cost-based business decision not to recall the engines equipped with the defective TU 76 nozzle guide vane, including the Life Flight 2 helicopter engine, to save millions of dollars. Evidence was elicited that TSA saved up to $48 million by not conducting a recall to replace the defective TU 76 nozzle guide vane. After a four week trial, the jury returned a single verdict on all claims against TSA and TEC and assessed damages at $70 million. The jury returned a verdict in favor of Rocky Mountain Helicopters.

I. SUBMISSION OF AGGRAVATING CIRCUMSTANCES CLAIM TO THE JURY

As their first point on appeal, TSA and TEC challenge the submissibility of aggravating circumstances. They contend that the trial court erred in overruling their motion for directed verdict at the close of all the evidence and in submitting the aggravating circumstances claim to the jury. They assert that the Letzes failed to prove (1) TSA and TEC knew or had reason to know there was a high degree of probability that the action would result in injury, (2) TSA and TEC knew of the allegedly defective condition of the TU 76 nozzle guide vane at the time it was sold or installed, or (3) TSA and TEC showed complete indifference to or a conscious disregard for the safety of others when they sold or installed the TU 76 nozzle guide vane. The Letzes argue that TSA and TEC have waived any objection they may have had to the submissibility of the aggravating circumstances claim.

A. Preservation of Issue

[1][2][3][4] To preserve the question of submissibility for appellate review in a jury-tried case, a motion for directed verdict must be filed at the close of all the evidence and, in the event of an adverse verdict, an after-trial motion for a new trial or to set aside a verdict must assign as error the trial court's failure to have directed such a verdict. *Browning v. Salem Memorial Dist. Hosp.*, 808 S.W.2d 943, 949 (Mo.App.1991). Failure to move for a directed verdict at the close of all the evidence

waives any contention that plaintiff failed to prove a submissible case. *Id.* Similarly, a motion for directed verdict that does not comply with the requirements of Rule 72.01(a) neither presents a basis for relief in the trial court nor preserves the issue in the appellate court. *Dierker Assocs., D.C., P.C. v. Gillis,* 859 S.W.2d 737, 743 (Mo.App.1993); *Kincaid Enters., Inc. v. Porter,* 812 S.W.2d 892, 895 (Mo.App.1991). Rule 72.01(a) directs that "[a] motion for a directed verdict shall state the specific grounds therefor." Rule 72.01. Where an insufficient oral or written motion for directed verdict has been made, a subsequent post-verdict motion is without basis and preserves nothing for review. *Gillis,* 859 S.W.2d at 743.

TSA and TEC failed to preserve the issue of submissibility of aggravating circumstances for appellate review. In their motions for directed verdict at the close of all ***164** the evidence, they asserted that the Letzes failed to prove their claims of negligence and strict liability in the design, manufacture, sale, or installation of the TU 76 nozzle guide vane. They did not raise the question of submissibility of aggravating circumstances in their motions. The motions for directed verdict, therefore, were insufficient to preserve the issue of submissibility of aggravating circumstances for appellate review.

B. Plain Error Review

An appellate court, however, may review for plain error affecting substantial rights under Rule 84.13(c). *Id.* Plain error review requires a finding that manifest injustice or a miscarriage of justice resulted from the verdict. Rule 84.13(c).

[5] To submit a case to the jury, every fact essential to liability must be predicated upon legal and substantial evidence. *Dildine v. Frichtel,* 890 S.W.2d 683, 685 (Mo.App.1994). "Substantial evidence is that which, if true, has probative force upon the issues, and from which the trier of fact can reasonably decide a case." *Id.* (quoting *Hurlock v. Park Lane Medical Ctr., Inc.,* 709 S.W.2d 872, 880 (Mo.App.1985)).

[6][7] In reviewing whether a plaintiff has made a submissible case, the evidence and all reasonable inferences to be drawn therefrom are viewed in the light most favorable to the verdict. *Dildine,* 890 S.W.2d at 685. A jury verdict will not be overturned unless there is a complete absence of probative facts to support it. *Id.*

[8][9] Under Missouri statutory law, damages are permitted in wrongful death actions, and

> [i]n every action brought under section 537.080, the trier of the facts may give to the party or parties entitled thereto such damages as the trier of the facts may deem fair and just for the death and loss thus occasioned, having regard to the pecuniary losses suffered by reason of the death, funeral expenses, and the reasonable value of the services, consortium, companionship, comfort, instruction, guidance, counsel, training, and support of which those on whose behalf suit may be brought have been deprived by reason of such death and without limiting such damages to those which would be sustained prior to attaining the age of majority by the deceased or by the person suffering any such loss. In addition, the trier of the facts may award such damages as the deceased may have suffered between the time of injury and the time of death and for the recovery of which the deceased might have maintained an action had death not ensued. ***The mitigating or aggravating circumstances attending the death may be considered by the trier of facts,*** but damages for grief and bereavement by reason of the death shall not be recoverable.

§ 537.090, RSMo 1994 (emphasis added). Aggravating circumstances damages are punitive in nature. *Elliot v. Kesler,* 799 S.W.2d 97, 103 (Mo.App.1990). Their purpose is to punish the defendant and deter future wrongdoing.[FN5] *Id.* To submit the issue of aggravating circumstances to the jury, willful misconduct, wantonness, recklessness, or a want of care indicative of indifference to consequences must be shown. *Wiseman v. Missouri Pac. R.R. Co.,* 575 S.W.2d 742, 752 (Mo. App.1978)(quoting *Williams v. Excavating & Foundation Co.,* 230 Mo.App. 973, 93 S.W.2d 123, 127 (1936)).

> FN5. Because punitive damages are extraordinary and harsh, the Missouri Supreme Court recently concluded that the higher "clear and convincing" standard of proof is required. *Rodriguez v. Suzuki Motor Corp.,* 936 S.W.2d 104, 111 (Mo. banc 1996). The clear and convincing standard of proof does not apply to this case, however, because the issue was not raised or preserved.

[10][11][12] In a negligence action, punitive damages may be awarded if the defendant knew or had reason to know a high degree of probability existed that the action would result in injury. *Stojkovic v. Weller,* 802 S.W.2d 152, 155 (Mo. banc 1991), *overruled on other grounds by Rodriguez v. Suzuki Motor Corp.,* 936 S.W.2d 104 (Mo. banc 1996); *Hoover's Dairy, Inc. v. Mid-America Dairymen Inc.,* 700 S.W.2d 426, 436 (Mo. banc 1985). To submit punitive damages to the jury in a strict liability case, a plaintiff must present evidence that the defendant placed in commerce an unreasonably dangerous*165 product with actual knowledge of the product's defect. *Sparks v. Consolidated Aluminum Co.,* 679 S.W.2d 348, 354 (Mo. App.1984). Under both theories, evidence must also be presented that the defendant showed a complete indifference to or conscious disregard for the safety of others. [FN6] *Id.; Stojkovic,* 802 S.W.2d at 155.

FN6. Both negligence and strict liability theories were submitted to the jury in this case.

[13] Substantial evidence adduced at trial established that TSA and TEC had actual knowledge of the defective condition of the TU 76 nozzle guide vane when it was installed in the Life Flight 2 helicopter in June of 1989. Furthermore, evidence was presented that TSA knew or had reason to know that a high degree of probability existed that the action would result in injury. TSA and TEC learned in 1985 after an in-flight engine failure in the Congo that TU 76 nozzle guide vanes in engines manufactured by TSA were cracking in the central hub and that the cracking could cause partial or total engine failure. In 1986, various comprehensive technical papers that thoroughly outlined the problem with the TU 76 were routed to TSA's highest corporate officials. In 1987, TEC mechanics began to discover and record cracks in the front and rear flanges of the central hub of TU 76 second stage nozzle guide vanes during routine engine inspections. TSA was also aware that at least three incidents of in-flight engine stoppages due to cracking of the TU 76 had occurred prior to the 1989 installation of the part by TEC in the Life Flight 2 helicopter engine. At least ten incidents of engine failure and loss of power because of TU 76 cracking and resulting disintegration occurred worldwide prior to the fatal Life Flight 2 accident. In the 1989 helicopter crash in Bolivia, four people were seriously injured after the stoppage of the helicopter engine due to a defective TU 76 nozzle guide vane.

Substantial evidence was also presented that TSA and TEC manifested indifference to or consciously disregarded the safety of others. TSA and TEC argue that the immediate undertaking of a redesign effort to produce a suitable replacement part after originally learning of the TU 76 cracking problems in 1985 and the issuance of several service letters warning of the possible problems with the TU 76 nozzle guide vane dispelled any notion that they were indifferent to the safety of others. After the development and certification of the TU 202 and TU 197 nozzle guide vanes, however, TSA and TEC made a conscious business decision not to immediately recall the defective TU 76. Instead, to save money, the companies chose to replace the defective part during the regularly scheduled overhaul of helicopter engines. Mr. Dennis Nichols, the president of TEC, acknowledged that the companies saved up to $48 million by not immediately recalling all helicopter engines equipped with the known defective part.[FN7] This decision was made despite internal company documentation that the TU 76 cracking problem had caused at least 13 in-flight engine failures or loss of power prior to the Life Flight 2 crash. These engine failures occurred during a time period in which TSA possessed a safe substitute nozzle guide vane.

FN7. See point four for a discussion of this evidence.

In May 1988, despite its knowledge of in-flight failures due to the cracking of the TU 76 nozzle guide, TSA actually increased the TBO, or time between overhaul, for the Arriel 1B gas turbine, Module 3 from 2000 to 2500 hours. This extension effectively increased the opportunity for in-flight engine failures caused by the defective TU 76. The engine in the helicopter that crashed, causing the death of Sherry Letz, had operated for over 2000 hours since it was last overhauled. Sufficient evidence, therefore, was offered by the Letzes to show TSA and TEC's knowledge of the defective part; the danger it posed in the Arriel 1B gas turbine engine; and the wantonness, recklessness, and indifference to the consequences of selling and failing to recall a defective engine part manifested by the companies. Manifest injustice, therefore, did not result from submission to the jury of the issue of aggravating circumstances. Point one is denied.

II. AGGRAVATING CIRCUMSTANCES INSTRUCTION AND VERDICT FORM

[14] TSA and TEC next claim that the trial court erred in submitting Instruction *166 No. 25 and Verdict Form A to the jury. They argue that the instruction and verdict form did not provide adequate due process safeguards in instructing the jury on aggravating circumstances damages. The Due Process Clause requires that adequate standards and controls be established to prevent a punitive damages award from constituting the arbitrary deprivation of property. *Call v. Heard,* 925 S.W.2d 840, 848 (Mo. banc 1996), *cert. denied,* 519 U.S. 1093, 117 S.Ct. 770, 136 L.Ed.2d 716 (1997). Instruction No. 25, patterned after MAI 5.01, the damage instruction for wrongful death actions, provided:

> If you find in favor of plaintiffs, then you must award plaintiffs such sum as you believe will fairly and justly compensate the survivors of Sherry Ann Letz for any damages you believe they and the decedent sustained and the survivors of Sherry Ann Letz are reasonably certain to sustain in the future as a direct result of the fatal injury to Sherry Ann Letz.

> In assessing damages you may take into consideration any aggravating circumstances attendant upon the fatal injury.

> You must not consider grief or bereavement suffered by reason of the death.

Verdict Form A did not separate actual damages from aggravating circumstances damages.

TSA and TEC argue that the instruction violates the Missouri Supreme Court's decision in *Bennett v. Owens-Corning Fiberglas Corp.,* 896 S.W.2d 464 (Mo. banc 1995), which was handed down less than two weeks after the jury verdict was rendered in this case. In *Bennett,* the Court held that aggravating circumstances damages under the wrongful death statute are punitive in nature and may only be awarded if accompanied by due process safeguards including proper narrowing jury instructions. *Id.* at 466-467. The Court found that the jury instructions based on MAI 5.01 and a modified version of MAI 10.04 failed to adequately guide the jury in awarding such punitive damages and were, therefore, unconstitutionally vague. *Id.* at 467-468. TSA and TEC contend that *Bennett* should be applied retroactively to this case thereby requiring a new trial on the issue of aggravating circumstances damages.

[15][16] The record discloses, however, that TSA and TEC did not properly preserve this issue for appellate review. To preserve a constitutional question for appellate review, it must be raised in the trial court at the earliest opportunity consistent with good pleading and orderly procedure and be further preserved in a motion for new trial. *Hatfield v. McCluney,* 893 S.W.2d 822, 829 (Mo. banc 1995); *Fahy v. Dresser Indus., Inc.,* 740 S.W.2d 635, 639 (Mo. banc 1987), *cert. denied,* 485 U.S. 1022, 108 S.Ct. 1576, 99 L.Ed.2d 891 (1988); *State v. Danforth,* 654 S.W.2d 912, 917 (Mo.App.1983). Rule 70.03 [FN8], which governs objections to instructions, provides:

FN8. Rule 70.03 became effective on January 1, 1994.

Counsel shall make specific objections to instructions considered erroneous. No party may assign as error the giving or failure to give instructions unless that party objects thereto before the jury retires to consider its verdict, stating distinctly the matter objected to and the grounds of the objection.
Rule 70.03. The rule also requires that the objections must be preserved in a motion for new trial in accordance with Rule 78.07. Furthermore, to be preserved, an objection to a verdict form must be raised either at the instruction conference or when the verdict is returned by the jury before it is accepted by the court. *Adams v. Children's Mercy Hosp.,* 848 S.W.2d 535, 541 (Mo.App.1993).

[17] TSA and TEC failed to specifically object to Instruction No. 25 and Verdict Form A prior to their submission to the jury. At the instruction conference, they sought to submit an alternative damage instruction to the trial court which omitted the aggravating circumstances paragraph. The instruction offered by TSA and TEC would not have submitted aggravating

circumstances in any form. They did not, however, distinctly claim that the damage instruction violated the Due Process Clause of the United States or Missouri Constitutions or that the instruction failed to inform the jury of the purpose ***167** or nature of aggravating circumstances damages. TSA and TEC did not object to the language of the instruction or to the joint submission of both actual and aggravating circumstances damages. They did not ask that the verdict form require the jury to separately list its actual and aggravating circumstances awards. TSA and TEC asked only that the aggravating circumstances damages language not be submitted. Not until their motion for a new trial did they claim that a separate submission for aggravating circumstances damages was required or that greater guidance to the jury regarding assessment of such damages was required. The alleged error in submitting the instruction and verdict form to the jury was not preserved for review.

TSA and TEC argue that objecting at trial to the instruction would have been a futile act because the trial court was required to submit the instruction based on the applicable MAI 5.01. They contend that a holding requiring an objection at trial to mandatory MAI instructions would effectively require parties to raise every conceivable objection in order to preserve a potential claim for review. This contention is without merit.

In *Bennett,* the defendant objected to the constitutionality of the submission of the aggravating circumstances instruction, and the trial court modified the MAI to separately submit actual and aggravating circumstances damages. *Bennett,* 896 S.W.2d at 467. Before considering defendant's argument that the trial court improperly instructed the jury regarding aggravating circumstances damages, the Missouri Supreme Court determined that an objection to the offending instruction was preserved. *Id.* It then approved the trial court's modifying the MAI to separately submit actual and aggravating circumstances damages. *Id.* at 467-468. The Supreme Court, however, reversed the judgment, not because the trial judge modified MAI 5.01 by incorporating language of MAI 10.04, but because he had not modified MAI 5.01 further. *Id.* at 468.

In the recent case of *Call v. Heard,* 925 S.W.2d 840, 847 (Mo. banc 1996), *cert. denied,* 519 U.S. 1093, 117 S.Ct. 770, 136 L.Ed.2d 716 (1997), the Missouri Supreme Court reaffirmed the requirement that a constitutional question, like others, must have been preserved for appellate review in order to determine the retroactive effect of the decision finding the offending instruction unconstitutional. The Court noted that the rule "is necessary in order to prevent surprise to the opposing party and to allow the trial court the opportunity to identify and rule on the issue." *Id.*

[18][19][20] One must object to instructions, even MAI instructions, in order to preserve objections to the giving of the instruction. Rule 70.03, cited by the Missouri Supreme Court in *Bennett,* requires, without exception, that objections to instructions must be made to preserve error for review. Rule 70.02 contemplates modification of an MAI instruction "where an MAI must be modified to fairly submit the issues in a particular case." Rule 70.02(b). Thus, the trial court has limited discretion in determining whether applicable MAI instructions "fairly submit the issues." Perceived imperfections of MAI instructions must be identified by objection in order to permit the trial judge to consider the issue and the requested deviation or the objection is waived.

[21][22] Although an applicable MAI must be given by a trial court to the exclusion of all others, *State ex rel. Missouri Highway and Transp. Comm'n v. Buys,* 909 S.W.2d 735, 739 (Mo.App.1995), an exception is that a court is not required to give an MAI instruction that violates the United States or Missouri Constitutions. If clear United States Supreme Court or Missouri Supreme Court precedent exists at the time of trial that an MAI breaches the federal constitution, the trial court need not submit the instruction to the jury. The Missouri Supreme Court has held that MAI and its Notes on Use are not binding to the extent they conflict with the substantive law. *State v. Carson,* 941 S.W.2d 518, 520 (Mo. banc 1997). If an instruction following MAI conflicts with the substantive law, any court should decline to follow MAI. *Id.* To require a trial court to submit an instruction clearly violative of the federal constitution because it was approved as an MAI prior to the ruling of the United States Supreme Court, would, ***168** if the issue were properly preserved, render the trial voidable and meaningless. It is this type of situation that Rule 70.02 contemplates as requiring MAI modification to "fairly submit the issues."

TEC and TSA failed to raise this constitutional issue at the earliest opportunity or to specifically object to the instruction before its submission to the jury. The question of retroactive application of *Bennett,* therefore, was not preserved for review. [FN9] Point two is denied.

FN9. The Eighth Circuit in *Baker v. General Motors Corp.,* 86 F.3d 811 (8th Cir.Mo.1996), *cert. granted,* 520 U.S. 1142, 117 S.Ct. 1310, 137 L.Ed.2d 474 (1997)(No. 96-653), addressed whether *Bennett* application is retroactive. Because the issue was not preserved, the issue is not addressed.

III. PHOTOGRAPH

As their third point on appeal, TSA and TEC claim that the trial court erred in refusing to grant a mistrial after the introduction of a photograph of Sherry's tombstone. They argue that the photograph was deceitfully introduced by the Letzes' counsel for the sole purpose of inciting juror sympathy.

During her direct examination, counsel for the Letzes questioned Sherry's mother about Sherry's interests, activities, and accomplishments before her death. Numerous exhibits were introduced into evidence such as award certificates, a videotape of Sherry with her children, and photographs depicting Sherry at different stages in her life. The various photographs were offered either individually or as a group on a photo board. Just prior to introduction of the photograph of Sherry's tombstone, the jury was shown, with accompanying narration by Mrs. Letz, a photo board on which numerous photos were affixed. The photographs depicted Sherry at summer camp, in her Brownie uniform, playing the violin, on prom night, graduating from high school, celebrating her son's first Christmas, playing golf, in the hospital at the birth of her second son, and on her last Christmas. Counsel and Ms. Letz then engaged in the following colloquy:

Q: Let me show you what's been marked as Plaintiffs' Exhibit 210, and do you recognize Plaintiffs' Exhibit 210?
A: Yes, I do.
Q: Is that a photograph taken on the occasion of her 21st birthday?
A: Yes, it was.

A photograph of Sherry's tombstone taken on the date that would have been her 21st birthday anniversary was offered into evidence. Sherry's death occurred before her 21st birthday anniversary. No objection was made to the introduction of the photograph, and it was passed to the jury.

TSA and TEC claim that the Letzes' counsel "engaged in a calculated ploy to expose the jury to evidence so completely irrelevant and prejudicial that diversionary tactics were required to avoid certain objection by defendants and rejection by the court." They argue that the prejudice resulting from the introduction of the photograph, which served only to incite the sympathy of the jury, and from counsels' misconduct can only be cured by reversal of the damages judgment.

The Letzes claim that TSA and TEC waived any claim of error regarding the introduction of the photograph. They contend that the companies failed to object to the photograph's admission into evidence when it was offered at trial or to seek a withdrawal instruction.

A. Preservation of Issue

[23][24][25] To preserve for appellate review an error regarding the admission of evidence, a timely objection must be made when the evidence is introduced at trial. *Kovacs v. Kovacs,* 869 S.W.2d 789, 792 (Mo.App.1994). If the objection is not made at the time of the incident giving rise to the objection, the objection may be deemed waived or abandoned. *McMillin v. Union Elec. Co.,* 820 S.W.2d 352, 355 (Mo.App.1991). Similarly, failure to make a timely request for further relief when an objection has been sustained may be deemed a waiver of further remedial relief. *Id.*

[26] In this case, the photograph was introduced into evidence and passed to the jury during the testimony of Mrs. Letz without objection. According to TSA and TEC, neither they nor the trial court saw the picture*169 before it was passed to the jury. The record reflects that TSA and TEC did not ask to see the photograph. The photograph was identified prior to trial as a numbered exhibit on the Letzes' list of exhibits and was available for review by TSA and TEC before the trial commenced. Defense counsel did not review the photograph either before trial or at trial before it was introduced.[FN10]

FN10. Exhibits 21 and 22 included a series of photographs of the decedent at various times of her life. TSA and TEC claim that the Letzes' counsel misidentified the photograph of the decedents headstone as Exhibit 210 when showing the photograph to the jury. The photograph was actually Exhibit 21-O. Exhibit 210 was a report. TSA and TEC assert that the misidentification was intentional and a part of a scheme to surreptitiously introduce the photograph and pass it to the jury by misleading defense counsel and court and concealing from them the contents of the photograph. The companies claim that this scheme was successful and is responsible for their failure to object to or ask to view the exhibit. When identifying the series of photographs and asking questions about them of Mrs. Letz, whether the Letzes' counsel identified the exhibit as 210 instead of 21-O is unclear. He did say, "Is this a picture taken on the occasion of her (the decedent's) 21st birthday?" The exhibit was obviously a photograph, not a report. Moreover, the photograph was introduced with numerous other photographs.

On the weekend following Mrs. Letz's testimony, counsel for TSA and TEC reviewed and compared the exhibits in the court file with their own notes and discovered the photo of Sherry's tombstone. They then brought the admission of the photograph to the court's attention and requested a mistrial. The court responded:

Let me advise both of you that it's proper procedure for you to show the Court the exhibits before you pass them to the jury or offer them in evidence so I can look at them and see if I have any reason to not receive them. You haven't been doing that and if I had seen this photograph marked as Exhibit 210, I would not have admitted it. It has no purpose in this case other than to provoke sympathy and to work on the sympathy to the jury and it's not admissible. If that was passed to the jury, I'm not going to declare a mistrial as requested. That is denied but I certainly will advise the jury in no uncertain terms that such evidence is not to be considered.

* * * * * *

I'm telling you that it doesn't make any difference whether there is any objection or not. Something that is improper is not to be tendered to the jury. I don't care whether it is something that you honestly did or whether you did it by design. I assume that you did it without knowledge that this would not be admitted, but I'm telling you that it is not admissible. It is prejudicial.

Whether it is prejudicial to the point where a mistrial should be declared is another question and I'm determining that it is not. I'm not going to declare a mistrial. That doesn't mean that at the end of this case if something happened that showed me that this jury had been swayed by passion or by prejudice or by some improper motive in returning a verdict, you couldn't lose your verdict. So I think you should be concerned about that.

Exhibit 210 is not admitted. It is withdrawn and I'll ask the defendant, how do you want me to handle it with the jury?

Because TSA and TEC failed to object to the photograph's admission when it was introduced at trial, the subsequent objection to the photograph was untimely, and any error regarding the photograph's admission was not preserved for review. The trial court, however, declared the photograph inadmissible and withdrew it from evidence despite the companies' untimely objection and offered to take corrective action. TSA and TEC requested a mistrial which the court declined. The alleged error regarding the court's refusal to grant a mistrial was preserved for review.

B. Denial of Mistrial

[27][28] A mistrial is a drastic remedy, and the decision to grant one for misconduct or the introduction of prejudicial evidence is largely within the discretion of the trial court. *Callahan v. Cardinal Glennon Hosp.*, 863 S.W.2d 852, 867-868 (Mo. banc 1993). The trial court is better able to determine the prejudicial effect of the improper evidence and to determine whether any resulting prejudice can be ameliorated by less ***170** drastic means than declaration of a mistrial. *State v. Sidebottom* 753 S.W.2d 915, 919-920 (Mo. banc 1988), *cert. denied*, 488 U.S. 975, 109 S.Ct. 515, 102 L.Ed.2d 550 (1988);

McMillin v. Union Elec. Co., 820 S.W.2d 352, 355-356 (Mo.App.1991). A reviewing appellate court will reverse only where there has been a manifest abuse of discretion. *Callahan,* 863 S.W.2d at 867-68. To establish manifest abuse, there must be a grievous error where prejudice cannot otherwise be removed. *Id.*

[29] The Letzes argue that the photograph of Sherry's gravestone was relevant to material issues such as the fact of her death and as a reminder of the finality of death. The parties, however, had stipulated to Sherry's death, and in closing argument the Letzes, through counsel, disclaimed any damages for funeral costs and burial expenses. Thus, while the photograph might have been relevant in other circumstances, it was not relevant in the circumstances presented. The photograph was offered merely to inflame the jury. Although the photograph was introduced for an improper purpose, prejudice so substantial to the opposing party to compel a mistrial does not automatically occur.

In determining the prejudicial effect of the photograph, the trial court considered the unique circumstances presented. It considered the impact of the introduction of the exhibit and the magnitude of the prejudice it engendered. In denying the motion for mistrial, the court concluded that introduction of the exhibit did not prejudice the jury to the companies' detriment.

[30] The trial court did not abuse its discretion in denying the motion for mistrial. Although the method used to introduce the photograph prompts criticism, the photograph contains nothing so offensive or inciting of passion as to produce prejudice. The scene is the decedent's gravestone, surrounded by flowers. Thus, the picture does not portray a scene so offensive or prejudicial by its content to warrant a mistrial. The jury observed the photograph for a few seconds during the four-week trial during which 45 witnesses testified in person or by deposition and during which 431 exhibits were admitted. Its consideration of the single photograph of the decedent's gravestone was not so outrageous and impacting an error that the trial court's decision not to grant a mistrial was an abuse of discretion so egregious as to necessitate a new trial. *See Callahan,* 863 S.W.2d at 867 (impact of jury questions was minimal at best where trial lasted three weeks and 26 witnesses testified).

The trial court did not abuse its discretion in refusing to grant a mistrial. Point three is denied.

IV. COST SAVINGS EVIDENCE

[31] In their fourth point, TSA and TEC claim that the trial court erred in admitting the deposition testimony of Dennis Nichols regarding the cost to recall and retrofit all TU 76 nozzle guide vanes in helicopters sold by the manufacturer and in flight status throughout the world. They also argue that the trial court erred in allowing the Letzes to use the "cost savings" evidence in arguing aggravating circumstances damages during closing argument. The deposition testimony was admissible, and the evidence presented at trial supported the Letzes' closing argument references to cost savings.

The following testimony from the videotaped deposition of Dennis Nichols, the President of TEC, was played for the jury. The questions were asked by John Risjord, who represented a party in a companion case.

Q. (By Mr. Risjord) Well, if Turbomeca, S.A. took the position when they learned of the problem and had the solution, let's assume that was in 1991, since that's the reference to-in the documents to it, they had some 2850 engines out in the world that needed either immediately or eventually that change, that improvement, right?

A. Yes.

Q. And we're told that the cost-do you know the cost of making the change?

A. No, I don't.

Q. We understand that it is in the area of $17,000 to correct this defect for one engine. Does that sound reasonable to you?

*171

A. Sounds reasonable.

Q. Yes, sir. And so if my mathematics is correct, it would cost the manufacturer, Turbomeca, S.A., or its parent corporation, some 48 million dollars just for the replacement of the defectively designed part?

A. (Witness nods his head.)

Q. You're nodding agreement with that. I take it that that's-

A. I agree with your arithmetic.

Q. And so if the French manufacturer takes the position that we're going to wait for overhaul and we're going to be able to charge the customer for the replacement of that defective part in the overhaul, then they save as of the time back in 1991, approximately, they save approximately 48 million dollars, don't they?

* * * * * *

Q. (By Mr. Risjord) Well, it's a matter of simple mathematics, not speculation. If the customer pays for it, Turbomeca, S.A. or their parent company Labinal saves 48 million dollars; isn't that correct?

* * * * * *

A. In the scenario that you have described which is somewhat hypothetical or speculative in nature, you're right, of course. I agree.

TSA and TEC contend that the cost savings evidence was speculative and without foundation and was not an appropriate method of measuring damages in a wrongful death action.

The Letzes first assert that TSA and TEC did not preserve these alleged errors for appellate review. They claim that the defendants failed to object to the questions and answers regarding the cost savings at the time of the deposition as required by Rule 57.07(d)(3)(B). Rule 57.07(d)(3)(b) requires that some, but not all, objections be made at the deposition of a witness, or those objections are waived. *Seabaugh v. Milde Farms, Inc.,* 816 S.W.2d 202, 210 (Mo. banc 1991). It provides:

(B) Errors and irregularities occurring at the oral examination in the manner of taking the deposition, in the form of the questions or answers, in the oath or affirmation, or in the conduct of the parties and errors of any kind which might be obviated, removed, or cured if promptly presented, are waived unless seasonable objection thereto is made at the taking of the deposition.

Rule 57.07(d)(3). "The rule serves to give questioning counsel an opportunity to rephrase the question, lay a better foundation, or clarify the question so that evidence will not be rejected at trial because of inadvertent omissions or careless questions." *Seabaugh,* 816 S.W.2d at 202.

Contrary to the Letzes' contention, the record reveals that counsel for TSA and TEC specifically objected to the form of the questions asked of Mr. Nichols and to his answers regarding the cost savings. The objections stated that the questioning lacked foundation, called for speculation, and misstated the evidence. The same objections were then made at trial. The objections were timely, and the issue of whether admission of Mr. Nichols's deposition testimony was error was preserved for review.

[32] The Letzes also claim that TSA and TEC failed to specifically object to their cost savings argument during closing arguments. Failure to object at trial to alleged improper argument preserves nothing for review on appeal. *Krenski v. Aubuchon,* 841 S.W.2d 721, 728 (Mo.App.1992), *overruled on other grounds by Rodriguez v. Suzuki Motor Corp.,* 936 S.W.2d 104 (Mo. banc 1996). The record confirms that TSA and TEC specifically objected to the use of cost savings to argue aggravating damages. Timely objections having been made, the alleged errors were properly preserved for review.

[33][34][35][36] The trial court has substantial discretion in ruling on the admissibility of evidence. *Graves v. Atchison-Holt Elec. Co-op.,* 886 S.W.2d 1, 3 (Mo.App.1994). Similarly, the regulation of closing arguments rests largely within the

sound discretion of the trial court. *Hagedorn v. Adams,* 854 S.W.2d 470, 478 (Mo.App.1993). "The permissible ***172** field of argument is broad and as long as counsel does not go beyond the evidence and issues drawn by the instructions or urge prejudicial matters or claim or defense which the evidence and issues do not justify, counsel is permitted wide latitude in his comments." *Id.* The trial court's rulings on evidence and arguments will not be disturbed on appeal absent an abuse of discretion. *Graves,* 886 S.W.2d at 3; *Hagedorn,* 854 S.W.2d at 478.

At trial, the Letzes claimed, as aggravating circumstances attending Sherry's death, that TSA and TEC knew the TU 76 nozzle guide vane was defective and the cause of several in-flight engine failures when the Life Flight 2 helicopter crashed. They also alleged that the knowledge of the defective part prompted the development and production of alternative nozzle guide vanes, the TU 197 and the TU 202, to replace the TU 76. The Letzes argued that TSA and TEC, however, did not immediately recall helicopters equipped with the TU 76 for retrofit with the safer nozzle guide vanes but, instead, waited to replace the defective parts during the helicopters' regularly scheduled overhaul to save money.

Dennis Nichols, President of TEC, and agent and representative of TSA, acknowledged during his deposition, portions of which were read to the jury, that the cost of replacing the TU 76 with a modified nozzle guide vane was approximately $17,000.[FN11] He stated in his deposition that the most effective and quickest means of remedying the defective engine part would have been to recall and retrofit the engines with the modified part. He also acknowledged that TSA did not recall the engines and elected to wait to replace the defective nozzle guide vane until the routine engine overhaul was performed to reduce the cost that would be incurred by the company. Mr. Nichols testified that TSA's policy was that defective nozzle guide vanes were replaced at the customer's cost when the engine was overhauled. Approximately 500 overhauls of engines containing the defective nozzle guide vane were performed by a repair facility owned by his company, TEC, and one other repair facility, both in North America, and, according to company policy, the customer was charged for each engine overhaul. The question posed to Mr. Nichols included the assumption that in 1991, 2,850 Arriel engines aboard helicopters needed either immediate or eventual replacement of the TU 76 nozzle vane guide.[FN12] Using these figures, the question was posed to Mr. Nichols whether TSA would have to expend $48 million to replace the defective TU 76 within engines manufactured by the company and existing in the world. He answered affirmatively.

> FN11. Answers to interrogatories provided by TEC state that replacing the TU 76 with the TU 197 required 52 hours and cost $17,107.25, and replacing the TU 76 with the TU 202 required 52 hours and cost $11,519.25.

> FN12. According to TSA technical note 9446, which was introduced at trial as Plaintiff's Exhibit 8, by December 1992, TU 76 nozzle guide vanes remained in 1769 engines of the entire TSA produced fleet. By the same time, twenty engines equipped with the TU 76 had been returned to TSA, and the TU 202 had replaced the TU 76 in 1056 engines of the fleet. The figure of 2850, therefore, is a reasonable figure for the number of engines in TSA's fleet worldwide that were equipped with the TU 76 nozzle guide vane in 1991 when the replacement TU 202 first became available.

The Letzes' premise was that the failure to immediately recall and replace the known defective TU 76 within helicopter engines manufactured by TSA and operating throughout the world was the consequence of a deliberate decision and was motivated by the desire to save the company $48 million. Among the evidence supporting the Letzes' argument was the deposition testimony of Alain Calemard, Vice-President for Engineering for TSA, that technical notes regarding the need to correct the defective TU 76 nozzle vain guide were written in 1986 and that six years elapsed before the company implemented the change into production engines. He stated that the commercial department of the company, responsible for determining whether TSA or the customer would pay for modification of engines, informed the engineering department that the customer could not be made to pay for the modification of the defective nozzle vain guide. The commercial department ***173** "blocked" implementation of the modification for some undetermined period of time.

TSA and TEC argue that no foundation existed for the $48 million figure argued by plaintiffs. Mr. Nichols, however, acknowledged the $17,000 amount as an approximate cost to replace a single defective TU 76 nozzle guide vane with a TU 202 model, and he expressly accepted that 2,850 engines sold required the change. Additionally, Dr. David Hoeppner, a professor of mechanical engineering and consultant in airworthiness and reliability engineering design and quality assurance engineering design, testified in behalf of plaintiffs and agreed with Mr. Nichols that the cost of $17,000 per engine to replace the defective nozzle vane guide with the improved part was correct. Thus, these figures were supported by evidence, and the mathematical computation provided a basis for the Letzes' argument that the company decided not to recall and replace the defective engine part because it wanted to save the money such a recall would cost.

Although the defendant offered evidence that it would not have charged all customers for the repairs if done during scheduled maintenance, the jury's duty included resolving the conflict in the evidence. The cost savings realized, whether $48 million or a substantial portion of that sum, was relevant to the issue of aggravating circumstances.[FN13] Mr. Nichols's testimony was directly related to the companies' motive for not repairing the defective part of the helicopter engine that ultimately caused Sherry's death and, thus, was admissible. Additionally, counsel's remarks during closing argument regarding the cost savings as a motive for failure or refusal to expedite replacement of the defective engine part, known to cause the engine to fail, were supported by evidence in the case. The cost savings evidence directly related to the issue of aggravating circumstances attending Sherry's death which was properly before the jury. Plaintiffs' counsel's argument, therefore, was permissible. Point four is denied.

> FN13. TEC, by the deposition testimony of Carey Brown, an employee of TEC, introduced testimonial evidence that in 1993, in the normal course of business, when TEC was repairing helicopter engines sold by it in which a TU 76 nozzle guide vane was located and the engine maintenance purchased by the owner of the helicopter required that the nozzle be exposed, the company replaced the nozzle with a TU 202 nozzle "free of charge." Additionally, Mr. Brown's testimony was, "If the TU 76 nozzle guide was replaced in the course of normal overhaul or repair of the engine, some concession would be made by TEC in the course of the replacement."

V. EVIDENCE OF FACSIMILES SENT TO FAA

TSA and TEC next claim that the trial court erred in admitting Exhibits No. 91, 248, and 250, facsimiles sent to the Federal Aviation Administration (FAA) by TSA after the Life Flight 2 accident, and in allowing witnesses to be questioned about the exhibits. The facsimiles were sent by TSA to the FAA in response to an inquiry made by the FAA in furtherance of the investigation of the cause of the Life Flight 2 crash and reported seven prior incidents/accidents caused by the TU 76 nozzle guide vane defect. TSA and TEC argue that the reports, filed after Sherry's death, were irrelevant to aggravating circumstances attending Sherry's death. They contend that the post-accident evidence was offered merely to portray the companies as misleading the United States Government regarding the number of in-flight failures the TU 76 nozzle guide had caused prior to the Life Flight 2 crash.[FN14]

> FN14. The Letzes assert that TSA and TEC did not preserve this issue for appellate review by failing to object to the introduction of the evidence at trial and in their motion for a new trial. The record does not support the claim. The record indubitably shows that TSA and TEC objected to the introduction of Exhibit No. 91 at trial as postaccident evidence:
>
> THE COURT: Do you have any objections to any of these exhibits?
> Defense counsel: Yes, Your Honor. I have objections to three of the exhibits and also we plan to offer two exhibits.
> THE COURT: Let's get to the ones you object to.
> Defense Counsel: I object to Exhibit No. 91.
> THE COURT: What is the exhibit?
> Defense Counsel: I believe it is a postaccident communication between Turbomeca and FAA; and the objection is that it is, in fact, postaccident evidence. It is not relevant to the issues.

Similar objections were made at trial to the introduction of Exhibit Nos. 248 and 250. Although the admission of Exhibit Nos. 248 and 250 was not raised in their motion for a new trial, the admission of Exhibit No. 91 was raised, and, therefore, the issue regarding Exhibit 91 is preserved for appellate review. Rule 78.07; *Brown v. Van Noy*, 879 S.W.2d 667, 671 (Mo.App.1994).

*174 [37][38][39] Evidence is relevant if the fact it tends to establish tends in turn to prove or disprove a fact in issue or to corroborate evidence which is relevant and which bears on the principal issue. *Guthrie v. Missouri Methodist Hosp.,* 706 S.W.2d 938, 941 (Mo.App.1986). An award for exemplary damages such as aggravating circumstances damages must have some reasonable relation to the injury inflicted and the cause thereof. *Id.* at 942; *Vaughn v. North Am. Sys., Inc.,* 869 S.W.2d 757, 759 (Mo. banc 1994). "Actions subsequent to those for which damages are sought may be relevant and 'admissible under an issue of exemplary damages if so connected with the particular acts as tending to show defendant's disposition, intention, or motive in the commission of the particular acts for which damages are claimed.' " *Guthrie,* 706 S.W.2d at 942 (quoting *Charles F. Curry & Co. v. Hedrick,* 378 S.W.2d 522, 536 (Mo.1964)).

[40] Exhibit No. 91, the facsimile sent by TSA to the FAA after the Life Flight 2 crash, was relevant to the issue of aggravating circumstances attending Sherry's death. TSA's report to the FAA of prior incidents/accidents involving the TU 76 nozzle guide vane tended to establish that TSA was aware of the defective condition and danger of the part prior to Sherry's death. Additionally, evidence that TSA and TEC may have under-reported prior accidents to civil authorities tended to show the companies' motive to save the cost of a recall. As discussed in the previous point, evidence was introduced at trial that TSA made a conscious decision not to immediately recall all helicopters equipped with the TU 76 nozzle guide vanes because the company would save money by delaying retrofitting the helicopters' engines with the improved part. Similarly, grounding all helicopters equipped with the TU 76 by the FAA for safety reasons after the Life Flight 2 crash would have been costly to TSA and TEC because the action would have compelled recall and the company probably would have lost sales. Although the report was sent to the FAA after the May 27, 1993 fatal crash that killed Sherry, the report disclosed other helicopter crashes that occurred prior to the accident where the helicopters involved had the TU 76 nozzle guide vanes as engine components. The report to the FAA, therefore, tended to strengthen the Letzes contention that the companies failed to repair a known defective and dangerous part with a safe available part in order to save money. The facsimile sent to the FAA, therefore, was relevant to the issue of aggravating circumstances and was properly admitted into evidence. Point five is denied.

VI. MOTION FOR NEW TRIAL OR REMITTITUR

In their final point on appeal, TSA and TEC claim that the trial court erred in overruling their motion for a new trial or remittitur. They argue that the $70 million wrongful death award to the Letzes (1) was grossly excessive; (2) was the product of misconduct by the Letzes' attorneys; (3) demonstrated bias, passion, and prejudice on the part of the jury; (4) exceeded fair and reasonable compensation for the Letzes' injuries; (5) was unsupported by the evidence; and (6) bore no relation to the damages authorized by the wrongful death statute, section 537.090, RSMo 1994.

[41][42][43][44] In a wrongful death case, the jury has extraordinarily wide discretion in awarding damages. *Cannada v. Moore,* 578 S.W.2d 597, 604 (Mo. banc 1979). Similarly, a trial court has great discretion in approving a verdict or setting it aside as excessive. *Callahan v. Cardinal Glennon Hosp.,* 863 S.W.2d 852, 872 (Mo. banc 1993). An appellate court, therefore, "will interfere only when the verdict is so grossly excessive that it shocks the conscience of the court and convinces the court that both the jury and the trial court abused their discretion." *Fust v. Francois,* 913 S.W.2d 38, 49 (Mo.App.1995). Abuse of discretion regarding the punitive damage award is established when the punitive damage award manifests "improper motives or a clear absence of the ***175** honest exercise of judgment." *Call v. Heard,* 925 S.W.2d 840, 849 (Mo. banc 1996), cert. denied, 519 U.S. 1093, 117 S.Ct. 770, 136 L.Ed.2d 716 (1997)(quoting *Beggs v. Universal C.I.T. Credit Corp.,* 409 S.W.2d 719, 724 (Mo.1966)).

A. Review for Jury Misconduct Requiring a New Trial

[45][46][47] An excessive verdict resulting from jury bias and prejudice requires a new trial. *Coulter v. Michelin Tire Corp.,* 622 S.W.2d 421, 436 (Mo.App.1981), *cert. denied,* 456 U.S. 906, 102 S.Ct. 1752, 72 L.Ed.2d 162 (1982). Entitlement to a new trial based on an excessive verdict requires a showing of trial court error. *Callahan,* 863 S.W.2d at 872; *Larabee v. Washington,* 793 S.W.2d 357, 359 (Mo.App.1990). The size of the verdict alone will not establish bias, passion, and prejudice by the jury. *Id.* The complaining party must show that the verdict, viewed in the light most favorable to the prevailing

party, was glaringly unwarranted and that some trial error or misconduct of the prevailing party was responsible for prejudicing the jury. *Id.*

TSA and TEC fail to demonstrate that trial error or misconduct of the Letzes was responsible for prejudicing the jury. They cite to alleged trial error in the admission and use of the cost savings evidence and Exhibit 91, the facsimile sent to the FAA and the prejudicial effect of Exhibit 21-O, the photograph of Sherry's tombstone. As previously discussed, the cost savings evidence and Exhibit 91 were relevant to the issue of aggravating circumstances and were admissible. Although introduction of the photograph was improper, it was not prejudicial and did not warrant a new trial.

TSA and TEC also refer to certain remarks made by the Letzes' counsel in closing argument regarding the failure of the companies' executives to testify live [FN15] and to the videotaping techniques used in the depositions in arguing that the excessive verdict was a result of jury passion and prejudice. Even assuming *arguendo* that these alleged errors or misconduct were improper, they were minor and could not alone have caused the jury bias and prejudice alleged by defendants. Having failed to show that the alleged misconduct was not responsible for the large verdict, TSA and TEC are not entitled to a new trial. The verdict is, therefore, reviewed for simple excessiveness.

FN15. Most of the company executives testified by deposition.

B. Review For Simple Excessiveness Requiring Remittitur

[48][49][50] Where the jury errs by awarding a verdict that is simply too bountiful under the evidence, injustice may be prevented by ordering a remittitur. *Larabee,* 793 S.W.2d at 360. The jury is culpable only of an honest mistake as to the nature and extent of the injuries, not of misconduct, and a new trial is not required. *Id.* Remittitur is appropriate "if, after reviewing the evidence in support of the jury's verdict, the court finds that the jury's verdict is excessive because the amount of the verdict exceeds fair and reasonable compensation for plaintiff's injuries and damages." § 537.068, RSMo 1994. The doctrine of remittitur is intended to produce equitable compensation, to bring jury verdicts in line with prevailing awards, and to eliminate the retrial of lawsuits. *Bishop v. Cummines,* 870 S.W.2d 922, 923 (Mo.App.1994); *Fust,* 913 S.W.2d at 49. Determination of excessiveness is made on a case-by-case basis. *Moore v. Missouri-Nebraska Express, Inc.,* 892 S.W.2d 696, 714 (Mo.App.1994).

As previously discussed in Point I, Missouri statutory law allows recovery for compensatory and aggravating circumstances damages in a wrongful death action. § 537.090, RSMo 1994. Aggravating circumstances awards are punitive in nature. *Bennett v. Owens-Corning Fiberglas Corp.,* 896 S.W.2d 464, 466 (Mo. banc 1995). The jury in this case returned a single verdict of $70 million after a joint submission of actual and aggravating circumstances damages. [FN16] Thus, *176 the lump sum verdict consisted of a compensatory element and a punitive element. Because the verdict did not differentiate between a compensatory award and a punitive award as now required by *Bennett,* this court has no way of knowing what amounts the jury apportioned to each element of damages. Nevertheless, the evidence related to each component of damages, compensatory and punitive, may be analyzed to determine whether the jury's $70 million verdict exceeded fair and reasonable compensation for Letzes' injuries and damages.

FN16. Since the *Bennett* decision in 1995, compensatory and punitive damages are separately determined, and juries are instructed that any award for aggravating circumstances is "to punish defendant and to deter defendant and others from like conduct." *Bennett,* 896 S.W.2d at 468.

C. Compensatory Damages

[51][52] In ascertaining the amount of compensatory damages the jury would have awarded in this case, the evidence applicable to the wrongful death statute is considered. Compensatory damages may be awarded based on the pecuniary losses suffered by reason of the decedent's death, funeral expenses, loss of services, consortium, companionship, and comfort, and the pain and suffering experienced by the decedent because of the defendants' misconduct. Pecuniary loss may be shown

through evidence of the decedent's health, character, talents, earning capacity, life expectancy, age and habits. *Kilmer v. Browning*, 806 S.W.2d 75, 81 (Mo.App.1991). Crucial factors in the computation of consortium and companionship damages to a parent for the loss of a child or to a child for the loss of a parent must include the physical, emotional, and psychological relationship between the parent and the child. *Id.; Morrissey v. Welsh Co.*, 821 F.2d 1294, 1300 (8th Cir.Mo.1987). The pain suffered by the decedent between the time of injury and death is also considered in awarding damages. *Morrissey*, 821 F.2d at 1301. The 1979 amendment to section 537.090 allows the jury to award "such damages as the deceased may have suffered between the time of injury and the time of death and for the recovery of which the deceased might have maintained an action had death not ensued."

[53] The evidence presented at trial on the issue of compensatory damages revealed that at the time of her death in 1993, Sherry was 20 years old, a mother of two young boys, Eric and Christopher, and the only daughter of Jodie Letz. She had a life expectancy of 60.3 additional years to age 80. The Letzes' economic expert presented evidence that the economic loss suffered by Eric and Christopher as a result of Sherry's death was $798,643. This loss included the cost of raising the children, the value of household services, the value of guidance and counseling and the value of future earnings provided to the children. Sherry's shared close relationship with her children and with her mother was also evident. Mrs. Letz testified that when Sherry was not working to provide for her children, she enjoyed spending time with them. Mother and children played together or went to the zoo or to a fair. Mrs. Letz described the relationship between Sherry and her as one of daughter and mother and of best friends. The evidence also revealed that Sherry suffered conscious physical pain between the time the helicopter crashed and her death as a direct result of the crash. The Letzes' medical expert explained that she suffered extreme breathlessness and the sensation of suffocating for up to three minutes before she died.

[54][55] Along with consideration of the evidence, it is also necessary to consider compensatory awards in similar death cases to determine the amount of compensatory damages the jury would have awarded. TSA and TEC have gathered in an appendix to their brief all wrongful death awards in Missouri since 1986, consisting of 44 cases. Review of these cases reveal that most damages awards in the last ten years have ranged from about ten thousand to hundreds of thousands of dollars. In a few cases, damages in the $1 to $2 million dollar range have been affirmed on appeal.[FN17] *See Bennett v. Owens-Corning Fiberglas Corp.*, 896 S.W.2d 464 (Mo. banc 1995)(death involving asbestos exposure, actual damages of $1,114,00 affirmed, aggravating circumstances damages reversed for a new trial); *Goff v. St. Luke's Hosp. Of Kansas City*, 753 S.W.2d 557 (Mo.1988)($2 million in total damages affirmed, amount of damages not appealed); *177 Nesselrode v. Executive Beechcraft Inc.*, 707 S.W.2d 371 (Mo. banc 1986)(man killed in plane crash, total damages of $1,500,000 affirmed); *Lockhart v. Middleton*, 863 S.W.2d 367 (Mo.App.1993), *cert. denied*, 511 U.S. 1131, 114 S.Ct. 2143, 128 L.Ed.2d 871 (1994)(murder, total damages of $1,350,000 affirmed); *Eagleburger v. Emerson Elec.* Co. 794 S.W.2d 210 (Mo.App.1990)($1,060,050 in total damages affirmed); *Blum v. Airport Terminal Services, Inc.*, 762 S.W.2d 67 (Mo.App.1988)(pilot killed in plane crash, total damages of $1,500,000, including aggravating circumstances damages, found not to be excessive); *Schiles v. Schaefer*, 710 S.W.2d 254 (Mo.App.1986)(wrongful death action against doctor, clinic, and hospital, $1,220,000 in total damages affirmed). In one case, *Call v. Heard*, 925 S.W.2d 840 (Mo. banc 1996), *cert. denied*, 519 U.S. 1093, 117 S.Ct. 770, 136 L.Ed.2d 716 (1997), a compensatory verdict of $5 million was approved on appeal. In *Call*, a drunken driver killed *three* members of one family, including the parent who was the family's principal source of income, leaving two survivors (mother and one daughter). The $5 million compensatory verdict upheld on appeal in *Call* was part of the verdict entered by the court in the judge-tried case. No reported Missouri case disclosed a jury verdict compensating a plaintiff for loss in a wrongful death case in a sum approaching $5 million.[FN18] A survey of all these cases and consideration of the evidence in this case in the light most favorable to the plaintiffs convinces this court that a compensatory award for the death of Sherry, if separately delineated, would not have exceeded $2.5 million.

FN17. The awards in these cases were not necessarily an issue on appeal.

FN18. In closing argument, plaintiffs' counsel attempted to persuade the jury that $48 million represented the value of Sherry's life because that was the potential amount TSA and TEC saved by avoiding a recall. Money saved by a defendant's conscious disregard for public safety is not a proper consideration for compensatory damages under section 537.090. The motivation to save $48 million in exchange for the continued risk to people transported by helicopters powered by engines containing the defective TU 76 nozzle guide vane was properly considered, however, as a matter of aggravating circumstances as discussed *infra* in section D.1.

D. Punitive Damages

[56][57][58][59][60][61][62] Having determined that the jury's compensatory damages award would not have exceeded $2.5 million, punitive damages awarded by the jury in this case necessarily amounted to $67.5 million. Punitive damages may properly be imposed to further society's interests of punishing unlawful conduct and deterring its repetition. *BMW v. Gore,* 517 U.S. 559, 567, 116 S.Ct. 1589, 1595, 134 L.Ed.2d 809 (1996). The imposition of a punitive award implicates Fourteenth Amendment due process concerns. *Honda Motor Co., Ltd. v. Oberg,* 512 U.S. 415, 114 S.Ct. 2331, 129 L.Ed.2d 336 (1994). "A decision to punish a tortfeasor by means of an exaction of exemplary damages is an exercise of state power that must comply with the Due Process Clause of the Fourteenth Amendment." *Id.* at 434, 114 S.Ct. at 2342. The constitutional concerns are both procedural and substantive. *See BMW,* 517 U.S. at 559, 116 S.Ct. at 1589. Procedurally, the "traditional common law approach," which includes proper jury instruction and review of a jury award by the trial court and an appellate court, generally satisfies due process. *See Pacific Mut. Life Ins. Co. v. Haslip,* 499 U.S. 1, 15, 111 S.Ct. 1032, 1041-1042, 113 L.Ed.2d 1 (1991). Substantively, when an award can fairly be categorized as "grossly excessive" in relation to the interests of punishment and deterrence, it penetrates the "zone of arbitrariness" that violates the Due Process Clause of the Fourteenth Amendment. *BMW,* 517 U.S. at 568, 116 S.Ct. at 1595. Although a "mathematical bright line" test does not exist to determine the constitutionality of a punitive damage award, limitations on the finder of fact's discretion and "general concerns of reasonableness...enter into the constitutional calculus." *Haslip,* 499 U.S. at 18, 111 S.Ct. at 1043. To satisfy the due process and reasonableness requirements, the amount of punitive damages should reflect the enormity of the defendant's offense and be related to actual or potential harm resulting therefrom. *BMW,* 517 U.S. at 575, 116 S.Ct. at 1599; *Call,* 925 S.W.2d at 848.

[63] In reviewing a punitive damages award for excessiveness, due process and reasonableness requirements compel consideration of the degree of reprehensibility of ***178** the defendant's conduct, the relationship between the punitive damages award and the harm or potential harm suffered by the plaintiff, and the difference between the award and the civil penalties authorized or imposed in comparable cases. *BMW,* 517 U.S. at 573-576, 116 S.Ct. at 1598-1599. Missouri courts have also considered the following additional factors [FN19] in determining the propriety of a punitive damages award: (1) aggravating and mitigating circumstances surrounding the defendant's conduct; (2) the degree of malice or outrageousness of the defendant's conduct; (3) the defendant's character, financial worth, and affluence; (4) the age, health, and character of the injured party; (5) the nature of the injury; (6) awards given and approved in comparable cases; [FN20] and (7) the superior opportunity for the jury and trial court to appraise the plaintiff's injuries and other damages. *Call,* 925 S.W.2d at 849; *Moore,* 892 S.W.2d at 714; *Larabee,* 793 S.W.2d at 360. Missouri's requirements for the imposition of punitive damages satisfy the due process concerns expressed by the Supreme Court of the United States in *Haslip. Call,* 925 S.W.2d at 850.

FN19. Not all of the factors are necessarily discussed in a particular case.

FN20. This factor is no longer the sole factor considered in evaluating the excessiveness of a jury award. *Larabee,* 793 S.W.2d at 360.

1. Degree of Reprehensibility of TSA and TEC

[64] The degree of reprehensibility of a defendant's conduct is, perhaps, the most important indicium of the reasonableness of a punitive damages award. *BMW,* 517 U.S. at 575, 116 S.Ct. at 1599. Substantial evidence of aggravating circumstances enveloping Sherry's death was introduced at trial. The top-level executives of TSA and TEC knew of the history of the TU 76 nozzle guide vane, its propensity to crack, and the risk of in-flight engine failures. They knew the TU 76 nozzle guide vane had failed during engine operation causing the affected engines to cease functions, and they knew that helicopters had crashed because the TU 76 nozzle had failed. Because they knew of the propensity of the part to fail, they developed and possessed a safe nozzle guide vane to replace the defective part. The companies, however, did not recall helicopter engines

to replace the defective TU 76 but, instead, delayed the retrofit until each engine was overhauled during regularly scheduled maintenance. Despite the companies' awareness of the defective part, the recommended length between overhauls was lengthened by the companies from 2,000 hours of engine use to 2,500 hours. The business decision to not immediately recall the helicopter engines for retrofit was influenced by the desire to save TSA and TEC millions of dollars-potentially as much as $48 million.

[65][66] A defendant's choice to wantonly disregard the interests of those to whom some duty is owed to avoid incurring a cost is considered in determining whether a punitive award is reasonably related to the goals of deterrence and retribution. *Haslip*, 499 U.S. at 22, 111 S.Ct. at 1045-1046. TSA and TEC's knowledge of the propensity of the TU 76 nozzle guide vanes to crack and fail, thereby causing the engine in which it was located to malfunction; their knowledge that the defective part had caused helicopter crashes; their failure or refusal to warn of the defective part and the potential consequences of its failure and to recall the engines containing the defective part or otherwise provide for its replacement; their extension of the length of time between overhauls of engines containing the part at which time the part would be replaced from 2,000 to 2,500 hours of engine operating time; and the death to Sherry Ann Letz resulting from the conscious indifference manifested by the policy decisions of the companies to save potentially as much as $48 million dollars by not repairing the defective part warrant a substantial punitive damage award.[FN21] Thus, based on the evidence of TSA's and TEC's indifference to the safety of others and the profitability of the company's wrongful conduct, an award *179 totaling millions of dollars is not unreasonable.

FN21. The conduct of defendants in places other than Missouri specifically impacted on residents of this state and directly resulted in the death of Sherry Ann Letz.

2. Ratio of Punitive Damages to the Actual Harm Inflicted on the Plaintiff

[67] Exemplary damages must bear a reasonable relationship to compensatory damages. *BMW*, 517 U.S. at 580, 116 S.Ct. at 1601. The ratio of punitive and actual damages is a commonly cited indicium of an unreasonable or excessive punitive damages award. *Id.* The United States Supreme Court has long endorsed the proposition that a comparison between the punitive award and the compensatory award is significant. *Id.* at 580-582, 116 S.Ct. at 1601-1602.

In *Haslip*, the United States Supreme Court concluded that a punitive damages award of "more than 4 times the amount of compensatory damages" was close to being excessive. *Id.* at ---, 116 S.Ct. at 1602 (quoting *Haslip*, 499 U.S. at 23-24, 111 S.Ct. at 1046-1047). It then refined its analysis of excessiveness in *TXO Production Corp. v. Alliance Resources Corp.*, 509 U.S. 443, 460, 113 S.Ct. 2711, 2721-2722, 125 L.Ed.2d 366 (1993), stating that the proper inquiry was "whether there is a reasonable relationship between the punitive damages award and the harm likely to result from the defendant's conduct as well as the harm that actually occurred." In *TXO*, the Court determined that it would not rule out a large ratio of punitive to compensatory damages (526 to 1) when the actual damages were relatively small ($19,000) because the misconduct was part of a large pattern of outrageous conduct and the harm likely to result from defendant's misconduct was much larger. *Id.* at 462, 113 S.Ct. at 2722-2723. Thus, the Court reasoned that the relative ratio of punitive award to likely harm was not more than 10 to 1. *Id.* In *BMW*, the Court continued to reject the concept that "the constitutional line is marked by a simple mathematical formula" but noted that "low awards of compensatory damages may properly support a higher ratio than high compensatory awards if, for example, a particularly egregious act has resulted in only a small amount of economic damages." *BMW*, 517 U.S. at ----, 116 S.Ct. at 1602.

In the present case, the verdict amounted to no more than $2.5 million for compensatory damages and at least $67.5 million for aggravating circumstances damages. Thus, the verdict represents a ratio of punitive sanction to compensatory award of at least 27 to 1, an arguably high ratio. The actual result of the conduct of TSA and TEC, the death of a passenger of a helicopter equipped with a defective TU 76 nozzle guide vane, was relatively proportionate to the harm likely to result from the conduct. This case, therefore, was dissimilar to *TXO*, where the defendants caused only a small part of the damage they would have caused if allowed to continue their scheme. Moreover, the economic or actual damages were not small as in *TXO*, but were large, up to $2.5 million. The amount of the compensatory award, therefore, did not arguably merit a higher ratio.

3. Review of Similar Cases

As with the compensatory award, examination of other cases and awards is helpful in determining whether the award of $67.5 million is excessive and shocks the conscience of the court. Because the maximum award permissible under the evidence of a given case cannot be calculated with a precise mathematical formula, *Kenton v. Hyatt Hotels Corp.*, 693 S.W.2d 83, 98 (Mo. banc 1985), comparison to similar cases where a defendant showed a conscious disregard for public safety to save money is helpful in determining what award would fairly and reasonably compensate the Letzes. In *Morrissey v. Welsh Co.*, 821 F.2d 1294 (8th Cir.Mo.1987), the Eighth Circuit, applying Missouri law, held that an award of $6.5 million in an action for wrongful death of plaintiff's 22-year old daughter who was killed when a building wall collapsed on her automobile was not so large to be deemed excessive as a matter of law. *Id.* at 1299. The court explained that where the wall collapsed due to poor maintenance over a long period of time and where the owners of the building decided not to incur an expenditure of $264,000 to repair the entire building because it would soon be sold, the jury could reasonably have allocated $6.5 *180 million to represent the aggravating circumstances present in the case. *Id.* at 1302.

In another comparable case, *Grimshaw v. Ford Motor Co.*, 119 Cal.App.3d 757, 174 Cal.Rptr. 348 (Cal.Ct.App.1981), a passenger, who suffered severe and permanently disfiguring burns on his face and entire body in an automobile accident, brought a products liability action against the manufacturer of the automobile, Ford Motor Company. *Id.* 174 Cal.Rptr. at 358. At the trial, evidence was presented that during the development of the automobile, the manufacturer knew of the fuel tank's vulnerability to puncture and rupture at low rear impact speeds creating a significant risk of death or injury from fire and had the technology to substantially reduce the risk. *Id.* at 360-361. Instead, the company elected to go forward with the production of the car based on the cost savings that would inure from omitting or delaying the "fixes." *Id.* at 361.

The jury awarded the plaintiff $2,516,000 in compensatory damages and $125 million in punitives. *Id.* at 358. The trial court ordered the plaintiff to file a remittitur of $121.5 million of the punitive damages as a condition of overruling Ford's motion for a new trial. *Id.* The California Court of Appeals held that remittitur of the punitive damages was not manifest abuse of discretion after consideration of the ratio of punitive damages to compensatory damages, the aggravating circumstances, and the wealth of the defendant and its profit generating capacity. *Id.* at 390. Other products liability actions were brought against Ford with similar results. *See, e.g., Ford Motor Co. v. Stubblefield*, 171 Ga.App. 331, 319 S.E.2d 470 (1984)(where $8 million award was an amount necessary to deter manufacturer from repeating its conduct of deferring implementation of safety devices in order to protect its profits).

4. Conclusion

[68] After careful consideration of the above cases, the ratio between punitive and compensatory damages, and evidence of the degree of malice and conscious disregard for the safety of others shown by TSA and TEC and all other aggravating circumstances surrounding the companies' conduct, this court finds that the jury's punitive verdict of $67.5 million is grossly excessive. *Fust*, 913 S.W.2d at 49. The amount of the verdict exceeds fair and reasonable compensation for plaintiffs' injuries and damages. § 537.068. The punitive award judgment for $67.5 million is excessive in the amount of $41 million.

[69] An appellate court may not compel remittitur; it may only order a party plaintiff to remit or experience the burden and expense of a new trial. *Milam v. Vestal*, 671 S.W.2d 448, 453 (Mo.App.1984). If the Letzes, therefore, enter a remittitur of $41 million of the judgment against TSA and TEC within fifteen days after the filing of this court's mandate, that judgment will stand affirmed for $29 million, representing $2.5 million in compensatory damages and $26.5 million in punitive damages, as of the date of its original entry; otherwise that judgment is reversed and the cause remanded for a new trial on the issue of damages only.

Table of Cases and Statutes

Statutes

Index